ECONOMIC INFORMATION, DECISION, AND PREDICTION

SELECTED ESSAYS: VOLUME I

THEORY AND DECISION LIBRARY

AN INTERNATIONAL SERIES

IN THE PHILOSOPHY AND METHODOLOGY OF THE

SOCIAL AND BEHAVIORAL SCIENCES

VOLUME 7

JACOB MARSCHAK

ECONOMIC INFORMATION, DECISION, AND PREDICTION

Selected Essays: Volume I

PART I

Economics of Decision

D. REIDEL PUBLISHING COMPANY
DORDRECHT : HOLLAND / BOSTON : U.S.A.
LONDON : ENGLAND

Library of Congress Catalog Card Number 74-81940

Volume I: ISBN 90-277-0544-5
ISBN 90-277-1195-X (pbk.)
Volume II: ISBN 90-277-0545-3
ISBN 90-277-1196-8 (pbk.)
Volume III: ISBN 90-277-0546-1
ISBN 90-277-1197-6 (pbk.)

Published by D. Reidel Publishing Company,
P.O. Box 17, 3300 AA Dordrecht, Holland.

Sold and distributed in the U.S.A. and Canada
by Kluwer Boston Inc., Lincoln Building,
160 Old Derby Street, Hingham, MA 02043, U.S.A.

In all other countries, sold and distributed
by Kluwer Academic Publishers Group,
P.O. Box 322, 3300 AH Dordrecht, Holland.

D. Reidel Publishing Company is a member of the Kluwer Group.

0-1195-0580-468
0-1196-0580-468
0-1197-0580-468

Printed in The Netherlands

CONTENTS

PART I: ECONOMICS OF DECISION

CONTENTS OF VOLUMES II AND III

VOLUME II

PART II: ECONOMICS OF INFORMATION AND ORGANIZATION

VOLUME III

PART III: MONEY AND OTHER ASSETS

PART IV: ECONOMIC MEASUREMENTS

PART V: CONTRIBUTIONS TO THE LOGIC OF ECONOMICS

FOREWORD

The papers of Jacob Marschak which follow in these volumes are an extraordinary combination of original and fruitful departures in economic and social thought, superb clarity of exposition, and sensitivity to the values of earlier work and even competing traditions. They make us marvel alike at their variety, their quantity, and their quality.

But they do not, even so, fully reflect Marschak's contributions to the development of social science. He has had an unusual influence as one who exercises leadership. In a formal, organizational sense, this role has been manifest in his capacity as Director of the Cowles Commission for Research in Economics, then at the University of Chicago, in that organization's most productive and influential period, and later in his central role in the Western Management Science Institute, at the University of California at Los Angeles. I can speak from first-hand knowledge about the first. His special capacities are, first, the recognition of promising new concepts and of promising young scholars, and, second, getting his colleagues to join him in developing the ideas and involving them fully in the necessary tasks. There was an unusual combination of strength and humility in his methods; a display of force in pushing the work along but a willingness, almost an insistence, on treating even the most junior associate as a fully equal colleague in intellectual development, whose criticism of himself was to be encouraged.

His leadership has been exercised in the absence of formal positions. It appears to me that his aim, in his papers, at least since about 1950, has virtually never been only the presentation of results interesting in themselves and displaying his abilities; the papers have always been aimed to persuade the reader of the intellectual importance of the tasks as well of the rewards they will receive in terms of interesting problems.

The more recent interests of Jacob Marschak have been increasingly deep and broad. They have revolved about the question, how do and should individuals and groups of individuals make decisions? These are issues that have been posed perhaps most sharply by economists and statisticians but clearly cover a far wider domain of social thought; his intended audiences (and actual audiences, for many of the papers presented here originated as lectures or presentations before learned societies) include social psychologists, logicians, biologists, organization theorists, and management scientists.

The interesting problems in decision theory arise under conditions of uncertainty. Bernoulli's expected-utility hypothesis of 1738, designed to explain why individuals bought insurance at actuarially unfair rates and to resolve the St. Petersburg paradox, had been given axiomatic underpinnings by Frank Ramsey and, independently, by John von Neumann and Oskar Morgenstern; and Ramsey had added an axiomatic argument that rational choice under uncertainty had to be based on subjectively-held probabilities, a conclusion again independently arrived at later by Bruno de Finetti and Leonard J. Savage. Marschak was quick to recognize the importance of these hypotheses, for in his pioneering work on the theory of demand for money, he had stressed the importance of the holding of money as a rational response to uncertainty (see especially his important Essay 37), and so was aware of the need for a convenient general theory of behavior under uncertainty. His expositions and developments contributed heavily to acceptance of the new viewpoints and greatly enriched their content. But he was equally interested in the errors that individuals make in choice, their random responses to identical conditions. His series of axiomatic and empirical analyses have clarified greatly the meaning of the alternative hypotheses and have shown clearly the need for models to make sense out of experiments in this field on the borderline of economics and psychophysics.

Most original and most important of all, in my judgment (this may reflect only my own interests, but they have been conditioned by Marschak's work), is the economics of information and organization, the theory of decision-making by collectivities. Not only do human beings have limited knowledge, but they have particular knowledge; the uncertainties of different individuals are not identical, for they are probability distributions conditioned on different sets of signals from the world about them. The distribution of information has implications for the rules by which individuals make decisions; further, like any other distribution of goods, it gives rise to the possibility of making everyone better off by transmitting information, though as Marschak so strongly emphasizes, only at a cost.

The aim of this introduction, like that of a good *apéritif*, should be to arouse the appetite for the feast ahead, not to allay it, and I do not propose to give potted summaries of the works ahead; nothing could replace the style and verve of the original. I cannot refrain, though, from simply calling the reader's attention to the Essays (48 and 49) on measurement in economics, which combine exposition of highly technical methods of economic statistics with deep insights into the epistemology of the social sciences and make these elements all of a piece; and at least the economist should study the remarkable combination of empirical and theoretical reasoning in Essay 47.

No doubt, by the time these volumes appear, Jacob Marschak will have added more of his wide-ranging applications and developments, perhaps to some still further field of human inquiry. We will all remain grateful for the example of rigorous thought illuminating the broad concerns of human individuality and society.

KENNETH J. ARROW

PREFACE

This collection of essays reflects discussions of the last three or four decades, and some changes in the thinking habits of economists. It also reflects a broadening of the author's concept of 'economics'. As time advanced his interests shifted from econometrics and monetary theory to problems of decision, information and organization. The actions considered and their outcomes may, but need not be, inputs and outputs of quantifiable and marketable production factors and products, or their prices. Nowadays, broader 'optimization problems' are pigeonholed as belonging to 'operations research,' 'management science,' 'systems analysis'. They occupy economists, engineers and (to the extent that applied probabilities are involved) statisticians as well. As 'benefit-cost analysis' these tools are also applied to problems of social policy no less than to military or medical planning. There is a promise of cross-fertilization with the evolutionary theories of life science and anthropology. And the decision-theoretical approach has recently taken a foothold in the philosophy of science. Some of the papers in this volume reflect such interdisciplinary efforts, unified by a broadly 'economic' point of view.

A collection of essays is not a book. The reader of a book chapter is familiar with concepts explained in preceding chapters. But an essay should be self-contained. Hence many overlappings occur. Also, a collection of essays portrays the development of ideas and methods over time – a very fast development in the fields whose results are covered here – while in a book not only earlier terminology but also all earlier results may be discarded. Finally, the present essays have been addressed to audiences with different backgrounds, and so they differ in language, some are more expository, others cover more new ground.

I did not attempt to reshape the material of these essays into a unified, fresh-vintage book. Some errors were noticed and corrected. A few (too few!) references were updated. Some cross-references were added. Is the undertaking presumptuous? Or will it provide some convenience, by assembling materials from various sources, not all equally accessible?

The collection is in five parts. A rigid demarcation of their fields was not possible. Some essays could be assigned in a different way. An Introductory Note to each part will indicate some of its relations to other parts. Still, a reader concentrating on a special problem may find the classification useful.

Within each of the five parts, the essays are arranged chronologically, with the date of the first publication given after the title.

Cordial thanks to my co-authors, both for inspiring and working with me in the past and for permitting now this use of our joint product. They are (with ten essay numbers in brackets): William Andrews (47), Kenneth Arrow (19), Gordon Becker (10, 12, 14, 15), H. D. Block (7), Donald Davidson (6), Morris DeGroot (10, 12, 14, 15), Ted Harris (19), Helen Makower (34), Koichi Miyasawa (29). Some of them are better mathematicians than the undersigned (Block, DeGroot, Harris, Miyasawa), others are more skilled experimenters (Davidson, Becker). These and all other co-authors have made distinct contributions. I was also helped and encouraged by other members of research groups in which I was privileged to work: the Oxford Institute of Statistics; the Cowles Commission (later, Foundation) for Research in Economics at the University of Chicago (later at Yale University); the Institute of Industrial Administration, Carnegie-Mellon University; and the Western Management Science Institute, University of California at Los Angeles.

JACOB MARSCHAK

Los Angeles, October 1974

ACKNOWLEDGEMENTS

Essay 1 first appeared in *Econometrica*, Vol. 18, No. 2, pp. 111–141 (April 1950) and is reprinted here by permission of Joseph E. Stiglitz, Reprint Editor.

Essay 2 first appeared in *Proceedings of the Second Symposium on Mathematical Statistics and Probability* (ed. by Jerzy Neyman), pp. 493–506 (1951). Originally published by the University of California Press; reprinted by permission of The Regents of the University of California.

Essay 3 first appeared in *Game Theory and Political Behavior* (ed. by Martin Shubik), pp. 22–32, Doubleday and Co., 1954. It was included in *Game Theory and Related Approaches to Social Behavior* (ed. by Martin Shubik), pp. 95–109, Wiley, New York, 1964; reprinted here by permission of John Wiley and Sons, Inc.

Essay 4 first appeared in *Mathematical Thinking in the Social Sciences* (ed. by Paul F. Lazarsfeld), pp. 166–215, The Free Press, 1954. The volume was re-issued by Russell and Russell, 1964; reprinted here by permission of Macmillan Publishing Co., New York.

Essay 5 first appeared in *Mathematical Models of Human Behavior – Proceedings of a Symposium*, pp. 45–53. Copyright, 1955, by Dunlap and Associates, Inc., Stamford, Conn. Permission granted by J. Fucigna, Executive Vice-President.

Essay 6 (co-author: Donald Davidson) first appeared in *Measurement: Definitions and Theories* (ed. by C. West Churchman and Philburn Ratoosh), pp. 233–269. First published by Wiley, New York, 1959, and reprinted here by permission of John Wiley and Sons, Inc.

Essay 7 (co-author: H. D. Block) first appeared in *Contributions to Probability and Statistics: Essays in Honor of Harold Hotelling* (ed. by I. Olkin, S. G. Ghuryé, W. Hoeffding, W. G. Madow, and H. B. Mann, pp. 97–132 (1960). Reprinted here with the permission of the publishers, Stanford University Press. © 1960 by the Board of Trustees of the Leland Stanford Junior University.

Essay 8 first appeared in *Mathematical Methods in the Social Sciences* (ed. by K. J. Arrow, S. Karlin, and P. Suppes), pp. 312–329 (1960). Reprinted here with the permission of the publishers, Stanford University Press. © 1960 by the Board of Trustees of the Leland Stanford Junior University.

Essay 9 first appeared in *Behavioral Science*, Vol. 9, No. 2, pp. 103–110 (April 1964) and is reprinted here by permission of James G. Miller, M.D., Ph.D., Editor.

Essay 10 first appeared in *Behavioral Science*, Vol. 8, No. 1, pp. 41–55 (January 1963) and is reprinted here by permission of James G. Miller, M.D., Ph.D., Editor.

Essay 11 first appeared in *Management Science*, Vol. 9, No. 4, pp. 517–526 (July 1963) and is reprinted here by permission of The Institute of Management Sciences.

Essay 12 (co-authors: G. M. Becker and M. H. DeGroot) first appeared in *Behavioral Science*, Vol. 8, No. 3, pp. 199–202 (July 1963) and is reprinted here by permission of James G. Miller, M.D., Ph.D., Editor.

Essay 13 first appeared in *Econometrica*, Vol. 31, No. 4; pp. 719–725 (October 1963) and is reprinted here by permission of Joseph E. Stiglitz, Reprint Editor.

Essay 14 (co-authors: G. M. Becker and M. H. DeGroot) first appeared in *Behavioral Science*, Vol. 8, No. 4, pp. 306–311 (October 1963) and is reprinted here by permission of James G. Miller, M.D., Ph.D., Editor.

Essay 15 (co-authors: G. M. Becker and M. H. DeGroot) first appeared in *Behavioral Science*, Vol. 9, No. 3, pp. 226–232 (July 1964) and is reprinted here by permission of James G. Miller, M.D., Ph.D., Editor.

Essay 16 first appeared in *International Encyclopedia of the Social Sciences* (ed. by David L. Sills), Vol. 4, pp. 42–55 (1968) and is reprinted here by permission of the Publisher. Copyright © 1968 by Crowell Collier and Macmillan, Inc.

Essay 17 first appeared in *Induction, Growth and Trade: Essays in Honor of Sir Roy Harrod* (ed. by W. A. Eltis, M. FG. Scott and J. N. Wolfe), pp. 38–54, Clarendon Press, Oxford, 1970. © Oxford University Press, 1970. Reprinted by permission of the publishers.

Essay 18 is to be included in a forthcoming Volume in Honor of Ralph W. Gerard (ed. by R. Grenell) and is here printed by permission.

RECENT PUBLICATIONS BY THE AUTHOR

A list of publications by the author for 1923–71 will be found in *Decision and Organization, a Volume in Honor of Jacob Marschak* (ed. by C. B. McGuire and R. Radner), pp. 337–41, North-Holland Publishing Co. For the subsequent years add:

1972

'Optimal Systems for Information and Decision', in *Techniques of Optimization* (ed. by A. V. Balakrishnan), pp. 355–70 (*Selected Essays*, 32).

'Interdisciplinary Discussion on Mathematics in Behavioral Sciences', in *Festschrift fuer Walter G. Waffenschmidt* (ed. by H. J. Niedereichholz), pp. 127–32, Verlag A. Hain (*Selected Essays*, 55).

1973

'Limited Role of Entropy in Information Economics', *5th Conference on Optimization Techniques*, Part II (ed. by R. Conti and A. Ruberti), pp. 264–71. (Revised, in *Theory and Decision*, Vol. 5, pp. 1–7).

'Intersubjektive Wahrscheinlichkeit', *Heidelberger Jahrbuecher*, Vol. 17, pp. 14–26.

1974

'Prior and Posterior Probabilities and Semantic Information', in *Information, Inference and Decision* (ed. by G. Menges), pp. 167–80. Theory and Decision Library, Vol. 1, D. Reidel.

'Information, Decision and the Scientist', *Pragmatic Aspects of Human Communication* (ed. by C. Cherry), pp. 145–78. Theory and Decision Library, Vol. 4, D. Reidel.

'Optimal Organization: Analytiker möchten sich mit Praktikern verständigen', *Zeitschrift fuer Betriebswirtschaftliche Forschung*, Vol. 26, pp. 283–97.

'Value and Cost of Information', in *Production Theory* (ed. by W. Eichhorn, R. Henn, O. Opitz and R. W. Shephard), pp. 335–58, Springer.

'Economics of Organizational Forms', *Proceedings of Conference on Man and Computer* (ed. by M. Marois), North-Holland Publishing Co.

1975

'Personal Probabilities of Probabilities', (with K. Borch, H. Chernoff, M. DeGroot, R. Dorfman, W. Edwards, T. S. Ferguson, K. Miyasawa, P. Randolph, L. J. Savage, R. Schlaifer, R. L. Winkler). *Theory and Decision*, Vol. 6.

PART I

ECONOMICS OF DECISION

INTRODUCTORY NOTE

The author's work on economics of decision, the subject of Part One of Selected Essays, has, in fact, started with studies of optimal balance sheets and of liquidity, covered in Part Three. Under uncertainty, to choose between decisions is to choose between 'prospects': the probability distributions of outcomes. In some of those earlier writings (Essays 33,34) it was deemed useful to express each distribution of monetary yields by its moments and to associate these with words of common usage (lucrativity, risk, long odds), an approach that has later proved, at the hands of H. Markowitz (1959), computationally convenient. If expected utility is maximized such description of decision presupposes a polynomial utility function of money, an assumption later discarded, for good reasons, by J. W. Pratt (1964) and K. Arrow (1965). However, expected utility came later. Thus in the analysis of liquidity under uncertainty (Essay 35) the principle of 'minimax regret' was used. This and various other competing principles were surveyed by R. Radner and J. Marschak (1954). Expected utility (of decisions with outcomes not necessarily monetary or numerical) is introduced in Essay 1 of Part One on the lines of J. von Neumann and O. Morgenstern (1944), with only 'objective' probability considered. Personal probabilities of F. Ramsey (1926), B. de Finetti (1937), L. J. Savage (1954) came in later, in Essays 3, 4, 15; the 'intersubjective' nature of 'objective' probabilities and their relation to observable frequencies is treated in Essay 17 and the author's Heidelberg paper (1973), and more rigorously in Chapter 2 of the *Economic Theory of Teams* (Marschak and Radner 1972). A 'Round Robin' on 'Personal Probabilities of Probabilities' was initiated by the author who later added some further comments in the publication (1974).

Models of actual behavior (Essays 9, 15), in particular 'stochastic' ones (Essays 6–8, 10, 12, 14) acknowledge limitations of men's 'rationality'. To ignore those limitations is not economical.

REFERENCES

Arrow, K. J. (1965), Lecture 2 in *Aspects of the Theory of Risk-Bearing*, Helsinki, Yrjö Johnssonin Säätio. Republished as Chapter 3 of Essays in the *Theory of Risk-Bearing*, Markham Publishing Co., Chicago 1971.

De Finetti, B. (1937), 'La prévision, ses lois logiques, ses sources subjectives'. Republished in English, with some revisions, in *Studies in Subjective Probabilities* (ed. by H. E. Kyburg and H. Smokler), J. Wiley, New York, 1964.

Markowitz, H. (1959), *Portfolio Selection*, Cowles Foundation Monograph, 16, New York, J. Wiley.

Marschak, J. (1973), Intersubjektive Wahrscheinlichkeit, *Heidelberger Jahrbuecher*, **17**.

Marschak, J. and Others (K. Borch, H. Chernoff, M. H. DeGroot, R. Dorfman, W. Edwards, T. S. Ferguson, K. Miyasawa, P. Randolph, L. J. Savage, R. Schlaifer, R. L. Winkler) (1974). 'Personal Probabilities of Probabilities', *Theory and Decision*, **6** (forthcoming).

Marschak, J. and Radner, R. (1972), *Economic Theory of Teams*, Yale University Press.

Pratt, J. W. (1964), 'Risk Aversion in the Small and in the Large', *Econometrica*, **32**, 122–136.

Radner, R. and Marschak, J. (1954), 'Note on Some Proposed Decision Criteria,' in *Decision Processes* (ed. by R. M. Thrall *et al.*), pp. 61–68, Wiley, New York.

Ramsey, F. P. (1926), 'Truth and Probability', republished in *Foundations of Mathematics and Other Logical Essays*, Humanities Press, New York, 1950.

Savage, L. J. (1954), *The Foundations of Statistics*, J. Wiley. Revised edition, Dover Publications, 1972.

Von Neumann, J. and Morgenstern, O. (1944), *Theory of Games and Economic Behavior*, esp. Appendix added in the 1948 edition.

RATIONAL BEHAVIOR, UNCERTAIN PROSPECTS, AND MEASURABLE UTILITY*

(1950)

ABSTRACT. After introducing some basic concepts and three postulates on rational choice, it is proposed to show that if the economists' theory of assets is completed by a fourth postulate on rational choice, then utility can be defined as a quantity whose mathematical expectation is maximized by the rational man. In this sense, utility is 'measurable' and 'manageable'. These results are inspired by von Neumann's and Morgenstern's discussion of utility in *Theory of Games and Economic Behavior*; an attempt is made to sketch some relations between their approach and the present one, It is shown in conclusion that while gambling is compatible with the four postulates, the 'love of danger' is not: and a property of the maximum mathematical expectation of utility is conjectured.

I. SOME BASIC CONCEPTS

1. *Rational Behavior: Description and Advice*

The theory of rational behavior is a set of propositions that can be regarded either as idealized approximations to the actual behavior of men or as recommendations to be followed.

This can be shown in the following proposition: "The rational man does not make logical and arithmetical errors." Or, to give three particular examples: "if $x=2$ and $y=0.005$, the rational man concludes that $xy=0.01$"; "if all *A* are *B*, the rational man concludes that all non-*B* are non-*A*, but he does not conclude that all *B* are *A*"; "if *P* follows from *Q*, he concludes that non-*Q* follows from non-*P*, but he does not conclude that *Q* follows from *P*." Now, a large proportion of people, especially when in a hurry to answer and to act, are apt to disobey those rules. Living men and women are apt to misplace their decimal points; they often conclude from the part to the whole; and they are not above confusing a sufficient condition with a necessary one. That is, they do not behave rationally. What is, then, the use of setting up the above propositions of arithmetic and logic? The use is twofold: to describe approximately the behavior of men who, it is believed, cannot be 'all fools all the time', and to give advice on how to reach 'correct' conclusions. These two aspects of the rules of logic and arithmetic can be called, respectively, the descriptive and the recommendatory aspect.

As an approximative description of actual behavior, the rules of logic and arithmetic may be regarded as hypotheses on the psychology of reasoning and calculating: hypotheses whose predictive power ('predict how many people of a certain age-group, etc., will make a certain kind of error') is susceptible of empirical tests. Viewed from their recommendatory aspect, as advice on how to reach 'correct' conclusions, the rules of logic and arithmetic are susceptible only to the test of internal consistency; in fact, the aggregate of these rules (including the rule of internal consistency itself) can be regarded as nothing but the definition of 'correctness' of conclusions.

Note, however, that 'correct' conclusions are often regarded as having, in addition, a 'utilitarian' virtue. The results of decisions based on 'correct' conclusions are, in some sense, 'preferable' to results of decisions based on incorrect ones. It is 'advisable' to follow the rules of logic and arithmetic. In dealing with his environment ('nature', which includes 'society') a man who often makes mistakes in his inferences and his sums is, in the long run, apt to fare less well than if he had been a better logician and arithmetician. Thus concepts of 'welfare' and of 'long run', or of utility and mathematical expectation, become involved. If advisable decisions must obey rules of logic and arithmetic, they are not themselves defined by those rules alone. The fulfillment of rules of conventional logic and arithmetic is a necessary but not a sufficient condition for a decision to be advisable. We need additional definitions and postulated rules, to 'prolong' logic and arithmetic into the realm of decision. We shall define rational behavior as that which follows those rules, in addition to the rules of logic and arithmetic. It will be seen (an experience common in logic and mathematics) that alternative sets of postulated rules may or may not lead to different implications.

Again (as in the case of the logico-arithmetical rules in the narrower sense) these postulates, and their implications, can be used in two ways: they can be conceived as approximate descriptions of actual behavior or they can be regarded as rules of behavior to be followed. Both the descriptive and the recommendatory aspects have practical use. For example, a government (or a firm) has to (a) choose the advisable course of its own responses to environment and (b) know, as a part of its environment, something about the actual behavior of tax-payers, consumers, competitors, etc.

Rational behavior is also called the behavior of a rational man. For brevity, we shall speak of 'the man,' to cover the rational consumer, the rational firm, the rational government, etc.

2. *Complete Information*

We have further to distinguish between two cases: the case when the man thinks he knows certain relevant probability distributions, and the case when the man does not think so. We call the former case *complete information*, and the latter, *incomplete information*.[1] The theory of rational behavior under incomplete information is not presented here. It would be related to the studies on the rationale of sampling, started by Neyman and Pearson [1] and developed particularly by A. Wald, e.g. [1, 2]. The case of complete information can (but need not) be represented as a limiting one: it is approached as the number of observations which have been made by the man increases. Alternatively, one can think of the probabilities used in the man's decisions as 'degrees of belief' not related to specific samples in any simple way, yet obeying the usual axioms on probabilities.

A special case of complete information is that of *certainty*: in this case all probabilities have values 0 or 1.

3. *Future Histories x; Commodity Space X*

At a given point of time the man considers a sequence of, say, τ future time intervals, up to a certain time point called horizon. The amounts of each commodity consumed during each interval and the stocks of various kinds available at the horizon point define one of the mutually exclusive 'future histories'. Each such history can be represented by a point x in the 'commodity space' X. Since, for the more remote future, the man may have a coarser classification of goods than for the immediate future (a point emphasized by Koopmans [1]), some commodities, or commodity groups, may have to be entered identically as zeros for some time intervals or for the horizon point; hence the dimensionality of X at most equals $\gamma(\tau+1)$, where γ is the number of commodities ever to be entered.

One can also interpret each point x more narrowly, as the development of a particular 'venture' ('play'), disregarding all other aspects of a man's future. Thus, a firm owner's choice between various uses of cash profits in his personal plans of consumption may be considered irrelevant (this diminishes γ); only the near future is considered (this makes τ small); and attention is paid only to a particular shop or ship, patent or contract. Note, however, that even if one is concerned only with a single money wager, the number of alternative points x (here the alternative amounts of money gains) may be large.

Inasmuch as the man may treat time and the amounts of goods as both discrete and bounded, we shall assume the number of points x finite, though, of course, as large as we like. We shall enumerate these points as $x^{(0)},\ldots, x^{(\nu)}$.[2]

4. *Prospects a; domain A*

We call a prospect a the vector (the distribution) of the probabilities $a_0,\ldots, a_\nu$, assigned respectively to all the mutually exclusive histories $x^{(0)},\ldots, x^{(\nu)}$. We can write $a=a(x)$, where x is a random vector.[3] We have

$$(4.1)\qquad \sum_{\mu=0}^{\nu} a_\mu = 1, \quad a_\mu \geqslant 0, \quad (\mu = 0,\ldots, \nu).$$

Accordingly, we can represent each prospect by a point $a=(a_1,\ldots, a_\nu)$ in the domain A of the Euclidian ν-space defined by the condition that A consists of all points a such that for every a,

$$(4.2)\qquad \sum_{\mu=1}^{\nu} a_\mu \leqslant 1, \quad a_\mu \geqslant 0, \quad (\mu = 1,\ldots, \nu);$$

we define a_0:

$$(4.3)\qquad 0 \leqslant a_0 = 1 - \sum_{\mu=1}^{\nu} a_\mu \leqslant 1.$$

Note that A is an infinite set regardless of whether ν is or is not infinite, because each probability can take all real values from 0 to 1 subject only to the restriction (4.1).

If a prospect promises one particular history, say $x^{(\mu)}$, $(\mu=0,\ldots, \nu)$, with certainty, we call it a *sure prospect* and denote it by $a^{(\mu)}$. Prospects which are not sure are called uncertain.

5. *Geometric Presentation: Boundary and Interior of A*

In Figure 1, $\nu=2$, and the sure prospect $a^{(0)}$ is chosen as the origin. The two other sure prospects $a^{(1)}$, $a^{(2)}$, lie on the two axes, each at unit distance from the origin. The lengths of segments $\overline{am}=a_0$, $\overline{an}=a_1$, $\overline{ap}=a_2$, indicate the component probabilities of the uncertain prospect a; and $a_0+a_1+a_2=1$.[4] All points in or on the rectangular isosceles triangle $a^{(0)}a^{(1)}a^{(2)}$ constitute the domain A, as defined by (4.2). For any ν, the sure prospect $a^{(0)}=(0,\ldots,0)$ is at the origin; while any other sure prospect, $a^{(\mu)}$, $\mu=1,\ldots,\nu$, will be at some other corner of the domain A; $a^{(\mu)}$ is a unit vector: each of its ν components $a_\pi^{(\mu)}(\pi=1,\ldots,\nu)$ is 1 or 0 according as $\pi=\text{or}\neq\mu$. Any prospect a for which at least one component is zero, lies on the boundary of A. Any prospect not on the boundary of A is called an interior point.

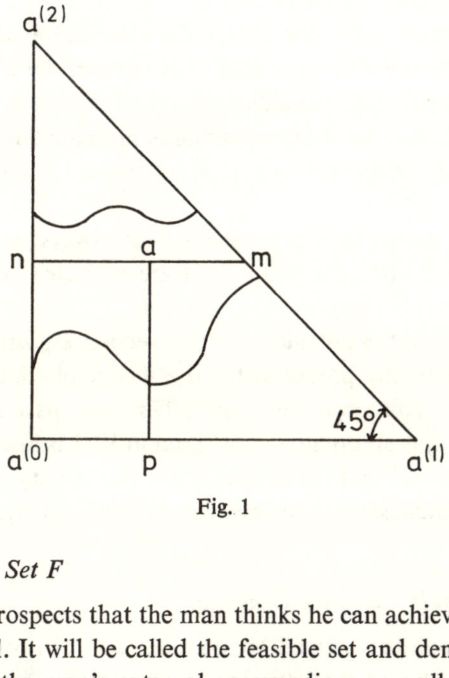

Fig. 1

6. *The Feasible Set F*

The set of all prospects that the man thinks he can achieve by his actions is a subset of A. It will be called the feasible set and denoted by F. It is determined by the man's external surroundings as well as his own endowment: the technology of his farm or factory, his ability to borrow, the market conditions, etc. Set F is not dependent on the man's 'tastes', to be defined in Section 8 below. In Figure 1, set F is indicated by the area bounded by, and including, the curved line and segments of axes. We shall always assume F to be a closed set.

II. THREE POSTULATES ON CHOICE

7. *Commodity Space X and Probability Space A*

The economic theory of choice was originally applied to alternative bundles of commodities, each promised with certainty, or to alternative combinations of this year's, next year's, third year's... flows of money (Fisher [2]) or of some other single commodity, again promised with certainty. We have called the set of such alternatives the space X. To treat uncertain prospects we have introduced the domain A of the ν-dimensional probability space, $\nu+1$ being the number of points in the commodity space X. The propositions (postulates, definitions, and derived propositions) on choice, formulated in this Part for points in the probability space, hold good also for the choice between commodity bundles or sequences of such bundles,[5] provided A is replaced by X. However, the following remarks should be made:

(1) The coordinates of A are continuous probabilities; if coordinates of X represented continuous quantities of goods, ν would be infinite. But see note 2.

(2) While the points in X are usually (not always) required to have nonnegative coordinates, the points in A are restricted more strongly by (4.2).

(3) In addition to the postulates of this section a postulate of 'monotonicity' is occasionally proposed for the theory of choice in the commodity space X. This postulate must differ from its counterpart in A and will deserve special discussion, in Section VIII below.

(4) It will be noted that for choices in the probability space, Postulate III introducing indifference surfaces can be replaced by a weaker one, III′ or III*.

8. POSTULATE I: *Complete Ordering*

One assumes a relation $\mathfrak{g}$ (read 'at least as good as') between elements $a, b, c\ldots$ of A, such that the following two postulates hold: Postulate Ia: *For any two* a, b, *at least one of the following holds*: $a\mathfrak{g}b$, $b\mathfrak{g}a$ (*comparability*). Postulate Ib: $a\mathfrak{g}b$, $b\mathfrak{g}c$ *together imply* $a\mathfrak{g}c$ (*transitivity*). Ia and Ib together state that $\mathfrak{g}$ is a *complete ordering* of A.

We define *tastes* by attaching the values 'true', 'false', to the statements $a\mathfrak{g}b$ applied to all pairs of points in A.

The *preference* and *indifference* relations, $\mathfrak{p}$ (read 'preferred to' or 'better than') and $\mathfrak{i}$ (read 'indifferent to' or 'equivalent to'), are defined as follows:

$$a\mathfrak{p}b \text{ means } a\mathfrak{g}b \text{ and not } b\mathfrak{g}a,$$
$$a\mathfrak{i}b \text{ means } a\mathfrak{g}b \text{ and } b\mathfrak{g}a,$$

where a, b are real vectors, and $a=b$ means, as usual, $a_\mu=b_\mu$, $\mu=1, \ldots, \nu$. It follows from the above postulates and definitions that $a=b$ implies $a\mathfrak{i}b$; $a\mathfrak{i}b$ implies $b\mathfrak{i}a$; and that $\mathfrak{i}$ and $\mathfrak{p}$ are transitive relations.

9. *Indifference Sets*; *Utility Indices*; *Utility Function*

For any a, we define its indifference set $J(a)$ as follows: $J(a)$ consists of all b's such that $b\mathfrak{i}a$. It follows that every a breaks up the set A into the following three pairwise disjunct subsets: $J(a)$; the region of all b's such that $b\mathfrak{p}a$; the region of all c's such that $a\mathfrak{p}c$.

It follows that the indifference sets can be uniquely arranged into a sequence. If a real number $u(a)$ is assigned to the indifference set $J(a)$, one can assign to any indifference set $J(b)$ a real number $u(b)$ such that $u(a)\geqslant u(b)$ means $a\mathfrak{g}b$. It follows that

$$u(a) > u(b) \text{ means } a\mathfrak{p}b,$$

and

$$u(a) = u(b) \text{ means } a\mathfrak{i}b.$$

The numbers $u(a), u(b), \ldots$ are called utility. indices or, briefly, utilities; and the function u on set A, a utility function. The class of all utility functions will be denoted by U.

A function $\phi(z)$ is said to be monotonically increasing if $\phi(z_1)>\phi(z_2)$ for $z_1>z_2$. Let $u(a)$ be a utility function. Then $\phi\,[u(A)]$ is a utility function if and only if ϕ is a monotonically increasing function.

10. *Maximizing Utility*

Define a subset F' of the feasible closed set F (Section 6 above) as follows: if d and b are in F' and if c is in F but not in F' then $d\,\mathfrak{i}\,b\mathfrak{p}c$. The set F' consists of the 'best feasible' prospects; and since F is closed, F' must contain at least one element (Arrow [1]). We study the case when F' has only one element (the best feasible prospect). Let u be a utility function. Then, under conditions just stated, $u(c)<u(b)=u(d)=\max\, u(a)$

over all a in F. To say that a certain function u is a utility function means that $u(a)$ is maximized with respect to a, subject to the condition that a is in the feasible set F.

11. *Internal and External Averages*

Let r be a real number, $0<r<1$. Then $b=ra+(1-r)\,c=\{[ra_0+(1-r)\,c_0], \ldots, [ra_\nu+(1-r)\,c_\nu]\}$ will be called an internal average of a and c; it is represented by a point on the straight line segment $\overline{ac}$. Let q be a real number, $q>1$. Then $d=qa+(1-q)\,c$ is called an external average of a and c and lies on the continuation of $\overline{ac}$ beyond a. Obviously, a is an internal average of d and c, with $q=1/r$.

12. POSTULATE II: *If* $a \mathfrak{p} b \mathfrak{p} c$, *then there exists* r, $0<r<1$, *such that* $b \mathfrak{i} [ra+(1-r)\,c]$. (*Continuity* of the preference relation.)

13. POSTULATE III: *For any* a *and* r, $0<r<1$, *there exists a prospect* b *such that not* $a \mathfrak{i} [ra+(1-r)\,b]$

That is, the neighborhood of any point a contains at least one point b in A which is not equivalent to a.

14. *Indifference Surfaces*

Postulates II and III imply together that the indifference set $J(a)$ forms a boundary between two regions of A: one containing all b's such that $b \mathfrak{p} a$; the other containing all c's such that $a \mathfrak{p} c$. In this case, $J(a)$ has one dimension less than the space, that is, $\nu-1$ dimensions, and is called an indifference surface. [Note that in special cases, e.g., for some points a on the boundary of A, the set $J(a)$ may have $<\nu-1$ dimensions: a may have either no b's ($b \mathfrak{p} a$) or no c's ($a \mathfrak{p} c$) in its neighborhood.] In any case, no two distinct indifference sets $J(a) \neq J(b)$ may intersect, since by the definitions in Section 8, $a \mathfrak{p} b$ is inconsistent with $a \mathfrak{i} b$.

15. Postulate III and its implication that indifference sets are, in general, surfaces forms an interesting link with tradition. But for the present purposes it can be replaced by one of the following two weaker postulates suggested, respectively, by Abraham Wald and Herman Rubin.

POSTULATE III*: *There exist two prospects* a *and* b *in the interior of* A *such that* $a \mathfrak{p} b$ *or* $b \mathfrak{p} a$.

POSTULATE III′: *There exist at least four distinct indifference sets.*

III. THE THEORY OF ASSETS

16. The theory of assets pointed out that the man chooses between achievable probability distributions. This proposition was just stated in Section 10. However, with exceptions that will be stated below, past writings on the theory of assets[6] did not represent each prospect by a point in the space of probabilities of mutually exclusive 'histories' x. They considered instead the joint probability distribution of the $\gamma(\tau+1)$ quantities of each commodity at each point of time (see Section 3). Each 'cell' of such a joint distribution corresponds to some history x. To a given distribution $a(x)$ of the histories x corresponds one joint probability distribution of the alternative commodity-amounts at various points of time. The latter distribution can be characterized by certain parameters, and writers on the theory of assets represented each prospect by a point in the space of these parameters; call this space P. For example, if only one commodity – say, money income – and one point of time are considered, so that the alternative histories x differ only by the amounts of money income, each prospect can be characterized by the mean, the variance, the skewness, etc., of the probability distribution of income; if more than one commodity or time-point is considered, say $\gamma(\tau+1)=\varepsilon$ quantities, each prospect may be characterized by ε means, ε variances, $\varepsilon(\varepsilon-1)/2$ correlations, etc. Each distribution parameter was regarded as being a 'good' (or possibly a 'bad') in the eyes of the man. Accordingly, each distribution was regarded as a bundle of 'commodities', subject to postulates which are analogous to Postulates I–III above. Tastes were described by indifference surfaces drawn in the parameter space P, and the empirical properties of these surfaces were discussed. For example, the risk-aversion (risk-discount), i.e., the rate of substitution between the mean and the variance of income, expressed by the relevant slope of an indifference surface, was stated to be positive. Opportunities were defined as a region of the space P (analogous to our region F of A). The boundary of this region – the 'opportunity surface' – was derived from the individual's initial possession of assets (physical goods and positive or negative claims), the prices or other conditions in the market of the assets (perfect or otherwise), and the production conditions. With opportunities

and tastes defined in the space of distribution parameters, the old theory of assets defined rational decision analogously to Section 10. (If all functions are well behaved, this will correspond to choosing the point of tangency between the opportunity surface and an indifference surface.) From here, the theory explained the market prices of assets in the same way in which prices of production factors are determined from the indifference maps of individuals, their initial possession of production factors, and the production functions for final goods. It also claimed to explain the determination of optimal balance sheets and plans, in the way the ordinary theory determines the equilibrium flows of consumption.

17. It was pointed out by Tintner[7] that the utility index might be considered, not as a function of distribution parameters but as a functional of the distribution function itself. This is tantamount to the use of the domain of probabilities, A, as in Part I above. To become more than a change in notation, this suggestion will need an additional postulate (Part IV). With the help of such a postulate, it will be shown in Part V that indifference sets in the A-space must be parallel hyperplanes. This will, in turn, imply the possibility of defining utility functions determined up to linear transformations. It will also imply that such a utility index of an uncertain prospect $a \equiv (a_0, \ldots, a_\nu)$ equals its 'expected utility', defined as the average of the utility indices of the sure prospects $a^{(0)}, \ldots, a^{(\nu)}$, weighted with the probabilities $a_0, \ldots, a_\nu$. This should also help to revise the theory of determination of optimal plans, defined as rational balance sheets or rational strategies.[8]

18. *The Mean vs Other Parameters*

It has been common among economists to insist that the means of the amounts of commodities are not the only parameters of their joint distribution that are relevant to the man's decisions, and possibly not the most important ones, and attempts were made to specify which additional, or alternative, parameters – e.g., the higher moments[9] – should be considered. These writers, e.g., Marschak [2], Tintner [1], often failed to make clear that the statement "the average *amounts of goods* are not alone relevant to the man's decision" does not contradict the statement that the average *utility* is maximized by him. The latter proposition permits, in fact, to relate 'risk-aversion', 'advantage of diversification', and similar concepts of the older asset theory to the properties of the utility function of sure prospects.[10]

IV. FOURTH POSTULATE ON CHOICE BETWEEN PROSPECTS

19. POSTULATE IV_1: *If* $a\,\mathrm{i}\,a'$ *and* $0<r<1$, *then* $a\,\mathrm{i}\,[ra+(1-r)\,a']$.

In words: If prospect a is equivalent to another prospect, a', then the prospect of obtaining either a or a' with certainty is equivalent to each of them. To illustrate this postulate, we can first interpret a, a' as sure prospects (Section 4 above), that is, as two mutually exclusive future sequences of events or, still simpler, as two mutually exclusive bundles of commodities. Suppose a man is indifferent as between a car and a \$1000 bill. Then he should be also indifferent as between a car, a \$1000 bill, and the ticket to a lottery in which the changes of winning a car or a \$1000 bill are, respectively, 0.2 and 0.8, say. The same applies if, for a car and \$1000, we substitute securities, or patents, or lottery tickets, etc., promising, respectively (if combined with the man's other assets), prospects such as those defined in Part I.

POSTULATE IV_2: *Let* a, a', b, *be three distinct prospects*; *let* $c=ra+$ $+(1-r)\,b$, *and* $c'=ra'+(1-r)\,b$, *where* $0<r<1$; *then* $a'\,\mathrm{i}\,a$ *implies* $c'\,\mathrm{i}\,c$.

In words: If two prospects a and a' are equivalent, then the prospect of having a or b with probabilities r, $1-r$, and the prospect of having a' or b with the same respective probabilities r, $1-r$, are equivalent. For example, suppose a \$1000 bill and a car are equivalent. Compare two lottery tickets, one promising a \$1000 bill or a house with probabilities 0.9 and 0.1, the other promising a car or a house, also with probabilities 0.9 and 0.1. Then there is no reason to prefer one of the two lottery tickets to the other.

For the geometry of these postulates see Figure 2, where $a'\,\mathrm{i}\,a$ and $\overline{a'a}\parallel\overline{c'c}$. Then by IV_1, the internal average $m\,\mathrm{i}\,a$; and by IV_2, $c'\,\mathrm{i}\,c$.

POSTULATE IV: *If* $a'\,\mathrm{i}\,a$ *and* $0<r<1$, *then for any* b, $[ra'+(1-r)\,b]$ $\mathrm{i}\,[ra+(1-r)\,b]$. This postulate summarizes IV_1 (for $b=a$) and IV_2 (for $b\neq a$).

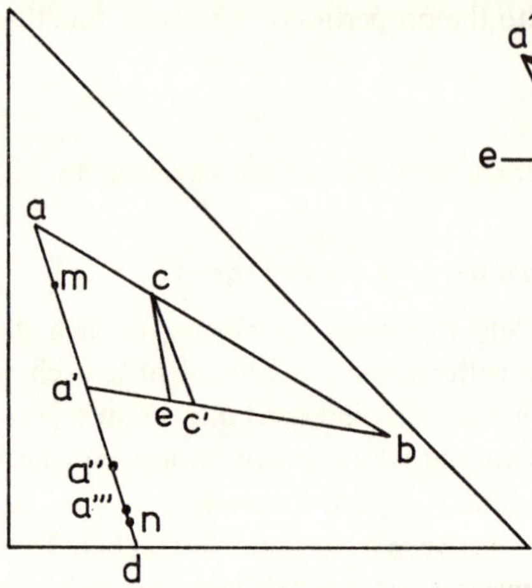

Fig. 2

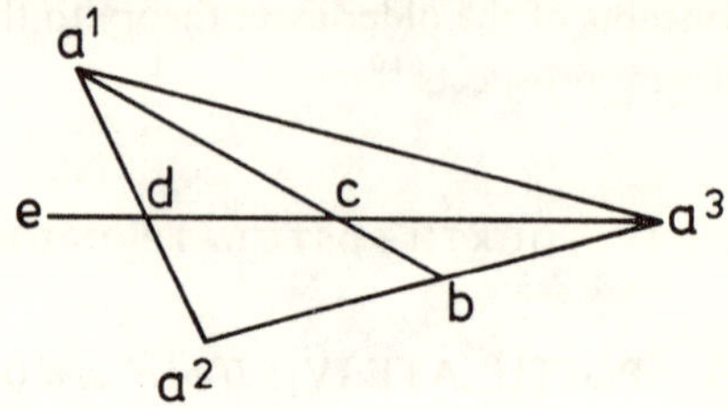

Fig. 3

20. While IV_1 states that the interval average (see Section 11 above) of two equivalent prospects is equivalent to them, the following lemma, implied in IV_1 and IV_2, extends this statement to external averages though under a restriction:

LEMMA 1: *If* $a\,\iota\,a'$, *and an interior point* p *is collinear with* a, a', *then* $p\,\iota\,a$.

Proof: Suppose p is between a and a': for example, $p=m$ in Figure 2; then the proposition follows directly from Postulate IV_1. Suppose now a' is between p and a: for example $p=n$ in Figure 2. Then continue the line $\overline{a'n}$ till its intersection d with the boundary of the domain. Define s, $0<s<1$, by the equation $a'=sd+(1-s)\,a$. Define $a''=sd+(1-s)\,a'$. Then $a\,\iota\,a'$ implies, by IV_2, $a''\,\iota\,a$. Define next $a'''=sd+(1-s)a''$, $a''''= =sd+(1-s)\,a'''$, etc. By applying IV_2 successively, every point a'', a''', a'''',... is shown to be in $J(a)$; and by IV_1 any point between a and a',..., a'''',... is also in $J(a)$. Therefore, since the distances $\overline{da'}$,..., $\overline{d''''}$,... approach zero, any point on the segment $\overline{ad}$ is in $J(a)$ except possibly d itself.

V. LINEAR UTILITY FUNCTIONS OF PROSPECTS

21. Part V will develop the implications of our four postulates. A particularly simple system of indifference sets – a family of parallel planes – will be shown to represent tastes with regard to prospects. It will then be proved that there exists a class of linear utility functions of prospects, and that the 'expected values' (properly defined) of such functions are maximized over the feasible set of prospects by the rational man (defined as one who follows the rules of logic and arithmetic and the four postulates of Part IV).

THEOREM 1: *The indifference sets $J(a)$ are parallel hyperplanes of $\leqslant \nu-1$ dimensions. For any interior a, $J(a)$ has $\nu-1$ dimensions.* This theorem will be derived from Postulates I, II, III*, IV; the results[11] would of course be valid if III* were replaced by a stronger Postulate III. (If, instead of Postulate III*, we admitted the stronger Postulate III and hence the existence of indifference hypersurfaces, Postulate IV would imply immediately that these surfaces must be parallel hyperplanes.)

To give a general idea of the proof we first confine ourselves to $\nu=2$ and to the interior of A only, and show that then (1) all indifference sets are straight lines and (2) all these lines are parallel. The general case will then be introduced in Section 22:1.

21:1. We first show that if three interior points a^1, a^2, a^3, are equivalent they must be collinear.[12] For suppose that, on the contrary, they are the vertices of a triangle, as in Figure 3. Then, by Lemma 1, any b on the triangle, any c within the triangle, and any interior point e outside the triangle are in $J(a^1)$; and this contradicts III*. Conversely, any interior point on the straight line containing a^1 and a^2 is in $J(a^1)$; this follows from Lemma 1.

21:2. Figure 2 shows that if $J(a)$ and $J(c)$ are straight lines containing the segments $\overline{aa'}$ and $\overline{cc'}$, then $\overline{aa'} \parallel \overline{cc'}$. For suppose that the line drawn through c parallel to aa' meets ba' in e. Then by IV_2, eic; and since cic', the points c, c', e, must be collinear, as shown in 21:1. Hence e must coincide with c'.

22:1. To prove for the whole domain A, of any dimension ν, that each set $J(a)$ is a hyperplane of $\leqslant \nu-1$ dimensions (of exactly $\nu-1$ dimensions if a is in the interior of A), Abraham Wald suggested the following set of lemmas. Denote by a' an interior point;[13] denote by $J'(a')$ the set of all interior points in $J(a')$.

22:2. LEMMA 2: *For any interior point a', the set $J'(a')$ consists of all the interior points of a hyperplane, $H(a')$ of $\leqslant \nu-1$ dimensions.* This follows from Lemma 1, as in 21:1, by proving that the vertices of a $(\nu+1)$-hedron cannot be equivalent, and that any interior point contained in the same hyperplane with ν equivalent points is equivalent to them.

22:3. LEMMA 3: *For any interior point a', $J(a')$ consists of $J'(a')$ and the intersection of $H(a')$ with the boundary of A.* To prove this, consider b'', a point on the boundary of A, and show that b'' is in $J(a')$ if, and only if, b'' is on the hyperplane $H(a')$.

22:3:1. *Necessity*: Suppose b'' is in $J(a')$ but not in $H(a')$. Then any interior point c' on the segment $\overline{b''a'}$ is not in $H(a')$; but on the other hand, by IV, c' is in $J(a')$ and hence in $J'(a')$ and, by Lemma 2, in $H(a')$. Because of this contradiction, b'' must be in $H(a')$.

22:3:2. *Sufficiency*: To show that if the boundary point b'' is on the hyperplane $H(a')$ it is also in the indifference set $J(a')$, distinguish three cases: (1) there exist two interior points c', d', such that $c'\mathfrak{p}a'\mathfrak{p}d'$; (2) thre is no interior point c' such that $c'\mathfrak{p}a'$; (3) thre is no interior point d' such that $a'\mathfrak{p}d'$.

In Case (1), by Lemma 2, neither c' nor d' is in $H(a')$. Suppose first (1α): that $b''\mathfrak{p}a'$; then $b''\mathfrak{p}a'\mathfrak{p}d'$, and, by Postulate II, there exists a point e' on segment $\overline{b''d'}$ such that e' is in $J(a')$; by Lemma 2, e' is in $H(a')$. But on the other hand, since b'' is in $H(a')$ while d' is not, e' on segment $\overline{b''d'}$ cannot be in $H(a')$. Because of this contradiction, the assumption (1α) that $b''\mathfrak{p}a'$ is false; so is, by symmetry, the assumption (1β) that $a'\mathfrak{p}b''$. Hence $a'\mathfrak{i}b''$.

In Case (2) there exists, by III*, an interior point d' such that $a'\mathfrak{p}d'$; and, by Lemma 2, d' is not in $H(a')$. Suppose first (2α): that $b''\mathfrak{p}a'$. Then $b''\mathfrak{p}a'\mathfrak{p}d'$, and, by II, there exists an interior point e' on segment $\overline{b''d'}$ such that e' is in $J(a')$ and hence, by Lemma 2, in H(a'). But on the other hand, since b'' is in $H(a')$ while d$'$ is not, e' is not in $H(a')$. Because of this contradiction, the assumption $b''\mathfrak{p}a'$ must be false.

Suppose next (2β): that $a'\mathfrak{p}b''$; and consider separately three subcases: ($2\beta\alpha$): $d'\mathfrak{p}b''$; ($2\beta\beta$): $b''\mathfrak{p}\ d'$; ($2\beta\gamma$): $b''\mathfrak{i}d'$. In ($2\beta\alpha$), $a'\mathfrak{p}d'\mathfrak{p}b''$ and hence, by II, there is a point e' on $\overline{a''b'}$ such that $e'\mathfrak{i}d'$; but then, since both a' and b'' are in $H(a')$, e' is in H(a'), while [as stated at the beginning of Case (2)] its equivalent d' is not in $H(A')$. This contradicts Lemma 2; hence ($2\beta\alpha$) is impossible. Subcase ($2\beta\beta$) is also impossible: for then $a'\mathfrak{p}b''\mathfrak{p}d'$ so that, by II, there exists a point e' on $\overline{a'd'}$ such that $e'\mathfrak{i}b''$ and e' is not in $H(a')$. Let $f'=re'+(1-r)\,a'$; $g'=rb''+(1-r)\,a'$; $0<r<1$. Then, by IV, $f'\mathfrak{i}g'$. But, by Lemma 2, this is impossible since g' is in $H(a')$ (because b'' is), while f' is not in $H(a')$ (because e' is not). There remains subcase ($2\beta\gamma$): $b''\mathfrak{i}d'$. This is also impossible since then $rd'+(1-r)\,a'\mathfrak{i}rb''+(1-r)\,a'$, $0<r<1$; yet the point to the right of $\mathfrak{i}$ is, and that to the left is not, in $H(a')$, thus contradicting Lemma 2.

Thus cases (2α): $b''\mathfrak{p}a'$, and (2β): $a'\mathfrak{p}b''$, are both impossible. There remains (2γ): $b''\mathfrak{i}a'$.

In Case (3), by a proof similar to that of Case (2), one shows again that $b''\mathfrak{i}a'$.

22:4. LEMMA 4: *If $b\mathfrak{p}a$, $0<r<1$, and $c=ra+(1-r)\,b$, then $b\mathfrak{p}c\mathfrak{p}a$.*

Proof: Since b, c, a, are collinear, it follows from Lemmas 2 and 3 that neither $a\mathfrak{i}c$ nor $b\mathfrak{i}c$ holds. If $a\mathfrak{p}c$ then by II the segment bc has an interior point d such that $a\mathfrak{i}d$. But this is impossible since, by IV, $b\mathfrak{p}a$ would then be false. One shows similarly that $c\mathfrak{p}b$ is impossible. Hence $b\mathfrak{p}c\mathfrak{p}a$.

By Lemmas 2 and 3 the indifference set $J(a')$ containing an interior point a' is a hyperplane, $H(a')$. We shall now prove

22:5. LEMMA 5: *If c is an interior point, $J(c)$ is a hyperplane of dimension $=\nu-1$.*

Proof: Suppose the set $J(c)$ [identical with $H(c)$] has $\nu-\alpha>0$ dimensions, and $\alpha>0$. Then $H(c)$ is determined by α independent linear equations. If $\alpha>1$, we can choose a 2-dimensional plane K through c that is determined by $\nu-2$ independent equations such that, when combined with the α independent equations of $H(c)$, they give ν independent equations determining c; that is, K and $H(c)$ intersect in a unique point c. But if $\alpha=1$, the intersection of $H(c)$ with any 2-dimensional plane is determined by at most $1+\nu-2=\nu-1$ independent equations, and hence has at least one dimension. We shall now show that $\alpha>1$ contradicts our previous lemmas. For if c is the only point common to both $H(c)$ and K, then, by Lemma 2, for no point a in K, distinct from c, is $a\,\mathfrak{i}\,c$. Choose three noncollinear points a^1, a^2, a^3, in K such that c is in the interior of the triangle $a^1a^2a^3$ (see Figure 3), Let $a^1\,\mathfrak{p}\,c$; then $a^2\,\mathfrak{p}\,c$, $a^3\,\mathfrak{p}\,c$; for if (for example) $c\,\mathfrak{p}\,a^2$ held, then by Postulate II, there would be a point d on segment $\overline{a^1a^2}$ such that $d\,\mathfrak{i}\,c$; but this is impossible since the plane K has only one point in common with $H(c)$. Hence either $a^i\,\mathfrak{p}\,c$ $(i=1,2,3)$ or $c\,\mathfrak{p}\,a^i$ $(i=1,2,3)$. The line a^1c intersects the segment $\overline{a^2a^3}$ in b, an internal average of a^2 and a^3. Hence $a^i\,\mathfrak{p}\,c (i=1,2,3)$ implies $b\,\mathfrak{p}\,c$ because both $a^2\,\mathfrak{p}\,c$ and $a^3\,\mathfrak{p}\,c$, and because either $a^2\,\mathfrak{i}\,a^3$ (in which case Lemma 1 applies) or not $a^2\,\mathfrak{i}\,a^3$ (in which case Lemma 4 applies); but by the same Lemma 4, $a^i\,\mathfrak{p}\,c$ $(i=1, 2, 3)$ implies $c\,\mathfrak{p}\,b$ because $a^1\,\mathfrak{p}\,c$. Hence the assumption $a^i\,\mathfrak{p}\,c$ was false. The assumption $c\,\mathfrak{p}\,a^i$ leads (by symmetry) to a similar contradiction; and $a^i\,\mathfrak{i}\,c$ was already ruled out. Hence the assumption $\alpha>1$ was false, and the lemma is proved.

22:6. LEMMA 6: *If a is on the boundary of A, $J(a)$ is a hyperplane of $\leqslant \nu-1$ dimensions.* For, if $J(a)$ contains an interior point a', $J(a)=J(a')=H(a')$ has $\nu-1$ dimensions by Lemma 5. If $J(a)$ contains boundary points only, then $J(a)$ is a hyperplane of $\leqslant \nu-1$ dimensions (facet, edge,...) forming part of the boundary of A.

23. To prove Theorem 1 (Section 2:1 above), it remains to be shown that all the indifference hyperplanes are parallel. This is done by the same reasoning as in 21:2, except that the lines $\overline{aa'}$, $\overline{cc'}$, $\overline{ce}$, have to be regarded as the intersections of the plane of the page with hyperplanes of dimension $\leqslant \nu-1$.

24. THEOREM 2: *If prospects a^1, a^2, a^3,... lie on a straight line in this order, and if $h>i$ and $j>k$, then $a^h\,\mathfrak{i}\,a^i$ implies $a^j\,\mathfrak{i}\,a^k$, and $a^h\,\mathfrak{p}\,a^i$ implies $a^j\,\mathfrak{p}\,a^k$.*[14] This follows immediately from the above lemmas.

25. Since all indifference sets J are parallel hyperplanes (Figure 4 for $\nu=2$), we can write an equation for any $J(a)$. Choose any sure prospect, e.g., $a^{(0)}$, as the origin, and let $d[a; a^{(0)}]$ be its distance from the plane $J(a)$ which contains the point a with the coordinates $a_1,..., a_\nu$. Then

$$(25.1)\qquad d\,[a;a^{(0)}]=\sum_1^\nu k_\mu a_\mu,\ \sum_1^\nu (k_\mu)^2=1\,,$$

where k_μ $(\mu=1,..., \nu)$ are real numbers (direction cosines) characteristic of $J(a)$ but independent of a and of $a^{(0)}$. In particular, if $a^{(\mu)}$ is another sure prospect, its coordinate a^ν_π $(\pi=1,..., \nu)=\delta_{\pi\mu}$, i.e., equals 1 when $\pi=\mu$ and 0 otherwise. Therefore the distance of $J[a^{(\mu)}]$ from $a^{(0)}$, $d[a^{(\mu)}: a^{(0)}]=\sum_{\pi=1}^\nu a_\pi^{(\mu)}k_\pi=\sum_{\pi=1}^\nu \delta_{\pi\mu}k_\pi=k_\mu$. If, in addition, we define

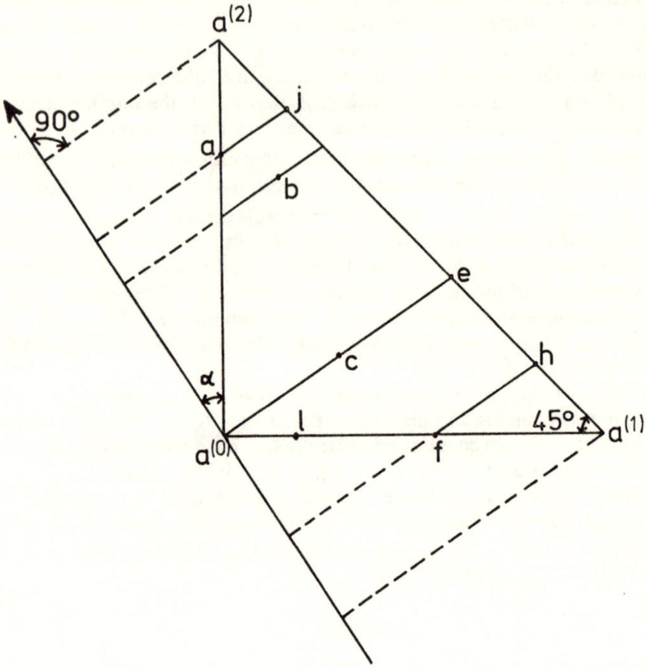

Fig. 4

$k_0 \equiv 0 = d[a^{(0)}; a^{(0)}]$, we have

$$d[a^{(\mu)}; a^{(0)}] = k_\mu, \quad (\mu = 0, \ldots, \nu). \tag{25.2}$$

If the origin is changed from $a^{(0)}$ to $a^{(\mu)}$, the distance of each indifference hyperplane from the origin is changed by the same constant k_μ. We can therefore replace $d[a; a^{(0)}]$ by the shorter symbol $d(a)$ with the understanding that $d(a)$ is determined up to an additive constant which depends on the arbitrary origin $a^{(0)}$. For further brevity, we shall write

$$d[a^{(\mu)}] \equiv d^{(\mu)}, \quad (\mu = 1, \ldots, \nu). \tag{25.3}$$

In this notation, and by (25.2), the equation (25.1) of an indifference plane $J(a)$ becomes

$$(25.4) \qquad d(a) = \sum_{0}^{\nu} a_\mu d^{(\mu)} .$$

26. We shall now show that the distance function $d(a)$ can be used as a utility function, as defined in Section 9 above. For this, we first prove the following lemma.

LEMMA 7: *If* $a \mathfrak{p} b \mathfrak{p} c$, *then either* $d(a) > d(b) > d(c)$ *or* $d(a) < d(b) < d(c)$.
Proof: By Postulate II there exists $b' = ra + (1-r)\,c$, $0 < r < 1$, such that b' is in $J(b)$. For each component of b', $b'_\mu = ra_\mu + (1-r)\,c_\mu$, $\mu = 0, \ldots, \nu$. Hence, by (25.4),

$$d(b) = d(b') = \sum b'_\mu d^{(\mu)} = r \sum a_\mu d^{(\mu)} + \\ + (1-r) \sum c_\mu d^{(\mu)} = rd(a) + (1-r)\, d(c),$$

thus proving the lemma: the plane $J(b)$ lies between the planes $J(a)$ and $J(c)$.

We can always define the positive direction for distances in such a way that the first and not the second alternative of Lemma 7 holds. We then have for any two prospects a, b:

$$(26.1) \qquad d(a) > d(b); \quad d(a) < d(b); \quad d(a) = d(b); \\ \text{according as } a \mathfrak{p} b; \quad b \mathfrak{p} a; \quad a \mathfrak{i} b.$$

Recalling the definitions in Section 9, we can therefore state as proven the following theorem.

THEOREM 3. *If positive direction is defined by* (26.1), *then the distances* $d(a)$, $d(b), \ldots$ *of the planes* $J(a)$, $J(b), \ldots$ *from the origin* $a^{(0)}$ *form a set of utility indices.*

27. Other statements of Theorem 3 are the following:
The distance function $d(a)$ *is a utility function.*
The man maximizes $d(a)$ *over the feasible set* F.
There exist $\nu+1$ *numbers* $k_1, \ldots, k_\nu$, *and* $k_0 = 0$, *such that for any a,b,* $\sum_0^\nu k_\mu a_\mu >$, $<$, *or* $= \sum_0^\nu k_\mu b_\mu$, *according as* $a \mathfrak{p} b$, $b \mathfrak{p} a$, *or* $a \mathfrak{i} b$.
The indifference sets in the space of prospects are parallel planes stacked up in the order of the man's preferences.

28. On the 'indifference map' in Figure 4, the arrow indicates positive

direction from the origin $a^{(0)}$. As always (compare with Figure 1), $\overline{a^{(0)}a^{(1)}} = \overline{a^{(0)}a^{(2)}} = 1$. Further, in this example

$$
\begin{aligned}
(28.1) \quad & a^{(2)}\,\mathfrak{p}\,a\,\mathfrak{p}\,b\,\mathfrak{p}\,a^{(0)}\,\mathfrak{i}\,c\,\mathfrak{p}\,f\,\mathfrak{p}\,a^{(1)};\\
& 0 < \alpha < \pi/2; \quad d^{(2)} = \cos\alpha > d(a) = \overline{aa^{(0)}}\cos\alpha > d(b) >\\
& \quad > d^{(0)} = 0 = d(c) = d(e) > d(f) = -\overline{fa^{(0)}}\sin\alpha =\\
& \quad = d(h) > d^{(1)} = -\sin\alpha, \quad \text{etc.}
\end{aligned}
$$

Note that the scale unit is determined by the fact that for any a, $\sum_0^\nu a_\mu = 1$, while the origin is fixed by choosing $d^{(0)} = 0$.

29. Theorems 1 to 3 are derived from Postulates I, II, III*, and IV on *rational* behavior. They cannot be tested by observation. But we can sketch out the following statements on *actual* behavior which, in principle, can be so tested:

(1) "Faced with a varying set of feasible prospects, Mr. Smith makes decisions which, with a probability p, do not deviate by more than a preassigned distance from the decisions consistent with Theorem 3." For example, with $\nu = 2$, let $a^{(0)}$, $a^{(1)}$, $a^{(2)}$ be the prospects of a sure life income of, respectively, \$2000, \$5000, and \$20000. The varying sets of feasible prospects can consist of various pairs or triplets, etc., of points marked in Figure 4. A set of decisions of Mr. Smith is inconsistent with the four postulates whenever it is inconsistent with relations (28.1), after fixing $d^{(0)} = 0$. A set of decisions indicating that there is no angle α such that $d^{(2)} = \cos\alpha$, $d(f) = -\overline{fa^{(0)}}\sin\alpha = d(h)$, would indicate deviations from rationality as defined by the postulates. The procedure of testing whether Smith is 'tolerably rational', i.e., whether p exceeds a certain limit, is a statistical one; so is the procedure of estimating the parameters of the indifference map (in our example, the angle α). The difficulties are obvious and stem from the economist's inability to make experiments. If Smith is made to answer questions on his decisions when faced with hypothetical sets of feasible prospects, the answers may involve a bias (and not merely a random deviation) when compared with his actual behavior. If, on the other hand, the sets of feasible prospects are those that have actually faced him in his life, they may not yield themselves to convenient simplification; moreover, Smith may have changed his tastes in the course of his life, although they had remained

consistent during each of several shorter periods. Some of these difficulties are obviated, but replaced by others, if the following hypothesis is tested:[15]

(2) "At least a fraction q of the buyers and sellers of real estate, securities, insurance policies, and other assets are tolerably rational (in the sense defined above); and the numbers characterizing their indifference maps (viz., their respective angles α, in the example of Figure 4) have such and such a frequency distribution."

30. The μth sure prospect can be denoted both as $a^{(\mu)}$ and as $x^{(\mu)}$; its utility will be denoted by

$$(30.1) \qquad u^{(\mu)} \equiv u\,[a^{(\mu)}] \equiv u\,[x^{(\mu)}].$$

$x^{(\mu)}$ is a particular value of the random vector x, and $u^{(\mu)}$ is a particular value of the random scalar $u(x)$. The expected value of $u(x)$ given the distribution $a(x)$ can be written[16] as

$$(30.2) \qquad \mathscr{E}u(x) \mid a(x) \equiv \sum_{\mu=0}^{\nu} u\,[x^{(\mu)}]\,a_\mu \equiv \sum_{\mu=0}^{\nu} u^{(\mu)}a_\mu \equiv \mathscr{E}u \mid a;$$

in the last form no dummy variables (x, μ) appear, thus making clear that the quantity in question depends only on the utility function u and the distribution ('prospect') a. The quantity $\mathscr{E}u|a$ can be regarded as the result of an operation which is performed upon the function u and depends on a; or as the result of an operation which is performed upon the prospect a and depends on u. According to the emphasis needed we may call $\mathscr{E}u|a$ the 'expected value of the utility function u', as well as the 'expected utility for a'.

31. In this notation and by Theorem 3, the distance function (25.4) has the following properties: $d(a)$ is a utility function; and $\mathscr{E}d|a=d(a)$. Consequently, $\mathscr{E}d|a$ is a utility function. That is, the man maximizes the expected value of utility function d. In Section 9 above, we have defined U, the class of utility functions. Now define a subclass V of U, consisting of all functions v with the following properties:

(α_1) $\quad \mathscr{E}v|a$ is in U,

(α_2) $\quad \mathscr{E}v|a$ is in V,

and

(α_3) $\mathscr{E}v|a = v(a)$.

Note that property (α_3) would suffice to define V, since (α_3) implies (α_2), and (α_2) implies (α_1). We have just shown that V contains at least one element, viz., the distance function d: it satisfies (α_3). We shall now prove the following theorem.

32. THEOREM 4: *V consists of all linear increasing functions of d.* That is, a function v is in V if and only if there exist two numbers l, m ($m>0$) such that for any a

(β) $v(a) = l + md(a)$.

Proof: Sufficiency: If (β) is true, then by (25.4) and the definitions (30.2),

$$\mathscr{E}v|a = \sum v^{(\mu)}a_\mu = l + m\sum d^{(\mu)}a_\mu = l + md(a) = v(a).$$

Thus (β) implies all three α-properties in Section 31.

Necessity: Suppose (α_1), the weakest of those three properties, is true. Then since both $\mathscr{E}v|a$ and $d(a)$ are in U, there exists a monotone increasing function ϕ, such that

$$(32.1)\qquad \mathscr{E}v|a = \phi\,[d(a)] \equiv \phi d(a)$$

(omitting brackets after ϕ for brevity). Put $a=a^{(\mu)}$. Then, since $\mathscr{E}v|a^{(\mu)} = v^{(\mu)}$, we have, by (32.1), $v^{(\mu)} = \phi d^{(\mu)}$; $\phi d(a) = \mathscr{E}v|a = \sum a_\mu v^{(\mu)} = \sum a_\mu \phi d^{(\mu)}$; thus

$$(32.2)\qquad \begin{cases} \sum a_\mu \phi d^{(\mu)} - 1\cdot\phi d(a) = 0\,; & \\ \sum a_\mu d^{(\mu)} - 1\cdot d(a) = 0 & \text{[by (25.4)];} \\ \sum a_\mu\cdot 1 - 1\cdot 1 = 0 & \text{[by (4.1)].} \end{cases}$$

The three equations (32.2) form a homogeneous linear system identical in $a_0, \ldots, a_\nu, -1$. Hence the rows

$$\begin{matrix} \phi d^{(0)}, \ldots, \phi d^{(\nu)}, \phi d(a) \\ d^{(0)}, \ldots, \phi d^{(\nu)}, \phi d(a) \\ 1, \ldots, 1, 1 \end{matrix}$$

are linearly dependent. Therefore ϕ is a linear function,

$$\phi d(a) = l + md(a)\,;$$

and $m>0$ since ϕ was already stated to be an increasing function. Thus (α_1) implies (β); and since (β) was shown (in the sufficiency proof) to imply (α_2) and (α_3), the proof is complete.

33. Thus V consists of all increasing linear functions of the probabilities $a_0, \ldots, a_\nu$:

$$(33.1) \qquad v(a) = l + m \sum a_\mu d^{(\mu)}.$$

We shall call the function $v(a)$ a *linear utility function* and the scalar $v(a)$ a *linear utility index* of prospect a. If Figure 4 represents an indifference map, and the utility index is measured perpendicularly to the plane of the page, then any plane whose intersection with the plane of the page is parallel would represent some element of V, or its negative.

The simplest linear utility function is the distance function $d(A)$ itself. In this case $l=0$, $m=1$. The distance function is a linear utility function unique up to an additive constant that depends on the choice of the origin such as $a^{(0)}$.

34. Immediately from (33.1) we obtain the well-known property of linear functions summarized in

THEOREM 5: *Let prospect a be a linear combination of ρ prospects,* $b^1, \ldots, b^\rho$: $a = \sum_1^\varrho r_\pi b^\pi$. *If v is a linear utility function, then and only then*

$$(34.1) \qquad v(a) = \sum_1^\varrho r_\pi v(b^\pi).$$

In particular, if a is an average, $a = r_1 b^1 + r_2 b^2$, $r_1 + r_2 = 1$,

$$(34.2) \qquad v(a) = r_1 v(b^1) + r_2 v(b^2)$$

and

$$(34.3) \qquad \frac{v(b^1) - v(a)}{v(a) - v(b^2)} = \frac{r_2}{r_1}.$$

Moreover, since $a = \sum_0^\nu a_\mu a^{(\mu)}$, we obtain again the property (α_3) in (31):

$$(34.4) \qquad v(a) = \sum_0^\nu a_\mu v^{(\mu)} = \mathscr{E} v \mid a \equiv \mathscr{E} v(x) \mid a(x).$$

35. On the other hand, the following property is not exclusive to linear utility functions: *If* v_1 *and* v_2 *are two linear utility functions, then there exist two numbers l, m* ($m>0$) *such that for any prospect a*,

$$(35.1) \qquad v_2(a) = l + mv_1(a).$$

That is, v_1 and v_2 are (increasing) linear transforms of each other; or, in other formulations, the function v is unique up to a linear transformation or up to two linear coefficients. This property follows from (33.1) but is obviously possessed also by any class W consisting of utility functions w such that for any a

$$(35.2) \qquad w(a) = l + m\phi_w d(a),$$

where $m>0$, and ϕ_w is a monotone increasing function, *not necessarily linear*; for example, ϕ_w may be the cubic function.

36. Another property which follows from (33.1) yet is possessed by certain classes of nonlinear utility functions is this: *If* v_1 *and* v_2 *are two linear utility functions, then*

$$(36.1) \qquad v_2(a) - v_2(b) = m[v_1(a) - v_1(b)],$$

where m is a positive constant independent of a, b. That is, the difference between the linear utilities of two prospects is unique up to a proportionality factor. This property follows from the property (35.1), and is therefore also shared by a class of nonlinear utility functions such as W defined in (35.2).

VI. MEASURABILITY AND MANAGEABILITY

37. The question has been often asked whether utility is 'measurable in the sense in which temperature is'.[17] Because temperature readings are nothing but distances (or angles or volumes depending on the design of the thermometer), and in order to avoid discussing the relation between the absolute and other scales of temperature, I prefer comparison with altitudes. The altitude of a point on the earth's surface is unique up to two constants (one positive) depending on the origin, such as the sea level, and the unit, such as the meter. The linear utility index of a prospect is also unique up to two constants (one positive), l and m in (33.1). In

this sense, altitudes expressed in meters, and linear utility indices, are equally strictly measurable.

38. This property they share, however, with altitudes expressed in cubes of their meter measurements, and with utility indices obtained from linear ones by substituting, say, $[d(a)]^3$ for $d(a)$; see Section 35. The property of being unique up to two constants is weaker than certain other properties of linear utility functions, for example, the property (34.4) of expected values of linear utility indices.

Numbers of meters, and not cubes of those numbers, are used in measuring altitudes because this simplifies certain important operations. One derives the altitude of point Y in meters from the altitude of point Z in meters and from the number of meters contained in the upward horizontal projection of the line connecting the two points, by forming an algebraic sum of the latter two numbers. If cubes of those numbers were used instead, one would have to cube the sum of two cube roots, a more complicated operation.

Money amounts are unique up to one positive proportionality factor depending on the currency unit. Their logarithms are also determined up to a single constant, an additive one. For additive operations, dollars are more manageable than logarithms. But the latter may be preferable when, as in constructing graphs of hyperinflation, one is interested in ratios; just as (I understand) it is convenient to use logarithms of time in discussing radioactive disintegration.

39. Thus, linear utility indices of prospects share with altitudes expressed in units of length not only the particular kind of measurability (viz., up to two constants, one positive) but also the 'manageability' with respect to certain, viz., linear, operations. In the case of utility indices of prospects, a particularly important kind of linear operations is the forming of averages as in (34.2), and especially the forming of expected values as in (34.4). For no other but linear utility indices is it true that the utility of a distribution (a prospect) is equal to the expected value of utilities of sure prospects, computed on the basis of that distribution.[18]

40. In Part V implications were derived from our four postulates on rational behavior. These results can be stated in two equivalent forms:

(α) The indifference surfaces in prospect space are linear and parallel (Theorem 1).

(β) There exist linear utility functions of prospects, with certain convenient properties (Theorems 3–5).

We have just shown that (α), (β) – and therefore our four postulates– are sufficient to derive measurable and manageable (in the defined sense) utility functions. To see whether these postulates are also necessary, we shall weaken (α) and study the implications. Suppose then that the indifference sets were not parallel planes [cf. (25.1)],

$$(40.1) \quad \sum_0^\nu k_\mu a_\mu = d(a), \quad k_0 = 0,$$

but would satisfy, instead, a more general equation

$$(40.2) \quad \sum_0^r k_\mu \psi(a_\mu) = d_\psi(a), \quad k_0 = 0, \quad k_\mu \geqslant 0, \quad (\mu = 1, \ldots, \nu),$$

where $d_\psi(a)$ is the utility index (a 'generalized distance') of $J(a)$, and ψ is a monotone increasing function such that $\psi(0)=0$, $\psi(1)=1$. [For example, if $\psi(z)=z^2$, then indifference surfaces are concentric ellipsoids.] Equation (40.2) is consistent with our postulates, except Postulate IV [unless $\psi(z)=z$]. Statements analogous to those in Section 25 and Section 26 would hold. Putting $a=a^{(\mu)}$, (40.2) becomes

$$(40.3) \quad k_\mu = d_\psi [a^{(\mu)}] \equiv d_\psi^{(\mu)},$$

say; substituting in (40.2), we find that the set $J(a)$ is defined by the utility index

$$(40.4) \quad d_\psi(a) = \sum_0^\nu \psi(a_\mu)\, d_\psi^{(\mu)}.$$

Define the operator $\mathscr{E}_\psi$ by

$$(40.5) \quad \mathscr{E}_\psi u \mid a \equiv \mathscr{E}_\psi u(x) \mid a(x) \equiv \sum_0^\nu \psi(a_\mu)\, u[a^{(\mu)}];$$

this is a generalization of the operator $\mathscr{E}$, each probability a_μ being replaced by its transform $\psi(a_\mu)$. Then, by (40.4),

$$(40.6) \quad d_\psi(a) = \mathscr{E}_\psi d_\psi \mid a.$$

Now, in analogy to the class V in Section 31, define a class V_ψ consisting of all utility functions v_ψ such that, for any a, $v_\psi(a) = \mathscr{E}_\psi v_\psi \mid a$. Then V_ψ consists of all products of the 'generalized distance' with arbitrary (and positive) constants, m. For, if $v_\psi = md_\psi$, the definition (40.5), with v_ψ substituted for u, implies $\mathscr{E}_\psi v_\psi \mid a = v_\psi(a)$. Conversely, if v_ψ is in V_ψ, and if ϕ is an unknown monotone function such that $\phi d(a) \equiv \phi\,[d(a)] = \mathscr{E}_\psi v_\psi a$, we obtain a system analogous to (32.2) but with only two instead of three equations (since the transforms of probabilities need not add up to unity):

$$\text{(40.7)} \qquad \begin{aligned} \sum_\mu \psi(a_\mu)\, \phi d_\psi^{(\mu)} &= \phi d_\psi(a), \\ \sum_\mu \psi(a_\mu)\, d_\psi^{(\mu)} &= d_\psi(a). \end{aligned}$$

We see that if Postulate IV were replaced in such a way as to lead to (40.2) instead of (40.1), it would be possible to define a utility function $v_\psi(a)$ unique up to a proportionality factor. Thus $v_\psi(a)$ is even more strictly 'measurable' than the function $v(a)$ derived with the aid of Postulate IV. In this sense, the virtue of that postulate does not consist in the 'measurability' of the function $v(a)$. Rather, it consists in the 'manageability' of $v(a)$, in the sense of property (34.4). In the case of the utility function $v(a)$ the expected value $\mathscr{E}v \mid a \equiv \sum v^{(\mu)} a_\mu$ is maximized; while in the case of the function $v_\psi(a)$, not the expected value, but a more complicated, usually nonlinear, expression $\mathscr{E}_\psi v_\psi \mid a \equiv \sum_\mu v_\psi^{(\mu)} \psi(a_\mu)$ is maximized.

41. This opens the question (to be taken up again in Part VIII) of still further, or of alternative, generalizations of (40.1) and, consequently, of the appropriate generalization of underlying postulates. Each such generalization would possibly define a nonlinear analogon – say $\mathscr{E}_*$ – of the operation $\mathscr{E}$ and an analogon – say V_* – of the linear subclass V of utility functions. V_* may be empty or consist of one element only, or of two or more functions which are, possibly nonlinear, transforms ϕ_* of each other. The possible nonlinearity of the operations $\mathscr{E}_*$ and ϕ_* that replace the operations $\mathscr{E}$ and ϕ of Section 30 will render the utility functions of prospects less 'manageable'. One might call them less 'measurable' if ϕ_* involved more parameters than ϕ; but in Section 40 we just had a case where the opposite was true.

VII. COMPARISON WITH VON NEUMANN AND MORGENSTERN

42. The word prospect is occasionally used in the *Theory of Games and Economic Behavior* (e.g., on top of page 18) essentially in the same sense as in this paper (see also Hicks [2]). More often the authors speak of a 'combination of events'. We call a prospect the probability distribution of the time sequences of all combinations of commodities (or, in fact, of any kinds of events), while von Neumann and Morgenstern take examples involving two or three commodities at one time point only. Since our time sequences are by necessity mutually exclusive, no confusion can arise in our formulations as to the effect of complementarity upon the choices. If proper wording is used, this is not an essential difference.

43. *Verbal Presentation: Utility Differences*

In the verbal presentation (Section 3.3) of the *Theory of Games*, the authors use as a behavior postulate the equivalent of our (34.3). In the present paper, on the other hand, (34.3) was derived from four postulates on rational behavior. Von Neumann and Morgenstern (in their verbal presentation) do not have Postulate IV but seem to have what amounts to Postulates I and II.

Our decision to introduce Postulate IV, rather than to start with (34.3) as a behavior postulate, is dictated by the desire to avoid behavior postulates which are neither immediately plausible nor show themselves as approximated by easily observable action. Postulates I and III* state essentially that man chooses between prospects; and we see men actually making choices – determining the balance sheet by buying or selling, or by abstaining from buying and selling, assets. Postulate II excludes discontinuities. Postulate IV is also a very weak (i.e., very plausible) one; it merely rules out behavior of a kind which most people would call absurd. The statement (34.3), on the other hand, is neither immediately plausible nor is it amenable to easy observation. True, a person when interviewed may make comparisons between two utility differences, but the comparison does not show itself in any choice except in the choice to answer a certain question in a certain way. However, H. Chernoff pointed out that such a check of utility comparison by an actual choice could be made in the following situation. According to L. J. Savage, the rational strategy in a one-person game under complete ignorance of circumstances might be defined as one that results in minimaxing 'regret', i.e., the difference between the utility actually realized and the utility that would have been realized if all circumstances were known. (See Marschak [6a] where this postulate was used.) That is, the strategy must be chosen so that even under circumstances which yield for this strategy a regret not smaller than under any other circumstances, this regret is not larger than for any other strategy.[19] Thus, a rational man playing the one-person game under ignorance of future circumstances has to base his choices on comparing differences between utilities.

44. *Mathematical Presentation: The Chain of Implications*

In their mathematical presentation, the authors of the *Theory of Games* do not actually make use of a behavior postulate on utility differences.[20] The behavior postulates used are set up in their Section 3.6, and we shall refer to them presently. An extensive appendix published in the second edition of the book shows that these postulates result in propositions (3:1:a) and (3:1:b) of the text (Section 3.5). The second of these implies, and is implied by, the linearity of what we called the utility functions of prospects, and appears thus equivalent to our Theorems 1–5. From this, the 'measurability' of utility is derived in (3:5:b) and (3:6) of the *Theory of Games*, in the sense that utility is unique up to a linear transformation: a property weaker than the preceding one, as shown in this paper (Sections 35–41 above).

44.1. *The axioms.*

The difference between the presentation in this paper and in the *Theory of Games* thus boils down to the difference between our Postulates I–IV, and the group of axioms (3:A), (3:B), (3:C), of the *Theory of Games*.[21] The 'entities' u, v, of the *Theory of Games* correspond to the various indifference sets – say J, J', in the present paper. The symbol $>$ defined in the authors' (3:A) is related to our $\mathfrak{p}$ as follows: if J contains a and J' contains a', and J, J' are distinct, we say $a \mathfrak{p} a'$ or $a' \mathfrak{p} a$; Von Neumann and Morgenstern say (replacing J, J' by u, v) $u>v$ or $v>u$. Moreover, $u=v$ corresponds to $J=J'$. As to the symbol $+$, and the operation $\alpha u+(1-\alpha)\, v=w$, the authors define it implicitly by the axioms (except that α is a real scalar, $0<\alpha<1$, identical with our r); while we use the symbol $+$ and the operation $ra+(1-r)a'$ in their usual meaning (addition, multiplication) as applied to the real vectors a, a'

and the scalar r. However, select element a from J, and a' from J'. Then the following operation on indifference sets can be defined: $rJ+(1-r)J'$ means $J[ra+(1+r)a']$. With this interpretation Axioms (3:A) and (3:B) of the *Theory of Games* will follow (with u, v, α replacing J, J', r) if the indifference sets are parallel hyperplanes, i.e., if our Postulates I, II, III*, and IV are fulfilled. In particular, the axiom (3:C:b) can be rendered as follows: "Let $0<r<1$, $0<q<1$; let a, b, c, e be prospects such that $b=ra+(1-r)e$, $c=qb+(1-q)e$. Then $c\,\mathfrak{i}\,[qra+(1-qr)e]$." This 'double mixing' is indeed implied in Postulate IV, as a succession of two single mixings discussed there.

I hesitate to say which (if any) is the stronger system of axioms. I find it easier to translate Postulate IV immediately into the language of observable decisions – see the examples in Section 19 above – than to do so with von Neumann and Morgenstern's (3:C:b), whether stated as it is in terms of entities not susceptible to ordinary arithmetical operations, or restated in the form I have just suggested. To use a phrase of von Neumann and Morgenstern, the approach used here seems to be more 'transparent', and its postulates have a more 'immediate intuitive meaning by which [their] appropriateness may be judged directly'.

44.2. *The proofs.* As already mentioned in Section 44, a part of the route, the part after establishing the proposition on the linearity of (certain) utility functions, is common to both presentations. But the previous part of the route, between the axioms and that proposition, is different. The present author does not claim to improve upon the minutiousness and rigor of the appendix to the second edition of the *Theory of Games*. The present paper consists essentially in applying the technique of indifference curves – as stated in our Postulates I –III– to prospects which are not sure. When Postulate IV is added, this technique yields in a simple way the Neumannian results. These are also obtained if III is replaced by a weaker Postulate III* (or III′).

VIII. LOVE OF DANGER INCOMPATIBLE WITH THE FOUR POSTULATES

45. THEOREM 6: *If* $a\,\mathfrak{p}\,b$ *and* $c=ra+(1-r)b$, *then* $a\,\mathfrak{p}\,c$ *for* $r>1$, $c\,\mathfrak{p}\,a$ *for* $r<1$. (That is, a is preferred to every point between a and b and to

every point on the prolongation of the segment *ab* beyond *b*; and every point on the prolongation of that segment beyond *a* is preferred to *a*.) This property of prospects follows directly from Theorems 2 or 4. In Figure 4, take any three points on a straight line not parallel to the indifference lines (planes)! The property may be called the monotonicity of the utility function of prospects $u(a)$, on the space A. It is different from the monotonicity assumption sometimes made for the utility function of commodities – say, $w(x)$ on the space X. This assumption is stated formally as follows (cf. Arrow [1]):

It is always possible to define final goods $x_1, \ldots, x_\varepsilon$ in such a way that if $x^{(\alpha)} \equiv (x^{(\alpha)}{}_1, \ldots, x_\varepsilon{}^{(\alpha)})$ and $x^{(\beta)} \equiv (x_1{}^{(\beta)}, \ldots, x_\varepsilon{}^{(\beta)})$ and if $x_\gamma{}^{(\alpha)} \geqslant x_\gamma{}^{(\beta)}$ for all γ and $x_\delta{}^{(\alpha)} > x_\delta{}^{(\beta)}$ for some $\delta (\gamma, \delta = 1, \ldots, \varepsilon)$, then $x^{(\alpha)} \mathfrak{p}\, x^{(\beta)}$.

That is, the addition of any final 'good' to (or subtraction of any final 'bad' from) a bundle of commodities (a history, a sure prospect) increases the utility of the bundle. More precisely, this assumption is taken to be valid not over the whole space X but only over a so-called effective region of it,[22] outside of this region the man is saturated with one or more of the 'goods', so that 'goods' become 'bad' or at least indifferent.

Obviously this form of monotonicity cannot apply to the prospect space A, because of restriction (4.1): it is impossible to increase the probability of one of the histories, say, the probability a_μ of $x^{(\mu)}$, without decreasing the probability of at least one of the other histories. Also, it would be impossible to classify each history – possibly a whole course of life – as either 'good' or 'bad' in the way we classify single final commodities such as bread and leisure or labor and sickness. The monotonicity assumption for commodities says: "The more of a good thing the better. If opportunities are unlimited, increase the quantity of every good thing until it ceases to be a good thing." The monotonicity assumption for prospects says: "If one alternative is better than another, increase the probability of the former at the expense of the latter.[23] If opportunities are unlimited, choose the prospect that promises the best history with 100% probability": the corner $a^{(2)}$ in Figure 4.

The monotonicity assumption for commodities is usually stated as an independent postulate or as the definition of the effective region. The monotonicity assumption for prospects (Theorem 6) follows from Postulates I, II, III (or III* or III′), and IV.

46. If our four postulates define rational behavior, the following actual behavior is not rational: many men, not at all bent on suicide, are enthusiastic mountain climbers and are elated, not (or not only) by exercise and scenery but by the very danger, in the following sense. Suppose the probability of fatal accident is 5%. The climber may prefer a survival chance of 95% to one of, say, 80% *but also* to one of 100%! The utility index of prospects reaches in this case its maximum at a point which is not a corner of domain A. (If in Figure 4, $a^{(0)}$ and $a^{(2)}$ are two ways of continuing to live, and $a^{(1)}$ is death, the highest utility will be not at $a^{(0)}$ or $a^{(2)}$ or a but, say, at j or l or b.)

47. Such behavior contradicts the monotonicity Theorem 6, and therefore at least one of our postulates. It is, therefore, in general inconsistent with the existence of linear utility functions for prospects. It also follows that the lover of danger does not, in general, maximize the expected value of the utility index. Not for him the linear utility functions of prospects, and the measurable and 'manageable' (Part VI) utility indices. Love of danger in this sense may very well be present also in what is usually considered economic decisions. The danger of loss including ruin, though probably shunned in the conservative code or cant of business, has quite possibly added to the zest and desirability of many an historically important venture, in the career of the leaders of mercenary armies, in the financing of great geographic discoveries or, closer to our time, in the financing of inventions and theater plays, and in stock and commodity speculation.

48. The 'love of danger' defined as nonmonotonicity of the utility function for prospects is to be carefully distinguished from the phenomenon alluded to in Part III: whether high variance of random income (or of the random quantity of any commodity) is or is not desirable depends on whether the marginal utility of mean income (or commodity) happens to be increasing rather than decreasing. Neither a positive nor a negative sign of the 'risk-discount' contradicts the monotonicity of the utility function for prospects (nor, of course, the monotonicity assumption for goods).[24]

The statement 'a man may desire to gamble' has thus two meanings.

If it means that the sign of the risk-discount is indefinite, the statement is consistent with rational behavior as defined by the four postulates. (In fact, it is well explained by implications from these very postulates.) If it means, however, that the man 'loves danger' so that his utility function of prospects is not monotonic along a straight line in space A, drawn at an angle to the indifference planes, then the statement is not consistent with the four postulates. Should one revise the postulates of rational choice in order to be able to include love of danger under rational behavior, then it would probably become impossible to attain manageable utility indices in the sense of Part VI. As indicated in Section 41, the operation of maximizing expected value would have to be replaced by a more general or more unwieldy one. The alternative is to stamp love of danger as nonrational, on a par with, say, the behavior of a man who prefers a to b and b to c and yet prefers c to a (denial of transitivity Postulate I); or a man to whom a car and a $1000 bill are equivalent and who yet prefers one of these things to a lottery ticket promising with certainty that either the one or the other thing will be obtained (denial of Postulate IV_1).

49. At this point we can only hint at what is probably the most important virtue of the advice to maximize expected utility and, hence, of the behavior postulates implied in this advice. We conjecture that, for a large class of distribution functions and utility functions, the following proposition is true: if every action is chosen in such a way as to maximize the expected utility, then, as the number of such actions is increased, the probability that the achieved utility differs from the maximum achievable utility by an arbitrarily small number, approaches unity. If this proposition is true, and if the logic of rational behavior is used as a tool of advice (see Section 1 above), it is best to exclude love of danger as irrational. If, on the other hand, rational behavior is used as an approximation hypothesis for the study of actual behavior, then again, love of danger may be considered as a departure from rationality. It is then a matter of empirical psychology and is important to economics in the same way in which inconsistency (intransitivity) of preferences, inability to measure, to imagine, to remember, are important. We treat it in the same way that we treat the fact that people make mistakes of arithmetic and infringe upon the rules of conventional logic.

NOTES

* Based on a Cowles Commission Discussion Paper, Economics No. 226 (hectographed), July, 1948, and a paper presented at the Madison Meeting of the Econometric Society, September, 1948, Marschak [4].

Acknowledgements are due to various present and former members of the Cowles Commission staff, especially Kenneth J. Arrow, Herman Chernoff, Nathan J. Divinsky, Clifford Hildreth, and Herman Rubin; to Leonard J. Savage, The University of Chicago and to Abraham Wald, Columbia University.

1 Uncertainty in Knight's [1] sense is presumably identical with incomplete information See also Marschak [5]; and Hart [1, 2].

2 The case of a possibly infinite ν has been treated by Rubin [1] with results substantially unchanged. The choice between ν finite or infinite is one of mathematical elegance rather than realism sugar is retailed by the pound, interests accrue daily, and horizons are limited.

3 We use letters $x, a, b, c, \ldots$, with or without superscripts for vectors, and $a_1, \ldots, a_\mu, \ldots, a_\nu$, for components of a. The letters $q, r, \ldots$, denote scalars. A line connecting two points is denoted thus: $\overline{ab}$. Capital letters A, F, J, U, V, X, are used for sets or classes

4 A more symmetrical but less familiar presentation would measure a_0, a_1, a_2 as the distances of a point a from each of the sides of an equilateral triangle.

5 Such propositions were discussed by Frisch [1, 2], Wold [1], Allen [2], Lange [1, 2], Samuelson [1], Arrow [2], and others.

6 Fisher [1], Appendix to Chapter XVI, p. 10. Pigou [1], Appendix 1. Hicks [1, 2]. Makower and Marschak [1]. Marschak [1, 2, 3]. This list is incomplete. See also note 9.

7 Tintner [1, 2, 3]; see also Hurwicz [1].

8 Marschak [7].

9 As a rival to the mean, the mode was suggested by Lange [3], As a measure of riskiness the standard deviation was suggested by I. Fisher [1] as early as 1906. This is in line with the actuarial theory of an individual insurance policy; Cramér [1], Part II. Another important parameter is the probability that a certain variable (cash reserve, annual profit, etc.) fall below a constant, for example, below zero. This occurs in the theory of the total risk of an insurance company: Cramér [1], Part III. According to a verbal communication of H. Somers, this may also be the meaning of a suggestion made by Fellner [1]. Unlike those of Cramér, the suggestions of Lange, Fellner, and other economists often intend to describe actual rather than advisable behavior (see Section 1, above).

10 See Marshall [1], Menger [1], Friedman and Savage [1], Marschak [4,7].

11 Rubin [1] has used Postulate III′ instead of III or III*. His proof applies to ν finite or infinite.

12 Superscripts indicate sure prospects only if in parentheses: $a^{(1)}$ not a^1; see Section V.

13 We shall denote interior points by single, boundary points by double, primes through Sections 22:1–22:4.

14 We shall encounter this theorem in Part VIII when discussing the 'monotonicity of utility functions of prospects'.

15 See in particular Friedman and Savage [1], Section 6; Vickrey [1]; and Törnqvist [1].

16 Henceforth all summations over μ will be from 0 through ν.

17 Allen [2], Lange [1], von Neumann and Morgenstern [1].

18 Compare Arrow [2], Chapter II, Section 1.

19 Contrast this with the two-person zero-sum game. There the rational player obtains the minimax utility, not the minimax difference between two utilities. (Von Neumann and Morgenstern [1], Sections 3–15.)
20 For sure prospects, R. Frisch [1] derived utility increments measurable up to a proportionality factor, by introducing postulates on the individual's choice between small displacements occurring in two different points of the commodity space.
21 We reprint these axioms from Section 3.6.1 (p. 26) of the *Theory of Games*; "*3.6.1*.., consider a system U of entities $u, v, w, \ldots$. In U a *relation* is given, $u > v$, and for any number α, $(0 < \alpha < 1)$, an *operation*

$$\alpha u + (1 - \alpha) v = w.$$

These concepts satisfy the following axioms:
(3:A) *$u > v$ is a complete ordering of U.*
This means: Write $u < v$ when $v > u$. Then:
(3:A:a) For any two u, v one and only one of the three following relations holds:

$$u = v,\ u > v,\ u < v.$$

(3:A:b) $u > v, v > w$ imply $u > w$.
(3:B) *Ordering and combining.*
(3:B:a) $u < v$ implies that $u < \alpha u + (1 - \alpha) v$.
(3:B:b) $u > v$ implies that $u > \alpha u + (1 - \alpha) v$.
(3:B:c) $u < w < v$ implies the existence of an α with

$$\alpha u + (1 - \alpha) v < w.$$

(3:B:d) $u > w > v$ implies the existence of an α with

$$\alpha u + (1 - \alpha) v > w.$$

(3:C) *Algebra of combining.*
(3:C:a) $\alpha u + (1 - \alpha) v = (1 - \alpha) v + \alpha u.$
(3:C:b) $\alpha[\beta u + (1 - \beta) v] + (1 - \alpha) v = \gamma u + (1 - \gamma) v$
where $\gamma = \alpha\beta$."
On what follows, I had the privilege of consulting Abraham Wald.
22 Allen [1], H. Wold [1].
23 This verbal proposition is easiest to visualize in the special case when the alternatives considered are sure prospects. Theorem 6 is more general since it holds for all prospects.
24 To show this, expand $\mathscr{E}u(x)$ about the mean of x, where x = income.

BIBLIOGRAPHY

Allen, R. G. D. [1] 'The Nature of Indifference Curves', *Review of Economic Studies* 1 (February, 1934) 110–121; [2] 'Note on the Determination of the Utility Function', *Review of Economic Studies* **2** (February, 1935) 155–158.

Arrow, K. J. [1] 'The Determination of Many-Commodity Preference Scales by Two-Commodity Comparisons', *Cowles Commission Discussion Paper* (hectographed), and to be published; [2] *Social Choice and Individual Values*, Cowles Commission Monograph No. 12, New York: John Wiley and Sons, forthcoming.

Cramér, H. [1] 'On the Mathematical Theory of Risk', *Försäkringsaktiebolaget Skandias Festkrift*, Centraltryckeriet, Stockholm, 1930, pp. 7–84.

Fellner, W. [1] *Monetary Policies and Full Employment*, University of California Press, Berkeley and Los Angeles, 1946, pp. 152–167.

Fisher, I. [1] *The Nature of Capital and Income*, The Macmillan Co., New York and London, 1906, 427 pp.; [2] *The Theory of Interest as Determined by Impatience to*

Spend Income and Opportunity to Invest It, The Macmillan Co., New York, 1930, 550 pp.

Friedman, M. and Savage, L. J. [1] 'The Utility Analysis of Choices Involving Risk', *Journal of Political Economy* **56** (August, 1948) 279–304.

Frisch, R. [1] 'Sur un problème d'économie pure', *Norsk Matematisk Forenings Skrifter*, Series 1, No. 16, 1926, pp. 1–40; [2] 'General Choice Field Theory', *Report of Third Annual Research Conference on Economics and Statistics, Colorado Springs*, Cowles Commission for Research in Economics, 1937, pp. 64–69.

Hart, A. G. [1] 'Anticipations, Uncertainty, and Dynamic Planning', *Journal of Business* **13** (October, 1940) (*Studies in Business Administration* **11**, No. 1, 98 pp.); [2] 'Risk, Uncertainty and the Unprofitability of Compounding Probabilities', *Studies in Mathematical Economics and Econometrics, in Memory of Henry Schultz* (ed. by O. Lange, F. McIntyre, T. O. Yntema), The University of Chicago Press, Chicago, 1942, pp. 110–118.

Hicks, J. R. [1] 'The Theory of Uncertainty and Profit', *Economica* (May, 1931), 170–189; [2] 'Application of Mathematical Methods to the Theory of Risk' (abstract), *Econometrica* **2** (April, 1934) 194–195; [3] 'A Suggestion for Simplifying the Theory of Money', *Economica*, New Series, Vol. 2 (February, 1935) 1–19.

Hurwicz, L. [1] 'Theory of Firm and of Investment', *Econometrica* **14** (April, 1946) 109–136; especially pp. 131–135.

Knight, F. H. [1] *Risk, Uncertainty, and Profit*, Houghton Mifflin Co., Boston and New York, 1921, 381 pp.

Koopmans, T. C. [1] 'Utility Analysis of Decisions Affecting Future Well-Being' (abstract), *Econometrica* **18** (April, 1950) 174–175.

Lange, O. [1] 'The Determinateness of the Utility Function', *Review of Economic Studies* **1** (June, 1934) 218–225; [2] *Review of Economic Studies* **2** (October, 1934) 75–77; [3] *Price Flexibility and Unemployment*, Cowles Commission Monograph No. 8, Principia Press, Bloomington, Ind., 1944, Chapter VI.

Makower, H. and Marschak, J. [1] 'Assets, Prices and Monetary Theory', *Economica*, New Series, **5** 1938) 261–268.

Marschak, J. [1] 'On Investment' (hectographed and privately circulated), 1935; [2] 'Utilities and Probabilities in Human Choice', *Report of Third Annual Research Conference on Economics and Statistics, Colorado Springs*, Cowles Commission for Research in Economics, 1937, pp. 79–82; [3] 'Money and the Theory of Assets', *Selected Essays*, 33; [4] 'Measurable Utility and the Theory of Assets' (abstract), *Econometrica* **17** (January, 1949) 63–64; [5] 'Von Neumann's and Morgenstern's New Approach to Static Economics', *Journal of Political Economy* **54** (April, 1946) 97–115; [6] 'The Role of Liquidity under Complete and Incomplete Information', *Selected Essays*, 39; [7] 'Optimal Investment of a Firm' (abstract), *Econometrica* **18** (April, 1950) 176–177.

Marshall, A [1] *Principles of Economics*, Macmillan and Co., London, 1920, Mathematical Appendix, Note IX.

Menger, K. [1] 'Das Unsicherheitsmoment in der Wertlehre', *Zeitschrift für Nationalökonomie* **5** (1934) 459–485.

Neumann, J. von and Morgenstern, O. [1] *Theory of Games and Economic Behavior*, Second Edition, Princeton University Press, Princeton, 1947, 641 pp.

Neymann, J. and Pearson, E. S. [1] 'Contributions to the Theory of Testing Statistical Hypotheses', *Statistical Research Memoirs* **1** (June, 1936).

Pareto, V. [1] *Manuel d'Economie Politique*, Second Edition, Giard, Paris, pp. 572–578.

Pigou, A. C. [1] *The Economics of Welfare*, Macmillan and Co., London, 1920, 176 pp.

Rubin, H. [1] 'An Axiom System for Measurable Utility' (unpublished).

Samuelson, P. A. [1] 'The Numerical Representation of Ordered Classifications and the Concept of Utility', *Review of Economic Studies* **6** (October, 1938) 65–70.

Tintner, G. [1] 'The Theory of Choice Under Subjective Risk and Uncertainty', *Econometrica* **9** (July–October, 1941) 298–304; [2] 'The Pure Theory of Production under Technological Risk and Uncertainty', *Econometrica* **9** (July–October, 1941) 305–312; [3] 'A Contribution to the Nonstatic Theory of Production', *Studies in Mathematical Economics and Econometrics, in Memory of Henry of Henry Schultz* (ed. by O. Lange, F. McIntyre, T. O. Yntema) The University of Chicago Press, Chicago, 1942, pp. 92–109.

Törnqvist, L. [1] 'On the Economic Theory of Lottery Gambles', *Skandinavisk Aktuarietidskrift* **28**, Nos. 3–4 (1945) 228–246.

Vickrey, W. [1] 'Measuring Marginal Utility by Reactions to Risk', *Econometrica* **13** (October, 1945) 319–333.

Wald, A. [1] 'Statistical Decision Functions Which Minimize the Maximum Risk, *Annals of Mathematics* **46** (April, 1945) 265–280; [2] 'Statistical Decision Functions', *Annals of Mathematical Statistics* (June, 1949) 165–205.

Wold, H. [1] 'A Synthesis of Pure Demand Analysis, Part II', *Skandinavisk Aktuarietidskrift* **26** (1943) 220–263.

2

WHY 'SHOULD' STATISTICIANS AND BUSINESSMEN MAXIMIZE 'MORAL EXPECTATION'?

(1951)

1. Introduction

1.1. The word 'should' in the title of this paper has the same meaning as in the following sentences: "In building a house, why should one act on the assumption that the floor area of a room is the product and not the sum of its length and width?"; "If all *A* are *B* and all *B* are *C*, why should one avoid acting as if all *C* were *A*?" People may often act contrary to these precepts or norms but then we say that they do not act reasonably. To discuss a set of norms of reasonable behavior (or possibly two or more such sets, each set being consistent internally but possibly inconsistent with other sets) is a problem in logic, not in psychology. It is a normative, not a descriptive, problem.

1.2. The phrase 'moral expectation' stems from the early students of probability who applied probabilities in their study of reasonable behavior of players in games of chance. Let the 'prospect' P, that is, the probability distribution $P(X)$ of a random 'outcome' X, depend upon a man's decision ('strategy') S:

$$(1.2{:}1) \quad P = P(X) = P(X; S).$$

Let the set $\mathscr{X}$ of all possible outcomes X be completely ordered by a relation $\mathfrak{g}$ ('read: as good as or better than'). Define a scalar function $u(X)$ on the set $\mathscr{X}$ as follows: for any pair, X_1 and X_2, in $\mathscr{X}$,

$$(1.2{:}2) \quad u(X_1) \geqq u(X_2) \quad \text{if} \quad X_1 \,\mathfrak{g}\, X_2 .$$

Then $u(X)$ is called the utility of X. It is a random variable whose distribution depends on the distribution P and hence on the strategy S. Its expected value,

$$(1.2{:}3) \quad Eu(X) \big| P(X; S) = \mu_u(S), \quad \text{say},$$

is called the moral expectation of X. Define a space $\mathscr{S}$ whose elements S represent possible strategies. The title of the paper asks whether it is reasonable always to choose as one's strategy an element S^* of $\mathscr{S}$ whenever

$$(1.2{:}4)\quad \mu_u(S^*) > \mu_u(S')$$

where S' is any element of $\mathscr{S}$ distinct from S^*.

1.3. The 'precept', always (that is, for any space $\mathscr{S}$) to maximize moral expectation, leads to inconsistent results unless all the utility functions considered are linear transforms of each other (in which case utility is sometimes said to be 'measurable'). This can be easily shown for the case of discrete probability distributions. Suppose X can only take values $X_0, \ldots, X_N$, and denote the corresponding probabilities by $p_0, \ldots, p_N$. Let u and v be two utility functions as defined in (1.2:2), and suppose the space $\mathscr{S}$ is such as to include a strategy for every distribution. In particular, let S' result in probabilities $p'_0, \ldots, p'_N$; and S^* in $p^*_0, \ldots, p^*_N$. Suppose that, following the 'precept,' S^* is not chosen in preference to S'; that is, by (1.2:4),

$$(1.3{:}1)\quad \mu_u(S^*) \leqq \mu_u(S'); \qquad \mu_v(S^*) \leqq \mu_v(S').$$

Suppose, in addition, that neither is S' chosen in preference to S^*. Then (1.3:1) becomes

$$\mu_u(S^*) = \mu_u(S'); \qquad \mu_v(S^*) = \mu_v(S');$$

$$\sum_0^N (p^*_n - p'_n)\cdot u(X_n) = 0 = \sum_0^N (p^*_n - p'_n)\cdot v(X_n) = \sum_0^N (p^*_n - p'_n)\cdot 1 .$$

This must remain true for prospects such that $p^*_n \neq p'_n$ for $n \leqq 2$ and $p^*_n = p'_n = 0$ for $n > 2$. Then the three equations

$$\sum_0^2 (p^*_n - p'_n)\cdot u(X_n) = \sum_0^2 (p^*_n - p'_n)\cdot v(X_n) = \sum_0^N (p^*_n - p'_n)\cdot 1$$

form a homogeneous linear system in the three $(p^*_n - p'_n)$, $n = 0, 1, 2$. Hence the $u(X_n)$, $v(X_n)$, 1 are linearly dependent, for any three arbitrarily chosen values of n. Therefore, there exist α, β such that

$$v(X_n) = \alpha + \beta u(X_n), \quad n = 0, \ldots, N.$$

The linear dependence of the utility functions follows thus from the linear nature of the operator E in (1.2:3). The following illustration may be useful. Suppose $\mathscr{X}$ consists of three alternative sums of money: \$$-1$, 0, 1. Let $w=M(u)$ and $v=L(u)=1+2u$ be, respectively, a nonlinear and a linear monotone increasing transform of a utility function $u(X)$. Let S' and S'' be two strategies resulting, respectively, in two different probability distributions of X, $P'(X)$ and $P''(X)$. In Table I the moral expectations,

TABLE I

	X	u	w	v		$P'(X)$	$P''(X)$
	-1	-2	-1	-3		$\frac{1}{2}$	0
	0	0	0	1		0	1
	1	1	2	3		$\frac{1}{2}$	0
$\mu(S')=$		$-\frac{1}{2}$	$\frac{1}{2}$	0	EX =	0	0
$\mu(S'')=$		0	0	1	$E(X-EX)^2=$	1	0
Best $S=$		S''	S'	S''			

$\mu(S')$ and $\mu(S'')$, are computed for the three different utility functions, u, w and v. Thus, of the two strategies S' and S'', S'' (resulting in a smaller variance of X) is chosen when the utility function is u or the linear transform v of u. But when the utility function is the nonlinear monotone transform w of u, a different strategy may be chosen – although the man maximizes his moral expectation.

1.4. Pascal's [9] immortality wager was an early application of the precept to maximize moral expectation. Essentially, Pascal made four propositions, with the first three of which we shall not quarrel. *First*, assume that, since chances for and against immortality are unknown, they are equal. *Second*, assume that, if there is immortality, then good life is followed by eternal bliss and bad life by eternal damnation. Regard these two sequences as outcomes X_1' and X_1'', respectively, and denote the outcomes 'good life followed by nothing' and 'bad life followed by nothing' by X_2' and X_2'', respectively. Consider 'good life' and 'bad life' as two strategies, S' and S''. In effect, Pascal computes the following two expected values:

$$\mu_u(S') = \tfrac{1}{2}u(X_1') + \tfrac{1}{2}u(X_2'),$$
$$\mu_u(S'') = \tfrac{1}{2}u(X_1'') + \tfrac{1}{2}u(X_2'').$$

Hence,

$$\mu_u(S') > \mu_u(S'') \quad \text{if} \quad u(X_1') - u(X_1'') > u(X_2'') - u(X_2').$$

For Pascal, the difference between the advantages of eternal bliss (following a short period of possibly tedious good life) and the disadvantages of eternal damnation (following a short though possibly not unpleasant bad life) exceeds the difference between the possible pleasures of sin and the possible inconveniences of virtue. These valuations (the utility function u) can be regarded as his *third* proposition and may be accepted. We shall be concerned with his *fourth* proposition: that, because $\mu_u(S')$ exceeds $\mu_u(S'')$, it is reasonable to choose S'.

1.5. In the particular case when the space $\mathscr{X}$ of outcomes consists of alternative sums of money (as in 1.3, table), the moral expectation of the gain, $Eu(X)$, is contrasted with its 'mathematical expectation', EX, which also depends on S. In the Petersburg game, there exists a strategy S', say, which makes EX infinite, yet a reasonable player would not choose S'. To explain the paradox, Daniel Bernoulli stated that a reasonable man maximizes $Eu(X)$ and not EX and that the function $u(X)$ has certain properties. See Menger [7].

1.6. In Section 2 of this paper, the precept to maximize $Eu(X)$ will be related to problems facing statisticians and businessmen and, in fact, to human decisions in general. Section 3 gives as a necessary condition for the precept a postulate which may be called the *Postulate of Substitution between Indifferent Prospects*. In an earlier paper [4], this postulate (jointly with certain other postulates) was shown to be a sufficient condition for the precept of maximizing $Eu(X)$, valid for a non-empty class of utility functions, each element of which is a linear transform of any of the others. This postulate appears, thus, to be logically equivalent to the moral expectation precept (provided the other postulates are admitted). It is also possibly equivalent to certain postulates of von Neumann and Morgenstern [8]. For a comparison, see [4, Section 7]. Finally, it is also equivalent to a postulate which Samuelson [11] recently formulated very succinctly and which he proposed to call *Special Independence Assumption*. A comparison between the postulate and the economist's concept of 'independence between consumption goods' is contained in Section 3 of the present paper.

1.7. In Section 4 a very rough outline of a different approach will be attempted. A rule of *Long Run Success* is formulated ('in the long run, it pays to be reasonable') by considering a strategy as a sequence of rules of action to be taken in response to future situations. It seems that the rule of Long Run Success is not equivalent to the precept to maximize moral expectation unless some further conditions are imposed upon the utility functions. No definitive results are available so far.

1.8. Note that the space $\mathscr{S}$ of strategies can be conceived as including among its elements, strategies consistent with the ordinary rules of logic and mathematics, and strategies not consistent with these rules. The distribution P of outcomes X and, therefore, the quantity $Eu(X)$ will depend on whether the decision maker is a good or a bad logician and arithmetician, on what kind of geometry he applies, etc. This kind of justification of a set of behavior norms including norms of thinking and counting was, I believe, occasionally attempted by pragmatist and evolutionary writers with some rule of long run success in mind: "If you act on the assumption that 2 times 2 equals 5, you (or your tribe or species) will, in some sense, fare worse in the long run than if you act on the assumption that 2 times 2 equals 4."

2. Some concrete cases

2.1. In recent years, the theory of statistical inference has taken a remarkably 'economic' turn. In choosing a rule for making observations (the design of a sample), money cost (C) is subtracted from what may be called the gross gain (G) derived by the statistician or his 'employer' from the knowledge acquired from the observations. G is conceived as a sum of money and is, in a simple case, the larger the smaller the error of the estimation based on the sample. The money sum $G-C=X$ is thus the outcome of the statistician's decision to choose a certain sample design. X is called the net gain or profit. X is to be maximized with respect to the variable under the statistician's control, that is, with respect to the design of the sample.

2.2. In a particular case when the sample designs under consideration differ only with respect to the size of the sample (number of observations) S, the best value $S=S^*$ must satisfy the approximate rule,

$$\frac{dG}{dS}=\frac{dC}{dS},$$

(provided G and C can be approximated by differentiable functions of S). This is the familiar rule of the economists: to equalize the marginal monetary product and the marginal monetary cost of the 'input' S. More generally one defines the space $\mathscr{S}$ of all possible sample designs and maximizes the scalar function $X(S)$ over this space.

2.3. However, the profit X is a random scalar since the gross gain G depends on the values that the observed random variables happen to take. (In addition, the cost C, too, may depend on observed values, as for example, when C depends on the location of individuals that happen to fall into a social survey sample or when the number of observations depends on observed values as in sequential sampling.) One cannot maximize the random variable X but one can maximize some quantity depending on its distribution, for example, its mean EX.

2.4. Both concepts, the sample design and the monetary profit, can be replaced by wider ones. As regards the first: the statistician can recommend not only the rule of making observations but also the decision to be taken after having collected them. This decision may be the choice of an estimate or of a hypothesis. More generally, it may be any decision that will influence the probability distribution of the gross gain G, for example, the decision to buy a certain quantity of a commodity. Generalizing the notation of 2.2, one defines $\mathscr{S}$ as the space of all possible 'strategies' S, each strategy being a certain rule for making observations *and* for taking decisions on the basis of these observations. The distribution of the random profit X – to be denoted by $P(X)$ – will depend on S and on the true distribution F of the observables. We can write

$$(2.4{:}1)\quad P(X) \equiv P(X; S, F), \qquad EX \equiv EX\big|(S, F) \equiv \mu_X(S, F), \quad \text{say}.$$

(In the simple case of 2.1, X depended on the estimation error, that is, the difference between a point estimate and the true value of the estimated parameter of the distribution of observables. This was obviously a special case of the one now stated.) The negative of the function μ_X just defined is identical with Wald's [12] 'risk function', with two differences: first, Wald always has $G \geqq 0$ (regarding $-G$, the 'loss suffered by the statistician', as a nonpositive quantity) – a trivial difference; second, Wald does not necessarily regard G, C and X as monetary quantities and presumably accepts the generalization that we are going to make now.

2.5. With the 'statistician' taking over entrepreneurial decisions, it becomes necessary to reconsider what is of concern to the businessman. To begin with, 'A full purse is not as good as an empty one is bad'. There exists a certain quantity K (possible zero) which depends on the firm's reserves and is such that, if $X \leqq K$, the firm is bankrupt and must be dissolved. It is reasonable that the probability of the occurrence of this situation should be made as small as possible. This objective may not be reached if the strategy chosen maximizes EX. On the other hand, suppose the firm tries to maximize the expression $Eu(X)$, where the 'utility function' $u(X)$ is defined as follows:

$$(2.5{:}1) \quad \begin{aligned} u(X) &= -v \quad \text{when} \quad X \leqq K, \\ u(X) &= X \quad \text{when} \quad X > K, \end{aligned}$$

where v is a positive constant. Let the probability density function of X, $X \neq K$, for a given strategy S be $p(X; S)$. Then the expected value of $u(X)$ given S is

$$(2.5{:}2) \quad Eu(X; S) = -\alpha(v + \beta) + \beta,$$

where

$$\alpha = \int_{-\infty}^{K} p(X; S)\, dX = \text{probability of bankruptcy},$$

$$\beta = \frac{\int_K^{\infty} Xp(X; S)\, dX}{\int_K^{\infty} p(X; S)\, dX}$$

$$= \text{profit averaged over all cases other than bankruptcy.}$$

Both α and β depend on S, and β is usually nonnegative. It follows from (2.5:2) that, for a given β, the firm's moral expectation is the larger the smaller is α, the probability of bankruptcy. The maximization of $Eu(X)$ would thus seem to describe reasonable behavior better than the maximization of EX.

2.6. Another example of the utility function of a random sum of money and of the effect of properties of this function upon the choice of strategy was given in Table I. A much discussed case has been that of a function $u(X)$ that is differentiable at least twice. If $u'(X)>0$ and $u''(X)<0$ for all values of X (the case of "decreasing and positive marginal utility of income"), then the individual who maximizes $Eu(X)$ will prefer, given the value of the mean profit EX, a prospect with a low variance to a prospect with a high variance of X. This is seen by expanding $Eu(X)$ into a Taylor series. See [6] and, for a somewhat more general case, [2].

2.7. More generally, the businessman is concerned not with a scalar quantity but with a vector: with the sequence of profits to be earned in successive years, the more distant ones being possibly of less import to the firm's decision (even if the joint probability distribution of the sequences is known exactly) than the more immediate ones; or, if he is a farmer, with a set of quantities earned, respectively, in the form of food, housing accommodation, etc. The fact that nonmonetary earnings and future earnings of any kind can be converted into current money at prices and interest rates prevailing in (perfect) markets does not dispose of the complication since these prices and interest rates themselves have to be explained by the strategies of the people that transact in these markets. However, the generalization from a scalar to a vector $X=\{x_i\}$ does not present difficulties. In particular, if $u(X)$ is twice differentiable, the results mentioned in 2.6 are easily generalized. Write vector

$$\mu \equiv \{Ex_i\}$$

and matrix

$$\sigma \equiv \|\sigma_{ij}\| \equiv \|E(x_i - \mu_i)(x_i - \mu_j)\|.$$

Then, if

$$u_{ij} = \frac{\partial^2 u}{\partial x_i \partial x_j}$$

exists for all i, j, we have by expanding about μ,

$$Eu(X) = u(\mu) + \tfrac{1}{2}\sum_{i,j} u_{ij}\sigma_{ij} + \cdots.$$

It follows that if $u_{ii}<0$ (decreasing marginal utility of the ith kind of commodity earned or of the ith year's money profit), then the individual will try to make the variance σ_{ii} as small as possible, given the other elements of μ and σ. A high correlation between the ith and the jth elements of the profit vector will be feared if $u_{ij}<0$ (the case of goods with negative complementarity); a high correlation between i and j will be desired if $u_{ij}>0$ (the case of positively complementary goods).

2.8. Note that the definition of complementarity just used is only possible because, as a corollary of the requirement to maximize moral expectation $Eu(X)$, all utility functions form a group of linear transforms. If a nonlinear transform of $u(X)$ – say the function $w(X)=f[u(X)]$, $f'>0$ – were admitted as a utility function, then, since a positive u_{ij} might be consistent with a negative w_{ij}, the sign of complementarity as just defined could not be ascertained.

2.9. In [5], the desirability of large or small variances of, or correlations between, inputs (production factors) of various kinds was studied on lines similar to 2.7. Rational advantages of 'pooling the risks' and of either specialization or diversification of production (depending on the sign of complementarity between factors of production) can be derived –always assuming that it is rational to maximize $Eu(X)$.

2.10. Certain things desired by the businessman – such as power or social position or reputation – are not quantities at all. It is therefore necessary to generalize further the concept of what is being maximized. This generalization was presented in 1.2. If the space $\mathscr{X}$ of 'outcomes' and the space $\mathscr{S}$ of strategies are defined, this permits us to take care of all human decisions, transcending conventional economics and including the private man's choice of profession or wife, the legislator's choice of election tactics or national policies or military and administrative decisions. This is of some interest to statisticians who, after all, are not all employed by profit making organizations.

2.11. Our question is, then, whether the following rule is reasonable: always choose a strategy S^* so as to obtain a prospect (a probability distribution)

$$P(X) \equiv P(X; S^*, F),$$

for which

$$\mu_u(S^*, F) \equiv Eu(X)\,|\,(S^*, F)$$

is larger than or equal to

$$\mu_u(S', F) \equiv Eu(X)\,|\,(S', F),$$

for any S'; where the scalar function $u(X)$ is defined over the space $\mathscr{X}$ of outcomes, S^* and S' are elements of the space $\mathscr{S}$ of strategies and F is the true distribution of the observables. In general, F is not (or not completely) known – in the case of the statistician as well as in the case of any other decision makers. The economist F. H. Knight [3] called the case of unknown F 'presence of uncertainty' and the case of known F (as in games of chance) 'presence of risk'. This terminology has been widely accepted among economists although it is not in line with general scientific usage of the word uncertainty. It would be better to speak of 'incomplete' versus 'complete' information. For the purpose of this paper, it is sufficient to deal with the case of complete information, that is, to assume F known. It is of no relevance to us here whether, in the case of F unknown, probabilities of the several alternatives have to be assumed equal before maximizing $\mu_u(S, F)$ with respect to S as was done by Pascal (1.4 above), or whether, following Wald and the authors of the *Theory of Games*, one should assume the least favorable distribution F, that is, minimize $\mu_u(S, F)$ with respect to F before maximizing it with respect to S. It is the latter, the maximization of μ_u with respect to S, that concerns us here: a problem common to the case of complete and to that of incomplete information and arising with Pascal as with Wald.

3. The Rule of Substitution between Indifferent Prospects

3.1. In [4], a certain set of behavior postulates, numbered I–IV, was shown by the author to imply the proposition that there exists a class of utility functions, linear transforms of each other, and such that for every utility function the expected value of utility is maximized. We shall presently restate these postulates and show that, if postulates I–III (which appear rather mild) are accepted, then postulate IV follows from the condition that $Eu(X)$ is maximized. A joint result of the two papers is, then, that under certain weak conditions, postulate IV and the rule of maximizing moral expectation are equivalent. Postulate IV will be called the 'rule of substitution between indifferent prospects'.

3.2. As in [4], we define a space $\mathscr{P}$ of prospects P (=probability distributions) for the case that the space $\mathscr{X}$ of outcomes consists of a finite number of elements, $X_0, X_1, \ldots, X_N$. (The case of N infinite was discussed by Rubin in [10] for the problem of [4].) Regard the probability that the particular outcome X_n will occur, $p(X_n)$, as a coordinate of the point P in the Euclidean N-space, $n=1, \ldots, N$. Since

$$(3.2{:}1) \quad 0 \leqslant \sum_{n=1}^{N} p(X_n) = 1 - p(X_0) \leqslant 1\,,$$

the space $\mathscr{P}$ of prospects is the domain of the N-space bounded by and including the surface of an $(N+1)$-hedron whose vertices are the origin $(0, 0, \ldots, 0)$ and the ends $(1, 0, 0, \ldots, 0)$, $(0, 1, 0, \ldots, 0), \ldots, (0, 0, 0, \ldots, 1)$ of the N unit vectors. These vertices represent the 'sure' prospects, each promising with certainty one particular outcome. Sure prospects will be denoted by $P^{(0)}, P^{(1)}, \ldots, P^{(N)}$. Using letters $P, Q, R, \ldots$ for prospects in general, we state the following postulates:

I. *The space $\mathscr{P}$ is completely ordered by the relation* $\mathfrak{g}$ (read 'as good as or better than'). Note: Whenever $P\mathfrak{g}Q$ we shall also write $u(P) \geqq u(Q)$. This defines a scalar 'utility function' $u(P)$ on the space $\mathscr{P}$. It is related in a simple way to the function $u(X)$ on the space $\mathscr{X}$, defined in 1.2 above, that is, we have $u(X_n) = u(P^{(n)})$, $n=0, 1, \ldots, N$, by definition. Furthermore, whenever $P\mathfrak{g}Q$ and not $Q\mathfrak{g}P$, we write $P\mathfrak{p}Q$ (read 'P preferred to Q') and have $u(P) > u(Q)$. Whenever $P\mathfrak{g}Q$ and $Q\mathfrak{g}P$, we write $P\mathfrak{i}Q$ (read 'P and Q are indifferent') and have $u(P) = u(Q)$.

II. $\mathfrak{g}$ *is continuous*, that is, if $P\mathfrak{g}Q\mathfrak{g}R$, then there exists a number r, $0 \leqq r \leqq 1$, such that if $Q' = rP + (1-r)\,R$ then $Q\mathfrak{i}Q'$. Note: We are using the symbols for addition, multiplication and equality in their ordinary meaning. Q' is the result of ordinary multiplication and addition performed on two vectors, P and R. Geometrically, Q' is a point on a straight line connecting P and R.

III. *There exist P and Q not on the boundary of $\mathscr{P}$, such that not* $P\mathfrak{i}Q$. Note: This is postulate III* of [4]. We refer to [4] for an alternative postulate and for a stronger one.

IV. *If* $P \mathfrak{i} Q$ *and* $0<r<1$ *and if* $P'=rR+(1-r)\,P$ *and* $Q'=rR+(1-r)\,Q$, *then* $P' \mathfrak{i} Q'$. Note: P' is the prospect of having either prospect P or prospect R with certain probabilities, $1-r$ and r. Q' is the prospect of having either Q or R also with probabilities $1-r$ and r. Postulate IV states that if P and Q are indifferent, so are P' and Q'. In a special case P and P' may coincide [4, postulate IVa]. Also, P or Q or R may be sure prospects.

3.3. In the language of the last section – see note to postulate I – the rule of maximizing $Eu(X)$ can be stated thus [writing for brevity $u(P^{(n)})=u^{(n)}$, which is independent of the prospects considered, and $P(X_n)=p_n$, $Q(X_n)=q_n$, etc.].

PROPOSITION 1. $Q \mathfrak{g} R$ *if and only if* $\sum_0^N u^{(n)} q_n \geqq \sum_0^N u^{(n)} r_n$.

We shall prove that this rule implies

PROPOSITION 2. *If* $P \mathfrak{p} Q \mathfrak{p} R$ *then the indifference sets* $J(P)$, $J(Q)$, $J(R)$ *are segments of three parallel* $(N-1)$*-dimensional hyperplanes, contained* in $\mathscr{P}$ *and stacked in the order* P, Q, R, *or its reverse*, where for any prospect P the indifference set $J(P)$ is defined as consisting of all prospects P' for which $P' \mathfrak{i} P$.

In fact, if $P \mathfrak{p} Q \mathfrak{p} R$ then, by the definition of the relations $\mathfrak{p}$ and $\mathfrak{i}$, proposition 1 implies that

$$\sum_0^N u^{(n)} p_n > \sum_0^N u^{(n)} q_n > \sum_0^N u^{(n)} r_n \,. \tag{3.3:1}$$

If, in addition, $P \mathfrak{i} P'$, $Q \mathfrak{i} Q'$ and $R \mathfrak{i} R'$, proposition 1 requires that

$$\sum_0^N u^{(n)} p_n = \sum_0^N u^{(n)} p_n' = a^* \quad \text{say,}$$

$$\sum_0^N u^{(n)} q_n = \sum_0^N u^{(n)} q_n' = b^* \quad \text{say,}$$

$$\sum_0^N u^{(n)} r_n = \sum_0^N u^{(n)} r_n' = c^* , \quad \text{say;}$$

where $a^* > b^* > c^*$. Write $v^{(n)} = u^{(n)} - u^{(0)}$, $n = 1, 2, \ldots, N$. Then the above equations become upon replacing p_0 by $1-\sum_1^N p_n$, etc. and upon replacing $a^*-u^{(0)}$ by a, etc.

$$(3.3{:}2)\quad \sum_1^N v^{(n)}p_n = \sum_1^N v^{(n)}p_n' = a\,,$$
$$\sum_1^N v^{(n)}q_n = \sum_1^N v^{(n)}q_n' = b\,,$$
$$\sum_1^N v^{(n)}r_n = \sum_1^N v^{(n)}r_n' = c\,.$$

The last two terms in the first line of (3.3:2) give the equation of a $(N-1)$-dimensional hyperplane which contains all P' such that $P'\mathfrak{i}P$. This hyperplane is therefore identical with the indifference set $J(P)$. Similarly, the other two lines in (3.3:2) provide the equations for the hyperplanes $J(Q)$ and $J(R)$. The three hyperplanes are parallel, each having the N direction cosines proportional to $v^{(n)}$, $n=1, 2,\ldots, N$. The distances of the three hyperplanes from the origin are proportional to a, b and c, respectively. Hence they are stacked in the order P, Q, R or its reverse.

3.4. Proposition 2 implies, in turn, postulate IV, provided postulates I–III are granted. In fact, in the notation used in the statement of postulate IV, prospects P and Q must both lie on $J(P)$, one of the parallel indifference planes revealed in proposition 2. Moreover, the indifference planes $J(P')$ and $J(Q')$ must be parallel to $J(P)$. On the other hand, P' and Q' must both lie on a plane parallel to $J(P)$ because $r=\overline{PP'}/\overline{PR}= =\overline{QQ'}/\overline{QR}$. And since in an Euclidean space there is only one plane through P' parallel to $J(P)$, we have $P'\mathfrak{i}Q'$.

The reasoning of this and the preceding sections presupposes the validity of postulates I–III. Postulate I excludes the case in which neither $P\mathfrak{g}Q$ nor $Q\mathfrak{g}P$ and this would rule out the existence of a function $u(P)$ on $\mathcal{P}$. Postulate II excludes the possibility of 'holes' in the indifference planes. Postulate III excludes the possibility that the whole interior of $\mathcal{P}$ might form a single indifference set.

We conclude that, given postulates I–III, postulate IV is not only a sufficient condition for proposition 1 (as was shown in [4]), but also a necessary condition. Thus, the two are equivalent, provided postulates I–III are granted. Postulates I–III seem indeed weak enough as a description of reasonable behavior. Postulate IV also seems reasonable to me and some further remarks in 3.5 may convince others. If, in addition, this postulate is taken to be intuitively more convincing than its logical equivalent, proposition 1, then the question asked in the title is answered.

3.5. In the discussion of the theory of choice between prospects, confusion seems to arise through the use of an ambiguous word, 'combination'. This word naturally expresses the operation '*and*', as in '*A and C*'. But it has also been applied to express the relation '*either–or*', as in '*either A or C*, with probabilities r and $1-r$'. Since prospects are always mutually exclusive, they cannot be 'combined' into an object of choice such as 'prospect A *and* prospect C' to be chosen in preference to another 'combination' such as 'prospect B *and* prospect C'. But they can be 'combined' in a different sense, namely, the combination 'either A or C, with probabilities r and $1-r$' can be formed and may be chosen in preference to the combination 'either B or C, with probabilities q and $1-q$'. Suppose, on the other hand, that A, B, C are objects that are not mutually exclusive. For example, A=country house, B=city house, C=car. Then the following rule of behavior would *not* be reasonable: "If I like A as well as I like B, then I like *A and C* as well as I like *B and C*." Such a rule would neglect the possibility that a car has more use in the country than in the city. But such a rule is *not* our postulate IV. The latter says, rather: "Call P the prospect of having the country house A and having, in addition, certain other things which will be held constant throughout the comparisons and which we shall call D; call Q the prospect of having the city house B and D. Then, if I like P as well as I like Q, I like the prospect of having either P or R as well as I like the prospect of having either Q or R, provided the odds are the same in each case." This is reasonable. The fact that the car is of better use when possessed jointly with a country house than when possessed jointly with a city house has no bearing on the choice between the prospects discussed, of which *none promises the joint possession of a car and a house*. To exclude more completely from our mind the logically illegitimate picture of a joint occurrence of mutually exclusive events, postulate IV might be illustrated most simply as follows: P=the career of a professor, Q=the career of a church minister, R=the career of a bus driver. Or, imagine that you have to choose between drawing from one or another of two urns; in each of them, 20 per cent of all tickets are inscribed 'car'; the remaining 80 per cent are inscribed 'country house' in the first urn and are inscribed 'city house' in the second urn. If you are indifferent between city house and country house, will you prefer one urn to the other, knowing that if you do get a car in any of the lotteries you will *not* get a house with it? The same applies naturally when P, Q and R are themselves nonsure prospects; for example, if they are tickets to three different lotteries.

3.6. It may be useful to refer to the notation of 2.7 where the outcome X was a joint occurrence of quantities $x_1, x_2, \ldots$ and was regarded as a vector $\{x_i\}$. The utility of X (or, in the language of prospects, the utility of the sure prospect that X occurs with certainty) is denoted by $u(x_1, x_2, \ldots)$. Disregard, as being kept constant, all x_i for $i > 3$. We say that commodity 3 is more complementary with commodity 1 than with commodity 2, over some defined intervals, if

$$(3.6:1) \quad u(x_1 + h_1, x_2, x_3) = u(x_1, x_2 + h_2, x_3)$$

and

$$u(x_1 + h_1, x_2, x_3 + h_3) > u(x_1, x_2 + h_2, x_3 + h_3),$$

where the h_i are positive. This definition of complementarity is in accord with the one used in 2.7 for the case when the x_i are continuous and u is twice differentiable. This is seen by expanding the function u into a Taylor series about x_1, x_2, x_3, and inserting into (3.6:1). On the other hand, in our example of the car and the two different houses, the three x_i can take the values 0 and 1 only. If, in the continuous case, the cross derivative $u_{13} = 0$ or if in the general case

$$u(x_1, x_2, x_3 + h_3) - u(x_1, x_2, x_3) = u(x_1 + h_1, x_2, x_3 + h_3) - \\ + u(x_1 + h_1, x_2, x_3),$$

we say that there is no complementarity (positive or negative) between commodities 1 and 3 or that the two are 'independent'. As stated in 2.8, these definitions presuppose that utility functions are linear transforms of each other.

To apply this concept to the choice between prospects, remember that we have then, as the argument of the utility function, not the vector of quantities of commodities but the probabilities of mutually exclusive events, $p_1, \ldots, p_N$ where, in particular, p_1 may be the probability that the vector of commodity quantities has a certain value and p_2 may be the probability that this vector has another value. It would be misleading to say that postulate IV asserts 'independence' (in the sense just stated) between any objects of choice themselves: the prospects $P, Q, \ldots$ are not (as the commodity quantities $x_1, x_2, \ldots$ are) coordinates of the space in which the indifference surfaces are drawn.

3.7. On the other hand, the probabilities $p_1, \ldots, p_N$ are indeed 'independent', in the sense that, if the precept of maximizing expected utility is always followed, then

$$\frac{\partial^2 u(p_1, p_2, \ldots, p_N)}{\partial p_m \partial p_n} = 0, \quad m, n = 1, \ldots, N,$$

because u is linear in its continuous argument, the vector $\{p_i\}$.

4. The Rule of Long Run Success

4.1. We shall now outline tentatively another proposition which may under certain conditions be implied by the rule of maximizing moral expectation and which appears (like postulate IV) intuitively more convincing than the rule itself.

For an integer $T > 0$, define a space $\mathscr{X}_{(T)}$, whose element $X_{(T)}$ represents a possible time sequence of situations $x_0, x_1, \ldots, x_T$ (for example, a sequence of annual profits or of balance sheets). Define a utility function $u_T(X_{(T)})$ such that if $X'_{(T)}$ and $X''_{(T)}$ are in $\mathscr{X}_{(T)}$, and $X'_{(T)} \mathrm{g} X''_{(T)}$ then $u_T(X'_{(T)}) \geqq u_T(X''_{(T)})$. Define a closed space $\mathscr{S}$, whose element S_T represents a possible strategy, defined as a sequence of functions, $s_0, s_1, \ldots, s_{T-1}$, where $s_t = s_t(x_0, x_1, \ldots, x_t)$. Thus S_T is a sequence of rules of how to respond at given times to a given sequence of past situations. Now define the probability that the strategy S^*_T will be at least as successful as S'_T:

$$(4.1{:}1) \quad Pr\{[u_T(X_{(T)}; S^*_T) \geqq u_T(X_{(T)}; S'_T)]\} = \pi_T(S^*_T, S'_T), \quad \text{say.}$$

Now let T increase and consider sequences such as

$$\mathscr{S}^* = (S^*_1, S^*_2, \ldots), \qquad \mathscr{S}' = (S'_1, S'_2, \ldots), \quad \text{etc.}$$

Suppose that there exists a limit

$$\lim_{T\to\infty} \pi_T(S_T^*, S_T') = \pi(\mathcal{S}^*, \mathcal{S}'), \quad \text{say},$$

for any two sequences $\mathcal{S}^*$ and $\mathcal{S}'$ and suppose that this limit

$$(4.1:2) \quad \pi(\mathcal{S}^*, \mathcal{S}') = 1.$$

Then the rule of long run success requires that the sequence $\mathcal{S}^*$ be chosen [or, if two or more values $\mathcal{S}^*$ exist that satisfy (4.1:2), one of them must be chosen]. This corresponds to the common sense definition, 'The best policy is the one that succeeds in the long run'.

4.2. We should like to know conditions under which the rule of maximizing moral expectation implies that the rule of long run success is satisfied. As a mere example that may start a discussion among those better qualified, we shall impose a (probably unnecessarily strong) condition upon the sequence of utility functions,

$$u_1(x_1), u_2(x_1, x_2), \ldots, u_T(x_1, x_2, \ldots, x_T)$$

with means

$$Eu_1, Eu_2, \ldots, Eu_T$$

and variances

$$\sigma_1^2, \sigma_2^2, \ldots, \sigma_T^2.$$

We do not assume the successive random variables $u_1, u_2, \ldots$ to be independent statistically. But we make the assumption that the variance σ_T^2 tends to zero as $T \to \infty$. Then u_T converges in probability to Eu_T. Therefore the difference,

$$u_T(X_{(T)}; S_T^*) - u_T(X_{(T)}; S\mathrm{x}),$$

converges in probability to

$$Eu_T(X_{(T)}; S\mathrm{x}) - Eu_T(X_{(T)}; S_T').$$

(See, for example, [1, especially pp. 253–255].) This difference is non-negative if the rule of maximizing moral expectation is followed, that is, if for every T a strategy S_T^* is chosen satisfying

$$Eu_T(X_{(T)};\, S_T^*) \geqq Eu_T(X_{(T)};\, S_T'),$$

where S_T' is another strategy in $\mathscr{S}_T$. Then

$$\pi(\mathscr{S}^*, \mathscr{S}') = 1$$

for every $\mathscr{S}'$ and the rule of long run success is satisfied.

We have used here, merely to illustrate the proposed approach, a crucial assumption that is hardly plausible: that the variance of the utility function of outcomes over a horizon T, tends to zero as the horizon increases. This assumption is also unnecessarily strong as it proves more than is required: for the limiting probability $\pi(\mathscr{S}^*, \mathscr{S}')$ to be equal to 1, it is not necessary that each of the two compared utilities converge separately to its respective expected value.

An alternative assumption might be that of statistical independence between utility functions over successive horizons, that is, between $u_1(x_1), u_2(x_1, x_2), \ldots$. But this is even less reasonable. It is possible that no plausible conditions exist under which the rule of maximizing moral expectation implies the rule of long run success as defined.

5. Summary

The rule of maximizing the expected value of utility was shown to imply that utility functions of prospects (that is, of alternative distributions of outcomes of strategies) are linear transforms of each other and are linear in the probabilities of outcomes. The rule is equivalent to the postulate that indifferent prospects are substituted for each other – provided certain other, weak postulates are granted. Finally, an attempt was made to relate the rule of maximizing the expected value of utility to a rule of aiming at a long run success. This required redefining outcomes, strategies and utilities as time sequences. The strategies discussed included those of statisticians and businessmen and can be conceived to include human decisions in general. At no point was it claimed that reasonable behavior is actually practiced by men: the paper is a study in consistent sets of norms, not an empirical study.

BIBLIOGRAPHY

[1] H. Cramér, *Mathematical Methods of Statistics*, Princeton University Press, Princeton, 1946.

[2] M. Friedman and L. J. Savage, 'The Utility Analysis of Choices Involving Risk', *J. of Political Economy* **56** (1948), 279–304.

[3] F. H. Knight, *Risk, Uncertainty, and Profit*, Houghton Mifflin, Boston and New York, 1921.

[4] J. Marschak, 'Rational Behavior, Uncertain Prospects, and Measurable Utility', *Selected Essays*, 1.

[5] J. Marschak, 'Optimal Investment of a Firm', *Selected Essays*, 39.

[6] A. Marshall, *Principles of Economics*, Macmillan, London, 1920. See Mathematical Appendix, Note IX.

[7] K. Menger, 'Das Unsicherheitsmoment in der Wertlehre', *Zeitschrift fuer Nationaloekonomie* **5** (1934), 459–485.

[8] J. von Neumann and O. Morgenstern, *Theory of Games and Economic Behavior*, 2nd ed., Princeton University Press, Princeton, 1947.

[9] B. Pascal, 'Article II: Qu'il est plus avantageux de croire que de ne pas croire ce qu'enseigne la religion chrétienne', *Pensées*, Garnier Frères, Paris, after the edition of 1670.

[10] H. Rubin, *Axiom System for Measurable Utility*, unpublished.

[11] P. A. Samuelson, *Measurement of Utility Reformulated*, unpublished.

[12] A. Wald, 'Statistical Decision Functions', *Annals ofMath. Stat.* **20** (1949), 220–263.

3

SCALING OF UTILITIES AND PROBABILITIES

(1954)

One strategy is better than another if it brings the player more. More of what? Clearly, one uses some criterion of 'utility', of something that is being maximized. Moreover, since the opponent's response or the future in general is uncertain, the player does not know a unique result of his strategy but rather expects various possible results, some with greater, some will smaller degrees of belief or '(subjective) probabilities'.

If utilities and probabilities could be merely ranked (like degrees of patriotism) but not also scaled (like degrees of temperature), the theory of games could say rather little. Accordingly, von Neumann and Morgenstern revived the eighteenth century concept of a player who is concerned with his subjective status (so called 'moral wealth' – the modern 'utility'), a number which, under uncertainty, is a random one, and whose average (the 'moral expectation' – the modern 'expected utility') the player tries to maximize. A lively discussion developed.[1] The most elegant restatement of the relevant postulates of rational behavior and a rigorous proof of the implied 'Bernoulli theorem' was given by Herstein and Milnor.[2] In this discussion, the necessarily subjective nature of the probabilities was somewhat neglected. But this latter aspect (actually also traceable back to the eighteenth century) was revived by Ramsey and De Finetti and in L. J. Savage's *Foundations of Statistics*.[3]

The following exposition tries to appeal to the reader's intuition and cater to his laziness more than it would be permissible in a mathematical paper. A proof is merely sketched. It may be added, however, that the substance of the proof, too, is simpler than in my earlier papers on the subject.[4]

I shall often use the second person pronoun. In discussing rational behavior as in discussing logic, appeal is made to the reader's reasonable self: given time to think, how would you decide? I don't deal with another, quite a different question (as different as psychology is from logic): how often do you decide hurriedly and foolishly?

I. THE CASE OF THREE OUTCOMES

Suppose you, the reader, have to choose between two decisions (actions): to build or not to build a bomb-proof shelter for yourself and your family. To make the example drastic, let us suppose that you are rich but that the shelter would cost you practically the whole of your fortune; and that such a shelter is both indispensable and sufficient for life preservation in the case of war. Thus your two alternative decisions and the two alternative states of the world (war or peace) combine into the following 'payoff matrix':

Decisions	States of World	
	Peace	War
Build shelter	Alive and poor (r_2)	Alive and poor (r_2)
Don't build shelter	Alive and rich (r_3)	Dead (r_1)

This is oversimplified indeed. Especially, we have neglected the difference between being alive and poor in peace, and being alive and poor in war (with shelterless neighbors dead). I need this particular simplification in order to have in my example just three possible outcomes. This will be a convenient introduction to more complicated cases. The three outcomes, or results, I have denoted by r_1='dead'; r_2='alive and poor'; r_3='alive and rich'. I suppose you prefer r_3 to r_2 and r_2 to r_1. This ranking of results is sufficient to determine your choice of action if you are certain about the future. If you are certain that there will be war, you choose to build the shelter (because you prefer r_2 to r_1); if you are sure that there will be peace, you choose not to build the shelter (because r_3 is better than r_2).

But suppose you do not know whether there will be war or peace. Yet you have to take a decision! You will still choose not to build a shelter if your *degree of belief* in peace and your *degree of preference* for wealth relative to survival are sufficiently large. (Note that we now speak of degrees and not of mere ranks! Summer is warmer than spring, and spring is warmer than winter: this is ranking; but we can also measure degrees of temperature in each of the three seasons.)

The statement I have just made, about the degrees of your beliefs and preferences that will make you decide not to build a shelter though you are uncertain about the future, must be made more precise. Denote the degrees of belief (also called subjective probabilities) that you assign to peace and war, respectively, by p and $1-p$. Calibrate your thermometer of preferences, or 'utilities' as follows: assign utility zero to the worst of the three outcomes, and utility one to the best. Thus

$$u(r_1) = 0; \qquad u(r_3) = 1.$$

Then, since r_2 is better than r_1 and worse than r_3,

$$0 < u(r_2) < 1$$

Subject to these inequalities, you are still free to assign any number $u(r_2)$ to the outcome r_2. I now suggest that you can, without incurring any logical contradiction, determine the number $u(r_2)$ in such a way as to satisfy the following principle: "*of any two decisions, the one you (the reader) choose is the one that, in your opinion, results in the higher, or at least not lower, average utility.*" The average utility that results from the decision 'don't build' is defined as the weighted average of $u(r_3)$ and $u(r_1)$, the weights being the corresponding degrees of belief, which we have denoted above by p and $1-p$, respectively. Thus the average utility that results from 'not building shelter' is

$$(1) \qquad u(r_3)\cdot p + u(r_1)\cdot(1-p) = 1\cdot p + 0\cdot(1-p) = p$$

On the other hand, the average utility that results from the decision 'to build' is

$$u(r_2)\cdot p + u(r_2)\cdot(1-p) = u(r_2)$$

Now, suppose you have chosen to build. According to the above principle of choosing in favor of the decision that results in the higher average utility, your actual choice will imply that, in your opinion [and still using the scale where one had fixed $u(r_3)=1$ and $u(r_1)=0$],

$$u(r_2) \geqslant p$$

On the other hand, if you had chosen not to build, the above principle would imply [still using the same scale]

$$u(r_2) \leqslant p$$

You can now perform on yourself a mental experiment, by varying the number p and asking: "with this degree of belief into persistence of peace, do I still prefer to build (or not to build)?" You may come close enough to a value of p, at which you will be *indifferent* between building and not building. Call this hypothetical value: $p=p_0$. Then both statements are true: $u(r_2)\geqslant p_0$ and $u(r_2)\leqslant p_0$. That is

$$u(r_2)=p_0$$

You have now attached numerical utilities to all three outcomes considered. You have also attached numerical average utilities to the two alternative decisions, to build and not to build. Call these two decisions (actions) a_1 and a_2, respectively. Thus

$$u(r_1)=0\,; \qquad u(r_2)=p_0\,; \qquad u(r_3)=1\,;$$
$$\text{average utility if } a_1 \text{ is taken} = p_0$$
$$\text{average utility if } a_2 \text{ is taken} = p$$

Remember that p is your actual degree of belief in peace; while p_0 is that degree of belief in peace that would make you indifferent between the two decisions. If you have decided to build, this implies that, in your opinion, $p\geqslant 0_0$. If you have decided not to build, this implies that, in your opinion, $p\leqslant p_0$.

We have had occasion to discuss your preferences between results (for example, better to be alive and poor than to be dead: choice between r_2 and r_1) as well as between decisions (better to build than not to build: choice between a_1 and a_2). It is thus natural to extend the concept of utility accordingly, and speak, not only of a utility of a result, but also of a utility of a decision. In fact a 'result' can be regarded as a special case of a 'decision,' viz., a decision which can have only one result. Such was in fact the decision a_1 in our example; its unique result was r_2. Accordingly we might simply assign to it the utility $u(a_1)=u(r_2)$. On the other hand, decision a_2 is identified with a bundle of results (r_3 and r_1), each with a respective degree of belief (p and $1-p$). We can call such a bundle a 'prospect': it is a (subjective) probability distribution of results, a lottery. A prospect promising – as in the case of a_1 – a single result, may be called a sure prospect. It is, in fact, *also* a (subjective) probability distribution, with one of the results having probability one. Thus, when you compared the two decisions, you did, in fact, compare the following two probability distributions (or prospects).

Decision:	Probability of		
	r_1	r_2	r_3
a_1	0	1	0
a_2	$1-p$	0	p

One can say that, of two decisions (or of two corresponding prospects), you have chosen the one with a higher, or at least not lower, utility. If you choose a_1, then $u(a_1) \geqslant u(a_2)$. The principle of choosing the decision that results in a higher average utility can, then, be rephrased as follows: "the utility of a decision is the higher, the higher the average utility resulting from it." It will therefore not contradict this principle if you simply equate $u(a_1)$ and $u(a_2)$ with the corresponding average utilities. That is

$$u(a_1) = p_0\,; \qquad u(a_2) = p$$

You have thus scaled the utilities of prospects, sure as well as non-sure ones:

$$u(r_1) = 0\,; \qquad u(r_2) = u(a_1) = p_0\,; \qquad u(a_2) = p\,; \qquad u(r_3) = 1$$

It will prove more convenient to use a notation that unifies the sure and non-sure prospects, by listing the alternative results and their corresponding probabilities. In this notation, the equations just given become

$$\begin{aligned} &u(r_1, r_2, r_3;\, 1, 0, 0) = 0\,; \\ &u(r_1, r_2, r_3;\, 0, 1, 0) = u(r_1, r_2, r_3;\, 1 - p_0, 0, p_0) = p_0 \\ &u(r_1, r_2, r_3;\, 1 - p, 0, p) = p\,; \\ &u(r_1, r_2, r_3;\, 0, 0, 1) = 1 \end{aligned}$$

It is easily checked that each of these equations satisfies the principle 'utility of a prospect equals its average utility', i.e., the average of the utilities of the component outcomes (sure prospects) promised by the prospect in question.

Note that the zero and the unit of the scale of utilities were chosen arbitrarily, by assigning utility 0 to the worst, and utility 1 to the best of the results considered. To this extent, the scale is arbitrary, just as is a temperature scale. If, for example, we had to put $u(r_1) = -10$ and $u(r_3) = +100$, the principle of choosing the decision with the higher average utility would yield [compare equations (1)]:

$$u(r_3) \cdot p + u(r_1) \cdot (1-p) = 100 \cdot p - 10 \cdot (1-p) = 110p - 10$$

as the average utility for the decision a_2; the latter we have also denoted by $(r_1, r_2, r_3; 1-p, 0, p)$. Thus if, as before, p_0 denotes the probability of peace that would make you indifferent between the two actions, our new scale will be (using both of the suggested notations):

$$\begin{aligned} u(r_1) &= u(r_1, r_2, r_3; 1, 0, 0) = -10; \\ u(r_2) &= u(a_1) = u(r_1, r_2, r_3; 0, 1, 0) = u(r_1, r_2, r_3; \\ &\qquad 1-p_0, 0, p_0) = 110p_0 - 10; \\ u(a_2) &= u(r_1, r_2, r_3; 1-p, 0, p) = 110p - 10; \\ u(r_3) &= u(r_1, r_2, r_3; 0, 0, 1) = 100 \end{aligned}$$

We see that, to convert from the old to the new utility scale, one has to perform a 'linear transformation': that is, to multiply by a constant (110) and to add a constant (−10); just as we do in converting from Fahrenheit degrees to centigrades or from altitudes measured in feet over Lake Michigan level to altitudes in meters over sea level. In this sense, the utility scale that interprets your choices among decisions is 'determinate up to an arbitrary linear transformation'. (Even, measurements of geometrical distances or of physical weights are determinate up to an arbitrary linear transformation, although in those cases only the multiplying constant is arbitrary: the 'unit of measurement'.)

So far, we have treated a case in which only three alternative outcomes (r_1, r_2, r_3) are possible. What have we shown? We have shown that your decisions are consistent with a scale of utilities that satisfies the following principle: *choose the decision that results, on the average, in the highest utility.* After fixing arbitrarily the utilities of two of the outcomes (assigning a higher utility to the better one), the application of this principle results in a definite utility number for the third outcome, and also in definite utility numbers for all prospects that promise the three outcomes with pre-assigned probabilities.

II. THE GENERAL CASE: BERNOULLI NORM

Let us now relax the strait jacket of 'three outcomes only'. Let there be any (finite) number of outcomes, also called 'sure prospects'. Let us generalize even further, by considering prospects which promise, with preassigned probabilities, not only certain outcomes, but possibly also prospects. The case where a prospect is a lottery promising certain outcomes rather than a lottery promising certain lotteries is clearly a special one, with certain probabilities shrinking to zeros.

So far, the letters a_1, a_2 stood for decision or action, and each corresponded to a certain prospect. We shall continue to denote prospects by $a_1, a_2, \ldots$, but it will be convenient also to use the subsequent letters of the alphabet ($b, c, \ldots$) and also x. For probabilities, we shall use, as before, p; but q and π will also be needed.

I want to convince the reader that it will be possible for him to set up a scale of his utilities of all prospects, sure and otherwise, this scale satisfying the following property: if a prospect x is a lottery promising the prospects $a_1, a_2, \ldots, a_n$ with subjective probabilities $\pi_1, \ldots, \pi_n$, then

$$(2) \qquad u(x) = \sum_{1}^{n} u(a_1)\, \pi_1$$

That is, again: the utility of a prospect should equal the average of promised utilities.

If it is possible to interpret your behavior as satisfying (2), we shall say that you obey the 'Bernoulli Norm': see 'Historical Note', below.

The technical term for 'average of values of a variable, weighted by probabilities of their occurrences' is 'mathematical expectation' of that variable, or, more briefly its 'expected value'. The expression on the right-hand side of (2) is, then, the 'expected value of utility of the prospect x', or, still more briefly, 'expected utility of x'. What we try to show is: there exists a numerical scale of utility for all prospects, with the following property: the utility of a prospect equals its expected utility. Since you will decide in favor of a prospect with higher utility in preference to one with lower utility, you will choose a decision that maximizes the utility of a prospect; and, by the principle just mentioned (and that we are going to prove), this implies that you maximize the expected utility of a prospect.

Let a and b be two prospects (either sure or uncertain) facing the reader, and let him regard b as better than a. Consider the following classes of prospects:

1. a and b
2. all prospects that promise a or b
3. all prospects that are not better than b and not worse than a [Obviously (1) and possibly (2) are included in (3).]
4. all prospects that are better than b
5. all prospects that are worse than a.

The utilities in class (1) will be assigned arbitrarily, except for the condition that a is worse than b. We put $u(a)=0$, $u(b)=1$. [If classes (4) and (5) were empty, a might stand for 'agony' and b for 'bliss'!]

The utilities in class (2) will all lie between (and excluding) 0 and 1, for the following reason: Let a lottery c promise b if a possible event s happens, and a if it does not happen. Therefore, if you acquire c and s happens, you get something better than a; while if s does not happen you get a. Hence c is better than a. Similarly, c is worse than b. For, if you acquire c and s happens you get b; but if s does not happen you have something worse than b. Hence $u(a)<u(c)<u(b)$ and therefore $0<u(c)<$ <1, i.e., $u(c)$ is some proper fraction.

Moreover compare two lotteries in class (2): c_1 and c_2, where c_i promises b if the event s_i happens. Let p_i be the probability of s_i and suppose $p_1<p_2$. Then $u(c_1)<u(c_2)$, for the following reason. The lottery c_2 promises b with larger probability than does lottery c_2; but with smaller probability than does a direct offer of b. Therefore c_2 can be conceived of as a lottery that promises c_1 and b with certain probabilities.[5] Hence, by a reasoning similar to the one made before, c_2 must be better than c_1 and worse than b.

It follows that you will rank the utilities of the various prospects in class (2) by assigning increasing proper fractions as the probability p of getting b increases.

It is permissible therefore to choose as the utility number for a lottery the fraction p if the lottery promises b with probability p. We have thus scaled all prospects of class (2), and this scale fits with the boundary values $u(a)=0$ and $u(b)=1$, since a and b can themselves be called lotteries, with $p=0$ and $=1$, respectively.

Before proceeding to the remaining classes of prospects, let us satisfy ourselves that our scale, so far, has the desired property. Let a prospect x

be a lottery promising prospects [belonging to classes (1) and (2)] $c_1, \ldots, c_n$ with probabilities $\pi_1, \ldots, \pi_n$. Show that

$$(3) \qquad u(x) = \sum_1^n \pi_i u(c_i)$$

To prove (3), we replace $u(x)$ by the probability with which the lottery x promises b. This probability is compounded from $p_1, \ldots, p_n$, where p_i is the probability with which c_i promises b. Hence $u(x) = \sum_1^n \pi_i p_i$. But we have seen that $u(c_i) = p_i$. Hence (3) is true.

Consider now the class (3) of prospects. It includes class (1); and we have seen that it also includes class (2); but it includes more. We have covered those of the members of (3), that are a or b or lotteries promising a or b; and we were able to assign to each of these lotteries a utility p equal to the probability with which that lottery promises b. Of course, p ranges from 0 (the utility of a itself) to 1 (the utility of b itself). Now the utility of any member of class (3) must lie between 0 and 1 since it consists of prospects that are not better than b and not worse than a. Hence, any member of class (3) – say, d_1 – that is not a lottery promising a or b has a utility that is equal to that of one of those lotteries – call it c_1 – i.e., to some p, $0 \leqslant p \leqslant 1$. If we now form a lottery y that promises various members $d_1, \ldots, d_n$ of class (3) with probabilities $\pi_1, \ldots, \pi_n$, then y has the same utility as the lottery x considered in Equation (3). For, the event s_1 (with probability π_1) will give the subject the prospect d_1 if he had chosen y; and the prospect c_1 if he had chosen x. And so for $s_2, \ldots, s_n$. But since we have seen each d_i to have the same utility as the corresponding c_i (this utility being equal to the probability with which c_i promises b), it follows that the subject is indifferent between y and x. Thus (3) is extended to all members of the class (3), since $u(y)$ can replace $u(x)$ and each $u(d_i)$ can replace $u(c_1)$.

This would complete the proof if we could assume that there exists for each subject a worst and a best prospect, 'agony' and 'bliss' (a and b). If this is not the case, i.e., utility is not bounded and classes (4) and (5) are not empty, Equation (3) still holds good. To show this, it suffices to pick the worst and the best prospect – say, a' and b' – among those composing the particular lottery x [i.e., a' and b' will be among the $c_1, \ldots, c_n$ in (3)], and use a' and b' in the same way in which a and b were treated previously; i.e., create a new scale of utilities – say, u' – with

$u'(a')=0$, $u'(b')=1$, $u'(a)=p<q=u'(b)$, where p and q are certain probabilities; a and b having, respectively, the same utilities as certain two lotteries, each promising a' or b'. We see by former reasoning, that in terms of this new scale, (3) will be valid, that is

$$(4) \qquad u'(x) = \sum \pi_1 u'(c_1)$$

But this latter equation remains valid also if the function u' is replaced by any linear transform of it, $\alpha u' + \beta$ (this can be easily verified by substitution). Now, the functions u' and u are, in fact, linear transforms of each other, with (for any c) $u'(c)=(q-p)\,u(c)+p$ [i.e., the scale u' is obtained from the scale u by shifting the origin by p and multiplying the utility unit by $q-p$]. Hence the validity of (4) entails the validity of (3) for any prospects,[6] i.e., the validity of (2).

III. HISTORICAL NOTE

Suppose that you apply the utility scale just described to various amounts of monetary wealth, and discover that, for you, the utility can be regarded as proportional to money amount. Should your tastes happen to be of this kind then (since you have agreed that your choices are as described by the Bernoulli Norm and you therefore maximize the mathematical expectation of utility) you are a maximizer of the mathematical expectation of monetary wealth. And remember that this mathematical expectation was computed on the basis of your subjective probabilities.

Now, the idea that a consistent decision-maker chooses a bet that gives him the maximum expected monetary wealth, computed on the basis of his subjective probabilities, can be traced back to Thomas Bayes (eighteenth century). Daniel Bernoulli who lived in that same century was not so clear about the subjective nature of the probabilities that can be said to underline human choice. He assumed people to know the true odds in a game, and neglected the case when a man has no sufficient theory or no large sample to compute the odds with precision. But, on the other hand, Bernoulli was emphatic (as Bayes was not: remember that Bayes dealt with money instead of utilities) about the subjective nature of preferences. Unless your tastes are of a peculiar character, utilities are not proportional to money amounts (and moreover they can and should be attached to many other objects of choice besides money!), and one must be careful to state that the consistent decision-maker maximizes his expected utility, not his expected monetary wealth. This is what we called the Bernoulli Norm. In stating it, we did describe the probabilities used as subjective and called them sometimes degrees of belief. But we did not say how they too (like the equally subjective utility numbers) can be derived as characterizing a consistent decision-maker's behavior. This was done by the late Frank Ramsey in 1926, and more recently by De Finetti and by L. J. Savage. Their approach will be outlined in our concluding section.

IV. THE RAMSEY NORM

I shall now try to convince you that your decisions, if consistent, can be interpreted in the following manner: there exist utility numbers, attached to outcomes of your actions, and there exist degrees of belief, attached to the future states of the world, with the following property: if for each of your possible actions the expected utility (i.e., the mathematical expectation of utility of outcomes) were computed on the basis of your degrees of belief, then the action chosen by you would be the one with the highest expected utility. We may call this the Ramsey Norm.

Imagine that the following eight actions $a_1, \ldots, a_8$ will have one of the two outcomes, Death (D) or Life (L), depending on whether the world will be in the state s_1 or s_2 or s_3 (mutually exclusive), as shown in the following table which, as you can convince yourself, exhausts all possible triplets of L- and D-symbols:

	States of World			Group
Actions	s_1	s_2	s_3	
a_1	D	D	D	1
a_2	L	D	D	2
a_3	D	L	D	2
a_4	D	D	L	2
a_5	D	L	L	3
a_6	L	D	L	3
a_7	L	L	D	3
a_8	L	L	L	4

I assume that you prefer Life to Death. Then you will prefer a_8 to a_7 because a_8 has a better outcome that a_7 in state s_3, and the same outcome as a_7 otherwise. By this reasoning, you will prefer the action a_8 to any of the actions in group 3; you will prefer any action in 3 and any one in 2 to the action a_1.

Now suppose, in addition, that you happen to be indifferent between a_2, a_3, and a_4. If this is the case we shall say that your degrees of belief in the occurrence of each of the states s_1, s_2, s_3 are $\frac{1}{3}$, $\frac{1}{3}$, $\frac{1}{3}$; and we shall assign to the occurrence of the state s_1 *or* s_2 (and similarly: of the state s_1 *or* s_3; and s_2 *or* s_3) the degree of belief $\frac{2}{3}$. Moreover: would it be reasonable for you to be indifferent within group 2 and not to be indifferent within group 3? Would this not mean that you grant the three possible future states of the world an equal degree of belief as long as rewards or punishments are attached to them in a certain way, but revise your beliefs when the rewards and punishments are interchanged? This would be unreasonable.

We thus have:

$$u(a_1) < u(a_2) = u(a_3) = u(a_4) < u(a_5) = u(a_6) = u(a_7) <$$
$$< u(a_8).$$

We now proceed to scale these utilities. We are free to fix the utility of Life (like the utility of 'bliss' in an earlier part of the paper) at 1, and the utility of Death at 0. Then the utilities of prospects will also fall in their places, being equal to the probability of Life as promised in a given prospect. That is, we obtain $u(a_1)=0$; $u(a_8)=1$; $u(a_2)=u(a_3)=u(a_4)=\frac{1}{3}$; $u(a_5)=u(a_6)=u(a_7)=\frac{2}{3}$. We shall find as before that this utility scale is consistent with your being a maximizer of expected utility.

Thus, not only your utilities but also your degrees of belief can be derived from your behavior – including the indifference which you have shown in choosing within group 2 of actions (and also – as consistency required – within the group 3 of actions).

We have thus shown that it was possible to interpret your choices as consistent with the existence of utilities and subjective probabilities and with the maximization of expected utility. Granted that the example was a special one. It can be easily extended to n (instead of 3) states of the world, and degrees of belief $0, 1/n, 2/n, \ldots, (n-1)/n, 1$ can then be defined – if one can catch you as being indifferent within a certain group of decisions.

How to arrange for a demarcation of states of the world that would make this possible requires a more complete and rigorous logical analysis. (This has been done by L. J. Savage.) Here we have had to content ourselves with a mere sketch.

NOTES

[1] For example, at the colloquium on risk in econometrics, held in 1952; its Proceedings published by the Centre National de la Recherche Scientifique, Paris, 1953.
[2] I. N. Herstein and John Milnor, 'An Axiomatic Approach to Measurable Utility', *Econometrica*, 1953.
[3] John Wiley and Sons, 1954.
[4] *Selected Essays*, 1, 2.
[5] Let these probabilities be q and $1-q$, respectively, q is easy to find (though it is not really necessary for our purpose) by posing

$$q \cdot p_1 + (1 - q) \cdot 1 = p_2$$

since p_2, the chance of obtaining b, must be equal to the chance (in the new lottery) of getting it by virtue of having gotten c_1, *plus* the chance of getting it directly. We have $q = (1 - p_2)/(1 - p_1)$.
[6] With $u(a) = 0$ and $u(b) = 1$, the utility $u(e)$ of a member of class (4) and the utility $u(f)$ of a member of class (5) are easily shown to be

$$u(e) = \frac{1}{q} > 1; \quad u(f) = 1 - \frac{1}{r} < 0$$

where q and r are probabilities defined as follows: the subject is indifferent between b and a lottery promising e or with respective probabilities q and $1 - q$; and he is indifferent between a and a lottery promising f or b with respective probabilities r and $1 - r$. It is easily verified that with these definitions,

$$u(e) \cdot q + u(a) \cdot (1 - q) = u(b)$$

and

$$u(f) \cdot r - u(b) \cdot (1 - r) = u(a)$$

4

PROBABILITY IN THE SOCIAL SCIENCES

(1954)

I. PROBABILITIES AND THE NORMS OF BEHAVIOR

Recently,[1] the U.N. forces in Korea faced the choice between two decisions: (I) to cross the 38° parallel or (II) not to cross it. Their commanders did not know whether, if the parallel were crossed, the Chinese adversary would or would not answer by counter-attacking in superior power, from across Korea's Northern border. In the language of current newspapers, our officers did not know whether the Chinese did or did not have 'aggressive intentions'. This is a vague term. The following table gives, however, an implicit definition that is precise enough. The intentions of the adversary are defined by their results, as follows:

TABLE I.1

	Our behavior	
Chinese behavior	(I) Cross the parallel	(II) Don't cross the parallel
(a) 'aggressive'	U.N.Losses	Stalemate
(b) 'non-aggressive'	U.N.Gains	Stalemate

We shall assume that, from the U.N. point of view, gains are preferable to stalemate, and stalemate is preferable to losses. We shall use the phrase 'probability is equal to one' as equivalent to 'it is certain'. Now suppose the probability of the Chinese being 'non-aggressive' is one. Then policy (I) produces a result (gains) preferable to the result (stalemate) of policy (II). The U.N. commander 'should' choose (I). If the probability of (b) were not one but zero – i.e., if the probability of (a) were one – he 'should' choose (II). Thus if we know that our commander was sure (rightly or wrongly) of his opponent's intentions and has done what he 'should' have done, then his opinion about those intentions – his assignment of probabilities to (a) and (b) – would be revealed by this action.

A similar inference from action to opinion, under the assumption that the acting person is doing what he 'should' be doing, can be made also in a more general case: namely, in the case when our commander is not necessarily sure as to the adversary's intentions, and thus associates them with probabilities that are not necessarily 1 or 0 but may be intermediate between 1 and 0. Such fractional probabilities we have not yet defined. Yet you have no doubt acted on the basis of judgments such as 'an assertion is almost certain to be true' (='is very probable'), 'almost certain to be untrue' (=has small probability), 'as likely as not to be true' (=has probability $\frac{1}{2}$).

Let us look into this more carefully. To avoid terminological confusion, let us call the probabilities assigned by our commander to the alternatives (a) and (b), his 'subjective probabilities'. We are not interested at present in how they originate – whether the commander derived them from some systematic observations, or based them on some vague experience, or even possibly on mere prejudice. We shall explore, instead, *whether these subjective probabilities can be defined in terms of his action.* The suspicion that this can be done is suggested by the following. Suppose our commander is 'almost certain' (subjective probability 'a little below one') that (b) is true; then, is it not right to say that he 'should' cross the 38° parallel? If he is 'almost certain' that (b) is not true (subjective probability 'a little above zero'), he 'should' not cross. One may therefore be tempted to say that there exists a certain critical level for the subjective probability of (b), with the following property: if the subjective probability of (b) is above this level, our commander chooses (I); if it is below, he chooses (II). 'Man is the measure' – if not of all things then, at least, of his own subjective probabilities, as revealed by his action.

A little reflection shows, however, that the commander's action cannot have been determined by his subjective probabilities, unless some – equally subjective – 'values' or 'utilities' had been attached to the outcomes of his actions – to the 'gains', 'losses' and 'stalemates' entered in our table. As a matter of fact, we had already made a statement about the utilities of these outcomes, when we said that gains are preferred to stalemate and stalemate is preferred to losses. If the three outcomes are thus 'completely ordered', we can attach to them 'utility numbers' which would be ordered in a corresponding fashion: for example, 7, 5, 1; or 6, 4, 2; or log6, log4, log2; – in short, any decreasing sequence of three numbers. If any such sequence is used to designate utility numbers, the outcome with a higher number will be preferred to one with a lower number. Yet such ordering of the outcomes is not sufficient to determine choice of action, even if the subjective probabilities of outcomes of a given action are fixed.

Suppose, for example, that two U.N. officers, an American and a South-Korean, agree that the Chinese are as likely as not to counter-attack if we cross 38° parallel. Yet the American may disfavor the crossing, while the South-Korean may advocate it. That is, the American may prefer a stalemate to a 50–50 chance of gains or losses; while the South-Korean (possibly reflecting his government's eagerness to re-unite the country) has an opposite preference. Thus, choice is determined by the complete ordering (the 'order of preferences') of probability distributions of outcomes, not by the complete ordering of the outcomes themselves.

The complete ordering of probability distributions is consistent with (though not necessarily equivalent to) assigning 'utility numbers' to probability distributions of outcomes, as well as to the outcomes themselves, according to the following rule: the utility number attached to a given probability distribution of outcomes equals the average of the utility numbers of the outcomes, weighted with the respective probabilities of those outcomes.[2]

In our example, both the American and the South-Korean may assign the same utility numbers to the best and the worst outcome: say 100 to 'gains', 0 to 'losses'. If they both want to maximize the expected utility, then their assumed disagreement about what to do reveals that, for the American, the utility of a stalemate is larger than 50 – namely, larger than $(\frac{1}{2})(100)+(\frac{1}{2})(0)$ – while for the South-Korean it is less than 50. One can, in fact, imagine an experiment in which a commander has to make (hypothetical) decisions, being faced not only with the choice 'a stalemate or a 50–50 chance of gains or losses', but also with choices such as 'a stalemate or a 60–40 chance of gains or losses', 'a stalemate or a 70–30 chance of gains or losses', etc. Suppose one would thus find a break-even point: for example, suppose that the commander has decided to cross the parallel if he felt that the chance of gains is larger than or equal to 65%; and not to cross if he felt the chance of gains is smaller than 65%. Then we can say that, for him, stalemate is equivalent to a 65–35 chance of gains or losses. Consequently, on a scale of utilities in which 100 and 0 are, respectively, assigned to gains and losses, the utility of stalemate (for that commander) will be 65, because (100) (65%) + (0) (35%) = 65. Thus, if we fix the '0' and '100' points in any arbitrary way (this is similar to the '0' and '212' points of the Fahrenheit scale, or the '0' and '100' of the centigrade scale of temperature), and if we assume that the man is 'doing what he should do' and that he 'should' maximize expected utility, then his actual responses to given probabilities of outcomes of his actions can be interpreted as revealing the utility numbers attached to each of those outcomes.[3]

Conversely, if the utilities attached by the decision-make to alternative outcomes are known, it is possible to infer from his decisions the subjective probabilities that he attaches to alternative outcomes – provided that he 'is doing what he should do' and that he 'should' always maximize expected utility.

It is historically interesting that Thomas Bayes, one of the founders of the theory of probability, used just this kind of inference in order to define probability: In his posthumous essay (famous for another reason) we read[4]

The probability of any event is the ratio between the value at which an expectation depending on the happening of the event ought to be computed, and the value of the thing expected upon its happening (Definition 5); and
'If a person has an expectation depending on the happening of an event, the probability of the event is to the probability of its failure as his loss if it fails to his gain if it happens' (Proposition 2).

Note Bayes' phrase 'ought to be computed'. His definition is a norm of behavior. To your gain (a_1 dollars, say) that is contingent upon an uncertain event, there 'ought to' correspond in your mind a smaller but sure gain (a dollars, say) such that you are indifferent between gaining a_1 upon the happening of the uncertain event, or gaining a with certainty. Hence, there is (or rather ought to be) in your mind also a ratio of these two numbers, $a/a_1 = p_1$, say. It is called by Bayes, probability of the event; while he calls a the 'expectation'. Suppose further that, if the event fails to happen, you neither gain nor lose. Then clearly $a = a_1 \cdot p_1 + 0 \cdot (1 - p_1)$ is the average of gain and loss, weighted with their respective probabilities. You 'ought to compute' this weighted average before making a choice. Of two uncertain gains choose the one with the higher value of expection.

In Bayes' second quoted statement the person must have chosen to conclude a fair bet – that is, the expection value $p_1 a_1 + p_2 a_2 = 0$, where the loss (taken as a positive number) equals to $-a_2$ and has probability $p_2(=1-p_1)$. Hence $p_1/p_2 = -a_2/a_1$.

No problem of ascertaining utility arises for Bayes because his gains and losses are money amounts. We can reformulate his definition of probability as the following normative statement (which we shall call 'Bayes' norm'):

Let the possible decisions be numbered $1,\ldots,n$; let the possible states of the world be numbered $1,\ldots,m$. Denote by a_{ij} the gain that the person will obtain if he takes the jth decision, and the world is in its ith state. Then, if the person behaves 'as he should', there exists a set of m non-negative numbers p_i which add up to unity

$$\sum_{i=1}^{m} p_i = 1$$

and have the following property: one decision (say the jth) is not preferred to another (say the kth) when and only when

$$\sum_{i=1}^{m} p_i a_{ij} \leqslant \sum_{i=1}^{m} p_i a_{ik} \quad (j, k = 1, \ldots, n) \tag{1.1}$$

A number p_i is called the (subjective) probability of the ith state of the world; the two sums in (1.1) are called expected gains associated with, respectively, the jth and the kth decision.

As an example (with $m=n=2$), the possible gains of a man who has decided between buying and not buying stocks are tabulated (See Table I.2.)

If the subject decides according to the norm thus postulated, then there must exist subjective probabilities p_1, $p_2(=1-p_1)$, with the following property: $p_1a_{11}+p_2a_{21} \leqslant p_1a_{12}+p_2a_{22}$ if the subject does not prefer buying to not buying; and such that $p_1a_{11}+p_{21}a_{21} \geqslant p_1a_{12}+p_2a_{22}$ if he does not prefer not buying to buying. Consequently, if he is indifferent between buying and not buying, both these relations are true so that

$$\begin{gathered} p_1a_{11} + p_2a_{21} = p_1a_{12} + p_2a_{22} \\ \frac{p_1}{p_2} = \frac{a_{22} - a_{21}}{a_{11} - a_{12}}, \quad \text{where} \quad p_1 + p_2 = 1. \end{gathered} \tag{1.2}$$

(Note that if we had put, for simplicity, $a_{12}=a_{22}=0$, we would obtain Bayes' 'Proposition 2'). Thus by confronting the subject with varying quadruplets of prospective gains one can estimate the subjective probabilities he assigns to the stocks' rise or fall, respectively. For example if (1.2) is satisfied for $a_{11}=-100$ dollars, $a_{21}=+300$ dollars, and $a_{12}=$ $=a_{22}=0$, then 'the odds are' $p_1:p_2=3:1$, in favor of falling stocks; or $p_1=\frac{3}{4}, p_2=\frac{1}{4}$.

TABLE I.2

States of the world $i=$	Decisions $j=$ 1. Buy	2. Don't buy
1. Stocks will fall	a_{11}	a_{12}
2. Stocks will rise	a_{21}	a_{22}

It is empirically ascertainable whether a subject's behavior is consistent with this norm. If it is, the subjective probabilities themselves are ascertainable. Consider, for example, the following "payoff matrices' – each being simply the Table 1.2, with captions omitted and letters a_{ij} replaced by dollar figures:

TABLE I.3

$$\begin{pmatrix}-100 & 0\\ 300 & 0\end{pmatrix};\quad \begin{pmatrix}-1 & 0\\ 3 & 0\end{pmatrix};\quad \begin{pmatrix}-2 & -1\\ 4 & 1\end{pmatrix};\quad \begin{pmatrix}-1 & 0\\ 2 & 0\end{pmatrix}.$$

Suppose that the subject is indifferent between buying and not buying when the gains are as in the first matrix. This is simply the case already studied; it has revealed subjective odds 3:1 in favor of falling stocks. Now, the norm implies that if he is indifferent between buying and not buying when faced with the first matrix, he should also be indifferent between buying and not buying when faced with the second and third matrices, but should not buy when faced with the fourth matrix of Table I:3: because not only

$$(-100)\left(\tfrac{3}{4}\right)+(300)\left(\tfrac{1}{4}\right)=(0)\left(\tfrac{3}{4}\right)+(0)\left(\tfrac{1}{4}\right)\quad\text{but also}$$
$$(-1)\left(\tfrac{3}{4}\right)+(3)\left(\tfrac{1}{4}\right)=(0)\left(\tfrac{3}{4}\right)+(0)\left(\tfrac{1}{4}\right)\quad\text{and also}$$
$$(-2)\left(\tfrac{3}{4}\right)+(4)\left(\tfrac{1}{4}\right)=(-1)\left(\tfrac{3}{4}\right)+(1)\left(\tfrac{1}{4}\right);\quad\text{while}$$
$$(-1)\left(\tfrac{3}{4}\right)+(2)\left(\tfrac{1}{4}\right)<(0)\left(\tfrac{3}{4}\right)+(0)\left(\tfrac{1}{4}\right).$$

Such empirical tests of consistency of a man's behavior with some given norm have been occasionally described as meaningless; with the consequence drawn that the (approximate) measurement of subjective probabilities has no meaning. The argument is as follows. Suppose the subject is indifferent between buying and not buying when faced with the first matrix of Table I.3, and also when faced with the fourth matrix. This need not imply that his behavior is inconsistent with Bayes' norm. The subject may have merely changed, during the time required by the experiments, his subjective odds, from 3:1 to 2:1 [since $(-1)(\frac{2}{3})+(2)(\frac{1}{3})=0$]. Suppose, on the other hand, that the subject, when faced with different payoff matrices, almost always makes the same choices as he would make if he maintained unchanged subjective odds and obeyed the Bayes' norm. Yet the subject may have behaved in contradiction with Bayes' norm; he may have changed his opinion about the odds, from experiment to experiment, in exactly such a fashion that the contradiction was masked.

This objection makes it necessary to reformulate every behavior norm by requiring that it should be 'approximately' valid during a specified period of time. But what is meant by 'approximate', and how to determine the time interval over which the norm is valid? This will depend on the use that has to be made of the norm in practice. The next two lectures give several illustrations of how the merely 'approximate' description of human behavior is used for prediction and policy.

What we called the Bayes' norm is quite innocent of the concept of utility. Herein lies its limitation. Most decisions do not result in monetary gains and losses. The military gain, or loss, in our Korean example (Table I.1) is not expressible, either as a money amount or as any other single quantity. It is, at best, a combination of quantities (a 'vector'): so and so many guns, prisoners, villages taken. To be sure (and this will help us later), even when the alternative outcomes differ only because of the presence or absence of some 'qualitative' attributes ('to live in the corn-belt', 'to die in New York') one can express them as a combination of quantities, each possibly having only a finite number of values: e.g., life or death = 1 or 2; corn-belt or New York or West Coast = 1 or 2 or 3; so that life in the corn-belt = vector (1,1). But this may be inconvenient. For our purposes, it is unnecessary. Our Korean example has shown, in a preliminary way, that we can interpret choices by assigning subjective 'utility numbers' to alternative events, the events themselves not having been expressed either as values of single numerical variables (such as the number of guns or of prisoners) nor as combinations of such values (the number of guns and of prisoners). We have seen that, *given the probabilities* of outcomes, one can infer from manifest decisions to underlying subjective utilities, provided the subject has chosen 'as he ought to'. To formalize this statement, let us replace Bayes' norm by the following one:

Let A be the set of all possible outcomes of the subject's decisions. Let a_{ij} $(i=1,\ldots m;\ 1,\ldots,n)$ be that element of A which he associates with the ith state of the world and his jth decision. If the probability assigned by the subject to the ith state of the world is

$$p_i (p_i \geqslant 0; \textstyle\sum p_i = 1; i = 1, \ldots, m)$$

and if he behaves 'as he should' then there exists a real valued function $u(a_{ij}) = u_{ij}$ such that one decision (say, the jth) is not preferred to another (say, the kth) when and only when

$$\sum_{i=1}^{m} p_i u_{ij} \leqslant \sum_{i=1}^{m} p_i u_{ik} \quad (j, k = 1, \ldots, n). \tag{3}$$

The function $u(\ )$ is called utility function; its value u_{ij} is called the utility of the outcome a_{ij}. The two sums in (3) are called expected utilities associated, respectively, with the jth and the kth decision.

The norm just stated presupposes that probabilities are given to the subject; and his actual decisions reveal his system of utilities.

This is, in a sense, opposite to Bayes' norm because if a subject acts according to Bayes' norm his actual decisions reveal his subjective probabilities; while the utilities are given, and are simply identical with amounts of money. We may call the norm just stated, the 'Daniel Bernoulli norm'.[5] His concept of 'moral expectation' is, in fact, identical with the 'expected utility' of the statement just formulated, at least for the special case when each a_{ij} is a number, viz., the monetary wealth of the subject. More generally, the a_{ij} may denote any kind of situation which the subject expects to be the result of a given decision of his.

To exemplify Bernoulli's norm we may use the captions of Table I.2 but replace monetary gains a_{ij} by utility numbers u_{ij}. We can, similarly, interpret the numbers entered in Table I.3 as utility numbers. Note that, in the case when these numbers measure the utilities associated with the monetary gains, it is the utilities not the dollar amounts that have, for example, in the first column of the first matrix, the ratio 1:3. If the person knows (or thinks he knows) the odds to be 3:1 in favor of stocks falling, he will be indifferent between buying and not buying if faced with the first three matrices; and will not buy if faced with the fourth.

If the probability estimates of the subject are known, and if he behaves according to the 'D. Bernoulli norm', it is possible to ascertain the utility numbers he assigns to various events, although only (as with centigrades and Fahrenheit degrees) up to two arbitrary constants. For example, suppose the subject is indifferent between buying and not buying stock when faced with the payoff matrix in dollars, given on the left part of the Table I.4.

TABLE I.4

Payoff in dollars		Payoff in utilities	
$a_{11} = -100$	$a_{12} = 50$	$u_{11} = u(-100) = 0$	$u_{12} = u(50) = ?$
$a_{21} = 200$	$a_{22} = 50$	$u_{21} = u(200) = 1$	$u_{21} = u(50) = ?$

Suppose (as before) that the odds are 3:1 in favor of the first row (falling stock prices). On the right side of Table I.4, we have fixed arbitrarily the zero and unity of the utility scale: 0 = utility of $-\$100$; 1 = utility of $200. What is, on this scale, the utility of $50? From the subject's indifference between the two decisions (represented, respectively, by the first and second column) we conclude, using D. Bernoulli's norm: $(0)\ (\frac{3}{4}) + $ $+ (1)\ (\frac{1}{4}) = u\ (50) = 0.25$. Thus, by varying the odds on which the subject is supposed to base his decision, and finding dollar payoff matrices such that the subject is indifferent between to decisions, one obtains the subject's utility scale for various outcomes of his decisions having arbitrarily fixed two points on this scale. This has been essentially the procedure of Mosteller and Nogee, already mentioned. The experimental difficulty includes, in particular, the ascertaining that the subject has 'learned' the odds that he is told are prevailing. Moreover, analogous to the discussion we had on the occasion of the Bayes' norm one has to meet the objection that the person may change his behavior parameters (his utility numbers, in the present case) during the experiment.

In the example just used, the outcomes a_{ij} were dollar amounts; it was shown that the utility number corresponding to any given dollar gain or loss – and thus the 'utility function of money gains' – can be ascertained from the actual choices of a subject assumed to obey a certain norm. Instead, the a_{ij} might equally well have been, not dollar gains or losses, nor the values of any other single variable (number of prisoners taken), but vectors of quantities, or 'qualitative' outcomes. Our example illustrates, incidentally, that Bayes' norm is not serviceable, not only because it has to deal with outcomes that are values of a single variable only, but also because it disagrees with the experience that people who can be expected to behave 'as they should' may have non-linear utility functions of money: the gain of $50 is half-way between −$100 and +$200; yet the choice has proved consistent with the utility of $50 being not half-way but one-quarter of the distance between −$100 and +$200. It seems that Bayes overlooked the reasons which had led his predecessors (Daniel Bernoulli, Cramer) to insist on the difference between 'physical wealth' and 'moral wealth': the latter not being, in general, proportional to the former. Present day economists call the latter, 'utility' (of a given monetary wealth or, more generally and precisely, of a given combination of goods in one's present and future possession). Even for the directors of a corporate firm, who decide on the basis of monetary profits and losses and not of ultimate 'pleasures and pains', it is not true that a dollar has the same weight in the decision regardless of the dollars already earned. A loss leading to bankruptcy subtracts more from the utility than a profit of equal size adds to it – the utility function is non-linear. For an attacker bent on destruction, the utility is not a linear function of the physical damage inflicted upon the enemy; rather, destruction beyond a certain point is useless to the attacker. And so on.

The D. Bernoulli norm, formulated in its essence around 1730, was accepted by modern economists like Alfred Marshall. But the assumption that a person computes and compares expected utilities associated with his alternative decisions may appear as complicated and artificial (not more or less, though, than does the computation of expected monetary gains which se med so evident to Bayes as to make him base on it his definition of probability!) In our days, von Neumann and Morgenstern, the authors of the *Theory of Games*, improved on their predecessors by providing a set of postulates, equivalent to, but in some sense simpler more appealing than the postulate of maximizing expected utility. More recent writers have tried to propose postulates that are still more 'transparent'.[6]

It is a remarkable psychological fact that a proposition may be equivalent to a set of intuitively appealing propositions and yet be not itself intuitively appealing. There would be otherwise no need for mathematical textbooks! This is a human limitation. For God, of course, the simplest axioms and the most difficult theorems are equally obvious, and their roles interchangeable. Let us, then, look at behavior postulates that are logically equivalent to but 'psychologically' simpler than the Bernoulli norm.

Let A, B, C,... denote probability distributions of outcomes; (in a special case a 'distribution' may assign probability 1 to one event, and 0 to all others; it is, in this case, identical with that single event). Denote by ABp the following probability distribution: 'probability p that the distribution is A; probability 1-p that the distribution is B'. Let $A \leqslant B$ mean 'A is not preferred to (or 'not better than') B'. '$A = B$' will be written instead of '$A \leqslant B$ and $B \leqslant A$' and will mean 'the subject is indifferent between A and B'. '$A < B$' will be written instead of '$A \leqslant B$ and not $B \leqslant A$' and will mean 'A is worse than B'. Then the subject 'should' obey the following rules:

I. The A, B, C,... are 'completely ordered' by the relation $\leqslant$; that is,
  (1) $A \leqslant B$ or $B \leqslant A$ ('comparability');
  (2) if $A \leqslant B$ and $B \leqslant C$ then $A \leqslant C$ ('transivity').

II. If $A = B$ then $CAp = CBp$.

III. If $A < B$ and $B < C$ then there exists a unique p such that $B = ACp$.

Rule I needs no explanation. A verbal comment on Rule II can be provided as follows. If A is not preferred to B and B is not preferred to C, I am indifferent as between the two. I am now offered two lotteries – one promising either C or A, with odds $p:(1-p)$, and the other promising either C or B, with the same odds. Thus the same outcome, C, with probability p, will occur on both lotteries; and if C does not occur then the first lottery will give me A, while the second will give me B. But I am indifferent between A and B. Hence, there is no reason for me to prefer one lottery to another.

Rule III asserts, in a rather strong form, the 'continuity' of the preference relation. Actually a milder formulation of Rule III, and also of Rule II would suffice to obtain the needed result, viz., the 'D. Bernoulli norm'. Our stronger formulation gives an easier, though more superficial, insight into the matter, although, even so, I shall have merely to hint at the proof. Note first that our rules permit us to 'calibrate' a utility scale as one does a thermometer. Choose three prospects A, B, C such that I am not indifferent between any two of them. Then, by Rule I, they can be ordered in a unique fashion. Suppose this order is: B is preferred to C, and C to A. On a horizontal straight line, plot them in the order (from left to right): A, C, B (Figure I.5). Call a number $u(A)$ the utility of A; this will be also the utility of all prospects A', A'', which, for me, are neither better nor worse than A. Similarly call $u(B)$ the utility of B and its equivalents. What number $u(C)$ shall we then have to assign to the utility of C and of its equivalents? By Rule III there exists a unique probability p such that, to me, C is equivalent to BAp. Call $u(C)$ the number equal to $pu(B)+(1-p)$ $u(A)$. In particular if we arbitrarily fix $u(A)=0$ and $u(B)=1$ then $u(C)$ is simply equal to p. We can now place C on our scale (Figure I.5), making the distance AB to represent one utility unit, and the distance AC to represent p utility units $(0<p<1)$. By Rule II, the number p will also measure the utility of all lotteries such as $A'Bp$, $AB'p$, $A'B'p$, where A' is equivalent to A and B' is equivalent to B. We can thus 'calibrate' the utility scale for all prospects which are not better than B and not worse than A: they will be expressed by appropriate numbers ranging from 0 to 1. If a prospect D is worse than A, then A lies on our scale between D and B. Suppose the odds (those required by the Rule III) which make A equivalent to a lottery promising B or D are $q:(1-q)$; that is, I am indifferent between A and BDq. Then call the utility of D, $u(D)$, a number such that $u(B)\cdot q+u(D)\ (1-q)=u(A)$. With $u(A)=0$ and $u(B)=1$ this makes $u(D)=-q/(1-q)$.

Outcomes: D	A	C	B	E
Utilities: $-q/(1-q)$	0	p	1	$1/r$

$$\overline{AC}:\overline{CB} = p:(1-p);\ u(C) = u(B)\cdot p+u(A)\cdot(1-p)$$

$$\overline{BA}:\overline{AC} = q:(1-q);\ u(A) = u(B)\cdot q+u(D)\cdot(1-q)$$

$$\overline{AB}:\overline{BE} = r:(1-r);\ u(B) = u(E)\cdot r+u(A)\cdot(1-r)$$

Fig. I.5

By an analogous procedure utility numbers are assigned to prospects – such as E in our figure – that are better than B. We have thus calibrated the utilities of all possible prospects. If we now assign the numbers 0 and 1 to the utilities not of A and B, but of some other pair of (non-equivalent) prospects, the origin and the unit of measurement of utilities is changed (just like we can measure the altitude of a mountain from the sea level as well as from a lake level, in yards as well as in feet). But in any case, the Bernoulli norm will follow. For, to take up first the case when a prospect involves only two alternative outcomes, we have seen (see Figure I.5) that the utility of such a prospect equals the sum of the utilities of the outcomes, multiplied by respective probabilities; i.e., the utility of a prospect equals its 'expected utility'. And since higher utilities are preferred to smaller ones, a prospect will not be preferred to another one unless its expected utility is higher. To extend this to the case of prospects involving more than two alternative outcomes is a matter of easy algebra. We shall skip it.

Our Figure I.5 could be also used to explain the approach of Bayes, if we reverse the problem and consider the outcomes as represented by given distances from the zero-point, measured in money units: $A=0$ dollars, $B=1$ dollar. Then Bayes defines the probability of, say, C, by the ratio of the distances $\overline{AC}:\overline{AB}$. This 'calibrates' probabilities.

We can say that in the Bayes norm the utilities were assumed objectively given (viz., identical with money amounts), and the probabilities were derived as parameters of the subject's behavior, as his 'degrees of belief'. Contrariwise, the Bernoulli norm assumes probabilities to be objectively given and derives subjective utilities. We had criticized Bayes' norm for its identifying the outcomes of decisions with the values of a single variable (such as the money gain) observable without reference to the subject. But a similar criticism applies to the Bernoulli norm. The probabilities on which the subject bases his action need not be identical with some objective properties of chance devices (cards, dice) which the experimenter uses. This was observed by the English mathematician and logician, F. P. Ramsey. He shows that manifest decisions can be thought of as revealing *both* the subject's probabilities *and* utilities. We can call 'Ramsey's norm' the following statement:

Let A be the set of all possible outcomes of the subject's decisions. Let a_{ij}

$(i=1,\ldots,m; j=1,\ldots,n)$ be that element of A which he associates with the ith state of the world and with his jth decision. If the subject behaves 'as he should', then there exists a unique set of numbers $p_i (p_i \geqslant 0; \sum p_i = 1; i=1,\ldots,m)$ and a real valued function $u(a_{ij}) = u_{ij}$ such that one decision (say, the jth) is not preferred to another (say, the kth) when and only when

$$(3) \qquad \sum_{i=1}^{m} p_i u_{ij} \leqslant \sum_{i=1}^{m} p_i u_{ik} (j, k = 1, \ldots, n).$$

The numbers p_i are called subjective probabilities (or degrees of belief). The function $u(a_{ij})$ is called utility function; its value u_{ij} is called the utility of the outcome a_{ij}. The two sums in (3) are called expected utilities associated, respectively, with the jth and the kth decision.

A set of behavior rules, equivalent to Ramsey's norm but 'psychologically' more appealing was proposed by Ramsey himself and, in our days, by De Finetti and, especially, by Savage.[7] It would be difficult to convey their proofs in this lecture. But it is possible to indicate that subjective probabilities can be defined on the basis of observable decisions of a subject, even if one rejects the identification (practised by Bayes) between utilities and money gains; and to indicate how this definition of probability is related to the norm requiring maximization of expected utility. Consider the matrix in Table I.6 of outcomes a_{ij}, with $m=n=2$. Suppose I am indifferent between the two decisions. Then Ramsey will define the degrees

TABLE I.6

States of the world (i)	Decisions (j) 1	2
1	α	β
2	β	α

of belief in (or the subjective probability of) each of the two states of the world as $p_1 = p_2 = \frac{1}{2}$. For example, suppose an urn contains white and red balls and I am given the choice between the following two options: (1) if I draw white, I die; if red, I live; (2) if I draw red, I die; if white, I live. If I am indifferent between the two options (but not between life and death) I have equal degrees of belief (defined as $\frac{1}{2}$) that the ball drawn will be white or red. We postulate that the subject has consistent degree of belief. That is, he will remain indifferent between any two options represented by the matrix of Table I.6, regardless of what meaning is given to the outcomes α and β. Having thus defined subjective probability$=\frac{1}{2}$ (but not yet any other probabilities) enables Ramsey to define a scale of measurable utilities, as follows. An outcome γ is said to be 'half-way' between α and β if the subject is indifferent between γ and the prospect of having α or β with subjective odds $\frac{1}{2}:\frac{1}{2}$. It is again postulated that the subject is consistent, in the sense that γ will remain 'half-way' between α and β regardless of the particular pair of the states of the world to which the subjective probabilities $\frac{1}{2}$, $\frac{1}{2}$ are attached. Now Ramsey can define the utility of α as zero, the utility of γ as 1, the utility of β as 2, and (with the help of some further axioms on order and continuity) he can construct the scale of utilities. This brings him to the same point at which Bayes had made the start, except that Bayes' money amounts are replaced by utility numbers. Like Bayes, Ramsey can now calibrate probabilities: these are ratios between certain differences between utilities – as on our Figure I.5. The norm that prospects with higher expected utilities should be preferred to those with lower ones follows immediately.

It is worth noting that the logic of connecting between 'measurable', (and not merely 'completely ordered') utilities as required by the Bernoulli and the Ramsey norm has been patterned, to a large extent, after Hilbert's 'Foundations of Geometry'[8] in which the relation was established between points ordered along a straight line and the real numbers measuring distances. In a more general sense, too, discussion of behavior norms is similar to that of foundations of geometry. Various geometries – various internally consistetn sets of axions and theorems – are possible. So are various sets of behavior rules. Such consistent systems do not assert anything about empirical reality – e.g., about physical or psychological phenomena. Yet they do help to order these phenomena, by comparing facts with ideals. The normative discussion of behavior shares this feature with mathematics and logics. In addition, it shares with logic another feature: certain modes of thinking *and* acting may be 'preferable' to others. For example, it is preferable, when one is told that all men are mortals, not to conclude that all mortals are men; and it is preferable, choosing A in preference to B, and B in preference to C, not to choose C in preference to A. We are warned against 'bad logic' as well as against 'inconsistent behavior' (the latter is even called sometimes 'illogical behavior'). The warning is of a pragmatic nature: bad logicians won't survive. In the last lecture, we shall return to this practical aspect of normative social science, and of probabilities in social science.

The approach of Ramsey and of D. Bernoulli is more congenial to social scientists than that of Bayes because Bayes confined himself to outcomes which are money gains. But still more important, the common feature of the approach of both Ramsey and Bayes, is particularly congenial to social scientists. It permits us to deal with 'probabilities of single events'. While the XVIII century Continentals, in Paris or Petersburg, indulged in dice and cards, and watched the frequencies of repeated events, the English seem to have thought more of horses and fighting cocks and wrestlers. The betting books of Oxford colleges are full of guesses such as 'Napoleon is dead' (dated November 1812) accompanied by the betting ratios – whether in guineas or in bottles of port. This is right after the social scientist's taste! He is often unable to observe repeated events.

But, then the following question arises: if I happen to be able to observe repeated events, how shall I use those observations in computing my 'degrees of belief', which are my guide in decision-making? Shall I, for example, equate my degree of belief in drawing a white ball from an urn, to the relative frequency of such drawings in the past, at least as an approximation? In short: *is there any relation between subjective probabilities and the statistical method*? Is there any sense in the statement: 'The chances that I shall survive the operation are the same as getting a royal flush'? (These questions are important for our future discussion because in the two remaining lectures, statistical methods will be applied to human and social phenomena and to policy decisions.)

These questions were, in essence, answered in the affirmative by Bayes himself, and again, in our time, by Ramsey. To justify the affirmative answer, one first shows that the 'law of large numbers', properly interpreted, does follow from the properties of subjective probabilities. To do this, it will be convenient to use the concepts of 'conditional probabilities' and of 'independence'. We shall define them as we proceed. (These concepts will also prove useful in Lectures 2 and 3.)

Let $\bar{W}$ be the negation of the state of the world W, and let $\bar{V}$ be the negation of the state of the world V; and suppose that the subject is indifferent between the following options:

$$\left.\begin{array}{l}\alpha \text{ if } \bar{W}\\ \beta \text{ if } W\\ \end{array}\right\} \text{ and } \left\{\begin{array}{l}\alpha \text{ if } \bar{W}\\ \beta' \text{ if } W \text{ and } V\\ \beta'' \text{ if } W \text{ and } \bar{V}\end{array}\right.$$

For example: let α=death, β=survival; β'=early arrival; β''=late arrival; $\bar{W}$=plane has engine trouble; V=plane is fast. Then the option on the left hand is: to die if the plane has engine trouble; to survive if it has not. The option on the right hand is: to die if the plane has engine trouble; to survive and arrive early if the plane has no engine trouble and is a fast one; to survive and arrive late if the plane has no engine trouble and is a slow one.[9] Our assumption is, then, that I am indifferent between the option on the left hand and the option on the right hand. That is, by Ramsey's postulate, the expected utility of the left-hand option is equal to that of the right-hand option. But the expected utility of the left-hand option is clearly

$$u(\alpha)\,p(\bar{W}) + u(\beta)\,p(W),$$

where $u(\alpha)$, $u(\beta)$ are the utility numbers attached to the outcomes α and β, respectively, and $p(\bar{W})$ and $p(W)$ are the probabilities of the alternative states of the world $\bar{W}$ and W respectively. In a similar notation, the expected utility of the right-hand option is

$$u(\alpha)\,p(\bar{W}) + u(\beta')\,p(W \text{ and } V) + u(\beta'')\,p(W \text{ and } \bar{V}).$$

Hence the indifference between the two options implies the equality of the two expressions we have written. This equality implies – since the term containing $u(\alpha)$ cancels out –

$$(1.3)\qquad u(\beta)\,p(W) = u(\beta')\,p(W \text{ and } V) + u(\beta'')\,p(W \text{ and } \bar{V}).$$

Let us now give the two quantities

$$\frac{p(W \text{ and } V)}{p(W)} \quad\text{and}\quad \frac{p(W \text{ and } \bar{V})}{p(W)},$$

the names 'conditional probability of V given W' and 'conditional probability of $\bar{V}$ given W'; and denote these two quantities, respectively, by

$$p(V|W) \quad\text{and}\quad p(\bar{V}|W).$$

Then our last equation becomes – dividing by $p(W)$ –

$$(1.4)\qquad u(\beta) = u(\beta')\cdot p(V|W) + u(\beta'')\cdot p(\bar{V}|W).$$

Now define 'independence' as follows. Suppose the state x_2 is 'irrelevant' to the state x_1 in the sense that the conditional probability of x_1 given x_2 is the same as the probability of x_1:

$$p(x_1 | x_2) = p(x_1).$$

By the definition of conditional probability this means

$$(1.5) \qquad \frac{p(x_1 \text{ and } x_2)}{p(x_2)} = p(x_1),$$
$$p(x_1 \text{ and } x_2) = p(x_1) \cdot p(x_2).$$

Thus the 'irrelevance' of x_2 for x_1 is equivalent to the relation (1.3), which will define 'independence' between x_1 and x_2. Since (1.3) is symmetrical in x_1 and x_2 the following are equivalent: independence between x_1 and x_2; irrelevance of x_2 for x_1; and irrelevance of x, for x_{21}. One can extend the concept of independence to, say, N events and define it by

$$(1.6) \qquad p(x_1 \text{ and } x_2 \text{ and } x_3 \ldots \text{ and } x_N) = p(x_1)\, p(x_2)\, p(x_3) \ldots p(x_N).$$

Thus if one tosses coins, one can compute the probability that the independent events $x_1, \ldots, x_N$ will be all 'heads'; or that the first two are heads and the rest tails; or that some other preassigned proportion of tosses be heads. These computations are a matter of arithmetic. As the result, one finds (one version of) the law of large numbers: if the 'probability of heads' equals p then the 'probability that the proportion of heads in a long sequence of independent throws will converge to p' equals 1. Remember that the probabilities in question (the numbers p and 1 in our last sentence) are subjective degrees of belief, defined as guides in choosing between actions.[10]

We shall now sketch out the proof that any 'preconceived' (or 'a priori') degrees of belief 'should' be modified in the light of experience, in a certain well-defined way, which is fundamentally the one at the basis of sampling statistics. (Note the 'should'! We are talking of norms!).

Suppose that my degree of belief in drawing a black ball from an urn, on condition that the world is in state W, is π. This quantity is also called the 'likelihood of the state W on the basis of an observed drawing of a black ball'. If the urn contains only black and red balls, then clearly the likelihood of W on the basis of an observed drawing of a red ball is $1-\pi$. Similarly, let us denote by $\bar{\pi}$ and $1-\bar{\pi}$, respectively, the likelihoods of the alternative state, $\bar{W}$, on the basis of an observed drawing of a black or of a red ball. Let x_i be the ith independent observation, and let '$x_i=b$' and '$x_i=r$' mean that this observation is the drawing of a black or a red ball, respectively. We can then rewrite our definitions as follows:

$$\pi = p(x_i = b \mid W); \quad 1 - \pi = p(x_i = r \mid W)$$
$$\bar{\pi} = p(x_i = b \mid \bar{W}); \quad 1 - \bar{\pi} = p(x_i = r \mid \bar{W}).$$

Consider in particular, the first observation, x_1, and write the degree of belief that the world is in the state W *and* that the first drawing will be 'black', thus:

$$p(W; \text{ and } x_1 = b).$$

On the other hand, denote separately the degrees of belief that the world is in state W (regardless of observations) and that the first drawing is black, by

$$p^0(W) \text{ and } p(x_1 = b),$$

respectively. If we now recall our definition of conditional probabilities, we have

$$p(W; \text{and } x_1 = b) = p(x_1 = b \mid W) \cdot p^0(W)$$

and also

$$p(W; \text{and } x_1 = b) = p(W \mid x_1 = b) \cdot p(x_1 = b).$$

The quantities $p^{\circ}(W)$ and $p(W \mid x_1=b)$ are called, respectively, the *a priori* and the *a posteriori* degree of belief in W; while $p(x_1=b \mid W)$ is, as we recall, the likelihood π. Comparing the last two equations, we obtain

$$p(W \mid x_1 = b) \cdot p(x_1 = b) = \pi \cdot p^0(W).$$

And similarly (replacing W by $\bar{W}$ and therefore π by $\bar{\pi}$)

$$p(\bar{W} \mid x_1 = b) \cdot p(x_1 = b) = \bar{\pi} \cdot p^0(\bar{W}).$$

Dividing the last equation into the preceding one, one obtains a simple form of the celebrated 'Bayes Theorem':

$$(1.7)\qquad \frac{p(W \mid x_1 = b)}{p(\bar{W} \mid x_1 = b)} = \frac{p_0^0(W)\cdot\pi}{p\ (\bar{W})\cdot\bar{\pi}}$$

In words: the *a posteriori* degree of belief in a certain state of the world, given a certain observation, is proportional to the product of the *a priori* degree of belief in that state of the world *times* the likelihood of that state of the world given the observation. In this way, the observation leads to modifying the *a priori* degree of belief. The likelihoods, π and $\bar{\pi}$, operate as 'correction factors'. If the observation x_1 were 'red' instead of 'black', the correction factors would be $1-\pi$ and $1-\bar{\pi}$, respectively.

Suppose now the process is repeated: we take N independent observations $x_1, x_2, \ldots, x_N$, each time using the previously corrected degree of belief, correcting it further in the light of the new observation. Suppose we drew a black ball n times, (and therefore a red ball $N-n$ times). Applying Bayes Theorem,

$$(1.8)\qquad \frac{p(\bar{W} \mid x_1, \ldots, x_N)}{p(W \mid x_1, \ldots, x_N)} = \frac{p^0(\bar{W})\cdot\bar{\pi}^n(1-\bar{\pi})^{N-n}}{p^0(W)\cdot\pi^n(1-\pi)^{N-n}}.$$

But, by the law of large numbers, as stated above, if the true state of the world is W, then the degree of belief is 1 that the proportion of black drawings, n/N will converge to π. Therefore, the number of black drawings, n, will converge to $\pi\ N$; and the ratio between the *a posteriori* degrees of belief into $\bar{W}$ and W, as given in our last equation, will approach

$$\frac{p^0(\bar{W})}{p^0(W)}\cdot\left(\frac{\bar{\pi}^{\pi}(1-\bar{\pi})^{1-\pi}}{\pi^{\pi}(1-\pi)^{1-\pi}}\right)^N.$$

We see that as the number N of observations increases, the role of the *a priori* degrees of belief into the two alternative states of the world, $p^0(\bar{W})$ and $p^0(W)$, diminishes, overshadowed by the results of observations. Furthermore simple calculus shows that the expression

$$\bar{\pi}^{\pi}(1-\bar{\pi})^{1-\pi},$$

considered as a function of a variable $\bar{\pi}$, has its maximum when $\bar{\pi}=\pi$. Hence, in (1.8), the quantity that is raised to the Nth power, is a ratio of a smaller positive number to a larger one; and its Nth power approaches 0 as N increases. Therefore, of the two *a posteriori* degrees of belief that form the fraction on the left side of (1.8), and that must add up to 1, the numerator converges to 0 and the denominator to 1. That is, the degree of belief that will be assigned to the true state of the world (W) will approach 1. Hence, the investigator who will repeatedly apply Bayes Theorem and choose his decisions on the basis of degrees of belief thus computed will in effect believe that he would obtain a better result than if he would not do so. Perhaps this is what writers on probability mean when they use the expression 'practically certain' or 'certain for all practical purposes',[11] – an expression we shall also have the opportunity for using in the next two sections.

II. PROBABILITIES AND DESCRIPTIVE SOCIAL SCIENCE

We shall concern ourselves now with the uncertainties encountered by the social scientist when he tries to predict the behavior of people. Such prediction is rarely exact. It is usually 'probabilistic' or statistical, even when the sample used is very large and even when the prediction is made, not about individuals, but about large aggregates of people. After discussing the probabilistic character of descriptive social science, I shall give examples illustrating an important methodological problem that has recently occupied statisticians as well as social scientists: that of identifiability of structural characteristics. This will throw some light on the following more general fact: whether statistical data can yield the desired prediction depends not only on the size of the sample and on the goodness of statistical formulae, but also on the nature and validity of the assumptions which the investigator had to make before collecting them. These assumptions (sometimes called 'a model') are, of course, based on formerly acquired knowledge. In the case of a social scientist, this is often the knowledge of 'plausible' or of 'meaningful' relations.

A. *Norms Versus Habits*

We discussed in the first lecture some norms 'recommended' to decision makers who face uncertainty. Those norms or behavior postulates were similar to the rules of logic or geometry. It was not asserted that such norms were fully obeyed by all or even a sizable proportion of men or women, in our own or any other civilization, just as logicians and mathematicians do not assert that all or the majority of their countrymen or of members of any other society are immune to errors of logic or arithmetic.

It is merely recommended that those errors be avoided. Recommended norms and actual habits are not the same thing.

As a matter of empirical psychology it may be interesting to find in what manner a given individual deviates from such norms: how often is he apt to fall victim to a particular sophism, or to have trouble with his sums, or – nearer to our field – to be inconsistent in his preferences. As a matter of social science in general, we may be interested in the ethical and social conditions which affect the frequency of deviations from norms of reasonable thinking, counting and choosing. This knowledge of conditions affecting people's behavior is, first, a matter of scientific curiosity. But is has also its practical side. If we know what makes people more or less illogical or mathematically inept or poor decision makers, we may also find how best to enable them to learn the 'recommended' type of behavior – how, for example, they can get the habit of 'stopping to think'. The normative and the descriptive analysis complete each other.

In the previous section, we did not specify the source of the uncertainty that faces the decision maker. It may be uncertainty about nature. It may be uncertainty about the actions of other men. In our initial example, the U.N. commander had to puzzle out whether his Chinese adversary is or is not 'aggressive' (in the well defined sense of producing certain observable results under specified circumstances). This is uncertainty about people. If our commander estimates (or acts as if he had estimated) that the odds for the Chinese command having 'aggressive' designs are such and such, he has done a bit of descriptive social science. It may happen that, in my best judgment, my adversary behaves as he 'should' behave according to the norms of reasonableness which I recommend to myself. Any application of the Theory of Games (in its present form) is based on the assumption that this symmetry of behavior norms is an actual fact. However, this need not always be the case, nor need it be a useful approximation to reality. It may be more useful to actually study my adversary, as I would study weather or soil or any other uncertain natural phenomenon – provided such study of other people's behavior is feasible and not too costly. A commander – or, for that matter, a diplomat, or a labor union representative – will combine the theory of games ('What would I reasonably do if I were in the other fellow's position?') with as good an intelligence system as his resources can afford, whether by sending spies or by employing anthropologists. And, of course, what was said for a problem arising in fighting an opponent is also true for problems arising in forming an alliance, in building and operating within a social organization – in short in making decisions whose outcome will depend on actions of my fellow men about whom my knowledge is uncertain.

B. *Prediction*

Uncertain knowledge is not ignorance. Nineteenth-century social scientists were fascinated by 'iron laws of nature', when they took eighteenth-century physics for their ideal. It was fashionable, a hundred years ago, to speak of the iron law of demand and supply or (with Karl Marx) to claim predictability for society's future. We have learned today – possibly reflecting some trends in physical sciences – to be quite happy when we can make a prediction only with some (specified) probability. For the 'reasonable' man of our last lecture, a decision maker who weighs utilities with probabilities and maximizes the weighted sum, this kind of knowledge is certainly not useless! At the same time, such knowledge is usually the best that we can ever hope to have, in the field of social sciences, where uncertainties of our physical environment are topped by the diversity and capriciousness of human nature.

Briefly, empirical social science consist of statements about probability distributions. As a trivial but useful example, suppose a social statistician is hired to find what makes people smoke much or little or not at all. Or he wants to find what makes people communists. Let x denote the number of cigarettes smoked by a certain man on a certain day (x may be 0, 1, 2,... a many-valued variable); or let x denote a certain man's being or not being a communist (here $x=0$ or 1: a two-valued variable). What is the probability that x will have a certain value? The tendency to believe in smoking, or in communism, will depend on certain individual characteristics among which one will expect to find the age, sex, education, occupation of the subject; but also his income, the characteristics of his parents and siblings... but possibly also his past income and occupation... but then also his whole past history and that of his ancestors, and, in fact, his whole genetic and cultural endowment. This is a long list of factors. Call them $z^{(1)}, z^{(2)}, \ldots, z^{(N)}$, with N very large. We could make the desired prediction with certainty, for a subject whose $z^{(1)}, \ldots, z^{(N)}$ are known, if we also knew which combinations of the values of those variables make $x=0$, which combinations make $x=1$, etc. That is, the social scientist can predict from $z^{(1)}, \ldots, z^{(N)}$ if there exists a function

$$x = \phi(z^{(1)}, \ldots, z^{(N)}) \tag{2.1}$$

(say) and if he has been able to find this function on the basis of his previous observations on $x, z^{(1)}, \ldots, z^{(N)}$ for each of a sufficient number and variety of persons. However, a complete list of factors that may influence the man's smoking habits or his political beliefs is hopelessly long! The social scientist picks out a smaller number of factors – say $z^{(1)}, \ldots, z^{(n)}$ – and replaces the assumption (2.1) of an 'exact' relationship by a 'probabilistic' assumption, as follows: The variable x is a random variable (also called a chance variable or a stochastic variable); and the probability with which it takes any given value is a function of the variables $z^{(1)}, \ldots, z^{(n)}$ only. In other words, there exists a 'conditional probability of x, given $z^{(1)}, \ldots, z^{(n)}$',

$$\text{(2.2)} \qquad \pi(x \mid z^{(1)}, \ldots, z^{(n)}),$$

say. With the assumption thus changed, the predictor's task is to find, not the function ϕ in (2.1) but the function π in (2.2), from the values of $x, z^{(1)}, \ldots, z^{(n)}$ that he had observed on a sufficient number and variety of individuals. He can then state, for some new individual, with given $z^{(1)}, \ldots, z^{(n)}$ but an unknown x, the probability distribution of x: "the probability that Tom Smith, elevator boy at the State Department, middle-aged and unmarried, is a communist is 0.001%"; "the probability that Mrs. Brown, fashion editor, divorced, smokes 0, 1, ..., 30 cigarettes per day is, respectively, 1%, 5%, ..., 0%."

A very special, but convenient and familiar, form of this assumption will serve as illustration. One assumes that there exist $n+2$ numbers $\mu, \sigma, \alpha_1, \ldots, \alpha_n$ with the following property: the difference (called 'disturbance')

$$\text{(2.3)} \qquad x - \sum_{i=1}^{n} \alpha_i z^{(i)}$$

is independent of the $z^{(i)}$ and has normal distribution with expectation (mean) μ and standard deviation σ. In this case, the conditional distribution (2.2) of x, given $z^{(1)}, \ldots, z^{(n)}$, is also normal.[12] Its expectation is

$$\mu + \sum_{i=1}^{n} \alpha_i z_i$$

and is called the 'explained part of x'. Its standard deviation, σ, is identical with that of the disturbance (2.3). The numbers α_i can be regarded as 'weights' (not necessarily all positive) attached to the n explanatory variables; each of those variables contributes an additive component $\alpha_i z^{(i)}$ of x. If one could find, on the basis of past observations on the x and the $z^{(i)}$ of a sufficient number and variety of individuals, then, for any new individual, with known $z^{(i)}$ but unknown x, one would be able to make a 'probabilistic' prediction such as, for example: the odds are 19:1 that this man's x lies in the interval

$$\mu + \sum \alpha_i z^{(i)} \pm 2\sigma \tag{2.4}$$

The looks of this interval are familiar enough from textbooks and routines of research workers in social science. I am afraid its understanding is often confused by complications irrelevant from our point of view. One complication is that the constants μ, σ, and the α_i cannot be determined exactly from a finite number of observations. One can only determine their 'estimates'. These are suitably chosen functions of a finite number of observed values of the variables x, $z^{(1)} \ldots, z^{(n)}$. Since these variables are [or at least x is – according to (2.2)] random, the estimates are also random variables (they are 'subject to sampling errors') so that the interval (2.4), computed from those estimates, it itself 'wobbly'. But this is beside the point. We are not interested in sampling theory today. We can assume today that the investigator has collected a very large sample indeed; and that he has used appropriate formulas to compute estimates that are practically certain to approach the estimated constants as the sample increases (such estimates are called 'consistent'). Our point is that, even using an infinite sample and consistent estimates, he will not be able to predict x from a finite number (n) of explanatory variables except in a 'probabilistic' fashion typified by the statement that 'x will fall within the interval (2.4) with probability 0.05'.

Another concept that we wish to disregard here is that of 'errors of observation', a term originating in observatories and physical laboratories There the number N of possible explanatory factors is supposed to be small enough to be manageable; and the fact that the exact, non-probabilistic assumption (2.1) is not satisfied is (or was till the advent of modern statistical physics) blamed upon the frailty of the observer's eye and of his other instruments. In social science, human frailty is shared between the observer and his object. After repeatedly asking a blindfolded man which of two weights is heavier, the psychologist may have to record a frequency distribution of contradictory statements: 'The first weight is heavier', 'It is lighter', or 'No difference'. The psychologist will have to formulate his conclusions and predictions in a probabilistic manner even if he is sure that his own errors of observation (confusing the weights or misunderstanding the subject's responses) are negligible. A 'random disturbance' originating in the observed person not in the observer will always be present. Furthermore, even if it should be possible to design laboratory conditions so as to make both the errors of observation and the random disturbance of the observed phenomenon negligible, this cannot be achieved with data collected outside of laboratory walls – like the data on the smoking or the communist persuasion of persons. The variables, immense in number (N-n), which the investigator of such a problem has decided to leave out of account, are supposed by him to show their joint effect in the random disturbance (2.3). For example, each of the subject's ancestors has contributed something to his make-up, but each only a little: just like each of the innumerable causes that determine an honest card deal contributes a little. Such joint effects of a large number of separately insignificant causes are empirical phenomena that have been idealized in the mathematical concept of a random variable and a probability. An error of observation and a random disturbance, as defined, may both have their origin in those numerous, separately insignificant causes. However, if you prefer to ascribe the randomness of errors and disturbances to the free will of individuals, you may do so. This will not affect the choice of investigation methods.

The selection of the n explanatory variables, and the assumption that the difference (2.3) is independent of z_i and has a normal probability distribution [or, more generally, that x has some probability distribution (2.2) for any fixed value of the n variables selected as explanatory ones] may be false. If it is, it will lead to probabilistic prediction statements that are false, even if they are based on consistent estimates from very large samples. This suggests, of course, that one should test predictions like (2.4) against new facts; and then revise the assumption (2.2) if necessary. For example, one may change the list of explanatory variables or replace the linearity and normality assumptions by other ones. Thus the selection of assumptions need not be entirely based on prescientific knowledge but can be helped by progressive experience.

C. *Aggregation*

Large parts of social science deal, not with single individuals but with averages or aggregates. It has been occasionally remarked that random variations of behavior from one individual to another (or, for the same individual, from one day to another) tend to 'cancel out' when one deals with masses of man. Tseretelli, a political leader of the pre-Communist period of the Russian revolution, even went so far as to say (in predicting the failure of Communists to win the masses!), 'Persons can err, masses never'; and social scientists are apt to quote Boyle's law of gases, which is exact enough, yet can be derived from the random behavior of billions of small particles. Do social scientists fool themselves when they appeal to this analogy, thus trying to reduce the prediction interval to a single point and to evade the inconveniences of probabilistic thinking?

As an example, let me refer to the economists' attempt at explaining the aggregate investment, i.e., the total money outlay on plant and equipment made in a year by all the firms of the country.

This outlay is, of course, the sum of the outlays of individual firms on *their* plant and equipment. One might try to explain the decision of a manager or a management board of an individual firm by those variables that are likely to influence the level of anticipated profits, thus making the expansion of the firm's activities in a given year a promising or a bad proposition. Thus, one would think of explanatory variables like the following: the profits that are already being made at the time of decision; the current demand for the firm's product; the interest rate at which money can be borrowed to expand the firm's plant and machinery; the cost of new machinery and building. Clearly, many other variables will be needed to describe the particular circumstances in which a given firm finds itself, and which will affect the manager's anticipations of the future of his particular market and his decision to build a new wing of the plant or, on the contrary, to sell parts of his machinery for scrap without replacing them by new ones. If the particular circumstances do not vary too strongly from one firm to another, one might be able to explain the annual change in the aggregate plant and equipment of the American industry (so called rate of aggregate investment) as a function of those general variables: the total profits of the past year; the total demand for all products (represented by total national income); the average interest rate, the average cost of machinery and building, etc. To do this, one would be able to utilize the published historical statistics, which gives for each year and even each quarter or month, the aggregate outlays on plant and equipment, the total profits, the interest rate, prices, etc. In this hope, various investigators have looked for a statistical relationship between the aggregate annual investment of the American industry and the several aggregate variables that we have mentioned. In particular, attempts have been made to construct prediction intervals like (2.4), where μ and σ are the mean and standard deviation of the estimate of annual aggregate investment; while the $z^{(i)}$ are the various mentioned explanatory variables, also of aggregative nature: total profits of the preceding year, total national income, average interest rate, etc. However, the standard error σ of the estimate, and hence the prediction interval, proved to be very large; or, what is the same thing, the 'unexplained residual', the 'disturbance' (2.3) – with x interpreted as the annual rate of aggregate investment – has a very large standard deviation. The meaning of the prediction interval being 'very large' is simply this: it is so large as to be useless.

For the social scientists, an interesting possible explanation of the strong random variability of the unexplained residual of some aggregative variables, is the phenomenon variously called 'leadership,' 'imitation', 'contagion', or 'Zeitgeist' or 'fashion'. The random disturbances in the response (e.g., in the decision to expand plant) of any pair of individual members of a human group to a given set of circumstances may be positively correlated, both disturbances being partly determined by unspecified common cause. If this is the case, the response of the corresponding aggregative variable to a given set of circumstances will be subject to more unpredictable random fluctuations than if that correlation were absent.

A mathematical illustration will help. Suppose p variables $v_1, \ldots, v_p$ have a joint normal distribution with a common expectation $Ev_j = 0$ and a common variance $Ev^2 = \sigma^2$. Let them also have a common correlation coefficient for any pair $j \neq k$, $Ev_j v_k / \sigma^2 = \rho > 0$. Thus

$$Ev_j v_k = \begin{cases} \sigma^2 & \text{when } j = k \\ \sigma^2 \rho & \text{otherwise.} \end{cases}$$

What is the distribution of $\bar{v}$, the average of these variables? $\bar{v}$ has normal distribution. Its expectation$=0$. And its variance

$$(2.5) \qquad E(\bar{v})^2 = E\left(\frac{v_1 + \cdots + v_p}{p}\right)^2 = \frac{1}{p^2} E \sum_j \sum_k v_j v_k =$$
$$= \frac{1}{p^2}\left[p\sigma^2 + p(p-1)\,\sigma^2\rho\right] = \sigma^2\left[\frac{1-\rho}{p}\right] + \rho\sigma^2.$$
$$E(\bar{v})^2 \to \sigma^2\rho \quad \text{as} \quad p \to \infty.$$

Thus, under our assumptions, the variance of the average tends to zero if and only if the correlation $\rho=0$. Applying this to our problem of averaging the individual responses (e.g., the investment decisions of a number of firms), we can interpret v_j as follows:

$$(2.6) \qquad v_j = x_j - \sum_{i=1}^{n} \alpha_i z_j^{(i)} - \mu (j = 1, \ldots, p)$$

where the α_i and μ have the same meaning as in (2.3), (2.4), and the subscript j indicates the particular firm; its response (investment) x_j is explained by the variables $z^{(1)}, \ldots, z^{(n)}$, except for a random disturbance $\mu + v_j$, which has mean μ and variance σ^2. The variable x_j has then also variance σ^2, the same for all firms. If, for all pairs of firms, the random disturbances are not correlated ($\rho=0$) then indeed the average of the responses of all firms tends to have zero variance as the number of firms increases. But this is not so if there is, pairwise, a positive correlation between the individual disturbances. In the extreme case, when all firms act in unison ($\rho=1$), the average has the same variance as any individual response: an obvious result.[13] This mathematical illustration might be made more general – for example we might admit positive correlation coefficients of different sizes for different pairs of firms. But our result suffices, to show how 'fashion' endangers predictability – a warning against the abuse of a misunderstood 'law of averages'. If the decision-makers, however numerous, follow a few leaders, then the personal circumstances, the ulcers or divorce proceedings of the leaders become important factors in predicting the average or aggregate of the decisions.

D. *Identification*

Suppose two random characteristics X_1 and X_2 are being measured on each person of a sample. For example, X_1 may be a person's consumption of cigarettes, and X_2 his consumption of cereals; or X_1 may be the person's answer to the question 'Do you prefer blondes?' and X_2 his answer to the question 'Do you feel comfortable with strangers?' Suppose that a parameter Z is known to exist which varies from person to person but is fixed for each person; and which influences X_1 and X_2 in a 'probabilistic' fashion. That is, the probability that a person's X_1 and X_2 will take a given pair of values (or fall within given intervals) depends on the value of the person's Z. Thus the joint distribution of the numbers of cigarettes and bowls of cereals consumed by a person during a week may depend on the person's income, Z. In the case of the two questions – about blondes and about strangers – Z may stand for some characteristic, such as 'ethnocentricity', of which the answers to the two questions are symptoms.[14] We shall denote the joint probability distributions of X_1, X_2, conditional upon Z, by

$$(2.7) \qquad \pi(X_1, X_2 | Z),$$

a function of three variables. It is analogous to (2.2), with the vector $(z^{(1)}, \ldots, z^{(n)})$ replaced by a single Z, and the number x replaced by the vector (X_1, X_2). [In a more general case, both the random variable to the left and the parameter to the right of the bar in (2.7) will be vectors.:]

Suppose one has succeeded in estimating the function π from a sample. This knowledge could then be used in two opposite ways, to answer questions about a person not in the sample:

Question 1: given this person's Z, predict his X's.
Question 2: given his X's, make statements about his Z.

Why either of these applications of our knowledge of the conditional probability function π should ever arise in practice, will belong into our third lecture (on policies). For the time being, we shall regard both questions as legitimate expressions of scientific curiosity.

If the sampled persons had lent themselves to the measurement, not only of their X, but also of their Z, the problem of estimating the function π from the sample, and of subsequently answering Questions 1 or 2 about a person not in the sample, would be a familiar one. For example, the main use of computing a regression equation from a sample is to answer Question 1, in the manner of (2.4); using a sample to answer Question 2 is also a problem well known to statisticians, a discrimination problem.[15]

However, a new twist is introduced by making Z a non-observable (at least not observable on the sampled individuals), a 'latent' characteristic. It is natural to expect that this loss of information must be made up by some additional information if the problem is to remain solvable.

The following simple hypothesis (which is itself a bit of 'additional information') will be used for the case of 'cigarettes and cereals': X_1 and X_2 are proportional to Z, subject to random percentage deviations, denoted by U_1 and U_2, respectively. That is, there exist two constants, Λ_1 and Λ_2 such that

$$X_i = \Lambda_i Z(1 + U_i), \quad (i = 1, 2).$$

Remember that X_1, X_2 have been measured on persons of the sample, but Z has not. (Collectors of family budget data are, in fact, able to ascertain single consumption items but have difficulty in finding the incomes!) It will be convenient to use logarithms. Write $\log Z = z$, $\log X_i = x_i$, $\log \Lambda_i = \lambda_i$, $\log(1 + U_i) = u_i$ $(i = 1, 2)$. Then

$$\text{(2.8)} \qquad x_i = \lambda_i + z + u_i, \quad (i = 1, 2).$$

We shall further assume that random deviations cancel out in a very large sample, in the sense that the expectations of u_1, u_2 vanish:

$$\text{(2.9)} \qquad Eu_i = 0 \quad (i = 1, 2);$$

assume also that u_1, u_2 are jointly normally distributed. We shall write $Eu_i u_j = \sigma_{ij} (i, j = 1, 2)$. Our hypothesis involves thus 5 unknown parameters λ_1, λ_2, σ_{11}, σ_{22}, σ_{12}. Can we determine them and use them to make a probabilistic prediction of x_1 and x_2 for any given z?[16]

The answer depends on what information is in our possession *before* we collect the data. The main purpose of the present example is to show how the character of this '*a priori* information' makes the problem determinate or indeterminate. With insufficient *a priori* information, the problem is indeterminate however large the sample.

Assume, for example – in addition to the assumptions already made [(2.8), (2.9) and normality of the distribution of u_1, u_2] – that we know the frequency distribution of z[17]: viz., normal with known mean and variance (ζ and ω, say), and independent of the disturbances u_1 and u_2; hence, $Ezu_1 = 0 = Ezu_2$. As before, we shall neglect sampling errors (by assuming our sample very large), so that the sample averages x_1, x_2 are almost equal to the corresponding expectations; then by (2.8), (2.9), approximately

$$\bar{x}_i = Ex_i = \lambda_i + \zeta\,; \tag{2.10}$$

hence

$$\lambda_i = \bar{x}_i - \zeta \quad (i = 1, 2)\,,$$

thus determining the two unknowns λ_1, λ_2[18]. Moreover, the sample moments (sample averages of squares and products) computed from the observed values of x_i in the (very large) sample, serve to determine σ_{11}, σ_{22}, σ_{12}, the parameters of the distribution of u_1, u_2. For, by (2.8), (2.9),

$$x_i - \bar{x}_i = z - \zeta + u_i\,;$$

therefore

$$\begin{aligned} E(x_i - \bar{x}_i)\,(x_k - \bar{x}_k) &= E(z - \zeta)^2 + Eu_iu_k + (z-\zeta)(Eu_i + Eu_k) \\ &= \omega + \sigma_{ik}\,; \quad (i, k = 1, 2)\,. \end{aligned}$$

Hence, in a very large sample, approximately

$$\begin{aligned} &\text{sample average of } (x_1 - \bar{x}_1)^2 = \omega + \sigma_{11} \\ &\text{sample average of } (x_2 - \bar{x}_2)^2 = \omega + \sigma_{22} \\ &\text{sample average of } (x_1 - \bar{x}_1)\,(x_2 - \bar{x}_2) = \omega + \sigma_{12}\,, \end{aligned} \tag{2.11}$$

where ω and the sample moments are known. The parameters σ_{11}, σ_{22}, σ_{12} thus estimated serve to determine (using the tables for bivariate normal distribution), the probability with which u_1 will fall into some given interval, and u_2 will fall, at the same time, into some given interval.

This would answer our Question 1. As to Question 2, I shall not go into details here. Suffice it to say that, once we know the conditional distribution of x_1, x_2 given z, we can also estimate the parameter z characterizing an individual, from values x_1, x_2 observed (once or in repeated observations) on an individual.

But suppose our *a priori* knowledge is less complete than in the example studied so far. For example, suppose we know the mean (ζ) of z (i.e., the geometric mean of average incomes of the U.S. population) but do not know its variance ω. We see from (2.10), (2.11) that we can then determine λ_1, λ_2 but not σ_{11}, σ_{22}, σ_{12}. Consequently we can predict x_i for a given z only in the sense of providing the conditional expectation of $x_i(=\lambda_i+z)$ but not of stating an interval into which the x_i should fall with preassigned probability. Nor shall we be able to estimate an individual's z from an observation on his x_1, x_2.

Or suppose we have the knowledge of both μ and ω, but have also a larger list of unknowns, because we are convinced that the assumption (2.8) is too special and should be replaced by a more general one:

$$(2.12) \qquad x_i = \lambda_i + \beta_i z + u_i{}^{19} \quad (i = 1, 2),$$

with β_1, β_2 unknown. Using this equation, we can again express – similarly to (2.10), (2.11) – the two sample means of x_1 and x_2 and their three sample moments in terms of the 7 unknowns. We shall be 2 equations short. The problem is indeterminate.

Consider, on the other hand, the case when we have fewer unknown constants than we have equations to determine them. Suppose again that we know both ζ and ω and let our hypothesis again be expressed by (2.8), (2.9). But, suppose, in addition, we know from other sources that $\sigma_{12}=0$, i.e., there can be, at any fixed income, no correlation between eating of cereals and smoking. We have then only four constants to determine (λ_1, λ_2, σ_{11}, σ_{22}), yet can derive from the observations the same five equations (2.10), (2.11) as in our first example, in which σ_{12} was unknown. If the hypothesis now used is correct, i.e., if (2.8), (2.9), as well as the assumed frequency distribution of z and the assertion $\sigma_{12}=0$, are all valid, then one of those equations derived from observations is redundant for the purpose of determining unknown parameters. But then it can be used to test the hypothesis. Indeed, the assertion $\sigma_{12}=0$ makes the last of the equations (2.11) into a relation between two known quantities, viz., between the observed cross-moment of x_1 and x_2 and the known variance ω of z. If this relation is not, in fact, satisfied, our hypothesis is wrong: e.g., (2.8) may be false, or z or u_1, u_2 are not distributed normally, or $w \neq$ variance of z, or $\sigma_{12} \neq 0$, etc.[20]

To sum up our examples: We started with a case in which all unknown constants could be determined from an equal number of (independent) equations obtained from observations – all constants were '*identifiable*'. By modifying the assumptions used or the kind of data available we obtained a case in which some of the constants, and another in which all of the constants were (however large the number of observations!) not determinable, '*nonidentifiable*'. Finally, we have had an example of '*over-identification*': observations yielded more (independent) equations than there are unknown constants; if these equations are inconsistent,[21] the hypothesis used must be rejected.

The term identifiability was suggested by T. C. Koopmans and the relevant mathematics were studied by the staff of the Cowles Commission for Research in Economics in considerable detail (see, e.g., the Commission's Monographs No. 10 and 14) because of the importance of the indentification problem in economics.[22] However, the problem seems to be present in other social sciences as well, e.g., in the Lazarfeld theory of latent structures and in Thurstone's factor analysis. In fact, my examples were chosen with the very purpose of providing a link between problems encountered in economics and those more familiar to a sociologist or psychologist, but, alas, less familiar to me. Let me, then, venture again to interpret x_1 and x_2 as answers to two questions asked of a person possessing an unknown degree z of some measurable characteristic. z is a parameter, changing from person to person. It is not a random variable.[23] The variables x_1 and x_2 can each take values 1 (for 'yes') or 0 (for 'no'). Assuming that a very large number of persons have been questioned, we want to determine the conditional joint probability

$$(2.13)\qquad \pi = \pi(x_1, x_2 | z).$$

This is the same as (2.2), with $n = 1$ and with x interpreted as a vector consisting of two components. Since x_1, x_2 can have only two values each, it is inappropriate to state an assumption about the distribution of a random 'unexplained residual', a continuous quantity such as (2.3), or the u_i in (2.8). Instead, we specify directly the function (2.13) of z, i.e., assume that the respective probabilities of the four possible alternatives [(1) $x_1 = x_2 = 0$; (2) $x_1 = x_2 = 1$; (3) $x_1 = 0, x_2 = 1$; (4) $x_1 = 1, x_2 = 0$] are determined by z in a specified fashion (Lazarfeld's 'trace lines') Suppose, for example, that the function π can be tabulated as follows (each cell corresponding to the probability of one combination of answers)

(2.14)

$x_1 \| x_2$	0	1
0	$\alpha_{00} + \beta_{00} z$	$\alpha_{01} + \beta_{01} z$
1	$\alpha_{10} + \beta_{10} z$	$\alpha_{11} + \beta_{11} z$

(This presupposes of course that z has an upper and a lower limit.) The α's and β's are unknown. Since the four probabilities must add up to 1 for any z, the α's must add to 1, and the β's to 0. We have thus 6 (not 8) unknown constants. Can we determine them from the sample? Call p_{ij} the proportion of people, in a very large sample, whose pair of answers is: $x_1=i$, $x_2=j$. Denote by ζ the mean of z in the sample. Then

$$(2.15) \qquad p_{ij} = \alpha_{ij} + \beta_{ij}\,\zeta \quad (i, j = 0, 1)\,.$$

ζ can be chosen as a unit of measurement of the z. The four proportions p_{ij} are all observable, but since they must add up to 1, only three of the four equations (2.15) are independent. This is not enough to determine the 6 unknowns. They are not identifiable.

But suppose we know with certainty the following property of our questionnaire: for any given person, the probability of answering the first question by yes is independent of whether he answers the second question by a yes or a no (though, of course, both probabilities vary from person to person, depending on z). Obviously, not every questionnaire satisfies this condition. This is a case of a 'pure test', in Lazarsfeld's terminology. The probability that a person answers with 'yes' the question 'Is your name John?' depends on how the same person answers the question 'Are you a woman?' If the probability of a person's being a man is 0.5, and the probability of a person's being called John is 0.1 (the average between the probability 0.2 of a man's being called John and the probability 0.0 of a woman's being called John), then the probability of a person's both being a man and being called John is not 0.5×0.1 (as it would be if these two events were independent) but 0.5×0.2.

Or consider two questions that are almost identical in content. Suppose the probability for the first question to be answered affirmatively by any person with z degrees of 'ethnocentricity' is q; the corresponding probability for the second question will then be near q; and the probability that a person with z degrees of ethnocentricity will answer both questions in the affirmative will be, not near q^2 but near q.

It may also be that the degree of dependence between the answers depends itself on z. An extreme ethnocentric may strongly associate dark hair with fast talk (and perhaps dislike both) while a man on the other end of the ethnocentricity scale will not have this ready image in his mind: thus a test may be 'pure' for some persons, not 'pure' for others.

Suppose, however, the investigator is sure to have formulated his questions so that, for a fixed z, the answers are completely independent; he is sure that all traces of possible associations, logical or otherwise, between the questions, have been weeded out. This *a priori* knowledge permits him to specify the function π more narrowly. For example, in the case (2.14) the assumption of independence will be expressed by the condition

$$(2.16) \qquad \frac{\alpha_{00} + \beta_{00} z}{\alpha_{10} + \beta_{10} z} = \frac{\alpha_{01} + \beta_{01} z}{\alpha_{11} + \beta_{11} z}.$$

Multiplying out and transferring all terms to one side, we obtain a quadratic expression in z which must vanish for any z. Hence each of its three terms vanishes, thus providing us with the three missing equations. Our 6 constants have now become identifiable.

In this example, the assumption of independence between answers (in the sense defined) has proved powerful enough to make an otherwise unidentifiable set of unknowns identifiable. The result can be used to estimate the latent characteristic z of a person outside the sample (the discrimination problem mentioned above): e.g., if his answer is 'no' to both questions, the maximum likelihood estimate of his z is obtained by maximizing with respect to z the probability π $(0, 0 | z)$. We therefore put $\alpha_{00} + \beta_{00} z = 1$. One can also estimate an appropriate confidence interval for z. If all the unknown constants α_{00}, β_{00}, etc. had been unidentifiable it would have been impossible to estimate z. We can say that non-identifiability would make the confidence interval for z infinite. It can be conjectured that if z is identifiable both with and without the assumption of independence, the appropriate confidence interval for z is shorter when this assumption is made than when it is not made.

Since the assumption of independence between questions can have such powerful implications, the investigator, in using or designing the questionnaire, will have to be very critical.[24] As in many other cases, the soundness of statistical results will much depend on the soundness of pre-statistical assumptions which prove inaccessible to statistical test.

III. PROBABILITY AND POLICY

In the first lecture we discussed the following rule of conduct: choose that decision which makes the 'moral expectation' (=the mathematical expectation of utility) as large as possible. This presupposes consistency in the decision-maker's system of preferences. A rational policy maker must 'know what he wants'. In addition (at least in the approaches of Bayes and Ramsey), he must 'know what he believes' – his system of subjective probabilites, too, must be consistent. To require these consistencies is on the same plane as to require that the policy maker do not make errors of logic and arithmetic: that he avoid contradictions. Logic is self-control, and this includes logic of decision. In Ramsey's words, one should be able to 'stop to think it out', rather than to act on the temporarily uppermost desire and belief. This is an ideal, a skill which good decision-makers possess in a higher degree than poor ones. A bad decision-maker tosses in bed and decides in a half-dream. A good decision-maker dresses up a payoff matrix (though not necessarily with pen on paper). I suspect this skill is not entirely inborn and can be acquired by training: a fruitful field for applied psychology.

We also found in our first lecture that the rule of maximizing moral expectation leads to the proposition that degrees of belief (which we needed to know in order to compute moral expectations) are, in the limit, equal to relative frequencies obtained from samples. Accordingly, we devoted our second lecture to showing how certain probability distributions that interest a social scientist are obtained from observations. The probability distributions that interest the social scientist must be usable for prediction of the behavior of people. In the concluding part of the second lecture, we found that certain probability distributions needed for such prediction may be inaccessible to estimation, no matter how large the sample. Certain parameters are 'non-identifiable'. Yet these parameters are often just the ones the social scientist is particularly curious about: he feels they constitute his 'theory', as distinct from 'mere description'. He is interested in 'structures', 'latent parameters', and not in mere 'empirical regularities' and must be disappointed whenever he finds that the goal cannot be attained with the available kind of data.

What are those 'latent' properties, those 'theories' behind the manifest data? Why are they interesting? And what makes them so elusive? My tentative answer will be: that 'theories' are sought for the sake of decision-making; and that the difficulty in getting at them is due to the difficulty of performing experiments.

To take up one of the examples of our second lecture: Why is a market research organization not interested in merely estimating from its data the bivariate distribution of the consumption of cigarettes and the consumption of cereals? That would permit them to predict the one from the other. But this is not interesting. Instead, there is lurking a theory that both smoking and the expenditure on cereals depend on the third variable, income, which happen to be difficult to ascertain and is thus 'latent' rather than 'manifest'. We have shown that under certain hypotheses it is possible and under other hypotheses impossible, to obtain from data on cereals and cigarettes consimed by a sample of people, a relationship that will predict cereals consumption from income and that is presumably more 'theoretical', more of a 'structure', than the relationship between the consumption of cereals and that of cigarettes. The relationship involves two kinds of knowledge: the 'prestatistical' hypotheses just mentioned and the numerical parameters estimated from the sample. E.g., the hypothesis may be: cigarettes and cereals are consumed in proportion to incomes, apart from a random percentage deviation for each of the two items, these deviations being distributed normally, with zero correlation. The numerical parameters to be estimated may have been, in this case, the unknown (geometric) mean of the ratios of each of the two expenditure items to the individual's income, and the variances of each of the two deviations. We have seen that if we know the correlation (e.g., zero) between the two deviations, and know the income distribution (though not the individual incomes) in the population from which the sample was taken, the set of parameters is identifiable. But some or all of them become non-identifiable if our *a priori* knowledge is less complete – for example, if we do not have grounds to assume that the average relation between income and smoking or cereal-eating is one of proportionality, or that the two deviations from proportionality are non-correlated (i.e., that a man's smoking beyond his means is compatible with over-eating as well as with under-eating cereals, compared with the average breakfast of his income group). In these cases, knowledge of the 'latent' relation between income and the consumption items becomes inaccessible, with the type of data we have assumed in our example.

Why hanker after this inaccessible knowledge? Why not be content – to continue with our example – with predicting cereal consumption from cigarette consumption or vice versa, which is perfectly possible on the basis of our data? Presumably because the market research organization does not expect the latter kind of prediction to be of much use in future practical situations. It does find it useful to predict consumption from income. Why? Because it visualizes the following situation: given a new market, with customers' income distribution known and different from that of the population previously studied, predict the demand for cereals or cigarettes. If the decision to face new markets would never have to be taken, research about the influence of income (or other such factors) on consumption would be unnecessary: it would suffice to know past consumption.

Similarly, if – in line with the last example of our previous lecture – the manifest data are answers to a questionnaire and the latent parameter deemed to underly those answers is the 'degree of ethnocentricity', the reason why we are interested in measuring the latter is, presumably, its potential usefulness. It is not useful to predict that a 'yes' answer to a certain question entails, with a certain probability, a 'no' answer to another question (with population the same as the sampled one). I presume that what is really wanted is to predict the action of some new individual or group. It is assumed *a priori* that, for example, the discourteous treatment of immigrants by an official is determined by his degree of ethnocentricity which also influences his answers to questionnaires and which (if 'identifiable') is revealed by those answers. One wants to use those answers of the aspirant to an office to predict the behavior of the future official. A convenient way to state the relation between the observable answers to the questionnaire and the virtually observable action of the official is *via* the 'degree of ethnocentricity' which influences both. It is assumed to be 'behind' those observables, just like the genetic make-up of an individual is 'behind' observable data on his and his ancestors' hereditary features, even though genes might never become observable through the strongest ultra microscope. The study both of genotype and of 'ethnocentricities' would not be called for if predictions of the effects of changed genotype and changed ethnocentricity (or their changed distribution within a population), as in problems of animal breeding or the administration of policies towards ethnical minorities, were never to be made.

Permit me to use an example from economics: a severely simplified variant of a 'Keynesian' model designed to discuss fiscal policy as an instrument for maintaining employment and stable prices.

Consider the dollar value of all goods and services produced during a year (not counting those used for repair or renewal of the existing stock).

This dollar amount can be called the (net) national product. It is composed of the dollar amounts – called incomes – paid out, in the course of production, to workers, factory-owners, capital-lenders. Thus net national product is identical with national income. Denote this quantity by y. Consider now another quantity: the dollar value of all goods and services demanded during a year (again not counting repair and renewal). This national demand is composed of three parts: (1) the demand of consumers for food, shelter, etc. – denote it by c; (2) the demand of businessmen for machines and other goods to increase their plants and inventories (a matter I had occasion to mention in the previous lecture) – denote it by b; (3) the demand of the government for the services of its employees and for public buildings, armament goods, etc. – we shall denote it (for reasons that will appear presently) by a Greek letter, ρ (for Roosevelt). In general the national demand $c+b+\rho$ is not identical with the national product (income) y. People who decide about production (and hence about the incomes disbursed) may or may not be able to quickly adjust production to demand. However in our context we need not discuss this adjustment process, its motives and form, except in a footnote later.[25] We shall assume that production is adjusted to demand instantaneously, so that always

$$(3.1) \qquad y = c + b + \rho\,.$$

Of these quantities, only ρ is directly controlled by the policymaker, the government. What determines the rest, namely b and c?

As to b, let us assume that businessmen feel encouraged to expand their plant when the current national income, y, is high; at least they feel so 'on the whole', i.e., apart from some random deviation. To fix the ideas, let us use a linear approximation:

$$(3.2) \qquad b = \beta y + v_b\,, \quad \beta > 0\,;$$

where β is a parameter characterizing businessmen's behavior and v_b is a normally distributed random variable; denote its mean and variance by the Greek letters μ_b and σ_{bb} respectively.

As to c, let us assume that people's consumption depends, apart from a random deviation v_c, only on the amount of income that remains in their hands after payment of taxes, and on nothing else. Using again a linear approximation,

(3.3) $c = \gamma(y - \tau) + v_c, \quad \gamma > 0;$

where γ is a parameter descriptive of consumers' behavior and τ denotes the tax collected. The mean and variance of v_c (assumed normal) will be denoted by μ_c and σ_{cc}, respectively. Since the random deviations in the behavior of consumers may or may not be correlated with those in the behavior of businessmen we need also a symbol σ_{bc} to denote their covariance.

Finally, we assume for simplicity that the government determines directly the tax collected, τ (and not, as is actually the case, the tax rates only).

Let us now marshall all our quantities:

government-controlled: ρ, τ;
noncontrolled parameters: $\beta, \gamma, \mu_b, \mu_c,$
$\sigma_{bb}, \sigma_{cc}, \sigma_{bc}$;
dependent variables: b, c, y;
random deviations: v_b, v_c.

We have three dependent variables and a system of three equations. We can solve for b, c, y. For example, Equation (3.4) below gives the solution for y. Since the system involves random deviations v_b, v_c, the dependent variables b, c, y are also random: they fluctuate with v_b, v_c. If the deviations v_b, v_c were observable, one could determine, for every pair v_b, v_c, the values that the dependent variables b, c, y would take, provided one knows the parameters ρ, τ, β, γ. Actually v_b, v_c are not observable but their probability distribution is fully determined by the parameters μ_b. μ_c, σ_{bb}, σ_{cc}, σ_{bc}. If one knows these parameters, one can find the probability distribution of b, c, y for any given set of values of the controlled parameters ρ, τ and of β, γ.

We are not concerned here with whether the model is economically sound. It is too crude. We merely use it as an example for our methodological discussion. The model's three equations, together with the probability distribution of the random deviations v_b, v_c, purport to 'explain' the observed distribution of the three dependent variables b, c, y. The model expresses a hypothesis about the behavior of consumers and businessmen, summarized by the non-controlled parameters – the Greek letters excluding ρ and τ. The policy problem is for the government to choose the best values of the controlled parameters ρ, τ, – the values that will maximize the government's 'expected utility', a term defined in our first lecture. If the government were concerned simply with the national income y (a dollar amount, as you remember) it would choose ρ and τ so as to maximize the expected value (the mean) of y – call it μ_y, one of the parameters of the distribution of y. How is the distribution of y determined by ρ and τ? The random variable y is related to ρ, τ in a linear fashion, as is seen by solving our three equations:

$$(3.4) \qquad y = \lambda(\rho - \gamma\tau) + \lambda(v_b + v_c),$$

where $\lambda = 1/(1-\beta-\gamma)$. Since $v_b + v_c$ is distributed normally, so is y. The mean of y is

$$(3.5) \qquad \mu_y = \lambda(\rho - \gamma\tau) + \lambda(\mu_b + \mu_c);$$

this is how μ_y is affffected by the government's choice of public expenditure ρ and tax revenue τ.

Note in passing that the policy-maker might be concerned, not only with a high mean national income but also with a high predictability of national income, as expressed by its variance, σ_{yy}. As the late Senator Arthur Vandenberg said in criticizing the New Deal: 'We don't want to live on a flying trapeze.' It is worthwhile to remark, as an exercise in the logic of these matters, that in our particular model the policy-maker is unable to affect σ_{yy}. The variance of y is not affected by adding to y a constant; it is, by (3.4), simply proportional to the variance of $(v_b + v_c)$ and is equal to

$$(3.6) \qquad \sigma_{yy} = \lambda^2(\sigma_{bb} + \sigma_{cc} + 2\sigma_{bc}).$$

Thus, the knowledge of the last three of the non-controlled parameters of our list above, is irrelevant for policy purposes if the policy goal depends on μ_y and/or σ_{yy}. If our model were nonlinear, the result might be different, and the knowledge of σ_{bb}, σ_{cc}, σ_{bc} important to the policy-maker concerned with high and/or reasonably predictable national income. In any case, this knowledge is necessary if one wants to 'predict', in the sense of our Lecture II, the random variable, income: i.e., if one wants to estimate the distribution of y. This is, in our example, described by μ_y and σ_{yy}, and to know σ_{yy} one has to know σ_{bb}, σ_{cc}, σ_{bc}. But such prediction may be of no concern to a practical policy-maker.

Continuing with a government bent on maximizing the expected value μ_y of national money income, return to our equation (3.5). We shall assume $\lambda > 0$, that is $\beta + \gamma < 1$. This assumption is not based on systematic statistical studies but on a general estimate of plausible behavior of consumers and businessmen and also on the observed 'stability' of a system, a consideration which we cannot discuss here in any detail.[26] If, then, $\lambda > 0$, the expected money incomes μ_y as determined in (3.5) is increased by raising ρ and cutting down τ. If there is an upper limit on government expenditure – say, ρ_{max} – and a lower limit on tax revenue – say, τ_{min} – then money income is highest with $\rho = \rho_{max}$ and $\tau = \tau_{min}$ (possibly zero). No knowledge about the behavior parameters β, γ is necessary to find these optimal values of the government-controlled parameters, except the validity of the assumption $\beta + \gamma - 1 < 0$.

This result is due to the fact that, under our assumptions, – as summarized in (3.5) – the expected money income μ_y changes monotonically (has no turning points) in response to changes in ρ and τ. Therefore y can achieve a maximum only at some boundary values of ρ and τ. If we introduced, for realism's sake, an upper limit on the deficit $\rho - \tau$, the same general result would remain true: no knowledge of the non-controlled parameters would be necessary to determine the policy (ρ, τ) that maximizes expected income (μ_y).

Let us now change our example so as to make it more up-to-date. To think of a government that tries to maximize the expected national income measured in dollars (the money income y) was possible in times of depression when prices were relatively stable, and a rise in money income was about equivalent to a rise in physical production and employment. In present inflationary times one has to think not only of the money income y but also of the price level, call it p. The physical production is $Y = y/p$; and the government is concerned with both Y and p. This is how we modify the previously assumed utility function of the policy maker. We have also to modify the model (3.1), (3.2), (3.3), by adding statements about what determines the dependent variables we have just added to our list, viz., Y and p.

One simple hypothesis is to assume that physical production Y cannot rise above a maximum, η (the 'full employment output'); and that the price level p is constant ($p = \pi$, say), as long as this maximum output is not reached. That is, our two additional dependent variables, Y and p, are determined as follows, in terms of our old dependent variable y and the parameters π and η:

$$(3.9)\qquad \begin{aligned} &Y = y/\pi, p = \pi &&\text{when} \quad y \leqslant \eta\pi \\ &Y = \eta, \quad p = y/\eta &&\text{when} \quad y > \eta\pi . \end{aligned}$$

Roughly, the first line corresponds to an unemployment situation and the second line to a full employment situation. In the former, money income y changes because of changes in physical output Y; in the latter, y changes because of changes in price level p. If we retain, in addition, our old Equations (3.1), (3.2), (3.3) and therefore also their implication (3.4) we see from (3.9) that the new dependent variables Y and p are random variables whose distribution depends on the same parameters as does the distribution of y, and, in addition, on the parameters η (maximum output) and π (constant price level during depression).

We can assume that the policy maker regards high physical output as desirable, and a strong rise in prices over their depression level as undesirable – e.g., because of the injustice that such a rise would inflict on certain people. Thus his utility function – $U(Y, p)$, say – is increasing in Y and decreasing in p, with $p \geqslant \pi$. As a simple example, we may have, as his utility

$$(3.10)\qquad u = U(Y, p) = Y - Ap, \quad A > 0, p \geqslant \pi .$$

The reader will notice that we use italicized capitals to indicate a new class of properties – not the parameters (controlled or non-controlled) of the model but the characteristics of the decisionmaker's valuations, his 'tastes'. In particular, A is the number of units of real income (e.g., billions of dollars with the purchasing power of the year 1940) that he thinks it worthwhile to sacrifice in order to avoid the rise of price level by one point, In assigning any pair of values to the controlled parameters ρ and τ, he will affect the distribution of Y and p, and hence the expected value of u, that is, his 'moral expectation', in the sense of our Lecture 1. Our assumptions (3.9), (3.10) will help as an illustration. Under these assumptions, the utility u is the following function of money income y:

$$(3.11)\qquad u = \begin{cases} \dfrac{y}{\pi} - A\pi & \text{when} \quad y \leqslant \eta\pi \\[2ex] \eta - \dfrac{Ay}{\eta} & \text{when} \quad y \geqslant \eta\pi . \end{cases}$$

This function is represented on Figure III.1 by a broken line consisting of two straight line segments: utility u rises with money income till the latter reaches $\eta\ \pi$; then u falls. Each bell-shaped curve (of which only two are drawn) indicates one of the possible normal distribution density functions of y, with a fixed variance [which, by (3.6), does not depend on policies] and a varying mean [which, by (3.5) does depend on ρ and τ]. (The two drawn curves have respective means μ_y'' and μ_y'.) Thus the policy (ρ, τ) determines the position of the bell-shaped curve, i.e., gives the probability that money income y will fall into any given (small) interval. If this probability

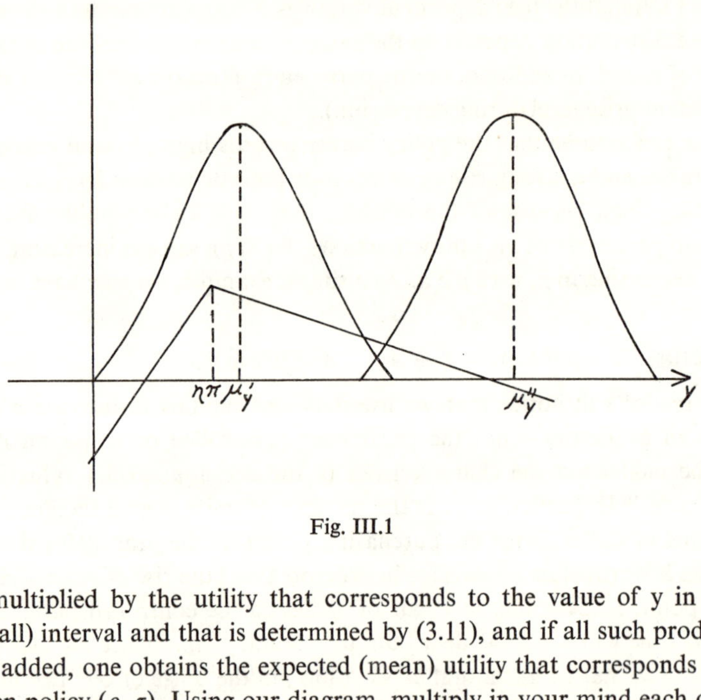

Fig. III.1

is multiplied by the utility that corresponds to the value of y in this (small) interval and that is determined by (3.11), and if all such products are added, one obtains the expected (mean) utility that corresponds to a given policy (ρ, τ). Using our diagram, multiply in your mind each ordinate of the bell-shaped curve by each corresponding ordinate of the broken line, and add all such products. Their sum is the expected utility. Clearly, as the bell-shaped curve moves too far to the right or to the left, the higher utilities (i.e., the ordinates of the broken line taken in the proximity of the full-employment point, $\eta\ \pi$) are multiplied with the lower probabilities (i.e., with the ordinates at the left or right 'tail' of the bell-shaped curve). Hence there exists some intermediate position of the bell-shaped curve – and hence some value of μ_y – that results in the highest expected utility.

To this optimal value of μ_y will correspond, by (3.5), an optimal value of $\rho - \gamma\tau$, given the non-controlled parameters. Hence the knowledge of those parameters (β, γ, μ_b, μ_c) is needed to find those pairs of value of the policy-parameters ρ and τ, that will maximize expected utility, given the 'taste-parameter' A of the policy-maker. Of course, the knowledge of the feasible limits such as $\tau_{\min}$, $\rho_{\max}$ will also have to be used, to sift out the non-feasible combinations of taxes and expenditures. But, unlike in our previous example, this knowledge will not suffice. It becomes necessary to estimate the parameters that characterize the behavior of consumers and businessmen.

We see thus that the need for the knowledge of certain parameters, and therefore for their identifiability (in the sense of Lecture 2), depends, in general, on the whole model in which these parameters occur; and on the utility function of the decisionmaker.

Does not this land us in a rather crass pragmatism? What about theory for its own sake, a theory that is not used to give advice, to choose, to act? A pragmatist will say that theory provides us with solutions which are potentially useful for a large class of decisions. It is welcome because we cannot foresee which particular decisions we shall have to take. Our decisions may or may not be such as to leave certain properties of the system unchanged. Hence, the more we know about its properties the better. If we merely want to know how long it takes to boil an egg, the best is to boil one or two without going into the chemistry of protein molecules. The need for chemistry is due to our want to do other and new things!

The word 'value' is more respectable than 'utility', yet means essentially the same. If the satisfaction of scientific curiosity is recognized by our culture as one of the major values, the search for facts as well as theories is justified even if no predictive uses can be seen for the results. Yet, an additional scrutiny in terms of other social values remains important. Especially in social science there has been a temptation to use statistical tools for laborious rediscovery of the trivial, or the recording of the useless. One should not brush away as 'utilitarian' or 'pragmatic' the reminder that we ought to help in the making of socially important decisions.[27]

NOTES

1 The lecture was given on 6 December 1950.

2 Such a weighted average of utilities has been called 'mathematical expectation of utility' or simply 'expected utility'. The founders of the theory of probabilities when speculating about gamblers' choices, called this weighted average the 'moral expectation' (= the mathematical expectation of 'moral' as distinct from physical', or 'monetary' wealth). The term 'military worth' (of a military situation or objective) encountered in military writings is presumably equivalent to 'utility'. It is likely that the often heard term, 'calculated risk' of a military enterprise, if the term has any meaning at all, means the negative of 'expected military worth', in the sense of an average of the utilities of the alternative outcomes of the enterprise, weighted with their respective probabilities.

3 Actual experiments of this kind were reported by F. Mosteller and P. Nogee in 'An Experimental Measurement of Utility', *Journal of Political Economy*, **59**, (1951) 371–404

4 'An Essay towards Solving a Problem in the Doctrine of Chances', *Phil. Trans. Royal Soc. of London* (1763) 370–418. (Facsimile edition by W. Edwards Deming, Washington, D. C., 1940.)

5 Daniel Bernoulli's 'Specimen theoriae novae de mensura sortis' was published in the 1730–31 volume of transactions of the St. Petersburg Imperial Academy of Sciences, pp. 175–192. A German translation by Alfred Pringsheim, is available: '*Die Grundlage der modernen Wertlehre. Versuch einer neuen Theorie von Glücksfällen*', Leipzig, 1896.

6 Recent studies by Savage and by Herstein and Milnor (to be published) have simplified or generalized the earlier formulations of von Neumann and Morgenstern, and of J. Marschak.

7 Frank Plumpton Ramsey 'Truth and Probability' (1926) and 'Further Considerations' (1928) published posthumously in *The Foundations of Mathematics and Other Logical Essays*, London 1931 (republished: The Humanities Press, New York, 1950). De Finetti, Bruno, La Prevision: ses lois logiques, ses sources subjectives', *Annales de l'Institut Henri Poincaré* (1937) 1–68. L. J. Savage, 'Notes on the Foundations of Statistics' (mimeographed), University of Chicago lectures, 1951.

8 David Hilbert, *Die Grundlagen der Geometrie*, Leipzig 1910.

9 Note that here and in what follows we are taking a more general view of a 'state of the world' than in our previous examples. A state of the world may now include more than one possibility; and each possibility can, in turn, be subdivided. Thus 'W' is a state of the world, and its subdivision, the alternatives 'W and V' and 'W and $\bar{V}$' are also states of the world.

10 However the arithmetical operations leading to the statement are independent of this interpretation of it. They are the same as those used by James Bernoulli (Daniel's kin) who possibly did not think of probabilities as subjective.

11 A rigorous analysis on these lines is contained in an unpublished study by Roy Radner on 'Consistent Decision Functions'.

12 In our example, this assumption can be used only as an approximation since normal distribution applies to a continuous (and therefore infinite-valued) variable whereas x(cigarettes, communism) is discrete. Such approximations are convenient. For example, in Lloyd Warner's studies, the variable x is social status measured on a 12-point scale on the basis of neighbors' opinions; the $z^{(1)}$, $z^{(2)}$... are, respectively, income, housing conditions (again a discrete variable) etc.; and 'weights' α_i are estimated, as well as μ and σ, by the method of 'multiple regression'. With two-valued variables, this appraisal degenerates into familiar 'tests of dual hypotheses' (chi-squared, analysis of variance).

[13] The problem may be posed somewhat differently. Given the joint distribution of the random disturbances v of the responses of individual firms (i.e., given μ, σ and ρ), what is the distribution of the disturbance of the sum (not of the average)? One may, for example, compare the constant ratio σ/μ (the 'coefficient of variation' of v) and the ratio between the following two constants: the standard deviation of the sum of random disturbances and the expectation of this sum. This ratio converges to $(\sigma/\mu)\sqrt{\rho}$. (A more difficult problem is to estimate the coefficient of variation of the sum: it is the expectation of a random ratio, not the ratio of two constants).

[14] Cf. Paul Lazarsfeld, 'The Logical and Mathematical Foundations of Latent Structure Analysis', 'The Interpretation of Some Latent Structures', *Measurement and Prediction* **4**, Studies in Psychology of World War II, Princeton University Press, 1950.

[15] See, for example, A. M. Mood, *Introduction to the Theory of Statistics*, New York 1950, pp. 299–301. To quote Mood's example, "Anthropologists... make measurements x on skulls, of known age z, then estimate the age z_0 of a skull of unknown age with measurements x'".

[16] The random variable $x_1 - z(= u + \lambda_1)$ corresponds thus to the expression (2.3), with $n = 1$ and all the α_i known. It is normally distributed (with mean $\mu = \lambda_1$), jointly with another random variable, $x_2 - z$.

[17] For example, although we cannot ascertain the incomes of families who tell us their consumption of cigarettes and cereals, we may know from some other source the distribution of those incomes; e.g., if our sample is large and we have reasons to regard it as representing the whole U.S. population, then the income distribution is known from income tax statistics.

[18] Remembering that λ_i, x_i, z stand for the logarithms of A_i, X_i, Z, this means that the unknown proportionality factor A_i in (2.7), can be estimated as the ratio of the geometric mean of X_i (observed in a large sample) to the (known) geometric mean of Z – a result that is not unexpected, in view of the multiplicative character of the random deviation $(1 + U_i)$.

[19] Implying that the consumption item X_i is (apart from random disturbances) proportional, not to the individual's income Z, but to some unknown power of it, Z^{β_i}.

[20] If the sample is not very large, the test procedure is more delicate, since the non-fulfillment of equations such as (2.11) may be due to sampling errors. The question asked then is whether the equation is 'significantly' unfulfiled. Further, redundant information (such as $\sigma_{12} = 0$ in our case) may be used, not to test the hypothesis, but to increase the precision of the estimate of the parameters.

[21] Rather, '*significantly*' inconsistent, unless the sample is infinite. See previous note.

[22] For the history and bibliography of the subject, see Olav Reiersøl and T. C. Koopmans, 'The Identification of Structural Characteristics', *Annals of Mathematical Statistics* **21** (June 1950) 165–181, esp. p. 167; T. C. Koopmans, 'Identification Problems in Economic Model Construction', *Econometrics* **17**, No. 2 (April 1949) 125–144, esp. p. 126; Jerzy Neyman, 'Existence of Consistent Estimates of the Directional Parameter in a Linear Structural Relation between Two Variables', *Annals of Mathematical Statistics* **22** (1951) 497–512.

[23] This characterization of z will simplify the exposition that follows presently, and also that of 'policies' to be discussed in lecture III.

[24] See also M. A. Girshick, 'Model Construction in the Social Sciences – An Expository Discussion of Measurement and Prediction', *The Public Opinion Quarterly* **14**, No. 4 (Winter 1950–51).

[25] See note 26 below.

[26] Suffice it to say that Equation (3.1), stating that production (mesured in dollars), y, is adjusted instantaneously to demand (measured in dollars), $b+c+\rho$, is merely an approximation of some equation that would state how this adjustment proceeds in time. For example, if one thinks that producers are stimulated by the excess of demand over supply one might try to replace (3.1) by the differential equation

$$\text{(3.7)} \qquad \mathrm{d}y/\mathrm{d}t = \alpha(b + c + \rho - y),$$

where t is time and α, a positive constant, is a behavior parameter measuring the speed of the producers' reaction to a unit discrepancy between demand and production. Using (3.2), (3.3), the Equation (3.7) becomes

$$\text{(3.8)} \qquad \mathrm{d}y/\mathrm{d}t = \alpha[y(\beta + \gamma - 1) + \rho - \gamma\tau + v_b + v_c];$$

if v_b and v_c were constant, (3.8) would imply that y grows exponentially ('explodes') through time if $\beta+\gamma-1>0$, and declines exponentially ('fades out') towards the 'equilibrium value' given in (3.4), if $\beta+\gamma-1<0$. Because of random fluctuations of v_b and v_c, these trends will be distorted somewhat but it remains true that the inequality $\beta+\gamma-1>0$ implies an 'explosive' rise in income (measured in dollars) such as was historically observed only in times of a few exceptional hyper-inflations. At least when one has to decide between small upward or downward variations of ρ and τ, the behavior of consumers and businessmen can be assumed to be such as to preclude explosive hyperinflation, and hence to preclude that $\beta+\gamma>1$, i.e., to preclude λ negative.

[27] See also the author's two papers on 'Statistical Inference from Non-Experimental Observations: An Economic Example' (in: *International Statistical Institute*, 25th Session, 1947. Volume III, Part A, pp. 289–301) and on 'Economic Measurements for Policy and Prediction', *Selected Essays*, 49.

5

NORMS AND HABITS OF DECISION MAKING UNDER CERTAINTY* **

(1955)

> Thinking is as unnatural and arduous an activity for human beings as walking on two legs is for monkeys.
>
> Arnold Toynbee (*Greek historical thought*, preface to 2d edition).
>
> Men must not allow themselves to be swayed by their moods, believing one thing at one moment and another at another.
>
> Bertrand Russell (*Conquest of happiness*)
>
> Industry is discovering that the man who can run one company can run another one making an entirely different product, because the qualities required for most top jobs are virtually identical – the ability... to make sound decisions quickly and firmly.
>
> *Time*, Oct. 12, 1953. ('The great man hunt: Industry needs more good executives').

I. NORMS, HABITS, TEACHING

We can *prescribe* norms, *describe* habits, and possibly, *teach* habits that approach norms. This applies to norms and habits of thinking as well as to norms and habits of decision making.

The rules of arithmetic, geometry and logic are norms. They may or may not be obeyed in fact when children or abnormal adults or primitive men do their sums, measure plots of land or draw conclusions from premises. As to normal adults in a modern society, they, too, make mistakes in mathematics and are often victims to crude logical fallacies, as many a column of Letters to the Editor will testify. Yet norms can be taught.

When Queen Dido of Carthage acquired land she took advantage of the seller who indiscriminately regarded a plot of land as small whether it was measured by its area (covered by an ox's hide) or by its perimeter (marked by narrow strips made out of the ox's hide). The knowledge that a rectangle's area is length times width, so useful to builders and surveyors, is comparatively recent. The arithmetic of compound interest is a mystery to the Indian peasant at the mercy of the loan shark. Nor is it much better understood, I am afraid, by some Americans who buy refrigerators on installments. According to *Life* magazine, number rackets in the South offer much less favorable odds than they do in the North – presumably because their Southern clientele is less sophisticated in matters of elementary probability calculus. The circular brass basin in King Solomon's temple was said to have a circumference three times as long as its diameter; centuries later Greek youth was taught a much better approximation to π.

Mathematics and logic are normative. But the way in which certain people count, measure and think is the subject of descriptive science – of psychology, I suppose. The methods by which the existing ways of counting, measuring and thinking can be changed and, especially, can be improved (i.e., brought nearer to given norms) is, I suppose, also a problem of psychology – of applied psychology, in this case. In fact, there has been research and teaching on 'How to teach mathematics' – how successful, I don't know.

Similarly, certain formal norms of good decision making have been formulated. They do not, in general, coincide with the habits of decision making among ordinary people in our or any other civilization. These habits can be studied empirically. Moreover, there may be a social need to bring these habits closer to the norms. It is important that at least people whose decisions involve the welfare of many others should fulfill certain norms of consistency, should know, for example, how to 'make up their minds': business administrators, public servants, military leaders. If so, the question of what are and how to change decision habits becomes one of great practical importance.

II. SURE VS. UNCERTAIN PROSPECTS

In general, the outcome of a decision depends not only on the decision itself, but also on the situation which will prevail when the decision becomes effective. Thus to each situation corresponds a set of outcomes, each depending on the decision taken. And to each decision corresponds a set of outcomes, one outcome for each possible situation. We may call this latter set of outcomes, attached to a given decision, a *prospect*. In general, one does not know which situation will prevail in the future. He has to choose among prospects, that is, among sets of outcomes, in the knowledge that each outcome corresponds to some specified situation. This general case is called uncertainty. One can regard the case of certainty as a special case. In this case the future situation is known, so that the decision maker has to choose among prospects each consisting of a single outcome only. These are '*sure prospects*'. Because of its comparative simplicity, it is useful to devote attention to this special case before proceeding to the general one. I shall thus limit the discussion to the norms and habits of decision making under certainty.[1]

We shall give a very rough and tentative sketch of a decision norm. We shall formulate it in such a way as to permit its comparison with habits, for example, with observable actions of a human subject in a laboratory, and not only with his verbal statements about hypothetical decisions. Given the set of alternative outcomes, the *first choice* can be observed as an action, but the second (third, etc.) choice, if stated in the form, 'If I could not obtain x I would try to get y', can be observed only as a verbal statement unless x is actually eliminated from the set of obtainable outcomes, in which case the subject can take y as a *first* choice, an action.

Moreover, since in real life one can never refuse to take a decision (such refusal is itself a decision), we are entitled to formulate the norms so as to exclude incomparability and indifference between any two outcomes.

Finally, since we deal with sure prospects only, we can speak interchangeably of a 'situation' and of a 'set of ourcomes', and identify a decision with the choosing of a single outcome out of a set.

We shall denote outcomes by $x, y, z, \ldots$ and state our norm in two parts:

(1) For any pair (x, y) of outcomes, the following shall be true: If out of a set including x and y the subject chooses x, then, if faced again with this or any other set including x and y, he shall not choose y.

(2) For all triples (x, y, z) of outcomes, the following shall be true: If, out of a set including x and y, the subject chooses x; and if, out of a set including y and z and not x, he chooses y; then, out of a set including x and z, he shall not choose z.

More formally: let X be the set of all outcomes $x, y, z, \ldots$; let X', X'', X''' be subsets of X. Denote by $f(X')$, $f(X'')$, $f(X''')$ the respective *first choices* among the outcomes contained in those subsets. Norm (1) states that if both X' and X'' include x and y and if $f(X')=x$ then $f(X'')\neq y$. Norm (2) states: if X' includes x and y; if X'' includes y and z but not x;

and if X''' includes x and z; then $f(X')=x$ and $f(X'')=y$ imply $f(X''')\neq z$.

In much of the current literature the decision maker is imagined to make choices among two members of a *pair* of outcomes, and a binary relation 'x is not worse than y' is defined that induces an ordering ('complete and weak') on the set of outcomes. It is understood that if x is not worse than y but not conversely, the subject chooses x. But if x is not worse than y and also y is not worse than x, the decision is indeterminate and the subject is said to be indifferent between x and y. However, this cannot be observed by an outsider unless verbal statements and not only actions of the subject are taken as observed facts and are used as data to predict future actual decisions.

The relation between the decision norms (1) and (2) and the properties of the ordering relation 'not worse than' that are usually assumed, explicitly or tacitly, seems to be as follows. Norm (1) is implied by three distinct properties of that ordering relation and by the above exclusion of indifference:

(α) *comparability*: all outcomes are comparable, i.e., for no two outcomes should it be impossible to state that one of them is not worse than the other;

(β) *irrelevance of additional alternatives*: whether x is or is not worse than y is independent of whether z is also available;

(γ) *constancy* of the ordering relation over time: if x is considered not worse than y at one time it should remain so at another.

As to decision norm (2), it is implied by the following property usually assumed about the ordering relation for outcomes:

(δ) *transitivity*: if x is not worse than y, and y is not worse than z, then x is not worse than z.

Norms (1) and (2) can be said to define *consistency of decisions*. In the literature the consistency concept has often been confined to (δ) only; but, no doubt, (γ) and (β) also deserve the name!

If norms (1) and (2) are fulfilled, it is possible to rank all outcomes so as to characterize a given individual by his consistent ranking of outcomes, in the following sense. As before, denote by f the operation of picking a first choice from a given set. Consider a finite set X_0 and let $x_0=f(X_0)$. Denote by $\bar{x}_i$ a set consisting of x_i only; then $X_0-\bar{x}_0$ is a set obtained by eliminating x_0 from X_0. Let $f(X_0 - \bar{x}_0) = x_1$, $f(X_0 - \bar{x}_0 - \bar{x}_1) = x_2$, and, in general,

$$f\left(X_0 - \sum_0^m \bar{x}_i\right) = x_{m+1}, \quad m = 0, 1, \ldots .$$

We obtain a complete and strong ordering: x_0 ranks before x_1, etc. We now state: the ranking $(x_0, x_1, \ldots, x_m, \ldots)$ will prevail for any subset X' of X_0. That is to say, if $x_h, x_i, x_j, \ldots$ are all included in X' and the subscript h is a number smaller than the subscripts of all other elements of X' then $x_h = f(X')$. This follows from our norms (1) and (2).

III. DECISION HABITS

If one investigates empirically whether a subject actually fulfills our decision norm and therefore has a consistent ordering of first choices, one will, I think, almost certainly find that the norm is not fulfilled. This may be blamed on observation errors – e.g., the experimenter's failure to replicate exactly a given set of outcomes or a specified subset of it.

As an alternative explanation, one may suspect with Polonius that "though this is madness it has method." For example, one may find that, for a certain man or even for all members of a group, x is *always* the first choice in (x, y, z) and y is *always* the first choice in (x, y, w), thus breaking norm (1) under well-defined conditions. Or one may find a constant trend over time (due to learning, fatigue, aging, etc.) so that, for example, from a constant set $(x, y, z, \ldots)$ of outcomes, a person *always* makes x his first choice on the first trial, y on the second, z on the third, etc. Thirdly, one may assume that the variation of the subject's ranking order of outcomes is a random variation, satisfying a certain probability distribution that can be estimated from observations. Should this be so, it would be possible to make a statistical prediction of the subject's future decisions in the sense that the scientist will be able to bet specified odds on how the subject will decide in given situations.

In any case, one will try to consider, as a verifiable model of actual decision habits of a person or a group, not the decision norm as stated, but possibly some weakened version of it. It is probably necessary to combine the three escapes just suggested: observation errors, deviations from the norm due to ascertainable causes, and random variations. Let us, for the sake of simplicity, confine ourselves to the third way out, and weaken the 'norms' into 'models of habits' merely by introducing random variations.[2]

In the last paragraph of the preceding section we described the ranking of outcomes by successive elimination of first choices.[3] Now, instead of assuming that this ranking order does not vary, let us assume that it varies according to some probability distribution. If there are altogether n outcomes, $n!$ rankings will be possible. Denote them by r_i, $i=1,\dots,n!$, and assume that a fixed probability $p_i=p(r_i)$ exists for each of them. Call this model M.

In a somewhat stronger model, one can add another restriction: assume that the set $p_1,\dots,p_n$ has a unique maximum, say p_m (that is, the ranking order r_m is more probable than all others), and that p_i becomes larger as the number of reversals[4] needed to obtain r_i from r_m become smaller. We may call this assumption M_1, and the resulting model (combination of M and M_1) MM_1.

Another possible restriction is that of transitivity in the following sense. Let R_{xy} be the set of all rankings such that x ranks before y. If we denote by p_{xy} the probability that one of these rankings will be observed, then, by definition, $p_{xy}=\sum_{r\in R_{xy}} p(r)=1-p_{yx}$. Our transitivity requirement for stochastic models (call it M_2) says: for any x, y, z, if $p_{xy}\geqslant\frac{1}{2}$ and $p_{yz}\geqslant\frac{1}{2}$. then $p_{xz}\geqslant\frac{1}{2}$.

Note that, in stochastic models, the concept of indifference becomes independent of the subject's verbal statements, provided the probabilities can be estimated. He is indifferent between x and y if $p_{xy}=\frac{1}{2}=p_{yz}$.

Condition M_2 restricts the class of possible probability distributions of rankings. As an example (due to Christopher Winsten), consider a subject presented with a set of three alternative outcomes x, y, z, and let the probabilities of the six possible rankings be, in an obvious notation,

$$p_{xyz}=p_{zxy}=p_{yzx}=\tfrac{1}{6}+\alpha$$
$$p_{yxz}=p_{zyx}=p_{xzy}=\tfrac{1}{6}-\alpha,$$

where $0<\alpha\leqslant\frac{1}{6}$. Then the probability (denoted by p_{xy}) that, in choices among three outcomes, x is ranked before y is

$$p_{xy}=p_{xyz}+p_{zxy}+p_{xzy}=\tfrac{1}{2}+\alpha>\tfrac{1}{2}.$$

Similarly $p_{yz}=p_{xyz}+p_{yzx}+p_{yxz}=\tfrac{1}{2}+\alpha>\tfrac{1}{2}.$

Yet

$$p_{xz} = p_{xyz} + p_{yxz} + p_{xzy} = \tfrac{1}{2} - \alpha < \tfrac{1}{2}.$$

That is, although x is, more often than not, ranked *before* y; and y *before* z; yet x is, more often than not, ranked *behind* z. We shall have to ask whether there exist probability distributions of rankings that are consistent with M_2. But before doing this, let us stop for some other more or less plausible hypotheses on decision making.

At the end of the preceding section, we stated as a consequence of our 'norm' that the ranking of outcomes obtained by successive elimination of first choices from the sets X_0, $X_0 - \bar{x}_0$, $X_0 - \bar{x}_0 - \bar{x}_1$, etc., shall prevail also in all subsets of X_0. In the current section, we have replaced a unique ranking of outcomes by a probability distribution of such rankings. We can now ask whether the subject who, more often than not, has ranked x before y within the large set X_0 will also, more often than not, rank x before y in each of the subsets of X_0 that contain both x and y. The simplest such subsets are the pairs contained in X_0. It can be asked for each of the $n(n-1)/2$ pairs whether the same ranking of the pair (in the sense of comparative probabilities) is maintained throughout all of the 2^{n-2} sets that contain the pair. Appropriately modified, the same question can be extended from pairs to triples, etc.

A still stronger proposition would be to require that not only should the probabilities of rankings maintain a consistent order when the subject is repeatedly faced with various sets of outcomes; but that the magnitudes of those probabilities should be consistent. That is, let us denote by $p_{xy} | x, y, z$ and by $p_{xy} | x, y$ the probabilities that x be ranked before y when the subject is presented, respectively, with a set of three, and the set of two elements containing x and y. We then require that

$$p_{xy} | x, y = p_{xy} | x, y, z,$$

and not only (as just before), that

$$p_{xy} | x, y \geqslant \tfrac{1}{2} \text{ when and only when } p_{xy} | x, y, z \geqslant \tfrac{1}{2}.$$

We may call these two propositions, M_4 and M_3, respectively.

We now proceed to a very special proposition on the form of the probability distribution of rankings. It is strong enough not only to imply the transitivity condition, M_2, but also to induce a measurement scale on the suitably defined 'utilities' of outcomes.

Consider a set X of n outcomes. It is then asserted that there exists a probability distribution F of n real random variables $U_1, \ldots, U_n$ with the following property: if a ranking r places the outcomes in the order x_1^r, $x_2^r, \ldots, x_n^r$, then its probability $p(r)$ equals the probability that the inequalities $U_1^r > U_2^r > \cdots > U_n^r$ between correspondingly arranged U_i's are satisfied. Call this assumption M_5.

The following special form of the distribution F is compatible with, and indeed implies, the transitivity condition M_2. Let F be normal with equal variances and equal covariances. Call this assumption M_6. That is, writing $\mu_i = EU_i$ and $\sigma_{ij} = E(U_i - \mu_i)(U_j - \mu_j)$, $i, j = 1, \ldots, n$, we assume $\sigma_{ij} = \sigma^2$ for $i = j$, and $\sigma_{ij} = \rho\sigma^2$ for $i \neq j$ (ρ is the correlation coefficient). Let us prove, for the case $n = 3$, that our assumptions imply transitivity, in the sense that if the three outcomes are x_1, x_2, x_3 and if p_{ij} is the probability that p_i is ranked before p_j then the following holds:

$$\text{if } p_{12} > \tfrac{1}{2} \text{ and } p_{23} > \tfrac{1}{2} \text{ then } p_{13} > \tfrac{1}{2}.$$

By M_5 (of which M_6 is a special case), $p_{12} = \text{Prob}\,(U_1 - U_2 > 0)$; and by M_6, $U_1 - U_2$ is distributed normally, with mean $\mu_1 - \mu_2$ and variance $\sigma_{11} + \sigma_{22} - 2\sigma_{12} = 2\sigma^2\,(1 - \rho)$. Hence $p_{12} > \frac{1}{2}$ if and only if $\mu_1 - \mu_2 > 0$. Similarly, $p_{23} > \frac{1}{2}$ if and only if $\mu_2 - \mu_3 > 0$. Hence $p_{12} > \frac{1}{2}$ and $p_{23} > \frac{1}{2}$ if and only if $\mu_1 - \mu_3 > 0$, and this is equivalent to $p_{13} > \frac{1}{2}$. We can now restate M_6 as follows. For any (finite) set of outcomes $x_1, \ldots, x_n$ there exists a set of real numbers $\mu_1, \ldots, \mu_n, \tau$ such that the probability p_{ij} of ranking x_i before x_j is equal to $G_{ij}(0)$, where G_{ij} is a normal (cumulative) distribution function with mean $\mu_j - \mu_i$ and variance τ^2. [τ^2 is, of course, equal to $2\sigma^2(1 - \rho)$, in terms of parameters of the n-variate distribution function F.] Thus, if the sample is large enough to estimate the probability p_{ij} from the frequency with which x_i was observed to be ranked ahead of x_j, then the mean $\mu_j - \mu_i$ can be read from the normal probability table, after fixing arbitrarily the origin (with $\mu_1 = 0$, say) and scale (with $\tau = 1$, say). Also, if the sample is large enough, the hypothesis itself can be disproved from observations: for the number $(n-1)$ of unknown parameters is smaller than the number $n(n-1)/2$ of estimated probabilities, p_{ij}, provided $n > 2$; and if rankings are performed not only on pairs but also on larger sets the difference between the number of knowns and of unknowns is still larger. Usually, the sample will be small, and many of the inconsistencies will be blamed on this smallness!

Assumption M_6 is used in the method of paired comparisons. (Louis Thurstone had originally restricted M_6 still further, by assuming $\rho=0$; F. Mosteller[5] showed this restriction to be unnecessary.) When applied to decisions, the means $\mu_1,\dots,\mu_n$ have been called utilities because of the property that $\mu_i>\mu_j$ if and only if x_i will, *more often than not*, be ranked ahead of x_j; this property being, of course, weaker than the property assigned to utilities in (non-stochastic) decision norms: the utility of x_i exceeds that of x_j if and only if x_i is *always* ranked ahead of x_j.

The assumption of normality, in M_5 and M_6, is an awkward one in the case – quite usual in economic life – of quantifiable 'goods' (and 'bads'). Suppose x_1 means one meal and x_2 means two meals. Then (unless the cost of throwing a meal away is considerable) we shall expect *with certainty* that the subject will rank x_2 ahead of x_1, with only pathological exceptions. This can be also extended to some outcomes consisting of pairs, or triples, etc., of goods: e.g., if $x_1=1$ meal and 1 theater ticket, $x_2=1$ meal and 2 theater tickets, and $x_3=2$ meals and 2 theater tickets, then the ranking will be, *with certainty*: x_3, x_2, x_1. Yet the assumption of a normal distribution $F(U_1,\dots,U_n)$ does not admit for any pair x_i, x_j that the probability $p_{ij}=\Pr(U_i-U_j>0)$ be 1 (or 0), unless all choices are non-random. Even a weaker assumption than that of normality is inconsistent with the certainty that more of a good will be chosen in preference to less. Any model that assigns an equal utility difference to all pairs (x_i, x_j), (x_h, x_i), etc., for which the probabilities of ranking p_{ij}, p_{hi} are equal, will lead to an absurd result. For suppose x_1, x_2, x_3 form a sequence of decreasing quantities of a good. Then $p_{12}=p_{23}=p_{13}=1$ and hence $\mu_1-\mu_2=\mu_2-\mu_3=\mu_1-\mu_3$ and therefore $\mu_1=\mu_2=\mu_3=0$, an absurd result.[6]

However, instead of normal distributions, one can use certain distributions in which probabilities are non-zero only for a certain range of values of a variable. In fact, the transitivity condition M_2 is satisfied by any distribution $F(U_1,\dots,U_n)$ which does not change when the sign of any deviate $(U_i-\mu_i)$ is reversed. If, in addition, F does not change when any two deviates $(U_i-\mu_i)$, $(U_j-\mu_j)$ are interchanged, a scale of utilities can be obtained.

Let me conclude by presenting a model (M_7) that may be used to scale utilities of quantifiable goods. Let a and b be variable *quantities* of two distinct goods, A and B, and let us observe the frequency with which the subject prefers b units of B to a units of A. For a large sample, this frequency will approach a probability to be denoted by $p(b, a)$. As in the method of paired comparisons, let us assume that $p(b, a)$ increases or at least does not decrease, as the difference of utilities of the two outcomes increases:

$$(M_7) \qquad p(b, a) = H[v(b) - u(a)]$$

where H is a monotone non-decreasing function with values between (but possibly excluding) 0 and 1, and $v(b)$ and $u(a)$ are, respectively, the utilities of b units of B and of a units of A. The functions v and u are monotone increasing and are called utility functions. Can we trace them? The observed variables are a, b, and, in a large sample, the probabilities $p(b, a)$. Suppose, then, we have estimated the surface $p(b, a)$. For example, we may have obtained a graph of lines of equal p's in the (a, b)-plane, as on Figure 1.

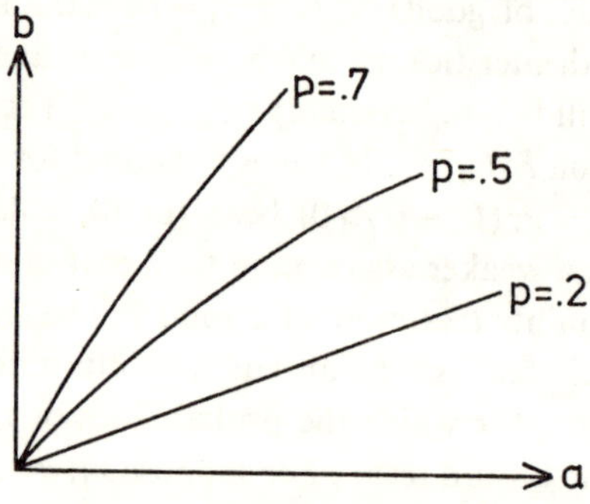

Fig. 1. Hypothetical probabilities of ranking b units of B ahead of a units of A.

The problem is to find a distribution function H such that its inverse should satisfy the condition (implied by M_7):

$$H^{-1}[p(b, a)] = v(b) - u(a) \quad \text{for all} \quad b, a;$$

this implies, for example, that, for any quadruple b, a, b', a',

$$H^{-1}[p(b, a)] - H^{-1}[p(b, a')] = \\ = H^{-1}[p(b', a)] - H^{-1}[p(b', a')].$$

Should such a function H exist, then the utility-differences $v(b)-u(a)$ can be derived for all b, a. And by fixing arbitrarily two values such as $v(b_0)=1$, $u(a_0)=2$, the two utility functions can be found. In practice, the data will, very likely, not admit the existence of a function H which will satisfy exactly the last displayed equation above. But, then, in practice, the sample will not be large enough to get the exact shape of the surface $p(b, a)$. This allows somewhat greater freedom. From the observed frequencies – one frequency for each observed pair b, a – one has to estimate the combined operator $H^{-1}[p(\ )]$, subject to the condition M_7 and consistent with the character of p as a proper fraction, H as a cumulative distribution function, and v and u as monotone increasing functions. While it would be tempting to assume H normal, the considerations given above against M_6 for the case of quantifiable goods warn against this assumption. Rather, ours seems to be a job for nonparametric statisticians.

NOTES

* Research under contract of Cowles Commission with the Office of Naval Research.

** With acknowledgments to Roy Radner and Christopher Winsten, Cowles Commission; T. W. Anderson, Columbia University; Ward Edwards, Johns Hopkins University; Conrad Oort, Fellow of Committee on Behavioral Sciences, University of Chicago.

1 The paper originally submitted to the Rye conference of 1954 included sections on uncertainty. Some of these have been, in the meantime, reproduced in an article: 'Scaling of Utilities and Probabilities', *Selected Essays*, 3. Rather than republishing the contents of the article and including other sections on uncertainty, the author has now expanded the originally terse and unreadable sections on certainty and hopes to present the rest of the materials on another occasion.

2 I have learned from Louis N. Thurstone that psychophysical experiments lead naturally to a stochastic interpretation of human responses to stimuli; and Thurstone himself, in his work on consumers' habits, is a pioneer in stochastic interpretation of decisions. Another pioneer was the late Hans Reichenbach, the logician, in an unpublished RAND paper dated August 1949. More recently, stochastic models for decisions under certainty were proposed in experimental studies of Professor Andreas Papandreou and his colleagues at the University of Minnesota (*A Test of a Proposition in the Theory of Choice*), 1954.

Leo Törnqvist (*A Model for Stochastic Decision Making*, Cowles Commission Discussion Paper, Economics 2100, March 1954) and Stephan Vail (*A stochastic model for utilities*, Seminar on the applications of mathematics to the social sciences, University of Michigan, 1953) have proposed appropriate axiomatics, as has done, for a related problem, Karl Menger (Probabilistic Theories of Relations', *Proc. Nat. Acad. Sci.* **37**, (1951), (178–180).

Though not explicitly so, a stochastic model is also in the background of the published experimental studies of F. Mosteller and P. Nogee ('An Experimental Measurement of Utility', *J. Polit. Econ.*, 1952), on decision making under uncertainty. See also p. 76

of Ward Edwards' experimental report ('The Reliability of Probability-Preferences', *Amer. J. Psychol.*, March 1954).

[3] It is probably easier, in performing experiments, to ask the subject to rank all the elements of a set than to ask him for a succession of decisions (i.e., of first choices). I do not insist on the former method, and what follows can equally be applied to both methods. But one should be aware of a smaller predictive value of verbal hypothetical statements compared with actual decision, when observed data are used to predict future actual decisions. Perhaps the second, third, etc., choices should be given smaller weights in statistical computations than is given to the first choice.

[4] See Kendall, M., *The Advanced Theory of Statistics*. Vol. I, p. 391.

[5] Remarks on the method of paired comparisons. I. *Psychometrika*, 1951, 1–9. In practice, Thurstone did not actually maintain the restriction ($\rho = 0$) introduced in his original article: 'A Law of Comparative Judgment', *Psychol. Rev.* (1927) 273–286.

[6] Although I have excluded from this paper the case of uncertainty, the following brief remark is in order. While maintaining the same property of utilities as assigned to the μ_i in the paired comparisons method (viz.: $\mu_1 \geqslant \mu_2$ if and only if $p_{12} \geqslant \frac{1}{2}$), it is possible to obtain another scale of utilities from observations on choices between bets, involving money sums (as in the cited experiments of Mosteller and Nogee) or any other outcomes, possibly all non-quantifiable. The additional proposition used in this case is the 'Bernoulli norm': the utility of a bet is equal to the sum of the utilities of its alternative outcomes, multiplied by respective probabilities (for the justification of this norm, see, for example, my article cited above). In the case of bets, even when the outcomes are not quantifiable goods, normal distribution is ruled out for similar reasons as above. If $\mu_1 > \mu_2$ then of any two bets promising x_1 or x_2, the one attaching greater probability to x_1 will be preferred with certainty. It would be interesting to find whether it is possible to formulate the assumptions of stochastic behavior that would be weak enough to yield a consistent scale of utilities by using bets as well as sure prospects.

6

EXPERIMENTAL TESTS OF A STOCHASTIC DECISION THEORY*

(1959)

Co-author: Donald Davidson

I. INTRODUCTION

Common experience suggests, and experiment confirms, that a person does not always make the same choice when faced with the same options, even when the circumstances of choice seem in all relevant respects to be the same. However, the bulk of economic theory neglects the existence of such inconsistencies; and the best known theories for decision making, for example, those of von Neumann and Morgenstern [1] or Savage [2], base the existence of a measurable utility upon a pattern of invariant two-place relations, sometimes called 'preference' and 'indifference'. This raises a difficulty for any attempt to use such theories to describe and predict actual behavior.

A number of ways of meeting the difficulty may be mentioned:

(1) It is possible to insist on the normative status of the theory and construe all deviations as evidence of error on the part of the subject.

(2) One may defend the descriptive accuracy of the theory and argue that it has been incorrectly interpreted; for example, by wrongly identifying two options (say winning $1 at time t and winning $1 at time $t+10$ minutes) as the same.

(3) One may interpret every case of inconsistency as a case of indifference: if the subject has chosen a rather than b but soon afterwards chooses b rather than a, this is interpreted as indifference between those two objects; if he chooses a rather than b, b rather than c, and c rather than a, this is interpreted as indifference between those three objects. In empirical application, this approach would probably make indifference all-pervasive.

(4) An alternative approach is to define preference and indifference in terms of probabilities of choice. Mosteller and Nogee, in testing the von Neumann and Morgenstern axioms, considered a subject indifferent between two options when he chose each option half the time [3]; Edwards

[4] has also used this method. In this approach probabilities of choice do not enter the formal axiomatic development.

(5) A fifth strategy, explored in this paper, incorporates probabilities of choice into the axiomatic structure and exploits their properties in scaling utilities.

II. PRIMITIVE AND DEFINED NOTIONS

We now introduce various concepts needed for the subsequent discussion. It should be emphasized that strictness has in many places been sacrificed to perspicuity; we trust that the knowing reader can make the corrections needed for formal accuracy. First we list the primitive notions:

Primitive 1

A set A of *alternatives*.[1] A may include wagers (choices involving risk) as well as sure outcomes. In this and the following section, we shall treat alternatives quite generally. In the section entitled 'Stochastic Theory of Choice Between Subjectively Even-Chance Wagers' we shall use special properties of wagers.

Primitive 2

The *probability* $P(a, b)$ that the subject, forced to choose between a and b, chooses a. We assume, in what follows, for every a and b in A:

(a) $P(a, b) + P(b, a) = 1$.
(b) $P(a, b)$ lies in the open interval $(0, 1)$.

In a fully formalized exposition these assumptions would appear as axioms or theorems; in this paper we shall sometimes leave these assumptions tacit. Under a natural interpretation Primitive 2(a) has empirical content: it implies that, when a subject is asked to choose between a or b, he always chooses a or b. Normally, we are not interested in testing Primitive 2(a); rather, we attempt to make it true by enforcing a choice. Therefore we may want to state our experimental hypothesis as follows: if Primitive 2(a) is true for a given subject, then the other axioms hold; if Primitive 2(a) fails for a subject, we then reject the subject, not the hypothesis. Or we may want to include Primitive 2(a) in the hypothesis and reject the hypothesis for a subject who refuses an offered choice.

For the experiments reported here, the issue is academic. All subjects were docile.

For the case where $a=b$, Primitive 2(a) has the consequence $P(a, a)= =\frac{1}{2}$. Formal convenience dictates that we not exclude this case although we give it no empirical meaning.

Before commenting on Primitive 2(b), it will be useful to give some definitions.

DEFINITION 1. a is *absolutely preferred* to b if and only if $P(a, b)=1$. This concept corresponds to the psychologists' 'perfect discrimination'.

DEFINITION 2. a is *stochastically preferred* to b if and only if $\frac{1}{2}< <P(a, b)<1$.

DEFINITION 3. a and b are *stochastically indifferent* if and only if $P(a,b) =\frac{1}{2}$. Since we use the word 'indifferent' in no other sense, we often omit the word 'stochastically'.

DEFINITION 4. c is a *stochastic mid-point* between a and b if and only if $P(a, c)=P(c, b)$.

In situations in which it is natural to apply the theory, it is obvious that cases of absolute preference occur, violating Primitive 2(b). In particular, one would expect that when a and b denote respectively 'receiving m dollars' and 'receiving n dollars' (or, for that matter, m or n units of some commodity), then $m>n$ implies $P(a, b)=1$. More generally, if m_1, n_1 are amounts of some commodity and m_2, n_2 are amounts of a second commodity, and $m_1>n_1$, $m_2 \geqslant n_2$, then the alternative consisting of receiving m_1 and m_2 will be absolutely preferred to the alternative n_1 and n_2. This extends also to bundles consisting of three or more commodities.

In the experimental testing of stochastic theories of choice, various devices may be used to avoid comparisons of alternatives which yield absolute preferences. Papandreou *et al.* [5], using appropriate commodity bundles, avoided cases of the sort just mentioned. The methods used for avoiding comparisons apt to generate absolute preference in the experiments reported here are discussed in what follows.

As long as the assumption stated in Primitive 2(b) remains in force, it is not enough merely to avoid comparing alternatives one of which is absolutely preferred to another; the set A of alternatives to which the theory applies must contain no two such alternatives. Although we have no solution on hand, we shall mention in the next section the possibility of modifying the formal system to eliminate dependence on the assumption in Primitive 2(b).

III. GENERAL STOCHASTIC THEORY OF CHOICE

An important aspect of a general stochastic theory of choice lies in the fact that, without specifically considering wagers, it is possible to obtain forms of measurement stronger than a mere ordering by imposing plausible conditions on probabilities of choice. When conditions of sufficient strength are satisfied, it is possible to interpret a comparison of probabilities as a comparison of differences in subjective value or utility. This idea is captured in a general form by the following definition:

DEFINITION 5. For a given subject, a real-valued function u is called a *utility function* on A (in the sense of Definition 5) if and only if, for every a, b, c, and d in A,

$$P(a, b) \geqslant P(c, d) \quad \text{if and only if} \quad u(a) - u(b) \geqslant u(c) - u(d).$$

The technique of building a subjective scale on the basis of frequency of discriminated differences is common in psychophysics since Fechner [6]; however, the emphasis in psychophysics on relating the subjective (sensation) scale to a physical continuum (which is not assumed in utility measurement) tends to obscure the analogy. Discussion of the relation between psychophysical scaling and utility measurement will be found in Marschak [7] and Luce [8, 9].

There is a much used adage in psychophysics which may be taken as suggesting the principle underlying Definition 5: "Equally often noticed differences are equal [on the sensation scale] unless noticed always or never" (ascribed by Guilford [10] to Fullerton and Cattell). The final phrase of this adage enters a caveat which is clearly as pertinent in utility as in sensation measurement for, in our terms, the caveat concerns the case of absolute preference. Consider the case where $P(6¢, 5¢)=1 =P(\$5000, \$0)$ and hence, by Definition 5, $u(6¢)-u(5¢)=u(\$5000)- -u(\$0)$, which is intuitively absurd. The difficulty created by the existence of absolute preferences is thus clear. The approach to a solution which suggests itself is to add to Definition 5 the caveat "provided neither $P(a, b)$ nor $P(c, d)$ is equal to 0 or 1." This would require modification of the axiomatic conditions needed to prove the existence of a utility function. We have not attempted to carry out this modification, which may well not be trivial.

We now consider what conditions are sufficient for the existence of a utility function (in the sense of Definition 5). Fortunately, in approaching this question, we are able to depend on previous work because any theory which makes essential use of a four-place relation comparing intervals may, with fairly trivial modifications, be reconstrued as a theory in which the atomic sentences are all of the form $P(a, b) \geqslant P(c, d)$, as demanded by Definition 5.[2]

What constitutes sufficient conditions for the existence of a utility function depends, in part, on the nature of the set A. We therefore consider several cases:

Case (*a*). The set A contains a known finite number n of alternatives, $a_1, \ldots, a_n$. In this case, it is always possible, although perhaps tedious, to stipulate conditions on the probabilities $P(a_i, a_j)$ necessary and sufficient for the existence of a utility function. A simple example (for $n=3$) will be treated fully later. In general, it suffices, because of Primitive 2(a), to consider those probabilities $P(a, b)$ that are $\geqslant \frac{1}{2}$; a given complete ordering of these numbers yields, by Definition 5, a sequence of $n(n-1)/2$ inequalities of the form

$$u(a_g) - u(a_h) \geqslant u(a_i) - u(a_k) \geqslant \cdots \geqslant 0$$

involving a set of only n distinct unknowns, viz., the utilities of the n alternatives. Whether these inequalities have a solution can be answered separately for each of the possible $[n(n-1)/2]!$ orderings of the probabilities.

Case (*b*). The set A contains an arbitrary number of alternatives which are equally spaced in utility [such that for every a, b, c, and d in A, if a and b are adjacent in utility[3] and c and d are adjacent, then $P(a, b)=P(c, d)$:. The axioms are an obvious modification of the axioms in Davidson, Suppes, and Siegel [11, p. 31:.

Case (*c*). It will be convenient to give two definitions. The first we owe to Professor Patrick Suppes.

DEFINITION 6. A set A of alternatives is *stochastically continuous* if and only if it meets the following three conditions for every a, b, c, and d in A:

(i) There exists a stochastic mid-point between a and b.

(ii) If $P(c, d) > P(a, b) > \frac{1}{2}$, then there exists a g such that $P(c, g) > > \frac{1}{2}$ and $P(g, d) \geqslant P(a, b)$.

(iii) (Archimedean condition.) If $P(a, b) > \frac{1}{2}$, then for every probability q such that $P(a, b) > q > \frac{1}{2}$, there exists a positive integer n such that $q \geqslant P(a, c_1) = P(c_1, c_2) = \cdots = P(c_n, b) > \frac{1}{2}$.

DEFINITION 7. The *quadruple condition* is satisfied if and only if, for every a, b, c, and d in A, $P(a, b) \geqslant P(c, d)$ implies $P(a, c) \geqslant P(b, d)$.

It follows immediately from Definition 5 that, if a utility function exists on A, then the quadruple condition is satisfied in A. However, we are now in a position to assert more:

THEOREM 1. *If A is stochastically continuous then a utility function exists if and only if the quadruple condition is satisfied.*

A proof of this theorem will not be given here. The general line of demonstration is as follows: Suppes and Winet [12] have given an axiomatization of utility based on a primitive concept which compares utility differences, and they have proved that, if certain axioms on a relation between two pairs of alternatives hold, then utility differences can be defined and, hence, a function analogous to a utility function (in the sense of Definition 5) exists. (See also Alt [13].) Suppes [14] has shown how to express these axioms in terms of relations between probabilities; the new axioms on probabilities (let us call them S) suffice to prove the existence of a utility function in the sense of Definition 5. The three conditions of Definition 6 are trivially equivalent to the continuity axioms of S. Finally, we have been able to prove that all the further axioms of S hold if the quadruple condition is satisfied [and provided, of course, the assumptions specified in Primitives 2(a) and (b) hold]. Hence we know that, if the continuity and quadruple conditions of Definitions 6 and 7 hold, S holds, and there exists a utility function.

Case (d) A result similar to Theorem 1 was obtained by Debreu [15] under a different definition of stochastic continuity properties. Debreu has shown that there exists a utility function on A if the following conditions are satisfied:

(i) If a, b, c are in A and $P(b, a) \geqslant q \geqslant P(c, a)$, then there is a d in A such that $P(d, a) = q$.

(ii) The quadruple condition holds for A.

Case (*e*). The set A contains an unknown number (possibly finite) of alternatives. For this case, no axiom system is known, and it has been conjectured by Scott and Suppes [16] that under certain natural restrictions on the form of axioms no axiomatization is possible.

It may be noted that in Cases (b), (c), and (d), the axiom systems adequate to prove the existence of a utility function (in the sense of Definition 5) are adequate to prove also that any such function is unique up to a linear transformation (i.e., the existence of cardinal utilities).

We can submit to direct experimental test a set of the kind described in Case (a) containing a small, known, finite number of alternatives (let us call the set of alternatives under test T). If the quadruple condition is satisfied for every quadruple of alternatives in T, and T is a sample drawn from a larger set A, we may conclude – with a degree of confidence depending among other things on the size of the sample – that the quadruple condition holds for A. If our hypothesis is that a utility function on A exists, then we need further information about A; for example, we may know the (finite) number of its elements, Case (a), or we may hold that A is stochastically continuous, Cases (c) and (d).

In the experiment reported here, one hypothesis is that a utility function exists for the set consisting of all money wagers of a certain sort. If we can assume that A is stochastically continuous in the sense of Cases (c) or (d), e.g., because the money amounts which enters the wagers are, approximately, continuous variables, and if, on the basis of our sample T, we have concluded that the quadruple condition holds for A, then we can conclude, by Theorem 1, that there exists a utility function on A.

Actually, we did not test for the quadruple condition on our sample T. Instead, we tested for certain implications of that condition: if T does not satisfy such an implication, we reject the hypothesis that T satisfies the quadruple condition. Those implications involve triples (not quadruples) of alternatives and will be referred to as stochastic transitivity properties.

Even for relatively small finite sets of alternatives, the existence of a utility function in the sense of Definition 5 implies more than is implied by the quadruple condition alone. This fact suggests a view of the relation between experimental evidence and hypothesis which differs slightly from the one outlined in the preceding paragraphs. For each sample T drawn from A, we may test *all* the conditions necessary and sufficient for the existence of a utility function on T [the general method is given above in the discussion of Case (a)]. We then consider confirmation of the existence of a utility function on T as inductive evidence for the existence of a utility function on A. As will be shown, the condition of strong stochastic transitivity about to be stated gives necessary and sufficient conditions for the existence of a utility function on a set consisting of three alternatives.

CONDITION 1.

(a) *Weak stochastic transitivity* holds in A if and only if, for all a, b, and c in A,

$$\text{if } P(a, b) \geqslant \tfrac{1}{2} \text{ and } P(b, c) \geqslant \tfrac{1}{2}, \text{ then } P(a, c) \geqslant \tfrac{1}{2}.$$

(b) *Strong stochastic transitivity* holds in A if and only if, for all a, b, and c in A,

$$\text{If } P(a, b) \geqslant \tfrac{1}{2} \text{ and } P(b, c) \geqslant \tfrac{1}{2}, \quad \text{then } P(a, c) \geqslant \max\,[P(a, b), P(b, c)].$$

These terms are due to S. Vail [17]. (We sometimes omit the word 'stochastic'.) Clearly Condition 1(b) implies 1(a), but 1(a) does not imply 1(b); both are implied by the existence of a utility function and are, therefore, necessary conditions for the existence of such a function. Condition 1(b) is equivalent to:

CONDITION 2.

$$\text{If } P(a, b) \leqslant \tfrac{1}{2}, \text{ then } P(a, c) \leqslant P(b, c).$$

Proof: To show that Condition 1(b) implies Condition 2, assume $P(a, b) \geqslant \frac{1}{2}$ and show that, by Condition 1(b), $P(a, c) \geqslant P(b, c)$ for each of the three possible cases:

1. $P(b, c) \geqslant \frac{1}{2}$; then $P(a, c) \geqslant \max\,[P(a, b), P(b, c)] \geqslant P(b, c)$.
2. $P(b, c) < \frac{1}{2} \leqslant P(a, c)$; then $P(a, c) \geqslant P(b, c)$.

3. $P(b, c) < \frac{1}{2}, P(a, c) < \frac{1}{2}$; then $P(c, a) > \frac{1}{2}$, hence $P(c, b) \geqslant \max[P(c, a), P(a, b)] \geqslant P(c, a), P(a, c) \geqslant P(b, c)$.

It may be left to the reader to prove the converse, i.e., that Condition 2 implies Condition 1 (b).

Consider three fixed alternatives, a_1, a_2, a_3 and label the three relevant probabilities $P(a_1, a_2)=p_1$, $P(a_2, a_3)=p_2$, $P(a_3, a_1)=p_3$. The two

TABLE I

Specimen stimulus cards
For testing transitivity of alternatives

	A	B
ZOJ	− 5¢	+36¢
ZEJ	−21¢	−38¢

	A	B
QUG	+36¢	−54¢
QUJ	−38¢	+22¢

	A	B
WUH	−54¢	− 5¢
XEQ	+22¢	−21¢

For testing transitivity of utility intervals

	A	B
ZOJ	− 6¢	+ 5¢
ZEJ	+24¢	+13¢

	A	B
QUG	+38¢	+31¢
QUJ	+13¢	+24¢

	A	B
WUH	+31¢	+38¢
XEQ	+5¢	− 6¢

kinds of transitivity condition applied to the set consisting of a_1, a_2, a_3 can then be expressed in the following symmetric form:

CONDITION 3

(a) *Weak transitivity*: p_1, p_2, p_3 not all $\geqslant \frac{1}{2}$ or $\leqslant \frac{1}{2}$ unless they are all $= \frac{1}{2}$.

(b) *Strong transitivity*:

$$p_1 \geqslant \tfrac{1}{2} \text{ if and only if } p_2 + p_3 \leqslant 1,$$
$$p_2 \geqslant \tfrac{1}{2} \text{ if and only if } p_3 + p_1 \leqslant 1,$$
$$p_3 \geqslant \tfrac{1}{2} \text{ if and only if } p_1 + p_2 \leqslant 1.$$

In the experiment reported in this paper, we are concerned with triples of alternatives. It is therefore interesting to note that, if the set of alternatives consists of exactly three elements a, b, c, then the condition of strong stochastic transitivity is not only necessary for the existence of a utility function (as mentioned in the foregoing) but also sufficient. For, under strong transitivity, we may assume without loss of generality that $P(a, c) \geqslant P(a, b) \geqslant P(b, c) \geqslant \frac{1}{2}$. The corresponding inequalities between utilities (Definition 5) are: $u(a) - u(c) \geqslant u(a) - u(b) \geqslant u(b) - u(c) \geqslant 0$. These inequalities are satisfied, for example, by the following numbers: $u(a) = 1$, $u(c) = 0$, $u(b) =$ any number between, and including, 0 and 1.

In Table I, the upper three cards show how we tested strong (and weak) transitivity experimentally. The subject made choices between the two columns on a card; the syllables on the left represent events determining the outcome of a wager. On the three cards there are altogether three alternatives (wagers) paired in each of the three possible ways. By testing whether Condition 3(b) holds for a sample consisting of a number of such triples of alternatives, we obtain evidence for or against the hypothesis that a utility function exists on the set of alternatives from which the sample is drawn.

IV. STOCHASTIC THEORY OF CHOICE BETWEEN SUBJECTIVELY EVEN-CHANCE WAGERS

In this section we deal with a special case of the stochastic theory of choice, exploiting some possible properties of choices between wagers of a special sort, namely, those created by chance events with a 'subjective probability of one half'. The theoretical and experimental importance of the nonstochastic theory of choice for such wagers was first pointed out by Ramsey [18]; a formalization of the theory applied to finite sets, and reports of several experimental applications (including one with stochastic aspects) are given in Davidson *et al.* [11].

We assumed in the foregoing section that the set A of alternatives might contain wagers as well as sure outcomes; however, the formal developments made no use of this assumption.

Some additional primitive notions are needed.

Primitive 3
A set X of *states of the world*. The subsets of X are called *events*, denoted by $E, F, \ldots$ and forming a set $\mathscr{E}$.

Primitive 4. If a, b are in A and E is in $\mathscr{E}$, then aEb is the wager which consists in getting a if E happens, and getting b if E does not happen.

Definitions 1 through 4 are applicable to wagers; for example, when $P(aEb, cFd)=\frac{1}{2}$, we say that aEb and cFd are (stochastically) indifferent. We may presume that in certain cases absolute preference occurs. In particular, if a_1, a_2, b_1, b_2 are in A and $P(a_1, b_1)=1=P(a_2, b_2)$, then for any event E in $\mathscr{E}$, $P(a_1Ea_2, b_1Eb_2)=1$.

DEFINITION 8. An event E in $\mathscr{E}$ is an *even-chance event* if and only if, for every a and b in A,

$$P(aEb, bEa) = \tfrac{1}{2}.$$

If E is an even-chance event, we call aEb an *even-chance wager*. It is obvious that the notion of even chance involved in this definition is *subjective*; it makes no appeal to the objective probability of E. The justification for our terminology is simple. Suppose a subject prefers a to b. If he thinks E is more likely to happen than not, he will choose aEb more often than bEa; if he thinks E less likely to happen than not, he will choose aEb less often than bEa. Hence he will choose aEb and bEa equally often if and only if he thinks E is as likely to happen as not, i.e., E has a 'subjectively even chance'.

DEFINITION 9. The subject is said to be *unbiased* if and only if, for any two even-chance events E and F and any a and b in A,

$$P(aEb, aFb) = \tfrac{1}{2}.$$

It is obvious that if this condition is satisfied and there exists a utility function u on A, then for any two even-chance events E and F and any a and b in A,

$$u(aEb) = u(bEa) = u(aFb) = u(bFa).$$

This justifies writing simply ab for aEb where E is any even-chance event;

since we explicitly consider no other events, symbols for chance events need not enter our formalism.

The chief concern of this section may be stated by giving a more restrictive version of Definition 5:

DEFINITION 10. A real-valued function u is an *even-chance wager utility function* (or a *utility function in the sense of Definition* 10) on A if and only if:

(a) u is a utility function on A in the sense of Definition 5;
(b) for every a and b in A and every even-chance event E, $u(aEb) = [u(a)]/2 + [u(b)]/2$.

Definition 10(a) and (b) together express in stochastic form the usual hypothesis that a subject prefers the wager with the higher expected utility (applying this hypothesis to the case of even-chance wagers). Clearly, these conditions imply that $u(aEb)$ has the same value for all even-chance events E in $\mathscr{E}$, and that the subject is unbiased.

Now we wish to state conditions sufficient for the existence of an even-chance wager utility function. To this end we define the following condition:

DEFINITION 11. The *even-chance mid-point* condition holds in A if and only if the subject is unbiased and, for every a and b in A,

$$P(a, ab) = P(ab, b).$$

(Definition 11 says ab is a stochastic mid-point between a and b; see Definition 4.)
We may now state a theorem analogous to Theorem 1:

THEOREM 2. *If A is stochastically continuous, then an even-chance wager utility function on A exists if and only if the quadruple condition* (*Definition* 7) *and the even-chance mid-point condition hold in A.*
Proof: Suppose A is stochastically continuous. Then a function u on A such that $P(a, b) \geqslant P(c, d)$ if and only if $u(a) - u(b) \geqslant u(c) - u(d)$ exists if and only if the quadruple condition holds (Theorem 1). Hence the quadruple condition is a necessary condition for the existence of an even-chance wage utility function. And if the quadruple condition is satisfied,

then a utility function in the sense of Definition 5 exists; hence:

$$P(a, ab) = P(ab, b) \quad \text{if and only if} \quad u(a) - u(ab) = u(ab) - u(b)$$

that is,

$$u(ab) = \frac{u(a)}{2} + \frac{u(b)}{2}.$$

Therefore the quadruple and even-chance mid-point conditions together are necessary and sufficient for the existence of a utility function in the sense of Definition 10, provided A is stochastically continuous.

An alternative statement of sufficient conditions may now be considered We define:

DEFINITION 12. The *even-chance quadruple condition* holds in A if and only if, for every a, b, c, and d in A,

$$P(a, b) \geqslant P(c, d) \quad \text{if and only if} \quad P(a, bc) \geqslant P(bc, d),$$

and assert:

THEOREM 3. *If A is stochastically continuous then a utility function on A in the sense of Definition 10 exists if and only if the even-chance quadruple condition holds in A.*

Proof. It follows directly from Definition 10 that, if a utility function in the sense of that definition exists, the even-chance quadruple condition holds. We prove the sufficiency of the even-chance quadruple condition by showing that it implies both the even-chance mid-point condition and the quadruple condition, and then applying Theorem 2. By the even-chance quadruple condition we have (replacing b by a, and c and d by b):

1. $P(a, a) = P(b, b)$ if and only if $P(a, ab) = P(ab, b)$.

The right side of (1) (i.e., the even-chance mid-point condition) is true since the left side is true by Primitive 2(a). Using the even-chance quadruple condition again and Primitive 2(a), the following steps lead to the quadruple condition:

2. $P(a, b) \geqslant P(c, d)$ if and only if $P(d, bc) \geqslant P(bc, a)$.
3. $P(d, bc) \geqslant P(bc, a)$ if and only if $P(a, c) \geqslant P(b, d)$.

We may now establish:

THEOREM 4. *If the even-chance quadruple condition holds in A, then for all a, b, c, and d in A,*

$$P(a, b) \geqslant P(c, d) \quad \text{if and only if} \quad P(ad, bc) \geqslant \tfrac{1}{2}.$$

We establish Theorem 4 by noting that, if the even-chance quadruple condition holds, then $P(a, b) \geqslant P(c, d)$ is equivalent to $P(a, bc) \geqslant P(bc, d)$, which in turn is equivalent to $P(ad, bc) \geqslant P(bc, ad)$.

We have seen (in the proof of Theorem 3) that the even-chance quadruple condition implies the quadruple as well as the even-chance midpoint condition. On the other hand, it seems a safe conjecture that these two conditions in conjunction do not imply the even-chance quadruple condition unless the assumption of stochastic continuity is made. With the assumption of stochastic continuity, the implication does hold, as is easily seen from Theorems 2 and 3.

Theorem 4 thus states a strong principle. In interlocks, in effect, the utility scales obtained by comparing differences in utility by two separate methods.

CONDITION 4

(a) *Weak stochastic transitivity for utility intervals* holds in A if and only if, for all a, b, c, d, e, and f in A,

$$\text{if } P(bf, de) \geqslant \tfrac{1}{2} \text{ and } P(ae, cf) \geqslant \tfrac{1}{2}, \text{ then } P(ab, cd) \geqslant \tfrac{1}{2}.$$

(b) *Strong stochastic transitivity for utility intervals* holds in A if and only if, for all a, b, c, d, e, and f in A,

$$P(bf, de) \geqslant \tfrac{1}{2} \text{ if and only if } P(ab, cd) \geqslant P(ae, cf).$$

The analogy between the transitivity conditions for alternatives (Condition 1) and transitivity conditions for intervals (Condition 4) may be brought out as follows. If a utility function in the sense of Definition 10 exists, then Condition 4(a) is equivalent to the statement (holding, identically, for any six numbers):

If

$$[u(b) + u(f)] - [u(d) + u(e)] \geqslant 0$$

and

$$[u(a) + u(e)] - [u(c) + u(f)] \geqslant 0$$

then

$$[u(a) + u(b)] - [u(c) + u(d)] \geqslant 0,$$

and hence to:

CONDITION 5

(a) If $u(b) - u(d) \geqslant u(e) - u(f)$ and $u(e) - u(f) \geqslant u(c) - u(a)$ then $u(b) - u(d) \geqslant u(c) - u(a)$.

Similarly, Condition 4(b) is equivalent to:

(b) $u(b) - u(d) \geqslant u(e) - u(f)$ if and only if $[u(b) - u(d)] - [u(c) - u(a)] \geqslant [u(e) - u(f)] - [u(c) - u(a)]$.

Now let the length of the utility interval $u(b) - u(d) = I$, $u(e) - u(f) = J$, and $u(c) - u(a) = K$. Then Conditions 5(a) and (b) become similar in form to Conditions 1(a) and 2:

CONDITION 6

(a) If $I \geqslant J$ and $J \geqslant K$, then $I \geqslant K$.
(b) $I \geqslant J$ if and only if $I - K \geqslant J - K$.

Thus Conditions 4(a) and (b) may be interpreted as stating conditions on utility intervals analogous to Conditions 1(a) and (b) for alternatives (whether or not these alternatives happen to be wagers). However, it should be emphasized that in testing the transitivity of intervals we must make use of wagers; although we did use wagers in testing the transitivity of alternatives, this is not essential to the theory.

From Conditions 5(a) and (b), it is clear that the transitivity conditions for utility intervals are necessary for the existence of a utility function in the sense of Definition 10.[4] To obtain evidence whether such a function exists for a limited set of outcomes consisting of winning and losing small amounts of money, we tested certain implications of Conditions 4(a) and (b) for sextuples of outcomes which may be regarded as samples from the total set of outcomes. Let us designate six specific money outcomes, a_1, a_2, a_3, a_4, a_5, a_6, arranged in ascending order by monetary value. For reasons given in the next section, we considered the following probabilities only:

$$p_1 = P(a_1a_4, a_2a_3) \qquad p_2 = P(a_6a_3, a_5a_4)$$
$$p_3 = P(a_5a_2, a_6a_1).$$

For these three probabilities the implications of Conditions (4)a and (b) are just:

CONDITION 7

(a) *Weak transitivity of utility intervals:* p_1, p_2, p_3 not all $\geqslant \frac{1}{2}$ or $\leqslant \frac{1}{2}$ unless they are all $= \frac{1}{2}$.

(b) *Strong transitivity of utility intervals*:

$$p_1 \geqslant \tfrac{1}{2} \quad \text{if and only if} \quad p_2 + p_3 \leqslant 1,$$
$$p_2 \geqslant \tfrac{1}{2} \quad \text{if and only if} \quad p_3 + p_1 \leqslant 1,$$
$$p_3 \geqslant \tfrac{1}{2} \quad \text{if and only if} \quad p_1 + p_2 \leqslant 1.$$

It will be noted that Conditions 7(a) and (b) are identical with Conditions 3(a) and (b) where, of course, the three relevant probabilities are differently defined. If a utility function for the six outcomes $a_1, \ldots, a_6$ exists, Conditions 7(a) and (b) will be satisfied; but the converse is not in general true. The existence of a utility function in the sense of Definition 10 implies, even for six outcomes, more than is implied by the transitivity of intervals condition (for example, Theorem 4 is implied by the existence of a utility function but not by the transitivity of intervals condition); and the transitivity of intervals condition alone implies more for six outcomes than is tested by checking the relations given in Conditions 7(a) and (b) and with p_1, p_2, p_3 as defined above.

The second line of specimen cards in Table 1 illustrates the method used in testing Conditions 4(a) and (b). Before the three pairs of wagers on these cards were offered to the subject, it was verified that the chance events underlying the designed money wagers were even-chance events in the sense of Definition 8.[5] This justified the assumption that all wagers on the cards were (for the given subject) even-chance wagers; therefore it could be tentatively assumed that, whenever the subject chose a wager (a column of a card), he could be interpreted as comparing two utility intervals, represented by the rows of the card. On the three cards illustrated, there are three pairs of identical rows: they correspond to the intervals *I*, *J*, and *K* in Conditions 6(a) and (b). (From Conditions 5(a) and (b) it is clear that interchange of rows or of columns in a given card does not matter, nor does the interchange of alternatives in one of the columns.)

V. EXPERIMENTAL DESIGN

The experiment to be described was designed to test the plausibility of the hypothesis that (for given individuals) there exists a utility function in the sense of Definition 10 (or at least, in the sense of Definition 5), defined over a set of alternatives consisting of winning and losing small amounts of money and of even-chance wagers constructed from the basic alternatives. The individuals were 17 students from an elementary logic class at Stanford University. The general hypothesis was tested by testing certain of its consequences: stochastic transitivity (weak and strong) of alternatives as applied to triples of alternatives (interpreted here as wagers), and stochastic transitivity (weak and strong) of utility intervals as applied to sextuples of alternatives.

The obvious way of testing a stochastic theory of choice is to estimate probabilities of choice from frequencies of choice observed when the subject is repeatedly offered the same alternatives. This method, common from psychophysical experiments, has been used with apparent success by a number of workers in decision theory. These workers (who include Mosteller and Nogee, Ward Edwards, and Papandreou) were, of course, aware of the memory effect, and used various techniques in the attempt to cope with it. In a pilot study for the present experiment, we found that, with wagers of the sort we wished to use, the subject almost always made the same choice when offered the same pair of alternatives; thus we would be forced to estimate almost every probability as 0 or 1. The wagers between which the subjects had to choose had the same actuarial value; the wagers could therefore be assumed to be close in subjective utility. Remarks by the subjects led to the suspicion that the cause of the unforeseen consistency was the subject's ability to remember his previous choices (although various masking procedures were attempted such as reversing the order in which the wagers in a pair were offered, and inserting other offers between repetitions of the identical pair of wagers). In psychophysical experiments, memory cannot have this effect since the subject is given no way of identifying the repetition of a stimulus.

To avoid the effect of memory, the same *pair* of wagers was never offered twice to a subject. The method used for testing our hypothesis under this restriction is explained in the next section.

Each subject was asked to make 319 choices; a choice consisted in a

TABLE II

Money amounts (wins and losses) used in constructing stimulus cards

Sequence	*a*	*b*	*c*	*d*	*e*	*f*	*g*
1	−17	−12	− 5	+ 2	+ 8	+17	+21
2	−20	−16	−11	− 4	+ 3	+10	+15
3	−12	− 5	+ 2	+ 9	+14	+19	+23
4	−22	−18	−14	− 9	− 2	+ 5	+12
5	−14	− 8	− 4	+ 5	+13	+20	+26
6	−36	−17	− 8	+ 2	+10	+21	+27
7	−13	− 8	− 5	− 1	+ 4	+ 7	+12
8	−35	−28	−22	−15	− 8	− 2	+ 6
9	−27	−16	− 4	+ 7	+21	+34	+47
10	− 6	+ 1	+ 8	+15	+22	+30	+34
11	−39	−25	− 9	+ 6	+23	+40	+56
12	−37	−22	− 6	+ 5	+21	+38	+54
13	− 7	− 4	− 1	+ 3	+ 6	+ 8	+11
14	−14	− 9	− 6	− 2	+ 3	+ 6	+11
15	− 6	+ 2	+12	+21	+29	+36	+42
16	−24	−20	−14	− 7	+ 1	+ 8	+13
17	−31	−17	− 5	+ 8	+21	+33	+46
18	−11	− 3	+ 4	+12	+19	+24	+28
19	−17	− 6	+ 5	+13	+24	+31	+38

verbal response (*A* or *B*) to a stimulus card of the kind illustrated in Table I. In 107 cases selected (with certain limitations to be mentioned later) at random, and unknown in advance to the subject, the response of the subject was followed by playing off the wager selected, and the subject lost or won the appropriate amount of money.

The 319 stimulus cards were designed as follows. Every card displayed four figures (positive or negative) representing a possible outcome consisting of losing or winning the amount of money shown. On the left were two nonsense syllables (*WUH* and *XEQ*; *ZOJ* and *ZEJ*; *QUJ* and *QUG*) which stood for chance events. The events were created by the subject tossing a die with one nonsense syllable on three faces and another nonsense syllable on the other three faces. In an effort to offset recency and memory effects three different dice were used. The two right-hand columns marked *A* and *B*, represent the wagers between which the subject was to choose.

For testing hypotheses concerning the existence of an even-chance wager utility function, it was necessary to ascertain whether the events created by the three dice were even-chance events. In practice, this was tested indirectly by assuming, for any money amounts m and n (in cents):

$$P(mEn, nEm) = \tfrac{1}{2} \quad \text{if and only if} \quad P(mEn, n-1\,E\,m) > \tfrac{1}{2}$$
$$\text{and} \quad P(mEn, n+1\,E\,m) < \tfrac{1}{2}.$$

Previous experiments had shown that, given this modified interpretation, subjects generally accepted the nonsense-syllable dice as generating even-chance events; therefore we tested each die only a few times with each subject [11, p. 56 and Table I, p. 57]. In all, 12 stimulus cards were used to test the dice; three additional cards were added to this group to familiarize the subject with other sorts of choices.

The remaining cards were intended to test the transitivity of alternatives and of intervals (Conditions 1 and 4). Thirty-eight sequences of seven money amounts were chosen such that the money amounts, in the light of previous experiments [3, 11], would be approximately evenly spaced in utility for most subjects. Table II gives the first 19 sequences; the other 19 sequences were produced from the first by reversing the signs (thus wins become losses and vice versa). This symmetry provides a simple guarantee that the actuarial value of the complete set of wagers is zero; why this is desirable will be explained below. Eight cards were made for each sequence of money amounts, yielding $8 \times 38 = 304$ cards in all. Using the letters at the top of Table II, the eight cards showed the following patterns:

1	2	3	4	5	6	7	8
$a\ b$ $d\ c$	$c\ d$ $f\ e$	$a\ b$ $f\ e$	$b\ c$ $e\ d$	$a\ c$ $f\ d$	$d\ e$ $g\ b$	$b\ c$ $g\ f$	$b\ d$ $g\ e$

It will be observed that the triads 3, 4, 5 and 2, 7, 8 each contain just three alternatives (wagers, represented as columns), and thus may be used to test the transitivity of alternatives. Triads 1, 2, 3 and 4, 6, 7 each compare, in effect, three intervals (represented by rows), and thus may be used to test the transitivity of intervals. Because of this overlap between triples, we have achieved some economy in the number of observations: the total of 304 cards yields 76 triples designed to test the transitivity of alternatives and 76 triples designed to test the transitivity of intervals.

The assignment of one of the three dice to a specific card was random. Because certain wagers (not cards) were repeated once, the column (*A* or *B*) on which a wager appeared was randomized; the row (top or bottom) assigned to an outcome in a wager was also randomized. Finally, the order in which the cards appeared was randomized, except that the 15 cards, used for learning and to test that the dice created even-chance events, preceded all others; and all three cards from a given triple appeared during the same session.

We may now make explicit two rules employed in limiting the offers appearing on the stimulus cards. No sure-thing alternatives were allowed on the ground that these might distort the results should there exist a specific utility or disutility of gambling. The second rule is intended to eliminate cases of absolute preference. In any given triple of cards, there are six distinct outcomes. Let us assign the numbers 1, 2,..., 6 to the six outcomes in order of monetary value; the number assigned to an outcome denotes its rank. The rule is this: on any given card, the sum of the ranks of the two outcomes in one wager must be equal to the sum of the ranks of the two outcomes in the other wager. Since the outcomes are chosen to be approximately evenly spaced in utility, the rule is designed to insure that two wagers that are compared shall not differ too strongly in expected utility. In application, no two wagers on one card differed by more than $4\frac{1}{2}$ cents in actuarial value. When the transitivity of intervals is tested for six outcomes, the two rules just mentioned limit the pairs of wagers to be compared to exactly three.

Of the 17 subjects 6 were women and 11 were men. Subjects were tested individually. Each subject came to three sessions, spaced a few days apart; two sessions were never on the same day for a given subject, nor more than five days apart. A session lasted between 35 and 55 minutes. Subjects were asked not to discuss the experiment during the testing; none of them had any detailed knowledge of game theory or decision theory.

At the beginning of the first session, a subject was shown the three nonsense-syllable dice and the game he was to play was explained. The subject was given $2 credit (in chips) and told that this was his stake for the three sessions. At the end of the three sessions, his chips would be redeemed in cash; if he had won, he would receive $2 plus his winnings; losses would come out of the $2; greater losses would have to be paid out of his own pocket.

The first stimulus cards have been described; of these, 12 tested whether the subject accepted the dice as creating even-chance events, and three were for learning purposes. In effect, every subject did accept the dice as 'fair'. All of the first 15 cards were played off. After the subject gave his response by choosing wager *A* or *B*, he put the indicated die in a leather cup, shook, and rolled. Depending on the outcome, the experimenter then collected from or paid out to the subject the appropriate number of chips. The rest of the first session consisted in responses to 88 more stimulus cards testing the two sorts of transitivity. Of these, 25 choices were played off; the subject did not, of course, know whether a card would be played until after he had made his choice. The cumulative expected win for a subject who always chose the wager with the higher actuarial value was +44 cents for the 25 cards which were played off. Subjects were urged to take as long as they wished to make a decision.

During the second session the subject was asked to make 112 decisions; of these, 36 were played off. The cumulative expected win for the actuarial chooser was +39 cents.

The last session called for 104 decisions of which 31 with an expected win of +55 cents were played off. During this last session, the experimenter could play off additional wagers to increase the winnings of an unlucky subject.

As mentioned above, the actuarial value of the total of all wagers offered was zero. Since the wagers between which a subject was to choose seldom had exactly the same actuarial value, a consistent 'actuarial chooser' could have expected to win if every choice had been played off. The cards chosen for playing had a small positive actuarial value for the 'random chooser' and a higher actuarial value for the actuarial chooser. The hope was that the average subject with average luck would slowly increase the sum at his disposal; its size would not vary enough to influence choices substantially. It may be doubted whether this hope was entirely realized. In any case, for many subjects the sum at their disposal changed fairly radically during the play, and verbal comments by subjects suggested that this influenced choices. The highest total win (for all three sessions) was $4.87 (including the original $2 stake); the least fortunate subject received a few cents less than $2. However, several subjects had their winnings 'artificially' increased during the last session by the experimenter naming for playoff certain cards on which both wagers had high positive actuarial value; unknown to the subject, it had been decided in advance that no subject would average less than \$1 an hour for his time.

VI. STATISTICAL DECISION RULES

Transitivity Regions. Consider the three related probabilities p_1, p_2, p_3 as defined for the statement of Conditions 3(a) and (b), or as defined for the statement of Conditions 7(a) and (b). Let us denote by $p^i = \langle p_1^i, p_2^i, p_3^i \rangle$ the ith ordered triple of probabilities so defined. p^i is a point in the unit cube U, since each component of p is between 0 and 1.

We now define two subregions of U:

Region W: p^i obeys Condition 3(a) [or 7(a)] (region of weak transitivity).

Region S: p^i obeys Condition 3(b) [or 7(b)] (region of strong transitivity).

Obviously, region S is included in region W. The hypothesis pairs to be tested may be stated:

Hypothesis H_w: For all i, p^i is in W.
Hypothesis H_w^0: There exists an i such that p^i is in $U - W$.
Hypothesis H_s^0: For all i, p^i is in S.
Hypothesis H_0: There exists an i such that p^i is in $U - S$.

Note that each of the hypotheses has two empirical interpretations; one concerns stochastic transitivity of alternatives, the other stochastic transitivity of utility intervals. We need not distinguish between the two interpretations in discussing the method of statistical testing.

Since a given choice was presented to a subject only once, it was impossible to estimate the probability triples p^i from observed frequencies. Corresponding to a given p^i, we made one observation consisting of the three responses of a subject to a triple of related stimulus cards. Suppose, for the sake of simplicity of exposition, that the pairs of wagers on a related triple of stimulus cards are arranged in the order suggested by the definitions of p_1, p_2, p_3 (pp. 141, 148); this has been done for the triples of cards shown in Table I. Then if the subject chooses column A on the first card, there is greater likelihood that $p_1 > \frac{1}{2}$ than that $p_1 < \frac{1}{2}$; if he chooses column A on the third card, there is greater likelihood that $p_3 > \frac{1}{2}$ than that $p_3 < \frac{1}{2}$. An *observation* is an ordered triple of reponses; there are just eight possible observations:

$$\begin{array}{ll} O_1 = \langle A, A, A\rangle & O_5 = \langle B, A, A\rangle \\ O_2 = \langle A, A, B\rangle & O_6 = \langle B, A, B\rangle \\ O_3 = \langle A, B, A\rangle & O_7 = \langle B, B, A\rangle \\ O_4 = \langle A, B, B\rangle & O_8 = \langle B, B, B\rangle \end{array}$$

In a nonstochastic theory, observations O_1 and O_8 would be cases of intransitivity. In a stochastic theory, they merely strengthen the evidence in favor of (stochastic) intransitivity. To avoid confusion we call such observations *cyclical* because, e.g., $\langle A, A, A\rangle$ means that a certain wager a was chosen in preference to b, b to c, and c in preference to a, thus forming a cycle.

In its strict formulation, our problem is analogous to the following simpler (one- instead of three-dimensional) problem: "Test the hypothesis that each coin made by a certain coin-making machine has a bias, not necessarily an equally strong one for all coins, in favor of falling heads. You are permitted to take a finite number of coins and to toss each coin just once." Each coin of this example corresponds to a triple of choices from three pairs of our wagers. The parameter space is, respectively, the unit interval (0, 1) or the unit cube U. The interval $(\frac{1}{2}, 1)$ which contains the probability of a biased coin falling heads corresponds to our transitivity region W (or S) which contains all probability triples if the subject satisfies the transitivity condition. Should this formulation be accepted, then, out of the infinite set of potential observations (coins, triples of choices) it would suffice for a single one to be outside of a specified region (the bias interval for coins, the transitivity region for response triples) to rule out the hypothesis in question. But such a fact cannot be ascertained empirically from a finite number of observations. The problem becomes accessible to empirical test if it is reformulated as follows: "A coin-making machine is characterized by an unknown probability distribution of the chance variable p (probability of a coin falling heads); one is permitted to toss coins, each only once, in order to get evidence about the distribution of p." The chance variable p corresponds, in the theory of stochastic choice, to the triple: $\langle p_1, p_2, p_3\rangle$ defined above.

For example, one might test the following hypothesis about the distribution of p: the proportion of coins (or of triples of wagers) whose p falls into a specified region is at least 95 per cent. This approach has been used in a later study, by H. D. Block and J. Marschak [20]; with regions like S, this statistical problem is rather complicated. In the present study, we chose a simpler though more arbitrary approach by adding the following assumption: p is uniformly distributed about an unknown region which is either the whole space of possible p's (the unit cube, in our case) or a specified region (such as W or S). We have thus two pairs of alternative hypotheses:

H_w: p^i is distributed uniformly over W, and $\text{Prob}(p^i \in W) = 1$.
H_0: p^i is distributed uniformly over U, and $\text{Prob}(p^i \in U) = 1$.
H_s: p^i is distributed uniformly over S, and $\text{Prob}(p^i \in S = 1$.
H_0: p^i is distributed uniformly over U, and $\text{Prob}(p^i \in U) = 1$.

It turns out that for testing the statistically reformulated hypotheses, all that matters (the 'sufficient statistic') is the number of cyclical observations. Computations yield the following probabilities of a cyclical observation:

	Probability of a Cyclical Observation
If H_0 is true	$\frac{20}{80}$ or 25.00%
If H_w is true	$\frac{15}{80}$ or 18.75%
If H_s is true	$\frac{11}{80}$ or 13.75%

The reasoning leading to the first figure (25 per cent) is obvious: if p^i is distributed uniformly over the unit cube, each of the eight possible observations $O_1, \ldots, O_8$ is equiprobable. Since two of these are cyclical, the probability that a given observation is cyclical if H_0 is true is $\frac{1}{4}$. The other two figures ($\frac{15}{80}$ and $\frac{11}{80}$) were obtained[6] by integrating over the specified region (W or S, respectively) the expression

$$p_1 p_2 p_3 + (1 - p_1)(1 - p_2)(1 - p_3)$$

(i.e., the probability that O_1 or O_8 will occur), and dividing by the volume of that region.

The *decision rule* used was this (we state if for H_w; that for H_s is analogous). Accept H_w if the number r of cyclical observations is less than c, where c (a number obtainable from tables of binomial distribution) is such that $\text{Prob}(r < c$, when H_0 is true$) = \text{Prob}(r \geqslant c$, when H_w is true$)$. The two probabilities just written are, respectively, that of committing the error of

TABLE III. Decision rules

	Number of Observations	
	$n=76$ (All Sessions)	$n=26$ (Session III)
Accept H_w if r is less than:	17	6
Significance level:	24 %	35 %
Accept H_s if r is less than:	15	5
Significance level:	10 %	23 %

TABLE IV

Number of cyclical observations for each subject

	Testing transitivity of alternatives				Testing transitivity of intervals			
Sessions	I	II	III	Total	I	II	III	Total
Number of triples offered	22	28	26	76	22	28	26	76
Expected number under uniform distribution over the region of:	Number of cyclical observations							
Unit cube	5.50	7.00	6.50	19.00	5.50	7.00	6.50	19.00
Weak transitivity	4.13	5.25	4.88	14.25	4.13	5.25	4.88	14.25
Strong transitivity	3.03	3.85	3.58	10.45	3.03	3.85	3.58	10.45
Subject								
A	4	0	0	4	0	0	1	1
B	3	5	2	10	1	6	3	10
C	5	3	3	11	6	5	5	16
D	4	7	0	11	4	5	2	11
E	1	0	0	1	0	3	3	6
F	3	6	0	9	5	10	2	17
G	2	1	2	5	3	0	0	3
H	2	1	1	4	4	2	1	7
I	1	2	1	4	3	3	0	6
J	2	9	5	16	3	3	6	12
K	4	2	2	8	3	5	3	11
L	1	1	0	2	1	1	0	2
M	2	2	1	5	7	5	1	13
N	6	3	7	16	2	0	3	5
O	4	2	1	7	3	2	0	5
P	1	3	3	7	2	1	3	6
Q	7	5	2	14	1	4	2	7
Average no. of cyclical observations	3.06	3.06	1.76	7.88	2.82	3.24	2.06	8.12
Proportion of cyclical observations	13.9%	10.9%	6.8%	10.4%	12.8%	11.6%	7.9%	10.7%

accepting H_w when H_0 is true, and that of committing the error of accepting H_0 when H_w is true. By making them equal, we make the larger of the two error probabilities a minimum. The significance level of test is equal to both of them. If instead of this 'minimax' principle that takes into account both kinds of error, we had followed the custom of merely 'testing the null hypothesis', the decision could have been made, given our number of observations, with a much lower probability of errors of Type I (called 'significance level'). The latter would then have been defined as the probability of rejecting H_0 when it is true. However, the nature of the problem forces us to treat the null hypothesis and its alternative symmetrically.

In the present experiment we made on each subject a total of 76 observations for each hypothesis; 26 observations for each hypothesis were made during the last session. Applying our computations and decision rule to these figures, we obtain Table III.

One obtains, of course, much lower significance levels if one is permitted to regard the responses of all subjects as belonging to the same statistical population, thus increasing the sample size by the factor of 17 (the number of subjects). Using the normal distribution formula, one can compute the decision rules at which the probabilities of errors of both kinds are equal. The rules are, for samples of this magnitude: reject H_w if and only if the proportion of cyclical observations is larger than 21.7 per cent; reject H_s if and only if this proportion is larger than 18.7 per cent (compare these figures with the last line of Table IV). The significance levels are as follows; for Session III, 0.055 for H_w and 0.001 for H_s; for the total of all sessions, 0.003 for H_w and negligible for H_s.

Finally, we observe that, if the proportion of cyclical observations falls very much below the probability indicated above for weak or strong transitivity, we shall presume that the assumption of uniform distribution over the (weak or strong) transitivity region is to be corrected: we shall have to assign lower weights to those points of the region that lie near its boundaries other than the facets of the unit cube.

As another and possibly preferable way of exploiting the information more fully, Herman Chernoff and Roy Radner[7] suggested computing the likelihood ratio for each pair of hypotheses and each possible set of observations. Let $P_0(r, n)$ be the probability that, out of n responses, exactly r are cyclical if H_0 is true. With a corresponding notation for the cases when H_w or H_s are true, we can use the ratios

$$L_w(r, n) = P_w(r, n)/P_0(r, n) \quad \text{and} \quad L_s(r, n) = P_s(r, n)/P_0(r, n)$$

to convey the confidence that one may attach, on the basis of observations, to the hypothesis H_w or H_s, each against the hypothesis H_0. Using the binomial distribution formulas, one derives from the probabilities of cyclical observations ($\frac{20}{80}$ for H_0, $\frac{15}{80}$ for H_w and $\frac{11}{80}$ for H_s), the two likelihood ratios

$$L_w(r, n) = (\tfrac{19}{13})^r \cdot (\tfrac{13}{12})^n \quad \text{and} \quad L_s(r, n) = (\tfrac{11}{23})^r \cdot (\tfrac{23}{20})^n$$

These numbers are tabulated in Table V, for $n=76$ and $n=26$ (with r ranging from 0 to respectively 17 and 7), and can be used to interpret, subject by subject, the results shown in Table IV for the total of observations and for Session III:[8]

TABLE V
Likelihood ratios (approximate)

No. of cyclical responses: $r =$	H_ω against H_0 $n=76$	H_ω against H_0 $n=26$	H_8 against H_0 $n=76$	H_8 against H_0 $n=26$
0	430	8.0	40000	38
1	300	5.5	20000	18
2	210	3.8	9300	8.7
3	140	2.7	4500	4.1
4	100	1.8	2100	2.0
5	69	1.3	1000	0.9
6	49	0.9	490	0.5
7	33	0.6	240	0.2
8	23	0.4	110	0.1
9	16		54	
10	11		26	
11	7.6		12	
12	5.3		5.9	
13	3.6		2.8	
14	2.5		1.3	
15	1.7		0.6	
16	1.2		0.3	
17	0.8		0.1	

VII. RESULTS OF EXPERIMENT

Table IV summarizes the main experimental findings. For a large majority of subjects, the number of cyclical responses falls far below the expected frequency under strong transitivity (both of alternatives and of intervals). Under the null hypothesis, one out of four triples could, on the average, be expected to be cyclical; this would result in 38 cyclical responses for the total of 152 triples, or 19 for the 76 triples which tested each of the two varieties of transitivity. The highest total number of cyclical responses for any subject was 28 (subject *J*), while subject *F* had the highest number of cyclical responses (17) for a set of 76 triples. The expected numbers of cyclical responses in 76 triples for H_w and H_s are 14.25 and 10.45 respectively. Two subjects (*J* and *N*) in the case of transitivity of alternatives, and two subjects (*C* and *F*) in the case of the transitivity of intervals, exceeded the number of cyclical responses expected on the assumption that H_w is true. The *average* number of cyclical responses for all subjects on the 76 triples testing transitivity of alternatives is 10.4; the average on the 76 triples testing transitivity of intervals is 10.7. These figures are close to the prediction of 10.45 cyclical responses if strong transitivity holds.

The last line of Table IV should be related to what was said about using the responses of *all* subjects as a sample from the same population (p. 158). On this basis (and under the assumptions of the foregoing section regarding *a priori* distribution), weak as well as strong transitivity, for both alternatives and intervals, should be accepted at a quite low (i.e., strict) significance level.[9]

Table VI applies the decision rules (Table III) to each subject (using the results from all sessions). For all subjects, Hypothesis H_w of weak transitivity had to be accepted with respect both to alternatives and to intervals (though at a very modest, i.e., high, significance level). For all but two subjects, strong transitivity had to be accepted (at a significance level of 10 per cent), but the two subjects were not the same for alternatives and for intervals. The correlation of 0.49 between behavior with respect to alternatives and behavior with respect to intervals is just significant at the 5 per cent level for 17 observation pairs; however, it should not be judged significant at that level if one considers the fact that some of the data were used in two ways as described on p. 151.

An interesting feature of the data displayed in Table IV is the change in

TABLE VI

All sessions (76 triads); distribution of subjects by the number of cyclical observations (correlation coefficient = 0.49)

No. of cyclical observations for alternatives	1	2	3	4	5	6	7	8	9	10	11	12	13	14	15	16	17	No. of subjects	
1						*E*												1	Accept strong and weak transitivity
2		*L*																0	
3																		3	
4	*A*					*I*	*H*											2	
5			*G*										*M*					0	
6																		2	
7					*O*	*P*												1	
8											*K*							1	
0																	*F*	1	
1										*B*								2	
1											*D*					*C*		0	
1																		0	
13																		1	
14							*Q*												
15																		0	Accept weak transitivity only
16					*N*							*J*						2	
17																		0	
No. of subjects	1	1	1	0	2	3	2	0	0	1	2	1	1	0	0	1	1		
	Accept strong and weak transitivity													Accept weak transitivity only					

the proportion of cyclical observations from session to session. Although not always evident for individual subjects, when the results for all subjects are averaged there is a systematic decrease in the percentage of cyclical observations from session to session both alternatives and for intervals. During the first session, the over-all proportion of cycles is 13.4 per cent; during the second session, 10.5 per cent; during the third 7.4 per cent.

For the third session, the decision rule indicates that the null hypothesis must be accepted for one subject (*N*) for transitivity of alternatives, and for one subject (*J*) for transitivity of intervals. There is also one subject in each category (subjects *J* and *C* respectively) for whom weak but not strong transitivity must be accepted. In every other case the hypothesis of strong transitivity may be accepted.

During the three sessions, there was an increase in the correlation between performance with respect to alternatives and performance with respect to intervals, as follows:

Session	I	II	III	Total
Correlation	0.00	0.52	0.58	0.49

The change from I to II is significant at the 5 per cent level.

VIII. DISCUSSION

Assuming that a utility function of money unique up to a linear transformation exists for a subject, it is possible to make some rough inferences from the data concerning the shape of the utility curve (a curve which plots utility against the money amount of the basic alternatives). Table VII classifies the responses of each subject to the 304 cards used to test transitivity. On 249 cards the two wagers had different actuarial values; the second and fifth columns in Table VII show in how many cases the subject chose the wager with the higher *actuarial value* ('actuarial responses') and in how many cases the subject chose the wager with the lower actuarial value ('counteractuarial responses'). On every card, one wager involved the highest and lowest of four money amounts, whereas the other wager involved outcomes of intermediate money value; see p. 148. Responses may therefore be classified according as the subjects chose the wager with the greater or the lesser *dispersion* (the dispersion of an even-chance

TABLE VII

Responses for each subject according to actuarial value and dispersion (total number of wagers = 304)

	Pairs of wagers of unequal actuarial value				Pairs of wagers of equal actuarial value		All pairs of wagers	
Subject	Actuarial responses	Counteractuarial responses						
		Dispersion chosen High	Low	Total	Dispersion chosen High	Low	Dispersion chosen High	Low
A	227	10	12	22	11	44	134	170
B	149	75	25	100	41	14	213	91
C	162	54	33	87	37	18	184	120
D	165	75	9	84	43	12	234	70
E	174	45	30	75	29	26	168	135
F	161	73	15	88	41	14	223	81
G	149	79	21	100	43	12	225	79
H	175	65	9	74	46	9	225	79
I	200	36	13	49	34	21	181	123
J	162	50	37	87	27	28	164	140
K	167	54	28	82	34	21	184	120
L	182	15	52	67	18	37	103	201
M	136	49	64	113	28	27	137	167
N	160	53	36	89	37	18	177	127
O	216	12	21	33	12	43	127	177
P	165	23	61	84	18	37	104	200
Q	145	58	46	104	34	21	169	135

wager is the difference in money value between the two outcomes). The second and third columns of figures in Table VII show how often the counteractuarial choices favored high or low dispersion. Fifty-five cards showed wagers of equal actuarial value; these responses are classified to indicate whether the high or the low dispersion wager was chosen. In evaluating the figures in Table VII, it is necessary to know that of the 249 cards with wagers of unequal actuarial value, 124 paired the higher actuarial value with the higher dispersion and 125 paired the higher actuarial value with the lower dispersion.

A subject for whom utility was linear in money and with absolute preferences between all pairs of wagers offered would always choose the wager with the higher actuarial value. There is no subject who did this.

Subjects *A* and *O* come closest with 22 and 33 counteractuarial answers. Both these subjects show some preference for low dispersion when they depart from the actuarial choice.

We may call a subject *conservative* who, when departing from the actuarial answer, more often than not chose the wager with the lower dispersion, for such a subject would, from an insurance point of view, be paying for the privilege of taking the smaller risk. In the same way we may call a subject *venturesome* who, when departing from the actuarial answer, more often than not chose the wager with the higher dispersion. Using this criterion, five subjects were conservative and twelve were venturesome. In the light of previous experimental results with college students [3, 11], the percentage of venturesome subjects is perhaps surprising. Part of the explanation may lie in the fact that the subjects were volunteers and knew, before they volunteered, that the experiment involved some financial risk.

A subject who invariably chose the higher or the lower dispersion would yield no cyclical observations (no pair of wagers showed the same dispersion, since this would lead to absolute preference), whereas the consistent actuarial chooser would be certain to show no more than six cyclical triads of responses (there were six triples of cards where each pair of wagers had the same actuarial value). It is therefore an interesting question to what extent the results obtained were caused by actuarial, conservative, or venturesome strategies (conscious or otherwise) on the part of the subjects. Table VII makes it obvious that no subject consistently followed any of the three policies. Comparison of Tables IV and VII brings out the fact that the four subjects with the largest number of cyclical observations (subjects *C*, *D*, *F*, and *J*) include none of the five subjects with the largest number of counteractuarial responses. On the other hand, subject *L*, with the lowest number (4) of cyclical triples, seems to owe this score in part to a conservative taste for low dispersion wagers, whereas subject *A*, with only five cyclical triples, has the fewest counteractuarial responses.

We may also ask whether the frequency of cyclical observations depends on the size of the differences in the actuarial values of each pair of wagers. One would expect cyclical observations to occur relatively more often in cases where these differences are small and thus provide no guidance, or only a weak one, for the choice between two wagers and

TABLE VIII

Actuarial characteristics of triples offered and the frequency of cyclical observations

	Character of triples offered[a]	Number of observations			Percentage of cyclical in total
		Total	Cyclical	Non-cyclical	
A	$d=0$ on all three cards	102	17	85	16.7
B	$0<d\leqslant\frac{1}{2}$¢ on all three cards	272	59	213	21.7
(A, B)	$0\leqslant d\leqslant\frac{1}{2}$¢ on all three cards	(374)	(76)	(298)	(20.3)
C	$d\leqslant 1$¢ on all three cards	442	49	393	11.1
D	All other triples	1768	147	1621	8.3
(C, D)	$d>\frac{1}{2}$¢ on at least one of the three cards	(2210)	(196)	(2014)	(9.3)
	Total	2548	272	2312	10.5

Variation of frequency between groups	χ^2	P	Significant?
A against B	1.3	>0.25	No
C against D	3.2	>0.05	Hardly
(A, B) against C	13.7	<0.005	Yes
(A, B) against (C, D)	43	<0.005	Yes

[a] $d=$ difference between actuarial values of the two wagers on a card.

the ranking of three wagers. In Table VIII, four groups – A, B, C, D – of triples are defined, the number of observations (i.e., the number of triples times 17, the number of subjects) is entered for each group, and the frequency of cyclical versus noncyclical observations is given. A finer grouping of triples was precluded by sample size limitations. In fact, the distinction between groups A and B proved to be statistically insignificant (and hence the unexpectedly *lower* percentage of cyclical observations in group A compared with group B is not statistically significant). Significant and interesting results are obtained by comparing group (A, B) (which is the union of A and B and thus consists of all triples with actuarial differences not exceeding $\frac{1}{2}$ cent on any/card) either with group C (actuarial differences not smaller than 1 cent on any card) or with the composite group (C, D) (actuarial difference exceeds $\frac{1}{2}$ cent on at least one card). These comparisons tend to confirm the hypothesis that small actuarial differences favor the occurrence of cyclical choices.

It may be asked whether the decrease in the proportion of cyclical observations from session to session was accompanied by an increase in the proportion of actuarial responses. The following figures show that it was.

	Sessions		
	I	II	III
Number of cards with wagers of different actuarial value	1241	1598	1394
Number of actuarial choices	810	1106	979
Percentage	65.3	69.2	70.2
Number of triples	748	952	884
Number of noncyclical observations	648	845	819
Percentage	86.6	89.5	92.6

The increase in the proportion of actuarial choices was statistically significant ($P<0.05$) from Session I to Session II and definitely not significant ($P>0.50$) from Session II to Session III. On the other hand, the proportion of noncyclical observations increased highly significantly ($P<0.01$) from Session II to Session III, although it did not increase significantly ($P>0.2$) from Session I to Session II. This suggests that, to the extent to which there was an increase in noncyclical observations, it should not be explained by the increase in actuarial choices. However, a more detailed analysis would be necessary to clarify this point.[10]

In the table just given, the proportion of noncyclical observations to the total number of triples of cards is, in each of the three sessions, consistently higher than the proportion of actuarial choices to the total number of cards. A formal test shows the difference between the proportions to be statistically highly significant. Thus, considering all subjects to belong to the same population, the probability that a subject's response to a triad of cards will be noncyclical is higher than the probability that his response to a single card will be actuarial.

Broadly speaking, the present experiment shows that in its context decisions are better explained by certain implications of a stochastic decision theory than by the assumption that choices are made at random. The interest of this result would be impugned if the same data could be as well or better explained by alternative hypotheses. For this reason, we have been considering the plausibility of the claim that, to the extent that subjects avoided cyclical triads of responses (and hence tended to verify the hypotheses under test), this was caused by the more or less consistent employment of actuarial, venturesome, or conservative policies by the subjects. In Table IX we attempt a direct comparison of three alternative theories as predictors of certain observed choices.

Assume that a related triple of cards was always arranged in the 'normal form', shown in Table I, and that the three cards were presented to the subject in order from left to right. If a subject chose one left and one right column for the first two cards, the hypotheses H_w (or H_s) as well as H_0 would predict equal probabilities of choice for each wager on the third card. The interesting cases arise when the left column or the right column is chosen on both the first two cards; then the hypotheses H_w and H_s will give the higher probability of choice to the opposite column on the third card (for example, if column A is chosen on each of the first two cards, column B is more apt to be chosen on the third card if the hypotheses are true).

The first two columns of figures in Table IX show how often the subject chose the more probable wager on the third card for those cases where both of the first two choices were wager A or wager B. The third and fourth columns show how often, for the same cards for which results are given in the first two columns, the subject chose the wager with the higher actuarial value. The total number of predictions is lower because some cards had two wagers with equal actuarial values. The last two columns show, for the same cards again, how often the subject chose in accord with his general tendency to favor low or high dispersion wagers. This tendency was determined from the figures in Table VII, showing how often the counteractuarial responses of the subject favored low or high dispersion.

At the bottom of Table IX, the three theories are compared with respect to the percentage of correct predictions. The expected utility theory is superior to the other two with 81.6 per cent correct predictions; the actuarial theory is slightly better than the dispersion theory with 72.2 per cent correct predictions as compared to 69.0 per cent correct predictions.

TABLE IX

Comparison of expected utility, actuarial, and dispersion theories as predictors

Subject	Expected utility theory		Actuarial theory		Dispersion theory	
	Correct	Incorrect	Correct	Incorrect	Correct	Incorrect
A	84	5	74	5	56	33
B	63	20	39	29	60	23
C	46	27	42	20	44	29
D	86	22	69	24	84	24
E	76	7	56	19	50	33
F	80	26	68	28	74	32
G	86	8	47	33	80	14
H	100	11	74	22	92	19
I	71	10	66	8	50	31
J	49	28	43	25	42	35
K	52	20	43	17	48	25
L	83	4	60	17	64	23
M	57	18	43	25	50	25
N	63	21	53	22	59	25
O	76	12	69	8	57	31
P	70	13	52	24	68	15
Q	70	21	41	35	48	43
Totals	1213	273	939	361	1026	460
Percentage correct	81.6		72.2		69.0	

Each of the differences between these proportions (taken pairwise) is statistically significant ($P<0.01$). It is also worth noting that for every individual subject, the expected utility theory predicted better than the dispersion theory; however, the actuarial theory was very slightly superior to the expected utility theory for two subjects (subjects *C* and *J*).

A remark is called for concerning the marked decrease in the proportion of cyclical observations from session to session. It seems attractive to call this a learning phenomenon. However, what was learned was certainly not connected with specific cards, wagers, money amounts, or triples of cards, for none of these was repeated in two sessions (specific cards and triples were not repeated even in the same session). The evidence indicates that the subjective probability of the chance events was firmly established from the start. We may say that the subject learned transitive behavior or that he learned to maximize expected utility (at least in the sense of our stochastic definitions of these terms). There is also evidence that some subjects learned to make actuarial choices. The matter seems worthy of fuller study, both theoretical and experimental.

IX. SUMMARY

The experiment was designed to test whether certain conditions hold which are necessary for the existence of a utility function over the set of money wagers as well as over the set of money amounts. Seventeen subjects were tested individually in three sessions each. Every choice involved a risk since subjects did not know in advance which choices would be played off, i.e., would result in actually paying (or receiving) money. The main results may be summarized as follows:

(1) For all subjects, the number of intransitive triads of responses (called 'cyclical observations') was, as required by the hypotheses, less than the number expected by chance.

(2) A statistical test, based on responses to nonrepeated choice situations, indicates the acceptance, for all subjects, of the hypotheses of weak stochastic transitivity of alternatives and weak stochastic transitivity of utility intervals.

(3) For 15 subjects in each case, the acceptance of the hypotheses of strong stochastic transitivity of alternatives and of intervals is indicated.

(4) Both in testing the transitivity of alternatives and the transitivity of intervals, there was a systematic decrease in the number of cyclical responses from session to session.

(5) A comparison shows the superior accuracy of a stochastic theory of decision in predicting certain choices as compared to two alternative theories. On the whole, the evidence does not appear to support the claim that the low number of cyclical observations can be wholly explained by simple policies based on the actuarial values of wagers or on the degree of risk (dispersion).

NOTES

* Research undertaken by the Applied Mathematics and Statistics Laboratory, Stanford University, under contract Nonr-225(17), NR 171-034, with the Office of Naval Research, and by the Cowles Commission for Research in Economics under contract Nonr-358(01), NR 047-006, with the Office of Naval Research.

The authors were helped by discussions with G. Debreu, E. Fels, L. Hurwicz, R. Radner, H. Raiffa, R. Summers, R. Savage, and P. Suppes.

[1] We use the word 'alternative', as is fairly common in the literature of decision theory, to mean one of two or more things or courses among which a person may choose.

[2] The modifications may allow for the special properties of probabilities, and for the fact that $P(a, b) \geqslant P(c, d)$ compares signed intervals whereas the quaternary relations taken as primitive in some theories compare unsigned intervals.

[3] Let $P(a, b) \geqslant \frac{1}{2}$; then a and b are said to be adjacent in utility if $P(a, b) \leqslant p(a, c)$ for every c with $P(a, c) \geqslant \frac{1}{2}$.

[4] We conjectured that, if the set of alternatives is stochastically continuous, then the conjunction of strong transitivity of alternatives and of strong transitivity of utility intervals is necessary *and sufficient* for the existence of a utility function in the sense of Definition 10. While this paper was in preparation, G. Debreu [19] proved a closely related theorem which seems particularly applicable to wagers in money amounts (or, more generally, in any continuous commodity amounts).

[5] A more precise statement of the procedure used will be given in the next section.

[6] With the help of Karol Valpreda Walsh and Robert C. Mercer, which we gratefully acknowledge.

[7] In an oral communication.

[8] Again, if we regard all subjects as belonging to the same statistical population, the likelihood ratios are naturally much higher; they are of the order of many thousands, for both H_w and H_s, even if the proportion of cyclical observations is as high as 15 per cent.

[9] The size of the sample used for the *joint* test of transitivity of alternatives *and* of intervals is somewhat reduced by the overlapping between the sets of cards used for these two tests separately (see p. 151); this raises the significance level somewhat.

[10] We are grateful to R. Rosett for computations and suggestions.

BIBLIOGRAPHY

[1] von Neumann, J. and Morgenstern, O., *Theory of Games and Economic Behavior*, 2nd ed., Princeton University Press, Princeton, 1947.

[2] Savage, L. J., *Foundations of Statistics*, John Wiley and Sons, New York, 1951. Revised, Dover, 1972.

[3] Mosteller, F. and Nogee, P., 'An Experimental Measurement of Utility', *Journal of Political Economy* **59** (1951) 371–404.

[4] Edwards, Ward, 'Articles on Probability Preferences', *American Journal of Psychology* **66** (1953) 345–364; **67** (1954) 56–67; **67** (1954) 68–95.

[5] Papandreou, Andreas G., with the collaboration of O. H. Sauerlander, Brownlee, O. H., Hurwicz, L., and Franklyn, W., 'A Test of a Stochastic Theory of Choice', *University of California Publications in Economics* **16**, No. 1 (1957) 1–18.

[6] Fechner, Gustav Theodor, *Elemente der Psychophysik*, Leipzig, 1859 and 1889.

[7] Marschak, Jacob, 'Norms and Habits of Decision Making Under Certainty', *Selected Essays*, 5.

[8] Luce, R. Duncan, 'A Probabilistic Theory of Utility', *Econometrica* **26** (1958) 193–224.

[9] Luce, R. Duncan and Raiffa, Howard, *Games and Decisions*, John Wiley and Sons, New York, 1957 (Appendix I, 'A Probabilistic Theory of Utility', pp. 371–384).

[10] Guilford, J. P., *Psychometric Methods*, New York, 1954.
[11] Davidson, Donald, Suppes, Patrick, and Siegel, Sidney, *Decision Making, An Experimental Approach*, Stanford University Press, 1957.
[12] Suppes, P. and Winet, M., 'An Axiomatization of Utility Based on the Notion of Utility Differences', *Management Science* **I** (1955) 259–270.
[13] Alt, Franz, 'Ueber die Messbarkeit des Nutzens', *Zeitschrift fuer National-oekonomie* **7**, No. 2 (1936) 161–169.
[14] Suppes, P., 'A Set of Axioms for Paired Comparisons' (dittoed), Center for Behavioral Sciences, 1956.
[15] Debreu, Gerard, 'Stochastic Choice and Cardinal Utility', *Econometrica* **26** [1958] 440–444.
[16] Scott, Dana and Suppes, P., 'Foundational Aspects of Theories of Measurement', *Journal of Symbolic Logic* **23** (1958).
[17] Vail, Stephan, 'A Stochastic Model for Utilities', Seminar on the Application of Mathematics to the Social Sciences, Ann Arbor, University of Michigan, 1953 (dittoed).
[18] Ramsey, Frank P., *The Foundations of Mathematics and* Other Logical Essays, Routledge and Kegan Paul, London, 1931.
[19] Debreu, Gerard, 'Cardinal Utility for Even-Chance Mixtures of Sure Prospects', *Review of Economic Studies* **26** (1958–1959).
[20] Block, H. D. and Marschak, Jacob, 'Random Orderings and Stochastic Theories of Responses', *Selected Essays*, 7.

7

RANDOM ORDERINGS AND STOCHASTIC THEORIES OF RESPONSES*

(1960)

Co-author: H. D. Block

I. THE PROBLEM

In interpreting human behavior there is a need to substitute 'stochastic consistency of choices' for 'absolute consistency of choices'. The latter is usually assumed in economic theory, but is not well supported by experience. It is, in fact, not assumed in empirical econometrics and psychology.

The stochastic approach brings out the affinity between the phenomenon of choice and the more general psychological phenomenon of response to physical stimuli or, for that matter, to questionnaires, or of the action of 'judges' who compare the performances of individuals.[1]

Let A be the set of all alternatives (or actions) ever to be considered by a given subject. Let F be a subset of A. Let $(a; F)$ denote a 'multiple choice' (also called 'first choice' out of a set), i.e., the following observed fact: When forced to choose one element of F, the subject chose a. In the theory of choice, F is called the feasible set. When F consists of 2, 3,... elements, the multiple choice is called binary, ternary,....

In another language, the set F is associated with a stimulus and consists of all possible responses of the subject to that stimulus; A is then interpreted as the set of all possible responses to all stimuli. In experiments on so-called preferences and attitudes, the stimulus consists in offering a list of alternative menus, alternative political candidates, alternative answers to an item in the questionnaire. This list is then the feasible set F. When a 'judge' makes paired comparisons, the set F is a pair of individuals. In experiments on perceptional discrimination, physical stimuli – sounds, lights, or weights – impinge upon the subject; his response consists in stating that one of those objects is louder, or brighter, or heavier than the other(s). The set F is then the set of the n possible responses (or $n+1$ if 'I don't know' statements are permitted).

Another example of F is the set of all family budgets open to a family with a fixed amount of money, given the prices of goods (see Hotelling [2]). Each element of F is a different way of allocating the money among different goods.

In this paper – subject only to some attempted generalizations in Section VII – we shall call the observed choice, or response, $(a; F)$ the *basic* or *direct observation*. These observations can be counted, and the constraints on (i.e., the relations among) the resulting numbers (which may possibly be only 1's or 0's) we shall call *conditions*. Some of these conditions we shall call *directly testable*. Only those conditions are directly testable which involve the basic observations only. We shall encounter conditions that are not directly testable because they involve certain entities (constructs) that are not directly observable. An important class of these constructs will be called *utilities* (identical with *sensations* in psychophysics, *values* in anthropology, ethics, and older economics). These will be defined in a variety of ways, but will always denote certain real numbers, constant or random, associated with the elements of the set A.

However, to involve basic observations only is a necessary but not a sufficient property of a directly testable condition. For example, if the set A of alternatives is finite but of a size unknown, or too large to be exhausted by experiment, a constraint involving all alternatives simultaneously – such as Condition (o) in Section IV and Condition (P_n) in Section V – cannot be tested.

The purpose of this paper is to study the logical relations between various conditions describing consistency of responses, and in particular the logical relations between certain conditions that are not directly testable and others that are. This will tell whether a given class of observational results would or would not justify the acceptance (or the rejection) of a theory.

Our particular way of defining the class of basic observations and, correspondingly, of the directly testable conditions is to some extent arbitrary. Depending on the range of possible experiments and other observations, it may be preferable to define the class more narrowly, e.g., by including binary choices only. Or we might define this class more broadly. Following the practice of psychologists, we might admit the ranking, by the subject, of three or more objects as an observable fact, although the subject's observed action consists in this case of a verbal statement. (In the case of two objects, ranking and choosing is the same thing.) We might even admit as observable the subject's verbal statements of the relative 'intensity' of his preferences.

Such variations of the domain of testability will be tentatively discussed in Section VII. In the rest of the paper, by using a particular demarcation of the class of directly testable conditions (the one most closely corresponding to the nature of economic observations), we are able to carry out a reasonably complete analysis of the relevant logical relations. The study may thus serve as a start when similar attempts are made under another definition of basic observations.

In particular, our operational approach seems to be unable to handle the following distinction that appears natural on grounds of common sense and may be important for predictions. If out of the pair $F=(a, b)$ of desirable objects a man chooses sometimes a and sometimes b, our introspection tells us that we may ascribe this to either or both of two different 'causes':

1. He may have difficulty in perceiving all the relevant characteristics of the objects, as when a and b are two 10-ton carloads of the same merchandise but the exact quantity (in pounds, net of package) or, for that matter, all the differences in quality cannot be ascertained.
2. Even if he knew exactly the differences in the characteristics of the two objects, he might find them almost equally 'desirable' or containing the promise of equal 'satisfaction', and he will vacillate as a result.

To disentangle the two 'causes' – call them 'perceptibility' and 'desirability' (anticipated 'satisfaction') – may be important if one wants to predict how people will act if perceptibility is kept constant while desirability varies, or vice versa. Economists in particular have mostly considered men's decisions under the assumption of perfect perceptibility, also called perfect information. In the more recent developments of economic decision theory, imperfect information is introduced, but a clear, and probably fruitful, distinction is kept between varying the nature of (so-called) information and varying the satisfaction (the 'payoff') attainable through the choice of action. Economists[2] use the term 'utility' as interchangeable with desirability (satisfaction), and thus independent of perceptibility. Our concept is coarser. All the various definitions of utility given in this paper will be related to the empirical entities, called 'alternatives'. Each of these is identified precisely but combines the two aspects, information and desirability, in some unknown though presumably not-too-changeable fashion. Thus when two carloads are offered again, and, say, the firm's quality-control facilities (or, in a similar example, a housewife's abilities to discriminate between cuts of meat) have not changed, predictions from previous behavior observations can be made. If discrimination is learned, through experience, in some more-or-less-determined manner, the model has to be modified, of course, but we have not attempted to bring in learning.

Stochastic theory introduces the probability $p(a; F)$ of the basic observation $(a; F)$, and it is assumed that inferences about constraints on these probabilities can be made from a finite number of basic observations. These constraints may be described with the help of parameters of certain distributions, and some of these parameters have been called, a century ago, sensations (Fechner [3], see especially pp. 70–103 of the 1889 edition). We shall call them *constant utilities.* Various types of constant utilities have been proposed. They will be studied in Section II. In addition, there emerge naturally the concepts of *random utilities* and *random orderings* to be treated in Section III. Sections IV and V continue the study of directly testable conditions necessary and/or sufficient for the existence of constant and random utilities (and random orderings), respectively. Section VI sums up the main logical relations between the random and the various forms of constant utilities, and includes a very incomplete attempt to relate our various models to the work of other authors. As already mentioned, a generalized experimental situation – the combination of ranking and choosing – will be formulated in Section VII. Section VIII discusses the memory effect and other difficulties of experiments on choice and ranking, difficulties perhaps encountered less in psychophysics proper. We shall postpone the description of Section IX until the end of the present introductory section. Section X deals tentatively with a special statistical problem: how to test statistically our directly testable conditions – i.e., the properties of the probabilities $p(a; F)$ – when (to avoid the memory effect and to avoid assuming that all subjects have identical distribution properties) each set F can be offered only a few times, possibly only once.

Clearly, non-stochastic theory is a special, strong form of stochastic theory. And whenever a theory of choices or responses is being submitted to a statistical test there is, explicitly or not, an underlying model of stochastic behavior of the subject (or possibly of the error-making observer).

We shall conclude this section with a brief examination of the non-stochastic, or absolute, theory of choice. We shall formulate it in terms of our 'basic observations', and not, as usual, in terms of the subject's verbal preference or indifference statements. Define[3] for all a, b in A:

(1.1) '$a > b$' (a preferred to b) means 'never (b; F) if F contains a',
'$a \gtrsim b$' means 'not: $b \succ a$',
'$a \sim b$' (indifference) means '$a \gtrsim b$ and $b \gtrsim a$'.

Thus, if the subject forced to choose between a and b chooses b nine (but not ten) times out of ten, the non-stochastic theory calls him indifferent. We have always $a \gtrsim b$ or $b \gtrsim a$ since the subject is forced to choose. Therefore the relation '$\gtrsim$' is said to induce complete weak ordering on A provided the following condition (testable by basic observations) is satisfied:

(1.2) if $a \gtrsim b$ and $b \gtrsim c$, then $a \gtrsim c$ (transitivity).

If, in addition, the set A is finite, $A = (a_1, \ldots, a_n)$, we can associate with each of its elements a_i an integer r_i, $1 \leqq r_i \leqq n$, called *rank*, such that

(1.3) $r_i \leqq r_j$ if $a_i \gtrsim a_j$.

The vector $r = (r_1, \ldots, r_n)$, which can also be regarded as an integer-valued function on the set of integers $N = (1, \ldots, n)$, is called a ranking on N. If by some arbitrary convention ties are excluded, all r_i's are different integers and r is a permutation. Clearly any strictly decreasing monotone function on the integers $r_1, \ldots, r_n$ induces a real-valued function ω on A which is order-preserving in the sense that

(1.4) $\omega(a_i) \geqq \omega(a_j)$ *if and only if* $a_i \gtrsim a_j$.

The function ω, called the ('*ordinal*') *utility function*, is unique up to increasing monotone transformations.

If the set A of alternatives is not finite, an order-preserving function ω on A need not exist. However, Debreu [5] proved that an order-preserving function exists if A and the ordering relation '$\succsim$' satisfy a certain rather weak condition[4] that may justify the assumption of ordinal utility functions over the space of commodity-bundles.[5]

In the stochastic models that will follow, the (testable) transitivity condition (1.2) and the 'ordinal' utility function ω made possible by it will be suitably generalized. But, in addition, some stronger testable conditions and, correspondingly, more strictly measurable utility functions will arise naturally.

A final remark: The case when the set A includes wagers so that choices are, in general, made under uncertainty, is more general than that of choices among sure alternatives. This case has been often treated, ever since Daniel Bernoulli [8] and, for that matter, Marshall (Note IX, p. 843, [9]), by ordering the wagers according to their 'expected utility'. This leads to a non-stochastic utility that is more strictly measurable than ω: It is unique up to increasing linear transformations. This model, too lends itself to stochastic generalizations, as will be briefly discussed in Section IX.

II. STOCHASTIC CONCEPTS OF CONSTANT UTILITIES

In general, $A=(a, b, \ldots)$ will continue to denote the set of distinct alternatives, and F the feasible subset. For mathematical ease, we shall assume A to be finite, unless otherwise stated, and identify it with $N=(1, \ldots, n)$. A feasible subset will be $M \subseteq N$. The probability that the subject forced to choose an element of M chooses i, denoted previously by $p(i; M)$, can be written more briefly thus: $i(M)$. Clearly

$$(2.1) \qquad i(M) \geqq 0\,; \qquad \sum_{i \in M} i(M) = 1\,.$$

When $M=(i, j, k, \ldots)$, $i(M)=i((i, j, k, \ldots))$ will be written simply $i(i, j, k, \ldots)$. Then $i(M)$ will be called the binary, ternary…, probability when M consists of 2, 3, …, distinct elements. The binary probability will be sometimes written in still shorter forms: $i(i, j)=ij$, $i \neq j$. It will prove convenient to define $ii=\frac{1}{2}$ so that, using (2.1), always

$$(2.2) \qquad ij + ji = 1\,,$$

whether i and j are distinct or not.

For easier reference, the various *conditions* will be labeled by (more-or less suggestive) letters, thus: (x). *A theorem* is an implication-relation between conditions (the 'hypothesis' and the 'conclusion'); by using arrows several theorems can be combined into one. In addition to the usual signs $\rightarrow$ ('implies') and $\leftrightarrow$ ('implies and is implied by'), we shall also use $\mapsto$ ('implies but is *not* implied by'). When $(x) \mapsto (y)$, (x), is said to be stronger than (y); rejection of (y) forces rejection of (x), but acceptance of (y) is inconclusive. We shall also use the sign $\leftarrow\!\!\!\mid$ for 'does not imply nor is implied by'.

Each of the following three conditions (w), (v), (u), arranged in a sequence of increasing strength, constrains the set of probabilities $i(M)$ by postulating the existence of some real vector of order n (a real-valued function on the set N), called utility vector (utility function), and denoted by w, v, u, respectively. The stronger the constraint, the more strict is the sense in which the utility vector in measurable; that is, the smaller is the group of transformations under which the vector remains indeterminate.

CONDITION (w). *There is a constant real vector* $w=(w_1, \ldots, w_n)$ *such that*

$$(2.3) \qquad w_i \geqq w_j \quad \textit{if and only if} \quad ij \geqq \tfrac{1}{2},$$

where w_i may be called the *weak* utility of i; and w the weak utility function on N.

CONDITION (v). *There is a constant real vector* $v=(v_1, \ldots, v_n)$ *and, associated with it, a distribution function* φ_v, *strictly increasing* [*except when its value is* 0 *or* 1][6], *such that*

$$(2.4) \qquad \varphi_v(v_i - v_j) = ij\,; \qquad \varphi_v(0) = ii = \tfrac{1}{2}.$$

Then v_i may be called a *strong* utility of i; and v, a strong utility function on N.

CONDITION (u). *There is a constant positive vector* $u=(u_1, \ldots, u_n)$ *such that for any* i, j *in* M

$$(2.5) \qquad u_i/u_j = i(M)/j(M), \quad \text{all} \quad M \subseteq N,$$

where u_i may be called the *strict* utility of i; and u the strict utility function on N.

Clearly the weak utility function w is *unique up to an increasing monotone transformation.* It is analogous to the function w of the non-stochastic model (Section 1), with '$a_i \gtrsim a_j$' interpreted as '$ij \geqq \frac{1}{2}$'. We can call the cases $ij > \frac{1}{2}$ and $ij = \frac{1}{2}$, stochastic preference and indifference, respectively. These concepts are implicitly used in experimental work as when, e.g., Mosteller and Nogee [10] define indifference as the case when the subject chooses one of the two offered alternatives half of the time. As in the non-stochastic model, (w) implies a testable

CONDITION (t) (transitivity).

(2.6) *If* $ij \geqq \frac{1}{2}$ *and* $jk \geqq \frac{1}{2}$, *then* $ik \geqq \frac{1}{2}$.

Since always $ij \geqq$ or $\leqq \frac{1}{2}$, transitivity guarantees a (complete weak) ordering on N: the alternative i is ranked above, below, or on the level of j according as $ij >$, $<$, or $= \frac{1}{2}$. Since N is finite we, have (as in Section I):

THEOREM 2.1. (w)$\leftrightarrow$(t) *provided the set of alternatives is finite.*

If we admit infinite sets of alternatives and redefine the condition (w) accordingly, we have (w) $\rightarrow$ (t). But if we denote by (D) Debreu's Condition (note 4) and replace '$a \gtrsim a'$' and '$ij \geqq \frac{1}{2}$' by '$aa' \geqq \frac{1}{2}$' we can write

THEOREM 2.2. $[(D), t] \mapsto (w) \mapsto (t)$.

Condition (v), the existence of 'strong' utilities, may be made plausible by a physical analogy. Because of random variations in the properties of the air, metals, and so forth, the lowest voltage needed to produce a spark in a given direction is random; assume then that the probability of the occurrence of the spark is the larger, the larger the voltage. Condition (v) has been used in psychophysics (and more recently in the scaling of attitudes) ever since Fechner [3]. It is stated in the psychologists' adage (Guilford, [11]): "*Equally often noticed differences* (on the 'sensation' scale) *are equal* [*unless noticed always or never*]." A similar thought might unify the recent attempts to measure the 'power' of person X over person Y: on the one hand, by the probability that Y obeys X; and on the other hand, by the difference in the payoff (utility) to Y in the case of his obeying, as compared with his disobeying, X.[7]

If (v) is satisfied by some v, φ_v, then clearly for *any increasing linear transform* $v' = \alpha + \beta v$ there exist a $\varphi_{v'}$ satisfying that condition. (If the set of alternatives is continuous, and the distribution φ_v strictly monotone, these are the only admissible transformations.[8]) The scale unit for v may be chosen by setting, for example, the quartile φ_v^{-1} (.25)=1; this or a similarly chosen unit is sometimes called the 'just noticeable difference', we believe. Moreover, because of (2.4), φ_v may be (and, in the continuous case, must be) so chosen that

$$(2.7) \qquad \varphi_v(\zeta) + \varphi_v(-\zeta) = 1$$

for all real ζ. Then φ_v is anti-symmetrical about the point $(0, \frac{1}{2})$; the median and the mean (if it exists) are zero. This is satisfied if φ_v is normal, as assumed by Fechner, whose test of normality was, however, rather crude. Normality of φ_v is also assumed in most textbooks; we do not know whether a formal test of this assumption has been developed. The 'logistic' distribution function $\varphi_v(\zeta)=1/(1+e^{-}\zeta)$ which, as we shall presently see, is required by the next stronger condition (u), also has the property (2.7).

THEOREM 2.3. $(v) \mapsto (w)$.

Proof. Sufficiency. Assume (v) and choose i, j with $v_i \geqq v_j$; then

$$ij = \varphi_v(v_i - v_j) \geqq \varphi_v(0) = \tfrac{1}{2};$$

hence (w) is satisfied, with $w=v$.

No necessity. Let $N=(1, 2, 3)$ and assume $12>13>23>\frac{1}{2}$. Then (w) is satisfied, with $w_1>w_2>w_3$; but no linear function of w will satisfy (v); for, by (v), if $\frac{1}{2}<23$ then $0=v_1-v_1<v_2-v_3$, $v_1-v_2<v_1-v_3$; hence, by (v), $12<13$, which contradicts the assumption.

As to the 'strict' constant utility condition (u), it has been postulated, and developed most fully, by R. D. Luce [15].[9] We shall now give some of his results. Because of (2.1), Condition (u) can be rewritten in the form

$$(2.8) \qquad i(M) = u_i / \sum_{j \in M} u_j, \quad \text{all} \quad M \subseteq N.$$

It follows that the vector u is *unique up to a positive factor* $\lambda = u_i/i(N)$. With N fixed, a convenient normalization is $\lambda = 1 = \sum_{i \in N} i(N)$; $u_i = i(N)$.

Putting $M=(i, j)$, $i(M)=ij$, we see that the probability of a binary choice is related to the ratio u_i/u_j by

$$(2.9) \qquad \psi(u_i/u_j) = ij, \quad \text{where} \quad \psi(x) = \begin{cases} x/(1+x), & x > 0, \\ 0, & x \leqq 0. \end{cases}$$

Clearly ψ is a distribution function, for it is increasing, and $\psi(-\infty)=0$, $\psi(\infty)=1$. It is analogous to φ_v of condition (v), with ratios replacing differences, but is restricted to a particular form. Moreover, by putting v_k equal to $\log u_k$, we recover condition (v) itself, with φ_v a 'logistic curve':

$$\text{(2.10)} \qquad \varphi_v(\zeta) = 1/(1 + e^{-\zeta}).$$

This proves

THEOREM 2.4. (u)$\mapsto$(v),
for (v) imposes constraints on binary choices only.

We shall now introduce two *directly testable* conditions equivalent to (u). First consider

CONDITION ($p.r$) (constancy of probability-ratios). *$i(M)>0$ for every i in M; and for every i, j in N, the ratio $i(M)/j(M)$ is constant over all sets $M \subseteq N$ that contain i and j.*

Condition ($p.\,r$) follows directly from (u); conversely, rewriting ($p.r$) as

$$\text{(2.11)} \qquad i(M)/i(N) = j(M)/j(N) = \sum_{k \in M} k(M)/\sum_{k \in M} k(N),$$

putting $k(N)=u_k$ and using (2.1), we obtain (u). Now consider

CONDITION ($c.p$) (probability of choice as a conditional probability).

$$\text{(2.12)} \qquad 0 < i(M) = i(N)/\sum_{k \in M} k(N) \quad \text{all } i \text{ in} \quad M \subseteq N.$$

The fraction on the right-hand side, is, of course, the conditional probability that the element i of N is chosen *when it is known that the element chosen belongs to the subset M of N*. On the other hand, the quantity on the left-hand side is the probability that the element i of N is chosen *when the subject is forced to make his choice from the subset M of N*. Clearly these two quantities are not identical; ($c.p$) is a verifiable, empirical proposition which may or may not have intuitive appeal.[10] Condition ($c.p$) follows directly from (u) written in the form (2.8); on the other hand, on replacing i by j in (2.12) and comparing the two equations, one obtains ($p.r$) which we have seen to be equivalent to (u). We summarize this and the previous results of this section in the following theorem, placing the directly testable conditions in the lower line:

THEOREM 2.5.

$$\begin{array}{ccc} (u) \mapsto (v) & \mapsto & (w) \\ \updownarrow & & \updownarrow \\ (p.r) \mapsto (c.p) & \mapsto & (t)\,, \end{array}$$

provided that the Debreu condition is satisfied. (This includes the case of a finite set of alternatives.)

III. RANDOM ORDERINGS AND RANDOM UTILITIES

In the non-stochastic theory briefly reviewed in Section I, the preference statement '$a_i \succ a_j$' assigns probability 1 to a certain class of choices. In the stochastic models of Section II, the corresponding statement '$ij > \frac{1}{2}$' merely sets a lower bound on that probability and is therefore weaker; however, some of those models are weaker than others.

A different way of weakening the non-stochastic theory consists in making the ('ordinal') utility function w a random one; i.e., by defining a probability measure on the space of all real-valued functions on A. In the case of the economic example of Section I, Wald's problem of evaluating the (non-stochastic) utility function w of consumers from their observed choices $(a; F)$ is replaced by the following more general one: Estimate the probability distribution P on the space of random utility functions U, using the probabilities $p(a; F)$ already estimated from the observations $(a; F)$, or using these observations directly. Any random utility function will be regarded as equivalent to any of its increasing monotone transforms.

However, the choice probabilities $p(a; F)$ may or may not be consistent with the existence of a random utility function. That is, the following condition (defining, in fact, that function) may or may not be fulfilled:

CONDITION (U) (existence of random utilities). *There is a random vector $U = (U_1, \ldots, U_n)$ unique up to an increasing monotone transformation and such that, for any i in $M \subseteq N$,*

$$(3.1) \qquad \Pr\{U_i \geqq U_j, \quad \text{all } j \text{ in } \quad M\} = i(M).$$

U_i is called *random utility of i*. Putting $M = (i, j)$,

$$(3.2) \qquad \Pr\{U_i \geqq U_j\} = ij.$$

By (2.2), it follows that, for all $i \neq j$,

$$\text{(3.3)} \qquad \Pr\{U_i = U_j\} = 0\,;$$

for if $\Pr\{U_i = U_j\} > 0$, then by (3.2) $ij + ji = \Pr\{U_i \geqq U_j\} + \Pr\{U_i \leqq U_j\} = \Pr\{U_i \geqq U_j\} + \Pr\{U_i < U_j\} + \Pr\{U_i = U_j\} > 1$, contradicting (2.2).

When the set of alternatives is finite, we can consider one particular monotone transform of U, the ranking $r = (r_1, \ldots, r_n)$ on the set $N = (1, \ldots, n)$. Because of (3.3), no ties will occur. Hence R, the set of all rankings on N, consists of the $n!$ permutations on N. We shall denote by i_r the element of N that has rank i when the ranking is r; i.e., $r_{i_r} = i$. Using this notation, we write a given ranking $r = (r_1, \ldots, r_n) = 1_r 2_r \ldots n_r$ (without commas and parentheses). Thus, if $n = 3$, the ranking $r = 312$ means that $r_1 = 2$, $r_2 = 3$, $r_3 = 1$, and is therefore identical with $r = (2, 3, 1)$.

Denote by R_{iM} the set of all rankings on N in which i is the first among all elements of $M \subseteq N$:

$$\text{(3.4)} \qquad R_{iM} = \{r \mid r_i \leqq r_j, \quad \text{all} \quad j \in M\} \quad i \in M\,.$$

For example, if $N = (1, 2, 3)$, $M = (1, 2)$, $i = 1$, then $R_{iM} = (123, 132, 312)$. Clearly, for every $M \subseteq N$,

(3.5) *R_{iM} and R_{jM} are disjoint for all $i \neq j$ in M;*

and if we denote by R^M the set of all permutations on M, we have

$$\text{(3.6)} \qquad \bigcup_{i \in M} R_{iM} = R^M\,; \qquad \bigcup_{i \in N} R_{iN} = R^N = R\,.$$

The following condition will be presently shown to be equivalent to (U).

CONDITION (P) (existence of a probability distribution of rankings consistent with probabilities $i(M)$). *There are $n!$ numbers $P(r)$ such that*

$$\text{(3.7)} \qquad P(r) \geqq 0\,, \qquad \sum_{R_{iM}} P(r) = i(M)\,, \qquad i \in M \subseteq N\,.$$

It follows, using (3.6), (2.1), that $\sum_R P(r) = 1$. We can call $P(r)$ the *probability of the ranking r*.

THEOREM 3.1. $(U) \leftrightarrow (P)$.

Proof. If we assume Condition (U) and define $P(r) = \Pr\{U_{1_r} > U_{2_r} > \cdots > U_{n_r}\}$, we obtain Condition (P). Conversely, assume (P) and define the random vector U thus: For any non-random real vector $s=(s_i, \ldots, s_n)$ let

$$\text{(3.8)} \qquad \Pr\{U=-s\}=\begin{cases} P(s), & s\in R, \\ 0, & s\notin R, \end{cases}$$

where R is the set of permutations on N. Then Condition (U) is satisfied.

THEOREM 3.2. *The existence of random utilities U does not imply the existence of weak constant utilities w, let alone the existence of strong or strict utilities, v or u.*

Proof. Let $N=(1, 2, 3)$ and $0<\alpha<\frac{1}{3}$. Let the probabilities of rankings $P(r)$ be

$$\begin{aligned} P(123) &= P(231) = P(312) = \tfrac{1}{6} + \alpha > 0, \\ P(321) &= P(213) = P(132) = \tfrac{1}{6} - \alpha > 0. \end{aligned}$$

(Then $\sum P(r)=1$.) Let the probabilities of choices $i(M)$, $M\subseteq N$, be

$$\text{(3.9)} \qquad \begin{aligned} 1(N) &= 2(N) = 3(N) = \tfrac{1}{3}, \\ 1(1,2) &= 2(2,3) = 3(1,3) = \alpha + \tfrac{1}{2}, \\ 2(1,2) &= 3(2,3) = 1(1,3) = -\alpha + \tfrac{1}{2}. \end{aligned}$$

Then $1(N)=P(123)+P(132)$, $1(1,2)=P(123)+P(132)+P(312)$, etc., and Condition ($P$)—or its equivalent, ($U$)—is satisfied. But Condition (t) is not: $1(1,2)>\frac{1}{2}$, $2(2,3)>\frac{1}{2}$, but $1(1,3)<\frac{1}{2}$. This proves the present theorem, using Theorem 2.5.[11]

We shall show that the following conditions are necessary for (P), and therefore for its equivalent, (U):

CONDITION (e) (effect of enlarging the feasible set). *If $L\subseteq M\subseteq N$, then*

$$\text{(3.10)} \qquad i(M) \leqq i(L).$$

CONDITION (e_3). *For any three elements i, j, k of N,*

$$\text{(3.11)} \qquad i(i,j) \geqq i(i,j,k); \text{ or, equivalently,}$$

$$\text{(3.11')} \qquad i(i,j,k) \leqq \min(ij, ik).$$

Clearly (e_3) is a special case of (e); it was exemplified numerically in (3.9), for $n=3$. Applying to (P) the fact that $R_{iM}=\{r\,|\,r_i\leqq r_j, j\in L\}\cap$

$\cap \{r \mid r_i \leqq r_j, j \in M - L\} \subseteq R_{iL}$, we obtain

THEOREM 3.3. $(P) \rightarrow (e) \mapsto (e_3)$.[12]

THEOREM 3.4. *The existence of random utilities U is not implied by the existence of strong constant utilities v, let alone by the existence of weak constant utilities w.*

Proof. Denote by x, y, z the distinct generic elements of $N=(1, 2, 3)$. There exist three numbers (for example, $v_1=0.2$, $v_2=0.1$, $v_3=0$) such that

$$\begin{aligned} 0 &< v_z - v_y + \tfrac{1}{2} = \beta_{xy} < 1, \\ 0 &< v_1 - v_2 = \gamma_1 < 1, \\ 0 &< v_2 - v_3 = \gamma_2 < 1, \\ 0 &< v_3 - v_1 + 1 = \gamma_3 < 1. \end{aligned}$$

Since $\beta_{xy}+\beta_{zx}=1=\sum_x \gamma_x$, we can put $x(x, y)=\beta_{xy}$, $x(x, y, z)=\gamma_x$. Then Condition (v) is satisfied, with $\varphi_v(\zeta)=\zeta+\frac{1}{2}$. But since $\gamma_3-\beta_{31}=\frac{1}{2}>0$, $3(1, 2, 3)>3(1, 3)$, Condition (e) and therefore also the stronger Condition (P) and its equivalent (U) are contradicted.

In the work of Thurstone [16] the following condition condition seems to be used:

CONDITION $(s.n)$ (symmetrical normal). *There is a normal random vector $U=(U_1, \ldots, U_n)$ that satisfies Condition (U) and has all variances equal ($\sigma_{ii}=\sigma^2$, say) and all covariances equal ($\sigma_{ij}=\rho\sigma^2$, say).*

Clearly this implies that both (U) and (v) are satisfied: let $v_i=EU_i$ and let φ_v, at all points $\zeta=v_i-v_j$, be normal, with mean zero and variance $2\sigma^2(1-\rho)$. Even the following, weaker condition is sufficient for the conjunction $[(U), (v)]$:

CONDITION (s) (symmetry of adjusted random utilities). *There is a random vector U satisfying Condition (U), and a constant vector $v=(v_1, \ldots, v_n)$ such that $V=U-v$ has a distribution function symmetric in its arguments.*

If U, v satisfy this condition, then any pair of increasing linear transforms $\alpha+\beta U$, $\alpha+\beta v$ (α, β scalars) will satisfy it. Clearly $(s.n) \mapsto (s)$. Moreover,

THEOREM 3.5. $(s.n) \mapsto (s) \mapsto [(U), (v)]$.

Proof. Sufficiency of (s). If (s) is true, so is (U); and $i(i,j)=\Pr\{U_i \geqq U_j\}=\Pr\{V_j - V_i \leqq v_i - v_j\}$ = the value of a distribution function at $v_i - v_j$; because of symmetry, this function is the same for all i, j and can be written as φ_v, satisfying (v).

No sufficiency of [(U), (v)]. Let $N=(1, 2, 3)$. Let $v_i = i+3$, and let V_1, V_2, V_3 be independently distributed with $\Pr\{V_i=3\}=p_i=1-\Pr\{V_i=-3\}$, where $p_1=1-p_3=p>\frac{1}{2}$, $p_2=\frac{1}{2}$. If $U=v+V$, then $\Pr\{U_1>U_3\}=p^2$; $\Pr\{U_1>U_2\}=p/2=\Pr\{U_2>U_3\}$; $\Pr\{U_1>U_2, U_2>U_3\}=p^2/2$, etc. Hence U satisfies Condition (U), if $1(1, 2)=2(2,3)=p/2$; $1(1, 3)=p/2$; $1(1, 2, 3)=p^2/2$, etc. Then Condition (v) is also satisfied, with

$$\varphi_v(v_1 - v_2) = \varphi_v(v_2 - v_3) = \varphi_v(-1) = p/2 > p^2 = \\ = \varphi_v(-2) = \varphi_v(v_1 - v_3).$$

Yet no linear transformation of v or monotone transformation of U can make the distribution of V symmetric, since the p_i are not all equal. If, on the other hand, the set of alternatives is continuous, let V have a joint normal distribution with zero mean and a constant variance τ^2 of differences $V_x - V_y$: $\tau^2 = \sigma_{zz} + \sigma_{yy} - 2\sigma_{xy}$, all x, y, where $\sigma_{11}=\frac{1}{2}$ and (for $x, y \neq 1$) $\sigma_{xz}=1$, $\sigma_{x1}=0$, $\sigma_{xy}=\frac{1}{4}$. If $U=V+EU$ satisfies condition (U), then (v) is also satisfied, with $v=EU$ and φ_v normal with zero mean and variance $\tau^2=\frac{3}{2}$. But no translation can make the distribution function of V symmetric in its arguments.

Mosteller [17] dropped Thurstone's symmetry assumption but maintained normality. We do not know whether tests have been developed for the joint condition [(U), (v)] in general, or for the special case of joint normality with constant variance of differences.

We shall now discuss another condition that is also stronger than the conjunction [(U), (v)] and is of particular interest, being equivalent to Condition (u) of Section II (existence of strict constant utilities). For a given permutation r of the set N define

$$\text{(3.12)} \qquad \pi(r) = \prod_{j=1}^{n-1} j_r(j_r, (j+1)_r, \ldots, n_r).$$

For example, $\pi(312)=3(1, 2, 3)\cdot 1(1, 2)$. Suppose this were the probability of the ranking 312. This would exemplify

CONDITION (π) (probability of ranking as the product of probabilities of successive first choices). *Condition* (P) *is true and, for every ranking* r *of* N, $P(r)=\pi(r)$ *as defined in* (3.12).

Substituting $\pi(r)$ for $P(r)$ in (3.7), we can put Condition (π) into a form involving the 'basic' probabilities (those of 'first choices') only:

$$i(M) = \sum_{r \in R_{iM}} \pi(r), \quad \text{for all } M \text{ and } i \in M. \tag{3.13}$$

THEOREM 3.6. $(u) \leftrightarrow (\pi)$.

Proof (outline). *Sufficiency of* (u). Define

$$\Omega(r) = \prod_{j=1}^{n-1} u_{j_r} / \sum_{k=j}^{n} u_{k_r}. \tag{3.14}$$

To prove that (u) implies (π), or (2.8) implies (3.13), is to prove the identity

$$\sum_{r \in R_{iM}} \Omega(r) = u_i / \sum_{h \in M} u_h, \tag{3.15}$$

for all $i \in M$, all $M \subseteq N$, and any positive numbers $u_1, \ldots, u_n$.[13] Without loss of generality let $M = (1, \ldots, m)$, $m \leqq n$, and, as in (3.6), denote by R^M the set of all permutations of M. Then $r^M = (r_1^M, \ldots, r_m^M) \in R^M$. The set $R = R^N$ is partitioned into m subsets of the form

$$R_{iM}^N = (r^N \mid r_i^N \leqq r_j^N; \quad \text{all} \quad j \in M), \quad i \in M;$$

the set R^N is also partitioned into $m!$ subsets of the form

$$R^N(r^M) = (r^N \mid r_i^N \leqq r_j^N \quad \text{if} \quad r_i^M \leqq r_j^M; \quad \text{all} \quad i. j \in M).$$

Similarly, R^M is partitioned into subsets $R^M(r^L)$, $L \subseteq M$. One obtains, by induction on m, first the identities

$$\sum_{r^M \in R^M} \Omega(r^M) = 1, \qquad \sum_{r^M \in R^M(r^L)} \Omega(r^M) = \Omega(r^L),$$

and then (3.15).

Necessity of (u). To show that (3.13) implies (2.8), let $u_i = i(N)$, all $i \in N$. Because of the identity (3.15), all numbers $i(M)$ that satisfy (3.13) also satisfy the system of equations

$$i(M) = \sum_{r \in R_{iM}} u_{1_r} \prod_{j=2}^{n-1} j_r(j_r, \ldots, n_r), \qquad \sum_{i \in M} i(M) = 1. \tag{3.16}$$

One then proves the uniqueness of this solution: Starting with $M = N$, then taking all sets M with $n-1$ elements, then with $n-2$ elements and so on, one can solve (3.16) for all $i(M)$ and one finds that they are all given by (2.8).

THEOREM 3.7. *If* (u) *is true, then* (P) *and* (U) *hold, with* $P(r)=\pi(r)=$ $=\Omega(r)$. This is clearly a corollary to Theorem 3.6, using Theorem 3.1.

Some interest attaches to a condition that, in effect, appears in the work of Luce [15]. In the same way as Condition (u) treats the probabilities of *first* choices, $p(i;\, M)=i(M)$, this new condition treats the probabilities of *last* choices. We may denote these by $p'(i;\, M)=i'(M)$ and remark that last choices are not 'basic observations' in our sense. (However, see Section VII on considering the rankings themselves, and hence also the last choices, 'observable'; see also Marschak [20], Section XI.)[14]

CONDITION (u'). *There exists a constant positive vector* $u'=(u_i',\ldots,u_n')$ *such that for any* i, j *in* M, $u_i'/u_j'=i'(M)/j'(M)$.

It is possible, however, to prove

THEOREM 3.8. *If* $n>2$, (u') *is inconsistent with* (u) *unless* $i(N)=i'(N)=$ $=1/n$ *for all* $i\in N$.

Proof (outline). Define, for each ranking $r=1_r2_r\ldots n_r$ the inverted ranking $r^*=n_r(n-1)_r\ldots 2_r1_r$ (hence $r^{**}=r$); and define

$$\Omega'(r)=\prod_{j=1}^{n-1} u_{j_r}'/\sum_{k=j}^{n} u_{k_r}'.$$

By Theorem 3.7. if (u) is true then $P(r)=\Omega(r)$. By the same theorem, if (u') is true then $P(r^*)=\Omega'(r)$, and hence $P(r)=P(r^{**})=\Omega'(r^*)$. Therefore if both (u) and (u') are true,

$$(3.18)\qquad \Omega(r)=\Omega'(r^*).$$

Define the ranking $s=2_r1_r3_r\ldots(n-1)_rn_r$. Since $\sum u_i=1=\sum u_i'$ without loss of generality, we have $\Omega(r)/\Omega(s)=(1-u_{2_r})/(1-u_{1_r})$; $\Omega'(r^*)/\Omega'(s^*)=$ $=u_{2_r}'/u_{1_r}'$. Since 1_r2_r are arbitrary, we have by (3.18) $u_i'/u_j'=(1-u_i)/(1-u_j)$; and summing on i, we find $u_j=1-(n-1)\,u_j'$. Now define $t=1_r2_r\ldots(n-2)_r$ $n_r(n-1)_r$; then by (3.18)

$$\Omega(r)/\Omega(t)=u_{(n-1)_r}/u_{n_r}=\Omega'(r^*)/\Omega'(t^*)$$
$$=(1-u'_{(n-1)_r})/(1-u_{n_r}');$$

and in general $u_i/u_j=(1-u_i')/(1-u_j')=[1-(n-1)\,u_i']/[1-(n-1)\,u_j']$; or $(n-2)\,u_i'=(n-2)\,u_i'$. Hence, for $n>2$, we have $u_i'=u_j'$ and $u_i=u_j$; so that $i(N)=i'(N)=1/n$ for all i.

THEOREM 3.9. $(u)\mapsto[(U,v)]\leftarrow\!\dashv(s)$.

Proof. We have $(u)\mapsto(U)$ by Theorems 3.6 and 3.1, since (π) is strictly stronger than (P). Moreover, $(u)\mapsto(v)$, and $(s)\mapsto(U,v)$ by Theorems 2.4 and 3.5. It remains to prove that (U,v) does not imply (u). Consider any normal distribution symmetric in its arguments. Then, by Theorem 3.5, (U) and (v) are both satisfied; and the corresponding φ_v is normal, contrary to the implication (2.10) of (u).

Some of the results of this and the preceding sections are worth summarizing in

THEOREM 3.10. 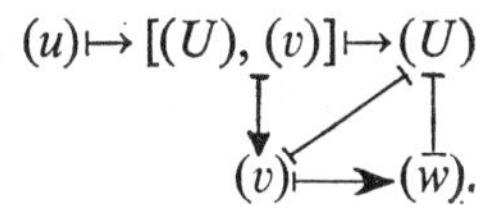

IV. FURTHER DIRECTLY TESTABLE CONDITIONS FOR THE EXISTENCE OF CONSTANT UTILITIES

We shall deal here with 'strong' utilities v only; directly testable conditions for the existence of 'strict' utilities u and 'weak' utilities w were given in Section II. Directly testable conditions for (v) – like those for (w) and unlike those for (u) – can, of course, involve binary choices only.

Unless otherwise stated, the set of alternatives will be assumed finite: $N=(1,\ldots,n)$. It is easy to see that we can rewrite

CONDITION (v). *There is a real vector* $v=(v_1,\ldots,v_n)$ *such that*

(4.1) *if* $hi\geqq jk$ *then* $v_k-v_i\geqq v_j-v_k$,

provided hi *and* jk *are not both* 0 *or* 1.

This implies that $hi\geqq\frac{1}{2}$ if, and only if, $v_k-v_i\geqq 0$. It is seen immediately that (v) implies each of the following conditions:

CONDITION (t) (transitivity). *If* $ij\geqq\frac{1}{2}$ *and* $jk\geqq\frac{1}{2}$, *then* $ik\geqq\frac{1}{2}$.

CONDITION (t_s) (strong transitivity). *If* $ij \geqq \frac{1}{2}$ *and* $jk \geqq \frac{1}{2}$, *then* $ik \geqq \max(ij, jk)$.

CONDITION (t_s^*). *If* $ij \geqq \frac{1}{2}$, *then* $ix \geqq jx$, *all* x *in* N.

CONDITION (t_s^{**}). *If there exists* k *such that* $ik \geqq jk$, *then* $ij \geqq \frac{1}{2}$.

CONDITION (6_w) (weak condition on 6-tuples). *If* $i_1 i_2 \geqq j_1 j_2$ *and* $i_2 i_3 \geqq j_2 j_3$, *then* $i_1 i_3 \geqq j_1 j_3$.

CONDITION (m_w) (weak condition on m-tuples). *For any* $m \leqq n$, *if* $i_k i_{k+1} \geqq j_k j_{k+1}$, $h=1,\ldots, m-1$, then $i_1 i_m \geqq j_1 j_m$.

CONDITION (q) (quadruple condition). *If* $hi \geqq jk$, *then* $hj \geqq ik$.

CONDITION (6_s) (strong condition on 6-tuples). *If* $i_1 i_2 \geqq i_2 j_3$ *and* $i_2 i_3 \geqq j_1 j_2$, *then* $i_1 i_3 \geqq j_1 j_3$.

THEOREM 4.1.
$$\begin{array}{ccccccccccc} (v) & \mapsto & (6_s) & \mapsto & (q) & \mapsto & (6_w) & \mapsto & (t_s) & \mapsto & (t) \\ & & & & & & \updownarrow & & \updownarrow & & \\ & & & & & & (m_w) & & (t_s^*) \leftrightarrow (t_s^{**}). & & \end{array}$$

Proof. Obviously (v) implies all the other conditions, and obviously $(t_s) \to (t)$. To prove $(t_s) \to (t_s^*)$, let $ij \geqq \frac{1}{2}$ and apply (t_s) to three cases: (1) $jx \geqq \frac{1}{2}$; (2) $jx < \frac{1}{2}$, $xi \geqq \frac{1}{2}0$ (3) $jx < \frac{1}{2}$, $xi < \frac{1}{2}$. To prove the converse, let $ij \geqq \frac{1}{2}, jk \geqq \frac{1}{2}$; by (t_s^*) $ix \geqq jx, jy \geqq ky$; put $x=k$, $y=i$. To prove $(t_s^*) \leftrightarrow (t_s^{**})$, apply a contradiction argument, using (2.2). To prove $(6_w) \to (t_s)$, let $ij \geqq \frac{1}{2}, jk \geqq \frac{1}{2}$ and apply (6_w) with $i=i_1, j=i_2=j_2, k=i_3$; and (1) $j_1=j, j_3=k$; (2) $j_1=i, j_3=j$. Condition (m_w) implies, and is itself obtained by successive application of (6_w). To prove $(q) \to (6_w)$ is straightforward. To prove $(6)_s \to (q)$, let $hi \geqq jk$, $i_1=h$, $j_1=i_2=i$, $i_3=j_2=j$, $j_3=k$.

The absence of implications is proved by counterexamples:[15] (t) does not imply (t_s) since, with $n=3$ and $12 > 13 > \frac{1}{2}$ and $23 > \frac{1}{2}$, (t) but not (t_s) is satisfied. To prove that (t_s) does not imply (6_w), let $n=4$ and $\frac{1}{2} < 43 < 32 < 21 < 31 < 42 < 41$. To prove that (6_w) does not imply (q), let $n=4$, and $\frac{1}{2} < 32 < 43 < 21 < 31 < 42 < 41$. To prove that (q) does not imply (6_s), let $n=5$ and $\frac{1}{2} < 21 < 54 < 32 < 43 < 53 < 31 < 42 < 41 < 52 < 51$. To prove that (6_s) does not imply (v), a counterexample (with $n=9$) was constructed, but must be omitted here.

All the conditions given so far are necessary but not sufficient for the existence of v. With the exception of (m_w), they all involve binary choices among elements of subsets of fixed size m; $m=3$ in (t) and (t_s); $m=4$ in (q); $m=6$ in (6_w) and (6_s). The exception (m_w) is only apparent as (m_w) is equivalent to (6_w). Therefore all those conditions can be applied even when the size of N (the number n of all alternatives) is unknown. The following two conditions can be applied only if the size of N is known.

CONDITION (m_s) (strong condition on m-tuples). *For any* $m \leqq n$, $i_1 i_m \geqq j_1 j_m$, *if* $i_k i_{1+k} \geqq j_{r_k} j_{1+r_k}$, $k=1,\ldots,m-1$, *where* $r=(r_1,\ldots,r_{m-1})$ *is any permutation of the set* $(1,\ldots,m-1)$.

CONDITION (o) (ordering of the probabilities of binary choices). *Arrange all the* $ij \geqq \frac{1}{2}$ *in a sequence of* $n(n-1)/2$ *inequalities (involving only* n *distinct alternatives):* $i_1 i_2 \geqq i_3 i_4 \geqq \cdots \geqq \frac{1}{2}$; *then the corresponding system of* $n(n-1)/2$ *inequalities in* n *distinct real numbers*

$$v_{i_1} - v_{i_2} \geqq v_{i_3} - v_{i_4} \geqq \cdots \geqq 0$$

must have a solution.

The following needs no proof.

THEOREM 4.2. $(v) \leftrightarrow (o) \rightarrow (m_s) \mapsto (6_s)$.

We have not investigated whether (m_s) implies (o).

Thus, for a finite set N of alternatives we have the condition (o) [perhaps also (m_s)?] sufficient and necessary for the existence of a strong utility vector v, and testable if N has known size. For finite N of unknown size our testable conditions are necessary only.

A summary of the main results of this section, assuming the set of alternatives finite, is given by

THEOREM 4.3.

$$\begin{array}{ccccccccccc} (v) & & & & & & & & (w) & & \\ \updownarrow & & & & & & & & \updownarrow & & \\ (o) & \rightarrow & (m_s) & \mapsto & (q) & \mapsto & (6_w) & \mapsto & (t_s) & \mapsto & (t). \end{array}$$

If the set of alternatives is ascribed some continuity properties (to be defined presently), some of the necessary testable conditions become also sufficient. We give two examples. Suppose one postulates

CONDITION $(s.c)$ (stochastic continuity). *For any elements a, b, c of the set A of alternatives such that* $ab<\lambda<ac$, *there is an element d in A with* $ad=\lambda$. Debreu [24] has proved

THEOREM 4.4. $[(s.c), (q)] \mapsto (v)$.

Or one may postulate a stronger

CONDITION $(d.b.p)$ (continuous differentiability of binary probabilities). *The set, A, of alternatives is representable by a real interval, and* $p(a, b)=p(a; (a, b))$ *is continuously differentiable with* $\partial p/\partial b<0$, $\partial p/\partial a>0$.

In Block and Marschak [21] proof was given of

THEOREM 4.5. $[(d.b.p), (6_w) \mapsto (v)$.

To show this, one first proves a

LEMMA. *Let* $x, y \in [0, 1]$ *and let* $f(x, y)$ *be continuously differentiable with* $\partial f/\partial y<0$, $\partial f/\partial x>0$. *Then, in order that f admit the representation* $f(x, y)= =h(u(x)-v(y))$, where *h, u, v are monotone increasing functions of one variable, it is necessary and sufficient that there exist functions* $\alpha(x)$, $\beta(y)$ *such that* $(\partial f/\partial x)/(\partial f/\partial y)=\alpha(x)/\beta(y)$.

V. FURTHER DIRECTLY TESTABLE CONDITIONS FOR THE EXISTENCE OF RANDOM ORDERINGS

Directly testable sufficient conditions for (U), the existence of random utilities (or, equivalently, for (P), the existence of random orderings), were given in Section III. It was shown, for example, that the probabilities $P(r)$ exist if the ratios $i(M)/j(M)$ do not depend on M. We have also shown that this condition is not necessary. On the other hand, the directly testable condition (e) is necessary: if the $P(r)$ exist, then $i(M) \leq i(L)$ for any $i \in L \subseteq M \subseteq N$. We shall presently show that this condition is not sufficient. We have not found directly testable conditions that are both sufficient and necessary for the existence of $P(r)$ on N. The following partial results may, however, prove useful. They still use finite sets of alternatives only, of known or unknown size. The case of continuous sets has not been explored.

Condition (e_3) defined in Section III (3.11), as a special case of Condition (e), can also be conveniently denoted by (P_3), being the first link in a sequence of Conditions (P_m), $m=3, \ldots, n$, which we shall state presently. Let us first state

THEOREM 5.1. *If* $n=3$, *then* $(P_3) \leftrightarrow (P)$.

Proof. Sufficiency of (P_3). Denote by x, y, z the generic distinct elements of $N=(1, 2, 3)$, define $Q(zxy)=x(x, y)-x(x, y, z)$, and assume ($P_3$) or its equivalent, ($e_3$). Then by (3.11), $Q(zxy) \geqq 0$; and by (2.2), (2.1), the sum of the six numbers $Q(zxy)$ is equal to $3-2=1$; hence (P) is satisfied, with $P(xyz)=Q(xyz)$.

Necessity of (P_3). By Theorem 3.3.

CONDITION (P_4). *For any four distinct elements* w, x, y, z *of* N,

$$w(w, x, y) \geqq w(w, x, y, z); \tag{5.1}$$

$$w(w, x) - w(w, x, y) \geqq w(w, x, z) - w(w, x, y, z). \tag{5.2}$$

THEOREM 5.2. $(P) \rightarrow (P_4) \mapsto (P_3)$.

Proof. Add (5.1) and (5.2) to obtain (P_3) ($=e_3$) from (P_4). The converse is clearly not true. Moreover, if (P) is true, then

$$w(w, x, y) - w(w, x, y, z) = P(zwxy) + P(zwyx), \tag{5.3}$$

$$\begin{aligned} w(w, x) - [w(w, x, y) + w(w, x, z)] - w(w, x, y, z) = \\ = P(zywx) + P(yzwx); \end{aligned} \tag{5.4}$$

since the expressions on the right-hand side are non-negative, (P_4) is satisfied. The converse is not true, since (P) may involve subsets with more than four elements.

THEOREM 5.3. *If* $n=4$, $(P_4) \leftrightarrow (P)$.

Proof. Sufficiency of (P_4). If x, y, z, w are generic distinct elements of $N=(1, 2, 3, 4)$, then (5.3), (5.4) is a system of 24 equations in as many unknowns, $P(r)$, non-negative and adding up to 1; the knowns being the $x(M)$, $M \subseteq N$. Each permutation r occurs exactly once in the set (5.3) and exactly once in the set (5.4). Thus the system breaks into six sets of four equations; each set involves exactly four permutations r (none of which appears in the other five sets) and is of the form

$$(5.5)\qquad \begin{aligned}\alpha &= P(r^{(1)}) + P(r^{(2)}),\\ \beta &= P(r^{(2)}) + P(r^{(3)}),\\ \gamma &= P(r^{(3)}) + P(r^{(4)}),\\ \delta &= P(r^{(4)}) + P(r^{(1)}),\end{aligned}$$

where the known $\alpha, \beta, \gamma, \delta$ are non-negative. They obey the restriction $\alpha+\gamma=\beta+\delta$, so that the four equations are linearly dependent. A non-negative solution for the four $P(r)$ is obtained by putting $0=P(r^{(4)})$ or $0=P(r^{(2)})$ according as $\beta>\gamma$ or not. One then verifies (P) for all $x(M)$ and obtains $\sum_R P(r)=1$.

Necessity of (P_4). By Theorem 5.2.

THEOREM 5.4. *When* $n=4$, $(P_4)\mapsto(e)$.

Proof. Sufficiency. By Theorems 5.3 and 3.3.

No necessity. (P_4) implies

$$(5.6)\quad w(w, x) - w(w, x, y) \geqq w(w, x, z) - w(w, x, y, z) \geqq 0\,;$$

when $n=4$, (e) is the pair of inequalities

$$(5.7)\qquad w(w, x) - w(w, x, y) \geqq 0,$$

$$(5.8)\qquad w(w, x, z) - w(w, y, z) \geqq 0,$$

which are implied by, but do not imply, (5.6).

Conditions (P_4) and (P_3) are special cases of

CONDITION (P_m). *Let* $y, z, x_1, \ldots, x_{m-2}$ *denote m generic distinct elements of a set M consisting of m elements,* $3\leqq m\leqq n$. *Then for any h,* $3\leqq h\leqq m$,

$$(5.9)\qquad \begin{aligned}S_h = y(y, z) &- [y(y, z, x_1) + y(y, z, x_2) + \cdots +\\ &+ y(y, z, x_{h-2})] + [y(y, z, x_1, x_2) + y(y, z, x_1, x_3) +\\ &+ \cdots + y(y, z, x_{h-3}, x_{h-2})] \ldots \pm y(y, z, x_1, \ldots, x_{h-2}) \geqq 0.\end{aligned}$$

THEOREM 5.5. $(P)\to(P_n)$, *with*

$$(5.10)\qquad S_m = \sum_r P(1_r 2_r \ldots (m-2)_r\, yz), \quad m = 3, \ldots, n\,;$$

the sum being taken over all permutations r of the m-element-set M which end in yz.

Proof. Assume (P) and count the number of times, with sign, that any particular permutation is included in S_m. A term of the type $\ldots y \ldots z \ldots$, where $k \geqq 1$ elements besides z follow y, has the coefficient

$$(5.11)\qquad 1-\binom{k}{1}+\binom{k}{2}-\ldots+\binom{k}{k}=(1-1)^k=0.$$

and so the only remaining terms will be as specified on the right-hand side of (5.10).

We have seen that, in addition, $(P_n)\rightarrow(P)$ for $n\leqq 4$. We do not know whether this is true for $n>4$. And we note that (P_n) is not testable if n is unknown.

An interesting condition involving binary choices only was formulated independently by several authors (perhaps first by Guilbaud [25]):

CONDITION (c_3) (a condition on cycles of 3 elements).[16] *For any three distinct elements i, j, k of N,*

$$(5.12)\qquad 1\leqq ij+jk+ki\leqq 2.$$

THEOREM 5.6. $(e_3)\mapsto(c_3)$.

Proof. Sufficiency. Let $M=(i,j,k)\subseteq N$. By (e_3), $ij\geqq i(M)$, $jk\geqq j(M)$, $ki\geqq k(M)$; add; apply (2.1), (2.2).

No necessity. Use the example of Theorem 3.4, where $ij+jk+ki=\frac{3}{2}$, so that the binary probabilities obey (c_3); but one of the ternary probabilities contradicts (e_3). We shall now prove

THEOREM 5.7. *Condition (c_3) is sufficient and necessary for the binary probabilities to be consistent with Condition (e_3).*

Proof. Sufficiency. Denote by x, y, z the generic distinct elements of $M=(i,j,k)\subseteq N$. We have to show that if the six binary probabilities xy satisfy (c_3), then there exist three numbers γ_z that have the properties required by (e_3) of the ternary probabilities, viz., $\sum_z\gamma_z=1, 0\leqq\gamma_z\leqq$ $\leqq\min(xy, xz)$ for all x. Clearly such numbers exist if

$$(5.13)\qquad s=\min(ij,jk)+\min(ji,jk)+\min(ki,)\,kj\geqq 1.$$

Let ij be minimal, and hence, by (2.2), ji maximal, among the six xy. If $kj<ki$, then, by (2.2), $s=ij+1\geqq 1$; if $kj\geqq ki$, then (c_3) implies $s\geqq 1$.

Hence, (c_3) guarantees the existence of the desired numbers γ_z (in general not unique).

Necessity. By Theorem 5.6.

Theorem 5.7 may be of importance if binary probabilities are the only observable ones (see Section VII). For the same reason, the following theorems, 5.8 and 5.9, will be of interest. We shall first state the relations between (e_3), (c_3), and the two transitivity conditions (t_s) and (t) of Section IV:

THEOREM 5.8.
$$\begin{array}{ccc}(t_s) & \vdash\!\!\!-\!\!\!\dashv & (e_3)\\ \downarrow & \times & \downarrow \\ (t) & \vdash\!\!\!-\!\!\!\dashv & (c_3).\end{array}$$

Proof. $(t_s)\mapsto(t)$, $(e_3)\mapsto(c_3)$ by Theorems 4.1, 5.6. To show that (t_s) implies (c_3) assume, for some i, j, k in N, $ij+jk+ki<1$, contradicting (c_3); then $ij+jk<1$, and by (2.2) $ij<kj$; so that, if (t_s) [and therefore, by 4.1, (t_s^{**})] holds, then $ik<\frac{1}{2}, ki>\frac{1}{2}$, and by symmetry $ij>\frac{1}{2}, jk>\frac{1}{2}$, hence $ij+jk+ki>\frac{3}{2}$, contradicting the assumption. To show that (c_3) does not imply (t), let alone (t_s), consider $N=(i, j, k)$, and make $ij=jk=ki=0.4$, thus satisfying (c_3) but not (t). On the other hand, the case $N=(i, j, k)$, $ij=jk=0.1$, $kj=0.6$ shows that (t) does not imply (c_3). Finally, to see that $(t_s) \vdash\!\dashv (e_3)$ and $(t) \vdash\!\dashv (e_3)$, note that (t_s) and (t) constrain only binary probabilities while (e_3) constrains ternary as well as binary ones, and its constraint on the latter is identical with (c_3), which was just shown not to imply (t_s) or (t).

The following condition on binary probabilities, due to Georgescu-Roegen [22], generalizes (c_3):

CONDITION (c_m). *For any $x_1, \ldots, x_m$ in N,*

$$1 \leqq x_1x_2 + x_2x_3 + \cdots + x_{m-1}x_m + x_mx_1 \leqq m-1. \tag{5.14}$$

A proposition stronger than (c_m) and – as will be proved presently – equivalent to (c_3) is

CONDITION (c^*). *(c_m) holds for all $m \leqq n$.*

THEOREM 5.9. $(c_3)\leftrightarrow(c^*)\mapsto(c_m)$.

Proof. We have only to prove that (c_3) implies (c^*) and is not implied by (c_m), $m>3$. First show that the conjunction $[(c_3), (c_{m-1})] \rightarrow (c_m)$: by (c_{m-1}),

$$(5.15) \qquad 1 \leqq x_1x_2 + x_2x_3 + \cdots + x_{m-1}x_1 \leqq m-2\,;$$

and, by (c_3)

$$1 \leqq x_{m-1}x_m + x_mx_1 + x_1x_{m-1} \leqq 2,$$

or, by (2.2)

$$(5.16) \qquad 0 \leqq x_{m-1}x_m + x_mx_1 - x_{m-1}x_1 \leqq 1\,;$$

adding (5.15) and (5.16), we obtain (c_m); now put $m=4, 5, \ldots$. To prove that (c_m) does not imply (c_3) let $m=n=4$; if the matrix $[x_ix_j]$ is

$$\begin{bmatrix} 0.5 & 0.8 & 0.2 & 0.5 \\ 0.2 & 0.5 & 0.8 & 0.6 \\ 0.8 & 0.2 & 0.5 & 0.6 \\ 0.5 & 0.4 & 0.4 & 0.5 \end{bmatrix},$$

then (c_4) is satisfied, but (c_3) is not, for $x_1x_2+x_2x_3+x_3x_1=2.4>2$.

The main results of this section can be summarized in

THEOREM 5.10. *If* $n \geqq m > 3$, *then*

$$\begin{array}{ccccccccccc} (P) & \rightarrow & (P_n) & \mapsto & (P_m) & \mapsto & (e_3) & \leftrightarrow & (P_3) & & \\ \downarrow\!\!\!\!\top & & & & & & \downarrow\!\!\!\!\top & & & & \\ (e) & \mapsto & (c_m) & \leftarrow\!\!\!\!\dashv & (c^*) & \leftrightarrow & (c_3) & \leftarrow\!\!\!\!\dashv & (t_s) & \mapsto & (t)\,; \end{array}$$

if $n=3$ *or* 4, *then* $(P) \mapsto (P_n)$.

VI. A SURVEY

Theorem 3.10 summarized the relations between conditions postulating the existence of random orderings, and of constant utilities of various degrees of strength. It is also useful to summarize the relations between Conditions (U), (u), (v), and (w) and some of the testable conditions, mainly from Sections IV and V:

THEOREM 6.1. *For A finite,*

$$\begin{array}{ccccccccccccc} (c.p) & \leftrightarrow & (u) & \mapsto & (v) & \mapsto & (q) & \mapsto & (t_s) & \mapsto & (t) & \leftrightarrow & (w) \\ \updownarrow & & \downarrow\!\!\!\!\top & \nearrow & & \searrow & & \nearrow & \downarrow\!\!\!\!\top & \nearrow & & & \\ (\pi) & \mapsto & (U) & \mapsto & & & (e) & \mapsto & (c_3). & & & & \end{array}$$

The following attempt to relate our various conditions to the hypotheses stated by earlier authors is very incomplete. Not only could we not do justice to the work of many psychologists; we have also failed to study thoroughly some of the statisticians' work.

In Section II, the ideas of R. D. Luce, imposing a very strong constraint on the probabilities of multiple choices of any order, were identified with Condition (u); it can also be found in an early unpublished paper of Törnqvist [26]; and was stated orally (but taken back as unrealistic) by Debreu. R. A. Bradley and M. E. Terry [27] and L. R. Ford [28] applied this condition to binary choices only; in this form it is studied by J. Marschak [20] in some detail. A weaker constraint on the probabilities of binary choices is that of Fechner [3], identified with Condition (v). This condition, the still weaker Condition (w), and an intermediate case [the 'strong transitivity', (t_s)], was also studied by C. Coombs [29]; H. Gulliksen [30]; the late S. Valavanis-Vail [31], to whom we owe the important Condition (t_s); W. Edwards [32]; A. G. Papandreou *et al.* [33]; K. May [34]; J. M. Davis [35]; and D. Davidson (in collaboration with one of the present authors) [36].

In Section III, we identified an idea of Thurstone's with our Condition ($s.n$) (somewhat weakened in the subsequent work of Mosteller): a special form of combining the model (v) of strong constant utilities with the model (U) of random orderings. Conditions which can be identified with (U) were studied by G. Th. Gilbaud [25], N. Georgescu-Roegen ([22], [37]), D. Rosenblatt [38], R. D. Luce [15], J. Marschak [39], and others.

M. G. Kendall [40], G. L. Mallows [41], I. R. Savage [42], E. L. Lehmann [43], H. D. Brunk [44] and other statisticians (we owe these references to Lehmann) have studied rank-order statistics, 'ranking models', and paired comparisons, starting with problems of statistical inference. For example, given a sample of binary choices, estimate the 'underlying' (constant) ranking (perhaps a vector-parameter of the distribution of our U?); or test the hypothesis that a certain parameter is higher with one than with another of a pair of parent populations. To our regret, we have not had the opportunity to do the important job of stating the relations (if any) between our network of conditions and the stochastic models that may underlie the work of these authors. We shall briefly deal with statistical inference in Section X.

VII. VARYING THE DOMAIN OF TESTABILITY

As remarked in Section I, the definition of the class of basic observations, and therefore also of the class of testable conditions, depends on the range of possible experiments and other observations. Moreover, Condition (o) of Section IV exemplifies the case of a constraint that involves all elements of the set of alternatives simultaneously; if this set is finite and of unknown size, such a condition is not testable, whatever the definition of the basic observation.

In this paper, the basic observations have been defined as $(a; F)$, the actual *choice* of a single element a out of a feasible subset F of alternatives. It was suspected that the subject's verbal statements about how he *ranks* the elements of a given subset of three or more alternatives were less reliable, for the characterization and prediction of actual behavior, than his actual choices. But this suspecion may have been unnecessary. Psychologists do ask their subjects to rank three or more objects, according to the subject's intensity of perception, or his preferences, etc. They also ask 'judges' to rank individuals according to some characteristics. Presumably some consistency is assumed to prevail among all the rankings of any offered subsets of alternatives, and also between these rankings and the actual choices from any offered subset. In a stochastic model involving a finite set of alternatives $N=(1, 2, 3, 4)$, this would mean that, for example, a subject who, *at a given time*, ranks N in the order 1234, *would*, if asked to rank the subset (2, 3, 4), produce the ranking 234; and if asked to choose from the subset (2, 3, 4), *would* choose 2. The experimenter's faith in such consistency may be increased if the subject is told that the verbal statement about ranking will commit his actual choice when he is later presented with a pair of alternatives (a procedure suggested in a non-stochastic context by W. A. Wallis as quoted by L. J. Savage [45]), or, for that matter, with any subset of alternatives.[17] With the rankings (on the set N of all alternatives) admitted as basic observations, our condition (P) can be reformulated as a testable one, with $P(r)$ indicating the probability of an *observable* ranking r; that is, P is a distribution about which inferences can be made from experiments on rankings.

TESTABLE CONDITION (P). *The numbers* $P(r)$ *have the property* (3.7).

Since ranking experiments can be made on any subset $K \subseteq N$, we may, denoting by $P(r^K)$ the probability of a ranking r^K of K, generalize (P) into the following

TESTABLE CONDITION (P^K). *The numbers* $P(r^K)$ *have the property* (3.7) *with K replacing N, and with* $M \subseteq K \subseteq N$.

Note that when the subset K consists of two elements, the choosing from the subset and its ranking are the same thing. But the observation of ranking within triples and larger subsets does provide additional testable constraints not covered in the previous sections.

Testability is extended still further if the following procedure is permitted. The subject is given a set $M \subseteq N$, where M consists of m objects, and is told to select l of them $(l \leqq m)$ and to rank these l objects. The ranking is denoted by $r^{L,M} = (r_{a_1} \ldots r_{a_l})$ where $L = \{a_1, \ldots, a_l\}$. The condition $(P_{l,m})$ is said to hold if there exist $n!$ non-negative numbers $P(r^{N,N}) = P(r)$ whose sum is unity such that, for each set M having at least l, but not more than m elements, and each subset L of M with l elements

$$(7.1) \qquad P(r^{L,M}) = \sum P(r),$$

the summation being over all rankings r such that $r_i \leqq r_j$ if either (1) $i \in L$ and $j \in M - L$, or (2) $i \in L$, $j \in L$, and $r_i^{L,M} \leqq r_j^{L,M}$.
Note: with $l = 1$, $(P_{1,n})$ *becomes the condition* (P) *of Section* 3, since (7.1) then becomes

$$i(M) = \sum_{r \mid r_i \leqq r_j,\, j \in M} P(r).$$

Thus $(P) \leftrightarrow (P_{1,n})$.

Clearly: $(P_{l,m}) \mapsto (P_{l,m-1})$, $(l < m)$; $(P_{m-1,m}) \leftrightarrow (P_{m,m})$. Moreover:

1. If $L = (i)$, then $P(r^{L,M}) = i(M)$.
2. If $L = (i)$, $M = (i, j)$, then $P(r^{L,M}) = P(ij)$.
3. If $L = (i, j)$, $M = (i, j)$, then $P(r^{L,M}) = P(ij)$.
4. If $L = N$ or $N - 1$, then $P(r^{L,N}) = P(r) = P(1_r 2_r \ldots n_r)$.

So far, we have discussed the possibility of extending the domain of testable conditions beyond the definition given in Section I. On the other hand, the observational possibilities may be such as to make even that definition too wide.

For example, they may be such as to make binary but not ternary, etc. choices observable. As remarked orally by H. Simon, to replace the experiment – in which the subject names the heaviest of two objects placed in his two hands – by a similar experiment with three objects (taken in successive pairs, or weighed on three fingers, etc.) may change experimental conditions so drastically as to invite inconsistencies. On the other hand, no such inconsistencies need be expected in experiments where the subject tells which of the two, or three, or possibly four lights is brighter. In the economics of the actual market, binary choices are often not observable where ternary or higher ones are; for example, a speculator will (1) buy, (2) sell, or (3) do neither of these.

When the testability domain is extended, some sufficient existence conditions become irrelevant. As a simple example let N consist of three elements and first assume that both binary and ternary choices are observable but rankings are not. Theorem 5.1 gives a necessary and sufficient condition for the existence of probabilities of rankings as defined in Condition (P) of Section III. But it does not say that these probabilities will be equal to the numbers $P(r)$ of the Testable Condition (P) of the present section, numbers about which inferences could be made if rankings were observable.

On the other hand, suppose that only binary choices among the three alternatives in N are observable, but neither ternary choice nor rankings are. Then Condition (c_3) ($1 \leqq xy + yz + zx \leqq 2$) becomes important; for, by Theorem 5.7, this condition is sufficient for the existence of the three ternary choice probabilities $i(x, y, z)$ and of the six probabilities of rankings $P(r)$; and nothing stronger can be stated with the observations at hand.

VIII. THE BOUNDARY CASE: PERFECT DISCRIMINATION OR PREFERENCE

The case when the binary probability $p(a; F)$, with $F=(a, b)$, takes the boundary values 1 or 0 is called, in psychology of perceptions, perfect (as distinct from imperfect) discrimination. In the language of the theory of choice there is then perfect (as distinct from imperfect, or stochastic) preference. The term can be extended to the case when the feasible set F contains any number of elements.

To take account of the boundary case, special provisos are needed to make conditions such as (t_s), (v), (u) consistent with empirical observations. To take the weakest of those conditions, (t_s) or its equivalent

(t_s^{**}): if there exists an element k of the set N of alternatives, such that $ik = jk$, then $ij = \frac{1}{2}$. Now, if three bodies i, j, k weigh, respectively, 1000, 10, and 6 grams, and xy is the probability that the subject says that x is heavier than y, then the observations will very likely show $ij = ik$; but they will very unlikely show $jk = \frac{1}{2}$. The conditions (t) and (w), both weaker than (t_s), are not endangered by this fact. But the stronger conditions (v) and (u) are. Without the proviso about boundary cases, made in Section II and again in Section IV, Condition (v) would imply, in our case of three bodies, $v_j = v_k$ for each of the lighter ones, because of the existence of the very heavy body i. Similarly, in Condition (u) all the (strict) utilities u_i had to be assumed positive to prevent any of the probabilities $i(M)$ from being 0 or 1.

Perfect discrimination is circumvented experimentally by presenting to the subject, at each trial, objects not too strongly differing from each other in the relevant physical dimension; and by keeping the subject uninformed of the physical dimension – for example, through blindfolding.

This approach is not sufficient, for experiments on choice, to the extent to which these are intended to reveal 'desirabilities,' with 'perceptibility' kept more or less constant (see Section 1). Ideally, one would like to give the subject all the physical information, making the choice dependent only on his 'desires'. Suppose, then, that two alternatives differ from each other, however slightly, with respect to a single characteristic which is easily identified by the subject and is completely ordered with respect to the subject's choices. He will then presumably show perfect preference. Thus, in particular, when a and b are quantities of an economic 'good' and a exceeds b, he will prefer a with probability 1, even if the difference in quantities is very small. (In fact, this may be regarded as the definition of a 'homogeneous' economic good.) Also, if a and b are two vectors of quantities of the same m goods, $a = (a_1, \ldots, a_m)$, $b = (b_1, \ldots, b_m)$, and if a dominates b, i.e., if $a_i \geqq b_i$ for all i and $a_j > b_j$ for some j, then a will be perfectly preferred to b. The same is true if the vectors a and b are interpreted as two money wagers, (where a_i and b_i are, respectively, the monetary gains awarded when event E_i happens) and a dominates b. On the other hand, if a and b are two vectors neither of which dominates the other, stochastic instead of perfect preference may occur. Accordingly, the pairs of commodity-bundles used in the experiments by Papandreou and others [33] and the pairs of wagers used in the experiments of Davidson and

Marschak [36] were such as to exclude domination.

The vacillation of the chooser between the alternatives has thus been ascribed by Simon [46] and by Quandt [47] to the presence, in each alternative, of several relevant characteristics that themselves are completely ordered, but to which the subject pays attention only one at a time. In general, we need not assume that every alternative is so reduced (albeit 'unconsciously') to a bundle of characteristics, each of them an ordered one, so that the businessman decomposes, as it were, the job-applicant into his 'personality factors', or considers a prospective plant site as a vector of numerical attributes. Yet in some important cases such vectorial representation is indeed manifest. This gives rise to disturbing discontinuities in applying our stochastic models. For example, denote by $a=(a_1, a_2)$, $b=(b_1, b_2)$, and $b'=(b'_1, b'_2)$, three pairs of 'homogeneous commodities' – apples and oranges, not factories and vice-presidents; let ε_1 and ε_2 be two small positive numbers, and let $b_1=b'_1=a_1+\varepsilon_1$, $b_2=a_2$, $b'_2=a_2-\varepsilon_2$. Then, very likely, the binary probability ba is 1; while $b'a$ may be quite close to $\frac{1}{2}$; this big jump in probabilities would result from a very small physical change in the alternatives offered.

For such reasons, the psychophysicist's proviso that the 'differences' should not be 'noticed always or never' is doubly important in designing and interpreting experiments on economic choices,[18] if one wants such experiments to throw light on desirabilities, as separated from the perceptibility aspect of the choice phenomenon.

IX. REMARKS ON CHOICE UNDER UNCERTAINTY

As visualized at the end of Section I, we shall now outline possible stochastic reformulations of the theory of choice under uncertainty, weakening in particular the 'expected utility' condition.

A wager associates each alternative (in the sense defined previously) $i=1,\ldots,n$ with an event. Denote by $q=(q_1,\ldots,q_n)$ any wager in which the event giving rise to alternative i has probability q_i (possibly zero). In its non-stochastic form, the expected utility condition says that there is a constant vector $\bar{\omega}=(\bar{\omega}_1,\ldots,\bar{\omega}_n)$, unique up to an increasing linear transformation, and such that

$$(9.1) \qquad \sum\bar{\omega}_i q_i \geqq \sum\bar{\omega}_i q'_i \quad \text{if and only if} \quad q \succsim q',$$

where $\gtrsim$ means 'preferred or indifferent'. Since the observer cannot be sure that two subjects behave as if they ascribed the same probability to any given event, not only the 'utility-numbers' $\bar{\omega}_i$ but also the probabilities q_i have to be interpreted in a subjective sense, thus: For a given subject, there exist a vector ω and, associated with each wager, a vector q such that (9.1) is satisfied.

It has been shown[19] that this condition is implied by other conditions (called 'axioms') that apparently appeal more immediately to what our intuition recommends as rational, or consistent. As we remarked at the beginning, consistency in an absolute sense is likely to be rejected by experience.[20] But it can be replaced by more general conditions, of stochastic consistency; these imply, or are implied by, or both, statistically testable hypotheses. In particular, each of the Conditions (w), (v), (u), (U) of our Sections II and III can be combined with the expected utility principle to yield a stronger condition to be denoted by $(\bar{\omega})$, $(\bar{v})$, $(\bar{u})$, $(\bar{U})$, respectively. In formulating these conditions, we shall denote by Q the set of all wagers (i.e., the set of all vectors q of order n, with $\sum q_i=1$, $q_i \geqq 0$, all i); the feasible set of wagers will be denoted by $F \subseteq Q$; the probabilities of choices will be denoted as before, e.g., $q(F)=p(q; F)$; $qq'=p(q; (q, q'))$.

CONDITION $(\bar{w})$. *There is a constant vector* $\bar{w}=(\bar{w}, \ldots, \bar{w}_n)$ *such that*

$$(9.2) \qquad \sum \bar{w}_i q_i \geqq \sum \bar{w}_i q_i', \quad \text{if} \quad qq' \geqq \tfrac{1}{2}.$$

CONDITION $(\bar{v})$. *There is a constant vector* $\bar{v}=(\bar{v}_i, \ldots, \bar{v}_n)$ *and, associated with it, a distribution function* $\varphi_{\bar{v}}$, *strictly increasing except at its values* 1 *and* 0, *such that*

$$(9.3) \qquad \varphi_{\bar{v}}\left(\sum \bar{v}_i q_i - \sum \bar{v}_i q_i'\right) = qq'.$$

CONDITION $(\bar{u})$. *There is a constant positive vector* $\bar{u}=(\bar{u}_1, \ldots, \bar{u}_n)$ *such that, for every* $F \subseteq Q$ *and every* q, q' *in* F,

$$(9.4) \qquad \frac{\sum q_i \bar{u}_i}{\sum q_i' \bar{u}_i} = \frac{q(F)}{q'(F)}.$$

CONDITION $(\bar{U})$. *There is a random vector* $\bar{U}=(\bar{U}_1, \ldots, \bar{U}_n)$ *such that for every* $F \subseteq Q$ *and every* q *in* F,

$$(9.5) \qquad q(F) = \Pr\{\textstyle\sum(q_i - q_i')\,\bar{U}_i \geqq 0\,; \quad \textit{all} \quad q' \text{ in } F\}\,.$$

Clearly $\bar{w}$ and $\bar{U}$ (unlike w and U) are unique up to an increasing linear transformation. So is $\bar{v}$ (by virtue of the continuity of the set Q; see note 8). And $\bar{u}$ is unique up to a positive multiplier (as is u).

The directly testable conditions of the previous sections – e.g., Conditions (t), (t_s), (q), etc. – can be appropriately reformulated, and some new ones added. A case most easily accessible to observations is that of even-chance wagers: i.e., the case when the subjective probabilities are $\frac{1}{2}$ for each of a pair of alternatives. Let *iEj* be the wager promising *i* if event *E* happens, and *j* otherwise; then the subjective probability of *E* (and therefore also each of the subjective probabilities q_i and q_j) is said to be equal to $\frac{1}{2}$ if the subject is indifferent between *iEj* and *jEi*. Or, using the stochastic interpretation and denoting by $(iEj\cdot jEi)$ the probability of choosing the first out of that pair of wagers, $q_i = q_j = \frac{1}{2}$ if $(iEj\cdot jEi) = \frac{1}{2}$. In principle this property is operationally ascertainable.[21] Consider an even-chance wager, with $q_1 = q_2 = \frac{1}{2}$, and another, $q_3' = q_4' = \frac{1}{2}$; the expressions $\sum q_i\bar{v}_i$ and $\sum q_i'\bar{v}_i$ in Condition $(\bar{v})$ become, respectively, $(\bar{v}_1 + \bar{v}_2)/2$ and $(\bar{v}_3 + \bar{v}_4)/2$; and so with similar expressions in $(\bar{u})$, $(\bar{w})$ and $(\bar{U})$. We can denote the even-chance wager *aEb* simply by $\overline{ab}$ (hence $\overline{aa} = a$), and the probability of choice between two such wagers by $(\overline{ab}\cdot\overline{cd})$. Then Condition $(\bar{v})$ can be rewritten – analogous to relation (4.1) and with the proviso that the considered probabilities of choice are not 1 or 0 – thus:

$$(9.6) \qquad \begin{array}{l} \textit{if} \quad (\overline{a_1a_2}\cdot\overline{b_1b_2}) \geqq (\overline{b_3b_4}\cdot\overline{a_3a_4})\,, \\ \textit{then} \quad v_{a_1} + v_{a_2} + v_{a_3} + v_{a_4} \geqq v_{b_1} + v_{b_2} + v_{b_3} + v_{v_4}\,. \end{array}$$

This clearly implies the following *directly testable* set of conditions:

CONDITION (8_E) (8-tuple condition on even-chance wagers). *If* $(\overline{a_1a_2}\cdot\overline{b_1b_2}) \geqq (\overline{b_3b_4}\cdot\overline{a_3a_4})$, *then* $(\overline{a_{r_1}a_{r_2}}\cdot\overline{b_{s_1}b_{s_2}}) \geqq (\overline{b_{s_3}b_{s_4}}\cdot\overline{a_{r_3}a_{r_4}})$, *where* (r_1, r_2, r_3, r_4) *and* (s_1, s_2, s_3, s_4) *are arbitrary permutations of* (1, 2, 3, 4).

THEOREM 9.1. $(\bar{v}) \rightarrow (8_E)$.

It can be shown that the set (8_E) of conditions is not only necessary but also sufficient for (9.6) provided the stochastic continuity condition (*s.c*) of Section 4 is satisfied with respect to the considered set of even-chance wagers.

If some of the eight alternatives in Condition (8_E) are made identical, weaker directly testable conditions arise, involving a smaller number of distinct alternatives, and necessary for Condition ($\bar{v}$). In certain conjunctions, and assuming stochastic continuity, they are also sufficient for ($\bar{v}$), over the considered set of even-chance wagers. They were studied by Davidson and Marschak [36]; Debreu's paper [54], though dealing with even-chance wagers in a non-stochastic context, is also relevant.

X. TESTING STOCHASTIC CONSTRAINTS WHEN REPLICATIONS ARE FEW[22]

All the considered conditions have been constraints on probabilities of certain responses of the subject to varying external conditions. More precisely, these probabilities have been in the form $p(a; F)$ although in Section VII more general forms were briefly discussed. These probabilities define the coordinates of the parameter space, and each directly testable condition ('hypothesis') defines a certain region of this space. The test consists in deciding, on the basis of observations, whether the parameter point – the set of probabilities $p(a; F)$ for all F – falls into that region.

A trial is easily replicated if the same feasible set F – the same set of stimuli – can be presented to a random sample of subjects *provided* it is reasonable to assume that each member of the parent population is characterized by the same relevant probability distribution of responses. This assumption has been made, in effect (with respect to choices of foods, birthday gifts, etc.) by Jones, Peryam, and Thurstone [55], Thurstone and Jones [56], and Gulliksen [57].

If this assumption of identical distributions is not justified, the hypothesis must be tested separately for each subject to find the proportion of the observed subjects that fail to satisfy certain strong conditions – such as (q) (see Section IV) and therefore (v); the proportion of subjects failing to satisfy weaker conditions – such as (t) and therefore (w); and so forth. One can thus estimate the frequency distribution of the various 'degrees of stochastic consistency' among the parent population, even though the probabilities $(a; F)$ are not the same for two persons with the same degree of consistency. Two persons may both obey (w) and both fail to satisfy (v), even though one of them tends to vegetarianism more than the other. In psychophysics, two persons may obey the Fechnerian condition (v)

and yet have different functions φ_v, e.g., have different quartiles or 'just noticeable' differences (see Section II). A frequency distribution of degrees of (stochastic) consistency, in a given culture, is a useful thing to know. One may be interested in training people towards greater consistency, because of its importance for decision-making and leadership. This is not the same thing as inculcating identical tastes.

The number of replications, *for the same subject*, of the same set F of stimuli is limited by the fact that, in the course of successive replications, the subject's characteristic probabilities $p(a; F)$ for a given F may change. Inasmuch as this may be due to fatigue, psychophysicists do not seem to have found it necessary to curtail replications too much; they regard relative frequencies with which given responses a are elicited by a fixed F (e.g., a fixed pair of sounds) as workable estimates of the probabilities $p(a; F)$.

True, in psychophysical experiments the subject must be prevented from identifying the stimuli and remembering them. For example, he must be blindfolded. If he were asked to choose the heavier of two objects (or the string producing the higher pitch) but were not blindfolded, the visual stimulus, added to that of the weight (or sound), might help him to identify and remember the objects and thus possibly influence him when the same object is presented again.

For a similar reason, successive replications may lack independence when subjects have to respond to verbal stimuli, as in questionnaires on attitudes or on voting preferences. Students of attitudes try therefore to repeat a question in a different form, preferably after a lapse of a little time. The same lack of serial independence is likely to occur in the case of choices between verbally stated economic alternatives such as commodities and wagers. It might not be true of 'blindfolded' choices between wines. But, as pointed out in Section I, the economic theorist wants to separate preferences from difficulties of perception; his ideal is to observe the decisions of people while giving them as complete information as possible.

Accordingly, experimenters on choices have used only a small number of repetitions of the same pair of alternatives (Papandreou *et al.* [33]) or have avoided such repetitions altogether (Davidson and Marschak [36]). This creates special problems in devising statistical tests of significance, and at any rate makes such tests relatively weak. To bring out the logical nature of the problem, we shall concentrate on the mathematically easiest (though empirically weakest) case when each set F is presented once only; and we shall limit ourselves to the simplest of our hypotheses, the weak stochastic transitivity condition (t).

During the course of experiment the subject is asked to choose one from each of the sets (a, b), (b, c), (a, c). Denote by p_a, p_b, p_c the binary probabilities ab, bc, ca. Then $p=(p_a, p_b, p_c)$ is a point in $[0, 1]^3$. Assume that the subject has a certain probability distribution $\mathscr{P}$ of choosing points in $[0, 1]^3$; the random choice of triples (a, b, c) leads to a random choice from $[0, 1]^3$ with the distribution $\mathscr{P}$ on it. Let $q_i=p_i-\frac{1}{2}$, $i=a, b, c$. The region of $[0, 1]^3$ where condition (t) is *not* satisfied (call it T) is characterized by the fact that all three q_i are $\geqq 0$ or $\leqq 0$ and are not all $=0$. That is, apart from a set of measure 0, all three q_i have the same sign. It is desired to estimate $\mathscr{P}(T)=\Theta$.

It may be useful to think of an analogous one-dimensional problem. A coin-making machine is characterized by an unknown probability distribution of the chance variable p (probability of a coin falling heads). One is permitted to toss coins, *each only a few times* (*perhaps only once*), in order to get evidence about the distribution of p; for example, one wants to test the hypothesis that the proportion of coins with $p>\frac{1}{2}$ (i.e., biased in favor of heads) is not more than a preassigned number. The region '$p>\frac{1}{2}$' clearly corresponds to our region T, and can be so denoted; the preassigned number is an upper bound Θ' on $\mathscr{P}(T)=\Theta$. Now, an infinite number of coins of which exactly 10% are biased for heads, would, if each is tossed once, show more than 5% (and not more than 55%) heads; hence, if out of a very large number of coins tossed, exactly $Z=5\%$ have fallen heads, all we can say is that the proportion of coins biased for heads is less than $\Theta'=10\%=2Z$. Thus, *regardless of the number of coins* we are able to toss (each once), we cannot in general make statements involving a pre-assigned upper bound Θ' on the proportion of coins belonging to a given region. If Θ' had been 15%, then we could assert $\Theta<\Theta'$, but if Θ' had been 7%, then we could not assert $\Theta<\Theta'$. Thus, if we want to be sure that we can make an assertion, we can choose Θ' only after the tossings have been observed; if we are willing to accept the possibility of making no assertion, we can preassign Θ'. Similarly, in testing the stochastic transitivity condition (t), we shall be able to post-assign but not always to pre-assign an upper bound Θ' on Θ; and this regardless of the number of triples (a, b, c) we can present – each once – to the subject. The situation there is further complicated by the fact that we have only a finite sample and we introduce other parameters t^0, t' to analyze the confidence level.

Furthermore, if each coin could be tossed twice, we would still be unable to guarantee an assertion with a pre-assigned upper bound to Θ, but the ratio $\Theta'/\bar{Z}$ of the post-assigned bound to the observed proportion of heads would become smaller. And a similar statement can be made about the consequences of duplicating the presentation of each triple (a, b, c) to the subject.

We shall now develop a test of Condition (t). Let

$$(10.1)\quad f(p) = p_a p_b p_c + (1 - p_a)(1 - p_b)(1 - p_c) = \\ = \tfrac{1}{4} + q_a q_b + q_b q_c + q_c q_a,$$

where $q_i = p_i - \frac{1}{2}$. If $p \in T$ then $f(p) \geqq \frac{1}{4}$. If $p \notin T$ then $f(p) \leqq \frac{1}{2}$, for if $q_a = -\alpha$, $q_b = \beta$, $q_c = \gamma$ (α, β, γ non-negative), $f(p) = \frac{1}{4} + \beta\gamma - \alpha(\beta + \gamma) \leqq \leqq \frac{1}{4} + \beta\gamma \leqq \frac{1}{2}$, and the other possibilities are covered by symmetry. Define three random variables X_a, X_b, X_c: $X_a = 1$ if a is chosen from (a, b) and $X_a = 0$ otherwise; $X_b = 1$ if b is chosen from (b, c) and $X_b = 0$ otherwise; $X_c = 1$ if c is chosen from (a, c) and $X_c = 0$ otherwise. Define

$$(10.2)\quad Z = X_a X_b X_c + (1 - X_a)(1 - X_b)(1 - X_c).$$

For a given vector p, $\Pr\{Z=1\} = f(p)$. Now $\Pr\{Z=1\} = \Pr\{Z=1 \mid p \in T\} \cdot \mathscr{P}(p \in T) + \Pr\{Z=1 \mid p \notin T\}\, \mathscr{P}(p \notin T)$. Hence $\Pr\{Z=1\} \geqq (\Theta/4) + 0$ and $\Pr\{Z=1\} \leqq \Theta + \frac{1}{2}(1 - \Theta) = \frac{1}{2} + (\Theta/2)$. Thus Z is a binomial chance variable with mean $\mu = \Pr\{Z=1\}$ where

$$(10.3)\quad (\Theta/4) \leqq \mu \leqq \tfrac{1}{2} + (\Theta/2).$$

Let $Z_1, \ldots, Z_m$ be independent observations on Z, each based on a different triple (a, b, c). Let $\bar{Z} = \sum_1^m Z_k/m$. Our first test is based on the following considerations:

(1) Let $0 < \Theta' \leqq 1$. If $\Theta \geqq \Theta'$ then $\mu \geqq \Theta'/4$. Let V' be a binomial chance variable with $\Pr\{V'=1\} = \Theta'/4$. Then $\Pr\{Z_k=0\} \leqq \Pr\{V'=0\}$. Let $t' \leqq \Theta'/4$. Then $\Pr\{\bar{Z} \leqq t'\} \leqq \Pr\{\bar{V}' \leqq t'\}$ where $\bar{V}'$ is the mean of m values of V'. If a confidence level α' is specified, one can choose m large enough so that $\Pr\{\bar{V}' \leqq t'\} \leqq \alpha'$. Hence:

$$(10.4')\quad \text{if}\quad \Theta \geqq \Theta',\ \Pr\{\bar{Z} \leqq t'\} \leqq \alpha'.$$

(2) Similarly, consider Θ^0, with $0 \leqq \Theta^0 < \frac{1}{2}$. If $\Theta \leqq \Theta^0$ then $\mu \leqq \frac{1}{2} + \Theta^0/2$. Let V^0 be a binomial random variable with $\Pr\{V^0 = 1\} = \frac{1}{2} + \Theta^0/2$. Then $\Pr\{Z_k = 1\} \leqq \Pr\{V^0 = 1\}$. Let $t^0 \geqq \frac{1}{2} + \Theta^0/2$. Then $\Pr\{\bar{Z} \geqq t^0\} \leqq \Pr\{\bar{V}^0 \geqq$ $\geqq t^0\}$ where $\bar{V}^0$ is the mean of m values of V^0. Again, with a specified confidence level α^0, we can choose large enough m to make $\Pr\{\bar{V}^0 \geqq t^0\} \leqq$ $\leqq \alpha^0$. Hence

$$(10.4^0) \quad \text{if} \quad \Theta \leqq \Theta^0, \Pr\{\bar{Z} \geqq t^0\} \leqq \alpha^0 .$$

Summarizing: If $\bar{Z} \geqq t^0$, we assert $\Theta > \Theta^0$; if $\bar{Z} \leqq t'$, we assert $\Theta < \Theta'$; if $t' < \bar{Z} < t^0$, we assert nothing. The consequences of this are shown in the following table of probabilities of occurrence:

Assertion	True state	
	$\Theta \leqq \Theta^0$	$\Theta \geqq \Theta'$
$\Theta > \Theta^0$	$< \alpha^0$	–
$\Theta < \Theta'$	–	$< \alpha'$
Nothing	–	–

where the dashes indicate probabilities that we have not estimated. This procedure protects us against extreme errors of classification, but leaves open the possibility of coming to no decision.

If m is large enough so that the normal approximation to the binomial may be used, then the constants involved in the test are determined by the following equations:

$$(10.5) \quad F(s^0) = 1 - \alpha^0, \quad F(s') = 1 - \alpha',$$

where F is the normal distribution function with zero mean and unit variance, and

$$(10.6') \quad s' = (\Theta' - 4t')\sqrt{m}\big/2\sqrt{\Theta'(1 - \Theta'/4)},$$

$$(10.6^0) \quad s^0 = (2t^0 - 1 - \Theta^0)\sqrt{m}\big/\sqrt{(1 + \Theta^0)(1 - \Theta^0)}.$$

The experimenter may specify the parameters $\Theta^0, \Theta', t^0, t'$ either before or after the experiment. Let us first discuss the case where the choice is made *after* he has the data. Suppose $\bar{Z}$ turns out to be quite high. He is then seeking to make an assertion $\Theta > \Theta^0$. He can do this with confidence level $1 - \alpha^0$ where α^0 is determined from (10.6^0), provided that $t^0 \leqq \bar{Z}$ and $\Theta^0 \leqq 2t^0 - 1$. He would like Θ^0 to be as high as possible and at the same time $1-\alpha^0$ to be as high as possible. As he takes Θ^0 closer to $2t^0-1$, s^0 tends to zero and α^0 tends to $\frac{1}{2}$, which is not a convincing confidence level. Thus to keep the confidence level $1-\alpha^0$ high he must take Θ^0 much less than $2t^0-1$; on the other hand, the smaller he takes Θ^0, the weaker the impact of his assertion $\Theta>\Theta^0$. Thus it is clear that he should choose t^0 as large as possible, namely $\bar{Z}$. Now if the experimenter wants to work with a fixed confidence level $1-\alpha^0$, he should adjust Θ^0 low enough so that he achieves, by (10.6^0), his desired confidence level. If, on the other hand, there is a fixed 'tolerance level' Θ^0 which the experimenter regards as the significant indicator of inconsistency, then he would use this fixed Θ^0 and again with $t^0=\bar{Z}$ find his confidence level by (10.6^0). More generally, he can strike what balance he wishes, pushing Θ^0 up while driving $1-\alpha^0$ down, keeping of course $t^0=\bar{Z}$. If, instead, $\bar{Z}$ is quite low, then he wishes to assert $\Theta<\Theta'$. Here he would like Θ' as small as possible and $1-\alpha'$ as large as possible. Considerations similar to those above, applied now to (10.6′), show that he should choose $t'=\bar{Z}$ and similarly make an arrangement between Θ' and $1-\alpha'$.

It may be, however, that the experimenter is doing many experiments and would like to have a fixed procedure, regardless of the data. He can specify t^0 and Θ^0 in advance, subject to $\Theta^0\leqq 2t^0-1$, and know that his confidence level is given by (10.6^0). (The larger $2t^0-1-\Theta^0$, the larger the confidence level, but the larger he takes t^0, the more likely he will have nothing to assert, while the smaller he takes Θ^0, the weaker are the assertions he does make; this balance he settles in advance.) Similarly he selects Θ', t' in advance. Now the data from many experiments can be handled by a fixed procedure; if $\bar{Z}\geqq t^0$ or $\bar{Z}\leqq t'$, an assertion is made, while if $t'<\bar{Z}<t^0$, no assertion is made. This procedure will be more convenient, but clearly it involves a loss of one or more of the following: confidence level, strength of assertion, and likelihood of making an assertion, as compared with the method of selecting the parameters after the experiment. However, if the experimenter is testing a large number of individuals in order to select a subset for further testing, he might find it better, as far as the data-processing is concerned, to fix the parameters in advance.

Our second method is to find a confidence interval for Θ. Let $0<\alpha<1$ and $0<\delta<1$ be given. Then it follows that for m sufficiently large $P(-\delta<\bar{Z}-\mu<\delta)>1-\alpha$; i.e., $P(\bar{Z}-\mu<\delta$ and $\bar{Z}-\mu>-\delta)>1-\alpha$, or $P(\bar{Z}<\delta+\mu$ and $\bar{Z}>\mu-\delta)>1-\alpha$; from (10.3) it follows that $P(\bar{Z}<\delta+$

$+\frac{1}{2}+(\Theta/2)$ and $\bar{Z}>(\Theta/4)-\delta)>1-\alpha$. Thus $P(2\bar{Z}-2\delta-1<\Theta<4\bar{Z}+$ $+4\delta)>1-\alpha$.

While it is true that the length of the confidence interval $(2\bar{Z}-2\delta-1,$ $4\bar{Z}+4\delta)$ is $2\bar{Z}+6\delta+1>1$, it is not centered at $\frac{1}{2}$. Hence, if $\bar{Z}$ is near zero or unity, the effective length of the interval may be quite small; e.g., if $\bar{Z}=0$, the conclusion is $-2\delta-1<\Theta<4\delta$, which has an effective length of only 4δ; while if $\bar{Z}=1$, the conclusion is $1-2\delta<\Theta<4+4\delta$, which has an effective length of 2δ. Since for a prescribed significance level $1-\alpha$ we do not know δ explicitly, we can use the estimate $\delta=k(\alpha)\,\sigma=k(\alpha)\cdot$ $\cdot(pq/m)^{1/2}\leqq k(\alpha)/2(m)^{1/2}$. Thus

$$P\left(2\bar{Z}-\frac{k(\alpha)}{\sqrt{m}}-1<\Theta<4\bar{Z}+\frac{2k(\alpha)}{\sqrt{m}}\right)>1-\alpha\,.$$

If the normal approximation for the binomial is used, $k(\alpha)$ is determined from the equation

$$F(k(\alpha))=1-\alpha/2\,, \tag{10.7}$$

where F is the normal distribution with zero mean and unit variance.

The confidence interval may also be used for making decisions; e.g. let $0<\Theta^*\leqq\Theta^{**}<1$. If the confidence interval is contained in the interval $(0,\,\Theta^*)$, assert that $\Theta\leqq\Theta^*$; if the confidence interval is contained in the interval $(\Theta^{**},\,1)$ assert that $\Theta\geqq\Theta^{**}$, otherwise assert nothing. In other words, if

$$\bar{Z}<\frac{\Theta^*}{4}-\frac{k(\alpha)}{2\sqrt{m}}\cdot$$

assert that $\Theta\leqq\Theta^*$; if

$$\bar{Z}>\tfrac{1}{2}\left(\Theta^{**}+1+\frac{k(\alpha)}{\sqrt{m}}\right),$$

assert that $\Theta\geqq\Theta^{**}$; otherwise assert nothing. We then get the following table of probabilities.[23]

Assertion	True state		
	$0\leqq\theta<\theta^*$	$\theta^*\leqq\theta\leqq\theta^{**}$	$\theta^{**}<\theta\leqq 1$
$\theta\leqq\theta^*$	–	$<\alpha$	$<\alpha$
$\theta\geqq\theta^{**}$	$<\alpha$	$<\alpha$	–
Nothing	–	–	–

NOTES

* Research carried out mostly under contracts of the Office of Naval Research with the Cowles Foundations for Economics at Yale University and with Columbia University. The paper was completed while Jacob Marschak was Ford Visiting Research Professor at the Graduate School of Industrial Administration, Carnegie Institute of Technology. We owe much to discussions with D. Davidson, G. Debreu, M. DeGroot, L. Hurwicz, and R. D. Luce.

1 While the stochastic approach uses measurable *probabilities*, another approach, also promising to give realism and unity to the understanding of choices and responses, makes use of the measurable *time-delay* of a choice or response. The shorter the delay, the larger is the difference between certain values said to be attached by the subject to two alternative responses. A very long delay reveals a state of (almost) indifference, the 'conflict-situation': Hamlet took a very long time to decide whether to kill his uncle. The logic of this approach and its combination with stochastic theories was treated by Cartwright and Festinger [1].

2 As pointed out by James Tobin in a private communication. *Added in 1974*: Tversky [59, p. 295] regards this distinction as amenable to his experiments on multi-attribute alternatives. See also [60].

3 Preferences thus defined are 'independent of irrelevant alternatives', a principle pointed out by Hotelling's pupil Arrow [4] and much used ever since. A better name for Arrow's principle is 'irrelevance of added alternatives'.

4 The condition is, *A is perfectly separable and is ordered by the relation* '$\succsim$'; *and for every a' in A the sets* $(a \mid a' \succsim a)$ and $(a \mid a \succsim a')$ *are closed.* The condition is trivially fulfilled by every finite set, for it is perfectly separable and all its, subsets are closed. Also, every subset of a finite-dimensional Euclidean space is perfectly separable, and it is reasonable to assume that the sets $(a \mid a' \succsim a)$ and $(a \mid a \succsim a')$ are closed when '$\succsim$' means a consumer's preference over the space of a finite number of commodities.

5 Thus Abraham Wald [6] has suggested a method to evaluate the consumer's ordinal utility function ω from the basic observations $(a; F)$ – purchases made as F varies with incomes and prices – assuming a non-stochastic model and not attempting a statistical estimate. More recently, H. Theil and H. Neudecker [7] gave a stochastic generalization of the same model, specifying, as did Wald, ω to be quadratic in the quantities of the goods consumed.

6 Regarding the proviso in brackets, see Section VIII.

7 These two points of view, the empirical and the game-theoretical, are represented in somewhat modified form by Dahl [12] and by Shapley and Shubik [13], respectively. If one accepts John Harsanyi's proposal to measure the power of X over Y by "how much difference it makes to Y between being X's friend or enemy," this difference between maxmax and maxmin payoffs (see, e.g., Luce and Raiffa [14]) might be related to the probability of Y's decision to be a friend.

8 For, suppose that $\varphi_{v}'(v'(x)-v'(y)) \equiv \varphi_v(v(x)-v(y))$. Then with $\phi = \varphi_{v'}^{-1}\ \varphi_v$ we have (i) $v'(x)-v'(y)=\phi(v(x)-v(y))$, (ii) $v'(y)-v'(z)=\phi(v(y)-v(z))$, and (iii) $v'(x)-v'(z)=\phi(v(x)-v(z))$. Adding (i) and (ii) and using (iii) we find, letting $a = v(x) - v(y)$, $b = v(y)-v(z)$, that $\phi(a+b)=\phi(a)+\phi(b)$. The only solution of this last equation which is not unbounded in every interval is, as is well known, $\phi(a)=\beta a$. Then from (i), with y fixed, we have $v'(x)=\beta v(x)+\alpha$.

9 Occasionally (in his Section 2.D.3, entitled 'A Generalization to Two or More Alternatives') Luce combines Condition (u) with another condition which we shall call (u')

(existence of strict *dis*utilities of *last* choices) and which is not generally consistent with (u): see our Theorem 3.8 below.

10 Luce tries to convey this appeal by an analogy with Arrow's (non-stochastic) principle which we called before the 'irrelevance of added alternatives'.

11 This counterexample is due to C. Winsten. Another interesting proof is due to P. Halmos. Three dice, A, B, C, are loaded so as to turn up with the following probabilities:

Face no.		1	2	3	4	5	6
Die:	A	0	0	.5	5	0	0
	B	0	.6	0	0	0	.4
	C	.4	0	0	0	.6	0

Let a, b, c (independent chance variables) be the number of spots turning up on A, B, C, respectively. Then (P) is satisfied: the probabilities of the six possible rankings of the numbers a, b, c according to magnitude, must be consistent with the probabilities that one of the numbers is the largest in a given pair or triple. But (t) is not satisfied: $\Pr\{a>b\}=.6>\frac{1}{2}$; $\Pr\{b>c\}=.64>\frac{1}{2}$; $\Pr\{a>c\}=.4<\frac{1}{2}$.

12 Whether or not (e) implies (P) will be left open until Section V.

13 Block and Marschak [18] searched for an appropriate urn model, and Debreu [19] found it, thus providing a shorter proof.

14 *Added in 1973*: See now Section 6.3., An 'Impossibility' Theorem, in Luce and Suppes [58].

15 For methods to construct these counterexamples see Block and Marschak [21]. Georgescu-Roegen [22] and Chipman [23] obtained a condition intermediate in strength between (t_s) and (t) by substituting min for max in (t_s). See Marschak ([20]), Section 7.)

16 Since (5.12) can be rewritten $ij+jk\geqslant ik$, this condition has also been called 'triangular'. Its further properties are studied in Marschak [20].

17 On the other hand, the following procedure will not do for our present purposes (it was suggested in an earlier paper of Marschak [39]): to construct the subject's ranking of a set by asking him to make a choice from it; then removing the alternative chosen, and asking him to make a choice from the remaining subset; and so on. In the stochastic case, the subject may shift during the procedure from one ranking to another ranking of the same set. In [39] the case was non-stochastic.

18 The case of absolute preferences is discussed by N. Georgescu-Roegen [22] in the context of the economic theory of demand (for homogeneous commodities). J. S. Chipman [23] drew attention to important anomalies in the case of statistical decisions.

19 This was done by J. von Neumann and O. Morgenstern [48], with q interpreted 'objectively'; their 'axioms' and proof were subsequently simplified by various writers, most concisely by I. N. Herstein and J. Milnor [49]. The 'subjective' interpretation of q was introduced by F. P. Ramsey [50] and made precise by L. J. Savage [45]. See also W. Edwards [32]. R. D. Luce [51] generalized the stochastic theory of choices under uncertainty by introducing random subjective probabilities.

20 See the examples of actual behavior found by M. Allais [52] and discussed also by L. J. Savage ([45], pp. 101–4.)

21 For still greater experimental ease, Davidson and Marschak [36], following the device used by Davidson, Suppes and Siegel [53], and guided by considerations of continuity, assumed that, when the alternatives i, j, i', j' are money amounts, then the

even-chance event E has also the following testable property:

$$(iEj \cdot j' Ei) = 1 = (jEi \cdot i' Ej),$$

provided $i - i' = j - j' = \varepsilon$, a small positive amount.

[22] *Added in 1974:* See now DeGroot [61].

[21] Naturally, much stronger tests are obtained if some *a priori* restrictions are admitted. Thus, in the Davidson and Marschak paper [36] two alternative hypotheses were formulated to test a stochastic constraint, viz., the transitivity condition (t) or (t_s): (1) The probability-triples (ac, bc, ca) are distributed uniformly over $[0, 1]^3$; (2) they are distributed over the region defined by Condition (t) or Condition (t_s) uniformly. Mathematical simplicity is about the only serious claim in favor of these restrictions unless one invokes Laplace's 'principle of ignorance'.

BIBLIOGRAPHY

[1] Cartwright, D. and Festinger, L., 'A Quantitative Theory of Decision', *Psychol. Rev.* **50** (1943) 595–621.

[2] Hotelling, H., 'Demand Functions with Limited Budgets', *Econometrica* **3** (1935) 66–78.

[3] Fechner, G. Th., *Elemente der Psychophysik*, Breitkopf & Härtel, Leipzig, 1859.

[4] Arrow, K. J., *Social Choice and Individual Values*, Wiley, New York, 1951.

[5] Debreu, G., 'Representation of a Preference Ordering by a Numerical Function', Chap. 11 in R. M. Thrall, C. H. Coombs and R. L. Davis (eds.), *Decision Processes*, Wiley, New York, 1954.

[6] Wald, A., 'The Approximate Determination of Indifference Surfaces by Means of Engel Curves, *Econometrica* **8** (1940) 144–75.

[7] Theil, H. and Neudecker, H., 'Substitution, Complementarity and the Residual Variation around Engle Curves', *Rev. Econ. Studies* **25** (1957) 114–23.

[8] Bernoulli, D., 'Exposition of a New Theory on the Measurement of Risk' (translated by Dr. Louise Sommer), *Econometrica*, **22** (1954) 23–36.

[9] Marshall, A., *Principles of Economics*, 8th ed. Macmillan, London, 1920.

[10] Mosteller, F. and Nogee, P., 'An Experimental Measurement of Utility', *J. Polit. Econ.* **59** (1951) 371–404.

[11] Guilford, J. P., *Psychometric Methods*, 2d ed., McGraw-Hill, New York, 1954.

[12] Dahl, R. A., 'The Concept of Power', *Behav. Sci.* **2** (1957) 201–15.

[13] Shapley, L. and Shubik, M., 'A Method for Evaluating the Distribution of Power in a Committee System', *Amer. Polit. Sci. Rev.* **48** (1954) 787–92.

[14] Luce, R. D. and Raiffa, H., *Games and Decisions*, Wiley, New York, 1957.

[15] Luce, R. D., *Individual Choice Behavior*, Wiley, New York, 1959.

[16] Thurstone, L. L., 'A Law of Comparative Judgment', *Psychol. Rev.* **34** (1927) 273–86.

[17] Mosteller, F., 'Remarks on the Method of Paired Comparisons', *Psychometrika* **26** (1951) 3–9, 203–6, 207–18.

[18] Block, H. D. and Marschak, J. 'An Identity in Arithmetic', *Bull. Amer. Math. Soc.* **65** (1959) 123–24.

[19] Debreu, G., 'On "An identity in arithmetic"', *Proc. Amer. Math. Soc.* **11** (1960) 220–21.

[20] Marschak, J., 'Binary Choice Constaints on Random Utility Indicators', *Selected Essays*, 8.

[21] Block, H. D. and Marschak, J., 'Random Orderings', Cowles Foundation Discussion Paper No. 42, Cowles Foundation, New Haven, Conn., 1957 (duplicated).

[22] Georgescu-Roegen, N, 'Threshold in Choice and the Theory of Demand', *Econometrica* **26** (1958) 157–68.

[23] Chipman, J. S. 'Stochastic Choice and Subjective Probability', Technical Report No. 2, School of Business Administration, Univ. of Minn., Minneapolis, Minn., 1958 (duplicated).

[24] Debreu, G., 'Stochastic Choice and Cardinal Utility', *Econometrica* **26** (1958) 440–44.

[25] Guilbaud, G. Th., 'Sur une difficulté de la théorie du risque', *Colloques internationaux du centre national de la recherche scientifique* (*économétrie*) **40** (1953) 19–25.

[26] Törnqvist, L., 'A Model for Stochastic Decision Making', Cowles Commission Discussion Paper, Economics 2100, Cowles Commission, Chicago, 1954 (duplicated).

[27] Bradley, R. A. and Terry, M. E., 'Rank Analysis of Incomplete Block Designs, I. The Method of Paired Comparisons', *Biometrika* **39** (1952) 324–44.

[28] Ford, L. R., 'Solution of a Ranking Problem from Binary Comparisons', *Amer. Math. Month.* **64** (1957) (Aug. suppl.), 28–33.

[29] Coombs, C., On the Use of Inconsistency of Preferences in Psychological Measurement', *J. Exp. Psychol.* **55** (1958) 1–7.

[30] Gulliksen, H., 'Paired Comparisons and the Logic of Measurement', *Psychol. Rev.* **53** (1946) 199–213.

[31] Valavanis-Vail, S., 'A Stochastic Model for Utilities', Seminar on the application of mathematics to social sciences, Univ. Michigan, Ann Arbor, 1957 (duplicated).

[32] Edwards, W., 'Probability Preferences in Gambling', *Amer. J. Psychol.* **66** (1955) 349–64.

[33] Papandreou, A. G. (with the collaboration of O. H. Sauerlender, O. H. Brownlee, L. Hurwicz, W. Franklin), 'A test of a Stochastic Theory of Choice, *Univ. Calif. Publ. in Econ.* **16** (1957) 1–18.

[34] May, K., 'Intransitivity, Utility and the Aggregation of Preference Patterns', *Econometrica* **22** (1954) 1–13.

[35] Davis, J. M., 'The Transitivity of Preferences', *Behav. Sci.* **3** (1958) 26–33.

[36] Davidson, D. and Marschak, J., 'Experimental Tests of Stochastic Decision Theories', *Selected Essays*, 6.

[37] Georgescu-Roegen, N., 'The Pure Theory of Consumer Behavior', *Quart. J. Econ.* **50** (1936) 545–93.

[38] Rosenblatt, D., 'On Some Stochastic Process Formulations of Individual Preference and Consumer Behavior (abst.)', *Econometrica* **24** (1956) 347–48.

[39] Marschak, J., 'Norms and Habits of Decision Making under Certainty', *Selected Essays*, 5.

[40] Kendall, M. G., 'Further Contributions to the Theory of Paired Comparisons', *Biometrics* **11** (1955) 43–67.

[41] Mallows, G. L., 'Non-Null Ranking Models, I', *Biometrika* **44** (1957) 114–30.

[42] Savage, I. R., 'Contributions to the Theory of Rank Orders', *Ann. Math. Stat.* **27** (1956) 590–615; **28** (1957) 968–77.

[43] Lehmann, E. L., 'Ordered Families of Distributions', *Ann. Math. Stat.* **26** (1955) 399–419.

[44] Brunk, H. D., 'Mathematical Models for Ranking from Paired Comparisons',

Technical Report No. 11, Air Force Office of Scientific Research, Department of Mathematics, University of Missouri, Columbia, Mo., Nov. 1958 (duplicated).

[45] Savage, L. J., *The Foundations of Statistics*, Wiley, New York, 1954. Revised, Dover, 1972.

[46] Simon, H. A., 'A Behavioral Model of Rational Choice', *Quart. J. Econ.* **69** (1955) 99–118.

[47] Quandt, R. E., 'A Probabilistic Theory of Consumer Behavior', *Quart. J. Econ.* **70** (1956) 507–36.

[48] Neumann, J. von and Morgenstern, O., *Theory of Games and Economic Behavior*, 2d ed. Princeton Univ. Press, Princeton N.J., 1947.

[49] Herstein, I. N. and Milnor, J., 'An Axiomatic Approach to Measurable Utility' *Econometrica* **21** (1953) 291–97.

[50] Ramsey, F. P., *The Foundations of Mathematics and Other Logical Essays*, Kegan Paul, London 1931.

[51] Luce, R. D., 'A Probabilistic Theory of Utility', *Econometrica* **26** (1958) 193–224.

[52] Allais, M., 'Le comportement de l'homme rationnel devant le risque: critique des postulats et axiomes de l'école américaine', *Econometrica* **21** (1953) 503–46.

[53] Davidson, D. and Suppes, P. (in collaboration with S. Siegel), *Decision Making: An Experimental Approach*, Stanford Univ. Press, Stanford, Calif., 1957.

[54] Debreu, G., 'Cardinal Utility for Even-Chance Mixtures of Pairs of Sure Prospects', *Rev. Econ. Studies* **26**(1958/9) 174–77.

[55] Jones, L. V., Peryam, D. R., and Thurstone, L. L., 'Development of a Scale for Measuring Soldiers' Food Preferences', *Food Research* **20** (1955) 512–20.

[56] Thurstone, L. L. and Jones, L., 'The Rational Origin for Measuring Subjective Values', *J. Amer. Stat. Assoc.* **52** (1957) 458–71.

[57] Gulliksen, H., 'Measurement of Subjective Values', *Psychometrika* **21** (1956) 229–44.

[58] Luce, R. D. and Suppes, P., 'Preference, Utility, and Subjective Probability', *Handbook of Mathematical Psychology*, Vol. III, Ch. 19, Wiley, 1965.

[59] Tversky, A., 'Elimination by Aspects: A Theory of Choice', *Psychological Review* **79** (1972) 281–99.

[60] Tversky, A., 'Intransitivity of Preferences', *Psychological Review* **76** (1969) 31–48.

[61] DeGroot, M. H., 'Optimal Allocation of Observations', *Annals of the Institute of Statistical Mathematics*, **18** (1966) 13–28.

8

BINARY-CHOICE CONSTRAINTS AND RANDOM UTILITY INDICATORS*

(1960)

I. THE PROBLEM

This paper contains suggestions for combining various available types of information on economic choice. There are in the main three types.

(i) Controlled experiments on choices from small sets (usually pairs) of alternatives.

(ii) Surveys of consumers' choices from large sets of alternatives, each set being determined by the market prices and by each consumer's monetary resources; similar surveys (*mutatis mutandis*) of producers' choices are also available, especially in the case of farmers.

(iii) Time series of total consumption (or production) of individual commodities, total incomes, and market prices, over a given geographical area.

Various researchers (Marschak [16], and more recently Tobin [19], Wold [22], and Farrell [9]) have tried to combine information on (ii) and (iii). The present paper deals with combining the materials in (i) and (ii), albeit only to the extent of outlining the general problem and of concluding with an example.

Suppose that, given a set of consumers' budgets at varying prices, we want to estimate a function on the commodity space that might be used as a utility indicator (defining a system of 'indifference surfaces') to describe the tastes of the sampled group of people. The desired statistical estimation will usually be preceded by the 'specification' of a class of eligible functions on the commodity space. The continuity and convexity ('diminishing marginal satisfaction') properties postulated in economic theory, partly in connection with its requirement of 'consumer's equilibrium', permit such specification only within very broad limits.

Suppose, however, that, in addition to the consumers' survey data, laboratory data are available that imply that the choices being made by people of a given socio-economic group obey certain constraints. The knowledge of these constraints might provide help in further restricting the set of eligible utility indicators.

It will be realistic to assume that a man's choice from a given set of alternatives is not unique but obeys some probability distribution. This agrees with the approach usual in psychometrics and psychophysics, and may also explain a part of the statistical variations in economic survey data. Accordingly, our approach will be 'stochastic' throughout. We shall study the logical connections between different behavior assumptions made in stochastic theories of decision.

II. BINARY-CHOICE PROBABILITIES

Unless specified to the contrary, all concepts in this paper are associated with a single given person, the 'subject' of experiments. The only experiments considered in this paper – except for cursory remarks on other kinds of experiments, especially in Sections IV, V, and XI – are *binary choices:* the subject is forced to choose one of the pair (x, y) of alternatives. On the other hand, the data resulting from a consumer survey are, of course, *multiple choices* since a consumer's monetary resources permit him, given the prices of goods, to choose from among more than a pair of alternative budgets.

The following notation will be used:

$\boldsymbol{X}$, the set of *alternatives*, with generic elements $x, y, \ldots,$.

n, the number of elements of $\boldsymbol{X}$ when $\boldsymbol{X}$ is finite; in this case the elements will be identified by integers: $\boldsymbol{X}=(1, \ldots, n)$.

$\boldsymbol{p}$, the class of functions p on $\boldsymbol{X} \times \boldsymbol{X}$ (or, with $\boldsymbol{X}$ finite, the set of matrices $p=[p_{xy}]$) such that

$$(1) \qquad p_{xy} = 1 - p_{yx} \geqq 0\,.$$

Hence $p_{xx}=\frac{1}{2}$. When $x \neq y$, the function p_{xy} is called the *probability of a binary choice, viz.*, of the choice of x out of the subset (x, y) of $\boldsymbol{X}$. A region $\boldsymbol{p}_C \subseteq \boldsymbol{p}$ defines a condition (C) on all $\boldsymbol{p}_{xy}$ and is called a *binary-choice constraint*. It will be convenient to identify such constraints, and other conditions, by symbols in parentheses, thus: (C).

Binary-choice constraints involving no other quantities but the p_{xy} are called *directly testable*: it will be assumed that they can be accepted or rejected, in the sense of statistical inference, on the basis of binary-choice experiments. (However, except in the case of finite X and very large samples permitting the approximation of each p_{xy} by the corresponding observed frequency, difficult statistical problems that cannot be treated here present themselves, but see [1, Section 10].) Constraints on the p_{xy} that are not 'directly testable' involve in particular the existence of the variously defined 'utilities', a theoretical construct. It will be important to find which of the 'directly testable' constraints imply or are implied by the existence of 'utilities' in the various senses of this term.

EXAMPLE. Let $X=(1, 2, 3)$. A function p is completely described by any six numbers p_{xy} obeying (1). The relation $1 \leqq p_{12}+p_{23}+p_{31} \leqq 2$ exemplifies a binary-choice constraint. It is 'directly testable' and is implied by certain 'utility' statements, as will be seen in Section VI.

III. RANDOM UTILITY INDICATOR

A probability measure on the set of real-valued functions on X defines a real-valued random function on X (a random vector if X is finite); its values are random numbers.

DEFINITION. $U^{(2)}$, *a real-valued random function on* X, *is called a* random utility indicator 'in the binary sense' *if, for every* $x \neq y$,

$$\Pr(U_x^{(2)} \geqq U_y^{(2)}) = p_{xy}. \tag{2}$$

(The idea goes back to Thurstone's 'law of comparative judgment' [18].)

It follows that if F is a random utility indicator in the binary sense, and G is a strictly increasing transform of F (that is, $F_x \geqq F_y$ if and only if $G_x \geqq G_y$, for all x, y), then G is also a random utility indicator in the binary sense.

The following theorem was suggested by M. DeGroot:

THEOREM 1. *If* $U^{(2)}$ *is a random utility indicator in the binary sense, then* $\Pr(U_x^{(2)} = U_y^{(2)}) = 0$ *for every* $x \neq y$.

Proof. Let $x \neq y$ and suppose $\Pr(U_x^{(2)} = U_y^{(2)}) > 0$. Then

$$\begin{aligned} p_{xy} + p_{yx} &= \Pr(U_x^{(2)} \geqq U_y^{(2)}) + \Pr(U_y^{(2)} \geqq U_x^{(2)}) = \\ &= \Pr(U_x^{(2)} > U_y^{(2)}) + \Pr(U_y^{(2)} > U_x^{(2)}) + \\ &\quad + 2\Pr(U_x^{(2)} = U_y^{(2)}) = \end{aligned}$$

$$\begin{aligned}&= \{\Pr(U_x^{(2)} > U_y^{(2)}) + \Pr(U_y^{(2)} > U_x^{(2)}) + \\ &\quad + \Pr(U_x^{(2)} = U_y^{(2)})\} + \Pr(U_x^{(2)} = U_y^{(2)}) = \\ &= 1 + \Pr(U_x^{(2)} = U_y^{(2)}) > 1,\end{aligned}$$

contradicting (1).

EXAMPLES. (i) Let $X=(1, 2, 3)$; then $U^{(2)}$ is a random utility indicator if the six numbers $\Pr(U_x^{(2)})$ are respectively equal to the six numbers p_{xy} which (or some constraints on which) are obtained from observations.

(ii) Let X denote the real m-space with generic point $x=(x_1,\ldots, x_m)$; let $T=(T_1,\ldots, T_m)$ be a random vector such that $0<T_i<1$ $(i=1,\ldots, m)$ and $\sum T_i=1$. Let

$$U_x^{(2)} = \prod_{i=1}^{m} x_i^{T_i} \tag{3}$$

(the 'Cobb-Douglas function' frequently used in economics, with X being the commodity space). If $\Pr(U_x^{(2)} \geqq U_y^{(2)})=p_{xy}$, then $U^{(2)}$ is a random utility indicator 'in the binary sense'. This example will be used again in Section XII.

CONDITION $(U^{(2)})$. The function p is such that $U^{(2)}$ exists.

IV. A REMARK ON MULTIPLE-CHOICE PROBABILITIES

The concepts and the condition just defined can be easily generalized to multiple-choice probabilities. For every $x \in X^*$ and $X^* \subseteq X$, one defines $p_x(X^*)$, obeying

$$p_x(X^*) \geqq 0, \qquad \sum_{x \in X^*} p_x(X^*) = 1. \tag{4}$$

The number $p_x(X^*)$ is interpreted as the probability that the subject, forced to choose from the subset X^*, will choose x. Clearly, p_{xy} is a special case, with $X^*=(x, y)$. The following condition exemplifies an important and plausible constraint that would be directly testable if multiple choices from subsets of various sizes were observable:

$$\text{if} \quad x \in X^{**} \subseteq X^* \subseteq X, \quad \text{then} \quad p_x(X^*) \leqq p_x(X^{**}). \tag{5}$$

In [1], Block and Marschak dealt with multiple-choice probabilities, and had accordingly used the following definition of the random utility indicator, stronger than the one given in Section III:

DEFINITION. *U, a random function on $\mathbf{X}$, is a* random utility indicator *if, for all $\mathbf{X}^* \subseteq \mathbf{X}$,*

$$\text{(6)} \qquad \Pr(U_x \geqq U_y, \quad y \in \mathbf{X}^*) = p_x(\mathbf{X}^*).$$

Correspondingly, Condition $(U^{(2)})$ is replaced by the stronger

CONDITION (U). The set of probabilities $p_x(\mathbf{X}^*)$, where $x \in \mathbf{X}^*$ and $\mathbf{X}^* \subseteq \mathbf{X}$ is such that U, in the sense of (6), exists.

Clearly, Condition (U) implies $(U^{(2)})$ and also implies (5).

Some other properties of U will be used later, in Section XI. However, because of experimental difficulties with large subsets of alternatives, it seems worthwhile to devote a special and intensive study to binary-choice probabilities. They cover much of the existing materials on human responses, and many practical situations ('pairwise comparisons'). Moreover, the following needs no proof:

THEOREM 2. *If the p_{xy} admit the existence of a function $U^{(2)}$ satisfying Condition $(U^{(2)})$, then, for every $x \in \mathbf{X}^*$* and *$\mathbf{X}^* \subseteq \mathbf{X}$, there exists a number $q_x(\mathbf{X}^*) \geqq 0$ such that, putting $p_x(\mathbf{X}^*) = q_x(\mathbf{X}^*)$ and $U = U^{(2)}$, condition* (6) *is satisfied.*

That is, Condition $(U^{(2)})$ guarantees the existence of numbers which, if they were the observed multiple-choice probabilities, would satisfy Condition (U).

Except in Section XI, it will not be assumed in this paper that constraints on non-binary-choice probabilities – such as (5) – can be inferred from observations.

V. PROBABILITY OF RANKING

Similarly, and possibly on still stronger grounds, no reference will be made in this paper to experiments in which the subject is requested, not to make an actual choice but to rank three or more alternatives according to his preferences (with two alternatives, choosing and ranking may be regarded as identical). It will not be assumed that responses obtained in such experiments are in any sense consistent with choices of single alternatives from subsets. To be sure, we shall use the term 'probability of ranking', but not to denote a number that is estimated (or, more generally, whose properties are inferred) from experiments on ranking. Rather, we give the following definition:

DEFINITION. *If* $U^{(2)}$ *is a random utility indicator, then, for any* $x_1, x_2, \ldots, x_m$ *in* $\boldsymbol{X}$, *the number*

$$(7) \qquad P(x_1 x_2 \ldots x_m) = \Pr(U^{(2)}_{x_1} > U^{(2)}_{x_2} > + > U^{(2)}_{x_m})$$

is called the probability of the ranking *(permutation)* $x_1 x_2 \ldots x_m$. *It follows that* $P(xy) = p_{xy}$.

THEOREM 3. *If* $(U)^{(2)})$ *is satisfied and* $\boldsymbol{X}^* = \boldsymbol{M} = (1, \ldots, m)$ *is a finite subset of* $\boldsymbol{X}$, *then for any* $i, j \in \boldsymbol{M}$,

$$(8) \qquad p_{ij} = \sum_{r \in R_{ij}} P(r),$$

where $\boldsymbol{R}_{ij}$ *is the set of all rankings r on* $\boldsymbol{M}$ *in which i precedes j.*

Proof. By (2), (7).

THEOREM 4. $(U^{(2)})$ *is satisfied for* $\boldsymbol{X}$ *finite,* $\boldsymbol{X} = \boldsymbol{N} = (1, \ldots, n)$, *if there is a non-negative function P on the set of rankings r on N such that equation* (8) *holds, provided* $\boldsymbol{R}_{ij}$ *is redefined as the set of all rankings on* $\boldsymbol{N}$ *in which i precedes j.*

Proof. Denote by $r = 1_r 2_r \ldots n_r$ the ranking in which the ith place is occupied by i_r. Then, by (7)

$$P(r) = P(1_r 2_r \ldots n_r) = \Pr(U^{(2)}_{1_r} > U^{(2)}_{2_r} > + > U^{2)}_{n_r},$$

and by (8) the condition (2) is satisfied.

VI. A CONDITION FOR EXISTENCE OF A RANDOM UTILITY INDICATOR

CONDITION (Δ) ['triangular']. For all x, y, z in $\boldsymbol{X}$,

$$(9) \qquad p_{xy} + p_{yz} \geqq p_{xz}.$$

By virtue of (1), this can be rewritten more symmetrically as

$$(9a) \qquad 1 \leqq p_{xy} + p_{yz} + p_{zx} \leqq 2.$$

Define

$$(10)\qquad \Delta_{xyz} = p_{xy} + p_{yz} + p_{zx} - 1\,;$$

then by (1), $\Delta_{xyz} + \Delta_{zyx} = 1$; and (9a) can be rewritten as

$$(9b)\qquad 0 \leqq \Delta_{xyz} \leqq 1\,.$$

Condition(Δ) was probably first noticed by Guilbaud [13].

THEOREM 5. ($U^{(2)}$) *implies* (Δ). [*And therefore, clearly,* (U) *also implies* (Δ).]

Proof. Denote by x, y, z the generic elements of the subset (1, 2, 3) of X. Then, by the definition (7), the six $P(xyz)$ add up to 1, and each is greater than or equal to 0. If ($U^{(2)}$) is true, then, by Theorem 3,

$$(11)\qquad \begin{aligned} p_{12} &= P(132) + P(123) + P(312)\,,\\ p_{23} &= P(123) + P(213) + P(231)\,,\\ p_{31} &= P(312) + P(231) + P(321)\,. \end{aligned}$$

In (11) the sum of the left sides is $\Delta_{123} + 1$; on the right side, the three off-diagonal terms of the symmetric matrix add up to s, say, where $0 \leqq s \leqq 1$; and all nine terms add up to $1 + s$. Hence

$$0 \leqq \Delta_{123} = s = P(123) + P(231) + P(312) \leqq 1\,,$$

and (9b) is satisfied.

THEOREM 6. *If* $X = (1, 2, 3)$, *then* (Δ) *implies* ($U^{(2)}$).[1]

Proof. Denote by x, y, z the generic elements of X. We shall show that, for any six numbers p_{xy} satisfying (1) and such that $0 \leqq \Delta_{123} = p_{12} + p_{21} + p_{31} - 1$, one can find six numbers $P(xyz)$, non-negative, adding up to 1, and satisfying (11). We have just seen that if $\sum_{xyz} P(xyz) = 1$, then (11) implies

$$(12)\qquad \Delta_{123} = P(123 + P(231) + P(312)\,.$$

Subtracting (12) from each of the equations (11), we obtain

$$(13)\qquad \begin{aligned} p_{12} - \Delta_{123} &= P(132) - P(231)\,,\\ p_{23} - \Delta_{123} &= P(213) - P(312)\,,\\ p_{31} - \Delta_{123} &= P(321) - P(123)\,. \end{aligned}$$

Put $0=P(231)$ or $P(132)$ according as $p_{12} \geqq$ or $\leqq \Delta_{123}$; put $0=P(312)$ or $P(213)$ according as $p_{23} \geqq$ or $\leqq \Delta_{123}$. Substituting into (13) and (12), one obtains the remaining four $P(xyz)$, non-negative and adding up to 1. Hence, by Theorem 4, $(U^{(2)})$ is satisfied.

AN ALTERNATIVE PROOF OF THEOREM 5. A probability distribution on the set of rankings on $\boldsymbol{X}=(1,\ldots,n)$ is a vector P whose components $P(r^k)$, where $k=1,\ldots,n!$, are non-negative and add up to 1. The set $\boldsymbol{P}$ of all such vectors is convex and has $n!-1$ dimensions and $n!$ vertices. The vertex P_k shall represent the distribution in which $P(r^k)=1$. Suppose $(U^{(2)})$ holds and let $[p_{xy}(P)]$ be the $n\times n$ matrix of binary probabilities generated by P in $\boldsymbol{P}$. Consider the vertex P_k of $\boldsymbol{P}$ and denote by r_x^k the rank assigned to x when the ranking is r^k. Then, for $x \neq y$,

$$p_{xy}(P_k) = \begin{cases} 1 & \text{if } r_x^k < r_y^k, \\ 0 & \text{if } r_x^k > r_y^k. \end{cases}$$

Let x, y, z be all distinct. Since $r_x^k < r_y^k$ and $r_y^k < r_z^k$ imply $r_z^k > r_x^k$, the triple

$$\{p_{xy}(P_k), p_{yz}(P_k), p_{zx}(P_k)\}$$

cannot consist of 1's only or of 0's only. Hence the sum of these three probabilities, for every ranking r^k, is either 1 or 2. Now, every vector P is a convex combination of the unit vectors P_k:

$$P = \sum P_k \cdot P(r^k) \qquad (\sum P(r^k) = 1; P(r^k) \geqq 0; k = 1, \ldots, n!)$$

and

$$p_{xy}(P) = \sum p_{xy}(P_k) \cdot P(r^k).$$

Hence every sum $p_{xy}(P)+p_{yz}(P)+p_{zx}(P)$ is a weighted average of the numbers 1 and 2, so that (Δ) is satisfied.

This proof was obtained after a conversation with Herman Chernoff, who had suggested the following way to prove (or disprove) the converse of Theorem 5.

CONVERSE OF THEOREM 5. Denote by $\boldsymbol{S_P}$ the set of all matrices $[p_{xy}]$ generated by the distributions P in $\boldsymbol{P}$; denote by $\boldsymbol{S_\Delta}$ the set of all matrices $[p_{xy}]$ satisfying (Δ). Each of these sets has $n(n-1)/2$ dimensions and is convex. $\boldsymbol{S_P}$ has $n!$ vertices, each corresponding to precisely one vertex of $\boldsymbol{P}$, and such that for x, y, z distinct, $p_{xy}=1$ or 0, and $p_{xy}+p_{yz}+$ $+p_{zx}=1$ or 2. Hence all vertices of $\boldsymbol{S_P}$ are elements and are, in fact vertices, of $\boldsymbol{S_\Delta}$, and (another way to state Theorem 5) $\boldsymbol{S_\Delta}$ contains $\boldsymbol{S_P}$. If it were possible to prove that all vertices of $\boldsymbol{S_\Delta}$ are vertices of $\boldsymbol{S_P}$, the converse of Theorem 5 would be proved for any n, thus extending Thcorem 6. We therefore register (but do not assert to be true!) the following

CONJECTURE 1. *For any finite* $\boldsymbol{X}$, *(Δ) implies* $(U^{(2)})$.[2]

While (Δ) is necessary for $(U^{(2)})$ and therefore for (U), and even if it were true that (Δ) is sufficient for $(U^{(2)})$, it is certainly not sufficient for (U) since (Δ) does not put any constraints on non-binary choices while (U) does [we have seen that (U) implies (5)]. Some sufficient conditions for $(U^{(2)})$ and (U), respectively, will be given in Sections X and XI.

VII. TRANSITIVITY OF STOCHASTIC PREFERENCES

DEFINITION. *Alternative* x *is* stochastically preferred (stochastically indifferent) *to* y *if* $p_{xy}>\frac{1}{2}$ $(p_{xy}=\frac{1}{2})$.

In what follows, the words 'transitivity of stochastic preferences' will be abbreviated to 'transitivity'.

CONDITIONS (t_w) [weak transitivity], (t_m) [mild transitivity], and (t_s) [strong transitivity.[3] If $\min(p_{xy}, p_{yz}) \geqq \frac{1}{2}$, then

$$p_{xz} \geqq \begin{cases} \frac{1}{2} & \text{Condition } (t_w), \\ \min(p_{xy}, p_{yz}) & \text{Condition } (t_m), \\ \max(p_{xy}, p_{yz}) & \text{Condition } (t_s). \end{cases}$$

Equivalently, by (1): if $\max(p_{xy}, p_{yz}) \leqq \frac{1}{2}$, then

$$p_{xz} \leqq \begin{cases} \frac{1}{2} & \text{Condition } (t_w), \\ \max(p_{xy}, p_{yz}) & \text{Condition } (t_m), \\ \min(p_{xy}, p_{yz}) & \text{Condition } (t_s). \end{cases}$$

A more symmetric equivalent form for (t_w) is, by (1),

$$\min(p_{xy}, p_{yz}, p_{zx}) \leqq \tfrac{1}{2} \leqq \max(p_{xy}, p_{yz}, p_{zx}).$$

THEOREM 7. *Condition* (t_s) *is equivalent to the following conditions: if* $p_{xy} \geqq \frac{1}{2}$, *then* $p_{xz} \geqq p_{yz}$, *for all* $z \in \boldsymbol{X}$; *and if* $z \in \boldsymbol{X}$ *and* $p_{xz} \geqq p_{yz}$, *then* $p_{xy} \geqq \frac{1}{2}$.

Proof. See [1], Theorem 4.1.

THEOREM 8. *Condition* (t_s) *is strictly stronger than* (t_m), *and* (t_m) *is strictly stronger than* (t_w).

Proof. Obvious.

THEOREM 9. *Condition* (t_w) *is neither sufficient nor necessary for* (Δ).

Proof. Let $n=3$, and $p_{13}=0.6$. If $p_{12}=p_{23}=0.9$, then (t_w) is satisfied but (Δ) is not. If $p_{12}=p_{23}=0.4$, then (Δ) is satisfied but (t_w) is not.

THEOREM 10. *Condition* (t_m) *is strictly stronger than* (Δ).

Proof. (i) Sufficiency. Consider $(1, 2, 3)\subseteq \boldsymbol{X}$. Using the notation of Section 6, we have to prove that (t_m) implies $0\leqq \Delta_{xyz}\leqq 1$. By (1) we can let $p_{12}\geqq p_{23}\geqq \frac{1}{2}\geqq p_{32}\geqq p_{21}$ without loss of generality; then

$$p_{12}+p_{23}\geqq 1\geqq p_{32}+p_{21}$$

$$p_{12}+p_{23}+p_{31}-1=\Delta_{123}\geqq 0,$$

$$1-\Delta_{123}=p_{21}+p_{32}+p_{13}-1=\Delta_{321}\leqq 1.$$

Now assume (t_m). Then

$$p_{31}\leqq \max(p_{32},p_{21})=p_{32},$$

$$\Delta_{123}\leqq p_{12}+p_{23}+p_{32}-1=p_{12}\leqq 1$$

and

$$p_{13}\geqq \min(p_{12},p_{23})=p_{12},$$

$$\Delta_{321}\geqq p_{21}+p_{32}+p_{12}-1=p_{32}\geqq 0.$$

(ii) No necessity. By Theorems 8, 9.

THEOREM 11. *Condition* (t_m) *is strictly stronger than the conjunction of* (t_w) *and* (Δ).

Proof. (i) Sufficiency. By Theorems 8, 10. (ii) No necessity. Let $\boldsymbol{X}=$ $=(1, 2, 3)$, $p_{12}=.8$. $p_{23}=.7$, and $p_{31}=.4$. Then (t_w) and (Δ) are satisfied. But since $p_{12}>p_{23}>.5$ while $p_{13}=.6<p_{23}$, Condition (t_m) is violated.

Write $\rightarrow$ for 'implies', $\leftrightarrow$ for 'implies and is implied by, $\mapsto$ for 'implies but is not implied by', $\vdash\!\dashv$ for 'does not imply nor is implied by'. Then our results can be summarized in

THEOREM 12.

$$\begin{array}{ccccccc} & & (t_s) & \mapsto & (t_m) & \mapsto & (t_w, \Delta) \\ & & & & & & \downarrow\!\!\!\!\!\!\!\;\bar{} \\ (\Delta; n=3) & \mapsto & (U^{(2)}) & \rightarrow & (\Delta) & \vdash\!\dashv & (t_w). \\ & & \uparrow & & & & \\ & & (U) & & & & \end{array}$$

In political science the fact that Condition ($U^{(2)}$) does not imply Condition (t_w) is interpreted as 'intransitivity of the majority rule'. It was pointed out by Kenneth Arrow. We have shown in [1, Theorem 3.2] that even the stronger Condition (U) does not imply (t_w).

VIII. WEAK UTILITY FUNCTION

DEFINITION. *A real-valued function* w *on* X *is called a* weak utility function *if* $w_x \geqq w_y$ when and only when $p_{xy} \geqq \frac{1}{2}$.

CONDITION (w). The function p is such that w exists. It follows that w is unique up to an increasing monotone transformation.

THEOREM 13. $(w) \mapsto (t_w)$.

Proof. (i) Sufficiency. Let $p_{ab} \geqq \frac{1}{2}$, $p_{bc} \geqq \frac{1}{2}$, $a, b, c \in X$. If (w) is true, then $w_a \geqq w_b \geqq w_c$ and $p_{ac} \geqq \frac{1}{2}$. (ii) No necessity, Let X be a real 2-space with generic points $x = (x_1, x_2)$ and assume that $p_{xy} > \frac{1}{2}$ when either $x_1 > y_1$ or $x_1 = y_1$ and $x_2 > y_2$ (lexicographical ordering). Compare Debreu [6].

CONDITION (D). X is perfectly separable (i.e., contains a countable and dense subset); and for every a in X, the sets $(x \mid p_{xa} \geqq \frac{1}{2})$ and $(x \mid p_{xa} \leqq \frac{1}{2})$ are closed. This is adapted from Debreu's paper just cited, which also contains, *mutatis mutandis*, the proof of

THEOREM 14. *If* (D) *is satisfied, then* (w) *and* (t_w) *are equivalent.*

REMARK. Condition (D) is trivially satisfied on X finite. Moreover, every subset of a finite-dimensional real space is perfectly separable; and it is reasonable to assume that Condition (D) is satisfied on a commodity space.

We summarize some of the previous results in

THEOREM 15.

$$\begin{array}{ccccccccc} (t_w;\, n \text{ finite}) & \mapsto & (t_w, D) & \mapsto & (w) & \mapsto & (t_w) & & \\ & & & & & & \updownarrow & & \\ (\Delta;\, n=3) & \mapsto & U^{(2)} & \rightarrow & (\Delta) & \leftarrow\!\shortmid & (t_w, \Delta) & \leftarrow\!\shortmid\, (t_m) & \leftarrow\!\shortmid\, (t_s) \end{array}$$

IX. STRONG UTILITY FUNCTION

DEFINITION. *A real-valued function* v *on* $\boldsymbol{X}$ *is called a* strong utility function *if there exists a monotone increasing function* ϕ_v *such that*

$$\phi_v(v_x - v_y) = p_{xy};\ \phi_v(0) = \tfrac{1}{2}. \tag{14}$$

CONDITION (v). The function p is such that v exists.

THEOREM 16. *If* $\boldsymbol{X}$ *is continuous and* ϕ_v *is strictly monotone, then* (i) v *is unique up to an increasing linear transformation, and* (ii) *for any real number* λ

$$\phi_v(\lambda) + \phi_v(-\lambda) = 1. \tag{15}$$

Proof. For (i), see [1, Section II]; (ii) is obvious.

Equation (15) implies that ϕ_v is anti-symmetrical about $(0, \frac{1}{2})$; the median and the mean (if it exists) are 0.

The strong utility v_x of alternative x corresponds to the 'sensation' produced by a stimulus x, as defined by Fechner [10] in 1859. It also corresponds to the relative position of a gene in the chromosome when inferred from the probability of a 'crossover': this generation of a real line from a set of probabilities was noticed by D. Hilbert.[4]

CONDITION (q) [quadruple condition]. For any x, y, z, t in $\boldsymbol{X}$,

$$\text{if} \quad p_{xy} \geqq p_{zt}, \quad \text{then} \quad p_{xz} \geqq p_{yt}. \tag{16}$$

THEOREM 17. *Condition* (v) *implies Condition* (q) [*Proof.* By monotonicity of ϕ_v]; *Condition* (q) *implies Condition* (t_s) [*Proof.* In (16) put $z=t$ and use Theorem 7]; *Condition* (v) *implies Condition* (w) [*Proof.* In (14), put $v=w$].

THEOREM 18. *If* $\boldsymbol{X}$ *is finite,* $\boldsymbol{X}=(1,\dots, n)$, *then* ($q$) *implies* ($v$) *only for* $n \leqq 4$.

Proof. See [1], Proof of Theorem 4. 1.

For $\boldsymbol{X}$ continuous it is useful to consider the following

CONDITION ($s \cdot c$) ['stochastic continuity']. If $p_{xy} < q < p_{xz}$, then there is a t in $\boldsymbol{X}$ such that $p_{xt} = q$. In [7] Debreu has proved

THEOREM 19. *If Condition* $(s \cdot c)$ *is satisfied, then* (q) *implies* (v).

If both $(U^{(2)})$ and (v) are satisfied, we can define a random function V_x by

$$(17) \qquad U_x^{(2)} = v_x + V_x, \qquad EV_x = 0,$$

and set up the following three conditions, each stronger than the preceding one:

There exist two functions on X, a real-valued v and a random-valued V, and a distribution function ϕ_v such that

$$p_{xy} = \phi_v(v_x - v_y), \qquad \Pr(V_y - V_x \leqq \lambda) = \phi_v(\lambda),$$

where

CONDITION (V): $\lambda = v_x - v_y$;

CONDITION (V'): $\lambda =$ any real number;

CONDITION (V''): $\Pr(V_x \leqq \alpha,\ V_y \leqq \beta) = \Pr(V_x \leqq \beta,\ V_y \leqq \alpha)$, $\lambda, \alpha, \beta =$ any real numbers.

In Condition (V) the distribution of the differences $V_x - V_y$ is defined only for each pair of alternatives (possibly finite in number); in (V') this distribution is defined for any real argument; in (V''), in addition, the (multivariate) distribution function of V is symmetrical in its arguments. From (17) and Theorem 16 one obtains

THEOREM 20.

$$(V'') \mapsto (V') \mapsto (V) \leftrightarrow (U^{(2)}, v) \quad \textit{if} \quad X \textit{ is finite};$$
$$(V'') \mapsto (V') \leftrightarrow (V) \leftrightarrow (U^{(2)}, v) \quad \textit{if} \quad X \textit{ is continuous}.$$

In the work of Thurstone and his school a condition even stronger than (V'') is used: the distribution function of V is assumed to be normal and symmetric (zero means, equal variances, equal covariances). Actually, a normal distribution of differences ϕ_v (as assumed by Fechner) is consistent also with a normal distribution of V non-symmetrical in its arguments.

For possible application to the commodity space some of our results can be summarized in

THEOREM 21. *If X is continuous and the conditions* (D) *and* ($s \cdot c$) *are satisfied, then*

$$\begin{array}{ccccccccccccc}
(V'') & \mapsto & (V') & \leftrightarrow & (U^{(2)}, v) & \mapsto & (v) & \leftrightarrow & (q) & \mapsto & (t_s) & \mapsto & (t_w) \\
 & & & & \downarrow & & & & & & \downarrow & & \updownarrow \\
 & & & & (U^{(2)}) & & \longrightarrow & & & & (\Delta) & \mapsfrom & (w).
\end{array}$$

X. STRICT UTILITY FUNCTION (IN THE 'BINARY' SENSE)

DEFINITION. *A* positive-valued function $u^{(2)}$ on X *is called a* strict utility function (in the 'binary' sense) *if.*

$$(18) \qquad p_{xy} = \frac{u_x^{(2)}}{u_x^{(2)} + u_y^{(2)}}.$$

Clearly, every positive multiple of a strict utility function is also a strict utility function.

CONDITION ($u^{(2)}$). The function p is such that $u^{(2)}$ exists. Applying (18) one obtains

THEOREM 22. *Condition* ($u^{(2)}$) *is true only if* (i) $0 < p_{xy} < 1$ *for every x, y in X, and* (ii) *for any subset* $(1, \ldots, m) \subseteq X$ $(m > 1)$, *the following equation holds*:

$$(19) \qquad p_{12} \cdot p_{23} \cdots p_{m-1,\, m} \cdot p_{m1} = p_{21} \cdot p_{32} \cdots p_{m,\, m-1} \cdot p_{1m}.$$

Note that (19) is 'directly testable'. Condition ($u^{(2)}$) was formulated by Törnqvist [20], Bradley and Terry [3], and L. R. Ford [11]. It is a weak form of a postulate that has been proposed by Luce [15] and that involves multiple-choice probabilities: see Section XI below.

THEOREM 23. $(u^{(2)}) \mapsto (v)$.

Proof. (i) Necessity. Put $u_y^{(2)} = e^{v_y}$; then by (18) $p_{xy} = \phi_v(v_x - v_y)$, where

$$(20) \qquad \phi_v(\lambda) = \frac{1}{1 + e^{-\lambda}},$$

the 'logistic curve'. (ii) No sufficiency. For X continuous, by the above proof of necessity (due to Luce) and by Theorem 16, we see that Condition

($u^{(2)}$) is not implied by (v), since ($u^{(2)}$) restricts the function ϕ_v to the form (20). For X finite, let

$$(21)\qquad X = (1, 2, 3); \qquad p_{12} = .6, \qquad p_{23} = .7, \qquad p_{13} = .8.$$

Then (v) is satisfied[5] by $v_1 = .3$, $v_2 = .2$, $v_3 = .0$, and $\phi_v(\lambda) = .5 + \lambda$. But (19), and therefore ($u^{(2)}$), is not.

THEOREM 24. *If X is finite, then ($u^{(2)}$) implies ($U^{(2)}$).*

Proof. We shall use an arithmetical identity proved in [1, Theorem 3.6] and [8]:

LEMMA. *Let $N = (1, \ldots, n)$ and denote by $r = (1_r 2_r \ldots n_r)$ the permutation on N in which the kth place is occupied by the element k_r; denote by R_{iM} the set of permutations on N in which i precedes all other elements of $M \subseteq N$. Then, for any positive $u_1, \ldots, u_n$,*

$$(22)\qquad \frac{u_i}{\sum_{h \in M} u_h} \equiv \sum_{r \in R_{iM}} \prod_{j=1} \frac{u_{j_r}}{\sum_{k=j}^{n} u_{k_r}}.$$

To prove Theorem 24 from this Lemma let $X = N$, $M = (i, j)$, $u_x = u_x^{(2)}$; then by (18) the left side of (22) becomes p_{ij}, and the set $R_{iM} = R_{ij}$, as defined in Theorem 3. Since each of the products on the right side is positive and they add up to p_{ij}, we can equate each of them to a probability of ranking in the sense of (7), so that, for any ranking r on N,

$$(23)\qquad P(r) = P(1_r 2_r \ldots n_r) = \frac{u_{1_r}}{u_{1_r} + + + u_{n_r}} \cdot \frac{u_{2_r}}{u_{2_r} + + + u_{n_r}} \cdots$$
$$\cdots \frac{u_{(n-1)_r}}{u_{(n-1)_r} + u_{n_r}}.$$

Since we interpret each u_i as $u^{(2)}$, then by Theorem 4 ($U^{(2)}$) is satisfied.

If X is continuous, the reasoning just used can be applied to any finite subset of X. Hence the following

CONJECTURE 2. *Theorem 24 applies to any X.*

Remark. The proof of Theorem 24 could be much simplified if Conjecture 1 (Section VI) were proved to be true. For it would then suffice to prove that ($u^{(2)}$) implies (Δ). This is indeed the case: for, writing

$u_y^{(2)}/u_x^{(2)}=a$, $u_z^{(2)}/u_y^{(2)}=b$, and $u_x^{(2)}/u_z^{(2)}=c$, we have $abc=1$, and by (10), (18), we obtain

$$(24) \qquad 0 < \Delta_{xyz} = \frac{1}{1+a} + \frac{1}{1+b} + \frac{1}{1+c} - 1 = \frac{1}{1+k} < 1,$$

where $k=(1+ab+bc+ca)/(1+a+b+c)>0$, since $a, b, c>0$.

THEOREM 25. *$(U^{(2)})$ does not imply $(u^{(2)})$.*

Proof: Consider again example (21). Since $p_{31}=.2$, it follows that $\Delta_{123}=.5$; hence Condition (Δ) and, by Theorem 6, Condition $(U^{(2)})$ are satisfied. But (19) is not.

Since example (21) was seen to satisfy (v), Theorem 25 can be replaced by the even stronger

THEOREM 26. *The conjunction of $(U^{(2)})$ and (v) does not imply $(u^{(2)})$.*

Some of the results of this and the preceding section can be summarized in

THEOREM 27. *For X finite,*

$$\begin{array}{ccccccccccccc} (u^{(2)}) & \mapsto & [(U^{(2)}),(v)] & \mapsto & (v) & \mapsto & (q) & \mapsto & (t_s) & \mapsto & (t_w) & \leftrightarrow & (w) \\ & & \swarrow & & & & & & & \updownarrow & & & \\ & (U^{(2)}) & & & \longrightarrow & & & & & (\Delta). & & & \end{array}$$

Remark on the commodity space. If Condition (D) is satisfied on the continuous commodity space and if Conjecture 2 is correct, Theorem 27 applies also to the commodity space; if, in addition, $(s \cdot c)$ is satisfied, then $(v) \leftrightarrow (q)$.

XI. SOME RESULTS ON MULTIPLE-CHOICE PROBABILITIES

In Section IV, the Condition (U) was stated. Clearly, (U) implies $(U^{(2)})$. Similarly, $(u^{(2)})$ can be replaced by the following stronger

CONDITION (u). There exists a positive-valued function u on $\boldsymbol{X}$ such that for any finite subset $\boldsymbol{M}=(x_1,\ldots, x_m)\subseteq \boldsymbol{X}$, the multiple-choice probability

$$(25) \qquad p_{x_i}(M) = \frac{u_i}{\sum_{j \in M} u_j}.$$

The function u may be called a *strict utility function in the multiple-choice sense.*

As was proved in [1], (u) implies that the probability of each ranking in the multiple-choice sense, defined as

$$P(r) = \Pr(U_{1_r} > U_{2_r} > \cdots > U_{n_r}), \quad \text{with} \quad \sum_{R_{iM}} P(r) = p_i(M),$$

exists and is precisely the expression on the right side of (23). For example, if $X = (1, 2, 3)$, then

$$(26) \qquad P(xyz) = \frac{u_x}{u_x + u_y + u_z} \cdot \frac{u_y}{u_y + u_z} = p_x(X) \cdot p_y(y, z),$$

by (25). Thus (u) implies (and, as shown in [1], is equivalent to) the proposition that the probability of a given ranking of a finite set of alternatives is the product of probabilities of multiple choices made successively, from the set itself, then from the subset remaining after eliminating the first choice, then from the subset remaining after eliminating the second choice, etc. Applying the Lemma of Section X we obtain, using (25),

THEOREM 28. $(u) \to (U)$ *when* X *is finite.*

This result is discussed in more detail in [1]. We can prove the even stronger

THEOREM 29. $(u) \mapsto [(U), (v)]$ *when* X *is finite.*

Proof. (i) Necessity. By Theorems 28 and 23, remembering that (u) of course implies ($u^{(2)}$). (ii) No sufficiency. Note that for $X = (1, 2, 3)$, condition (u) implies, by (19) and (26) respectively,

$$(27) \qquad p_{12} \cdot p_{23} \cdot p_{31} = p_{13} \cdot p_{32} \cdot p_{21},$$

and

$$(28) \qquad P(123) \cdot P(231) \cdot P(312) = P(213) \cdot P(132) \cdot P(321).$$

Moreover, (U) implies $p_{xy} = P(xyz) + P(xzy) + P(zxy)$ and $p_x(X) = P(xyz) + P(xzy)$. It is easy to construct examples satisfying (v) and (U) but not (27) or (28). For example, use (21), which we have seen satisfies (v) and which contradicts (27); and put, in addition, the following values: for the probabilities of ranking, $P(123) = P(132) = .3$, $P(231) = P(213) = .2$, $P(312) = P(321) = 0$; for the ternary probabilities, $p_1(X) = .6$, $p_2(X) = .4$, and $p_3(X)=0$. The foregoing results, together with some obtained in the previous section, can be summarized in

THEOREM 30.

$$\begin{array}{ccccc} (u) & \mapsto & [(U),(v)] & \mapsto & (U) \\ \downarrow & & \downarrow & & \downarrow \\ (u^{(2)}) & \mapsto & [(U^{(2)}),(v)] & \mapsto & (U^{(2)}) \\ & & \downarrow & & \downarrow \\ & & (v) & \mapsto & (\Delta) \end{array}$$

Luce [15] proposed a condition still stronger than (u), being a conjunction of (u) and the following

CONDITION (u'). Denote by $p'_x(X^*)$ the probability that x is the *last* choice out of the subset $X^* \subseteq X$. There exists a real-valued function u' on X such that for any finite subset $M=(x_i, \ldots, x_m) \subseteq X$, the probability

$$p'_{x_i}(M) = \frac{u'_i}{\sum_{j \in M} u'_j}.$$

The function u' may be called a *strict disutility function.* However, apart from trivial cases, the functions u and u' cannot both exist:

THEOREM 31. *Conditions* (u) *and* (u') *can both hold only if all first choices are equally probable and all last choices are equally probable, or if* X *has only two elements.*

Proof. If $n \geqq 3$, let $M \subseteq X$ consist of three elements, to be denoted generically by x, y, z. Assume both Conditions (u) and (u'). Without loss of generality, let $u_x+u_y+u_z=1=u'_x+u'_y+u'_z$, so that $p_x(M)=u_x$, $p'_x(M)=u'_x$, for all x in M. Then

$$u_x \cdot \frac{u'_z}{1-u'_x} = u'_z \cdot \frac{u_x}{1-u_z}, \quad \text{all} \quad x, z \text{ in } M,$$

since both the left and the right side express the probability of the same event, viz., of x being the first, and z the last choice. Hence $u'_x=u_z$, $p'_x(M)=p_z(M)$ for any pair x, z of the arbitrary three-elements subset M. Interchanging variables x, y, z, and applying (u), (u'),

$$p'_x(X)p_y(=X) = p'_y(X) = p_x(X), \quad \text{all} \quad x, y \text{ in } X.$$

This proves the Theorem for $n \geqq 3$. When $n=2$, the same reasoning yields trivially the identity $p_x(x, y) = p'_y(x, y)$. For a more detailed proof see [1, Theorem 3.8].

It has been pointed out by Luce (in private correspondence) that while in experiments on choices the probabilities of last choices may or may not be accessible to observations, they definitely are in experiments on perceptions: the subject's decision as to which is the loudest of three sounds is as observable as his decision as to which sound is the softest. If one accepts (u), symmetry requires one to accept (u') also. But, as we have shown, these two conditions are mutually inconsistent.

Therefore, we must limit ourselves to the weaker Condition ($u^{(2)}$). It involves binary choices only, so that, when identifying the loudest sound, the subject identifies also the softest. That is, if the subset $\boldsymbol{X}^*$ consists of two elements, then Conditions ($u^{(2)}$), (u), and (u') are identical. A strict utility function in this limited sense – $u^{(2)}$ rather than u – is compatible with the existence of the corresponding strict disutility function and of a random utility indicator $U^{(2)}$ involving binary choices only. *Added in* 1973: See now Luce and Suppes [23], especially p. 358.

XII. BINARY-CHOICE CONSTRAINTS AND THE FORM OF THE RANDOM UTILITY INDICATOR

Consider Example (ii) of Section III, and let $m=2$, $0 < T_1 = A < 1$, and $T_2 = 1 - A$. Then

$$(29) \qquad U_x^{(2)} = x_1^A x_2^{1-A};$$

the function $U^{(2)}$ is monotone increasing in x in the sense that if $x = (x_1, x_2)$, $y = (y_1, y_2)$, $x_1 \geqq y_1$, and $x_2 > y_2$, then $U_x^{(2)} > U_y^{(2)}$ is a random function depending on the random parameter A.[6] If $U^{(2)}$ is a utility indicator in the 'binary' sense of (2), then $p_{xy} = \Pr(U_x^{(2)} \geqq U_y^{(2)} = \Pr(y_1^A y_2^{1-A} \leqq \leqq x_A^1 x_2^{1-A})$. Let $y_1 > x_1$ and $y_2 < x_2$ (so that x does not dominate y, and conversely). Then $\log(y_1/x_1) > 0$, $\log(x_2/y_2) > 0$, and

$$p_{xy} = \Pr\left(\frac{A}{1-A} \leqq \frac{\log(x_2/y_2)}{\log(y_1/x_1)}\right) = F(\mu_{xy}),$$

where $\mu_{xy} = \log(x_2/y_2)/\log(y_1/x_1)$ and F is a monotone non-decreasing function depending on the distribution of A. We shall now show that the form (29) of the random utility indicator is not consistent with some binary-choice constraints:

THEOREM 32. *If the random utility indicator has the form* (29), *then the strong transitivity condition* (t_s) *is, in general, not satisfied.*

Proof. Consider three points x, y, z with $z_1 > y_1 > x_1$ and $z_2 < y_2 < x_2$. Then

$$p_{xy} = F(\mu_{xy}), \qquad \mu_{xy} = (\log x_2 - \log y_2(/(\log y_1 - \log x_1),$$
$$p_{yz} = F(\mu_{yz}), \qquad \mu_{yz} = (\log y_2 - \log z_2)/(\log z_1 - \log y_1),$$
$$p_{xz} = F(\mu_{xz}), \qquad \mu_{xz} = (\log x_2 - \log z_2)/(\log z_1 - \log x_1),$$
$$\mu_{xz} = \frac{\mu_{xy}(\log y_1 - \log x_1) + \mu_{yz}(\log z_1 - \log y_1)}{(\log y_1 - \log x_1) + (\log z_1 - \log y_1)},$$

a convex combination of μ_{xy} and μ_{yz}. Hence min $(\mu_{xy}, \mu_{yz}) \leqq \mu_{xz} \leqq$ max (μ_{xy}, μ_{yz}); and since F is non-decreasing, min $(p_{xy}, p_{yz}) \leqq p_{xz} \leqq \max(p_{xy}, p_{yz})$. This is consistent with the Weak and the Mild Transitivity Conditions, (t_w) and (t_m) of Section VII, but not with the Strong Transitivity Condition (t_s). All three conditions are directly testable.

Thus (29) is in general inconsistent with the existence of strict or strong utility functions, since those imply strong transitivity (Theorems 17 and 27).

Consider now another random form of the 'Cobb-Douglas function':

(30) $\qquad U_x^{(2)} = x_1^{\alpha} x_2^{1-\alpha} + V_x,$

where α is a constant, $0 < \alpha < 1$, and V is a random function on $\boldsymbol{X}$. If $U^{(2)}$ is a random utility indicator, then

$$p_{xy} = \Pr(U_x^{(2)} \geqq U_y^{(2)}) = \Pr(V_y - V_z \leqq x_1^{\alpha} x_2^{1-\alpha} - y_1^{\alpha} y_2^{1-\alpha}).$$

Suppose we have found V such that $\Pr(V_y - V_x \leqq \lambda) = \phi(\lambda)$ for any real λ, with ϕ being a distribution function independent of x, y. Then Condition (V') of Section IX is satisfied, and

(31) $\qquad U_x^{(2)} - V_x = v_x = x_1^{\alpha} x_2^{1-\alpha}$

is a strong utility function consistent with the assumed random utility indicator.[7]

If we could accept the still stronger condition (V''), i.e., let the (infinite-dimensional) distribution of V be symmetrical in its arguments $(x, y, \ldots)$, we would have to search for such distributions. However, the symmetry assumption is hardly realistic: for example, in the case of normality it implies that deviations from the average budget composition have not only the same variances everywhere but also the same correlations for any two points of the X-plane, however close or remote in relation to each other.

The examples used in this section have the purpose merely of illustrating the problem: to find a class of random utility indicators consistent with a given set of binary-choice constraints.

NOTES

* Dedicated to Ragnar Frisch, an old and esteemed friend, on the occasion of his sixty-fifth birthday.

The paper was completed during a year's visit at the Carnegie Institute of Technology, The research was carried out partly under a contract of the Office of Naval Research with the Cowles Foundation for Research in Economics at Yale University, Task NR047-006. Previous collaboration with H. D. Block and discussions with Herman Chernoff, Gerard Debreu, Morris DeGroot, Tjalling Koopmans, and R. Duncan Luce were most helpful.

1 See also [1], Theorems 5.7, 5.1.

2 I am told by Professor T. Motzkin that he has proved the conjecture for $n \leqq 5$. Because of applications to the commodity space or to the space of wagers, the continuous case (as in Theorems 19 and 14) would deserve study.

3 Conditions (t_w) and (t_s) were formulated by S. Valavanis-Vail [21] and originated in his work with C. Coombs. Condition (t_m) was formulated by N. Georgescu-Roegen [12] and by John Chipman [4]. Experimental tests of stochastic transitivity conditions were undertaken by Papandreou *et al.* [17] and by Davidson and Marschak [5].

4 In a paper [14] pointed out to me by Hans Rademacher.

5 It is noteworthy that for $n = 3$, Condition (t_s) is not only necessary but also sufficient for (v). This follows from Theorems 17 and 18.

6 Maximizing $U_x^{(2)}$ with respect to x, subject to the constancy of income $x_1 + x_2$, we see that A is the (random) proportion spent on the 1th commodity. Hence the observed frequency distribution of this proportion should help to estimate the distribution of A – assuming that members of the sampled population were characterized by the same random function $U^{(2)}$. (But we shall not pursue this matter here.)

7 One may want to use indifference lines to picture some relevant aspect of a given random utility indicator, and in particular, its mean. In the case just discussed, described by (30) and (31), we may choose V to have 0 expectation; then $EU_x^{(2)} = v_x$. Accordingly, an indifference line through x consists of all points y, with $v_y = v_x$ and $p_{yx} = \phi_v(0) = \frac{1}{2}$ as in (14); it is then the common boundary of the two sets used in Condition (D), Section VIII. On the other hand, if the random utility indicator is described by (29), equation $EU_y^{(2)} = EU_x^{(2)}$, or possibly $E \log U_y^{(2)} = E \log U_x^{(2)}$, gives quite a different representation.

BIBLIOGRAPHY

[1] Block, H. D. and Marschak, J., 'Random Orderings and Stochastic Theories of Responses', *Selected Essays*, 7.

[2] Block, H. D. and Marschak, J., 'An Identity in Arithmetic', *Bulletin of the American Mathematical Society* **65** (1959), 123–24.

[3] Bradley, R. A. and Terry, M. E., 'Rank Analysis of Incomplete Block Designs. I. The Method of Paired Comparisons', *Biometrika* **39** (1952), 324–44.

[4] Chipman, J. S., 'Stochastic Choice and Subjective Probability' (abstract), *Econometrica* **26** (1958), 613.

[5] Davidson, D. and Marschak, J., 'Experimental Tests of Stochastic Decision Theories', *Selected Essays*, 6.

[6] Debreu, G., 'Representation of a Preference Ordering by a Numerical Function', in R. M. Thrall, C. Coombs, and R. L. Davis (eds.), *Decision Processes*, John Wiley and Sons, New York, 1954, pp. 159–66.

[7] Debreu, G., 'Stochastic Choice and Cardinal Utility', *Econometrica* **26** (1958), 440–44.

[8] Debreu, G., 'On An Identity in Arithmetic', *Proceedings of the American Mathematical Society* **11** (1960) 220–21.

[9] Farrell, M. J., 'The Demand for Motor-Cars in the United States'. *Journal of the Royal Statistical Society, A* **117** (1954), 171–93.

[10] Fechner, G. Th., *Elemente der Psychophysik*, 1859 (see especially pp. 70–103 of the 1889 edition).

[11] Ford, L. R., 'Solution of a Ranking Problem from Binary Comparisons', *American Mathematical Monthly* **64** (1957), No. 8 (supplement), 28–33.

[12] Georgescu-Roegen, N., 'Threshold in Choice and the Theory of Demand', *Econometrica* **26** (1958, 157–68.

[13] Guilbaud, G., 'Sur une difficulté de la théorie du risque', *Colloques Internationaux du Centre National de la Recherche Scientifique* (*Econométrie*) **40** (1953), 19–25.

[14] Hilbert, D., 'Naturerkenntis und Logik', *Gesammelte Abhandlungen* **3** (1935), esp. pp. 379–80.

[15] Luce, R. D., *Individual Choice Behavior*, John Wiley and Sons, New York, 1959.

[16] Marschak, J., 'Money Illusion and Demand Analysis', *Selected Essays*, 46.

[17] Papandreou, A. G. (with the collaboration of O. H. Sauerlender, O. H. Brownlee, L. Hurwicz, W. Franklin), 'A Test of a Stochastic Theory of Choice', *University of California Publications in Economics* **16** (1957), 1–18.

[18] Thurstone, L. L., 'A Law of Comparative Judgment', *Psychological Review* **34** (1927), 273–86.

[19] Tobin, J., 'A Statistical Demand Function for Food in the U.S.A.', *Journal of the Royal Statistical Society A* **113** (1951), 113–49.

[20] Törnqvist, L., 'A Model for Stochastic Decision Making', *Cowles Commission Discussion Paper*, Economics 2100, 1954 (duplicated).

[21] Valavanis-Vail, S., 'A Stochastic Model for Utilities', seminar on the application of mathematics to social sciences, University of Michigan, 1957 (duplicated).

[22] Wold, H. (with L. Jureen), *Demand Analysis*, John Wiley and Sons, New York, 1953.

[23] Luce, R. D. and Suppes, P., 'Preference, Utility, and Subjective Probability', *Handbook of Mathematical Psychology*, Vol. III, Ch. 19, Wiley, 1965.

9

ACTUAL VERSUS CONSISTENT DECISION BEHAVIOR*

(1964)

I. PURPOSE

Like any other specialist in decision-making, the manager expects science to answer two questions:

(1) What is the manager's optimal (effective, efficient) behavior, in the face of a given task? That is, how should *he* impinge upon Nature (including humans) to achieve, on the average, results that are best from his point of view? (*Normative science*: engineering, operations research, medicine and other 'know-how' sciences).

(2.) How does Nature (including humans) behave? (*Descriptive science*: physics, psychology, biology).

Normative science develops methods that use the findings of descriptive science to predict results from actions, and thus choose optimal actions.

One particular subject of descriptive sciences of behavior is the study of the *limitations of men's capacities* for finding optimal decisions; or, more generally, the study of the *cost of decision-making*, in a society with a given supply of, and demand for, decision-making skills. The normative science of management must take these limitations and costs as described by behavioral science into account, and seek optimum results of decisions *feasible* under limited decision capacity, and *net* of decision cost. Also, descriptive behavioral science may help to determine optimal strategies for training decision-makers.

The 'humans' in the two questions above are the manager's customers, competitors, coworkers, etc., including himself. Three particular (and not exhaustive) classes of managerial action are:

(1) to assign decisions to men in an optimal way;

(2) to remedy the failure of some men (including himself) to optimize their actions; and

(3) to exploit the failure of other men to optimize *their* actions.

Each class calls for contributions of descriptive behavioral science. In particular, Class 1 calls for measurement of relevant variables (dimensions of decision-making capacity, e.g., speed, memory, and size and frequency of deviations from optimum under varying conditions such as cultural background, business experience, and stress.

Class 2 calls for the study of the behavior of *successful* optimizers. The study (by simulation or otherwise) of traditional, possibly outdated decision routines and habits of average managers is of smaller practical value. Besides the study of successful decision techniques, Class 2 calls also for the study of processes of learning and training.

By contrast, Class 3 calls for the study of average and below-average types of decision-makers: installment buyers who fail to compute the true interest rates, or housewives fascinated by 'economy-size' packages.

In the next section some general hypotheses of decision behavior will be stated. They are, at least in part, mutually exclusive: if actual behavior confirms one hypothesis it may contradict another one.

Finally, the concluding section will contain suggestions of possible experiments to test the hypotheses. Few of these experiments have been carried out on a convincing scale. Tentative explorations performed by the author over a number of years on his own graduate students, or by these students on their wives or friends, do supply some preliminary evidence which deserves to be tested in a more rigorous way. It would be worthwhile to peform such experiments on mature executives (in business or in public agencies) rather than on students.

II. GENERAL HYPOTHESES

The following general hypotheses, or some of their implications, will be considered.

A. *Hypothesis 1. 'Rational' or 'Consistent' Behavior*

The subject's actions (choices) are consistent with a constant system of numerical utilities (attached by him to the possible outcomes of his actions, and characterizing his 'tastes') and of numerical subjective probabilities (attached by him to events that he does not control and characterizing his 'beliefs'). These numbers, constant over some reasonably long period of time, have the following property: out of any set of feasible actions, the subject always chooses one with the highest average of utilities of outcomes, weighted by the subjective probabilities of events. This average is called 'mathematical expectation of utility' or simply 'expected utility'. This 'expected utility principle' follows, by ordinary rules of logic, from much simpler, basic postulates. These I shall state presently. Later, I shall illustrate them, as well as some of their logical implications, by appropriate experiments. Note, however, that a person whose behavior conforms with these postulates in simple experimental situations may or may not, when faced with more complex situations, obey the logical implications of these postulates, such as the expected utility principle. For it may be a stiff requirement for a man to be logical! This was, in fact, proved by some of the experiments.

An action is defined by the different outcomes it yields when different, specified events occur. In this sense, 'not to act' (e.g., 'not to invest', i.e., to keep cash) is also an action. Thus, any subject is forced to decide between actions; but he can find himself indifferent. In what follows, the case of indifference is sometimes omitted to simplify presentation. In this and several other respects our presentation, sufficiently precise for its purpose, is not precise enough for complete logical analysis. This will be found in Savage (1954). Roughly, our Postulate I is his P1; our Postulate 2 is his P3; and out Postulate 3 is his P2 and P4. An elementary exposition will be found in Marschak and Radner (1963). Most of the logical work deriving the expected utility principle from some basic postulates was done by F. Ramsey in the 1920's, B. de Finetti in the 1930's, J. Von Neumann and O. Morgenstern in the 1940's, and L. J. Savage in the 1950's.

1. *Postulate of consistent preferences between actions.* If the subject prefers action *A* to *B*, and *B* to *C*, he prefers *A* to *C*. It follows that outcomes of actions are also ranked consistently, since a given outcome (e.g., a 'job') can be identified with an action (viz., 'choosing the job') that yields this outcome with certainty whatever the external events. Choice under certainty is a special case of choice under uncertainty. In fact, Postulate 1 suffices for the economic theory of certainty; but to tackle economics of uncertainty, it is to be supplemented by Postulates 2 and 3 which follow.

2. *Admissibility postulate.* Suppose two actions, *A* and *B*, would result in

the same outcomes if certain events would occur; and that otherwise *A* results in an outcome that is preferable to *B*'s outcome. Then *A* itself is preferable to *B*. (Laws that threaten the death penalty for desertion from the battlefield utilize, in effect, this postulate!)

3. *Postulate of independence of tastes and beliefs.* If the subject's choice among actions reveals that, in his view, one event is more probable than another, then, in the absence of new information, his subsequent choices must be consistent with this view, regardless of the outcomes. One should neither think wishfully nor be subject to persecution mania!

The experiments that follow below tend to confirm that the basic postulates are actually obeyed when and only when stress is absent (e.g., memory is not overloaded, ample time is provided, etc.) and, above all, when and only when the structure of the problem is very simple and is laid bare, by the use of lucid syntax, tabular presentation, etc.

Thus, Roger Crane, a member of a nationally known accounting firm, reports the use of 'Payoff Tables' in his attempt to make the discussions at Corporation Board meetings more orderly and fruitful, and even to apply the expected utility principle. Uncontrolled events (e.g. the future possible states of the market) head the columns of the table; the available actions (whether to merge with firm *A*, *B*, *C*, or not at all) head the rows of the table; and the outcome of a given action and a given event is entered in the appropriate cell of the table.

Under stress, or if the problem is complex, or has not been prestructured ('predigested') for the subject' use, the 'rational' hypothesis seems to be rarely satisfied; it is not good descriptive psychology. Other hypotheses present themselves.

B. *Hypothesis 2. Learning Theory*

As trials are repeated, the subject approaches asymptotically a stable behavior (which is, in general, not the rational one). In particular, his decision may depend on the success or failure (possibly measured from some 'aspiration level') of his previous decision; and the degree of this dependence – the 'reinforcement parameter' – determines the speed of learning characterizing a given subject (Bush and Mosteller, 1955; Estes, 1950).

C. *Hypothesis 3. Stochastic Decision Theory*

The subject's choices are described by probability distributions which can be construed as weak (i.e., generalized) forms of rational behavior (Becker *et al.*, 1963; Block and Marschak, 1960; Luce, 1959; Marschak, 1960; and Restle, 1961). For example, a very weak postulate of stochastic behavior is this: "If the subject is more likely to prefer, than not to prefer, A to B; and is more likely to prefer, than not to prefer, B to C; then he is more likely to prefer, than not to prefer, A to C." On the other hand, a very strong postulate of stochastic behavior ('Luce's Axiom') is this: "If, when presented with the triple (A, B, C) the subject chooses A or B or C with relative frequencies in proportion $p_A : p_B : p_C$; then, if presented with the pair (A, B), he will choose A or B with relative frequencies in proportion $p_A : p_B$." This leads to a new definition of utilities (viz., numbers proportionate to $p_A, p_B, p_C \ldots$).[1] A stochastic behavior postulate of intermediate strength has been used by the late L. L. Thurstone and his followers who, in essence, equate utility with 'subjective sensation', taken from Fechner's psychophysics (1859). Still another postulate (also weaker than Luce's Axiom) assumes that the subject's ranking of all considered alternative actions varies according to some probability scheme.

D. *Hypothesis 4*

This is a combination of Hypotheses 2 and 3 (Estes, 1960; Luce, 1959; Suppes and Atkinson, 1960, Ch. 11).

E. *Hypothesis 5. Application of Gestalt Theory*

The subject has *sudden insight* into the rational structure of a decision problem ('Aha!').

F. *Hypothesis 5. Effect of Training*

The subject's insight can be brought about or accelerated by appropriate training strategies.

III. EXPERIMENTS

A. *Experiments 1. Consistent Ranking of Actions*

Experiment 1a. Complex objects such as 'a patent', 'a labor contract', 'plant', etc., each described in detail, each fraught with uncertainties, and none having a market price, are presented in pairs, without cost to chooser (or with cost counted in), in the following order:

the (A, B)-pairs: $(A_1, B_1); (A_2, B_2); \ldots; (A_m, B_m)$;
the (B, C)-pairs: $(B_1, C_1); (B_2, C_2); \ldots; (B_m, C_m)$;
the (C, A)-pairs: $(C_1, A_1); (C_2, A_2); \ldots; (C_m, A_m)$.

The subject is not consistent if he prefers A_i to B_i, and B_i to C_i, yet also prefers C_i to A_i, for some i.

Experiment 1b. If for a given number (m) of trials (A_i, B_i, C_i), the subject has behaved consistently in Experiment 1a, he is now made to choose from a set such as $(A_1\ B_1, C_2)$. He is not consistent if he prefers A_1 when presented with the pair (A_1, B_1), yet prefers B_1 when presented with the triplet (A_1, B_1, C_2). We invariably laugh at the story of the man who chose steak from a menu containing steak and fish; but changed his choice to fish when told that chicken was also available! (The story is Luce's; its principle was first stated by Arrow.)

Experiment 1c. Finally, the subject is asked to rank all $3m$ alternatives. The ranking is tested against his preferences as exhibited in Experiment 1a.

Preliminary evidence. Experiments on my own students suggest that they satisfied the Postulate of Consistent Preference if, in Experiment 1a, m, the number of triads used, was small; e.g., $m=5$. Inconsistencics arose more often in Experiments 1b and 1c. However, the objects considered were those appropriate for the experience of (married) graduate students, rather than businessmen: jobs, trips, apartments, house furnishings, investment information, medical care, etc.

In other experiments, on students of logic and mathematics at Stanford University, the weak stochastic hypothesis mentioned above under Hypothesis 3 was satisfied by almost all subjects; but not the Fechnerian hypothesis. The objects considered were small monetary wagers (see Davidson and Marschak, 1959).

B. *Experiments 2. Admissibility Principle*

Experiment 2a. "You may get a job in a foreign country or an equally good one at home. If a revolution in a foreign country occurs you lose the job; but it can't happen here. Your choice?"

Experiment 2b. "Write down, but don't tell me, the *cash value* (v) of your property to you: that is, the smallest acceptable price. Then name your asking price (a); after this, I (your broker) shall draw at random a number (b) as the buying price. If b exceeds a you'll get b. Otherwise you will keep your property. Now name your asking price."

Experiments performed in my class on my students, and by them on their friends or wives, tend to suggest the following evidence:

In Experiment 2a the foreign job is rejected, in accordance with the admissibility principle. But in Experiment 2*b* the admissibility principle is applied only if the experimenter "untwists" the problem by presenting and explaining a formula, a table, or a diagram, for example: Suppose the value of the property to you is $v = 25$. It is arranged that if $b > a$ you receive b; if $b \leqq a$, you keep v. Hence the payoff will depend on a (which you control) and b (which you don't control) in the following way:

	b: 10	20	30	40
a:	Outcomes, when $v = 25$			
15	25	20	30	40
25	25	25	30	40
35	25	25	25	40

Clearly the only admissible action is to name an asking price a equal to 25, i.e., to the value of the property to you (v). If you ask more or less than 25, you lose (compared with the admissible action) whenever b happens to fall between a and v, and you fare equally well otherwise. Honesty is (in this case at least) the best policy! Instead, most subjects named an asking price in excess of the value of the property to them. Perhaps they assumed, albeit unconsciously, that some bargaining will ensue, although this was explicitly excluded under the conditions given in the experiment.

(Later the experiment was modified to free it from associations with the real estate market. Here v equaled the money amount entered on a check or I.O.U. signed by the experimenter and picked up by the subject at random from an urn filled with such checks, each with a different value. In this modified situation the admissibility postulate was transgressed less frequently.)

C. *Experiment 3. Independence of Tastes and Beliefs*

Consider the following events, not controlled by you:

X: Democrats win in 1964
$\bar{X}$: they do not win
Y: next card drawn is a spade
$\bar{Y}$: it is not.

We consider now 6 actions (bets) A, B, C, A', B', C', and tabulate their outcomes (gains and losses) which depend on the events, as follows:

Events:	X	$\bar{X}$		$\bar{X}$	X		Y	$\bar{Y}$
Actions:								
A:	\$100	\$ 0	B:	\$100	\$ 0	C:	\$100	\$ 0
A':	\$ 50	\$−50	B':	\$ 50	\$−50	C':	\$ 50	\$−50

If you prefer A to B (i.e. bet on the Democratic candidate rather than on his rival); and B to C (i.e. bet on the non-Democratic candidate rather than on spades); then we usually say that you think X is more probable than $\bar{X}$, and that $\bar{X}$ is more probable than Y. This is the common English use of the subjective probability concept. The experiment consists in finding whether a subject retains this ranking of the three probabilities also when the stakes are changed: on bets A', B', C', instead of gaining \$100 or nothing, he now will gain or lose \$50. If his beliefs and tastes are independent, this change of outcomes should not affect his ranking of events according to their probabilities: X should, as before, appear to him more probable than $\bar{X}$, and $\bar{X}$ more probable than Y, and this should be reflected in his choice of action. Hence he should prefer A' to B', and B' to C'.

When the conditions are presented in tabulated form as above, few subjects show inconsistency. But would they remain consistent if the job of structuring had been left to them?

Experiment 3 verifies, or refutes, the independence of tastes and beliefs. We have seen that if such independence prevails, a probability ranking of events will express the subject's beliefs. Moreover, if Postulates 1, 2, and 3 are verified, and, in addition, the subject follows rules of logic, then it can be shown that his beliefs can be expressed by assigning to the events not only probability ranks, but actual numbers which we can call (subjective) probabilities because they have the same mathematical properties as those established in the classical theory of probabilities. In particular, if two events X and Y are mutually exclusive the subjective probability assigned to the event 'X or Y' is the sum of the probability of X and of that of Y (the 'additivity law'). The logical grounds for the existence of such numerical subjective probabilities can be roughly illustrated in the context of the following experiments.

D. *Experiment 4. Numerical Subjective Probabilities*

Denote by '*D.J.*' the 'Dow-Jones stock price average at this year's end', and by x some positive number. Consider two actions (bets) A and B such that:

> if you choose A you will get \$100 if *D.J.* exceeds x, and you will get \$0 otherwise;
> if you choose B you will get \$0 if *D.J.* exceeds x, and you will get \$100 otherwise.

By definition, if your beliefs and tastes are independent, your preference ranking as between the two actions will remain the same if the pair of outcomes (\$100, \$0) is replaced by some other pair (O_1, O_2) such that O_1 is better than O_2. Your choice as between A and B will indicate whether you consider the event '*D.J.* exceeds x' more or less probable than its negation. Therefore, if we adopt the useful convention that the probabilities of an event and of its negation add up to 1, we shall say that the subjective probability of the event '*D.J.* exceeds x' is larger than $\frac{1}{2}$ if you prefer A to B; smaller than $\frac{1}{2}$ if you prefer B to A; and equal to $\frac{1}{2}$ if you are indifferent between A and B. Hence, by adjusting the variable x upward and downward we can find a value of x such that your subjective probability of the event '*D.J.* exceeds x' is equal to $\frac{1}{2}$.

We can find in a similar way two numbers y_1 and y_2 such that you will be *indifferent* between three following bets C, D, E:

> If you choose C you will get \$100 if *D.J.* is less than y_1, and \$0 otherwise;
> if you choose D you will get \$100 if *D.J.* is y_1 or more, but less than y_2, and \$0 otherwise;
> if you choose E you will get \$100 if *D.J.* is y_2 or more, and \$0 otherwise.

Or, in tabular form:

	I	II	III
	0	y_1	y_2
C	$100	$ 0	$ 0
D	$ 0	$100	$ 0
E	$ 0	$ 0	$100

Your indifference between *C*, *D*, *E* will indicate that you deem the three mutually exclusive events (the three intervals I, II, III on the *D.J.* scale) to be equally probable. In other words, their subjective probabilities are $\frac{1}{3}$, $\frac{1}{3}$, $\frac{1}{3}$ – *provided* your (the subject's) tastes and beliefs are independent. This can be tested by finding whether you are also indifferent between the following three bets (with the same meaning of y_1, y_2):

	I	II	III
	0	y_1	y_2
C′	$100	$ 0	$100
D′	$ 0	$100	$100
E′	$100	$100	$ 0

(your indifference between *C* and *D* revealed that, for you, events I and II are equally probable; this belief should not be changed if the outcome of either action in case of event III is changed from $0 to $100; hence you should be indifferent between *C′* and *D′*; and similarly between *D′* and *E′*) On the other hand, any of the actions *C′ D′*, *E′* is better than any of the actions *C*, *D*, *E*, by the admissibility principle. Accordingly, having assigned probabilities $\frac{1}{3}$ to each of the events I, II, III, we may assign probabilities $\frac{2}{3}$ to the events 'I or II', 'II or III', 'I or III', thus at the same time satisfying the additivity law for probabilities. And if we call $100, $0, 'success' and 'failure' respectively we see that you prefer that action which has a higher subjective probability of success. Again, this agrees with usual English.

Using three mutually exclusive and exhaustive events, we have defined subjective probabilities $\frac{1}{3}$ and $\frac{2}{3}$ as revealed by a consistent subject's preferences between actions. This reasoning can be extended to any number – 4, 5,..., *n* of events, and leads to the definition of any subjective probability expressed by a rational fraction m/n; and, in fact, as expressed by any number (whether rational or irrational) between 0 and 1. If each of two actions A_1 and A_2 can yield either 'success' or 'failure', and if A_1 is preferred (or indifferent) to A_2, then the probability of success, p_1, of A_1 is larger than (or equal to) the probability of success, p_2, of A_2, as viewed by the subject.

Let us agree to assign utility$=0$ to failure (and to an action that always leads to failure). Then the utility of success (and of an action that always leads to success) must be larger; let it be$=1$. By the admissibility principle, any action that yields possibly success, and possibly failure, is better than sure failure and worse than sure success. Therefore its utility must be assigned a number between 0 and 1. In particular, to a lottery (action, bet, venture) A_i that succeeds with probability p_i, we may assign the utility p_i: this will agree with our previous statement that A_i is preferred to (hence is utility is larger than that of) A_2 if $p_1 > p_2$. Now note that *such an assignment of utilities agrees with the expected utility principle*; for indeed

$$p_i \cdot 1 + (1 - p_i) \cdot 0 = p_i .$$

Consider now a "mixed" lottery. It yields a ticket of A_1 with subjective probability π_1, a ticket of A_2 with subjective probability π_2, etc. Since the ordinary probability laws are obeyed, such a mixed lottery will yield success with subjective probability $p_1\pi_2 + p_2\pi_2 + \cdots$. And since we have agreed to equate a lottery's utility with its chance of success we see that the utility of the mixed lottery is the weighted average of the utilities of the component lotteries that are its outcomes. Again, *this agrees with the expected utility principle.*

As a further step, extend this reasoning to *any* outcomes that are not better than the 'success' and not worse than the 'failure' defined so far. The consistent man will be indifferent between such an outcome and some lottery which has probability p_i (say) of success; hence this outcome's utility can be set equal to p_i. And an action which yields, with respective probabilities $\pi_1, \pi_2, \ldots$, objects whose utilities are $p_1, p_2, \ldots$, will be equivalent, in that man's view, to the mixed lottery whose utility we have seen to be $p_1\pi_1 + p_2\pi_2 + \cdots$. *This agrees again with the expected utility principle.*

A complete and rigorous proof that the expected utility principle follows from the three basic postulates by ordinary rules of logic is more lengthy and cannot be given here. Indeed this logical process, though elementary, does not seem to correspond to the behavior of an untrained, unprepared, or inexperienced 'average' man of our culture. This is illustrated by the following experiment.

E. *Experiment 5. Existence of a Utility Function*

Consider the following four lottery tickets:

Lottery ticket	If Heads, you get:	If Tails, you get:	Cash equivalent?
A	\$100	\$0	\$*a*
B	\$100	*A*	\$*b*
C	\$0	*A*	\$*c*
D	*B*	*C*	\$*d*

We either assume that the subjective probabilities of Heads and Tails are equal (i.e., that the subject is indifferent between betting something on Heads or betting the same thing on Tails) or we test this assumption by actual trials. (This was done by Davidson and Suppes [1957] who painted one nonsense syllable on three sides of a die and another nonsense syllable on the three remaining sides, and tested whether the subject who chose to bet on the first nonsense syllable changed the choice when the rewards on that bet were lowered very slightly.) Under Hypothesis 1, the hypothesis of consistent behavior, the subject assigning a winning chance $\frac{1}{2}$ to A should also assign:

a winning chance $(\frac{1}{2})\cdot(1) + (\frac{1}{2})\cdot(\frac{1}{2}) = \frac{3}{4}$ to B;
a winning chance $(\frac{1}{2})\cdot(0) + (\frac{1}{2})\cdot(\frac{1}{2}) = \frac{1}{4}$ to C; and therefore
a winning chance $(\frac{1}{2})\cdot(\frac{3}{4}) + (\frac{1}{2})(\frac{1}{4}) = \frac{1}{2}$ to D. Consequently he should declare $b > d = a > c$.

Moreover, if he is consistent and 'averts risk' – so that, for him, money has 'decreasing marginal utility' – he would name $a<50$, $b<(100+a)/2$, $c<a/2$. The three cash amounts a, b, c permit us to estimate three non trivial points on the curve representing his utility function of money gains and monetary wagers $u(g)$, *provided his consistency has been confirmed* by his naming $d=a$. For we are free to fix two points arbitrarily (as when 'calibrating' a thermometer scale): say, $u(\$100)=1$, $u(\$0)=0$. Then, $u(a)=u(A)=(1+0)/2=.5$; $u(b)=u(B)=(1+.5)/2=.75$; $u(c)=u(C)= =(0+.5)/2=.25$.

In experiments with students they usually failed to name $d=a$, unless they stated values $a=d=50$, $b=75$, $c=25$. In this case we suspect that they have parrot-like followed the rule (which they have heard somewhere) of computing actuarial values, and did not name their genuine subjective cash equivalent. To check this, and educate them for later experiments, we have asked them whether they are really indifferent between 'gain \$100, lose \$100 on the toss of a coin' and 'gain a dime, lose a dime on the toss of a coin', thus dispelling the learned myth of actuarial values.

Experiment 5 can be generalized to the case when the subjective odds are not necessarily 1:1, and indeed are unknown to the experimeter (Becker *et al.*, 1963; the point was also made by Jacques Drèze). Instead of 'Heads–Tails', we may use the events: 'The next student to speak to me in this classroom will be less (not less) than 25 years old' (if the experiment is performed in a graduate classroom). Note that the choices (B) and (C) may imply a second, and choice (D) even a third trial. Now, a consistent man will behave as if he assigned to the alternative events some probabilities, p and q, say, with $p+q=1$. Moreover, if as before (without loss of generality) the utility scale is calibrated so that $u(\$100)=1$, $u(\$0)=0$, then a consistent man will behave as if he assigned to the four lottery tickets of the experiment the following utilities:

$$\begin{aligned} u(A) &= p\cdot u(\$100) + q\cdot u(\$0) = p \\ u(B) &= p\cdot u(\$100) + q\cdot u(A) = p + qp \\ u(C) &= p\cdot u(\$0) + qu(A) = 0 + qp \\ u(D) &= p(p + qp) + q(qp) = p, \end{aligned}$$

since $p+q=1$. And since $p\geqslant 0$, $q\geqslant 0$, we obtain the following ranking of utilities: $u(B)\geqslant u(A)=u(D)\geqslant u(C)$; accordingly the consistent man should name cash-equivalents of the four lotteries, ordered thus: $b\geqslant a=d\geqslant c$. If neither event is judged impossible by the consistent man, i.e., if $p>0$, $q>0$, the ranking is exactly the same as before, viz. $b>a=d>c$.

Gordon Becker collected evidence that in some cases the subject's cash-equivalents do gradually approach a consistent pattern as the experiment is continued (a lottery E is formed: D if Heads, \$100 if Tails; etc.). It is not clear whether such subjects 'learn' in the sense of Hypothesis 2 or have a sudden insight ('Aha!)') as in Hypothesis 5. To decide this, appropriate significance tests need to be developed.

NOTES

* Based on studies carried out at the Western Management Science Institute, University of California at Los Angeles, partially supported by the Office of Naval Research, Task 047-041 and by the Ford Foundation.

[1] Think of the opinion-polled housewife in the *New Yorker* cartoon (November 14, 1959): "I'd say I'm about 42 percent for Nixon, 39 per cent for Rockefeller, 19 per cent undecided!"

BIBLIOGRAPHY

Becker, G. M., DeGroot, M. H., and Marschak, J., 'Stochastic Models of Choice Behavior', *Selected Essays*, 10.

Becker, G. M., DeGroot, M. H., and Marschak, J., 'Measuring Utility by a Single-response Sequential Choice', *Selected Essays*, 15.

Block, H. D. and Marschak, J., 'Random Orderings and Stochastic Theories of Response', *Selected Essays*, 7.

Bush, R. R. and Mosteller, C. F., *Stochastic Models for Learning*, Wiley, New York, 1955.

Crane, R. R. and Wanthal, A. E., 'An Approach to the Problem of Growth by Company Acquisition', Paper read at the Orientation Seminar Appraising Corporation Mergers and Acquisitions, American Management Association (Mimeo).

Davidson, D. and Marschak, J., 'Experimental Tests of a Stochastic Decision Theory', *Selected Essays*, 6.

Davidson, D. and Suppes, P., *Decision Making: an Experimental Approach*, Stanford Univ. Press, Stanford, Calif., 1957.

Estes, W. K., 'Toward a Statistical Theory of Learning', *Psychol. Rev.* **57** (1950) 94–107

Estes, W. K., 'A Random Walk Model for Choice Behavior' in K. Arrow *et al.* (eds.), *Mathematical Methods in the Social Sciences*, Stanford Univ. Press Stanford, Calif., 1960.

Fechner, G. T., *Elemente der Psychophysik*. Breitkopf & Haertel, Leipzig, 1859.

Luce, R. D., *Individual Choice Behavior*, Wiley, New York, 1959.

Marschak, J., Binary Choice Constraints on Random Utility Indicators', *Selected Essays*, 8.

Marschak, J. and Radner, R., *Economic Theory of Teams*, Ch. I, Working Paper No. 67, Center for Research in Management Science, Univ. of California, Berkeley, 1963 (Mimeo). *Added in 1974*: Now in book form, Yale University Press, 1972.

Restle, F., *Psychology of Judgment and Choice: a Theoretical Essay*, Wiley, New York, 1961.

Savage, L. J., *Foundations of Statistics*, Wiley, New York, 1954.

Suppes, P. and Atkinson, R. C., *Markov Learning Models for Multiperson Interactions*, Stanford Univ. Press, Stanford, Calif., 1960.

10

STOCHASTIC MODELS OF CHOICE BEHAVIOR*

(1963)

Co-authors: G. M. Becker and M. H. DeGroot

I. INTRODUCTION

Let S denote a finite set of n objects, or rewards, which can be thought of as being numbered serially, $1, 2, \ldots, n$. An *offered set* is a nonempty subset of S. We will be concerned with experiments in which a subject chooses a reward from each of several offered sets. The word 'rewards' is used here to describe the objects in S in order to convey the notion that the subject will choose the reward that he prefers from any offered set. Thus, if the subject knows he will receive the reward that he chooses, presumably he will choose the reward that he would most like to possess.

From these considerations it would seem plausible to postulate the existence of an ordering (by preference) of the n objects in S such that from any offered set the subject will choose that object which ranks highest in the ordering. The existence of an ordering of this type implies that the subject's choices from various offered sets will be consistent in a very strong sense. For example, if a subject chooses object x from the offered set $\{x, y\}$ containing the two objects x and y, and if he chooses y from $\{y, z\}$, then he must choose x from $\{x, z\}$. Furthermore, if he is presented with the offered set $\{x, y\}$ at two different times under similar conditions, then his choice should be the same at both times.

It is not difficult to envisage situations in which the subject's choices would be consistent in the sense just described. If, for example, the objects in S were different amounts of money, presumably the subject would always choose the largest amount present in any offered set. On the other hand, simple experiments reveal that if S comprises different commodity bundles, or different lottery tickets whereby the subject receives a random amount of money according to some probability distribution, or indeed any objects for which there is no 'natural' simple ordering, then the subject's choices will very often not be consistent.[1] In order to account for these inconsistencies it is convenient to introduce what is called a stochastic model.

A *stochastic model* is a specification, for each offered set M and each object $x \in M$, of the probability that the subject will choose x from M. This probability is denoted by $x(M)$. Clearly, under any stochastic model it must be true that $0 \leqslant x(M) \leqslant 1$ and $\sum_{x \in M} x(M) = 1$ for all x and all M.

II. RANDOM UTILITY MODELS

A large class of stochastic models, called the random utility models, can be derived from the following considerations.

Each object $x \in S$, no matter how simple it might appear, has many attributes. For each $x \in S$, let Ω_x denote the set of all attributes of x. To simplify the following discussion it is assumed that each set Ω_x is finite. When making a choice from among the objects in S a subject does not necessarily consider all of the attributes of all of the objects. Rather, he may consider for each $x \in S$ some subset A_x of its attributes that happens to come to mind and seems to be particularly relevant at the time that he must make a choice. Thus, for each object, we can think of the subset of attributes that the subject considers at a given time as being randomly chosen according to some probabilistic law. Let $Pr\{A_x; x \in S\}$ denote the probability that the subject considers the subset A_x, $x \in S$. Finally, for each $x \in S$, there is a number $U_x(A_x)$ associated with each subset A_x of attributes. This number can be thought of as the utility of x with respect to the given subset A_x. The subject, when choosing from S, considers a subset A_x of attributes for each $x \in S$ that is determined by the probability distribution $Pr\{A_x; x \in S\}$ and chooses that object x from S for which $U_x(A_x)$ is largest.

When choosing from an offered set M, other than S, the subject chooses that object $x \in M$ for which $U_x(A_x)$ is largest among all objects in M. In making this statement we are, in effect, assuming that the subsets of attributes that the subject considers are always determined by the probability distribution $Pr\{A_x; x \in S\}$ regardless of the offered set from which the subject is choosing. A more elaborate theory in which the probability distribution of subsets of attributes depends on the offered set could be given, but it does not seem worthwhile to do so at this stage of development. Since the subsets of attributes that the subject considers are randomly chosen, it follows that the utilities U_x, $x \in S$, constitute a random vector. Furthermore, if the subject considers a certain subset of attributes of one of the objects in S, then it is likely that he will consider subsets of similar attributes of the other objects. In other words, it is not necessarily true that $Pr\{A_x;\, x \in M\}$ and $\prod_{x \in M} Pr\{A_x\}$ are always equal. Thus, the random utilities U_x, $x \in S$, need not be independent random variables.

To clarify these notions consider the following simple example (see also Quandt, 1956). A person is trying to decide which of three suits of clothes, x, y, and z, to wear on a certain occasion. When making this decision he might: (1) consider the style of a suit of primary importance and the material secondary; (2) consider the material of primary importance and the style secondary; or (3) consider style and material of equal importance. Let us say that the occurrence of (1) means that the person considers the subsets A_x, A_y, and A_z of attributes of x, y, and z; the occurrence of (2) means that he considers the subsets B_x, B_y, and B_z; and the occurrence of (3) means that he considers C_x, C_y, and C_z.

Suppose that $Pr\{A_x, A_y, A_z\} = \frac{3}{8}$, $Pr\{B_x, B_y, B_z\} = \frac{1}{8}$, and $Pr\{C_x, C_y, C_z\} = \frac{4}{8}$. These are the probabilities of occurrence of (1), (2), and (3).

Suppose also that $U_x(A_x) > U_y(A_y) > U_z(A_z)$, $U_z(B_z) > U_y(B_y) > U_x(B_x)$, and $U_y(C_y) > U_x(C_x) > U_z(C_z)$. Then, x is preferred when (1) occurs; z is preferred when (2) occurs; and y is preferred when (3) occurs.

It follows that when the subject chooses from the set S containing all three suits, the probabilities of choice are $x(S) = \frac{3}{8}$, $y(S) = \frac{4}{8}$, and $z(S) = \frac{1}{8}$. If suit z is being cleaned at the time of decision so that the choice is restricted to the set M containing only x and y, then $x(M) = \frac{3}{8}$ and $y(M) = \frac{5}{8}$.

The following formal definition was given by Block and Marschak (1960). (The term 'random utility indicator' is used in Marschak [1960].) A stochastic model is said to be a *random utility model* if there exists a random vector $(U_1, \ldots, U_n)$ such that, for all offered sets M and all $x \in M$,

$$(1) \qquad x(M) = Pr\{U_x \geqslant U_y \quad \text{for all} \quad y \in M\}.$$

It is an easy consequence of this definition and is proved in Block and Marschak (1960) that under any random utility model

$$(2) \qquad Pr\{U_x = U_y\} = 0 \quad \text{for all} \quad x \neq y.$$

In effect, this means that every time the subject makes a choice from an offered set it is possible for him to strictly order the objects by their utilities, although this ordering is random and may change for the next choice the subject makes. The possibility that two objects have equal utility could be admitted at the expense of a more complicated definition instead of Equation (1). This will not be done here.

III. LUCE OR STRICT UTILITY MODELS

We now define a special class of stochastic models originally introduced by Luce (1959). A stochastic model will be called a *Luce or strict utility model*[2] if there exist positive constants $u_1, \ldots, u_n$ such that

$$(3) \qquad x(M) = \frac{u_x}{\sum_{y \in M} u_y},$$

for all offered sets M and all $x \in M$. It is easily seen that this is equivalent to the requirement that $x(S) > 0$ for all $x \in S$ and

$$(4) \qquad x(M) = \frac{x(S)}{\sum_{y \in M} y(S)},$$

for all M and all $x \in M$. The following theorem is stated and proved in Block and Marschak (1960).

THEOREM I. Every Luce model is a random utility model.

The meaning of this theorem is that if the probabilities $x(M)$ are given by Equation (3) for some set of positive numbers $u_1, \ldots, u_n$, then there exists a random vector $(U_1, \ldots, U_n)$ with an appropriate multivariate distribution such that the probabilities $x(M)$ are also given by Equation (1). Thus, the Luce models form a subclass of the random utility models.

We will now give two characterizations of this subclass, but before doing so it is convenient to introduce some notation. For a given random utility model and any two offered sets $L \subset M$, let $E(L, M)$ denote the event that there exists an object $x \in L$ such that $U_x \geqslant U_y$ for all $y \in M$. Thus, $E(L, M)$ is the event that the object with largest utility among all the objects in M belongs to the subset L. When $x \in M$, and L contains only the object x, we write $E(x, M)$ instead of $E(L, M)$. If $x \in L \subset M$ then $E(x, M) \subset E(L, M)$, $E(x, M) \subset E(x, L)$ and $Pr\{E(L, M\} = \sum_{y \in L} y(M)$.

THEOREM II. A random utility model is a Luce model if and only if $x(S)>0$ for all $x \in S$ and

$$(5) \qquad x(M) = Pr\{E(x, S) | E(M, S)\}$$

for all M and all $x \in M$.

Proof. If $x(S)>0$ for all $x \in S$ then

$$(6) \qquad Pr\{E(x, S) \mid E(M, S)\} = \frac{Pr\{E(x, S) \cap E(M, S)\}}{Pr\{E(M, S)\}} = \\ = \frac{Pr\{E(x, S)\}}{Pr\{E(M, S)\}} = \frac{x(S)}{\sum_{y \in M} y(S)}.$$

Hence, if $x(S)>0$ for all $x \in S$ and Equation (5) holds, then

$$(7) \qquad x(M) = x(S) / \sum_{y \in M} y(S),$$

and these are the defining properties of a Luce model.

Conversely, if the random utility model is a Luce model, then by definition, $x(S)>0$ for all $x \in S$ and Equation (7) holds. Consequently, so do Equations (6) and (5).

THEOREM III. A random utility model is a Luce model if and only if $x(S)>0$ for all $x \in S$ and, for every offered set M,

$$(8) \qquad Pr\{E(x, S) | E(x, M)\} = k_M, \quad \text{a constant, for all} \quad x \in M.$$

Proof. If $x(S)>0$ for all $x \in S$ then

$$(9) \qquad x(S) = Pr\{E(x, S)\} = Pr\{E(x, S) \cap E(x, M)\} \\ = P\{E(x, S) | E(x, M)\} \, Pr\{E(x, M)\} \\ = P\{E(x, S) | E(x, M)\} \, x(M),$$

for all M and all $x \in M$.

Hence, if $x(S)>0$ for all $x \in S$ and Equation (8) holds, then

$$(10) \qquad x(S) = k_M x(M)$$

and

$$(11) \qquad \sum_{x \in M} x(S) = k_M \sum_{x \in M} x(M) = k_M.$$

Thus

$$(12) \qquad x(M) = \frac{x(S)}{k_M} = \frac{x(S)}{\sum_{y \in M} y(S)}$$

and the model is a Luce model.

Conversely, if the random utility model is a Luce model, then by definition, $x(S) > 0$ for all $x \in S$ and Equation (7) holds. Hence, from Equation (9),

$$(13) \qquad Pr\{E(x, S) \mid E(x, M)\} = \frac{x(S)}{x(M)} = \sum_{y \in M} y(S),$$

which is constant for all $x \in M$. This concludes the proof.

IV. FECHNER OR STRONG UTILITY MODELS

In many experiments each of the offered sets from which a subject must choose contains exactly two of the objects in S. An experiment of this type is called a *binary experiment* and an offered set containing exactly two objects is called a *binary offered set*. Binary experiments have been discussed in detail by Marschak (1960). In such experiments the specification of the probabilities $x(M)$ for offered sets M containing more than two objects is irrelevant, since no pertinent experimental data can be obtained. A specification of the probabilities $x(M)$ for all binary offered sets M is called a *binary model.*

Clearly every stochastic model can be thought of as a binary stochastic model simply by considering only those probabilities $x(M)$ that refer to binary M. Thus, all random utility models and, in particular, all Luce models are binary stochastic models when the defining Equations (1) and (3) are restricted to binary M. These restricted models will be called *binary random utility models* and *binary Luce models*. A binary model is called a *strong utility or Fechner model* if there exist constants $v_1, \ldots, v_n$ and a nondecreasing real-valued function $\Phi(r)$ defined for all real numbers r, such that for every binary offered set $M = \{x, y\}$,

$$(14) \qquad x(M) = \Phi(v_x - v_y).$$

Since (14) restricts the values of $\Phi(r)$ at only a finite number of values of

r and since $x(M)+y(M)=1$, it is easily seen that $\Phi(r)$ can be chosen to be a continuous, non-decreasing function such that

$$(15)\qquad \lim_{r\to-\infty}\Phi(r)=0,\qquad \lim_{r\to\infty}\Phi(r)=1,\quad\text{and}\quad \Phi(r)+\Phi(-r)=1\quad\text{for all}\quad r.$$

The following derivation of the Fechner models, in the same spirit as the derivation given for the random utility models, is sometimes helpful. The function $\Phi(r)$ can be thought of as the distribution function of a continuous random variable ε, with a symmetric distribution around the value 0. For each object $x\in S$, the number v_x represents, in some appropriate sense, the utility, or value, of x to the subject. Thus, when presented with a choice from $\{x, y\}$, the subject would ideally want to choose x if $v_x-v_y>0$ and y if $v_x-v_y<0$. However, because of some inherent limitations in the choice-making process (e.g., not being able to consider all attributes of both x and y) the subject cannot calculate v_x-v_y exactly, but rather can calculate only $v_x-v_y+\varepsilon$, where ε is the random variable just defined. He then chooses x if $v_x-v_y+\varepsilon>0$ and y otherwise. This leads to Equation (14).

We now mention some relations between the Fechner, binary Luce, and binary random utility models.

THEOREM IV. Every binary Luce model is a binary random utility model, but not conversely.

THEOREM V. Every binary Luce model is a Fechner model, but not conversely.

Calling a Luce model strict and a Fechner model strong is justified by Theorem V, the word 'strict' conveying the greater restriction. Correspondingly, the constants $u_1,\ldots,u_n$ are called strict utilities, and the constants $v_1,\ldots,v_n$ are called strong utilities, both distinct from the random utilities $U_1,\ldots,U_n$ which are random variables, not constants.

Proofs are given in Block and Marschak (1960). (Indeed, Theorem V is proved by choosing $\Phi(r)$ as in Equation (17) below.) It is also shown there that not every binary random utility model is a Fechner model, but it is not known whether every Fechner model is a binary random utility model. However, the following theorem shows that at least a large class of Fechner models are also binary random utility models.

THEOREM VI. Every Fechner model such that $\Phi(r)$ is the distribution function of the difference of two independent and identically distributed random variables is a binary random utility model.

Proof. Define the random vector $(U_1,..., U_n)$ by

$$U_i = v_i + \varepsilon_i, i = 1,..., n$$

where $\varepsilon_1,..., \varepsilon_n$ are independent and identically distributed random variables such that $\Phi(r)$ is the distribution function of $\varepsilon_i - \varepsilon_j$ for all $i \neq j$, and $v_1,..., v_n$ are the constants appearing in the Fechner model. Then, for any $M = \{x, y\}$,

$$(16) \qquad x(M) = Pr\{U_x \geqslant U_y\} = Pr\{v_x + \varepsilon_x \geqslant v_y + \varepsilon_y\} = \\ = Pr\{\varepsilon_y - \varepsilon_x \leqslant v_x - v_y\} = \Phi(v_x - v_y).$$

It follows from this theorem that, for example, any Fechner model in which $\Phi(r)$ is a normal distribution function is also a binary random utility model.

V. STATISTICAL ANALYSIS OF EXPERIMENTAL DATA

Consider an experiment in which a subject makes choices from several offered sets. It is assumed throughout this paper that the subject's choices in such an experiment are independent. That is, it is assumed that for any finite collection $M_1,..., M_k$ of the offered sets presented in the experiment, the probability that the subject will choose object x_i from M_i, $i=1,..., k$, is $\prod_{i=1}^{k} x_i(M_i)$. This assumption excludes the possibility that the subject undergoes some learning process in the course of the experiment whereby his choice from an offered set depends on the previously offered sets from which he has already chosen and on his choices from those offered sets. The reason for making the assumption of independence of choices is that it yields an explicit, simple probabilistic model for a wide variety of situations. However, in order that the assumption be satisfied in an experiment, it is very often essential that the subject does not make a choice from any particular offered set more than a few times. Indeed, if some offered set is to be presented to the subject more than once during the experiment it is important that sufficient precautions are taken to insure that when the subject is presented with the offered set for the second time he has forgotten his earlier choice.

In general, the purpose of performing an experiment and observing the subject's choices is to gain information about the probabilities $x(M)$, which are typically not completely known to the experimenter (or to the subject). The questions about the probabilities $x(M)$ that the experimenter wants to answer can very often be classified either as questions of testing some hypotheses about the stochastic model or as questions of estimating some parameters appearing in the stochastic model. To the authors' knowledge, the only relevant statistical methods that have thus far appeared in the literature are concerned with Fechner models for binary experiments.

Consider a Fechner model in which the function $\Phi(r)$ is the logistic function

$$\Phi(r) = \frac{1}{1+e^{-r}}. \tag{17}$$

(Fechner models in which $\Phi(r)$ is of the form of Equation (17) are also binary Luce models. We will return to this relationship below.) Berkson (1955, 1957) has used this function in problems of bioassay. His approach can be slightly generalized as follows. Suppose that on each of a sequence of trials one observes either a success or a failure. Suppose that the probability p of observing a success on a given trial is

$$p = \frac{1}{1 + Exp\left\{-\sum_{i=1}^{n} c_i v_i\right\}}, \tag{18}$$

where $v_1, \ldots, v_n$ are unknown parameters and $c_1, \ldots, c_n$ are known constants whose values are fixed by the experimenter on each trial. The problem is to estimate the parameters $v_1, \ldots, v_n$ from observations made at several sets of constants $c_1, \ldots, c_n$. Berkson has derived the maximum likelihood and other estimates of $v_1, \ldots, v_n$ and Cox (1958) has suggested some further techniques. Their methods obviously apply to experiments on binary choices by regarding the presentation of the offered set $\{x, y\}$ as the assignment of the values $c_x = 1$, $c_y = -1$, $c_i = 0$ for $i \neq x$, $i \neq y$, and regarding the choice of x from $\{x, y\}$ as the observation of a success. However, the known properties of their estimates are large sample properties, and no evaluation has been made when none of the sets of constants $c_1, \ldots, c_n$ are repeated in the experiment.

If, in a Fechner model, $\Phi(r)$ is given by Equation (17), then it is readily verified that the model is also a binary Luce model, with the relation between the constants $u_1, \ldots, u_n$ of the Luce model and the constants $v_1, \ldots, v_n$ of the Fechner model given by

$$(19) \qquad u_i, = e^{v_i}, \quad i = 1, \ldots, n.$$

Maximum likelihood estimation of the parameters $u_1, \ldots, u_n$ has been discussed by Abelson and Bradley (1954), Bradley (1954a, 1955), Bradley and Terry (1952), and Ford (1957) in the context of paired comparisons, but again this is a large sample technique. The maximum likelihood estimates of $u_1, \ldots, u_n$ and of $v_1, \ldots, v_n$ are related by Equation (19), just as the parameters are, but the work dealing with the logistic function and that dealing with paired comparisons seem to have developed independently of each other.

Brunk (1960) has presented a technique for computing the maximum likelihood estimates of the parameters $v_1, \ldots, v_n$ in a Fechner model when the function $\Phi(r)$ belongs to an exponential family of distribution functions.

Bradley (1954b) has derived a test of goodness-of-fit for testing whether a binary stochastic model is a binary Luce model, but the distribution of his test statistic is known only when each binary offered set is presented many times.

To summarize, no statistical techniques have as yet been given for other than binary experiments, and for binary experiments the existing techniques depend on repetitions of the offered sets. Such repetitions should not be essential since if S contains n objects there are $2^n - n - 1$ distinct offered sets containing at least two objects, and $\binom{n}{2}$ distinct binary offered sets. Hence, if the stochastic model is known except for the values of n parameters, then even though no offered set is presented to the subject more than once during the experiment, the number of choices that the subject makes will still be much larger than the number of unknown parameters when n is not too small. In this situation one would still expect to be able to find good estimates of the parameters, but as yet no general techniques are known.

VI. WAGERS

In many situations, each of the objects in an offered set from which a subject must choose contains some degree of uncertainty, in the sense that even after having chosen one of the objects from the offered set, the actual reward that the subject will receive is a random variable. In such situations, by choosing an object from an offered set, the subject is in fact choosing a probability distribution for the reward that he will receive. The offered set is simply some set of possible (or available) probability distributions. We now make this notation precise.

As before, let S denote a finite set of n rewards numbered $1, 2, \ldots, n$. Let $E_1, \ldots, E_t$ denote a finite class of mutually exclusive and exhaustive events. (For example, in simple experiments the events $E_1, \ldots, E_t$ might be the various possible outcomes when a card is drawn from a deck of some specified composition.) For convenience we assume that each of the events $E_1, \ldots, E_t$ has positive probability. A *wager* $\mathbf{w}=(w_1, \ldots, w_t)$ is a vector such that each component w_i, $i=1, \ldots, t$, is one of the integers $1, 2, \ldots, n$. In other words, a wager associates with each of the events E_i a reward w_i in S. An *offered set* is a nonempty, finite subset of the set of all wagers.

The interpretation is as follows. A subject must choose one of the wagers from a given offered set. If he chooses the wager $\mathbf{w}=(w_1, \ldots, w_t)$ then he receives one of the rewards $w_1, \ldots, w_t$ depending on which of the events $E_1, \ldots, E_t$ occurs. Thus, the subject's preferences among the rewards in S will lead to preferences among the wagers in the offered set.

For any wager $\mathbf{w}$, let $p_i(\mathbf{w})$ be the probability of receiving reward i, $i=1, \ldots, n$. Thus, $p_i(\mathbf{w})$ is the total probability of those events E_j for which $w_j=i$. Let $\mathbf{p}(\mathbf{w})$ denote the vector $(p_1(\mathbf{w}), \ldots, p_n(\mathbf{w}))$, and consider two wagers $\mathbf{w}$ and $\mathbf{w}'$ such that $\mathbf{p}(\mathbf{w})=\mathbf{p}(\mathbf{w}')$. Since the probabilities of receiving the various rewards are identical for both of the wagers $\mathbf{w}$ and $\mathbf{w}'$, it seems reasonable to assume that a subject would be indifferent when making a choice between them. In order for this assumption to be reasonable it is essential that the occurrence of any of the events $E_1, \ldots, E_t$ does not affect the worth of any of the rewards to the subject. In other words, it is essential that the only features of the events $E_1, \ldots, E_t$ that are relevant to the subject's choice are the probabilities of the events. For this reason it is convenient to think of the events $E_1, \ldots, E_t$ as outcomes of some gambling device such as a deck of cards or a pair of dice.

We make full use of this argument by assuming that if $\mathbf{p}(\mathbf{w}) = \mathbf{p}(\mathbf{w}')$ then the wagers $\mathbf{w}$ and $\mathbf{w}'$ are interchangeable in the sense that we can replace one of them by the other in any offered set without changing the chances of any of the wagers in the offered set being chosen. Indeed, the stochastic models for wagers to be presented in the next section depend on the wagers in an offered set only through the vectors $\mathbf{p}(\mathbf{w})$.

Consider now the situation in which the n rewards in the set S are n different amounts of money. Suppose that reward i is the amount a_i, $i=1, \ldots, n$, and suppose that the rewards have been numbered so that $a_1 < a_2 < \cdots < a_n$. It seems reasonable to assume that any subject, when asked to choose from among different amounts of money, will always choose the largest amount.

Let $\mathbf{w} = (w_1, \ldots, w_t)$ and $\mathbf{w}' = (w'_1, \ldots, w'_t)$ be two wagers such that $w_i \geqslant w'_i$, $i = 1, \ldots, t$, and $w_i > w'_i$ for at least one value of i. We then say that $\mathbf{w}$ *dominates* $\mathbf{w}'$. It follows that a subject will never choose the wager $\mathbf{w}'$ if the wager $\mathbf{w}$ is also available in the offered set. This is so because no matter which event E_i occurs, the subject will receive at least as much money from $\mathbf{w}$ as from $\mathbf{w}'$, and might receive more from $\mathbf{w}$.

It is convenient to make the following definition. The wager $\mathbf{w}$ is said to be *absolutely preferred* to the wager $\mathbf{w}'$ if, for every offered set M containing both $\mathbf{w}$ and $\mathbf{w}'$, $\mathbf{w}'(M) = 0$. Thus, if $\mathbf{w}$ dominates $\mathbf{w}'$ then w is *absolutely* preferred to w'.

Suppose then that

$$(20) \qquad w_i \geqslant w'_i, \; i = 1, \ldots, t.$$

Since, regardless of which event occurs, the reward received from $\mathbf{w}$ is at least as large as the reward received from $\mathbf{w}'$, it follows that for any amount of money a, the probability of receiving at least a is at least as large for $\mathbf{w}$ as it is for $\mathbf{w}'$. Thus,

$$(21) \qquad \sum_{j=x}^{n} p_j(\mathbf{w}) \geqslant \sum_{j=x}^{n} p_j(\mathbf{w}'), \; x = 1, \ldots, n,$$

and if inequality holds in (20) for at least one value of i, then inequality holds in (21) for at least one value of x.

Furthermore, it can be shown that if (21) holds for some pairs of wagers

w and **w**′ with inequality for some value of x then there exist wagers **w**″ and **w**‴ such that $\mathbf{p}(\mathbf{w}'')=\mathbf{p}(\mathbf{w})$, $\mathbf{p}(\mathbf{w}''')=\mathbf{p}(\mathbf{w}')$, and $w_i'' \geqslant w_i'''$, $i=1,\ldots,t$, with inequality for some value of i. Thus, **w**″ dominates **w**‴ and, hence, **w**″ is absolutely preferred to **w**‴. Since, **w** and **w**″ are interchangeable and **w**′ and **w**‴ are also interchangeable, it follows that **w** is absolutely preferred to **w**′. Hence, we conclude that if **w** and **w**′ satisfy (21) with inequality for some value of x, then **w** is absolutely preferred to **w**′.

All of this can be illustrated with an example. Suppose that the ten events, $E_1,\ldots,E_{10}$, are equally probable, and consider the wagers $\mathbf{w}^1$, $\mathbf{w}^2$, and $\mathbf{w}^3$ associating rewards (integers representing amounts of money) with outcomes as follows:

	E_1	E_2	E_3	E_4	E_5	E_6	E_7	E_8	E_9	E_{10}
$\mathbf{w}^1$:	3	1	4	2	2	5	3	4	4	2
$\mathbf{w}^2$:	4	2	4	3	2	5	3	4	5	2
$\mathbf{w}^3$:	2	4	2	4	5	1	4	3	2	3

It is immediately seen that for every event the reward from $\mathbf{w}^2$ is at least as large as the reward from $\mathbf{w}^1$. Hence, $\mathbf{w}^2$ dominates $\mathbf{w}^1$ and is absolutely preferred to $\mathbf{w}^1$. Since the rewards from $\mathbf{w}^2$ are simply a permutation of the rewards from $\mathbf{w}^1$ (and all E_i are equally probably), $\mathbf{w}^3$ and $\mathbf{w}^1$ are interchangeable, and hence $\mathbf{w}^2$ is also absolutely preferred to $\mathbf{w}^3$. In an actual experiment a subject might easily note that $\mathbf{w}^2$ dominates $\mathbf{w}^1$ and would never choose $\mathbf{w}^1$. However, since $\mathbf{w}^3$ yields larger rewards than $\mathbf{w}^2$ for some events, a subject might at times choose $\mathbf{w}^3$ in preference to $\mathbf{w}^2$. If, as is done in the stochastic models that will now be presented, a wager **w** is characterized simply by the vector $\mathbf{p}(\mathbf{w})$, it must be reasonable to assume that such violations of interchangeability do not occur. This assumption is very often reasonable when dealing, for example, with fewer than ten events, or when the subject has ample time to consider his choice.

VII. STOCHASTIC MODELS FOR WAGERS

As discussed in the preceding section, we now represent a wager as an n-dimensional vector $\mathbf{p}=(p_1,\ldots,p_n)$ such that $p_i \geqslant 0$, $i=1,\ldots,n$, and $\sum_{i=1}^{n} p_i=1$. The interpretation is that if a subject chooses the wager $p=(p_1,\ldots,p_n)$ from some offered set then he receives reward i with probability p_i, $i=1,\ldots,n$. (An offered set is accordingly to be thought of as a finite set of vectors of the above form.)

For reasons similar to those given in the Introduction (and which are no doubt even more compelling when dealing with wagers), it is again convenient to introduce a stochastic model for subjects' choices.

A *stochastic model for wagers* is a specification, for every offered set M and every wager $\mathbf{p}\in M$, of the probability that $\mathbf{p}$ will be chosen from M. This probability is denoted by $\mathbf{p}(M)$. Clearly, under any stochastic model for wagers it must be true that $0\leqslant\mathbf{p}(M)\leqslant 1$ and $\sum_{\mathbf{p}\in M}\mathbf{p}(M)=1$.

The celebrated von Neumann-Morgenstern (1947) concept of utility provides a very special type of model for a subject's choices. A model for wagers is said to be a *von Neumann-Morgenstern* model if there exist constants $t_1,\ldots,t_n$ with the property that, for any offered set M and any wager $\mathbf{p}\in M$, $\mathbf{p}(M)=0$ whenever there exists $\mathbf{q}\in M$ with

$$\sum_{i=1}^{n} q_i t_i > \sum_{i=1}^{n} p_i t_i .$$

The constant t_i is called the *utility of reward* i, $i=1,\ldots,n$, and $\sum_{i=1}^{n} p_i t_i$ is called the *utility of the wager*, $\mathbf{p}$. Thus, the von Neumann-Morgenstern model says that the utility of a wager is the expected utility of the reward received from the wager, and the subject always chooses, from any offered set, a wager of maximum utility.

Except for those offered sets in which more than one wager has maximum utility (in this case nothing has been said about the subject's choice from among them), the above model is nonstochastic in the sense that it exactly specifies the subject's choices. Consequently, it is desirable to develop models that admit more randomness in these choices. The stochastic models for wagers that will now be presented attempt to combine the stochastic models given in the earlier sections of this paper with the von Neumann-Morgenstern concept of the utility of a wager.

A stochastic model for wagers is said to be a *random utility model for wagers* if there exists a random vector $(U_1,\ldots,U_n)$ such that, for any offered set M and every $\mathbf{p}\in M$,

$$\text{(22)}\qquad \mathbf{p}(M) = Pr\left\{\sum_{i=1}^{n} p_i U_i \geqslant \sum_{i=1}^{n} q_i U_i \quad \text{for all} \quad \mathbf{q}\in M\right\}.$$

A wager $\mathbf{p}$ such that $p_i=1$ for some value of i is said to be a *sure thing*:

in this case the subject is certain of the reward that he will receive from this wager. Clearly, if the only wagers that appear in the offered sets presented to the subject are sure things, then these models[3] reduce to the random utility models presented in the section on Random Utility Models. Analogous to (2), it follows from Equation (22) that

$$(23) \qquad Pr\left\{\sum_{i=1}^{n} p_i U_i = \sum_{i=1}^{n} q_i U_i\right\} = 0 \quad \text{for all} \quad \mathbf{p} \neq \mathbf{q}.$$

A stochastic model for wagers is said to be a *Luce model for wagers* if there exist constants $u_1, \ldots, u_n$ and a positive, strictly increasing function $h(r)$ defined for all real numbers r, such that

$$(24) \qquad \mathbf{p}(M) = \frac{h\left(\sum_{i=1}^{n} p_i u_i\right)}{\sum_{q \in M} h\left(\sum_{i=1}^{n} q_i u_i\right)}$$

for all M and every $\mathbf{p} \in M$. Again, if the only wagers appearing in an experiment are sure things, then these models reduce to the Luce models presented earlier, with u_i as defined there equal to $h(u_i)$ as defined here, $i = 1, \ldots, n$.

An offered set containing exactly two wagers is a *binary offered set.* An experiment in which the only offered sets presented to the subject are binary is a *binary experiment.* A stochastic model for wagers that specifies the probabilities $\mathbf{p}(M)$ only for binary M is a *binary stochastic model for wagers.* The *binary random utility models for wagers* and *binary Luce models for wagers* are obtained by restricting the definitions of Equations (22) and (24) to binary M.

A binary stochastic model for wagers is said to be a *Fechner model for wagers* if there exist constants $v_1, \ldots, v_n$, a strictly increasing function $k(r)$, and a nondecreasing function $\Phi(r)$, defined for all real numbers r, such that for every binary $M = \{\mathbf{p}, \mathbf{q}\}$,

$$(25) \qquad \mathbf{p}(M) = \Phi\left(k\left(\sum_{i=1}^{n} p_i v_i\right) - k\left(\sum_{i=1}^{n} q_i v_i\right)\right).$$

Clearly, $\Phi(r)$ can be chosen so that

$$(26) \qquad \Phi(r) + \Phi(-r) = 1$$

for all r. Again, if the only wagers considered are sure things, then the Fechner models for wagers reduce to the Fechner models defined earlier, with v_i as defined there equal to $k(v_i)$ as defined here, $i=1,\ldots,n$.

VIII. RELATIONSHIPS AMONG THE MODELS

In the section on Fechner Models we discussed various inclusion relations between the stochastic models. Not surprisingly, some of these relations no longer hold between the corresponding stochastic models for wagers. Indeed, the class of Luce models for wagers is not contained in the class of random utility models for wagers. This is seen by considering four wagers

$$\text{(27)} \qquad \mathbf{p}^j = (p_1^j, \ldots, p_n^j),\ j = 1, 2, 3, 4,$$

such that

$$\text{(28)} \qquad p_i^1 - p_i^2 = p_i^3 - p_i^4,\ i = 1, \ldots, n.$$

It follows from (22) that under any random utility model for wagers,

$$\begin{aligned} \text{(29)} \qquad \mathbf{p}^1(\{\mathbf{p}^1, \mathbf{p}^2\}) &= Pr\left\{\sum_{i=1} p_i^1 U_i \geqslant \sum_{i=1}^{n} p_i^2 U_i\right\} = \\ &= Pr\left\{\sum_{i=1}^{n} (p_i^1 - p_i^2)\, U_i \geqslant 0\right\} = \\ &= Pr\left\{\sum_{i=1}^{n} (p_i^3 - p_i^4)\, U_i \geqslant 0\right\} = \\ &= \mathbf{p}^3(\{\mathbf{p}^3, \mathbf{p}^4\}). \end{aligned}$$

Clearly, this equality need not hold under a Luce model for wagers. Furthermore, since the only offered sets used in this demonstration were binary, we can conclude that the class of binary Luce models for wagers is not contained in the class of binary random utility models for wagers.

THEOREM VII. Every binary Luce model for wagers is a Fechner model for wagers.

Proof. Consider a binary Luce model for wagers defined by constants $u_i, \ldots, u_n$ and the function $h(r)$. A Fechner model for wagers is characterized by the constants $v_i, \ldots, v_n$ and the functions $k(r)$ and $\Phi(r)$. It is readily checked that if these are defined by

$$(30)\qquad \begin{aligned} v_i &= u_i,\ i = 1, \ldots, n, \\ k(r) &= \log h(r), \\ \Phi(r) &= \frac{1}{1 + e^{-r}}, \end{aligned}$$

then the two models yield the same values for all $\mathbf{p}(M)$.

It follows from Theorem VII and the comments preceding it that the class of Fechner models for wagers is not contained in the class of binary random utility models for wagers. Finally, it can be easily checked that no inclusion relationships in the reverse direction hold.

IX. ABSOLUTE PREFERENCES AND STOCHASTIC MODELS

Let us now return to the situation discussed under Wagers, where the set S of rewards comprise different amounts of money. Reward i is the amount a_i, $i=1,\ldots, n$; and

$$a_1 < a_2 < \cdots < a_n.$$

It was argued there that if the wagers $\mathbf{p}=(p_1,\ldots, p_n)$ and $\mathbf{q}=(q_1,\ldots, q_n)$ satisfy the relations

$$(31)\qquad \sum_{j=x}^{n} p_j \geqslant \sum_{j=x}^{n} q_j,\ x = 1, \ldots, n,$$

with inequality for at least one value of x, then $\mathbf{p}$ is absolutely preferred to $\mathbf{q}$. That is, the probability that $\mathbf{q}$ will be chosen from an offered set that also contains $\mathbf{p}$ is 0.

However, it is important to recognize that no provision has been made for this property in the Luce and Fechner models for wagers as presented above. Indeed, in the Luce model for wagers as given by Equation (24) it is readily seen that, since $h(r)>0$ for all values of r, every wager in any offered set has positive probability of being chosen. In the Fechner model for wagers as given by Equation (25), it is quite possible for two wagers $\mathbf{p}$ and $\mathbf{q}$ to satisfy Equation (31) and still have a very small difference,

$$k\left(\sum_{i=1}^{n} p_i v_i\right) - k\left(\sum_{i=1}^{n} q_i v_i\right).$$

Thus, in conducting an experiment relating to these models, special treatment is required for offered sets containing a pair of wagers satisfying (31).

Finally, we point out that the concept of absolute preference between wagers can be naturally injected into the random utility models for wagers. In fact, the statement that a subject always prefers a larger amount of money to a smaller amount is precisely the statement that the distribution of the random vector $(U_1, \ldots, U_n)$ satisfies the condition.

$$(32) \qquad Pr\{U_1 < U_2 < \cdots < U_n\} = 1 .$$

It then follows easily that if $\mathbf{p}$ and $\mathbf{q}$ are two wagers such that (31) holds, then

$$(33) \qquad Pr\left\{\sum_{i=1}^{n} p_i U_i \geqslant \sum_{i=1}^{n} q_i U_i\right\} = 1 ,$$

and, hence, $\mathbf{p}$ is absolutely preferred to $\mathbf{q}$.

X. SOME PROPERTIES OF THE MODELS

In this section we will derive a few special properties of the stochastic models for wagers that were presented earlier. These properties make it possible to test certain hypotheses about the models on the basis of observations of the subject's choices from a limited number of offered sets.

Consider a Luce model for wagers, defined by the constants $u_1, \ldots, u_n$ and the function $h(r)$, and suppose that $h(r) = r$ for all real numbers r. Then, for any offered set M and any wager $\mathbf{p} \in M$,

$$(34) \qquad \mathbf{p}(M) = \frac{\sum_{i=1}^{n} p_i u_i}{\sum_{q \in M} \sum_{i=1}^{n} q_i u_i} ,$$

where the constants $u_1, \ldots, u_n$ are necessarily positive.

Let M^* be an offered set containing the $m+1$ wagers

$$(35) \qquad \mathbf{p}^j = (p_1^j, \ldots, p_n^j), j = 1, \ldots, m + 1 ,$$

and suppose that

$$(36) \qquad p_i^{m+1} = \frac{1}{m} \sum_{j=1}^{m} p_i^j, \; i = 1, \ldots, n ;$$

that is, the wager p^{m+1} is the average of the other m wagers in M^*. It then follows from (34) and (36) that

$$\text{(37)} \qquad \mathbf{p}^{m+1}(M^*) = \frac{\sum_{i=1}^{n} p_i^{m+1} u_i}{\sum_{j=1}^{m} \sum_{i=1}^{n} p_i^j u_i + \sum_{i=1}^{n} p_i^{m+1} u_i} = $$

$$= \frac{\frac{1}{m} \sum_{i=1}^{n} \sum_{j=1}^{m} p_i^j u_i}{\sum_{j=1}^{m} \sum_{i=1}^{n} p_i^j u_i + \frac{1}{m} \sum_{i=1}^{n} \sum_{j=1}^{m} p_i^j u_i} =$$

$$= \frac{1}{m+1}.$$

Thus, $\mathbf{p}^{m+1}(M^*) = 1/(m+1)$ regardless of the values of $u_1, \ldots, u_n$. This provides an obvious test of the model (34) as follows. If a subject is presented with several distinct offered sets, each having the form of M^* (i.e., each containing an 'average wager'), then under this model the distribution of the number of times the subject chooses the average wager is binomial with parameter $1/(m+1)$.

Furthermore, if in a Luce model for wagers the function $h(r)$ is convex, then it can be shown that $\mathbf{p}^{m+1}(M^*) \leqslant 1/(m+1)$ for all values of $u_1, \ldots, u_n$. If $h(r)$ is concave then $\mathbf{p}^{m+1}(M^*) \geqslant 1/(m+1)$ for all values of $u_1, \ldots, u_n$. These remarks indicate that the usual 1-tailed or 2-tailed test of the hypothesis that $\mathbf{p}^{m+1}(M^*) = 1/(m+1)$ would be appropriate for testing the linearity of h.

We now consider the same probability $\mathbf{p}^{m+1}(M^*)$ under a random utility model for wagers. From Equation (22),

$$\text{(38)} \qquad \mathbf{p}^{m+1}(M^*) = Pr\left\{\sum_{i=1}^{n} p_i^{m+1} U_i \geqslant \sum_{i=1}^{n} p_i^j U_i \text{ for } j = 1, \ldots, m\right\}.$$

But

$$\text{(39)} \qquad \sum_{i=1}^{n} p_i^{m+1} U_i = \frac{1}{m} \sum_{i=1}^{n} \sum_{j=1}^{n} p_i^j U_i = \frac{1}{m} \sum_{j=1}^{m} \left(\sum_{i=1}^{n} p_i^j U_i\right);$$

that is, $\sum_{i=1}^{n} p_i^{m+1} U_i$ is the average of the m quantities $\sum_{i=1}^{n} p_i^j U_i, j = 1, \ldots, m$. Hence,

$$(40)\qquad \sum_{i=1}^{n} p_i^{m+1} U_i \leqslant \max_{j=1,\ldots,m} \sum_{i=1}^{n} p_i^j U_i,$$

and equality holds if and only if the quantities $\sum_{i=1}^n p_j^i U_i, j=1,\ldots, m$, are all equal. But it follows from (23) that

$$(41)\qquad Pr\left\{\sum_{i=1}^{n} p_i^1 U_i = \ldots = \sum_{i=1}^{n} p_i^m U_i\right\} = 0.$$

Hence,

$$(42)\qquad Pr\left\{\sum_{i=1}^{n} p_i^{m+1} U_i < \max_{j=1,\ldots,m} \sum_{i=1}^{n} p_i^j U_i\right\} = 1$$

and, from (38),

$$(43)\qquad p^{m+1}(M^*) = 0.$$

Equation (43) provides a test of the random utility models[4] for wagers: if the 'average wager' is ever chosen from an offered set of the form M^* the stochastic model cannot belong to this class.

The results of an experiment testing both the Luce and the random utility model for wagers will be published in a separate paper. Consider now a Fechner model for wagers defined by the constants $v_1, \ldots, v_n$ and the functions $k(r)$ and $\Phi(r)$. Then for every binary offered set $M = \{\mathbf{p}, \mathbf{q}\}$,

$$(44)\qquad \mathbf{p}(M) = \Phi\left[k\left(\sum_{i=1}^{n} p_i v_i\right) - k\left(\sum_{i=1}^{n} q_i v_i\right)\right].$$

Suppose that the n rewards in S are different amounts of money, numbered in order of increasing amount. It is then reasonable to assume that in the Fechner model for wagers, $v_1 < v_2 < \cdots < v_n$. Consider c binary offered sets $M^j = \{\mathbf{p}^j, \mathbf{q}^j\}$, $j = 1, \ldots, c$, where the wagers $\mathbf{p}^j = (p_1^j, \ldots, p_n^j)$ and $\mathbf{q}^j = (q_1^j, \ldots, q_n^j)$, $j = 1, \ldots, c$ have been chosen so that

$$(45)\qquad p_j^i - q_j^i = d_i, j = 1, \ldots, c;\ i = 1, \ldots, n,$$

and

$$(46)\qquad \sum_{l=x}^{n} q_l^j \geqslant \sum_{l=x}^{n} q_l^{j'},\ x = 1, \ldots, n,$$

whenever $j > j'$.

As examples of such wagers, suppose that $n=3$ and define

$$\text{(47)}\qquad \begin{array}{ll} \mathbf{p}^1 = (.8, 0, .2), & \mathbf{p}^2 = (.7, 0, .3), \\ \mathbf{p}^3 = (.6, .1, .3), & \mathbf{p}^4 = (.4, .2, .4), \\ \mathbf{q}^1 = (.7, .3, 0), & \mathbf{p}^2 = (.6, .3, .1), \\ \mathbf{q}^3 = (.5, .4, .1), & \mathbf{q}^4 = (.3, .5, .2). \end{array}$$

The binary offered sets $M^j = \{\mathbf{p}^j, \mathbf{q}^j\}, j=1, 2, 3, 4$, satisfy (45) and (46), and it should be clear from (47) how this list could be made arbitrarily long.

It follows from (44) and (45) that

$$\text{(48)}\qquad \mathbf{p}^j(M^j) = \Phi\left[k\left(\sum_{i=1}^{n} q_i^j v_i + \sum_{i=1}^{n} d_i v_i\right) - k\left(\sum_{i=1}^{n} q_i^j v_i\right)\right],$$

and from (46) that

$$\text{(49)}\qquad \sum_{i=1}^{n} q_i^1 v_i < \sum_{i=1}^{n} q_i^2 v_i < \cdots < \sum_{i=1}^{n} q_i^c v_i .$$

Hence, if $k(r)$ is a convex function of r, then either $\mathbf{p}^1(M^1) \leqslant \cdots \leqslant \mathbf{p}^c(M^c)$ or $\mathbf{p}^1(M^1) \geqslant \cdots \geqslant \mathbf{p}^c(M^c)$, depending on whether $\sum_{i=1}^{n} d_i v_i \geqslant 0$ or $\sum_{i=1}^{n} d_i v_i \leqslant 0$. A similar statement can be made if $k(r)$ is concave. In particular, if $k(r)$ is linear, then $\mathbf{p}^1(M^1) = \cdots = \mathbf{p}^c(M^c)$. These equalities would also hold if $\sum_{i=1}^{n} d_i v_i = 0$, but since the experimenter typically has at least a rough idea of the magnitudes of $v_1, \ldots, v_n$, he can choose $d_1, \ldots, d_n$ so that the chance that $\sum_{i=1}^{n} d_i v_i = 0$ is negligible.

We can then test the hypothesis that $k(r)$ is linear against the alternative that it is strictly convex or concave as follows.

Record the subject's choices from the offered sets $M^1, \ldots, M^c$ as a sequence of *p*s and *q*s. Then conditionally on the observed number of *p*s and *q*s in the sequence, all sequences with these numbers are equally likely if $k(r)$ is linear, whereas there is a greater chance that the *ps* will be grouped at one end and the *qs* at the other if $k(r)$ is strictly convex or concave. Thus, the usual runs test would be appropriate. If $k(r)$ is linear, the number of runs of *p*s and *q*s in the sequence has the distribution that results when all sequences are equally likely; if $k(r)$ is strictly convex or concave, we would expect to observe fewer runs.

Finally, it is easily seen from Equations (22) and (45) that under any binary random utility model for wagers,

$$\mathbf{p}^j(M^j) = Pr\left\{\sum_{i=1}^{n} d_i U_i \geqslant 0\right\}, j = 1, \ldots, c. \tag{50}$$

Hence, $\mathbf{p}^1(M^1) = \cdots = \mathbf{p}^c(M^c)$, and rejection of this hypothesis implies rejection of the binary random utility models for wagers.

XI. THE SIGN TEST

The following situation arises quite often in analyzing experiments of the type we are considering in this paper. Let $(R_1, T_1), \ldots, (R_m, T_m)$ be m independent pairs of random variables. (This does not assume that R_j and T_j are independent.) Suppose that each of the random variables R_j, T_j, $j=1, \ldots, m$, takes only the values 0 and 1, and let

$$\begin{aligned} &Pr\{R_j = 1, T_j = 1\} = \pi_{11}^j, \\ &Pr\{R_j = 1, T_j = 0\} = \pi_{10}^j, \\ &Pr\{R_j = 0, T_j = 1\} = \pi_{10}^j, \\ &Pr\{R_j = 0, T_j = 0\} = \pi_{00}^j, j = 1, \ldots, m. \end{aligned} \tag{51}$$

Define $D_j = R_j - T_j$, $j = 1, \ldots, m$. Then

$$\begin{aligned} &Pr\{D_j = 1\} = \pi_{10}^j, \\ &Pr\{D_j = 0\} = \pi_{11}^j + \pi_{00}^j, \\ &Pr\{D_j = -1\} = \pi_{01}^j, j = 1, \ldots, m. \end{aligned} \tag{52}$$

Suppose that we are interested in testing the hypothesis

$$H_0: \pi_{10}^j = \pi_{01}^j, j = 1, \ldots, m, \tag{53}$$

against one of the hypotheses

$$\begin{aligned} &H_1: \pi_{10}^j > \pi_{01}^j, j = 1, \ldots, m, \\ &H_2: \pi_{10}^j < \pi_{01}^j, j = 1, \ldots, m, \\ &H_3: \text{Either } H_1 \text{ or } H_2. \end{aligned} \tag{54}$$

It follows from (52) that

$$Pr\{D_j = 1 \mid D_j \neq 0\} = \frac{\pi_{10}^j}{\pi_{10}^j + \pi_{01}^j} \gtreqless \tag{55}$$

$$\gtreqless \tfrac{1}{2} \quad \text{according as} \quad \pi_{10}^j \gtreqless \pi_{01}^j.$$

Let

$$m^* = \sum_{j=1}^{m} |D_j|, \tag{56}$$

$$(56) \qquad D^* = \tfrac{1}{2} \sum_{j=1}^{m} D_j(1 + D_j);$$

that is, m^* is the number of nonzero observations D_j, and D^* is the number of D_j such that $D_j = 1$. It follows from (53) and (55) that if H_0 is true, the conditional distribution of D^*, given the value of m^*, is a binomial distribution with parameter $\frac{1}{2}$, and a 1-tailed or 2-tailed test is appropriate depending on which of the alternative hypotheses H_1, H_2, or H_3 is of interest. Furthermore, if for each conditional value of m^* a test of size α is used, then the over-all test of H_0 has size α.

We now give two examples of the use of this test. The first example is based on a comment of Debreu (1960); the second deals with the problems of predicting subjects' choices. The examples do not deal with wagers explicitly, and so we revert to the term 'objects' to denote the alternatives in an offered set.

Consider m pairs of offered sets, $M_j = \{x_j, y_j\}$ and $M_j' = \{x_j, y_j, y_j'\}$, $j = 1, \ldots, m$, where the objects y_j and y_j' are essentially identical (or indistinguishable) in each pair, $j = 1, \ldots, m$. There are (at least) two points of view regarding the probabilities $x_j(M_j)$ and $x_j(M_j')$. One point of view is that since y_j and y_j' are essentially identical objects, adding y_j' to the offered set M_j should not affect the probability that x_j is chosen; that is, $x_j(M_j) = x_j(M_j')$, $j = 1, \ldots, m$. The second point of view – as would be true, for example, under the Luce model – is that adding another object to the offered set M_j should reduce the probability that x_j is chosen; that is, $x_j(M_j) > x_j(M_j')$, $j = 1, \ldots, m$.

Let $R_j = 1$ if x_j is chosen from M_j and let $R_j = 0$ otherwise; let $T_j = 1$ if x_j is chosen from M_j' and let $T_j = 0$ otherwise. Then assuming all choices are independent,

$$(57) \qquad \begin{aligned} Pr\{D_j = 1\} &= \pi_{10}^j = [x_j(M_j)]\,[1 - x_j(M_j')], \\ Pr\{D_j = -1\} &= \pi_{01}^j = [1 - x_j(M_j)]\,[x_j(M_j')]. \end{aligned}$$

It is readily checked that the hypothesis that $x_j(M_j) = x_j(M_j')$, $j = 1, \ldots, m$, is the hypothesis H_0 of Equation (53), and the hypothesis that $x_j(M_j > > x_j(M_j')$, $j = 1, \ldots, m$, is the hypothesis H_1 of (54).

An experiment testing these two hypotheses will be reported in a separate paper.

As a second example, consider two techniques, A and B, for predicting a subject's choices from offered sets. Suppose that each technique is used to predict the choices from offered sets M_j, $j=1,\ldots,m$. Let $T_j=1$ if A predicts the correct choice from M_j and let $R_j=0$ otherwise; let $R_j=1$ if B predicts the correct choice from M_j and let $T_j=0$ otherwise. Suppose that one person claims that $Pr\{R_j=1\}=Pr\{T_j=1\}$, $j=1,\ldots,m$, and another claims that $Pr\{R_j=1\}>Pr\{T_j=1\}$, $j=1,\ldots,m$. That is, one person claims that both techniques have the same chance of being correct on each offered set and another claims that A has a better chance than B of being correct. Note that R_j and T_j are not necessarily independent, since A and B are predicting the choice from the same offered set. Since

$$(58)\qquad \begin{aligned} Pr\{R_j=1\} &= \pi_{10}^j + \pi_{11}^j, \\ Pr\{T_j=1\} &= \pi_{01}^j + \pi_{11}^j, \end{aligned}$$

it is easily seen that the two claims correspond to the hypotheses H_0 and H_1 of (53) and (54).

XII. HETEROGENEOUS POPULATIONS

Very often an experiment on choice behavior is performed not just with one subject but with a random sample of subjects from some population. In this situation the experimenter is typically interested not only in deciding whether the choice behavior of each subject satisfies a certain condition but also in making some inference about the proportion of individuals in the population whose choice behavior satisfies the condition. It is this problem that will now be considered.

Suppose that a random sample of s subjects is selected from some population and the choices of each subject from several offered sets are observed. Denote the probability distribution of the choices of the jth subject by f_j, $j=1,\ldots,s$. Suppose that we want to decide for each subject in the sample whether his probability distribution f_j satisfies a certain condition C (written $f_j\in C$) or not ($f_j\in' C$). Assume that for each subject in the sample we perform a test of the hypotheses

$$(59)\qquad \begin{aligned} &H_0: f_j\in C \\ &H_1: f_j\in' C, \end{aligned}$$

of size α. That is, for each subject the probability of rejecting H_0 when it is true is at most α.

Let π represent the proportion of individuals in the entire population whose probability distribution f of choices satisfies the hypothesis $f \in C$. Suppose we are also interested in testing the hypotheses

$$(60) \qquad \begin{aligned} &H_0' : \pi \geqslant 1 - \delta \\ &H_1' : \pi < 1 - \delta , \end{aligned}$$

where δ is a fixed (typically small) positive number. Intuitively, if we reject H_0 too many times when testing each individual in the sample, then we will want to reject H_0'. More precisely, let β denote the probability that H_0 will be rejected for a subject drawn at random from the population. Then

$$(61) \qquad \begin{aligned} \beta = &Pr\{\text{Rej. } H_0 | f \in C\} \, Pr\{f \in C\} + \\ &+ Pr\{\text{Rej. } H_0 | f \in' C\} \, Pr\{f \in' C\} \leqslant \\ &\leqslant \alpha\pi + (1 - \pi) = 1 - (1 - \alpha)\,\pi . \end{aligned}$$

If H_0' is true, then $\pi \geqslant 1 - \delta$ and

$$(62) \qquad \beta \leqslant 1 - (1 - \alpha)(1 - \delta) = \alpha + \delta - \alpha\delta .$$

Thus, under H_0' the number of subjects in the sample for whom H_0 is rejected has a binomial distribution with parameter $\beta \leqslant \alpha + \delta - \alpha\delta$. Thus, we can test the hypotheses (60) with the usual 1-tailed test of a binomial parameter.

NOTES

* This paper is one of a series resulting from the co-operation of the three authors at the Western Management Science Institute, University of California at Los Angeles, in 1960-1961. The work was supported in part by the Ford Foundation, the Behavioral Research Service, General Electric Company, and a contract with the Office of Naval Research, Task Number 047-041.

1 If the objects in S are commodity bundles, lottery tickets, or other objects that can be represented as vectors, then there is a natural partial ordering of the objects, and a subjects choices from among the objects in a simply ordered subset of S would typically be consistent. Thus, if every component of commodity bundle a is larger than the corresponding component of commodity bundle b, then a subject would typically always choose a rather than b. Situations of this type are discussed in the section on Wagers.

2 Luce admitted the further possibility that $x(M)$ might be 0 or 1, in which case Equation (3) need not hold. The general question that this raises is discussed in the section on Wagers.

3 It should be noted that in Equation (22) only a single realization of the random vector $(U_1 \ldots, U_n)$ is needed. Under an alternative class of models one might assume that independent realizations of $(U_1, \ldots, U_n)$ are made for each wager in M. When choosing from offered sets containing sure things, these models would not reduce to the

ones presented in the section on Random Utility Models unless the components of $(U_1, \ldots, U_n)$ were independent.

[4] Under the alternative models mentioned in note 3, $\mathbf{p}^{m+1}(M^*)$ need not be 0.

BIBLIOGRAPHY

Abelson, R. M. and Bradley, R. A., 'A 2 × 2 Factorial with Paired Comparisons', *Biometrics* **10** (1954) 487–502.

Berkson, J., 'Maximum Likelihood and Minimum χ^2 Estimates of the Logistic Function', *J. Amer. Statist. Assoc.* **50** (1955) 130–162.

Berkson, J., 'Tables for the Maximum Likelihood Estimate of the Logistic Function', *Biometrics* **13** (1957) 28–34.

Block, H. D. and Marschak, J., 'Random Orderings and Stochastic Theories of Response', *Selected Essays*, 7.

Bradley, R. A., 'Rank Analysis of Incomplete Block Designs. II. Additional Tables for the Method of Paired Comparisons', *Biometrika* **41** (1954) 502–537. (a)

Bradley, R. A., 'Incomplete Block Rank Analysis: on the Appropriateness of the Model for a Method of Paired Comparisons', *Biometrics* **10** (1954) 375–390. (b)

Bradley, R. A., 'Rank Analysis of Incomplete Block Designs. III. Some Large Sample Results on Estimation and Power for a Method of Paired Comparisons', *Biometrika* **42** (1955) 450–470.

Bradley, R. A. and Terry, M. E., 'Rank Analysis of Incomplete Block Designs. I. The Method of Paired Comparisons', *Biometrika* **39** (1952) 324–345.

Brunk, H. D., 'Mathematical Models for Ranking from Paired Comparisons', *J. Amer. Statist. Assoc.* **55** (1960) 503–520.

Cox, D. R., 'The Regression Analysis of Binary Sequences', *J. Royal Statist. Soc., Series B* **20** (1958) 215–242.

Debreu, G., 'Review of R. D. Luce's *Individual Choice Behavior*', *Amer. Econ. Rev.* **50** (1960) 186–188.

Ford, L. R., Jr., 'Solution of a Ranking Problem from Binary Comparisons', *Amer. Math. Monthly* **64** (1957) 8 (suppl.), 28–33.

Luce, R. D., *Individual Choice Behavior*, Wiley, New York, 1959.

Marschak, J., 'Binary-Choice Constraints and Random Utility Indicators', *Selected Essays*, 8.

von Neumann, J. and Morgenstern, O., *Theory of Games and Economic Behavior*', Princeton Univ. Press, Princeton, N.J., 1947.

Quandt, R. E., 'A Probabilistic Theory of Consumer Behavior', *Quart. J. Econ.* **70** (1956) 506–536.

11

ON ADAPTIVE PROGRAMMING*

(1963)

In general, it is non-optimal to estimate, on the basis of past experience and as a basis for present action, an *a posteriori* statistical parameter other than the optimal action itself.

I. PURPOSE OF THIS NOTE

'Adaptive programming' consists in finding the best sequence of rules of action when properties of the relevant probability distribution, to be used in choosing an action, have to be inferred from the effects of previous actions.

This note proposes to drive home a point about 'adaptive programming' which, while obvious, often seems to be misunderstood. It is often stated that, in the case of adaptive programming, each action in the sequence is determined in 'two steps' of data processing: (1) re-estimating the probability-distribution *a posteriori*, and (2) computing the action on the basis of the new estimate.

In this general form, the statement is correct. But it is misunderstood whenever the estimation of the *a posteriori* probability distribution is reduced to estimating some of its parameters (such as the mean) chosen by statistical habit and convenience without reference to the givens of the problem. These givens include, in particular, the transformation function (which relates the state resulting from an action to the state preceding it) and the utility, or criterion, function (the maximand expressed as a function of the final state). To justify the reduction of an *a posteriori* distribution to its mean (say) rather than to some other parameter(s), one would have to assume a very special class of transformation and criterion functions.

One way to make the statement both specific and correct is to say: the optimal action, as a function of the previous states and all other information currently available to the decision maker, is itself a parameter of the probability distribution. It is this parameter that one has to estimate on the basis of current information.

The misunderstanding is particularly glaring when one recalls that the usually recommended theoretical estimators of a parameter are themselves chosen on the basis of their 'optimal properties'. An estimator is recommended because it maximizes a likelihood function, or minimizes the sum of squares of residuals, or the variance of the difference between the estimate and the true value of a parameter, etc. Thus, once having decided, for whatever reason, to represent the *a posteriori* distribution by a certain parameter, the two-steps procedure would first minimize the sum of squares of residuals (for example), to obtain the estimate of the parameter; it would then insert the estimate into the expression for expected utility and then perform a second extremization – viz., that of the expected utility with respect to action. But the decision maker's goal is fully expressed by his utility function! To maximize the latter under the constraint that the sum of squares of residuals also be maximized, will in general depress the utility obtained and thus decrease the efficiency of programming.

I do not believe the pioneering books of Abraham Wald [1] and of Richard Bellman [2], [3] contain the misleading statement. As only few problems in adaptive programming have so far received specific treatment, the statement is mostly heard as a general and somewhat vague prescription. A field in which students have indeed come to grips with the question raised here, and where the misleading statement has been made and contested, and has been, in fact, prevalent in practice, is that of economic policy to be derived, given the utility function, from a system of stochastic simultaneous equations. A rather full analysis of this case was given recently by Walter Fisher in [4], where some earlier literature is also discussed.

This note deals with a particular class of transformation and utility functions. However, the class is broad enough to illustrate the statement that it is not, in general, optimal to reduce the *a posteriori* distribution to a particular parameter, or set of parameters, unless these parameters happen to be the ones called for by the particular transformation and utility functions. Thus, in a particular case (in this note, the case of a quadratic transformation function) one will indeed need to compute and recompute the mean. But this does not apply in general.

To give better insight, the adaptive model will be preceded by a corresponding stochastic model (probability distribution known) and this, in turn, will be preceded by a corresponding deterministic model.

II. GENERAL FORMULATION

Define:

$[x_t]$, $t=0, 1, \ldots, T$: the sequence of *states*.

$[y_t]$, $t=0, 1, \ldots, T-1$: the sequence of *actions*.

In a programming problem, *given* are:

(1) x_0, the *initial state*.

(2) ψ, the *utility function* of the final state's utility $u=\psi(x_T)$.

(3) a *transformation function* g such that

$$x_{t+1} = g(x_t, y_t), \quad t = 0, 1, \ldots, T-1 .$$

To find: the value $[y_t^*]$ of $[y_t]$ such that

(1) for every $t(=0, 1, \ldots, T-1)$, y_t^* depends at most on $(x_0, x_1, \ldots, x_t)$, and

(2) the expectation of utility is maximized. The sequence $[y_t^*]$ is called *optimal program.*

III. ASSUMPTIONS OF THIS NOTE

In general, each x_t and each y_t is a vector or, even more generally, an element of some abstract set. For present purposes, x_t, y_t will be real numbers.

As we are not interested here in the asymptotic properties of long sequences of actions, we shall put $T=2$, to achieve the greatest possible simplicity without loosing the essence. For the same purpose we shall assume that

$$u = x_T = x_2 \, ; \tag{3.1}$$

and that

$$x_{t+1} = g(x_t, y_t) = x_t - f(y_t - x_t - a_t), \quad t = 0, 1, \tag{3.2}$$

where f is a twice differentiable function satisfying appropriate second-order conditions (these may vary from model to model and will not be stated explicitly) to ensure that a finite maximum of expected utility is achieved when its first derivatives with respect to actions vanish.

The term a_t may be random. If it is, we shall assume that a_0 and a_1 have identical independent distributions.

It will be convenient to define

$$z_t \equiv y_t - x_t\,;$$

then

$$(3.3) \qquad x_{t+1} = x_t - f(z_t - a_t), \qquad y_t = x_t + z_t\,;$$

and we can replace the search for the optimal sequence (y_0^*, y_1^*) by the search for the optimal sequence (z_0^*, z_1^*).

In each of the three models, the quadratic case

$$(3.4) \qquad x_{t+1} = x_t - (z_t - a_t)^2/2$$

will be presented first, to exploit its elementary properties.[1] (Also, in this case, the reader will easily prove that the required second-order conditions are satisfied in each model). This will be followed by the general case (3.3). We shall also briefly contrast the quadratic case with the slightly more general one:

$$(3.5) \qquad x_{t+1} = x_t - h\,[(z_t - a_t)^2/2]\,,$$

where h is a positive-valued function. For example, when $h(r) = e^{-r}$, the quadratic case is replaced by that of a Gaussian one (both occur in practice).

IV. DETERMINISTIC MODEL

To start with the quadratic case (3.4), let $a_t = a$, a known constant. Then

$$(4.1) \qquad x_1 = x_0 - (z_0 - a)^2/2$$

$$(4.2) \qquad u = x_2 = x_1 - (z_1 - a)^2/2\,.$$

Clearly, from (4.2),

$$(4.3) \qquad z_1^* = a\,; \qquad y_1^* = x_1 + a\,;$$

inserting into (4.2)

$$\max\nolimits_{z_1} u = x_1\,,$$

so that, by (4.1),

$$\max\nolimits_{z_1} u = x_0 - (z_0 - a)^2/2\,,$$

(4.4) $z_0^* = a\,; \qquad y_0^* = x_0 + a\,.$

The maximum utility is

(4.5) $\max_{z_0 z_1} u = x_0\,.$

Of course we could obtain the same result by simply maximizing u simultaneously with respect to z_0 and z_1, after inserting x_1 from (4.1) into (4.2). But we wanted to exhibit the procedure of 'advancing backward', characteristic of dynamic programming in more complicated cases.

The same optimal actions would be also found in the case (3.5) such as the 'Gaussian' case. But this similarity will break down in the stochastic and deterministic models.

Now, in the more general case of our deterministic model (3.3),

(4.6) $x_1 = x_0 - f(z_0 - a)$

(4.7) $u = x_2 = x_1 - f(z_1 - a)\,.$

Since we have assumed f to fulfill the second order condition for the maximum of u, we obtain z_0^*, z_1^* by differentiation.

Again, we use the 'advancing backward' method, starting with the final action, z_1:

(4.8) $\partial u/\partial z_1 = 0 = -f'(z_1 - a), \quad \text{when} \quad z_1 = z_1^*\,.$

Denote by f^D a function such that

(4.9) $f'(r - a) = 0 \quad \text{when} \quad r = f^D(a)\,.$

f^D is '*the Transform of f appropriate for the Deterministic model*'. Then, from (4.6), (4.8),

(4.10) $z_1^* = f^D(a)\,; \quad y_1^* = x_1 + f^D(a)\,.$

Inserting into (4.6), then into (4.7)

(4.11) $\max_{z_1} u = x_0 - f(z_0 - a) - f\,[f^D(a) - a]\,.$

The last term on the right side depends only on a and on the function f (from which f^D is derived). Hence, differentiating (4.11) with respect to z_0:

$$f(z_0^* - a) = 0\,,$$

so that by the definition of f^D in (4.9)

(4.12) $z_0^* = f^D(a)\,; \qquad y_0^* = x_0 + f^D(a)\,.$

The results (4.3), (4.4) of the quadratic case are, of course, recovered, since in that case $f'(r-a)=r-a, f^D(a)=a$.

V. STOCHASTIC MODEL

We shall confine ourselves to the simple case when the successive random disturbances a_0, a_1 have identical and independent distributions. More particularly, assume

(5.1) $\Pr(a_t = 1) = \alpha\,; \qquad \Pr(a_t = 0) = \beta\,, \quad t = 0, 1\,,$

where α is known and $\alpha+\beta=1$. For any function ϕ of (a_0, a_1) we shall denote by $E_{a_t}\,\phi$ its expectation taken over the values of a_t. Hence

$$E_{a_1}\phi(a_0, a_1) = a\phi(a_0, 1) + \beta\phi(a_0, 0)$$

(5.2) $$E_{a_0}\phi(a_0, a_1) = \alpha\phi(1, a_1) + \beta\phi(0, a_1)$$

$$E_{a_1}E_{a_0}\phi = E_{a_0}E_{a_1}\phi$$

(5.3) $$E_{a_t} = \alpha\,; \qquad E_{a_t}(a_t - \alpha)^2 = \operatorname{Var} a_t = \alpha\beta\,, \quad t = 0, 1$$

However, we shall omit the subscript under E whenever ambiguity is absent. We want to maximize expected utility defined as

(5.4) $U = E_{a_1}E_{a_0}u = E_{a_0}E_{a_1}u\,.$

In the quadratic case (3.4)

(5.5) $$\begin{aligned} x_1 &= x_0 - (z_0 - a_0)^2/2 \\ u &= x_1 - (z_1 - a_1)^2/2 \end{aligned}$$

'Advancing backward' find z_1^* first, noting that

$$\partial u/\partial z_1 = -(z_1 - a_1)\,.$$

Then by (5.4),

(5.6) $$\partial U/\partial z_1 = E_{a_1}E_{a_0}(\partial u/\partial z_1) = E_{a_1}[-(z_1 - a_1)] = -(z_1 - \alpha) = = 0\,,$$

when $z_1=z_1^*$: for we have assumed in Section III that the second order conditions, appropriate to the model considered, are satisfied. Hence

(5.7) $z_1^* = \alpha\,, \qquad y_1^* = x_1 + \alpha\,.$

Inserting into (5.6), we obtain, for $z_1 = z_1^*$,

$$u = x_0 - (z_0 - a_0)^2/2 - (\alpha - a_1)^2$$
$$\partial u/\partial z_0 = -(z_0 - a_0)$$
$$\partial U/\partial z_0 = E_{a_0} E_{a_1}(\partial u/\partial z_0) = -(z_0 - \alpha) = 0$$
$$(5.8) \qquad z_0^* = \alpha\,, \qquad y_0^* = x_0 + \alpha\,.$$

The results (4.3), (4.4) of the corresponding deterministic model (with $a=1$) are recovered putting $\alpha = 1$. Note also that the maximum expected utility, in the stochastic case, is, by (5.4)

$$\max U = x_0 - \operatorname{Var} a_t = x_0 - \alpha\beta\,,$$

to be compared with (4.5). Thus, in the quadratic stochastic case, the loss due to uncertainty is equal to the (known) variance of the random disturbance.

Note also that, in the stochastic model, the solution in the Gaussian case is different from the solution in the quadratic case: (5.6) is replaced by

$$-\partial U/\partial z_1 = \alpha \cdot (z_1 - 1) \cdot e^{-(z_1 - 1)^2/2} + \beta \cdot z_1 e^{-z_1{}^2/2} = 0\,.$$

Now to the general case (3.3):

$$(5.9) \qquad u = x_1 - f(z_1 - a_1)$$

$$(5.10) \qquad x_1 = x_0 - f(z_0 - a_0).$$

We want to maximize expected utility U, defined in (5.4). As in (5.6),

$$\partial E_{a_1}(u)/\partial z_1 = E_{a_1}(\partial u/\partial z_1) = -E_{a_1} f'(z_1 - a_1)\,.$$
$$(5.11) \qquad -E_{a_1}(\partial u/\partial z_1) = \alpha f'(z_1 - 1) + \beta f'(z_1)\,.$$

Let f^S be a function such that

$$(5.12) \qquad af'(r-1) + \beta f'(r) = 0 \quad \text{when} \quad r = f^S(\alpha)\,.$$

f^S is '*the Transform of f appropriate for the Stochastic Model*'. Then, since the appropriate second-order condition is assumed fulfilled, we have, by (5.11), (5.12)

$$(5.13) \qquad z_1^* = f^S(\alpha)\,, \qquad y_1^* = x_1 + f^S(\alpha)\,.$$

Inserting into (5.10), we obtain by the same reasoning

$$(5.14) \qquad z_0^* = f^S(\alpha)\,, \qquad y_0^* = x_0 + f^S(\alpha)\,.$$

In the quadratic case, for example, $f^S(\alpha)=\alpha$, yielding (5.7), (5.8). And the results of the general deterministic case (4.6), (4.7), with $a=1$ are also recovered, by putting $\alpha=1$ so that (5.12) becomes (4.9).

VI. ADAPTIVE MODEL

We shall retain the assumptions and notations of the stochastic model, but assume that not α itself but only an *a priori* distribution p^0 of α is known before action y_0 is taken. We shall confine ourselves to the case when this distribution is finite:

$$\text{(6.1)} \qquad \textit{A priori} \quad \Pr(\alpha=\alpha_k)=p_k^0>0 \quad \text{if} \quad k=1,\ldots,K \\ =0 \text{ otherwise}$$

Thus p^0 is positive-valued only on a specified finite subset $(\alpha_1,\ldots,\alpha_K)$ of the interval [0, 1]. We conjecture, however, that our results can be extended to a continuous distribution p^0 defined on the whole unit interval so that the specification of the α_k is unnecessary.

For a given action y_0 the resulting state x_1 has a $1-1$ relation to the value actually taken by the random disturbance a_0:

$$\text{(6.2)} \qquad x_1=x_1(a_0)=\begin{matrix} x_0-f(z_0-1) \\ x_0-f(z_0)\end{matrix} \quad \text{according as} \quad a_0=\begin{matrix}1, \\ 0\end{matrix}$$

where, of course, x_0 and f have been known from the beginning; $z_0=y_0-x_0$ characterizes the action already taken (and presumably remembered); and x_1 has been that action's result. The knowledge of a_0 inferred by (6.2) is used to replace the *a priori* distribution

$$p^0\equiv\{p_k^0\}\equiv(p_1^0,\ldots,p_K^0)$$

by an *a posteriori* distribution depending on a_0 and denoted thus:

$$p^1(a_0)\equiv\{p_k^1(a_0)\}\equiv(p_1^1(a_0),\ldots,p_K^1(a_0)).$$

By Bayes' theorem and (5.1),

$$\text{(6.3)} \qquad \textit{A posteriori} \quad \Pr(\alpha=\alpha_k\,|\,a_0)\equiv p_k^1(a_0) \begin{matrix} =\alpha_k p_k^0/\sum\alpha_j p_j^0 \text{ if } a_0=1; \\ =\beta_k p_k^0/\sum\beta_j p_j^0 \text{ if } a_0=0.\end{matrix}$$

Here the summation is over $j=1,\ldots,K$. It will be convenient to denote by E_{p^0} and $E_{p^1(a_0)}$, respectively, the expectations taken when the *a priori* distribution p^0 or the *a posteriori* distribution $p^1(a_0)$ is used. Therefore, for example, because of (5.3),

$$(6.4) \qquad E_{p^1(a_0)}[E_{a_1}(a_1)] = E_{p^1(a_0)}(\alpha) = \sum p_k^1(a_0)\cdot a_k.$$

On the basis of the knowledge of a_0 we shall have to choose y_1 (or, equivalently, z_1) so as to maximize the expected utility given a_0

$$U(a_0) \equiv E_{p^1(a_0)}E_{a_1}[u(a_0)],$$

where, in the quadratic case which we want to handle first,

$$u(a_0) = x_1(a_0) - (z_1 - a_1)^2/2.$$

But $\partial U(a_0)/\partial z_1$ vanishes if and only if $z_1 = z_1^*$ (since the second order conditions are easily shown to be fulfilled). Hence,

$$0 = E_{p^1(a_0)}[E_{a^1}(z_1^* - a_1)] = z_1^* - E_{p^1(a_0)}(a_1);$$

and by (6.4), (6.3)

$$(6.5) \qquad z_1^* = \sum \alpha_k p_k^1(a_0) \begin{cases} = \sum \alpha_k^2 p_k^0 / \sum \alpha_j p_j^0 & \text{if} \quad a_0 = 1; \\ = \sum \alpha_k \beta_k p_k^0 / \sum \beta_j p_j^0 & \text{if} \quad a_0 = 0. \end{cases}$$

Hence the maximum expected utility, given a_0, is

$$(6.6) \qquad U^*(a_0) \equiv \max_{z_1} U(a_0) = E_{p^1(a_0)}[E_{a_1} u^*(a_0)]$$

where by (6.5)

$$u^*(a_0) \equiv x_1(a_0) - [\sum \alpha_k p_1^k(a_0) - a_1]^2/2,$$
$$x_1(a_0) = x_0 - (z_0 - a_0)^2/2,$$

so that

$$(6.7) \qquad \partial u^*(a_0)/\partial z_0 = -(z - a_0) = E_{p^1(a_0)}[E_{a_1}\partial u^*(a_0)/\partial z_0],$$

because a_0, a_1 are independent. We use this result to maximize, with respect to z_0, the *a priori* expectation of utility, written as

$$(6.8) \qquad U^* \equiv E_{p^0}E_{a_0}U^*(a_0) = \sum p_k^0[\alpha_k U^*(1) + \beta_k U^*(0)]$$

(compare (5.2)). Now by (6.6), (6.7)

$$(6.9) \qquad \partial U^*(a_0)/\partial z_0 = E_{p^1(a_0)}[E_{a_1}\partial u^*(a_0)/\partial z_0] = -(z_0 - a_0).$$

Now since, again, the second order conditions are known to be fulfilled,

$$\partial U^*/\partial z_0 = 0 \quad \text{when} \quad z_0 = z_0^*;$$

so that by (6.8), (6.9)

$$(6.10) \qquad \begin{aligned} 0 &= \sum p_k^0 [\alpha_k(z_0^* - 1) + \beta_k z_0^*] \\ z_0^* &= \sum \alpha_k p_k^0 . \end{aligned}$$

It is seen from (6.10), (6.5) that, in the quadratic case, the optimal values z_0^*, z_k^1, do turn out to be the means of the unknown parameter α computed on the basis of the *a priori* distribution p^0 or the *a posteriori* distribution $p^1(a_0)$, respectively. The optimal actions $y_t^* = x_t + z_t^*$, $t=0, 1$, are chosen on the basis of those means.

Now let us turn to the general case (5.9), (5.10) [but with α unknown]:

$$\partial u/\partial z_1 = -f'(z_1 - a_1),$$

so that

$$\partial U/\partial z_1 = E_{p^1(a_0)}[E_{a_1} f'(z_1 - a_1)],$$

the value of a_0 having been inferred from x_1 as in (6.2). Hence, since the appropriate second order conditions for maximum expected utility have been assumed to be fulfilled by the function f,

$$\begin{aligned} 0 &= \sum p_k^1(1) [\alpha_k f'(z_1^* - 1) + \beta_k f'(z_1^*)] \quad \text{if} \quad a_0 = 1 \\ 0 &= \sum p_k^1(0) [\alpha_k f'(z_1^* - 1) + \beta_k f'(z_1^*)] \quad \text{if} \quad a_0 = 0 . \end{aligned}$$

Denote the solution of each of these two equations by

$$(6.11) \qquad z_1^* = f^A(p^1(a_0)); \quad a_0 = 1, 0 .$$

The function f^A is, then, the '*Transform of f appropriate to the Adaptive Model*'. Check for the quadratic case: then

$$f'(z_1^* - 1) = z_1^* - 1, \quad f'(z_1^*) = z^*,$$

and we recover the solution (6.5). To continue with the general case, retaining the definition (6.6), we obtain, instead of (6.7),

$$\begin{aligned} u^*(a_0) &= x_1(a_0) - f[f^A(p^1(a_0)) - a_1] \\ x_1(a_0) &= x_0 - f(z_0 - a_0), \end{aligned}$$

$$\partial u^*(a_0)/\partial z_0 = \partial x_1(a_0)/\partial z_0 = -f'(z_0 - a_0) = \partial U^*(a_0)/\partial z_0,$$

since a_1, a_0 are independent. Moreover

$$\begin{aligned} U^* &\equiv E_{p^0}E_{a_0}U^*(a_0) = \sum p_k^0[\alpha_k U^*(1) + \beta_k U^*(0)] \\ \partial U^*/\partial z_0 &= \sum p_k^0 \cdot [\alpha_k \cdot \partial U^*(1)/\partial z_0 + \beta_k \cdot \partial U^*(0)/\partial z_0] \\ &= -\sum p_k^0 [\alpha_k f'(z_0 - 1) + \beta_k f'(z_0)] = 0, \end{aligned}$$

when $z_0 = z_0^*$. Hence, by the above definition of f^A,

$$z_0^* = f^A(p^0) \tag{6.12}$$

We can, in fact, consider z_1^* in (6.11) and z_0^* in (6.12) as the relevant parameters of the *a posteriori* and the *a priori* distributions, respectively: relevant, that is, to the particular problem characterized by the function f. Suppose that, instead of using the transform f^A of f, we would have proceeded as follows: after inferring a_0 from x_1 exactly by (6.2), and constructing the *a posteriori* probability distribution $p^1(a_0)$ of the a_k, compute the mean

$$\sum \alpha_k p_k^1(a_0) = \bar{\alpha}(a_0),$$

say. Insert this into the stochastic *non-adaptive* model of Section V, to replace α in (5.1), (5.13), obtaining

$$f^S(\bar{\alpha}(a_0)) = \bar{z}_1, \quad \text{say}.$$

This would be perhaps a '2-step procedure', in the (misleading) sense described in our introductory section. It is not clear what $\bar{z}_0$ would be. Perhaps it is obtained by inserting $\bar{z}_1$ into the utility expectation U computed on the basis of the *a priori* probability distribution p^0, and then maximizing U with respect to z_0? Or perhaps $\bar{z}_0$ is computed by assuing

$$\alpha = \bar{\alpha}^0(a_0) \equiv \sum \alpha_k p_k^0,$$

and assuming, as was done with z_1, that the model is a non-adaptive one?

Any such solution would be non-optimal except in special cases.

[*Added in* 1973. With adaptive programming implying the knowledge of prior probabilities it is, in fact, formally identical with stochastic programming. (See 'Proposition 1' in Koichi Miyasawa [9].) In terms more general than those of our text, let $a = (a_1, \ldots, a_T)$ be a time sequence of random (and not necessarily additive and independent) shocks, with a belonging, for simplicity, to a countable set. In stochastic programming, the probability $p(a)$ is assumed known. In adaptive programming, there exists an unknown distribution of the sequence a, characterized by an unknown parameter α (possibly a vector, or a point in the space of all distributions of a). But a prior distribution $F(\alpha)$ is known and so is the conditional probability $q(a \mid \alpha)$ (say). Then

$$p(a) = \int q(a \mid \alpha) \, \mathrm{d}F(\alpha).$$

Hence the givens, (q, F), of an adaptive problem determine also the given, p, of the stochastic problem. Thus maximizing expected utility of a strategy, given (q, F), is the same as to maximize it, given p. (A strategy is defined as a sequence of decision functions, each associating the information available at a given time with the action to be taken at that time.)]

VII. CONCLUDING REMARK

In pure as distinct from applied research one usually does not know in advance what the applications will be. When estimating a planetary orbit Gauss [6] argued for maximizing what is today called the likelihood function of observations. Under his assumption that observation errors are normally distributed this implied the least squares method. Later, he justified the method differently (see Neyman [7]): by the need to minimize the expected loss due to estimation errors admitting that the loss function quadratic in these errors is merely the simplest of the infinitely many other loss functions that might be considered. Whatever the justification, he could not know what particular use will be made of his estimate. Perhaps it is not too far fetched to suggest that, when making more precise estimates of the position of the moon for the landing of a modern astronaut, one should maximize the now relevant criterion function (which may depend on the date and safety of landing, etc.) simultaneously with respect to the estimate *and* to the structural characteristics of the spaceship.

Some time ago, Sir Ronald Fisher [8] deplored the recent Russian "ideal that research in pure science can and should be geared to technological performance" and the American tendency "to confuse the process appropriate for drawing correct conclusions with those aimed at... saving money." Yet, I do not know whether an all-purpose scientific induction criterion has ever been constructed or even proved to exist. Perhaps we must share Gauss' latter and resigned view that any such criterion is arbitrary, apart from simplicity. Be it as it may. Problems of programming are always applied ones. And even though disagreement may exist as to the precise criterion function that the program has to maximize, we have seen that on formal grounds it will be, in general, inefficient to separate the estimation procedure from the determination of optimal rules of action.

NOTES

* Supported by the Office of Naval Research under task number NR-047-041, by the Electronic Systems Division, Systems Design Laboratory under contract number AF 19(628)-31, and by a grant from the Ford Foundation to Western Management Science Institute.

1 Analogous results are obtained in a multi-variate quadratic case studied by Joseph and Tou [5].

BIBLIOGRAPHY

[1] Wald, Abraham, *Statistical Decision Functions*, 1950.

[2] Bellman, Richard, *Dynamic Programming*, 1957.

[3] Bellman, Richard, *Adaptive Control Processes*, 1961.

[4] Fisher, Walter D., 'Estimation in the Linear Decision Model', *International Economic Review*, **3**, No. 1 (January 1962), 1–29.

[5] Joseph, Peter D. and Tou, Julius T., 'On Linear Control Theory', *Applications and Industry*, publ. by American Institute of Electrical Engineers, September 1961.

[6] Gauss, Carl Friedrich, *Aus der Theorie der Bewegung der Himmelskoerper* (1809), 2. Buch, 3. Abschnitt, Sec. 176–179. Translation from Latin in selected *Abhandlungen zur Methode der kleinsten Quadrate* (A. Boersch and P. Simon, eds.), Berlin 1887, pp. 99–104.

[7] Neyman, Jerzy, 'Note on an Article by Sir Ronald Fisher', *Journal Royal Stat. Soc.* **B18** (1956), 288–294. Neyman quotes from Gauss' *Theorie der... Combination der Beobachtungen* (1821), Sec. 6, also included in the *Abhandlungen...*, (see preceding footnote), pp. 5–6.

[8] Fisher, Sir Ronald, 'Statistical Methods and Scientific Induction', *Journal Royal Stat. Soc.* **B 17** (1955), 69–78.

[9] Miyasawa, Koichi, 'Information Structures in Stochastic Programming Problems', *Management Science* **14** (1968) 5, esp. p. 276.

12

AN EXPERIMENTAL STUDY OF SOME STOCHASTIC MODELS FOR WAGERS*

(1963)

Co-authors: G. M. BECKER and M. H. DEGROOT

In this paper we report the results of an experiment designed to test the appropriateness of certain models for choices among wagers. These models and the test procedure to be used have previously been described in this journal in some detail (Becker *et al.*, 1963), but for convenience we will briefly restate them here. The reader should, however, refer to Becker *et al.* (1963) for precise statements of the basic concepts of rewards, wagers, offered sets, and stochastic models for wagers, and for proofs of theorems.

Two particular models of choice among wagers will be studied here. For easier explanation, we shall briefly recall the two corresponding models of choice among objects that are not necessarily wagers. Let all the objects used in a series of experiments belong to a finite set S of n objects; these can therefore be thought of as numbered from 1 to n. The probability that object i will be chosen from the subset M of S, offered in a given trial, is denoted by $i(M)$.

In the *strict utility* (*or Luce*) *model*, this probability $i(M)$ is assumed to be proportional to a positive constant characterizing the object i and called its *strict utility* u_i, fixed for a given person.

In the *random utility model*, on the other hand, the choice of a particular object i from an offered subset M of S is thought to depend on the way in which the person has ranked, at the time of making the choice, all objects in S. Each ranking (permutation of S) is assumed to have a probability, fixed for a given peson. That is, the set $S=(1, \ldots, n)$ of objects is associated with a vector $(U_1, \ldots, U_n)$ of random utilities, whose joint probability distribution is such that, for example, $Pr(U_{i_1} > U_{i_2} > \ldots > U_{in})$ is the probability that the elements $i_1, i_2, \ldots, i_n$ of S are ranked in that order.[1] The object chosen is the one ranked highest. Hence $i(M)=Pr(U_i \geqslant U_j$, all j in $M)$.

In applying these two models to the special case when the choice is among wagers, we exploit the additional hypothesis that such choice depends on the 'expected utility' of the wager, a concept that must be defined in a different way in each of the two models. We shall assume that all of the rewards used in the experiment form a finite set. We shall now denote this set of all rewards used (not the set of all wagers used) by $S=(1,\dots,n)$. Any wager p can then be represented as an n-dimensional vector $\mathbf{p}=(p_1,\dots,p_n)$, where p_i is the probability of receiving reward i, for $i=1,\dots,n$. For any offered set M (i.e., any finite set of wagers) and any wager $\mathbf{p}\in M$, $\mathbf{p}(M)$ is the probability that a subject will choose $\mathbf{p}$ from M.

By u_i and U_i $(i=1,\dots,n)$ we denote, as before, the strict and the random utility of the reward i. This yields two alternative definitions of expected utility of a wager $\mathbf{p}$ in a stochastic model: viz., the weighted averages $\sum_{i-1}p_iu_i$ and $\sum_{i-1}p_iU_i$.

In the *strict utility* (*or Luce*) *model for wagers*, the probability $\mathbf{p}(M)$ of choosing wager $\mathbf{p}$ from an offered subset M is proportional to that wager's 'strict utility', a quantity that is the greater, the greater $\sum p_iu_i$. In the *random utility model for wagers* the probability $\mathbf{p}(M)$ is equal to the probability that $\mathbf{p}$ is ranked higher than other wagers in M; the wagers being ranked according to their 'random utilities', $\sum p_iU_i$. Let us state this more precisely.

A stochastic model for wagers is said to be a *strict utility* (*or Luce*) *model for wagers* if there exist positive constants $u_1,\dots,u_n$, and a positive, strictly increasing function h, defined for all real numbers r in some interval containing all the values $u_1,\dots,u_n$, such that

$$(1)\qquad \mathbf{p}(M)=\frac{h\left(\sum_{i=1}^{n}p_iu_i\right)}{\sum_{q\in M}h\left(\sum_{i=1}^{n}q_iu_i\right)}$$

for every M and every $\mathbf{p}\in M$.

A model is a *random utility model for wagers* if there exists a random vector $(U_1,\dots,U_n)$ such that

$$(2)\qquad \mathbf{p}(M)=Pr\left[\sum_{i=1}^{n}p_iU_i\geqslant\sum_{i=1}^{n}q_iU_i\quad\text{for all}\quad \mathbf{q}\in M\right]$$

for every M and every $\mathbf{p}\in M$.

Let M^* be an offered set containing the $m+1$ distinct wagers

$$(3)\qquad \mathbf{p}^j=(p_1^j,\dots,p_n^j),\ j=1,\dots,m+1,$$

where

$$(4)\qquad p_i^{m+1} = \frac{1}{m}\sum_{j=1}^{m} p_i^j,\ i = 1, \dots, n;$$

that is, $\mathbf{p}^{m+1}$ is the average of the other m wagers in M^*. Let $p = \mathbf{p}^{m+1}$ (M^*). It has been shown (Becker *et al.*, 1963) that under any strict utility model for wagers and any values of $u_1, \dots, u_n$, $p \leqslant 1/(m+1)$ if h is a convex function and $p \geqslant (1/(m+1)$ if h is a concave function. In particular, $p = 1/(m+1)$ if h is a linear function. Furthermore, it was shown (Becker *et al.*, 1963) that under any random utility model for wagers, $p=0$.

Suppose that it is possible to observe a subject's choices from each of several distinct offered sets, each having the form of M^* (i.e., each containing one wager that is the average of the others). The above remarks indicate how one might test (1) the hypothesis that the appropriate stochastic model describing the subject's choices is a strict utility model for wagers with a linear function h against a class of alternatives that includes the strict utility models with a strictly convex or concave function h; or (2) the hypothesis that the appropriate stochastic model is a random utility model for wagers.

I. EXPERIMENT

Let (w_i, x_i, y_i, z_i), $i = 1, \dots, 25$, denote 25 distinct quadruples of monetary rewards, ordered so that for each value of i, $w_i < x_i < y_i < z_i$. From each of the quadruples (w_i, x_i, y_i, z_i), $i = 1. \dots, 25$, an offered set M_i^* was constructed as follows. Let $\mathbf{A}_i$ be the wager that yields the rewards w_i and z_i, each with probability $\frac{1}{2}$. Let $\mathbf{B}_i$ be the wager that yields the rewards x_i and y_i, each with probability $\frac{1}{2}$. Let $\mathbf{C}_i$ be the wager that yields each of the rewards w_i, x_i, y_i and z_i, with probability $\frac{1}{4}$. Then, for $i = 1, \dots, 25$, the wager $\mathbf{C}_i$ is the average of the wagers $\mathbf{A}_i$ and $\mathbf{B}_i$, in the sense of the preceding section, and the offered set M_i^* containing the three wagers $\mathbf{A}_i$, $\mathbf{B}_i$, and $\mathbf{C}_i$ is of the same form as the offered set M^* described above (with $m=2$).

In Table I the actual rewards used in the experiment are shown. Thus, e.g., wager $\mathbf{A}_1$ yields the reward 3 or 89, each with probability $\frac{1}{2}$; $\mathbf{B}_1$ yields the rewards 31 or 65, each with probability $\frac{1}{2}$; and $\mathbf{C}_1$ yields the rewards 3, 31, 65, or 89, each with probability $\frac{1}{4}$.[2]

Subjects were 62 students registered in a course in introductory psychology. Students in the course were required to serve six hours as experi-

TABLE I

Rewards and offered sets in the experiment

i	A_i		B_i	
1	3	89	31	65
2	0	72	17	51
3	1	45	13	37
4	10	62	20	54
5	60	88	72	78
6	20	56	30	54
7	2	44	11	33
8	2	80	17	63
9	22	78	35	63
10	3	87	29	57
11	29	61	41	55
12	4	45	18	42
13	8	50	19	35
14	16	84	18	72
15	6	90	21	73
16	14	88	53	57
17	23	55	39	49
18	21	93	27	73
19	4	62	24	36
20	6	76	12	72
21	2	98	26	80
22	3	71	33	37
23	16	42	24	38
24	2	32	10	28
25	0	36	7	25

mental subjects or else to write a term paper. Each student who participated in our experiment received one hour credit toward fulfilling this requirement.

Each subject received a test booklet containing the 25 offered sets M_i^*, $i=1,\ldots,25$, as well as 100 other offered sets designed for another purpose, together with instructions.

In 31 of the test booklets, the instructions informed the subject that the rewards represented dollars, and the subjects were encouraged to win as much money as possible. These subjects (the Score group) did not expect to be actually rewarded with the amount they won. The other 31 subjects (the Pay group) were informed that the rewards represented pennies and that they would actually be paid as much as they won from some of the wagers that they chose. The subjects were divided into the two groups at random.

Each reward in a wager was associated with the drawing of a card from a deck containing four cards labelled ZEJ, ZOJ, XEH, and XIH. In each offered set M_i^*, the wagers $\mathbf{A}_i$ $\mathbf{B}_i$, and $\mathbf{C}_i$ (although not identified as such to the subjects) appeared in a random order. Thus, for example, the offered set M_1^* appeared in the printed test booklet as follows:

ZEJ	3	31	3
ZOJ	89	65	31
XEH	3	31	65
XIH	89	65	89

The subject was asked to choose one of the three columns. He would then receive the reward appearing in the row corresponding to the card that would be drawn from the deck.

II. RESULTS AND ANALYSIS

As noted above, the statistic of interest is, for each subject, the number of times that he chose the wager $\mathbf{C}_i$ from the 25 offered sets M_i^*, $i=1,\ldots, 25$. Table 2 gives the distribution of subjects according to the number of times the 'average wager' $\mathbf{C}_i$ was chosen. Thus, for example, nine of the subjects in the Score group chose the wager C_i from exactly seven of the 25 offered sets.

A chi-square test did not reveal any significant difference between the distributions of the Pay and Score groups, and hence we studied only the last column of Table II, which gives the distribution of all subjects participating in the experiment.

One striking result to be noted immediately is that 60 of the 62 subjects chose the 'average wager' $\mathbf{C}_i$ at least once. Thus, the random utility model for wagers must be rejected for these 60 subjects.

Now suppose that the strict utility model for wagers is appropriate for some subject. If h is a linear function, then the distribution of the number N of times the 'average wager' is chosen by the subject is binomial with

TABLE II

Distribution of subjects according to the number of times C_i was chosen from the 25 offered sets

Number of choices of C_i	Pay group	Score group	All subjects
0	2	0	2
1	1	1	2
2	1	3	4
3	0	3	3
4	4	3	7
5	3	2	5
6	1	1	2
7	2	9	11
8	3	4	7
9	2	0	2
10	6	2	8
11	2	0	2
12	1	0	1
13	1	1	2
14	0	0	0
15	1	0	1
16	0	0	0
17	0	1	1
18	0	0	0
19	1	1	2
20 or more	0	0	0
Total	31	31	62

parameter $p=\frac{1}{3}$. Using a 2-tailed test of level of significance $\alpha=.088$ (a natural significance level resulting from the discreteness of the binomial distribution), the hypothesis that h is linear (i.e., that $p=\frac{1}{3}$) should be rejected if $N\leqslant 4$ or $N\geqslant 13$. It is readily found from Table II that performing this test on each of the 62 subjects leads to the rejection of the hypothesis for 24 of the subjects.

Suppose that for a given subject, after rejecting the hypothesis that the stochastic model is a strict utility model with linear h, it was desired to classify the stochastic model determining the subject's choices as either a Luce model with a strictly convex function h or a Luce model with a strictly concave function h. It follows from the remarks made earlier that a reasonable procedure would be to decide that h is strictly convex if $N\leqslant 4$ and that h is strictly concave if $N\geqslant 13$. From Table II it is seen that of the

24 subjects for whom the hypothesis that h is linear is rejected, 18 would be classified as having a strictly convex h and 6 as having a strictly concave h.

If we consider the 62 subjects as forming a random sample from some population, it is possible, by a technique described in Becker *et al.* (1963, p. 55), to obtain a confidence interval for the proportion of the population for whom the Luce model with linear h is not appropriate. The construction of a confidence interval with confidence coefficient .99, based on the observation that this model was rejected for 24 of the 62 subjects in the sample, leads to the statement that for at least 18 per cent of the population the Luce model with linear h is inappropriate.

Thus, in the experiment described above, neither the random utility model for wagers nor the strict utility model for wagers with linear h is adequate for describing the chice behavior of a large proportion of the population under study.

NOTES

* The work described in this paper was sponsored by the Western Management Science Institute, University of California at Los Angeles, under grants from the General Electric Company and its Behavioral Research Service, the Ford Foundation, and a contract with the Office of Naval Research, Nonr 233(75).

1 It can be proved that $Pr(U_i \geqslant U_j) = 0$ for all $i \neq j$. In this sense, the random utility model excludes ties. See Equation (2), Becker *et al.* (1963), and Block and Marschak (1960).

2 The expected monetary rewards are larger for A_i than B_i in twelve cases, and smaller in thirteen cases. The standard deviations of monetary rewards are $(z_i - w_i)/2$ and $(y_i - x_i)/2$, for every A_i and B_i, respectively, and the former is larger than the latter. In this sense, A_i is more 'risky' than B_i, for every i, as pointed out by a referee.

BIBLIOGRAPHY

Becker, H. M., DeGroot, M. H., and Marschak, J., 'Stochastic Models of Choice Behavior', 1963, *Selected Essays*, 10.

Block, H. D. and Marschak, J., 'Random Orderings and Stochastic Theories of Response', 1960, *Selected Essays*, 7.

13

THE PAYOFF-RELEVANT DESCRIPTION OF STATES AND ACTS*

(1963)

Typically, a problem in information economics consists of choosing simultaneously an optimal pair: (1) an information channel producing messages, and (2) a decision rule associating each message with an act. The givens of the problem are: the probability distribution on the states of the world, and the utility yielded by each combination of act and state, taking account of message costs.

Whatever the costs, probabilities, and utilities, a preliminary step consists in formulating a given information problem with just as much detail as neccessary. In particular, two descriptions of possible states and acts, one detailed and one less detailed, may be such as to lead to exactly the same physical outcomes or the same amounts of utility; yet it can be assumed that the more detailed description should be avoided. The situation is similar to that of optimal production programs: the set of possible programs is reduced to an efficient subset on the basis of the sole proposition that 'large inputs are bad, large outputs are good', regardless of a specific objective function on the set of programs.

Accordingly, this Note will deal with the reduction of descriptions of states and acts to relevant ones.[1] Another paper[2] will develop the concepts used in the first paragraph.

I. DESCRIPTIONS OF STATES AND ACTS

Consider the set $\{Z\}$ consisting of all possible partitions $Z=\{z\}$, $Z'= =\{z'\}$,... of a fundamental set of *states*, $X=\{x\}$. Each partition Z is called a set of (mutually exclusive and exhaustive) *state descriptions*.

Similarly, consider the set $\{C\}$ consisting of all partitions $C=\{c\}$, $C'=\{c'\}$,... of a fundamental set of *acts*, $A=\{a\}$. Each partition C is called a set of (mutually exclusive and exhaustive) *act descriptions*.

A binary relation '$\leqslant$' is defined on $\{Z\}$ and, similarly, on $\{C\}$ as follows:

(1) DEFINITION: $Z \leqslant Z'$ (*Z is finer than Z'*; or equivalently, *Z' is coarser than Z*) *if*, for every z in Z, there is a z' in Z' with $z \subseteq z'$.

The relation '$\leqslant$' induces a strict partial ordering on $\{Z\}$ and, similarly on $\{C\}$. Moreover, $\{Z\}$ is a lattice possessing a (unique) finest element, $\{(x)\}$, the finest partition of X, and a (unique) coarsest element (X), the coarsest partition of X. Similarly $\{C\}$ is a lattice, with $\{(a)\}$ and (A) as its (unique) finest and coarsest elements.[3]

II. OUTCOME CONDITION

Define a function from $X \times A$ to the set of *outcomes* $O = \{o_{xa}\}$; that is, to each pair (x, a) there corresponds one element o_{xa} in O. For a given pair Z in $\{Z\}$, C in $\{C\}$, define an *outcome function* from $Z \times C$ to the set of all subsets of O; thus

$$w_{ZC}(z, c) \subseteq O\,; \quad z \text{ in } Z,\, c \text{ in } C.$$

To simplify notation we shall consistently denote by $z, z' \ldots$ (possibly with a subscript) an element of $Z, Z', \ldots$, respectively; and similarly for $c, c', \ldots$ and $C, C', \ldots$. This will often permit us to drop the subscripts under w, as its domain $Z \times C$ is indicated unambiguously by the lower case letters in the argument. Moreover, we shall sometimes write x, a instead of $(x), (a)$; and X, A instead of $\{(x)\}, \{(a)\}$ without danger of ambiguity.

A set W of outcome functions w_{ZC}(all Z in $\{Z\}$, all C in $\{C\}$) is called an *outcome condition* if the following consistency requirement is satisfied:

$$(2) \qquad w_{ZC}(z, c) = \bigcup_{x \text{ in } z} \bigcup_{a \text{ in } c} (o_{xa}), \quad \text{all } z \text{ in } Z,\, c \textit{ in } C.$$

III. SUFFICIENTLY FINE DESCRIPTION SETS

DEFINITION: A *pair of sets* (Z, C) *is sufficiently fine* (*s.f.*) *for* W if every value of every outcome function in W consists of a single element of O.

By (2) this means that

$$(3) \qquad w(z, c) = (o_{xa}), \quad \text{all } x \text{ in } z,\, a \text{ in } c,\, z \text{ in } Z,\, c \text{ in } C.$$

DEFINITION: A set Z is *s.f.* for W if the pair (Z, A) is *s.f.* for W.

By (3) this means that

$$(4.1) \qquad w(z, a) = (o_{xa}), \quad \text{all } x \text{ in } z,\, a \text{ in } A,\, z \text{ in } Z.$$

Similarly,

DEFINITION: A set C is *s.f.* for W if

(4.2) $w(x, c) = (o_{xa})$, all a in c, x in X, c in C.

This language is justified by

THEOREM I: *If* Z *(or, respectively,* C*) is s.f., and* $Z' \leqslant Z$ *(or, respectively,* $C' \leqslant C$*) then* Z' (C') *is s.f.*

Proof. By (1), (2).

We also have

THEOREM II: (Z, C) *is s.f. for* W *if and only if* Z *and* C *are s.f. for* W.

Proof of sufficiency. From (4.1), (4.2) using (2). *Proof of necessity.* In (3) replace c, C, z, Z by a, A, x, X.

IV. EQUIVALENT STATES (ACTS) AND SUFFICIENTLY COARSE DESCRIPTION SETS

DEFINITION: z_1, z_2, in Z are *W-equivalent given* C if

(5.1) $w(z_1, c) = w(z_2, c)$, all c in C.

(It is easily seen that W-equivalence is a genuine equivalence relation.)

DEFINITION: c_1, c_2 in C are *W-equivalent given* X *if*

(5.2) $w(z, c_1 = w(z, c_2)$, all z in Z.

DEFINITION: A *pair of sets* (Z, C) *is sufficiently coarse (s.c.) for* W if no distinct elements of Z are W-equivalent given C; and no distinct elements of C are W-equivalent given Z.

That is (using (5.1), (5.2)), for all z_1, z_2 in Z and all c_1, c_2 in C

(6.1) $w(z_1, c) = w(z_2, c)$ for all c in C implies $z_1 = z_2$;

and

(6.2) $w(z, c_1) = w(z, c_2)$ for all z in Z implies $c_1 = c_2$.

DEFINITION: A *set* Z *is sufficiently coarse for* W if no distinct elements of Z are W-equivalent given A; that is (using (6.1)), for all z_1, z_2 in Z,

$$w(z_1, a) = w(z_2, a), \quad \text{all } a \text{ in } A, \text{ implies } z_1 = z_2. \tag{7.1}$$

Similarly,

DEFINITION: A *set* C *is sufficiently coarse for* W if, for all c_1, c_2 in C,

$$w(x, c_1) = w(x, c_2), \text{ all } x \text{ in } X, \text{ implies } c_1 = c_2. \tag{7.2}$$

This language is justified by

THEOREM III: *If the pair of sets* (Z, C) *is s.c. for* W *then* Z *and* C *are s.c. for* W (but the converse is not true: see Note below).

Proof. Suppose (Z, C) is s.c. for W. To prove that Z is s.c. let $z_1 \neq z_2$ be two elements of Z. Then by (2), (6.1),

$$\bigcup_{a \text{ in } c_0} \bigcup_{x \text{ in } z_1} (o_{xa}) \neq \bigcup_{a \text{ in } c_0} \bigcup_{x \text{ in } z_0} (o_{xa}) \quad \text{for some } c_0 \text{ in } C;$$

$$\bigcup_{a \text{ in } c_0} w(z_1, a) \neq \bigcup_{a \text{ in } c_0} w(z_2, a) \quad \text{for some } c_0 \text{ in } C;$$

$$w(z_1, a_0) \neq w(z_2, a_0) \quad \text{for some } a_0 \text{ in } A;$$

hence $z_1 \neq z_2$ implies $w(z_1, a_0) \neq w(z_2, a_0)$ for some a_0 in A; and this is equivalent to (7.1). One proves similarly (using (2), (6.2), (7.2)) that C is s.c. for W.

Note. Theorem III is analogous to the necessity part of Theorem II; but, unlike Theorem II, no sufficiency part holds. A counter-example is instructive as an exercise. Let O be the set of integers and consider the following matrix $[o_{xa}]$:

	x_1	x_2	x_3	x_4
a_1	1	2	1	3
a_2	3	4	2	4

Let $c = (a_1, a_2)$, $z_1 = (x_1, x_2)$, $z_2 = (x_3, x_4)$ so that $z_1 \neq z_2$. Then the pair (Z, C) is not sufficiently coarse, for the outcome function $w(z, c)$ is as follows:

$w(z, c)$

	z_1	z_2
c	(1, 2, 3, 4)	(1, 2, 3, 4)

Yet both Z and C are sufficiently coarse, for the outcome functions $w(z, a)$ and $w(x, c)$ are represented by the following two matrices:

$w(z, a)$	z_1	z_2
a_1	(1,2)	(1,3)
a_2	(3,4)	(2,4)

$w(x, c)$	x_1	x_2	x_3	x_4
c	(1,3)	(2.4)	(1,2)	(3,4)

V. UNIQUENESS AND EXISTENCE OF AN OUTCOME-RELEVANT PAIR (Z, C)

DEFINITION: *A pair* (Z, C) *is called outcome-relevant for* W *(or, briefly,* W*-relevant) if* (Z, C) *is both sufficiently fine and sufficiently coarse for* W.

THEOREM IV: *There is one and only one* W*-relevant pair.*

Proof of uniqueness. Suppose (Z, C) and (Z', C') are two W-relevant pairs. Then, by Theorems II and III, Z, C, Z', C' are sufficiently fine and sufficiently coarse. We shall show that $Z=Z'$ which means that

(8) $\quad$ for any z in Z, z' in Z', either $z \cap z' = \phi$ or $z = z'$.

Let $z \cap z' \neq \phi$. Then, since Z, Z' are s.f. for W, we have by (4.1),

(9) $\quad w(z, a) = (o_{xa}) = w(z', a),\quad$ all x in $z \cap z'$, all a in A.

Further, suppose x_0 is in z and hence by (4.1), (9),

(10) $\quad (o_{x_0a}) = w(z, a) = w(z', a),\quad$ all a in A;

it follows that x_0 is in z'. For, let x_0 in z_0' in Z'; then by (4.1), (10)

$$(o_{x_0a}) = w(z_0', a) = w(z', a),\quad \text{all } a \text{ in } A;$$

and, since Z is sufficiently coarse for W, $z_0'=z_0$ by (7.1). Thus x_0 in z implies x_0 in z'. By symmetry of reasoning, x_0 in z' implies x_0 in z. Hence $z=z'$, proving (8). Hence $Z=Z'$. By similar argument, $C=C'$.

Proof of existence. Let z^W be a class of all x that are w-equivalent, given A. Accordingly, define $Z^W=\{z^W\}$, a partition of X, as follows:

(11.1) $\quad Z^W = \{z^W : x_1, x_2 \text{ in } z^W \quad \text{if and only if}$

$$o_{x_1a} = o_{x_2a},\quad \text{all } a \text{ in } A\}.$$

Define similarly C^W, a partition of A:

(11.2) $C^W = \{c^W : a_1, a_2 \text{ in } c^W \quad \text{if and only if}$
$$o_{xa_1} = o_{xa_2}, \quad \text{all } x \text{ in } X\}.$$

Clearly Z^W is sufficiently fine, with

(12) $w(z^W, a) = (o_{xa}), \quad \text{all } a \text{ in } A, \text{ all } z^W \text{ in } Z^W.$

Similarly with C^W. Hence (Z^W, C^W) is sufficiently fine. Now, to show that (Z^W, C^W) is sufficiently coarse, suppose

(13.1) $w(z_1^W, c^W) = w(z_2^W, c^W), \quad \text{all } c^W \text{ in } C^W,$

and suppose

(13.2) $w(z^W, c_1^W) = w(z^W, c_2^W), \quad \text{all } z^W \text{ in } Z^W;$

and let x_1 in z_1^W, x_2 in z_2^W; then by (12) and (13.1)

$$(o_{x_1a}) = w(z_1^W, c^W) = w(z_2^W, c^W) = (o_{x_2a}), \quad \text{all } a \text{ in } A.$$

Hence by the definition of z^W in (11.1), z_2^W and z_1^W are identical equivalence sets. Thus (13.1) implies $z_1^W = z_2^W$. Similarly, (13.2) implies $c_1^W = c_2^W$. Hence (Z, C) is sufficiently coarse. Hence (Z^W, C^W) is W-relevant.

COROLLARY: *The only W-relevant pair is* (Z^W, C^W) *defined in* (11.1), ((11.2). *Accordingly,* Z^W *and* C^W *can be called the unique outcome-relevant description sets.*

VI. PAYOFF-RELEVANT DESCRIPTION SETS

A *utility function* $u(.)$ maps O into the set R of real numbers: $u(o)$ is the utility of an outcome o. Hence, with each $Z \times C$ and each outcome condition W is associated a subset of R:

$$u[w_{ZC}(z, c)] \equiv v_{ZC}(z, c) \subseteq R.$$

The function v_{ZC} just defined, a composition of w_{ZC} and u, is called the *payoff function.* A consistent set V of payoff functions is defined analogously to W in (2): V consists of all functions v_{ZC} such that

$$v_{ZC}(z, c) = \bigcup_{x \text{ in } z} \bigcup_{a \text{ in } c} (u(o_{xa})).$$

Again, we can often omit the domain index ZC without ambiguity. The concepts of sufficiently fine and coarse sets or pairs of sets, defined previously for W can be redefined for V in analogous fashion. In addition, $v(z, c)$ being, in general, a subset of real numbers, *a domination* relation between real-valued functions can be exploited: whenever, for a c_0 in C and all z in Z, there exists a c_1 in C such that (1) $v(z, c_0) \neq v(z, c_1)$, and (2) no element of $v(z, c_0)$ is larger than any element of $v(z, c_1)$, we say that c_0 is inadmissible. By eliminating all inadmissible elements from each set C, we obtain a smaller set of act descriptions, and the set $\{C\}$ of all such sets is redefined correspondingly.

A *payoff-relevant pair* (Z^V, C^V) defined analogously to (Z^W, C^W) exists and is unique by the same reasoning as in the proof of Theorem V. We give without proof

THEOREM V: *For any W, v and $u(.)$,*

(1) *if (Z, C) is sufficiently fine for W it is s.f. for V; but not conversely;*
(2) *if (Z, C) is sufficiently coarse for V it is s.c. for W; but not conversely;*
(3) $Z^W \leqslant Z^V$; $C^W \leqslant C^V$.

VII. SUMMARY

The domain $Z \times C$ of a payoff function is the product of a set of state descriptions and a set of act descriptions; the range of a payoff function is the power set of the set of real numbers (utilities). The domain is called payoff-relevant if it is both sufficiently fine (i.e., the payoff function is real valued everywhere) and sufficiently coarse (i.e., the payoff function is not constant for any fixed element of Z or of C). Given a consistent set V of payoff functions, there is one and only one payoff-relevant domain, $Z^V \times C^V$.

This result is derived from a more general one. An outcome function maps $Z \times C$ into the power set of a set O of ('physical') outcomes. An outcome-elevant domain is defined appropriately. Given a consistent set W of outcome functions there is one and only one outcome-relevant domain, $Z^W \times C^W$.

NOTES

* Supported by the Office of Naval Research under task number NR-047-041 and the Western Management Science Institute under its grant from the Ford Foundation.

[1] Thanks are due to J. MacQueen and T. Ferguson who have helped to outline some of the questions, and to Ray Radner and Zivia Wurtele who helped to outline some of the proofs.

[2] J. Marschak [1963].

[3] See Birkhoff [1948], especially p. 2, Example 6; p. 17, Example 4; p. 107, Theorem 8. The relation 'finer than' is closely related to Savage's [1954] relation 'extension of'; the latter is not anti-symmetric and induces a partial *pre*-ordering on X.

BIBLIOGRAPHY

[1] Birkhoff, G., *Lattice Theory* (2nd ed.), American Mathematical Society, New York, (Colloquium Publications, Vol. 25), 1948.

[2] Marschak, J., 'Problems in Information Economics' (1963), *Selected Essays*, 25.

[3] Savage, L. J., *The Foundations of Statistics*, Wiley and Sons, New York, 1954. Revised, Dover, 1972.

14

PROBABILITIES OF CHOICES AMONG VERY SIMILAR OBJECTS: AN EXPERIMENT TO DECIDE BETWEEN TWO MODELS*

(1963)

Co-authors: G. M. BECKER and M. H. DEGROOT

The purpose of this paper is to report an experimental investigation of individual choice behavior in certain situations suggested by Debreu (1960) in his review of Luce's book (1959). Let T denote the set of all possible alternatives from among which a subject might be required to choose. For any finite subset S of T (we call S the 'offered set') and any alternative x in S, let $x(S)$ denote the probability that the subject, when choosing among the alternatives in S, will choose x. Thus $x(\{x, y\})$ is the probability that the subject will choose from the pair $\{x, y\}$ the alternative x rather than y. When $x(\{x, y\})=1$, or equivalently $y(\{x, y\})=0$, we say that x is absolutely preferred to y. The Luce model[1] as presented in his book (1959) states that if no element of T is absolutely preferred to another element of T, then every element x of T is associated with a positive number $v(x)$ (which we have called 'strict utility of x') such that, for every offered subset S of T,

$$x(S) = \frac{v(x)}{\sum_{y \in S} v(y)};$$

(that is, the elements of any offered set are chosen with probabilities proportional to their strict utilities).

We will assume throughout this paper that $x(\{x, y\})$ is neither 0 nor 1 for every pair x, y in T. Then it follows from the Luce model that for any alternatives x, y, z in T, $x(\{x, y, z\})<x(\{x, y\})$. Debreu has criticized this property of the Luce model, contending that if the alternatives y and z are in some sense equivalent, then the addition of z to the set $\{x, y\}$ should not reduce the probability that x will be chosen. Indeed, the Luce model can lead to the result that although a person is more likely to choose coffee than to choose tea from a tray containing one cup of coffee and one cup

of tea, he is more likely to choose tea than to choose coffee from a tray containing one cup of coffee and two cups of tea. Specifically, suppose that x is a cup of coffee and y and z are cups of tea. Suppose further that $y(\{y, z\})=\frac{1}{2}$, therefore $v(y):v(z)=1:1$; and that $x(\{x, y\})=\frac{3}{5}$, therefore $v(x):v(y)=3:2$. Then $v(x):v(y):v(z)=3:2:2$ and hence $x(\{x, y, z\})=\frac{3}{7}$. Thus $x(\{x, y\})>\frac{1}{2}$ but $x(\{x, y, z\})<\frac{1}{2}$. Debreu suggests that in a situation of this type $x(\{x, y\})$ and $x(\{x, y, z\})$ should be more nearly equal, if not precisely equal. If Debreu's criticism is valid then the use of the Luce model must be restricted to distinct, dissimilar alternatives. This, of course, raises the delicate question as to when two alternatives should be considered to be dissimilar. In the example given above, if the two cups containing tea were easily distinguishable should they be considered as dissimilar alternatives?

In experiments to be described here, the above problem was investigated in situations where the alternatives from among which a subject must choose were wagers yielding monetary rewards.

Let $E_1, E_2, \ldots, E_t$, $t \geqslant 2$, be mutually exclusive and exhaustive events. A *wager* $\mathbf{W}$ is a vector $\mathbf{W}=(W_1, \ldots, W_t)$ where each W_i, $i=1, \ldots, t$, is a real number representing an amount of money. The interpretation is that if a subject chooses the wager $\mathbf{W}=(W_1, \ldots, W_t)$ from some offered set, then he will be rewarded with the amount W_i if the event E_i occurs, $i=1, \ldots, t$.

When a set of alternatives is presented to a subject, the alternatives must be presented in some media and in some order. Each wager must also be displayed in some configuration, i.e., the events and rewards must be arranged in some spatial or temporal configuration. A person's reaction to a set of wagers may be influenced by such configurations. For example, if the list of available wagers is sufficiently long, the person may select a wager before examining all of the alternatives on the list. Similarly, if the wagers depend upon a large number of events (i.e., if t is large), the subject may pay attention to only a few of the events and ignore others. In the experiments to be described here, an effort was made to ensure that these influences would be absent.

Suppose that the events $E_1, \ldots, E_t$ are equiprobable (as is the case in the experiments to be described here). We then say that the wagers $\mathbf{W}= =(W_1, \ldots, W_t)$ and $\mathbf{W}'=(W_1', \ldots, W_t')$ are *similar* if the rewards $(W_1', \ldots, W_t')$ are simply a permutation of the rewards $(W_1, \ldots, W_t)$. Thus, in particular, if $\mathbf{W}=\mathbf{W}'$ (i.e., $W_i'=W_i$, $i=1, \ldots, t$) then $\mathbf{W}$ and $\mathbf{W}'$ are similar;

in this case we say **W** and **W′** are similar and identical.

If the offered set of wagers from which a subject must choose is presented to him as a printed list it is possible that the list contains duplications. In other words, it is possible that a given wager appears more than once in the list. Accordingly, it is permissible to speak of an offered set containing the three alternatives **W**, **W′**, and **W** repeated again. In fact, offered sets of precisely this form are of interest in the present paper.

Let M be an offered set containing two dissimilar wagers, **A** and **B**, and let M' be an offered set containing the three wagers **A**, **B**, and **C**, where **B** and **C** are similar. In some of the experiments that were carried out, **C** was actually identical with **B**, and in others **B** and **C** were similar but not identical. In either case it is not unreasonable to interpret Debreu's comments as stating that $\mathbf{A}(M)=\mathbf{A}(M')$, whereas under the Luce model, $\mathbf{A}(M)>$ $>\mathbf{A}(M')$. (Recall that $\mathbf{A}(M)$ is the probability that **A** is chosen from M.)

Let $M_j=\{\mathbf{A}_j, \mathbf{B}_j\}$ and $M_j=\{\mathbf{A}_j, \mathbf{B}_j, \mathbf{C}_j\}$, $j=1,\ldots,n$, be n pairs of offered sets, each pair having the same form as the pair M and M' just described. (The wagers $\mathbf{A}_j$, $\mathbf{B}_j$ and $\mathbf{C}_j$ may, however, vary with j.)

It is known (see, e.g., the last two sections of Becker *et al.* [1963a]) that for a given subject, the hypotheses

$$H_0: \mathbf{A}_j(M_j)=\mathbf{A}_j(M_j'), j=1,\ldots,n,$$
$$H_1: \mathbf{A}_j(M_j)>\mathbf{A}_j(M_j'), j=1,\ldots,n,$$

can be tested as follows.

Let n^* denote the number of pairs, M_j and M_j', such that $\mathbf{A}_j$ is chosen from either M_j or M_j' *but not from both*. Let D^* denote the number of these pairs such that $\mathbf{A}_j$ is chosen from M_j but not from M_j'. Then, for a given value of n^*, the probability distribution of D^* is binomial with parameter $p=\frac{1}{2}$ if H_0 is true, whereas larger values of D^* are more probable if H_1 is true. Thus, the usual 1-tailed test of the hypothesis that the binomial parameter $p=\frac{1}{2}$ is appropriate.

Furthermore, suppose that this test has been carried out, at level of significance α, on each subject in a random sample of N subjects drawn from some population of interest. (α is the probability of rejecting H_0 for a given subject when it is, in fact, true.) Let π denote the proportion of the population for whom H_0 is true, and suppose that it is desired to test the hypothesis $H_0':\pi\geqslant 1-\delta$, where δ is some given number, $0<\delta<1$. If H_0' is true, then Y, the number of subjects in the sample of N for whom H_0 was rejected, has a binomial distribution with parameter $p \leqslant \alpha + \delta - \delta\alpha$. Thus, H_0' can be tested by a 1-tailed binomial test based on Y or equivalently, an upper confidence limit for π can be computed from Y.

I. EXPERIMENTAL DESIGN[2]

Let the events E_1, E_2, E_3 and E_4 be the four possible outcomes when one card is drawn from a deck of four cards. Each of the four cards is labeled

TABLE I

Amounts used in the experiment

i	w_i	x_i	y_i	z_i
1	19	9	7	1
2	18	11	9	4
3	36	18	12	4
4	40	26	10	0
5	58	36	22	2
6	52	28	22	8
7	70	35	25	0
8	74	51	27	6
9	68	43	33	12
10	86	66	18	8
11	87	64	32	11
12	98	79	15	0
13	100	75	25	2
14	86	52	48	18
15	91	66	26	11
16	92	74	44	28
17	94	67	51	28
18	96	70	50	34
19	93	76	62	47
20	94	69	67	46
21	96	73	59	46
22	97	81	77	63
23	98	82	76	64
24	93	81	73	71
25	99	95	85	83

with a different nonsense syllable and the deck is shuffled, so it is reasonable to assume that the four events are considered to be equiprobable by each of the subjects.

TABLE II

Experimental data

	Hypothesis pair											
	1			2			3			4		
Subject	n^*	D^*	Sig. level	n^*	D^*	Sig. level	n^*	D^*	Sig. level	n^*	D^*	Sig. level
1 SB	10	5		14	9		11	7		13	7	
2 PF	8	1		10	2		6	1		7	2	
3 PF	3	2		5	5	.031	5	5	.031	2	2	
4 SB	4	2		8	3		10	5		7	4	
5 SF	2	1		1	1		3	3	.125	2	2	
6 PF	12	6		9	3		7	2		10	5	
7 SC	6	1		5	1		9	3		6	1	
8 PB	0	0		0	0		2	0		3	1	
9 SB	6	3		7	3		6	3		7	4	
10 SB	3	0		1	0		3	1		3	0	
11 SF	11	6		12	5		11	6		8	6	.145
12 PB	13	6		9	5		12	5		13	4	
13 SB	6	4		4	2		4	3		7	6	.008
14 SF	0	0		0	0		0	0		0	0	
15 PF	1	0		1	0		0	0		1	0	
16 PF	12	7		11	8	.113	19	15	.010	18	13	.048
17 PB	5	3		8	6	.145	10	4		7	2	
18 SF	14	6		8	6	.145	13	6		13	3	
19 SF	5	3		4	2		3	1		4	2	
20 SB	13	9	.133	11	10	.006	12	11	.003	10	8	.055
21 PF	10	3		9	4		9	5		8	3	
22 PB	9	5		12	5		11	5		14	8	
23 SB	3	1		3	2		6	4		6	3	
24 PF	11	4		12	7		12	5		11	2	
25 PB	0	0		0	0		0	0		0	0	
26 PB	6	3		9	5		8	3		8	3	
27 SB	8	7	.008	7	6	.062	10	8	.055	11	9	.033
28 SF	5	1		4	1		7	3		6	2	
29 PB	5	1		6	3		8	4		10	4	
30 PF	9	9	.002	5	4		4	3		10	9	.001
31 SF	9	0		8	3		5	2		10	1	
32 SF	10	5		7	4		10	6		10	6	
33 PF	4	0		6	0		8	0		6	0	
34 PB	1	0		0	0		1	0		1	0	
35 SB	0	0		0	0		0	0		0	0	
36 SF	10	5		14	6		9	6		12	8	
37 PB	9	5		6	3		6	3		11	6	
38 SB	11	6		10	5		7	3		11	5	
39 PB	11	1		12	4		12	3		16	3	

TABLE II

Experimental data (*Continued*)

	Hypothesis pair											
	1			2			3			4		
Subject	n^*	D^*	Sig. level	n^*	D^*	Sig. level	n^*	D^*	Sig. level	n^*	D^*	Sig. level
40 PF	8	4		10	5		11	5		9	4	
41 PF	17	5		13	7		18	12	.119	10	4	
42 PB	7	1		9	3		9	5		7	3	
43 PF	8	3		9	3		5	1		4	1	
44 SF	9	5		8	5		11	6		10	5	
45 SB	1	0		1	0		2	1		2	1	
46 SF	1	1		1	1		2	1		2	1	
47 SB	10	4		11	4		9	4		13	7	
48 PB	10	5		8	2		10	7		12	10	.019
49 PB	11	6		8	7	.035	12	20	.019	11	7	
50 PB	10	7		10	9	.011	11	11	.000	9	8	
51 SF	12	6		8	5		9	4		13	5	
52 PB	9	2		13	5		14	5		9	2	
53 SB	12	11	.003	11	9	.033	12	8		11	9	
54 SB	5	3		5	2		4	2		4	3	
55 SF	14	9		13	9	.133	15	11	.059	12	9	.073
56 PF	9	7	.090	13	11	.011	12	10	.019	13	9	.133
57 SF	0	0		0	0		1	0		1	0	
58 SF	8	3		8	5		6	4		10	4	
59 PB	8	4		8	5		5	3		5	2	
60 PF	12	7		13	9	.133	10	8	.055	9	6	
61 PB	5	3		6	4		7	5	—	5	3	
62 PF	5	3		8	2		6	1		7	4	

Note: The symbols P or S, and F or B, following the subject serial number indicate whether the subject belonged to the Pay or Score, and Fore or Back, groups.
The significance levels are those for a 1-tailed binomial test. Only values less than .15 are listed.

The sets of wagers from among which the subjects must choose are constructed as follows. For each i, $i=1, 2, \ldots, 25$, let $S_i=\{w_i, x_i, y_i, z_i\}$ be four amounts of money such that $w_i>x_i>y_i>z_i$. Define the wagers $\mathbf{T}_i$, $\mathbf{U}_i$, and $\mathbf{V}_i$ to be $\mathbf{T}_i=(w_i, w_i, z_i, z_i)$, $\mathbf{U}_i=(x_i, x_i, y_i, y_i)$ and $\mathbf{V}_i=(y_i, y_i, x_i, x_i)$. In other words, in the wager $\mathbf{T}_i$ the reward is w_i if the event E_1 occurs, w_i if E_2 occurs, z_i if E_3 occurs, and z_i if E_4 occurs, and similarly for the wagers $\mathbf{U}_i$ and $\mathbf{V}_i$. Finally, define the offered sets L_i, L_i', L_i'', L_i'''

to be $L_i = \{\mathrm{T}_i, \mathrm{U}_i\}$, $L'_i = \{\mathrm{T}_i, \mathrm{U}_i, \mathrm{U}_i\}$, $L''_i = \{\mathrm{T}_i, \mathrm{U}_i, \mathrm{V}_i\}$, and $L'''_i = \{\mathrm{T}_i, \mathrm{V}_i\}$. Thus L_i and L'''_i are binary sets (pairs), while L''_i and L'_i are ternary sets (triples).

Thus, from each of the 25 sets S_i of monetary amounts, four different offered sets of wagers were constructed. Accordingly, each subject in the study chose one wager for each of 100 offered sets.

The monetary amounts used in the experiment are shown in Table I. The sets were presented in booklet form, approximately eight offered sets on each page. The order of presentation was essentially random, except that all of the binary offered sets, L_i and L'''_i, $i = 1, \ldots, 25$, were presented either before or after the entire group of ternary offered sets L'_i and L''_i, $i = 1, \ldots, 25$. Furthermore, care was taken to try to eliminate the possibility of the relative position of the wagers having an influence on the subjects' choices.

II. SUBJECTS AND EXPERIMENTAL GROUPS

Sixty-two students registered in an introductory psychology course volunteered as subjects for this experiment. Each student received one hour credit toward completion of a course requirement of six hours spent as an experimental subject. Students who did not complete this requirement were required to write a term paper.

Half of the subjects were told that they would be paid whatever they won from some of the wagers that they chose (the Pay group). To these subjects, the amounts appearing in the wagers were described as pennies. The other subjects (the Score group) were told that they would not be paid, but were instructed to win as much money as they could. The payoffs for the Score group were described as dollars. The same wagers were presented to both groups with only the instructions in the first part of the booklet varying. Also, half of the subjects chose from the 50 ternary offered sets first and then chose from the 50 binary offered sets (the Fore group). The other half of the subjects (the Back group) made their choices in the reverse order.

The subjects were randomly assigned to one of the four groups (Pay or Score, Fore or Back) according to the test booklet they received at the beginning of the session. All subjects were tested in a single group session that lasted approximately 45 minutes.

III. RESULTS

Referring to the definitions of the offered sets L_j, L'_j, L''_j and L'''_j, $j=1,\ldots,25$, it is seen that there are several possible pairs that could be chosen to play the role of the offered sets M_j and M' in the hypotheses H_0 and H_1 presented earlier. Thus, it would be reasonable to let (1) $M_j=L_j$ and $M'_j=L'_j$, or (2) $M_j=L_j$ and $M'_j=L''_j$, or (3) $M_j=L'''_j$ and $M'_j=L''_j$, or (4) $M_j=L'''_j$ and $M'_j=L'_j$. For any one of these definitions (1), (2), (3), or (4), we could carry out the test of the hypotheses H_0 and H_1 described above. Ideally, of course, it would be best to develop one composite test that would subsume all of these individual pairings, but it did not seem worthwhile to investigate such a test at the present stage of study.

The observed values of n^* and D^* for each of the subjects and each of the above four pairs of hypotheses are given in Table II. A simple tabulation from Table II will give, for any level of significance $\alpha \leqslant .15$, and any one of the four pairs of hypotheses, the number of subjects for whom H_0 would be rejected. This tabulation is given in Table III. Since there did not appear to be any significant difference between the Pay and Score, and Fore and Back groups, only the totals for all subjects are given.

Let us now regard the 62 experimental subjects as a random sample from some population of interest, and let π be the proportion of this

TABLE III

Number of the 62 subjects for whom H_0 is rejected

	Hypothesis pair			
	1	2	3	4
$\alpha = .15$	5	12	11	11
$\alpha = .05$	3	6	6	7

population for whom Debreu's comments are valid; i.e., π is the proportion of the population for whom H_0 is true. As described earlier, it is possible to use any single entry in Table III to obtain an upper confidence limit for π. A simple computation yields the following results, for confidence coefficient .90. The upper confidence limit for π corresponding to the observed result for $\alpha=.05$ and hypothesis pair 4 is .968. All other entries in Table III yield an upper limit 1 for π.

Thus, the observed data provide no reason to doubt that Debreu's comments are valid for most of the population.

NOTES

* The work described in this paper was supported by the Western Management Science Institute, University of California at Los Angeles, under its grant from the Ford Foundation, a grant from the General Electric Company, and a contract with the Office of Naval Research, Task Nonr 233(75). The statistical computations were carried out at the Western Data Processing Center, University of California at Los Angeles.

1 The Luce-Debreu controversy submitted here to an empirical test was briefly considered by the authors of the present article in the section 'The Sign Test' of their theoretical article (Becker *et al.*, 1963a). In that article, the 'Luce model' was also called 'strict utility model'. The notation in the present article follows Luce's book (1959) in some respects, thus slightly differing from the notation in Becker *et al.* (1963a).

2 It was possible to carry out this experiment in the same session with that described in Becker *et al.*, (1963b).

BIBLIOGRAPHY

Becker, G. M., DeGroot, M. H., and Marschak, J., 'Stochastic Models of Choice Behavior', (1963) (a) *Selected Essays*, 10.

Becker, G. M., DeGroot, M. H., and Marschak, J., 'An Experimental Study of Some Stochastic Models for Wagers', (1963) (b) *Selected Essays*, 12.

Debreu, G., 'Review of R. D. Luce, *Individual Choice Behavior*', *Amer. Econ. Rev.* **50** (1960) 186–188.

Luce, R. D., *Individual Choice Behavior*, Wiley, New York, 1959.

15

MEASURING UTILITY BY A SINGLE-RESPONSE SEQUENTIAL METHOD

(1964)

Co-authors: G. M. BECKER and M. H. DEGROOT

The purpose of this paper is to describe a sequential experiment that provides, at each stage in the sequence, an estimate of the utility to the subject of some amount of a commodity (e.g., money), and to present a few experimental results obtained with the method. The procedure is based upon the following well-known 'expected utility hypothesis'. For each person there exist numerical *constants*, called *utilities*, associated with the various possible outcomes of his actions, given the external events not under his control. If, for a given subject, we could know the values of these constants and the ('personal') probabilities he assigns to the various external events we could, according to this model, predict his choice from among any available set of actions. He will choose an action with the highest expected utility; i.e., with the highest average of utilities of outcomes, weighted by the probabilities he assigns to the corresponding events. He will be indifferent between any two actions with equal expected utilities. Note that (by the nature of weighted averages) the comparison between expected utilities does not depend on which two particular outcomes are regarded as having zero-utility and unit-utility.

Other models of choice behavior, called *stochastic models*, do not predict the actual choices of a subject from each given set of available actions but rather they make statements about the *probabilities* that the scientist might assign to the various actions being chosen by the subject. It is assumed that these probabilities do not change during the time period under consideration, thus precluding learning or any systematic change of behavior. Relations between these probabilities of choice and the expected utilities described above are postulated.

One such postulate (associated with the name of Fechner) specifies that, for a given subject, action A has a larger expected utility than action B if and only if, when forced to choose between A and B, the probability that he chooses A is larger than the probability that he chooses B. It follows that if a choice between A and B is made many times under identical conditions, the person will choose the action with the larger expected utility more than half of the time. If he is indifferent he will choose each action 50 per cent of the time.

Mosteller and Nogee (1951), in what was perhaps the first laboratory measurement of utility, based their experiment on the Fechner postulate. They offered a subject choices of the following type: either accept a wager $(a, p, -b)$ in which you will win a dollars with probability p and you will win $-b$ dollars (i.e., lose b dollars) with probability $1-p$, or do not bet at all. They repeated the same offer several times, thereby obtaining the proportion of times that the subject decided to accept the wager. By holding p and b constant and varying a they were able to estimate the amount of money a_0 at which this proportion was 50 per cent. Then by assumption the subject was indifferent between accepting the wager $(a_0, p, -b)$ and not betting at all. Hence, these two actions have equal expected utilities. Therefore, denoting by $u(x)$ the utility of gaining x dollars,

$$u(0) = pu(a_0) + (1 - p)\, u(-b).$$

As stated above, one can arbitrarily fix $u(0)=0$ and $u(-b)=-1$. Then

$$u(a_0) = (1 - p)/p.$$

By keeping b constant and using the above technique for seven different values of p, Mosteller and Nogee estimated seven points on the subject's 'money-gain utility curve (function)', which represents the relation between money gains and their utilities.

The experiment just described depends heavily on the assumption that the subject's probabilities of choice remain constant throughout the many times that he is choosing from the same available set of actions, and also on the assumption that each of the seven values of p used in the experiment is 'understood' by the subject: i.e., that his personal probability of winning a dollars in a given wager is in fact p.

The procedure to be presented here differs from that of Mosteller and Nogee in several respects. No choice is repeated, but a check on the subject's consistency, or on his learning process, is provided. This is achieved by letting each set of available actions depend on the subject's previous responses in a manner that leads to repeated estimates of the same points on his utility curve. Some of these checks for consistency would be applicable even if the personal probabilities p of the subject were not known to the experimenter. However, the only odds used in our experiment were 1:1 and 3:1, and it did not seem unreasonable to assume that the simple probabilities $\frac{1}{2}$ and (to a lesser extent) $\frac{3}{4}$ were 'understood' by the subject.

I. THE SEQUENTIAL PROCEDURE

Let p be the probability of an event E, and let (y, p, z) be a wager in which one wins the amount y if the event E occurs and one wins the amount z if E does not occur. If a subject is indifferent between accepting the wager (y, p, z) and accepting a certain monetary gain of amount x, we shall call x his cash-equivalent of (y, p, z). Thus, $u(x)=pu(y)+(1-p)\,u(z)$.

Let a and b, with $a<b$, be two convenient amounts of money and fix arbitrarily $u(a)=0$, $u(b)=1$. In the next section we shall describe a method for determining a subject's cash-equivalent of any given wager. For the moment let us assume that we know how to do this. Then, if x_1 is the cash-equivalent of the wager (a, p, b), we have

$$u(x_1) = pu(a) + (1 - p)\,u(b) = 1 - p\,.$$

Similarly, if x_2 is the cash-equivalent of (b, p, a), then

$$u(x_2) = pu(b) + (1 - p)\,u(a) = p\,.$$

The amounts x_1, x_2, a, and b can now be used in later stages of a sequential experiment to form ten new wagers, (a, p, x_1), (x_2, p, b), etc., and the cash-equivalents of each of these wagers can also be determined.

If we define $u^*(y, p, z)=pu(y)+(1-p)\,u(z)$ to be the utility of the wager (y, p, z) then it is easily verified that

$$\begin{aligned}
u^*(x_1, p, a) &= u^*(a, p, x_2) = p(1 - p)\,,\\
u^*(x_2, p, b) &= u^*(b, p, x_1) = 1 - p + p^2\,,\\
u^*(a, p, x_1) &= (1 - p)^2\,,\\
u^*(x_1, p, b) &= 1 - p^2\,,\\
u^*(x_2, p, a) &= p^2\,,\\
u^*(b, p, x_2) &= p(2 - p)\,,\\
u^*(x_1, p, x_2) &= 2p(1 - p)\,,\\
u^*(x_2, p, x_1) &= 1 - 2p + 2p^2\,.
\end{aligned}$$

It is seen from these equations that, regardless of the value of p, the wagers (x_1, p, a) and (a, p, x_2) have the same utility and consequently they also have the same cash-equivalent. Similarly, (x_2, p, b) and (b, p, x_1) have the same cash-equivalent. Thus the determination of a subject's cash-equivalents of the wagers (x_1, p, a) and (a, p, x_2), say, provides a check on whether the subject is behaving in a manner consistent with a well-defined utility functions as specified by the utility model. If p is known, further checks of this kind can be established, as will be seen later.

The same general procedure can be followed throughout the experiment using at each stage a different probability p' selected so that some of the wagers formed with p' will have the same utilities as some of the wagers formed with p.

II. DETERMINING THE CASH-EQUIVALENT OF A WAGER

The following method can be used to determine the cash-equivalent of a wager (y, p, z) for a given subject. The subject is told that he will be rewarded from the wager (y, p, z); i.e., that he will receive the amount y if the event E of probability p occurs and he will receive the amount z otherwise.

The subject is then told that as an alternative to receiving this random reward from the wager he has the privilege of trying to sell the wager for cash. Accordingly, he is asked to state the smallest amount s that he will accept (his *selling price*) in lieu of being rewarded from the wager. The understanding is that if a buyer can be found who is willing to pay an amount $b \geqslant s$ then the subject will receive b. If no buyer can be found who is willing to pay at least s then the subject retains the wager and receives the random reward, either y or z, as specified by the wager.

Let s be the subject's selling price and let e be his cash-equivalent of the wager. Let b be the maximum amount that any buyer is willing to pay. It is assumed that b does not depend on s, but the method of generating b is otherwise irrelevant. If $b \geqslant s$, the subject will receive the amount b. If $b < s$, the subject will receive a random reward as specified by the wager.

We claim that it is to the subject's advantage for his selling price to be precisely his cash-equivalent of the wager; that is, to have $s = e$. This can be seen as follows.

From the definition of e, $u(e) = u^*(y, p, z)$ and, hence, receiving the certain cash amount e is equivalent to the subject to receiving a random reward from the wager. Now suppose $s>e$. If $b<e$ or $b \geqslant s$, the subject's fortune changes just as it would had his selling price been $s=e$. However, if b is such that $e \leqslant b<s$, the subject does not sell the wager and he receives a random reward whose cash-equivalent is e. Had his selling price been $s=e$, then for the same value of b he would have received the amount $b \geqslant e$. Thus, for all possible values of b, the expected utility of the subject's reward is at least as large when his selling price is $s=e$ as it is when $s>e$, and for some values of b it is strictly larger.

To complete the argument, suppose $s<e$. If $b<s$ or $b \geqslant e$, the subject's fortune changes just as it would had his selling price been $s=e$. However, if $s \leqslant b<e$, the subject receives the amount b whereas had his selling price been $s=e$ he would not sell the wager and would receive a random reward with cash-equivalent $e>b$. Thus, again, for all values of b the expected utility of the reward is at least as much when $s=e$ as it is when $s<e$, and for some values of b it is strictly larger. This demonstrates that the subject's optimal selling price is $s=e$. It brings him the highest expected utility.[1]

III. EXPERIMENTAL PROCEDURE

At the ith stage ($i=1, 2, \ldots, 24$) of the sequential experiment, the subject was presented with a wager from which he would receive the amount A_i if a number X_i selected at random from a rotating bingo basket containing balls with the integers 1 through 100 was less than or equal to C_i, and he would receive the amount B_i if X_i was greater than C_i. (In the notation of the preceding sections, this is the wager $(A_i, C_i/100, B_i)$ if we make the assumption that all integers between 1 and 100 have the same probability of being selected.) After each selection the ball was put back into the basket.

Before X_i was selected, the subject named his selling price s_i for the wager. A random integer Y_i was then selected from the basket. If $Y_i \geqslant s_i$, the subject received the amount Y_i. In effect, he had sold the wager for the amount Y_i. If $Y_i \leqslant s_i$, the subject did not sell the wager, X_i was observed, and the subject received either A_i or B_i, according as $X_i \leqslant C_i$ or $X_i > C_i$.

The amounts A_i, B_i, C_i used at each of the 24 stages of the sequential experiment are shown in Table I together with the utilities of the wagers under the arbitrary assignment of the two values $u(0)=0$ and $u(100)=1$.

TABLE I

Experimental design

Stage, i	A_i	B_i	C_i	s_i	$u(s_i)$
1	0	100	50	s_1	1/2
2	0	100	75	s_2	1/4
3	0	100	25	s_3	3/4
4	s_1	100	50	s_4	3/4
5	0	s_1	50	s_5	1/4
6	s_2	s_3	75	s_6	3/8
7	s_2	s_3	25	s_7	5/8
8	100	s_3	25	s_8	13/16
9	s_5	100	50	s_9	5/8
10	s_5	s_1	50	s_{10}	3/8
11	0	s_3	25	s_{11}	9/16
12	s_2	100	75	s_{12}	7/16
13	s_4	100	50	s_{13}	7/8
14	s_7	s_8	75	s_{14}	43/64
15	s_5	s_4	50	s_{15}	1/2
16	s_9	100	50	s_{16}	13/16
17	s_6	s_7	75	s_{17}	7/16
18	s_9	s_{13}	50	s_{18}	3/4
19	s_{11}	s_8	75	s_{19}	5/8
20	0	s_{13}	50	s_{20}	7/16
21	s_1	s_4	50	s_{21}	5/8
22	s_{11}	s_8	25	s_{22}	3/4
23	0	s_4	50	s_{23}	3/8
24	s_{11}	100	75	s_{24}	43/64

It should be noted that several of the 24 wagers have the same utility; e.g., $u(s_3)=u(s_4)=u(s_{18})=u(s_{22})=\frac{3}{4}$.

Moreover, even if the subject does not feel that all integers have the same probability of being selected, it is still true that

$$\begin{aligned} u(s_3) &= u(s_{22}), \\ u(s_7) &= u(s_{19}), \\ u(s_9) &= u(s_{21}), \\ u(s_{10}) &= u(s_{23}). \end{aligned}$$

To see why this is so, we will prove, for example, that $u(s_3)=u(s_{22})$.

Let p be the probability that the number selected at random will be at most 25. Then it is seen from Table I that $u(s_{22})=u^*(s_{11}, p, s_8)= =pu(s_{11})+(1-p)\,u(s_8)$. But it is also seen from Table I that $u(s_{11})=$

$=u^*(0, p, s_3)=(1-p)\ u(s_3)$ and $u(s_8)=u^*(100, p, s_3)=p+(1-p)\ u(s_3)$. Furthermore, $u(s_3)=u^*(0, p, 100)=1-p$. Thus, $u(s_{22})=p(1-p)\ u(s_3)+$ $+p(1-p)+(1-p)^2\ u(s_3)=1-p=u(s_3)$.

The selling price s_i at a given stage is sometimes used as one of the rewards in the wagers presented at later stages. It should be noted that the subject can increase the utility of wagers presented at later stages by naming a higher selling price for wagers presented at earlier stages. In order to prevent the subject from recognizing that he had such control, his earlier selling prices were not used until several stages later.

In order to avoid changing the total capital of the subject during the sequence, the subject was not paid on any trial during the experiment and in fact was told that he would be paid on only one of the 24 trials. This trial was determined by drawing a number between 1 and 24 at random at the end of the session.

IV. INSTRUCTIONS

The subjects were instructed as follows:

Stage 1 only. "In this game we will draw a number between 1 and 100. If the number is equal to or less than 50, you will win nothing. If the number is greater than 50 you will win 100 cents. How much are you willing to accept instead of playing the game? After you tell me how much you are willing to take for the game, I will draw a number between 1 and 100. If the number I draw is equal to or greater than the price you asked, I will pay you whatever number I drew and you will not play the game. If the number I draw is less than the price you ask, you will play the game and win nothing if the next number I draw is equal to or less than 50, or you will win 100 cents if that number is greater than 50.

Do you have any questions?

What is the lowest amount you are willing to take for the game?"

Stages 2 through 24. "This time you will win the amount A_i if the number is equal to or less than C_i or you will win B_i if the number is larger than C_i.

Do you have any questions?

What is your lowest price for the game?

Subjects. Two male students were obtained through the Yale Student Placement Office to serve as subjects in an economic experiment being conducted at the Cowles Foundation for Economic Research, Yale

University. Subject 1 was an undergraduate in the Department of Psychology. Subject 2 was a graduate theology student. Each subject was guaranteed $1.25 per session (i.e., for his responses to the full sequence of 24 stages) and each subject participated in three sessions. In addition the subject received a bonus each session consisting of his winnings at one of the stages in the sequence. As already described, the subject was not told which stage would be used to determine his bonus until the end of the session.

V. RESULTS

Since each subject participated in three sessions the data provide an opportunity for the study of the change in the subjects' behavior as they grew familiar with the task.

Their selling prices for the wagers at each stage of each session, and the actuarial value of each wager (i.e., the expected monetary reward $(C_i/100) A_i+(1-C_i/100) B_i$) are shown in Table II. (Note that the selling prices named by Subject 1 were always multiples of 5 cents. Although such rounding violates the assumption of a strictly monotonic utility function, the effects of the violation are negligible here.)

As discussed earlier, $u(s_3)=u(s_{22})$, $u(s_7)=u(s_{19})$, $u(s_9)=u(s_{21})$, and $u(s_{10})=u(s_{23})$, regardless of the value of p used in computing the utilities of the wagers. Thus, if the subjects' behavior is consistent with the expect, ed utility model their selling prices should be such that $s_3=s_{22}$, $s_7=s_{19}$, $s_9=s_{21}$, and $s_{10}=s_{23}$. The observed differences $s_{22}-s_3$, etc., are shown in Table III. Since most of these differences are nonzero the data are not consistent with an expected utility model.

It should also be noted, however, that the differences in prices decrease, on the average, from session to session, indicating that behavior does become, in some sense, more consistent with an expected utility model as the subject becomes more familiar with the task. Thus, despite the fact that the model does not precisely fit the behavior of the subjects, there is some indication that it approximates such behavior and that the model becomes more appropriate as the subject becomes more familiar with the experiment.

Now let us again assume that the values $\frac{1}{2}$, $\frac{1}{4}$, and $\frac{3}{4}$ are in fact the subjects' personal probabilities of the relevant events (i.e., we assume that, for the subjects, all integers are equally probable of being selected). The

TABLE II

Selling prices of the wagers

Stage	Subject 1			Subject 2		
	Session 1	Session 2	Session 3	Session 1	Session 2	Session 3
1	65 (50)	45 (50)	50 (50)	60 (50)	80 (50)	65 (50)
2	40 (25)	25 (25)	25 (25)	50 (25)	55 (25)	45 (25)
3	80 (75)	80 (75)	75 (75)	80 (75)	90 (75)	75 (75)
4	70 (83)	65 (73)	65 (75)	100 (80)	92 (90)	80 (83)
5	30 (33)	25 (23)	30 (25)	24 (30)	65 (40)	54 (33)
6	40 (50)	25 (39)	50 (38)	65 (58)	75 (64)	79 (53)
7	60 (70)	65 (66)	60 (63)	75 (73)	80 (81)	65 (68)
8	75 (85)	90 (85)	75 (81)	95 (85)	98 (83)	87 (81)
9	45 (65)	40 (63)	40 (65)	75 (62)	80 (83)	75 (73)
10	40 (48)	30 (35)	40 (40)	40 (42)	70 (73)	55 (55)
11	60 (60)	65 (60)	50 (56)	75 (60)	80 (68)	60 (56)
12	50 (55)	40 (44)	50 (44)	80 (63)	75 (66)	70 (59)
13	65 (85)	65 (83)	75 (83)	100 (100)	99 (96)	95 (90)
14	65 (64)	75 (71)	60 (64)	90 (80)	95 (85)	82 (71)
15	40 (50)	40 (45)	50 (48)	60 (62)	78 (79)	70 (63)
16	55 (73)	60 (70)	65 (73)	90 (88)	95 (90)	90 (88)
17	45 (45)	45 (35)	55 (53)	75 (70)	79 (76)	70 (76)
18	50 (55)	55 (53)	60 (60)	95 (88)	98 (90)	93 (85)
19	65 (64)	70 (71)	60 (56)	85 (80)	95 (85)	75 (67)
20	25 (33)	45 (33)	50 (38)	50 (50)	60 (50)	63 (48)
21	65 (68)	55 (55)	60 (58)	75 (80)	89 (86)	78 (73)
22	65 (71)	80 (84)	70 (69)	90 (90)	97 (94)	82 (80)
23	25 (35)	45 (33)	45 (33)	50 (50)	55 (46)	55 (40)
24	65 (70)	65 (74)	60 (63)	90 (81)	98 (91)	80 (70)

Note: The figures given in parentheses are the actuarial values of the wagers.

TABLE III

Differences in selling prices of wagers of equal utility

	Subject 1			Subject 2		
	Session 1	Session 2	Session 3	Session 1	Session 2	Session 3
$s_{22} - s_3$	−15	0	−5	10	7	7
$s_{19} - s_7$	5	5	0	10	15	10
$s_{21} - s_9$	20	15	15	0	9	3
$s_{23} - s_{10}$	−15	15	5	10	−15	0

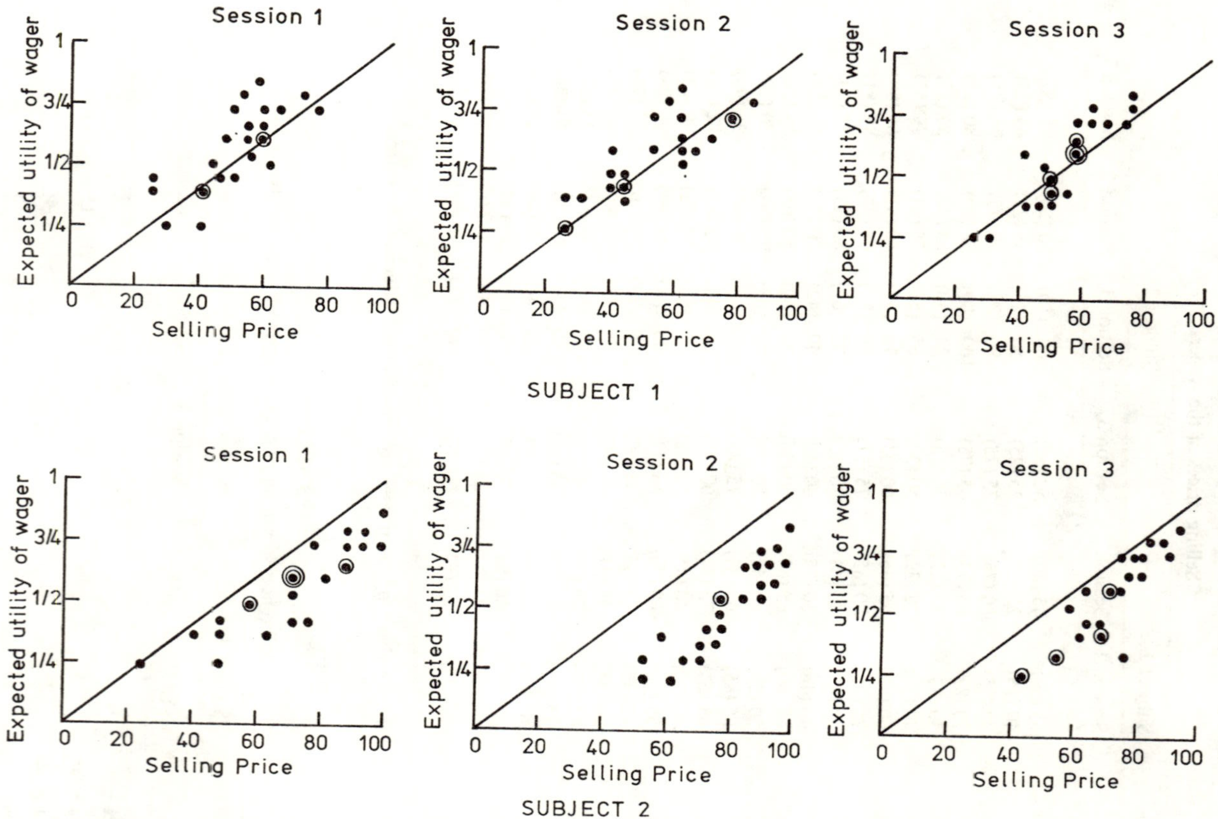

Fig. 1. Scatter Diagram of Subjects' Selling Prices Plotted against the Utilities of the Wagers. A circled dot indicates two coincident points. A twice-circled dot indicates three coincident points.

utilities of the wagers used in the experiment are given in Table I and, since the optimal selling price of a wager is its cash-equivalent, the selling prices named by a subject provide estimates of the amounts of money having these utilities. Thus, a scatter diagram of the selling prices named by a subject plotted against the utilities of the wagers should provide some suggestion of the subject's utility curve. These diagrams are given in Figure 1.

When viewing these diagrams it should be kept in mind that at each stage the utility of the wager was fixed and the selling price was the observed variable. Hence, the horizontal spread of points with the same utility is indicative of the inconsistency of the subjects' responses. In attempting to fit utility curves to these points, either 'by eye' or by some more refined method, the horizontal distances should perhaps be given primary consideration. Nevertheless, this discussion is not intended to minimize the relevance of the vertical spread of the utilities of wagers with the same selling price.

Because of the sequential nature of the experiment there is a dependence among the observations that makes a precise statistical analysis along traditional lines impractical. Accordingly, we content ourselves here with giving just a few general comments.

For both subjects, the horizontal spread of the points obtained in Session 3 at the fixed utility levels is relatively small. Thus, there is a trend toward the adoption of response patterns consistent with a set of constant utilities.

For a given wager, the larger the selling price named by a subject, the more willing he is to take risks. The selling prices named by Subject 1 were, in general, largest in Session 3. The linear (or actuarial) utility curve provides a not unreasonable fit to the observed points for this subject, although he is slightly more willing to take risks with small amounts and less willing with large amounts.

The observed points for Subject 2 in Session 3 lie below the linear utility curve, indicating the subject's willingness to take risks. For each subject, it is felt, a reasonable estimate of his utility curve can be sketched.

VI. CONCLUSIONS

An attempt has been made to measure the utility of money. Estimates of the amounts of money having been given, preselected utilities were obtained in a sequential procedure. At each stage of the procedure the subject stated the lowest price he would accept in lieu of a wager in his possession. It was shown that under the utility model this selling price will be the subject's cash-equivalent of the wager.

The inconsistency of the response of two subjects led to the rejection of the model. However, as the subjects became more familiar with the task their experience appeared to lead to more consistent behavior and less deviation from the results specified by the utility model. Thus, despite the rejection of the model in the strict sense, it is felt that it does, at least, approximate the observed behavior.

It is also our feeling that the procedure used here might provide useful data for the study of specific stochastic models of choice behavior, such as those given by Becker *et al.* (1963), and that it might be possible to use this procedure, alone or in combination with others, to estimate both personal probabilities and utilities of an experienced subject.

NOTE

[1] *Added in 1973.* Whether subjects do actually choose the optimal selling price was discussed by Marschak (1964) ('Experiment 2b') and (1968, p. 388). Further applications were suggested by Savage (1971), especially pp. 785–786.

BIBLIOGRAPHY

Becker, G. M., DeGroot, M. H., and Marschak, J., 'Stochastic Models of Choice Behavior' (1963), *Selected Essays*, 10.

Mosteller, F. and Nogee, P., 'An Experimental Measurement of Utility', *J. Polit. Econ.* **59** (1951) 371–404.

Added in 1973:

Marschak, J., 'Actual versus Consistent Decision Behavior' (1964), *Selected Essays*, 9.

Marschak, J., 'Decision Making: Economic Aspects' (1968), *Selected Essays*, 16.

Savage, L. J., 'Elicitation of Personal Probabilities and Expectations', *J. Amer. Statist. Assn.* **66** (1971) 783–801.

16

DECISION MAKING: ECONOMIC ASPECTS

(1968)

The distinction between prescriptive and descriptive theories of decision is similar to that between logic – a system of formally consistent rules of thought – and the psychology of thinking. A logical rule prescribes, for example, that if you believe all *X* to be *Y*, you should also believe that all non-*Y* are non-*X*, but not that all *Y* are *X*; and if you believe, in addition, that all *Y* are *Z*, you should believe all *X* to be *Z* (a logical rule known as transitivity of inclusion). Here, *X*, *Y*, and *Z* are objects or propositions. Such prescriptive rules do not state that all people of a given culture, social position, age, and so forth, always comply with them. If, for example, the links in a chain of reasoning are numerous, the rule of transitivity will probably be broken, at least by children or by unschooled or impatient people.

Descriptions, and consequently predictions, of 'illogical' behavior, as indeed of all human behavior, are presumably a task for psychologists or anthropologists. Such predictions are obviously important to practicing lawyers, politicians, salesmen, organizers, teachers, and others who work with people, just as predictions of the behavior of metals and animals are important to engineers and dairy farmers. These practitioners are well advised to know the frequencies of the various types of illogical behavior of their clients, adversaries, or students. But they are also well advised to avoid logical errors in their own behavior, as when they apply their knowledge of men (and of all nature, for that matter) to win lawsuits or elections or to be successful in organizing or teaching. For example, their propositions *X*, *Y*, and *Z* may be about another's madness, yet should obey the rule of transitivity of inclusion. Moreover, if you want to train future lawyers, statesmen, or businessmen, you are well advised to learn, from your own or other people's experiences, the techniques needed to make your pupil not only knowledgeable about other men's logical frailties but also strong in his own thinking and able to solve the brain twisters his future will offer. These pedagogical techniques are, of course, objects of descriptive study.

To illustrate the prescriptive-descriptive distinction in the domain of decisions, let us consider one of the rules proposed by prescriptive decision theory. We choose the rule called transitivity of preferences (other proposed rules will be discussed below) because of its special similarity with transitivity of inclusion. If you prefer *a* to *b* and *b* to *c*, you should prefer *a* to *c*. Here, *a*, *b*, and *c* are, in general, your actions with uncertain outcomes, although in the special case of 'sure actions', the outcome, e.g., gaining or losing an object, is unique, in which case preferring action *a* is, in effect, the same as preferring the outcome of action *a*. If an individual disobeys the transitivity rule and prefers *a* to *b*, *b* to *c*, and *c* to *a*, we would say that he does not know what he wants. Surely we would advise or train a practitioner to develop the ability for concentrated deliberation, weighing advantages and disadvantages in some appropriate way. This should result in a consistent ranking, from the most to the least preferable, with ties (i.e., indifference between some alternatives) not excluded, of alternative actions from which the decision maker may be forced to choose.

The statement that "given a set of feasible alternatives the 'reasonable' (rational) man should choose the best" and the parallel statement that "an actual man does choose the best (and if the best is not feasible, the second best, etc.)" are both empty if the ranking order is not supposed to be stable over a period long enough to make the statements of practical relevance. If the ranking order is stable, economics as the study of the best allocation of available resources becomes possible.

The boundary between descriptive and prescriptive economics did not worry early writers. Gresham's law, Ricardo's explanations of rent and of the high postwar price of bullion, and Böhm-Bawerk's theory of interest are deductions from the assumption of consistent ranking of alternatives by reasonable men. But those authors also practiced induction and looked for historical facts that confirmed their deductions. The two approaches are not inconsistent if one assumes that in the cultures considered, housewives and adult, gainfully occupied men have by and large been 'reasonable', at least when deciding not on wars and divorces but on matters of major interest to the economists of the time – for example, quantities such as prices, demands, and outputs, as well as less quantifiable choices such as location and internal organization (division of labor) of a plant. These matters were studied under the assumption of a tolerably well-known future.

The descriptive and prescriptive approaches became more clearly distinguished as more attention was directed to economic decisions under uncertainty (Fisher, 1906; Hicks, 1939; Hart, 1940) and, stimulated by the *Theory of Games and Economic Behavior* (von Neumann and Morgenstern, 1944), to nonquantifiable decisions traditionally assigned to political and military science or to sociology. In search of tools for their descriptive work, economists were also influenced by modern statistical decision theory. It then appeared that the reasonable man was not sufficiently approached even by the *ideal type* of an industrial entrepreneur, who evidently must be aided by a sophisticated hypothesis tester, a statistician, or, more recently and generally, an expert in operations research. As such experts, armed with computers, do indeed progressively penetrate the economic world, predictive and descriptive economics (e.g., the prediction of aggregate inventories) may again become closer to what can be deductively derived from rational decision rules.

To return to the analogy between theories of thinking and of decision, prescriptive theories of thinking and decision are concerned with formal consistency between sentences or decisions, not with their content. If one believes that Los Angeles is on the Moon and that Moon is in Africa, it is logical for him to believe that Los Angeles is in Africa, although none of the three statements is true. Similarly, if a man prefers killing to stealing and stealing to drinking strong liquor, he should prefer killing to drinking, although none of these actions is laudable or hygienic. Hicks (1939) used Milton's 'reason is also choice' as a motto to the theory of consumption. Ramsey (1923–1928) called his theory of decision an extension of logic, an attitude adopted more recently by other logicians, for example, Carnap (1962), von Wright (1963), and Jeffrey (1965). The mutual penetration of logic and decision theory will appear even more founded and urgent when we come to discuss the cost of thinking and deciding (Section VIII).

In Sections I, III, IV and V we shall discuss some prescriptive decision rules and outline some simple experiments whose outcomes determine whether the subject did or did not comply with these rules. Whenever such experiments or similar ones have actually been performed, we shall refer to available descriptive evidence, namely, the frequency of subject's obeying these rules or obeying some other stated behavior patterns, such as the probabilistic decision models of Section II. In Section VI the expected utility theorem implied by the prescriptive rules is discussed. Sections VII and VIII point to unsolved problems on the frontier of decision theory.

I. COMPLETE ORDERING OF ACTIONS

Before we consider the notion of a complete ordering of alternative actions or decisions (we need not distinguish between the two here), it is convenient to restate the *transitivity* of preferences by defining the relation 'not preferred to' or 'not better than', written symbolically as $\leqslant$. If $a \leqslant b$ and $b \leqslant c$, then $a \leqslant c$. It is a *reflexive* relation, i.e., $a \leqslant a$. A relation that is transitive and reflexive is called an *ordering* relation. When $a \leqslant b$ and $b \leqslant a$, we write $a \sim b$ and say that the decision maker is indifferent between a and b, even though a and b are not identical. For example, an investor may be indifferent between two different portfolios of securities. Thus '$\leqslant$' (unlike the relation 'not larger than' applied to numbers) is a *weak ordering* relation. Further, when $a \leqslant b$ and not $b \leqslant a$, we write $a < b$ and say that b is preferred to, or is better than, a.

Shall we say that a reasonable man always either prefers b to a or a to b or is indifferent? Or can he, in addition, refuse to compare them? If he can, the ordering of the actions by the relation 'not better than' is only a *partial* one. This position has been taken, for example, by Aumann (1962), Chipman (in Interdisciplinary Research Conference, 1960), and Wolfowitz (1962). But can one escape choosing? As in Pascal's (1670) famous immortality bet, *'Il faut parier!'* The avoiding of choice itself is a decision. Like other decisions, it is made more or less desirable by the prizes and penalties it entails. If this is granted, the transitive relation '$\leqslant$' is also *connective* and induces a *complete ordering*. Then any subset of actions can be arranged according to their desirabilities (with ties not excluded). Rank numbers, also called *ordinal utilities* (priorities), can then be assigned to the alternative actions provided that certain weak conditions are satisfied (Debreu, 1959, section 4, note 2, and section 4.6).

Tests of transitivity of preferences. As a matter of descriptive theory we ask whether people (of a given culture, etc.) do act as if there exist complete orderings of their actions by preferences. In actual experiments the penalty for refusing to choose was assumed to be strong enough to force subjects to make genuine choices in the form of verbal statements of preferences or, in some cases, actually to stake money on one wager rather than another. With connectivity of the preference relation thus assured and its reflexivity assumed by definition, the transitivity of the relation remained to be tested. The alternative actions were represented by multidimensional objects – a bundle of tickets to various shows (Papandreou, 1957), marriage partners classified by three three-valued characteristics (May, 1954; Davis, 1958), a monetary wager (Edwards, 1953; Davidson and Marschak, 1959), a price policy affecting both the firm's rate of return and its share of the market, an air trip varying in both cost and duration (MacCrimmon, 1965), and so forth. The subject responded by a triad of binary choices – *a* or *b*? *b* or *c*? *c* or *a*? – but in most experiments these choices were separated in time by choices from other triads, that is, '*a* or *b*?' was/followed by '*a'* or *b'*?' rather than by '*b* or *c*?' Moreover, neither of the two actions 'dominated' the other (see Section III), and no subject could use paper and pencil.

In all experiments, the transitivity rule was violated with varying frequencies. The proportion of the number of violations by all subjects to the maximum theoretical number of intransitive triads that were possible in the given experimental designs ranged from .04 in MacCrimmon's tests of business executives to .27 in May's tests of students. Since the experiments record actual choices and not preferences, intransitivity might be exhibited by a person who, although consistent, is strictly indifferent among three alternatives. (To approach, more generally, the case of 'near indifference', the hypothesis tested must be rephrased in probabilistic terms. This will be discussed in Section II.) Thus the outcome of an experiment depends on the nature of the alternatives offered, making the experiments mentioned not quite comparable.

It would also be of great interest to study the effects of the passage of time and the effects of learning, especially if different methods of training are applied, such as 'post-mortem' discussion (a domain opened by MacCrimmon), sequential modifications of the list of choices, etc. In fact, what would be the effect of supplying the subjects with paper and pencil and training them to use these prerequisites of our culture to tabulate the decision problem in an 'outcome matrix' as in Table I (p. 337) below?

It has been suggested (Quandt, 1956; Simon, 1957) that intransitivities of decisions occur when the subject is unable to pay simultaneous attention to the several dimensions of each object of choice. This is somewhat analogous to the psychophysical finding that discrimination is greater between sounds differing in pitch but of equal loudness than between sounds differing in both (Pollack, 1955). This suggests that the probabilistic approach common in psychophysics might be tried in a description of decision behavior. As to prescriptive theory, one may recall Benjamin Franklin's suggestion to score the pros and cons of each decision or the practice of adding scores when grading students or judging young ladies in beauty contests. Again, these or any other ways of overcoming the multidimensionality of decisions through deliberate and simultaneous marshaling of all the dimensions will in general require paper and pencil.

II. PROBABILISTIC ORDERING OF ACTIONS

Since the prescriptive rule of transitivity is often violated, it is necessary to recast descriptive decision theory in different terms. The hypothesis that transitivity of decisions may be achieved by learning or training has already been mentioned. It is also traditional in experimental psychology, especially since Fechner's (1860) studies of perception, to describe behavior by probability distributions. Economists, by contrast, have succeeded in the past in making useful predictions of the aggregate behavior of large numbers of individuals based on the assumption that individuals are, by and large, 'reasonable'. The probabilistic approach is rather new in economics, perhaps as young as the econometricians' attempts to test aggregate economic models statistically and to relate these models to observable behavior of sampled individual households and firms.

Luce and Suppes (1965) have comprehensively surveyed the literature and the experimental evidence relevant to probabilistic orderings. One model that implies all the others suggested so far is that presented by Luce (1959). Fixed positive numbers $v_a, v_b, v_c, \ldots$, called *strict utilities*, are attached to the alternative actions $a, b, c, \ldots$. The set of actions includes all alternatives that may ever be offered to a given subject. The strict utilities are assumed to have the following property: if the subject must choose from a particular subset of alternatives, he will choose each with a probability proportional to its strict utility. For example, suppose $v_a:v_b:v_c:v_d = 1:2:3:4$. Then, if asked to choose from the subset (a, b, c), the subject will choose a, b, or c with repective probabilities $\frac{1}{6}, \frac{2}{6}, \frac{3}{6}$; if he must choose from the pair (a, b), he will choose a or b with respective probabilities $\frac{1}{3}$, $\frac{2}{3}$. The hypothesis can be tested at least 'in principle' (i.e., assuming that representative samples from the universe of all choice situations can be obtained). One would observe the relative frequencies of choices from various subsets and infer, for example, that the ratio of the probability of choosing a to the probability of choosing b from the pair (a, b) does or does not change if a third alternative is also offered.

In another model, constants u_a, u_b, $u_c, \ldots$, called *strong utilities*, are associated with the alternatives $a, b, c, \ldots$. The strong utilities are assumed to have the following property: in the binary choice between a and b, the probability $p(a, b)$ of choosing a is an increasing function of the difference $u_a - u_b$ (except when $p(a, b)$ is equal to 1 or 0). It follows that $p(a, b) \gtreqless \frac{1}{2}$ according as $u_a \gtreqless u_b$. Note that the case $p(a, b) = \frac{1}{2}$ provides an operational definition of 'indifference' based on actual choices rather than on the verbal statement 'I am indifferent'. This model was used, in effect, in Thurstone's discussion of public opinion and of soldiers' food preferences (1927–1955). It is analogous to Fechner's perception model, which associates a physical stimulus a with a subjective 'sensation' u_a; the subject perceives a to be heavier (or louder or brighter) than b with a probability $p(a, b)$ that increases with the difference $u_a - u_b$ (provided $p(a, b)$ is neither 0 nor 1).

It can be shown that if strict utilities exist, then strong utilities also exist (putting $u_a = \log v_a$, etc.), but not the converse. The strong utility model implies, in turn, the still less restrictive *weak utility* model, which assigns the ordinal numbers w_a, w_b, $w_c, \ldots$ to the alternatives $a, b, c, \ldots$, such that $p(a, b) \gtreqless \frac{1}{2}$ according as $w_a \gtreqless w_b$. Clearly, if the strong utilities exist, so do the weak utilities (putting $w_a = u_a$, etc), but not the converse since differences between ordinal numbers are undefined. Both the weak utility model and the strong utility model can be tested in principle for possible rejection, for they have implications that involve choice probabilities only, avoiding the intervening utility concept. In particular, the models imply, respectively, the *weak stochastic transitivity*,

$$\text{if } p(a, b) \geqslant \tfrac{1}{2} \text{ and } p(b, c) \geqslant \tfrac{1}{2}, \text{ then } p(a, c) \geqslant \tfrac{1}{2},$$

and the *strong stochastic transitivity*,

$$\begin{aligned}&\text{if } p(a, b) \geqslant \tfrac{1}{2} \text{ and } p(b, c) \geqslant \tfrac{1}{2},\\ &\text{then } p(a, c) \geqslant \max\,[p(a, b), p(b, c)].\end{aligned}$$

Of these two forms of stochastic transitivity, the strong implies the weak one: it is, in turn, implied by the exact transitivity rule treated in Section I if the choice probabilities are assumed to take on only three values: 0, $\frac{1}{2}$, and 1, corresponding to the preference relations $a<b$, $a\sim b$, and $b<a$.

Another probabilistic model also implied by, and less restrictive than, Luce's strict utility model is the *random utility* model. It does not imply, nor is it implied by, the strong or the weak utility model. It asserts, for a given subject, the existence of a fixed probability distribution on the set of all preference orderings of all alternatives, so that for a set of N alternatives, a probability is attached to each of their $N!$ permutations. In the nonprobabilistic economics of consumer's choice the (ordinal) utility function that attaches a constant rank to each commodity bundle is a fixed one. In the random utility model this function is, instead, visualized as drawn at random from a set of such functions, according to a probability distribution that is fixed for the given subject. Thus the word 'utility' designates here a random number, not a constant as in the other probabilistic models described.

What relevance do these (and related) models have for a prescriptive theory of decision? Just as not all men are always consistent, not all men are always in good health. Doctors and nurses are busy measuring the temperatures and blood pressures of the sick ones. The probability distributions supposed to characterize a 'stochastic decision maker' may vary in the degree of their closeness to the ideal limit – consistency. For example, consistency is approached in the strong utility model as the values of $p(a, b)$ concentrate near 1 or 0 or $\frac{1}{2}$. We can thus trace the path of progress of learning or training for consistency.

III. INADMISSIBILITY OF DOMINATED ACTIONS

An action's result (outcome) depends, in general, not only on the action but also on the 'state of the world (nature or environment)', which is not in the decision maker's control. For our purposes an action (called an act by Savage [1954]) can be defined by the results it yields at various states of the world. Thus an action is a function from the set of states to the set of results. (This function has constant value if the action is a 'sure action'.) In a decision situation, only some such functions are available; their 'feasible set' (the 'offered set of alternatives' of Section II) depends, for example, on the decision maker's resources, technology, and market as he views them.

An *event* is a subset of the states of nature. In particular, the subset consisting of all states that, for any given feasible action, result in the same outcome is called an *outcome-relevant event*. In a decision situation the set of states is partitioned into such events, with all irrelevant details omitted.

Even if the well-disciplined decision maker can consistently rank multidimensional results according to his preferences, action under uncertainty remains multidimensional because of the multiplicity of events. Actions are bets, or wagers. Yet it seems reasonable to prescribe (as in Section 1) that bets be ordered; indeed, some authors prescribe that bets be completely ordered (Ramsey, 1923–1928; Savage, 1954; de Finetti, 1937). It will be shown in Section VI that a complete ordering corresponds to that of numerical 'expected utilities' of actions *provided* that the decision maker is consistent in the sense of obeying both the traditional rules of logic and certain postulates that are plausible enough to qualify as extensions of logic. These postulates will be discussed in this and subsequent sections, essentially following Savage.

Action a is said to dominate action b if the results of a are sometimes

TABLE I

An outcome matrix (in dollars)

Action	Event	
	Z_1	Z_2
a	1000	1500
a'	999	1500
b	1000	1000

(i.e., when some events take place) better than the results of b and are never worse. Is it not reasonable that you should prefer the dominating action? Any action that is dominated by some feasible action is thus inadmissible. Consider, for example, the actions listed in Table I. If action a is taken and the state of the world is Z_1, a gain of \$1000 will be realized; if action a is taken and the state of the world is Z_2, a gain of \$1500 will be realized; and so on. Such a table is called an *outcome matrix*.

The inadmissibility postulate would order these actions as follows:

$a' < a$, $b < a$. It does not, by itself, induce complete ordering of the actions. Thus, it is silent about the preference relation between actions a' and b in Table I. The 'expected utility' rule of Section VI will determine this relation roughly in the following manner: depending on the 'probabilities' of events and on the 'utilities' of results, the \$500 advantage of a' over b if Z_2 happens may or may not outweigh its \$1 disadvantage if Z_1 happens. This appeals to common sense but remains vague until, with help of other postulates, we define the concepts of 'probability' and 'utility'.

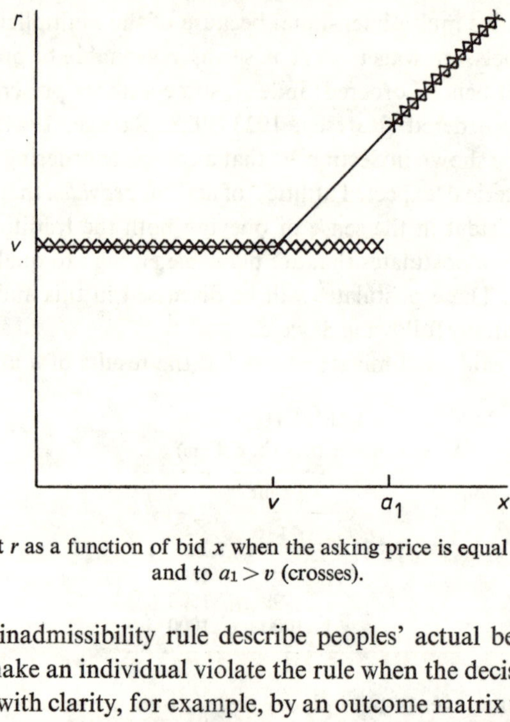

Fig. 1. Result r as a function of bid x when the asking price is equal to v (solid line) and to $a_1 > v$ (crosses).

Does the inadmissibility rule describe peoples' actual behavior? It is difficult to make an individual violate the rule when the decision situation is presented with clarity, for example, by an outcome matrix whose entries have an obvious ordering (sums of money, as in Table I, or good health, light illness, and death). But consider the following experiment. A subject is given an envelope containing v dollars; he is permitted to convince himself that the envelope does contain v dollars. He writes, but does not tell the experimenter his asking price, a, for the envelope and its contents. He will then receive a bid of x dollars. If x exceeds a, he will receive x dollars; otherwise, he will keep the v dollars. There will be no further negotiations.

Subjects often ask more than the true value, setting $a=a_1>v$. In Figure 1, the stipulated result r of such action is plotted against possible levels of the bid x (state of nature). Comparison with the corresponding plot for the 'honest' asking price, $a=a_0=v$, shows that a_1 is dominated by a_0. In fact, an asking price $a_2<v$ (not shown in Figure 1) is also dominated by a_0. Hence the honest asking price is the only admissible one. It seems that some subjects expect further negotiations despite the explicit warning. We surmise that they would waive uncalled-for associations and habits if trained to plot or tabulate payoffs.

IV. IRRELEVANCE OF NONAFFECTED OUTCOMES

Table II presents a matrix of outcomes measured in per cent of return on a firm's investment. We may interpret a, b, a', and b' as the firm's investing in the development of alternative products. The outcomes of these actions depend on the mutually exclusive events (say, business conditions) Z_1, Z_2, and Z_3. Suppose the firm prefers a to b. This preference cannot be due to any difference in the outcomes if the event Z_1 happens, for these outcomes are identically 5. Therefore, the firm's preference of a to b must be due to its preferring the wager '-200 if Z_2, 100 if Z_3' to the return of 5 with certainty. But then the firm should also prefer a' to b', for again, if Z_1 happens, the outcome (-200) is not affected by the firm's choice. Its preference as between a' and b' must depend on its preference as between the wager '-200 if Z_2, 100 if Z_3' and the certainty of 5, just as in the previous case. By the same reasoning, if the firm is indifferent between a and b, it should be indifferent between a' and b'. The rule enunciated here can be regarded as a generalization of the admissibility rule of the

TABLE II

Outcome matrix for the return on a firm's investment (per cent)

Action	Event Z_1	Z_2	Z_3
a	5	−200	100
b	5	5	5
a'	−200	−200	100
b'	−200	5	5

previous section, with wagers admitted as a form of outcomes so that, for example, action *a* is described as follows: if Z_1 happens, you get 5; otherwise you get a lottery ticket, losing 200 if Z_2 happens and gaining 100 if Z_3 happens.

Tests of the irrelevance rule. Most business executives violated the irrelevance rule when MacCrimmon (1965) *verbally* gave them the choices in Table II – first *a* versus *b*, then *a'* versus *b'*. However, a large majority of my students, who also never heard of the irrelevance principle but knew how to draw up a matrix of outcomes, complied with the rule. Allais (1953) performed a similar experiment, but instead of describing the three events as alternative business conditions, he gave them numerical probabilities (an extraneous notion in the present context), the probability of one of the events being only .01. Most of his respondents, including some decision theorists, violated the principle (but see Savage's pungent introspective discussion of his own second thought [1954, Section 5.6g]).

The following type of experiment has been discussed widely. Funnel 1 contains an equal number of red and black balls, and the subject is invited to convince himself of this; but he is not permitted to look into funnel 2, which he only knows to contain one or more balls whose colors are either black or red. When a handle is pulled, each funnel will release only the bottom ball. In the following bets, he will win either $100 or nothing:

Bet 1*R*: bottom ball in funnel 1 is red.
Bet 1*B*: bottom ball in funnel 1 is black.
Bet 2*R*: bottom ball in funnel 2 is red.
Bet 2*B*: bottom ball in funnel 2 is black.

The outcomes are as indicated in Table III, where, for example, event *RB* is 'bottom ball in funnel 1 is red, bottom ball in funnel 2 is black'. Suppose

TABLE III

Outcome matrix for the funnel experiment (in dollars)

	Event			
Bet	*RB*	*BR*	*RR*	*BB*
1*R*	100	0	100	0
2*R*	0	100	100	0
2*B*	100	0	0	100
1*B*	0	100	0	100

the subject always prefers to use funnel 1 rather than funnel 2, that is, he prefers bet $1R$ to $2R$ and also bet $1B$ to $2B$. He will thus treat the results unaffected by his choice – namely, those earned when events RR and BB occur – as *relevant* to his choice! Yet similar experiments performed by Chipman (see Interdisciplinary Research Conference 1960) and Ellsberg (1961) suggest that many people do indeed prefer funnel 1 to funnel 2. Some of my student subjects who did so motivated their choice by stating the sharp distinction between 'risk' (funnel 1) and 'uncertainty' (funnel 2), a distinction taught to economists since Knight (1921). Others stated that they could base their bets on more information when using funnel 1 than when using funnel 2. But information, although never harmful, can be useless. In experiments of Raiffa (1961) and Fellner (1965), subjects were, in effect, willing to pay for such useless information.

V. DEFINITIONS OF PROBABILITIES

Having defined events $Z_1, Z_2, Z_3, \ldots$ as subsets of the set X of all states of nature, it is consistent with current mathematical language and current English to require that any numbers, $\mathrm{p}(Z_1)$, $p(Z_2)$, $P(Z_3), \ldots$, claimed to be the probabilities of these events, satisfy the following conditions: (1) they should be nonnegative; (2) for any two mutually exclusive events, say Z_1 and Z_2, the number assigned to the event 'Z_1 or Z_2' (meaning the occurrence of either Z_1 or Z_2) should equal the sum of $P(Z_1)$ and $P(Z_2$; (3) $P(X)$, i.e., $P(Z_1$ or Z_2 or Z_3 or ...), should be equal to one.

Personal probabilities. The numbers $P(Z_1)$, $P(Z_2)$, $P(Z_3), \ldots$ are an individual's personal probabilities of these events if, in addition to having the mathematical properties just stated, they describe his behavior in the following sense: whenever $P(Z_1) > P(Z_2)$, for example, he will prefer betting on Z_1 to betting on Z_2, assuming he wants to win the bet. This, too, is consistent with ordinary English – he will prefer betting on the victory of the Democrats in the next election to betting on the truth of the proposition that California is longer than Norway if and only if he considers winning the former bet 'more probable' than winning the latter one. Here, 'betting on Z_1' means taking an action that yields a result s (for success) if Z_1 occurs, a result that is more desirable than the result f (for failure) if Z_1 does not occur. The probabilities of events must depend on the events only, i.e., the individual's preferences between bets must be the same for all pairs of results s, f (\$100, \$0; *status quo*, loss of prestige; etc.) provided only that s is better than f. This postulate of *independence of beliefs on rewards* must be added to those of Sections I, III, and IV. Will the subject reverse his judgment about the comparative chances of any two events – as revealed by his choices between two bets – if the prizes are changed? If not, he satisfies the postulate. It seems to be satisfied by practically all subjects asked to rank several bets according to their preferences, the rewards being first a pair s, f, then a different pair s', f'.

Suppose a subject is indifferent to bets on any of the eight horses running a race. His preferences would thus imply that $P(Z_1)=P(Z_2)=\cdots=$ $=P(Z_8)$, where Z_i is the event that the ith horse wins (ties are excluded for simplicity). The nonnegativity property is satisfied if we put $P(Z_i)=\frac{1}{8}$ for all i. What about the other two mathematical properties required? Suppose the subject considers double bets with the same prizes s, f as for single bets. He will prefer every double bet, e.g., the bet on the event 'Z_1 or Z_2', to any single bet (here he has, in effect, applied the inadmissibility postulate), and he will be indifferent between any two double bets (here the postulates of irrelevance and of intransitivity apply). Similarly, he will prefer triple bets to double bets and will be indifferent between any two triple bets, and so on. Consistent with these preferences, we can put

$$P(Z_i \text{ or } Z_j) = \tfrac{2}{8} = P(Z_i) + P(Z_j)$$

for any two horses i and j,

$$P(Z_i \text{ or } Z_j \text{ or } Z_k) = \tfrac{3}{8} = P(Z_i \text{ or } Z_j) + P(Z_k)$$

for any three horses i, j, and k, and so on. In general, we can assign probability $P(Z)=m/8$ to the event Z that one of the m specified horses will win (where $1 \leqslant m \leqslant 8$). Then the numbers $P(Z)$ are the subject's personal probabilities, for they agree with his preferences between bets and also satisfy the three mathematical requirements stated at the beginning of this section.

Instead of a horse race, a subject is asked to imagine a dial divided into n equal sectors. Suppose the hand of the dial is spun and comes to rest in the ith sector. We define this occurrence as event Z_i. If the subject is convinced that the dial's mechanism is 'fair', i.e., that the events $Z_1, Z_2, \ldots,$ Z_n are symmetrical (exchangeable), he will be indifferent among bets on any one of these n events. Following Borel (1939, chapter 5), he can then assess his personal probability of any event T, say, 'rain tomorrow', by finding a number m $(1 \leqslant m \leqslant n)$ such that betting on T is not more desirable than betting on 'Z_1 or Z_2 or ... or Z_m' and is not less desirable than betting on 'Z_1 or Z_2 or ... or Z_{m-1}'. Then his personal probability of T, $P(T)$, satisfies the inequality

$$\frac{m-1}{n} \leqslant P(T) \leqslant \frac{m}{n}.$$

By making n arbitrarily large, one can assess $P(T)$ arbitrarily closely, and by using dial arcs which represent any fraction, rational or irrational, of the dial's circumference, one can define personal probabilities ranging continuously from 0 to 1. Note that such assessments of personal probabilities, when determined in an experiment, are based not on the subject's verbal statement of numbers he calls probabilities but on his actual choices. They may therefore be useful in predicting actions provided that the subject is consistent. If he is not consistent, his violations may or may not be similar in principle to those incurred in any instrument readings – a theme of probabilistic psychology touched upon in Section II.

Objective probabilities. As a special case, personal probabilities of some real-world events may be 'objective', i.e., the same for different people. This is particularly the case when there is agreement that the events come sufficiently close, for all practical purposes of those involved, to fulfilling certain symmetry requirements. Approximate symmetry is assumed for the positions of a roulette dial like Borel's and for the occurrences of death among many similar males of age 20. Such requirements are strictly satisfied only by idealized, mathematically defined events – events that are never observed empirically. *A* 'fair' coin, a 'fair' roulette dial, a 'homogeneous' population of males aged 20 (or a 'random' sample from such a population) are all mathematical constructs. The mathematical theory of probability applies rules of logic to situations in which strict symmetry and the three properties stated at the beginning of this section hold (refining property 2 in order to accommodate the case of an infinite X). If decision makers agree that certain events are approximately symmetric, and if they apply logical rules, then their choices between betting on (predicting) any two events will agree; their personal (in this case also objective) probabilities will coincide with those given by mathematical theory. Clarity requires us, however, to distinguish between mathematical probabilities and objective probabilities assigned by decision makers to empirical events, just as we distinguish between a geometric rectangle and the shape of an actual sheet of paper.

VI. EXPECTED UTILITY

The four postulates discussed thus far – complete ordering of actions, inadmissibility of dominated actions, irrelevance of nonaffected outcomes, and independence of beliefs on rewards – appear about as convincing as the rules of logic (and about as subject to transgression by people not trained in untwisting brain twisters). Together with a 'continuity' postulate (to be introduced presently), they imply the following rule, which is more complicated and less immediately convincing: The consistent man behaves as if he (1) assigned personal probabilities $P(Z)$ to events Z, (2) assigned numerical utilities $u(r)$ to the results r of his actions, and (3) chose the action with the highest 'expected utility'. The expected utility $\omega(a)$ of action a is the weighted average

$$\omega(a) = \sum_r u(r)\cdot P(Z_{ra}),$$

where the event Z_{ra} is the set of all states for which action a yields result r.

The rule is trivially true when the choice is among sure actions; if action a always yields result r, then $P(Z_{ra})=1$, so that $\omega(a)=u(r)$.

Consider now actions with two possible results – success s and failure f. This is the case, for example, when actions are two-prize bets (as in Section V) or when the decision maker is a 'satisficer' (Simon, 1957) for whom all outcomes below his 'aspiration level' are equally bad and all others equally good. In Section V we saw that of two two-prize bets, a consistent decision maker prefers the bet that has the higher probability of success. Since s is better than f, we can assign numerical utilities

$$u(s) = 1 > 0 = u(f),$$

and we see that the expected utility $\omega(b)$ of a two-prize bet b coincides with its probability of success $P(Z_{sb})$, since

$$\omega(b) = 1\cdot P(Z_{sb}) + 0\cdot P(Z_{fb}) = P(Z_{sb}).$$

Thus the satisficer maximizes the probability of reaching his aspiration level.

As the next step, we compute the probability of success and hence the expected utility $\omega(c)$ of a bet c compounded of n simple two-prize bets or lottery tickets $b_1,\ldots,b_n$ on n different (but not necessarily mutually exclusive) events $T_1,\ldots,T_n$. Lottery ticket b_i is a bet on the event T_i, and the subject will receive ticket b_i if Z_i happens. The events $Z_1,\ldots,Z_n$ are mutually exclusive events one of which must happen, and the events 'Z_i and T_i' (the occurrence of Z_i and T_i) are pairwise independent in the sense that

$$P(Z_i \text{ and } T_i) = P(Z_i)\cdot P(T_i).$$

We can thus regard ticket b_i as the result yielded by action c when Z_i happens. Hence $P(Z_i)=P(Z_{b_ic})$ in the present notation. Moreover, we have just shown that the expected utility of a simple two-prize bet can be measured by its probability of success, so that $P(T_i)=\omega(b_i)$. Clearly, the probability of success of the compound bet c is the probability of the event '(Z_1 and T_1) or (Z_2 and T_2) or... or (Z_n and T_n)'; by mathematical property 2 of probabilities (Section V), this is equal to $\sum_i P(T_i)\cdot P(Z_i)$. Hence,

$$\omega(c) = \sum_i \omega(b_i)\cdot P(Z_{b_ic}),$$

i.e., the expected utility rule is valid for the special case where each result of an action is a two-prize bet.

To extend this in a final step to the general case, let s be the best and f the worst of all results of an action. In the preference notation of Section I, $f\leqslant r\leqslant s$ for any result r. Consider the continuous range of all bets b whose two prizes are s and f and whose success probabilities take all the values between (and including) 1 and 0. Then, for any $b, f\leqslant b\leqslant s$, and for a given r, $r\leqslant b$ or $b\leqslant r$ depending on the bet's success probability. A plausible *continuity postulate* asserts, for each r, the existence of a bet, say b_r, such that $r\sim b_r$. We can therefore assign to r a utility $u(r)=\omega(b_r)$. A decision maker should then be indifferent between an action a that yields various results r with respective probabilities $P(Z_{ra})$ and a bet c compounded of the corresponding two-prize bets b_r just described entering with the same probabilities $P(Z_{ra})$. That is to say, $P(Z_{b_rc})=P(Z_{ra})$. The expected utility rule follows, since

$$\begin{aligned}\omega(a) = \omega(c) &= \sum_r \omega(b_r)\cdot P(Z_{b_rc})\\ &= \sum_r u(r)\cdot P(Z_{ra}).\end{aligned}$$

Some insight into this derivation of the expected utility rule is provided to the trainee in decision making by letting him rank his preferences among the tickets to four lotteries. Each ticket is described by prizes contingent on two alternative events, one of which must occur. An example of such a decision problem is presented in Table IV, where p is written for $P(Z)$ for brevity. If the event Z is 'a coin is tossed and comes up heads' (we refer below to this event simply as 'heads') and the subject regards the coin as 'fair', then $p=\frac{1}{2}$. But Z may also be, for example, "the next sentence spoken in this room will contain the pronoun 'I'." In any case, when the inadmissibility postulate is applied, it is evident from the last column of Table IV that ticket a is better than c and worse than b. Furthermore, the decision maker should be indifferent between tickets a and d.

Cash equivalents and numerical utilities. Let us define the *cash equivalent* of ticket a, denoted $k(a)$, as the highest price the decision maker would offer for ticket a; $k(b)$, $k(c)$, and $k(d)$ are defined similarly. If asked to name his cash equivalent for each lottery ticket in Table IV, the decision maker should name amounts such that $k(b)>k(a)=k(d)>k(c)$. If he fails to do this, he is inconsistent, and no scale of numerical utilities can describe his behavior. If he is consistent, and if the event Z is 'heads', the following utilities for some money gains can be ascribed to him:

$$\begin{aligned}\omega(\$100) &= 1\,;\\ \omega\,[k(b)] &= \tfrac{3}{4}\,;\\ \omega\,[k(a)] = \omega\,[k(d)] &= \tfrac{1}{2}\,;\\ \omega\,[k(c)] &= \tfrac{1}{4}\,;\\ \omega(\$0) &= 0\,.\end{aligned}$$

Some but not all subjects conform with the required ranking of the lottery tickets. Therefore, in any empirical estimation of a subject's utilities and personal probabilities, one must check whether the subject is consistent, at least in some approximate sense. As pointed out in the simpler context of section 2, probabilistic models of decision and of learning to decide are needed for any descriptive theory, and they too may fail.

Behavior toward risk. Again suppose that the event Z in Table IV is 'heads'. If the subject has named cash equivalents $k(a)=k(d)=\$50$, $k(c)=\$25$, and $k(b)=\$75$ (and similarly for further, easily conceived compound lotteries with utilities $\frac{1}{8}, \frac{3}{8}, \ldots, \frac{1}{16}, \ldots$), we would infer that over the observed range he is indifferent between a 'fair bet' and the certainty of

TABLE IV

Decision problem involving lottery tickets

Lottery ticket	Prize if event Z happens	Prize if event Z does not happen	Probability of gaining \$100
a	\$100	\$0	p
b	Lottery ticket *a*	\$100	$p^2 + 1 - p > p$
c	Lottery ticket *a*	\$0	$p^2 < p$
d	Lottery ticket *b*	Lottery ticket *c*	$p(p^2+1-p)+(1-p)\,p^2=p$

getting its expected gain. We would say that he is 'indifferent to risk'. His utility function of money gain is a straight line. On the other hand, if he has named cash equivalents $k(a)=k(d)<\$50$, $k(c)<\frac{1}{2}k(a)$, and $k(b)<$ $<\frac{1}{2}[100+k(a)]$, his utility function of money gain will be a concave curve (any of its chords will lie below the corresponding arc), and we would say that he is 'averse to risk'. If the inequality signs in the preceding sentence are reversed, the utility function is convex (chords are above arcs), and we would say that over the observed range the subject 'loves risk'. When the utility function is either concave or convex, the decision maker maximizes the expected value, not of money gain, but of some nonlinear function of money gain.

Daniel Bernoulli (1738) pointed out that the utility function is concave in the case of the 'Petersburg paradox'. Marshall (1890) also assumed risk aversion as an economic fact (or perhaps as a prescription from Victorian morals) equivalent to that of 'decreasing marginal utility of money'. Some economic implications of risk aversion were given by Pratt (1964) and Arrow (1965). It should be noted that this assumption is inconsistent with the behavior of a satisficer for whom utility is a step-function of money gain and the behavior of a merchant for whom the disutility of bankruptcy is the same regardless of the amount owed.

The maxmin rule. In competition with the expected utility rule (and the postulates underlying it) is the 'conservative' or 'maxmin' rule, which states that the decision maker should maximize the minimum payoff; that is to say, the maxmin rule proposes that preferences among actions be based on each action's worst result only. Thus in the case of Table I the maxmin rule would prescribe that $a' < b$ even if Z_1 has the probability of, say, an earthquake, and presumably $b \sim a$, contradicting the inadmissibility postulate. However, because of the strong appeal of the inadmissibility postulate, it is usually proposed that the maxmin rule be applied only when domination is absent; this leads to the ordering $a' < b < a$ rather than $a' < b \sim a$. This proposal is not too satisfactory since it violates a plausible continuity principle (Milnor, 1954). A small modification in outcomes – by $1 in Table I, or by 1 cent for that matter – can make or break domination and thus reverse the preference ordering. Indeed, should we advise people not to live in San Francisco or Tokyo because of possible but not very probable earthquakes? Should we advise pedestrians never to cross streets because of the possibility of being struck by an auto? Such considerations compel us to balance the advantages against the disadvantages of competing decisions, weighing them by appropriately defined probabilities – the expected utility principle.

A historical note. Early theories prescribing maximization of expected utility were confined to special cases. Two types of restrictions were imposed. First, the decision maker was advised to maximize the expected value of his money wealth or gain, i.e., utility was in effect identified with a money amount or some linear function of a money amount. Some other quantifiable good, such as the number of prisoners taken or the number of patients cured, might play the same role as money, but nonquantifiable rewards and penalties of actions were unnecessarily excluded from the set of results. Second, probabilities were restricted to objective ones – a special case of personal probabilities.

It is difficult to imagine that an experienced Bronze Age player who used dice that had 'tooled edges and threw absolutely true' (David, 1962) would bet much more than 1:5 on the coming of the ace. Cardano's efforts in computing the gambler's odds (Ore, 1953) suggest at any rate that by the sixteenth century the rule of maximizing average money gains computed on the basis of objective probabilities was taken for granted.

We have already cited Bernoulli and Marshall as having proclaimed utility a nonlinear function of money, thus lifting the first of the above restrictions. Marshall also applied the utility concept to commodity bundles. Von Neumann and Morgenstern (1944) extended it further to all possible results of actions and derived the expected utility rule from simple consistency postulates. This was simplified by others, especially Herstein and Milnor (1953). All these writers dealt only with objective probabilities, leaving out the important cases in which symmetries between relevant events are not agreed upon.

Bayes (1764) can be credited with the idea of personal probabilities. He thought of them as being revealed by an individual's choices among wagers – not just on cards and coins, but on horses and fighting cocks as well! Thus Bayes removed the second restriction, but he retained the first in assuming that utility was in effect identified with money gains, so that betting 9 guineas against 1 implies a corresponding ratio of probabilities. In 1937, de Finetti provided mathematical rigor for this approach.

In 1926, Ramsey (1923–1928) stated, perhaps for the first time, simple consistency postulates that imply the existence of both personal probabilities (of any events, regardless of symmetries) and utilities (of any results of actions, quantifiable or not). Savage (1954) restated the consistency postulates and, partly following de Finetti and von Neumann and Morgenstern, proved that they imply the expected utility rule. For an original exposition, see Pratt *et al.* (1964).

Reviews of the works of other contemporary authors are found in Arrow (1951), Luce and Suppes (1965), Ozga (1965), and Fishburn (1964). Surveys and bibliographies as well as much original material by 21 leading authors on both the prescriptive and descriptive aspects of decision theory are found in Shelly and Bryan (1964).

VII. STRATEGIES

The existence of numerical utilities describing a decision maker's 'tastes' and of probabilities describing his 'beliefs' has been shown to follow from rules of consistency. To formulate and solve the problem of choosing a good decision, both tastes and beliefs must be assumed fixed over some given period of time (but see Koopmans [1964] on 'flexibility'). In general, the probabilities the decision maker assigns at any time to the various states of nature and thus to the results of his actions depend on his information at that time. New information may also uncover new feasible actions. We shall generalize the decision concept accordingly in several steps.

A *strategy* (also called a decision function or response rule) is the assignment, in advance of information, of specific actions to respond to the different messages that the decision maker may receive from an information source. If, more generally, messages, actions, and results form time sequences (the case of 'earning while learning'), we have a *sequential strategy* (also called an extensive or dynamic strategy). To each possible sequence of future messages, a sequential strategy assigns a sequence of actions (see, for example, Theil, 1964). An optimal sequential strategy maximizes the weighted average of utilities assigned to all possible sequences of results, possibly taking into account 'impatience' by means of a discount rate (Fisher, 1930; Koopmans, 1960). The weights are personal *joint* probabilities of sequences of events *and* messages. This amounts to the same thing as saying that the probabilities of events are revised each time a message is received.

It is still more general to redefine action in order to include in it the choice of information sources to be used and thus of 'questions to be asked' at a given time. The resulting problem of finding an optimal *informational strategy* is a task of economic theories of information and organization and also of statistical decision theory (e.g., Raiffa and Schlaifer, 1961) where events and information sources correspond to hypotheses and experiments, respectively.

Finally, if we allow the decision maker to receive messages about the feasibility and outcomes of actions he has not formerly considered, we obtain the still more general concept of *exploratory strategy*. True, it has been almost proverbially tenuous to assign probabilities to the results of industrial or scientific research; yet these undertakings are not different in principle from many other ventures and bets, such as those discussed in Section V.

The complex strategies noted here are hardly maximized by the actual entrepreneur, although the penetration of industry by professionals may again bring descriptive and prescriptive economics to their pristine closeness. Today many descriptive hypotheses in this field use the concept of aspiration level – the boundary between success and failure. The actual decision maker is said to revise his aspiration level upward or downward depending on whether he has or has not reached it by previous action; exploration for actions not previously considered is triggered by failure (Simon, 1957). The sequence of actions generated by the dynamic aspiration-level model will, in general, differ from that prescribed by dynamic programming. Yet, with utilities assigned to results of actions in a particular way, it is possible that the aspiration-level mechanism is indeed optimal. It has been inspired, in fact, by adaptive feedbacks observed in live organisms; such feedbacks presumably have maximized the probability of the survival of species.

VIII. COST OF DECISION MAKING

One action or strategy may appear better than another as long as we disregard the toil and trouble of decision making itself, i.e., the efforts of gathering information and of processing it into an optimal decision. The ranking of actions may be reversed when we take these efforts into account and deal, in this sense, with 'net' rather than 'gross' expected utilities of actions. A small increase in expected profit may not be worth a good night's sleep. In statistics, we stop sequential sampling earlier the higher the cost is of obtaining each observation. As an approximation to some logically required, but very complicated, decision rule, we may use a linear decision rule (e.g., prescribe inventories to be proportional to turnover) in order to lessen computational costs. The 'incrementalism' observed and recommended by Lindblom (1965) in the field of political decisions corresponds to the common mathematical practice of searching for a global optimum in the neighborhood of a local optimum or possibly in the neighborhood of the *status quo*. How many local search steps one should undertake and how often he should jump (hopefully) toward a global optimum will presumably depend on the costs of searching (see, for example, Gel'fand and Tsetlin, 1962). Indeed, some strategies may be too complex to be computable in a finite amount of time, even though they respond to each message by a feasible action. There is, after all, a limit on the capacity of computers and on the brain capacity of decision makers. Hence, some strategies may have infinite costs.

The net utility of an action is often represented as the difference between 'gross utility' and 'decision cost'. A prescriptive theory would presumably require that personal probabilities be assigned not only to the outcomes of the actions but also to the efforts of estimating the outcomes and of searching for the action with the highest expected utility.

On a more general level, it is not strictly permissible to represent net utility as a difference between gross utility and decision cost. Even if the two were measurable in dollars, say, utility may be a nonlinear function of money gains. Yet the assumption that net utility is separable into these components simplifies the theory – it reduces the cost of thinking! Almost all prescriptive theory to date deals with gross utility only. Little attention has been given to decision costs that might be subtractable and thus definable in arriving at a net utility concept. Still less attention has been given to a net utility concept that cannot be decomposed into gross-utility and decision-cost components.

The elements for a theory of the expected cost of using inanimate computers, given the (statistical) population of future problems, are probably available. However, the current classification of computation problems as 'scientific' and 'business' (differing in their comparative needs for speed and memory) is certainly much too rough. A theory of mechanical computation costs would resemble the theory of the cost of manufacturing with complex equipment and known technology when capacities and operations are scheduled optimally. On the other hand, so little is known about the 'technology' of human brains! If economists would join forces with students of the psychology of problem solving, insights would undoubtedly be gained into both the descriptive and prescriptive aspects of decision making.

BIBLIOGRAPHY

Allais, M.: 1953, 'Le comportement de l'homme rationnel devant le risque: Critique des postulats et axiomes de l'école americaine', *Econometrica* **21**, 503–546.

Arrow, Kenneth J.: 1951, 'Alternative Approaches to the Theory of Choice in Risk-taking Situations', *Econometrica* **19**, 404–437.

Arrow, Kenneth J.: 1958, 'Utilities, Attitudes, Choices: A Review Note', *Econometrica* **26**, 1–23.

Arrow, Kenneth J.: 1963, 'Utility and Expectation in Economic Behavior', pp. 724–752 in Sigmund Koch (ed.), *Psychology: A Study of a Science*, Volume 6: 'Investigations of Man as Socius: Their Place in Psychology and the Social Sciences', McGraw-Hill, New York.

Arrow, Kenneth J.: 1965, *Aspects of the Theory of Risk-Bearing*, Academic Bookstore, Helsinki.

Aumann, Robert J.: 1962, 'Utility Theory Without the Completeness Axiom', *Econometrica* **30**, 445–462. Corrections in Volume 32 of *Econometrica.*

Bayes, Thomas: (1764) 1958, 'An Essay Towards Solving a Problem in the Doctrine of Chances', *Biometrika* **45**, 296–315.

Bernoulli, Daniel: (1738) 1954, 'Exposition of a New Theory on the Measurement of Risk', *Econometrica* **22**, 23–36. First published as 'Specimen theoriae novae de mensura sortis'.

Borel, Émile: 1939, *Valeur practique et philosophie des probabilités*, Gauthier-Villars, Paris.

Carnap, R.: 1962, 'The Aim of Inductive Logic', pp. 303–318 in International Congress for Logic, Methodology, and Philosophy of Science, Stanford, California, 1960, *Logic, Methodology, and Philosophy of Science: Proceedings* (ed. by Ernest Nagel, Patrick Suppes, and Alfred Tarski), Stanford Univ. Press.

Chernoff, Herman and Moses, Lincoln E.: 1959, *Elementary Decision Theory*, Wiley, New York.

David, Florence N.: 1962, *Games, Gods and Gambling: The Origins and History of Probability and Statistical Ideas From the Earliest Times to the Newtonian Era*, Hafner, New York.

Davidson, Donald and Marschak, Jacob: 1959, 'Experimental Tests of a Stochastic Decision Theory', *Selected Essays*, 6.

Davis, John M.: 1958, 'The Transitivity of Preferences', *Behavioral Science* **3**, 26–33.

Debreu, Gerard: 1959, *Theory of Value*, Wiley, New York.

De Finetti, Bruno: (1937) 1964, 'Foresight: Its Logical Laws, Its Subjective Sources', pp. 93–158 in Henry E. Kyburg and Howard E. Smokler (eds.), *Studies in Subjective Probabilities*, Wiley, New York. First published in French.

Edwards, Ward: 1953, 'Probability-Preferences in Gambling', *American Journal of Psychology* **66**, 349–364.

Ellsberg, Daniel: 1961, 'Risk, Ambiguity, and the Savage Axioms', *Quarterly Journal of Economics* **75**, 643–669.

Fechner, Gustav T.: (1860) 1907, *Elemente der Psychophysik*, 2 vols. (3d ed.) Breitkopf & Härtel, Leipzig. An English translation of Volume 1 was published by Holt in 1966.

Fellner, William: 1965, *Probability and Profit*, Irwin, Homewood, Ill.

Fishburn, Peter C.: 1964, *Decision and Value Theory*, Wiley, New York.

Fisher, Irving: 1906, 'The Risk Element', pp. 265–300 in Irving Fisher, *The Nature of Capital and Income*, Macmillan, New York.

Fisher, Irving: (1930) 1961, *The Theory of Interest*, Kelley, New York. Revision of the author's *The Rate of Interest* (1907).

Franklin, Benjamin: (1772) 1945, 'How to Make a Decision'. p. 786 in *A Benjamin Franklin Reader* (ed. by Nathan G. Goodman), Crowell, New York. A letter to J. Priestly.

Gel'fand, I. M. and Tsetlin, M. L.: 1962, 'Some Methods of Control for Complex Systems', *Russian Mathematical Surveys* **17**, 95–117.

Hart, Albert G.: (1940) 1951, *Anticipations, Uncertainty and Dynamic Planning*, Kelley, New York.

Herstein, I. N. and Milnor, John: 1953, 'An Axiomatic Approach to Measurable Utility', *Econometrica* **21**, 291–297.

Hicks, John R.: (1939) 1946, *Value and Capital: An Inquiry Into Some Fundamental Principles of Economic Theory* (2d ed.), Clarendon, Oxford.

Interdisciplinary Research Conference, University of New Mexico: 1960, *Decisions, Values and Groups: Proceedings* (ed. by D. Willner), Pergamon, New York. See especially the article by J. S. Chipman, 'Stochastic Choice and SubjectiveProbability'.

Jeffrey, Richard C.: 1965, *The Logic of Decision*, McGraw-Hill, New York.

Knight, Frank H.: (1921) 1933, *Risk, Uncertainty and Profit*, London School of Economics and Political Science Series of Reprints of Scarce Tracts in Economic and Political Science, No. 16. London School of Economics.

Koopmans, Tjalling: 1960, 'Stationary Ordinal Utility and Impatience', *Econometrica* **28**, 287–309.

Koopmans, Tjalling: 1964, 'On Flexibility of Future Preference', pp. 243–254 in Maynard W. Shelly and Glenn L. Bryan (eds.), *Human Judgments and Optimality*, Wiley, New York.

Lindblom, Charles E.: 1965, *The Intelligence of Democracy: Decision Making Through Mutual Adjustment*, Free Press, New York.

Luce, R. Duncan: 1959, *Individual Choice Behavior: A Theoretical Analysis*, Wiley, New York.

Luce, R. Duncan and Raiffa, Howard: 1957, *Games and Decisions: Introduction and Critical Survey*. A study of the Behavior Models Project, Bureau of Applied Social Research, Columbia University, Wiley, New York. First issued in 1954 as *A Survey of the Theory of Games*, Columbia University, Bureau of Applied Social Research, Technical Report No. 5.

Luce, R. Duncan and Suppes, Patrick: 1965, 'Preference, Utility, and Subjective Probability', Volume 3, pp. 249–410 in R. Duncan Luce, Robert R. Bush, and Eugene Galanter (eds.), *Handbook of Mathematical Psychology*, Wiley, New York.

MacCrimmon, K. R.: 1965, 'An Experimental Study of the Decision-Making Behavior of Business Executives', Ph. D. dissertation, Univ. of California at Los Angeles.

Marschak, Jacob: 1950, 'Rational Behavior, Uncertain Prospects, and Measurable Utility', *Selected Essays*, 1.

Marschak, Jacob: (1954) 1964, 'Scaling of Utility and Probability', *Selected Essays*, 3.

Marshall, Alfred: (1890) 1961, *Principles of Economics* (9th ed.), Macmillan, New York. See especially the Mathematical Appendix, note 9.

May, Kenneth O.: 1954, 'Intransitivity, Utility and the Aggregation of Preference Patterns', *Econometrica* **22**, 1–13.

Milnor, John: 1954, 'Games Against Nature', pp. 49–60 in Robert M. Thrall, C. H. Combs, and R. L. Davis (eds.), *Decision Processes*, Wiley, New York.

Neyman, Jerzy: 1950, *First Course in Probability and Statistics*, Holt, New York.

Ore, Oystein: 1953, *Cardano, the Gambling Scholar*, Oxford Univ. Press. Princeton Univ. Press. Includes a translation by Sidney Henry Gould from the Latin of Cardano's *Book on Games of Chance*.

Oźga, S. Andrew: 1965, *Expectations in Economic Theory*, Weidenfeld & Nicolson, London.

Papandreou, Andreas G.: 1957, *A Test of a Stochastic Theory of Choice*, University of California Publications in Economics, Vol. 16, No. 1. Univ. of California Press. In collaboration with O. H. Sauerlender, O. H. Brownlee, L. Hurwicz, and W. Franklin.

Pascal, Blaise: (1670) 1961, *Pensées: Notes on Religion and Other Subjects*, Doubleday, New York. See especially Section 3: 'De la nécessité du pari'.

Pollack, Irwin: 1955, 'Sound Level Discrimination and Variation of Reference Testing Conditions', *Journal of the Acoustical Society of America* **27**, 474–480.

Pratt, John, W.: 1964, 'Risk Aversion in the Small and in the Large', *Econometrica* **32**, 122–136.

Pratt, John W., Raiffa, Howard, and Schlaifer, Robert: 1964, 'The Foundations of Decision Under Uncertainty: An Elementary Exposition', *Journal of the American Statistical Association* **59**, 353–375.

Quandt, Richard: 1956, 'A Probabilistic Theory of Consumer Behavior', *Quarterly Journal of Economics* **70**, 507–536.

Raiffa, Howard: 1961, 'Risk, Ambiguity, and the Savage Axioms: Comment', *Quarterly Journal of Economics* **75**, 690–694.

Raiffa, Howard and Schlaifer, Robert: 1961, *Applied Statistical Decision Theory*, Graduate School of Business Administartion, Studies in Managerial Economics, Harvard Univ., Boston, Division of Research.
Ramsey, Frank P.: (1923–1928) 1950, *The Foundations of Mathematics and Other Logical Essays*, Humanities, New York. See especially Chapter 7, 'Truth and Probabilities', and Chapter 8, 'Further Considerations'.
Savage, Leonard J.: 1954, *The Foundations of Statistics*, Wiley, New York. Revised, Dover, 1972.
Shackle, L. S.: (1949) 1952, *Expectation in Economics* (2d ed.), Cambridge Univ. Press.
Shackle, L. S.: 1955, *Uncertainty in Economics and Other Reflections*, Cambridge Univ. Press.
Shackle, L. S.: 1961, *Decision, Order and Time in Human Affairs*, Cambridge Univ. Press.
Shelly, Maynard W. and Bryan, Glenn L. (eds.): 1964, *Human Judgments and Optimality*, Wiley, New York.
Simon, Herbert A.: 1957, 'A Behavioral Model of Rational Choice', pp. 241–260 in Herbert A. Simon, *Models of Man*, Wiley, New York.
Simon, Herbert A.: 1959, 'Theories of Decision-Making in Economics and Behavioral Science', *American Economic Review* **49**, 253–283.
Theil, Henri: 1964, *Optimal Decision Rules for Government and Industry*, North Holland Publishing, Amsterdam; Rand McNally, Chicago.
Thurstone, Louis L.: (1927–1955) 1959, *The Measurement of Values*, Univ. of Chicago Press. Selections from previously published papers.
von Neumann, John and Morgenstern, Oskar: (1944) 1964, *Theory of Games and Economic Behavior* (3d ed.), Wiley, New York.
Wald, Abraham: (1950) 1964, *Statistical Decision Functions*, Wiley, New York.
Wolfowitz, J.: 1962, 'Bayesian Inference and Axioms of Consistent Decision', *Econometrica* **3**, 471–480.
Wright, Georg H. von: 1963, *The Logic of Preference*, Edinburgh Univ. Press.

17

THE ECONOMIC MAN'S LOGIC*

(1970)

I

The contributors to this volume want to honour an economist. He is also the author of *Foundations of Inductive Logic.*[1] I shall relate induction to the making of decisions under uncertainty. This will be recognized by economists as a natural extension of the problem facing a producer, consumer, investor (or, for that matter, a government agency) under uncertainty. It is also in the spirit of some modern logicians. Ramsey (1926, 1928) and von Wright (1963) have, in a sense, extended deductive logic by adding axioms of preference. Ramsey has used these axioms as the very foundations of probabilities and thus, presumably, of induction. Harrod, whose preface acknowledged Ramsey's moral support, has gone on to discoveries of his own. But I shall ask later whether Harrod's fundamental principle of 'continuity' of experience is at all related to De Finetti's (1937) 'exchangeability'. This concept is used by some of those working in Ramsey's spirit, in order to understand the relation between the probabilities that the maker of decisions (including predictions) uses, and the frequencies he has observed. Harrod refers at length and, on balance, critically to Carnap's duality of 'probability$_1$' and 'probability$_2$'. The latter is defined as a frequency. The former is closer to, or identical with, the concept to be presented here. This closeness is more evident now than it was at the time of Harrod's writing. For in 1962 Carnap explained some changes in his views, starting with a statement that will be acclaimed by those approaching probabilities via the logic of decisions.[2]

II

Both logicians and economists are wont to distinguish between prescribing and describing. Logic prescribes. Psychology describes. So do other 'behavioural sciences'. To illustrate: if objects x and y are identical, and objects y and z are also identical, the *homo logicus*, obeying the formal norms (consistency rules) of ordinary logic, will recognize x and z as identical too. But the 'brain-twister' puzzle at the end of the weekly paper will present these three objects in such a way that even a well-rested, college-educated reader may fail to recognize the identity between x and z; let alone a tired or sick man, a child, a drunk. And how often does a political speaker conclude in good faith that A implies B when his sole premiss was that A is a necessary condition for B; and how often, and how many people go along with his reasoning! Cognitive psychology[3] or, for that matter, anthropology may study the frequency of such aberrations among subjects with given physical and cultural characteristics, given the type of objects ('stimuli') considered.

Similarly, the consistent decision maker, the *homo economicus*, is not the actual, real man. For example: just like the non-logical (yet real) man may fail to obey the norm of transitivity of the identity relation between objects, the non-economic (yet real) man may fail to conform with the norm of transitivity of the indifference relation between actions: though indifferent between actions a and b, and between b and c, he may prefer a to c, say. And the empirical study may usefully occupy itself with recording the frequency of such behaviour, and its dependence on the characteristics of the man as well as of the actions considered. I say 'usefully' because such records can lead to predictions of practical importance.

It is of some consequence to extend our example of intransitive identity and indifference relations from man to an electronic computer. Because of its limited memory, or its limited speed (and a limited amount of available time), the computer must round off the results of its additions and multiplications. It will happen therefore, from time to time, that although the numbers x and y, and the numbers y and z are defined as pairwise equal, yet the computer's print-out will show x and z as not equal.[4]

Thus, an economic question arises, which I shall not try to answer here. The question applies, in fact, to men and machines alike. How much rationality, consistency, precision can one afford? What price logic? It was Ramsey (1926) who pointed to the 'reluctance to bother about trifles'. Indeed, we are free to proclaim weaker or stricter systems of consistency norms. Some of those which are weaker and which bother less 'about trifles' may turn out to be more 'rational'[5] if, as befits us economists, we take account of cost and limited resources, appropriately defined. The boundary between prescriptive and descriptive studies of human thought and decision is thus fluid.

Whatever this boundary, the study of the choice between conclusions from premises is usually regarded as the business of the logician (if prescriptive) or as the business of the cognitive psychologist (if descriptive).[6] The *description* of choices between actions (or decisions) is also usually regarded as the business of psychologists with their experiments,[7] but also of other students of human behaviour: anthropologists and sociologists with their interviews and questionnaires, economists with their attempts to estimate statistically the effect of various factors upon the (individual or aggregate) demands for goods, securities, foreign currencies....

But what about the *prescriptive* norms, the consistency rules for choices between decisions? In general, action must be decided upon under uncertainty about its results. Or, in an equivalent formulation, under uncertainty about the state of the world, which will affect the action's result. We are led to discussing something called 'probabilities', to be assigned by the decisionmaker to the several possible results of a given action of his, in a manner consistent, in some formal sense, with his preferences between actions. Or, in an equivalent formulation, he is thought to assign appropriate probabilities to the several possible events, each being a set of states of the world that determine the results of actions. In short, we discuss formal consistency rules that lead to judgments which are themselves not judgements about formal consistency but about material truth. And this, I suppose, is the proper domain of inductive logic. But note that, presented here in its relation with decision making, this logic involves, in addition to 'probability judgements' that the decider makes about the world, also his preferences between, his 'utility judgements' about, the compared actions and their results. (Thus both truth and goodness seem to be involved, and the post-Aristotelian wall between logic and ethics seems to be breached. Was not, in Socrates' eyes, the wise and the virtuous the same man?)

III

A set of decision norms or axioms, shaped up by De Finetti and by Savage (1954), is equivalent to the 'expected utility theorem'. We shall give the theorem as a purely mathematical statement. This will be followed by its interpretation, (viz., by translating symbols into corresponding entities relevant to decision making) and by the statement of the axioms.

Define a set A of functions a from the set $X=\{x\}$ to the set $C=\{c\}$. If the binary relation $\succcurlyeq$ on A satisfies axioms 1, 2,..., then, and only then, there exists a probability measure P on X and there exists a real-valued function u on C, such that, for any a_1, a_2 in A,

$$a_1 \succcurlyeq a_2 \quad \text{if and only if} \quad w(a_1) \geqslant w(a_2);$$

where by definition,

$$w(a) = \sum_c u(c)\, p_a(c),$$
$$p_a(c) = P\{x: a(x) = c\}.$$

(X assumed here finite for convenience). This is a purely mathematical statement, and so are the axioms 1, 2,.... But before we talk about the axioms, let us give the *interpretations* for the symbols, and some names:

A = set of *actions* a; X = set of *states* x; C = set of *consequences* (results) c. Thus typically $c=a(x)$: given the state, the action determines the consequence.

$a_1 \succcurlyeq a_2$ reads 'a_1 *is not worse than* a_2'. Depending on whether it is or is not the case that, in addition, also $a_2 \succcurlyeq a_1$, we write, respectively, $a_1 \sim a_2$ ('equally desirable', 'indifferent') or $a_1 \succ a_2$ ('better', 'preferred').

$u(c)$ is called the *utility* of c. P is a *measure* on X, in the usual sense. That is (roughly), P is a real-valued function on the set of subsets Z of X (called events) which is (1) non-negative, (2) additive, i.e., for any disjoint Z_1, Z_2, $P(Z_1 \text{ or } Z_2) = P(Z_1) + P(Z_2)$. Moreover the function P is a *probability measure*, for, in addition to the properties (1) and (2) it has the property (3), $P(X)=1$.

$p_a(c)$, as defined above, is then the probability assigned to the set of all states which make action a result in consequence c; and $w(a)$, as defined above, is the expectation (i.e., the average) of utilities of consequences of action a; in a rather unfortunate abbreviation, $w(a)$ is called *expected utility* of a.

This is, then, the theorem's interpretation. Utilities of consequences and probabilities of events are defined, for a given decision-maker, as numerical variables whose sum of products he maximizes, given the set of actions (decisions) available to him. But these variables exist if, and only if, he is 'consistent', in the sense that his preferences between all conceivable actions (i.e., all functions from the set of states to the set of consequences) satisfy certain axioms.

These axioms need to be stated only because the theorem as just interpreted in terms of decisions may appear less plausible, convincing, 'transparent' (an expression used in just such a context by Von Neumann and Morgenstern, 1947, p. 25) than those simple axioms, similarly interpreted. Mathematically, they are jointly equivalent to the theorem. To a god who sees this equivalence immediately, there is no virtue in the axioms' greater 'transparency': a psychological rather than logical category, a tribute to human weakness. Elsewhere,[8] I have tried to assemble fragmentary evidence on the extent to which responses of some men conform with Savage's axioms, at least when the subject is trained to 'stop and think' (Ramsey, 1928, p. 201): to 'untwist', e.g., to tabulate a verbally confused decision problem. This was followed by a rough outline of the proof (less rigorous than that of Savage, 1954) that the axioms do imply the theorem (the converse is rather obvious); and again, by a proposed test of compliance with the theorem itself.

Axiom 1 asserts that the relation 'not worse than' completely orders the set A of conceivable actions. The economists' well-known partitioning of the set of conceivable commodity bundles, *under certainty*, into equivalence sets called 'indifference surfaces' is a special case. Clearly, there is a 1–1 correspondence between the set C of consequences and that subset of A consisting of 'sure actions' only (i.e., such that $a(x)=c$ is a constant). Hence C itself can be said to be completely ordered by the relation 'not worse than'.

This permits a brief statement of *Axiom* 2: if $a(x)$ is not worse than $a'(x)$ for all x, and is better than $a'(x)$ for some x, then a is better than a'. This principle of 'inadmissibility of dominated actions' has guided statisticians long since (see, e.g., Wald, 1950). As a matter of sheer common sense it surely has guided all practical people who 'stopped to think'.

Axiom 3 can be interpreted as 'irrelevance of consequences that are not affected by the choice between two actions': if, for all x in the subset Z of X, $a_1(x)=a_2(x)$ and also $a_1'(x)=a_2'(x)$, and if, for all x not in Z, $a_1(x)=$ $=a_1'(x)$ and also $a_2(x)=a_2'(x)$, then a_1' is not worse than a_2', provided a_1

is not worse than a_2. I submit that an attentive reader who would care to tabulate a simple example of the premiss of this axiom (with Z and non-Z each consisting just of two elements) might 'convince' himself of the conclusion.[9]

Axiom 4 can be interpreted as 'independence of beliefs on rewards'. Let $a(x)=c=a'(x')$ for all x in Z, x' in Z'; let $a(x)=\bar{c}=a'(x')$ for all x in non-Z, x' in non-Z'; and let c be better than $\bar{c}$. Thus a and a' can be interpreted as two bets, with the same prizes, on the two events Z and Z', respectively. It is a remarkable feature of ordinary English that, when asked why he prefers to bet on Z rather than Z', many a subject says 'because Z is more probable'; and he says this regardless of whether those events are or are not repeatable. Now, Axiom 4 says that this 'belief' (as revealed by preferring a to a', say) remains unchanged when the pair of prizes ('rewards') $c \succcurlyeq \bar{c}$ is replaced by some other pair, $d \succcurlyeq \bar{d}$, say.

The proof of the existence of the numerical utility function $u(.)$ on the set C of consequences is of less interest to us here, than the existence of a probability measure P on X, underlying the 'expected utility' of each action. In fact, Axiom 4 makes it possible to discuss probabilities of events while considering just two consequences, c and $\bar{c}$ ('success' and 'failure'), with utilities 1 and 0 attached to them arbitrarily and with no loss of generality. Then the expected utility $w(a)$ becomes simply equal to the probability with which action a will result in success. In particular, the discussion may be, and is often, confined to the case when the action consists in predicting; its success is 'correct prediction' and its failure is 'wrong prediction'.

This may be also the place to remark that some authors have confined the set of considered consequences to monetary gains and losses only. By tacitly assuming, in addition, a constant marginal utility of money wealth they were able to identify probability with a 'fair betting coefficient'. This is the case with many passages of Carnap and with the original treatment by De Finetti.[10] It seems to me that this approach goes as far back as the Rev. T. Bayes himself![11] The sophistication about marginal utility of money, unleashed by Bayes's contemporary Daniel Bernoulli and taken up by economists, makes the 'fair bets' an insufficient device to reveal the probabilities that guide bettors. A more complicated device, Borel's dial, will be presented in Section V.

IV

Our axioms suffice to prove the existence of a probability measure P on X, such that $P(Z) \geqslant P(Z')$ whenever a bet on Z is judged as not worse than a bet on Z'. Familiar properties such as 'if Z contains Z' then $P(Z) \geqslant P(Z')$' and '$P(Z)+P(\text{non-}Z)=1$' are then guaranteed.

It is important to note that the axioms also imply corresponding properties of 'conditional probabilities', written $P(Z_1 | Z_2)$, read 'probability of Z_1, given Z_2', and defined by considering 'conditional bets'. Such a bet is called off if Z_2 does not occur; and the bet yields c or $\bar{c}$ (where, as before, c is better than $\bar{c}$), according to whether 'Z_2 and Z_1' happens. A conditional bet on Z_1 given Z_2 is not worse than one on Z_1' given Z_2 if and only if $P(Z_1 | Z_2) \geqslant P(Z_1' | Z_2)$. For a fixed Z_2, the function $P(Z_1 | Z_2)$ has again the three properties of a probability measure. Moreover, the axioms entail the following relation between the 'joint probability' $P(Z_1$ and $Z_2)$ (which we shall assume non-zero) and the conditional and non-conditional probabilities:

$$P(Z_1 \text{ and } Z_2) = P(Z_2).P(Z_1 | Z_2) = P(Z_1).P(Z_2 | Z_1).$$

Consequently

$$P(Z_2 | Z_1) = P(Z_2).P(Z_1 | Z_2)/P(Z_1);$$

and similarly, replacing Z_2 by some other event, Z_2',

$$P(Z_2' | Z_1) = P(Z_2').P(Z_1 | Z_2')/P(Z_1).$$

Dividing the last equation by the preceding one (no zeros are involved!),

$$\frac{P(Z_2 \mid Z_1)}{P(Z_2' \mid Z_1)} = \frac{P(Z_2)}{P(Z_2')} \cdot \frac{P(Z_1 \mid Z_2)}{P(Z_1 \mid Z_2')}.$$

Sometimes the events Z_2 and Z_2' are interpreted as two mutually exclusive 'hypotheses', and the event Z_1 as 'evidence'. For later use it will be convenient to denote the latter by E and the two hypotheses by H and H' (replacing Z_2 and Z_2'). We have then

$$\frac{P(H \mid E)}{P(H' \mid E)} = \frac{P(H)}{P(H')} \cdot \frac{P(E \mid H)}{P(E \mid H')}.$$

In this equation, a convenient form of the Bayes Theorem,[12] the ratio on the left-hand side is called 'posterior odds' and is, thus, equal to the product of so-called 'prior odds' to the 'likelihood ratio with respect to evidence E'. If you are consistent and if you assign constant marginal utility to money in the range of the prizes considered, these three ratios, as constrained by the above equation, represent the least favourable odds at which you will accept each of the following three bets: (1) the conditional bet on H given E, against H' given E; (2) the bet on H against H'; and (3) the conditional bet on E given H against E given H'. If constant marginal utility of money is not assumed, the 'Borel dial' to be described in the next section would reveal, as precisely as it can, that you assign to the six events in question just the probabilities consistent with the equation.

The theorem of Bayes, understood in this manner is, then, along with the expected utility theorem, entailed by the axioms of consistent decision making. The theorem will help us to explain why the consistent decision-maker whose evidence consists of a (properly defined) 'large sample' will (almost) maximize his expected utility if he assigns to a hypothesis a posterior probability equal to the relative frequency of certain observations.

I shall reason on lines consistent with Savage and De Finetti, I believe; and also with Carnap's treatment of the 'estimation' of his 'probability$_1$' (which is logically derived, not from frequencies but from betting decisions), given the observed frequencies. This approach seems to be different from Harrod's for whom (p. 47) 'The probability relation is ... essentially and by definition a relation of frequency', although he does not regard 'probability numbers as derived from or reflections of statistical frequencies in nature.' The difference between the two approaches will turn out to depend on the difference, if any, between Harrod's principle of 'continuity' (Chapter III) and the 'exchangeability' concept which we shall now present.

V

Although I had each axiom accompanied by its interpretation in terms of decisions, they, and the consequent existence of a probability measure on X, can be regarded as purely mathematical propositions about a binary relation called 'not worse than'. Now, the properties defining a probability measure form only the beginning of the calculus of probabilities. As pointed out by De Finetti (1937), a further premiss for the body of that calculus is the existence of 'exchangeable' subsets (events) of the set on which the probability measure is defined. For example, let X be partitioned into subsets Z and non-Z such that the decision-maker is indifferent between betting on either: each of these two actions is 'not worse than' the other. The two events are then 'exchangeable' and the partition itself, i.e., the pair 'Z, non-Z' is sometimes called a 'fair coin' (with Z and non-Z then called 'heads' and 'tails'). It corresponds to the gross physical reality of minted coins only in the same way in which the straight line of pure geometry corresponds to the edge of the paper page now facing you, my reader. There may or may not be agreement between people as to how closely this page approximates the ideal rectangle; and similarly, whether one should be indeed indifferent between betting on a particular physical coin's falling heads or falling tails up; or between betting on any of the 52 cards of a given (not necessarily well-shuffled) deck. But if you are indeed indifferent between those 52 bets, and, in addition, obey the consistency axioms, you will be also indifferent between betting on any of the four suits, and on either of the two colours. The probabilities of success in each of these three sets of equally desirable bets will, then, respectively be: $\frac{1}{52}, \frac{1}{4}, \frac{1}{2}$. It will also follow that you should be indifferent between betting on any specified set of (say) seven cards, the probability of success of any such bet being the same.

Probabilities as revealed by preferences between bets with the same pairs of prizes (c, $\bar{c}$ of our Axiom 4), were so described already by Borel (1924) in his review of Keynes (1921). Accordingly, I would like to call a 'Borel dial' the following device, designed to elicit a man's estimate of the probability of 'rain tomorrow', say. First, ascertain that the subject is indifferent between receiving 10 dollars if the twirled arrow stops within one or another of any two equal sectors of the dial. (This is, itself, an induction on the observer's part, in a sense which will become clear.) Then let him choose between receiving $10 if it rains tomorrow (and receiving nothing if it does not), and receiving $10 if the arrow stops between the noon position and the four o'clock position on the dial (and receiving nothing if it does not). If he prefers the former bet, we say that the probability he assigns to tomorrow's rain exceeds $\frac{1}{3}$. We then ask him to choose between receiving $10 only if it rains tomorrow, and receiving $10 only if the arrow stops between the noon and the six o'clock position.

If he now prefers the latter bet, his 'personal probability' of rain tomorrow is between $\frac{1}{3}$ and $\frac{1}{2}$. This method of evaluation of probabilities, says Borel (who by the way, uses dice, not a continuous dial) 'has exactly the same characteristics as the evaluation of prices.... If one desires to know the price of a ton of coal, it suffices to offer greater and greater prices to the person who possesses the coal; at a certain price he will decide to sell it.' Economists are aware, of course, that price theory and Walras's '*prix criés... dans le marché*' idealize gross reality. So does Borel's device, idealizing the consistency of bettors.

VI

Is there any relation between probabilities as revealed by a Borel dial applied to a consistent bettor, and the frequencies of observations in statistical samples, the very heart of scientific induction? To answer this, let us first add another case of exchangeability as a property of certain subsets ('events') of the set X (of 'states' x), on which a probability measure is defined. We shall consider the case called 'repeated and independent trials,' viewed again as a mathematical, not physical object. This case will prove to be much more important than that typified by the mathematical objects called 'fair coin', 'well-shuffled deck', etc. In their physical interpretation the latter objects are those illustrating the 'Principle of Indifference', and I agree with Harrod that it is of little consequence for the understanding of induction. By contrast, the exchangeability of 'repeated and independent trials', should its physical interpretation prove justifiable, would indeed entail important consequences for the problem of induction; and I believe it would correspond to Harrod's[13] weighty 'fair sampling postulate'.

Let, then, the generic element of the set X of states be the sequence (temporal or no, no matter) $x=(x_1, x_2, \ldots)$. Define the set T_i to consist of subsequences in which the component x_i is omitted. For simplicity let each component in each sequence or subsequence have just two possible values, denoted conveniently by 1 ('success') or 0 ('failure'). Define the event Z_i as the set of all those sequences x in which the ith component is a success: $Z_i=\{x:x_i=1\}$. Suppose a consistent man's indifference between conditional bets (as explained in Section IV) reveals that the conditional probability $P(Z_i|T_i)$ is the same for all T_i and all i, so that we can write

$P(Z_i|T_i)=P(Z_i)=p$, say. Then X is called a set of sequences of repeated and independent trials: the same probability is assigned to each trial, and this regardless of whether any other trial results in success or in failure.

Again, it may be a matter of disagreement whether a particular physical phenomenon has approximately the properties of such a set of sequences: whether, for example, successive experiments performed or to be performed in a certain laboratory under assertedly 'controlled conditions' do indeed possess the property that $P(Z_i|T_i)$ is the same for all i, and for all subsequences in T_i. Will everybody be indifferent between betting on a particular outcome of the first such experiment, given all others, and of the tenth, given all others?

We are now ready to establish a relation between probabilities assigned to given events by a consistent decision maker and the frequencies of those events he has observed. Let the states x in X be sequences he believes (as is revealed by his bets) to be sequences of repeated independent trials. That is, his assignment of probability of success, if evaluated on a Borel dial, will be the same for all trials, $i=1, 2, \ldots$, whether observed or not, and each independently of the outcomes of other trials. Now denote by $Z^{(p)}$ and $Z^{(p')}$, respectively, two subsets of X, each consisting of all sequences x such that, for all i, $P(Z_i|T_i)=P(Z_i)=p$ or $=p'$ (where $p \neq p'$). In the present context, $Z^{(p)}$ and $Z^{(p')}$ are two rival hypotheses corresponding to the H, H' of the Bayes theorem as formulated in our Section IV. If one of them, say $Z^{(p)}$, is accepted by the decision-maker, we say that his estimate of $P(Z_i)$ is p for all trials, viz., for all the (n, say) observed ones as well as for the non-observed ones, $i=n+1, \ldots$. This will be revealed by his betting behaviour; he will be indifferent between betting on the $(n+1)$th trial being a success, and betting on a fraction p of the circumference of the Borel dial. [Moreover, if the marginal utility of money were, for him, constant over the range of prizes considered, he would also accept a bet with odds $p:(1-p)$ or better.]

We shall now define that subset of X [i.e., that set of sequences $x=(x_1, \ldots, x_n)$] which will play the role of 'evidence'. First denote by $f_n=(x_1+\cdots+x_n)/n$ the relative frequency of 'successes' (i.e. of 1s rather than 0s). Now consider the set of all sequences $x=(x_1, \ldots, x_n, x_{n+1}, \ldots)$ such that f_n is within a distance δ from p. We can denote this set by

$$Z^{(p, \delta, f_n)} = \{x : p - \delta < f_n < p + \delta\}.$$

The set, $Z^{(p, \delta, f_n)}$, will play the role of evidence, E, in the Bayes theorem which we can now rewrite, for our present purposes, thus:

$$\frac{P(Z^{(p)} \mid Z^{(p, \delta, f_n)})}{P(Z^{(p')} \mid Z^{(p, \delta, f_n)})} = \frac{P(Z^{(p)})}{P(Z^{(p')})} \cdot \frac{P(Z^{(p, \delta, f_n)} \mid Z^{(p)})}{P(Z^{(p, \delta, f_n)} \mid Z^{(p')})}.$$

We shall consider the last of these three ratios: the likelihood ratio of the two hypotheses, $Z^{(p)}$ and $Z^{(p')}$ with respect to the evidence $Z(p, \delta, f_n)$; and shall apply to it the ('weak') 'law of large numbers'. This latter is a purely mathematical theorem. Its premises are the three properties defining any probability measure on any set, combined with the definition of a set of infinitely long sequences, each component of a given sequence having the same probability distribution of its values. The theorem is therefore valid independently of any particular interpretation of the probability concept in terms of natural (including human) phenomena.[14] This theorem says that, for any positive number δ,

$$P(Z^{(p, \delta, f_n)} \mid Z^{(p)}) \rightarrow 1$$

as n increases. That is: given that the probability of success in each of the indefinitely long sequence of trials is p, the conditional probability of the average number's f_n of successes in n trials being within an arbitrarily small distance δ of p tends towards certainty as n increases.[15]

Now, the conditional probability just specified is the numerator of the *likelihood ratio* we have proposed to consider. It follows from the theorem just stated that this ratio increases beyond all bounds (that is, towards 1:0) as n increases. What, then, about the *posterior odds*? Provided that the prior $P(Z^{(p)})$ is not zero, which, roughly, means that $Z^{(p)}$ is not impossible – the Bayes theorem as last rewritten and the property of our likelihood ratio as just stated imply that the posterior odds of $Z^{(p)}$ against $Z^{(p')}$ will also increase beyond all bounds. In words (roughly): if, as the number of observations increases, the relative frequency of successes is found to remain close to the number p, then the odds in favour of the hypothesis that this number is the probability of successes in each of the indefinite sequence of trials increase beyond all bounds; provided this hypothesis was not judged impossible to begin with. With this proviso, the effect of prior odds will be 'washed out', 'swamped' by the increasing likelihood ratio derived from observations. On the other hand, zero prior odds will never be overcome.[16]

It must be recalled that we interpret the odds in terms of decision-making. Indeed, one can derive from our premises directly that, for any δ, choices between bets, if based on the estimate $P(Z_{n+1})=f_n \pm \delta$ will yield, as the number n of observations increases, an increasingly higher expected utility relative to other choices between the same bets; where, it will be recalled, $P(Z_{n+1})$ is the probability that the $(n+1)$th trial will yield a success, i.e., that $x_{n+1}=1$.[17] This holds not only for the special case when the decision-maker is a 'predictor' (with utility$=1$ if right, $=0$ if wrong), but also in the general case, with utility depending on x_{n+1} and an action in any manner whatsoever. As before, in the limiting case where a certain value of the success probability is *a priori* impossible, it remains so *a posteriori*.

In addition to the proviso of non-zero prior odds, we must remind the reader most emphatically of a more important one: it has been assumed throughout that all of the indefinitely long sequence of trials have the same probability of success. Without this premiss of 'repeated independent trials' the conclusion of the Law of Large Numbers does not obtain, nor does therefore the conclusion about posterior odds of the considered hypothesis against an alternative.

Let me conclude this section with a side issue which, however, will help us, in the next section, to ask questions about Harrod's position compared with the present one. He rightly declares (p. 59) that the so-called Law of Succession[18] 'is derived from assigning equal prior probabilities' and notes

> that the gross and flagrant fallacies to which the application of the Law of Succession leads, all arise ... in the case of short runs.... If the principles by which the Law of Succession is derived were correct, then it ought to apply to very short runs, as well as to longer runs; no one, to my knowledge, has shown why on these principles this should not be so.'

Harrod remarks that his approach, too, 'does not apply to short runs' and that it has 'some family resemblance to the much abused Law of Succession' although its logical basis is quite different.

Now, we have seen that in the 'long run', that is, with a large number of observations, the effect of *any* prior probabilities, whether assumed equal or not, tends to be 'swamped' by the effects of observed frequencies. Thus the position presented here is consistent with the fact, observed by Harrod, that the applications of the Law of Succession, so flagrantly fallacious in the case of short runs, are less so for long runs.

VII

The reader will have noted that the emphasis on short *versus* long runs when it comes to estimating from observations is common to the present position and to that of Harrod. Now, mark our important provision: the decision-maker was made to assume that the many trials he has observed are 'exchangeable', both among themselves and with future trials. Harrod, on the other hand describes his Principle of Experience (Chapter III) as one of 'continuity' of a path partly traversed and still to be journeyed on. Is there a family resemblance between 'continuity' in Harrod's sense and our (and De Finetti's) 'exchangeability'? At any rate: what is the relation between these two concepts?

To me, this is the most important of all the numerous questions that I would have to answer before being sure that I have understood Harrod's book. Even if I had answered them I could not convey to the reader of this essay the depth, the vigour, and the beauty of Harrod's thought. As one can see by comparing the literature cited in the book and in this essay, the backgrounds are different even though we are both economists. Perhaps just this difference of backgrounds makes a comparison of the two approaches, and thus my main question as just stated, not altogether useless.

For better understanding, it is worth remarking that in most though not all of Harrod's reasoning, the relative frequency of successes in observed trials (f_n in my notation above) is, in effect, equal to 1. See, for example, the description of the continuous journey in the important Chapter III on the Principle of Experience.[19] I do not believe that this concentration on a special case weakens Harrod's argument. What is essential for Harrod is that some features observed during the journey are likely to be observed as the journey continues; the more likely the longer you have travelled.

Nor is it a matter of consequence (it seems to be more a matter of nomenclature) that, like Einstein, Harrod seems disinclined to believe that God plays dice. When Harrod says (p. 242) that 'Most of induction ... is not concerned to establish statistical frequencies, but to establish uniformities, laws or particular facts', I infer from the context that he has in mind deterministic laws and that, while he is indeed concerned with evaluating probabilities of hypotheses, these hypotheses are not themselves probability distributions. Modern statistics as a tool of inductive inference, and much of modern decision theory, takes a more general view. One does assign a posterior probability, for example, to the statement that this person has such and such probability of dying within a year if not operated upon, and a different probability if a particular operation is performed. And this may be more useful to the decision-making surgeon than the statement 'the patient has cancer for sure'. I said this approach is more general because 'probability $=1$ for a certain value of the variable' is a special case of a probability distribution. Thus, statisticians are apt to use distribution parameters to describe the 'state of the world'. Again, I do not believe that Harrod's 'deterministic' nomenclature makes a decisive difference.

Mostly, the hypotheses considered by Harrod are statements of the type 'If P is the case, then Q is the case' rather than simply 'Q is the case'. Again, this is not essential for our comparison of the two approaches. Harrod's interest in the conjoint occurrence of two events can be taken care of, in the other approach, by considering some conditional probability of Q, given P, as the hypothesis, and testing it by recording the conditional frequency of observed Q, given observed P.

In trying to establish a relation between Harrod's 'continuity' and the 'exchangeability of repeated independent trials' defined here, it is not decisive, either, that Harrod first proposes (pp. 89–90) a 'sampling postulate' (also called 'fair sampling postulate'), then shows it to be unnecessary for induction, replacing it by a proposition on the properties of our observations, not of nature itself (pp. 116–17). For both interpretations are consistent with the definition of repeated independent trials (observed as well as not yet observed) by stating:

$$P(Z_i) \text{ is the same for } i = 1, \ldots, n, n+1, \ldots$$

where $P(Z_i)$ is the probability of success in the ith trial and n is the number of observations already performed.

Nor does it seem to me that the emphasis on decision separates us Ramseyites from Harrod (and, in this respect, from most of traditional literature on logic) in a really important manner. As already pointed out, prediction is a special case of decision. Harrod's book is full of references to the usefulness of correct predictions, for cavemen and others. To be sure there may be disagreement about utilities in detail but hardly any about the need to survive. Moreover, it is presumed (or alleged) for the case of pure scientists that in their case there is intersubjective agreement about the two-valued utility of prediction (e.g., 1 if right, 0 if wrong). This makes expected utility identical with the probability of correct prediction so that, again, induction logic reveals itself as a special case of decision logic.[20]

What does then make the difference, if any, between the two approaches? In Section II, I pointed out that the boundary between prescription and description is fluid. How relaxed, or how restricted shall be the prescriptive norms of logic including the logic of decision? I have mentioned, for example (in Section II) those who relax the norms by denying transitivity of indifference (between actions, or between their consequences). Others have restricted the norms by prescribing, for example, aversion to risk. As far as I know, even some logicians of deduction are more 'relativistic' than others; although less so than the students of ethics, among whom Natural Right and the self-evident truths of 1776 are in disrepute, merited or not. But this is precisely why Harrod's ideas are so attractive. It is impossible not to share his aversion against 'defeatism' and 'escapism' (p. 20). There must be a fixed point somewhere!

The mathematical deductions – from premisses to conclusions – of De Finetti and others are without blemish. If a given sequence consists of repeated and independent trials, relative frequency approaches probability, and actions should be chosen accordingly. Here the sequences, and the actions themselves, are mathematical objects. But how do we know that a given sequence of actual observations, performed and to be performed in the world of phenomena, can be assumed, albeit approximately, to consist of repeated and independent components? How can we establish intersubjective agreement on these matters (even though agreement on other matters such as prior probabilities is not needed when the sample is large)? Or, in Harrod's language, how do we know that, with respect to a particular physical characteristic of events, we are on a continuous path? In the language of statisticians: how do we know that this and this and another item belong 'to the same population'? Who tells us that, in estimating the mortality rate, separation by age and sex is important but separation by alphabet is less so?

True, Harrod does not answer specific questions like these. But remember: he has not set out to write a treatise for practising statisticians. He has asked the philosopher's question: how has it been, how is it, possible to discover laws of nature? His answer: because the world (or our observation of the world) has regular, 'non-Heraclitean' features – although admittedly it is another matter to specify those features. In another language: yes, indeed, there are sequences sufficiently close to be treated as repeated and independent.

Harrod deplores 'shallow doctrines of a pragmatic kind'. If to be pragmatic is to relate truth to action, the adjective is, to me, a compliment. Separating prediction from decision only makes our thinking more special and thus poorer in results. But 'shallow' is another matter. When Harrod searches for grounds for induction (and thus for decision) he searches in depth.

NOTES

* Acknowledgements to the National Science Foundation and the Office of Naval Research for the support of the Western Management Science Institute, University of California at Los Angeles; and to James McQueen for criticisms.

1 Harrod, 1956, for all subsequent citations of his work.

2 Here is the statement from Carnap, 1962, p. XV:

'A. *The meaning of logical probability* (probability$_1$) was informally explained in ... several ways: (a) as the degree to which a hypothesis h is confirmed or supported by the evidence e; (b) as a fair betting quotient; and (c) as an estimate of relative frequency. Even at that time I regarded (a) as less satisfactory than (b) or (c); today I would avoid formulations of the kind (a) because of their ambiguity....'

'Although the concept of logical probability in the sense here intended is a purely logical concept, I think that the meaning of statements like "the probability of h with respect to e is 2/3" can best be characterized by explaining their use, *in combination with the concept of utility, in the rule for the determination of rational decisions* (my emphasis J. M.).... The explanation of probability as a betting quotient is a simplified special case of this rule.'

See also Carnap, 1962a. Carnap's student Jeffrey (1965) proceeded to systematize the approach characteristic of Ramsey (rather than that of De Finetti, or of Savage (1954), which I shall mostly follow here).

3 Abelson and Rosenberg, 1958.

4 Hamming, 1965; Rotstein, 1965. In application to human decisions see Kramer, 1968, and, of course, Simon, 1957, 1959. In application to probabilities, see many passages in Harrod's book. For example on p. 35: 'The reason why we cannot specify ... [a precise probability number] is simply that we have not had time, nor, perhaps, inclination, to make the count that would be required for [its] evaluation....' See also his numerous remarks on feasible limits of tolerance.

[5] Indeed, some recent thinking about decision norms (in particular, some yet unpublished work of P. Fishburn and of A. K. Sen) has stated important implications of depriving the economists' indifference relation of the transitivity property usually ascribed to it. This is the very reason why I chose to discuss this property as an example for the (moving) boundary between prescriptive and descriptive theory.
[6] Bruner *et al.* (1956).
[7] Edwards and Tversky (ed.), 1967.
[8] Marschak (1968). See also Luce and Suppes, (1965); Edwards and Tversky (1967).
[9] See, for example, Koopmans (1957), pp. 157–9.
[10] But Carnap's rule R_5 is more general: see the last sentence in the extensive quotation given by me in an earlier note. And De Finetti provides the necessary corrective note, with due reference to Ramsey, in his later, English edition: Kyburg and Smokler 1963, p. 102, note (a).
[11] Bayes (1764), Definition 5 and Proposition 2. See their interpretation in Marschak (1954), pp. 169–70.
[12] In the notation of Harrod (p. 15 footnote), $P(H)=p_2$, $P(H')=p_2$, $P(E|H)=q_1$, $P(E|H')=q_2$. If, as is assumed in his example, the two hypotheses are exhaustive, then $P(H|E)+P(H'|E)=1$, hence $P(H|E)=p_1q_1/(p_1q_1+p_2q_2)$; the formula he uses.
[13] To quote: 'The Principle of Indifference makes an assumption about nature.... If one defines probability by frequency, this implies that nature manifests each alternative an equal number of times. By contrast, the sampling postulate has nothing to do with the composition of nature, but is concerned only with our investigation of nature. It makes the assumption that the relative frequencies of our observations bear a relation to the relative frequencies of different kinds of observables; this requirement entails no assumption regading the composition of nature itself' (pp. 102–3). This passage is introduced by Harrod's observing 'that the Bayes-type argument would require, *in addition* [his italics; J.M.] to some such assumption as the Principle of Indifference, a sampling postulate'. If so, the argument that will follow in my text is not 'Bayes type'. It will use Bayes's theorem and a premiss akin to Harrod's sampling postulate but it will not use the Principle of Indifference since it will nowhere assume 'equal prior probabilities'.
[14] Therefore the theorem called here (and in textbooks on mathematical probability) the Law of Large Numbers cannot be identical with what Harrod (p. 74) calls the Law of Large Numbers and which he 'cannot regard as a universal law of nature *a priori*'. For the mathematical theorem does not claim to describe nature. It is another matter whether or not a particular interpretation of the theorem's premiss and conclusion, i.e., their translation into terms of natural phenomena, can be accepted with any degree of approximation. The same distinction will be made regarding the theorem we are going to discuss now, about estimating posterior probabilities by frequencies.
[15] The proof given in essence 200 years ago is based on combinatorial arithmetic such as that used by Harrod in a similar context (p. 88, footnote).
[16] The latter is the case of Pigou (1929) and the Archbishop of Canterbury, whom Pigou would maintain to be honest even if the Archbishop had dealt himself in one evening three hands each containing four aces, four kings, and four queens. I owe this reference to W. A. Wallis (1942, p. 236).
[17] See also Marschak and Radner (1972), Ch. II, Sections 8–11.
[18] The premiss of this ancient theorem is, more precisely, the uniform prior distribution on the set of values of the probability of success, i.e., on the interval between 0 and 1. One of its conclusions is that, in our notation, $P(Z_{n+1})=(1+nf_n)/(2+n)$.

This, of course, approaches f_n as n increases. See, e.g. Uspensky (1937), p. 69.
[19] Or, at the beginning of Chapter IV, on Inverse Probability: 'If property Q is not in fact almost always conjoined with property P, is it not a very curious thing that out of all the thousands, perhaps hundreds of thousands, of times that P has been seen, it has *always* [J. M.'s emphasis] been seen in conjunction with Q ' (p. 79).
[20] For a more general view see now Marschak (1974).

BIBLIOGRAPHY

Abelson, R. P. and Rosenberg, M. J., 'Symbolic Psycho-Logic', *Behavioral Science* 3 (1958) 1–13.

Bayes, Th., 'An Essay towards Solving a Problem in the Doctrine of Chances', 1764, now in *Biometrika* **45**, 296–315.

Borel, E., 'Apropos of a Treatise on Probability', 1924, reproduced in Kyburg and Smokler, 1964.

Bruner, J. S., Goodnow, J. J., and Austin, G. A., *A Study of Thinking*, New York 1956.

Carnap, R., *Logical Foundations of Probability* (Second ed.), Chicago 1962.

Carnap, R., 'The Aim of Inductive Logic', 1962a, in E. Nagel *et al.* (eds.), *Logic, Methodology and Philosophy of Science*, Stanford 1962, pp. 303–18.

De Finetti, B., 'Foresight: Its Logical Laws, its Subjective Sources', 1937. Translated from the French and provided with some additional notes of the author, in Kyburg and Smokler (1964).

Edwards, W. and Tversky, A. (eds.), *Decision Making: Selected Readings*, Penguin Books, 1967.

Hamming, R. W., 'Numerical Analysis vs. Mathematics', *Science*, (1965) 473–5.

Harrod, R., *Foundations of Inductive Logic*, London 1956.

Jeffrey, R. C., *The Logic of Decision*, New York 1965.

Koopmans, T. C., *Three Essays on the State of Economic Science*, New York 1957.

Kramer, G. H., 'An Impossibility Result concerning the Theory of Decision-Making', in J. L. Bernd (ed.), *Mathematical Applications in Political Science*, University of Virginia Press, 1968, Vol. III, pp. 39–51.

Kyburg, H. E. and Smokler, M. E., *Studies in Subjective Probability*, New York 1964.

Luce, R. D. and Suppes, P., 'Preference, Utility, and Subjective Probability', in *Handbook of Mathematical Psychology* (R. D. Luce *et al.*) New York 1965, Vol. 3, pp. 249–410.

Marschak, J., 'Probabilities in the Social Sciences', 1954, *Selected Essays*, 4.

Marschak, J., 'Decision-Making: Economic Aspects', 1968, *Selected Essays*, 16.

Marschak, J., 'Information, Decision, and the Scientist', in C. Cherry (ed.), *Pragmatic Aspects of Human Communication*, D. Reidel, Dordrecht, 1974, pp. 145–78.

Marschak, J. and Radner, R., *Economic Theory of Teams*, Yale University Press, 1972.

Pigou, A. C., 'The Function of Economic Analysis', Sidney Ball Lecture, reprinted in A. C. Pigou and D. H. Robertson, *Economic Essays and Addresses*, London 1931.

Ramsey, F. P., 'Truth and Probability', 1926. 'Further Considerations', 1928. Both Papers in *The Foundations of Mathematics and Other Logical Essays* (ed. by R. B. Braithwaite), New York 1950. The paper of 1926 also reproduced in Kyburg and Smokler 1964.

Rothstein, J., 'Numerical Analysis: Pure or Applied Mathematics?', *Science* (1965) 1049–50.

Savage, L. J., *The Foundations of Statistics*, New York 1954. Revised: Dover, 1972.

Simon, H. A., *Models of Man*, New York 1957.

Simon, H. A., 'Theories of Decision-Making in Economics and Behavioral Sciences,, *American Economic Review* **49**, 253–83.

Uspensky, J. V., *Introduction to Mathematical Probability*, New York and London 1937.

Von Neumann, J. and Morgenstern, O., *Theory of Games and Economic Behavior*, Princeton 1947.

Wald, A., *Statistical Decision Functions*, New York 1950.

Wallis, A. W., 'Compounding Probabilities from Independent Significance Tests', *Econometrica* (1942) 229–48.

Wright, G. H. von, *The Logic of Preference*, Edinburgh 1963.

18

ECONOMICS OF ACTING, THINKING, AND SURVIVING*

(1974)

I

The idealist philosophers of some 150 years ago have been accused of pan-logism. Quite likely, they would not mind. The present writer, an economist, will briefly indulge in pan-economism, if only to satisfy the editor of this volume who has encouraged the contributors to be 'as provocative as possible'.

Economics will be understood in the sense in which one speaks of 'Economy of Nature': not in the sense in which so-called 'material' (and sometimes measurable) items – food and shelter, and dollar bills – are contrasted with things lovable and beautiful. "Economics is about economizing" (Charles Hitch). "Economics is about the best use of scarce resources". Better still (because scarcity of resources might, unnecessarily, imply measurability): economics is about the best choice between available alternatives. Prudence would also be an adequate term.

II

These days, journalists and politicians and college administrators talk about 'priorities': we cannot do everything, let us make clear what we should do in the first, second, third place.... Clarity about the ranking of alternative actions is indeed a feature of economic thinking. It is an 'extension of logic' (F. P. Ramsey). Actual men are not 'economic men' nor are they, more broadly, 'logical men'. But illogical thinking can be distinguished from logical thinking. A sequence of choices that are capriciously inconsistent with any ranking can be distinguished from consistent, hence economic, choices.

Ranking, ordering can be applied to any set of possible actions, with the best at the top, the worst at the bottom. Psychologically speaking, to achieve consistent ranking, some soul-searching, some process of trial and error may be necessary.

No numerical characteristics are, in general, needed, to choose, for example, between one menu and another. To be sure some people count their calories. So-called 'criteria' – usually numerical ones – may indeed help. This is simple if there is just one such criterion: more rice is better than little rice. Usually there are several criteria. In a beauty contest, various scores are weighted and added to achieve a convincing ranking. We add, somewhat mysteriously, a student's numerical grades before he gets a *cum*, rather than a *summa cum laude*. The listing of pros and cons by Ben Franklin [5], and on Richard Nixon's pad inspected by Joseph Alsop [1], is of the same nature.

This assumed additivity of numerical criteria is often doubtful, a mere tribute to our weakness or laziness. I understand that some supervisors of airplane designs weigh and add the criteria 'speed, in miles per hour' and 'number of passenger seats'. Yet the airline's profit clearly depends not on the sum (weighted or not) of these quantities but on their product, namely on passenger-miles per hour (or year). Anyhow, additivity simplifies, and thus economizes on our thinking. It is simple, in particular, to think of the result of an action as additively separable into (viz., as the difference between) 'benefit' and 'cost': another current habit, giving some precision to the question: "is this worth while"?

III

I have now touched, in fact, on the 'economics of thinking'; yea, on the prudence of thinking lazily. What's the use of carrying many digits, of paying attention to third-order errors, if the added precision is not likely to cause a shift in the ranking of our actions and to call for a different choice of action.

Perhaps, then, the balancing of benefits and costs is applicable, not only to acting but also to thinking, both inductive and deductive? Recently, some logicians moved in this direction; notably those who tried to clarify and use the concept of probability. The logic of induction has received some inspiration from a new approach to probabilities, which relates statistical inference to the choice of action. And some logicians of deduction have applied probability to the domain of propositions, having been inspired by ideas of communication engineers who have related information to the number of symbols needed to store or transmit it, and thus to the probabilities of alternative occurrences.[1]

IV

The new approach to probabilities is perhaps more in the nature of a revival. For, around 1750, the Rev. Thomas Bayes [2] thought of probabilities as being revealed by the ratio of a bettor's possible gain to his possible loss. Around 1950, Rudolf Carnap [3] took essentially the same attitude. But to bet is to act, is it not?

For reasons to be stated later, we prefer a somewhat different – actually, a less restrictive – approach. Choose between betting on tomorrow's being a sunny day in Cambridge, Massachusetts or in Irvine, California. If you prefer the latter bet and are asked why, you will perhaps answer – and this answer will agree with ordinary English usage: "because a sunny day is a more probable event in California than in the Northeast." Note that the consequences of either bet – your possible gain and loss – need not be sums of money but can be any pair of things of which one – e.g., a vacation – is preferable to another – e.g., a prison term.

Further: are you indifferent, or not, between betting on one or any other particular card being drawn from a well-shuffled deck? And, accordingly, will you not say – again in agreement with ordinary English – that these 52 events are all equally probable? Your belief that a deck of cards is 'well shuffled' (or, for that matter, a coin is 'fair', a pair of dice 'unbiased') is, in fact defined by this, your indifference between certain bets. F. Ramsey [9] the logician, B. De Finetti [4] the actuary, L. J. Savage [10] the statistician, took up this line of thought. They extended the traditional logic of rational thought to include some postulates of rational, consistent action. Consistent preference ranking of actions, of which I spoke earlier, is one of these postulates. All of them are in the nature of plausible logical norms rather than psychological descriptions of actual behavior of hurried or tired men. The postulates imply, it turns out, that the 'probabilities' revealed by those consistent bets (on weather or cards, in our examples) – or, generally, by consistent actions under uncertainty – have about all the properties by which the concept of 'probability measure' is defined by mathematicians. Thus, a consistent bettor will not only, by definition, prefer to bet on those events to which he assigns higher probabilities. His bet will also reveal, for example, that (in accord with the 'additivity property' of the mathematical probability measure) he assigns probability $\frac{3}{52}$ to the event of drawing one of three specified cards, – provided he is indifferent between bets on any one card in the deck.

'Personal' probabilities as revealed by your choice of bets can, then, apply to non-repeatable events. For you can choose, for example, between betting on Julius Caesar's having died on a Monday or during the rest of the week. There would seem to be a gap between the Ramseyan probability and the frequency of successful outcomes of a repeated experiment.

Suppose, however, that you are indifferent between bets on the success of any one of a sequence of repeated trials. That is, you think the experiment is 'well-controlled' (similar to our 'well-shuffled' deck of cards). The following can then be proved from those postulates of consistent action: you will be well advised to assign to the success of any future trial a probability equal to the proportion of successes in a *large number* of already observed trials; and to choose your bets in accordance with the probability thus computed (the 'law of large numbers' is a purely mathematical step in the proof of this recommendation). The so-called 'objective' probabilities based on long-run observed frequencies are thus identical with the 'personal' ones; they presuppose, in fact, your personal indifference between bets on the success of any of repeated trials: your belief that the experiment is 'well-controlled'. See also [8] on the 'Economic Man's Logic'.

V

The consistency postulates applied to bets with just a pair of outcomes (success, failure) entail the existence of 'personal probabilities'. These satisfy the mathematical definition of probability measure and are revealed by the bettor's choices. Applied to any actions under uncertainty, with any number of outcomes, those postulates entail, furthermore, the existence of numerical 'utilities' of those outcomes. These numbers are defined by the following property: Suppose the sum of the utilities of the outcomes of one action, each utility being weighted (i.e., multiplied) by the outcome's probability, is smaller than the corresponding weighted sum for another action; then the latter action will be ranked higher on your scale of preferences. The word utility is borrowed from Jeremiah Bentham but its present meaning is much clearer, and is operational. It is also older. When the outcome is a money amount, its utility is the 'moral wealth' – so called by the founding fathers of probability calculus. They pointed out, in effect, that the risk-averting gambler or investor will not play a game with 50:50 chance (though he might accept a 60:40 chance, say) of winning or losing a hundred *louis d'or*. This is why we have, earlier in this essay, dismissed Bayes' concern with odds in terms of the ratio of money gained and lost. So did, in fact, De Finetti and Carnap when they revised their earlier writings.

We have mentioned earlier the simplifying – though not always justifiable – assumption that the preference rank of an action can be derived as a difference between benefit and cost. Correspondingly, the average utility (the weighted sum of utilities) of the outcomes of an action would be the difference between average benefit and average cost. Prudent laziness in induction, in empirical research, would then prescribe: do not increase the number of experiments unless the consequent change in action will result, on the average, in added benefits exceeding added cost.

VI

If, in matters of deductive logic, we follow J. Hintikka [6], it appears that personal probabilities – possibly again derived from choices between bets – can be applied to alternative possible sentences whose truth values are to be established by deduction. (I was often astonished to hear mathematicians say: 'This conjecture is very probable....") The larger the number of competing sentences, and the more equal their probabilities, the larger is the 'information' that the deductive steps will yield. The number of steps needed (the 'depth' of the true sentence, e.g., a theorem) is said to be a matter of logic, not psychology. This means (I presume) that although the most difficult theorem is immediately obvious to God, there is a minimum number of steps that Man (a logical ideal) must make to prove it. In the language of the present essay, this number might correspond to the 'cost', and the information yielded to the 'benefit' of a deductive job.

VII

I mentioned earlier the Economy of Nature. Ralph Gerard and his fellow biologists who, with this writer and others, want to honor Ralph by their contributions to this volume, will have guessed by now what I am driving at. Economics of surviving, placed along with the economics of acting and of thinking, means this to me: an interpretation of the process of selection as a continuing betting on those organic features that have comparatively great probability to survive in a given environment. A tautology seems to have provided guidance to most fruitful descriptive research. "What has a high probability to survive will survive, with high probability," is a tautology. But it has directed creative attention to the question: why – in terms of known physics and chemistry, say – has such-and-such feature of an organism a higher probability to survive in such-and-such environment, than this-and-this other feature?

As I understand, anthropologists, too, have derived useful insights from the question: what is the 'survival function'[2] of this particular social institution or tribal custom? In my own field – as was pointed out by S. Winter [11] – the description of competing sizes and structures of business organizations is well guided by a similar question. Strictly speaking, the question requires statements in probability terms – unless we are all-knowing. And such statements mean, essentially, comparisons between bets.

I hope – and fear – this essay has become sufficiently provocative without my dwelling further on things I know so little about – be it deductive logic or the theory of evolution.

NOTES

* This contribution to a volume in honor of Ralph W. Gerard was completed in 1970 but was still in press at the time of his death, February 1974.

[1] *Added in 1974.* But see now Marschak [8a].

[2] See Marschak [8b].

BIBLIOGRAPHY

[1] Alsop, Joseph, in *Newsweek*, 1 June 1970.

[2] Bayes, Thomas, 'An Essay Towards Solving a Problem in the Doctrine of Chances', 1764; now in *Biometrika* **45**, 296–315.

[3] Carnap, Rudolf, *Logical Foundations of Probability*, University of Chicago Press (first ed. 1950). In the Second Edition, 1962, see in particular p. XV.

[4] De Finetti, Bruno, 'La Prévision: ses Lois Logiques, ses Sources Subjectives', 1937. Now in English, and provided with additional notes by the author, in Kyburg and Smokler (eds.) [7], pp. 95–158.

[5] Franklin, Benjamin, 'How to Make a Decision', (a letter to J. Priestley), 1772; in *A Benjamin Franklin Reader* (ed. by N. G. Goodman), Crowell, New York, 1945, p. 786.

[6] Hintikka, Jaakko, 'Information, Deduction, and the *a priori*', *Nous*, 1970.

[7] Kyburg, Henry, E. and Smokler, Howard E. (eds.), *Essays in Subjective Probability*, Wiley, New York, 1964.
[8] Marschak, Jacob, 'The Economic Man's Logic', *Selected Essays*, 17.
[8a] Marschak, Jacob, 'Information, Decision, and the Scientist', *Pragmatic Aspects of Human Communication* (C. Cherry, ed.), pp. 145–178. D. Reidel, 1974.
[8b] Marschak, Jacob, 'Economics of Language', *Selected Essays*, 27.
[9] Ramsey, Frank P., 'Truth and Probability', 1926. Now in Kyburg and Smokler (ed.) [7], pp. 63–92.
[10] Savage, Leonard J., *The Foundation of Statistics*, Wiley, New York, 1954. Revised, Dover, 1972.
[11] Winter, Sidney, 'Economic 'Natural Selection' and the Theory of the Firm', *Yale Economic Essays* (1964).

INDEX OF NAMES

INDEX OF SUBJECTS

THEORY AND DECISION LIBRARY

An International Series in the Philosophy and Methodology of the Social and Behavioral Sciences

Editors:

GERALD EBERLEIN, *University of Saarland*

WERNER LEINFELLNER, *University of Nebraska*

1. GÜNTER MENGES (ed.), *Information, Inference, and Decision.* 1974, viii + 195 pp.
2. ANATOL RAPOPORT (ed.), *Game Theory as a Theory of Conflict Resolution.* 1974, v + 283 pp.
3. MARIO BUNGE (ed.), *The Methodological Unity of Science.* 1973, viii + 264 pp.
4. COLIN CHERRY (ed.), *Pragmatic Aspects of Human Communication.* 1974, ix + 178 pp.
5. FRIEDRICH RAPP (ed.), *Contributions to a Philosophy of Technology. Studies in the Structure of Thinking in the Technological Sciences.* 1974, xv + 228 pp.
6. WERNER LEINFELLNER and ECKEHART KÖHLER (eds.), *Developments in the Methodology of Social Science.* 1974, x + 430 pp.

ECONOMIC INFORMATION, DECISION, AND PREDICTION

SELECTED ESSAYS: VOLUME II

THEORY AND DECISION LIBRARY

AN INTERNATIONAL SERIES
IN THE PHILOSOPHY AND METHODOLOGY OF THE
SOCIAL AND BEHAVIORAL SCIENCES

VOLUME 7

JACOB MARSCHAK

ECONOMIC INFORMATION, DECISION, AND PREDICTION

Selected Essays: Volume II

PART II

Economics of Information and Organization

D. REIDEL PUBLISHING COMPANY
DORDRECHT : HOLLAND / BOSTON : U.S.A.
LONDON : ENGLAND

Library of Congress Catalog Card Number 74-81940

Volume I: ISBN 90-277-0544-5
ISBN 90-277-1195-X (pbk.)
Volume II: ISBN 90-277-0545-3
ISBN 90-277-1196-8 (pbk.)
Volume III: ISBN 90-277-0546-1
ISBN 90-277-1197-6 (pbk.)

Published by D. Reidel Publishing Company,
P.O. Box 17, 3300 AA Dordrecht, Holland.

Sold and distributed in the U.S.A. and Canada
by Kluwer Boston Inc., Lincoln Building,
160 Old Derby Street, Hingham, MA 02043, U.S.A.

In all other countries, sold and distributed
by Kluwer Academic Publishers Group,
P.O. Box 322, 3300 AH Dordrecht, Holland.

D. Reidel Publishing Company is a member of the Kluwer Group.

0-1195-0580-468
0-1196-0580-468
0-1197-0580-468

Printed in The Netherlands

CONTENTS

CONTENTS

CONTENTS OF VOLUMES I AND III

VOLUME I

VOLUME III

PART III: MONEY AND OTHER ASSETS

PART IV: ECONOMIC MEASUREMENTS

ACKNOWLEDGEMENTS

Essay 19 (co-authors: K. J. Arrow and T. E. Harris) first appeared in *Econometrica*, Vol. 19, No. 3, pp. 250–272 (July 1951) and is reprinted here by permission of Joseph E. Stiglitz, Reprint Editor.

Essay 20 first appeared in *Decision Processes* (ed. by R. M. Thrall,, C. H. Coombs, and R. L. Davis), pp. 187–220, Wiley, New York, 1954, and is reprinted here by permission of John Wiley and Sons, Inc.

Essay 21 first appeared in *Management Science*, Vol. 1, No. 2, pp. 127–137 (January 1955) and is reprinted here by permission of The Institute of Management Sciences.

Essay 22 first appeared in *Modern Organization Theory* (ed. by M. Haire), pp. 137–143, Wiley, New York, 1959, and is reprinted here by permission of John Wiley and Sons, Inc.

Essay 23 first appeared in *Contributions to Scientific Research in Management*, pp. 79–100, being a collection of papers presented at the inauguration of the Data Processing Center, and published by the Division of Research, Graduate School of Business Administration, University of California, Los Angeles, 1959. Reprinted here by permission of George A. Steiner, Director, on behalf of the Study Center for Research, Graduate School of Business Administration, University of California, Los Angeles.

Essay 24 was presented at a meeting of the American Economic Association, and first appeared in *American Economic Review*, Vol. 50, No. 2, pp. 541–548 (May 1960) and is reprinted here by permission of the American Economic Association.

Essay 25 was presented at a Conference on Management Controls at Stanford University and appeared in *Managment Controls: New Directions in Basic Research* (ed. by C. P. Bonini, R. K. Jaedicke, and H. M. Wagner), Chapter 3, pp. 38–90, McGraw-Hill, New York, 1964, and is reprinted here by permission of McGraw-Hill Book Company and the editors concerned.

Essay 26 first appeared in *Behavioral Science*, Vol. 1, No. 1, pp. 69–78

(January 1956) and is reprinted here by permission of James G. Miller, M.D., Ph.D., Editor.

Essay 27 first appeared in *Behavioral Science*, Vol. 10, No. 2, pp. 135–140 (April 1965) and is reprinted here by permission of James G. Miller, M.D., Ph.D., Editor.

Essay 28 first appeared in *Social Research*, Vol. 33, No. 2, pp. 151–159 (1966) and is reprinted here by permission of *Social Research*. The original issue of *Social Research* was dedicated to Adolph Lowe and Hans Neisser.

Essay 29 (Co-author: Koichi Miyasawa) first appeared in *International Economic Reyiew*, Vol. 9, No. 2, pp. 137–174 (June 1968) and is reprinted here by permission of the editor, Phoebus J. Dhrymes.

Essay 30 was the Richard T. Ely Lecture and was first printed in *American Economic Review*, Vol. 58, No. 2, pp. 1–18 (May 1968) and is reprinted here by permission of the American Economic Association.

Essay 31 first appeared in *Journal of the American Statistical Association*, Vol. 66, No. 333, pp. 192–219 (March 1971) and is reprinted here by permission of the American Statistical Association.

Essay 32 was presented at the Fourth Conference on Optimization Techniques sponsored by the International Association for Information Processing and led by A. V. Balakrishnan. It was first printed in *Techniques of Optimization* (ed. by A. V. Balakrishnan), pp. 355-370, Academic Press, New York, 1972, and is reprinted here by permission of the Academic Press.

PART II

ECONOMICS OF INFORMATION AND ORGANIZATION

INTRODUCTORY NOTE

"Shall I refill my oil tank?" This will depend on how much oil is left: a 'decision rule' now known as $S-s$ policy (Essay 19), an early form of what became, in greater depth and for wider fields, 'dynamic programming': Bellman (1957), Arrow *et al.* (1958), followed by many others. The topic is also touched upon in Parts One and Three (e.g., Essays 11, 37), but the emphasis of Part Two is on the problem of an 'organizer', a 'meta-decider': on what kind of information shall he base decisions? In Essays 23, 25, 29–32 (and also in Marschak (1971)) organization is a 'single-person team'. The more general problem of optimally assigning the tasks (inquiring, communicating, deciding) and incentives to a network of persons is treated in Essays 20–22, 24 and in the author's more recent work (1974a, b). In the book by Marschak and Radner (1972), the 'Epilogue' takes up the case of a stable non-team organization: a game-theoretical problem since some tasks and incentives are subject to bargaining; see also Radner (1972).

The 'bounds of rationality' (Simon, 1972) which, in Part One, led to tests of stochastic decision models are stated in Part Two as a 'cost of decision-making', both in economic and in interdisciplinary contexts (Essays 26–28). The relation of communication costs (but not of other costs to the team, nor of its benefit) to the 'entropy' formulas was further developed by the author (1973, 1974e). He also pointed out the possibly non-decreasing nature of 'marginal returns to information', properly defined: his only contribution to the study of the 'information market', a field of important recent studies by economists.

Recently, the 'semantic information' concept of some logicians led the author to apply to their field some results of information economics (1974c, d).

REFERENCES

Arrow, K. J., Karlin, S. and Scarf, H. (1958), *Studies in the Mathematical Theory of Inventory and Production*, Stanford University Press.

Bellman, R. (1957), *Dynamic Programming.*

Marschak, J. (1971), 'Optimal Symbol-Processing: A Problem in Individual and Social Economics', *Behavioral Science*, **16**, 3, 202–17.

Marschak, J. (1973), 'Limited Role of Entropy in Information Economics', in *5th Conference on Optimization Techniques*, Part II (ed. by R. Conti and A. Ruberti), pp. 264–71, Springer.

Marschak, J. (1974a), 'Optimale Organisation', *Zeitschrift fuer Betriebswirtschaftliche Forschung*, **26**, 283–97.

Marschak, J. (1974b), 'Economics of Organizational Forms', *Man and Computer* (ed. by M. Marois), North-Holland.

Marschak, J. (1974c), 'Information, Decision, and the Scientist', in *Pragmatic Aspects of Human Communication* (ed. by C. Cherry), pp. 145–78, D. Reidel, Dordrecht.

Marschak, J. (1974d), 'Prior and Posterior Probabilities and Semantic Information', in *Information, Inference and Decision* (ed. by G. Menges), D. Reidel, Dordrecht.

Marschak, J. (1974e), 'Entropy, Economics, Physics', Working Paper No. 221, Western Management Science Institute (presented at Econometric Society meeting, December).

Marschak, J. and Radner, R. (1972), *Economic Theory of Teams*, Yale University Press.

Radner, R. (1972), 'Normative Theories of Organization: an Introduction', in *Decision and Organization* (ed. by C. B. McGuire and R. Radner), pp. 177–88, North-Holland.

Simon, H. A. (1972), 'Theories of Bounded Rationality', in *Decision and Organization* (ed. by C. B. McGuire and R. Radner), pp. 161–76. North-Holland.

19

OPTIMAL INVENTORY POLICY*

(1951)

Co-authors: K. J. ARROW and T. HARRIS

ABSTRACT. Optimal inventory policy is first derived for a simple model in which the future (and constant) demand flow and other relevant quantities are known in advance. This is followed by the study of uncertainty models – a static and a dynamic one – in which the demand flow is a random variable with a known probability distribution. The best maximum stock and the best reordering point are determined as functions of the demand distribution, the cost of making an order, and the penalty of stock depletion.

I. INTRODUCTION

We propose to outline a method for deriving optimal rules of inventory policy for finished goods. The problem of inventories exists not only for business enterprises but also for nonprofit agencies such as governmental establishments and their various branches. Moreover, the concept of inventories can be generalized so as to include not only goods but also disposable reserves of manpower as well as various stand-by devices. Also, while inventories of finished goods present the simplest problem, the concept can be extended to goods which can be transformed, at a cost, into one or more kinds of finished goods if and when the need for such goods arises. The following notes prepare the way for a more general future analysis of 'flexible planning'.

We shall call 'net utility' the quantity that the policymaker seeks to maximize. In the case of profit-making enterprises this is conveniently approximated by profit: the difference between gross money revenue and money cost. A nonprofit agency such as a hospital may often be able to compute directly its money cost, and has to assign an approximate monetary value to the 'gross utility' of the performance of its tasks; it corresponds to the 'gross revenue' of an enterprise run for profit.[1]

The net utility to any policymaker is, in general, a random variable depending on certain conditions (i.e., on variables or on relations between variables). Some of these conditions he can control, others he cannot. The former are policy means (rules of action, strategies). The noncontrolled conditions are, in general, defined by a joint probability distribution of certain variables. Rational policy consists in fixing the controlled conditions so as to maximize the expected value of net utility, given the probability distribution of noncontrolled conditions. When this probability distribution degenerates into a set of nonrandom variables we have the case of 'certainty'. In this limiting case, net utility itself is a nonrandom variable, to be maximized by the policymaker.

In the present paper, the policymaker is the holder of inventories. At most one of the noncontrolled conditions will be regarded as a random one: the rate of demand for the policymaker's product. Other noncontrolled conditions will be regarded as constants, or as relations with constant parameters: the pipeline time; the cost of making an order; the relation between storage cost and the size of inventory; the price paid or its relation to the size of order (the 'supply function'); the gross revenue (or, more generally, the gross utility) obtained. (Speculative inventories are thus excluded from consideration.)

As to controlled conditions, we shall assume that the policymaker can control only the size of the orders he makes (at discrete points of time). This eliminates, for example, such policy means as the fixing of the selling price, or the use of advertising, to influence demand, and any bargaining with buyer(s) or competitor(s).

We believe our specialized formulation is a workable first approximation. By regarding the order size as the only controlled condition, and the demand as the only random noncontrolled condition, we do take account of most of the major questions that have actually arisen in the practice of business and nonprofit organizations.[2]

II. THE CASE OF CERTAINTY

A. Let x be the known constant rate of demand for the product of the organization, per unit of time. Let the gross utility (i.e., utility before deducting cost) obtained by the organization through satisfying this demand be, per unit of time,

$$ax + a_0 .$$

With a nonprofit organization, a_0 expresses the value of its 'being' (word coined for the British Navy). If the organization is a commercial firm, a is the selling price; otherwise a is the value to the organization of a unit of its operations. In general, a is a function of x. It will be sufficient, for our purposes, to assume a constant, and $a_0=0$. Denote by $b=b(q)$ the purchasing price of one unit when the size of order is q. We shall assume that $q \cdot b(q)$ is an increasing function of q, and that $b'(q) \leqslant 0$ (possible economy of large scale orders). Let K be the cost of handling an order, regardless of its size. Let the cost of carrying a stock z over one unit of time be

$$c_0 + 2cz,$$

where c_0 is the overhead cost of storage. In general, c_0 varies with the maximum amount stocked, and c varies with the current stock z and also (because of spoilage, leakage, and obsolescence) with the prices paid. However, we shall assume c_0 and c constant.

B. With K positive a continuous flow of orders would be infinitely expensive. Hence orders will be given at discrete time intervals. Let the first ordering date be 0. Let the length of the ith time interval be θ_i. Then the delivery during that interval is $x\theta_i$. See Figure 1a, where the common slope of all slanting lines is the demand flow, x.

We shall show that, under certain conditions, optimal policy will be as shown in Figure 1b: the intervals, possibly excepting the first one, will have the same optimal length and the same optimal highest and lowest stock levels.

We shall first assume that orders are fulfilled immediately. Then the

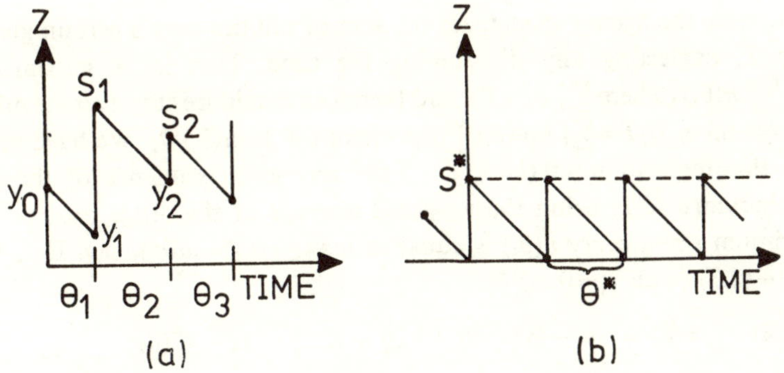

Fig. 1.

amount ordered at the beginning of the ith interval,

$$q_i = S_{i-1} - y_{i-1} \geqslant 0,$$

where S_{i-1} and y_{i-1} denote, respectively, the stocks available at the beginning of the ith interval after and before the replenishment. Since the delivery during that interval is

$$x\theta_i = S_{i-1} - y_i,$$

therefore

$$(2.1) \qquad q_i = x\theta_i + y_i - y_{i-1} \quad (i = 1, 2, \ldots),$$

while the average stock during the ith interval is

$$(2.2) \qquad \bar{z}_i = (S_{i-1} + y_i)/2 = (x\theta_i + 2y_i)/2 \quad (i = 1, 2, \ldots).$$

The net utility achieved during the ith interval (not allowing for a time discount) is

$$(2.3) \qquad u(\theta_i) = ax\theta_i - q_i \cdot b(q_i) - 2c\bar{z}_i\theta_i - K.$$

By (2.1), (2.2), this is a decreasing function of $y_i \geqslant 0$. Hence, for given θ_i and y_{i-1}, $u(\theta_i)$ has its maximum when $y_i = 0$. Further, we can put $y_0 = 0$: if the agency begins its operations with a stock $y' > 0$, its best policy is not to place orders till the stock runs down to zero, y'/x time units later; and this time point can be regarded as the origin. Then, by (2.3), $u(\theta_1)$ is largest, for a given θ_1, when $y_1 = 0$; and for any given sequence of interval lengths $\theta_1, \ldots, \theta_n$, the sum $U = \sum_1^n u(\theta_i)$ will have its maximum at $y_1 = \cdots = y_n = 0$.

Suppose the agency maximizes the sum of utilities over a certain given time T, neglecting any discounting for time. That is, it maximizes $U = \sum_1^n u(\theta_i)$ (where $\sum_1^n \theta_i = T$), and therefore maximizes the average utility over time, $U/T = \sum_1^n \theta_i v(\theta_i)/\sum \theta_i$, where $v(\theta_i) = u(\theta_i)/\theta_i$. We have seen that this requires $y_i = 0$ $(i = 1, 2, \ldots)$ for any given sequence of the θ_i. Furthermore U/T, being the weighted average of the $v(\theta_i)$, reaches its maximum when every $v(\theta_i)$ is equal to $\max_{\theta_i} v(\theta_i) = v(\theta^*)$, say. But, by (2.1)–(2.3) (with $y_i = 0$, $i \geqslant 0$),

$$(2.4) \qquad v(\theta) = ax - [xb(x\theta) + cx\theta + K/\theta] = ax - C(\theta),$$

The expression in square brackets being the total cost per time unit,

$C(\theta)$. If $v(\theta)$ has a maximum and $C(\theta)$ has a minimum at $\theta=\theta^*$, then

$$C'(\theta^*) = 0 = x^2 b'(x\theta^*) + cx - K/(\theta^*)^2 . \tag{2.5}$$

The optimal interval θ^* between orders can thus be computed as depending on the cost parameters, c and K, and the purchasing price function, $b(q)$ – provided the policymaker maximizes the sum of utilities over time, U, without any discounting for futurity during which the initial stock will last.

We obtain thus (as in Figure 1b), for the case in which orders are fulfilled immediately (pipeline time $=0$), a periodically repeated change from maximum stocks

$$S^* = x\theta^* \tag{2.6}$$

to minimum stocks

$$y = 0,$$

where the period, θ^*, satisfies (2.5).

C. We shall assume the purchase price function linear, so that $b''(q)=0$ identically and

$$b(q) = b_0 - b_1 q,$$

say, with $b_1 \geqslant 0$. Then, by (2.5),

$$\theta^* = \sqrt{K/x(c - b_1 x)}. \tag{2.7}$$

It is seen from the second-order conditions for maximum $v(\theta)$ in (2.4) that the expression under the root sign is always positive (i.e., there would be no positive and finite storage period if the ordering of one more unit decreased the price of the commodity by more than it increased the cost of storing one unit). Using (2.6), the optimal maximum stock is

$$S^* = \sqrt{Kx/(c - b_1 x)}. \tag{2.8}$$

Hence, as should be expected, the optimal order size, and therefore the optimal ordering interval, is larger, the larger the cost K of handling an order, the smaller the unit (marginal) storage cost c, and the larger the effect b_1 of the size of order upon the unit price.

We believe this is, in essence, the solution advanced by R. H. Wilson [1–4], formerly of the Bell Telephone Company, and also by other writers; see Alford and Banks [1]. We have proved the validity of Figure 1b (usually accepted intuitively) and have shown how to evaluate the optimal storage period.

D. If we now introduce a constant pipeline time, $\tau > 0$, elapsing between order and delivery, this will not affect S^* or θ^*, but the time of issuing the order will be shifted τ time units ahead. The order will be issued when the stock is reduced, not to zero, but to $x\tau$ units.

E. The policymaker may not have full control of the length of the time interval between any two successive orders. Transportion schedules or considerations of administrative convenience may be such as to make ordering impossible at intervals of length other than, say, $\theta^0 \neq \theta^*$. For example, θ^0 may be one business day or week, or it may be the period between two visits of a mail boat to an island depot. θ^0 is thus the 'scheduled' or 'smallest feasible' period between two non-zero orders. Denote the 'best feasible period' by θ', an unknown multiple integer of θ^0. As before, θ^* is the best (but possibly a non-feasible) period. By considering the expression $C(\theta)$ defined in (2.4) as total cost, one finds easily that: (1) if $\theta^0 > \theta^*$, then $\theta' = \theta^0$; (2) if $\theta^* > \theta^0$, then $\theta' = \theta^*$, provided θ^* is an integer multiple of θ^0; (3) if θ^* is larger than θ^0 but is not an integer multiple of θ^0, then define the integer $\bar{n} < \theta^*/\theta^0 < \bar{n}+1$; the best feasible period θ' is, in this case, either $\bar{n}\theta^0$ or $(\bar{n}+1)\,\theta^0$, whichever of the two results in a smaller cost when θ' is substituted in (2.4). In our hectographed paper, Arrow, Harris, and Marschak [1, Section IIE–F], this was treated in more detail, and an extension was made to the case in which ordering at nonscheduled times is not impossible but merely costly than ordering at scheduled times.

For reasons of space we omit here the problem of aggregation, also treated in that paper [1, Section II G–I] and, from a more general viewpoint, in Marschak [2]. We assume that there is only one commodity, or that the characteristic parameters for all commodities are such as to yield the same optimal period θ^* for all. We also assume that there is only one giver of orders (depot) and one receiver of orders (manufacturer); on this, see Tompkins [1].

III. A STATIC MODEL WITH UNCERTAINTY

A. Suppose an organization wants to choose the level $S \geqslant 0$ that the stock of a certain commodity should have at the beginning of a given period, in order to provide for the demand (requirements) that will occur during that period. We shall choose the time unit to be equal to the length of this period and shall use the notations of Section II. Thus $x \geqslant 0$ will denote the demand during the period. However, x will now be regarded as a random variable. We shall suppose that the organization knows the cumulative distribution of demand, $F(x)$. The gross utility, to the organization, of delivering ξ units of its product will be

$$a\xi + a_0 \quad (a, a_0 \text{ constant}). \tag{3.1}$$

The delivery during the period is a random variable: ξ equals x or S, whichever is smaller. Hence the expected gross utility is

$$aS[1 - F(S)] + a \int_0^S x \, dF(x) + a_0 \,. \tag{3.2}$$

We shall assume that the amount to be spent in purchasing S units is

$$S(b_0 - b_1 S) + K; \quad b_0 > 0, \quad b_1 \geqslant 0, \tag{3.3}$$

so that, as in Section IIC, the purchase price is either constant or linearly decreasing with the amount purchased. As before, the cost of handling and order is denoted by K but this term will not play any further role in the static model. We assume here that the whole stock S is to be purchased and that no utility is derived from satisfying demand after the period's end. Finally, the cost of carrying over our period the stock which has level S at the beginning of the period will be assumed to be

$$\text{const.} + cS \,. \tag{3.4}$$

Then, apart from a 'depletion penalty', which we shall introduce in Section IIIB, the net expected loss (the negative of net expected utility) is

$$\text{const.} + S(c + b_0 - b_1 S) - aS[1 - F(S)] - a \int_0^S x \, dF(x) \,. \tag{3.5}$$

B. We now define π, the depletion penalty, as follows: If $x \leqslant S$, there is no unsatisfied demand, and $\pi = 0$; but if $x > S$, the organization would be willing to pay an amount $\pi > 0$ to satisfy the excess, $x - S$, of demand over available stock.

We assume the penalty function as given. The organization – whether commercial or noncommercial – has a general idea of the value it would attach to the damage that would be caused by the nonavailability of an item. It knowns the cost and the poorer performance of emergency substitutes. The penalty for depleted stocks may be very high: "A horse, a horse, my kingdom for a horse," cried defeated Richard III.

C. Note that, in the case of a commercial enterprise, an independent penalty function, $\pi = \pi(x - S)$, need not be introduced. It can be replaced by considerations of 'losing custom', as in the following model. Let F_t be a Poisson distribution of demand for the period $(t, t+1)$, with the following interpretation. Its mean, μ_t, is proportional (a) to the probability that a member of a large but finite reservoir of customers will want to buy during that period, and (b) to the number of customers. μ_t equals μ_{t-1} if the demand during $(t-1, t)$ was satisfied. But, if that demand was in excess of the then available stock, μ_t is smaller than μ_{t-1} by an amount proportional to the unsatisfied demand, as some of the disappointed customers will drop out of the market. The problem is to maximize total expected utility over a sequence of periods (0, 1), (1, 2),..., if the initial distribution F_0 is given. (Such a dynamic model would be different from the one we are going to treat in Sections IV–VII.)

D. We shall assume

$$\pi = A + B(x - S) \quad \text{if} \quad x > S,$$
$$\pi = 0 \quad \text{otherwise},$$

where A, B are nonnegative constants, not both zero. Then π is a random variable, with expectation

$$(3.6) \qquad (A - BS)\,[1 - F(S)] + B \int_S^\infty x\, dF(x).$$

Accordingly, the expected net loss, taking account of the expected penalty, is the sum of expressions (3.5) and (3.6) and equals, apart from a constant,

$$(3.7) \qquad S(c + b_0 - b_1 S) + A\,[1 - F(S)] - (B + a)\, S\,[1 - F(S)] + \\ - (B + a) \int_0^S x\, dF(x) = L(S),$$

say. The stock level $S=S^*$ is optimal if $L(S^*)\leqslant L(S)$ for every S. Suppose the distribution function $F(x)$ possesses a differentiable density function, $f(x)\equiv dF(x)/dx$. If the absolute minimum of L is not at $S=0$, it will be at some point satisfying the relations

$$dL(S^*)/dS = 0, \qquad d^2L(S^*)/dS^2 > 0,$$

which imply that

$$\text{(3.8)} \qquad [c + b_0 - 2b_1 S^*] - Af(S^*) - (B + a)\,[1 - F(S^*)] = 0,$$

$$\text{(3.9)} \qquad -2b_1 - Af'(S^*) + (B + a) f(S^*) > 0.$$

E. In the economist's language, the first bracketed term in (3.8) is the 'marginal cost' (of buying and carrying an additional unit in stock); the remaining two terms yield the 'marginal expected utility.'

It is seen from (3.8) that the optimal stock S^* is determined by the following 'noncontrolled' parameters: (1) the demand distribution function, $F(x)$; (2) certain utility and cost parameters, $(c+b_0)$, b_1, A, and $(B+a)$. If, in particular, $b_1=0$ (i.e., the economy of big-lot purchases is negligible), these parameters reduce to two: $A/(c+b_0)$ and $(B+a)/(c+b_0)$. To simplify further, for the sake of illustration, suppose also that $B=a=0$, (that is, the penalty is either zero or A, independent of the size of the unsatisfied demand) and that utility derived from the functioning of the organization does not depend on the amounts delivered. Then (3.8), (3.9) become

$$\text{(3.10)} \qquad f(S^*) = (c + b_0)/A, \quad f'(S^*) < 0.$$

A graphical solution for this case is shown in Figure 2. (Note that $f'(S^*)<0$ but $f'(S')>0$; S^* is the best stock level, but S' is not.)

F. In some previous literature (Fry [1], Eisenhart [1]) the decision on inventories was related, not to utility and cost considerations, but to a preassigned probability $[1-F(S)]$ that demand will not exceed stock. The choice of the probability level $1-F(S)$ depends, of course, on some implicit evaluations of the damage that would be incurred if one were unable to satisfy demand. In the present paper, these evaluations are made explicit. On the other hand, since parameters such as A, B, a can be estimated only in a broad way (at least outside of a purely commercial

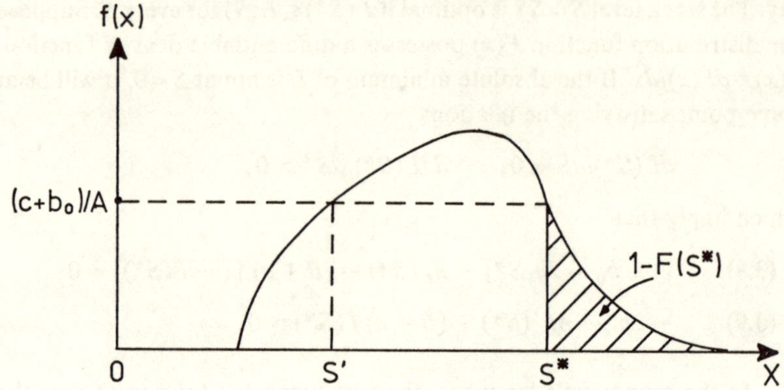

Fig. 2.

organization, where utility equals dollar profit and where models such as that of Section IIIC can be developed), it is a welcome support of one's judgment to check these estimates by referring to the corresponding level of probability for stock depletion. For example, if the distribution in Figure 2 were approximately normal, then to assume that penalty A is 100 times the marginal cost $c+b_0$ would be approximately equivalent to prescribing that the shaded area measuring the depletion probability should be 0.3%; to assume that $A=10(c+b_0)$ would be approximately equivalent to making depletion probability equal to 5%, etc.

G. In the more general case, when $B+a>0$ (but still $b_1=0$), a given optimal stock level S^*, and consequently a given probability of depletion $1-F(S^*)$, is consistent with a continuous set of values of the pair of parameters, $A/(c+b_0)=A'$, $(B+a)/(c+b_0)=B'$, such as would satisfy the linear equation (3.8). For example, if $F(x)$ is approximately normal, then an optimal stock exceeding the average demand by two standard deviations of demand (and, consequently, a depletion probability of approximately 2.3%) will be required by any pair of values of A', B' lying on the straight line intersecting the A'-axis at 13 and intersecting the B'-axis at 44; while an optimal stock exceeding the average demand by three standard deviations (and, consequently, a depletion probability of 0.1%) will correspond to a straight line intersecting those axes at 228 and 740, respectively. Thus a set of contour lines helps to choose an interval of optimal stock values consistent with a given region of plausible values of parameters describing penalty and gross utility.

IV. A DYNAMIC MODEL WITH UNCERTAINTY: PROBLEM

A. The model described in Section III may be called a static one. We shall now present a dynamic model. In this model the commodity can be reordered at discrete instants $0, \theta_0, \ldots, t\theta_0, \ldots$, where θ_0 is a fixed constant. We can therefore use θ_0 as a time unit. Let x_t (t integer) be the demand over the interval $(t, t+1)$. Assume the probability distribution of demand $F(x)$ to be independent of t. Denote by y_t the stock available at instant t, not including any replenishment that may arrive at this instant. Denote by z_t the stock at t including the replenishment. Denote by q_t the amount ordered at time t. Let the time between the ordering and the receiving of goods (pipeline time) be τ, an integer. Then

$$y_t = \max(z_{t-1} - x_{t-1}, 0) \quad (t = 1, 2, \ldots), \tag{4.1}$$

$$z_{t+\tau} = y_{t+\tau} + q_t \quad (t = 0, 1, \ldots). \tag{4.2}$$

In general, τ is a nonnegative random variable. We shall, however, assume $\tau=0$ to simplify the analysis at this stage. Then (4.2) becomes

$$z_t = y_t + q_t. \tag{4.3}$$

Choose two numbers S and s, $S>s>0$, and let them define the following rule of action:

$$\begin{aligned} &\text{If } y_t > s,\ q_t = 0 \quad (\text{and hence } z_t = y_t);\\ &\text{if } y_t \leqslant s,\ q_t = S - y_t \quad (\text{and hence } z_t = S). \end{aligned} \tag{4.4}$$

S and s are often called, respectively, the maximum stock and the reordering point (provided $\tau=0$).

Figure 3 shows the sort of curve that might be obtained for stock level as a function of time if such a rule is adopted. Figure 4 shows z_t as a function of y_t.

B. We shall assume (as we have done in Sections II and III) that the cost of handling an order does not depend on the amount ordered. Let this cost be K, a constant. Let the depletion penalty be A, a constant [compare Section IIID, with $B=0$]. Let the marginal cost of carrying

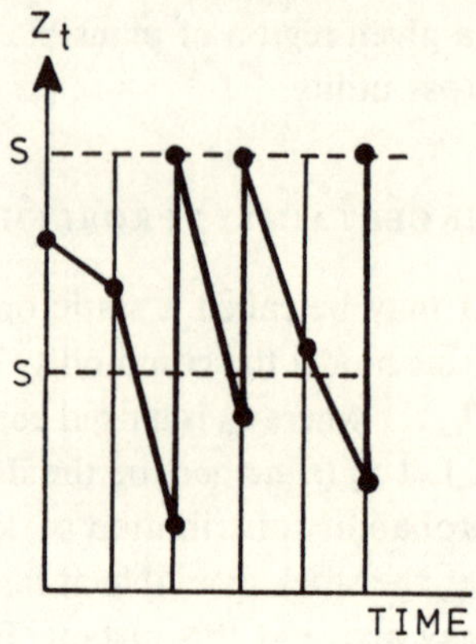

Fig. 3.

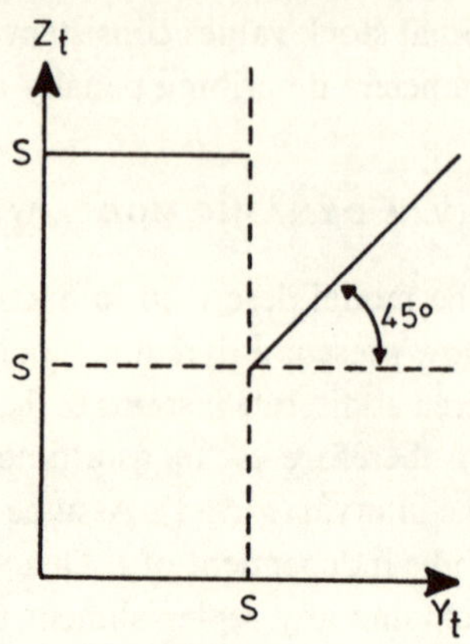

Fig. 4.

stock during a unit of time be c, as in (3.4). Assume the purchasing price per unit of commodity to be independent of the amount bought and equal to the marginal utility of one unit (i.e., in the notation of Section IIIA, $b_1=0$, $b_0=a$). That is, the utility of operations of the agency, in excess of the expenses paid for these operations, is assumed constant, apart from the cost of storage and of handling orders. In the notation of Section IIIA, this constant is a_0, while K and c denote, respectively, the cost of handling an order (of any size) and the marginal cost of storage. Our assumption is an admissible approximation in the case of some nonprofit agencies. It would certainly be both more general and more realistic to make the marginal utility of an operation differ from its purchasing price, as was the case in our static model. But this will require further mathematical work (see Section VIIA).

C. If y_0 is given and values S and s are chosen, the subsequent values y_t form a random process which is 'Markovian'; see Feller [2, Chapter XV]. That is, the probability distribution of y_{t+1}, given the value of y_t, is independent of $y_{t-1}, \ldots, y_0$. During the period $(t, t+1)$ a certain loss will be incurred whose conditional expectation, *for a fixed value of* y_t, we denote by $l(y_t)$. Under the simplifying assumptions of Section IVB,

$$l(y_t) = \begin{cases} cy_t + A[1 - F(y_t)] & \text{for } y_t > s, \\ cS + A[1 - F(S)] + K & \text{for } y_t \leqslant s. \end{cases} \tag{4.5}$$

Thus the function $l(y_t)$ involves S and s as parameters and is constant for $y_t \leqslant s$. Note that

$$(4.6) \qquad l(0) = l(S) + K.$$

The unconditional expectation of the loss during $(t, t+1)$, that is, the expectation of $l(y_t)$, with y_t as a random variable, will be denoted by

$$(4.7) \qquad l_t = l_t(y_0).$$

We shall write $l_t(y_0)$ rather than l_t only when we need to emphasize the dependence of l_t on the initial stock level. Clearly $l_0(y) = l(y)$ for every value y of y_0.

Figure 5 shows a *possible* type of graph for $l(y_t)$.

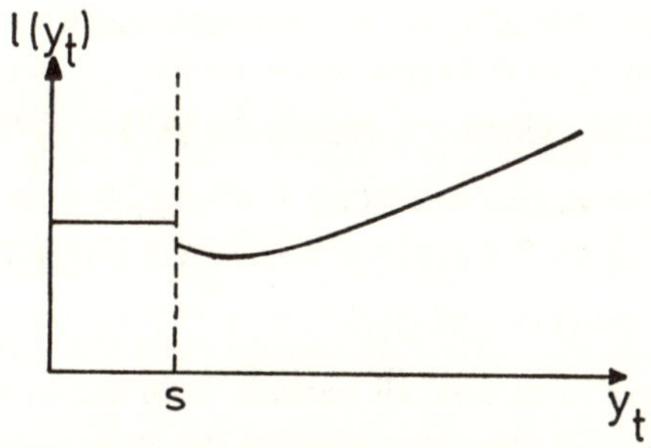

Fig. 5.

D. We now introduce the concepts of a discount factor, α, and of the 'present value' of a loss. If the value of y_{t_0} is given, the present value at time t_0 of the expected loss incurred in the interval (t_0+t, t_0+t+1) is $\alpha^t \mathscr{E}\,[l(y_{t_0+t})] = \alpha^t l_t(y_{t_0})$. When maximizing expected utility, the policymaker takes into account the present values of losses, not their values at the time when they are incurred. In commercial practice, α is equal to $1/(1+\rho)$, where ρ is an appropriate market rate of interest. In nonprofit practice, α would have to be evaluated separately (see also note 1). Later, however, it will be shown (see Section VB) that, under certain conditions, the optimal values of the parameters S, s can be found for α essentially equal to 1.

If we now define the function

$$L(y) = l_0(y) + \alpha l_1(y) + a^2 l_2(y) + \cdots,$$

we see from definition (4.7) that $L(y_t)$ is the present value at time t of the total expected loss incurred during the period $(t, t+1)$ and all subsequent periods when y_t is given. By definition, $L(y)$ involves the parameters S and s; and the policymaker fixes these parameters so as to minimize $L(y_0)$.

E.[3] Now suppose y_0 is given. For a fixed value of y_1, the present value of the total expected loss over all periods is

$$l(y_0) + \alpha l(y_1) + \alpha^2 \mathscr{E}_{y_1}[l(y_2)] + \alpha^3 \mathscr{E}_{y_1}[l(y_3)] + \cdots, \tag{4.8}$$

where we have used $\mathscr{E}_{y_1}[l(y_r)]$ to denote the conditional expectation of $l(y_r)$, given the fixed value y_1. Now

$$\mathscr{E}_{y_1}[l(y_r)] = l_{r-1}(y_1) \quad (r = 1, 2, \ldots)$$

because of the fact that, if y_1 is fixed, the subsequent value y_r $(r=1, 2, \ldots)$ is connected with y_1 in the same manner that y_{r-1} is connected with y_0 if y_1 is not specified. Therefore, expression (4.8) is equal to

$$\begin{aligned} l(y_0) + \alpha l_0(y_1) + \alpha^2 l_1(y_1) + \alpha^3 l_2(y_1) + \cdots &= \\ = l(y_0) + \alpha [l_0(y_1) + \alpha l_1(y_1) + \alpha^2 l_2(y_1) + \cdots] &= \\ = l(y_0) + \alpha L(y_1). & \end{aligned} \tag{4.9}$$

The total expected loss over all periods from the beginning, which by definition is $L(y_0)$, is the expectation of the expression in (4.9), with y_1 regarded as a random variable. Hence

$$L(y_0) = l(y_0) + \alpha \mathscr{E}[L(y_1)]. \tag{4.10}$$

To express the expected value of $L(y_1)$ as a function of y_0 we note that, if $y_0 \leqslant s$, then $z_0 = S$ and $y_1 = \max(S - x_0, 0)$; while, if $y_0 > s$, then $z_0 = y_0$ and $y_1 = \max(y_0 - x_0, 0)$. Thus

$$\begin{aligned} \mathscr{E}[L(y_1)] &= \int_{0-}^{S} L(S-x)\, dF(x) + L(0)[1 - F(S)] \text{ for } y_0 \leqslant s, \\ \mathscr{E}[L(y_1)] &= \int_{0-}^{y_0} L(y_0 - x)\, dF(x) + L(0)[1 - F(y_0)] \text{ for } y_0 > s. \end{aligned} \tag{4.10$'$}$$

[Notice that from the way we have defined the rule of action, $L(y)$ is constant for $0 \leqslant y \leqslant s$ so that $L(0)$ is unambiguously defined.] Putting

$y_0 = y$ we obtain from (4.10) and (4.10′) the equations

$$(4.11)\qquad L(y) = l(y) + \alpha \int_{0-}^{S} L(S) - x)\, dF(x) + \alpha L(0)\,[1 - F(S)] \qquad \text{if} \quad y \leqslant s,$$

$$(4.12)\qquad L(y) = l(y) + \alpha \int_{0-}^{y} L(y-x)\, dF(x) + \alpha L(0)\,[1 - F(y)] \qquad \text{if} \quad y > s.$$

Our problem is to find the function $L(y)$ that satisfies (4.11), (4.12) and to minimize $L(y_0)$ with respect to S, s.

V. A DYNAMIC MODEL: METHOD OF SOLUTION

A. In treating Equations (4.11) and (4.12) we drop for the time being the assumption that $F(x)$ has a density function and assume only that the random variable x cannot take negative values. In order to take care of the possibility that $F(x)$ has discontinuity at $x=0$ (i.e., a positive probability that $x=0$), we adopt the convention that Stieltjes integrals of the form $\int_0^{(\,)} (\,)\, dF(x)$ will be understood to have 0^- as the lower limit. We continue to assume that $l(y)$ is given by (4.5), but it is clear that a similar treatment would hold for any nonnegative function $l(y)$ that is constant for $0 \leqslant y \leqslant s$ and satisfies certain obvious regularity conditions.

Since $l(y)$, and therefore also $L(y)$, is independent of y for $0 \leqslant y \leqslant s$, equation (4.11) tells us simply that

$$(5.1)\qquad L(0) = l(0) + \alpha \int_0^S L(S-x)\, dF(x) + \alpha L(0)\,[1 - F(S)],$$

while putting $y = S$ in (4.12) gives

$$(5.2)\qquad L(S) = l(S) + \alpha \int_0^S L(S-x)\, dF(x) + \alpha L(0)\,[1 - F(S)].$$

Substracting (5.2) from (5.1) we obtain, using (4.6),

$$(5.3)\qquad L(0) - L(S) = K,$$

an expression which is in fact obvious since if the initial stock is 0 we immediately order an amount S at a cost K for ordering. We shall solve Equation (4.12) for the function $L(y)$ considering $L(0)$ as an unknown parameter, and then use (5.3) to determine $L(0)$.

On the right side of (4.12) we make the substitution

$$(5.4)\qquad \int_0^y L(y-x)\, dF(x) = \int_0^{y-s} L(y-x)\, dF(x) + L(0) \int_{y-s}^{y} dF(x);$$

the last term follows from the fact that $L(y-x) = L(0)$ when $0 \leqslant y - x \leqslant s$. Now make the change of variables,

$$(5.5)\qquad \begin{aligned} y - s &= \eta, \\ L(y) &= L(\eta + s) = \lambda(\eta). \end{aligned}$$

Putting (5.4) and (5.5) in (4.12) gives

$$(5.6)\qquad \lambda(\eta) = l(\eta + s) + \alpha L(0)\,[1 - F(\eta)] + \alpha \int_0^\eta \lambda(\eta - x)\, dF(x), \quad \eta > 0.$$

Equation (5.6) is in the standard form of the integral equation of renewal theory; see, for example, Feller's paper [1]. The solution of (5.6) can be expressed as follows. Define distribution functions $F_n(x)$ $(n = 1, 2, \ldots)$ [the convolutions of $F(x)$] by

$$(5.7)\qquad \begin{aligned} F_1(x) &= F(x), \\ F_{n+1}(x) &= \int_0^x F_n(x - u)\, dF(u). \end{aligned}$$

Define the function $H_\alpha(x)$:

$$(5.8)\qquad H_\alpha(x) = \sum_{n=1}^{\infty} \alpha^n F_n(x), \quad 0 \leqslant \alpha \leqslant 1.$$

It is obvious that the series converges if $0 \leqslant \alpha < 1$, and in fact it can be seen from Feller's article [1] that it converges if $\alpha = 1$, a fact we shall need in the sequel. Putting

$$(5.9)\qquad R(\eta) = l(\eta + s) + \alpha L(0)\,[1 - F(\eta)],$$

we can write the solution of (5.6) as

$$(5.10)\qquad \begin{aligned} \lambda(\eta) &= R(\eta) + \int_0^\eta R(\eta - x)\, dH_\alpha(x) \\ &= R(\eta) + \sum_{n=1}^{\infty} \alpha^n \int_0^\eta R(\eta - x)\, dF_n(x). \end{aligned}$$

This is the only solution which is bounded on every finite interval. In terms of L and l, (5.10) gives

$$(5.11)\qquad \begin{aligned} L(y) &= l(y) + \alpha L(0)\,[1 - F(y - s)] \\ &\quad + \int_0^{y-s} \{l(y - x) + \alpha L(0)\,[1 - F(y - x - s)]\}\, dH_\alpha(x), \quad y > s. \end{aligned}$$

From (5.3) and (5.11) we have

$$(5.12)\qquad \begin{aligned} L(0) - K &= l(S) + \int_0^{S-s} l(S - x)\, dH_\alpha(x) \\ &\quad + \alpha L(0) \left\{ 1 - F(S - s) + \int_0^{S-s} [1 - F(S - s - x)]\, dH_\alpha(x) \right\} \end{aligned}$$

In (5.12) we have a linear equation which we can solve for the unknown quantity $L(0)$ which has, as we shall show, a nonvanishing coefficient in (5.12) as long as $\alpha < 1$. This gives us the value of $L(y)$ for $y \leqslant s$, and we can obtain $L(y)$ for $y > s$ from (5.11) since every term on the right side of that equation is now known.

The coefficient of $L(0)$ in (5.12) is

$$(5.13) \qquad 1 - \alpha \left\{ 1 - F(S-s) + \int_0^{S-s} [1 - F(S-s-x)]\, dH_\alpha(x) \right\}$$

$$= 1 - \alpha \left\{ 1 - F(S-s) + H_\alpha(S-s) - \int_0^{S-s} F(S-s-x)\, dH_\alpha(x) \right\}$$

$$= 1 - \alpha \left\{ 1 - F(S-s) + \sum_{n=1}^{\infty} \alpha^n F_n(S-s) - \sum_{n=1}^{\infty} \alpha^n F_{n+1}(S-s) \right\}$$

$$= (1-\alpha)\,[1 + H_\alpha(S-s)].$$

Using (5.13) we obtain

$$(5.14) \qquad L(0) = \frac{K + l(S) + \int_0^{S-s} l(S-x)\, dH_\alpha(x)}{(1-\alpha)\,[1 + H_\alpha(S-s)]}.$$

Knowing $L(y)$ from (5.11) and (5.14), the next step is to find, for a given initial stock y_0, the values of s and S which minimize $L(y_0)$. We shall consider only the minimization of $L(0)$, although the procedure could be worked out to minimize $L(y_0)$ for any initial stock y_0. The procedure of minimizing $L(0)$ is not quite so special as it may appear. Suppose that for a given y_0 the values of s and S which minimize $L(y_0)$ are denoted by $s^*(y_0)$ and $S^*(y_0)$. If $s^*(0) > 0$ and if $s^*(y_0)$ and $S^*(y_0)$ are uniquely determined continuous functions of y_0 (a point which we have not investigated mathematically), then $s^*(y_0) = s^*(0)$, $S^*(y_0) = S^*(0)$ for sufficiently small y_0. To see this we write

$$L(y) = L(y; s, S)$$

to indicate the dependence of L on s and S. Let a be a number such that $0 < a < s^*(0)$. Suppose y_0, $0 < y_0 < a$, is sufficiently small so that $s^*(y_0) > a$. Then

$$L(y_0; s^*(y_0), S^*(y_0)) = \min_{s > a,\, S \geq s} L(y_0; s, S) =$$

$$= K + \min_{s > a,\, S \geq s} L(S; s, S),$$

which is minimized independently of y_0; Q.E.D.

In Section V B an optimization criterion will be given which is independent of the initial level y_0.

We now reintroduce the assumption that $F(x)$ has a probability density which is continuously differentiable,

$$F(x) = \int_0^x f(t)\, dt.$$

We recall from (4.5) that $l(y)$, for $y > s$, is given by

$$l(y) = A[1 - F(y)] + cy.$$

Consider the minimization of (5.14) with respect to s and S. First we consider the case where $S-s$ is fixed. The denominator of (5.14) involves S and s only as a function of $S-s$. We therefore have to minimize the numerator of (5.14) with respect to S, subject to the constraint that S is at least as great as the fixed value of $S-s$. If the minimum value does not occur for $S=S-s$ (i.e., $s=0$), it occurs at a value of S for which the conditions

$$c - Af(S) + \int_0^{S-s} [c - Af(S-x)]\, dH_\alpha(x) = 0, \tag{5.15}$$

$$-Af'(S) - \int_0^{S-s} Af'(S-x)\, dH_\alpha(x) > 0, \tag{5.16}$$

hold. It should be noted that K does not enter into (5.15) and (5.16).

If we drop the requirement that $S-s$ be fixed, then s^* and S^*, provided they satisfy the condition $0<s^*<S^*$, occur at a point where equation (5.15) holds, together with the equation obtained by setting the derivative of (5.14) with respect to $S-s$ equal to 0 and taking the appropriate second-order conditions into account. We also need here the assumption that $H_\alpha(x)$ is the integral of a function $h_\alpha(x)$,

$$H_\alpha(x) = \int_0^x h_\alpha(t)\, dt.$$

Then differentiation of (5.14) with respect to $S-s$ gives, setting the derivative equal to 0 and integrating by parts,

$$A[F(S) - F(s)] = c(S-s) + K + \int_0^{S-s} [c - Af(S-x)]\, H_\alpha(x)\, dx. \tag{5.17}$$

Presumably the minimization of (5.14) would be accomplished in practice by numerical methods.

B. So far we have considered α as an arbitrary parameter. It is clear that if we let $\alpha \to 1$, keeping s and S fixed, the quantity $L(0)$ becomes infinite. However, as we shall see, the quantity $(1-\alpha)\, L(0)$ approaches a finite limiting value whose significance can be explained as follows. Suppose that levels s and S have been fixed and that y_0 is given. We have mentioned that the quantities y_t then form a Markovian random process. Moreover, under assumptions on $F(x)$ [which are not of practical importance] the probability distribution of y_t, as $t \to \infty$, approaches a fixed limiting distribution which is independent of y_0. When $F(x)$ is a step function,[4] we are dealing with a Markov chain with a denumerable number of states. If $F(x)$ is not a step function this theory can still be applied indirectly. The 'age' of the stock at any given time (i.e., the length of time since the last order was placed) has a distribution of the discrete type which approaches a limit, and from this it follows that y_t has a limiting distribution. This implies that l_t, the expected loss in the interval $(t, t+1)$ approaches a limiting value l_∞ which is independent of y_0. (The losses during successive time intervals form a sequence of bounded random variables.) As we shall see, we can find the value of l_∞. Then if we do not want to use a discount factor α, one way to proceed is to pick s and S so as to minimize l_∞. This is almost equivalent to minimizing the total expected loss over a long finite time interval.

Another way to look at the situation is as follows. The limiting distribution of y_t for large t is a 'stationary distribution'; i.e., if y_0 has this distribution, instead of being fixed, then y_t has the same distribution for every t. The expected loss during $(t, t+1)$, if y_t has this distribution, is just l_∞.[5]

Since

$$L(0) = l_0(0) + \alpha l_1(0) + \alpha^2 l_2(0) + \cdots$$

and $l_t(0) \to l_\infty$ as $t \to \infty$, we have

$$L(0)(1-\alpha) = l_0(0) + \alpha[l_1(0) - l_0(0)] + \alpha^2[l_2(0) - l_1(0)] + \cdots. \tag{5.18}$$

The series

$$l_0(0) + [l_1(0) - l_0(0)] + [l_2(0) - l_1(0)] + \cdots$$

converges to the value l_∞ and therefore, by a standard result of analysis, we have, from (5.18),

$$\lim_{\alpha\to 1} L(0)(1-\alpha) = l_\infty.$$

In order to determine l_∞, we can then multiply the right side of (5.14) by $(1-\alpha)$ and let $\alpha \to 1$, obtaining

$$l_\infty = \frac{K + l(S) + \int_0^{S-s} l(S-x)\, dH(x)}{1 + H(S-s)}, \tag{5.19}$$

where $H(x)$ is defined by

$$H(x) = \lim_{\alpha\to 1} H_\alpha(x) = \sum_{n=1}^{\infty} F_n(x).$$

(It is not hard to see that the step

$$\lim_{\alpha\to 1} \int_0^{S-s} l(S-x)\, dH_\alpha(x) = \int_0^{S-s} l(S-x)\, dH(x)$$

is justified.)

We can then minimize the function in (5.19) with respect to s and S. It should be noted that l_∞ is, of course, independent of the initial stock y_0.

VI. A DYNAMIC MODEL: EXAMPLES

We consider now some examples for a particular function $F(x)$. It is advantageous to use a function whose convolutions can be written explicitly. From this point of view, functions of the form

$$F(x) = \frac{\beta^k}{(k-1)!} \int_0^x u^{k-1} e^{-\beta u}\, du, \quad k > 0, \quad \beta > 0, \tag{6.1}$$

are convenient [$(k-1)!$ is $\Gamma(k)$ if k is not an integer] since by proper choice of β and k we can give any desired values to the mean $(= k/\beta)$ and variance $(= k/\beta^2)$ of x, and since $F_n(x)$ is then given by

$$F_n(x) = \frac{\beta^{nk}}{(nk-1)!}\int_0^x u^{nk-1}\, e^{-\beta u}\, du.$$

The function $H_\alpha(x)$ is then given by

$$H_\alpha(x) = \int_0^x e^{-\beta u}\left\{\sum_{n=1}^{\infty}\frac{\beta^{nk}\alpha^n u^{nk-1}}{(nk-1)!}\right\} du. \tag{6.2}$$

If k is an integer, the summation in (6.2) can be performed explicitly, giving

$$H_\alpha(x) = \frac{\beta\alpha^{1/k}}{k}\int_0^x e^{-\beta u}\left(\sum_{j=1}^{k}\omega_j e^{\omega_j \alpha^{1/k}\beta u}\right) du, \tag{6.3}$$

where $\omega_1, \ldots, \omega_k$ are the kth roots of unity. For example, if $k=2$, we have $\omega_1 = -1$, $\omega_2 = 1$, so that

$$H_\alpha(x) = \frac{\beta\sqrt{\alpha}}{2}\int_0^x e^{-\beta u}(e^{\beta u\sqrt{\alpha}} - e^{-\beta u\sqrt{\alpha}})\, du.$$

It is instructive to find the value of l_∞ for the simple case $f(x) = e^{-x}$. In this case $\beta = k = 1$; $F = 1 - e^{-x}$; and, from (6.3),

$$H(x) = \int_0^x e^{-u}(e^u)\, du = x$$

and we have

$$\begin{aligned} l_\infty &= \frac{K + l(S) + \int_0^{S-s} l(S-x)\, dx}{1+S-s} \\ &= \frac{K + cS + Ae^{-S} + \int_0^{S-s}[c(S-x) + Ae^{-S+x}]\, dx}{1+S-s} \\ &= \frac{K + cS + Ae^{-S} + cS(S-s) - \frac{c}{2}(S-s)^2 + Ae^{-S}(e^{S-s}-1)}{1+S-s} \\ &= \frac{K + cS + Ae^{-s} + \frac{c}{2}(S^2 - s^2)}{1+S-s}. \end{aligned}$$

Letting $S - s = \Delta$, we see that this expression, for a fixed value of Δ, has its minimum (unless it occurs when $s = 0$) when

$$S = \log_e(A/c) - \log_e(1+\Delta) + \Delta.$$

VII. FURTHER PROBLEMS AND GENERALIZATIONS

To make the dynamic model more realistic certain generalizations are necessary. We shall register them in the present section as a program for further work.

A. Of the several cost and utility parameters used in the certainty model of Section II and in the static uncertainty model of Section III, we have retained in the dynamic uncertainty model only three: c, the marginal cost of storage; K, the constant cost of handling an order; and A, the constant part of the depletion penalty. We have thus dropped the parameters a, b_0, b_1 and B. The meaning of the first three of these was discussed in Section IVB. It can be presumed from Equation (3.8) of the more developed static model that if we similarly developed the dynamic model, c could be easily replaced by $(c+b_0)$ but that $(B+a)$ would form an additional parameter altogether excluded from our simple dynamic model. Difficulties of another kind will occur when $b_1>0$, i.e., when there are economies of big-lot buying, which are due, not to the advantage of handling one order instead of many, but to the cheapness of transporting (and producing) large quantities. This will obviously modify the rule of action (4.4), as the loss that we intend to minimize will depend on $(S-y_t)$, the size of the replenishment order.

B. We have assumed the distribution $F(x)$ of demand per unit period to be known, presumably having been estimated from previous samples. Actual estimations of this distribution were carried out by Fry and Wilson for the Bell Telephone Company, and by Kruskal and Wolf [1, 2] with the material of the medical branch of the U.S. Navy.

Instead of estimating the distribution $F(x)$, once and for all, and fixing constant values for S and s, one may vary S and s as new observations on demand are obtained. The problem is one of expressing the best values of S and s for the time t as functions of the sequence of observations available up to that time – say $S_t(x_1, \ldots, x_{t-1})$ and $s_t(x_1, \ldots, x_{t-1})$. More generally, one has to find a sequence of functions $q_t(x_1, \ldots, x_{t-1})$ giving the best amounts to be ordered, a sequence not necessarily restricted by conditions (4.4). We do not propose to attack this problem here.[6]

NOTES

* This paper was prepared in the summer of 1950 at the Logistics Conference of The

RAND Corporation, Santa Monica, California. It will be reprinted as Cowles Commission Paper, New Series, No. 44.

The authors express gratitude for remarks and criticism of staff members of the Cowles Commission for Research in Economics and, in particular, for detailed and helpful comments and suggestions by Gerard Debreu. Criticisms by Herbert A. Simon, Carnegie Institute of Technology, and discussions with Allen Newell, of The RAND Corporation, and with Joyce Friedman, Joseph Kruskal, and C. B. Tompkins, of the Office of Naval Research Logistics Project, George Washington University, have also proved stimulating.

The authors regret that the important work of Pierre Massé [1] did not come to their attention before this article was completed.

1 The head of a nonprofit organization, just like the head of a household, has to arrange the outcomes of alternative actions in the order of his preferences. Moreover, if choices can be made between alternative 'lotteries' each characterized by a different probability distribution of outcomes, then – as proved by von Neumann and Morgenstern [1] – numerical 'utilities' can be assigned to the outcomes in such a way that the chosen lottery is the one with the highest expected utility.

An important problem arises as to the decisions of a sub-agency of a profit or nonprofit organization. The head of a sub-agency has to take decisions that would maximize expected utility or revenue not to himself but to the superior organization. He cannot calculate the effect of his action upon this utility or revenue because he does not know the actions of other sub-agencies. However, the superior organization can, instead, inform its subordinates of a certain set of 'intrinsic prices'. This set has the following property: If each sub-agency maximizes *its* 'net revenue' computed in those 'prices' (i.e., if it maximizes the algebraic sum of inputs and outputs, present or future, each multiplied by its 'price'), then the utility for the superior organization is also maximized. The ratios between any two 'intrinsic prices' are equal to the ratios at which the corresponding in- or outputs can be substituted for each other without making the superior organization worse off (its resources and technology being given). See Koopmans [1, 2], Debreu [1].

Whenever direct monetary calculation appears not to be feasible, we shall, throughout this paper, use the words 'utility' and 'revenue' as interchangeable; the 'revenue' of a sub-agency being understood to be computed at the 'intrinsic prices' set up by the superior organization.

2 Before formulating the problem, a study was made of the existing business literature on inventory control, using freely the comprehensive bibliographies that were compiled by T. H. Whitin [1] of Princeton University, and by Louise B. Haack [1] of George Washington University, for projects of the Office of Naval Research at those universities.

3 The following intuitive summary of the argument of Section IV E has been kindly suggested by a referee: During the first period, the expected loss is $l(y)$ and demand is x with probability $dF(x)$; the stock remaining will be $S-x$ or $y-x$ as the case may be, with a forward-looking expected loss of, respectively, $L(S-x)$ or $L(y-x)$. In the former case, the expected future loss at the end of the first period is $\int_0^S L(S-x)\,dF(x) + {}$ $+ L(0)\,[1-F(S)]$, all of which needs only to be multipled by α to be discounted back to the beginning of the first period where it can be added to the original $l(y)$. This yields Equation (4.11). The companion Equation (4.12) is obtained similarly for the case when the stock remaining at the end of the first period is $y-x$.

4 See Feller [2, Chapter XV], for the case when $F(x)$ is a step function.

[5] This stationary distribution can be found explicitly and, as pointed out by H. Simon, gives an alternative means of finding l_∞.

[6] See Wald [1]; Arrow, Blackwell, and Girshick [1]. If judgment were available on the a priori probabilities of alternative distributions $F(x)$, the expected loss could be averaged over all possible $F(x)$ and minimized with respect to the unknown functions q_t or S_t, s_t. In the absence of such judgment, one might think of minimizing the maximum expected loss. In an appropriately modified form suggested by L. Savage [1], the latter principle was applied to a problem in investment decisions by Marschak [1], and its applicability discussed by Modigliani and Tobin. See also Niehans [1]. Other criteria have been proposed by Hurwicz [1].

A different approach was suggested by Herbert A. Simon [1].

BIBLIOGRAPHY

Alford, L. P. and Banks, John R. (eds.), [1] *Production Handbook*, Ronald Press, New York, 1944, 1639 pp. (especially pp. 394–403, where formulas by Norton and by Davis are given in addition to an example of numerical minimization of cost).

Arrow, K. J., Blackwell, D., and Girschick, M. A. [1] 'Bayes and Minimax Solutions of Sequential Decision Problems', *Econometrica* **17** (July–October, 1949) 214–244.

Arrow, K. J., Harris, T., and Marschak, J. [1] 'Optimal Inventory Policy' (hectographed), George Washington University Logistics Papers, Issue No. 4, Appendix 1 to Quarterly Progress Report No. 5, 16 November 1950–15 February 1951.

Debreu, Gerard, [1] 'The Coefficient of Resource Utilization', *Econometrica* **19** (July, 1951) 273–292.

Eisenhart, Churchill, [1] 'Some Inventory Problems' (hectographed), National Bureau of Standards, Techniques of Statistical Inference A2.2, Lecture 1, January 6, 1948, 14 pp.

Feller, W., [1] 'On the Integral Equation of Renewal Theory', *Annals of Mathematical Statistics* **12** (September, 1941) 243–267.

Feller, W., [2] *Introduction to Probability Theory*, John Wiley and Sons, New York, 1950, 419 pp.

Fry, Thornton C., [1] *Probability and Its Engineering Uses*, D. van Nostrand, New York, 1928, 476 pp. (especially pp. 229–232).

Haack, Louise B., [1] 'Selected Supplementary Bibliography of Publications on Inventory Control' (hectographed), The George Washington University Logistics Papers, Appendix 1 to Quarterly Progress Report No. 2, 16 February–15 May 1950.

Hurwicz, Leonid, [1] 'A Class of Criteria for Decision-Making under Ignorance' (hectographed), Cowles Commission Discussion Paper, Statistics No. 356, February 9, 1951, 3 pp.

Koopmans, T. C., [1] 'Analysis of Production as an Efficient Combination of Activities', in *Activity Analysis of Production and Allocation*, Cowles Commission Monograph 13, John Wiley and Sons, New York, 1951, pp. 33–97.

Koopmans, T. C., [2] 'Efficient Allocation of Resources' (submitted for publication in *Econometrica*).

Kruskal, J. B., Jr and Wolf, J. J., [1] 'Consumption as a Random Variable' (hectographed), Logistics Papers, Issue No. 2, Appendix 1 to Quarterly Progress Report No. 2, 16 February–15 May 1950, Office of Naval Research, Project NR 047001.

Kruskal, J. B., Jr. and Wolf, J. J., [2] 'Protection from Depletion of Supply in the

Bureau of Medicine and Surgery' (hectographed), Logistics Papers, Issue No. 2, Appendix 1 to Quarterly Progress Report No. 2, 16 February–15 May 1950, Office of Naval Research, Project NR 047001.

Marschak, Jacob, [1] 'Role of Liquidity under Complete and Incomplete Information', *Papers and Proceedings, American Economic Review* **39** (May, 1949) 182–195, with discussion by F. Modigliani and J. Tobin. (Abstracts in *Econometrica* **17** (April, 1949) 180–184).

Marschak, Jacob, [2] 'Optimal Aggregation of Inventories under Certainty' (hectographed), Cowles Commission Discussion Paper, Economics No. 2015, March 30, 1951.

Massé, Pierre, [1] *Les Réserves et la régulation de l'avenir dans la vie économique*, Hermann, Paris, 1946; Vol. I, *Avenir déterminé*, 148 pp.; Vol. II, *Avenir aléatoire*, 229 pp.

Neumann, John von and Morgenstern, O., [1] *Theory of Games and Economic Behavior* (second edition), Princeton University Press, Princeton, 1947, 641 pp.

Niehans, Dr. Jurg, [1] 'Zur Preisbildung bei Ungewissen Erwartungen', *Schweizerische Zeitschrift fuer Volkswirtschaft und Statistik* **84** (1948) 433–456, especially p. 445.

Savage, L. J., [1] 'The Theory of Statistical Decision', *Journal of the American Statistical Association* **46** (March, 1951) 55–67.

Simon, Herbert A., [1] 'An Exploration into the Use of Servomechanism Theory in the Study of Production Control' (submitted for publication in *Econometrica*).

Tompkins, C. B., [1] 'Allocation between Assignments to Planned Consumption and to Safety Allowance' (hectographed), George Washington University Logistics Papers, Appendix 1 to Quarterly Progress Report No. 3, 16 May–16 August 1950.

Wald, A., [1] *Statistical Decision Functions*, John Wiley and Sons, New York, 1950, 179 pp.

Whitin, T. H. (ed.), [1] 'Inventory Control Bibliography' (hectographed), The George Washington University Logistics Papers, Appendix 1 to Quarterly Progress Report No. 1, 28 November 1949–15 February 1950.

Wilson, R. H., [1] *Scientific Control of Stockroom Inventories*, Midwest Quality Control Conference, 1947.

Wilson, R. H., [2] 'Stockroom Purchasing', *Purchasing* **10** (February, 1941) 47–50.

Wilson, R. H., [3] 'A Universal System of Stock Control', *Purchasing* **11** (September, 1941) 80–88.

Wilson, R. H., [4] 'A Scientific Routine for Stock Control', *Harvard Business Review* **13** (October, 136) 116–128.

20

TOWARDS AN ECONOMIC THEORY OF ORGANIZATION AND INFORMATION*

(1954)

INTRODUCTION

The statement of Laplace [9] that the theory of probabilities is at bottom merely common sense reduced to calculus[1] and the saying of Schumpeter [18] that, to a layman, economics must appear *halb unverstaendlich, halb selbstverstaendlich*, have similar meanings. Both men said, in effect, that their respective disciplines formalized certain concepts and propositions of pre-scientific practice. Surely this did not lead them to think that their disciplines were useless. In fact, both disciplines have been fairly successful.

The present paper is conceived in the same spirit; and it happens to touch on both economic theory and probabilities. It can be interpreted as extending the economic theory of a rational firm into the domain of uncertainty, giving special regard to the character of a firm as a team. All criticisms leveled against economic theory can therefore be also raised against the type of work represented by this paper. In particular, in concentrating on the typically 'economic' question of the most efficient rules of action and communication for group members, I have pursued a line different from those who are interested in the description of existing modes of behavior within human groups. Yet, I do feel the two lines of research will meet some time, and that communication between the two types of workers is fruitful. When time comes for second approximations of the economic, normative approach, limitations on human rationality emphasized by descriptive workers will have to be properly formalized and introduced into the theory as a factual constraint. On the other hand, the criterion of efficiency of a team or of a foundation should be helpful in describing those human groups which have been created for a purpose: just as this same criterion of efficiency is a major guide in describing human artifacts such as machines or ships. The history of ships is no doubt fascinating and full of suggestions. But to buy or build a ship, it is also useful to know what makes a ship safe and fast. There is a history of political constitutions. There is also the question, What makes a constitution suitable for its task? There are many histories of business corporations. There is also the question, Which structures and procedures make a business organization profitable?

1. Teams, Foundations, Coalitions

1.1. *Preference Orderings*

Human groups can be classified according to whether a group goal exists and according to the relation between the group goal and the goals of group members. A more formal and convenient phrase for 'goal' is '*preference ordering of states of the world*'; or simply '*ordering*', or '*interests*'. The relation sG_is' will be read: 'from the point of view of i, the state s is at least as good as the state s'.' The binary relations G_i, $i=1, 2,\ldots, n$ will denote the orderings by individuals (individual interests), and G_0 the ordering from the point of view of the group (group interest). Groups will be classified according to which combinations of the following propositions are valid (S will denote the set of all states):

A. *For every i* ($i=1,\ldots, n$), *there exists a complete ordering* G_i *on* S. [that is, every group member has a preference ordering]:[2] *Rationality of members.*

B. *There exists a transitive ordering* G_0 *on* S. [That is, the states can be ordered for the group, at least partially: see note to A]: *Transitivity of group interests.*

C. *For any* s, s' *in* S, *if* sG_is' *for all* $i=1,\ldots, n$, *then* sG_0s'. [That is, if s is not worse than s' for any member of the group, it is not worse than s' for the group itself]: The so-called *Pareto optimality principle.*

D. *For any* s, s' in S, sG_0s' *or* $s'G_0s$. [That is, for no pair of states is it impossible to say which is preferable for the group, unless the two are equally desirable]. *Completeness of group preferences.* (Note that B and D imply together complete ordering.)

E. *For all* $i=1,\ldots, n$, sG_is' *if and only if* sG_0s'. [That is, all individuals have identical interests among themselves and with the group]: *Solidarity.*

If A is satisfied we call the n group members rational.

If A, B and C are satisfied the group is a *coalition*.

If A, B, C and D are satisfied we call it a *foundation*.
If A, B, C, D and E are satisfied we call it a *team*.

1.2. *Utility Functions*

The same concepts can be defined (somewhat more narrowly[3]), if the individual complete ordering G_i $(i=1,\dots,n)$ is replaced by a numerical function y_i on S, the so-called satisfaction or utility function. The group members are called rational if for every $i=1,\dots,n$ there exists a numerical function $u_i(s)$ such that $u_i(s)\geqq u_i(s')$ if and only if sG_is'. The corresponding group utility function $u_0(s)$, if it exists, may or may not be a numerical one. If $u_0(s)$ is numerical, then $u_0(s)\geqslant u_0(s')$ if and only if sG_0s'. In the case of *coalitions* other than foundations, $u_0(s)$ is the vector $[u_1(s),\dots,u_n(s)]$ (vectors are partially ordered). In the case of *foundations*, $u_0(s)$ is numerical and is a monotone non-decreasing function of $u_1(s)$, $u_2(s),\dots,u_n(s)$. In the case of *teams*, $u_0(s)=u_1(s)=\cdots=u_n(s)$.

1.3. *Incentives; Bargaining*

To sum up: an individual is rational if his preferences are *consistent*. A group of such individuals is a coalition if, whenever a state is worsened for one individual and is unchanged for all others, it is considered as worsened for the group. A coalition is a foundation if all states can be compared from the point of view of group interest. A foundation is a team if group interest coincides with the interest of each member.

A team may be regarded as the simplest form of a group. If a group is a foundation but not a team, the group has a goal separate from the individual goals. This gives rise to the problem of individual *incentives* that would best serve the group goal. If a group is a coalition but not a foundation, there is no 'group interest' to help in making all choices: when any state is reached where no member can be made better off without making another member worse off, further choices are determined by *bargaining*, and problems of 'relative power' arise. If a group of rational men is not a coalition, there arises the general problem of a (generally non-constant-sum) game.

1.4. *Some Recent Literature*

In recent literature the paper of Herbert Simon [20] on the Employment Relationship, dealt with a coalition (in our sense) between an employer and a worker. The work of Bavelas [1] and his group deals with foundations: a group goal exists (some task is to be achieved in shortest time with least error, etc.) but there need not be complete solidarity; some of Bavelas' mathematical problems (to find the minimal number of messages needed to fully equalize the state of information among n members) are team problems. In von Neumann-Morgenstern's *Theory of Games* [16], coalitions have the same meaning as here; foundations do not seem to occur; teams occur, e.g., in the case of a pair of bridge partners. The process of bargaining within a coalition, and the process of forming and dissolving coalitions within a general game is not treated in the *Theory of Games*. A theory of bargaining has been presented by J. Nash [12], [13]. It is possible that such problems require postulates additional to that of the existence of consistent individual preferences. Such postulates were developed in models such as R. Bush's [3] and N. Rashevsky's [15].

This paper represents a part of the work on teams by the author and other members of the Cowles Commission, especially Beckmann [2] and Radner [12], [14]. This work included also some preliminary attempts to deal with the problem of foundations: ([10], Part III; Faxèn [6]), but such attempts will not be made here.

2. Activities: observations, messages, actions

2.1. *Events and Actions*

Each state s of the world which, as discussed in 1, is compared with other states of the world from the point of view of the team's interests, can be regarded as depending on two classes of variables: (1) variables that are controlled by the n members; we shall call them actions and denote them by $a_1,\ldots, a_n$; (2) variables that are not controlled by the members; we shall call them 'states of environment' or 'external variables'; and summarize them by the letter x. Since the team's satisfaction depends on the state of the world s, and s depends on $a_1,\ldots, a_n$ and on x, we can denote the team's satisfaction by

$$(2.1.1) \quad u = u(a, x),$$

where $a=(a_1,\ldots, a_n)$. (Because of 'solidarity' of team members we have omitted the subscript under u). u is also called payoff or gain. The environment x will be considered random, with a known distribution function.

2.2. *Activities*

To each individual i corresponds an action variable a_i. Moreover, to each individual i corresponds a set X_i of the values of the variable (possibly a group of variables) that he can observe, and the value he has actually observed can be denoted by $x_i \in \mathsf{X}_i$. For example, x_1 = economic conditions, x_2 = political conditions, etc. Thus $x = (x_1, \ldots, x_n)$. We can distinguish three kinds of activities of i:

(1) To make an *observation* x_1 on the external world

(2) To perform an *action* a_i upon the external world

(3) To send to a co-member j a *message* (report) m_{ij}, i.e., a statement about the external world, of the form

$$x_i \in X_{ij} \subseteq \mathsf{X}_i ;$$

that is, a report states that the observation x_i made by the reporter belongs to a subset X_{ij} of X_i. The report can thus be identified as the set X_{ij}. Two extreme cases are: an 'exact (or most detailed) report' when X_{ij} consists of a single element, $X_{ij} = \{x_i\}$; 'no report' when $X_{ij} = \mathsf{X}_i$. We can write $X_{ii} = \mathsf{X}_i$.

2.3. *Cost of Message*

Thus in general a message m_{ij} is a subset of X_i. A non-negative number $c_i(m_{ij})$ will measure the *cost* of the message. We have

$$c_i(\{x_i\}) \geqslant c_i(\mathsf{X}_i) = 0 ,$$

while 'inexact messages' (i.e., messages where X_{ij} consists of more than one, but not of all elements of X_i) have intermediate cost. In special cases, c_i may be regarded as a non-increasing function of the measure of set X_{ij}.

2.4. *Examples*

(1) Let x_i = vector (x_i', x_i''), e.g., x_i' = leather price, x_i'' = shoe price. Then a report to j, giving values of x_i' *and* x_i'' (so that X_{ij} = a point in the x_i', x_i''-plane), is more 'exact' and more costly than one giving the value of x_i' only (so that X_{ij} = a line in the x_i', x_i''-plane) or of x_i'' only.

(2) Let x_i = price and let the report X_{ij} state a subinterval $\alpha \leqslant x_i \leqslant \beta$; then the report is the more exact and costly the smaller $\beta - \alpha$.

2.5. *Three-Phase Team*

We shall consider three-phase teams only:

Phase I : Observations made.
Phase II : Messages sent and received.
Phase III: Actions performed.

Actual teams may have, of course, many more phases. Messages will occur that do not fall under the definition of our Section 2.2.: e.g., reports transmitting a third member's message. In the present paper, after Phase I, the member i has information x_i. After Phase II his information is the logical product

$$\{x_i\} \cap X_{1i} \cap \cdots \cap X_{ni}.$$

2.6. *Best Rules*

We shall be concerned with determining the *best rules of action and communication*. A *rule* states, for a member i, the 'response' he should make to a given 'stimulus'. In Phase II, the stimulus consists of the observation x_i, and the response consists in sending the n-tuple of messages, $(m_{i1}, \ldots, m_{in}) = m_i'$ (a row vector). The rule for Phase II is a function R_i^{I} such that

$$(2.6.1) \quad m_i' = R_i^{\mathrm{I}}(x_i),$$

involving a communication cost $c_i(m_i^{\mathrm{I}})$, say. In Phase III, the stimulus of i consists of the observation x_i *and* of the n-tuple of messages received by him, $(m_{1i}, \ldots, m_{ni}) = m_i$, a column vector. The response is the action a_i, and the rule for Phase III is a function R_i^{II} such that

$$(2.6.2) \quad a_i = R_i^{\mathrm{II}}(x_i, m_i).$$

We shall write $x, m', m, a, R^{\mathrm{I}}, R^{\mathrm{II}}$ for the corresponding n-tuples $(x_1, \ldots, x_n)$, $(m_1', \ldots, m_n')$ etc., and denote by $c(m)$ the cost incurred when the matrix of messages sent is $[m_{ij}]$. From now on, we shall call $u(a, x)$ the *gross gain* of the team. The *net gain* of the team is

$$(2.6.3) \quad v = u(a, x) - c(m) = v(x; R^{\mathrm{I}}, R^{\mathrm{II}}; u, c),$$

a quantity depending on x; on the rules that determine m as a function of

x, and a as a function of x and m; and on the functions u and c that measure the team satisfaction and the cost of messages.

We have assumed that in the opinion of the organization or team a probability measure on the set X of the states x of environment exists and is known to them. This distribution of x will be denoted by $F(x)$. The expected value of the net gain is

$$\int_{\mathsf{X}} v(x; R^{\mathrm{I}}, R^{\mathrm{II}}; u, c)\, dF(x) = V(R^{\mathrm{I}}, R^{\mathrm{II}}; u, c, F), \tag{2.6.4}$$

say. We want to find the rules $R^{\mathrm{I}} = \hat{R}^{\mathrm{I}}$ and $R^{\mathrm{II}} = \hat{R}^{\mathrm{II}}$ that will maximize V. Clearly they will depend on the functions u, c and F. We want to study this dependence. What properties of the functions u, c and F make for more or for less frequent and detailed communication between a given pair of members? What conditions make it profitable to cut off direct communication between i and j?

2.7. *Maximizing Expected Utility*

In Section 1, a decision-maker was called rational if the states of the world at his choice were completely ordered (ranked) by his preferences. This ordering was represented by a numerical utility function. In the present Section, the preferences must be conceived in a manner that allows for the uncertainty of outcome of a decision. The decision-maker is pictured as assuming a certain probability distribution $F(x)$ of the environment. Therefore the outcome of each decision is a probability distribution of outcomes, a 'prospect'; though in a special case the distribution may degenerate into a sure outcome. The set S of 1.1 is to be reinterpreted as a set of prospects. A rational decision-maker has a complete ordering of prospects. A numerical utility function can be attached to prospects so that $u(s') \geqq u(s'')$ whenever prospect s' is preferred or equivalent to prospect s''. That is, the rational man chooses that prospect s for which $u(s)$ is a maximum.

However, the concept of rationality which we shall use is stronger than the one just stated. The rational decision-maker is defined as being able to represent his preferences by a numerical utility function possessing the following property. Denote by $(s_1, \ldots, s_m; p_1, \ldots, p_m)$ a prospect consisting of the anticipation of prospects (possibly, sure outcomes) $s_1, \ldots, s_m$ with respective probabilities $p_1, \ldots, p_m$. Then $u(s_1, \ldots, s_m); p'_1, \ldots, p'_m) \geqslant u(s_1, \ldots,$

$s_m; p''_1, \ldots, p''_m)$ if and only if

$$\sum_1^m p'_i u(s_i) \geqslant \sum_1^m p''_i u(s_i).$$

In other words: if we regard $u(s_1), \ldots, u(s_m)$ as alternative values of a random variable $u(s)$, the choice between two prospects characterized by the probability vectors $\{p'_i\}$ and $\{p''_i\}$ respectively depends on the values of a single parameter of the two considered distributions of $u(s)$, viz., on its expectation (mean). In this sense, the rational man is defined as maximizing expected utility. This definition was used in 2.6 where we ask for the rules of action and communication that would maximize the team's expected net gain.

This definition of rational decision under uncertainty goes back to Daniel Bernoulli and has been recently much discussed, under the impact of certain behavior postulates formulated in the Theory of Games. Here we shall not discuss these, or similar, postulates in detail.[4] Instead, it will suffice to show, in heuristic fashion, a way to assign to one's prospects a utility scale possessing the required property; and to claim that a system of preferences permitting such a scale does characterize an ideally consistent decision-maker, e.g. an ideal organizer and legislator for a team.

Assume provisionally that there exists for such a decision-maker a 'worst' and a 'best' state of the world. Denote them to by s_0 and s_1, respectively. Assign them utility numbers $u(s_0)=0$ and $u(s_1)=1$, and proceed to 'calibrate' on this scale the utilities of all other states. To begin with, consider a prospect promising s_1 with probability π and s_0 with probability $1-\pi$. In the notation just proposed above, such a prospect will be denoted by $(s_1, s_0; \pi, 1-\pi)$. The decision-maker – you, the reader, for example – will (a postulate is hidden here!) consider such a prospect better than s_0 and worse than s_1. Therefore you will assign to it a utility number between 0 and 1. The probability is itself such a number. It is therefore permissible to choose a utility function u such that $u(s_1, s_0; \pi, 1-\pi)=\pi$, for any π between 0 and 1, including 0 and 1 themselves [since $u(s_1, s_0; 0, 1)=u(s_0)=0$ and $u(s_1, s_0; 1, 0)=1$].

Consider next some prospect s that is neither s_0 nor s_1 nor the promise of s_1 or s_0 with some probabilities. If the decision-maker is indifferent between s and s_1, or, alternatively, between s and s_0, then, of course, $u(s)=0$ or 1, respectively. There remains the case when he considers s

better than s_0 but worse than s_1. In this case, by scanning all possible prospects of the type $(s_1, s_0; \pi, 1-\pi)$, with π ranging continuously from 0 to 1, one will find (a postulate is hidden here!) one such prospect that the decision-maker will be indifferent between it and the prospect s. That is, there will be a π such that $u(s)=u(s_1, s_0; \pi, 1-\pi)$. And since, on the utility scale chosen above, $u(s_1, s_0; \pi, 1-\pi)=\pi$, we shall have $u(s)=\pi$. Thus we have assigned utility numbers to all prospects.

To show that this utility scale possesses the required property, compute the utility of the prospect $s=(t_1, t_2,..., t_m; p_1, p_2,..., p_m)$, where $t_1,..., t_m$ are prospects (possibly sure ones) and $p_1,..., p_m$ their probabilities. Let the utility of each t_i be measured on our scale; that is, $u(t_i)=\pi_i$ if the decision-maker is indifferent between t_i and $(t_1, t_0; \pi_i, 1-\pi_i)$. Then the decision-maker is indifferent between the prospect $(t_1,..., t_m; p_1,..., p_m)$ and the prospect $[s_1, s_0; \pi_1, 1-\pi_1), (s_1, s_0; \pi_2, 1-\pi_2),..., (s_1, s_0; \pi_m, 1-\pi_m); p_1,..., p_m]$, (actually a postulate is hidden here). But the latter prospect is nothing but the promise of s_1 with probability $p_1\pi_1+p_2\pi_2+\cdots p_m\pi_m=\sum_1^m p_iu(t_i)$; and of s_0 with probability $1-\sum_1^m p_iu(t_i)$. Now, on our scale, the utility of such a prospect is simply equal to the probability of s_1. Hence

$$u(t_1,..., t_m; p_1,..., p_m) = \sum_1^m p_iu(t_i);$$

the expression on the right is the 'expected utility' of the prospect $(t_1,..., t_m; p_1,..., p_m)$. Hence, if two prospects $(t_1,..., t_m; p'_1,..., p'_m)$ and $(t_1,..., t_m; p''_1,..., p''_m)$ are compared, the preferred one will have the higher expected utility.

The provisional assumption that there exist a best and a worst states can be dropped. We can assign utilities 1 and 0 to any two states, s_1 and s_0 of which the former is preferred to the latter; and assign, as before, utility numbers π $(0\leqslant\pi\leqslant 1)$ to all prospects which are not better than s_1 and not worse than s_0. To assign a utility number to a prospect (say s_2) that is better than s_1, we first form a number π $(0<\pi<1)$ such that the decision-maker is indifferent between s_1 and $(s_2, s_0; \pi, 1-\pi)$; and let, accordingly, $u(s_2)$ satisfy the condition $\pi\cdot u(s_2)+(1-\pi)\,u(s_0)=u(s_1)$, and hence $\pi\cdot u(s_2)=1$, $u(s_2)=1/\pi>1$. Similarly, if s_2 is worse than s_0, we find a number π such that the decision-maker is indifferent between s_0 and $(s_1, s_2; \pi, 1-\pi)$, and define $u(s_2)$ by $u(s_0)=\pi\cdot u(s_1)+(1-\pi)\cdot u(s_2)$; and hence $u(s_2) = -\pi/(1-\pi) < 0$. It is easy to see that this utility scale, now extended beyond the interval $[s_0, s_1]$, will still possess the required property. Of course, the numbers in the scale will change linearly as s_0, s_1 – the prospects chosen to have zero-utility and unit-utility – are changed; but the required property is preserved.

The postulates tacitly used in this observation of utility-scaling can be roughly listed as follows:

(1) Numerical function $u(s)$ exists, such that $u(s_1) \geqslant u(s_2)$ if and only if s_1 is preferred or equivalent to s_2.

(2) If $u(s_1) > u(s_2)$ then, for any s_3 and any probability p, $u(s_1, s_3; p, 1-p) \geqq u(s_2, s_3; p, 1-p)$.

(3) If $u(s_1) > u(s_2) > u(s_3)$ then there exists a probability p such that $u(s_2) = u(s_1, s_3; p, 1-p)$.

2.8. *Unknown and Subjective Probabilities*

A natural objection against formulations like ours is to say that in reality the probability distribution F of external conditions is not known. In this case the problem becomes one of statistical inference, invoking principles like 'known *a priori* distribution on the space of F's', 'minimax', etc. For the case of a 'one-person team' (when activities consist only of observations and actions, no messages being sent) one might refer to works like Dvoretsky-Kiefer-Wolfowitz' second article on Inventories [5].

The assumption of a known *a priori* probability distribution is particularly germane to our problem, whether in the simple case of three-phase-teams or in more complicated cases. In a three-phase-team, there is no opportunity to acquire or improve the knowledge of the distribution F in the course of the team's operations. In this case, and if F is not known from appropriate statistical manipulation of data collected in the past, we shall still say that a rational decision-maker, if he makes at all choices among actions, has to make consistent assumptions about the probabilities of outcomes of the actions just as he has a consistent scale of the utilities of those outcomes. A postulational basis for the simultaneous existence of subjective utilities and probabilities, extending in a plausible way the postulates of 2.7, was proposed by Frank Ramsey, and more recently by L. J. Savage.[5]

If the operations of a team form a sequence of more than three phases, it is still useful to obtain the benefit of subjective probabilities. The rational decision-maker will start with some subjective probabilities. Even if they are mere hunches roughly summarizing his previous experience they will help him to lay down a plan as to how best to respond to any given sequence of future observations by an appropriate sequence of actions and communications. His actions, in this case, may but need not include data manipulation to provide progressively improved estimates of the distribution F of observables.

2.9. *Orders*

In 2.2 all messages were defined as statements (reports) about the external world. Reports are different in verbal content (and therefore differ in cost) from 'orders' or 'task assignments'. It seems, however, that by introducing orders no essential change will be introduced in our problem, at least at the present stage of analysis.

For example, suppose the relevant features of the world are characterized by two variables, x_1 and x_2. Let team member 1 observe x_1 and team member 2 observe x_2, and let the respective observed values be x_1^0 and x_2^0. Consider first the following rules: R^{I} consists of R_1^{I} only viz.: 1 tells 2 the observed value x_1^0; R^0 consists of R_2^{II} only, viz.: 2 chooses $a_2 = a_2^0$ that will minimize $u(a_2, x_1^0, x_2^0)$. In this case, member 1 is a mere 'reporter'. The payoff function $u(a_2, x_1, x_2)$ – a function of *three* variables – is fully known to member 2, but need not be known to member 1.

Now suppose, instead, that it is the member 1 who knows the function $u(a_2, x_1, x_2)$, and let the rule $R^{\mathrm{I}} = R_1^{\mathrm{I}}$ be as follows: 1 shall communicate to 2, not the observed value x_1^0, but the 'task', i.e., the function of *two* variables that is to be maximized,

$$u_0(a_2, x_2) = u(a_2, x_1^0, x_2).$$

Member 2 then proceeds to accomplish the task. That is, the rule $R^{\mathrm{II}} = R_2^{\mathrm{II}}$ is: member 2 (who had observed $x_2 = x_2^0$) shall choose $a_2 = a_2^0$ so as to maximize $u_0(a_2, x_2^0)$. In this case, member 1 is the 'boss': he determines, in the light of his knowledge of $x_1 = x_1^0$, the special task that member 2, the 'subordinate', has to fulfill – i.e., the specialized payoff function u_0 that 2 has to maximize. In military terminology, 1 is in charge of strategy, while 2 is in charge of tactics. The observable x_1 may consist of information about the overall plans of the enemy (plus the information received by the commander during his training), while x_2 may be a local situation. The distinction between reports and orders will not be pursued further in this paper.[6]

2.10. *Non-Additive Costs*

The definition of net gain in (2.6.3) is quite appropriate when the amount to be maximized is the expected net money gain. In more general cases, one cannot represent the maximand as the difference between (expected) gain and (expected) cost and will use some more general function to describe net gain. However, (2.6.3) will help us fix the ideas.

2.11. *A Remark on the General Multi-Phase Case.*[7]

The three-phase case can be generalized by constructing, for every phase $t=1,\ldots, T$, the following matrix with $n+1$ rows and columns (regarding a_i as a set of values):

a_{ij}^t means: 'what i tells j' (a subset of X_i or a_j)
a_{io}^t means: 'what i does to the outside world' (an element of a_i)
a_{oi}^t means: 'what i observes in the outside world' (an element of X_i)
a_{ii}^t, a_{oo}^t are empty.

Then $a_i^t = i$th column $= i$'s recently acquired information,

$a_i^t =$ sequence $(a_i^t, a_i^{t-1}) = i$'s state of information,
$a_{i'}^t = i$th row $= i$'s messages and actions.

In a stationary team there exists a set of rules $R=(R_1,\ldots, R_n)$, independent of time, such that

$$a_{i'}^t = R(a_i^{t-1}), \quad i=1,\ldots, n.$$

The team's gross gain for the period ending at T depends on the sequence of external events, a_o^T; and on the sequence of actions taken, $a_{o'}^T$; but since the latter depend on a_o^T and on the rule R, the gross gain is $u(a_o^T, R)$, say. The cost of communications will also depend on a_o^T, R. Hence the net gain is $v(a_o^T, R)$, say. The distribution of external states a_o^t depends, in general, on the sequence of previous states as well as on the sequence of previous actions ('controlled stochastic process'). Hence the distribution of the sequence a_o^T depends on the initial state a_o^o and on the rule R. Write this distribution as $F(a_o^T; a_o^o, R)$. Then the expected net gain (integrated over the space of all sequences a_o^T) is

$$\int v(a_o^T, R)\, dF(a_o^T; a_o^o, R) = V(R; a_o; v, F),$$

say. The rule $R = \hat{R}$ that maximizes this expression will depend on a_0, v and F. As in the three-phase case, the problem is to find how certain classes of rules (certain networks and procedures) correspond to certain classes of tasks – or, more generally, to certain classes of net gain functions – and to certain classes of distribution of external conditions.

2.12. *Procedures and Networks*

In the problem defined so far, one seeks to determine what each member has to do or to communicate in response to observations he makes and to messages he receives. Which are the members from whom he can receive and to whom he can send messages is a given not an unknown of this problem. The unknown of the problem is, in other words, the best *procedure* (the rule R), given the *network* of communication. The other givens are the cost c of sending a message; the gross payoff function u depending on certain action variables and observables; and the probability distribution F of the observables.

In a more complete team problem (it may be called the problem of the team's *constitution*), the network is not given. In addition to the cost c of sending a message over an existing network (cost of using the network) there is the cost $C = C(N)$ of constructing a network N. More precisely, if the team is a three-phase-team, $C(N)$ is the cost of maintaining and amortizing communication facilities per period of time needed to go through its three phases. The cost C depends on the nature of the network N – involving, for example, one-way communications (letters), two-way communications (telephone), many-way communications (conferences) between certain members. C does not depend on whether certain communication lines are or are not being used, i.e., on whether a message is or is not actually sent.

Given, then, the cost c of sending a message; given the function $C(N)$ determining for each network the cost of maintaining and operating it; and given the functions u and F, the constitutional problem seeks to find simultaneously the best pair (N, R), i.e., the network and the procedural rule such that the expected net payoff be a maximum. The procedural rule R consists, in three-phase teams, of the communication rule R^{I} and the action rule R^{II}. The unknowns of the complete team problem are: N, R^{I} and R^{II}.

Note that the concept of network does not confine itself to the physical communication plant. The description of a given network (also called 'organization chart') states all the permanent 'positions' within the team, thus including all long-term employment contracts, all regularly occurring conferences (but not emergency conferences), periodical reports (but not *ad hoc* reports), etc. The number of team members is thus itself a characteristic of the team, and the optimal size of a team for a given task – i.e., for a given function $u(a, x)$ – is a part of the constitutional problem.

The distinction between network and procedure is analogous to the economists' distinction between long-run decisions (such as building a plant) and short-run decisions (such as buying a certain amount of fuel). Although important intermediate cases exist, the distinction is useful at the present stage of analysis.

One way to study the complete team problem is to start with 'pure network problems' and 'pure procedural problems'. In pure procedural problems, the network is given. Hence the function $C(N)$ (costs of maintaining a network) is not involved, but the cost c of sending a message is. The unknowns of the pure procedural problem are (in three-phase teams): the communication rule R^{I} and the action rule R^{II}.

In pure network problems, on the other hand, the network N is not given, and the cost c of sending a message is assumed negligible. Therefore, any communication line if it exists can be assumed to be used, so that R^{I} is uniquely defined for each N. The unknowns of the pure network problem are (in three-phase teams): the action rule R^{II} and the network N.

Section 3 of the present paper can be said to deal with a pure network problem, although in a very rudimentary form. A somewhat more detailed analysis of pure network problems and of complete team problems has been attempted elsewhere: see [12], [14]. Section 4 starts with a pure procedural and ends with a constitutional problem of a very simple nature.

3. Buying Information

3.1. *The Value of an Inquiry*

Some important aspects of the team problem are brought out in the following simple case. A person's profit (utility) is $u(a, x)$ where a is his action and x is the state of environment (an element of the set X). The person knows the distribution $F(x)$. Assuming that he tries to maximize expected profit, how much should he be willing to pay for exact information on x?

Compare the maximum expected profit U under two alternatives: when the person has not inquired, and when he has inquired about the actual value of x. If he has not inquired, he will choose an action which is independent of x and which will maximize the expectation of the profit. This expectation will therefore be

$$U = U_0 = \max_a Eu(a, x).$$

If, on the other hand, the person has inquired about the actual value of x he will be able to choose an action that will maximize the actual profit. The action chosen will depend on x. The actual profit will be $\max_a u(a, x)$. The expectation of profit will be

$$U = U_1 = E \max_a u(a, x).$$

The difference $U_1 - U_0$ can be called w, the value of inquiry:

$$w = E \max_a u(a, x) - \max_a Eu(a, x) \geqslant 0, \tag{3.1.1}$$

for U_1 can never be smaller than U_0.[8]

The statement that an inquiry can never have negative value ('no damage in knowledge!') is easily confirmed as follows. Consider first the case when inquiry has been made. Then to each observed value of x will correspond a best value $\hat{a}$ of the action variable a, viz., the value of a that maximizes $u(a, x)$ for the observed value of x. The relation between x and $\hat{a}$ we can write as $\hat{a}=\hat{\alpha}(x)$. We call the function $\hat{\alpha}$ the best rule of action. Since in applying this rule of action one obtains the highest value of $u(a, x)$ consistent with the observed value of x, the result of applying this rule of action for every x is to obtain a higher expected value of $u(a, x)$ than in applying any other rule of action. We can thus write

$$U_1 = \max_\alpha Eu(\alpha(x), x) = Eu(\hat{\alpha}(x), x),$$

to indicate that the expected utility has been maximized with respect to the *function* α. Note that in the equations just written the symbol a does not appear; the utility u was expressed as depending on x and on the rule of action, α.

Now consider the case when inquiry has not been made. This time the unknown function $\alpha(x)$ degenerates into a single unknown constant, since expected utility has now to be maximized in ignorance of x. We can write

$$U_0 = \max Eu(\alpha(x), x) \quad \text{where} \quad \alpha(x) = \text{unknown constant.}$$

Thus U_1 and U_0 are both obtained by maximizing the same quantity over a set of functions, but in the case of U_0 this set is restricted by the condition that $\alpha(x)$ be a constant. It is clear that if one is restricted in the choice of the rule of action one can never obtain a better result than if one is not so restricted. That is, $U_1 \geqslant U_0$.

3.2. *Example I: 'Guessing the Color'*

The player knows that an urn contains a proportion $p \geqslant \frac{1}{2}$ of black balls, the other balls being red. A ball is drawn from the urn. It is not shown to the player but may be shown to his agent. The player has to state the color of the ball. He wins a dollar if his statement is correct, loses a dollar if it is wrong. How much should he be willing to pay the agent for informing him about the actual drawing?

Solution: If the player would not employ an agent his best action would be to bet on black. This would yield him an expected gain $U_0 = p \cdot 1 + (1-p)(-1) = 2p-1$ dollars. If, on the other hand, he employs an agent, his expected gain is $U_1 = 1$. Hence the player should be willing to pay the agent any amount up to $w = U_1 - U_0 = 2 - 2p$. We call w 'the value of inquiry'.

3.3. *Example II: 'A Monopolist'*

A monopolist sets the price a of his product and produces just enough for the demand. At price a the demand is $hx - ka$ where x is a random variable depending on the public's taste, and k is a positive coefficient. The mean μ and the variance σ^2 of x are both known to the monopolist. For greater convenience, and without loss of generality, the coefficients h and k can be made equal to 2 and 1, respectively, by appropriate choice of units. Then the profit is equal to $a(2x - a)$ minus the cost of production. Assume this cost to be independent of the amount produced. How much can the monopolist pay a market research agency for keeping him informed of current public tastes, i.e., of the actual value of x? (We shall assume that, for the monopolist, utility and profit are identical, i.e., he maximizes expected profit.)

Solution: Since cost is independent of his decision, the monopolist can disregard it. He will maximize the expectation of the quantity $u=a(2x-a)$. If he is ignorant of the actual value of x he chooses the price a so as to maximize $Eu=Ea(2x-a)=a(2\mu-a)$; the chosen price will be $a=\mu$, resulting in an expected profit (disregarding constant cost) $U_0=\mu^2$. If, on the other hand, the monopolist is informed of the actual value of x, he will choose every time the price a so as to maximize $u=a(2x-a)$; i.e., his best best rule of action will be: $a=x$. This yields an expected profit (disregarding cost) $U_1=Ex^2=(\mu^2+\sigma^2)$. Hence the value of inquiry is $w=U_1-U_0=\sigma^2$. Thus the services of the market research agency are the more valuable the stronger the variability of tastes; (although, if the demand were not a linear function of price, the approximate measure of variability would turn out to be not σ^2 but some other parameter of the distribution of x). I shall not subscribe to a newspaper if the news does not vary much from day to day!

3.4. *Example III: 'A Speculator'.*

Suppose a speculator cannot buy or sell more than one unit of a commodity. Let x be the difference between tomorrow's and today's price. The speculator knows that x is distributed uniformly between $\mu-\rho$ and $\mu+\rho$. How much is it worth for him to foresee exactly the price change, x?

Solution: Suppose first that he is ignorant of x. If the mean, μ (known to him!) is positive his best action is to buy one unit; if μ is negative, the best action is to sell one unit. The expected gain is $U_0=|\mu|$. If, on the other hand, he is informed of the actual value of x his best rule of action is: to buy one unit if x is positive, to sell one unit if x is negative. This yields him a gain $|x|$. To compute the expected gain $U_1=E|x|$ distinguish two cases: (1) if $|\mu|\geqslant\rho$, x has always the same sign and $U_1=E|x|=|\mu|=U_0$; (2) if $|\mu|\leqq\rho$, we have

$$U_1 = E|x| = \frac{1}{2\rho}\left(\int_0^{\mu+\rho} x\,dx + \int_{\mu-\rho}^{0} -x\,dx\right) =$$

$$= \frac{1}{2\rho}\left(\frac{(\mu+\rho)^2}{2} + \frac{(\mu-\rho)^2}{2}\right) = \frac{\mu^2+\rho^2}{2\rho}.$$

Therefore the value of inquiry is

$$(3.4)\qquad w = U_1 - U_0 = \begin{cases} 0 & \text{if } |\mu| \geqslant \rho \\ (|\mu| - \rho)^2/2\rho & \text{if } |\mu| \leqslant \rho. \end{cases}$$

Thus, inquiry is the less valuable the stronger is the known bias $|\mu|$ of the distribution of the price difference x; and the smaller is the range 2ρ of its variation. (See Figure 1.) This is as would be expected on intuitive grounds.

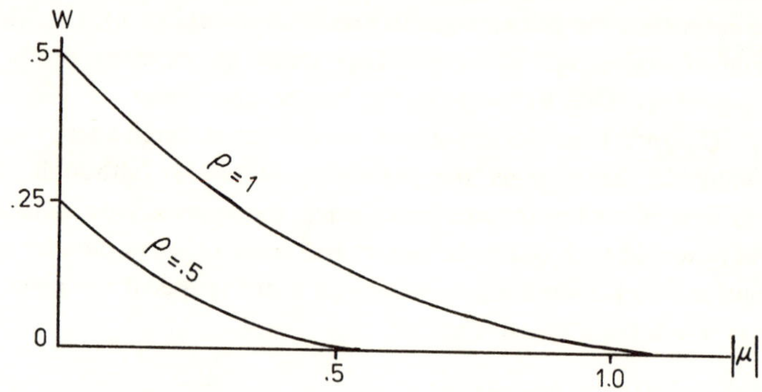

Fig. 1. The 'speculator's case'. Value (w) of inquiry when x is distributed uniformly with mean μ and range 2ρ.

3.4.1. It may be noted that the 'speculator's case' as defined has a more general application than it might appear. Instead of interpreting the extreme values of a as 'buy or sell one unit' one might regard them as 'do or don't'. In fact, any two-valued set of decisions, so frequently occurring in practice, would fit the example, provided u is linear in a; and, only for the sake of simplifying the computations, x, or some transform of it, is assumed to be uniformly distributed. For example $a = +1$ may mean 'attack', $a = -1$ 'don't attack', and x = difference between our forces and those of the enemy. In all these interpretations, since $u = ax$, positive x makes $a = 1$ advisable, and negative x makes $a = -1$ advisable. Clearly, with u linear in a, the choice of action that will maximize the expected value of ax is not affected if the pair $(-1, +1)$ is replaced by $(0, 1)$ or by any other pair of numbers of which the first is smaller than the second.

3.5. *Value of Inquiry and 'Amount of Information'*

Let us now summarize our examples using our general notation.

In the 'monopolist's case', $u=a(2x-a)$ and $F(x)$ has known mean μ and variance σ^2. One obtains

$$U_0 = \max_a Eu = \mu^2\,; \quad (\text{best } a = \mu)\,;$$

$$U_1 = E \max_a u = (\mu^2 + \sigma^2)\,; \quad (\text{best rule of action: } a = x)\,;$$

$$w = \sigma^2\,.$$

In the 'speculator's case', $u=ax$; $-1 \leqslant a \leqslant 1$; $F(x)$ is uniform, the lowest and highest values of x being, respectively, $\mu-\rho$ and $\mu+\rho$. The quantities U_0, U_1, w were evaluated in 3.4 above.

The case of 'guessing the color' is a variant of the speculator's case; $u=ax$; a and x have each only one pair of values (-1 and 1).

Thus, the value of inquiry, w, depends on both the distribution $F(x)$ and the payoff function $u(a, x)$. The amount of information as defined by Shannon [19] (or its negative, the 'entropy' or 'uncertainty' or 'randomness') depends on $F(x)$ only, as does the amount of information defined by R. A. Fisher [7]. As a result, the value of an inquiry, for a given payoff function, need not coincide with, or be related in any simple way to, the amount of uncertainty in Shannon's sense. For example, in 3.2, the value of inquiry (permitting now p to be smaller than $\frac{1}{2}$ and writing $q=1-p$) is $w=1-|p-q|$, while Shannon's uncertainty in the case of binomial distribution is proportionate to the logarithm of $1/p^p q^q$. Note that both expressions have a maximum when $p=\frac{1}{2}$ (maximum uncertainty) and a minimum when $p=1$ or 0 (certainty). If x is uniformly distributed with mean μ and range 2ρ, Shannon's entropy depends on ρ only; while the 'value of inquiry' in the case of such a distribution and assuming the payoff to depend linearly on a bounded action variable a, depends also on the mean, μ, as in (3.4) above. Finally, in our example of 3.3, the value of inquiry is proportional to the variance σ_x^2, for any distribution, while entropy is related to variance in a simple way in the case of normal distribution but not in general.

The concepts of value of inquiry and of amount of information are thus different. They serve different purposes.

4. One observer, one actor: network, procedure, constitution

4.1. *The Problem of 'Buying Information' as a Network Problem*

In 2.13, we distinguished between 'pure network problems', 'pure procedural problems', and complete or 'constitutional' problems. In Section 3 we have dealt with a simple (perhaps the simplest possible) pure network problem. The decision always to obtain information or never to obtain it was supposed to be taken once for all. Such decision defines a network. If the decision is never to receive information, the network chosen is that of a team consisting of a single man, an 'actor', who takes no observations, but always acts in a certain way, that is the best on the average: a 'traditional' or 'routine' system. If the decision is always to receive information, the network chosen can be interpreted in two ways:

(1) as a team consisting of a single man ('observer-actor') who is provided with more or less costly physical facilities for observations, or uses a non-negligible part of his time for observations;

(2) as a two-man team – an actor and an observer – with more or less costly physical facilities for observation *and* communication; in this case, the cost of using the communication line, once such a line is established (or once a fixed, non-negligible part of the team's time is set aside for communication), is negligible, so that the observed value of x is always communicated by the observer to the actor, regardless of the observed value of x (e.g., regardless of whether there is or there is no 'emergency').

4.2. *A Procedural Problem*

Let us, now, consider as given the following network: One member of the team (the 'observer') makes observations on the external world. There is a one-way communication line between him and the other member (the 'actor'). After having made the observation the observer may either communicate or not communicate it to the actor. In the former case, a cost, c dollars, is charged to the team, and the actor chooses his action on the basis of the observation communicated to him. In the latter case no communication cost is charged, but the actor has to choose his action without knowledge of the actual state of the external world. Of course, the probability distribution of the states of the world is assumed to be known in each case.

The problem is: (1) to find the rule of communication for the observer, i.e., to determine conditions (observed states of the world) under which he shall or shall not report to the actor; and (2) to find the rule of action for the actor, i.e., to determine which actions he shall perform upon receiving certain communications or upon receiving none.

Denote as before by X the set of all states of the world x. Let $X \subseteq \mathsf{X}$ be the subset of X such that if the observed state belongs to X, the observer shall send no report. Thus, not to send a report is tantamount to telling the actor that x is in X. The rule of communication can be written as follows (with X yet to find):

$$
\text{(4.2.1)} \quad \begin{aligned} R(x) &= X \quad \text{if} \quad x \in X \quad \text{(no report sent)}; \\ &= x \quad \text{if} \quad x \in \mathsf{X} - X \quad \text{(report sent)}. \end{aligned}
$$

The function R corresponds to R^{I} of Section 2.6. Its value $R(x)$ is the information made available to the actor. The rule of action can be written as follows:

$$
\text{(4.2.2)} \quad \begin{aligned} &\text{Action } a^0 \quad && \text{if} \quad R(x) = X, \quad x \in X \\ &\text{Action } \alpha(x) \quad && \text{if} \quad R(x) = x, \quad x \notin X. \end{aligned}
$$

The action a^0 and the function α are yet to find. a^0 is the action that maximizes the conditional expectation of gross payoff, given that x belongs to X:

$$
\text{(4.2.3)} \quad \max_a \int_X u(a, x)\, dF(x) = \int_X u(a^0, x)\, dF(x).
$$

Thus a^0 does not depend on x. It depends on the set X that the team chooses in advance of observation. We can write $a^0 = a^0(X)$. On the other hand, $\alpha(x)$ is the action that maximizes $u(a, x)$ for given x:

$$
\text{(4.2.4)} \quad \max_a u(a, x) = u[\alpha(x), x], \quad x \in \mathsf{X} - X.
$$

The function α together with the constant a^0 correspond to R^{II} of Section 2.6. Clearly, it is advantageous for the team to have the report withheld whenever the observed x is such that $u[a^0(X), x]$ is larger than $u[\alpha(x), x] - c$. That is, the net expected gain is maximized if X, a^0 and α satisfy the following condition:

$$
\text{(4.2.5)} \quad X = \{x \mid u[a^0(X), x] > u[\alpha(x), x] - c\}.
$$

[This intuitive result can be easily obtained formally by expressing the net expected gain through combining (4.2.3) and (4.2.4).]

4.3. *Example: the Procedural Aspect of the 'Speculator's Problem'*

As in Section 3.4, let $u=ax$, $-1 \leqslant a \leqslant 1$. Then u takes its maximum when a is either -1 or $+1$. $a=1$ may mean 'buying one unit' and $a=-1$ 'selling one unit'. The observable x may mean the predicted price change, and u the profit. Therefore a negative x makes $a=-1$ advisable; a positive x makes $a=+1$ advisable. [As remarked in 3.4.1 above, $a=1$ may also mean 'attack', $a=-1$ may mean 'don't attack', and x may mean 'difference between our forces and those of the enemy'.] To simplify computations, x is assumed to have uniform probability distribution.

The pure network aspect of the team problem given by the described nature of a, x and u was discussed in 3.4 above. We shall now deal with the procedural aspect of the same problem and, later (in 4.5) present the solution of the complete problem of 'best constitution' when a, x and u are as described.

4.4. In our example, the observer finds the actual value of x and may or may not communicate it (at cost c) to the actor who, in either case, has to decide whether to buy or sell one unit. What are the best rules for communication and action, given the (uniform) probability distribution of x? To simplify the problem we shall first assume the mean $\mu=0$, so that $-\rho \leqq x \leqq \rho$.

The communication rule can belong to one of two classes:

r^+: call only if the desirable action $= 1 (=$ 'buy')
r^-: call only if the desirable action $= -1 (=$ 'sell').

Let us first look for the best rule in r^+. Then, if the actor is called, he will choose $a=1$; if he is not called, he will choose $a=-1$. In the notation of Section 4.2,

$$a = \alpha(x) = 1, \quad x \notin X$$
$$a = a^0 = -1, \quad x \in X.$$

Since $u=ax$, condition (4.2.5) defines the best set X as follows: X (the set of observations that are not communicated) shall consist of all x such that

$$-x > x - c, \quad \text{i.e.,} \quad x < c/2.$$

Hence the best communication rule belonging to the class r^+ is: to call whenever $x \geqslant c/2$. The corresponding best action rule is: buy if called, sell if not called.

We find by a similar reasoning that the best communication rule belonging to the class r^- is: to call whenever $x \leqslant -c/2$. The corresponding best action rule is: sell if called, buy if not called.

Using now the known distribution of x, we have to compute the net expected gains (V^+ and V^-, say) obtained under these two competing rules, and choose the rule yielding the higher net expected gain. In our case, we have

$$V^+ = \frac{1}{2\rho}\left[\int_{-\rho}^{c/2} - x\,dx + \int_{c/2}^{\rho} (x-c)\,dx\right], \quad \frac{c}{2} \leqslant \rho$$

$$= 0 \qquad\qquad , \quad \frac{c}{2} \geqslant \rho .$$

$$V^- = \frac{1}{2\rho}\left[\int_{-\rho}^{-c/2} (-x-c)\,dx + \int_{-c/2} x\,dx\right], \quad \frac{c}{2} \leqslant \rho$$

$$= 0 \qquad\qquad , \quad \frac{c}{2} \leqslant \rho .$$

Hence

$$V^+ = V^- = \left(\rho - \frac{c}{2}\right)^2 \Big/ 2\rho, \quad c \leqslant 2\rho$$

$$= 0 \qquad , \quad c \geqslant 2\rho .$$

Thus in our case both rules are equally good and can be summed up as follows: if the cost of communication exceeds or is equal to the range 2ρ of the observable, the observer shall never communicate, and the actor shall take any action he pleases (since the expected gain $=0$ in any case); if the cost of communication is less than 2ρ, then either (1) the observer shall call whenever $x > c/2$, and the actor shall buy whenever called; or (2) the observer shall call whenever $x < -c/2$, and the actor shall sell whenever called. We shall call these rules (1) and (2).

4.5. If we had not assumed uniform distribution of x to be symmetrical (midpoint $\mu = 0$) the two rules would not turn out to be equivalent. In this, more general, case the solution is as follows: If $c/2 \geqq \rho - |\mu|$, never call; buy (sell) if $\mu>0$ (<0), always yielding the expected gain $|\mu|$. If $c/2 \leqq (\rho - |\mu|)$, then apply rule (1), or rule (2) above depending on whether μ is negative or positive (See Figure 2.) This agrees with common sense. If $\mu<0$, then a large positive $x(\geqslant c/2)$ is less likely to occur than a numerically large negative $x(\leqslant -c/2)$; and it is, of course, preferable to pay for signalling rarely rather than frequently.

If, as suggested in 3.4.1, $a=+1$ means 'do' (e.g., 'attack') and $a=-1$ means 'don't', then rule (1) becomes: 'call to encourage doing whenever the situation is very favorable relative to cost of communication ($x>c/2$)'; rule (2) becomes: 'call to warn against doing, whenever the situation is very unfavorable relative to the cost of communication ($x<-c/2$)'. Roughly, if favorable situations are less likely to occur ($\mu<0$), apply rule (1); otherwise, apply rule (2).

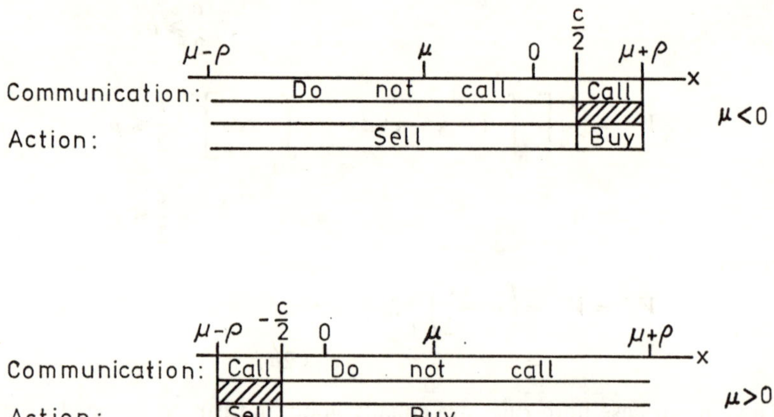

Fig. 2. The 'speculator's case' with one observer. Rules of action and communication ('call' region shaded) when x is distributed uniformly with range 2ρ and with mean μ, negative (above) or positive (below).

If $\mu \neq 0$ and the best appropriate rule is applied, a reasoning similar to that in 4.4 yields the following net expected gain:

$$(4.5.1)\quad V = |\mu| + \left(|\rho - \mu| - \frac{c}{2}\right)^2 \Big/ 2\rho \quad \text{if} \quad \frac{c}{2} \leqslant \rho - |\mu|;$$

$$= |\mu| \qquad \text{otherwise}.$$

4.6. *The 'Constitutional' Problem*

Let the cost of having an observer (per time period needed for one decision) be C. We have now the choice between two networks: one without, the other with observer. In each network the best appropriate rules will be applied. We have thus to choose between two 'constitutions': I) not to have an observer, and let the actor use the best action; II) to have an observer, and to let him apply the best rule of communication while letting the actor apply the best rule of action.

Under Constitution I, the best action is: $a=-1$ if $\mu<0$, $a=1$ if $\mu>0$. This results in a net expected gain $Eax=aEx=a\mu=$

$$V_{\text{I}} = |\mu| .$$

Under Constitution II, the expected gain obtained under the best rules of communication and action was shown in (4.5.1), where the cost c of sending a message but not the cost C of maintaining an observer (per period of time needed for each decision) was taken into account. The expected gain, correcting for this latter cost, is therefore

$$\begin{aligned} V_{\text{II}} &= -C + |\mu| + \left(\rho - |\mu| - \frac{c}{2}\right)^2 \Big/ 2\rho \quad \text{if} \quad \frac{c}{2} \leqslant \rho - |\mu| ; \\ &= -C + |\mu| \quad \text{otherwise}. \end{aligned}$$

Therefore the difference $V_{\text{II}} - V_{\text{I}}$ is positive, and hence Constitution II is preferable to I if the parameters ρ, $|\mu|$, c *and* C obey the conditions

$$\left(\rho - |\mu| - \frac{c}{2}\right)^2 \geqq 2C\rho , \qquad \rho - |\mu| - \frac{c}{2} \geqq 0 ;$$

hence (taking the positive square root because of the second inequality and dividing by ρ):

$$\frac{|\mu|}{\rho} + \frac{c}{2\rho} + \sqrt{\frac{2C}{\rho}} \leqslant 1 .$$

That is, if best rules of action and communication are used, the team shall have an observer only if, relative to the variability (measured by ρ) of external events x, (1) the costs c and C are small and (2) the expectation μ of x is not too far from zero (i.e., if favorable events are not much more, and not much less, likely to occur than unfavorable ones). (See Figure 3.)

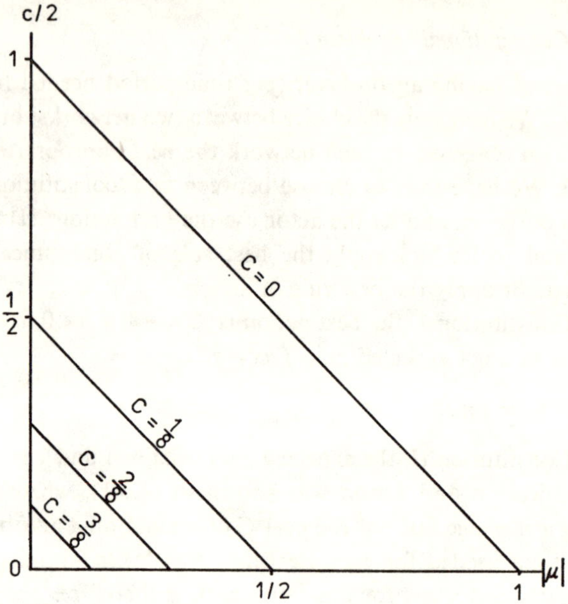

Fig. 3. The 'speculator's case'. Region (triangular) where use of observer is advisable. (With $\rho = 1$ and $C = 0, \frac{1}{8}, \frac{2}{8}, \frac{3}{8}$.)

5. Optimal inexact information

5.1. In Sections 3 and 4 the observer could send either an exact report or none at all. In Section 2, however, the problem was defined more generally. Information can be given with varying degrees of precision.

The organizer of the team can determine in advance a partitioning p of the set X of states of nature into disjoint subsets (possibly infinite in number) which we shall denote by

$$X_p^{(1)}, X_p^{(2)}, \ldots .$$

The observer finds that x belongs to $X_p^{(m)}$, say. He communicates to the actor the index m. This index will thus depend on x, the actual state of nature; and on p, the partitioning chosen in advance. The actor chooses then an action a that will maximize the conditional expectation

$$E\{u(a,x)\mid x\in X_p^{(m)}\}=\frac{\int_{X_p(m)} u(a,x)\,dF(x)}{\int_{X_p(m)} dF(x)},$$

the denominator being the probability that x falls into the subset $X_p^{(m)}$. Hence to the partition p and to the given functions u and F will correspond an expected payoff

$$U=U(\mathsf{p};u,F)=\sum_m \max_a \int_{X_p(m)} u(a,x)\,dF(x).$$

The quantities U_1 and U_0 defined in 3.1 were extreme cases. $U=U_1$ if every $X_p^{(m)}$ consists of a single element of X ('exact information'). $U=U_0$ ('no information') if $X_p^{(1)}=\mathsf{X}$; therefore $U_0=\max_a \int_{\mathsf{X}} u(a,x)\,dF(x)$. We can now define the value of an inquiry corresponding to a particular partition p as

$$w(\mathsf{p})=U(\mathsf{p})-U_0.$$

The actor will be informed into which subset $X_p^{(m)}$ x falls, only if such communication costs less than $w(\mathsf{p})$.

5.2. *Code*

A given partition p determines a 'code', according to which an observed state x will induce a signal $m=m(x)$. The function $m(x)$ may be called a 'code'. The code studied in Section 4 was a two-valued one: either 'call' or 'no call' depending on whether x falls into the one or the other of the two intervals into which X was partitioned. (Figure 2.) A call as well as the absence of a call conveyed to the actor a certain information. We have seen that in order to implement the code two kinds of cost had to be borne: a constant cost C of maintaining the network and a (random) variable cost of using it. The variable cost had two values, c and zero, depending on which of the two signals ('call', 'no call') was used. In a more general case, the variable cost may have more values: at most as many as there are subsets $X_p^{(m)}$.

With the cost thus defined the 'constitutional' problem of Section 4 can be extended as follows: how many observers shall there be in the team, and what codes shall they use? We shall not touch in this paper on a still more general extension that would introduce two or more actors.

Two types of optimal partitions p of the set X present special interest: (1) an optimal system of intervals for each of a given number of observables; (2) an optimal set of observables.

5.3. *Optimal System of Intervals*

If x is a real number, and X an interval, X may be partitioned into subintervals. These may or may not be of equal length. If they are, their number n measures the precision of information. For example, if $n=10^k$, k integer, variations of precision are expressed by the number k of decimal digits. We have then a sequence of partitions: p_k, $k=0, 1,\ldots$. On the lines of (3.1.1) the gross expected utility will increase, or at least not decrease, with increasing precision of information; while the costs of both maintaining and using the network will presumably also increase or at least not decrease. The problem is to find the optimal value of k.

5.3.1. If x is a real vector of, say, d dimensions, $x=(x_1,\ldots, x_d)$, the same principle applies: about each – say the i-th – of the d components, an inquiry of precision k_i can be made. The expected gross payoff as well as the cost will depend on the vector $(k_1,\ldots, k_d)$; and the vector maximizing expected net payoff will be chosen.

5.3.2. As pointed out by L. Törnqvist the optimal code will, in general, consist, for each real variable, of intervals of unequal rather than equal length. (The unequal 'brackets' of published income statistics provide a well known example.) Thus the maximization of net expected payoff will be performed, not with respect to a precision measure k but rather with respect to the code function $m(x)$, as defined in 5.2.

5.4. *Optimal Set of Observables*

Another concept of precision of an inquiry concerning a d-dimensional state of nature $(x_1,\ldots, x_d)$ is determined by the components – not necessarily real numbers – about which information is sought, this information being exact. For example, if x_1 represents future weather and x_2 represents future prices, a farmer may wish to inquire about none or one or both of these, before making a decision on what to plant. Presumably both the gross expected payoff and the cost of maintaining and using the network will increase (or at least not decrease) if, to a given set of observables, an additional observable is added.

5.4.1. If some of the components $(x_1, \ldots, x_d)$ are real numbers, the principles of 5.4 (choosing the variables about which information is sought) can be combined with those of 5.3 (choosing the best system of intervals for each of these variables). If all components are real numbers, 5.3.1 embraces both principles: $k_i = 0$ means that no information is given about the ith component.

5.5. *An Example of Buying Precision*

Consider again the 'monopolist's case' of 3.3:

$$(5.5.1) \quad u = a(2x - a).$$

We have seen that $U_0 = \mu^2$, $U_1 = U_0 + \sigma^2$. To simplify our illustration assume in addition that x is distributed uniformly over the interval $0 \leqq x \leqq \rho$. Then $\mu = \rho/2$, $\sigma^2 = \rho^2/12$, $U_0 = \rho^2/4$, $U_1 = \rho^2/3$. Let us investigate the 'buying of precision', in the sense of 5.3, but without confining ourselves to the case when n, the number of sub-intervals, is 10^k (or 2^k, etc.), where k = the number of decimal (or binary, etc.) digits used. The observer informs the actor about the interval into which x falls. That is, the observer gives the integer m, such that

$$(5.5.2) \quad 1 \leqslant m \leqslant n \quad \text{and} \quad \frac{m-1}{n} \rho \leqslant x \leqslant \frac{m}{n} \rho .$$

Thus m depends on n and x; m is the smallest integer not exceeded by nx/ρ. Upon learning m, the actor chooses an action in the midpoint of the interval: $a = a(m, n) = \rho(m - \frac{1}{2})/n$, since, under our assumptions, this maximizes the conditional expectation

$$E\{u(a, x) \,|\, m - 1 < nx/\rho \leqq m\}$$

which then takes the value

$$U(m, n) = [a(m, n)]^2 = (m - \tfrac{1}{2})^2 \cdot \rho^2/n^2 .$$

Hence, the (non-conditional) expectation of payoff that the actor has if he chooses a degree n of precision is

$$U(n) = \sum_{m=1}^{n} U(m, n)/n =$$
$$= \frac{\rho^2}{n^3}\left[\frac{n(n+1)(2n+1)}{6} - \frac{n(n+1)}{2} + \frac{n}{4}\right] =$$
$$= \rho^2\left(\frac{1}{3} - \frac{1}{12n^2}\right).$$

This agrees with the two extreme cases computed above:

$$U(1) = U_0 = \rho^2/4 \quad \text{(case of 'no inquiry')};$$
$$U(\mathrm{M}) = U_1 = \rho^2/3 \quad \text{(case of 'exact inquiry')}.$$

If the 'value of precision'

$$w(n) = U(n) - U(1) = \rho^2\left(1 - \frac{1}{n^2}\right)\Big/12$$

falls short of the cost of inquiry, inquiry will not be made with that precision.

We might develop our example further by assuming that both the cost and the precision depend on the size of a sample.

5.6. *An Extension to Several Observables*

Let

$$(5.6.1) \qquad u = a\left(2\cdot\sum_{i=1}^{d} \gamma_i x_i - a\right),$$

an extension of (5.5.1), with x_i being distributed uniformly and independently over the interval $0 < x_i \leqslant \rho_i$. Thus γ_i (a positive number) signifies the importance of and ρ_i the uncertainty about the variable x_i. The actor chooses, for each i, the precision n_i: i.e., he asks about the value of m_i that satisfies

$$(5.6.2) \qquad \frac{m_i - 1}{n_i} < x_i \leqslant \frac{m_i}{n_i}\rho_i, \quad i = 1, \dots, \quad .$$

In particular, if $n_i = 1$, no inquiry is made about x_i. Thus we have the situation described in the last sentence of 5.4.1. By a reasoning extending that of 5.5, one can show that the precision n_i for the variable x_i becomes more valuable as its uncertainty ρ_i and/or its importance γ_i increase.

5.7. *The Role of Statistical Dependence*

It can be further conjectured that, the larger the statistical dependence between x_1 and x_2, the smaller is the advantage of learning about both over learning about only one of them. In the example that follows, we drop the assumption of independent distribution of the x's; and we consider only the case – 5.4 – where each variable can be learned either exactly or not at all. Let, as in (5.6.1) (but with γ's all equal)

$$u = a(2x_1 + 2x_2 - a),$$

and assume x_i to be two-valued, with the following probability distribution:

$$(5.7.1)\qquad \begin{array}{c|cc} x_1 \backslash x_2 & 1 & 0 \\ \hline 1 & p_{11} & p_{12} \\ 0 & p_{21} & p_{22} \end{array}$$

If the determinant $p_{11}p_{22}-p_{21}p_{12}$ is denoted by d, and the marginal probabilities by $p_1=p_{11}+p_{12}=1-q_1, p_2=p_{11}+p_{21}=1-q_2$, then the above matrix of probabilities is equal to

$$(5.7.2)\qquad \begin{bmatrix} p_1p_2+d & p_1q_2-d \\ p_2q_1-d & q_1q_2+d \end{bmatrix}.$$

p_iq_i measures the 'uncertainty' about x_i; (it has its maximum for $p_i=\frac{1}{2}$, minimum for $p_i=1$ or 0). d^2 measures the statistical dependence between x_1 and x_2.[9]

Denote the maximum expected payoff by

U_{00} if no inquiry is made
U_{11} if inquiry is made on x_1 and x_2
U_{10} if inquiry is made on x_1 only
U_{01} if inquiry is made on x_2 only.

Then $$U_{00}=\max_a Eu=[E(x_1+x_2)]^2=(p_1+p_2)^2$$

$$(5.7.3)\qquad U_{11}=E\max_a u=E(x_1+x_2)^2=U_{00}+p_1q_1+p_2q_2+2d.$$

To compute U_{10}, write

$$\max_a a[-a+2E(x_1+x_2 \mid x_1=1)] = [E(x_1+x_2 \mid x_1=1)]^2 = u_1;$$

$$\max_a a[-a+2E(x_1+x_2 \mid x_1=0)] = [E(x_1+x_2 \mid x_1=0)]^2 = u_0,$$

say. Then $U_{10}=u_1p_1+u_0q_1$ and therefore

$$(5.7.4) \quad U_{11} = U_{10} + p_2q_2 - \frac{d^2}{p_1q_1}.$$

We see from (5.7.3) that the value of inquiring about both variables, compared with no inquiry at all, is the larger the larger the uncertainty p_iq_i about each variable. We see from (5.7.4) that the advantage of inquiring about both variables, compared with inquiring about one only is the larger the larger those uncertainties and the smaller the statistical dependence (d^2) between the two variables. I am not going to subscribe to a second newspaper if it mainly repeats what the first paper says, or if it always says the opposite! [As to the role of the algebraic value of d in (5.7.3), and, hence, of positive vs. negative correlation, this has probably to do with the concave nature of the assumed payoff function u with respect to a. But this is only a conjecture.]

6. Concluding Remark

The results obtained in our various examples seem to agree with common sense, but, I think, only with common sense revealed by hindsight, except possibly for those 'exact minds who feel by a sort of instinct' who appeared in the quotation from Laplace in note 1 of this paper. I may remind the reader that the problems solved here surely belong to the simplest team problems that one can imagine. As the networks and the payoff functions become more complex, as statistical dependence between observables is introduced, as non-additive costs are admitted, as the simple three-phase models are abandoned in favor of models permitting feedbacks, etc., unarmed common sense will become more and more powerless, and precise logical analysis more and more necessary. Even though such analysis will always have to use simplified models while reality includes many "things that cannot be submitted to calculus, it gives the surest hints that can guide us in our judgment... and teaches us to avoid illusions that ofttimes confuse us."

NOTES

* Research undertaken by the Cowles Commission for Research in Economics under contract Nonr.-358 (01), NR 047-006 with the Office of Naval Research. The bulk of the paper was written in December 1952. Its revision in August 1953 was part of the author's work at the Institute for Numerical Analysis under a contract between the National Bureau of Standards and the University of California, supported in part by the Air Research and Development Command, USAF.

Acknowledgments are due to Gerard Debreu, Roy Radner, and Leo Törnquist, of the Cowles Commission staff. The author owes much to earlier discussions with Alan Newell, Joseph Kruskal, and C. B. Tompkins.

1 Laplace adds: "it makes us appreciate with exactitude that which exact minds feel by a sort of instinct without being able ofttimes to give a reason for it... . Even in the things that cannot be submitted to calculus, it gives the surest hints that can guide us in our judgment... and teaches us to avoid the illusions that ofttimes confuse us."

2 Note: an ordering G_i on **s** is said to be complete if it has the following two properties: (a) if s, s', s'' are in **s** then sG_is' and $s'G_is''$ imply sG_is'' (transitivity); (b) if s and s' are in **s** then sG_is' or $s'G_is$ (completeness). If (a) but not (b) is satisfied, the ordering G_i is said to be partial.

3 See G. Debreu [4].

4 See [14], [10].

5 See [17], [10].

6 In an earlier paper a different definition of orders was given. An order was defined as a message restricting the actions of the subordinate to a certain subset of possible actions. The present definition resulted from discussions with Roy Radner and Herbert Simon.

7 See L. Hurwicz [8].

8 This is easily shown formally for the case when x takes discrete values x_i with probabilities p_i ($i=1, 2, \ldots$). By definition

$$\max_a u(a, x_i) \geqq u(a, x_i) \quad \text{for all} \quad a, i.$$

Multiplying by p_i (all non-negative) and summing over i:

$$\sum_i p_i \max_a u(a, x_i) \geqslant \sum_i p_i\, u(a, x_i) \quad \text{for all} \quad a$$

$$E \max_a \; u(a, x) \geqslant E\, u(a, x) \quad \text{for all} \quad a.$$

The last relation holds also when a on the right side takes the value that maximizes $Eu(a, x)$. This proves (3.1.1). Briefly, the average of maxima cannot be smaller than the maximum average.

9 A suggestion by R. Radner.

BIBLIOGRAPHY

[1] Bavelas, A., 'Communication Patterns in Task-Oriented Groups', *Policy Sciences* (ed. by H. D. Lasswell and D. Lerner).

[2] Beckmann, M., 'On Marschak's Model of an Arbitrage Firm', Abstract in *Econometrica* (April 1953), 347 (see also [21] below).

[3] Bush, R., Hays, and McEachern, A. W., 'A Mathematical Model for Two-Person Interactions', December 5, 1951. Laboratory of Social Relations, Harvard University (mimeographed).
[4] Debreu, G., 'Representation of a Preference Ordering by a Numerical Function'.
[5] Dvoretzky, A., Kiefer, J., and Wolfowitz, J., 'The Inventory Problem: II. Case of Unknown Distributions of Demand', *Econometrica* (July 1952).
[6] Faxèn, K., 'Incentive Functions and the Arbitrage Firm', *Cowles Commission Discussion Paper* Economics 2059, November 24, 1952 (hectographed). See also abstract in *Econometrica*, April 1953, p. 346.
[7] Fisher, R. A., 'The Logic of Inductive Inference', *Journal of the Royal Statistical Society* (1935). (Reprinted in R. A. Fisher's *Contributions to Mathematical Statistics*, New York 1950.)
[8] Hurwicz, L., 'Theory of Economic Organization', *Econometrica*, (July 1951) p. 54. Abstract of paper.
[9] Laplace, 'A Philosophical Essay on the Theory of Probabilities', Translation by Truscott and Emory. 1902. p. 196.
[10] Marschak, J., 'Probability in the Social Sciences', 1954, *Selected Essays*, 4.
[11] Marschak, J., 'Organized Decision-Making', *Colloques Internationaux du Centre National de la Recherche Scientifique* **40**, Econometrie, Colloque du Mai 1952, pp. 201–211. Paris, 1953.
[12] Nash, J., 'The Bargaining Problem', *Econometrica* (April 1950).
[13] Nash, J., 'Two-Person Cooperative Games', *Econometrica* (January 1953).
[14] Marschak, J. and Radner, R., 'The Firm as a Team', *Cowles Commission Discussion Paper* Economics 2093 (hectographed).
[15] Rashevsky, N., *Mathematical Biology of Social Behavior*, p. 33.
[16] von Neumann, J. and Morgenstern, O., *Theory of Games and Economic Behavior*, 1944.
[17] Savage, L. J., *Foundations of Statistics*, John Wiley and Sons, 1954.
[18] Schumpeter, J., *Hauptinhalt und Wesen der theoretischen Nationaloekonomie*, 1908.
[19] Shannon, C. and Weaver, W., *The Mathematical Theory of Communication*, 1949.
[20] Simon, H., 'A Formal Theory of Employment Relationship', *Econometrica* (1951) 293–305.
[21] Kiefer, J. and Orey, P., 'On the Arbitrage Problem', *Cowles Commission Discussion Paper*, Economics 2068, February 1953.

21

ELEMENTS FOR A THEORY OF TEAMS*

(1955)

1. The problem of organizations

Organizations have been often compared with machines: armies and navies have been called 'fighting machines'. A machine is built to fulfill a task. So is a military organization, a government, a business firm.

Living organisms have also been compared with machines, each having presumably the task of achieving a high probability of survival and of reproduction. The organic forms which are by and large best fit for a given environment have been selected in the course of millions of years. Man-made organizations are much younger, and changes in their environment have been rapid. It is hard to believe that these machines, the human organizations as they exist today, could not be fitted better to their environment. To construct and improve machines, is the subject of technology: a normative and not merely descriptive science.

Just as the technology of ordinary machines (and, for that matter, the technology of organisms: e.g. medicine) is helped by the use of well-defined scientific concepts, so might be the technology of human organizations. The modern naval vessel as a highly efficient inanimate machine would not exist if Newton had not, 250 years ago, laid down his clear definitions of mass and force, to supersede the vague and confused concepts of so-called common sense. But what about the 'animated' part of the ship, the group of men that decide what to do with those bits of metal and rubber? Is it possible to analyze the ship's organization (and also the organization in charge of its logistic support, and, in principle, any other organization) by hitting upon a system of concepts that is truly essential and, ultimately, useful? No one trained in science or engineering can get much satisfaction from the analysis of complicated organization problems as they are presented in an administration manual or a business school textbook even when the author is a practical genius of organization. Practical intuition is not teachable: genius cannot be transmitted. But science can be taught and transmitted.

Just as pre-Newtonian physicists talked of 'force' in terms of confused common sense, so do we today talk of 'line vs. staff', 'communication vs. command', 'authority and responsibility' – concepts that are ambiguous just because everyone thinks he understands them, and everyone understands them differently. Chemistry would not have advanced if it had used the language of cookbooks. Of the social sciences, economics owes its progress and usefulness to the (comparative!) clarity of its concepts.

Recent attempts to analyze organization problems in a scientific manner were stimulated by the classical economic theory of the firm (Walras, Marshall) and by the newer theories of statistical decision functions (Neyman, Wald), the theory of games (von Neumann and Morgenstern), and the theory of communications (Wiener, Shannon). The Office of Naval Research, and especially its Logistics Branch, has encouraged this development.[1] The task is big and can be carried out only step by step. The first step has been to study a particularly simple form of organization which we call a team.

2. Teams

We define a team as a group of persons each of whom takes decisions about something different but who receive a common reward as the joint result of all those decisions.

In a business firm, for example, one of the executives is in charge of production, another is in charge of sales, or of personnel, of financing and so on. Their separate decisions in these various fields result jointly in the firm's profit. In a fleet or a civilian government agency, the joint result of the decisions of the several officers is the larger or smaller success score in accomplishing a task.

In discussing teams, we abstract from special interests of its members. We thus eliminate, at this stage of our inquiry, the difficult problems of bargaining and of incentives, problems raised but not solved by the young theory of games between two or more persons. [In fact, in terms of that theory, our 'team' (for example, a pair of partners in the game of bridge) is a single person!]

Clearly, the team's success score depends not only on the members' decisions but also on the external situation not under their control. A table that describes how the score is determined by all decisions and all external conditions is called 'gross score table' (or gross score function, a function of as many variables as there are decision makers plus the number of situation variables). It is exemplified in Table I, below.

3. Information

Further, it is clear that people should be able to take better (or at least not worse) decisions, if they know much about the external situation than if they know little. But to keep each member of the team in precise knowledge about everything that is relevant to the team as a whole, the team would have to incur heavy costs of information. For it would have to maintain and operate a vast network of observation posts and communication links (besides running the risks of garbling and interception of messages, and of congestion of data on the desk or in the head of the decision maker; these we shall not discuss here, or shall consider included in the 'cost').

Accordingly, when each executive of a business firm makes his decision he bases it not only on those facts known to them all, such as, for example, the data on the general financial prospects of the firm, as circularized from a center or pieced together at a conference. He bases his decision also on his special or local information. Moreover, some data he needs to know precisely; others, only approximately. I presume (as a layman) the same is true of a fleet. It is not necessary for every officer to be informed about everything.

This is precisely the problem that faces the organizer of a team: How to balance the advantages of fuller information against its cost. The more information at the disposal of each member the higher is the *gross* success score of the team. From this, the cost of information is to be deducted. A team is efficient if the *net* score is maximized.

Further: The information at the basis of each decision may be the knowledge of some *constants* – e.g., of the laws of physics or of naval tactics, learned by the engineer or admiral, in school and through experience. But, in addition, one needs information about the ever *varying situation*: for example, about tomorrow's weather and market prices, in the business of farming; about local requirements for gasoline, in the logistic problem of multi-branch storage; about the weather and the enemy dispositions in various parts of the sea, in the business of naval fighting.[2]

In this article, we shall concentrate on information in the sense of those day-to-day random variations. We shall assume that the organizer of the team knows all the relevant physical (or military) constants. This implies that he knows with what *probabilities* the weather or prices of local gas requirements, or enemy's dispositions, etc. will be such-and-such rather than so-and-so – as exemplified in Table II. He also knows the gross score table (such as Table I, already mentioned). Therefore he can compute the *expected gross score*. This is the gross score that would be obtained in the long-run average, if each team member would be given a certain specified part of the information and would respond to it according to some specified *decision rule* ('do this if you learn that'). He also knows the *cost* of conveying those specified parts of information (a cost that, too, may depend on the external situation). Thus, the *expected net score* can be computed for any given system of communication and any given set of decision rules.

Hence the *team problem*: find the best communication system and the best decision rules, given the gross score table, the probabilities of situations, and the cost of communication.

4. Scoring

We have assumed that the success of the team can be scored on the scale that has the following property: a higher expected net score is to be preferred to a lower one. Such a scale is called 'utility scale' by economists; while, I believe, soldiers and sailors speak of 'military worth'. In the simplest case the scale may have just two points: '1' for success (however large), '0' for failure (however disastrous). In this case the expected score is identical with the probability of success (because it is equal to 1 times this probability, *plus* 0 times the probability of failure). But more detailed scales are in use by decision-makers and organizers of teams, albeit often only semi-consciously. They are mostly guided by some numerical facts, taken singly or in combination: dollars; casualties; weapons or territory taken or lost; finally the estimated gain or loss in the 'posture' – i.e., in the probability of success of some super-team such as the nation itself, – for example in the probability of national victory.

In this short paper the author will permit himself to skip the difficult problem of actual scoring, and of how to train responsible people to think in scores. He states the hope that tables expressing the score as a function of decisions and situations will become a recognized tool.

5. Simple models

In the meantime, let us construct such tables hypothetically, and study their implications, step by step. Admittedly, such simple models are highly unrealistic. Bodies falling in a vacuum or deprived of dimensions were simple models too. To calculate the capacity of a bridge represented by a web of geometric lines seems also unrealistic. Yet, such abstractions have created useful clarity where there was confusion. This is encouraging.

6. A two-member team

Let a team consist of just two members (call them I and II), each having to decide whether 'to act' in some unique way, or "not to act": for example, whether or not to attack the enemy. We thus have two two-valued *decision-variables*. Further, let x_1 and x_2 be two *situation variables*: for example, the strength of enemy forces near the first and near the second team member, respectively. Finally, suppose that each situation variable can take three values: 'unfavorable to us' (denoted by $-$), 'favorable to us' (denoted by $+$), and 'medium' (denoted by 0); thus, $-$, $+$, and 0 may correspond to the enemy in a given locality being strong, weak, or of medium strength. A particularly simple gross score function is represented on Table I.

Since we shall have to compute expected scores, we need to know the probability with which each of the $3 \times 3 = 9$ situations can occur. On Table II a probability distribution is assumed that will make our computations and our reasoning simple and without tears.

Clearly, if each member were informed about the enemy forces in *both* locations, the team's expected score would be highest if negative scores were avoided altogether, each member obeying the following *decision rule*: 'act only if the situation is $(+, +)$ or $(+, 0)$ or $(0, +)$', the first sign in each pair referring to the first, and the second sign to the second situation variable (in words: 'act if at least one of the variables is favorable'). We call this a *good decision rule* because it earns the highest expected gross score, viz. (multiplying scores in Table I with probabilities in

TABLE I[a]

Gross scores without interaction

x_1		x_2					
		II doesn't act			II acts		
		−	0	+	−	0	+
I doesn't act	−	0	0	0	−20	−10	0
	0	0	0	0	−10	0	10
	+	0	0	0	0	10	20
I acts	−	−20	−10	0	−40	−20	0
	0	−10	0	10	−20	0	20
	+	0	10	20	−20	20	40

[a] The algebraically inclined reader will have noticed that we have assumed the gross score to be equal to $(d_1 + d_2)(x_1 + x_2)$, where the d's stand for decision variables and can take values 0 and 1, and the x's stand for situation variables and can take values −10, 0 and +10. I chose this very special function (and generalize it only slightly in Table VI by adding an 'interaction' term), to make the exposition easy. Much insight into the general nature of the team problem has been obtained by Radner who studied the implications of a score function quadratic in the '*decision vector*' $(d_1, \ldots, d_m)$, with coefficients depending on a random '*situation vector*' $(x_1, \ldots, x_n)$.

TABLE II

Probability distribution of situations

x_1	x_2: −	0	+
−	.1	.1	.1
0	.1	.2	.1
+	.1	.1	.1

Table II):

$$(40)(0.1) + (20)(0.1) + (20)(0.1) + (0)(0.7) = 8 .$$

No decision rule is better though some are as good, e.g. the rule 'don't act if the situation is (−, −), (−, 0) or (0, −)'.

This was easy. So is the opposite extreme case, when, instead of both commanders being all-knowing, they are both fully ignorant of the situation. Then the following rules are both good: 'always act', and 'never act'. Both earn the same expected gross score, zero.

These were special cases. Generally each team member has information different from the other's. Each can be informed on: (1) x_1 and x_2; (2) x_1 only; (3) x_2 only; (4) nothing. There are thus $4 \times 4 = 16$ '*information structures*', each defined by 'who knows what'. For each information structure, a good decision rule for each member has to be found, and thus the maximum expected gross score computed for the team.

This is simple when the score table is like Table I, where the team's score can be regarded as the sum of partial scores contributed by the members independently of each other (the scores earned by both members' acting are simply the double of those earned by a single member's acting). In such a case we say that there is *no interaction between decisions*. Table III states, accordingly, a good decision rule and the maximum expected partial score for any of the two members taken separately.

We can use these results to obtain, in Table IV, the total gross expected score for the team, in the case of each of the 16 possible information structures.

TABLE III

When the member knows:	Then a good decision rule is:	And his partial expected gross score is:
Nothing	Never act	0
x_1	Act if $x_1 = +$	$(10)(0.1) + (20)(0.1) = 3$
x_2	Act if $x_2 = +$	$(10)(0.1) + (20)(0.1) = 3$
x_1 and x_2	Act if x_1 or $x_2 = +$	$(10)(0.1) + (20)(0.1) + (10)(0.1) = 4$

TABLE IV

Team's gross expected score for each of the 16 information structures
(Each entry shows the two contributions and their sum)

If I Knows:	And if II Knows			
	Nothing	x_1	x_2	x_1 and x_2
Nothing	$0+0=0$	$0+3=3$	$0+3=3$	$0+4=4$
x_1	$3+0=3$	$3+3=6$	$3+3=6$	$3+4=7$
x_2	$3+0=3$	$3+3=6$	$3+3=6$	$3+4=7$
x_1 and x_2	$4+0=4$	$4+3=7$	$4+3=7$	$4+4=8$

We have now to allow for the *cost of information.* In our simplest model, we shall identify the communication system with a *network* consisting of two (or one, or none) observation posts, each attached to one of the team members, and of a communication link (one-way, or two-way or none) between the team members. As information cost we consider, at the present stage, simply the expense of maintaining the necessary personnel and equipment, regardless of how often it is used. In particular take the case where it is prohibitively costly, or impossible, for member I to observe x_2 and for member II to observe x_1; while the observation cost of x_1 by I, and of x_2 by II, is the same. In that case, only six out of the 16 information structures of Table IV need to be considered; the other 10 being either the mirror-images of the six (our assumptions on score function, probabilities, and costs being symmetrical) or being prohibitively expensive. These six are generated by networks listed in Table V, where an arrow → indicates the direction of one-way communication (mail), and ↔ indicates two-way communication (telephone); '□' means 'no observation' and '×' means 'observation', the left of each pair of symbols corresponding to member I and variable x_1, and the right to II and x_2. Thus '× □' means 'I observes x_1, II observes nothing'; and '× → □' means 'I observes x_1 and tells II; II observes nothing'. The resulting information structure is given in the second and third column of Table V.

Thus, in our model (as also summarized in the last column of Table VIII), to add one observation post, i.e. to replace (a) by (b) or (b) by (c), will pay only if it costs less than 3 score units. To set up a one-way communication line from a team member who has an observation post to

TABLE V

Six simple networks

Network	Information structure: I knows	Information structure: II knows	Gross expected score (from Table IV)
(a) □ □	Nothing	Nothing	0
(b) × □	x_1	Nothing	3
(c) × ×	x_1	x_2	6
(d) × → □	x_1	x_1	6
(e) × → ×	x_1	x_1 and x_2	7
(f) × ↔ ×	x_1 and x_2	x_1 and x_2	8

another who has none, i.e. to replace (b) by (d), will only pay if a one-way communication line costs less than 3 units. But if both have observation posts, the advantage of setting up a one-way communication between them, replacing (c) by (e), is only 1 unit; and the advantage of replacing one-way (e) by two-way (f) communication is also 1 unit.

7. Interaction between Decisions

A more general and realistic model will take account of the usual advantage of coordination between members, the disadvantage of their being out of step. To put it more precisely: the effect of one man's decision on the team's score depends on what the other man has decided to do. We call this dependence, *interaction*. The Score Table VI is constructed from Table I by adding 4 units to the team's score when both members act (e.g., attack) or both don't; otherwise, the team pays a penalty of 4 units.

How will the presence of interaction affect the choice of the most efficient network? To answer this, we have again to find the good decision rules. They are given in Table VII, where the expected gross score for the team is shown, assuming as before the probabilities from Table II (the

TABLE VI[a]

Gross scores (with interaction)

	x_1	x_2					
		II doesn't act			II acts		
		–	0	+	–	0	+
I doesn't act	–	4	4	4	–24	–14	–4
	0	4	4	4	–14	–4	6
	+	4	4	4	–4	6	16
I acts	–	–24	–14	–4	–36	–16	4
	0	–14	–4	6	–16	4	24
	+	–4	6	16	4	24	44

[a] We can now generalize the formula for the score function given in the footnote to Table I. In both Tables, I and VI, the gross score $=(x_1+x_2)(d_1+d_2)+C.(d_1-\frac{1}{2})(d_2-\frac{1}{2})$, with $C=0$ in Table I, and $C=16$ in Table VI. Thus interaction has shown itself through the presence of a product of the decision variables in the score function; and the coefficient C expresses the strength of interaction.

TABLE VII

Effect of interaction

Network	When coordination premium $= \pm 4$ (as in Table III)			When coordination premium $= 0$ (as in table I): Gross expected score (from Table V)
	Good decision rule		Gross expected score	
	Member I shall act	Member II shall act		
(a) □ □	Never	Never	4.0	0.0
(b) × □	Only if $x_1 = +$	Never	4.6	3.0
(c) × ×	Only if $x_1 = +$	Only if $x_2 = +$	6.8	6.0
(d) × → □	Only if $x_1 = +$	Only if $x_1 = +$	10.0	6.0
(e) × → ×	Only if $x_1 = +$	Only if $x_1 = +$ or $x_1 = 0$, $x_2 = +$	10.2	7.0
(f) × ↔ ×	Only if $x_1 = +$ or $x_2 = +$ or both $= 0$	Only if $x_1 = +$ or $x_2 = +$ or both $= 0$	12.0	8.0

TABLE VIII

Advantage of setting up:	Explanation	Case of interaction	Case of no interaction
First observation post	(b)–(a)	.6	3
Second observation post	(c)–(b)	2.2	3
One-way communication line	(d)–(b)	5.4	3
One-way communication line	(e)–(c)	3.4	1
Second-way communication line	(f)–(e)	1.8	1

reader will be able to check), and is compared with the corresponding score in the absence of interaction. The interesting thing is to see (on Table VIII) how the presence of interaction affects the importance of certain changes in the network. The role of communication is increased, that of direct observations diminished.

8. Dependence between situation variables

The need for communication would be also enhanced through another kind of change in the conditions of the problem. If the dependence between the situation variables was decreased (so that it would be more difficult to predict x_2 on the basis of information on x_1, than in our model so far), then communications would become more worthwhile. In fact, on Table II, the variables were not independent: if $x_1=0$, the chance that x_2 also $=0$ is $\frac{1}{2}$; but if x_1 is not $=0$, the chance that $x_2=0$ is only $\frac{1}{3}$. We leave to the reader to show that communication becomes more profitable if Table II is replaced by Table IX (where the variables are completely independent) and less profitable if it is replaced by, for example, Table X (where there is a stronger dependence between variables than in II). This, of course, is what common sense would expect.

Three probability distributions

x_1 \ x_2	TABLE IX			TABLE II (repeated)			TABLE X		
	–	0	+	–	0	+	–	0	+
–	$\frac{1}{9}$	$\frac{1}{9}$	$\frac{1}{9}$	.1	.1	.1	.2	.1	0
0	$\frac{1}{9}$	$\frac{1}{9}$	$\frac{1}{9}$	.1	.2	.1	.1	.2	.1
+	$\frac{1}{9}$	$\frac{1}{9}$	$\frac{1}{9}$	.1	.1	.1	0	.1	.2

9. Degree of uncertainty about a variable

Another common sense hunch would also be easy to confirm numerically: if a variable fluctuates only little, it is not worthwhile to pay for observing it. The reader may check this if he interprets Table I as follows (see footnote to that table): each man's action contributes to the team's score the amount x_1+x_2, where x_1 and x_2 can each take the values: $-10, 0, 10$. Suppose now that x_1 can still take the same values, but the values of x_2 have doubled and are: $-20, 0, 20$. The spread of x_2, the average error in predicting it, has increased. Then the worth of knowing x_2 becomes larger than that of knowing x_1; whereas on Table III (and IV) they were equal.[3]

10. Good network vs. good code

So far our team problem was: given the gross score table, the probabilities of situations and the cost of various networks, find simultaneously a good network and a good set of decision rules appropriate to it: see, for example, Table VII. In this problem, the team economizes on some information costs by keeping its members informed possibly of some but (in general) not all situation variables: see the 16 different 'information structures' of Table IV. However, the concept of information structure can be enlarged, to mean that the team members' knowledge is, in general, not only not complete (i.e., does not embrace all situation variables relevant to the team) but also not precise. For example: 'the wind is in NW direction', rather than 'so and so many degrees, minutes and seconds'. We may call such communication a 'coded' one: a code replaces a whole set of values (in our case, all the directions contained in a 45° angle) by a single symbol. Coding may mean economy. Our problem becomes: to find simultaneously a good network, a good code and a good decision rule.

For example, assume again the score function of Table I, and suppose two observation posts and a two-way communication line (telephone) exist already (and therefore cost nothing) but it costs the commanders' valuable time to use the line. Each of them upon having observed 'his' situation variable can either act on his own, or not act, or call up the other member; in the latter case, the two decide either to act or not to act. Note the 'coding': if member I does not call up, this very fact conveys some information to II, at no cost to the team. The question is: *when* shall each partner call up, or not call up (and, in the latter case, shall he act or not)?

What would your common sense tell you: shall he phone to warn (when the situation on his front is bad)? Or to encourage (when it is good)? Or to inquire (when it is intermediate)? Try it on your friends: you will receive widely different answers. Common sense does not seem to help here. The author addressed himself to C. B. Tompkins who, with the help of the SWAC computer of the Institute for Numerical Analysis (then with the National Bureau of Standards), has found the following good rules of decision and communication (Table XI, with 'mirror-images' eliminated).

11. Towards greater realism

Of the necessary extensions of the problem, the extension to an arbitrary number of team members and of situation variables, and to general score functions and probability distributions is mathematically feasible.[4] More serious is the lack of a theory of determination of costs of networks and codes.[5]

A realistic theory of teams would be dynamic. It takes time to process

TABLE XI[a]

Good rules as to when a member shall 'Act', do nothing ('not') or phone ('ph')

	If the communication											
	costs 4 or more						costs 4 or less					
	I shall, whenever $x_1=$			II shall, whenever $x_2=$			I shall, whenever $x_1=$			II shall, whenever $x_2=$		
	–	0	+	–	0	+	–	0	+	–	0	+
Rule 1	not	not	act	not	not	act	not	not	ph	not	not	act
Rule 2	not	not	act	not	act	act	not	act	ph	ph	not	act
Rule 3							not	ph	act	not	ph	act
Rule 4							ph	ph	act	act	act	act
Rule 5							ph	act	act	ph	act	act

[a] The assumed probability distribution was that of Table I (thus x_1 and x_2 are assumed independent). A solution, though not a quite complete one, of the analogous case, when x_1 and x_2 are continuous and thus can take *any* values (with equal probability) within a given interval, was obtained by J. Kiefer and S. Orey, Cowles Commission Discussion Paper, Economics 2068 (mimeographed).

and pass messages along a chain of team members; and messages must include not only information on external variables but also information on what has been done by other members of the team. Problems of feedback (with 'checking-up' or 'inspection' as an important variety) may arise. Further, probability distributions, score functions, and costs are seldom known at the time when the team is set up; rather, knowledge about them is acquired gradually, while the team already proceeds with decisions.

These facts make the dynamic team problem similar to those in cybernetics and in sequential statistical analysis. Earlier in this paper we have also mentioned the game-theoretical nature of the problems that would arise if we had not deliberately abstracted from the diversity of interests of the individual members of an organization: another gap to be filled by a realistic theory.

Theory apart, much empirical work is needed to get an insight into the constants of the problem, such as the score functions, the probability distributions, the communication costs that do occur in real organizations. In addition, those organizations that can be presumed to have already developed into approximately efficient ones, through the experience, clear thinking, and intuition of their leaders, may provide not only the constants but also the (approximate) solutions of their team problems. Thus theory can be checked against facts. Most likely the leaders of efficient organizations are not averse to an articulate and unambiguous language of the serious research worker and would cooperate in the task of putting empirical flesh on the bones of abstraction.

NOTES

* Research undertaken by the Cowles Commission for Research in Economics under contract Nonr-358(01), NR C47-006 with the Office of Naval Research. Read before the first national meeting of the Institute of Management Sciences, Oct. 21–22, 1954.

[1] The author is aware, in particular, of the pioneering ideas of C. B. Tompkins and J. Kruskal, formerly at the Logistics Research Project of ONR, George Washington University, in collaboration, at that time, with A. Newell of RAND. The present paper is mainly based on the work of the author carried out, in collaboration with R. Radner and others, within the ONR Project on Decision-Making under Uncertainty at the Cowles Commission for Research in Economics, University of Chicago.

[2] I submit that, by and large, '*staff*' officers know the constants, while '*line*' officers have information on the values taken by random variables.

[3] In terms of the footnote to Table I, one can also say that the score function $(d_1 + d_2)(x_1 + x_2)$ is replaced by $(d_1 + d_2)(x_1 + 2x_2)$, while x_1 and x_2 take the same values as before, viz., -10, 0, 10. That is, the '*importance*' of the situation variable x_2 has doubled. Again, it is commonsense to expect that this will increase the worth of knowing x_2.

[4] See footnote to Table I.

[5] The ONR project on task-oriented groups carried out at MIT by A. Bavelas, D. Luce and others, has, however, contributed much to the understanding of the communication cost inasmuch as it depends on the number of transmissions necessary to spread information among the team-members.

22

EFFICIENT AND VIABLE* ORGANIZATIONAL FORMS**

(1959)

If several persons agree to follow a certain set of rules, we shall say – just for the purpose of this paper and without quarreling with other existing definitions – that they are members of an *organization*. We shall call this set of rules the *organizational form* or *constitution*.

The rules that the members are supposed to obey deal with their actions, mutual communications, and observations. Typically such a rule (also called 'role' by sociologists, I believe) states what a given member *should do* when he receives information.

Doing means here either:

(1) impinging on the world outside of the group of people forming the organization; we call this *action*; or

(2) sending to or receiving a message from another member; we call this *internal communication* (and for brevity often omit the word 'internal'); or

(3) receiving messages from the outside world; we call this *observation*.

For example, an action may consists in adding fuel to a heater, in driving a truck, or in writing to a client. A communication may consist in giving an order to a subordinate, a report to the boss, a speech at the board meeting. An observation may consist in reading a newspaper, a client's letter, the report of a market-research agency.

It is convenient to extend the term 'communication with another member' to 'communication with one's own memory': committing a received message to one's memory ('filing'), or digging out past information. A cross section of what is being done within an organization during a given period of time is schematically represented by a matrix (Table I) which may clarify the logic of our concepts.

The cell (1, 2) would be filled with the description of messages sent by member 1 to member 2; the cell (2, 1) would contain messages in the opposite direction. The row and the column marked 'zero' represent the outside world; hence the observations being made by member 1 would

TABLE I

A matrix of actions, observations, and internal communications

	Receiver 0	1	2	...
Sender 0	(0, 0)	(0, 1)	(0, 2)	
1	(1, 0)	(1, 1)	(1, 2)	
2	(2, 0)	(2, 1)	(2, 2)	
⋮				

be entered in the cell (0, 1), and the actions of member 1 (interpreted as 'messages to the outside world') would be entered in (1, 0). Each diagonal cell – (1, 1), (2, 2)... – is filled with communications between a member and his memory; with the exception of the cell (0, 0), which naturally summarizes all those external events that do not impinge upon, nor in any way reflect, the organization's doings.

In general, an organization member acts or communicates or observes in a given period of time in response to some 'message' that he has received from the outside world or from a member (possibly himself), in the preceding period(s). As we have indicated at the beginning, the organizational form consists of rules that prescribe 'who should do what in response to what information?' Schematically, the rules state that if the cells of the matrix in Table 1 had certain contents during a given week, they should be filled in a certain fashion in the next week.

The workings of an organization might be better understood if, instead of the usual 'organizational chart', one could have the description – if only very rough – of 'who does what in response to what information?'

A description of the rules of action and communication that are in actual use in a given organization (though possibly not the officially proclaimed ones) would help to *improve* them. The set of rules can be good, less good, bad. One set of rules is better – or more efficient – than another if, *on the average*, it is more conducive to achieving certain *goals*.

Let us discuss in more detail this evaluation of rules, and hence of organizational forms, according to their efficiency. As so often, it helps to begin with a simple, limiting case: the one-man organization, the rules for a single decision-maker. They prescribe what he shall do in response to a given information. One rule is more efficient than another if, *on the average*, it is more likely to further the decision-maker's goals.

I have just said 'on the average' because the outcome of a person's doings depends, of course, on the chance events of the outside world, and not only on his manner of acting. No soldier or farmer claims the gift of prophecy. Every businessman knows that business involves gambling. He acts on the basis of more-or-less well-founded ideas of how likely it is that the demand for his product will rise or fall; or how likely is an invention to succeed or to fail; and so on. In short, he acts on the basis of some approximate knowledge of, or some hunches about, the probabilities of possible events. More or less consciously he estimates, in effect, the *probability* with which a given decision of his will lead to one result rather than to another.

The decision-maker cannot control the external events, such as the public's demand in a widely competitive market, or the government policies that lead to inflation or deflation; he can only estimate the probabilities of such events. But he can control his own decisions. He chooses, from among several decisions open to him, that decision which – measured on his goals – leads, on the average, to better (or, at least, not worse) results than other possible decisions. One calls such decisions good, or *optimal*, decisions (avoiding the term 'best decision', since two decisions may be equally good); or efficient decisions. (We shall use *decision* and *action* interchangeably.)

The description just given presupposes the simple, but rather exceptional case of 'one-shot decision': the case when no consideration is given to the fact that today's decision may affect the outcome of tomorrow's decision. Yet little thought suffices to extend the concept of efficient decisions also to the more interesting, more usual, and more general case when the phrase 'sufficient unto the day is the evil thereof' is not valid. In this more general case one makes 'decisions about future decisions', one chooses 'maxims of behavior', also called 'sequential decisions', strategies, or, in our terminology, *decision rules*. Faced with an unknown sequence of future events, the decision-maker chooses not only what to do today, but also (more or less roughly) how to respond to each of the various possible events of tomorrow and of the day after, and of a still later day. In this choice he is guided by some (more-or-less vague, more-or-less conscious) estimates of probabilities; so that, again, an efficient decision rule is one that, on the average, produces good results, in terms of the decision-maker's goals.

Clearly this is an idealized picture, a norm, a piece of logic not of psychology. To prefer efficiency to inefficiency is itself a norm. Is it therefore a useless exercise? I don't think so. Psychologists tells us how often, and by what kind of people, certain logical – or, for that matter, arithmetical – errors are made; this does not make arithmetic and logic useless. In fact, we do try to teach children arithmetic. We are concerned when our students lack logic. And, I suppose, teachers of Business or of Military Art are rather anxious to inculcate the ability of efficient decision.

Our picture of efficient decision-making is unpsychological in another important way; it is not true that a man has consistent goals, or values (on which to measure efficiency). It is an idealization to say that a businessman (as such) tries to make, on the average, a large profit, and that the military man tries to act so as to make victory as probable as possible. Again, I believe this idealization is not useless (measured on the goals of those who try to improve the workings of businessmen or of generals).

We now return to the general case, the several-man organization. The extension to this case of the concept of decision rules just defined for the special case, the one-man organization, is obvious: the 'rule' is replaced by a 'set of rules' (one for each member); and the concept of internal communication is widened to the scope given it at the very beginning of the paper. It is the concept of the goals (or values) that seems to present difficulties. If, psychologically, even a single man may lack consistency of values, what to say of a group of several?

Nonetheless, it is possible to evaluate the efficiency of an organizational form, for a given goal. A business concern may be inefficient in profit-making but efficient in making its executives love each other. Once the goal is stated, the same logical tools apply. If the goal is defined by an 'aspiration level' we can say that the decision's outcome has two values: 0 if 'failure' (below the aspiration level); 1 if 'success' (above the aspiration level); and the *average* value of the outcome = (1 × Probability of success) + (0 × Probability of failure) = Probability of success.

One empirically useful approach is to estimate the efficiency of an organizational form by taking as the goal a high chance of survival. A census of existing organizational forms in some centuries-old field (e.g., that of religious organizations, or of small handicraft, or of family farming), may confirm that certain rules of action and communication, in this particular field, are more viable than others; they have, in the anthropologists' language, a higher 'survival value'. Such empirical confirmation on evolutionary grounds is, however, true only if one has the right to assume that the environment (that is, the probability distribution of the relevant external conditions) has not changed significantly in the course of time.

Whether the investigator chooses viability or some other goal as the criterion to compare the efficiency of organizational forms in a given field of activity, this goal need not coincide with the goals of any of the members of the organization. Such coincidence is improbable, if only because the individual goals are, in general, not identical among themselves.

This independence of the organizational goal (as chosen by the investigator) from the individual goals does not, by any means, make the efficiency judgments meaningless. It is certainly possible to judge the efficiency of a business corporation in terms, say, of its aggregate profits over the next two generations, without postulating this to be the goal of any of the executives or stockholders. Nor does the frequent praise of the efficiency of the Roman Catholic Church necessarily imply that it has served well the individual aims of all its popes, bishops, and laity.

This raises the problem of *incentives*. Organization rules can be devised in such a way that, if every member pursues his own goal, the goal of the organization is served. This is exemplified in practice by bonuses to executives and the promise of loot to besieging solders; and in theory, by the (idealized) model of the *laissez-faire* economy. And there exist, of course, also negative incentives (punishments).

I shall have to leave the problem of incentives aside. In what follows, we shall not be concerned with individual goals. If they still lurk in your mind, inhibiting our understanding of each other, you may make the assumption (actually unnecessary for what follows) that the members of the business organization I am going to discuss are partners sharing the profits equally, or that some perfect system of incentives is operating. In short, he may think of a *team*. My main purpose is to illustrate how various organizational forms can be compared, and an optimal one chosen, given a goal.

Suppose a shipbuilding firm has *two docks*: an old one and a new, mechanized one. The former has higher operational costs (mainly labor) and the difference depends on the dockworkers' wage rates, assumed to be the same in both docks. Suppose further the firm has *two sales representatives*, each in a different market. We shall call the two markets East and West. Each representative receives price offers (orders for ships) in his market: this is his piece of information. The production manager on the other hand, knows the current wage rate and hence the production *costs*. Suppose the operational costs per ship are

in the new dock: 20
in the old dock: 35

(we neglect capital charges and other non-operational, fixed costs as they must be paid in any case and therefore cannot affect the choice of a decision). Suppose the *price* offered by a client to a salesman are

in the East: 29
in the West: 21

Clearly if the production manager and the two sales representatives sit in conference they will take the following decision as the best one: use the new dock for the Eastern client (making a profit of $29-20=9$), reject the Western offer, leave the old dock idle. Instead of having a conference, they might also reach this same decision by each salesman's first reporting the local price to the production manager and then receiving from him the instruction to accept or reject the offer.

But conferences and other forms of extensive communications take time and money, especially in the form of salaries to busy executives. We ask therefore: Is it always best to 'centralize' all decisions, i.e., base them on all *available information* collected at some conference or headquarters? Under what circumstances is such centralization justified? When is it, on the contrary, more economical to let the local, or the specialized, persons go ahead on the basis of their own *limited information* even if this may involve occasional risks? And what should this limited information be? Should, in our example, a sales representative be constantly informed of the fluctuations in production cost, though not of the fluctuations in markets other than his own? Or could one leave him without even the cost information? Furthermore, each type of information can be used in a variety of ways, applying different *rules of action*. For example, if each salesman knows the production costs in both docks and has the power to accept or reject offers in ignorance of prices in markets other than his own, at what prices should he accept offers, so as to minimize the risk of forcing the firm into the use of the old dock at too small a profit or even at a loss?

In spite of its artificial simplicity, our example may throw light on a fairly large class of practical problems. These arise whenever several decision-makers share the same limited facilities, and the unit cost to the firm increases with output. Instead of two docks, one might think of several plants; or one can replace the 'new dock' by 'operations during the normal working day of the wage earners', and the 'old dock' by 'overtime work at extra pay'. Also, instead of 'local prices' one might think, for products like bread, of 'expected local demand' (as with the sales organization of bakeries, a problem that has been studied by C. B. McGuire[1] at the Cowles Foundation, Yale University, and that has in part suggested the example I use here). Thus, many aspects of our 'shipyard' example carry over into other fields.[2]

To return to our problem: We want to find, for each system of communications, an optimal set of rules of action for the sales representatives, i.e., that set of rules of action which results in the highest average profit attainable with this communication system. We may call this the *maximum average gross profit*. Deducting the average communication cost (i.e., mainly the executives' salaries chargeable to communications) necessary to maintain and operate the particular communication system, one obtains the *maximum average net* profit of the organizational form that is characterized by the communication system.

If, for example, the average profit of a 'centralized' decision system is only slightly higher than that of some 'decentralized' system (assuming that appropriate optimal rules of action are used in each case), then the centralized system will have to be rejected, unless the added communication costs that it requires are also slight.

To illustrate, assume that the operational costs in the two docks (20 and 35, respectively) are constant; it is only the prices offered that vary. To figure out in advance the best rules of action, one needs to have an idea of the likely price situations. For simplicity, assume that the prices in the two markets obey the law of chance of Table II. That is, with prob-

TABLE II

Probability distribution of prices offered in two markets

		East		
		High (=39)	Low (=21)	Total probability
West	High (=31)	.4	.1	.5
	Low (=29)	.1	.4	.5
	Total probability	.5	.5	1.0

	Average price	Price spread
East	30	18
West	30	2
	Correlation coefficient	=.6

ability .4 both prices are high; with probability .4 they are both low; with probability .1 the Eastern price is high and the Western low; finally, with probability .1 the price is high in the West and low in the East. (Thus markets are supposed to be more likely to move in the same than in opposite directions.) We have further supposed that while the average price is the same (=30) in both markets, the Eastern price jumps more violently: from the 'low' of 21 to the 'high' of 39; whereas the Western 'low' is 29 and its 'high' is 31 (no intermediate prices in any market; this simplifies the arithmetic).

Under the centralized system the head office will clearly choose the following rule as optimal: a ship will be built in the new dock, for the Eastern client if his price is high, for the Western client if the Eastern price is low; the old dock will lie idle (at least as long as the assumed costs remain unchanged). This rule and the resulting profits are shown in Table III on the following page.

In the table: The average profit=(19) (.4)+(19) (.1)+(11) (.1)+ +(9) (.4)=14.2. It is easy to see that any other rule, under a centralized system, will yield a lower average profit.

Now, assuming the same cost and price conditions, consider the following form of a '*decentralized*' system: each sales representative accepts or rejects local offers in ignorance of the price in the other market. Clearly there are four possible rules for each sales representative (see Table III).

TABLE III

Optimal decision rule in a centralized firm

Prices:		Offer Accepted	Profit	Probability
East	West			
39	31	East	$39-20=19$	.4
39	29	East	$39-20=19$	.1
21	31	West	$31-20=11$	.1
21	29	West	$29-20=\ 9$	.4

Average Profit: 14.2

(1) accept only if the price offered to you is high; (2) accept only if that price is low (a paradoxical yet reasonable rule, as we shall see!); (3) accept at either price; (4) never accept – i.e., go fishing. Hence there are $4 \times 4 = 16$ possible pairs of rules for the pair of salesmen. For each pair of rules one can compute, as before, the average profit.

It may seem a *paradox*, but the following pair of rules turns out to be optimal: the Eastern salesman should accept offers at the high price only; but the Westerner should accept offers *at the low price only.* With these rules, the average profit is (19. (.4)+(13) (.1)+(0) (.1)+(9)(.4)=12.5, computed as shown in Table IV.

TABLE IV

Optimal decision rule in a decentralized firm

Prices:		Offer Accepted	Profit	Probability
East	West			
39	31	East	$39-20=19$	.4
39	29	East and West	$39+29-35$ $-20=13$	.1
21	31	None	0	.1
21	29	West	$29-20=\ 9$	.4

Average Profit: 12.5

Similar computations show that the next-best pair of rules is for the Easterner to accept at high prices only and for the Westerner to accept in any case (average profit = 12). The rule that ranks third (with average profit = 10) is: either the East or the West agency should close shop, the other should accept an offer at any price. The ranking of such rules would turn out to be a different one if I had not purposely chosen numbers that lead to a 'paradox' – i.e., to a correct solution that may not seem right at first sight. It serves to illustrate the need for some formal thinking and reckoning. The solution becomes plausible if you remember that under our assumption a low Western price of 29 is likely (with odds as high as 4:1) to be accompanied by a still lower Eastern price of 21; while a high Western price of 31 is likely (with high odds again) to be accompanied by a still higher Eastern price of 39. This justified, on the average, the Westerner's acceptance of a low-price offer to insure that the efficient dock will be used, and his rejection of a high-price offer to diminish the risk of forcing the firm into using the second, inefficient dock at a loss.

We thus find that the 'decentralized' system (as defined) yields, under the best rules, an average profit that is 1.7 (=14.2 – 12.5) below the highest average profit attainable under the 'centralized' system. Therefore, if the additional *communication* cost implied in the centralized system exceeds 1.7, we shall reject it; if it is less than 1.7, we accept centralization.

The answer to every problem depends on the 'givens' of the problem. In every team problem, the 'givens' are: (1) the 'payoff function,' i.e., the formula that shows how profit depends on the decisions (in our case the decisions to accept or reject an offer) and on the external states (in our case the two prices) as shown, for example, in the 'profit' column of the last two tables; (2) the *probability function*: it states the probabilities with which the various possible external states are likely to occur; and (3) the *organization cost function* which attaches a cost to each of the organizational forms under consideration.

With regard to the *payoff function*, one can say, in general, that more communication is justified when the payoff function involves '*complementarity*' between the members' actions, in the following sense: the effect of one member's action depends on what his colleague is doing. This was certainly so in our example, because of the high production cost in the old dock. If the two docks were equally efficient the need for communication and, hence, the advantage of centralization would be smaller. There is a high complementarity, and therefore strong need for communication, among the station-masters of a railroad; but, I presume, little complementarity between the branch managers of Sears Roebuck.

Another property of the payoff function which, if present, calls for communication is the existence of '*multiple optima*'. It is equally good for all to drive on the right side of the road, or for all to drive on the left side (as they do in England); but someone has to play the role of a *coordinator*. Time-schedules for group work are often of the same nature; we needed an organizer to have all participants of this symposium to come to this place at this time, although some other place and time might be equally good.

In our case, I had mentioned a pair of rules of action under which one of the two salesmen – *regardless* which – should accept all offers (at least as long as production costs remained as they were), while the other should not accept any. This pair of rules ranked third, but it would become an optimal one under different numerical assumptions. But then there would be actually two pairs of rules to choose between: either the Westerner or the Easterner should be the one always to accept offers. Thus a coordinator is needed because there are two equally good solutions.

We have also seen how the *probability distribution* of non-controlled events (prices, in our case) affects the solution. Our 'paradoxical' solution was due to a high correlation between the two prices and to the fact that one of them had a higher spread or variance than the other. Common sense can add a few more guesses about the way in which the nature of the probability distribution affects the choice between various forms of communication. I am willing to pay a lot for information on future prices of stocks, not of bonds; for the higher the *variability* of a thing, the more useful it is to learn about its state. Further, I am not willing to pay much for special information about the price of a stock, if it is strongly correlated with some other price which I know anyhow.

To obtain other useful theorems about the way in which the payoff function and the probability distribution may affect the ranking of various organizational forms, one has to dig deeper, gathering factual knowledge about live organizations (see my earlier remarks on the deficiency of mere 'organization charts') and interpreting it logically and mathematically.

One important gap has to be closed: our ignorance of the *communication costs*. We need measurements of the executives' efficiency in using their time – a subject on which, I think, psychologists are working. What we need is something corresponding to, but more appropriate than the I.Q. We need a special 'E.Q.' (executive quotient). The I.Q. scale is essentially nothing but the statistical distribution of a large sample of

American children with respect to their performance of certain tasks. For example, 'I.Q. = 100' is a set of tasks that fifty percent of all children can perform (the 'median' performance). We need, similarly, a statistical distribution of American executive abilities, as measured by performance truly relevant to efficient communication and decision-making.

On Figure 1, the three *given* functions – the probability function, the payoff function, and the organizational cost function – are represented by boxes: they are 'operators' transforming 'inputs' into 'outputs' as indicated by arrows. These three functions, or operators, are *given*; that is, they are not controlled by the organizer. But two other operators (boxes) – the information rule and the action rule – are chosen by him, rather than given to him; the investigator can compare them with other rules for greater or smaller efficiency. Each input or output is an element of some set, represented by a circle. For example, a particular 'external state' is operated upon in three places: first, together with a particular 'action' it determines the particular gross payoff, depending on the payoff function; second, the external state has its probability depending on the given probability function; third, depending on the chosen information rule, the external state will result in a given state of information. The information rule and the action rule can be chosen each out of a set of such rules – represented by dotted circles (thus the two boxes drawn are typical only of other elements of the sets of possible rules of action and information). The two rules are chosen so as to make the *net average payoff* as high as possible; it is the difference between *average gross payoff* and *average organization cost*; the circles representing these two variables (sets) are distinguished by an aura to emphasize that they are 'goal' variables, in the light of which the efficiency of rules is judged.

There is no need here to expand on the differences between a 'model' and the 'reality', and on the usefulness of models for both understanding and improving practical solutions. My 'shipyard' model is easily made more realistic and more complicated. Its solutions would then transgress simple arithmetic, needed for a presentation like this one, and call for more powerful mathematics and machines. (In fact, the 'bakery' problem mentioned above turns out to be one in linear programming.)[3] Even then, the main service one can expect from organization models is to clarify the general logical lines of a practical problem. This clears the ground for the more subtle aspects of the practical problem that escape formalization

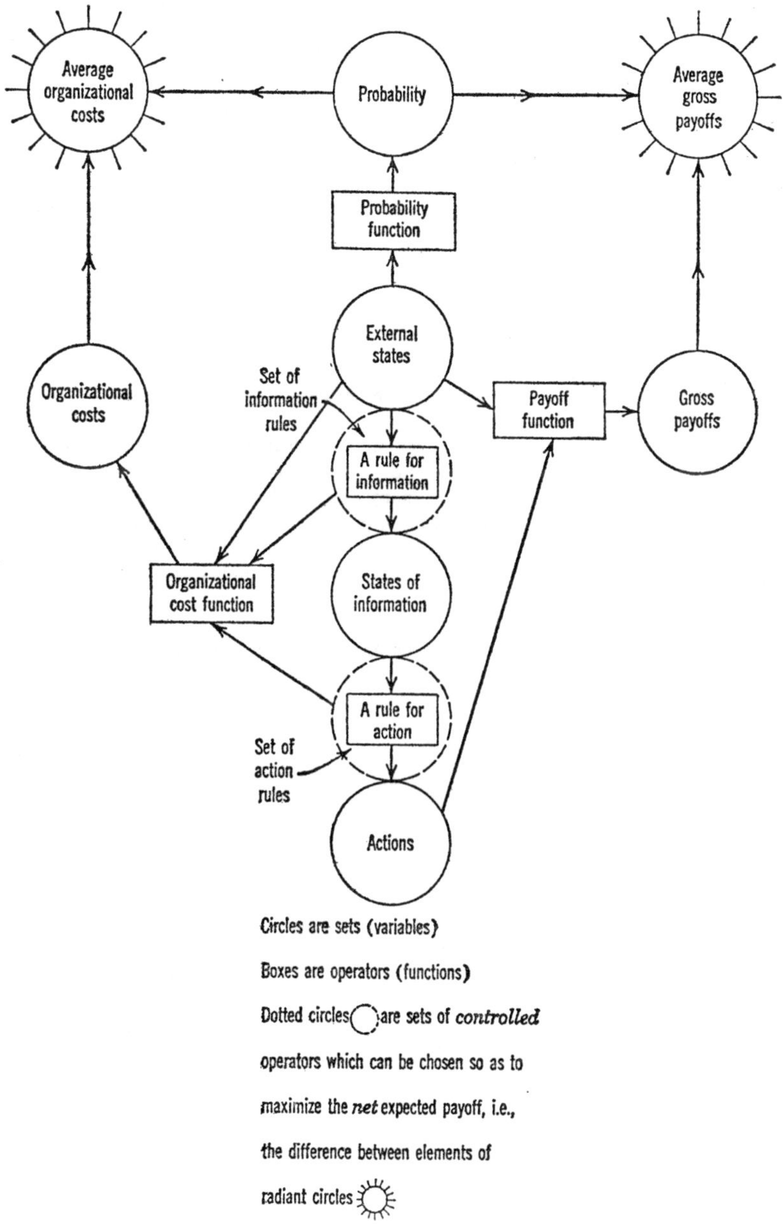

Fig. 1. Determination of average gross payoff and average organizational costs.

and call for so-called intuitive judgment. Even the best biochemist will not replace a good restaurant chef. Yet biochemical analysis has, in fact, improved our food.

NOTES

* Viability stems from French *vie* not from Latin *via*: see Webster.

** A draft version of the paper, prepared under a contract of the Office of Naval Research with the Cowles Foundation for Research in Economics at Yale University, was presented at a Symposium of the Research Committee on Organization Planning of the American Institute of Industrial Engineers, New York, March, 1958. The paper was expanded and completed when the author was visiting research professor at the Carnegie Institute of Technology, 1958–1959. Reprinted from *Modern Organization Theory* (Mason Haire, ed.), Wiley, New York, 1959.

1 C. B. McGuire, 'Some Team Models of a Sales Organization', *Management Science*, 7 (1961), 101–130.

2 In collaboration with Roy Radner, now at the University of California, the author has attempted to classify various models of teams on the basis of their mathematical properties. Such models are relevant to many aspects of business, such as production, promotion of sales, speculation, etc. A book on the economic theory of teams is being prepared. See also the author's 'Elements for a Theory of Teams', *Selected Essays*, 21, and 'Towards an Economic Theory of Organization and Information', *Selected Essays*, 20.

3 For a different problem, see Roy Radner, 'The Application of Linear Programming to Team Decision Problems', *Management Science* 5, No. 2 (January, 1959).

23

REMARKS ON THE ECONOMICS OF INFORMATION*

(1959)

The words 'amount of information', 'value of information', 'cost of information', 'piece-wage to the informant' have been much in use recently, but the relations between these quantities are not always made clear. Perhaps an attempt at clarification is in order. Though for some listeners it will elaborate the obvious, the attempt seems to be justified by the existing state of discussion.[1]

1. On criteria

This paper was prepared as an address to a group of engineers, economists, and mathematicians, gathered to inaugurate a scientific center dedicated to the joint work of these three professions. In deciding between alternative devices, instruments, processes, it is natural for an engineer to look for purely physical criteria, goals that are independent of the needs of the human user. The economist's criteria are rooted in human needs and tastes, profits and utilities, and this makes him a nuisance. To compute the number of calories produced and consumed by a society is a neat job; the maximization of the energy output is a goal that can be stated clearly enough. (It was, in fact, so stated by the technocracy movement.) The economist messes it all up by his reminder that some individuals are happier with a fatless diet. For the society as a whole the economist computes a complicated criterion such as 'national income in deflated dollars'; but even this he does only half-heartedly, troubled by his knowledge that the markets in which dollar prices are made are imperfect so that many human wants remain incomparable.

The engineer designing a privately owned power station strives to achieve a high quotient of kilowatt-hours per ton of coal. The economist reminds him that the stockholders are more interested in profits and these are impaired by the high interest charge on the investment in a physically efficient but costly generator. Charles Hitch [1958], head of RAND's economic division, gave this other example: a handy criterion occasionally suggested to direct decisions in anti-submarine warfare is the ratio of enemy U-boats destroyed to our merchant ships sunk. This ratio is high when our convoys consist of many destroyers and very few (zero if possible) merchant ships. If this criterion had been used in the last war, we would have shuttled destroyers across the ocean but would have failed to transport the men and supplies to Europe needed to win the war.

This *Streit der Fakultäten* is, as usual, a conflict of nomenclatures, definitions. The third profession present here today, the mathematician, specializes in precise and consistent definitions, and may thus help the other two; provided the formal similarity of mathematical expressions does not prevent us from distinguishing between their various possible physical, or economic, interpretations.

A statistical distribution parameter called entropy, $H(X) = -\sum p_x \log p_x$ (where the probabilities p_x are defined on a set X of n states x) measures, in some sense, the 'degree of uncertainty'. It also has mathematical properties that enables Shannon (1948) to use it as a measure of the amount of information.

This parameter clearly does not depend on the particular uses to which the information will be put. If, on the other hand, the user asks 'How much is the information worth to me?', 'How much am I willing to pay for it?', it is natural that the answer about this quantity (for which the term 'value of information' suggests itself) will vary from user to user. This certainly complicates matters, and attempts have been made to show that if the value, or worth, of information to its receiver is defined in some appropriate way it can yet be made independent of the user; more than that, it will be measured precisely by the entropy formula.

In trying to clarify the terms, we have met problems that are not merely linguistic, but actually reveal separate classes of important and measurable quantities. It turned out that writers who tried to define a value of information independent of the user have sometimes used the word to denote such quantities as the cost to the seller of information (similar to the cost of production), or the piece-wage to be paid to the informant to increase his reliability.

2. Demand and Supply Price of Information

It is agreed that for technical purposes the word 'information' never denotes a single message but rather a set of potential messages associated with a given instrument (source or channel) of information. The man who buys a newspaper does not know beforehand what will be in the news. He acquires access to potential messages belonging to a set called news.

Information is demanded and supplied, and we can speak of a demand price and a supply price of information as we do in the case of commodities.

A person's demand price for information is the highest price that he is willing to pay for it. This price clearly depends on how useful or important are, for that particular person, the messages that he will obtain from the given information instrument. The horse-race fan will pay much for the newspaper with the latest racing results; weather services are of greater value to farmers, airlines, and the tourist trade than to the steel industry; and some people don't care even for the highest-fidelity radio sets.

To an economist, it seems natural to call value of information the average amount earned with the help of that information. Moreover, if I already have access to a certain kind of information which earns for me, on the average, the amount V_0; and if the access to some other kind of information will help me to a greater average earning, V_1; then my demand price for that information is $V_1 - V_0$.

The supply price of information, on the other hand, is the lowest price its supplier is willing to charge. It cannot, in the long run, fall below the cost to the supplier or he will lose the motive to supply it.

In a market of comparable information instruments (e.g., newspapers), with numerous and freely competing buyers and sellers, a market price would emerge. It will be actually paid by all buyers and accepted by all sellers, excepting those (and only those) buyers whose demand price is lower, and those (and only those) sellers whose supply price is higher, than the market price. These ('submarginal') buyers and sellers will abstain from transaction. In the more usual and interesting case when a large and free market for comparable information instruments does not exist, this 'classical' economic model does not apply and the analysis becomes more difficult. But the concepts of demand price (related to the value of information) and the supply price (related to the cost of information) remain fundamental.

What is the relation of information value and information cost to the concept of information amount, which has been developed for the uses of the industry of communication devices and has been fruitfully transferred to various sciences? The amount of information does not depend on the needs of any particular buyer of information. Hence it is not identical with the value of information just shown to determine the demand price. But it is presumably related to the cost, and hence the supply price, of information as we shall presently see.

3. A SIMPLE CASE: EQUIPROBABLE FAULTLESS MESSAGES

If the set whose information amount is being measured consists of n potential messages that have equal probabilities, $p_x = 1/n$, the information amount $H(X) = -\sum_{x=1}^{n} p_x \log p_x = -n \cdot (1/n)\,[\log(1/n)] = \log n$ is simply defined so as to increase with the number of distinct potential messages. It is also usual to say that the larger this number the more precise is the information instrument: this is a definition. And the more precise the instrument, the costlier is the instrument and its operation: this is, or is asserted to be, an empirical fact. The increase of cost with increasing precision is associated with the fact that larger precision means (by the definition just given) a larger number of symbols needed at a minimum to distinguish the messages: as for example, when each message consists of a numerical variable given to the nearest tenth, or hundredth, or thousandth of a unit. It takes more time to transmit more symbols.[2] And presumably it takes more labor and other resources to produce an instrument capable of transmitting more symbols per unit of time. The minimum number of symbols needed – e.g., the number of digits in the example just given – increases in proportion to the logarithm of the number of potential messages; so that (roughly?) cost is proportional to the amount of information. Moreover, if every potential message reports, not on a single variable, but on two independent variables (e.g., temperature and humidity), the total number of potential messages is the product of the numbers of potential messages associated with each variable; but the total number of symbols needed is the sum of the number of symbols needed for each variable. And this again corresponds (roughly) to the behavior of the cost: the cost of introducing a second variable is simply added to the cost of giving messages about the single one.

4. An illustration[3]

While still confining ourselves to the simple case of equiprobable messages we shall illustrate in more detail the fact that information value and information amount do not necessarily go together.

Suppose the price of a stock can change from this to the next week, by any amount between +6 and −6 points with equal probability. Suppose you can use the services of either of two informants, each a faultless predictor of stock prices. Informant A sends only two kinds of messages: (1) stock will rise; and (2), stock will not rise. Informant B is more precise in that his messages can be of three kinds: (1) stock will rise by 2 points or more, (2) stock will fall by 2 points or more, (3) stock will move by less than 2 points in either direction. If, as we shall assume for a while, there are no transaction costs (brokerage charges, etc.), a good rule for your action on the basis of information from A is: 'buy stock when A predicts rise, sell otherwise'; and, on the basis of information from B: 'buy stock when B predicts rise of 2 points or more, sell when he predicts fall of 2 points or more, do nothing otherwise'. Thus informant A enables you to take advantage of every price change while B is useless whenever price change is moderate. You will prefer A. Yet A is the less precise of the two: A uses only two equiprobable potential messages while B uses three! The amounts of information are in the ratio $\log 2 : \log 3 = 1 : 1.6$ approximately. But the values of information are in the ratio $9:8 = 1:0.9$ approximately. For, applying to the information from A your good rule of action, you will gain an average of $(6+0)/2$ points per share on purchases of rising stock, and obtain the same average gain on sales of falling stock; and since both cases have equal probabilities, your expected gain will be

$$\left(\frac{1}{2}\right)\left(\frac{6+0}{2}\right)+\left(\frac{1}{2}\right)\left(\frac{6+0}{2}\right)=3$$

points per share. On the other hand, B will help you to only

$$\left(\frac{1}{3}\right)\left(\frac{6+2}{2}\right)+\left(\frac{1}{3}\right)(0)+\left(\frac{1}{3}\right)\left(\frac{6+2}{2}\right)=2\tfrac{2}{3}$$

points per share.

We can also conceive of a third informant B′, who exerts himself to give even more precise messages than B: he breaks up the whole range of possible price-changes into a large *odd* number of intervals of which the middle one is centered around zero. The amount of information in his set of messages will exceed by far that of A's and B's messages, making B′ a very expensive information instrument indeed. But the value of his information to you, while exceeding the value of B's information, will still fall short of the value of A's information (although it will approach it): because B′ fails and A does not fail to make the useful distinction between rises and declines of stock when they are within the middle interval. As so often, the brand least costly to make is the best for the buyer.

Instead of measuring the amount of information in the set of potential equiprobable messages we might regard the informant as a channel of communication whose output is the message and whose input is some event (the price-change, in our case). This will enable us to introduce – albeit in a trivial application – the concept of transmission rate which we shall need later.[4] The probability distribution of price-changes characterizes the 'source' of information: a distribution on the set X, consisting of events x; X is the whole range of possible price-changes. The distribution of messages characterizes the 'channel': this is a distribution on the set Y, consisting of messages y, each corresponding to one of m equal intervals into which X is partitioned. Let us approximate the assumed continuous uniform distribution on X by a discrete one, by breaking up each interval y of X into an indefinitely large number k of equal subintervals, and associating each with a different event x. There are then km equally probable events x, and the amount of information needed to identify x is equal to $H(X) = \log km$. We can say that $H(X)$ measures the uncertainty about x that prevails before a message is received. We shall now measure the uncertainty about x that remains, on the average, after a message is received; this is denoted by $H(X|Y)$ and is called the equivocation of the channel Y with respect to the source X; and the difference $R(Y, X) = H(X) - H(X|Y)$ is naturally called the transmission rate of Y with respect to X. The function R is symmetrical: $R(Y, X) = R(X, Y)$.

To obtain $H(X|Y)$ we first compute $H(X|y)$, the uncertainty remaining after a given message y is received. This is defined as $-\sum p(x|y) \log p(x|y)$ where $p(x|y)$ is the conditional probability of x given y. To compute $H(X|y)$, note that the joint probability $p(x, y) = 1/km$ when x is in the interval y; and $=$ zero otherwise; and the probability of each y is $p_y = 1/m$.

Hence, each of the non-zero conditional probabilities $p(x|y)=p(x, y)/p_y= =1/k$. Hence $H(X|y)=\log k$, the same for all y. Therefore the (average) equivocation $H(X|Y)$ is also $=\log k$, and the transmission rate $R(Y, X)= =\log km-\log k=\log m$. Thus the transmission rate is (in our case) the same as the amount of information in the set of potential messages; and the ordering of channels according to their transmission rates (given the source) is not the same as the ordering according to their information value to the speculator.

5. The payoff-function

In our example, you have used A's or B's information on stock prices in order to buy or sell. Your actual gain (or loss) from each action was determined by both the action and the actual price change, according to the following 'payoff function': if the price changes by $+x$ points, and you buy (sell), you gain (lose) x points per share; if the price changes by $-x$ points, your gains from buying or selling are, respectively, $-x$ and $+x$ points. If we denote the three-valued action variable by a, with $a=+1$ (buying), $a=-1$ (selling), and $a=0$ (do nothing) then the gain u is equal to xa. We shall use Greek ω as a symbol for a payoff function, and the corresponding Latin letter u, for the value of this function. In our case (see figures 1 and 2),

$$(1) \qquad u=\omega(x, a)=xa.$$

It is important to make explicit an assumption tacitly made so far: the decision-maker maximizes the expected payoff. In our example the payoff was measured in money. It is more general to define as the payoff that function of the action and the state of the world, whose expected value is being maximized by the decision-maker. That such a function (defined on all possible outcomes of actions, whether these outcomes be money amounts or not) exists is an assumption about the decision-maker's behavior. It was shown by Von Neumann and Morgenstern (1948) that it follows from certain simple maxims of consistent behavior which it is reasonable to advise a person to use. The 'payoff function' and the 'criterion function' are the same thing.[5]

Under conditions of our example, the payoff function (1) resulted in your preferring informant A to informant B. But we can change the payoff

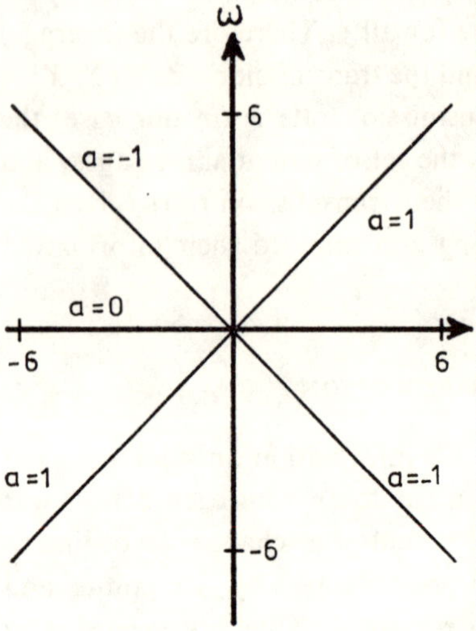

Fig. 1: $4 = \omega(x, a)$

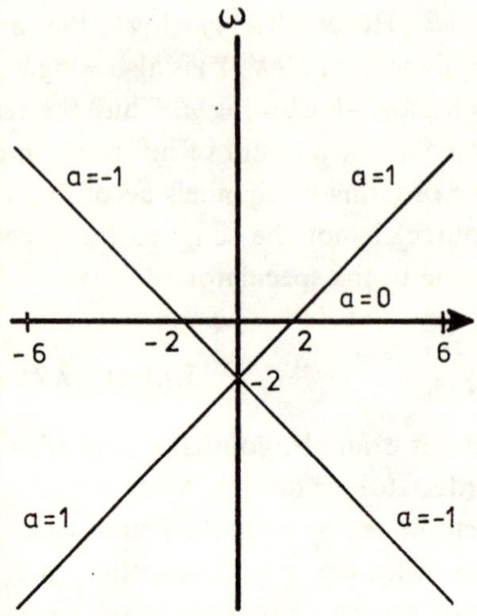

Fig. 1*: $u = \omega^*(x, a)$

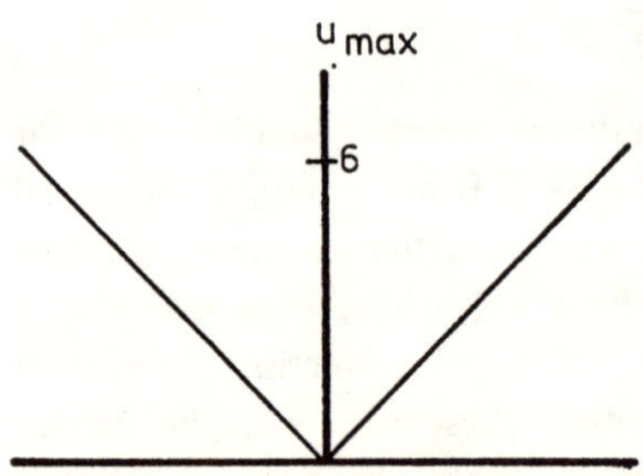

Fig. 2: $u_{max} = \max_a \omega(x, a)$

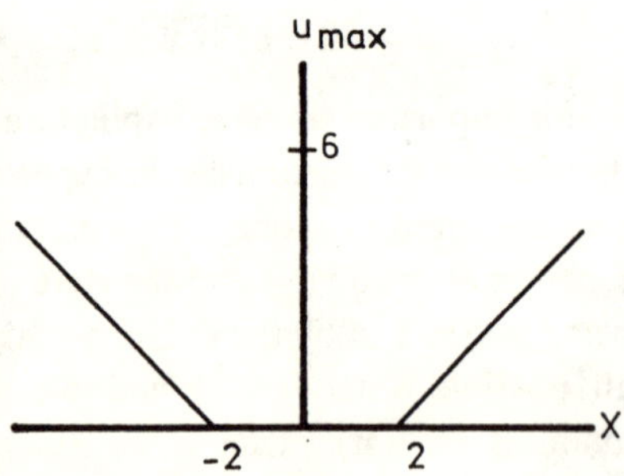

Fig. 2*: $u_{max} = \max_a \omega^*(x, a)$

function so as to reverse your preferences. Instead of assuming transaction costs negligible, let us assume you have to pay (in brokerage fees, taxes, etc.) 2 points per share on each purchase or sale. Figure 1* shows this new payoff function, ω^*:

$$(2) \qquad u = \omega^*(x, a) = \begin{matrix} xa - 2, & a \neq 0 \\ 0, & a = 0. \end{matrix}$$

Figure 2* shows that it becomes advantageous for you to abstain from transaction whenever the price is predicted to change by less than 2 points. B enables you to apply such a rule. But A does not. As a result, A will help you to an expected profit of $3-2=1$ point per share. But B will help you to more, viz., to

$$\left(\frac{1}{3}\right)\left[\frac{6+2}{2} - 2\right] + \left(\frac{1}{3}\right)(0) + \left(\frac{1}{3}\right)\left[\frac{6+2}{2} - 2\right] = 1\tfrac{1}{3}$$

points per share. The value of information from B has now become larger than that from A.

6. Information Structure

What is the explanation for this switching of the comparative values of the two information instruments? Let X denote the whole set of possible price-changes, i.e., the whole interval between, and including, -6 and $+6$. Thus $X=[-6, +6]$. Consider its following subsets:

$$X_1 = [-6, -2); \qquad X_2 = [-2, 0); \qquad X_3 = [0, +2); \qquad X_4 = [+2, +6].$$

Informant A, in fact, partitions X into two subsets, one message corresponding to each subset: one subset consists of X_1 and X_2, and the other subset consists of X_3 and X_4. Informant B partitions X into three subsets: X_1; X_4; and 'X_2 and X_3'. When the payoff function is ω of Equation (1) (the case of zero transaction costs), the client's choice of action is influenced by whether the predicted price change belongs to 'X_1 and X_2' or to 'X_3 and X_4'; but it is not important for him to distinguish between X_1 and X_2, as both will dictate the same appropriate action ('sell'); similarly, the distinction between X_3 and X_4 is unimportant. Hence the greater value of A when payoff function is ω. But when it is the function ω^* of Equation (2) (i.e., transaction costs = 2), the distinction between X_1 and X_2, and also between X_3 and X_4, becomes important enough to make B a more valuable information instrument than A.

Thus each information instrument is characterized by the way it partitions the set X of all possible states of the environment. We call each way of partitioning (or, briefly, each partition) of X an 'information structure'. We have seen that, whether a particular information structure yields a greater expected payoff than another structure depends in general on the payoff function, as our example has shown. Thus, in general, the ranking of information structures (and instruments) according to their value is a 'subjective' matter, inasmuch as it depends on the usefulness of information for a given user.

The question arises naturally whether there are pairs of partitions such that the ranking of their values is not influenced by the payoff function. It is easily seen that such ('objective') ranking is possible *if and only if one partition is a sub-partition of the other* in the sense that each of the subsets in the former partition is contained in some subset of the latter. For example, suppose informant C uses four messages, corresponding to the partition of X into the 4 subsets X_1, X_2, X_3, X_4 given above. This partition is a sub-partition of the two-set partition used by A as well as of the three-set partition used by B. And it is clear that any client of C has all the knowledge that a client of A or B has. Hence, for any client, whatever his payoff function, the information value of A or B can never exceed that of C (with the particular payoff function ω used above, information value of C is strictly larger than that of B and equals that of A; under ω^*, the positions of A and B are interchanged). Thus if one information structure is a subpartition of another, their values are ranked independently of the payoff function. The converse is also true. For (as pointed out by Roy Radner), if one partition is not a sub-partition of another, then there will be two states x_1, x_2 such that, under the first partition, x_2 belongs into the same subset with x_1; while under the second partition, x_2 belongs to a different subset from x_1. The second partition will then have greater information value for a payoff function in which it is most important to distinguish x_2 from x_1. Thus consider, in our example, three price changes: -3, -1, $+1$. A's information structure is not a subpartition of B's, nor conversely; and this shows up in the fact that A permits to distinguish -1 from $+1$ but not from -3; while B permits to distinguish -1 from -3

but not from $+1$. When the payoff function is ω (transaction cost nil) it is the former distinction that matters; when the payoff function is ω^*, it is the latter.

We can also regard each partition, or information structure, as a function (operator) η, that translates each state of environment – i.e., each element x of X – into a message $y=\eta(x)$ (y is the value of the function η). For a particular y, all those states $x_1, x_2, \ldots$, for which $\eta(x_1)=\eta(x_2)= =\cdots=y$, form a particular one of the subsets generated by the information structure η.

Let P be the probability distribution on X. (When X is finite we can write p_x for the probability that a particular state x obtains.) It is clear that the distribution P, together with the information structure η, will determine the probability distribution over the set of messages y. And since the amount of information is a property of the probability distribution of messages, it is a property of the pair (P, η). In our example, the (uniform) distribution P of price-changes, and the information structures – say, $\eta^A, \eta^B, \ldots$, characterizing the informants A, B, ... – were such as to generate the distribution of messages: $(\frac{1}{2}, \frac{1}{2})$ in the case A; $(\frac{1}{3}, \frac{1}{3}, \frac{1}{3})$ in the case B, ... Even more: P and η taken together determine completely the joint distribution of the messages and of the states of the world; and, hence, also the conditional probability that the world is in a given state if the message received is a given one. This remark will become somewhat less trivial later when we drop our assumption that the informants were faultless.

We can now summarize our concepts formally: Write X=set of states of the world; x=a particular state; P=probability distribution on X [when X is finite, p_x is the probability of a given x]; a=action (=decision); u=payoff, ω=payoff function, η=information structure, y=message, α=rule of action, i.e., a function associating a message y with an action a.

Then $y=\eta(x)$; $a=\alpha(y)$; and $u=\omega(x, a)$. Hence $u=\omega(x, \alpha(y))=\omega(x, \alpha(\eta(x))$: the payoff depends on the state of the world and will vary with the three functions ω, α, and η. The expected payoff is $U=E_x u= =E_x\omega(x, \alpha(\eta(x)))$ [in the case of finite X, $U=\sum_x p_x \omega(x, \alpha(x)))$]. Thus the expected payoff depends on the functions ω, α, η, and P. We can write $U=U(\alpha, \eta; \omega, P)$, separating by a semicolon the functions the decision-maker can choose (α and η) from those he cannot: the payoff function and the distribution function of the states of the world.

If the rule of action is a good one, $\alpha=\alpha^*$, say, U is maximized over the set of all possible action rules. That is, $U(\alpha^*, \eta; \omega, P) = \max_\alpha U(\alpha, \eta; \omega, P) = V(\eta; \omega, P)$, say, is the maximum expected payoff achievable with the information structure η, given ω and P. We call $V(\eta; \omega, P)$ the *information value* of η and want to emphasize that, in general, it depends on ω. On the other hand, the probability distribution of messages, or (more comprehensively) the joint probability distribution of messages and states of the world, depends on η, P but is independent of ω.

If I am in possession of an information instrument characterized by structure η^0 of information, I shall be willing to offer the *demand price* $V(\eta^1; \omega, P) - V(\eta^0; \omega, P)$ for the instrument with information structure η^1 if the difference is positive. In particular η^0 may mean 'no information': a degenerate partition of X into a single subset (itself).

7. Non-equiprobable faultless messages

In our examples so far, a faultless informant sent equiprobable messages. But our results apply to more general case: it remains true that the value of a given information structure, and the ranking of the values for different information structures, depend on the payoff function.

On the other hand, the amount of information is independent of the payoff function. In particular, the information is highest, regardless of the payoffs, when the messages are equiprobable, and hence remove the "highest degree of uncertainty." Consider the following type of payoff functions, ω, and the following probabilities p_x of two alternative states of nature:

State of nature $x=$	1	2
Action		
$a=1$	r_1	0
2	0	r_2
Probability $p_x=$	p_1	p_2,

where $p_1 + p_2 = 1$ and the rewards r_i are positive. How much will you pay to the informant who tells you without fault the actual state of nature? Call this information structure η^1. With its help you will always choose the appropriate action, $a = x$, and earn, on the average, $V_1(\eta^1; \omega, P) = p_1 r_1 + p_2 r_2$. If you act without the knowledge of the actual state (we shall then say you possess information structure η^0), your expected reward is p_1r_1 or p_2r_2 depending on the action you choose once for all (or is between these two amounts if you randomize your actions). In this case, the highest expected reward is $V_0 = \max(p_1r_1, p_2r_2)$. Hence, assuming (without loss of generality) $p_2r_2 \geqq p_1r_1$, the demand price for η^1 is

$$V_1 - V_0 = (p_1r_1 + p_2r_2) - p_1r_1 = p_2r_2 .$$

This quantity reaches its maximum, not when "the degree of uncertainty" is highest ($p_1 = p_2 = \frac{1}{2}$) but when $p_2r_2 = p_1r_1$, $p_1 = r_2/(r_1 + r_2)$; this is $\neq \frac{1}{2}$ unless $r_1 = r_2$.

Similarly, while, for a three-message set, the information amount is highest when $p_i = \frac{1}{3}$ $(i = 1, 2, 3)$, in the following example the demand price is highest at other probability distributions of messages. Consider two payoff functions, ω' and ω''; and assume a probability distribution P (with $p_2 = \frac{1}{3}$):

ω'			
$x =$	1	2	3
$a = 1$	r_1	0	0
2	0	r_2	r_2
$p_x =$	p_1	$\frac{1}{3}$	p_3

ω''			
$x =$	1	2	3
$a = 1$	r_1	r_1	0
2	0	0	r_2
$p_x =$	p_1	$\frac{1}{3}$	p_3

Thus, if the payoff function is ω' it is unimportant to distinguish between the states 2 and 3; the demand price is the same as in the two-states example just used. Accordingly, it reaches its maximum when $p_1 = r_2/(r_1 + r_2)$. Similarly, when the payoff function is ω'', maximum demand price is reached when $p_3 = r_2/(r_1 + r_2)$. And in the particular case when $r_1 = r_2$, the probability distribution resulting in the highest demand price is, in the case of each of the two payoff functions: $(\frac{1}{2}, \frac{1}{3}, \frac{1}{6})$ and $(\frac{1}{6}, \frac{1}{3}, \frac{1}{2})$, respectively, not $(\frac{1}{3}, \frac{1}{3}, \frac{1}{3})$! The 'highest degree of uncertainty' does not correspond to the highest demand price for information dispelling it.

There are of course many parameters of the probability distribution P on the (finite) set $X = (x_1, \ldots, x_n)$ of states of nature, that have the property of reaching the maximum when $p_1 = p_2 = \cdots = p_n$. Of such parameters, the entropy measure, $-\sum p_i \log p_i$, has the further property that it increases with the minimum number of symbols needed to distinguish messages about long sequences of states of nature. To see this, compute the number of distinct sequences of length T. Each sequence in which $x_1, \ldots, x_n$ occur

$t_1, \ldots, t_n$ times respectively $(\sum t_i = T)$ has the probability $p_1^{t_2} p_2^{t_2} \ldots p_n^{t_n}$; and since, with T large, it is practically certain that $t_i = Tp_i$, each such sequence has the probability $(p_1^{p_1} p_2^{p_2} \ldots p_n^{p_n})^T$. The reciprocal, $(p_1^{p_1} p_2^{p_2} \ldots p_n^{p_n})^{-T}$ is therefore the number of distinct sequences; and its logarithm, $-T \sum p_i \log p_i$ is proportional to the number of digits needed to distinguish between messages about such sequences. As in our earlier exposition (of the special case when the states of nature are equiprobable and $T=1$, and therefore the messages are equiprobable), the number of digits can be taken to be roughly proportional to the cost of transmitting information about T successive states. Hence the average cost per transmitted occurrence is proportional to $H = -\sum p_i \log p_i$, the entropy. This quantity has its maximum when all p_i are equal $(=1/n)$.

Changing our terminology we can also regard the set $X = (x_1, \ldots, x_n)$ as a vocabulary, and each state of nature as a sequence of words describing it. For each word, the probability of its occurrence will, in general, depend on its predecessors in the sequence; but we omit this complication for the present discussion, for our main conclusion remains valid: the cost of information increases roughly with the number of symbols needed and this is measured by the amount of information defined as the entropy, a statistical parameter characterizing the set of potential messages and independent of the payoff function. But the value of information, and its demand price, do depend on the payoff function.

8. Special classes of payoff-functions

The binary relation 'η' is a sub-partition of η''' induces a partial ordering on all partitions of the set X. We have seen that

$$(3) \qquad V(\eta'; \omega, P) \geqq V(\eta''; \omega, P) \quad \text{for all} \quad P, \omega$$

if and only if η' is a sub-partition of η''. If two information structures are not related by sub-partitioning, it is possible to reverse the comparative ranking of their information values by changing the payoff function. However, we may consider restricting the payoff function to some special class Ω such that, for all payoff functions in Ω, the ranking of information values depends on η and P only. For example, we may define some numerical function $K(\eta, P)$ such that

$$(4) \qquad V(\eta'; \omega, P) \geqq V(\eta''; \omega, P) \quad \text{for all} \quad \omega \text{ in } \Omega$$

if and only if $K(\eta', P) \geqq K(\eta'', P)$. In particular, since the probability distribution of messages is determined by η and P, the number $K(\eta, P)$ may be chosen to be a parameter of that distribution – for example, the entropy characterizing it. Is there such a class Ω?

9. Faulty information

A particularly important class Ω of payoff functions is defined by the concept of faulty information (i.e., 'noise' *and* 'loss' in the channel). Let us regard the variable, state of nature x as a pair (x^e, x^i) where x^e denotes the *e*xternal or *e*nvironmental state, and x^i the *i*nternal state (i.e., the state of the *i*nformation *i*nstrument). Internal state is a variable with the following property: it influences the message but not the payoff. The message is $y = \eta(x^e, x^i) = \eta(x)$ as before; but the payoff function depends now only on x^e and the action variable a. That is, there exists a function $\bar{\omega}$ such that the payoff

$$u = \omega(x, a) = \omega(x^e, x^i, a) = \bar{\omega}(x^e, a). \tag{5}$$

A simple question which, on the face of it, seems to put our previous results in doubt, will illustrate these concepts. Suppose an expert offers to predict which of two things will happen (e.g., whether a stock will rise or fall). Won't you be willing to pay him more (certainly, not less!) if you know him to be right 90 per cent of the time than if you know him to be right only 60 per cent of the time? If so, the information value is larger (or at least not smaller) in the former than in the latter case, regardless of how important the event predicted is for you, i.e., regardless of how it (together with any given action of yours) affects your profit. No change in the payoff function will alter the ranking of information values. Note, moreover, that if the probability of the expert's being right is, say, 40 per cent, he is as good as if he were right 60 per cent of the time since you can always replace his message by its opposite. Thus the information value is smallest when the probability of error is $= 50$ per cent.

To check the intuition, let $x^i =$ state of the instrument $= +1$ or -1 according to whether the informant is right or wrong; and denote the two values of x^e, the external variable in question, by $+1$ and -1. With this notation the message y is the product $x^e x^i$ of two independent random variables:

$$y = x^e x^i = \eta(x^e, x^i) \tag{6}$$

The information structure η thus defined is the partition of the set X of pairs (x^e, x^i) into two subsets, with $x^e x^i = +1$ and -1, respectively. By the conditions of the problem, there are two possible actions, $a = +1$ and -1 (say) such that $a = +1$ is the appropriate (i.e., the most profitable) action when the external state $x^e = +1$; and $a = -1$ is appropriate when $x^e = -1$. That is, if we denote the four possible payoffs $u = \varpi(x^e, a)$ by

$$(7) \qquad \varpi(+1, +1) = r_1\,; \qquad \varpi(-1, -1) = r_2\,;$$
$$\varpi(-1, +1) = s_2\,; \qquad \varpi(+1, -1) = s_1\,,$$

then

$$(8) \qquad r_1 \geqq s_1,\, r_2 \geqq s_2\,.$$

This property of ϖ, a special case of the independence of ω on x^i, defines the class Ω of admitted payoff functions. We now ask whether, if the information structure η is defined as in (6), then the ranking of the information values $V(\eta; \omega, P)$ for varying P is the same for all payoff functions in Ω.

For a given message y, the action $a = a^*(y)$ is optimal if it yields the maximum conditional expected payoff. For example, $a^*(1) = 1$ or $= -1$ according as

$$(8a) \qquad r_1 Pr(x^e = 1 \,|\, y = 1) + s_1 Pr(x^e = -1 \,|\, y = 1) \geqq \text{or} \leqq$$
$$s_2 Pr(x^e = 1 \,|\, y = 1) + s_1 Pr(x^e = -1 \,|\, y = 1)\,.$$

Writing

$$Pr(x^e = 1) \equiv p^e \equiv 1 - q^e\,,$$
$$Pr(x^i = 1) \equiv p^i \equiv 1 - q^i\,,$$
$$A \equiv p^e(r_1 - s_1) > 0\,, \qquad B \equiv q^e(r_2 - s_2) > 0\,,$$

we obtain from (8a):

$$a^*(1) = 1 \quad \text{or} \quad = -1 \quad \text{according as} \quad p^i/q^i \geqq \quad \text{or} \quad \leqq B/A\,.$$

Similarly, we obtain from a relation analogous to (8a), with $y = -1$:

$$a^*(-1) = -1 \quad \text{or} \quad = 1 \quad \text{according as} \quad p^i/q^i \geqq \quad \text{or} \quad \leqq A/B\,.$$

Combining these results we find the conditions on p^i, under which each of the four possible decision rules $\alpha^*(y)$ is optimal

1. if $|p^i - \frac{1}{2}| \geqq \frac{|A-B|}{2(A+B)}$,

then $\alpha^*(y)=y$ or $=-y$ according as $p^i \geqq \frac{1}{2}$ or $\leqq \frac{1}{2}$;

2. if $|p^i - \frac{1}{2}| \leqq \frac{|A-B|}{2(A+B)}$,

then $\alpha^*(y)=1$ or $=-1$ according as $A \geqq B$ or $\leqq B$.

Thus, you should always obey (always disobey) your informant in case 1, i.e., in the case when the probability p^i of his being right is not too close to $\frac{1}{2}$, whereas the ratio $A/B=(p^e/q^e)\cdot(r_1-s_1)/(r_2-s_2)$ is close to 1. The ratio A/B approaches 1 as your uncertainty about the true state increases, i.e., as $p^e=Pr(x=1)$ approaches $\frac{1}{2}$; and as the advantage (r_1-s_1) of taking the right action when $x=1$ approaches the corresponding advantage (r_2-s_2) when $x=-1$. In case 2, on the other hand, you should pay no attention to the informant: for then p^i is close to $\frac{1}{2}$, p^e is close to 1 (or 0), and the advantage (r_1-s_1) is much larger (smaller) than the advantage (r_2-s_2), justifying your keeping your action constant at $a=1$ (or $=-1$).[6]

Hence the expected payoff of case 2 is equal, in our notation, to V_0: the maximum expected profit when no information is used. After computing the maximum expected profit for case 1, we obtain the demand price of information:

$$\text{(8b)} \qquad V_1 - V_0 \begin{cases} = 0 & \text{if } |p^i - \frac{1}{2}| \leqq \dfrac{|A-B|}{2(A+B)} \\ = |p^i - \frac{1}{2}|\,(A+B) - \frac{1}{2}|A-B| & \text{otherwise}. \end{cases}$$

On the other hand, consider the informant as a channel whose input is the two-valued variable x^e, and whose output is the two-valued variable $y=x^e \cdot x^i$. The transmission rate as defined in Section 4 is, by symmetry, $R(Y, X^e)=-H(Y|X^e)+H(Y)$ where

$$\begin{aligned} -H(Y|X^e) = -H(X^i) &= p^i \log p^i + q^i \log q^i, \\ H(Y) &= (p^e p^i + q^e q^i)\log(p^e p^i + q^e q^i) + \\ &\quad + (p^e q^i + q^e p^i)\log(p^e q^i + q^e p^i). \end{aligned}$$

When the probability distribution of the source is such that the transmission rate reaches its maximum, the achieved transmission rate is called the capacity of the channel. In our case, of the two components of $R(Y, X^e)$, only the second, $H(Y)$, depends on p^e. Its maximum is log2, achieved when $p^e = q^e = \frac{1}{2}$. Hence the capacity of the channel is

$$(9) \qquad C(Y) = p^i \log p^i + \log q^i + \log 2 .$$

If we compare informants with various probabilities p^i of being right, we see that $C(Y)$ is zero when $p^i = \frac{1}{2}$, and increases with the absolute value $|p^i - \frac{1}{2}|$.

Hence by (8b) the demand price of information is a non-increasing function of the channel capacity C: the demand price remains zero as long as $|p^i - \frac{1}{2}|$, and hence C, does not exceed a certain critical level; the demand price then rises as a non-linear function of C. Both the critical level and the non-linear function do *depend* on the parameters r_1, r_2, s_1, s_2 that distinguish one element of the class Ω from another.

In a 'fair bet' with a fixed stake s we would have, in particular, by (8b):

$$s_1 = s_2 = -s; \qquad r_1/s = q^e/p^e; \qquad r_2/s = p^e/q^e;$$
$$V_1 - V_0 = 2s|p^i - \tfrac{1}{2}| .$$

This last result will be compared with the one of the next section.

10. A case when information value coincides with channel capacity

This interesting case was constructed by J. R. Kelly, Jr. (1956) of Bell Telephone Laboratories. In presenting it, we shall find it logically instructive to continue the use of our formal notation even though it is made to look incongruous by the intuitive simplicity of the problem. The problem retains all the characteristics of our very last example (fair bet) except that the set of actions and the payoff functions are defined differently. The stake s varies from bet to bet, the gambler having decided in advance that he will bet a fixed proportion l of the capital available after the previous bet. Thus the action a is now described by a pair of variables, with k denoting the direction of the bet:

$$a = (k, l); \qquad k = +1, -1; \quad 0 \leqq l \leqq 1 .$$

For simplicity, assume $p^e = \frac{1}{2}$ (however, Kelly obtains his result also for an arbitrary p^e). Denoting by c the capital before the bet, the money losses and gains become:

$$s_1 = s_2 = -cl; \qquad r_1 = r_2 = cl.$$

However, the payoff u, i.e., the random variable whose expected value is maximized, is assumed to be, not the money gain or loss, but the exponential rate of growth of capital, i.e., the logarithm of the ratio between the capital after and before the bet:

$$\text{(10)} \qquad u = \begin{cases} \log(1+l) & \text{if gambler wins} \\ \log(1-l) & \text{if gambler loses}. \end{cases}$$

With $p^i \geqq \frac{1}{2}$ (no loss of generality), a good rule requires that the informant's advice be followed. This makes the expected payoff[7] equal to

$$Eu = p^i \log(1+l) + q^i \log(1-l),$$

which has maximum when $l = 2p^i - 1$. Hence the expected payoff

$$\text{(11)} \qquad V_1 = \max_l Eu = p^i \log p^i + q^i \log q^i + \log 2$$

is by (9) equal to $C(Y)$, the channel's capacity. This is also equal to the demand price since the maximum expected payoff obtained without information is

$$V_0 = \max_l \left(\tfrac{1}{2}\log(1+l) + \tfrac{1}{2}\log(1-l)\right) = 0.$$

At the risk of being pedantic, it will be helpful to relate the results to our concepts. We have as in the preceding section

$$x = (x^e, x^i); \qquad y = \eta(x) = x^e x^i.$$

Moreover:

$$a = \alpha(y) = (k, l) = [\mathrm{K}(y), l], \quad \text{say};$$
$$u = \omega(x, a) = \bar{\omega}(x^e, a) = \bar{\omega}(x^e, k, l) = \log(1 + klx^e);$$
$$\alpha^*(y) = (y, l^*)$$
$$V_1 = \max_\alpha E_x u = \max_l \max_{\mathrm{K}} E_x \log(1 + K(y)\, lx) =$$
$$= \max_l E_x \log(1 + ylx^e) = \max_l \sum_{x^i} \sum_{x^e} p(x^i, x^e) \log(1 +$$
$$+ (x^e)^2\, lx^i);$$

since x^i and x^e are independent and $(x^e)^2 = 1$, we have, denoting by $p(x^i)$ $(=p^i$ or $q^i)$ the (marginal) probability of x^i

$$V_1 = \max_l \sum_{x^i} p(x^i) \log(1 + lx^i) =$$
$$= \max_l [p^i \log(1 + l) + q^i \log(1 - l)] = C$$

To use Kelly's summary (p. 926): "If a gambler bets on the input symbol to a communication channel and bets his money in the same proportion each time a particular symbol is received, his capital will grow (or shrink) exponentially. If the odds are consistent with the probabilities of occurrence of the transmitted symbols (i.e., equal to their reciprocals[8]), the maximum value of this exponential rate of growth will be equal to the rate of transmission of information."

In constructing his example, Kelly was motivated (pp. 917–918) by the desire to attach "a value measure to a communication system" *without using* a function "defined on pairs of symbols which tells how bad it is to receive a certain symbol when a specified symbol is transmitted." Kelly calls this function "a cost function." In our notation, it is the function $\bar{\omega}$ in the definition of the payoff: $u=\bar{\omega}(x^e, a^*(y))$ where $\bar{\omega}$ is the payoff function (independent of the state x^i of the information instrument), and where $\alpha^*(y)$ is the action appropriate to the received symbol; that is, the action rule α^* maximizes the expectation Eu:

$$\max_\alpha E\bar{\omega}(x^e, \alpha(y)) = E\bar{\omega}(x^e, \alpha^*(y)).$$

This interpretation of Kelly's term 'cost function'[9] is confirmed by his further reference to the "utility theory of Von Neumann" and to a property of the "cost function," *viz.*, "it must be such that... a system must be preferable to another if its average cost is less." Kelly believes that the "cost function approach" "is too general to shed any light on the specific problems of communication theory. The distinguishing feature of a communication system is that the ultimate receiver (thought of here as a person) is in a position to profit from any knowledge of the input symbols or even from a better estimate of their probabilities. A cost function, if it is supposed to apply to a communication system, must somehow reflect this feature."

In this weak form, Kelly's requirement is, in fact, satisfied by *any* payoff function. For, by the definition of maximum, if a^* maximizes $\omega(x, a)$ and b^* maximizes $\omega(y, b)$ then $\omega(x, a^*) \geqq \omega(x, b^*)$: the profit is not diminished by an action chosen in full knowledge of the true state x. And similarly with ω replaced by its expectation, x by its distribution P, y by some estimate of P, and the action variable a by α, the rule of action.

It seems however that Kelly has in mind one or both of the following two stronger requirements. One of them is: *given* any payoff function, capacities of different channels should be *ordered* according to the expected payoffs associated with these channels. A still stronger requirement would be, that the maximum expected payoff be equal or proportional to, or an increasing linear function (or some other fixed increasing function) of the channel capacity *independent* of the payoff function; so that channel capacity is a *measure* (up to a fixed increasing transformation) of the expected payoff. We may call these two requirements the ordering and the measuring requirements, respectively.

We have seen in Section 9 on faulty information, that the *ordering* requirement is satisfied by any payoff function, for the case when the channel transmits two alternative symbols (messages) only. The stronger, or measurement, requirement is not, in general, satisfied; we have seen in Section 9 that it is not satisfied even for 2-message channels.

Suppose, for example, the gambler would have to pay a progressive income tax on his gains. The exponential rate of growth of capital would then be, not $\log(1+lx^i)$, but $\log f(1+lx^i)$, with f a concave function. And the result (11) would not obtain.

This agrees with Kelly's own result. Although he declared the intention (p. 918) "to take some real-life situation which seems to possess the essential features of a communication problem, and to analyze it without the introduction of an arbitrary cost function," he concludes that the particular criterion followed by his gambler – and resulting in the information value being equal to channel capacity – is related to the particular assumptions made: the results would be different, writes Kelly, if we "for example, suppose the gambler's wife allowed him to bet one dollar each week but not to reinvest his winnings."

The re-investment feature of Kelly's example has attracted the attention of R. Bellman and R. Kalaba (1957), who regarded it as a case in dynamic programming, a good program being characterized by an optimal constant l^*. These writers are quite clear that the coincidence in this case, of information value and channel capacity, is due to the logarithmic nature of the payoff function chosen.

11. Incentive Fee to Forecaster

In an article 'Measures of the Value of Information', John McCarthy (1956) attaches to this term still a different meaning. Generalizing a concept due to I. J. Good (1952, p. 113) he defines what we might call an *efficient incentive fee function.* Good speaks of a "fair fee" and McCarthy – more appropriately, we think – speaks of "a payoff rule to keep the forecaster honest." The payoff in question is *not* the value of information in our sense. It is not the worth of information to its user.

The question raised by both Good and McCarthy is extremely interesting and, in fact, opens up a new field of problems in the economics of information. Yet an incentive fee to the expert is not the same thing as the value of his service to the client. If I am in a hurry and am aware that exactly 25 cents added to the taxi driver's tip will suffice to make him skillfully avoid the traffic lights, I shall conditionally promise him exactly an extra quarter; though by arriving in time for my appointment I shall gain $1000. If on this basis, the expected values of his gain and of my gain are computed, two quite different numbers will result. The same applies to the services of a forecaster.

Good's problem, presented by him rather casually in a single paragraph, can be stated as follows. Denote by $p=(p_1,\dots,p_n)$ the vector of the probabilities of alternative events $k=1,\dots,n$. The client does not know p but has an *a priori* expectation $Ep=(Ep_1,\dots,Ep_n)=(\bar{p}_1,\dots,\bar{p}_n)$. The expert will tell the client an estimate y of p, $y=(y_1,\dots,y_n)$, and receive a fee $f(y_k)$ if the event k happens. We shall call the function f an efficient incentive function if f has the following properties:

(a) the expected fee $F=F(y)=\sum p_k f(y_k)$ is largest when $y=p$ (i.e., when the expert's estimates are perfect):

$$F(y)=\sum p_k f(y_k)\leqq \sum p_k f(p_k)=\max_y F(y)=F^*,\quad \text{say}. \tag{12}$$

(b) the expected fee is nil if the expert does not know more than the client:

$$\sum \bar{p}_k f(\bar{p}_k)=0. \tag{13}$$

Good states that both requirements are satisfied by

$$f(y_k)=A\log y_k+B,\quad A>0;\quad k=1,\dots,n. \tag{14}$$

To see that (12) is satisfied when f has this form,[10] we can maximize $\sum p_k \log y_k$ with respect to the y_k subject to $\sum y_k = 1$; and then check that the maximizing vector y is non-negative. A little more insight is gained if we remember that $\log y_k$ is a concave function of y_k; if $z_k > 0$ for all k and $\sum z_k = s$, then

$$\log(\sum p_k \cdot z_k/s) \geqq \sum p_k \log(z_k/s),$$
$$\log \sum p_k z_k \geqslant \sum p_k \log z_k; \quad \text{let} \quad z_k = y_k/p_k;$$
$$0 \geqq \sum p_k \log y_k - \sum p_k \log p_k;$$

hence if $A > 0$ then

$$\sum p_k (A \log p_k + B) \geqq \sum p_k (A \log y_k + B) \quad \text{for any} \quad B.$$

Hence, the logarithmic incentive function satisfies (12). It yields the maximum expected fee

$$F^* = \max_y F(y) = A \sum p_k \cdot \log p_k + B, \tag{15}$$

a linearly decreasing function of the entropy parameter that characterizes the true probability distribution of the external events. By the very nature of the problem, the comparative importance of the events and of client's actions for the client's welfare, and hence the payoff function to the client, does not enter the function f, nor the maximum expected fee F^*. This latter quantity is *not*, as McCarthy seems to assert, "a good measure of what it is worth to be given these probabilities." It does measure, not the *worth* to the client, but the (expected) *cost* to the client if, to stimulate the expert's efforts to give a good forecast, the client has agreed to pay him according to an efficient incentive fee formula.

On the other hand, as Good remarks, his result is affected by the money utility function of the *expert* (not the client): if the expert maximizes the expectation, not of his money fee but, say, of its logarithm, the efficient fee schedule ceases to be related to entropy as in (15). Thus, the payoff function *to the expert* (the function whose value the expert tries to maximize) does affect the expected cost (not the expected payoff) to the client.

The result is also influenced by the client's 'beliefs' (not by his uses or tastes, as expressed in his payoff function): for it is easily seen that in order for the incentive function (14) to satisfy the second efficiency property, (13), the number B must be

$$B = -\sum \bar{p}_k \log \bar{p}_k \cdot A.$$

As to the parameter A: it is an item for bargaining between the client and the expert, as McCarthy has correctly remarked in a more general context.

In the particular case when, *a priori*, all events are equally probable, all $\bar{p}_k = 1/n$, $B = A \log n$. And if $n=2$, $F^* = A(p_1 \log p_1 + p_2 \log p_2) + \log 2$.

Thus Kelly's result in (11) is formally a special case of Good's result. But the content is quite different. Kelly's maximand is the expected payoff to the client; the variable with respect to which it is maximized is the decision of the client, *viz.*, the choice of the optimal fraction l to be reinvested; and p_1, p_2 are characteristics of the expert (the 'channel'), *viz.*, the probabilities of his being right or wrong; p_1, p_2 are known to the client. Good's maximand, on the other hand, is the expected payoff to the expert; it is maximized with respect to the expert's decision, *viz.*, the effort to make a better estimate of the p's; and the p's are characteristics (unknown to the client) of the external environment (the 'source'), not of the expert. Kelly's quantity is related to the demand price, Good's to the supply price, of information.

McCarthy has generalized Good's problem as follows: instead of looking for a single efficient incentive function f, the same for all y_k, and depending on one variable only, he looks for n functions $f_1, \ldots, f_n$, each depending on the vector $y = (y_1, \ldots, y_n)$ of the expert's estimates. If the event k happens, the expert receives $f_k(y)$. The set $(f_1, \ldots, f_n)$ of functions is an efficient incentive function (or, in McCarthy's words, a payoff rule that keeps the forecaster honest) if, regardless of the value of $p = (p_1, \ldots, p_n)$ the expected fee $\sum p_k f_k(y)$ is maximized if and only if $y = p$, i.e., if $y_k = p_k$ for each k. McCarthy then states, without proof, that the set $(f_1, \ldots, f_n)$ is efficient if and only if $f_k(y) = (\partial/\partial y_k)\, \phi(y)$, where ϕ is a convex function homogeneous of the first degree.[11]

Granting at least the sufficiency part of this theorem of McCarthy, it would follow that the logarithmic incentive function is not the only efficient one. Beckmann's function (14*) in a previous footnote seems to confirm this for Good's special case. Consequently, the maximum expected fee does not have to be related to the entropy formula.

We may question moreover whether the client is really interested in the efficient incentive function defined as the one that 'keeps the expert honest', i.e., encourages him to bring every y_k as close to p_k as possible. For different values of k, the (signed) error $y_k - p_k$ may be of different importance to the client.

Some tantalizingly short remarks of McCarthy give the promise of a fruitful analysis of the non-zero sum game between the expert and the client, and of the expert's effort. In this approach, the entropy formula loses its significance; and the payoff functions of the expert and the client must gain in significance.

NOTES

* *Author's note*: The paper, completed during the author's year on a rotating visiting research professorship at Carnegie Institute of Technology, was started under a contract of the Office of Naval Research with the Cowles Foundation for Research in Economics. Acknowledgments are due to my colleagues at the Cowles Foundation, M. Beckmann, G. Debreu, C. B. McGuire, J. Harsanyi, and R. Radner, and to a correspondence with C. B. Tompkins. See also the author's earlier paper [1954] and, of course, L. J. Savage's book [1954], especially Chapters 6–7.

1 As pointed out to me by George A. Miller of Harvard to whom I owe many of the references to the literature used here.

2 See, for example, Gilbert [1958].

3 Taken from Marschak and Radner [1958], Chapter 3.

4 We follow some comments of McGuire [1959], and the discussion of Feinstein [1958].

5 Here is an example of non-monetary payoffs: To compare the information values of a slow and a fast military communication system Thornton Page [1957] assumed that the lack of information – due to communication delay – on each of the relevant external variables 'degrades the decision' in a given way. In our terminology, the best decision possible on the basis of delayed information results in a diminished payoff. The information values computed by Page are, in effect, the expected payoffs under each of the compared communication systems.

6 *Added in 1973*. See Figures 3s, 5s in *Selected Essays*, 31.

7 Kelly justifies the result in a different way, trying to avoid the concept of a criterion (payoff) function whose *expectation* is being maximized. He uses the time-sequence involved in his problem: the sequence of capital amounts, c_t after the t-th bet. He computes the *probability limit* of the average

$$\frac{1}{T}\sum_{t=1}^{T} \log(c_t/c_{t-1}),$$

where $c_t = c_0(1+l)^{W_t}(1-l)^{L_t}$, and W_t = number of wins, L_t = number of losses in the first t bets, and $W_t + L_t = t$. This does, in effect, amount to assuming the criterion function (10); although the proof seems formally to duplicate the reasoning establishing the entropy formula for the transmission of a long sequence of messages about varying states of nature, Section 7 above.

8 This is the case of fair odds, with p^e arbitrary; but Kelly treated also the case when odds are not fair.

[9] The word 'cost' stands presumably for the *negative* difference between two payoffs of which the smaller one is due to poorer information. This should not be confused with our use of the word cost, as the cost to the seller of information.
[10] McCarthy refers to an unpublished proof by Gleason, of the uniqueness of the logarithmic solution (14). Martin Beckmann constructed the following counterexample, with $n=2$:

$$(14^*) \qquad f(y_k) = \int_{1/2}^{y_k} \frac{g(|t-1/2|)}{t}\,dt, \quad k=1,2,$$

where g is an arbitrary positive-valued function. The expression $p_1 f(y_1)+(1-p_1)$ $f(1-y_1)$ is maximized when $y_1=p_1$.
[10] *Added in 1973.* For $n>3$, a proof was given by Aczél and Pfanzagl in 1966. See D. H. Krantz, R. D. Luce, P. Suppes and A. Tversky, *Foundations of Measurement*, Vol. I, pp. 401, 406, Academic Press, 1971.
[11] However, Good's case seems to provide a counter-example showing that the homogeneity property does not seem to be necessary. We know that if, for every $h, f_h(y)=$ $=A\log y_h+B$ then F is an efficient incentive function. Find $\phi(y)$ such that, for every h,

$$f_h(y) = \partial\phi/\partial y_h = A\log y_h + B\,;$$

then $\partial^2\phi/\partial y_h\,\partial y_j=0,\ h\neq j$; hence $\phi(y)$ is a sum:

$$\phi(y) = \Sigma\int f_h(y)\,dy_h = A\Sigma y_h(\log y_h - 1) + B\Sigma y_h + C = \\ = A\Sigma y_h\log y_h + K,$$

where $K=B+C-A$.

It is easily seen that $\phi(y)$ is indeed convex. But it is not homogeneous of first degree: for $\phi(ry)-r\phi(y)=K(1-r)+Ar\log r$; this cannot vanish for all r and fixed K, A.

Added in 1973. The intended meaning of McCarthy's homogeneity condition has been clarified by A. D. Hendrickson and R. J. Buehler, 'Proper Scores for Probability Forecasters', *Annals of Math. Stat.* **42** (1971) 1916–1921. See also L. J. Savage, ''Elicitation of Personal Probabilities and Expectations', *J. Amer. Stat. Assn.* **66** (1971) 783–801.

BIBLIOGRAPHY

Bellman, R. and Kalaba, R., 'Dynamic Programming and Statistical Communication Theory', *Proc. Nat. Acad. Sci.* **43** (1957) 749–751.

Feinstein, A., *Foundations of Information Theory*, New York, 1958.

Gilbert, E. N., 'An Outline of Information Theory', *The American Statistician* **12** (1958) 13–19.

Good, I. J., 'Rational Decisions', *J. Royal Stat. Soc., B.* **14**, No. 1 (1952) 107–115, especially p. 112.

Hitch, C. J., 'Economics and Military Operations Research', *Rev. Ec. Stat.* **50** (1958) 199–209.

Kelly, J., 'A New Interpretation of Information Rate', *Bell Syst. Tech. J.* **35** (1956) 917–926.

Marschak, J., 'Towards an Economic Theory of Information and Organization', 1954, *Selected Essays*, 20.

Marschak, J. and Radner, R., *Economic Theory of Teams*, Chapters 2 and 3 (mimeo.), Cowles Foundation Discussion Paper No. 59, 1958. *Added in 1973.* Book with same title, Chapter 3, Yale University Press, 1972.

McCarthy, J., 'Measures of the Value of Information', *Proc. Nat. Acad. Sci.*, **42** (1956) 654–655.

McGuire, C. B., *Comparison of Information Structures* (mimeo.), Cowles Foundation Discussion Paper No. 71, 1959, Revised and published later as Chapter 5 of *Decision and Organization*, North-Holland Publ. Co., 1972, pp. 101–130.

Page, Thornton, 'The Value of Information in Decision-Making', *Proceedings of the First International Conference on Operations Research* (Oxford, 1957). Operations Research Society of America, 1957, 306–314.

Savage, L. J., *The Foundations of Statistics*, New York, 1954. Revised: Dover, 1972.

Shannon, C., *A Mathematical Theory of Communications*, *Bell Syst. Tech. J.*, 1948, pp. 379–423, 623–656.

Von Neumann, J. and Morgenstern, O., *Theory of Games and Economic Behavior* (2nd ed.), 1948.

24

THEORY OF AN EFFICIENT SEVERAL PERSON FIRM*

(1960)

The firm of the classical theory is managed by a single person, the entrepreneur; he has complete knowledge of his present and future environment and is efficient in the special sense that he chooses plans maximizing his profit. More recent studies deal with a firm that is led by one or more persons. Each of them decides on the basis of partial information; and the decision may or may not be efficient.

Efficiency. In one respect, my exposition will not be quite so general. For I shall confine myself to the efficient firm, although in a broader sense. The firm will be assumed to have a consistent order of preferences. Its goal need not be maximum profit.

Our Chairman today, Richard Cyert, is one of those who have searched for significant theorems about inefficient behavior of firms. I submit that the analysis of efficient business firms, while less general and less closely portraying reality, is also useful, for two reasons: (1) It may well be that, on the whole, the efficiency assumption is not a bad approximation, especially for organizations that have survived over a long time; they have behaved as if they had pursued the goal of maximizing the chance of survival (not the profit); (2) we are often asked, not to describe how badly business people have solved their problems in the past, but to solve a business problem, as best we can; to act like engineers, not to engage in comparative zoology.

Subjective Probabilities and Utilities. Strictly speaking, the manager of A. Marshall's theory, if he did not know the environment with certainty, knew the probability distribution characterizing it; and he computed and maximized the actuarial value (the mathematical expectation) of utility accordingly. When Frank Knight showed that relevant future events are, in the main, not repetitive, it was concluded that the theory of probability is of no interest to the theory of the firm. This made the analysis of decisions somewhat inarticulate. Yet in recent years the practical needs of business and military decision-makers made it necessary to take a second look. Modern statisticians, asked to advise on action without being able to collect large samples, have approached the problem in the economist's spirit, as one of efficient behavior. Somewhat simplifying, we can say that the 'personalistic' view of L. J. Savage and others has revived the concepts and behavior postulates made in the eighteenth century by Thomas Bayes, a founder of the theory of probability; thus: (1) if, for whatever reason, you bet 9 guineas against 1 on one of two alternative events, you behave as if you were assigning at least .9 probability to one of them, and were choosing that action (viz., to bet rather than not to bet) which maximizes the actuarial value of your gain; (2) if the trials are repeated, you will achieve maximum actuarial gain by raising, after each trial, the odds in favor of that event which has just occurred.

The definition of (subjective) probabilities given in the first clause reminds the economist of the definition of the consumer's subjective utilities: if, and only if, the decision-maker is consistent do those numbers, or ranks, exist; i.e., can be ascertained from his behavior. And because of the second clause, the subjective probabilities will approach the relative frequencies, and hence approach the objective probabilities, as repetitions become more numerous. Knight's risk – the case when probabilities are known to the decision-maker – is thus a limiting case.

The main step beyond Bayes made by modern thinkers (beginning with F. P. Ramsey) consists in replacing money by utility. This brings us, in fact, back to Marshall's view of gambling, but with probabilities reinterpreted subjectively. If business is gambling (as Mr. Baruch asserted against squeamish J. P. Morgan), it is less like roulette than like betting on horses.

The efficient man, then, behaves as if there existed two sets of numbers called, respectively, utilities (attached to the states of the decision-maker) and probabilities (attached to the states of the environment), whose sum of products (the expected utility) he maximizes. This takes care of the manager who is cautious in the sense that he assigns an almost infinite negative utility to bankruptcy; or a manager who merely aspires to survive, or to achieve some other 'level of aspiration' or who is interested, not only in profits, but also in power or status. No tautology is involved, since consistency may be contradicted by facts.

By incorporating subjective probabilities, economic theory of choice becomes a theory, not only of consistent tastes, but also of consistent beliefs. On this basis, a large number of business problems have been submitted to analysis: inventory control, production planning, portfolio selection, quality control. Let me point out some important concepts and relations fundamental to these studies and to the theory of the several-person firm, and not so clearly perceived in older theory.

Pay-off Function. The action of the decision-maker, given the environment, determines his future state. Therefore, depending on the particular criterion applied – profit, sales, status, survival, or power, or any combination of these – action and environment jointly determine the utility, or pay-off. The table showing the pay-off for each action in each environment is called pay-off function. If, for example, a competitive firm is judged by the simple criterion of profits, the pay-off function coincides with the classical profit function, which essentially reflects production technology and market conditions. The actions are, in this case, the inputs of raw materials, labor, etc.; and the product and input prices constitute the environment.

Decision Rule. Under uncertainty, the firm has to determine not an optimal action but an optimal decision rule. The rule tells how to adjust action to information. To be sure, in the extreme case of uncertainty, when the man cannot learn anything beyond the probability distribution he believes in, he can do no better than fix some optimal *routine* – a constant action that maximizes expected pay-off. For example, the expected profit of a firm may be maximized by fixing output so that, on the average, marginal revenue and cost are equal, the actual prices being unknown. In general, uncertainty is not that extreme. The firm can adjust its action to varying information even though information is not a complete or precise statement about the environment (but may merely help to estimate it). An optimal decision rule calls for an action that maximizes the expected conditional pay-off, given the information; for then the absolute (nonconditional) expected pay-off will be, in the long run, higher than if information were ignored. In the previous example, the optimal decision rule would become: given the information, choose an input level at which the conditionally expected marginal cost and revenue are equated.

A particularly important case of partial information was pointed out by Albert Hart, the economist. In general, the firm's profit depends upon a time-sequence of actions; but the firm's best plan is not a time-sequence of actions but, more flexibly, a time-sequence of decision rules, each making the action at a given future time depend on the partial information that will be available at that time. In the theory of games a sequence of decision rules is called 'strategy' (as distinct from a single action or move). In statistics it is called 'sequential decision function'. Its name in the current literature on operations research is 'dynamic program'. For brevity we shall use the term 'decision rule' (in singular) to denote the whole sequence of such rules.

Information Cost. Information is not costless. A firm which, not contented with a rough idea of averages, bases its decision on a very close continual study of various markets, has to pay for it. The closer the information to the true state of the environment, the better will be the best action chosen, in the sense of a higher expected utility of the outcome. That this gain may be offset by the cost of gathering information was first emphasized in statistical decision theory: large samples are expensive. Similarly all research activities of a firm, and also its internal communications, are costly, because they claim the manager's limited time or because a delayed decision may be ill-suited to a changed environment.

Information Rule. We shall call an 'information rule' the schedule that tells, for each state of the environment, what the firm will know about it. Suppose the relevant aspect of the environment is the set of prices of all raw materials and products of the firm and its competitors. Under one information rule, the firm might learn all these prices daily, to the nearest half-cent. Under another information rule, the firm might learn some of these prices weekly, others monthly and with less precision, and still others not at all. The former information rule may contribute more to the expected profit but will also presumably cost more.

Decision Cost. Cost is also attached to each decision rule. The processing of information into decision may be a difficult mental task; it is the more costly the larger its claims on the available capacity of the manager, and the larger the loss resulting from delay.

Organizational Form. We shall define organizational form as a pair of two rules: the decision rule and the information rule. A schedule showing the cost of each organizational form may be called the 'organizational cost function'.

If information and decision were costless, the efficient firm's problem would be to find a decision rule that bases action on all available information and maximizes expected utility. Since information and decision are not costless, the problem consists in finding simultaneously the decision rule and the information rule – i.e., in finding the organizational form – that will maximize expected utility net of organizational cost.

The solution of the problem – the optimal organizational form – will depend on the given circumstances. And what are these givens of the problem? They are, of course: the pay-off function; the probability distribution of the states of the environment; and the organizational cost function. For remember that each information rule translates environment into (usually partial) information, and each decision rule translates information into action. Hence each organizational form translates environment into action. But the action and the environment determine jointly the achieved utility, in a manner described by the pay-off function. Now, if information and decision were costless, the utility achieved in a given environment would depend on the pay-off function and the organizational form. Therefore the expectation of utility, i.e., its average taken over all possible states of the environment would depend on (1) their probabilities, (2) the pay-off function, and (3) the organizational form. The net expected utility depends, in addition, on (4) the organizational cost function. This cost function, the pay-off function, and the probability distribution are not under the firm's control. Given these three out of the four factors determining the net expected pay-off, the firm can choose the fourth – the organizational form – so as to maximize the net expected pay-off.

Illustrations. To illustrate the effect of the probability distribution on the optimal organizational form, suppose an external variable is subject only to small variations; then it may not pay to get information about them and to adjust one's actions to this information. Or suppose two variables are strongly correlated; then it may suffice to get information about one of them.

To illustrate the effect of the pay-off function, suppose that two purchased inputs are mutually strong complements or close substitutes; i.e., the marginal pay-off due to one of them strongly depends on the amount of the other. Then the firm benefits from knowing the variations in the prices of both; it will increase one input not only whenever the price of that input falls but also whenever the price of its complement falls (or that of its substitute rises).

To illustrate the effect of organizational cost: If it is large, the firm may prefer to pursue routine policy (mentioned by me earlier), and not to be kept informed about the variations of any of the external variables. It is because of high decision cost that a retailer uses a mechanical markup rule. It is because of high information cost that he does not spy on his competitors more extensively, and judges the market on the basis of his sales only.

Several-Person Firm. How is the problem modified if the firm consists of several – say, n – decision-makers (executives)? Each of them decides about different things and on the basis of different information. Our concept of organizational form has to be generalized. There are now n information rules, each translating true environment into some different, partial information, available to a different executive; and n decision rules, each translating the information of a given executive into his action. The set of n information rules – who learns what? – is generated by a communication network and the rules of operating it: Who talks to whom and when? Again, decision and information cost will mainly consist of claims on the executives' time and of losses due to delayed decisions. It is mostly a fixed cost inasmuch as these persons are usually on long-term contracts.

To choose a good network of communication and good rules of operating it may require difficult analysis in any particular case. Economic theory never does more than establish some general results. Even these are, so far, fragmentary rather than systematic.

Suppose an outsider wants to organize or reorganize a firm according to his own criteria and beliefs. How will his choice of organizational form depend on his views of the pay-off function, the probability distribution, and the schedule of organizational costs? How do these factors affect the need for more or less communication between executives?

Properties of Pay-off Function: Complementarity. The allotted roles of two executives may be such that, with communication, they can increase each other's effectiveness; without communication, they may step on each other's toes. At first sight, there seems to be more complementarity, and hence more need for communication, when the different operations must be performed in succession – e.g., along a conveyor or at successive stops of an airline (studied by M. Beckmann)[1] – than in the case of 'parallel coupling' as among branch managers of a hotel chain. However, simultaneous operations may also imply high complementarity, if the branches have to compete for a limited capacity of some central facility, as with the salesmen of a bakery (studied by C. B. McGuire)[2]. Finally, a special case (emphasized in the theory of non-constant-sum games) occurs when the pay-off function has several maxima; e.g., two or more timetables are often equally good, but some 'co-ordinator' has to choose one.

Person-by-Person Maximization. In the case of some pay-off functions, the maximizing decision rules can be found by step-wise approximations, person by person. This is true of the smooth pay-off functions beloved of classical economic theory: the summit of a smooth hill can be reached step-wise by moving due north and stopping at the highest point on that route; moving due east from there, and finding the highest point on that route; moving north from there, etc. Yet the hill representing the pay-off function may have a 'ridge', as when, e.g., the sales of a nonstorable product are proportional to production or to demand, whichever is smaller; alternate adjustments by the manager of production and that of promotion will lead to one of the many points where production equals demand, but this need not be the highest one.

Properties of the Probability Distribution. We have already mentioned, for the single-person case, the effect of variances and of correlations. The extension is obvious. As another example, suppose that the branch manager of a bank has power to decide on his own, except in emergencies; e.g., he can grant a loan only below a certain limit. Clearly, the optimal limit will depend both on the relative cost of the central and local officers' time and on the probabilities of applications for loans of various amounts.

Incentives and Leadership. So far, we discussed the goodness of alternative organizational forms chosen on the basis of the goals and beliefs of some outsider: an 'organizer', a management consultant. The goals and the beliefs of the several executives themselves will, in general, differ. E.g., the goal of the owner-manager is not that of his officers. Goal divergence is diminished by appropriate incentives – positive such as a bonus or negative such as the threat of dismissal. A decision rule takes the form: Upon receiving information, proceed so as to maximize the actuarial value of utility to yourself, using as much additional information as you possess or can gather on your own. But even a complete identification of goals would not make beliefs identical. And an action optimal when the actuarial values are computed on the basis of one set of probabilities is not optimal under another such set. A leader is that member of the organization who imposes his goals and beliefs on the choice of the organizational form; he does so by setting incentives and thus controlling the actions of other members.

No theory is possible when concepts are vague. Yet an economist who takes seriously the multipersonal nature of the modern firm has at his disposal only ill-defined traditional concepts such as leadership, power, authority, co-operation, centralization. He is used to clearer ones; like 'complementarity between factors of production'. The present paper attempts to point a way to the necessary clarification.

NOTES

* Prepared under a contract of the Office of Naval Research, Task NR 047-006, with the Cowles Foundation for Research in Economics at Yale University. The main contents of this expository paper resulted from the author's long collaboration with Roy Radner.

[1] Beckmann, M., 'Decision and Team Problems in Airline Reservations', *Econometrica*, **26** (1958), 134–145.

[2] McGuire, C. B., 'Some Team Models of a Sales Organization', *Management Science*, **7** (1961), 101–130.

25

PROBLEMS IN INFORMATION ECONOMICS*

(1964)

INTRODUCTION

Problems in information economics consist in characterizing optimal 'information systems'. The microeconomics of information, an extension of the usual theory of the firm, a household, or a government agency considers a single decider with fixed tastes, beliefs, and resources. It is concerned with the choice of an optimal information system under those fixed conditions. An information system may be a simple instrument for collecting observations of the environment, or a complex network (an 'organization') of men and machines who make observations, process them, and send messages to each other and finally to those who perform actions impinging on the environment and thus yielding a 'payoff'. In this complex case, the chooser of the optimal information system can be visualized as the 'organizer' (e.g., a management consultant). For brevity, we shall designate all information systems simply as 'channels'.

Corresponding to our description of micro-economics of information, we can regard the macro-economics of information as an extension of the theory of welfare economics, or public policy. It would attempt to characterize a socially optimal allocation of channels, given the distribution of tastes and beliefs, and given the society's total resources and their initial distribution.

After introducing, in Sections 1 to 6, some useful concepts and propositions, we shall apply them in the rest of the paper to focus on a special micro-economic question, of much relevance to any future macro-economic theory of information. This question is: is there, in any sense, a 'law of decreasing returns to information?' In the case of land, labor, and capital, the question is known to be crucial in the discussion of optimal resource allocation methods in a market or a planned economy, at least in a somewhat weaker form, as the 'assumption of non-decreasing returns to scale' (rather than to a particular factor of production), also known as the assumption of convexity of the set of possible production plans:

see, for example, Debreu [1]. If that assumption is not satisfied the optimal allocation may be a 'boundary solution' (rather than an 'interior solution'): so that it may be best to use a resource to the limit.

In the case of land, labor, and capital, the discussion of decreasing returns would be simplified if one could, without affecting the results too strongly, replace 'bundles' of land plots, of working individuals, and of assets and liabilities, by appropriate aggregates called 'factors of production' and represented by real numbers (instead of vectors). But this is possible only in special cases. The same is true of channels, or information systems. As we shall see, a channel is essentially characterized by a joint probability distribution of 'messages' and 'events'. To replace the distribution by a single parameter (e.g., some single measure of 'information capacity') will, in general, vitiate the results, that is, provide non-optimal solutions. The analogy is particularly strong between economics of information and economics of capital, the latter being a bundle of assets and liabilities characterized essentially by the joint probability of their yields. In fact, an attentive reader will be able to broaden at will the interpretation of our terms in this article, so as to embrace the general question: to find conditions for the optimality of any given arrangement of men, materials and machines, including men, materials, and machines used in gathering, processing, and communicating data. The recent development of 'automation' has perhaps added some realism to this generalization of the economic problem.

To familiarize the reader with the relevant concepts and propositions, we shall use very simple examples and accompany them by economic interpretations. In the main 'Example 1', more and more assumptions are made as the discussion progresses. They permit us to by-pass the aggregation problem and, in Part II of the paper, to discuss explicitly an important case of increasing returns to information.

I. GENERAL PROBLEM

1. *Acts, States, Channels*

Given: $A=\{a\}$, the set of possible *acts* of the decision maker; $X=\{x\}$, the set of possible *states* of his environment. Any partition of A will be called a set of *act descriptions*; any partition of X will be called a set of *state descriptions*.

Given: $H=\{h\}$, a set of *channels* available to the decision maker; and, for each channel h, a set $Y^h=\{y^h\}$ of state descriptions called signals or *messages* (these are messages that can be received by the decision maker). Thus y^h is a subset of X.

EXAMPLE 1. Let

(1) $x=(x_1,\ldots,x_n)\in X;\quad X=\text{real } n\text{-space}$

(2) $m\leqslant n;$

the following channels will be considered with appropriate interpretations:

(3.1) $h' : y^{h'} = (x_1, \ldots, x_m)$ thus $Y^{h'} = \text{real } m\text{-space}$

(3.2) $h : y^h = \sum_1^m x_i$ thus $Y^h = \text{real line}$

(3.3) $h^* : y^{h^*} = \begin{cases} 1 & \text{if } \sum_1^m x_i > 0 \\ -1 & \text{otherwise} \end{cases}$ thus Y^{h^*} consists of 2 points

The following INTERPRETATIONS may be useful to fix ideas:

(a) $x_i (i=1,\ldots,n)$ is the (possibly non-positive) change in the unit price of a security over the next month. Channel h' makes (infallible) predictions of price changes for m selected securities. h predicts the total (possibly non-positive) gain on a portfolio composed of these securities, one unit of each. h^* predicts whether this gain is positive or not; it is a 'binary channel'. [Instead of a portfolio of securities, we might also consider a list of prices of selected goods and services demanded by the nation, and a price-index based on such a list.]

(b) $x_i (i=1,\ldots,n)$ is the score (measured from some norm) on the ith test of a prospective employee, $y^{h'}$ is a list of m scores, y^h is their sum, y^{h^*} tells whether the norm is, on the average, exceeded.

Note that of the three partitions $Y^{h'}$, Y^h, Y^{h^*} of X, the first is *finer* than the second, and the second is *finer* than the third in the following sense:

DEFINITION. Let Z and Z' be partitions of X. Z is said to be *finer than* Z' (or alternatively, Z' to be *coarser than* Z) if for every z in Z there is a z' and Z' with $z\subseteq z'$.

The relation 'finer than' (the words 'a subpartition of' are also used[1]) induced a partial ordering on the set $\{Z\}$ of all partitions of X. Moreover, $\{Z\}$ is a lattice possessing a (unique) finest element, $\{(x)\}$, and a (unique) coarsest element, (X).

2. *Payoff-Relevant Sets of State Descriptions and Act Descriptions*

We shall continue to denote by $Z=\{z\}$ a partition of X; and we shall denote by $C=\{c\}$ a partition of A. In general, the decision maker associates with a given pair 'state description z and act description c' a set of one or more physical outcomes (e.g., the possession of several alternative lots of land) and he may or may not attach to these outcomes the same payoff in terms of 'utility' (a real number). If he does not, we say that the set $Z \times C$ of the pairs (z, c) is 'too coarse'. On the other hand $Z \times C$ is 'too fine' if, for every c in C, some pairs (z_1, c), (z_2, c) yield identical sets of utilities although $z_1 \neq z_2$; or for every z in Z, some pairs (z, c_1), (z, c_2) yield identical sets of utilities although $c_1 \neq c_2$. In the following example (Exhibit 3-1), $Z \times C$ is both too coarse and too fine (the entries are sets of utility-numbers).

EXHIBIT 3-1

A payoff matrix

Act descriptions	State descriptions		
	z_1	z_2	z_3
c_1	(1, 2)	(1, 2)	(1)
c_2	(1, 2)	(1, 2)	(1)
c_3	(3)	(3)	(0)

We can assume that the handling of too fine descriptions of states and acts induces a cost (lowers utility) to the decision maker; while too coarse descriptions of states and acts make it generally impossible to make choices, either under certainty or uncertainty.

We must therefore search for a *payoff-relevant* pair $Z \times C$, i.e., one that (if it exists) is not too coarse and not too fine. This search is preliminary to the search for a (jointly) best act description and best channel; just like the search for the efficient boundary (Irving Fisher's 'Opportunity Line': [4]) of a given feasible set is preliminary to the search for its optimal point.

The concepts will be formalized as follows, remembering that a function (a payoff function in our case) is changed when we change its domain ($Z \times C$ in our case). For a closer discussion see [5].

Given: for every partition Z of X and every partition C of A, a set $\Omega = \{\omega_{ZC}\}$ called *payoff condition*, with the following three propties:

(i) Each element ω_{ZC} of Ω is a function (called *payoff function*) from $Z \times C$ to the set of all subsets of the real line R; thus if $z \in Z$, $c \in C$, then

$$(4) \qquad \omega_{ZC}(z, c) \subseteq R$$

(ii) If $Z = \{(x)\}$ and $C = \{(a)\}$, (these are, of course, the finest partitions of X and A, respectively), then

$$(5) \qquad \omega_{ZC}\{(x), (a)\} \equiv (u_{xa}) \quad \text{is a single-element set.}$$

The number u_{xa} is called the utility of act a at state x. The function ω_{ZC} obeying (5) is called *basic payoff function.*

(iii) All payoff functions in Ω are *consistent* in the sense that

$$(6) \qquad \omega_{ZC}(z, c) = \bigcup_{x \in z} \bigcup_{a \in c} (u_{xa}) \quad \text{all} \quad z, c$$

The components z and c of the argument of a payoff function ω_{ZC} will be called, respectively, an *event* and an *action.* Hence an action is an act description. An event is a state description. A message (Section 1 above) is also a state description, and differs from an event in that a message does not, in general, enter the argument of a payoff function. Rather, it is the argument of the decision function, to be defined in Section 4.

DEFINITIONS. $Z \times C$ is sufficiently fine (or, equivalently, 'not too coarse'), given Ω, if and only if

$$(7) \qquad \omega_{ZC}(z, c) = (u_{xa}) \quad \text{all} \quad x \in z, a \in c, z \in Z, c \in C$$

$Z \times C$ is sufficiently coarse (='not too fine'), given Ω, if and only if, for every $z_1, z_2 \in Z$, $c_1, c_2 \in C$,

$$(8.1) \qquad \omega_{ZC}(z_1, c) = \omega_{ZC}(z_2, c) \quad \text{for all} \quad c \in C \quad \text{implies} \quad z_1 = z_2$$

and

$$(8.2) \qquad \omega_{ZC}(z, c_1) = \omega_{ZC}(z, c_2) \quad \text{for all} \quad z \in Z \quad \text{implies} \quad c_1 = c_2$$

$Z \times C$ is *payoff-relevant*, given Ω, if and only if $Z \times C$ is not too coarse and not too fine, given Ω.

THEOREM I. *There is one and only one payoff-relevant pair, $Z \times C$, given* Ω, (it will be sometimes denoted by $Z^{\Omega} \times C^{\Omega}$). The proof is given in [5].[2]

EXAMPLE 1 (Continued). As before, let X=real n-space, $x=(x_1, \dots, x_n)$. Let

$$(9) \qquad A = \text{real interval } (-1 \leqslant a \leqslant 1)$$

By (6), we can define two alternative payoff conditions Ω, Ω' by giving the utilities (u_{xa}, u'_{xa}, say) of each act at each state. Accordingly, define

$$(10) \qquad \Omega : u_{xa} = a \cdot \sum_1^n x_i$$

$$(10') \qquad \Omega' : u'_{xa} = \delta\left(a \sum_1^n x_i\right)$$

where δ is the *sign function* in the sense that, for any real r,

$$\delta_r \equiv \delta(r) = \begin{cases} 1 & \text{if } r > 0 \\ -1 & \text{otherwise} \end{cases}$$

[We shall retain this definition and notation for the sign function through the rest of the paper.] Now consider the following sets of state descriptions, each set being an element of the set $\{Z\}$ of all partitions of X:

$$Z^0 = \{(x)\}$$

$$Z^{\mathrm{I}} = \left\{z^{\mathrm{I}} : x \in z^{\mathrm{I}} \Leftrightarrow \sum_1^n x_i = z^{\mathrm{I}}\right\}$$

$$Z^{\mathrm{II}} = \left\{z^{\mathrm{II}} : x \in z^{\mathrm{II}} \Leftrightarrow \delta\left(\sum_1^n x_i\right) = x^{\mathrm{II}}\right\}$$

and the following set of act descriptions (actions), each an element of the set $\{C\}$ of all partitions of A:

$$C^0 = \{(a)\}$$

$$C^{\mathrm{II}} = \{c^{\mathrm{II}} : a \in c^{\mathrm{II}} \Leftrightarrow \delta(a) = c^{\mathrm{II}}\}$$

In the payoff condition is Ω as in (10), then clearly $Z^0 \times C$ is too fine, for all C in $\{C\}$, since there exists x, x^*, such that $x \neq x^*$ and yet $\sum_1^n x_i = \sum_1^n x_i^*$, and hence $u_{xa} = u_{x^*a}$, for all a. But $Z^{\mathrm{II}} \times C$ is too coarse for all C in $\{C\}$, since there exist x, x^* in X with $\sum x_i > \sum x_i^* > 0$. And

$Z \times C^{\mathrm{II}}$ is too coarse, for all Z in $\{Z\}$, for there exist $a > a^* > 0$ in A. It is easily seen that $Z^{\mathrm{I}} \times C^0$ is the pair relevant with respect to Ω.

If, on the other hand the payoff condition is Ω' as in (10′) then the pairs $Z^0 \times C$ and $Z^{\mathrm{I}} \times C$ are too fine, for all C in $\{C\}$; the pair $Z \times C^0$ is too fine, for all Z in $\{Z\}$; and it is easily seen that $Z^{\mathrm{II}} \times C^{\mathrm{II}}$ is relevant with respect to Ω'.

INTERPRETATION: 'Speculator' vs. 'sign-matcher'.

Every $z^0 \equiv (x)$ in Z^0 is some list of price-changes predicted for the month's end for each of n securities making up a portfolio. Every $c^0 \equiv (a)$ in C^0 is some number of portfolio-units, sold (if $a > 0$) or bought (if $a < 0$) today to be repurchased or resold at month's end. The *speculator's* payoff is u_{xa} in (10) if his utilities are proportional to his money gains. If a is in the interval $[-1, +1]$ it is easily seen that he need not consider other values of a than -1 or $+1$.

The professional adviser to the speculator will be rewarded or penalized, by receiving $+1$ or -1 money units depending on whether he has succeeded or failed to match the sign of the recommended action a with the sign of $\sum_1^n x_i$. The *sign-matcher's* payoff is u'_{xa} in (10′) if his utilities are proportional to his money gains.

A Corollary to Theorem I, proved with it in [5], shows how the payoff-relevant pair Z^Ω, C^Ω of partitions can be constructed when X, A and Ω are known. So far, we have evaded the question whether the decider is assumed to know the sets X and A, i.e., to be able to identify every most detailed description of states and acts. In our interpretation of Example 1 the investor's chosen dinner menu was not mentioned as an attribute of an act description, nor was the position of the planetoid Vesta mentioned among the attributes of a state description. These and many other details were tacitly judged irrelevant to the payoff that consisted of, or depended on, the profit earned on the investor's portfolio, and nothing else. We shall take up this question in Section 5.

It will be understood (because of Theorem I) that to give a payoff condition Ω implies giving a payoff function $\omega_{Z^\Omega C^\Omega}$ that maps a well defined payoff-relevant pair (Z^Ω, C^Ω) of description sets into the set of real numbers (utilities).

DEFINITIONS. Consider a payoff condition $\Omega = \{\omega_{ZC}\}$, and hence the basic payoff function u_{xa}, as given. If a_1, a_2 are two acts in A, then a_1 is said to *dominate* a_2 if $u_{xa_1} \geqslant u_{xa_2}$ for all x in X, and $u_{xa_1} > u_{xa_2}$ for some x in X. The subset $A(\Omega) = \{a(\Omega)\}$ of A consisting of all non-dominated acts $a(\Omega)$, and also every partition $C(\Omega)$ of $A(\Omega)$, will be called *efficient* with respect to Ω. Since, by definition, the decider maximizes utility, one must consider only these efficient sets (of acts or actions, respectively). Replacing every partition C of A by a partition $C(\Omega)$ of $A(\Omega)$, entails replacing the payoff condition $\{\omega_{ZC}\} \equiv \Omega$ by $\{\omega_{ZC(\Omega)}\} \equiv (\Omega)$ (say). With all the non-efficient action sets eliminated, some pairs $Z \times C$ which are too fine for Ω are not too fine for (Ω). The pair $Z^{(\Omega)} \times C^{(\Omega)}$ 'relevant' with respect to (Ω) may be called 'efficiently relevant' with respect to Ω. It will, in general, differ from the pair $Z^{\Omega} \times C^{\Omega}$ simply 'relevant' with respect to Ω.

EXAMPLE 1 (continued). Clearly, if the payoff condition is Ω as in (10), the efficient set of acts is $A(\Omega) = \{a(\Omega)\} = \{\delta_a\} = (1, -1)$, and its finest partition $C^0(\Omega) = ((1), (-1))$ is the efficient set of actions. The pair $Z^{(\Omega)} \times C^{(\Omega)}$ efficiently relevant with respect to Ω is $Z^{\text{I}} \times C^0(\Omega)$. If, on the other hand, the payoff condition is Ω' as in (10′) the efficient set of acts is $A(\Omega') = C^{\text{II}}$, and the efficiently relevant pair is $Z^{\text{II}} \times C^{\text{II}}$.

3. *Probabilities of Messages and Events*

Given: A probability measure P defined on the set X of states. (The 'personal' nature of P will be discussed below, Section 5.)

With P given, the probability distribution over any partition Z of X is determined. In particular, P determines, for a given payoff condition Ω, the probability distribution over the set Z^{Ω} of payoff-relevant state descriptions. Also, given a channel h, P determines the probability distribution over the set Y^h of potential messages that may be received by the decider.

More strongly: the probability measure P on X determines the multivariate distribution over the product space of all partitions Z of X. Therefore P determines the bivariate distribution for each pair of such partitions. In particular, the measure P on X determines the bivariate distribution of (Z^{Ω}, Y^h), for every payoff condition Ω and every channel h.

For simplicity of presentation, we shall assume X finite. The probability $P(x \in z)$ that x falls into the subset z of X, i.e., into the element z of partition Z of X, might be denoted by $p_Z(z)$, as distinguished from $p_{Z'}(z')$

where $z' \subset Z'$. But we shall be able to omit the domain index (Z, Z') if we are careful in denoting the argument of the function by appropriate lower-case letters (z, z') and write $P(x \in z) = p(z)$, $P(x \in z') = p(z')$, it being understood that $z \in Z$, $z' \in Z'$ etc. Thus, we shall define the marginal probabilities

$$(11.1) \quad p(z^{\Omega}) = P(x \in z^{\Omega}) = \sum_{x \in z^{\Omega}} p(x)$$

$$(11.2) \quad p(y^{h}) = P(x \in y^{h}) = \sum_{x \in y^{h}} p(x);$$

the joint probability:

$$(12) \quad p(z^{\Omega}, y^{h}) = P(x \in z^{\Omega}, x \in y^{h}) = \sum_{x \in z^{\Omega} \cap y^{h}} p(x);$$

and the conditional probability:

$$(13) \quad p(z^{\Omega}) | y^{h}) = p(z^{\Omega}, y^{h}) / p(y^{h})$$

All state descriptions with which we shall deal will be either *messages* received by the decider and denoted by y^h; or they will affect the payoff, i.e. occur in the argument of a payoff function $\omega_{ZC}(z, c)$. In the latter case we call them *events*, z. Thus (13) defines the conditional probability of an event, given a message.

The events z will be usually payoff-relevant, and denoted by z^{Ω}; but we shall sometimes be able to remove the superscript Ω for brevity. Also for brevity, we can omit the domain index ZC of a payoff function ω_{ZC}, it being indicated by the corresponding lower-case letters in the argument.

For example, let there be exactly 8 *states* x, labelled 1, 2,..., 8, and write $p(x) \equiv p_x$. Exhibit 3-2 gives the joint distribution $p(z, y)$ of *events* z (defined in the headings of rows) and of *messages* y (defined in the headings of columns):

EXHIBIT 3-2

Joint distribution $p(z, y)$

z: \ y:	(2, 3)	(4, 5)	(6, 1)	(7, 8)
(1, 2)	p_2	0	p_1	0
(3, 4)	p_3	p_4	0	0
(5, 6)	0	p_5	p_6	0
(7, 8)	0	0	0	p_7+p_8
$p(y)$	p_2+p_3	p_4+p_5	p_1+p_6	p_7+p_8

From this, the conditional distribution $p(z|y)=p(z, y)/p(y)$ can be derived. For example, $P[z=(1, 2)|y=(2, 3)]=p_2/(p_2+p_3)$.

SUB-EXAMPLE 1.1. (*A finite set of states*). Define the set X of *states* as in Example 1, with $n=2$. Let each co-ordinate of x have 3 values (so that X consists of $3^2=9$ points), and be distributed independently, identically, and symmetrically (in fact, binomially) about the origin, as in Exhibit 3-3. The sets Z^{I} and Z^{II} of *events* defined in Section 2, Example 1 (continued) will be designated, without danger of ambiguity, as random variables $z^{\mathrm{I}}=x_1+x_2$ (five-valued) and $z^{\mathrm{II}}=\delta(z^{\mathrm{I}})$ (two-valued). The distributions of z^{I} and z^{II} are determined by that of x as shown on Exhibit 3-3, where probability numbers corresponding to points in sets are grouped into appropriate subsets.

The distribution of messages y^h and messages y^{h*} also determined by that of states x, is shown in a similar way on Exhibit 3-4. Finally Exhibits 3-5 and 3-6 show the bivariate distributions of events and messages considered, and corresponding conditional distributions of events, given the messages. All these distributions are derived from that of states.[3]

EXHIBIT 3-3

Distributions of states $x=(x_1, x_2)$; events $z^{\mathrm{I}}=(x_1+x_2)$; and events $z^{\mathrm{II}}=\delta(z^{\mathrm{I}})$.

$P(x_i=0)=1/2$; $P(x_i=1)=1/4=P(x_i=-1)$; $p(x_i, x_j)=p(x_i)\cdot p(x_j)$

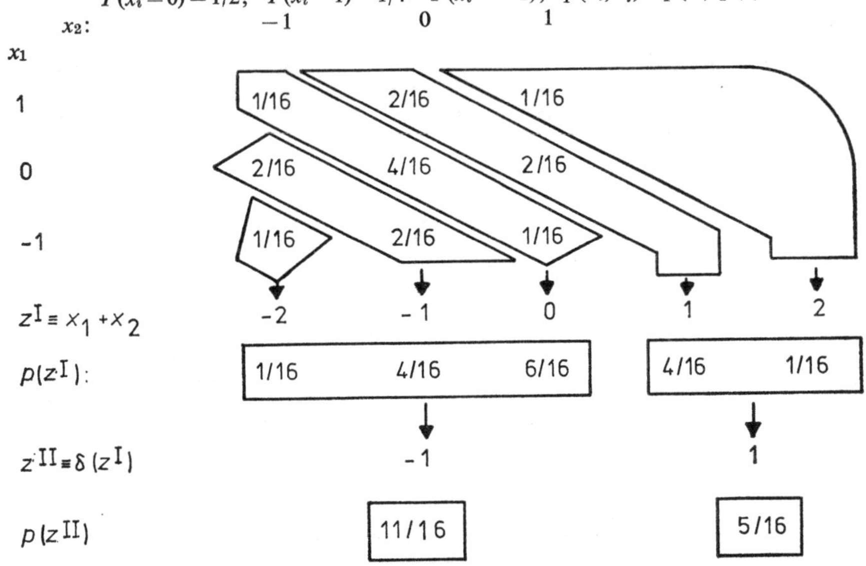

With our definition of states, events and messages, to state an 'error' in a message y – for example, to measure an observation or transmission error – is to make a comparison between the *state description* y and the *state description* (event) z; not between y and the *state* x. The state of the observation or transmission instrument, associated with the error, is itself one of the attributes of the state x of the world. This idea has been effectively stressed by R. Radner.

EXHIBIT 3-4

Distributions of states $x=(x_1, x_2)$; messages $y^h=(x_1)$; and messages $y^{h*}=\delta(y^h)$.

x_2: / x_1	-1	0	1	y^h	$p(y^h)$	y^{h*}	$p(y^{h*})$
1	1/16	2/16	1/16	→ 1	4/16	→ 1	4/16
0	2/16	4/16	2/16	→ 0	8/16	→ -1	12/16
-1	1/16	2/16	1/16	→ -1	4/16		

EXHIBIT 3-5

Distribution of events z^{I}, jointly with, or conditional on, messages y^h, y^{h*}.

y^h:	1	0	-1	1	0	-1	y^{h*}:1	-1	1	-1
z^{I}		$p(z^{\mathrm{I}}, y^h)$			$p(z^{\mathrm{I}} \mid y^h)$		$p(z^{\mathrm{I}}, y^{h*})$		$p(z^{\mathrm{I}} \mid y^{h*})$	
-2	0	0	1/16	0	0	1/4	0	1/16	0	1/12
-1	0	2/16	2/16	0	1/4	2/4	0	4/16	0	4/12
0	1/16	4/16	1/16	1/4	2/4	1/4	1/16	5/16	1/4	5/12
1	2/16	2/16	0	2/4	1/4	0	2/16	2/16	2/4	2/12
2	1/16	0	0	1/4	0	0	1/16	0	1/4	0
Sum	1/4	2/4	1/4	1	1	1	1/4	3/4	1	1

EXHIBIT 3-6

Distribution of events z^{II}, jointly with, or conditional on messages y^h, y^{h*}.

y^h:	1	0	-1	1	0	-1	y^{h*}:1	-1	1	-1
z^{II}		$p(z^{\mathrm{II}}, y^h)$			$p(z^{\mathrm{II}} \mid y^h)$		$p(z^{\mathrm{II}}, y^{h*})$		$p(z^{\mathrm{II}} \mid y^{h*})$	
-1	1/16	6/16	4/16	1/4	3/4	1	1/16	10/16	1/4	5/6
1	3/16	2/16	0	3/4	1/4	0	3/16	2/16	3/4	1/6
Sum	1/4	2/4	1/4	1	1	1	1/4	3/4	1	1

4. *Feasible and Optimal Action Rules*

We use the brief term *action* for the act description c that occurs in the argument of a payoff function. Usually any action we shall deal with will be relevant, c^{Ω}, or efficiently relevant, $c^{(\Omega)}$; but these superscripts will be often omitted. [The difference will not matter: any action that maximizes expected payoff will turn out to be efficient.] Any function $\gamma_{h,\Omega}$ from the set Y^h of messages (received through channel h) to a set C^{Ω} of payoff-relevant actions is called a *decision function* (or *action rule*). Thus

$$(14)\qquad c^{\Omega} = \gamma_{h,\Omega}(y^h) \quad c^{\Omega} \in C^{\Omega}, \quad y^h \in Y^h$$

The payoff of a given action and given event is then

$$(15)\qquad \omega(z^{\Omega}, c^{\Omega}) = \omega\,[z^{\Omega}, \gamma_{h,\Omega}(y^h)]$$

It follows from (14) that each pair (h, Ω) – a given channel and a given payoff condition – is associated with a unique set $\Gamma_{h,\Omega}$ of action rules. The average payoff of an action rule will be called its payoff, to be denoted by $u(\gamma_{h,\Omega})$. By (15)

$$(16)\qquad \begin{aligned} u(\gamma_{h,\Omega}) &= E\omega(z^{\Omega}, c^{\Omega}) = E\omega\,[z^{\Omega}, \gamma_{h,\Omega}(y^h)] \\ &= \sum_{y \in Y^h} \sum_{z^{\Omega} \in z^{\Omega}} \omega\,[z^{\Omega}, \gamma_{h,\Omega}(y^h)] \cdot p(z^{\Omega}, y^h) \end{aligned}$$

so that by (13)

$$(17)\qquad u(\gamma_{h,\Omega}) = \sum_{y \in Y^h} p(y^h) \sum_{z^{\Omega} \in Z^{\Omega}} \omega\,[z^{\Omega}, \gamma_{h,\Omega}(y^h)] \cdot p(z^{\Omega} \mid y^h)$$

The second sum in (17) is the expected payoff conditional upon the message y^h received, and depending on the action rule. The payoff of the action rule is the average of the conditional expected payoffs, taken over all the messages of the channel h. Equation (17) implies that, to maximize $u(\gamma_{h,\Omega})$ over the set $\Gamma_{h,\Omega}$ of action rules, we can maximize separately the expected payoffs conditional upon each of the messages y^h. That is: if $\gamma^*_{h,\Omega}$ is optimal, i.e., if it has maximum utility for a given (h, Ω) then

$$(18)\qquad u(\gamma^*_{h,\Omega}) = \sum_{y^h \in Y^h} p(y) \max_{\gamma \in \Gamma_{h,\Omega}} \sum_{z^{\Omega} \in Z^{\Omega}} \omega\,[z^{\Omega}, \gamma(y^h)]\, p(z^{\Omega} \mid y^h$$

or, still simpler (see [14]),

$$(19)\qquad u(\gamma^*_{h,\Omega}) = \sum_{y^h \in Y^h} p(y^h) \max_{c \in C^{\Omega}} \sum_{z^{\Omega} \in Z^{\Omega}} \omega(z^{\Omega}, c)\, p(z^{\Omega} \mid y^h)$$

that is, the payoff of action rule is maximized by choosing, for each message y^h an optimal action, i.e., one that will maximize the expected payoff conditional upon this message; the set of pairs 'message, optimal action' determines then the optimal action rule, given the channel h and the payoff condition Ω.

The formulations in this section do not differ in spirit or content from those used in the current work in decision theory. The notations are almost identical with those used in the economic theory of teams,[4] except for the lavish use of the indices h and Ω, necessitated by the particular focus of this paper.

5. *Beliefs, Tastes and Resources*

So far, an optimal rule of action $\gamma^*_{h,\Omega}$ has been defined formally in (18) as that element of the set $\Gamma_{h,\Omega}$ of action rules which maximizes the expected payoff expressed in (16). We assume the decider to be *consistent*, in the following sense: if the channel h and the payoff condition Ω vary, he will choose an appropriately varying optimal rule of action. This is, in fact, implied in the meaning of 'personal probabilities' and 'utilities': they are numbers which are assigned, on the one hand, to events and, on the other, to outcomes of a consistent man's actions, and which have the property that he will always choose the action maximizing the sum of products of these numbers, i.e., the expected utility. The existence of such numbers follows, by logic and mathematics, from a few simple postulates of choice (of which the rules of transitivity and of admissibility are two) which the consistent man will regret not to have obeyed just as he would regret to have disobeyed the rules of logic and arithmetic (see Savage [3]).

Under certainty, an optimal action of a consistent man is determined by two conditions: (1) his *resources*, i.e., the set of feasible actions (e.g., the consumer's resources are given by his assets and the market prices, and the producer's resources are given by his assets and technology); (2) his *tastes*, i.e., the preference ordering on the set of all actions.

In the more general case of uncertainty the preference ordering, or *tastes*, of a consistent man must satisfy the following conditions: there exists a function ω_{XA} on $X \times A$ and a probability function $p(x)$ on X such that, for all a_1, a_2 in A,

(20) a_2 is not preferred to a_1 if

$$\sum_{x \in X} \omega_{XA}(x, a_1)\, p(x) \geqslant \sum_{x \in X} \omega_{XA}(x, a_2)\, p(x)$$

The two compared averages are called utilities of a_1, a_2, respectively, although this word is sometimes confined only to acts a with $\omega(x, a)$ constant over X. (Note also that in the special case of certainty, $\omega(x, a)$ is indeed constant over X, for every a.) The function p on X can then be said to describe the decider's *beliefs*.[5]

The decider's *resources* under uncertainty can be described as the set H of available channels, and the set $\Gamma_{h,\Omega}$ of available action rules, with due attention to the fact that, in general, channels and action rules are not costless. The *cost* of using a channel will depend, in general, on the channel, and on the message actually sent. Accordingly, we define a cost function, κ, from the set Y^h of messages associated with channel h to the set of real numbers (utilities). Henceforth we shall call the payoff $\omega(z^\Omega, c^\Omega)$ of action c^Ω its gross payoff, given the event z^Ω. From the gross payoff, the cost $\kappa(y^h)$ is deducted to obtain the net payoff of the action, given the event and the message. The net payoff is, by (15)

$$(21) \qquad \omega[z^\Omega, \gamma_{h,\Omega}(y^h)] - \kappa(y^h)$$

Correspondingly the maximum average payoff $u(\gamma^*_{h,\Omega})$ defined in (18) can be called the *gross payoff of channel h, given* Ω. It depends on h and Ω and can be conveniently denoted by

$$(22) \qquad v(h, \Omega) \equiv u(\gamma^*_{h,\Omega}) = E_y\{\max_c E_z[\omega(z, c) \mid y]\} \qquad z \in Z^\Omega, \quad c \in C^\Omega, \quad y \in Y^h$$

As explained in Section 4, $v(h, \Omega)$ is the average (over all y) of the conditionally expected payoffs obtained under the optimal action rule.
The *net payoff of channel h, given* Ω, is then

$$(23) \qquad w(h, \Omega) = v(h, \Omega) - E_y\kappa(y^h)$$

To choose an optimal channel is to maximize $w(h, \Omega)$ over the set H of available channels. This operation is preceded by finding the action rule $\gamma^*_{h,\Omega}$ optimal over the set of available action rules.[6]

Regarding the set of available action rules, remember that in Section 4 we have defined the whole set $\Gamma_{h,\Omega}$ of functions obtained by associating each possible payoff-relevant action c^{Ω} with each possible message y^h. In general, only some *feasible subset* of $\Gamma_{h,\Omega}$ will have to be considered, either because some actions are physically incompatible with some messages or because some action rules are difficult to specify or to implement. For example, to specify an optimal decision function of numerical messages may be very difficult unless one limits oneself to the class of linear decision functions. In the last analysis the feasible subset of action rules is chosen on grounds of cost (with infinite cost for physically unfeasible rules). Accordingly, one might redefine the cost $\kappa(y^h)$ to be dependent on the pair $(y^h, \gamma_{h,\Omega})$ and thus to represent the *combined cost of information and of decision making*. This cost, $\kappa(y^h, \gamma_{h,\Omega})$ would replace $\kappa(y^h)$ in (21) and (23). We could go further and interpret h as an instrument that not only produces messages statistically dependent on events, but also transforms messages into decisions. This would take fuller account of automation and of its analogies in the organization problem, but we shall not make this step here. We shall, instead, neglect the cost of decision-making.

6. *Sufficient Channels*

In an important case, the ordering of gross channel payoffs is independent of the payoff condition. We give without proof the following Theorem (see also [10]):

THEOREM II. $v(h, \Omega) \geqslant v(h^*, \Omega)$ *for all* Ω *and all* P *on* X *if and only if* Y^h *is finer than* Y^{h*}.

This is useful in connection with the following definition and postulate:

DEFINITION. A channel h^* is said to be sufficient with respect to the payoff condition Ω if, for any available Y^h that is finer than Y^{h*}, $v(h, \Omega) = v(h^*, \Omega)$.

POSTULATE. If Y^h is finer than Y^{h^*}, the expected channel cost to the decider is larger (or at least not smaller) for h than for h^*. (This postulate is to be added to those on consistent behavior of the decider.)

It follows that, if channel h^* is sufficient, it cannot be worse than any available channel that is finer or coarser than h^*. (The relation to sufficient statistics, a special case, is obvious. See also [12, 13].)[7]

II. A SPECIAL CLASS OF PROBLEMS (SUB-EXAMPLE 1.2)

7. *Continuous vs. Two-Valued Messages*; *Continuous vs. Two-Valued Linear Payoffs.*

As before, we define a *state* $x \in X$ as a real vector

$$x = (x_1, \dots, x_n)$$

We shall consider two sequences, H and H^*, of *channels*; and two alternative payoff conditions, Ω and Ω'. As before, we define a sign function δ of any real number r thus:

$$\delta_r \equiv \delta(r) = \begin{cases} 1 & \text{if } \; r > 0 \\ -1 & \text{otherwise} \end{cases} \tag{24}$$

The sequence $H = (h_1, \dots, h_n)$ of channels is defined thus: for every $m(\leqslant n)$, the message obtained through the channel h_m is

$$y^{h_m} = \sum_1^m x_i = y_m, \quad \text{say}. \tag{25}$$

Thus Y^{h_m} is the real line.

The sequence $H^* = (h_1^*, \dots, h_n^*)$ of channels is defined thus: for every $m(\leqslant n)$

$$y^{h^*m} = \delta(y_m). \tag{25*}$$

Thus Y^{h^*m} consists of two points.

In either case messages are about some property of the sub-vector $(x_1, \dots, x_m)$. In the case H the message is a continuous random variable $y_m = \sum_i^m x_i$. In the case H^* the message is a two-valued random variable: $y_m^* = +1$ or -1. *Note*: *Clearly h_m is finer than h_m^*!*

INTERPRETATION: If we interpret x as the list of future price changes of n securities, a message y_m gives the sum (or, with properly chosen units, the mean) of such changes for a sample consisting of $m(\leqslant n)$ securities. A message y_m^*, on the other hand, merely states whether the sum (or mean) of the m prices is or is not going to rise. In a more general interpretation, x is a finite population, y_m is the sample mean, and $\delta(y_m) \equiv y_m^*$ is its sign.

We shall sometimes write $y_m = y$ for brevity.

As in (9), (10) and (10′), we define the act a as a point in the real interval

(26) $\quad -1 \leqslant a \leqslant 1$

and we define two alternative payoff conditions:

(27) $\quad \Omega : u_{xa} = a \cdot \sum_1^n x_i \qquad \Omega' : u'_{xa} = a \cdot \delta \left(\sum_1^n x_i \right).$

[INTERPRETATION: As before, Ω characterizes a 'speculator' with continuous profit variable, and Ω' a 'sign-matcher', with a 2-valued profit-variable.]

We have seen (Section 2) that the efficiently relevant pairs of description sets are, in this Example, for the two payoff functions Ω, Ω', respectively:

State descriptions (set of payoff-relevant events):

$$Z^{(\Omega)} = Z^{\mathrm{I}} = \left\{ z^{\mathrm{I}} : x \in z^{\mathrm{I}} \Leftrightarrow \sum_1^n x_i = z^{\mathrm{I}} \right\};$$

$$Z^{(\Omega')} = Z^{\mathrm{II}} = \left\{ z^{\mathrm{II}} : x \in z^{\mathrm{II}} \Leftrightarrow \delta \left(\sum_1^n x_i \right) = z^{\mathrm{II}} \right\}$$

We shall henceforth write $z^{\mathrm{I}} \equiv z$, for brevity. Then

$$Z^{(\Omega)} = \{z\} \qquad Z^{(\Omega')} = \{\delta_z\}$$

Act description (set of efficient payoff-relevant actions):

$$C^{(\Omega)} = C^{(\Omega')} \equiv \{(\delta_a)\} = (1, -1)$$

We shall henceforth write $c = \delta_a$. Then by (27) the two payoff functions to consider are:

(28) $\quad \omega(z, c) = z \cdot \delta_a \quad$ and $\quad \omega'(z, c) = \delta_z : \delta_a$

where $z = \sum_1^n x_i$.

EXHIBIT 3-7

Four cases

Payoff condition:	Channels	
	h_m: message $= y_m = \sum_1^m x_i$	h^*_m: message $= \delta(y_m)$.
Ω: (payoff $= \delta_a \cdot z$)	Case 1	Case 2
Ω': (payoff $= \delta_a \cdot \delta_z$)	Case 3	Case 4

The two payoff conditions Ω, Ω', combined with the two channel sequences H, H^*, result in four cases which we shall number as on Exhibit 3-7.

In all 4 cases, the linear nature of the payoff conditions (27) requires that the set of acts be bounded, as in (26); so that the decider's best action is one of two extremes, $c = +1$ or -1 (e.g., 'sell or buy the maximum possible amount').

In Cases 3 and 4, the decider's payoff function is two-valued (the 'sign-matcher' case), while in Cases 1 and 2 it is continuous. As to channels: in cases 2 and 4 they send only two-valued ('yes, or no') messages while in cases 1 and 3 the messages are continuous.

For any probability distribution on X we shall characterize the gross channel payoffs on Exhibit 3-8, obtained on the lines of (18), (19), (22), by the following reasoning:

If the payoff condition is Ω [as defined in (27)] and therefore the payoff function is ω [see (28)] then, for any channel h, the conditionally expected payoff, given the message y^h, is

$$\begin{aligned} E_z[\omega(z, c) \mid y^h] &= \sum_z \delta_a z \cdot p(z \mid y^h) \\ &= \delta_a \sum_z z \cdot p(z \mid y^h) = \delta_a E_z(z \mid y^h); \end{aligned}$$

hence optimal action c is $+1$ or -1 according as the conditional expectation $E(z \mid y^h)$ is or is not positive. Therefore

$$\max_c E_z[\omega(z, c) \mid y^h] = |E(z \mid y^h)|,$$

the *absolute value* of $E(z \mid y^h)$. Hence, by (19), (22), the gross channel payoff is

$$(29) \qquad v(h, \Omega) = E_{y^h}\{|E(z \mid y^h)|\}$$

By similar reasoning, if the payoff condition is Ω' then, for any h,

$$(29') \qquad \begin{aligned} &\max_c E_z[\omega(z, c) \mid y^h] = |E(\delta_z \mid y^h)| \\ &v(h, \Omega') = E_{y^h}\{|E(\delta_z \mid y^h)|\} \end{aligned}$$

Inserting the definitions of channels h and messages y^h from (25), (25*) we obtain Exhibit 3-8, with the understanding that the inner E-symbol means averaging over events (z or δ_z, as the case may be), while the outer

E-symbol means averaging over messages (y_m or δ_{y_m}, as the case may be); and remembering that $z=\sum_1^n x_i$, and that δ is the sign function defined in (24).

EXHIBIT 3-8

Gross channel payoffs v

Payoff condition	Channels	
	h_m (message: y_m)	h^*_m (message: δ_{y_m})
	Case 1	Case 2
Ω: (payoff $=\delta_a \cdot z$)	$E\{\lvert E(z \mid y_m)\rvert\}$	$E\{\lvert E(z \mid \delta_{y_m})\rvert\}$
	Case 3	Case 4
Ω': (payoff $=\delta_a \cdot \delta_z$)	$E\{\lvert E(\delta_z \mid y_m)\rvert\}$	$E\{\lvert E(\delta_z \mid \delta_{y_m})\rvert\}$

8. *Conditions for Sufficiency of Binary Channels*

In our example so far, we have not yet specified the probability distribution of states, or the probability measure P on X. We shall see in this section that, under a rather weak specification of P, the coarser sequence H^* of (binary) channels becomes sufficient with respect to the continuous payoff condition Ω; and that under a somewhat stronger specification of P, H^* becomes sufficient also with respect to the binary payoff condition Ω'. The results of this Section will be utilized in the next two sections, enabling us to discuss channel costs relevant to the problem and then, assuming a more special (viz., the normal) distribution of states, take up the question of 'decreasing marginal returns', and determine the optimal channel for given channel cost conditions. A similar study was made by McGuire [11].

Our weak specification is this: assume the co-ordinates x_i of the state vector x are statistically independent,

(I) $\qquad p(x_i \mid x_j) = p(x_i)$

and they have zero means,

(II) $\qquad Ex_i = 0 \quad i = 1 \ldots, n$

We want to show that, under this assumption,

$$v(h_m, \Omega) = v(h_m^*, \Omega)$$

where [see Exhibit 3-8, cases 1 and 2]

(30) $v(h_m, \Omega) = E\{|E(z|y_m)|\}$

(30*) $v(h^*_m, \Omega) = E\{|E(z|\delta_{y_m})|\}$

Since the x_i are independent, and $Ex_i = 0 (i = 1, \ldots, n)$,

$$E(x_j \mid x_i) \begin{cases} = Ex_j = 0 & \text{if } i \neq j \\ = x_i & \text{if } i = j \end{cases}$$

Hence, writing $y_m \equiv y$ for brevity,

(31) $$E(z \mid y) = E\left(y + \sum_{m+1}^{n} x_j \mid y\right) = y$$

$$|E(z \mid y)| = |y|$$

Hence by (30)

(32) $v(h_m, \Omega) = E(|y|)$

On the other hand, to evaluate $v(h^*_m, \Omega)$ of (30*), note that

$$E(z \mid \delta_y) = \begin{cases} E(y \mid y > 0) \\ E(y \mid y \leqslant 0) \end{cases} \text{when } \delta_y = \begin{cases} +1 \\ -1 \end{cases}$$

$$|E(z \mid \delta_y)| = \begin{cases} E(y \mid y > 0) \\ E(-y \mid y \leqslant 0) \end{cases} \text{when } \delta_y = \begin{cases} +1 \\ -1 \end{cases}$$

Hence $|E(z|\delta_y)| = E(|y|)$, a constant.

$$v(h^*_m, \Omega) = E\{E|y|\} = E(|y|)$$

so that, by (32),

(33) $v(h^*_m, \Omega) = E(|y|) = v(h_m, \Omega) \equiv v_\Omega(m)$

Thus when the payoff condition is Ω and the probability assumptions (I), (II) hold, both the coarser and the finer channel yield the same payoff, to be denoted by $v_\Omega(m)$. The coarser channel h^*_m is sufficient with respect to the payoff condition Ω.

Turning now to the binary payoff condition Ω' (cases 3 and 4 of Exhibit 3-8) we shall show that

$$v(h_m, \Omega') = v(h^*_m, \Omega')$$

(so that the binary channel h_m^* is sufficient with respect to Ω') if we replace our previous specifications (I), (II) of the state distribution, by stronger ones: assume all the co-ordinates x_i of x have the same distribution G_1 (say); that is, for any η,

(III) $\quad G_1(\eta) = P(x_i \leqslant \eta) \quad i = 1, \ldots, n$

Also assume G_1 is symmetrical about the origin, i.e.,

(IV) $\quad G_1(\eta) + G_1(-\eta) = 1$

It follows from (III) that the sum of any r distinct co-ordinates has the same distribution G_r. Thus in particular

$$P\left(\sum_{m+1}^{n} x_i \leqslant \eta\right) = P\left(\sum_{1}^{n-m} x_i \leqslant \eta\right) = G_{n-m}(\eta)$$

$$P(y \leqslant \eta) = P\left(\sum_{1}^{m} x_i \leqslant \eta\right) = G_m(\eta);$$

it then follows from (IV) that every G_r is symmetrical about the origin:

(34) $\quad G_r(\eta) + G_r(-\eta) = 1 \qquad dG_r(\eta) = dG_r(-\eta) \quad r = 1, \ldots, n$

and since G_r is a non-decreasing function,

(35) $\quad G_r(\eta) \gtreqless \frac{1}{2}$ if $\eta \gtreqless 0, \quad r = 1, \ldots, n$

In this notation,

$$\begin{aligned} P(z \leqslant 0 \mid y = \eta) &= P\left(y + \sum_{m+1}^{n} x_i \leqslant 0 \mid y = \eta\right) = \\ &= P\left(\eta + \sum_{m+1}^{n} x_i \leqslant 0\right) = \\ &= P\left(\sum_{m+1}^{n} x_i \leqslant -\eta\right) = \\ &= G_{n-m}(-\eta) = 1 - G_{n-m}(\eta) \end{aligned}$$

so that

(36) $\quad P(z > 0 \mid y = \eta) = G_{n-m}(\eta) = P(z \leqslant 0 \mid y = -\eta) \geqslant \frac{1}{2}$ when $\eta \geqslant 0$

$\quad P(z \leqslant 0 \mid y = \eta) = 1 - G_{n-m}(\eta) = P(z > 0 \mid y = -\eta) < \frac{1}{2}$ when $\eta < 0$

We can now compute the probabilities for each of the four pairs of values of (δ_z, δ_y). Denote $P(\delta_z=1, \delta_y=1)$ by $p_\delta(1, 1)$ etc. Then

$$p_\delta(1, 1) = P(z > 0, y > 0) = \int_0^\infty P(z > 0 \mid y = \eta)\, dG_m(\eta) =$$

$$= \int_0^\infty G_{n-m}(\eta)\, dG_m(\eta) \equiv g_{m,n}, \quad \text{say}$$

Since, for η non-negative, both $G_{n-m}(\eta)$ and $G_m(\eta)$ are $\geqslant \frac{1}{2}$, $g_{m,n} \geqslant \frac{1}{4}$. When $m=n$, $P(z>0, y>0)=P(z>0)=\frac{1}{2}$. Thus we can make the following definition of $g_{m,n}$ (or g, for brevity)

$$\text{(37)} \qquad g \equiv p_\delta(1, 1) \equiv \begin{cases} \int_0^\infty G_{n-m}(\eta)\, dG_m(\eta) & m = 1, \ldots, n-1 \\ \frac{1}{2} & m = n \end{cases}$$

The quantity g measures the *probability volume over the positive quadrant of the bivariate distribution* of (z, y). The distribution of (δ_z, δ_y) is:

$$\text{(38)} \qquad \begin{aligned} &\tfrac{1}{4} \leqslant p_\delta(1,1) = g = p_\delta(-1, -1) \leqslant \tfrac{1}{2} \\ &0 \leqslant p_\delta(1, -1) = \tfrac{1}{2} - g = p_\delta(-1, 1) \leqslant \tfrac{1}{4} \end{aligned}$$

Now, to evaluate

$$\text{(39)} \qquad v(h_m, \Omega') = E\{|E(\delta_z \mid y)|\}$$

we note that

$$E(\delta_z \mid y) = 1 \cdot P(z > 0 \mid y) - 1 \cdot P(z \leqslant 0 \mid y) = 2P(z > 0 \mid y) - 1$$

and by (36), (35):

$$E(\delta_z \mid y) = 2G_{n-m}(y) - 1 \left.\begin{matrix} \\ \\ \end{matrix}\right\} \begin{matrix} > 0, & y > 0 \\ \leqslant 0, & y \leqslant 0 \end{matrix}$$

$$|E(\delta_z \mid y)| = \begin{cases} 2G_{n-m}(y) - 1, & y > 0 \\ 1 - 2G_{n-m}(y) = 2G_{n-m}(-y) - 1, & y \leqslant 0 \end{cases}$$

Hence $|E(\delta_z \mid y)| = 2G_{n-m}(|y|) - 1 \geqslant 0$

and by (39)

$$(40)\qquad v(h_m, \Omega') = \int_{-\infty}^{\infty} [2G_{n-m}(|y|) - 1]\, dG_m(y)$$

$$= -1 + 2\int_{0}^{\infty} 2G_{n-m}(y)\, dG_m(y)$$

$$v(h_m, \Omega') = 4g - 1 \geqslant 0,$$

g being as defined in (37). On the other hand, to evaluate

$$(41)\qquad v(h^*_m, \Omega') = E\{|E(\delta_z | \delta_y)|\}$$

we note that

$$E(\delta_z | \delta_y) = P(\delta_z = 1 | \delta_y) - P(\delta_z = -1 | \delta_y) = \\ = 2P(\delta_z = 1 | \delta_y) - 1$$

$$E(\delta_z | \delta_y) = \begin{cases} 2P(z > 0 | y > 0) - 1 & \delta_y = 1 \\ 2P(z > 0 | y \leqslant 0) - 1 & \delta_y = -1. \end{cases}$$

Now by (38)

$$P(z > 0 | y > 0) = [P(z > 0, y > 0)/P(y > 0)] = \\ = 2P(z > 0, y > 0) = 2g$$

$$P(z > 0 | y \leqslant 0) = [P(z > 0, y \leqslant 0)/P(y \leqslant 0)] = \\ = 2P(z > 0, y \leqslant 0) = 1 - 2g$$

$$E(\delta_z | \delta_y) = \begin{cases} 4g - 1 > 0 & \delta_y = 1 \\ 1 - 4g < 0 & \delta_y = -1 \end{cases}$$

$$|E(\delta_z | \delta_y)| = 4g - 1 \quad \text{a constant.}$$

And by (41), (40)

$$(42')\qquad v(h^*_m, \Omega') = 4g - 1 = v(h_m, \Omega') \equiv v_\Omega(m)$$

where g is defined as in (37). Thus, under assumptions (III)–(IV), the coarser channel h^* is sufficient with respect to the payoff condition Ω'.

Under the same assumptions (III)–(IV) and the payoff condition Ω, the gross revenue of either channel, evaluated in (33), becomes [8]

$$(42)\qquad v(h^*_m, \Omega) = 2\int_{0}^{\infty} y\, dG_m(y) = v(h_m, \Omega) = v_\Omega(m)$$

9. *Channel Costs*

Because of our initial, broad definition of a channel as an instrument for gathering, processing, and (not only!) communicating data the expected channel costs $E\kappa(y)$ as defined in Section 5 should include the costs of observing the world, and of formulating (computing, coding) a message and transmitting it.

The theory of information has established a measure of the minimum channel capacity which is required to handle messages at a given rate, when the joint distribution on the set of the channel's inputs (the 'source') and the set of its outputs (the set of messages) is known. Presumably channel cost increases with capacity; or, given the capacity, longer time is required per message, and this is again reflected in cost. (See [10].) This seems to be true, however, only if the channels considered are comparable in some sense, still to be defined. Two data-processing instruments of the same capacity are not necessarily associated with the same expected cost per message. Just as two land plots of equal acreage do not necessarily cost the same. Neither acreage nor information capacity solve the aggregation problem present in each case. The channels cannot be, in general, identified by a single (scalar) variable.

However, in the particular case of our example, all sufficient channels h_m^* belong to the sequence H^*, ordered according to the unique parameter m, the number of observed co-ordinates x_i of the state vector $x=(x_i \ldots, x_n)$ $(m \leqslant n)$. The distribution of x is given, and the joint input-output distributions, and hence the required capacities associated with the several channels, differ only with respect to the free parameter m. In this sense, the aggregation problem is bypassed. We can study the problem of increasing of decreasing returns (marginal gross payoffs) to a single information channel parameter which itself increases with cost: just as we can study the problem of increasing or decreasing returns to a single quantitative input (or to a fixed mix of inputs) in a given industry.

The function relating the number m of observations to the minimum required capacity of channel h_m^* will depend on the distribution of the state vector x. It is not necessary to characterize this function explicitly.[9] It is simpler to associate channel cost of h_m^*, not with its capacity, but directly with the number of observations. On empirical grounds, we may know how the cost of observations depends on their number, and we shall regard other contributions to channel cost as fixed.

We shall assume the cost per observation to be constant[10] and denote it by k. Then the net payoffs are:

$$(43) \qquad w_\Omega(m) = v_\Omega(m) - km \quad w_{\Omega'}(m) = v_{\Omega'}(m) - km.^{11}$$

The gross revenues v_Ω, $v_{\Omega'}$, evaluated in (42), (42′) depend only on the functions G_m, G_{n-m}. These, in turn, are derived from some given distribution of states which obeys assumptions (I)–(IV). We shall therefore be able, given any distribution satisfying (I)–(IV), to obtain the functional relationship between the unit cost k of observation and the optimal number of observations, separately for each of the two payoff conditions considered. We can denote these functions by

$$m_\Omega(k) \quad \text{and} \quad m_{\Omega'}(k)$$

respectively.

However, to make these two functions comparable, we must standardize the units. For the speculator (case Ω), the profit unit is \$1. For the sign-matcher (case Ω') profit unit is the fixed money amount gained as reward or lost as penalty. These are also utility units. To compare the functions $m_\Omega(k)$ and $m_{\Omega'}(k)$, relating optimal channel to the cost k per observation, we shall choose as a unit of gain (and of cost) the profit that is yielded by a single observation. That is, we shall impose the standardizing convention,

$$(44) \qquad v_\Omega(1) = 2\int_0^\infty y\,dG_1(y) = 1 \quad \text{using (42)}$$

$$(44') \qquad v_{\Omega'}(1) = 4\int_0^\infty G_{n-1}(y)\,dG_1(y) - 1 = 1 \quad \text{using (42'), (37)}.$$

(Note that in the latter case, the money unit will depend on n.) With the money unit thus standardized, k will measure the cost per observation, expressed as its proportion to the revenue yielded by a single observation.

10. *The Case of Normal Distribution of States*

We shall analyze completely, not the case of rather weak restrictions (I)–(IV) of Section 8, but only a more special case: the normal distribution

We assume, then, the state vector $x=(x_1,\ldots, x_n)$ to be distributed normally with zero-means and zero-covariances, thus satisfying all restrictions (I)–(IV). For convenience, we measure each x_i in units such that all variances $E(x_i^2)=1$. To summarize:

$$(45) \qquad x_i \text{ normal}, \quad E(x_i)=0=E(x_ix_j) \quad i\neq j$$
$$E(x_i^2)=1 \quad i=1,\ldots,n$$

Since $z=\sum_1^n x_i$, $y=y_m=\sum_1^m x_i$, z and y are jointly normal with

$$(46) \qquad E(z)=0=E(y) \qquad E(z^2)=n\geqslant 1 \quad E(y^2)=m\geqslant 1$$

so that the standard deviations are

$$\sigma_z=\sqrt{n}\geqslant 1 \qquad \sigma_y=\sqrt{m}\geqslant 1$$

The covariance between z and y is

$$E(zy)=E\left[\left(y+\sum_{m+1}^{n} x_j\right)y\right]=$$
$$=E(y^2)+\sum_{1}^{m}\sum_{m+1}^{n} E(x_ix_j)=m\geqslant 1$$

Hence the correlation, ρ, between z and y is always positive:

$$(47) \qquad \rho=E(zy)/\sigma_z\sigma_y=m/\sqrt{mn}=+\sqrt{m/n}, \quad 0<\rho\leqslant 1$$

The gross revenue under the (continuous) payoff condition Ω is obtained immediately from (42). Since $G_m(y)$ is now normal with mean$=0$ and $\sigma_y^2=m$,

$$v_\Omega=+\sqrt{2m/\pi}$$

or, expressed in standard units defined in (44):

$$(48) \qquad v_\Omega=+\sqrt{m}=v_\Omega(m)$$

On Exhibit 3-9 the function (48) is plotted for m continuous over the domain $[0, n]$, although only integer values will occur. The function is concave in m; the marginal returns to the number m of observations are decreasing throughout. To find the optimal channel, we maximize the net revenue

$$(49) \qquad w_\Omega=\sqrt{m}-km$$

with respect to m, subject to the condition that m is zero or a positive integer not exceeding n. For n large we can treat m as approximately continuous, and let dw_Ω/dm vanish for $m \geqslant 0$. The optimal number of observations is then,

$$m_\Omega(k) = \begin{cases} 0 & k > \frac{1}{2} \\ 1/(4k^2) & 1/(2\sqrt{n}) \leqslant k \leqslant \frac{1}{2} \\ n & k < 1/(2\sqrt{n}). \end{cases} \tag{50}$$

This function is plotted on Exhibit 3-10 for $n = 100$.

We turn now to determining the gross revenue under the (binary) payoff condition Ω'. By (42′), this requires evaluating g, the probability volume of the bivariate distribution over the positive quadrant. It does not depend on scale. The function G_r defined in Section 8,

$$G_r(\eta) = P\left(\sum_1^r x_i \leqslant \eta\right) \quad r = 1, \ldots, n$$

EXHIBIT 3-9

Gross profit $v(m)$ to channel h_m

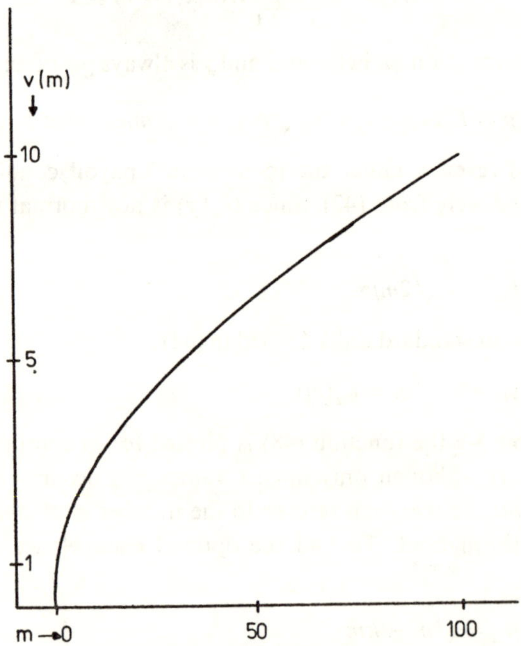

EXHIBIT 3-10

Optimal $m(=m_k)$ at unit cost k
(Channel h_m)

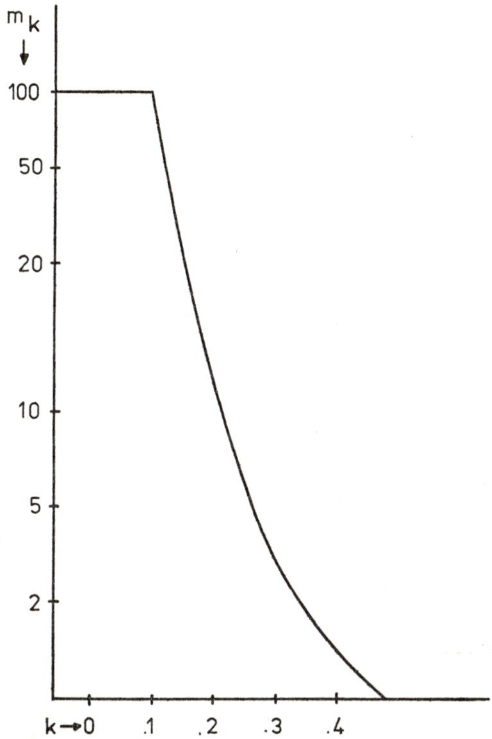

becomes, under the assumptions (45), the normal distribution function with mean=0 and variance=r. Therefore, by changing scales appropriately, we can express g in terms of the unit-normal distribution function $N=G_1$:

$$g = \int_0^\infty G_{n-m}(y)\, dG_m(y) = \int_0^\infty N(\tau y)\, N'(y)\, dy \tag{51}$$

where

$$\tau = \sqrt{m/(n-m)} = \rho/\sqrt{1-\rho^2} \quad \text{by (47)} \tag{52}$$

Differentiate g with respect to τ:

$$dg/d\tau = \int_0^\infty N'(\tau y)\, yN'(y)\, dy$$

$$= \int_0^\infty e^{-(y^2/2)-(\tau^2 y^2/2)}(y/2\pi)\, dy$$

$$= (1/2\pi) \int_0^\infty e^{-y^2(1+\tau^2)/2}\, y\, dy$$

Substitute $t = y\sqrt{1+\tau^2}$; then $y\, dy = t\, dt/(1+\tau^2)$;

$$dg/d\tau = (1/2\pi) \int_0^\infty e^{-t^2/2} t\, dt/(1+\tau^2) = (1/2\pi)\cdot[1/(1+\tau^2)]\cdot 1$$

$$dg = (1/2\pi)\,(1/1+\tau^2)\, d\tau\,;$$

integrate:

$$g = (1/2\pi) \int d\tau/(1+\tau^2) = (1/2\pi) \arctan\tau + C$$

If we define an angle q by

$$\rho = \sin q$$

then by (52)

$$\tau = \tan q$$

(53) $$q = \arcsin\rho = \arctan\tau$$

$$g = (1/2\pi)\arcsin\rho + C = g(\rho)$$

say. To determine C, put $\rho = 0$. Then $q = 0 = \tau$, and by (51)

$$g(0) = \int_0^\infty N'(y)\, N(0)\, dy = (\tfrac{1}{2}) \int_0^\infty N'(y)\, dy = \tfrac{1}{4}$$

hence

(54) $$g(\rho) = (\tfrac{1}{4}) + (1/2\pi)\arcsin\rho$$

This gives the probability $g = P(z>0, y>0)$ for *any*[12] bivariate normal distribution with zero-means and correlation ρ: for we have not yet used the only restriction (47) on ρ that is imposed in our particular case, viz $\rho > 0$, making $g > \frac{1}{4}$.

Now, by (42′) and (54)

$$v_{\Omega'}(m) = 4g_{m,\,n} - 1 = (2/\pi)\arcsin\rho \geqslant 0 \quad \rho = \sqrt{m/n}, \quad 0 \leqslant m \leqslant n \tag{55}$$

if we regard m, from now on, as continuous over the whole interval $[0, n]$. Since n is fixed, it is convenient to regard as the variable the ratio $\mu = m/n$ of sample to population size. Then, with q defined as before,

$$\begin{aligned} \rho &= \sqrt{\mu} = \sin q \quad 0 \leqslant q \leqslant \pi/2 \\ \mu &= \sin^2 q = (1 - \cos 2q)/2 \\ \frac{d\mu}{dq} &= \sin 2q\,. \end{aligned} \tag{56}$$

With n fixed, the gross revenue will be denoted by

$$V \equiv V(\mu) \equiv v_{\Omega'}(m) = (2/\pi)\arcsin\sqrt{\mu} = (2/\pi)\,q \tag{57}$$

When $\mu = 0, \quad q = 0, \quad V = 0;$

$\mu = \frac{1}{2}, \quad q = \pi/4, \quad V = \frac{1}{2};$

$\mu = 1, \quad q = \pi/2, \quad V = 1;$

Moreover,

$$dV/d\mu = (2/\pi)/\sin 2\text{q} \geqslant 0 \tag{58}$$

$$d^2V/d\mu^2 = (-\,4/\pi)\,\text{ctn}\,2q/\sin^2 q \begin{Bmatrix} < \\ = \\ > \end{Bmatrix} 0 \quad \text{when} \quad \mu \begin{Bmatrix} < \frac{1}{2} \\ = \frac{1}{2} \\ > \frac{1}{2}, \end{Bmatrix} \tag{59}$$

since $\text{ctn}\,2q = (1 - 2\sin^2 q)/2\sin q\cos q = (1-2\mu)/2\sqrt{\mu(1-\mu)}$. By (58), the function $V(\mu)$ is monotone non-decreasing. By (59), it is concave at $\mu < \frac{1}{2}$, has inflexion at $\mu = \frac{1}{2}$, and is convex above this point. Thus we have decreasing marginal returns for low proportion of sample to population, but increasing returns when the proportion is high! Doubling the number of observations may more than double the payoff!

On Exhibit 3-11, gross revenue is plotted against the channel variable $\mu = m/n$, when the payoff condition, Ω', is a binary one: the 'sign-matcher's' case. To compare with the corresponding Exhibit 3-9, where the assumed payoff condition, Ω, was a continuous one, (the 'speculator's' case) we have expressed the revenue in standard units as defined in (44′). Let

(60) $\quad v = 1/\arcsin\sqrt{1/n} = \text{approx.}\ \sqrt{n}$ for n large. By (55)

(61) $\quad V_{\Omega'}(1) = 4g_{1,n} - 1 = (2/\pi)\arcsin\sqrt{1/n} = 2/v\pi\,.$

Dividing this quantity into the payoff expression of (57), we obtain the standardized payoff, denoted by $v(\mu)$:

(62) $\quad v(\mu) = v\cdot\arcsin\sqrt{\mu} = \text{approx.}\ \sqrt{n}\cdot\arcsin\sqrt{\mu}\quad$ for n large.

On Exhibit 3-11, $v(\mu)$ is plotted with n fixed at 100, so that $v = 10$ approximately, and 100 μ = the percentage of sample to population size.

EXHIBIT 3-11

Gross profit $v(m)$ to channel h^*_m.
(Slope of straight line = critical cost $\bar{k} = 1.38$.
Vertical segments: net profit at $\bar{k}$.)

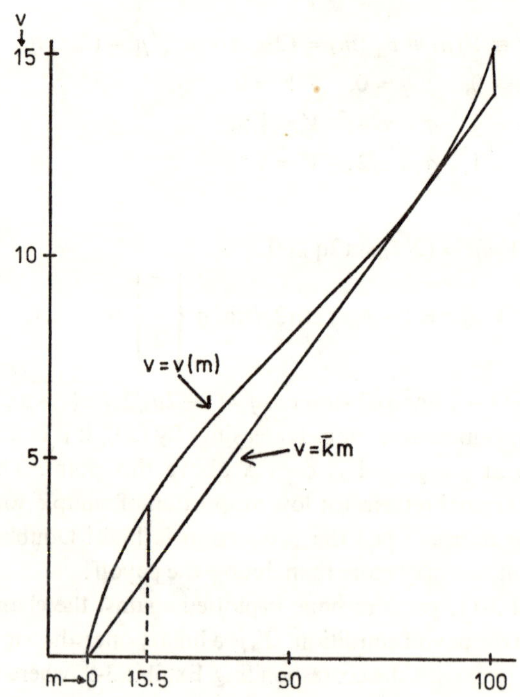

EXHIBIT 3-12

Optimal $m(=m_k)$ at unit cost k.
(Channel h^*_m)

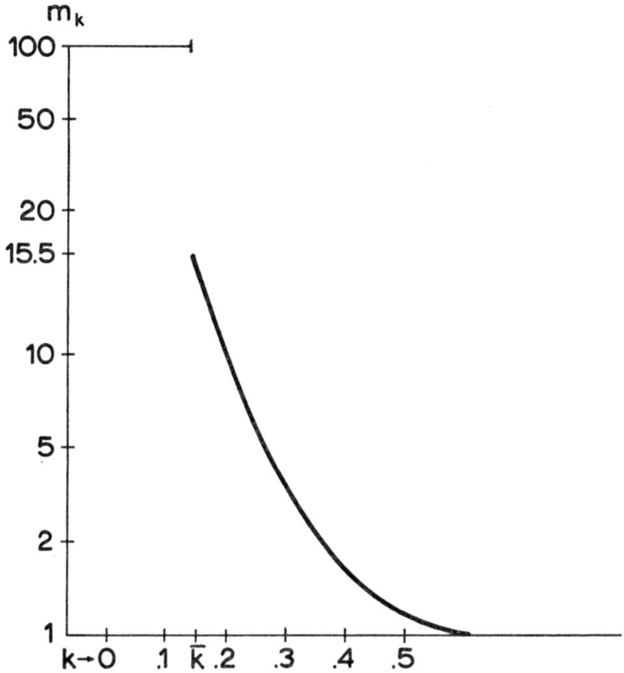

Because of the convex shape of $v(\mu)$ over the upper half of its domain, the optimal value of μ, at sufficiently low unit costs of observation, will not be found anywhere in the interior of the interval $0 \leqslant \mu \leqslant 1$, but rather at its upper boundary, $\mu = 1$: a case of 'convex programming'.

The function

$$\mu_k = m_{\Omega'}(k)/n$$

will express, for n fixed, the effect of varying the (standardized) unit cost k of observations upon the optimal proportion μ_k of sample to population when the payoff condition is Ω': the 'sign-matcher's' case. This function is plotted in Exhibit 3-12. It is to be compared with Exhibit 3-10, plotted correspondingly for the 'speculator's' case, Ω. In both cases, we fix $n = 100$.

On Exhibit 3-10, the optimal number of observations, $m_k = n\mu_k$ is determined – as long as the unit cost k is not prohibitive – by equalizing marginal revenue and unit cost. This follows from the concave shape of the gross revenue function of the channel, which guarantees maximum of the net revenue at its stationary value. When k exceeds the value at which $\mu_k = 1/n$, $m_k = 1$, it becomes prohibitive: m_k falls to 0.

On Exhibit 3-12, by contrast, it is optimal to use the greatest possible number of observations, $\mu_k = 1$, $m_k = n$, for a whole range of unit costs k of observation, reaching from 0 to a certain critical value. Only above this value of k, the 'law of decreasing returns' becomes effective, and the optimal decision is obtained by equating marginal return and unit cost; as long, of course, as k remains nonprohibitive.

To plot μ_k (or $m_k = n\mu_k$) as on Exhibit 3-12, we have to maximize the net payoff

$$(63) \qquad w(\mu) = v(\mu) - kn\mu$$

with respect to μ for given k, over the range $0 \leqslant \mu \leqslant 1$. We denote by μ_k the optimal value of μ and by v_k, w_k the corresponding gross and net revenues. We know that, when k is at or below the critical point $\bar{k}$ (say), then

$$(64) \qquad \begin{aligned} &\mu_k = 1, \qquad v_k = v(1) = \nu \cdot \arcsin 1 = \nu\pi/2 \quad \text{by (62)} \\ &w_k = (\nu\pi/2) - kn \quad k \leqslant \bar{k} \end{aligned}$$

On the other hand, when $k \geqslant \bar{k}$, the optimal value $\mu_k = \mu_k^*$ (say) must satisfy the stationarity condition which by (63) is

$$(65) \qquad [dw(\mu)/d\mu]_{\mu=\mu^*k} = [dv(\mu)/d\mu]_{\mu=\mu^*k} - kn = 0$$

The maximum net payoff is, by (64), (65) the following function of k:

$$(66) \qquad \begin{aligned} w_k &= \frac{\nu\pi}{2} - kn && k \leqslant \bar{k} \\ & v(\mu_k^*) - kn\mu_k^* && k \geqslant \bar{k} \end{aligned}$$

where μ_k^* is defined by (65), and the critical value $\bar{k}$ is determined by setting

$$(67) \qquad (\nu\pi/2) - \bar{k}n = v(\mu_k^*) - \bar{k}n\mu_k^*$$

We shall now extend the results to the case of a general (linear or non-linear) differentiable non-decreasing utility function v of money. The question of whether marginal returns to information can be increasing

(Exhibits 3-9 and 3-11) must be replaced by the more general question of whether at sufficiently low information costs, the expected channel utility Υ (see note 6) can achieve its maximum when the number of observations is highest (Exhibits 3-10 and 3-12). It can only if $d\Upsilon/dm \geqslant 0$ at $m=n$, and $d\Upsilon/dm>0$ in the proximity of n. Again the answer will be 'no' in the 'speculator' case, and 'yes' in the 'sign-matcher' case.

The '*speculator's*' best action rule is $\gamma^*(y)=\delta_y$, and hence his money profit $=z\delta_y$. Since the monetary channel cost is $=km=kn\rho^2$, the expected channel utility is

$$(68) \qquad \Upsilon \equiv Ev(z\delta_y - kn\rho^2) \equiv \Upsilon_q,$$

say, where $q=\arcsin\rho$. Define a function of z and q:

$$(69) \qquad \Phi_q(z) \equiv v(z - kn\rho^2)$$

Since v is differentiable and non-decreasing, and excluding the trivial case $v=\text{const.}$,

$$(70) \qquad \begin{aligned} &\Phi'_q(z) \equiv \partial\Phi_q(z)/\partial z > 0 \quad \text{for almost all } z \\ &\Phi_q(z) - \Phi_q(-z) > 0 \quad \text{for almost all positive } z \end{aligned}$$

Denote by $f(y,z)=f(-y,-z)$ the joint density of y, z; and by $f(z)$, $f(y|z)$ a marginal and conditional density. With the distribution parameters as given at the beginning of this section, and using the notation of (51) we note that

$$(71) \qquad Pr(y>0\,|\,z) = \int_0^\infty f(y\,|\,z)\,dy = N(z\tau)$$

where $\tau=\rho/\sqrt{1-\rho^2}=\tan q$. Then by (68), (69)

$$\begin{aligned} \Upsilon_q &= \int_{-\infty}^{\infty} dz \left[\int_0^\infty \Phi_q(z)\,f(y,z)\,dy + \int_{-\infty}^{0} \Phi_q(-z)\,f(y,z)\,dy\right] \\ &= 2\int_{-\infty}^{\infty} \Phi_q(z)\,f(z)\left[\int_0^\infty f(y\,|\,z)\,dy\right] dz \\ &= 2\int_{-\infty}^{\infty} \Phi_q(z)\,N'(z)\,N(z\tau)\,dz \quad \text{by (71)} \end{aligned}$$

Now $d\Upsilon_q/dq = I_q + J_q$ where

$$\tfrac{1}{2}I_q = \int_{-\infty}^{\infty} (\partial\Phi_q/\partial q)\cdot N'(z)\, N(z\tau)\, dz =$$

$$= -\, kn\cdot \sin 2q\cdot \int_{-\infty}^{\infty} \Phi_q'(z)\, N'(z)\, N(z\tau)\, dz$$

$$\tfrac{1}{2}J_q = \int_{-\infty}^{\infty} \Phi_q(z)\, N'(z)\cdot [dN(z\tau)/dq]\, dz =$$

$$= (1/\cos^2 q)\cdot \int_{0}^{\infty} [\Phi_q(z) - \Phi_q(-z)]\, zN'(z)\, N'(z\tau)\, dz$$

When $0<m<n$, $0<q<\pi/2$, $I<0$, $J>0$, by (70). Let $q=\frac{1}{2}\pi-\varepsilon$, ε small positive. Then approximately (neglecting ε^2 and higher powers) $\rho=1$, $\cos q=\varepsilon$, $\sin 2q=2\varepsilon$, $\tau=1/\varepsilon$, $N(z\tau)=1$, and

$$I_{(\pi/2)-\varepsilon} = -\, kn\cdot 2\varepsilon \int_{-\infty}^{\infty} \Phi_q'(z)\cdot N'(z)\, dz < 0$$

$$J_{(\pi/2)-\varepsilon} = (1/\varepsilon^2\sqrt{2\pi})\cdot \int_{0}^{\infty} [\Phi_q(z) - \Phi_q(-z)] \times$$

$$\times\, z \exp[-\, z^2(1+\varepsilon^{-2})/2]\, dz > 0$$

As $\varepsilon \to 0$, both I and J approach zero, J faster than I (because of the exponential term) so that at $q=\frac{1}{2}\pi-\varepsilon$, $d\Upsilon_q/dq<0$. Hence at $q=\frac{1}{2}\pi$, $m=n$, Υ has a (local) minimum, not a (global) maximum.

The '*sign-matcher*' has the same best action rule and the same channel cost as the 'speculator'; but since his money profit$=\delta_z\delta_y$, the expected channel utility is

$$\Upsilon_q = Ev(\delta_z\delta_y - kn\rho^2)\,;$$

then by (69)

$$(72)\qquad \Upsilon_q = \Phi_q(1)\,Pr(\delta_z = \delta_y) + \Phi_q(-1)\,Pr(\delta_z \neq \delta_y) =$$
$$= \Phi_q(1)\,(\tfrac{1}{2} + q\pi^{-1}) + \Phi_q(-1)\,(\tfrac{1}{2} - q\pi^{-1}) \quad \text{by (54)}$$
$$\frac{d\Upsilon_q}{dq} = -\,kn\cdot\sin 2q\cdot[\Phi_q'(1)\,(\tfrac{1}{2} + q\pi^{-1}) + \Phi_q'(-1)\,(\tfrac{1}{2} - q\pi^{-1})] + \pi^{-1}\,[\Phi_q(1) - \Phi_q(-1)]$$

By (70), this is positive both when $q=\pi/2$ and when $q=0$. Hence, at $m=n$, Υ has a local, and possibly global, maximum. When kn is large the global maximum may be at $m<1$ so that no observations will be made. On the other hand,

$$\lim_{kn\to 0} \Upsilon_q = \upsilon(1)\,(\tfrac{1}{2} + q\pi^{-1}) + \upsilon(-1)\,(\tfrac{1}{2} - q\pi^{-1}) \begin{cases} < \upsilon(1) & q < \pi/2 \\ = \upsilon(1) & q = \pi/2 \end{cases}$$

$$\lim_{kn\to 0} (\Upsilon_{\pi/2} - \Upsilon_q) > 0 \quad q < \pi/2$$

so that, for kn sufficiently small, the channel with $q=\pi/2$, $m=n$ may be optimal.

Similar results were also obtained for a non-differentiable utility function of a 'satisficer': $\upsilon(r)=1$ or 0 as $r \geqslant$ or $< A$, a constant (the 'aspiration level'). If this utility function is attributed to the 'speculator' it has been shown[13] that Υ_q has a local minimum at $m=n$. But in the case of the 'sign-matcher' this utility function results in a global maximum for Υ_q at $m=n$, if and only if $kn \leqslant 1-A$.

NOTES

* Supported by the Western Management Science Institute under its grant from the Ford Foundation and a contract with the Office of Naval Research, NONR 233(75). In the Proceedings containing this paper it is followed by comments of Thomas A. Marschak and Stanley Reiter.

1 Birkhoff [2]. Savage's [3] relation 'extension of' is also pertinent.

2 Actually, in [5] the author first proves a somewhat stronger theorem. Instead of the *payoff condition*, Ω (denoted there by V), a more general, *outcome condition*, W, is defined: it is a (consistent) set of 'outcome functions', from $Z \times C$ to the set of subsets of (physical) outcomes, which are not necessarily real numbers. The uniqueness and existence of an 'outcome-relevant' domain $Z^W \times C^W$, given W, is then proved. A real valued utility function u, on the set of outcomes, is then introduced.

3 y^{h*} and z^{II} are each distributed asymmetrically (Exhibits 3-4 and 3-3) because of the way the sign function was defined. This would become less pronounced if each coordinate x_i took a larger number of values, thus approaching continuity and making the probabilities $P(\Sigma_1{}^m x_i = 0)$, $P(\Sigma_1{}^n x_i = 0)$ approach zero.

[4] For example McGuire [6], Marschak [7], Radner [8]. In [9] Radner states the relation to the concepts of statistical decision theory.

[5] We can now offer at least a conjectural answer to a question raised at the end of Section 2. It is not required that the decider be able to specify the most detailed set of state descriptions and of act descriptions, and the corresponding payoff and probability function. But it is required that consistency be preserved between the different coarser description sets and corresponding payoff and probability functions, that will vary from one decision situation to another and will obey the (appropriately modified) preference condition (20). The sets and functions must be such as to admit the existence of some (unknown), X, A, ω_{XA}, $p(X)$ satisfying the consistency conditions (6) and (12). If such consistency is preserved then it is possible, given a collection of sets $Z, Z', \ldots$, of events on the one hand, and a collection of sets $C, C', \ldots$ of actions on the other, to construct the two sets X^* and A^* consisting, respectively of all the intersections

$$x^* \equiv z \cap z' \cap \ldots \quad \text{all} \quad z \in Z, z' \in Z', \ldots$$
$$a^* \equiv c \cap c' \cap \ldots \quad \text{all} \quad c \in C, c' \in C', \ldots$$

and to use X^*, A^* as if they were the most detailed sets X, A, in order to find the payoff-relevant sets Z^{Ω}, C^{Ω} for a given payoff condition Ω, as in [5], Corollary to Theorem I.

[6] An unpublished statement by K. Arrow prompts the following important remark. To define the net payoff of an action as a difference (21) *between two utility amounts* and to define, accordingly, the net payoff of a channel (i.e., the maximand!) as a difference (23) *between two utility amounts* is justified in the case when the outcomes of actions and the costs of messages are expressed in money, but only if the utility function of money is linear.

At the end of this paper, we shall interpret Ω as the payoff condition in terms of money, not of utility: that is, $\omega(z^{\Omega}, c^{\Omega})$ is the money profit. Similarly, $\kappa(y^h)$ is the (non-negative) monetary cost of a message. We shall denote by υ a general (linear or non-linear) non-decreasing utility function of money. To choose an optimal channel is, then, to maximize, over the set H of available channels, the *expected channel utility* defined as

$$(23^*) \qquad Y \equiv Y(h, \Omega) \equiv E\upsilon[\omega(z^{\Omega}, c^{\Omega}) - \kappa(y^h)]$$

where the action $c^{\Omega} \equiv \gamma^*_{h\Omega}(y^h)$, and where (since υ is non-decreasing and κ is non-negative) the best action rule γ^* has been chosen so as to maximize the conditionally expected money profit, given the message y^h.

It would be still more general – but more meager in results – not to assume any monetary measurements and to apply general utility function to the set of outcomes of all feasible pairs of channels and of action rules.

Added in 1973. See now Section 3 of K. J. Arrow, 'The Value of and the Demand for Organization', *Decision and Organization*, ed. by C. B. McGuire and R. Radner, North Holland, 1972.

[7] The results of this section are not affected in substance by the remark in the previous note if gross channel payoff $v(h, \Omega)$ is redefined as $Y(h, \Omega)$ of (23*), putting $\kappa(y^h) = 0$ and remembering that the money utility function υ is non-decreasing. Similarly, expected channel cost is redefined as $Y(h, \Omega)$, putting $\omega = 0$ and remembering that κ is non-negative.

[8] SUB-EXAMPLE 11, continued. Note that the distribution on X given in Exhibit 3-3 satisfies condition (III) of the present section; it also satisfies the symmetry condition, though not in the continuous form (IV). Putting $z^{\mathrm{I}} = z$, $z^{\mathrm{II}} = \delta_z$, $y^h = y$ (with $m = 1$), $y^{h*} = \delta_y$, we can use Exhibits 3-5 and 3-6 to compute directly the gross channel payoffs for each of the 4 cases of Exhibits 3-7 and 3-8.

Cases 1 and 2: $v(h, \Omega) = v(h^*, \Omega) = \frac{1}{2}$
Cases 3 and 4: $v(h, \Omega') = v(h^*, \Omega') = \frac{5}{8}$

Thus, in this discrete sub-example, too, the binary channel (h^*) is sufficient under either payoff condition considered.

9 If $x = (x_1, \ldots, x_n)$ is considered the input, and $y^*_m = \delta(\Sigma_1^m x_i)$ the output of the channel h^*_m, the minimum required capacity of h^*_m is defined as the difference between U_0 ('uncertainty at source') and U_1 ('uncertainty retained') where

$$U_0 = -\sum_{\xi} P(x = \xi) \log P(x = \xi)$$

$$-U_1 = P(y^*_m = 1) \sum_{\xi} P(x = \xi \,|\, y^*_m = 1) \log P(x = \xi \,|\, y^*_m = 1)$$

$$+ P(y^*_m \,|\, -1) \sum_{\xi} P(x = \xi \,|\, y^*_m = -1) \log P(x = \xi \,|\, y^*_m = -1)$$

and ξ is a value of the (finite-valued) vector x. The difference $U_0 - U_1$ is called the 'transmission rate' associated with (x, y^*_m). It is conjectured that it approaches a simple function of m as the distribution of x approaches normal distribution.

10 The unit cost of 'search' to the consumer is assumed constant by Stigler [14] in a simple market problem, but he allows non-linearity of cost in another context.

11 As indicated in note 5, both sides of each of these equations are measured in utility units, and a linear utility function of money is assumed. A more general case will be studied at the end of the next section.

12 The result (54) can also be obtained directly from the bivariate normal distribution formula, using auxiliary variables q, u, τ, with:

$$\rho = \sin q \qquad z = u \cos q + y \sin q \qquad \tau = \tan q$$

This leads to (51) and (54). See also [15], [16] for other proofs.

13 In collaboration with T. Ferguson. For our definition of 'satisficing' see [5a, pp. 140–141].

BIBLIOGRAPHY

[1] Debreu, Gerard, *Theory of Value*, Wiley, New York, 1959.

[2] Birkhoff, Garrett, *Lattice Theory* (2d ed.), American Mathematical Society, New York, (Colloquium publication), Vol. 25, 1949.

[3] Savage, Leonard J., *The Foundations of Statistics*, Wiley, New York, 1954, Revised: Dover, 1972.

[4] Fisher, Irving, *The Theory of Interest*, Kelley, New York, 1930.

[5] Marschak, Jacob, 'The Payoff-Relevant Description of States and Acts', *Selected Essays*, 13.

[5a] March, James G. and Herbert A. Simon with the collaboration of Harold Guetzkow, *Organizations*, Wiley, New York, 1958.

[6] McGuire, C. B., 'Some Team Models of a Sales Organization', *Management Science* **7** (1961) 101–130.

[7] Marschak, Jacob, 'Towards an Economic Theory of Organization and Information', *Selected Essays*, 20.

[8] Radner, Roy, 'The Evaluation of Information in Organizations', *Proceedings of the 4th Berkeley Symposium on Mathematical Statistics*, Vol. 1, pp. 491–530, Berkeley, 1961.

[9] Radner, Roy, 'Team Decision Problems', *Annals of Mathematical Statistics* **33** (1962) 857–881.

[10] Marschak, Jacob, 'Remarks on the Economics of Information', *Selected Essays*, 23.

[11] McGuire, C. B., 'The Marginal Productivity of a Fully Exploited Bit', (mimeogr.) RAND D-8947, 1961.

[12] Raiffa, Howard and Schlaifer, Robert, *Applied Statistical Decision Theory*, Division of Research, Graduate School of Business Administration, Harvard University, Boston, 1961.

[13] Feinstein, Amiel, *Foundations of Information Theory*, McGraw-Hill, New York, 1958.

[14] Stigler, George J., 'The Economics of Information', *Journal of Political Economy* **69** (1961) 213–225.

[15] Gupta, Shanti S., 'Probability Integrals of Multivariate Normal and Multivariate *t*', Technical Report No. 64, *Applied Mathematics and Statistics Laboratory, Stanford University*, 1962. Accepted for publication in *Annals of Mathematical Statistics.*

[16] Cramér, Harold, *Mathematical Methods of Statistics*, Princeton, Princeton, N.J., 1946, p. 290.

26

THE COST OF DECISION MAKING: AN INTERDISCIPLINARY DISCUSSION

(1956)

*Formal Models Seminar, March 30, 1954 and April 13, 1954**

Participants (at time of the discussion, all associated with the University of Chicago except as indicated): Jay B. Best, physiology; Robert I. Crane, history; Donald W. Fiske, psychology; George R. Flowers, biology; H. G. Landau, mathematical biology; Jacob Marschak, economics; Robert S. Merrill, anthropology; James G. Miller, psychiatry and psychology; Andreas Papandraeou (University of Minnesota), economics; Anatol Rapoport, mathematical biology; Marianne Simmel (University of Illinois), psychology; and Burton Stein, history.

Marschak: What is the value of the information we may obtain, say, from a spy or from a scientist? What relations can be found between value and amount of information?

Take the case of making even-money bets that a blue ball will be extracted from an urn containing red and blue balls. We may simply use our knowledge of the probability that the ball will be blue, or we may supplement this knowledge by using a spy. Let p = the probability of getting a blue ball; then $1-p$ = the probability of a red ball. Set the amount of one dollar to be gained or lost per decision. Let

$$p > \tfrac{1}{2}.$$

Without the informer, we shall always bet on blue; with the informer, we shall always gain a dollar. Compare the two average gains:

The value, $U_0 = (+1)\,p + (-1)\,(1-p) = 2p - 1$ (without the informer).

The value, $U_1 = 1$ (employing the spy)

The *value of information*, then, is

$$V = U_1 - U_0 = 1 - (2p - 1) = 2(1 - p)$$

Figure 1 is a plot of the situation when the spy is reliable.

Suppose the spy is unreliable. Let q = the probability of his telling the

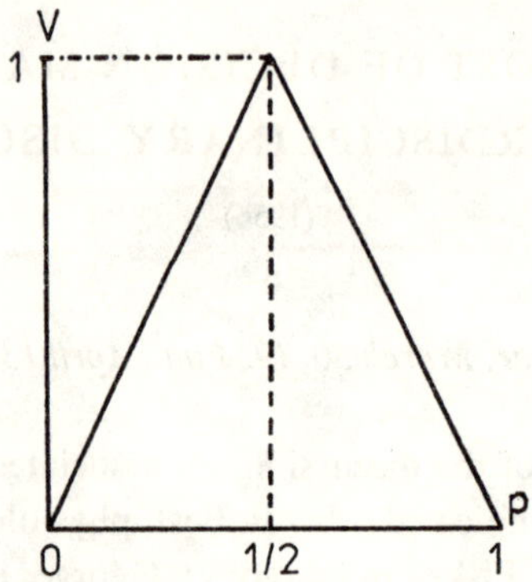

Fig. 1. Value of information when spy is reliable.

truth. Then

$$U_0 = 2p - 1$$
$$U_1 = (+1)\,q + (-1)\,(1 - q) = 2q - 1$$

Therefore, $V = 2(q - p)$ of which the previous formula for V was a special case with $q = 1$. See Figure 1.

Further, the net value gained by using the spy is

$$U_1 - U_0 - c$$

where c is the cost paid to the spy.

Some spies, or other sources of information, are more costly than others Some are more reliable than others. We are thus faced with choices among various net values:

No spies: $2p - 1 - c_0$
Spy No. 1: $2q_1 - 1 - c_1$
Spy No. 2: $2q_2 - 1 - c_2$

Note that if the spy is paid only when he's right, then the net gain is $2q_1 - 1 - c_1 q_1$, etc. (A suggestion of A. Rapoport.)

We have seen the *value of information* from a completely reliable spy is $2(1 - p)$. This is different from the *amount of information* (Shannon). The amount of information doesn't depend on the economic value to the decision maker. It depends entirely on the properties of the probability distribution and is defined as

$$-[p \log p + (1 - p) \log(1 - p)].$$

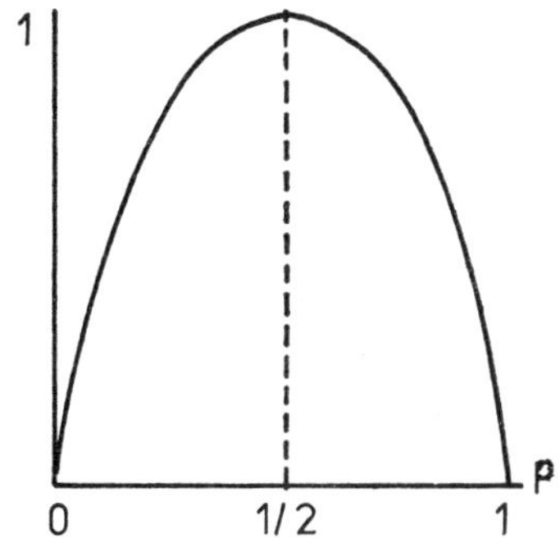

Fig. 2. Shannon's information plotted against p.

Shannon's formulation plots into Figure 2. Thus, in our case, value and amount of information coincide for the case of $p=0$, 1, and $\frac{1}{2}$, but not for the intermediate cases.

A farmer is faced with the problem of how many acres to cultivate. The concept of action will be introduced here. At this point, action and decision will be considered as identical.

Let $a =$ acreage, or action

$\mu =$ mean price of grain

$x =$ deviation from μ

Then price $=\mu+x$ and $Ex=0$ (that is, the expected deviation is zero). Write $Ex^2=\sigma^2$ ($=$variance).

Let $u(a, x)=$profit.

Let us say that in Condition 0 the farmer has no information, i.e., he doesn't know the price; in Condition 1 the farmer does have a source of information. (A good farmer actually 'employs two statisticians': one for the market, one for the weather.) Let us assume yield/acre is always $=1$. We shall compare the highest expected profit (highest long-run average profit) that can be achieved in either of these two conditions, and compute the value of information:

$$V = E \max_a u(a, x) - \max_a Eu(a, x).$$

The revenue will be $a(\mu+x)$. Suppose he farms different acres at a

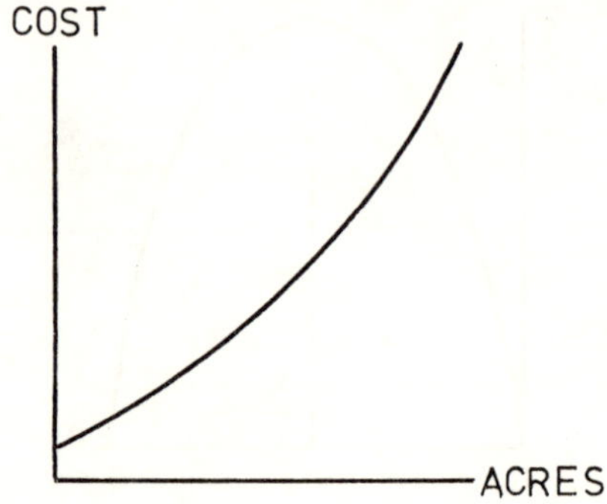

Fig. 3. Total cost depends on number of acres.

different expense. On Fig. 3 we have assumed his total cost$=\frac{1}{2}a^2+\beta a+\gamma$. The derivative of this $a+\beta$; that is, the additional cost of adding acres increases with the number already under cultivation. The profit, u=revenue less cost.

Now consider Condition 0, wherein the farmer has no information:

$$Eu \text{ (or long-run average profit)}$$
$$= Ea(\mu + x) - (\tfrac{1}{2}a^2 + \beta a + \gamma);$$
$$(1) \qquad Eu = -\tfrac{1}{2}a^2 + a(\mu - \beta) - \gamma \quad (\text{since } Ex = 0)$$

The derivative of this is: $-a+\mu-\beta=0$, if Eu is at its maximum with respect to a.

$$U_0 = \max_a Eu = \frac{(\mu - \beta)^2}{2} - \gamma,$$

which is the maximum average profit that can be obtained when x is unknown.

Now let's consider Condition 1, wherein the farmer has information on prices. First, find

$$\max_a u(a, x)$$

He tries to maximize u, given x, by choosing the best decision a. We have $u=-\frac{1}{2}a^2+a(\mu+x-\beta)-\gamma$. This is similar to the right-hand side of Equation (1) except that $(\mu+x)$ is substituted for μ. In this second case, differentiation gives us:

$$-a + \mu + x - \beta = 0,$$

when u is at its maximum with respect to a.

Then

$$\max_a u(a, x) = \frac{(\mu + x - \beta)^2}{2} - \gamma.$$

Now we want to find the expected value of this maximum profit

$$U_1 = E\frac{(\mu + x - \beta)^2}{2} - \gamma = \frac{(\mu - \beta)^2}{2} - \gamma + \frac{\sigma^2}{2}.$$

(The last term is one-half the variance of price.)

What is the value of information?

$$V = U_1 - U_0 = \frac{\sigma^2}{2}$$

Rapoport: The result would be some other multiple of σ^2 if Marschak had not chosen $\frac{1}{2}$ for his original equation.

Marschak: Yes. In any case, the value of information is related to the variance (expected square deviation) if profit is quadratic in the 'decision variable' a. This result is independent of the distribution of the 'nature variable' x. But notice that when this distribution is normal, Shannon's measure of the *amount* (not the *value*) of information about x is also related to the variance of x.

Landau: The acreage is actually finite; $a \leqslant A$, say.

Marschak: In this case, the optimal a is the same as in my case, or is equal to A, whichever is smaller.

Miller: What is the relationship of what you've said to organization theory?

Marschak: I have taken a simple case with one actor and one observer (several observers – spies – in the case of the urn). In the general case, the problem is whether or not we should maintain a given line of communication, that is, when does its cost exceed its value? Later we'll get into cases with multiplicity of actors. You may be interested in today's problem in its relation to the evolution of the brain. The value of information may be nil to a species that lives in an environment with very low 'variance,' e.g. receives its food always floating in the same direction. Such a species need not have sensory organs.

Best: My comments here stem from the discussion by Marschak in the formal models seminar of March 30, 1954. A certain price per decision was exacted by a 'seer' or observer with regard to the number of acres a farmer should plant in order to 'win' in the face of changing market conditions, etc. It was assumed that the observer was not always correct but merely had a higher probability of being correct than the farmer trusting to chance would have. Viewing animals as an economic structure in which the brain and sensory organs would be analogous to the seer and the metabolic requirements for their maintenance the cost, Marschak raised the question of whether animals that were susceptible to impinging stimuli from all sides, such as those that live in the sea or calm water, did not have larger brains than those that live in a stream where all significant stimuli come from upstream.

As a rule which seems to be fairly valid, those organisms which obtain their food by foraging, i.e., moving about and seeking out other organisms to prey on and eat, have developed the largest brains and head ganglia with the most highly specialized and differentiated receptor systems. An example of this is that the Cephalopods in the phylum of Molluscs, by an entirely independent evolutionary route from that of the vertebrates, have chosen a predatory and highly motile mode of existence with concomitant development of the head ganglion into a fairly respectable brain and eyes that closely resemble those of vertebrates. This development stands in contrast to that of the other molluscs who lead more sessile existences and have much less extensively developed receptor, conductile and integrative tissues.

The biological question posed by Marschak might be approached by rephrasing the problem slightly from the form chosen in the seminar discussion. An animal, by virtue of the fact that it goes abroad in search of food, is confronted with a larger domain of possible events, both profitable (nutritious) and dangerous, than if it follwed a more sessile pattern of behavior. One might suppose that an organism is faced with n_0 decision situations *per unit time* if it sits still, and $n_0 + M$ decisions per unit time if it is moving about, where M would be some monotone function of its speed and range of movement. Suppose further that

p_0 is the probability of a correct decision by 'chance'.
$1-p_0$ is the probability of a wrong decision by 'chance'.
w is the amount the animal 'wins' on a correct decision.
L is the amount the animal 'loses' on a wrong decision.

If the animal has a brain we might suppose it to make correct decisions with a probability of p_1 and wrong decisions with a probability of $(1-p_1)$ and that $p_1 > p_0$. The metabolic cost of maintenance *per unit time* of such a brain will, however, be g, and this will, in general, take more the form of a 'fixed overhead' cost rather than an assessment per decision for the animal. Then for a motile animal with no brain the net nutritional gain per unit time would be

$$U_0 = wp_0(n_0 + M) - L(1 - p_0)(n_0 + M)$$

with the sessile existence being represented by the special case in which $M=0$. For a motile animal with a brain, however, the net nutritional gain per unit time would be

$$U_1 = wp_1(n_0 + M) - L(1 - p_1)(n_0 + M) - g.$$

The nutritional gain by virtue of having a brain is then just

$$U_1 - U_0 = (w + L)(p_1 - p_0)(n_0 + M) - g,$$

so that possession of a brain will represent a handicap unless

$$(w + L)(p_1 - p_0)(n_0 + M) \geqslant g.$$

One may look upon the ratio

$$E = g/(p_1 - p_0)$$

as a kind of 'extravagance index' associated with the possession of a brain. Then a brain will represent a handicap unless

$$(w + L)(n_0 + M) \geqslant E.$$

Thus, one has the common-sense result that the higher the stakes $(w+L)$ and the more the animal 'gets around', the more it can afford to pay metabolically for being intelligent.

Miller: Instead of defining p as the probability of the correctness of decision, we might define it as the probability of an adequate defense made by an organism in resistance to environmental stresses. This makes it a somewhat more general formulation. For a subsystem dealing with stress to be worthwhile, $U_1 - U_0$ must be greater than zero. If not, the subsystem is extravagant. Examples would be an FBI turning into a Gestapo, automatic headlight-dimming devices in automobiles which discharge batteries etc.

Marschak: A better title for Best's discussion would be 'Gain and Cost Due to Decisions and Observations'. But this is not very important. It seems to me very striking that this group readily accepts Best's notion of *molluscus economicus* while it resists that of *homo economicus*! There were objections when I spoke of humans as entrepreneurs maximizing something (such as dollars), but there have been no objections today to dealing with molluscs in this way! I was interested to learn from Best's talk that biologists do think in terms of what may be called the economics of evolution. Best, you talk as if animals were trying to economize on energy?

Best: Yes. But I like to view this process from the standpoint of the species rather than of the single animal. For a species which has a high rate of division and growth, it actually may be more economical to take a loss in indivudual lives so that the species may evolve. But this is by no means a unique way of doing business. Humans, for instance, have an elaborate nervous system for protection of *individuals* in the species. Still other survival processes are also successful. I think species maximize probability of survival of their genetic descendants through adopting a mode of life best suited to this end. Suppose an animal has adopted a particular mode of life: Is it then useful or not for it to have a brain? Best strategy for the mollusc involves getting as much food as is necessary. Those who do this best will survive.

Marschak: In the simple case of either surviving or not surviving, you may say the utility function is two-valued. In this case, to maximize the probability of survival is formally identical with maximizing the expected utility, where the utility is two-valued: utility of survival $=1$, utility of nonsurvival $=0$, expected utility $=p\cdot 1+(1-p)\cdot 0=p$.

Best: I wasn't talking about a decision. Suppose you start off with a group of molluscs from which equal numbers of different evolutionary strains will be drawn. Those which enjoy the greatest net caloric intake will survive.

Marschak: Would you say that you can interpret evolution by saying that species maximize the rate of population increase? The balance of births over deaths should be, precentagewise, as high as possible. It does not follow that the more complex organisms will be those that survive. Have they, in fact, increased their share in total living matter?

Best: I think it is Dr. Gerard who is interested in the idea of survival of more complicated forms. I think one can point to evolutionary development towards less complicated forms, e.g., the evolution of parasitic forms from animals which were once free-swimming.

Miller: I think Dr. Gerard has modified his thinking about this notion during the past year. He would probably say, though, that probably the more complicated organisms came after the less complicated organisms. It doesn't mean necessarily that less complicated forms will disappear; if environmental stresses are minimal, they will survive. In general, however, when mutations occur, you can state that there are three possibilities: (a) a less complicated structure mutates to a more complex one, (b) a structure mutates to one of equal complexity (or efficiency), (c) a structure mutates to one of lesser complexity (or efficiency). Actually, complexity and efficiency don't necessarily correspond, so perhaps there are six rather than three possibilities: more complexity with either more or less efficiency, and so on. Increasing complexity in evolution must be considered in relation to the nature of the environment, to determine whether it will lead to survival. A human being is capable of surviving in a more complex environment than an amoeba.

Marschak: Probably you include our social institutions, e.g., our municipal transportation, among our 'organs'. But, then, are we not more helpless than animals in a changing environment, as when elevators and water heaters stop functioning in a war or a strike?

Miller: Most discussions I've read of social evolution have been nonsensical because they deal with vague analogies rather than with precise study of the mechanisms. I think it is possible, however, to talk sensibly about social evolution. If an individual can't handle stresses, and has become a specialized part of a group, he is now more vulnerable. But he has gained many advantages. A good analogy to the Marschak-Best model is the assignment of sentry functions in a wagon train passing through Indian territory; it is a more effective organization than any individual can be.

Simmel: Simpson uses an interesting analogy on evolution. Rocks, stones, and grains of sand are placed in a bin. The large rocks are pace-setters; after they are put into the bin, there are still spaces for the smaller stones, and thereafter for the sand. If there are changes in the properties of the pace-setters, then perhaps 'mutants' in other categories have better chances of 'survival'.

Marschak: Thus, species form an environment for each other.

Best: An example is that a species dependent upon photosynthetic plants for food can't multiply out of proportion to a certain rate of photosynthesis.

Merrill: To go back to Best's model: No account was taken of the overhead on the locomotor system (as well as the brain). Could this model be modified to include the matter of change, say, between the locomotor system and the brain? In anthropology, the current view is that locomotor change (e.g. man's emergence as a bipedal animal) is prior to the brain change.

Best: Actually, locomotor system is involved in my term M.

Crane: In the illustration of the pioneer group in Indian territory, one must weigh the advantages of such an organization against the advantages of the passage of a single scout through this territory: he can remain unseen by the enemy.

Miller: This is analogous to defenses of a biological organism: a small, weak organism can be camouflaged – not so a larger, stronger organism.

Crane: I took it that Best viewed this evolutionary process as one of maximizing the probability of survival of the larger number of offspring.

Best: Usually by successful survival one means that the species has existed for a long time.

Crane: Some species are so successful in maintaining their existence and in breeding that eventually their numbers increase to a point where sufficient food is unavailable. Consider the lemmings. Such success is illusory.

Best: If there are so many lemmings that the only place to put them is in the ocean, then lemmings are successful. I would view as successful up to the present all lemmings that you find. (In answer to Marschak) No, I wouldn't consider success in terms of total mass or number or health of organisms.

Fiske: Rather the number of generations the species has kept going.

Best: Yes. Probability of survival of their lineal descendants.

Fiske: Using this criterion, what you are maximizing is not rate of growth of the population but the chances of the rate staying positive.

Best: That's right. We got off into a subcorollary of this: Does increase of the total number tend to increase the probability of continued survival over a long period of time?

Marschak: You're interested in the integral of population over time: the total number of moluscs that have lived until now. You have tried to maximize this.

Best: It would be a question whether you would want to take the integral over all those that have existed or wished to count the total time over which they have continued to exist.

Flowers: I'm wondering about what you mean by correct decision by which the animal 'wins' the amount W. Do you consider that he has a net gain of energy after his correct decision or that he made a correct decision in that he got his prey but may or may not have a net gain of energy?

Best: If the prey is too small, perhaps there's no gain.

Flowers: He may intercept the prey but nutrition may be insufficient.

Marschak: What is Best's payoff matrix? Is it like this? In the case of motile animal we have (denoting, as before by a the decision, or action, variable, and by x the nature variable, or environment):

	$x=1=$ Danger	$x=2=$ Food
$a=1=$ run	$W-g$	$L-g$
$a=2=$ grab	$L-g$	$W-g$

Now consider the sessile organism:

	$x=1=$ Danger	$x=2=$ Food
$a=0=$ sit	L	W

Flowers' objection is that the situation is more differentiated than the two symbols W and L permit us to describe. There are more than only two possible outcomes.

Flowers: Yes. Moreover, the organism doesn't have information to know whether he's going to spend more energy than he's going to take in.

Marschak: Would you suggest that there are more than two actions in the first case and more than one in the second case? You would complicate this further?

Best: This is not a pretentious model but merely a reformulation of the mathematical statements made by Marschak.

Simmel: One difficulty with the model is that it defines payoff of a single individual decision. But what matters is the payoff over a long time for the whole species. If the organism grabs when there's danger, its fate is settled once and for all, while if the organism runs toward food or away from danger on a single decision, its fate is not settled once and for all.

Marschak: Yes. This matrix may be considered set up for one unit of time. A more complete model would assign a payoff to each sequence of outcomes. In business, you compute the sum of discounted values of future profits, and maximize this. However, Best will form a sum of payoffs, not only for each individual over time, but also compute the sum of such sums over all individuals of the species.

Miller: Coming back to the discussion between Crane and Best, I'd like to raise a *caveat* about a word like success. Success is a value term and as such must be carefully inspected. Perhaps to the biologist, continuation of the species is the most successful accomplishment; however, to others, continuation of the individual is more important. It may well be that one is incompatible with the other. It may also be that a lemming would not consider himself successful in Best's terms. Propagation might go on so rapidly in India, say, that the next generation would not have the same opportunity to propagate as the last generation simply because there wouldn't be enough food to sustain them. This suggests another conception of success. We may have at least five or six different values implied in the word success.

Marschak: Best's concern was only with prediction. He is not concerned with the mortality rate of Indian babies or of fish eggs, offset by large birthrate. He will say the Indians are all right as long as there are 400 million of them and as longs as this number is stable. In fact, he is only interested in this number. He is able to predict that fish or people with a particular kind of device (high birth- *and* death-rate) maintain themselves. Perhaps it is sound for Best to stick to his particular criterion of survival probability as a tool of prediction even though Crane might rightfully object to it as a moral value.

Landau: The criterion of survival explains the direction of evolution, but the fact we seem worried about is that there are a lot of different ways of surviving. I would like to suggest that there may be a difference between organic evolution and social evolution. An organism doesn't really have a choice: If a mutation occurs, it may or may not be successful and consequently may or may not survive. And there may be several possible ways to survive; sessile and mobile molluscs both have survived. When Miller spoke of the division of labor among people crossing the prairie, it occurred to me that the humans would be more successful perhaps if each individual could perform all these functions (sentry, fighting, working) by himself. However, this would require mutation, and we have no control over this. The important difference, then, it seems to me, is that in social evolution we have some choice, or so it appears.

Marschak: To this extent, social institutions are artifacts, like machines. In order to achieve a purpose, you choose the best machine, i.e., one that maximizes something, e.g., profits. At the turn of the 18th-19th century intellectuals were busy discussing various political constitutions among which they had choice: see the Federalist papers.

Stein: I was wondering after Flowers' question if the item food might not be considered net caloric gain. Perhaps this is closer to what Best was thinking of. If so, perhaps one of the prime functions of the added brain is to make the fairly subtle decision about whether there will be a net gain.

Best: Yes. Net caloric gain is closer to what I meant. But this makes the model less simple.

Marschak: Can you supply numbers for the matrix? Nobody will criticize you if they're not absolutely right. How about:

	Danger	Food
Run	$-1-g$	$-1-g$
Grab	$-100-g$	$+50-g$

If you run away from enemy or food, all that happens is tha‿ you've expended a little energy, say one unit; and g, in Best's terms, is the energy cost of maintaining the brain.

Miller: Perhaps Danger-Grab should be minus infinity. Though perhaps not if you consider the species as a whole.

Landau: It would only make sense in terms of evolution of species as a whole.

Marschak: You have to cumulate over time and over all individuals.

Landau: Anyone who could fill values into this matrix at all realistically would be making a major discovery.

Papandraeou: A question concerning the predictive value of this model. You indicated that prediction was the primary objective of it. In economics, where we also speak of maximization, our primary objective is to predict the signs of rates of change of variables with respect to parameters. For instance, if there is an increase in the wage rate by the union, the fact that the firm maximizes profits permits us to predict, given some other assumptions, that somebody will be fired. Now, what kind of prediction concerning pure behavior of the molluscs can you make from a model of this sort?

Best: One common-sense result mentioned was that the more the animal gets around and forages for prey, the more valuable a brain will be. At least among the molluscs, this happens to be so. The more active, predatory ones have so developed. It's admittedly a hindsight prediction.

Marschak: As in Papandraeou's wage example: If parameter g (brain's 'wages') increases, brain becomes a waste. Another parameter is p_0, a property of the environment. If p_0 is $\frac{1}{2}$, then it pays very much to have an added sensory organ. When it is near 1 or 0, then it will not pay.

Best: I set up my probability slightly differently than yours. This is the probability of obtaining food if it grabs at random. In your case, didn't you have an over-all climatological probability?

Miller: In answer to Mr. Papandraeou's question about what empirical studies can follow from this model: Another study would be the inheritance of acquired information – Lamarckianism vs. Darwinianism. One might study different generations of molluscs to determine the respective probabilities with which each generation grabs and runs. Perhaps the present generation would grab vs. run with the same probability as a previous generation, or maybe they would grab vs. run with a chance probability at first and gradually change as time went by. (McDougall did experiments on this problem a decade or so ago.) The question, then, is: Do you have a 'spy' who gives you the information on the basis of which you decide to grab vs. run? Or is this information gained through inheritance or observation of parent's responses?

Crane: If it costs a sizable amount for a mollusc to maintain a brain and since there are the two types of molluscs – motile and sessile – why did the motile ones become motile and develop brains while the sessile oysters, for instance, got along all right?

Best: You have mutations occurring all the time. If you want to know how many ways there are of surviving, you can count the number of species there are on earth.

Landau: Simpson's rocks and pebbles analogy is pertinent here. Different mutant forms survive in different environments.

Miller: One may use a very simple figure of speech. If you have enough income so that you don't have to work, and then you added another subsystem known as your mother-in-law, you have several possible courses of action: You can starve to death, or you can go to work, or you can send your mother-in-law out to work for you. So a mutation presents new species that evolve with new problems of survival and perhaps new assets for survival.

Marschak: I'd like to continue my answer to Mr. Papandreaou, by interpreting Best's results in terms of our previous two sessions. We ask how the variations in parameters affect the choice of the organization. We have to distinguish here two groups of parameters. One group describes nature, in terms of probabilities of its possible states. In Best's model, this was represented by p_0. Another group consisted of parameters characterizing the payoff, as a function of the decision (action) and the state of nature. To review:

Payoff function: $u(a, x)$, as represented by the matrix.

Here

$a =$ decision (it has, in our example, two values: run and grab)
$x =$ state of nature (also two values: damage and food).

If the mollusc has a brain, its rule of action, $a=\alpha(x)$ is as follows: 'if $x=$damage, than $a=$run; if $x=$food, then $a=$grab',

Best also mentioned that from the point of view of the species, it is the long-run average that matters. In his formulas, he multiplied each caloric payoff by its probability, and added. Clearly this long-run average (or 'expected payoff') depends on: (a) these probabilities; (b) the payoff function; (c) the rule of action.

In the case of the mollusc with brain, the action a depends on information about x; but in the case, 'without brain', the action (viz., sitting still) does not depend on x. It is, in fact, constant. We have thus two information structures' each having one row and one column:

Without brain:

	x
a	0

(Action doesn't depend on the state of nature.)

With brain:

	x
a	1

(Action does depend on the state of nature.)

Here 0 stands for 'independence of a from x', 1 stands for dependence. In my example of a farm given last time, there might have been two action variables: a_1=decision about amount of grain and a_2= decision about amount of livestock; and three nature variables were x_1=the price of grain, x_2=the price of livestock, and x_3=the weather. A hypothetical information structure might be: to base planting on the knowledge of grain prices and of weather; and to base livestock raising on the knowledge of livestock prices:

	x_1	x_2	x_2
a_1	1	0	1
a_2	0	1	0

With this information structure the rule of action will be of the following kind:

$$a_1 = \alpha_1(x_1, x_3); \qquad a_2 = \alpha_2(x_2).$$

Among the various possible functions α_1, α_2 there will be some that are best. When they are used, the expected payoff less the cost of information equals the value of the above information structure.

The case of Best has an additional complication. He assumes an 'imperfect spy'; his p_1 is less than 1. The case of the imperfect spy was discussed in my first session. In general, decisions aren't based on the true state of nature but rather what the decider thinks the state of nature to be.

Let

y = information available to the decision maker, and
x = true state of nature.

Then $y=\eta(x)$, where the function η may be called the coding function. It depends on the organs or methods available to learn about the state of nature. The personnel manager of a firm observes the labor market, but he does not communicate all his observations in detail to, say, the president. He'll make use of averages to give a more compact statement, which is, presumably, cheaper to communicate and easier to act upon. Thus, the rule of action is, in general, not $a=\alpha(x)$ but, rather, $a=\alpha(y)$, where $y=\eta(x)$.

In the case of an imperfect spy, $\eta(x)$ is a random function, viz.:

$$\eta(x) = x \text{ with probability } p_1\text{; non-}x \text{ with probability } 1-p_1\,,$$

where p_1 has the same meaning as in Best's model. There may be a choice of the best, or cheapest, coding function, given the other conditions. It may not be worthwhile to get all information exactly. We ask: What kind of information is it important to require observers to communicate? Sometimes it is better to know a shorthand summary. For example, sometimes the decisions of the high levels of government depend on national income, the general price level, etc. All these are averages ('index-numbers') or totals, not details. Thus $\eta(x)$ is not equal to x. This is also the case when, for reasons of economy, one decides to accept a certain amount of 'noise', by hiring an 'unreliable' spy.

To take account of this generalization, we must describe the information structure of a given network by giving, for each decision variable (say, a_i), not – as I have done earlier – the list of nature variables that are exactly known to the ith decision maker; but, rather, by giving, more generally, the coding function $\eta_i(x)$ that indicates how the information available to the ith decision maker is formed from nature variables. The information structure is the n-tuplet $\eta_1(x),\ldots,\eta_n(x)$, if there are n decision variables. Clearly the previous definition of information structure is a special case: to pick out some of the nature variables and leave the others out as irrelevant to a particular decision, is a special case of coding.

In any case, our problem is to compare between two or more competing networks, each characterized by a cost and a certain information structure and, hence, characterized (given the payoff function and the nature's probabilities) by certain best rules of action. On this basis the net values of networks are compared. This was discussed in the previous session and has been also done, in essence, in Best's formulas.

NOTE

* This discussion was held at the University of Chicago by members and guests of the Committee on Behavioral Sciences. The discussion on March 30 was initiated by Jacob Marschak and on April 13 by Jay B. Best.

27

ECONOMICS OF LANGUAGE*

(1965)

I. AN OPTIMAL COMMUNICATION SYSTEM

A group of engineers were designing the communication system of a small fighter plane. They were told to keep the communication equipment as light as possible so as not to impair the plane's speed and maneuverability, or the load of fuel and ammunition it can carry. Every pound saved on communication hardware would improve the plane's performance. The different messages that the pilot may have to exchange with his gunner or with other planes or with the ground, and that provide for all the contingencies of navigation and fighting, are not numerous. No need for verbal messages, a telephone. A small set of dials and off-on signals would do.

A psychologist was called in to study the available records of communications in actual combat, and to perform mock-combat tests. The group's final recommendation: restore the telephone. Men in mortal danger, or approaching or escaping it, need to hear and talk to other men, with plenty of redundancy, and not even always confining the talk to the task in hand. Without the relief of verbal, voiced exchange, tension might become intolerable, sometimes to the point of nervous breakdown, and would in any case lead to diminished performance during the same or the next mission. A reminiscence, some banter, a cheer, perhaps a whistled tune, any effective sharing of experience could help. But this requires a richer, a more habitual language than the primitive and exotic dictionary of buttons and dials. Jokes coded in advance are notoriously un-funny.

Thus, nervous relief for the plane's crew is 'worth' a couple of pounds of communication equipment. 'Worth' is an economic term. This does not mean that "worth" is measured in money. Nor can we subtract pounds from, say, microwatt-seconds of nervous exertion. What we do measure is the probability of success of the plane's mission. Adding to a given communication vocabulary tends to decrease this probability (by adding to the plane's load), but also to increase it (by improving the crew's mental state). When the advantages and disadvantages are so balanced that the probability of success of the mission is the highest achievable, we say that the system is optimal, or (equivalently) is efficient, or economical.

The present writer does not know whether the recommendation of the psychologist and his colleagues was accepted, and telephones were kept in those fighter plane designs. But he is an economist, and the story impressed him as a problem in the Economics of Language. He apologizes to those of his fellow economists who might prefer to define their field more narrowly, and who would object to this (not at all unusual) identification of economics with the search for optimality in fields extending beyond, though including, the production and distribution of marketable goods. Being ignorant of linguistics, he apologizes even more humbly to those linguists who would scorn the designation of a simple dial-and-buttons system as a language. He does think, however, that his story deals with the essential stuff of economics, in particular the economics of uncertainty that characterizes problems of human information, communication, and organization. See, for example, Marschak (1954, 1959, 1964).

At the same time, the author suspects that these problems are indeed not without pertinence to the phenomenon of language, or at least put them in a perspective worth exploring. With all the reluctance befitting a curious layman he submits this sketch of an article as a question to linguists. He asks them whether their work to date contains building materials for any future economics of the most developed and most fully studied system of communications within human organizations: the language, spoken or written.

II. EFFICIENCY AND VIABILITY

The story of the fighter plane illustrates, however, only one, the *normative* (or *policy*, or *efficiency*) branch of communication economics, namely, the search for communication systems best suited to a given goal; or, more generally, best suited to a given scale of values ('utilities' is the economist's term). It searches for a system that would maximize the average achieved value; it being understood that the average is weighted by the probabilities of the various contingencies. This policy rule goes back to the eighteenth century's idea of maximizing the 'moral value of wealth'

(Daniel Bernoulli, 1738). It was shown more recently that this rule is logically implied by a few plausible axioms of consistency so that it can be regarded, in the words of F. P. Ramsey (1926), as 'an extension of logic'. Still more recent developments, in the theory of games, of statistics, and 'operations research', have brought about a rich literature on the logic of the 'average utility rule', e.g., L. J. Savage (1954).

In the simple case when the value scale has only two points, of which one ('goal attained') is preferable to the other ('goal failed'), maximizing average utility is identical with maximizing the probability of achieving the preferable result (i.e., of attaining the goal), as in our fighter case.

Another branch of communication economics would be the *explanatory* one. It asks: Why are the known languages of the present and the past what they are or were? This is equivalent to asking: Why has any observed trait, or set of traits, of a communication system survived for as long a time as it has, in fact, survived? It will be seen that this is, in turn, equivalent to the following question: Given the environment, what determines the probability that a set of traits will remain in existence for a given length of time? Logically, surviving is a special case of 'attaining a goal'. Viability is thus a special case of efficiency. This goes for language as well as for other aspects of human organization (and thus, of 'culture' if I may use the word). Therefore, explanatory economics of language (as of 'culture' in general) can be regarded, formally, as a special case of the normative, or policy, study: as if the scale of values of a (fictitious) policy-maker consisted in preferring long to short durations of survival of a set of characteristics. To be sure, the historical records of survivals and extinctions of linguistic forms reflect also the efforts of actual, non-fictitious policy-makers, whose scale of values may or may not have been the conservative one.

To exemplify the distinction between a normative and explanatory approach in another branch of anthropology, Kluckhohn and Leighton (1946, pp. 176–177) pointed out that witch-killing seems to benefit a tribe's cohesion; but Michael Polanyi (1965) using his, or our, scale of values could not help expressing his disgust at such a statement. According to Darwin (1872), Goethe, in 1794–5, "pointedly remarked ... that the future question for naturalists will be how, for instance, cattle got their horns, and not for what they are used": an explanatory, nonnormative approach, we would say.

III. POLICY

When the *Académie Française* debates its Dictionary, it is engaged in policy-making. A word, a rule is accepted, rejected on the basis of some scale of values. I have not followed the debates but imagine something like the following criteria might be used. One of them may be logical consistency: try to avoid too many exceptions to a rule, ban illogical sentences. Another criterion may be the aesthetics of sounds and cadences, as well as of some meanings: avoid vulgar associations. Perhaps more important is the goal of preserving national unity: defend tradition, yet adapt judicially to the new needs, and the changing degrees of influence of various portions of the people, possibly caused by some identifiable change in the environment. Any such criteria need not be, but sometimes are, mutually inconsistent. Then the decision finally made will reflect – and a set of such decisions will indeed define – the relative power of the contestants, as studied, for example, by Harsanyi (1962a, b) in this journal. In this, the *Académie* is presumably not unlike any other legislative body.

In the United States, there is no language legislation. Several dictionaries compete with each other in the market, and they also compete with show business, the schools, the press, the political orators, and the pulpit. There exists nonetheless a public debate on language policy, and it is possible to identify the underlying criteria: see, for example, Sledd and Ebbit (1962) on *Webster's Third* (controversial) *Edition.* As a non-native, therefore self-conscious, user of English, and a reader of both British and American publications and manuscripts (including students' essays), I offer one class of cases that may illustrate further the possible value scales of competing language policies. It seems that, *pace* Dickens, the adjectives 'mutual' and 'common' are treated as interchangeable except possibly in legal and scientific literature. Interchangeable – in the U.S.A. but I think not in England – are also 'present' and 'current'. Some critics of the new *Webster* have pointed out that it equates 'uninterested' with 'disinterested' (which latter should properly mean 'impartial'), thus making "*two words do the work of one.*" For a scientist or lawyer such many-to-one correspondence between words and concepts is surely uneconomical for it may leave some concepts wordless. It is vital for the economist that the reader of the expression "national income of 1933 in dollars of current purchasing power" should unequivocally understand "purchasing power of 1933," not of 1965. Also, superfluous words are apt to create pseudoconcepts empty of content and repugnant to the realist. Precisely in this context, Lotka (1924), the scientist, quotes Goethe, the sage: "*Gewoehnlich glaubt der Mensch, wenn er nur Worte hoert,/Es muesse sich dabei auch etwas denken lassen.*"[1]

Yet, to have some 'two words do the work of one' is not uneconomical for people whose tasks and needs do not ordinarily call for distinguishing between the particular concepts in question. Such people may include teen-agers, and lazy reporters. But poets and orators, too, may indulge in, yes be in vital need of, a hoard of synonyms.

Another type of what is sometimes called economy of language may also be actually noneconomical, with respect to some scale of values. The short sentence of some ancients – '*Eo rus*!' '*I*' – is aesthetically appealing as are the sparse brush strokes of an early Chinese drawing. But surely, as we have noted, the aesthetic criterion is not the only one admitted in language policy. Nor is it true that thriftiness is the only criterion in arts, poetry, or literary style – or even in economics (in the narrower sense). Schopenhauer stated his aversion to brevity of style as explicitly as Keynes deplored the public dangers of private thrift. (When the economist Veblen advocated austerity – using, by the way, rather luxuriant language – his criterion was still another one: the moral criterion.) It is possible, to be sure, that economy of effort was operating in the process of language evolution. If so, economy of effort would define just one of the language characteristics that satisfy the survival criterion. We shall return to this in the next section.

Surely the present article does not contain any new linguistic facts. So far its purpose has been to present language as an object of choice, of policy, in exactly the same sense in which the communication system of the fighter plane had to be chosen. "To govern is to choose" (Kennedy, 1963). This presupposes the existence of the chooser's scale of values, the consistency of his 'tastes'. In the case of the fighter plane, the 'tastes' are defined by its mission. The maker of language policies may have to spend some effort to arrive at a consistent scale of values. With the future environment uncertain he must also arrive at consistent 'beliefs' about its probabilities. The actual policy-making, outside of engineering, possibly medicine and some business and administrative, notably military, activities, is certainly far from the ideal concept of consistent policy-making. As Ramsey (1926) remarked, people do not always follows logical rules unless they make an effort ('stop to think'). Indeed, logic is not psychology! The data available to linguistic politicians in particular (or, to *épater* them in another way: linguistic engineers), for checking and rechecking their tastes and beliefs, are, I fear, quite rough. Yet the present attempt to sketch a relation between their task and the logic of policies in general may help to understand the debates and debaters of dictionaries and grammars.

IV. EVOLUTION

If, in a given environment *E*, a trait *X* has survived longer than has trait *Y*, we usually infer: it is probable that '*X* is better adapted to *E* than is *Y*'. The expression in quotation marks again involves probabilities since it usually means something like the following: 'Given *E* and given any time length *T* (in years, say), *X* is not less likely, and for some values of *T* is more likely, to survive beyond *T* years, than is *Y*'. The double use of probabilities is made necessary, at the first step, by the fewness of available observations ('sampling error'), and, at the second step, by the inherent uncertainty of the phenomenon, presumably due to individually insignificant but numerous, unidentifiable factors. Note also that environment itself must be usually defined, not as a constant, but, instead, as a variable obeying a fixed probability distribution. For example, 'a country is exposed to invasions' or 'to unpredictable weather' means that the probability of invasion, or the variance of temperature, is and remains high.

In brief, what has survived had probably a higher probability of survival than what has not. Like all mathematical statements this is a tautology. Like some of them, it is useful in guiding empirical research – in our case, the search for factors that have, in fact, endowed various traits with higher or lower survival probabilities in given environments.

We have called this section 'Evolution', but only in the sense of the survival of traits best fitted to an environment; not at all in the sense of any progress or improvement or rising complexity. For, as pointed out by Darwin (1859, Ch. IV),

> ... natural selection, or the survival of the fittest, does not necessarily include progressive development – it only takes advantage of such variations as arise and are beneficial

to each creature under its complex relations of life. And it may be asked what advantage, as far as we can see, would it be to an infusorian animalcule – to an intestinal worm – or even to an earthworm, to be highly organized. If it were no advantage, these forms... might remain for indefinite ages in their present lowly condition.

Whether, or in what environments, there is a change towards a richer or a poorer, a more or a less logical, a more or a less complex language – whatever these general categories may mean – cannot be deduced from the above tautology alone. But empirical research tells whether, or under what conditions, certain directions of change under those general categories have in fact prevailed. A step has then been made toward an explanation, and therefore a prediction, of the form: "such and such an environment will, will not, favor the survival of such and such general property of language." For example, if greater complexity of language means its ability to express a greater variety of situations, and the environment tends to fluctuate strongly and frequently, a complex (or shall we say *flexible*?) language will have a higher chance of survival.

The reader will have noticed that, in our terminology, evolution, in the sense of survival of the fittest characteristics, is the object of 'explanatory economics'. It compares the various alternative traits with respect to their optimality in the sense of maximum survival chance, not in the sense of any other scale of values. It is a question of fact, and depends on the properties of the environment, whether the surviving traits have been also optimal with respect to some other scale such as the degrees of complexity. One will also expect, in particular, that the language reflects the scale of values of the socially dominant group so that, for example, the multiplicity of forms of address would be about coeval with an aristocratic society, etc. I am sure anthropologists and sociologists of culture have their card files full of such observations. Thus W.S. Laughlin (1963, pp. 640–641) compares arctic tribes of different longevity:

...people who lived in the more harsh arctic environments died earlier... the greater overlap between generations associated with greater longevity provides more time for transfer of information. The experience of older people is stored in accessible form for a longer period in more 'storage cells'... artistic expression and the larger number of public ceremonies and myths are among the correlative benefits of greater longevity and greater population.

One would like to know how these differences are reflected in the language.

An exciting study in explanatory economics of language is furnished by 'Zipf's Law' (Zipf, 1949), a class of statistical distributions of words according to the frequencies of their occurrences. The economist recognizes in 'Zipf's Law' the 'Pareto Law', of doubtful empirical validity, of the distribution of incomes by size, and is tempted to transfer his doubts from the one to the other. To my knowledge, neither model has been submitted to appropriate statistical tests, which would compare its 'goodness of fit' with that of other proposed classes of skew distributions. But it is not the empirical validity that we are going to discuss here. G. K. Zipf has intuitively (but vaguely) related this empirical regularity to a 'principle of least effort'. Mandelbrot (1953) has shown that the observed regularity does indeed follow from the assumption of minimum average 'cost' of communication, given the (appropriately defined) rate of information flow, and assuming that a word's 'cost' increases when a letter is added. Mandelbrot's model, described also in Colin Cherry's (1957) well-known book, is wider than Zipf's: it allows (as we shall presently see) one characteristic of the word-distribution to vary from language to language.

Considerations of 'effort' or 'cost' give Mandelbrot's analysis an economic flavor. But this is not all. To understand its evolutionary meaning we note, first, that replacing 'automobile' by 'car' does indeed save one's breath! This is not trivial. If very many such replacements occur, correspondingly more energy or time is left for other uses that are important for the maintenance of the individual's life or of the social fabric in his generation and beyond. Moreover, communication delays make decisions obsolete in the face of quickly changing situations; the brevity of the great leaders' commands has had not only aesthetic value. A language does not survive if its carrier, the society, disintegrates.

Second, the information rate measures, roughly speaking, the variety of potential messages, the degree of precision, of conceptual discrimination. Certain properties of the evironment – technological, forensic, cultic, – may be such that the benefit of greater precision achieved by frequent use of some long words outweighs the disadvantages of effort and delay. These benefits and disadvantages are ultimately measured, not in units of time or energy or in information bits (we must not subtract eggs from apples) but as additions to, and subtractions from, the probability of survival of a given language structure. For remember that Mandelbrot minimizes average 'cost', *keeping the information rate fixed.* The information rate – the degree of variety, precision, discrimination – appears therefore as a parameter of Zipf's distribution (in fact, a slope of a certain line on his diagram). This parameter can itself vary, adapting to the environment. That is, the probability of survival in a given environment is maximized simultaneously (1) over the set of classes of word-distributions (Mandelbrot's is one such class), and (2) over the set of possible information rates (each rate defining one member of Mandelbrot's class).

Viewed in this way, the Zipf-Mandelbrot model, whether empirically valid or not, illustrates our methodological point: to explain why a language is what it is one must show why its properties are, on the balance, conductive to its survival.

NOTES

* A contribution to *Orbis Scriptus: Dmitry Tschiževskij zum 70. Geburtstag* (W. Weintraub *et al.* (eds.), Eidos Verlag, Munchen), revised for this journal with the permission of the volume's publisher. It is a part of a research project on Individual and Organized Decision Making, carried out at the Western Management Science Institute, University of California at Los Angeles, and supported in part by the Office of Naval Research (Contract No. 233-75) and the Ford Foundation. The author was greatly stimulated by discussions at the Conference on Speech, Language, and Communication sponsored in November, 1963 by the Brain Research Institute, U.C.L.A., and the U.S. Air Force Office of Scientific Research. He owes much to the contributions of P. Garvin, H. Hoijer, S. M. Lamb, and F. A. Lounsbury.

1 Freely translated, "One hears mere words but believes each has a meaning." This goes also for sentences. "*Und so erscheint uns die Evidenz dieses Satzes in ihrer ganzen Notwendigkeit*": a young German philosopher had this in the tentative outline of his proposed Oxford thesis, some 30 years ago. In an effort to translate it into English, the sentence had to be successively pruned to its shorter equivalents, and ultimately to nothing. *Added in 1973.* He was the late Th. Adorno.

BIBLIOGRAPHY

Bernoulli, D., *Specimen Theoriae Novae de Mensura Sortis.* 1738. English translation by Louise Sommer, *Econometrica*, **22** (1954) 23–36. See especially, on page 33, a letter of Gabriel Cramer written in 1724.

Cherry, C., *On Human Communication*, Wiley, New York, 1957.

Darwin, C. (1), *The Origin of Species*, 1859. (2) 'An Historical Sketch of the Progress of Opinion on the Origin of Species', *The Origin of Species* (6th ed.), Preface. 1872. Both reprinted as a Mentor Book, 1958.

Harsanyi, J. C., 'Measurement of Social Power, Opportunity Costs, and the Theory of Two-Person Bargaining Games', *Behav. Sci.* **7** (1962) 67–80. (a)

Harsanyi, J. C., 'Measurement of Social Power in *n*-Person Reciprocal Power Situations', *Behav. Sci.* **7** (1962) 81–91. (b)

Kennedy, J. F., 'Speech at the United Nations', August, 1963.

Kluckhohn, C. and Leighton, Dorothea, *The Navaho*, Harvard Univ. Press, Cambridge, 1946.

Laughlin, W. S., 'Eskimos and Aleuts: Their Origins and Evolution', *Science* **142** (1963) 633–645.

Lotka, A. J., *Elements of Physical Biology*, 1924. Reprinted as *Elements of Mathematical Biology*, Dover Publications, New York, 1956.

Mandelbrot, B., An Information Theory of the Structure of Language Based upon... Statistical Matching of Messages and Coding, in W. Jackson (ed.), *Proceedings of Symposium on Applications of Communication Theory*, Butterworth Scientific Publications, London, 1953.

Marschak, J., 'Towards an Economic Theory of Information and Organization', 1954, *Selected Essays*, 20.

Marschak, J., 'Efficient and Viable Organizational Forms', 1959, *Selected Essays*, 22.

Marschak, J., 'Problems in Information Economics', 1964, *Selected Essays*, 25.

Polanyi, M., 'On the Modern Mind', *Encounter* **24** (1965), 5, 12–20.

Ramsey, F. P., *Truth and Probability*, 1926. Reprinted in H. E. Kyburg and H. Smokler (eds.), *Studies in Subjective probability*, Wiley, New York, 1964.

Savage, L. J., *The Foundations of Statistics*, Wiley, New York, 1954. Revised: Dover, 1972.

Sledd, J. and Ebbit, Wilma, *Dictionaries and that Dictionary*, Scott, Foresman, Chicago, 1962.

Zipf, G. K., *Human Behavior and the Principle of Least Effort*, Addison-Wesley, Cambridge, Mass. 1949.

28

ECONOMIC PLANNING AND THE COST OF THINKING*

(1966)

We shall call economic planning the process of arriving at an optimal decision. A decision, or action, is called optimal if, in the decision-maker's well-considered view, and allowing for the cost of making the decision, its results will be, on the average, not worse than those of any other available action. The set of available actions is called his 'resources'. Economic planning is, in this sense, concerned with the 'best use of resources'.

To be sure, the word 'economic' has also another, narrower meaning. Economists focus most of their attention on decisions about bundles of quantifiable and infinitely divisible 'commodities'. This excludes from consideration decisions such as 'firing Mr. X, an executive'. Presumably evaluation of such decisions is passed on to sociologists or political analysts. This specialization is extremely useful for certain purposes but it bars the access to some fruitful general principles. In what follows we shall use both the wide and the narrow interpretation of 'economic'.

On the other hand, the word 'planning' suggests broadening the concept of decision into that of 'multi-stage decision', also called 'strategy' ('dynamic program'): a time sequence of rules specifying how the action to be taken at each future instant should depend on the information then available. In the special case of quantifiable commodity bundles the problem is met by considering, for example, the commodity 'sugar to be received on May 1 if a certain event happens' as different from sugar at another date or contingency.

The decision-maker, or actor, introduced in our definition of economic planning is, of course, an idealized one. His choosing between decisions by comparing the average goodness of their respective results presupposes that he consistently attaches probabilities to the possible external events that will determine the result of each action. These probabilities are the actor's own 'beliefs' and become 'objective' only when other reasonable people agree on the similarity (repetitiveness) of certain events such as statistical samples. Furthermore, the choosing of decisions according to the average goodness of their results presupposes a consistent scale of 'utilities' attached to those results and describing the actor's 'tastes'.

Presuppositions of this sort are conceptual idealizations[1] such as have been inevitable ever since Socrates discussed wisdom and pleasure. Will this approach prove useful? Only if the attentive reader ends by finding that it has helped him to articulate some important problems of the real world with greater clarity than he would without such help.

The idealized decision-maker may be a private person, a business corporation, a local or national public agency, or the national government itself. I shall ask questions on the *organizational* economics of planning. Roughly, this means asking: how may we best use given resources in obtaining and processing information in order to determine and carry out optimal strategies?

To state this question in the context of national multi-stage planning of commodity bundles, remember the following economic theorem, vaguely anticipated by Adam Smith and rigorously stated and proved by Arrow and Debreu for the general case of multi-stage decisions:[2] If no producer or consumer can influence commodity prices, and if each does what he thinks is best for himself, and if producers' returns and consumers' tastes obey so-called 'convexity' conditions (roughly, the 'laws' of non-increasing physical marginal returns for producers, and of non-increasing marginal utilities for consumers) then there exists a set of prices at which (1) demand equals supply for each commodity, and (2) a 'Pareto-optimum' is reached, that is, with existing resources, nobody can be made better off without hurting someone else.

Now compare this with the result that can be achieved by a national government, informed of the physical conditions of each production establishment and of the tastes of each consumer. In principle, such information can indeed be processed into a plan that will achieve a Pareto-optimum, regardless of whether laws of non-increasing returns and utilities apply. In particular, it would make full use of large-scale economies ('increasing marginal returns') of a plant, with no fear of monopolies. It would also fully use large-scale economies of every community of plants and households – a city, for example; and it would minimize the mutual nuisance that individual producers and consumers create for each other when left to themselves. Or, if the government wishes, it will achieve and enforce a plan optimal from its own point of view, free of delusions and unpatriotic or unhygienic sins of individual citizens.

But this comparison is not complete. It disregards the *organizational* cost and efficiency (concepts still to be defined). In the Adam Smith case, the Pareto-optimal set of prices is achieved through the process of raising (lowering) a price if demand is larger (smaller) than supply. This haggling in markets – both 'spot' and 'futures' – is done by specialized brokers in Wall, LaSalle and Montgomery Streets, and by other specialists, the salesman and buyers in the individual firms. All of them collect, process, and transmit information.[3] Soviet-type planning has also been done by specialists, but with information of different – in fact, more detailed – nature. Instead of price bids and counterbids data are transmitted to the central brain, stating the production possibilities of each plant as well as the potential demands. At least in principle, the central brain processes these data into a national economic plan and transmits it to the plants which, presumably, have sufficient incentives to carry it out.

If both these systems of information processing were equal in cost and efficiency there would be little to choose between them from the point of view of Pareto-optimality; and something could be said for the centralized system from the point of view of national goals, especially if these did not include individual liberty and initiative as goods in themselves.

The importance of organizational economics is thus clear, I hope. In general, the problem involves a collection of people – between two persons and 500 million, say – and is a multi-stage one. Yet it is useful to present the simplest possible case as a start. We shall show latter how to generalize it.

In a single-person, single-stage case, the economic organization problem degenerates into the problem of choosing an optimal information system. An information system is a set of potential 'messages' which the decision maker will use by responding to each message with some action. An action is appropriate (or optimal) with respect to a message if, given the message, the actions' result is, on the average, not worse than that of any other available action. For example: my suceess or failure in keeping an appointment at the other end of the continent, but also my survival itself, depends on (1) my decision to fly or not to fly and (2) on tomorrow's weather. My wall barometer tells me today's air pressure. Whether the appropriate response to the message 'pressure low' is to fly or not to fly depends on (1) the utilities attached to 'keeping appointment', 'failing appointment but surviving', and 'crash'; and (2) the probability of good flying conditions tomorrow, given that today's air pressure is low. We are thus interested in the strength of the statistical relation between the 'payoff relevant' event (viz., tomorrow's weather) and the message belonging to the 'information system' used. In our example, the latter is associated with the barometer. The utility achieved, on the average of all messages of this system, if each is responded to by an appropriate action, may be called the 'gross value' of an information system. Very likely the evening newspaper with its weather forecasts has a greater gross information value than my barometer. The adjective 'gross' is needed to suggest that some costs must be subtracted before deciding whether or not to buy the newpaper. We shall return to this.

So far we have, in effect, characterized an information system by the joint probabilities of messages and events. We shall call one system *more informative* than another, with respect to a given set of alternative events, if the former system has a larger gross value to any maker of decisions the results of which depend on those events. To this extent, economic comparison can be made for some, though not all, pairs of information systems without specifying the tastes and resources of a particular user.

An important case when such comparison can be made occurs when all users believe that one system of messages, to be called 'primary', is related to another, 'secondary' system, by 'garbling', in the following sense: given a primary message (e.g., a patrol's report to the commander), the probabilities of all secondary messages (the commander's possible reports to his chief) are determined uniquely, regardless of the actual event (which will determine the result of the chief's decision). The following is easy to prove, and seems intuitively plausible. The gross value of the secondary system is equal to the average utility that the primary system would yield if each of the primary messages were responded to, not by an action appropriate to it (and hence optimal), but by an action appropriate to some message of the secondary system, received at random with a probability that depends on the primary message. It follows that the secondary system never has a higher gross value, and (since this is true for any user) is never more informative than the primary system.

A special, limiting case of garbling is that of coarsening, condensing information: certain details are suppressed, i.e., they are left unspecified. Thus to each primary ('fine') message corresponds a unique secondary ('coarse') one: a many-to-one correspondence also called 'information loss without noise', As in the case of garbling, each primary message will uniquely determine the probabilities of all secondary messages. But now, more specifically, one of these probabilities is equal to 1, the rest to zero. As one would expect, coarsening, suppression of details, can never increase gross information value.

To delay information is sometimes (but by no means always) tantamount to coarsening or garbling it. Suppose the result of my action on May 1 depends on the sequence of events up to May 1, but I have to act knowing only their curtailed sequence – up to, say, April 1. The events of April constitute then a 'suppressed detail' and I suffer the damage due to coarsened information; and a delay of two months would be still worse. Or suppose the result of my action depends only on what will happen in May, but the probabilities of the events of any month are uniquely determined by what has happened in the preceding month, regardless of all earlier events; the events are then said to constitute a Markov chain. Complete information about March events can then be regarded as being garbled (in the sense of our definition) from complete information about April events; so that again delay decreases (or at any rate cannot increase) gross information value. Moreover, longer delays are worse than short ones.

However, these cases are far from general. A longer delay may be preferable if events constitute an (almost) periodic process (rather than a Markov chain). Before going out on a Sunday, I prefer to know various restaurants' preceding Sunday menus, rather than those of last Friday. Also, when events change slowly and the available information about old events is much more reliable (e.g., based on a larger sample) than the available information about recent events, I may prefer delayed information.[4]

The coarsening, the garbling, and sometimes the delaying of information cannot increase and may decrease gross information value. But it is the net, not the gross, value that must decide the choice between information systems. In a simple case this means subtracting the cost (both fixed and variable) of obtaining 'messages', whether through direct observations of the world or by a hook-up to some receptor. We must also estimate and subtract the cost of decision making itself: the efforts of finding the action appropriate to a given message received. Such subtraction presupposes that utility can be represented as a difference between 'revenues' and 'costs', as in the special case of the 'risk-indifferent' investor –

that is, one who maximizes average money gain. The general, less tractable case involves direct estimation of the average utility, a function of all the advantageous and disadvantageous characteristics of an information system. Alternatively, we may content ourselves with measuring those characteristics in physical units ('fixed cost in dollars', 'speed of transmission', a set of measures of garbling) in order to select, from all available information systems, the list of 'efficient' ones, in the following sense (reminiscent of 'Pareto optimum'): no system is available that is in all respects better than some of the listed systems.

We can extend the problem to an organization consisting of several members, assuming at first that they have identical tastes and beliefs (a 'team'). An organizational system is defined by the sets of messages that can be received by the different members, and by the members' rules of action. It states 'who should do what in response to what messages'. The concept of doing (action) is here extended to include the sending of messages to one's fellow members, and the (partial) solving of the fellow-members' problem of finding optimal action. Moreover the actions of an 'organizer' (or 'sub-organizer') will consist in improving the organization system itself.

The disadvantages of coarsening, garbling and (possibly) delaying information would then apply directly, in a manner that, superficially, seems paradoxical. Suppose a 'decentralized' organization is defined, and contrasted with a 'centralized' one, by the fact that in the former each member decides on the basis of his own information, while in the latter every decision is based on the combined information of all. If so, centralization is characterized by a 'finer' information system, and consequently can have greater, never smaller, gross value. Considerations of gross value would then suggest that all members except one should be mere 'reporters'. Such considerations would also suggest that every intermediary link in an organization is damaging or at least superfluous: for it can only coarsen or garble (and possibly delay) information. Such conclusions, however, while suggestive, cannot be final. We have still to take account of the 'costs'. These may possibly be infinite, in the sense that some arrangements are not feasible. For example, brains able to retain certain detailed information, or to transmit it, or to process it into an approximately optimal decision within preassigned limits of error and delay, may not exist. Or they may be very rare or expensive. It is the organizer's job to consider the increments of net, not of gross, organizational value to be effected by the possible changes he might suggest. Taken in its full complexity, no precise solution can be found for an organizer's problem sufficiently promptly so that the solution may be useful; not even if the data of the problem (resources, probabilities, costs) were all assembled. At best, approximate solutions subject to quick changes can be looked for.

Now we may introduce the diversity of the members' tastes and beliefs, but retain the organizer's problem as one of maximizing average utility according to *his* tastes and beliefs. He will use his messages to communicate conditions, commonly called 'incentives', such that, when each member maximizes his average utility subject to these conditions, the average utility as conceived by the organizer is maximized. Overtime premiums and salesmen's bonuses are examples of this. Their closer determination is the outcome of bargaining: a problem in game theory that, I believe, is not fully solved, or even formulated satisfactorily.

Finally, we can ask for the conditions under which a given system of messages and incentives, optimal from the organizer's point of view, is also Pareto-optimal. A dictator might be able to ascertain the tastes and beliefs of his subjects and devise an allocation of tasks (including the tasks of communicating and making decisions) and a system of incentives that would be Pareto-optimal – if the cost of ascertaining tastes and beliefs were nil.

Almost certainly, this cost is formidable. And, as we have hinted, sacrifice of liberty may, too, be counted as an organizational cost, a lowering of utility to almost all citizens, probably in many cultures and certainly in ours. But this does not remove the need to 'join the debate'[5] as to how to reap the advantages of liberty and of informational economy (lower 'cost of thinking') in the market society, free of monopolies, while also utilizing large-scale economies of plants, households, and communities, prevented from harming one another. The debate is far from concluded.

NOTES

* Author's note. This is an attempt to give a non-mathematical version of a paper presented at the Interdisciplinary Symposium on the Mathematical Bases of Economic Planning, American Association for the Advancement of Science, Berkeley, California, December 1965. (Prepared at the Western Management Science Institute under a con-

tract with the Office of Naval Research.) Thanks are due to Professor J. Hirshleifer for many comments.

[1] On idealization in the social sciences see Section 7 of Hans Neisser's *On the Sociology of Knowledge* (Heineman, New York, 1965). For the particular idealization of the decision-maker used here, in contexts both prescriptive and descriptive, see the present author's forthcoming 'Decision-Making: Economic Aspects' *Selected Essays*, 16.

[2] K. J. Arrow, 'The Role of Securities in the Optimal Allocation of Risk-Bearing,' *Review of Economic Studies* **31** (1964), 91–96; original publication in French, 1953. G. Debreu, *Theory of Value* Wiley, (New York, 1959).

[3] 'No doubt the stimulus-response relations as described in the Law of Supply and Demand represent an effective communication system,' says Adolph Lowe (*On Economic Knowledge*, Harper & Row, New York, 1965, p. 35) and proceeds to study those limitations on this system's effectiveness that are due to the uncertainty about the future.

[4] For more precise statements see 'Economics of Information Systems', *Selected Essays*, 31.

[5] George J. Stigler, 'The Enjoined Debate', *Chicago Today* **3** (1966) (published by the University of Chicago) 2–9. F. M. Bator, 'The Anatomy of Market Failure', *Quarterly Journal of Economics* **72** (1958), 351–379. Thomas A. Marschak, 'Economic Theory of Organization', *Handbook of Organizations* (ed. by James G. March), Rand McNally, 1965, pp. 423–450.

29

ECONOMIC COMPARABILITY OF INFORMATION SYSTEMS*

(1968)

Co-author: KOICHI MIYASAWA

1. INTRODUCTION

An information system is a set of potential messages to be received by the decision maker. It is characterized by the statistical relation of the messages to the payoff-relevant events, and also by the message cost.[1] Neglecting this cost, the (gross) value of an information system for a given user is the (gross) payoff that he would obtain, on the average, if he would respond to each message by the most appropriate decision. Thus (gross) information value depends not only on the statistical relation between messages and events but also on the payoff function. The latter expresses the user's 'tastes' and 'technology'. The ordering of statistically defined information systems by their values is therefore at most a partial one. This contrasts with the complete ordering of information systems (channels) by their equivocation (a statistical parameter used in the classical information theory that disregards variation of payoff functions from user to user).

Indeed, if 'noise' is defined to increase with equivocation[2] a 'noisy' information system may be more valuable to a given user than a noiseless one: the betting sports fan may have reason to prefer the sports page of a newspaper to its society page even though both pages have the same number of English words and the sports page has misprints, the society page none.

The partial ordering of information systems by their (gross) values will be studied. In particular, conditions, sufficient or necessary, will be stated under which two systems are comparable, so that one of them is 'more informative' than the other in the following sense: one of them can never have smaller value than the other for any payoff function defined on a given set of events. The ordering of information systems according to their informativeness has applications in the economics of information and organization; and also, as shown by D. Blackwell, in statistics (where messages and events correspond, respectively, to observations and hypotheses).[3]

Sections 1–5 will define concepts useful for the statement of our problem of finding conditions for the comparability of information systems. The remaining sections seek to solve this problem and to prove inclusion relations between the various conditions studied.

2. Events and decisions

For a given actor (decision-maker), we define a set X of *states* x of the environment (not controlled by the actor[4]), a set C of *Consequence* c. Each function from X to C is called an act by Savage [16]. However, not all acts thus defined are feasible. Define the set A consisting of all feasible acts, a. These we shall call actions.[5] The set A can be thought of as the resources or technology available to the particular actor. Each action a maps X into C

$$a(x) = c.$$

This is, in general, a many-to-one mapping, for each state x may describe the environment in unlimited detail, and some of this detail may be irrelevant in the following sense. Two distinct states, x and x' may be such that $a(x)=a(x')$ for every a in A. We shall then say that x and x' are equivalent with respect to A. We can partition X into equivalence sets of the form

$$\text{(2.1.A)} \quad z_x^A \equiv \{x' \in X : a(x') = a(x), \quad \text{all} \quad a \in A\}.$$

Denote this partition by Z^A. Each equivalence set z^A in Z^A may be called an event, relevant with respect to technology A; or, briefly, an A-relevant event.

EXAMPLE. Suppose X is an n-tuple of variables, some of them continuous, with n arbitrarily large; the consequences of any action of yours are not affected by many of these variables (political situation in Uganda) or by minor variations of the remaining ones (seconds of daily sunshine).

The set of states of the environment can be 'coarsened' still further if we pay attention, not only to the actor's technology but also to his tastes. It would suffice for this purpose, to replace in (2.1.A) the equality sign between $a(x')$ and $a(x)$ by some symbol representing the actor's indifference between these two consequences. There is no need to use numerical utilities. But since the numerical utility concept will be needed soon anyway, denote by u the actor's utility function, a function from C to the set of the reals, and write

$$(2.2) \qquad \omega(x, a) \equiv u(a(x)) \equiv u(c);$$

the function ω from $X \times A$ to the reals is called the *payoff function.* Now partition X into equivalence sets of the form

$$(2.1.\omega) \quad z_x^\omega \equiv \{x' \in X : \omega(x', a) = \omega(x, a), \quad \text{all} \quad a \in A\}.$$

This partition, denoted by Z^ω, is clearly coarser than Z^A (i.e., Z^A is a sub-partition of Z^ω). We shall call z^ω, a typical equivalence set in Z^ω, an *event, relevant with respect to the payoff function* ω; or briefly, an ω-relevant event.

EXAMPLE. Suppose each consequence of any of your actions is a triple (c_1, c_2, c_3) where c_1 and c_2 are your profits of this and of the next year, measured in cents; and c_3 is the amount of air pollution created by your plant. Suppose you are indifferent between $c \equiv (c_1, c_2, c_3)$ and $c' \equiv \equiv (c_1', c_2', c_3')$ because you are not concerned with differences less than \$1, or because you are willing to trade off a part of this year's profit for a profit increase in the next year; and because air pollution results only in other people's discomfort. Then $u(c) = u(c')$; and if, for all actions a in A, $a(x) = = c$ and $a(x') = c'$, then the states x and x' belong to the same payoff-relevant event z^ω.

Considerations of 'taste' induce also a coarsening of the set of actions. It may happen that, for two distinct actions a and a', and for all x in X,

$$u(a(x)) = u(a'(x)); \quad \text{that is,} \quad \omega(x, a) = \omega(x, a').$$

Let us, then, define a partition D^ω of A into equivalence sets of the form

$$(2.3) \qquad d_a^\omega \equiv \{a' \in A : \omega(x, a') = \omega(x, a), \quad \text{all} \quad x \in X\}.$$

For convenience we shall call D^ω the set of *ω-relevant decisions*; its typical element d^ω will sometimes be denoted briefly as d.

EXAMPLE. Let each consequence be a triple (c_1, c_2, c_3) defined in the previous example; suppose you are indifferent to air pollution and that two methods of production, a and a', always yield (i.e., for every x) the same profits but different amounts of air pollution. Then a and a' belong to the same ω-relevant decision d^ω.

Observing that ω is constant on $z^\omega \times d^\omega$, we may write without ambiguity $\omega(z^\omega, d^\omega)$ where ω is defined over the domain $Z^\omega \times D^\omega$ instead of $X \times A$.

In what follows we shall be interested in varying the payoff function ω subject to a constraint depending on an arbitrarily fixed partition Z of X into *events* z. Given a payoff function ω, Z is called *ω-adequate* if it is a sub-partition of *ω-relevant* partition Z^ω, see Marschak-Radner [12, (Chapter 2)]; for example, Z^A (relevant with respect to technology but not necessary with respect to tastes) is ω-adequate. Then every $z \in Z$ is a subset of exactly one $z^\omega \in Z^\omega$ and we can write, without danger of ambiguity, $\omega(z, d^\omega)$, where the function ω is defined over the domain $Z \times D^\omega$. Now let Ω_z be the set of all payoff functions ω for which Z is ω-adequate. Given a fixed set Z of events we shall vary the payoff function ω over the set Ω_z. In the terminology of Marschak [11] an adequate partition is 'sufficiently fine'.

It has been shown – see Savage [16] – that certain plausible, quasi-logical postulates imply for a consistent decision-maker: (a) the existence of a numerical function u on the set C of consequences; hence a numerical function ω on $Z \times D^\omega$; and (b) the existence of a probability measure $\mathscr{P}$ on X; hence of a probability function $p(z)$ on Z, with the following property: given two decisions d and d' in D^ω, a consistent actor will not prefer d' to d if (assuming Z finite for simplicity)

$$(2.4) \qquad \sum_{z \in Z} \omega(z, d)\, p(z) \geqq \sum_{z \in Z} \omega(z, d')\, p(z).$$

The two compared averages are called the (expected) utilities of the decisions d and d', respectively. The proposition just stated is called the expected utility theorem. Roughly, it says that an actor conforming with certain consistency postulates (and with the rules of ordinary logic) maximizes the expected utility of decision.

We stated above that the set $A = \{a\}$ of actions (i.e., feasible acts) represents the actor's technology, and that the utility function u on the set C represents his tastes; hence the payoff function $\omega(x, a) \equiv u(a(x))$ reflects both. We can now add his beliefs, represented by the probability measure $\mathscr{P}$ on X. In what follows we shall consider $\mathscr{P}$ and Z fixed; and we shall permit ω to vary over the set Ω_Z for which Z is ω-adequate. This will enable us to discuss the 'informativeness' of information systems for an arbitrary set of their users: see Example in Section 5. [*Added in 1973*: in a later paper, Marschak [17], the probability measure $\mathscr{P}$ on X is permitted to vary.]

3. Information systems

An *information system* Y is a set consisting of (potential) *messages* y. We shall regard Y as another partition of the set X of states x. Unlike partition Z of X into payoff-adequate events z, the partition Y of X into messages y is not associated with the feasibility of actions and the indifference among their results. Instead, Y is associated with some object – an instrument – that produces messages. See Figures 1a–c. Example: The state x may be such that (a) my barometer shows low pressure: this is message y and that (b) the visibility at the airport is low, thus affecting the success of a decision to fly: this is event z.

In the language of information theory, a set Z of events would be called 'source' and a set Y of messages, a 'channel'. In the language of statistical inference, Z represents a set of alternative hypotheses, and Y represents the set of outcomes of an experiment and is itself called an experiment.

If a probability measure $\mathscr{P}$ is defined on X, the joint probability function on $Z \times Y$ is determined. In fact, given a set $(Y, Y', Y'', \ldots)$ of *available information systems*, the multivariate distribution on $Z \times Y \times Y' \times Y'' \times \cdots$ is defined. We shall write, using the same symbol $p(\ )$ for probability functions over different domains, yet without risk of ambiguity:

probability of event,

$$\Pr(x \in z) \equiv p(z);$$

probability of message,

$$\Pr(x \in y) \equiv p(y),$$

$(p(z)$ and $p(y)$ are all positive since z and y are non-empty);

joint probability of event and message,

$$\Pr(x \in z \cap y) \equiv p(z, y);$$

posterior probability of event, given the message,

$$p(z, y)/p(y) \equiv p(z \mid y);$$

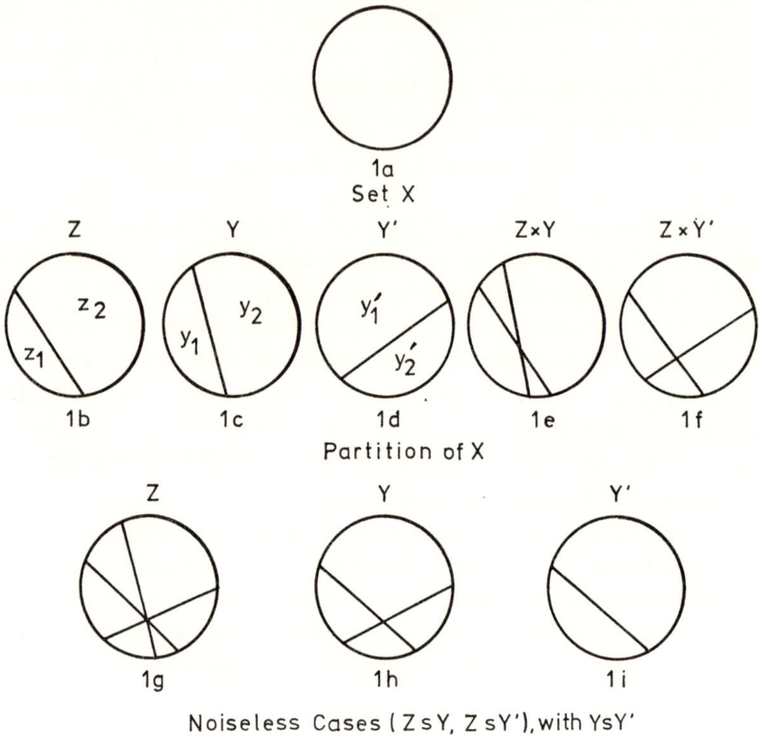

Fig. 1. Set X and its partitions.

likelihood of message, given the event,

$$p(z, y)/p(z) \equiv p(y|z).$$

When comparing two information systems Y and Y' we shall also use expressions like the following:

probability of joint occurrence of massage $y \in Y$ and $y' \in Y'$,

$$\Pr(x \in y \cap y') = p(y, y');$$

probability of joint occurrence of event z and messages y, y',

$$\Pr(x \in z \cap y \cap y') = p(z, y, y');$$

probability of y', given y,

$$p(y, y')/p(y) \equiv p(y'|y);$$

posterior probability of event z, given messages y, y',

$$p(z, y, y')/p(y, y') \equiv p(z \mid y, y');$$

and so on.

For simplicity of reasoning, we have assumed the set Z of events and the sets $Y, Y', \ldots$, of messages *finite*. (No such assumption will be made about X, the set of states, except in Theorem 11.4.) Specifically,

$$Z \equiv (z_1, \ldots, z_m); \qquad Y \equiv (y_1, \ldots, y_n); \qquad Y' \equiv (y'_1, \ldots, y'_{n'});$$
$$m, n, n', \ldots \geqq 2.$$

The generic elements z of Z, y of Y, y' of $Y', \ldots$, can be regarded as random variables taking, respectively, the values

$$z_i (i = 1, \ldots, m); \qquad y_j (j = 1, \ldots, n); \qquad y'_k (k = 1, \ldots, n'); \ldots.$$

In most of our discussion Z will be fixed, and the effects of varying Y (i.e., of replacing it by Y', say) will be studied – see Figures 1b–f – using for the three marginal probabilities the following vectors (the various alternative notations will be used according to convenience):

$$\begin{aligned}
&\text{the } (m \times 1)\text{-vector } [p(z)] \equiv [p(z_i)] \equiv [r_z] \equiv [r_i] \equiv r \\
&\text{the } (n \times 1)\text{-vector } [p(y] \equiv [p(y_j)] \equiv [q_j] \equiv q^Y \equiv q \\
&\text{the } (n' \times 1)\text{-vector } [p(y')] \equiv [p(y'_k] \equiv [q'_k] \equiv q^{Y'} \equiv q'.
\end{aligned}$$

For the joint probabilities of events and messages; the posterior probabilities of events (given the message in Y); and the likelihoods of those messages (given the events in Z), we use the $(m \times n)$-matrices

$$\begin{aligned}
&[p(z, y)] \equiv [p(z_i, y_j)] \equiv [p_{zy}] \equiv [p_{ij}] \equiv P^Y \equiv P \\
&[p(z \mid y)] \equiv [p(z_i \mid y_i)] \equiv [\pi_{zy}] \equiv [\pi_{ij}] \equiv \Pi^Y \equiv \Pi \\
&[p(y \mid z)] \equiv [p(y_j \mid z_i)] \equiv [\lambda_{zy}] \equiv [\lambda_{ij}] \equiv \Lambda^Y \equiv \Lambda
\end{aligned}$$

and the corresponding $(m \times n')$-matrices for Y'

$$P^{Y'} \equiv P'; \qquad \Pi^{Y'} \equiv \Pi'; \qquad \Lambda^{Y'} \equiv \Lambda'.$$

By definition (writing henceforth $\sum_y, \sum_z$ for summation over sets Y, Z)

$$\text{(3.1.1)} \quad \sum_z p_{zy} = q_y > 0, \qquad \sum_y p_{zy} = r_z > 0, \qquad \pi_{zy} \geqq 0, \qquad \lambda_{zy} \geqq 0$$

(3.1.2) $$p_{zy} = \lambda_{zy} r_z = \pi_{zy} q_y \geqq 0$$

(3.1.3) $$1 = \sum_y q_y = \sum_z r_z = \sum_y \lambda_{zy} = \sum_z \pi_{zy} = \sum_y \sum_z p_{zy} .$$

Moreover, with Z fixed, r is fixed and we have for any Y, Y'

(3.2) $$\Pi q = r = \Pi' q' .$$

We shall also use the $(n \times n')$-matrix

(3.3) $$[p(y' \mid y)] \equiv [p(y'_k \mid y_j)] \equiv [\gamma_{yy'}] \equiv [\gamma_{jk}] \equiv \Gamma .$$

Clearly,

(3.4) $$\gamma_{yy'} \geqq 0 ; \qquad \sum_{y'} \gamma_{yy'} = 1 ;$$

(3.5) $$q' = \Gamma_{(\tau)} q ,$$

where $\Gamma_{(\tau)}$ is the transpose of Γ. Similarly, we define the $(n' \times n)$-matrix

(3.3′) $$[p(y \mid y')] \equiv [p(y_j \mid y'_k)] \equiv [\gamma'_{yy'}] \equiv [\gamma'_{jk}] \equiv \Gamma' ,$$

(3.4′) $$\gamma'_{yy'} \geqq 0 ; \qquad \sum_y \gamma'_{y'y} = 1 ,$$

(3.5′) $$q = \underset{(\tau)}{\Gamma'} q' .$$

Let T and T' be two partitions of X. T is said to be a *subpartition* of (or *finer than*) T' (or, equivalently, T' is coarser than T),

(3.6) $$T \, s \, T'$$

if each t in T is contained in one of the t' in T'; or equivalently, there is a many-to-one correspondence $T \to T'$. Condition (3.6) implies – and, in case of X finite, is equivalent to – the following: for any $t \in T$, $t' \in T'$,

(3.7) $$p(t' \mid t) = \begin{cases} 1 & \text{if} \quad t \subset t' \\ 0 & \text{otherwise} . \end{cases}$$

In particular, if the set Z of events is finer than the information system Y, (see Figures 1g, 1h)

(3.8) $$Z \, s \, Y ,$$

we shall say that Y is *noiseless* (with respect to Z). In this case there is a *many-to-one correspondence* $Z \to Y$; and it will follow that

$$p(y \mid z) \equiv \lambda_{zy} = \begin{cases} 1 & \text{if} \quad z \subset y \\ 0 & \text{otherwise}. \end{cases} \tag{3.9}$$

Thus each row of Λ^Y consists of one 1 and $n-1$ zeros if Y is noiseless.[6]

In Section 11, we shall consider the case when the two compared information systems, Y and Y' are both *noiseless* (see Figures 1g, 1h, 1i):

CONDITION (N): $Z s Y$, $Z s Y'$.

If two information systems Y and Y' (noiseless or not) are such that Y is finer than Y', and thus Y' *coarser* than Y we write

CONDITION (C): $Y s Y'$.

In this case we can also say that Y' is obtained from Y by *collapsing*, or *condensing*, several messages in Y into a single message in Y'. Under condition (C) there is a many-to-one correspondence $Y \to Y'$, and (C) will imply, as in (3.7) that

$$p(y' \mid y) \equiv \gamma_{yy'} = \begin{cases} 1 & \text{if} \quad y \subset y' \\ 0 & \text{otherwise}. \end{cases} \tag{3.10}$$

4. Information values: gross and net

The actor associates each message in Y with some decision in D^ω. This mapping will be called a *decision rule*, δ^ω, an element of a set Δ^ω. Without danger of ambiguity we shall often omit the superscript ω. Thus

$$\begin{aligned} d &= \delta(y), \\ \omega(z, d) &= \omega(z, \delta(y)); \qquad z \in Z, \quad y \in Y, \quad d \in D, \quad \delta \in \Delta. \end{aligned} \tag{4.1}$$

Thus, given the payoff function ω, the utility of the result depends on the event z, the message y and the decision rule δ.

The utility amount $\omega(z, \delta(y))$ may be interpreted by expressing the economic effect (i.e., the effect upon the utility to the decision-maker), not only of decision $\delta(y)$, given event z, but also of the decision rule δ itself. For example, a simple (e.g., linear) decision rule is less costly to apply than a complicated one. Moreover, a decision rule from Y to D, where D consists of feasible decisions (actions), may itself be non-feasible – for example, if it is so complicated as to exceed the decision-making capabilities of available men or machines. Strictly speaking, we should define a feasible subset Δ_φ of Δ, for use in any further economic discussion of information systems. For the sake of simplicity we shall neglect in most of the following both the cost and the possible non-feasibility of decision rules and assume $\Delta_\varphi = \Delta$.

An optimal decision rule δ^* in Δ maximizes the utility averaged over all messages y in Y. The maximum expected utility thus achieved will be denoted by $U(P^Y; \omega)$ for it will depend on the joint probability P^Y of y and z (with Z fixed) and on the payoff function ω:

$$(4.2) \qquad U(P^Y; \omega) \equiv \sum_y \sum_z \omega(z, \delta^*(y))\, p_{zy} \geqq \sum_y \sum_z \omega(z, \delta(y))\, p_{zy}$$

for all δ in Δ. Then, since $p_{zy} = q_y \pi_{zy}$, we have

$$(4.3) \qquad \begin{aligned} U(P^Y; \omega) &\equiv \max_{\delta \in \Delta} \sum_y q_y \sum_z \pi_{zy} \omega(z, \delta(y)) \\ &\equiv \sum_y q_y \max_{d \in D} \sum_z \pi_{zy} \omega(z, d) \\ &\equiv \sum_y q_y \sum_z \pi_{zy} \omega(z, d_y) \equiv \sum_y \sum_z p_{zy} \omega(z, d_y), \end{aligned}$$

thus defining $d_y \equiv \delta^*(y)$ as the optimal decision in response to message y:

$$(4.4) \qquad \sum_z \pi_{zy} \omega(z, d_y) \geqq \sum_z \pi_{zy} \omega(z, d), \quad \text{all} \quad d \in D.$$

In order to guarantee the achievement of a maximum in (4.3), (4.4), we shall henceforth assume that the set of real numbers $\omega(z, d)$, $d \in D^\omega$, is bounded from above and closed and that ω is continuous.

A more appropriate and precise name for the quantity $U(P^Y; \omega)$ would be *gross* value of Y, in contrast to its *net* value. So far, we have neglected those economic effects of an information instrument that are due not to decision based on messages received through the instrument but to its other properties, roughly called 'cost of information'. For example, one of two compared instruments may be more expensive, or it may send messages that while related to events by the same probability distribution are more time-consuming. Strictly speaking, these two instruments produce two different partitions of X: for the occurrence of a particular message belongs to the detailed description of a state x; and the consequence may depend, not only on decision d and event z but also on the manner in which the message received through a particular instrument affects the user's resources and well-being, through the expenditure of time, money and effort involved in the process of receiving the message. Equation (2.2) should be replaced by a more general one

$$(4.5) \qquad u(c) \equiv u(d(z), y) \equiv \omega_Y(z, d, y)$$

say, where y belongs to a set Y of messages associated with a particular instrument. The new function ω_Y may be called the *net payoff function.* In a simple but important case

$$(4.6) \qquad \omega_Y(z, d, y) = \omega(z, d) - \varkappa(y),$$

where, for example, $\varkappa(y)$ is the monetary cost associated with message y, $\omega(z, d)$ is the ('gross') monetary profit from decision d when event z occurs, and utility is linear in money: see Raiffa and Schlaifer [15, (Section 4)]. In general the net value of an information system Y can be written as

$$(4.7) \qquad U_Y(Y) \equiv \max_{\delta \in \Delta} \sum_z \sum_y \omega_Y(z, \delta(y), y)\, p_{zy}$$

so that in the special, additive case (4.6) we have,

$$(4.8) \qquad U_Y(Y) = U(P^Y; \omega) - \sum_y \varkappa(y)\, p(y).$$

In what follows we shall indeed assume (4.6), hence (4.8). This will permit us to study the economic effect of statistical properties of an information system, separated from the system's cost properties. But remember that in the general case (4.5), (4.7), the net value of an information system cannot be decomposed into gross payoff and cost as additive components.

5. Comparison of (gross) information values

We shall compare the (gross) values of two information systems, Y and Y', having fixed the set Z of events and thus the vector $r = [r_z]$ of marginal probabilities of events and the set Ω_Z of considered payoff functions.

EXAMPLE. To expand further the flight passenger's case of Section 2: We can ask whether a barometer or a hygrometer (with messages referring to humidity) is preferable to a user who has a ranch, an airplane, or both. The uses considered will define the set Z of payoff-adequate weather descriptions which will permit the necessary comparison.

In the ('Bayesian') spirit of the expected utility theorem, the two joint distributions P^Y and $P^{Y'}$ (also denoted as P and P') are known to the decision maker. He knows therefore also the pairs

$$(\Pi_*, q_*) \quad \text{and} \quad (\Pi'_*, q'_*),$$
$$(\Lambda_*, r_*) \quad \text{and} \quad (\Lambda'_*, r_*),$$

indicating by the star subscript (as it will be sometimes useful to do) that those matrices and vectors are known. Such knowledge is usually assumed in operations research problems – including the most general ones of sequential decision making, in which one starts with an initial distribution of states seen as time sequences and conditional upon the sequence of decisions: see Miyasawa [14]. The knowledge of r_* is also often assumed in information theory: for each channel Y, the joint distribution $p(z, y)$ is known, permitting one to compute, for a given source Z, the equivocation characterizing the channel Y[7]

$$H(Z \mid Y) = -\sum_y p(y) \sum_z p(z \mid y) \log p(z \mid y). \tag{5.1}$$

(Compare this with (4.3)!)

Also, $U(P^Y; \omega)$ and $U(P^{Y'}; \omega)$ can sometimes be ordered, for all ω considered, without the knowledge of the distributions P^Y and $P^{Y'}$ and only knowing the process that produces Y and Y' and imposes certain general restrictions on the trivariate distribution of z, y, y'. Such will be, in fact, the content of Sections 6 and 7.

It is also useful to consider cases where the comparison between information values of Y and Y' is made by someone who uses the knowledge of $\Pi = \Pi_*$ and $\Pi' = \Pi'_*$ (ignoring or being ignorant of q, q'); or who uses the knowledge of $\Lambda = \Lambda_*$ and $\Lambda' = \Lambda'_*$ (ignoring or being ignorant of the value of r). Such cases of limited knowledge will be considered because they may simplify the procedure of comparing information values. In addition, an actor may have knowledge of posterior probabilities π_{zy} associated with each message y, but have trouble ascertaining the probability q_y of each message: this makes the comparison of Π with Π' interesting. (Note, however, that the probability vectors q, q', r even though ignored or not known are constrained by identity (3.2).)

Finally the ignorance of the (prior) distribution of hypotheses is maintained in non-Bayesian statistics, making it impossible to use other than the likelihood matrices $\Lambda = \Lambda_*$ and $\Lambda' = \Lambda'_*$.

Whenever P^Y, $P^{Y'}$ are known (hence r, Λ, Λ', Π, Π' have known values r_*, Λ_*, etc.) and are such that

$$(5.2) \qquad U(P^Y;\omega) \geqq U(P^{Y'};\omega), \quad \text{all} \quad \omega \text{ in } \Omega_Z,$$

we shall write

CONDITION (P): $P^Y > P^{Y'}$ (or briefly: $P > P'$),
and say: 'Y is more informative[8] than Y' as revealed by their joint distributions P, P' with Z' or simply '*P is more informative than P'*'. Note that (5.2) can be rewritten thus

$$(5.2.1) \qquad U(\Pi_*, q_*;\omega) \geqq U(\Pi'_*, q'_*;\omega), \quad \text{all} \quad \omega \text{ in } \Omega_Z; \quad \text{or}$$
$$(\Pi_*, q_*) > (\Pi'_*, q'_*),$$

or

$$(5.2.2) \qquad U(\Lambda_*, r_*;\omega) \geqq U(\Lambda'_*, r_*;\omega), \quad \text{all} \quad \omega \text{ in } \Omega_Z; \quad \text{or}$$
$$(\Lambda_*, r_*) > (\Lambda'_*, r_*).$$

If r is ignored or not known, we may ask whether

$$(5.3) \qquad U(\Lambda_*, r;\omega) \geqq U(\Lambda'_*, r;\omega), \quad \text{all} \quad \omega \text{ in } \Omega_Z \quad \text{and all} \quad r;$$

and, if so, write (omitting the stars for brevity)

CONDITION (Λ): $\Lambda > \Lambda'$
and say: 'Y is more informative than Y' as revealed by the likelihood matrices Λ and Λ'', or simply: '*Λ is more informative than Λ'*'.

Finally, it may also be of interest to ask whether or not

$$(5.4) \qquad U(\Pi_*, q;\omega) \geqq U(\Pi'_*, q';\omega) \quad \text{for all} \quad \omega \text{ in } \Omega_Z \text{ and all}$$
$$q, q' \quad \text{such that} \quad \Pi_* q = \Pi'_* q'.$$

This question arises naturally when the marginal probabilities q, q', r are ignored or not known. Since Z, hence r, is the same for both information systems, $\Pi_* q = \Pi'_* q'$ by (3.2). When (5.4) is satisfied we shall say (omitting stars for brevity) that 'Y is more informative than Y' as revealed by the posterior probabilities Π, Π''; or briefly '*Π is more informative than Π'*', and write

CONDITION (Π): $\Pi > \Pi'$.

The binary relation '$>$' defined above on the set of all matrices P, or all matrices Π, or all matrices Λ, as the case may be, induces in all cases at most a partial ordering on the P (or the Π or the Λ), hence on any set of available information systems. For, in general, there will be some pairs (P, P') or (Π, Π') or (Λ, Λ') for which there exist two payoff functions, ω and ω' in Ω_Z, such that the inequality in (5.2) or (5.3) or (5.4) is valid for ω but not for ω'. In contrast, the equivocation (5.1) used in information theory does not depend on the payoff function and thus induces complete (and weak) ordering. It will be shown that lower equivocation is necessary but not sufficient for higher informativeness: see Section 12.

Since q, q' and r are all fixed (at starred values) in condition (P) but not in condition (Λ) nor in condition (Π), condition (P) is weaker than either of the other two, and we have

THEOREM 5.1. $(\Lambda) \Rightarrow (P)$; $(\Pi) \Rightarrow (P)$.

We shall now prove that (Λ) and (P) are equivalent.

THEOREM 5.2. $(P) \Leftrightarrow (\Lambda)$.

Proof. By Theorem 5.1, it will be enough to prove $(P) \Rightarrow (\Lambda)$. Let $P^Y \equiv (\Lambda, r)$, $P^{Y'} \equiv (\Lambda', r)$ and assume that, as in (5.2.2) but with stars omitted for brevity, condition (P) holds. From (3.1.2) and (4.3), for any payoff function $\omega \in \Omega_Z$ from $D^\omega \times Z$ to the reals,

$$(5.5) \qquad U(P^Y; \omega) \equiv U(\Lambda, r; \omega) \equiv \sum_y \max_{d \in D^\omega} \sum_z r_z \lambda_{zy} \omega(z, d).$$

For any given $r = \bar{r}$ define a new payoff function $\bar{\omega}$ in Ω_Z by

$$(5.6) \qquad \bar{\omega}(z, d) = \frac{\bar{r}_z}{r_z} \omega(z, d); \; D^{\bar{\omega}} = D^\omega.$$

Then, replacing ω by $\bar{\omega}$ in (5.5),

$$(5.7)\qquad U(P^Y;\bar{\omega}) = \sum_y \max_{d\in D^\omega} \sum_z \bar{r}_z\lambda_{zy}\omega(z,d) = U(\Lambda, \bar{r}; \omega).$$

By similar reasoning,

$$(5.7')\qquad U(P^{Y'};\bar{\omega}) = U(\Lambda', \bar{r}; \omega).$$

From condition (P), we know

$$(5.8)\qquad U(P^Y;\bar{\omega}) \geqq U(P^{Y'};\bar{\omega}).$$

Therefore by (5.7), (5.7′) and (5.8),

$$(5.9)\qquad U(\Lambda, \bar{r}; \bar{\omega}) \geqq U(\Lambda', \bar{r}; \omega),$$

where $\bar{r}$ and ω are arbitrary, so that (5.3) is satisfied. Thus (P) implies (Λ).

It follows from Theorem 5.2 that, if one system is more informative than another as revealed by their respective likelihood matrices, no further knowledge is added by knowing the prior probabilities of events. On the other hand, we shall show in Section 9, Theorem 9.3 that (P) implies (Π) only under certain conditions. Anticipating this result we state a summarizing

THEOREM 5.3. $(\Pi) \mapsto (P) \Leftrightarrow (\Lambda)$,
using here and henceforth the symbol $\mapsto$ for 'implies but is not implied by'.

We conclude this section by remarking that it is not possible to apply the relation 'more informative than' to net rather than gross information values. Modifying the notation of (4.7) in an obvious way, suppose that the net payoff functions ω_Y and ω_{Y}, defined respectively on $Z\times D\times Y$ and $Z\times D\times Y'$ are such that for some positive number k

$$(5.10)\qquad k > U_Y(Y;\omega_Y) - U_{Y'}(Y';\omega_{Y'}) \geqq 0;$$

then there exists another pair of net payoff functions, $\bar{\omega}_Y$ and $\bar{\omega}_{Y'}$, such that

$$U_Y(Y;\bar{\omega}_Y) - U_{Y'}(Y';\omega_{Y'}) < 0:$$

for example, let

$$\bar{\omega}_Y(z,d,y) = \omega_Y(z,d,y) - \tfrac{1}{2}k;$$
$$\bar{\omega}_{Y'}(z,d,y') = \omega_{Y'}(z,d,y') + \tfrac{1}{2}k.$$

In particular, when the net payoffs can be decomposed into gross payoffs and information costs as in (4.6), it is always possible to imagine information cost functions $\kappa(y)$, $\kappa'(y')$ that would reverse the second inequality in (5.10).

6. Garbled information

For any joint distribution of three variables z, y, y' the following identities hold:

$$(6.1)\qquad \frac{p(y' \mid y, z)}{p(y' \mid y)} \equiv \frac{p(z \mid y, y')}{p(z \mid y)} \equiv \frac{p(y, y' \mid z)}{p(y \mid z)\cdot p(y' \mid y)},$$

since each of these three ratios is equal to

$$\frac{p(z, y, y')\cdot p(y)}{p(z, y)\cdot p(y, y')}$$

We shall say that, for a given set Z of events, the information system Y in *garbled* into Y' when, for all $z \in Z$, $y \in Y$, $y' \in Y$ the following condition holds:

CONDITION (*G*): *Each of the three ratios in* (6.1) *is equal to* 1.

(G) can therefore be written in three equivalent forms. Each seems to agree with the ordinary usage of the term garbling.[9]

$$(G_1)\qquad p(y' \mid y, z) = p(y' \mid y),$$

i.e., given a message y of the original information system Y, the conditional probability of message y' of the garbled system Y' does not depend on event z.

$$(G_2)\qquad p(z \mid y, y') = p(z \mid y),$$

i.e., the posterior probability of event z given the original message y, does not depend on the garbled message y'.

$$(G_3)\qquad p(y, y' \mid z) = p(y \mid z)\cdot p(y' \mid y):$$

this describes the generation of the pair of messages, y and y': while in general $p(y, y' | z) = p(y | z)\cdot p(y' | y, z)$, this identity becomes in the garbling case, (G_3), because of (G_1).

The following condition that is implied, but does not imply[10] condition (G), is obtained by summing (G_3) over y

$$p(y' \mid z) \equiv \sum_y p(y, y' \mid z) = \sum_y p(y \mid z)\, p(y' \mid y), \qquad \text{all} \quad z \in Z,\ y' \in Y';$$

or, in the notation of Section 2,

$$\lambda'_{zy'} = \sum_y \lambda_{zy} \gamma_{yy'} . \tag{6.2}$$

Using matrix notation we rewrite this as

CONDITION (Γ): $\Lambda' = \Lambda\Gamma$,
and obtain

THEOREM 6.1. $(G) \mapsto (\Gamma)$.

A row-stochastic, or Markov, matrix is one with non-negative elements only, and with all row-sums $=1$. Denote the class of all Markov matrices of order $n \times n'$ by $\mathcal{M}$, and the class of their transposes, i.e., of all 'column-stochastic' matrices of order $n' \times n$, by $\mathcal{M}_{(\tau)}$. Then obviously

$$\Gamma \in \mathcal{M},\ \Gamma' \in \mathcal{M}_{(\tau)} . \tag{6.3}$$

In honor of David Blackwell, we have called the following condition

CONDITION (B): There exists a matrix $B = [\beta_{jk}]$ such that

$$\begin{array}{ll} (B_0) & B \in \mathcal{M} \\ (B_1) & \Lambda' = \Lambda B . \end{array} \tag{6.4}$$

Condition (B) is implied by the garbling condition (G), but not conversely[11]; for we can prove

THEOREM 6.2. $(G) \mapsto (\Gamma) \mapsto (B)$.

Proof. By (6.3), (Γ) implies (B). The converse is not necessarily true (see Section 9). Hence our theorem follows from Theorem 6.1. We shall now prove the important

THEOREM 6.3. $(B) \Rightarrow (\Lambda)$.

Proof. For any $(\Lambda, r) \equiv (\Pi, q)$ and ω, define for every message y_j the optimal decision d_j; that is, by (4.4),

$$(6.5) \qquad \sum_{i=1}^{m} \pi_{ij}\omega(z_i, d_j) \geqslant \sum_{i=1}^{m} \pi_{ij}\omega(z_i, d), \quad \text{all} \quad d \in D^{\omega};$$

or, omitting the summation limits for brevity and writing

$$(6.6) \qquad \begin{aligned} &\omega(z_i, d_j) \equiv u_{ij}, \\ &\sum_i \pi_{ij}u_{ij} \geqq \sum_i \pi_{ij}\omega(z_i, d), \quad \text{all} \quad d \in D^{\omega}, \end{aligned}$$

$$(6.7) \qquad \sum_i r_i\lambda_{ij}u_{ij} \geqq \sum_i r_i\lambda_{ij}\omega(z_i, d), \quad \text{all} \quad d \in D^{\omega},$$

by (3.1.2). Then by (4.3)

$$(6.8) \qquad \begin{aligned} U(P;\omega) &\equiv U(\Lambda, r;\omega) \equiv U(\Pi, q;\omega) \\ &= \sum_{i,j} q_j\pi_{ij}u_{ij} = \sum_{i,j} r_i\lambda_{ij}u_{ij}. \end{aligned}$$

Similarly, for $(\Lambda', r) \equiv (\Pi', q')$, we define $d'_k \in D^{\omega}$ and $u'_{ik} \equiv \omega(z_i, d_k)$ so that

$$(6.6') \qquad \sum_i \pi'_{ik}u'_{ik} \geqq \sum_i \pi'_{ik}\omega(z_i, d), \quad \text{all} \quad d \in D^{\omega},$$

$$(6.7') \qquad \sum_i r_i\lambda'_{ik}u'_{ik} \geqq \sum_i r_i\lambda'_{ik}\omega(z_i, d), \quad \text{all} \quad d \in D^{\omega},$$

and we have

$$(6.8') \qquad \begin{aligned} U(P';\omega) &\equiv U(\Lambda', r;\omega) \equiv U(\Pi', q';\omega) \\ &= \sum_{i,k} q'_k\pi'_{ik}u'_{ik} = \sum_{i,k} r_i\lambda'_{ik}u'_{ik}. \end{aligned}$$

Suppose (B) holds. Then by (6.8′), (6.7), (6.8) we have, for any r, ω,

$$\begin{aligned} U(\Lambda'; r; \omega) &= \sum_k \beta_{jk} \sum_{i,j} r_i\lambda_{ij}u'_{ik} \\ &\leqq \sum_k \beta_{jk} \sum_{i,j} r_i\lambda_{ij}u_{ij} = \sum_{i,j} r_i\lambda_{ij}u_{ij} \\ &= U(\Lambda, r; \omega). \end{aligned}$$

This proves that (B) implies (Λ). In Section 8 we shall prove the converse, so that (B)⇔(Λ).

From Theorems 6.1, 6.2 and 6.3 we immediately obtain

THEOREM 6.4. *If Y is garbled into Y' then Y is more informative than Y' as revealed by their likelihood matrices Λ and Λ'.*

The following theorem summarizes the inclusion relations stated in this and the preceding section:

THEOREM 6.5. $(G) \mapsto (\Gamma) \mapsto (B) \Leftrightarrow (\Lambda) \Leftrightarrow (P) \Leftarrow\!\!| (\Pi)$.

The proof of this theorem will be complete when, as mentioned before, it is shown that (Λ) implies (B) (Section 8) and that (B) does not imply (Γ) nor does (Γ) imply (G) (Section 9). Pending these proofs we have proved so far only the weaker

THEOREM 6.6. $(\mathrm{G}) \Rightarrow (\Gamma) \Rightarrow (B) \Rightarrow (\Lambda) \Leftrightarrow (P)$.

7. Collapsing Information and Joining Information

The case in which Y' is condensed from Y was defined at the end of Section 3 as

$$\text{(C)} \qquad Y \,\mathrm{s}\, Y',$$

i.e., each y in Y is contained in one y' in Y'. Hence by (3.7)

$$\begin{array}{llll} \text{either} & y \subset y', & p(y' \mid y) = 1, & p(y, y' \mid z) = p(y \mid z) \\ \text{or} & y \not\subset y', & p(y' \mid y) = 0, & p(y, y' \mid z) = 0. \end{array}$$

In either case, (G_1) is satisfied. Hence (C) implies (G); but the converse is obviously not true. Collapsing information is thus a special case of garbling. We state this as

THEOREM 7.1. $(C) \mapsto (G)$.

Let every message in Y be obtained by *joining* a message in Y' with a message belonging to a third information system, T. Since Y, Y', T are partitions of X, we have (see, e.g., Halmos [8])

CONDITION (J): $Y = Y' \times T = \{(y' \cap t)\}, y' \in Y', t \in T.$

Clearly Y is finer than Y', so that (J) implies (C); but the converse is, of course, not true, and we have

THEOREM 7.2. $(J) \mapsto (C)$.

We can combine these results with those of Sections 5 and 6 into

THEOREM 7.3. $(J) \mapsto (C) \Rightarrow (G) \mapsto (\Gamma) \mapsto (B) \Rightarrow (\Lambda) \Leftrightarrow (P)$.

Thus Y' is less informative than Y when Y' is garbled or condensed from Y; or when Y is formed by joining Y' with a message from a third information system. Garbling and condensing information occurs when an intermediate node is inserted in a communication network – as, for example, when reports are processed into commands. Joining information occurs when information is centralized. It follows that inserting an intermediate node never increases, and centralizing information never decreases, the gross expected payoff. But the *net* payoffs may be ordered differently. For example, the cost of centralizing information may offset its advantages (see remarks at the end of Section 5) or such centralization may call for rules that are not feasible (cf. Section 4).

8. Equivalence of Conditions (B), (Λ), (P) and (θ)

THEOREM 8.1. $(B) \Leftrightarrow (P) \Leftrightarrow (\Lambda)$.

Proof. Because of Theorem 5.2 and 6.3, it will suffice to prove (P)⇒(B). We shall first prove the following:

LEMMA. If (P) holds, then for any real $(n' \times m)$-matrix $V = [v_{ki}]$ there exists a matrix $M = [m_{ki}] \in \mathcal{M}_{(\tau)}$ such that

$$(8.1) \qquad \sum_{i,k,j} m_{kj} r_i \lambda_{ij} v_{ik} \geqq \sum_{i,k} r_i \lambda'_{ki} v_{ki}.$$

To prove the lemma let us define, for a given matrix $V = [v_{ki}]$ the payoff function ω as follows: $D^{\omega} = \{d_1, \ldots, d_{n'}\}$, and

$$(8.2) \qquad \omega(z_i, d_k) = v_{ki}, \quad i = 1, \ldots, m; \quad k = 1, \ldots, n'.$$

Now define, for each message y_j in Y, the optimal decision $d_{k(j)} \in D^{\omega}$ by

$$(8.3) \qquad \sum_i r_i \lambda_{ij} \omega(z_i, d_{k(j)}) \geqq \sum_i r_i \lambda_{ij} v_{ki}, \quad k = 1, \ldots, n'; \quad j = 1, \ldots, n;$$

then by (4.3), (3.1.2)

$$(8.4) \qquad U(P^Y; \omega) = \sum_{i,j} r_i \lambda_{ij} v_{k(j)i}.$$

Now, for any matrix $T=[t_{kj}]\in\mathscr{M}_{(\tau)}$, we have by (8.3)

$$\sum_{i,j,k} t_{kj}r_i\lambda_{ij}v_{k(j)i}=\sum_{i,j} r_i\lambda_{ij}v_{k(j)i}\geqq\sum_{i,j,k} t_{kj}r_i\lambda_{ij}v_{ki}, \tag{8.5}$$

since $t_{kj}\geqq 0$, $\sum_k t_{kj}=1$. That is

$$U(P^Y;\omega)\geqq\sum_{i,j,k} t_{kj}r_i\lambda_{ij}v_{ki}. \tag{8.6}$$

Now by definition,

$$U(P^{Y'};\omega)\geqq\sum_{i,k} r_i\lambda'_{ik}\omega(z_i,d_k),\quad\text{all}\quad d_k\in D^\omega,\ \text{i.e.,} \tag{8.7}$$

$$U(P^{Y'};\omega)\geqq\sum_{i,k} r_i\lambda'_{ik}v_{ki}. \tag{8.8}$$

If condition (P) holds then,

$$U(P^Y;\omega)\geqq U(P^{Y'};\omega). \tag{8.9}$$

Let our matrix T be such that

$$t_{kj}=\begin{cases}1 & \text{if}\quad k=k(j)\\ 0 & \text{otherwise}.\end{cases}$$

Then (8.6) becomes an equality. Therefore by (8.8) and (8.9) T has the properties of the matrix M required in the lemma.

To complete the proof of the theorem, let $\mathscr{V}$ be the set of all $(n'\times m)$-matrices $V=[v_{ki}]$ such that $0\leqq v_{ki}\leqq 1$; as before, let $M=[m_{kj}]$ belong to $\mathscr{M}_{(\tau)}$; and define a function $\Psi(M,V)$ on $\mathscr{M}_{(\tau)}\times\mathscr{V}$ by

$$\Psi(M,V)=\sum_{i,j,k} m_{kj}r_i\lambda_{ij}v_{ki}-\sum_{i,k} r_i\lambda'_{ik}v_{ki}. \tag{8.10}$$

Then Ψ is a bilinear function of M and V; and the factors $\mathscr{M}_{(\tau)}$ and $\mathscr{V}$ of its domain are both closed, bounded and convex sets in $(n'\times n)$- and $(n'\times m)$-spaces, respectively. Therefore, by a saddle point theorem – see, e.g., Karlin [9, (II, theorem 1.51)], there exists a pair $[m^0_{kj}]\equiv M^0\in\mathscr{M}_{(\tau)}$ and $V^0\in\mathscr{V}$ such that

$$\Psi(M,V^0)\leqq\Psi(M^0,V^0)\leqq\Psi(M^0,V), \tag{8.11}$$

for all $M\in\mathscr{M}_{(\tau)}$ and $V\in\mathscr{V}$.

Suppose (P) holds. Applying our lemma to $V=V^0$, we see that there exists a matrix $M\in\mathscr{M}_{(\tau)}$ such that $\Psi(M,V^0)\geqq 0$. Therefore by (8.11)

$\Psi(M^0, V^0) \geqq 0$ and thus

$$(8.12) \qquad \Psi(M^0, V) \geqq 0, \quad \text{all} \quad V \in \mathscr{V}.$$

Define $V^{(ki)} \in \mathscr{V}$ as a matrix whose (k, i)-th element is 1 and all other elements are 0. Then by (8.10), (8.12)

$$\Psi(M^0, V^{(ki)}) = \sum_j m^0_{kj} r_i \lambda_{ij} - r_i \lambda'_{ik} \geqq 0,$$

and since all $r_i > 0$ by (3.1.1), we have

$$(8.13) \qquad \sum_i m^0_{kj} \lambda_{ij} \geqq \lambda'_{ik}, \quad i = 1, \ldots, m; \quad k = 1, \ldots, n'.$$

If in (8.13) at least one of the inequalities is strict, we obtain a contradiction

$$(8.14) \qquad \sum_{i, j, k} m^0_{kj} \lambda_{ij} = \sum_{i, k} \lambda_{ij} = m > \sum_{i, k} \lambda'_{ik} = m,$$

since $\sum_k m^0_{kj} = \sum_j \lambda_{ij} = \sum_k \lambda'_{ik} = 1$. Therefore

$$(8.15) \qquad \sum_j m^0_{kj} \lambda_{ij} = \lambda'_{ik}, \quad i = 1, \ldots, m; \quad k = 1, \ldots, n',$$

$$(8.16) \qquad \Lambda' = \Lambda M^0_{(\tau)}$$

where $M^0_{(\tau)}$ is the transposed matrix of M^0, hence

$$(8.17) \qquad M^0_{(\tau)} \in \mathscr{M}.$$

Now put $B = M^0_{(\tau)}$. Then B fulfills the conditions (6.4). This proves that (P)⇒(B) and completes the proof of our theorem.

We shall now show that the following condition (which will prove useful in Section 9) is equivalent to (B) and thus to (P) and (Λ):

CONDITION (θ): There exists a matrix $\theta \equiv [\theta_{jk}]$ such that

$$(8.18) \qquad \begin{aligned} &(\theta_0)\colon \ \theta \in \mathscr{M}_{(\tau)} \\ &(\theta_1)\colon \ \Pi' = \Pi\theta \quad \text{and} \\ &(\theta_2)\colon \ q = \theta q'. \end{aligned}$$

Note that (θ) is a property of the joint distributions P, P', while (B) is a property of the likelihoods Λ, Λ' only.

THEOREM 8.2. $(B)\Leftrightarrow(\theta)$.

Proof. By definition (see Section 3)

$$q_j = \sum_i r_i \lambda_{ij} > 0, \quad q'_k = \sum_i r_i \lambda'_{ik} > 0 \tag{8.19}$$

$$q_j \pi_{ij} = r_i \lambda_{ij} \geqq 0, \quad q'_k \pi'_{ik} = r_i \lambda'_{ik} \geqq 0. \tag{8.20}$$

Suppose (B) is true: that is, there exists $B \equiv [\beta_{jk}]$ such that

$$\lambda'_{ik} = \sum_j \lambda_{ij} \beta_{jk}; \quad \beta_{jk} \geqq 0, \quad \sum_k \beta_{jk} = 1. \tag{8.21}$$

Then by (8.19)

$$q'_k = \sum_{i,j} r_i \lambda_{ij} \beta_{jk} = \sum_j q_j \beta_{jk}. \tag{8.22}$$

Given the matrix B define a matrix $[\theta_{jk}] \equiv \theta$ by the following equations:

$$\theta_{jk} q'_k = \beta_{jk} q_j, \quad \text{all} \quad j, k. \tag{8.23}$$

It is easily verified that θ is in $\mathscr{M}_{(\tau)}$ (using (8.22)); that $q = \theta q'$ (using (6.4) and (8.23)); and that $\Pi' = \Pi\theta$ (using (8.20), (8.21), (8.23)). Hence (B)$\Rightarrow(\theta)$. To prove the converse, note that condition (θ_1) implies, by (8.20)

$$\begin{aligned} \pi'_{ik} &= \frac{r_i \lambda'_{ik}}{q'_k} = \sum_j \pi_{ij} \theta_{jk} = \sum_j \frac{r_i \lambda_{ij}}{q_j} \theta_{jk}, \\ \lambda'_{ik} &= q'_k \sum_j \frac{\theta_{jk}}{q_j} \lambda_{ij}. \end{aligned} \tag{8.24}$$

Define $B \equiv [\beta_{jk}]$ by (8.23). Then by (θ_2)

$$\sum_k \beta_{jk} = \frac{1}{q_j} \sum_k \theta_{jk} q'_k = \frac{q_j}{q_j} = 1; \quad \beta_{jk} \geqq 0,$$

hence $B \in \mathscr{M}$; moreover by (θ_1) and (8.23), $\Lambda' = \Lambda B$. Thus B satisfies both conditions in (6.4), and we have proved that $(\theta)\Rightarrow$(B). This completes the proof.

Combining Theorems 8.1 and 8.2, we have

THEOREM 8.3. $(P)\Leftrightarrow(\Lambda)\Leftrightarrow(B)\Leftrightarrow(\theta)$.

Using the matrix $\Gamma' \equiv [p(y|y')]$ defined in (3.3′) we introduce

CONDITION (Γ'): $\Pi' = \Pi\Gamma'$.
Then we have

THEOREM 8.4. $(G) \Rightarrow (\Gamma') \Rightarrow (\theta)$.

Proof. Consider the identities

$$p(y, z \mid y') = p(y, y', z)/p(y') = p(z \mid y, y') \cdot p(y, y')/p(y')$$
$$p(y, z \mid y') = p(z \mid y, y') \cdot p(y \mid y');$$

summing over y

$$p(z \mid y') = \sum_y p(z \mid y, y') \cdot p(y \mid y').$$

This becomes, if (G_2) holds,

$$p(z \mid y') = \sum_y p(z \mid y) \cdot p(y \mid y')$$
$$\Pi' = \Pi\Gamma'.$$

This proves $(G) \Rightarrow (\Gamma')$. It is clear that if ($\Gamma'$) holds, then ($\theta$) is satisfied with $\theta = \Gamma'$. This completes the proof.

If a matrix B, and therefore also matrix θ, exists, it is possible to interpret the information systems Y and Y' *as if* Y were garbled into Y', although it is not known whether or not the trivariate distribution on $Z \times Y \times Y'$ satisfies condition (G).

EXAMPLE. As in Section 2, let z be the visibility at the airport. Let y be the true atmospheric pressure, and y' be the reading on a barometer. Then presumably condition (G) is satisfied, and by the proof of Theorems 6.5 and 8.4, conditions (B) and (θ) are satisfied by matrices $B = \Gamma$ and $\theta = \Gamma'$ (and possibly also other matrices). If, on the other hand, we interpret y', not as a reading on a barometer, but as, say, the true level of humidity, then we have no reason to suppose that Y is garbled into Y' (or conversely). If the bivariate distributions on $Z \times Y$ and $Z \times Y'$, respectively, happen to satisfy condition (B), hence (θ), it may be useful to interpret the matrix θ *as if* it were identical with Γ' (and B with Γ). That is, we can conceive of the messages y_j as follows: given y'_k, the message y_j will be produced, using a random device, with probability $p(y_j \mid y'_k) = \theta_{jk}$, $j = 1, \ldots, n$.

9. Comparative informativeness revealed by posterior probabilities only: the case of independent Π matrix

Let π_j and π'_k be the jth column of Π and the kth column of Π' respectively. Now, π_j and π'_k can be interpreted as m-dimensional vectors or points in m-dimensional space. Accordingly Π and Π' can be interpreted whenever it is convenient – as two sets of vectors: $\Pi \equiv \{\pi_1, \ldots, \pi_n\}$, $\Pi' \equiv \{\pi'_i, \ldots, \pi'_{n'}\}$. Let S^{m-1} be the simplex defined by the set of all points $v = (v_1, \ldots, v_m)$ such that $v_i \geqq 0$, $\sum v_i = 1$. Clearly both Π and Π' are subsets of S^{m-1}.

Define the following condition: the set Π' is contained in the convex hull $K(\Pi)$ of the set Π:

CONDITION (K): $\Pi' \subset K(\Pi)$.

This is represented by Figures 2a, 3a, 3b, 4, but not by Figures 2b, 3d. Clearly (K) is equivalent to the following condition: there exists a matrix M such that

$$(9.1) \qquad M \in \mathscr{M}_{(\tau)}; \quad \Pi' = \Pi M:$$

(9.1) is identical with conditions (θ_0) and (θ_1) of Section 8. Hence (θ) which requires, in addition, (θ_2), implies but is not implied by (K). We have thus

THEOREM 9.1. $(\theta) \Vdash\!\!\!\Rightarrow (K)$.

In this section we shall consider the case when the columns of the matrix Π (but not necessarily of Π') are linearly independent, that is:

CONDITION (I_π): (rank of Π) $= n$.

This condition will be later shown to apply in two important cases: the binomial case ($n=2$) of Section 10 and the noiseless case of Section 11.

Similarly we introduce

CONDITION (I_Λ): (rank of Λ) $= n$.

Noting that the r_i and q_j are all >0 it is easy to prove

THEOREM 9.2. $(I_\pi) \Leftrightarrow (I_\Lambda)$.

Now we shall prove

THEOREM 9.3. *If conditions* (I_π) *and* (θ) *(hence also condition* (B)*) are true, then* (B) *and* (θ) *are satisfied by a unique pair of matrices* B, θ *related by the equations*

$$(8.23) \qquad \theta_{jk}q'_k = \beta_{jk}q_j, \quad all \quad j, k.$$

Proof. By the hypothesis, we have

$$(\theta_1): \Pi' = \Pi\theta, \qquad (\mathrm{B}_1): \Lambda' = \Lambda B,$$

and Π consists of linearly independent columns. Then by Theorem 9.2,

Figures 2, 3, 4 – Simplex representation of posterior probabilities

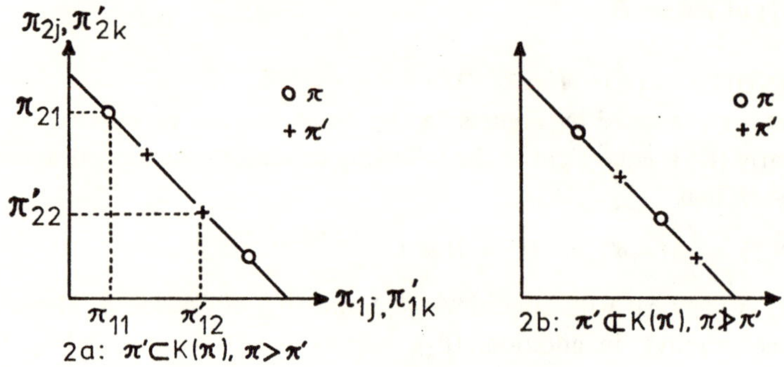

Fig. 2. $m = 2$; Y, Y' binary: $m = 2 = n = n'$.

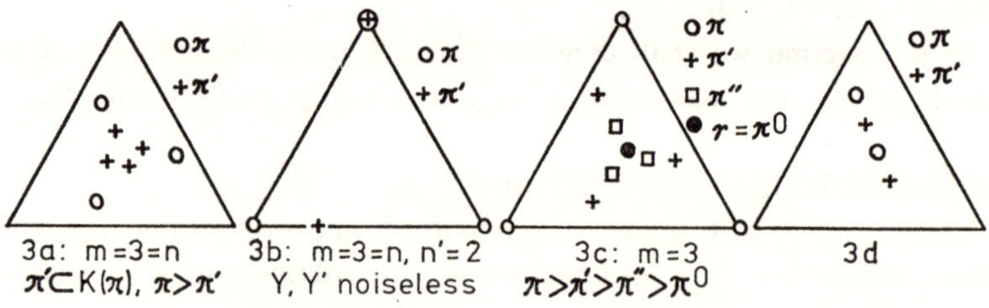

Fig. 3. $m = 3$.

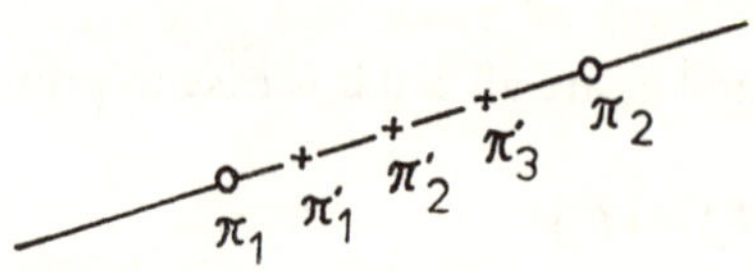

Fig. 4. $m \geqq 2$; Y binomial; $n = 2$.

Λ also consists of linearly independent columns. Therefore, in the above relations (θ_1) and (B_1), θ and B are unique. Now in proving Theorem 8.2 we have shown that if a matrix B satisfying condition (B) exists then a matrix θ defined by equations (8.23) will satisfy condition (θ); and conversely. Hence the unique pair B, θ satisfying (B), (θ) respectively must also satisfy equations (8.23). Stronger than Theorem 9.3 is

THEOREM 9.4. *$[(I_\Lambda)$ and $(B)] \Leftrightarrow [(B)$ with unique $B] \Leftrightarrow [(\theta)$ with unique $\theta]$.*

Proof. By Theorems 9.2 and 9.3, it is sufficient to prove that, when (B) holds and B is unique, then (I_Λ) holds. Suppose (B) holds, with unique $B \equiv [\beta_{jk}]$ but (I_Λ) does not hold. Let $g < n$ and let $\lambda_1, \ldots, \lambda_g$ be linearly independent, while $\lambda_{g+1}, \ldots, \lambda_n$ are linearly dependent on $\{\lambda_1, \ldots, \lambda_g\}$. That is

$$\lambda_h = \sum_{l=1}^{g} a_{hl}\lambda_l, \quad h = g+1, \ldots, n. \tag{9.2}$$

By condition (B) and (9.2)

$$\lambda'_k = \sum_{j=1}^{n} \beta_{jk}\lambda_j = \sum_{l=1}^{g} \left(\beta_{lk} + \sum_{h=g+1}^{n} a_{hl}\beta_{hk}\right)\lambda_l, \quad k = 1, \ldots, n'. \tag{9.3}$$

Let us define a matrix $\Delta \equiv [\delta_{jk}]$ as follows:

$$\delta_{j1} = \beta_{j1} + \varepsilon_j \tag{9.4}$$

$$\delta_{js} = \beta_{js} - \frac{1}{n'-1}\varepsilon_j, \quad s = 2, \ldots, n'; \quad j = 1, \ldots, n, \tag{9.5}$$

where $\varepsilon_j, j = 1, \ldots, n$ are numbers such that

$$\varepsilon_l + \sum_{h=g+1}^{n} a_{hl}\varepsilon_h = 0, \quad l = 1, \ldots, g. \tag{9.6}$$

We shall prove our theorem for the case in which all $\beta_{jk} > 0$. Clearly it is possible to choose all $\varepsilon_j, j = 1, \ldots, n$ which satisfy (9.6) and have arbitrarily small absolute values. Then, for $\beta_{jk} > 0$ and $|\varepsilon_j|$ sufficiently small, we have by (9.4), (9.5)

$$\delta_{jk} \geqq 0, \qquad \sum_k \delta_{jk} = \sum_k \beta_{jk} = 1. \tag{9.7}$$

By (9.4), (9.5), (9.6),

$$(9.8) \qquad \delta_{lk} + \sum_h a_{hl}\delta_{hk} = \beta_{lk} + \sum_h a_{hl}\beta_{hk}.$$

Therefore by (9.2), (9.3), (9.8),

$$(9.9) \qquad \lambda'_k = \sum_{l=1}^{g} \left(\delta_{lk} + \sum_h a_{hl}\delta_{hk}\right)\lambda_l = \sum_{j=1}^{n} \delta_{jk}\lambda_j.$$

Then it follows from (9.7) and (9.8) that $\Delta \in \mathcal{M}$, $\Delta \neq B$, and $\Lambda' = \Lambda\Delta$. The part of the theorem involving θ is proved similarly.

We shall now show that, under condition (I_π), if Y' is obtained by garbling Y – see Section 6 – then the matrices B and θ are identical, respectively, with the matrices $\Gamma \equiv [\gamma_{jk}]$ and $\Gamma' \equiv [\gamma'_{jk}]$ defined in Section 3:

$$\gamma_{jk} \equiv p(y'_k \mid y_j); \qquad \gamma'_{jk} \equiv p(y_j \mid y'_k).$$

THEOREM 9.5. $[(I_\pi)$ *and* $(G)] \Rightarrow (B = \Gamma, \theta = \Gamma')$.

Proof. By Theorem 6.5 and 8.2, condition (G) implies that

$$\Lambda' = \Lambda\Gamma, \qquad \Lambda' = \Lambda B, \qquad \Pi' = \Pi\theta.$$

Hence $\Lambda(\Gamma - B) = 0$. Let (I_π) hold. Then by Theorem 9.2, Λ consists of independent columns, and therefore $\Gamma = B$, i.e.:

$$\gamma_{jk} \equiv p(y'_k \mid y_j) = \beta_{jk}, \quad \text{all} \quad j, k.$$

By Theorem 9.3, θ is uniquely defined by

$$\theta_{jk} = \beta_{jk} q_j / q'_k = p(y'_k \mid y_j)\, p(y_j) / p(y'_k) = p(y_j \mid y'_k);$$

hence

$$[\theta_{jk}] = [\gamma'_{jk}], \quad \theta = \Gamma'.$$

We shall now prove that (Γ) does not imply (G), nor does (B) imply (Γ). Condition (Γ) means

$$(9.10) \qquad p(y' \mid z) = \sum_y p(y \mid z)\, p(y' \mid y).$$

On the other hand we have identically

$$(9.11) \qquad p(y' \mid z) = \sum_y p(y, y' \mid z) = \sum_y p(y \mid z)\, p(y' \mid z, y).$$

If Π is linearly dependent, then by Theorem 9.4, Equations (9.10), (9.11) are consistent with the inequality

$$p(y' \mid y) \neq p(y' \mid z, y),$$

as contrasted with (G_1). Hence (G) does not necessarily follow from (Γ). Similarly we can prove that (B) does not imply (Γ).

We shall now show that the independence condition (I_π) is both sufficient and necessary for the equivalence of the conditions (P), (Π) and (K). We shall start with

THEOREM 9.6. $(I_\pi) \Rightarrow ((K) \Leftrightarrow (P))$.

Proof. By Theorems 8.3 and 9.1, we always have (P)$\Rightarrow$(K). Therefore we need only prove that (K)$\Rightarrow$(P) if the linear independence condition (I_π) holds; i.e., that

$$(9.12) \qquad (I_\pi) \Rightarrow ((K) \Rightarrow (P)).$$

Let Y and Y' be two information systems with known $P^Y \equiv (\Pi_*, q_*)$ and $P^{Y'} \equiv (\Pi'_*, q'_*)$ respectively, where by (3.2)

$$(9.13) \qquad \Pi_* q_* = \Pi'_*, q'_*.$$

Suppose (K) holds; that is, there exists a matrix M satisfying (9.1) with $\Pi = \Pi_*$, $\Pi' = \Pi'_*$. Then by (9.13)

$$(9.14) \qquad \Pi_*(q_* - Mq'_*) = 0.$$

If (I_π) holds for Π_*, then, the linear independence of its columns implies

$$(9.15) \qquad q_* = Mq'_*,$$

so that, by (9.1), all three components of condition (θ) hold. Hence by Theorem 8.3, (P) holds. This proves that

$$(9.16) \qquad (I_\pi) \Rightarrow ((K) \Rightarrow (P)).$$

We shall now prove

THEOREM 9.7. $(I_\pi) \Rightarrow ((P) \Leftrightarrow (\Pi))$.

Proof. Since by Theorem 5.1, (Π) always implies (P), we need only to prove that (P) implies (Π) if (I_π) holds; i.e., that

$$(9.17) \qquad (I_\pi) \Rightarrow ((P) \Rightarrow (\Pi)).$$

First note that since (P) is equivalent to (θ) by Theorem 8.3, condition (Π) is by definition equivalent to the following: for any q, q' such that

$$(9.18) \qquad \Pi_* q = \Pi'_* q'$$

there exists a matrix θ such that

$$(9.19) \qquad \begin{aligned} &\theta \in \mathscr{M}_{(\tau)}, \\ &\Pi'_* = \Pi_* \theta, \\ &q \;\; = \theta q'. \end{aligned}$$

The last three conditions correspond to the three components of condition (θ), applied here to all q, q' consistent with (9.18), and not only (as in (9.13)) to a particular q_*, q'_*.

Suppose (P), or equivalently (θ), holds for the known (starred) distributions; that is, there exists a matrix θ_* (say) such that

$$(9.20.0) \quad \theta_* \in \mathscr{M}_{(\tau)},$$

$$(9.20.1) \quad \Pi'_* = \Pi_* \theta_*,$$

$$(9.20.2) \quad q_* \;= \theta_* q'_*.$$

Thus, under condition (P), there exists at least one triple (q, q', θ) which satisfies (9.19), viz., the triple (q_*, q'_*, θ_*). Now let q, q' be undetermined except for the constraint (9.18). Then by (9.20.1),

$$(9.21) \qquad \Pi_*(q - \theta_* q') = 0.$$

If the columns of Π_* are linearly independent then (9.21) implies $q = \theta_* q'$; i.e., (P) then implies (Π) with $\theta = \theta_*$. Therefore

$$(9.22) \qquad (I_\pi) \Rightarrow ((P) \Rightarrow (\Pi)).$$

This completes the proof.

Combining Theorems 9.6 and 9.7, we have

THEOREM 9.8. $(I_\pi) \Rightarrow ((K) \Leftrightarrow (P) \Leftrightarrow (\Pi))$.

EXAMPLE. Let $m = n = n' = 3$. Figure 3c shows a sequence of triangles (with vertices representing the matrices Π, Π', Π'', Π^0), nestling in each other and containing the point r; the largest triangle coincides with the simplex itself, and the sequence shrinks to the point r as its lower bound. The vertices of any of these triangles represent the set $\Pi = \{\pi_1, \pi_2, \pi_3\}$ of some information system Y, and the triangle itself is $K(\Pi)$. If the triangle corresponding to Y' is nestled in the triangle corresponding to Y, then $\Pi' \subset K(\Pi)$; and since the vertices are not collinear, condition (I_π) is satisfied. Hence by Theorem 9.2, $\Pi > \Pi'$: the system Y is more informative than Y', as revealed by the posterior probabilities alone. Note that the vertices of the largest triangle in the sequence, i.e. of the simplex itself, give perfect information; while the lower bound represented by point r is just as informative as 'null information', i.e. the knowledge of the prior probabilities alone, without any messages. The sequence is ordered according to informativeness, and so is any other sequence of nestling triangles. The set of all triangles is a lattice, partially ordered by the relation 'more informative than', with 'complete information' as the maximum element, and 'null information' as the infimum.

10. Binomial and Binary Information Systems

The numbers m, n, n' are always $\geqq 2$. Following Blackwell and Girshick [4] the case $m=2$ will be called *dichotomy*. If information system Y consists of 2 messages, $n=2$, it is called *binomial*; and when $m=n=2$, the information-theoretical literature – e.g., Feinstein [7] – calls the channel (the information system) Y, *binary*. We shall denote these conditions thus:

$$\text{(d)}: \; m = 2\,; \qquad \text{(b)}: \; n = 2\,; \qquad \text{(b')}: \; n' = 2\,.$$

Thus a binary channel is defined by (b) and (d).

Since always $m \geqq 2$, condition (b) implies that the columns of the matrix Π are linearly independent. Thus (b) implies (I_π), but of course, not conversely. Hence by Theorem 9.8

THEOREM 10.1. $(b) \mapsto ((K) \Leftrightarrow (\Pi) \mapsto (P))$.

The case is illustrated on Figure 4, where the points π_1, π_2 representing Y, and the points π_1', π_2', π_3' representing Y' are all arranged on a straight line in a space of m dimensions (arbitrary $m \geqq 2$), and all π_k' lie *between* π_1 and π_2.

The more special case $n = n' = m = 2$ – i.e. (b), (b') and (d) – occurs in the testing of simple hypotheses and in comparing 'binary channels'. After labelling the two events z_1 and z_2 arbitrarily, let us label the two messages in Y so that

$$(10.1) \qquad \pi_{11} \geqq \pi_{12}.$$

Then condition (K) takes the form

$$(10.2) \qquad \begin{aligned} \pi_{11} \geqq \pi'_{11} \geqq \pi_{12}, \\ \pi_{11} \geqq \pi'_{12} \geqq \pi_{12}, \end{aligned}$$

and by Theorem 10.1, we have

THEOREM 10.2. *Let Y and Y' be two binary channels (i.e., let $m=n==n'=2$); then Y is more informative than Y' if and only if the posterior probabilities satisfy the relation* (10.2); *provided the two messages in Y are labelled so as to make $\pi_{11} \geqq \pi_{12}$.*

This criterion (usable only when the posterior probabilities are known) is simpler than the one provided by Blackwell-Girshick [4, (section 12.5)] and based on the likelihood matrix Λ.

11. Comparison of Noiseless Information Systems

Let Y be a noiseless information system, i.e. $Z \mathrm{s} Y$ (see Section 2). Then $\lambda_{ij} \equiv p(y_j|z_i) = 1$ or 0, all i, j. In general, $\sum_j \lambda_{ij} = 1$ and $\sum_i r_i \lambda_{ij} = q_j > 0$. Therefore, if Y is noiseless, then each row of its Λ matrix contains one and only one non-zero ($=1$) element and each column contains at least one non-zero ($=1$) element. Now $\pi_{ij} = r_i \lambda_{ij} / q_j$. Hence, whenever $\lambda_{ij} = 1$ or 0, then $\pi_{ij} = r_i / q_j$ (>0) or 0, respectively. Therefore;

(11.1) *If Y is noiseless, then each row of its Π matrix contains one and only one non-zero* (>0) *element and each column contains at least one non-zero* (>0) *element.*

Using (11.1) we shall prove the following property of condition (N) defined in Section 3:

THEOREM 11.1. *$(N) \mapsto ((I_\pi)$ and $(I_{\pi'}))$.*

Proof. Suppose Y is noiseless and let

$$(11.2) \qquad \sum_{j=1}^{n} g_j \pi_{ij} = 0, \quad \text{all} \quad i = 1, \ldots, m,$$

for some real numbers $g_1, \ldots, g_n$. We shall then show that $g_j = 0$, for all j, i.e., the columns of Π are linearly independent. We note that by (11.1), for any fixed j, say $j = j_1$, there is at least one i, say $i = i_1$, such that $\pi_{i_1 j_1} > 0$. Then by (11.1), $\pi_{i_1 j} = 0$, for all $j \neq j_1$. Therefore, for $i = i_1$, (11.2) becomes $g_{j_1} \pi_{i_1 j_1} = 0$. Since $\pi_{i_1 j_1} > 0$, we have

$$(11.3) \qquad g_{j_1} = 0\,, \quad j_1 = 1, \ldots, n\,;$$

that is, (I_π) holds. Similarly, for Y' noiseless, we have $(\mathrm{I}_{\pi'})$. The converse obviously does not hold.

Using Theorems 9.7 and 11.1, we have

THEOREM 11.2. $(N) \mapsto ((P) \Leftrightarrow (\Pi) \Leftrightarrow (K))$.

In Section 2, we defined condition (C); and by Theorem 7.3, $(\mathrm{C}) \mapsto (\mathrm{P})$. Hence by Theorem 11.2, we have

THEOREM 11.3. $(N) \mapsto ((C)) \Rightarrow (\Pi) \Leftrightarrow (P) \Leftrightarrow (K))$.

Thus, if both Y and Y' are noiseless, and Y is finer than Y', then Y is more informative than Y', as revealed by posterior probabilities of events

$$(11.4) \qquad \Pi' = \Pi M\,, \quad M \equiv [\mu_{jk}] \in \mathscr{M}_{(\tau)}\,,$$

which is, of course, our condition (K).

Remark 1. The matrix $M \equiv [\mu_{jk}]$ in (11.4), with $Z \text{ s } Y \text{ s } Y'$, $\Pi' = \Pi M$, has the following interpretation:

$$M = \Gamma' \equiv [\gamma'_{jk}] \equiv [p(y_j \mid y'_k)]\,,$$

since by Theorems 11.1, 11.3, 7.1, 9.5, we have $\theta = \Gamma' = M$.

EXAMPLE. Let $Z \text{ s } Y \text{ s } Y'$, so that by Theorem 11.3 and Remark 1, $\Pi' = \Pi M$, $\mu_{jk} = p(y_j \mid y'_k)$; let the posterior probability matrices be as follows (with $0 < \pi'_{11} = 1 - \pi'_{21} < 1$);

$$\Pi = \begin{matrix} 1 & 0 & 0 \\ 0 & 1 & 0 \\ 0 & 0 & 1 \end{matrix} \qquad \Pi' = \begin{matrix} \pi'_{11} & 0 \\ \pi'_{21} & 0 \\ 0 & 1. \end{matrix}$$

Then $y'_1 = y_1 \cup y_2$, $y'_2 = y_3$. Since Π is the identity matrix I, we have

$\Pi' = \Pi M = IM = M = \Gamma'$. The case is illustrated in Figure 3b, where the point π'_1 divides the base of the triangle in proportion $\pi'_{21} : \pi'_{11} = = p(y_2 | y'_1) : p(y_1 | y'_1)$.

Now we shall prove the following

THEOREM 11.4. $(N) \models ((C) \Leftrightarrow (K) \Leftrightarrow (\Pi) \Leftrightarrow (P))$, *when* X *is finite.*

Proof. By Theorems 11.2 and 11.3, it will suffice to prove that

$$(\mathrm{N}) \models ((K) \Rightarrow (C)), \quad \text{when} \quad X \text{ is finite.}$$

Let us assume (N) and (K): that is, $Z \,\mathrm{s}\, Y$, $Z \,\mathrm{s}\, Y'$ and (11.4) holds, so that

$$(11.5) \qquad \pi'_{ik} = \sum_j \pi_{ij} \mu_{jk}, \quad \text{all} \quad i, k.$$

For any fixed k, say $k = k_1$, let $z_i \in Z$ be contained in y'_k (remember that Z is a sub-partition of the noiseless information system Y'.) Then $\lambda'_{i_1 k_1} = 1$, and

$$(11.6) \qquad \pi'_{i_1 k_1} > 0.$$

Since Y is noiseless, by (11.1) the i_1th row of Π contains one and only one non-zero element, say $\pi_{i_1 j_1} > 0$. Then

$$(11.7) \qquad \pi_{i_1 j_1} > 0, \qquad \pi_{i_1 j} = 0, \quad \text{for all} \quad j \neq j_1.$$

In (11.5), let $i = i_1$ and $k = k_1$; then by (11.7),

$$(11.8) \qquad \pi'_{i_1 k_1} = \pi_{i_1 j_1 k_1};$$

hence

$$(11.9) \qquad \mu_{j_1 k_1} > 0,$$

by (11.6), (11.7), (11.8). Suppose X is finite. Then $\pi_{i_1 j_1} > 0$, (i.e., $\lambda_{i_1 j_1} = 1$) implies $z_{i_1} \subset y_{j_1}$; therefore, (11.7) admits of the following interpretation:

(11.10) *For any fixed* $k = k_1$, *and any* $z_{i_1} \subset y'_{k_1}$, *there exists at least one* y_{j_1} *such that* $z_{i_1} \subset y_{j_1}$.

Now, for this y_{j_1}, let $z_{i'} \in Z$ be contained in y_{j_1}. Then $\lambda_{i' j_1} = 1$ and

$$(11.11) \qquad \pi_{i' j_1} > 0, \qquad \pi_{i' j} = 0, \quad \text{for all} \quad j \neq j_1,$$

by (11.1). Then, for $i = i'$ and $k = k_1$ (11.5) becomes

$$(11.12) \qquad \pi_{i' k_1} = \pi_{i' j_1} \mu_{j_1 k_1},$$

so that by (11.9), (11.11) and (11.12), $\pi_{i'k_1}>0$, $\mu_{i'k_1}=1$. When X is finite this implies $z_{i'}\subset y'_{k_1}$. This proves that

(11.13) *For any* y_{j_1} *such that* $y_{j_1}\cap y'_{k_1}\neq\varnothing$, $y_{j_1}\subset y'_{k_1}$.

From (11.10) and (11.13), we conclude that, if (N) and (K) hold and X is finite, then any y'_k is a union of disjoint y's, i.e., $Y \mathrm{s} Y'$, viz., (C) holds. This completes the proof.

Remark 2. Let Y be noiseless: If the columns of Π' are linear combinations of Π, that is, if there exists a $n\times n'$ matrix $A=[\alpha_{jk}]$ such that $\Pi'=\Pi A$, i.e.,

$$(11.14)\quad \pi'_{ik}=\sum_j \pi_{ij}\alpha_{jk},\quad \text{all}\quad i,k,$$

then $A\in\mathcal{M}^{(c)}_{n\times n'}$; hence (K) holds.

To prove, sum both sides of (11.14) with respect to i; then $\sum_j \alpha_{jk}=1$, all k (since $\sum_i \pi'_{ik}=\sum_i \pi_{ij}=1$). It remains to prove that $\alpha_{jk}\geqq 0$ for all j, k. Fix $j=j_1$, $k=k_1$, and let $i=i_1$ be such that $\pi_{i_1j_1}>0$. Since Y is noiseless, we have by (11.1), (11.14)

$$\pi'_{i_1k_1}=\pi_{i_1j_1}\alpha_{j_1k_1}.$$

Since $\pi_{i_1j_1}>0$, if $\pi'_{i1k_1}>0$ we have $\alpha_{j_1k_1}>0$; and if $\pi'_{i_1k_1}=0$, then $\alpha_{j_1k_1}=0$. Hence $\alpha_{jk}\geqq 0$, all j, k, completing the proof.

12. Convex operators on posterior probabilities: the equivocation parameter

For any payoff function ω, we shall define a function v_ω on the simplex S^{m-1} (i.e., on the set of all vectors $\xi\equiv(\xi_1,\ldots,\xi_m)$ such that $\xi_i\geqq 0$, $\sum\xi_i=1$) as follows:

$$(12.1)\quad v_\omega(\xi)\equiv\max_{d\in D^\omega}\sum_{i=1}^{m}\omega(z_i,d)\,\xi_i.$$

Then by (4.3), we have

$$(12.2)\quad U(P;\omega)\equiv\sum_{j=1}^{n} q_j v_\omega(\pi_j),$$

where π_j is the jth column of Π. Consider a pair of probability distributions (Π, q), (Π', q') with the following property:[12]

CONDITION (φ): For any convex function φ on S^{m-1}

$$\sum_{k=1}^{n} q_j\varphi(\pi_j) \geqq \sum_{k=1}^{n'} q_k\varphi(\pi'_k). \tag{12.3}$$

We shall prove

THEOREM 12.1. (P)$\Leftrightarrow$(φ).

Proof. First we shall prove (φ)$\Rightarrow$(P). We have by (12.1), for any two vectors $\xi_1 \equiv (\xi_{11}, \dots, \xi_{m1})$, $\xi_2 \equiv (\xi_{12}, \dots, \xi_{m2})$, both in S^{m-1}, and letting $0 \leqq \alpha \leqq 1$,

$$\begin{aligned} v_\omega(\alpha\xi_1 + (1-\alpha)\,\xi_2) &\leqq \alpha \max_{d \in D^\omega} \sum_i \omega(z_i, d)\,\xi_{i1} + \\ &\quad + (1-\alpha) \max_{d \in D^\omega} \sum_i \omega(z_i, d)\,\xi_{i2} = \\ &= \alpha v_\omega(\xi_1) + (1-\alpha)\,v_\omega(\xi_2). \end{aligned} \tag{12.4}$$

That is, v_ω is a convex function on S^{m-1}. Therefore, using expression (12.2) for $U(P;\omega)$ and a similar one for $U(P';\omega)$, condition (φ) is seen to imply that $U(P;\omega) \geqq U(P';\omega)$, all ω, i.e., condition (P).

Next we shall prove (P)$\Rightarrow$(φ). By Theorem 8.3, (P)$\Leftrightarrow$(θ). Therefore, if (P) holds, then there exists

$$\theta = [\theta_{jk}]$$

such that

$$\theta_{jk} \geqq 0, \quad \sum_j \theta_{jk} = 1, \tag{12.5.0}$$

$$\pi'_k = \sum_j \pi_j\theta_{jk}, \quad \text{all} \quad k, \tag{12.5.1}$$

$$q_j = \sum_k \theta_{jk}q'_k, \quad \text{all} \quad j. \tag{12.5.2}$$

Hence for any convex function φ on S^{m-1}, we have

$$\begin{aligned} \sum_j q_j\varphi(\pi_j) &= \sum_k q'_k \sum_j \theta_{jk}\varphi(\pi_j) \\ &\geqq \sum_k q'_k\varphi\left(\sum_j \theta_{jk}\pi_j\right) = \sum_k q'_k\varphi(\pi'_k); \end{aligned} \tag{12.6}$$

hence (P)$\Rightarrow$(φ), completing the proof of the theorem.

Let φ^* be a particular convex function on S^{m-1}, and suppose

CONDITION (φ^*): $\sum_{j=1}^{n} q_j\varphi^*(\pi_j) \geqq \sum_{k=1}^{n'} q'_k\varphi^*(\pi'_k)$.
Clearly (φ^*) cannot be a sufficient but is a necessary condition for (φ). Thus, by Theorem 12.1, (φ^*) is a necessary condition for (P). Thus

THEOREM 12.2. $(P) \Leftrightarrow (\varphi) \mapsto (\varphi^*)$.

An important special case is that of the equivocation parameter $H(Z \mid Y)$ of classical information theory, defined in (5.1) or, in another notation, by

$$(12.7) \qquad H(Z \mid Y) \equiv -\sum_j q_j \sum_i \pi_{ij} \log \pi_{ij}\,.$$

The function

$$-H(\xi) \equiv \sum_i \xi_i \log \xi_i\,,$$

where $\xi \equiv (\xi_1, \ldots, \xi_m) \in S^{m-1}$, is well known to be convex.[13] Therefore, if we introduce

CONDITION (H): $H(Z \mid Y) \leqq H(Z \mid Y')$.
we can replace, Theorem 12.2, (φ^*) by (H) and obtain

THEOREM 12.3. $(P) \mapsto (H)$:
i.e., lower equivocation is necessary but not sufficient for higher informativeness.

13. Some relations with Blackwell's results[14]

Using our terminology and notation we can say that in Blackwell [2], an information system Y is defined by its likelihood matrix Λ without referring to the probability distribution on Z. Given an information system Y and a payoff function ω, we shall define a set W_Y^ω in m-dimensional space as follows. Let D^ω be the set of decisions relevant to ω and let Δ_Y^ω be the set of all decision rules δ from Y to D^ω. Corresponding to each $\delta \in \Delta_Y^\omega$, define a point

$$(13.1) \qquad w(\delta) \equiv (w_1(\delta), \ldots, w_m(\delta))$$

in m-dimensional space by

$$(13.2) \qquad w_i(\delta) \equiv \sum_y w(z_i, \delta(y))\, p(y \mid z_i), \quad i = 1, \ldots, m.$$

Then the set W_Y^ω is defined as follows

$$(13.3) \qquad W_Y^\omega \equiv \{w(\delta);\, \delta \in \Delta_Y^\omega\}.$$

The set $W_{Y'}^\omega$ is defined similarly. Assume that both W_Y^ω and $W_{Y'}^\omega$ are closed sets. In Blackwell's definition,[15] Y is said to be more informative than Y', if the convex hull of W_Y^ω, $K(W_Y^\omega)$, contains $W_{Y'}^\omega$ for all ω. We shall call

CONDITION (W): $K(W_Y^\omega) \supset W_{Y'}^\omega$, for all ω.

Blackwell [3] and Blackwell-Girshick [4] have proved

THEOREM 13.1. $(W) \Leftrightarrow (B)$.

From this theorem and our Theorem 8.3, we immediately obtain

THEOREM 13.2. $(P) \Leftrightarrow (\Lambda) \Leftrightarrow (W) \Leftrightarrow (B) \Leftrightarrow (\theta)$.

Here we shall give a direct proof of the equivalence of three conditions (P), (Λ) and (W) without going through condition (B)

$$(13.4) \qquad (\mathrm{P}) \Leftrightarrow (\Lambda) \Leftrightarrow (\mathrm{W}).$$

First note that $U(P; \omega)$ can be expressed by means of the set W_Y^ω defined in (13.3)

$$\begin{aligned} U(P; \omega) \equiv U(\Lambda_*, r_*; \omega) &= \max_{\delta \in \Delta^\omega{}_Y} \sum_i r_{*i} \sum_y \omega(z_i, \delta(y))\, p(y \mid z_i) \\ &= \max_{\delta \in \Delta^\omega{}_Y} \sum_i r_{*i} w_i(\delta), \end{aligned}$$

$$(13.5) \qquad U(P; \omega) \equiv U(\Lambda_*, r_*; \omega) = \max_{w \in W^\omega{}_Y} \sum_i r_{*i} w_i, \qquad \text{where} \quad w = (w_1, \ldots, w_m).$$

Similarly, we have

$$(13.6) \qquad U(P'; \omega) \equiv U(\Lambda'_*, r_*; \omega) = \max_{w \in W^\omega{}_{Y'}} \sum_i r_{*i} w_i.$$

Suppose (W) holds, i.e., $K(W_Y^\omega) \supset W_{Y'}^\omega$, for all ω. Then for any r,

$$(13.7) \qquad \max_{w \in W^\omega{}_Y} \sum_i r_i w_i \geqq \max_{w \in W^\omega{}_{Y'}} \sum_i r_i w_i , \quad \text{for all} \quad \omega .$$

By (13.5) and (13.6), the relation (13.7) is equivalent to

$$(13.8) \qquad U(\Lambda_*, r; \omega) \geqq U(\Lambda'_*, r; \omega), \quad \text{for all} \quad r, \omega .$$

Hence (W) implies (Λ). And since clearly $(\Lambda) \Rightarrow$ (P), we have proved that $(\mathrm{W}) \Rightarrow (\Lambda) \Rightarrow (\mathrm{P})$.

Next, we shall prove that (P) implies (W); that is, if

$$(13.9) \qquad U(\Lambda_* r_*; \omega) \geqq U(\Lambda'_*, r_*; \omega), \quad \text{for all} \quad \omega ,$$

then (W) holds. (The proof is similar to that of Theorem 8.1.) Let $(g_1, \ldots, g_m)$ be an arbitrary set of m real numbers; define

$$(13.10) \quad h_i \equiv g_1 / r_{*i} \quad i = 1, \ldots, m .$$

For any payoff function ω, we define a payoff function $\bar{\omega}$ by $D^{\bar{\omega}} = D^\omega$ and

$$(13.11) \quad \bar{\omega}(z_i, d) = h_i \omega(z_i, d), \quad d \in D^\omega, \quad i = 1, \ldots, m .$$

Then it is clear that

$$(13.12) \quad \bar{w}_i(\delta) \equiv \sum_y \bar{\omega}(z_i, \delta(y)) \, p(y \mid z_i) = h_i w_i(\delta), \quad i = 1, \ldots, m ,$$

where $\delta \in \Delta_Y^\omega \equiv \Delta_Y^{\bar{\omega}}$, and $w_i(\delta)$ is defined by (13.2).

Let us define a linear transformation T from m-space to m-space by $Tw \equiv T(w_1, \ldots, w_m) = (h_1 w_1, \ldots, h_m w_m)$. Then from (13.12) we have $\bar{w}(\delta) \equiv \equiv (\bar{w}_1(\delta), \ldots, \bar{w}_m(\delta)) = Tw(\delta)$, for all $\delta \in \Delta_Y^\omega \equiv \Delta_Y^{\bar{\omega}}$. Therefore W_Y^ω defined by (13.3) and $W_Y^{\bar{\omega}}$ defined similarly with respect to $\bar{\omega}$ are related by

$$(13.13) \quad W_Y^{\bar{\omega}} = T W_Y^\omega .$$

From (13.5) and (13.13), we have

$$(13.14) \quad U(\Lambda_*, r_*; \bar{\omega}) = \max_{w \in W^\omega{}_Y} \sum r_{*i} w_i = \max_{w \in W^\omega{}_Y} \sum r_{*i} (Tw)_i$$

where $(Tw)_i$ is the ith coordinate of the point Tw, that is, from the definition of T and (13.10),

$$(13.15) \quad (Tw)_i = h_i w_i = \frac{g_i}{r_{*i}} w_i, \quad i = 1, \ldots, m.$$

Therefore, from (13.14) and (13.15), we have

$$(13.16) \quad U(\Lambda_*, r_*; \bar{\omega}) = \max_{w \in W^{\omega}_Y} \sum_i g_i w_i.$$

Similarly

$$(13.16') \quad U(\Lambda'_*, r_*; \bar{\omega}) = \max_{w \in W^{\omega}_{Y'}} \sum_i g_i w_i.$$

From (13.9), (13.16) and (13.16′) we have

$$(13.17) \quad \max_{w \in W^{\omega}_Y} \sum_i g_i w_i \geqq \max_{w \in W^{\omega}_Y} \sum_i g_i w_i,$$

where $(g_1, \ldots, g_m)$ and ω is any set of m real numbers and ω is any payoff function. Therefore (13.17) implies

$$K(W^{\omega}_Y) \supset W^{\omega}_{Y}, \quad \text{for all} \quad \omega,$$

that is, (W). Accordingly (P)⇒(W) is proved. This completes a proof of the equivalence relation (13.4) which includes Theorem 5.2 as a part of it.

14. Dichotomies: $m = 2$

In the dichotomy case, Z consists of two events z_1 and z_2:$m=2$. As in (9.19), let

$$(14.1) \quad \Pi_* q = \Pi'_* q' (= r),$$

where Π_*, Π'_*, but not q, q', r are fixed. Henceforth we shall omit the asterisk without ambiguity.

With respect to an information system Y, define two functions $G_Y(t)$ and $F_Y(t)$ on [0, 1] as follows:[16]

$$(14.2) \quad G_Y(t) \equiv \sum_{\pi_{1j} \leqq t} q_j,$$

$$(14.3) \quad F_Y(t) \equiv \int_0^t G_Y(u)\, du.$$

$G_{Y'}(t)$ and $F_{Y'}(t)$ are defined similarly with respect to Y'. Clearly $G_Y(t)$

is a monotone non-decreasing step function with a jump of q_j at $t=\pi_{1j}$, $j=1,\ldots,n$.

From the consistency condition (14.1),

$$F_Y(1) = \int_0^1 G_Y(t)\,dt = 1 - \sum_j q_j\pi_{1j} = 1 - r_1 = r_2,$$

$$F_{Y'}(1) = \int_0^1 G_{Y'}(t)\,dt = 1 - \sum_k q'_k\pi'_{1k} = 1 - r_1 = r_2.$$

Therefore

$$(14.4)\qquad F_Y(1) = F_{Y'}(1) = r_2.$$

It will become clear that the relation (14.4) is a key point in our proof of Theorem 14.3 below. Now we shall introduce

CONDITION (F): $F_Y(t) \geqq F_{Y'}(t)$, all t, $0 \leqq t \leqq 1$.

Then, following a reasoning similar to that of Blackwell-Girshick [4, (theorem 12.4.1)], it is easy to prove[17]

THEOREM 14.1. *When* $m=2$, $(\varphi) \Leftrightarrow (F)$.

Then by Theorems 12.1 and 14.1, we have

THEOREM 14.2. *When* $m=2$, $(\Pi) \Leftrightarrow (F)$.

Referring to the definition of points π_j, π'_k in S^{m-1}, we shall introduce the following condition for $m=2$.

CONDITION (c): *All points* π'_k *of* Π' *lie between two consecutive points of* Π. (See Figure 5a).

On Figure 6a, the graphs of the functions $G_Y(t)$ and $G_{Y'}(t)$ are drawn on the same interval [0,1]. The interval [0, 1] is partitioned into sub-intervals by points $\pi_{11},\ldots,\pi_{1n}$ and $\pi'_{11},\ldots,\pi'_{1n'}$. Among these sub-intervals, the ones where

$$(14.5)\qquad G_Y(t) > G_{Y'}(t)$$

shall be denoted by $I_+^{(1)}, I_+^{(2)},\ldots$, and the ones where

$$(14.6)\qquad G_Y(t) < G_{Y'}(t)$$

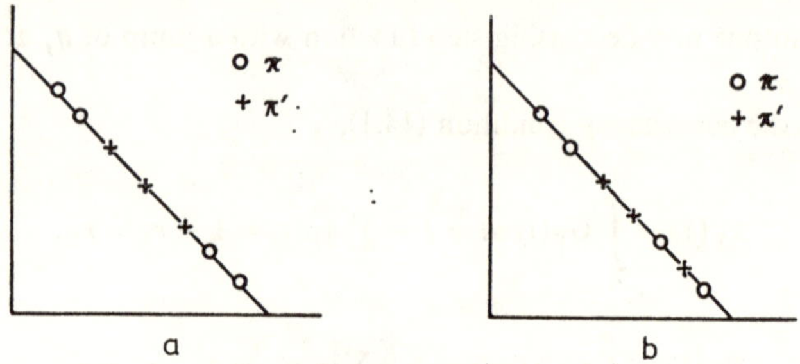

Fig. 5. Dichotomies: $m=2$.

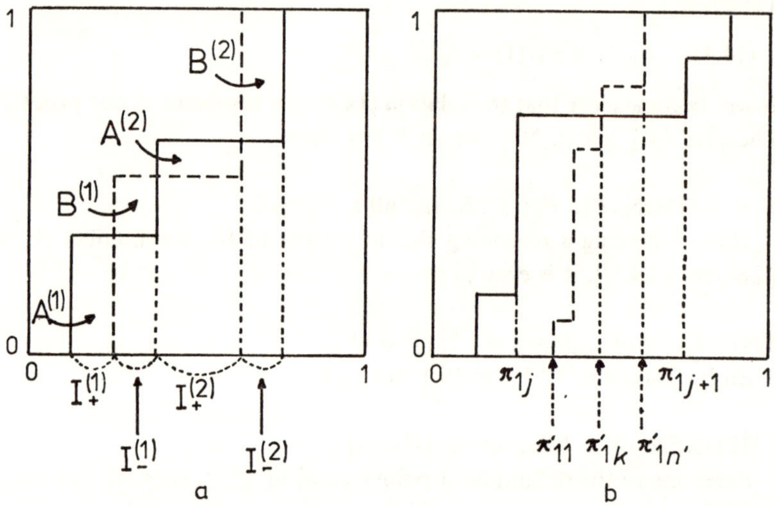

Fig. 6.

shall be denoted by $I_-^{(1)}, I_-^{(2)}, \ldots$. (Note that $G_Y(t)-G_{Y'}(t)$ and $G_{Y'}(t)-$ $-G_Y(t)$ are constant positive numbers on $I_+^{(\alpha)}$ and $I_-^{(\beta)}$ respectively.) The length of those intervals will also be denoted by $I_+^{(\alpha)}$, $I_-^{(\beta)}$, respectively.

Define the positive real numbers $A^{(1)}, A^{(2)}, \ldots$ and $B^{(1)}, B^{(2)}, \ldots$ by

$$(14.7) \qquad A^{(\alpha)} \equiv I_+^{(\alpha)}(G_Y(t) - G_{Y'}(t)), \quad t \varepsilon I_+^{(\alpha)},$$

$$(14.8) \qquad B^{(\beta)} \equiv I_-^{(\beta)}(G_{Y'}(t) - G_Y(t)), \quad t \in I_-^{(\beta)}.$$

Then by (14.4),

$$(14.9) \qquad A^{(1)} + A^{(2)} + \cdots = B^{(1)} + B^{(2)} + \cdots.$$

The following theorem gives a simpler characterization of 'greater informativeness' than Blackwell-Girshick's Theorem 12.4.1 [4].

THEOREM 14.3. *When* $m=2$, $(\Pi)\Leftrightarrow(c)$.

Proof. Without loss of generality, let $\pi_{11}<\pi_{12}<\cdots<\pi_{1n}$ and $\pi'_{11}<\pi'_{12}<\cdots<\pi'_{1n'}$. First, we shall prove (c)$\Rightarrow$(Π). For a unique j, we have by condition (c)

$$\pi_{1j}\leqq\pi'_{11}<\cdots<\pi'_{1n'}\leqq\pi_{1j+1}\,. \tag{14.10}$$

Let q, q' be any vectors such that (14.1) holds. Then $G_Y(\pi_{1j})<1=G_{Y'}(\pi'_{1n'})$. Therefore, there exists an index k such that

$$G_{Y'}(\pi'_{1k-1})\leqq G_Y(\pi_{1j})\leqq G_{Y'}(\pi'_{1k})\,, \tag{14.11}$$

(where, when $k=1$, we consider only the right-hand inequality). Then from the monotonicity of $G_Y(t)$ and $G_{Y'}(t)$ (see Figure 6b)

$$\begin{aligned} &G_Y(t)\geqq G_{Y'}(t)\,, \quad 0<t<\pi'_{1k}\,,\\ &G_{Y'}(t)\leqq G_Y(t)\,, \quad \pi'_{1k}\leqq t\leqq 1\,. \end{aligned} \tag{14.12}$$

Therefore, all intervals $I_+^{(1)}, I_+^{(2)},\ldots$ are located on the left-hand side of π'_{1k} and all the intervals $I_-^{(1)}, I_-^{(2)},\ldots$ are located on the right-hand side of π'_{1k}. Therefore by (14.9) and the definitions of $F_Y(t)$ and $F_{Y'}(t)$, clearly, condition (F) holds. Then by Theorem 14.2, it follows that (c)$\Rightarrow$(Π).

Next, in order to prove that (Π)$\Rightarrow$(c), suppose that (c) does not hold. Then there exists at least one pair of points among $\pi'_{11},\ldots,\pi'_{1n'}$, – say π'_{1k} and π'_{1k+1} – such that the interval (π'_{1k}, π'_{1k+1}) contains at least one point of $\{\pi_{11},\ldots,\pi_{1n}\}$ – say $\pi_{1j},\ldots,\pi_{1j+s}$, $s\geqq 0$. We shall show that there exists a pair of vectors $q\equiv(q_1,\ldots,q_n)$, $q_j>0$, $\sum q_j=1$ and $q'\equiv(q'_1,\ldots,q'_{n'})$, $q'_k>0$, $\sum q'_k=1$ such that

$$\Pi q=\Pi' q'\,, \tag{14.13}$$

and for the two corresponding information systems Y and Y', the respective functions $F_Y(t)$ and $F_{Y'}(t)$ do not satisfy condition (F). Then by Theorem 14.2, we can conclude $(\Pi, q)\not\succ(\Pi', q')$, i.e., (Π) does not hold.

We can choose $q\equiv(q_1,\ldots,q_n)$ and $q'\equiv(q'_1,\ldots,q'_{n'})$ so as to satisfy (14.9) and the following conditions (14.14.1)–(14.14.5):

$$(14.14.1)\quad 0 < q_g \ll q_h, \quad g = 1, \ldots, j-1, j+1, \ldots, j+s-1, j+s+1, \ldots, n, \quad h = j, j+s,$$

$$(14.14.2)\quad \sum_{g=1}^{n} q_g = 1$$

$$(14.14.3)\quad 0 < q'_g \ll q'_h, \quad g = 1, \ldots, k-1, k+2, \ldots, n', \quad h = k, k+1,$$

$$(14.14.4)\quad \sum_{h=1}^{n'} q'_h = 1,$$

$$(14.14.5)\quad \sum_{g=1}^{j-1} q_g < \sum_{h=1}^{k} q'_h < \sum_{g=1}^{j+s} q_g,$$

where for two positive numbers a and b, $a \ll b$ denote that a is infinitesimally small compared to b. Now, in numbering the intervals $I_+^{(\alpha)}$ and $I_+^{(\beta)}$, let us define $I_+^{(1)}$ and $I_-^{(1)}$ by $I_+^{(1)} \equiv [\pi_{1j+s}, \pi'_{1k+1}]$, $I_-^{(1)} \equiv [\pi'_{1k}, \pi_{1j}]$. Then

$$(14.15)\quad A^{(1)} \equiv (\pi'_{1k+1} - \pi_{1j+s})(G_Y(t) - G_{Y'}(t)), \quad \pi_{1j+s} \leqq t \leqq \pi'_{1k+1},$$

$$(14.16)\quad B^{(1)} \equiv (\pi_{1j} - \pi'_{1k})(G_{Y'}(t) - G_Y(t)), \quad \pi'_{1k} \leqq t \leqq \pi_{1j}.$$

Then in addition to (14.9), by (14.14.1) and (14.14.3), we have

$$(14.17)\quad A^{(2)} + A^{(3)} + \cdots \ll A^{(1)},$$

$$(14.18)\quad B^{(2)} + B^{(3)} + \cdots \ll B^{(1)}.$$

Now, by (14.9)

$$(14.19)\quad A^{(1)} - B^{(1)} = (B^{(2)} + B^{(3)} + \cdots) - (A^{(2)} + A^{(3)} + \cdots).$$

Therefore, by (14.17), (14.18), $A^{(1)} - B^{(1)}$ is almost zero. Accordingly by (14.17)

$$(14.20)\quad A^{(2)} + A^{(3)} + \cdots \ll B^{(1)}.$$

This implies that we cannot have $F_Y(t) \geqq F_{Y'}(t)$ over the whole sub-interval (π'_{1k}, π_{1j}). We have thus shown that if (c) does not hold, then (F) does not hold and by Theorem 14.2, (Π) cannot hold. Hence (Π)⇒(c), completing the proof of the theorem.

15. Summary

Given the set X of states of nature, described in unlimited detail and with a probability measure defined on it, we consider its partitions: Z (set of events z) and $Y, Y', Y'', \ldots$ (information systems, i.e., sets of mutually exclusive messages denoted by y in Y, y' in Y' etc.). The set Ω_Z consists of all payoff functions ω for which Z is a payoff-adequate (i.e., not too coarse) partition of X. Let the set of feasible decisions d entering the argument of ω be D^ω; thus ω is a real valued function on $Z \times D^\omega$. The (gross) expected payoff of an information system Y is

$$U(Y; \omega) = \sum_{z, y} \Pr(x \in z \cap y) \cdot \omega(z, d_y),$$

where d_y is a decision responding optimally to message y; that is,

$$\sum_z \Pr(x \in z \cap y) \left[\omega(z, d_y) - \omega(z, d)\right] \geqq 0, \quad \text{all} \quad d \in D^\omega.$$

A class of partially ordering relations is defined on the set of information systems $Y, Y', \ldots$, as follows: Y is said to be more informative than Y', as revealed by a given property of the distribution on $Z \times Y \times Y'$, if this property implies that

$$U(Y; \omega) \geqq U(Y'; \omega), \quad \text{all} \quad \omega \in \Omega_Z.$$

In particular, greater informativeness of Y relative to Y' may be revealed by comparing the (bivariate) distributions on $Z \times Y$ and on $Z \times Y'$; by comparing the matrix of likelihoods $\Lambda \equiv [\lambda_{zy}] \equiv [\Pr(x \in z \cap y)/\Pr(x \in z)]$, with the correspondingly defined matrix Λ'; or by comparing the matrix of posterior probabilities, $\Pi \equiv [\pi_{zy}]$ $[\Pr(x \in z \cap y)/\Pr(x \in y)]$, with the correspondingly defined matrix Π. The latter comparison is the strictly stronger one (Theorem 5.3) except in the important case when the messages of the more informative system (each message being represented by a column of Π, or of Λ) are linearly independent: Theorems 9.5, 9.7. The numerical criteria for comparison of informativeness, given in Theorem 13.2 are all equivalent, and are strictly stronger than that of Theorem 9.1; but they are all equivalent in the case of linear independence between messages. This case applies in particular to information systems that are noiseless with respect to – i.e., are sub-partitions of – the set Z of events

(Section 11); or are binomial – the case of two messages, – or binary – the case of two messages and two events (Section 10). Furthermore, for the 'dichotomy' cases (i.e., the case of only two events), a certain property of posterior probabilities is proved to be necessary and sufficient for Y to be more informative than Y' (Section 14). The 'equivocation' parameter of classical information theory, as well as its generalization to any other convex operator on posterior probabilities, is shown to be a necessary but not sufficient criterion of comparative informativeness; but a stronger criterion involving *all* convex operators on posterior probabilities is shown to be both sufficient and necessary (Section 12).

Statements on comparative informativeness can also be derived from the knowledge, not of the numerical properties of the probability distribution of events and messages, but of the process by which messages constituting one information system are generated from those of another system. Thus it is shown that 'garbling', of Y into Y', a well-defined property of some distributions on $Z \times Y \times Y'$, can never make Y' more informative than Y. A special case of garbling is 'collapsing' information, and a still more special case is dis-'joining' it: Theorem 7.3. Moreover, in the case of garbling of linearly independent messages, the Markov matrices used in some of the criteria of informativeness and relating the distribution on $Z \times Y$ to that on $Z \times Y'$ receive an insightful interpretation in terms of conditional probabilities of the messages of one system, given the message of another: Theorem 9.3.

To use our results for a definitive economic comparison of information systems one would have to know information costs. Unless these are additive, one would have to discard the concept of gross payoff functions (Section 4). One should, moreover, characterize the feasible set Δ_φ of decision rules (rather than the set D^ω of feasible decision), and take account of the cost which is associated with a decision rule; this cost, too, is in general non-additive, thus calling for a further re-definition of (net) payoffs.

In addition to these open questions of an economic nature, the mathematician will notice that by confining ourselves to finite sets of events and messages, we have neglected measure-theoretical difficulties which were attacked by other authors (see note 14).

More general studies are therefore necessary. We hope the present study contributes to stimulating and preparing them.

NOTES

* This work was supported partly by the office of Naval Research under Task 047-041 and partly by the Western Management Science Institute under a grant from the Ford Foundation. Reproduction in whole or in part is permitted for any purpose of the United States Government. During 1964/5, Koichi Miyasawa, Professor of Statistics at the University of Tokyo, was post-doctoral Fellow under a Ford Foundation Grant to the University of California.

The article is the product of very close collaboration although a few of the sections are predominantly the results of the work of one of the two authors (e.g., Sections 1–7 in the case of Marschak and Sections 8, 13, 14 in the case of Miyasawa). We owe thanks to Dr. Leif Appelgren, Stockholm, for constructive criticisms and to Professor Arthur Geoffrion of the Western Management Science Institute for many corrections and improvements.

1 This cost will be assumed additive. We shall thus treat a special case only: see Section 4.

2 See note 7 on the textbook terminology regarding 'noiselessness' and 'equivocation'.

3 Blackwell [2], Blackwell and Girschick [4], also McGuire [13].

4 Thus, in the case of sequential decisions, a state x would describe the time-sequence of external conditions. The sequence of states in the language of systems theory and dynamic programming corresponds (with the exception of the initial state) to a consequence in our terminology.

5 In an earlier paper (Marschak [11]) the existence and uniqueness of the sets of payoff-relevant actions and events was proved, using a set of physically distinct feasible actions.

6 This agrees with the terminology of Feinstein [7]; however, Abramson [1] calls the case (3.9) a 'deterministic channel', and reserves the adjective 'noiseless' for the case when the correspondence $Z \to Y$ is one-to-many, hence in our notation,

$$p(z \mid y) = \Pi_{zy} = \begin{cases} 1 & \text{if } y \subset z \\ 0 & \text{otherwise}, \end{cases}$$

so that each column of Π^Y consists of 1 one and $m-1$ zeros. In this case, however, it should be easy (i.e., costless) for the user to consider all messages corresponding to the same event, as one and the same message; this establishes a *one-to-one* correspondence between the set of messages (thus redefined) and the set of events. This is sometimes called perfect information. Then Π and Λ are the same (permutation) matrix:

$$\lambda_{zy} = \pi_{zy} = \begin{cases} 1 & \text{if } z = y \\ 0 & \text{otherwise}. \end{cases}$$

It seems to us therefore that the case called 'noiseless' by Abramson is of little interest: it collapses into the case of perfect information which is a special case of noiseless information, in Feinstein's and our sense.

7 The equivocation $H(Z \mid Y) = 0$ if and only if all $p(z \mid y) \equiv \pi_{zy} = 1$ or 0, i.e., if and only if Y is noiseless in the sense of Abramson and not in the sense used by Feinstein and ourselves. On the other hand, Y is noiseless in the latter sense, i.e., all $p(y \mid z) \equiv$ $\equiv \lambda_{zy} = 1$ or 0, if and only if the expression

$$H(Y \mid Z) \equiv -\sum_z p(z) \sum_y p(y \mid z) \log p(y \mid z) = 0\,.$$

Following Abramson, the latter expression might be called equivocation of Y with respect to Z.

[8] Strictly speaking, the term 'not less informative' would be more appropriate. We have chosen terms that will be shown to harmonize with those of Blackwell: see Section 13.

[9] This is called 'cascade' in information theory; e.g., Abramson [1, (section 5.9)].

[10] A rigorous proof will be given in Section 9.

[11] It is therefore called 'quasi-garbling' in a later paper, 'Optimal Systems for Information and Decision', *Selected Essays*, 32.

[12] In DeGroot's [6] definition of an information amount $I[Y; r; \varphi]$ it is reasonable to require that $I[Y, r; \varphi] \geqq 0$ for all Y and r. He proves that an (uncertainty) function φ is concave on S^{m-1} is a necessary and sufficient condition for that.

[13] Since $d^2(\xi_i \log \xi_i)/d\xi_i^2 = 1/\xi_i > 0$ for non-negative ξ_i, the matrix of second derivatives of $-H(\xi)$, which is diagonal, is positive definite – a sufficient condition for convexity.

[14] Compare also Blackwell-Girshick [4]. While that book is restricted to finite sets of messages and of events, earlier work of Blackwell [2, 3] extends also to cases when the set of messages are continuous. Accordingly our conditions (B), (W), (φ), all equivalent to (P), are generalized into ($\tilde{\text{B}}$), ($\tilde{\text{W}}$), ($\tilde{\varphi}$), say. Blackwell [3] proved that ($\tilde{\text{B}}$)⇒ ($\tilde{\text{W}}$) and also ($\tilde{\text{B}}$)⇒ (φ); compare also DeGroot [6]. We do not know whether, conversely, corresponding to our theorems for finite information systems, one also has ($\tilde{\text{W}}$)⇒ ($\tilde{\text{B}}$) and ($\tilde{\varphi}$)⇒ ($\tilde{\text{B}}$).

[15] A definition of more informativeness by condition (W) was originally proposed by Bohnenblust, Shapley and Scherman [5].

[16] Compare $G_Y(t)$ and $F_Y(t)$ with $F_P(t)$ and $C_P(t)$ in Blackwell-Girschick (4, (theorem 12.4.1)]. If $r_1 = r_2 = 1/2$, then our $G_Y(t)$, $F_Y(t)$ become equal to Blackwell-Girshick's $F_P(t)$, $C_P(t)$ respectively.

[17] We shall show that Theorem 14.1 can be proved by almost the same device as given by Blackwell-Girshick [4] in their proof of their Theorem 12.4.1. When $m = 2$, condition (φ) is equivalent to the following condition: For any convex function φ on [0, 1],

$$\sum_{j=1}^{n} q_j \varphi(\pi_{1i}) \geqq \sum_{k=1}^{n'} q_k \varphi(\pi'_{ik}) .$$

Defining a function $f_t(u)$ on [0, 1] for each t, $0 \leqq t \leqq 1$, by.

$$f_t(u) = \begin{cases} t - u, & \text{for } 0 \leqq u \leqq t \\ 0, & \text{for } t \leqq u \leqq 1 , \end{cases}$$

any (continuous) convex function φ on [0, 1] can be uniformly approximated by a function of the form

$$g(u) = \sum_s c_s f_{t_s}(u) + au + b ,$$

where $c_s \geqq 0$. Now without loss of generality, we assume that

$$\pi_{11} < \pi_{12} < \cdots < \pi_{in} \quad \text{and} \quad \pi'_{11} < \pi'_{12} < \cdots < \pi'_{1n'} .$$

Then it is clear that we have

$$F_Y(t) = \sum_{j=1}^{n} q_j f_t(\pi_{1j}) , \qquad F_{Y'}(t) = \sum_{k=1}^{n'} g'_k f_t(\pi'_{1k}) .$$

Then

$$\sum_j q_j g(\pi_{1j}) = \sum_s c_s F_Y(t_s) + ar_1 + b ,$$

$$\sum_k q'_k g(\pi'_{1k}) = \sum_s c_s F_{Y'}(t_s) + ar_1 + b ,$$

since

$$\Sigma q_j \pi_{1j} = \Sigma q_k \pi'_{1k} = r\,.$$

Therefore condition (φ) is equivalent to condition (F), since $c_s \geqq 0$.

BIBLIOGRAPHY

[1] Abramson, Norman, *Information Theory and Coding*, McGraw-Hill, New York, 1963.

[2] Blackwell, David, 'Comparison of Experiments', in J. Neyman (ed.), *Proceedings of the Second Berkeley Symposium on Mathematical Statistics and Probability*, University of California Press, Berkeley, 1951, pp. 93–102.

[3] Blackwell, David, 'Equivalent Comparisons of Experiments', *Annals of Mathematical Statistics* **24** (June, 1953), 265–73.

[4] Blackwell, David, and Girshick, M. A., *Theory of Games and Statistical Decisions*, John Wiley and Sons, New York, 1954.

[5] Bohnenblust, H. F., Shapley, L. S., and Sherman, S., 'Reconnaissance in Game Theory', Research Memorandum RM-208, The RAND Corporation, 1949.

[6] DeGroot, M. H., 'Uncertainty, Information and Sequential Experiments', *Annals of Mathematical Statistics* **33** (1962), 404–419.

[7] Feinstein, Amiel, *Foundations of Information Theory*, McGraw-Hill, New York, 1958.

[8] Halmos, Paul R., *Measure Theory*, Van Nostrand, Princeton, N.J., 1950.

[9] Karlin, Samuel, *Mathematical Methods and Theory in Games, Programming, and Economics*, Vol. II, Addison-Wesley, Reading, Mass., 1959.

[10] Marschak, Jacob, 'Remarks on the Economics of Information', *Selected Essays*, 23.

[11] Marschak, Jacob, 'The Payoff-Relevant Description of States and Acts', *Selected Essays*, 13.

[12] Marschak, Jacob, and Radner, R., *Economic Theory of Teams*, Chapter II, Yale University Press, 1972.

[13] McGuire, C. B., 'Comparisons of Information Systems', Cowles Foundation Discussion Paper No. 71 (1959), revised in: *Decision and Organization* (ed. by C. B. McGuire and R. Radner), Chapter 5, North-Holland, 1972.

[14] Miyasawa, Koichi, 'Information Structures in Stochastic Programming', *Management Science* **14** (January, 1968), 215–291.

[15] Raiffa, Howard and Schlaifer, R., *Applied Statistical Decision Theory*, Harvard University Press, Cambridge, Mass. 1961.

[16] Savage, Leonard J., *The Foundations of Statistics*, John Wiley and Sons, New York 1954.

30

ECONOMICS OF INQUIRING, COMMUNICATING, DECIDING*

(1968)

We hear much of today's 'informational revolution'. We are also told of the rapid growth of the 'knowledge industry'. Informational revolution is exemplified by TV pictures of the moon surface and also by robotized stock market transactions and, hopefully, by computerized professors. Fritz Machlup defined the knowledge industry to include education and research as well as publishing and broadcasting. He estimated its share in the gross national product of 1958 at 23 percent to 29 percent, and its growth rate at about 10 percent, or twice that of the GNP. Projecting to the present, the share of the knowledge industry would then appear to straddle the 40 percent mark!

There is a suspicious overlap between these activities and those which Adam Smith and Karl Marx called 'unproductive' and which include the work of kings and professors, none of whom add to the vendible and visible stocks of the nation. To be sure, recent analysis – for example, by T. W. Schultz and C. C. v. Weizsaecker – found it both convenient and feasible to define human capital and thus to consider education as investment. But the notable fact remains that professors and kings or the modern equivalent of kings – managers, both public and private – are strongly involved in those trends: informational revolution and growing knowledge industry.

Professors and managers, but also computers and TV sets, are involved in still another trend relevant to my talk. A growing proportion of both manhours and machine-hours is not employed for using large amounts of energy (muscular or otherwise) to transform or transport matter. Instead, so-called 'brains' (human or otherwise) are employed to manipulate symbols. A sequence or network of such symbol manipulators uses up a minute amount of energy to eventually release, trigger-like, large amounts of energy through the more brutal medium of generators, muscles, and machine tools. In a modern assembly or disassembly plant (sawmill, meat packing), a growing majority of people, wearing white collars, or blue denims as well, do the brain work of inspecting, deciding, reporting

– shunting, pushing buttons – and not the muscular work of shaping or carrying material masses; and a growing proportion of machines, called control mechanisms, are also busy with inspecting, reporting, deciding, and not with transforming or transporting matter and energy.

My topic is the economics of what I shall call the services of inquiring, communicating, deciding. Data are gathered. They are communicated to the decision-maker. He, on the basis of the message received, decides upon the action to be taken. A higher-order decision must have been made previously. Someone representing the interests of the economic unit considered – its head, leader, organizer – must have chosen a particular combination of these three services from all those available in their respective markets. The maker of this higher-order decision (the 'meta-decider', sometimes called 'the organizer') may happen to be the same person who will decide upon acting. Or more generally, the organizer will hire the services of the decision-maker – who, in appropriate cases, may be just a robot.

I might also call my topic the economics of the instruments, or devices, human or otherwise, for inquiring, communicating, and deciding. For it is not relevant, for my purposes, to distinguish between purchased instruments and hired services, provided the length of the hire contract is specified. In any case, I shall be concerned with symbol manipulators, human or otherwise, rather than with processors or transporters of matter or energy.

Here is what I plan to do. I shall present, in turn, from the user's point of view, the successive links in the sequence of symbol-manipulating services: inquiry, or data gathering; communication of messages; and deciding upon actions on the basis of messages received. It will turn out, in fact, that the link called 'communication' must be broken into two distinct services: on the one hand, the service of 'encoding and decoding' which, at the present state of arts and in the most numerous and socially most important cases, is best supplied by men; and on the other hand, the service of 'transmission' which is best supplied by inanimate equipment. As to the *supply* conditions of services of inquiry, or data production, and of decision making, I shall be able to submit nothing but crude illustrations, I am afraid. As to the *demand* side, economists will not be surprised that to make an economical – that is, optimal, efficient – choice the user must choose those links, or components, simultaneously (just as a manufacturer cannot choose between rail and road as means of bringing him fuel without making up his mind, at the same time, whether the fuel should be coal or oil). Hence, the jointness of demand for services of inquiry, communication, and decision.

To be sure, current engineering science finds it convenient to isolate a pure theory of communication – a theory of efficient coding and transmission alone, essentially created by Claude Shannon and streamlined by Jack Wolfowitz. At the other extreme, statistical decision theory culminating in the work of David Blackwell leaves out the communication component and only analyzes, from the point of view of a perfect decision-maker, the optimal choice of inquiry, or data producing, services, also called 'experiments'. I shall later state the implicit tacit assumptions made in each case. If they are not satisfied, the user guided by those subtheories will have suboptimized. This is not to say that we ought not to break up a complex problem into subproblems, assuming them independent as a provisional first approximation. Given our human limitations, this may even be the optimal research strategy. It just happens that the economist is aware of interdependencies: he calls them complementarity and substitutability of goods. He is also traditionally permitted – as is the philosopher – to attack complexities with ridiculously simple examples in order to get directly to the general and fundamental.

Let me, then, go ahead with a simple example. I must decide this Thursday night whether to fly West next Saturday morning. Visibility and winds along the airplane's route the day after tomorrow will determine whether, if I do fly, I shall arrive in time for an important appointment or shall be killed in a crash. If I don't fly, I miss the appointment. But I cannot know what the weather will be. Instead, I may look tonight at the hotel barometer; or I may rely on the radio reports of other, more numerous and accurate barometer readings; or I may rely on the *Farmer's Almanac*. If the cost of these various services were equal, I would choose the one which gives data most closely reflecting (in some sense) the actual event I am interested in: the weather on Saturday. But perfection is costly, and I shall choose a service that is known not to mislead too grossly or too frequently, yet will be relatively cheap.

Take another example. A store's profit will be influenced by its inventory policy, given the actual future demand for its merchandise. Lacking the knowledge of this demand, the firm will have to choose between various services of market forecasters differing in precision and accuracy but also in the fees charged.

So much about services that inquire; i.e., produce data. These data are not identical with, yet do reflect in some sense the events that are relevant to, the result of a decision. Now, the decision-maker may or may not be able to obtain such data directly. Another service called 'communication' will bring to him, not those data, but a message, possibly delayed or distorted, about those data. He must decide on the basis of such a message, which is now twice removed, in a sense, from the actual, result-relevant event: weather on Saturday, demand next month, and so on.

The inventory example illustrates also the nature of decision services. Inventory policy is a rule stating whether and how much to reorder when the stock at hand is at a given level and you have some – usually imperfect – knowledge related to the prospective demand of your customers. One policy is similar to the one you use when you decide whether to refill your car's oil tank up to a certain upper level (this you will do whenever oil is below a certain lower level) or to leave it alone. Except that in the inventory case the two critical levels themselves are not fixed but should depend on what the store has learned – however imperfectly – about future demand; that is, on the message it has received about the data produced by a market forecast. Such a decision rule or strategy – a rule of how to respond to the message – may require the sophisticated services of a specialist or a computer. Contrast with this a simple routine rule: to refill the inventory every Monday to a constant level. This can be handled by an unskilled clerk or a cheap robot. The more sophisticated, flexible, nonroutine rule would be preferable if it were not for its higher cost.

To state more precisely the problem facing the user of the data producing, communication, and decision services, it is convenient to represent each service as a transformer of inputs into outputs. (Transformer, transformation, and function mean essentially the same thing.) A data producing service such as a barometer is a transformer whose input is the result-relevant event (weather next Saturday) and whose output is an observed value, a datum (the barometer reading tonight). We say that the data service is both precise and reliable if to each result-relevant event corresponds one observation or datum, and conversely.

But this perfection is almost never attained. Generally, each event may be reflected in various alternative observed values, with some alternatives more likely than others. We have here the case of an 'unreliable' (probabilistic, stochastic, noisy) transformer. For example, suppose that if Saturday's weather is going to be good, the chance that the barometer shows high pressure tonight is 80 percent. We say that the likelihood of the observation 'high pressure', given the event 'good weather', is 80 percent. Suppose the likelihood of low pressure if the weather is going to be dangerous is also 80 percent. Suppose that on a second barometer both these likelihoods are lower: 60 percent and 60 percent, say. If you have access to both barometers at the same cost or effort, you will prefer to be guided by the first one. For, in an obvious sense it is more reliable (more informative, in Blackwell's terminology). Indeed, in the case of perfect reliability the two likelihoods would be 100 percent and 100 per-

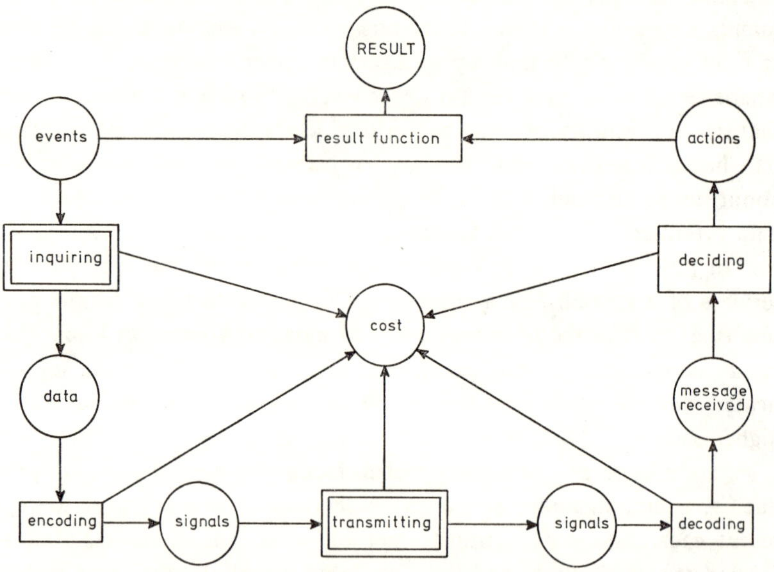

○ Circles = variables (generally random).

□ Boxes = transformers (noisy if double-framed). User maximizes average result minus cost (assuming additive utilities).

Note: In statistical theory, the lower row encoding→…→ decoding is omitted so that messages received = data. In communication theory, data = events; actions = = messages received; and result = 'bad' or 'good' according as message received is or is not identical with datum.

cent; and clearly our first barometer (with 80 percent, 80 percent) comes closer to this perfection than the second (with 60 percent, 60 percent). In fact, the second comes closer than the first to the other extreme: likelihoods 50 percent, 50 percent, in which case the barometer would be useless.

Or consider a consumer survey conducted by a government agency. The success of the government decision to undertake one or another administrative action depends on the attitudes of all consumers. But only a certain number are sampled. The larger the sample the more reliable is the estimate of people's attitude. But also the more expensive. It is not different with research into the laws of physics or biology. What I called 'result-relevant events' the statisticians call 'hypotheses'. The data producing service (e.g., a sampling) they call 'experiment', and the data are called 'observations'.

Unfortunately, it is not always possible to compare two data producing services on the basis of the likelihoods only. How does our first barometer, with the 80 percent likelihood of high pressure given good weather, and 80 percent likelihood of low pressure given dangerous weather compare with the following one: if the weather is going to be good, the barometer will show high pressure for sure, i.e., with likelihood 100 percent; but given dangerous weather, it will show high or low pressure, not with 80:20 but with 50:50 chances. Thus, whenever the new barometer shows low pressure, it gives you absolute certainty that the weather cannot be good. But when it shows high pressure you are left guessing, and you might be better off with the original barometer. Which barometer should guide you?

Here I must remind you that, just as economists are Keynesians or non-Keynesians, the statisticians are Bayesians or non-Bayesians. The Bayesians, having given serious thought to our problem, tell me to consult two further items: (1) the approximate, so-called 'prior', probabilities that I would assign to dangerous versus good weather for next Saturday – in the absence of any barometer, e.g., on the basis of my previous experience with December weather; (2) the utilities that I assign to various results of my actions and whose actuarial value I would like to be as high as possible. In our case, the best result is: surviving and making the appointment. The second best is: surviving but missing the appointment. The worst is death. What matters is the ratio of the disadvantage of missing the appointment (but staying alive) to the disadvantage of death. Now, unless a barometer is useless, I would fly if it shows high pressure and not fly otherwise (or vice versa). The probabilities of these pressure readings depend on my prior probability of the two states of weather and on the likelihoods characterizing each of the two barometers. Therefore, those pressures will be read on the two barometers with different probabilities. Hence the average utility of the results of actions dictated by each barometer and weighted by the probabilities of its readings will differ as between the two barometer. I prefer the one whose dictation will yield, on the average, the higher utility.

Suppose, then, the prior probability of bad (i.e., deadly dangerous) weather is, in my judgment, about 10 percent. Should I use the 'old' barometer (whose likelihoods are 80 percent and 80 percent) or the 'new' barometer (whose likelihoods are 100 percent and 50 percent), still assuming that the costs are equal. It turns out that I should stick to the old barometer as long as I judge the disadvantage of missing the appointment (while staying alive) to be less than one-seventh of the disadvantage of death. This is surely my case!

I believe this business of assigning prior probabilities to events and of utilities to results is a headache familiar to cost-benefit analysts, certainly present in this very room! It surely requires some soul-searching to appraise and reappraise the subjective probabilities ('beliefs') and utilities ('goals', 'values', 'tastes') of your government agency. You will presumably try out various plausible assumptions and see whether your boss likes the decisions derived from them; and whether under repeated trials of this kind his choices reveal a consistency of his beliefs and of his tastes. Or perhaps such trials will gradually train him toward consistency – toward learning what he wants and believes.

So far, we have seen how the consistent user should choose between available inquiry services when their costs are equal. This has required, for some though not all pairs of such services, to take account of the user's utilities and prior probabilities in order to compute the average utility attainable on the basis of an inquiry. If costs are not equal, the knowledge of prior probabilities and utilities becomes necessary in all cases. For simplicity, a tacit assumption is made. One assumes, in terms of our example, that it is possible to represent the utility of, say, "having made the appointment and having my wealth diminished by the dollar cost of a particular inquiry" as a sum of two utilities. In other words, utility is assumed to be additive and to be commensurable with dollars. Under this assumption, one may call the average utility of results of actions guided by an inquiry simply its dollar value to the user, his demand price. He compares it with the dollar cost, which is the supply price. The additivity assumption is implicitly made by statisticians. They assume in effect that the disutility of a result of action based on a sampling survey is measured by the size of the error of an estimate, and then vaguely compare its average with the dollar cost of the sampling survey. Engineers indulge in similar practices, as we shall see. Not so the economists. Sophisticated in matters of substitution, income elasticity, and risk aversion – all of which question the assumption of additive utility – they raise a warning finger. They do so at least when they talk theory and are not themselves engaged in the practical pursuits variously called 'management science', 'operations research', 'system analysis', 'cost-benefit analysis'.

My barometer case – with just two alternative events, two possible observations, and two actions – is probably the simplest nontrivial problem in statistical decision theory. As I said before, this theory neglects the communication link. Result-relevant events, each having some prior probability, are transformed into data by a transformer called an 'inquiry', or an 'experiment' (like a barometer, or a sampling survey). Data flow directly into the transformer called 'decision-maker', who applies a decision rule (e.g., 'fly if barometric pressure high') and puts out actions. Finally, events and decisions are joint inputs of a transformer which may be called 'result function': its output is a result. Assuming additive utility, a dollar amount can be attached to each result. And the probability of each result is determined by the prior probability of each event, by the array (characteristic of the data producing service) of the likelihoods of the data, given each event, and by the decision rule (characteristic of the given decision service) transforming data into actions. The probabilities of the results thus derived serve as weights to obtain the average of their utilities. This average may be called the 'gross value', to a given user, of the given pair of data producing and decision-making services. It is the maximum demand price offered by their user. Their combined cost asked by the suppliers is the minimum supply price. The difference may be called 'the net combined value of these two services to the user'. He will choose the combination with highest net value.

This net value depends, then, on the one hand, on the choice of services made by their user. On the other hand, it depends on conditions outside of his control: viz., his utilities and prior probabilities and the costs of available services. His problem is to maximize the net value of the data producing and decision-making services, given those noncontrolled conditions.

Those familiar with what has been called 'information theory' in the last two decades will have noticed that, so far, we have not used the concept of amount of information, measured in units called 'bits'. My uncertainty about a set of alternative events is the same as the amount of information that I would receive if that uncertainty were completely removed; that is, if I would know exactly which particular event does happen. Roughly speaking, this uncertainty is measured by the smallest average number of successive yes-and-no answers needed to completely remove uncertainty. This number depends roughly on the prior probabilities of events. Suppose, for example, that the following four events have equal probabilities (one-quarter each): the bride at the neighborhood church next Saturday will or won't wear a mini-dress, and her dress will or won't be white. To learn the color of the dress I need one yes-or-no question; so my uncertainty about color measures one bit. For the same reason, my uncertainty about both color and style is two bits since I need two yes-and-no answers to answer it. Thus the uncertainty, measured in bits, about those two mutually independent sets of events is the sum $(1+1=2)$ of the uncertainties about each of them. The number of bits is, in this sense, additive: a property that we require of every genuine measure, such as that of time, distance, volume, energy, dollar income, and dollar wealth.

If the four bridal events were not equally probable – for example, if the odds for a maxi-dress were not 1:1 but 9:1 (while a dress of each style were still as likely as not to be white) – the average necessary number of yes-and-no questions and thus the number of information bits would be smaller in the long run, i.e., over a long sequence of such events: for we can then profitably identify the more probable sequences (i.e., those mostly consisting of maxi-dresses) by asking a few questions only – as any skilled player of the '20 questions game' knows. As before, the count of bits agrees remarkably with the intuitive use of the English word uncertainty: for when the odds are 9:1 I am almost certain, and with odds 1:1, I am fully ignorant, am I not?

Now suppose you have the choice between learning both the style and the color of the bride's dress and learning, with equal speed and for the same fee, the future price of your stocks. Suppose the price is as likely to rise as to fall. Depending on your selling or purchasing now, you may lose or double your fortune. A service that will tell you correctly whether the stock price will rise or fall conveys only one bit of information; whereas the service telling you correctly both the style and the color of the dress provides two bits. Yet you will prefer to learn about the stocks, not about the dress. There is, thus, no relation between the number of bits conveyed and the gross value of the data producing service. Nor does there seem to be a relation between the number of bits and the cost of a data producing service. For example, the cost of a sampling survey depends on its size, and this is not clearly related to the number of bits involved.

On the other hand, the number of yes-and-no symbols involved is clearly relevant to the performance and the cost of the transmission service regardless of whether these symbols refer to the length of the bridal skirt or to the trend of prices of your stock. To the economist, the contrast between production and transmission of data is strikingly analogous to the contrast between production and transportation of goods. A gallon of whiskey is more valuable than a gallon of gasoline: their costs to the producer and their values to the buyer are quite different. Yet to transport one gallon over one mile costs about the same for any liquid.

When, some twenty years ago, those elusive things labeled by the vague English words 'uncertainty' and its negative, 'information', were harnessed, subjected to genuine measurements (as was energy some hundred years ago, and mass and force much earlier), it was easy to understand the enthusiasm of people in elusive fields such as psychology. But also, to some extent, in statistics and in mathematics, where it was partly due to deep and beautiful theorems developed in this context. It is remarkable that C. Shannon who first proposed these theorems clearly limited their application to communications.

Statistical decision theory deals only with the choice of experiments and of decision rules; that is, with the choice of data producing and of deciding services. It omits the lower row of the chart reproduced earlier: encoding of data into signals, transmitting signals through a 'communication channel', and decoding them back into messages that the decider would understand. In other words, for the statistician the decision is taken on the basis of a message which is simply the same thing as the data produced by the inquiry or experiment.

Not so with the communication engineer. His responsibility is to construct channels for the fast and reliable transmission of signals. (It all started in the telephone industry!) He is therefore also interested in devising appropriate codes which translate ordinary English into signals and signals back into English. But, to concentrate his mind on pure communication economics he makes, in effect, the following simplifying assumptions: First, events and data are identical, for he is not interested in the imperfections of the data producing service. Second, deciding is the same thing as decoding; so that action is simply the same thing as the message received. Third, as we have observed for the case of non-equiprobable events (which is, of course the usual case), the count of bits presupposes, in general, long sequences of events; and, as we shall see, such long sequences are also essential to make the crucial concept of 'channel capacity' useful. Fourth, in most though not all[1] of their work, communication engineers assume an extremely simple result function. There are only two results: bad (say, minus one), when the decoded, received message is not identical with the datum sent; good (say, zero), when the two are identical. That is, all errors are equally important, have the same disutility, whether an inch is taken for a mile or merely a colon is taken for a semicolon. Finally, utility is assumed to be additive; i.e., it is conceived as the sum of certain measurable advantages and disadvantages, appropriately converted into dollars. We have seen that statisticians make the same assumption when they compare the sampling error with the dollar cost of the sample. The economist who detects and warns against this assumption is somewhat of a purist. The assumption is surely convenient for practical purposes and its removal is perhaps not that urgent.

Indeed this last assumption permits the engineer to ask the following economic question on behalf of the user of transmission channels and of coding services. Given the dollar costs of available channels, what is the best combination of the following evils: the probability of error (any error); the cost of the channel; the average time delay, which depends both on the length of signal sequences transmitted at a time and on the size of the code's vocabulary. That is, disutility is thought of, in effect, as a sum of dollars that buy a given channel; plus the dollar-equivalent of an error (any error); plus the dollar-equivalent, to a given user, of each time delay arising in the coding and transmission of a given datum. The user's problem is to choose that combination of channel and code which will minimize the sum of the averages of these amounts, weighted by appropriate probabilities. What do these probabilities depend on? On the uncertainty about data (=events); on the likelihood array characterizing the channel's reliability (the array of conditional probabilities of output symbols given an input symbol); and on the coding and decoding procedures.

Clearly, an appropriately redundant code can almost overcome the lack of reliability of the channel; that is, it can almost eliminate the occurrence of errors. For example, the encoder just lets every 'yes' or 'no' to be repeated many times, and the decoder takes 'no' for the answer if he has received more 'no''s than 'yes''s. 'Don't! – repeat, don't! – repeat, don't shoot!' If I have heard two don'ts and only one do, I shan't shoot. However, we may need great redundancy of the code if the channel is very unreliable; and this will cause long delays if the channel is slow. But a channel that is fast and reliable is expensive.

If the user can afford to wait for a long sequence of data to flow in before they are encoded, the problem of choosing between channels is simplified, for their variety is reduced as follows. Instead of a whole array of likelihoods (of channel output symbols, given each input symbol) it becomes sufficient to use a single reliability measure (in bits per input symbol) which, multiplied by the channel's speed of transmission (in input symbols per time unit), gives the channel's 'capacity', in bits per time unit.[2] Provided this capacity is larger than the number of bits per time unit that characterizes the uncertainty and speed of the flow of data, it has been shown that the user can achieve any desired probability of errors, however small, by using an appropriate, though redundant, code. Assuming that such codes have indeed been constructed (quite a difficult problem, solved only to a small part), it would be for the user to weigh against each other the disadvantages of errors, of time delays and of the high costs of high-capacity channels.

To avoid errors in our mutual understanding, let me be redundant, mindful of my low transmitting capacity and of your limited memory. I said a short time ago that engineers have isolated the pure communication problem by not concerning themselves with the services that produce data and that decide on acting; and also by usually refusing to distinguish between important and unimportant errors. I also pleaded, a longer time ago, on behalf of economists who emphasize that the demand for all services, all the transformers on my chart, is a joint one. Indeed, the user can improve the reliability of messages on which decisions are based by improving the communication service, but also by improving the data producing service which he is free to choose. Similarly, the user (the 'meta-decider') is free to choose the deciding service; for example, he may prefer not to burden the unskilled but inexpensive decider with messages written in a vocabulary that is too rich and fine. Moreover, depending on the user's result function, he may fear some errors of communication but be indifferent to others. He may be indifferent to the music of the voice at the other end of the telephone; so he does not really need a high-fidelity telephone.

On the other hand, statisticians have isolated their problem, also essentially an economic one, by omitting the communication components. As I said before, this may be a good research strategy. I am told that in the early space vehicles rectangular pieces of equipment were used although the vehicles had circular cross-section. That is, the problem of building a good battery (say) was solved separately from, not jointly with, the problem of building a fast vehicle. Our problem-solving (decision-making) capacity is limited to only a few good solutions per manhour. To take up all problems at once is desirable but not cheap and perhaps not feasible. However, as time goes on the joint approach should be tried. Hence this economist's appeal to both statisticians and engineers.

I have just said that the limitation of the research capacity of all of us explains and possibly justifies the fact that engineers and statisticians have broken up the economics of symbol manipulation into separate sections, neglecting the essential complementarity of the several services from the point of view of the demand by the user.

However, this separation seems to be partly justified also by the economics of the services themselves; viz., by the supply side. I mean in particular the conditions for the production, and therefore for the supply, of inanimate transmission channels, such as telephones, the broadcasting apparatus, perhaps even the products of the old-fashioned printing press.

To be sure, you may not be anxious to learn about the bridal dress and be very much interested in the stock market. Yet your morning newspaper will bring you both a society page (which you will throw away) and a stock market page. Any page costs as much to print as any other page. The cost depends on the number of symbols on the page, and this corresponds to the number of bits transmitted by the printed messages. And the cost per bit turns out to be smaller if every subscriber receives both the social page and the stock market report and the sports page and the political news, regardless of his special tastes. Similarly, I am forced to subscribe to a high-fidelity telephone service although I am not interested in the music of the other person's voice. I suppose this is due to the economies of mass production. It is cheaper to produce instruments that will minimize the probability of transmission error – any error, however unimportant to me personally – than to custom-make instruments which would suit people's individual preferences. Remember that, in this country at least, with its large total demand for clothing and for food, consumers do find it advantageous to buy ready-made suits and standardized groceries. To go to a Bond Street tailor or to buy fancy foods is slightly more satisfactory but so much more expensive!

The problem is familiar to operations researchers as that of optimal assortment. It is also known to social and economic statisticians, editors of census volumes, and makers of production indices. They call it 'optimal aggregation'. What indeed is the most economical way to break down a collection of items into groups, each to be treated as if it were homogeneous, when every detail suppressed involves some sacrifice, yet also saves cost?

Thus, it is just possible that, for the purposes of large markets (but not, I would think, for the purpose of building a particular satellite!) the isolated theory of transmission channels that minimize the probability of error – any error – is exactly what one needs. Yet, to be sure of this, we ought to have at least an approximate idea as to whether the services immediately complementing the transmission, that is, the services of coding, also exhibit advantages of mass production; and that the imperfections of available data producing and decision-making services are indeed negligible as to their economic effects.

Inanimate transmission channels do display the advantages of mass production. This makes it useful, when studying their supply conditions, to apply the pure theory of communication and to derive economically significant results from measuring information in bits. But what about other symbol-manipulating services: inquiry, coding, deciding? What can we say, in particular, about those supplied not by machines but by humans?

Before commenting on this most fascinating question, let us remind ourselves of the principles of the analysis of demand, supply, and the markets, and apply them, in particular, to the markets of symbol-manipulating services.

The demands of individual users are aggregated into the total demands for various data-providing services: total demands for weather forecasters and market prophets; for the output of research laboratories, for services of spies and detectives – given the prices of each of these services. Similarly with the total demands for various communication services – television, telephones, post office, newspapers, but also schools! – given, again, the prices of each. And so also with the demand for deciders – inventory clerks and vice-presidents for finance, and humble robots. Some of these services are substitutes for one another: for example, TV, radio and newspapers; telephone and mail. Some are mutual complements: the demand for weather data and for radio sets boosts each other.

Now, to explain the 'given prices' in the markets and the kind and volume of transactions that actually come about, we need to know also the supply conditions. What does it cost to produce a market survey; to print a mass-circulation paper or a professional periodical; or to run a school? And to rear and train a vice-president or to build an automatic pilot? Again, the supply conditions are interrelated, although perhaps not as closely as the demand conditions. An automatic pilot combines the services of inquiring and of deciding, and it might be more costly to produce these services separately.

At any rate, the supply of a given service or a bundle of services – at given prices! – will depend on the costs of producing various kinds and amounts of them. Under competition the price will, then, equate demand and supply.

Is this not classroom economics? Yes indeed. But it should include the more advanced parts of it which allow for oligopoly, uncertainty, and other such things, mildly called 'imperfections'. Particularly important are the facts of indivisibility, or more precisely, the lack of homogeneity, of standardization of many of the symbol manipulators. There exist almost unique, irreplaceable research workers, teachers, administrators; just as there exist unique choice locations for plants and harbors. The problem of unique or imperfectly standardized goods is not peculiar to the economics of inquiring, communicating, and deciding. But it has been indeed neglected in the textbooks.

Let us return to the comparison of services supplied by men and by machines. The subject has seriously worried the most creatively imaginative pessimists of science fiction – from Karel Čapek to Ray Bradbury. It has also fascinated, and has led to some serious work of, psychologists and computer scientists. The results of this work, however tentative, are of great interest to us economists.

To begin with, humans are very poor transmission channels. "Indeed," says George Miller, a leading psycholinguist, "it is an act of charity to call a man a channel at all. Compared to telephone or television channels, man is better characterized as a bottleneck. Under optimal conditions it is possible for a skilled typist or piano player to transmit 25 bits per second.... We shall have to regard 25 bits per second as near the upper limit." More usually, the transmission capacity of an average person in our culture is only 10 bits or less, that is, we are unable to identify a stimulus without error when the stimulus is selected from more than 2^{10}, i.e., about a thousand equiprobable alternatives (that is, when the identification logically requires at least ten yes-or-no questions). As to the so-called 'short memory', an important accessory of many transmission instruments, George Miller says that "no self-respecting photographic plate would even bother to sneer at us."

But what about the other symbol-manipulating services? Take coding. The lady who is typing the almost illegible manuscript of this lecture has an uncanny gift of recognizing the intended meaning of letters and words. I think she does this mostly by looking at the context of a whole sentence, or even of the whole paper itself. This we can interpret either by saying that she has the ability of encoding almost without errors the data presented in longhand into the symbols of the typewriter alphabet; or that she decodes the longhand symbols given to her, into messages, and these into actions; viz., into pressing the keys, mostly in such a way that no error occurs. As you know, the computer industry has just begun to construct machines that may one day match the human ability to recognize simple visual patterns such as hand-written individual letters (not whole sentences!). But some people believe it will take a very long time (generations or centuries, Y. Bar-Hillel thinks) until a machine can conduct 'intelligent conversation' with a man or with another machine. The key words are 'heuristic' and 'intuition'. They are as vague as 'pattern recognition', 'Gestalt', and 'context', and all these words are perhaps intended to have the same meaning. It is remarkable, in fact, in this very context, that you and I vaguely understand each other as to what the word 'context' is intended to mean. We understand each other not letter by letter, not even word by word, but by grouping symbols into large chunks – letters (or rather, phonemes) into words, and words into sentences, and even into larger entities, each including all sentences with the same so-called 'meaning'. The chunks forming the vocabulary of a human coder or decoder are of course much less numerous than the ensemble of all possible combinations of a given number of letters, say. The use of chunks diminishes therefore the flow of signals through the channel; it is more efficient, more economical. Consider the three letters C, O, W. They can be combined in six possible ways. But only one of the six combinations occurs in your vocabulary: cow. And, remarkably, it invokes not just the few properties listed by taxonomists who define a cow, but a whole image of shapes and sounds and colors and the tail waving the flies away. A most efficient, economical code – the living human language!

Most important, when you, a man, talk to a fellow human you adjust your code to the receptor, and keep readjusting it, sensitive to his feedback responses. Is this not what characterizes a good teacher? James Boswell, young and smug, wrote in his diary:

> Health, youth, and gold sufficient I possess;
> Where one has more, five hundred sure have less.

He could as well have said: my wealth is at the uppermost $\frac{1}{5}$ percentile. This would be economical if you would address income statisticians: you would utilize a 'subroutine' that has been educated into them! But when you address other people, better recite a poem.

Even the talking to computers is better done by men, at least today. The encoding, or programming, of a difficult problem for a computer is said to be an art, not a science. People who say this probably mean precisely this: the activity of programming cannot be delegated by men to machines, at least not in serious cases and not in the present state of technology. Hence the very large proportion (one-half, I understand) that the human activity of programming contributes to the value added by computing organizations.

To turn from coding to inquiring services. A biochemist (J. Lederberg) and a computer scientist (E. Feigenbaum) have told a computer how to generate the graphs of all imaginable organic compounds of a certain class, and also how to match them with certain empirically observed spectra. This was essentially a job of mathematical routine. But now comes the heuristics! The biochemist had accumulated enough experience and a flair to eliminate as unrealistic all but a few patterns from the thousands that the computer had printed. Yet the human being, a Nobel laureate, was not able to articulate his flair, although he did learn in this direction from the cooperation with the computer. Given the abilities and the technologies, there is some optimal way of allocating the tasks between men and machines – as economists have known long ago. And we must not be too hard on the computer: its hardware is certainly much less complex than the man's genetic endowment, and the computer's short babyhood is not rich in experience.

Finally, the service of decision making or problem solving. How to allocate tasks of this nature among executives and machines? A delicate problem! It involves all echelons of a corporation, up to, but of course not including, the president, who cannot fire himself. I had better skirt this subject!

But let me remind you of the distinction I have made earlier, between decision making and the higher-order activity of choosing who or what should provide a given service of decision making or of inquiring or of coding or transmitting. The man in charge was called the 'leader' or 'organizer'. It is his judgment of prior probabilities and utilities, his 'beliefs' and his 'tastes' (or 'values', in other words), that are used among the 'givens' of the organizer's problem. He cannot delegate them, either to men or machines.

His problem may be, in fact, much, much larger than my chart suggests at first glance. The economic problem of organization is that of allocating numerous kinds of tasks, symbol manipulating as well as physical, to numerous transformers, arranged in a complex yet efficient network. And further complications, of a different kind, arise when a single organizer is replaced by several. Their beliefs and utilities are not the same. They engage in a nonconstant sum game. The economist's problem is then shifted from the search for optimality to the search for stability: he tries to explain, as does the biologist or anthropologist, why certain arrangements, certain allocations of tasks and incentives (rewards) have a greater chance to survive over a given period than other arrangements, and under what conditions.

The criterion of survival, viability, stability guides the social scientist who describes, and tries to explain, the existing institutions. Yet not everything that is stable is desirable. Some wicked dictatorships have been quite stable. Along with the stability criterion, the economist uses a weak collective optimality criterion, a modest common denominator on which people might agree in spite of their divergent utilities and beliefs: an arrangement of tasks and incentives is optimal in this modest sense if there is no feasible arrangement that would be better or at least not worse for all members of the organization.

What, then, if we consider the whole society as an organization? How should incentives and tasks be allocated in a way that is stable or is collectively optimal, or, if possible, both? Further, some of us cannot help but smuggle in our own values, in particular a high valuation of liberty and equity. I suppose 'public policy', 'public good', in our tradition, mean somehow to reconcile the criteria of stability and of collective optimality with those of liberty and equity. Though the economic theorist prefers to hide behind the technical term 'welfare economics', he means not just Secretary Gardner's Department of Health, Education and Welfare, but much more, the whole public policy. Nor is our special concern only education, even if taken in the broad sense of the communication of what my chart calls 'data', to the whole or some parts of the public. For research, inquiry has been also our concern here. Public policy problems in the field of symbol manipulation are crudely exemplified by questions such as, "When, if at all, should the government subsidize or protect research and teaching and the dissemination of news?"

As far as I know, welfare economics of symbol manipulation is at its beginning. Special problems, such as the theory of patents and of public versus private broadcasting and, most importantly, of the economics of education, have been studied and the names of Silberston, Coase, Gary Becker come to mind.

On the more abstract level, a basic distinction exists between the information about external facts and the information conveyed to a member of society about the doings of others. A preliminary analysis of economic policy of information about external facts has been made by my colleague Hirshleifer. If correct, his conclusions on teaching and research are quite relevant to the California battle of tuition fees, although Hirshleifer's analysis had to be based on some extreme, simplifying assumptions. To analyze the economics of information of people about other people is even harder. Game theorists have provided some building blocks. Ozga has worked on 'imperfect markets through lack of knowledge' and Stigler on the information in the labor market. It is just one year ago that Leijonhufvud told this Association that Keynesian unemployment may be mostly due to lack of information. We know very little about the technology of such information; for example, about the optimal language. Indeed, many believe that the run on gold is dammed, not by verbal announcements in English or even in French, but by actually selling gold to all comers. And Radner has penetratingly pointed to the setup cost of information which makes for increasing returns to scale and makes it difficult to apply the classical theory of free markets, which reconciles optimality and stability.

All this discussion, mostly by young members of our Association, is recent, very exciting, and, I believe, very important. The informational revolution is upon us, and the manipulation of symbols dominates our lives more and more. I do hope we shall soon understand how to harness and benefit from those trends in our culture.

NOTES

* Supported by a grant from the Ford Foundation to the Graduate School of Business Administration, University of California at Berkeley, and administered through the Center for Research in Management Science. Facilities of the Western Management Science Institute, Univ. of California at Los Angeles (supported by grants or contracts of the National Science and the Ford Foundations and of the Office of Naval Research) were used in preparing the present revised version of the Richard T. Ely lecture, American Economic Association.

1 Not, in particular, in Claude E. Shannon's work on a 'fidelity criterion,' which does correspond to a general result function.

2 For example, two channels with equal transmission speeds and each characterized by the same array of likehoods as, respectively, the old and the new barometer of our previous illustration have approximately equal capacities, in bits per second.

31

ECONOMICS OF INFORMATION SYSTEMS*

(1971)

ABSTRACT. In an information-processing chain, only the initial inputs ('environment') and the terminal outputs ('actions') affect directly the benefit to the user who maximizes its expected excess over cost. All intermediate flows ('symbols') affect directly only costs and delays. Delays affect benefit non-additively, through 'impatience' and, possibly, 'obsolescence.' Traditionally, statistical theory disregards delays and decision costs; and communication theory treats delays as costs. A more complete, unifying approach is proposed, and it is asked whether convexity conditions (e.g., 'decreasing marginal returns') required for competitive market equilibrium are satisfied.

1. INTRODUCTION

1.1. *The Economist's General Information Problem*

Out of several pushbuttons, each of a different color, you select one. A slight push, and massive amounts of energy are released and are transformed in the manner you have prescribed. The button colors which you have perceived and from which you have selected, exemplify signs, symbols. Your 'manipulation of symbols', equally vaguely called 'handling of information' (or somewhat more precisely, 'sorting') has involved little energy but has discharged and directed a large amount. You have done 'brain work'. No economist will deny that a large part of our national product is contributed by symbol manipulation – telephoning orders, discussing in conferences, shuffling papers, or just performing some of the humble tasks required of the inspector, or even an ordinary worker, on the assembly line.[1]

The economist asks, first: what determines the demand and supply of the goods and services used to manipulate symbols. This may help him, second, to understand how social welfare is affected by the manner in which resources are allocated to those goods and services.

A prerequisite is to define concepts and study their interrelations in a way that would prove useful for answering these questions. The economist begins by assuming that those who demand and use, and those who produce and supply, the goods and services considered, make choices that are 'economical' (='rational') in some usefully defined way, and are made under well defined constraints. The constraints may include limitations on the choosers' memories and other mental abilities. The economic theorist leaves the door open to psychologists, sociologists, historians, and to his own 'institutionalist' colleagues in the hope they will help to determine the values of underlying parameters.

1.2. *The User's problem, Viewed by Non-Economists*

Besides its interest to economists, the manipulation of symbols, or information processing, has been the domain of philosophers and linguists; of computer scientists, control theorists and communication engineers; and of statisticians. The latter, following the path of J. Neyman and A. Wald, have become more and more concerned with the economical manner of obtaining 'information', and have discovered much that is useful to the economist. Engineers have proposed a 'measure of information' based on probability relations between classes of arbitrary signs. This arose out of practical, 'economic' needs of the communication industry. My task will be, in part, to see how those results fit into the general economics of symbol-manipulating goods and services, – including, for example, the services of statisticians, and of men who design or handle computers and control mechanisms. – Finally, attempts have been made on the part of linguists and philosophers to apply the engineers' measure of information to the probabilities of sequences of signs in a natural language [40]; or to define a measure of 'semantic information', a 'content measure' – essentially by substituting for an arbitrary class of sign sequences its partition into equivalence classes consisting of sequences with identical 'meaning' [9], [57], [58].

In recent years, the approach *via* economic rationality (i.e., *via* the expected utility to the decision-maker) has begun to penetrate the work of both engineers and philosophers. An important, though still not sufficiently well known step was made by pioneer C. Shannon himself [51] when he removed his earlier tacit assignment[2] of equal penalty for all communication errors. He introduced, instead, a 'fidelity criterion'. This corresponds to the 'benefit', a component of the economists' 'utility' albeit confined as we shall see to the context of communication only and therefore defined on a very special class of actions and events. And Ronald A. Howard [22] writes, in a broader context:

... The early developers stressed that the information measure was dependent only on the probabilistic structure of the communication process. For example, if losing all your assets in the stock market and having whale steak for dinner have the same probability, then the information associated with the occurrence of either event is the same.... No theory that involves just the probabilities of outcomes without considering their consequences could possibly be adequate in describing the importance of uncertainty to the decision maker.'

He concludes his analysis of a neat model with a challenge to his profession (and perhaps to mine as well):

If information value and associated decision theoretic structures do not in the future occupy a large part of the education of engineers, then the engineering profeession will find that its traditional role of managing scientific and economic resources for the benefit of man has been forfeited to another profession.

And philosopher R. Carnap whom we have mentioned as one of the early proponents of a 'semantic' information measure ('content measure') wrote in a more recent [11] paper:

When I consider the application of the concept of probability in science then I usually have in mind in the first place the probabilitity of predictions and only secondarily the probability of laws or theories. Once we see clearly which features of prediction are desirable, then we may say that a given theory is preferable to another one if the predictions yielded by the first theory possess on the average more of the desirable features than the prediction yielded by the other theory....

He then proceeds to show that if 'a practically acting man

bases his choice either on content measure alone or on probability alone, he will sometimes be led to choices that are clearly wrong. We should choose that action for which the expectation value of the utility of outcome is a maximum (pp. 252, 253–4, 157).[3]

1.3. *Individual Demand for Information Services*

Thus encouraged by the spread of understanding of the economic approach to information use, I shall proceed with my task, a more special one than the general economic information problem outlined at the beginning. I shall study the rational choice-making of an individual from among available information systems, or available components of such systems. The availability constraint specifices, in particular, the costs and the delays associated with given components (or with chains or networks of components) of information systems. As is familiar to students of the market, the available set depends on the choices made by suppliers. In last effect, joint choices by demanders and suppliers would determine which information systems are in fact produced and used under given external conditions. These conditions include the technological knowledge of those concerned.

I shall not be able to make more than casual remarks on the supply. The first of the two general questions to be asked by the economist, the joint determination of demand and supply, will therefore receive only a partial answer. And the second question, that of socially optimal allocation of resources to informational goods and services, is pushed away still farther. This is not to say that the allocation question cannot be studied till the demand and supply of informational goods and services is fully understood. Significant work of Hurwicz [23], Stigler [52, 53], Hirshleifer [21], Radner [43, 44] testifies to the contrary.

2. Processing

2.1. *Processing P is Defined as*

$$P = \langle X, Y, \eta, \beta, \tau \rangle,$$

where

$X =$ set of inputs x

$Y =$ set of outputs y

η = transformation from X to Y, including the case of stochastic transformation (see below)

κ = transformation from X to non-negative reals, measuring cost (in cost units)

τ = transformation from X to non-negative reals, measuring delay (in time units).

X, Y are, generally, random sets. η, in a special case called 'deterministic' or 'noiseless', is an ordinary function, i.e., it associates every x in X with a unique $y = \eta(x)$ in Y. However, we must consider the more general case, called 'stochastic' or 'noisy', in which, instead, η associates every x in X with some ('conditional') probability distribution on Y. For simplicity of presentation we shall usually (except for some economically interesting examples) assume X and Y finite,

$$X = (1, \ldots, m), \qquad Y = (1, \ldots, n),$$

so that $\eta_{ij} = \text{Prob}(y = j \mid x = i)$. Hence $\eta = [\eta_{xz}]$ is a $m \times n$ Markov matrix, i.e., all $\eta_{xy} \geqslant 0$ and $\sum_y \eta_{xy} = 1$ for all x.[4] Clearly, the special, deterministic case occurs if one element in each row of the matrix $[\eta_{xy}]$ is $=1$; then we can write

$$(2.1.1)\quad \eta_{xy} = \genfrac{}{}{0pt}{}{1}{0} \text{ if } y \genfrac{}{}{0pt}{}{=}{\neq} \eta(x).$$[5]

As to κ: we shall assume $\kappa(x)$, the cost of processing a given input x, to be constant. We thus forego the discussion of a more general, stochastic case, in which $\kappa(x)$ is a probability distribution of costs, given x. Similarly, we assume that the time $\tau(x)$ required to process a given input x is constant.

2.2. *Cost-Relevant Inputs*

In important cases, exemplified by processings called 'storage' and 'transportation', two otherwise different inputs, $x=i$ and $x=i'$, say, are such that $\kappa(i)=\kappa(i')$. (It costs about the same to transport, over 100 miles, a gallon of whiskey or of gasoline; but see Section 8.1.) It is then convenient to replace the original set X by a reduced set X/κ consisting of equivalence classes x/κ such that all elements of the same class are associated with the same cost.

2.3. *Available (Feasible) Processings*

For given X, Y, not all triples (η, κ, τ) are available. For example, to implement a given transformation η at lowered delays $\tau(x)$ for all x may require raised costs $\kappa(x)$. The set of available processings will be denoted by $\mathscr{P}$.

2.4. *Purposive Processing*

Consider a case in which the y in Y [now to be rewritten as a in $A=(1,\dots,n)$] can be interpreted as the *actions* (decisions) of a person who obeys certain axioms of decision logic,[6] and the inputs x in X [now to be rewritten as $Z=(1,\dots,m)$] are events beyond his control. Then there exists a probability distribution $\pi=$vector $[\pi_z]$ and a bounded real-valued 'utility function' $\omega(a, z, \kappa(z), \tau(z))$ such that, given two available processings

$$P' = \langle Z', A', \eta', \kappa', \tau' \rangle; \qquad P'' = \langle Z'', A'', \eta'', \kappa'', \tau'' \rangle,$$

the chooser of a processing will choose P' only if

$$U_{\pi\omega}(P') \geqslant U_{\pi\omega}(P''),$$

where, for any processing P, its (expected) utility is

$$(2.4.1) \quad U_{\pi\omega}(P) = \sum_{za} \pi_z \eta_{za} \omega(a, z, \kappa(z), \tau(z)).$$

It follows that, given the characteristics of the chooser (viz., π, ω, listed in the subscript under U for convenience) and given the available set $\mathscr{P}$, processing P^* will be chosen only if

$$P^* \in \mathscr{P}, \qquad U_{\pi\omega}(P^*) \geqslant U_{\pi\omega}(P), \quad \text{all} \quad P \text{ in } \mathscr{P}.$$

2.5. *Timing*

Utility depends on action. Accordingly, we consider that the utility is 'earned', and the action a is taken, at the same time. But the cost $\kappa(z)$ is incurred $\tau(z)$ time units earlier.

2.6. *Continued Purposive Processing*

It is often necessary to reinterpret the output a and input z as time-sequences, with a 'horizon' $\equiv T$, possibly infinite:

$$(2.6.1) \quad a = \{a_t\}, \qquad z = \{z_t\}, \qquad t = 1, \ldots, T.$$

An element η_{za} of the transformation η is then the conditional probability of a particular sequence of T actions, given a sequence of T events. Using the results of Koopmans [26], implied by some plausible axioms he has suggested, the utility $\omega(a, z, \kappa(z), \tau(z))$ entering the definition (2.4.1) of the utility of processing can be decomposed thus:

$$(2.6.2) \quad \omega(a, z, \kappa(z), \tau(z)) = \sum_{t=1}^{T} v(\bar{a}_t, \bar{z}_t, \kappa(z_t))\, d^{\Sigma_{s=1}^{T} \tau(z_s)},$$

where the 'discount constant' $d (0 < d \leqslant 1)$ and the function v are independent of time and where $\bar{a}_t$, $\bar{z}_t$ are, respectively, the 'histories' up to t:

$$(2.6.3) \quad \bar{a}_t = (a_1, \ldots, a_t), \quad \bar{z}_t = (z_1, \ldots, z_t).$$

2.7. *Additive Costs and Discounted Benefits*

A convenient though rather special assumption is often tacitly made in practice. It is assumed that, given any distribution π, the utility of processing, $U_{\pi\omega}(P)$ increases with the 'expected discounted benefit', B, and decreases with 'expected cost', K. Before defining B and K precisely, let us state the assumption in two other, obviously equivalent, forms:

(1) of all processings with the same K, the one with highest B has highest utility; and

(2) the efficient subset of $\mathscr{P}$ consists of all those available processings for which the pair $(-K, B)$ is not dominated by any other such available pair.

If, on the other hand, the assumption does not hold, then a processing may exceed in utility, and hence be preferable to, another processing, even though the latter has lower expected cost and higher expected discounted benefit. It will be shown that the stated tacit assumption implies that the utility function ω is decomposable in a certain sense.

More precisely, we define

$$K \equiv K_\pi(\kappa) \equiv \textstyle\sum_z \pi_z \kappa(z), \tag{2.7.1}$$

$$B \equiv B_{\pi\beta d}(\eta, \tau) \equiv \textstyle\sum_{zy} \beta(a, z)\, d^{\tau(z)} \pi_z \eta_{zy}, \tag{2.7.2}$$

where β is the 'benefit function' from $Z \times A$ to reals, and d is the discount constant. [Similar to (2.4.1), subscripts under K, B convey the relevant characteristics of the decision maker.] Note that d occurs in (2.7.2) but not in (2.71). This is because of the assumption on timing in Section 2.5; this difference will be removed when we study processing chains, as in Section 2.9.

It follows from the general theorem on multi-criterion decisions (Appendix A) that $U_{\pi\omega}$ is monotone increasing in B and in $-K$ if and only if there exists a function β and constants d and c such that

$$\omega(a, z, \kappa(z), \tau(z)) = -\, c\kappa(z) + \beta(a, z)\, d^{\tau(z)}\,; \quad c > 0\,; \tag{2.7.3}$$

(c is a conversion factor, fixing the choice of units.) It then follows by (2.4.1) that the utility of processing is monotone in $-K$ and B (for all π), if and only if it is a linear combination,

$$U = -\, cK + B, \quad c > 0\,.^7 \tag{2.7.4}$$

2.8. *Benefit-Relevant Sets of Events and Actions*

It is convenient to define Z and A in such a manner that

$$\beta(a, z) = \beta(a, z'), \quad \text{all} \quad a \in A, \quad \text{only if} \quad z = z',$$

and

$$\beta(a, z) = \beta(a', z), \quad \text{all} \quad z \in Z, \quad \text{only if} \quad a = a'.$$

Thus if Z and A are finite, so that β can be represented as a 'benefit matrix'

$$\beta = [\beta_{az}],$$

then no two columns and no two rows are identical. (Returning to Section 2.2, we note that z and z' may be equivalent with respect to costs but not equivalent with respect to benefits.) And no generality is lost if all the *dominated rows are deleted.*

2.9. *Processing Chains*

Define a sequence

$$P^1, \ldots, P^N,$$

where

$$P^k = \langle X^k, X^{k+1}, \eta^k, \kappa^k, \tau^k \rangle, \quad k = 1, \ldots, N. \tag{2.9.1}$$

Let X^k have n_k elements, so that η^k is of order $n_k \times n_{k+1}$. Such a sequence is equivalent to a processing

$$P = \langle X^1, X^{N+1}, \eta, \ldots \rangle, \tag{2.9.2}$$

where

$$\eta_{x^1 x^{N+1}} = \sum_{x^2 \ldots x^N} \eta_{x^1 x^2} \eta_{x^2 x^3} \cdots \eta_{x^N x^{N+1}},$$

so that

$$\eta = \prod_{k=1}^{N} \eta^k. \tag{2.9.3}$$

With P in (2.9.2) equivalent to the sequence (2.9.1), the utility achieved by P and by that sequence should be, in a purposive case, equal. This makes it impossible, in general, to fill the places indicated by dots in (2.9.2) by single real-valued functions. Rather, the utility of P (if P is purposive) would depend on the sequences $\{\kappa^k\}$, $\{\tau^k\}$, $k = 1, \ldots, N$. This is easily seen by applying the decomposition of utility over time as in (2.6.2) to the case (2.7.3) of additive costs and benefits.

2.10 *Networks*

More general than a chain is a network, in which each transformation may have several input and output variables, some possibly shared with other transformations. We shall not pursue this here, see [38].

3. Symbols as Outputs and Inputs

3.1. *A Purposive Processing Chain*

Consider a chain (2.9.1) consisting of N successive processing links, with

$$X^{N+1} = \text{set } A \text{ of actions } a,$$
$$X^1 = \text{set } Z \text{ of events } z,$$

where a and z are typical arguments of the benefit function $\beta(a, z)$. Each may be a time-sequence as in (2.6.1). Some physical processes cause an action and event to jointly yield some physical consequence (again possibly a time-sequence, e.g., a sequence of annual monetary profits), to which a benefiit number is attached. But we shall not be concerned with these physical processes, and the chains (or networks) that they form.

The intermediate inputs and outputs, $X^2, \ldots X^N$ do not enter the benefit function. As in Section 2.2, two elements x_1^k, x_k^2 of the set X^k, $k=2, \ldots, N$, can be considered equivalent if their processing costs are equal:

$$\kappa^k(x_1^k) = \kappa^k(x_k^2).$$

It will be convenient to reserve the term 'symbols' for the 'benefit-neutral' but 'cost-relevant' inputs and outputs. Thus the links $P^2, \ldots, P^N$ will be said to process symbols onto symbols. Typical examples are: translation (e.g., encoding, decoding) of messages, transmission of messages over distances, and their storage over time. On the other hand, an event or an action (even that of a painter or composer) will not be called a symbol; but processing link P^1 will be said to transform event into a symbol; and P^N will be said to transform a symbol into action.

3.2. *Choosing the Chain: a Meta-Decison*

The action, or decision, $a \equiv x^{N+1}$, the output of the last link in the purposive chain must be distinguished from the decision to choose one rather than another chain. The difference between expected benefit and cost is maximized by the chooser of the chain. The chooser may hire men or machines to perform the successive processings, including the ultimate one, viz., the choice of action, or decision. If this ultimate processing link is called deciding, the choice of it and of other links of the chain may be called meta-deciding.

3.3. *Some Information Systems*

A purposive processing chain is often called an information system, the word information presumably bearing some relation to transformations from and into symbol sets. Information about a physical fact is not the fact itself but some 'symbols' (e.g., words) associated with it. Historically, two kinds of 'shortened' chains have been considered by specialists:

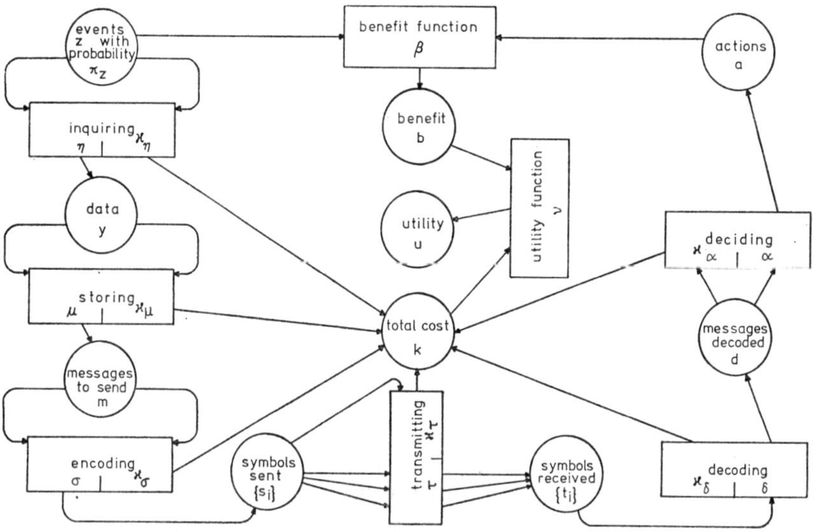

Greek letters $\eta, \mu, \sigma, \tau, \delta, \alpha, \beta, \nu,$ for processors;
corresponding Latin letters $y, m, s, t, d, a, b, u,$ for their outputs.
The cost functions are $\varkappa_\eta, \varkappa_\mu, \varkappa_\sigma, \varkappa_\tau, \varkappa_\delta, \varkappa_\alpha,$ with k as joint output.

Fig. 1. Inquiring, communicating, deciding.

statisticians on the one hand, and communication engineers on the other. They are:

(a) a two-link chain, with

$X^1 = Z =$ events $\qquad P^1 =$ experiment, inquiry
$X^2 = Y =$ data, $\qquad P^2 =$ strategy
$\quad =$ observations
$X^3 = A =$ actions,
$\quad$ decisions

(b) a four-link chain, with

$X^1 = Z =$ messages to be sent	$P^1 =$ storing
$X^2 =$ long stored sequences of messages	$P^2 =$ encoding
$X^3 =$ encoded messages	$P^3 =$ transmission
$X^4 =$ received messages	$P^4 =$ decoding
$X^5 = A =$ decoded messages.	

The chains (a) and (b) are linked together in Figure 1.

To suit special applications, some special assumptions are usually made, different in (a) and in (b), regarding the sets of inputs and outputs, the sets of available processings, the cost and delay functions κ and τ, and the benefit function β. We shall indicate some of those assumptions and the implications of removing them, in due course.

Both (a) and (b) can be considered as special cases of a longer chain. It seems that such longer chains are necessary to describe, in their full richness, the operations of a computer (including problem-solving, simulation, pattern recognition, etc.). The popular description of these operations as 'information processing' would then appear a felicitous one. This would include, for example, programmed navigation, see [12].

In the following four sections we deal with the two-link chain (a), and study the consequences of some simplifying assumptions used in the literature of 'statistical decision theory'. These results are applicable also to information systems consisting of any number of links, with actions based, not directly on observations (outputs of the 'inquiring' link), but on the outputs of subsequent processings (e.g., encoding, transmitting) of observations. By (2.9.3), the system's transformation matrix η is the product of the successive transformation matrices, η^k. Only the product of all but the last one need to be specified if the assumptions listed in Section 4 are made. Accordingly, in the next four sections, η will be called, interchangeably, the inquiry matrix or simply inquiry; or, to be more general, the transformation matrix of an information system or, briefly, information matrix. Of the assumptions to be listed in Section 4 that of additive cost is perhaps least offensive and is at the same time fruitful, for it permits focus on the properties of the information matrix η. On the other hand, the question of successive delays (operation speeds and capacities at successive links), mostly neglected in the two-links theory and introduced in our Section 6 in general terms only, will become a serious one when the processing chain is lengthened by inserting links that implement the communication between the observer and the decision-maker.

4. Inquiring and Deciding in Statistical Theory

4.1. *The Two-Link Chain*

Link P^1 in the two-link chain (a) of Section 3.3 has been variously called 'experiment', 'taking observations', also 'making a diagnosis'. Link P^2, 'strategy', has been also called 'decision rule'. Reflecting certain aspects of statistical practice, the usual analysis of the two-link chain makes tacitly some restrictions which do not appear necessary or justifiable in the broader context of economic comparison of purposive processings. In particular, the delays $\tau^1(z)$, $\tau^2(y)$ are neglected; and so are frequently the constraints on strategies, and their cost, $\kappa^2(y)$.[8]

4.2. *Neglecting Delays*

While, as will be shown, the speed of processing is accorded great importance by communication engineers who study the several-link chain (b) described in Section 3.3, processing speed is completely neglected in the statistical theory of the two-link chain (a). No explicit attention is paid to whether it takes an hour or a month to collect a sample, or to apply a given decision rule. Accordingly the question of 'overloaded capacity' of an observation equipment or decision-making equipment is not, to my knowledge, treated explicitly in statistical literature. It is assumed in effect that for all processing chains considered, $\tau^1(z)$ is the same constant, and $\tau^2(y)$ is the same constant; so that, when comparing the values of two processings, one can assume for both, without loss of generality,

$$(4.2.1) \quad \tau^1(z) = \tau^2(y) = 0\,.$$

No doubt this assumption is not made in actual statistical practice. If the expected benefit can be strongly diminished when decisions are based on obsolete data (see Section 6), the chooser of the experiment and the strategy will give preference to accelerated ones, costs permitting. Moreover, it is not economical to accelerate the experiment if this results in piling up unused data because decisions are taken too slowly. Such considerations surely arise in industrial quality control, in marketing research, in the preparation of economic indices for public policy, and, very likely also in much of scientific laboratory and clinical work: see, for example, [1].

4.3. *'Statistical Decision Problem'*

With delays out of the way, the '*statistical decision problem*' takes the following form. Changing notations somewhat, write:

$$(4.3.1)\quad \begin{aligned} \eta^1_{zy} &= p(y \mid z) = \eta_{zy}; & \kappa^1(z) &= \kappa_z; & P^1 &= \langle \eta, \kappa \rangle \\ \eta^2_{ya} &= p(a \mid y) = \alpha_{ya}; & \kappa^2(y) &= \delta_y; & P^2 &= \langle \alpha, \delta \rangle . \end{aligned}$$

In this context, $\eta = [\eta_{zy}]$ is often called the matrix of likelihoods, and $\alpha = [\alpha_{ya}]$ is called a (randomized, mixed) strategy. The sets Z and A are regarded as fixed; this and the fact that Y is the range of η and the domain of α justifies the above abbreviated definition of the links P^1, P^2. Then the processing chain (P^1, P^2), if available, can be written as

$$(4.3.2)\quad P \equiv (\eta, \alpha, \kappa, \delta) \in \mathscr{P},$$

where $\mathscr{P}$ is the feasible set. We assume additive cost as in Section 2.7 but postpone till later (Section 6) the consideration of continued processing introduced in Section 2.6. The chooser then, maximizes, subject to the constraint (4.3.2), the expected utility U which is the difference between expected benefit B (no discounting for delay need be considered) and expected cost K, where [9]

$$(4.3.3)\quad B = B_{\pi\beta}(P) = \textstyle\sum_{zya} \beta(a, z)\, \pi_z \eta_{zy} \alpha_{ya},$$

$$(4.3.4)\quad K = K_\pi(P) = \textstyle\sum_z \pi_z \kappa_z + \sum_{zy} \pi_z \eta_{zy} \delta_y,$$

$$(4.3.5)\quad U = U_{\pi\beta}(P) = B_{\pi\beta}(P) - K_\pi(P).$$

As in Section 2.7, the subscripts under B, K, U characterize the chooser. Together with the feasible set $\mathscr{P}$, they form the givens of the chooser's problem. Hence the optimal chain P^* is a function of π, β, $\mathscr{P}$. So is the efficient set, which consists of all elements of $\mathscr{P}$ for which the pair $(-K, B)$ is not dominated by any other such feasible pair.

4.4. *Action as a Subset of Events*

In general, there is no need to assume any formal, logical relation between Z and A. For example, Z may be the set (cancer, no cancer), and A may be the set (surgery, radiotherapy, no treatment). The benefit function β would then assign a value to each of the $2\times 3=6$ pairs (a, z). In statistical literature, an action that can be considered relevant to the benefit of the statistician's 'employer', can be identified with the choice of one of disjoint subsets ('alternative hypotheses') of the set of benefit-relevant events. Such actions cannot be more numerous than events. *Added in 1974*: See now [58].

True, the action of the statistician is, in other cases, said to consist in choosing from a set of overlapping subsets of events, e.g., in naming an interval.[10] He is then supposed to use choice criteria relevant to his own, not his employer's, benefit.

For purposes of economics of information, it is more useful to say that the statistician's task is to derive, from observations y, the likelihoods η_{zy} for all events z relevant to his employer's benefit. Given the prior probabilities π_z, one can then determine the joint probabilities $\pi_z\eta_{zy}$ or, for that matter, the posterior probabilities $(\pi_z\eta_{zy}/\sum_t \pi_t\eta_{ty})$. The employer or his operations research man (possibly identical with the statistician) will combine these probalities with the benefits yielded to the employer by *his* actions, given the events, and choose the action that maximizes expected benefit.

Accordingly, we shall permit the employer's (user's) actions to be more numerous than events. This will lead to interesting results in the economics of comparing information systems, see Section 7.5.

To be sure, a problem of communication arises. It is, in fact, the problem of optimal encoding, in the sense of our Section 8. It may be costly or even non-feasible to communicate in all detail the posterior or the joint probability distributions involved, to the employer, or to his operations research man, or to a low-echelon decision-making man or machine. With this in mind, a condensed message may be used: for example, the posterior probability that z lies in a particular interval. The choice of the interval will then depend, not on the statistician's 'tastes', but on the 'meta-decider's' judgment as to the contributions of alternative codes to *his* benefit and cost.

4.5. *Neglecting the Constraints and Costs of Deciding*

In important parts of statistical literature decison-making is, in effect, assumed costless and unconstrained. This strong assumption has led to a fruitful discussion of 'comparative informativeness' of the matrices $\eta = [\eta_{zy}]$. We shall pursue it in some detail in Sections 5 and 6.

The assumption of costless and unconstrained deciding is too strong to have been actually accepted in practice. For example, in the case where observations y and decisions $a = \alpha(y)$ are both real-valued, attention was paid, quite early, to a special class of decision rules, viz., to the class of *linear* α, presumably because linear functions require less computational effort. (The theorem that, among unbiased *linear* estimators the least-squares estimator is best, goes back to Gauss, I understand.) The search for good 'robust' statistics is motivated by the low prior probabilities of narrowly specified models. But it is also due to considerations of computational economy, I suppose; as is, of course, the rounding-off of digits in the computational process.

4.6. *Value of Information*

With decision undelayed, costless and unconstrained, and inquiry undelayed, the problem of the chooser of a two-link chain P is simplified. Denote by $\{\alpha\}$ the set of *all* stochastic transformations from Y to A (remember that any such transformation was assumed feasible) and let $\{\eta, \kappa\}$ be the set of feasible pairs of inquiry transformations η and inquiry cost functions κ. Then the constraint (4.3.2) is relaxed into

$$(4.6.1) \quad P \equiv (\eta, \alpha, \kappa) \in \{\alpha\} \times \{\kappa, \eta\},$$

since $\delta = 0$. Further, Equation (4.3.3) is unaffected, but in (4.3.4) the term involving δ vanishes. Therefore, (4.3.5) can be rewritten as

$$(4.6.2) \quad U = U_{\pi\beta}(\eta, \alpha, \kappa) = B_{\pi\beta}(\eta, \alpha) - K_\pi(\kappa)$$

where

$$(4.6.3) \quad B_{\pi\beta}(\eta, \alpha) = \textstyle\sum_{zya} \beta(a, z)\, \pi_z \eta_{zy} \alpha_{ya}$$

$$(4.6.4) \quad K_\pi(\kappa) = \textstyle\sum_z \pi_z \kappa_z .$$

Define the '*information value*' of η:

$$(4.6.5)\quad V_{\pi\beta}(\eta) \equiv \max_{\alpha \in \{\alpha\}} B_{\pi\beta}(\eta, \alpha) \equiv B_{\pi\beta}(\eta, \alpha^*),$$

say; then, to maximize expected utility U with respect to η, α, κ over their feasible set, given π, β, is equivalent to

$$(4.6.6)\quad \max_{\eta} V_{\pi\beta}(\eta) - \min_{\kappa} K_{\pi}(\kappa),$$

subject to the cost constraint

$$(4.6.7)\quad (\kappa, \eta) \in \{(\kappa, \eta)\}.$$

With the meta-decider's problem reduced to (4.6.6) and (4.6.7), it is useful to consider the expected cost $K_{\pi}(\kappa)$ as fixed and to compare various information matrices $\eta, \eta', \ldots$, according to their values $V_{\pi\beta}(\eta)$, $V_{\pi\beta}(\eta')$,...

4.7. *Appropriate Action, a_y; Value of Observation, V_y*

The optimal decision rule α^* defined in (4.6.5) depends only on η and π, β. Now, for each η, given π and β, there will exist a deterministic optimal decision rule; for it is well known that, in a one-person game, there exists a pure optimal strategy (the average of several quantities cannot exceed every one of them). Thus, no generality is lost if we define $\{\alpha\}$ as the set of all mappings from Y to A. The assumption of costless and non-restricted decisions excludes the case when the hired (and presumably cheap) decision-making man or machine uses a non-optimal deterministic rule; and also the case when he (it) makes 'random errors', unless they happen to constitute an optimal random strategy.

With $\{\alpha\}$ reduced to the set of all *pure* strategies, i.e., all functions α from Y to A, we can write $a = \alpha(y)$ so that [similar to (2.1.1)]

$$(4.7.1)\quad \alpha_{ya} = \begin{matrix} 1 \\ 0 \end{matrix} \quad \text{if} \quad a \begin{matrix} = \\ \neq \end{matrix} \alpha(y),$$

and denote the action that is 'appropriate' (i.e., optimal) in response to y by

$$a_y = \alpha^*(y);$$

that is, for a given y,

$$(4.7.2)\quad \max_{a \in A} \sum_{z} \beta(a, z)\, \pi_z \eta_{zy} \equiv \sum_{z} \beta(a_y, z)\, \pi_z \eta_{zy} \equiv V_y(\eta),$$

say. $V_y(\eta)$ may be called 'value of the observation y'. Later, it will prove convenient to define

$$(4.7.3) \qquad \gamma_z(a) \equiv \pi_z \beta(a, z),$$

the benefit of action a at event z, *weighted* by that event's probability. Then (4.7.2) becomes

$$(4.7.4) \qquad V_y(\eta) \equiv \max_a \sum_z \gamma_z(a)\, \eta_{zy} = \sum_z \gamma_z(a_y)\, \eta_{zy}.$$

By (4.6.3), (4.7.1) and (4.6.5), the value of an inquiry is

$$(4.7.5) \qquad V(\eta) = \sum_y V_y(\eta).$$

Note that $\sum_z \gamma_z(a)$ is the 'prior expectation of benefit' of action a.

4.8. *Labelling of Observations*

It is clear from (4.6.3), (4.6.5) that $V(\eta)$ is invariant under interchange of columns in η. Therefore, if η is of order $m \times n$ and P a permutation matrix of order n, we shall agree that

$$(4.8.1) \qquad \eta \quad \text{and} \quad \eta P \text{ are equivalent.}$$

Thus if (with $m=n=2$), $z=1$ means 'stock will rise' and $z=2$ means 'stock will not rise', then the datum 'my broker says stock will rise' can be labelled, indifferently, as $y=1$ or as $y=2$. There is no loss of generality in choosing any one particular labelling.

Also, no generality is lost if we agree to eliminate any column of η that consists of 0's only, and thus designates (with Y finite, as we recall!) an observation that never occurs.

It is seen from (4.7.4) that two observations $y=j, k$, whose conditional probabilities, given any event z, are pairwise equal, yield the same appropriate action $a_j = a_k$ and the same value $V_j = V_k$. It is convenient therefore, and involves no loss of generality, to redefine every such inquiry by adding any two identical columns, and thus to make every inquiry matrix η to consist of non-identical columns only.

4.9. *Null-Information*

Null-information is said to be provided by any matrix η^0 whose rows are identical, so that we can write

$$\eta^0_{zy} = \lambda_y, \quad \text{all} \quad z\,; \qquad \sum_{y=1}^{n} \lambda_y = 1\,.$$

Then by (4.7.4), (4.7.5)

$$\text{(4.9.1)} \qquad \begin{aligned} V_y(\eta^0) &= \lambda_y \max_a \sum_z \gamma_z(a) \\ V(\eta^0) &= \max_a \sum_z \gamma_z(a) = \sum_z \gamma_z(a^0), \end{aligned}$$

say. Thus action a^0 is optimal, independently of observations; and all null-inquiries have the same value. As their canonical form we can conveniently choose the $(m \times 1)$ matrix with all elements $\eta^0_{z1} = 1$, $z = 1, \ldots, m$. That is, the same unique observation is obtained, with certainty, whatever the event. Then η^0 is the column vector of order m, with all elements $=1$: a 'sum vector', sometimes denoted by $\eta^0 = \mathbf{1}$. It will be shown in Section 5.3 that no inquiry can have a value smaller than that of a null-inquiry. This justifies writing[11]

$$\text{(4.9.2)} \qquad V(\eta^0) = V(\mathbf{1}) = V^{\min}\,.$$

4.10 *Essential Set of Inquiry Matrices*

Let H_m be the set of all Markov matrices with m rows and with all columns non-zero and not pairwise identical. Summarizing the conventions made in Section 4.8, the essential set of inquiries about m events is defined as the partition H_m/e into equivalence classes; where η and η' in H_m are equivalent, $\eta = [\eta_{zy}] e \eta' = [\eta'_{zy'}]$, if $\eta' = \eta P$ for some permutation matrix P or if every η_{zy}, $\eta'_{zy'}$ is independent of z.[12] Accordingly, when η and η' are both noiseless, then $\eta e \eta'$ means that the sets Y and Y' are permutations of each other.

4.11. *Perfect Information*

Perfect information will be said to be provided by a matrix η of order $m \times m$ such that the correspondence between Z and Y is one to one. That is, one element in each row of η is $=1$ [and hence the other elements in the row are 0 and η is noiseless, as in (2.1.1)]; and, moreover, in each column one element is 1 and all other elements are 0. Thus η is a permutation matrix, $\eta = Q$, say. Its transpose Q^T is clearly a permutation matrix, too,

$Q^T = P$, say; and it is well known that

$$I = QP,$$

where I is the identity matrix. Then by (4.8.1), I and Q will be considered equivalent: without loss of generality, perfect information will be represented by the identity matrix I as its canonical form.

4.12. *Useless Inquiries*

Given π, β (and, thus, given γ) an inquiry η is called useless *if an optimal action, the same for all observations, exists:* for all y, $a_y = a^*$, say. Clearly all null-inquiries are useless. But the converse is not, in general, true, as will be seen in Sections 7.4, 7.5. Furthermore, using (4.9.2), we have the following

THEOREM: $V(\eta) = V^{\min}$ if and only if η is useless.

To prove sufficiency, let a^* be optimal for a useless inquiry η^*. That is, $a_y = a^*$ for all y:

$$V_y(\eta^*) = \Sigma_z \gamma_z(a^*)\, \eta^*_{zy} \geqslant \Sigma_z \gamma_z(a)\, \eta^*_{zy}, \quad \text{all } a, \quad \text{all } y;$$

summing over y we have, by (4.7.5) and since $\Sigma_y \eta^*_{zy} = 1$,

$$V(\eta^*) = \Sigma_z\, \gamma_z(a^*) \geqslant \Sigma_z\, \gamma_z(a), \quad \text{all} \quad a;$$
$$V(\eta^*) = \max_a \Sigma_z\, \gamma_z(a) = V^{\min}.$$

To prove necessity, suppose

$$V(\eta) = V^{\min};$$

that is,

$$V(\eta) = \max_a \Sigma_z\, \gamma_z(a) = \Sigma_z\, \gamma_z(a^*),$$

say. Then a (not necessarily unique) optimal strategy is

$$a_y = a^*, \quad \text{all} \quad y;$$

that is, η is useless.

4.13. *Convexity of the Function $V_{\pi\beta}(\eta)$*

It follows by (4.6.3) and a well-known theorem (see, e.g., [25, Appendix

B.4]), that the information value

$$V_{\pi\beta}(\eta) = \max_{\alpha} B_{\pi\beta}(\eta, \alpha)$$

is a convex function of η; it is represented by the upper envelope of a family of hyperplanes.[13] The same is true of V_y in (4.7.2)

5. Comparative Informativeness

The assumptions of statistical theory set out in the preceding section will be maintained here and in Sections 6 and 7. In particular, deciding is assumed unconstrained so that, for given sets Y, A, the feasible set of strategies consists of all functions from Y to A; and the cost of deciding is zero (or, more generally, constant).

5.1. *Definition*

We say, following Blackwell[14] that η is more informative than η', and write $\eta > \eta'$, if and only if

$$V_{\pi\beta}(\eta) \geqslant V_{\pi\beta}(\eta') \quad \text{for all} \quad \pi, \beta,$$

where π, β are defined on fixed sets Z and $A \times Z$, respectively. By fixing these sets rich enough, we can apply the definition of 'more informative than' to an arbitrarily large set of meta-deciders concerned with the choice among information matrices.

Clearly '$>$' is a transitive and reflexive relation, and thus induces an ordering on the set of information matrices. It is a partial ordering on this set: for it is easy to construct cases when, depending on π, β the information matrix η has a larger or a smaller value than η'. Clearly the relation '$>$' induces also a partial ordering on the essential set H_m/e defined in Section 4.10. In particular, when $\eta e \eta'$ then obviously both $\eta > \eta'$ and $\eta' < \eta$. But the converse is not true; see note 18 to Section 5.6.

5.2. *Garbling*

Consider an information matrix $\eta = [\eta_{zy}]$ and suppose that, whenever the observation $y (=1, \ldots, n)$ is made, the decision-maker does not learn it; instead, a random device is used such that, given the observation y, he will receive, with probability $g_{yy'}$, a signal $y' = 1, \ldots, n'$. Clearly $g_{yy'} \geqslant 0$,

$\sum_{y'} g_{yy'}=1$. The random device is thus characterized by a Markov matrix $G=[g_{yy'}]$, of order $n\times n'$. It follows that, given the event $z=1,\ldots,m$, the decision-maker receives signal y' with probability

$$(5.2.1)\quad \sum_y \eta_{zy} g_{yy'} = \eta'_{zy'},$$

say, where $\eta'_{zy'}\geqslant 0$, $\sum_{y'} \eta'_{zy'}=1$. In effect, he has used an information matrix $\eta'=[\eta'_{zy'}]$ of order $m\times n'$ such that

$$(5.2.2)\quad \eta' = \eta G.$$

It seems to agree with common usage, to say that η' is obtained from η by *garbling*.[15] And it is intuitively clear that a garbled information matrix cannot exceed in value the original one: for the decision-maker receiving a 'garbled' signal will, at best, choose an action appropriate to that signal, not to the original observation. Formally, we have

THEOREM: If η, η', G are Markov matrices with $\eta'=\eta G$, then $\eta>\eta'$.
Proof: By (4.7.4), (4.7.5), (5.2.1)

$$\begin{aligned} V(\eta') &= \Sigma_{y'z}\, \gamma_z(a_{y'})\, \eta_{zy'} = \Sigma_{y'z}\, \gamma_z(a_{y'})\, \Sigma_y\, \eta_{zy} g_{yy'} = \\ &= \Sigma_{y'}\, g_{yy'}\, \Sigma_{yz}\, \gamma_z(a_{y'})\, \eta_{zy} \leqslant \\ &\leqslant \Sigma_{y'}\, g_{yy'}\, \Sigma_{yz}\, \gamma_z(a_y)\, \eta_{zy} = 1\cdot V(\eta). \end{aligned}$$

5.3. *Maximal and Minimal Information Matrices*

THEOREM:

$$(5.3.1)\quad \begin{aligned} I_m &> \eta \\ \eta &> \mathbf{1}_m, \end{aligned}$$

where η has m rows and I_m and $\mathbf{1}_m$ (identity matrix and sum vector of order m) correspond to perfect and to null-information (Sections 4.11, 4.9).

Proof: Verify that

$$\eta = I_m \eta, \qquad \mathbf{1}_m = \eta \mathbf{1}_n,$$

for any η of order $m\times n$; then, noting that η and $\mathbf{1}_n$ are Markov matrices, apply the Theorem of Section 5.2 on 'garbling'.

Thus the canonical forms of the perfect information and the null-information matrices constitute, respectively, the maximal and minimal elements of the lattice in which the essential set of information matrices is partially ordered by the relation 'more informative than'.

5.4. *Comparative Coarseness*

Suppose the garbling matrix G in (5.2.2) is noiseless, i.e., analogous to (2.1.1),

$$(5.4.1) \quad g_{yy'} = \begin{matrix} 1 \\ 0 \end{matrix} \quad \text{if} \quad y' \begin{matrix} = \\ \neq \end{matrix} g(y),$$

for all y, y'. That is, G is reduced to a many-to-one mapping g, from $Y = (1, \ldots, n)$ to $Y' = (1, \ldots, n')$; and clearly $n' \leqslant n$. Then it seems to agree with common usage to say that Y' is *coarser* than Y (or, equivalently, Y is *finer* than Y'). For example, two elements y_1 and y_2 may be real numbers (or vectors), identical except for the last digit (or the last component), and this digit (or component) is omitted in the element $y'_1 = g(y_1) = g(y_2)$ of Y'. 'Some details are suppressed' or more generally (to include the limiting case $G = I_n$, $n' = n$), 'no details are added'. Applying (5.4.1) to (5.2.1),

$$\eta'_{zy'} = \sum_{y \in S_{y'}} \eta_{zy}, \quad \text{where} \quad S_{y'} = \{y \mid g(y) = y'\}:$$

an intuitively obvious result.[16] It follows from the theorem of Section 5.2 that

(5.4.2) if η' is coarser than η then $\eta > \eta'$.

This confirms the intuitive assertion that adding detail (at no cost!) cannot do damage, since the detail can be ignored.

5.5. *Blackwell's Theorem*

We give this name to the proposition that

$$\eta > \eta' \quad \text{if and only if} \quad \eta' = \eta G \quad \text{for some Markov matrix } G.$$

The sufficiency part was proved in Section 5.2. For proof of necessity, see [6] or [37].

5.6. *The Case of Noiseless Information*

THEOREM: If η and η' are noiseless then $\eta > \eta'$ if and only if η' is coarser than η.

Proof: Sufficiency follows from (5.4.2). Necessity follows from Blackwell's theorem, noting that if $\eta' = \eta G$ and η, η' are noiseless then by (5.2.1) every entry in G is either 1 or 0, i.e., G is noiseless.[17]

It follows that *two noiseless inquiries η and η' have equal information value for any given π, β if, and only if, they are identical up to a permutation of columns.* The sufficiency part of this proposition is obvious. The necessity part follows from the previous theorem: for if $\eta > \eta'$ and $\eta' > \eta$, and hence each of the two inquiries is coarser than the other, then to each y in Y corresponds a unique y' in Y', and conversely. Hence the correspondence between Y and Y' is one-to-one.

Thus the partial weak ordering induced by the relation 'more informative than' is a strong one over the noiseless subset of the essential set H_m/e of inquiries defined in Section 4.10.[18]

6. Informativeness of Systems over Time

6.1. *Environment, Action, and Observation as Time-Sequences*

One or both of the arguments a, z of the benefit function β can be interpreted as time-sequences, as in (2.6.1), assuming additive costs as in Section 2.7. With z a time-sequence, it will be convenient (changing our terminology somewhat) to call z the *environment* and to reserve the term '*successive events*' for the components of the sequence $z = \{z_t\}$, $t = t_1, \ldots, t_T$; to give unit-length to each of the intervals (t_i, t_{i+1}), $i = 1, \ldots, T-1$; and sometimes to make $t_1 = 1$, so that $t = 1, \ldots, T$. Each component a_t of a will be called successive action. If the benefit can be represented as a sum of discounted 'successive benefits'

$$(6.1.1) \quad \beta(a, z) = \sum_{t=1}^{T} d^t \beta^* (a_t, z_t),$$

say (as would be implied by the assumption (2.6.2) combined with (2.7.3)), then it is important to agree that a_t and z_t need not 'physically' occur simultaneously, e.g., a_t may be 'sell stock short today' and z_t may be 'stock price a month from today'.

A successive action a_t is taken, using the decision rule α_t, in response to $\bar{y}_t$, where $\bar{y}_t$ is the *remembered past history of successive observations,*

$$(6.1.2) \quad \bar{y}_t = (y_{t-\mu}, \ldots, y_{t-1}, y_t);$$

the time-length μ measures the *length of memory*. Again, the subscript t in $\bar{y}_t$ means only that the action taken at time t is based on $\bar{y}_t$; it does not necessarily mean that y_t, the last component of $\bar{y}_t$, was 'physically' observed at time t.

In this interpretation, π becomes a distribution on the set Z of sequences z. The information matrix η transforms (stochastically, in general) the environment z into a sequence of remembered histories,

$$(6.1.3) \quad y = (\bar{y}_{t-\mu}, \ldots, \bar{y}_T) \in Y;$$

that is, η_{zy} is the probability of the sequence y of remembered histories, given a particular environment (i.e., a particular sequence of successive events), $z=(z_1, \ldots, z_T)$. A strategy α is a sequence of functions $\alpha_1, \ldots, \alpha_T$, where $a_t = \alpha_t(\bar{y}_t)$, thus α is a function from Y to the set A of action-sequences. With these generalizing interpretations, the results of Section 5 apply.

6.2. *Effect of Memory Length on Informativeness*

Let $\mu' < \mu$; let inquiry η' yield remembered history

$$(6.2.1) \quad \bar{y}'_t = (y_{t-\mu'}, \ldots, y_t)$$

whenever inquiry η yields remembered history

$$(6.2.2) \quad \bar{y}_t = (y_{t-\mu}, \ldots, y_{t-\mu'}, \ldots, y_t);$$

clearly η' is coarser than η. Hence by (5.4.2) η is more informative than η'.

6.3. *Delayed vs Prompt Perfect Information*

Prompt perfect and delayed perfect information are defined, respectively by

$$\begin{array}{lll} y_t = z_t, & t = 1, \ldots, T; & y_t \in Y; \\ y_t = z_{t-\theta}, & t = \theta + 1, \ldots, T; & y'_t \in Y'. \end{array}$$

θ is the delay, an integer with $0 < \theta < T$. Now, there is a one-to-one correspondence between the set Z of environments z (sequences of successive events) on the one hand, and, on the other, the set, $\bar{Z}$ (say) of sequences $\bar{z} = (\bar{z}_1, \ldots, \bar{z}_T)$ of past histories $[\bar{z}_t = (z_1, \ldots, z_t)]$ of successive events: for $\bar{z}_{t+1} = (\bar{z}_t, z_{t+1})$. Replace Z by $\bar{Z}$ and redefine β and π accordingly. Then prompt perfect inquiry, a mapping η from Z to Y, is represented by the identity matrix I; but delayed perfect inquiry, a mapping η' from Z to Y', is not. Hence $\eta > \eta'$, by (5.3.1). A delay cannot improve perfect information.

However, if prompt information is not perfect, its value can be exceeded by that of delayed (perfect or imperfect) information. Thus, detailed survey data, even when two years old, may be more valuable (because less 'coarse': see Section 5.4) than those of a less detailed survey made at the time the action is taken.

6.4. *Perfect Information with Long vs Short Delay When the Environment is Markovian*

Given the distribution π on the set of environments (sequences of successive events) we can derive the conditional probability of the event z_t given the preceding past history,

$$\bar{p}_t \equiv p(z_t | \bar{z}_{t-1}),$$

and also the conditional probability of z_t given z_{t-1},

$$p_t \equiv p(z_t | z_{t-1}).$$

The environment z is said to be Markovian if

$$\bar{p}_t = p_t. \tag{6.4.1}$$

THEOREM. If z is Markovian then a perfect inquiry with shorter delay is more informative than a perfect inquiry with longer delay.

We omit the proof because of its simplicity.

Shorter delay is not necessarily advantageous if the environment is not Markovian but is, for example, periodic. Restaurant menus do not vary much as between Sundays, and also, in Catholic countries, as between Fridays. And both differ from each other and from the menus of other days of the week. In a Catholic country, before deciding on a Thursday where to eat next Sunday, it is best to know next Sunday's menu ($\theta = 0$, as in Section 6.3); but the next best is to learn the menu, not of next Friday ($\theta = 2$ days) but of the previous Sunday ($\theta = 7$ days)!

6.5. *Obsolescence and Impatience*

The discount constant d, as used in Sections 2.6 and 2.7, reflects a feature of the utility function sometimes called impatience. It is one reason why delays diminish the value of an inquiry (and, more generally, of information systems, see end of Section 3.3). We see now another reason, which, when it is applicable, may be more powerful: the obsolescence of the inputs to the decision-making.[19]

6.6. *Sequential Inquiries and Adaptive Programming*

The concept a_t of a successive action (decision) can be usefully extended to include decisions about the observations to be taken at the next point of time. Thus

$$(6.6.1) \quad a_t = (a_t', \eta_{t+1}),$$

where a_t' may be called, successive action in the ordinary sense (it enters the benefit function) and η_{t+1} is 'inquiry at time $t+1$'. Both are chosen simultaneously, on the basis of remembered history, $\bar{y}_t$. Sequential sampling in statistics is a special case, in which a_t' includes among its values the null-action: 'do nothing that would directly influence the benefit', and η_{t+1} includes among its values the null-inquiry $\mathbf{1}$; a_t' is null, (i.e., ordinary action is postponed) and η_{t+1} is non-null (i.e., further observations are taken), till some point τ (say) such that $\eta_{\tau+1}$ is null (observations cease) and a_τ' is non-null ('terminal action'). The more general case is 'earn while you learn'.

Inquiring and deciding over time, including the general, sequential case just discussed is sometimes called adaptive programming. This is sometimes described as a sequence of step-wise revisions of the probability distribution of the environment, starting with the prior distribution π and replacing it with posterior distributions, given past histories, $p(z \mid \bar{y}_t)$, $t=1,\ldots$. This description can lead to misapplications, if the researcher estimates each of these successive distributions by some conventional parameters (means, variances, for example). The parameter actually needed is the optimal action a_t^* (say) itself! Also, a misleading distinction is sometimes made between 'stochastic programming' in which the distribution of z is known, and 'adaptive programming' in which it is gradually learned. But actually, once the knowledge of the prior distribution π is admitted the mathematical processes needed to compute the optimal sequence of actions [including inquiries as in (6.6.1)] are equivalent.[20]

7. Optimal inquiries[21]

7.1. *Binary Inquiries as an Example*

The 'likelihood matrix' $\eta = [\eta_{zy}]$ is called binary if it is of order 2×2, so that $Z = (1, 2)$, $Y = (1, 2)$ and we can denote the likelihoods by

$$(7.1.1)\quad \begin{aligned} \eta_{11} &= 1 - \eta_{12} = p_1 \\ \eta_{22} &= 1 - \eta_{21} = p_2 . \end{aligned}$$

(This notation makes the subscripts of the p_i conveniently symmetrical.) To avoid triviality, we assume the probabilities π_z of the two events to be both positive:

$$(7.1.2)\quad 0 < \pi_2 = 1 - \pi_1 < 1 .$$

Binary inquiries are widely used in statistics. In testing against a null-hypothesis, the 'error probabilities of first and second kind' are related to η_{11}, η_{22} or their complements (see Section 7.6). Binary 'channel matrices' are much used in the theory of communication. We shall look to both fields for examples when later, in Section 7.8–7.10, we search for the optimal inquiry, i.r., one that maximizes the difference between expected benefit and expected cost, and shall use sampling costs as well as the cost of a transmission channel.

The analysis carried out in this section will exploit the simple properties of a binary inquiry or its even simpler, symmetric sub-case ($p_1 = p_2$). Perhaps the insight gained can be later used to handle non-binary inquiries; some beginnings will be attempted in Section 7.7.

7.2. *Informativeness of Binary Inquiries*

Given the inquiry matrix

$$(7.2.1)\quad \eta = [\eta_{zy}] = \begin{pmatrix} p_1 & 1 - p_1 \\ 1 - p_2 & p_2 \end{pmatrix}, \qquad 0 \leqslant p_i \leqslant 1, \quad i = 1, 2,$$

there is no loss of generality in permuting the columns so as to make the determinant $|\eta|$ non-negative:

$$(7.2.2)\quad |\eta| = p_1 + p_2 - 1 \geqslant 0 .$$

Note that $|\eta|=0$ is the case of null-information, see Section 4.9. Define the two *likelihood ratios*

$$(7.2.3)\quad \lambda_1 = p_1/(1-p_2)\,; \qquad \lambda_2 = p_2/(1-p_1)\,.$$

Then under the convention (7.2.2),

$$(7.2.4)\quad \lambda_1 \geqslant 1\,, \qquad \lambda_2 \geqslant 1\,.$$

Denote by p_i', λ_i' $(i=1, 2)$, respectively, the two likelihoods and two likelihood ratios characterizing another inquiry, η'. Write for brevity

$$\lambda > \lambda' \quad \text{when} \quad \lambda_1 \geqslant \lambda_1' \quad \text{and} \quad \lambda_2 \geqslant \lambda_2'\,,$$
$$p > p' \quad \text{when} \quad p_1 \geqslant p_1' \quad \text{and} \quad p_2 \geqslant p_2'\,.$$

The relation denoted by '$>$' induces a partial ordering on the set of pairs $\lambda=(\lambda_1, \lambda_2)$ and on the set of pairs $p=(p_1, p_2)$ as it does on the set of inquiries η. When neither $\eta>\eta'$ nor $\eta'>\eta$ we write $\eta \| \eta'$; and a similar meaning attaches to $\lambda \| \lambda'$ and $p \| p'$ (as when, for example, $p_1>p_1'$ and $p_2'>p_2$).

THEOREM. (1) If $\lambda>\lambda'$ then $\eta>\eta'$ and conversely.
(2) If $p>p'$ then $\eta>\eta'$ but the converse is not true.

Proof of (1). By definition of λ_1, η, η',

$$(7.2.5)\quad \lambda_1 - \lambda_1' \equiv (\eta_{11}\eta_{21}' - \eta_{11}'\eta_{21})/\eta_{21}\eta_{21}' \geqslant 0$$

if the numerator $\geqslant 0$. Now suppose $\eta>\eta'$. Then by Blackwell's theorem (Section 5.5)

$$\eta_{ij}' = \eta_{i1}g_{1j} + \eta_{i2}g_{2j} \quad (i=1, 2; j=1. 2)\,,$$

where g_{kj} is an element of a 2×2 Markov matrix. The numerator in (7.2.5) becomes, in the notation of (7.2.1)

$$g_{21}(p_1 + p_2 - 1) \geqslant 0\,;$$

hence by (7.2.2), $\lambda_1' \geqslant \lambda_1$; and by symmetry of subscripts, $\lambda_2 \geqslant \lambda_2'$. This proves the 'converse' part of (1):

$$\text{if } \eta > \eta' \quad \text{then } \lambda > \lambda'\,.$$

Hence, interchanging η and η',

$$\text{if } \eta' > \eta \quad \text{then } \lambda' > \lambda\,;$$

and if $\eta \parallel \eta'$ then neither $\lambda > \lambda'$ nor $\lambda < \lambda'$, and therefore

$$\text{if } \eta \parallel \eta \quad \text{then } \lambda \parallel \lambda'.$$

Since these three possibilities are exhaustive, it follows that

$$\text{(7.2.6)} \quad \text{if } \lambda > \lambda', \quad \text{then } \eta > \eta',$$

completing the proof of part (1) of the theorem. On Figure 2, the region

$$R_\eta^+ = \{\eta' : \eta' > \eta\} = \{\eta' : \lambda' > \lambda\}$$

is bounded from below by two straight lines,

$$\{\eta' : \lambda_1' = \lambda_1\} \quad \text{and} \quad \{\eta' : \lambda_2' = \lambda_2\}$$

which go through the point $\eta = (\eta_{11}, \eta_{22})$ and (0, 1) or (1, 0), respectively. [The content of Section 5.3 is readily illustrated, with perfect information represented by the point (1, 1), and null-information by any point on the main diagonal.]

As to part (2) of the Theorem, it follows from (7.2.5), (7.2.1), (7.2.6) that $p > p'$ implies $\lambda > \lambda'$ and hence also $\eta > \eta'$. But the converse is not true: for let

$$p_1 - p_1' > p_1 p_2' - p_2 p_1' > p_2' - p_2 > 0\,;$$

then $\lambda > \lambda'$ but $p \parallel p'$. On Figure 2, the sets

$$\{\eta' : p' > p\} \quad \text{and} \quad \{\eta' : p > p'\}$$

would be represented, respectively, by the upper-right and lower-left rectangles (not shown on Figure 2) bounded by lines through η, parallel to the axes. Clearly, these rectangles are *proper* subregions of R_η^+ and R_η^-, respectively (except trivially at the vertices of the unit square). This illustrates (2): it is possible to increase informativeness by increasing the error probability of one kind, provided the error probability of the other kind is sufficiently decreased. Here the error probabilities are interpreted as in (7.6.1) later.

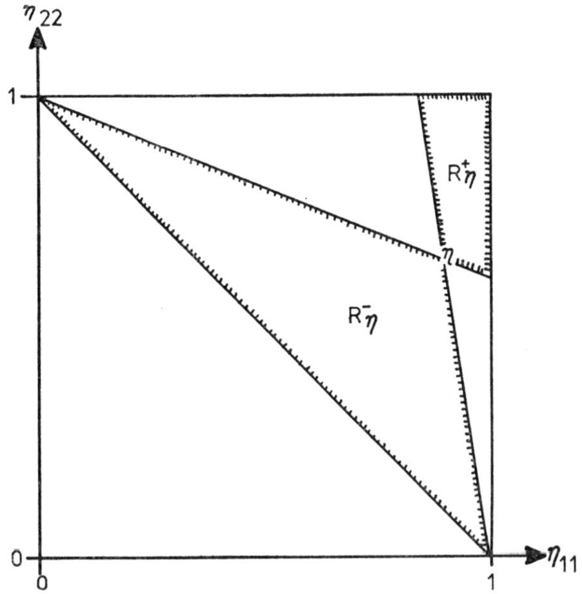

Fig. 2. Regions of binary information matrices, more ($R_\eta{}^+$) and less ($R_\eta{}^-$) informative than η.

7.3. *Symmetric Binary Information Matrices*

This is a special case of (7.2.1), with

$$p_1 = p_2 = p\,,$$

say (thus p will denote here a scalar, not a pair). The convention (7.2.2) becomes

$$p \geqslant \tfrac{1}{2}\,,$$

and it follows from the theorem of the preceding section that informativeness increases as p increases: an intuitively obvious result. On Figure 2, the symmetric matrices would be represented by the line (not drawn) connecting $(\tfrac{1}{2}, \tfrac{1}{2})$ and $(1, 1)$.

7.4. *Value of Binary Inquiry: the Case of Two Actions*

As stated in Section 2.8, no two rows and no two columns of the benefit matrix $\beta = [\beta_{az}]$ are identical; and any action represented by a dominated row is eliminated. Suppose that after such elimination there remain two rows, i.e., $A=(1,2)$. Then there is no loss of generality in writing

$$\text{(7.4.1)}\quad \beta=[\beta_{az}]=\begin{pmatrix} b_1 & b_2-r_2 \\ b_1-r_1 & b_2 \end{pmatrix},$$
$$r_z>0,\quad z=1,2;$$

the r_z are often called 'regrets' (about not having used the action $a=z$, optimal under certainty). This benefit matrix is, in effect, used in statistics when the two actions are: 'reject the hypothesis' and 'accept it'; the r_z are then penalties for committing an error of first or second kind.

The value of information is, by (4.7.5)

$$\text{(7.4.2)}\quad V(\eta)=V_1(\eta)+V_2(\eta);$$

and by (4.7.4), writing $\pi_z\beta_{az}=\gamma_z(a)=\gamma_{az}$ ('weighted benefits'),

$$\text{(7.4.3)}\quad \begin{aligned} V_1(\eta)&=\max(\gamma_{11}\eta_{11}+\gamma_{12}\eta_{21},\gamma_{21}\eta_{11}+\gamma_{22}\eta_{21})\\ V_2(\eta)&=\max(\gamma_{11}\eta_{12}+\gamma_{12}\eta_{22},\gamma_{21}\eta_{12}+\gamma_{22}\eta_{22}).\end{aligned}$$

Write $s_z\equiv\pi_z r_z$ ('weighted regrets'). Then by (7.4.1), (7.1.2)

$$\text{(7.4.4)}\quad [\gamma_{az}]=\begin{pmatrix} \pi_1 b_1 & \pi_2 b_2-s_2 \\ \pi_1 b_1-s_1 & \pi_2 b_2 \end{pmatrix},$$
$$s_z>0,\quad z=1,2.$$

And since always

$$\max(g_1,h_1)+\max(g_2,h_2)$$
$$=\max(g_1+g_2,h_1+h_2,g_1+h_2,h_1+g_2),$$

we obtain from (7.4.2)–(7.4.4)

$$\text{(7.4.5)}\quad V(\eta)=\pi_1 b_1+\pi_2 b_2$$
$$-\min(s_1,s_1\eta_{12}+s_2\eta_{21},s_1\eta_{11}+s_2\eta_{22},s_2).$$

When information is perfect, $\eta_{12}=\eta_{21}=0$; and since both $s_z>0$, then by (5.3.1)

$$\text{(7.4.6)}\quad V^{\max}=\pi_1 b_1+\pi_2 b_2.$$ [22]

Since the labelling of events z is arbitrary, let, without loss of generality and using (7.4.4),

$$\text{(7.4.7)}\quad s_2\geqslant s_1>0.$$

Then with the observations y labelled to yield (7.2.2), $\eta_{11}+\eta_{22}\geqslant 1$, we have

$$s_1\eta_{11}+s_2\eta_{22}\geqslant s_1\,.$$

The loss due to the imperfection of η becomes then, by (7.4.5), (7.4.6),

$$L(\eta)=V^{\max}-V(\eta)=\min(s_1,s_1\eta_{12}+s_2\eta_{21})\,. \tag{7.4.8}$$

By (5.3.1), maximum loss, $L^{\max}$ obtains at null-information, i.e., when the rows of η are identical. Then

$$\eta_{12}+\eta_{21}=1\,, \tag{7.4.9}$$

and hence $s_1\eta_{12}+s_2\eta_{21}$ is a weighted average of s_1, s_2 so that by (7.4.7),

$$s_1\eta_{12}+s_2\eta_{21}\geqslant s_1\,. \tag{7.4.10}$$

Therefore by (7.4.8)

$$L^{\max}=s_1\,.$$

Clearly (7.4.9), while sufficient, is not necessary for (7.4.10). All inquiries satisfying (7.4.10) have the same information value

$$\begin{aligned}V^{\min}&=V^{\max}-L^{\max}\\&=\pi_1b_1+\pi_2b_2-s_1\,,\end{aligned}$$

equal to the value of null-information. They constitute the 'useless indifference set', H^0:

$$\begin{aligned}H^0&=\{\eta:s_1\eta_{12}+s_2\eta_{21}\geqslant s_1\}\,;\quad\text{hence}\\H^0&=\{\eta:s_1\eta_{11}+s_2\eta_{22}\leqslant s_2\}\,.\end{aligned} \tag{7.4.11}$$

If η is not in H^0 then by (7.4.8)

$$L(\eta)=s_1\eta_{12}+s_2\eta_{21}=s_1+s_2-(s_1\eta_{22})\,.$$

In general, then [but with the z and y labelled as stated above and using the notations of (7.2.1), (7.4.4)]

$$V(p_1,p_2)=\pi_1b_1+\pi_2b_2-\begin{matrix}s_1\\{[s_1(1-p_1)+s_2(1-p_2)]}\end{matrix} \tag{7.4.12}$$

$$\text{as}\quad p_1/(1-p_2)\begin{matrix}\leqslant\\ \geqslant\end{matrix}s_2/s_1\,.$$

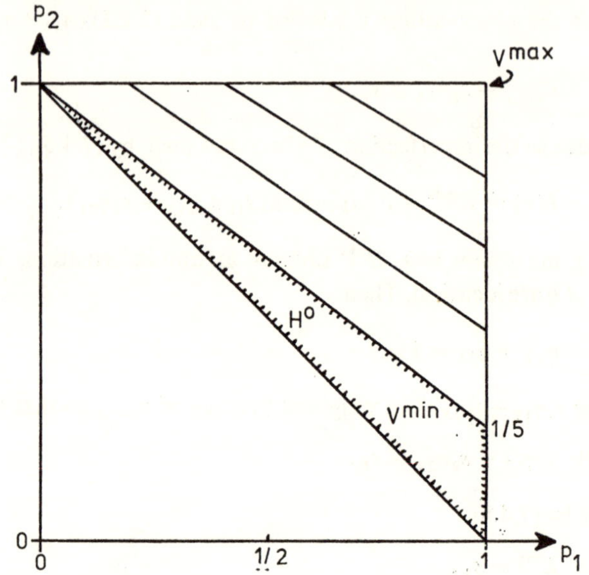

Fig. 3. Indifference sets of binary information matrices: the case of two actions.

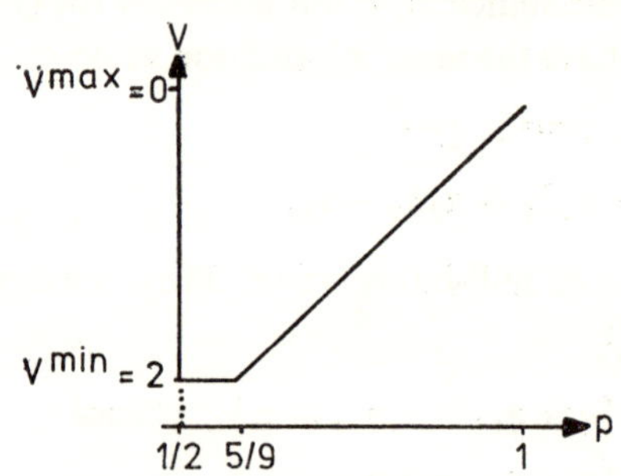

Fig. 3s. Values of symmetric matrices of Figure 3.

Figure 3 is drawn in the (p_1, p_2)-plane assuming $s_1 = 4$, $s_2 = 5$. The useless set H_0 consists of the points in and on the triangle bounded by the main diagonal, the p_2-axis and the straight line

(7.4.13) $s_1 p_1 + s_2 p_2 = s_2$.

All other indifference sets are straight lines parallel to (7.4.13). If the convention (7.2.2), but not (7.4.7), were dropped the indifference sets below the main diagonal would replicate those of Figure 3 in an obvious way, preserving the slope $-s_1/s_2$.

Note that all users with the same ratio s_1/s_2 of 'weighted regrets' have the same system of difference sets of binary inquiries (in the case of two actions).

If η is symmetrical (as in Section 7.3), $\eta_{11}=\eta_{22}=p=1-q\geqslant\frac{1}{2}$, (7.4.12) becomes

$$V(\eta)=\pi_1b_1+\pi_2b_2-\frac{s_1}{(s_1+s_2)\,q}\quad\text{as}\quad p/q\lesseqgtr s_2/s_1\,.$$

Thus the information value of a symmetric binary information (in the case of two actions), if plotted against the probability $p\geqslant\frac{1}{2}$, consists of a 'useless' horizontal segment till p reaches a certain bound; and is a positively sloped straight line for larger p. On Figure 3s the information value is plotted, assuming $b_1=b_2=0$ and, as before, $s_1=4$, $s_2=5$, and illustrating the statement of Section 4.13: the function $V(p)$ is convex.

7.5. *Binary Inquiries with More Than Two Actions*[23]

If the number of non-dominated, benefit-relevant actions exceeds two the convex function $V_{\pi\beta}(\eta)$, where η is a binary inquiry, may but need not retain the shape just derived for the case of two actions. In particular, $V_{\pi\beta}$ may become a *strictly* convex function of η.

We shall write

$$\beta(a,z)=\beta_z(a)\,;\quad \pi_z\beta_z(a)=\gamma_z(a);\quad z=1,2\,;\quad a\in A\,.$$

Let a and a' be two distinct elements of A. Then

$$(7.5.1)\qquad \beta_1(a)>\beta_1(a')\quad\text{implies}\quad\beta_2(a)<\beta_2(a')$$

lest a' be dominated by a. The case $\beta_1(a)=\beta_1(a')$, $\beta_2(a)=\beta_2(a')$ is also eliminated since A was defined as benefit-relevant (Section 2.8). We can therefore order all actions completely and strongly by the values of $\beta_1(a)$. Moreover, we shall consider A to be closed. If A is finite we can index its N elements a^i so that

$$(7.5.2)\qquad \beta_1(a^{i+1})>\beta_1(a^i)\,;\qquad \beta_2(a^{i+1})<\beta_2(a^i),\quad i=1,\ldots,N-1\,.$$

When A is not countable we shall represent it by the interval $A=[0,1]$, with $\beta_1(a)$ strictly increasing and $\beta_2(a)$ strictly decreasing in a. If, in particular, these two functions are differentiable, it follows that

$$(7.5.3)\qquad \beta_1'(a)>0\,,\qquad \beta_2'(a)<0\,,$$

and we say that the 'marginal benefits' are, respectively, positive or negative, given z.

We shall consider the case of 'increasing or constant marginal benefits' as well as the economically more plausible case of 'decreasing marginal benefits'. If $\beta_z(a)$ is 'smooth' (twice differentiable) the two cases are, respectively:

$$(7.5.4) \quad \text{(I) } \beta_z''(a) \geqslant 0\,; \qquad \text{(II) } \beta_z''(a) < 0\,; \quad z = 1.\,2.$$

More broadly, the two cases can be interpreted for any continuous function $\beta_z(a)$ by requiring it to be convex or strictly concave, respectively. And stretching the definitions still further we may let A be finite, arrange and label its elements as in (7.5.2) and be concerned with the signs of second differences instead of second derivatives. That is, writing

$$\Delta_{zi}^2 = [\beta_z(a^{i+1}) - \beta_z(a^i)] - [\beta_z(a_i^i) - B_z(a^{i-1})],$$

the two cases in (7.5.4) are replaced, respectively by

$$(7.5.5) \quad \text{(I) } \Delta_{zi}^2 \geqslant 0\,; \qquad \text{(II) } \Delta_{zi}^2 < 0\,;$$
$$z = 1, 2 \quad i = 2, \ldots, N-1\,.$$

(Moreover, it can be shown that we can put $\beta_1(a^1)=0=\beta_2(a^N)$ without loss of generality.) This would apply to our example of Section 4.4, with cancer absent or present and with three treatments available; see also end of Section 7.5.

Here is, on the other hand, an example of a smooth benefit function which we shall use later. A farmer wishes to maximize the amount harvested. He must decide on how to allocate his total acreage $(=1)$ between two crops, the 'wet' crop being favored by wet weather (denoted by $z=1$), and the 'dry' crop by dry weather $(z=2)$. The action a is the acreage allotted to the *wet* crop. Denote the harvest from x acres of the wet crop when the weather is or is not favorable to it by, respectively, $f_w(x)$ and $g_w(x)$, $0 \leqslant x < 1$. Correspondingly $f_d(x)$ and $g_d(x)$ are the dry crop harvests. Thus,

$$f_w(x) > g_w(x)\,, \qquad f_d(x) > g_d(x)\,,$$

and these four functions have positive first derivatives. The combined harvest of the two crops is

$$(7.5.6)\quad \begin{aligned}\beta_1(a) &= f_w(a) + g_d(1-a) \text{ in wet weather}\\ \beta_2(a) &= g_w(a) + f_d(1-a) \text{ in dry weather}.\end{aligned}$$

If no action is dominated, we have by (7.5.3)

$$(7.5.6')\quad \begin{aligned}\beta_1'(a) &= f_w'(a) - g_d'(1-a) > 0,\\ \beta_2'(a) &= g_w'(a) - f_d'(1-a) < 0.\end{aligned}$$

Now, if the farming of each crop obeys the 'law of decreasing marginal returns to land' the second derivatives of all the four functions $f_w, g_w\, f_d, g_d$ are negative and therefore

$$(7.5.6'')\quad \begin{aligned}\beta_1''(a) &= f_w''(a) + g_d''(1-a) < 0,\\ \beta_2''(a) &= g_w''(a) + f_d''(1-a) < 0;\end{aligned}$$

and the inequality signs are reversed if the marginal returns to land are increasing.

To express the value of inquiry, V, in the general case, denote by $B_y(a)$ the expected benefit of an observation y when action a is taken:

$$(7.5.7)\quad B_y(a) = \gamma_1(a)\eta_{1y} + \gamma_2(a)\,\eta_{2y},\quad y = 1, 2.$$

By (4.7.4) the value of observation y is

$$(7.5.8)\quad \begin{aligned}V_y(\eta) &= \gamma_1(a_y)\,\eta_{1y} + \gamma_2(a_y)\,\eta_{2y}\\ &\geqslant \gamma_1(a)\,\eta_{1y} + \gamma_2(a)\,\eta_{2y},\quad a \in A;\end{aligned}$$

and the value of inquiry is

$$V(\eta) = V_1(\eta) + V_2(\eta).$$

If the functions $\beta_z(a)$ are both *convex*, then so are the functions $\gamma_z(a)$ and consequently their increasing linear combination $B_y(a)$ is convex. Hence $B_y(a)$ will be maximized by one of the extreme values of a; this is, by (7.5.2),

$$a_y = a^1 \quad \text{or} \quad a^N,\quad y = 1, 2.$$

The case of convex benefit functions is thus reduced to that of two actions (Section 7.4), so that the function $V(p_1, p_2)$ is again as represented on Figures 3 and 3s. The same applies to the case of A finite and appropriately ordered, with first differences increasing or constant as in (7.5.5), (I).

We shall show, on the other hand, that if the two benefit functions $\beta_z(a)$ are *smooth and strictly concave* then V is *strictly convex* in p_1, p_2. Note that, if $\beta_z''(a)<0$ then $\gamma_z''(a)<0$ since $\pi_z>0$. Define

$$V_y' \equiv \left.\frac{dB_y(a)}{da}\right]_{a=a_y}; \qquad V_y'' \equiv \left.\frac{d^2B_y(a)}{da^2}\right]_{a=a_y}; \quad y=1,2.$$

Then by (7.5.8) we have, for $y=1, 2$,

$$(7.5.8') \quad V_y' = \gamma_1'(a_y)\,\eta_{1y} + \gamma_2'(a_y)\,\eta_{2y} = 0$$

since, with $\gamma_z''(a)<0$,

$$(7.5.8'') \quad V_y'' = \gamma_1''(a_y)\,\eta_{1y} + \gamma_2''(a_y)\,\pi_{2y} < 0.$$

Note that under these conditions all useless inquiries are null-inquiries. For let η be useless as defined in Section 4.12. Then $a_1=a_2=a^*$, say; and by (7.5.8′)

$$(7.5.9) \quad \begin{aligned} &\gamma_1'(a^*)\,\eta_{11} + \gamma_2'(a^*)\,\eta_{21} = 0 \quad \text{[repeated in the equation} \\ &\gamma_1'(a^*)\,\eta_{12} + \gamma_2'(a^*)\,\eta_{22} = 0]; \quad \text{hence} \\ &\eta_{11}/\eta_{21} = -\,\gamma_2'(a^*)/\gamma_1'(a^*) = \eta_{12}/\eta_{22}, \\ &\eta_{11}/(1-\eta_{22}) = \eta_{22}/(1-\eta_{11}), \\ &\eta_{11} + \eta_{22} = 1. \end{aligned}$$

The set of useless inquiries, $\{\eta : V(\eta) = V^{\min}\}$ is therefore represented by the main diagonal of the unit square provided both benefit functions are strictly concave and smooth.

Strict convexity of V in p_1, p_2 when the $\gamma_z(a)$ are strictly concave and smooth, can be proved without solving equation (7.5.8′) explicitly. It suffices to show – as is done in Appendix B – that

$$(7.5.10) \quad w_{11} > 0, \quad \begin{vmatrix} w_{11} & w_{12} \\ w_{21} & w_{22} \end{vmatrix} > 0,$$

where

$$(7.5.11) \quad w_{ij} \equiv \partial^2 V/\partial p_i \partial p_j.$$

However, for the sake of illustration and to construct Figure 4, we shall derive an explicit solution by assuming the benefit function quadratic and concave. Specifically,[24] let

$$(7.5.12)\quad \begin{aligned}\gamma_1(a) &= (1 + 4a - 2a^2)/4\,;\\ \gamma_2(a) &= (3 - 2a^2)/4\,.\end{aligned}$$

Differentiating with respect to a, substituting onto (7.5.8′) and solving, we obtain

$$a_1 = p_1/(p_1 + q_2), \qquad a_2 = q_1/(q_1 + p_2),$$

where $p_i = 1 - q_i = \eta_{ii}$. Then by (7.5.8), (7.5.12)

$$(7.5.13)\quad V = V_1 + V_2 = 1 + \frac{1}{2}\cdot\frac{p_1p_2 + q_1q_2}{(p_1 + q_2)(p_2 + q_1)},$$

symmetric and strictly convex in p_1, p_2. The contour lines over the unit square are portions of ellipses, V=const., whose major axis is the main diagonal (the line $p_1 + p_2 = 1$) and whose minor axes range in length from zero to $\sqrt{2}$. The former extreme corresponds to the set of useless inquiries, which is represented by the main diagonal and thus coincides with the set of null-inquiries, agreeing with the result just stated for all strictly concave smooth benefit functions. At the other extreme, the indifference set is reduced to two points, (1, 1) and (0, 0): perfect information. If, applying the convention (7.2.2), i.e., eliminating the half-square below the main diagonal, we qualify the likelihoods, p_1, p_2 as 'goods' then the indifference sets (except at the extremes) are represented by strictly concave curves: see Figure 4.

When the binary inquiry is symmetric, write $p_1 = p_2 = p$, and (7.5.13) becomes

$$(7.5.14)\quad V = \tfrac{3}{2} - p + p^2,$$

a convex parabola with a minimum at $p = \frac{1}{2}$, the only useless inquiry. If p is a 'good', $p \geqslant \frac{1}{2}$, V is rising and strictly convex in p. See Figure 4s.

We return now briefly to the case of *A finite*. Condition (7.5.8) applies, so that again the information value is

$$(7.5.15)\quad \begin{aligned} V(\eta) &= V_1 + V_2 = \\ &= \max_a(\gamma_{a1}\eta_{11} + \gamma_{a2}\eta_{21}) + \max_a(\gamma_{a2}\eta_{21} + \gamma_{a2}\eta_{22}),\end{aligned}$$

writing $\gamma_{az} = \gamma_z(a)$.

Corresponding to the case of *strictly concave* smooth benefit functions,

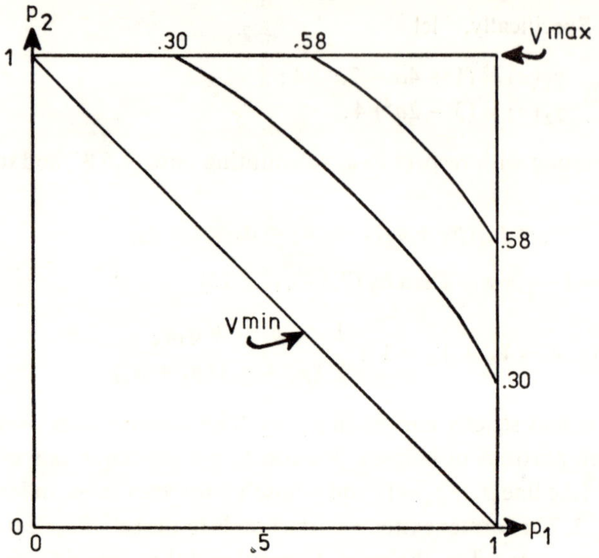

Fig. 4. Indifference sets of binary information matrices: a case of a continuum of actions.

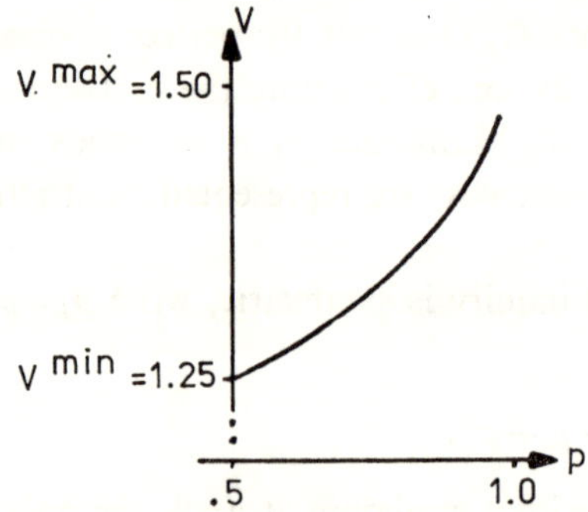

Fig. 4s. Values of symmetric matrices of Figure 4.

(7.5.4, II) that we have just studied, is now condition (7.5.5, II) on the second differences. The surface $V(\eta)$ is then again convex and non-linear. It is piecewise linear. The contour lines for $V > V^{\min}$ are piecewise linear; and they are again concave over the region $p_1 + p_2 > 1$. But, different from the case of smooth benefit functions, the set of useless inquiries ($V = V^{\min}$) is now not confined to the main diagonal (i.e., to null inquiries) but is represented by a flat region. As an example Figure 5 is drawn for the case of 3 actions, $A=(1, 2, 3)$, with the matrix of weighted benefits

$$[\gamma_{az}] = \begin{pmatrix} 5 & 0 \\ 4 & 2 \\ 0 & 3 \end{pmatrix}$$

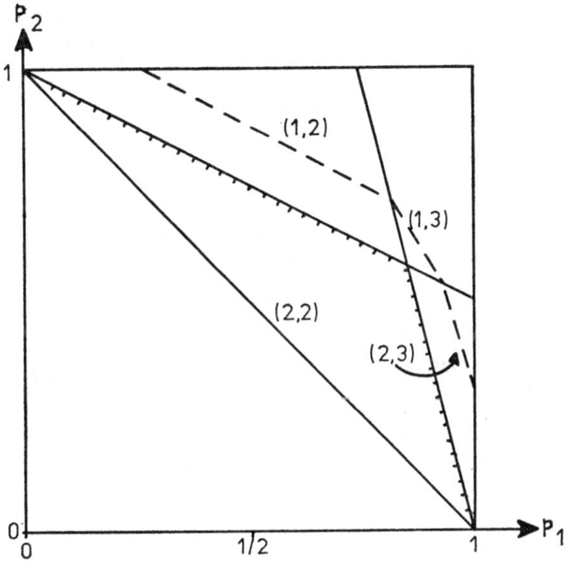

Fig. 5. Indifference sets of binary information matrices: a case of three actions.

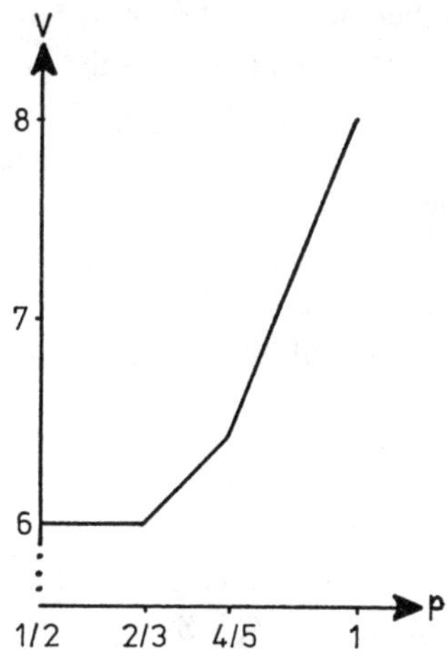

Fig. 5s. Values of symmetric matrices of Figure 5.

Applying (7.5.15) in the region $p_1+p_2 \geqslant 1$ and writing $q_i = 1-p_i$, we have

$V_1 = \max(5p_1, 4p_1+2q_2)$, corresponding to the appropriate actions
$a_1 = \quad 1, \quad 2$. Similarly,
$V_2 = \max(5q_1, 4q_1+2p_2, 3p_2)$, corresponding to
$a_2 = \quad 1, \quad 2, \quad 3$. Hence, omitting dominated values,
$V = \max(p_1+2p_2+4,\ 5p_1+3p_2,\ 6,\ 4p_1+p_2+2)$, corresponding to the optimal strategies $\alpha^* = (a_1, a_2)$:
$\alpha^* = \quad (1, 2), \quad (1,3), (2,2), \quad (2, 3)$.

Perfect information ($p_1=p_2=1$) yields $V^{\max}=\max(6, 8, 6, 7)=8$. Information is useless when $a_1=a_2=2$, hence $V^{\min}=6$. The useless region is bounded, on Figure 5, by the shaded piecewise linear concave curve, and its optimal strategy (2, 2) is indicated. The regions corresponding to the other three optimal strategies are indicated similarly; and the broken line – also piecewise linear and concave – is the contour line for $V=6\frac{1}{4}$.

When only symmetric inquiries are considered, $p_1=p_2=p \geqslant \frac{1}{2}$, and

$$V = \max(6, 3p + 4, 8p),$$

as plotted on Figure 5s: V is piecewise linear and convex in p, with a horizontal 'useless' portion.

7.6. *On Indifference Sets of Binary Inquiries*

In the case of two actions, the results of Section 7.4 and Figure 3 are consistent with the indifference lines drawn by Savage [49] in the space of the 'error probabilities of two kinds'. In the spirit presented here, he defines an error probability as that of '*doing the wrong thing*' if one of the two possible events, hypotheses, obtains; rather than by the usual, non-operational phrase, 'probability of *rejecting*' a true hypothesis. He also points out that these two probabilities depend on the experiment (characterized, in our notation, by the matrix η) *and* on the decision rule used. Note that, if this rule is optimal, the error probability takes, in our notation, the form

$$(7.6.1) \quad 1 - \Pr(a = a_y | z) = 1 - p(y|z) = 1 - \eta_{zy},$$

provided that for each datum y there is a distinct appropriate action, a_y. The space of error probabilities is then essentially identical with the space of likelihoods as on our Figures 3, 4, 5. Savage states, correctly but without proof, that (consistently with our Figure 3 for the case of two actions) the slope of the parallel straight indifference lines is the negative of the "personal odds... when the two errors are equally expensive." (The 'useless' region H^0 is not mentioned.)

However, he avoided such concepts when providing 'an imperfect and special demonstration' for a (perhaps 'non-Bayesian') audience. This demonstration leads to parallel straight indifference lines *regardless of the number of actions*. This contradicts our Section 7.5 and Figures 4 and 5.

The demonstration considers, in effect, three inquiry matrices η, η', η'' where

$$\eta = k\eta' + (1-k)\,\eta'', \quad 0 < k < 1,$$

so that the points representing the three inquiries are collinear. Now denote by

$$g \equiv (\eta', \eta''; k)$$

a gamble which yields the inquiries η' and η'' with respective probabilities k and $1-k$. Clearly an inquirer indifferent between η' and η'' is also indifferent between them and g. Therefore, if g and η *were identical objects* it would indeed follow that the straight line containing η, η', η'' is an indifference line. Moreover, for any η^*, our inquirer must be indifferent between the gambles

$$g' \equiv (\eta', \eta^*; k) \quad \text{and} \quad g'' \equiv (\eta'', \eta^*; k);$$

and again: should these two gambles be, respectively, *identical* with the inquiries whose matrices are the convex combinations

$$k\eta' + (1-k)\,\eta^* \quad \text{and} \quad k\eta'' + (1-k)\,\eta^*,$$

then it would further follow that the indifference lines must be parallel, regardless of the number of available actions.

This conflict with the results of our Section 7.5 is explained if we realize that gamble g is in general *not identical* with inquiry η (and similarly, the other two gambles are not identical with the associated convex combinations of inquiries). For action a_y, appropriate to the outcome y of experiment η, may be quite different from the actions a'_y and a''_y (say) that are appropriate to the same outcome y of experiments η' and η'' which are yielded by gamble g. This makes the demonstration inapplicable whenever more than two actions are available.[25]

7.7. *A Remark on Non-Binary Inquiries*

With non-binary inquiries obvious difficulties arise. For example, with $m \geqslant 2$, the elimination of dominated actions fails to yield an ordering of actions as in (7.5.2), with its simple implications for the case of convex benefit functions. Methods of mathematical programming are called for, especially when the benefit functions are non-smooth.

It is interesting to note some properties of the sets of useless and of null-inquiries. In the case of strictly concave smooth benefit functions, the two sets coincide when $m = n = 2$. But in general the useless set may have higher dimensionality than the set of null-inquiries. To see this, note that, since

$$\sum_{y=1}^{n} \eta_{zy} = 1, \quad z = 1, \ldots, m,$$

the set of all inquiries can be represented by a unit-cube of

$$m(n-1) \text{ dimensions}.$$

The set of all null-inquiries obeys in addition the $(m-1)\,(n-1)$ equations

$$(7.7.1) \quad \eta_{1y} = \cdots = \eta_{my}, \quad y = 1, \ldots, n-1,$$

and is therefore represented by a hyperplane of

$$m(n-1) - (m-1)\,(n-1) = n-1 \text{ dimensions},$$

going through a diagonal of the unit cube. On the other hand, the set of useless inquiries is defined by the $(n-1)$ equations

$$(7.7.2) \quad a_1 = \cdots = a_n.$$

The dimensionality of that set is therefore $= (m-1)\,(n-1) > n-1$ if $m > 2$.

In particular, if the $\gamma_z(a)$ are smooth and strictly concave, the $n-1$ Equations (7.7.2) defining the useless set can be rewritten as

$$(7.7.3) \quad \textstyle\sum_z \gamma_z'(a^*)\,\eta_{zy} = 0, \quad y = 1, \ldots, n-1.$$

Therefore, if the $\gamma_{z1}(a)$ are concave and quadratic, then Figure 4 is generalized as follows: the indifference surfaces are portions of hyper-ellipsoids and the set of useless inquiries is a hyperplane (7.7.3) of higher order than, and embedding, the set of null-inquiries.

7.8. *Cost and Feasibility Conditions*

So far, we have explored, at least for the case of binary information matrices, the behavior of the information value function $V(\eta)$ which associates each η with the maximum expected benefit. If utility can be represented as the difference between benefit and information cost, an optimal matrix η maximizes the difference between $V(\eta)$ and the expected information cost, subject to a constraint on feasible pairs (η, κ) of inquiries and cost functions (Section 4.6),

$$(\eta, \kappa) \in \{(\eta, \kappa)\}.$$

A simple assumption is to associate each η with just one cost function $\kappa_z(\eta)$, viz., the one giving the lowest expected cost [as in (4.6.6], for a given η. In addition we shall make $\kappa_z(\eta)$ independent of z:

$$\kappa_z(\eta) = \kappa(\eta),$$

say. Thus, if η is obtained by a sampling survey of families the cost $\kappa(\eta)$ will depend on the size of the sample needed to obtain η (i.e., to attain some preassigned error probabilities); but not on the properties of the families – disregarding, for example, the fact that households of certain types may require second visits.

Under these assumptions, expected utility is simply

$$U(\eta) = V(\eta) - \kappa(\eta).$$

Often cost is considered to be bounded from above so that the feasible set of inquiries has the form

$$\{\eta : \kappa(\eta) \leqslant \text{const.}\}. \tag{7.8.1}$$

Still confining ourselves to binary information matrices, we shall give examples illustrating the possible behavior of the cost functions $\kappa(\eta)$. An important question is: under what conditions does the expected utility, as a function of η, and thus of p_1, p_2

$$U(p_1, p_2) = V(p_1, p_2) - \kappa(p_1, p_2) \tag{7.8.2}$$

behave in such a way that the optimal information matrix is an 'interior solution'. If it does not, optimal information may be null-information; or we may have $p_1 = 1, p_2 = 1$, a case of 'large scale economies'.

7.9. *Cost Increasing in Channel Capacity*

The capacity $C=C(p_1, p_2)$ of a channel transmitting one digit per time unit (see below, Section 8.4) is given, in the binary case, by[26]

$$
\begin{aligned}
&2^C = 2^{L_1} + 2^{L_2}, \quad \text{where}\\
&L_1 = (q_1 H_2 - p_2 H_1)/|\eta|\,;\\
(7.9.1)\quad &L_2 = (q_2 H_1 - p_1 H_2)/|\eta|\,,\\
&|\eta| = p_1 + p_2 - 1\,, \qquad q_i = 1 - p_i\,,\\
&H_i = -\,(p_i \log_2 p_i + q_1 \log_2 q_i)\,, \quad i = 1, 2\,.
\end{aligned}
$$

C is quasi-convex in (p_1, p_2). The contour lines of equal capacity are strictly concave for $p_1 + p_2 > 1$; all points on the straight line $p_1 + p_2 = 1$ have equal capacity $C=0$; and maximum capacity is $C(1, 1)=1$, see Figure 6.

Suppose that the contour lines of equal information value are strictly concave, as in the 'farmer's case' of Section 7.5 and Figure 4. Suppose further that the 'observations' $y=1, 2$ are messages ('wet', 'dry') received

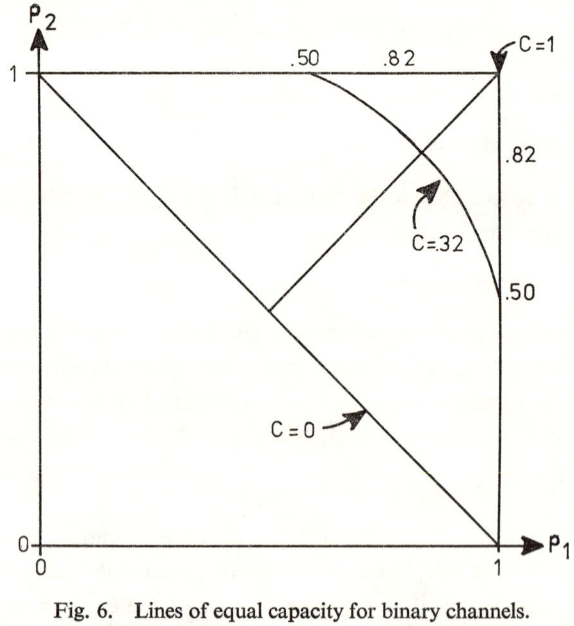

Fig. 6. Lines of equal capacity for binary channels.

through a channel whose inputs are the 'true' events (viz. actual future weather), $z=1, 2$. And suppose information cost strictly increases with channel capacity. If, as in (7.8.1), the maximum cost is fixed, so is then the capacity $C=C_0$, say. An optimal information system (consisting in this case of the channel and nothing else) is an 'interior' optimum if the contour line of equal information value tangent to the contour line of capacity C_0 has, at the point of tangency, a lesser curvature. This happens to be so in the case of our farmer,[27] but need not happen if a different benefit function is given.[28]

If the information cost is not fixed then under our assumption and by (7.8.2)

$$U(p_1, p_2) = V(p_1, p_2) - f\,[C(p_1, p_2)],$$

where f is a strictly increasing function. An interior solution will exist if U is quasi-concave; and this will depend on f. This can be illustrated in the symmetric case, $p_1=p_2=p\geqslant\frac{1}{2}$. Then

$$C = 1 + p\log_2 p + (1-p)\log_2(1-p),$$

increasing and strictly convex in p since $C''(p)>0$. Using the strictly convex information value (7.5.14) of our farmer's case, it is easily seen that $U=V-f(C)$ is maximized at $p=\frac{1}{2}$ or 1 (so that no interior solution exists) if f is linear; but f strictly convex may yield an interior solution.

7.10. *Cost of Inferring Sign of Mean of Finite Population from Sign of Mean of Sample*

Suppose n random variables u_i $(i=1,\ldots, n)$ are jointly normal, with

$$E(u_i) = 0, \quad E(u_i u_j) = {1 \atop 0} \text{ if } j {= \atop \neq} i.$$

Define the events z and the 'observations' (usually called 'statistics') y by

$$z = {1 \atop 2} \text{ if } \sum_1^n u_i {< \atop \leqslant} 0; \quad y = {1 \atop 2} \text{ if } \sum_1^m u_i {> \atop \leqslant} 0 \quad 1 \leqslant m \leqslant n;$$

thus m is the size of the sample, and n is the size of the population. Then (see [13, p. 290]) the joint distribution of z and y is given by

$$\Pr(z=1, y=1) = \Pr(z=2, y=2) = \tfrac{1}{4} + (\arcsin\rho)/2\pi$$
$$\Pr(z=1, y=2) = \Pr(z=2, y=1) = \tfrac{1}{4} - (\arcsin\rho)/2\pi,$$

where $\rho = \sqrt{m/n}$.[29] Hence η is binary symmetric, with

$$\begin{aligned} \eta_{11} &= \Pr(y=1 \mid z=1) = \tfrac{1}{4} + \arcsin \sqrt{m/n}/2\pi \\ dm/dp &= 2\pi n \sin \pi (4p-1) \\ d^2m/dp^2 &= 8\pi^2 n \cos(4p-1) \gtrless 0 \quad \text{if} \quad p \lessgtr \tfrac{3}{8}. \end{aligned}$$

The sample size m is thus an increasing function of p, convex for small (and hence less informative: Section 7.3) values of p, and concave for larger ones. So is the cost of information (sampling cost) if we assume it to increase linearly with m.

8. Economics of Communication

8.1. *The Fidelity Criterion as Benefit*

In the preceding three sections, the benefit $\beta(a, z)$ depends on the 'action' a in A and the 'event' (or hypothesis)[30] z in Z. A probability function π is defined on Z. Event z is transformed into 'observation' y by a processing η; and y is transformed into a by a subsequent processing called strategy (these processings are possibly stochastic).

Now let us interpret, instead, z in Z as a 'message sent', occurring with probability π_z. Interpret processing η as 'communication' (to be specified later as a chain: storing, encoding, transmitting): it transforms message z into y, the latter to be interpreted as some signals received by the decision-maker. An important restriction is this: *the set A of actions a is identical with the set Z of messages sent.* The strategy α consists then in a rule of 'decoding' the received signals y, i.e., in prescribing which element a of Z (or which conditional distribution of a) should be associated with a given y. The information system of our Figure 1 is reduced to its 'communication' segment.

The early writings on communication theory – most importantly the pioneering work of Shannon [50] – impose in effect a further restriction, by assuming equal penalty for all communication errors, so that 'a miss is as bad as a mile'. That is, the benefit function is taken to be simply

$$(8.1.1) \quad \beta(a, z) = \begin{matrix} 0 \\ -1 \end{matrix} \quad \text{if} \quad a \begin{matrix} = \\ \neq \end{matrix} z.$$

Then the expected benefit is, by (4.6.3),

$$(8.1.2)\quad B_{\pi\beta}(\eta,\alpha) = \Sigma_{zya}\beta(a,z)\,\pi_z\eta_{zy}\alpha_{ya} = \\ = -\sum_{z\neq a}\sum_{ya}\pi_z\eta_{zy}\alpha_{ya} = -\,p_e,$$

where p_e denotes the 'probability of error'. For a given set Z (characterized by π), p_e depends then only on the properties of the communication processing η and the decoding strategy α.

To be sure, the special assumption (8.1.1) was abandoned in the last chapter of Shannon's early work [50] for the case when, in our notation, Z is the real line. In this case exact communication ($p_e=0$) is practically impossible and, in fact, not needed. This property of 'continuous sources' moved Shannon to suggest various measures of a (possibly non-metric) 'distance' between the message sent and message received. "It measures how undesirable it is ... to receive" (p. 76) a when z is sent. Thus Shannon's 'distance' would correspond to our 'penalty', the negative of our 'benefit': a function that can take more than just two values. Later, Shannon [51] extended the idea to 'discrete' sources, presumably recognizing its general importance. He defined the 'fidelity criterion' (and its negative, the 'distortion'), as a general real-valued function of the message sent and the message decoded. This function is identical with our general benefit function that maps $Z\times A$ into reals; except for the restriction (mentioned earlier) that replaces $Z\times A$ by $Z\times Z$. A fidelity criterion does, then, assign different penalties (negative benefits) to different errors of communication and decoding. To use Shannon's example: it is more dangerous to mistake the emergency signal for 'all's well' than conversely.[31]

There is an important analogy between communicating information, on the one hand, and, on the other, the storing and transporting of physical commodities. By and large (as indicated in Section 2.2), the costs and delays involved in storage and transportation of commodities are independent of the cost of producing and of the use to be made of them. Similarly, the costs and delays in retaining and transmitting knowledge are, by and large, independent of the cost of producing and the value of using it. *Added in 1974*: And they are additive, see [59].

This justifies the interest in measuring the 'amount' (as distinct from cost and value) of information: it would correspond to the physical volume or weight of goods in warehouses and in transit. Essentially it should measure the *number of symbols* needed to store and transmit a message: for, the larger the collection of symbols – a spoken or written English or coded sentence, a picture – the more time or effort or equipment is required to handle it. And, under assumption (8.1.1), the number of required symbols is independent of the benefit function of the ultimate user, – the 'meta-decider' (Section 3.2) as distinct from the decoder.

However (to return to our analogy), the storage and transportation costs of a commodity are not completely independent of its value in use. The more valuable a commodity the greater will be the diminishment of profit due to breakage or leakage, per pound or gallon. Similarly, some distortions of messages are more dangerous, diminish the benefit more, than others. They require a larger number (for example, a repetition) of symbols to mitigate the resulting damage. Shannon's fidelity criterion, replacing the simple assumption (8.1.1) takes account of the benefit function. The number of symbols needed is recomputed, still considering the information system of our Figure 1 as consisting of its communication segment only.

8.2. *Capacity of Noiseless Channel*

We mentioned in Section 4.2 that statistical decision theory neglects delays in processing. Communication theory does not neglect them. Concepts like the speed of processing (thruput per time unit), and the maximum of this speed, achievable with a given processing instrument arise naturally. As a simple case, imagine a noiseless transmission channel. Its inputs are sequences of symbols such as dots and dashes, or numerical digits. Let us call them digits. They are the outputs of the preceding processing link, the encoding, to be discussed next, in Section 8.3. The digits are transmitted through the channel one by one and received at the other end with no distortion. If the channel is a cable consisting of several wires, several symbols can be transmitted simultaneously. We can therefore diminish delays by increasing the number of wires, which thus measures the channel's capacity: the maximum number of digits that can be transmitted per unit of time, analogous to the capacity of a pipeline.

Channel capacity – already in the noiseless case – is economically significant for two reasons. First, if the inflow of input digits per time unit exceeds the channel capacity, untransmitted, and therefore useless, inputs will pile up indefinitely, with an obvious detriment to the expected benefit.

Second, any further increase of capacity, in excess of the inflow of inputs, will diminish the delay between input and output of the channel.

Why delays can diminish expected benefit, is due to 'impatience' (preference for early results of actions) as well as to the obsolescence of data – i.e., in our case, of the channel outputs – on which the choice of action is based. This was discussed in Section 6.5.

While increased channel capacity thus increases expected benefit, it will, in general, also require an increase in cost.

Expected benefit is diminished by delay. But benefit is not necessarily a linear function of delay. Hence (see Appendix A) expected utility (difference between expected benefit and expected cost) need not be monotone in expected delay. Therefore, it is not correct to present the economics of communication – even in the simplest case of a noiseless channel – as that of minimizing expected cost for a given expected delay, or at given expected speed of transmission. Yet, just this seems to be done, in this or similar contexts, in much of the literature, where, essentially, the problem is presented as that of determining an efficient set in the space of expectations of various 'criteria'.[32]

8.3. *Minimum Expected Length of Code Word, as the 'Uncertainty at Source'*

If only two possible messages z (=1 or 0, say) can be sent, each can be encoded as a single binary digit, to be transmitted through the (noiseless) channel. However, if a time sequence of T such two-valued messages is to be communicated, less than T digits (and hence less than one digit per message) will be needed on the average if one uses 'code words' (binary sequences) with few digits for the more probable and with more digits for the less probable sequences of messages. For example, if one uses this principle and if the odds for z taking its two values are 9:1, then, even if the sequences of messages occur independently ('have no pattern'), it is possible to devise codes which will use, on the average, approximately only .64 or .53 digits per message when $T=2$ or $T=3$, respectively. In general, as established in the 'Fundamental Theorem for a Noiseless Channel' by Shannon [50], the minimum expected length of the code word converges toward the (never negative) quantity

$$(8.3.1) \qquad -\sum_{z \in Z} \pi_z \log_2 \pi_z \equiv H(\pi), \quad \text{also written as} \quad H(Z)$$

and called entropy. This limit is valid not only for the case of two-valued messages (as in our example, with $H(\pi)=.47$) but for a set Z of any size m. Since $H(\pi)$ increases with m and, furthermore, since $H(\pi)$ is largest when all the m elements of Z are equiprobable [so that every $\pi_2=1/m$, and $H(\pi)=m$], the name 'amount of uncertainty' (about z) occasionally given to $H(\pi)$ does agree with English usage. Alternatively, one says that $H(\pi)$ units of information are gained if this uncertainty is removed (by learning the actual value of z). Indeed $H(\pi)$ has been proposed as a '*measure*' *of uncertainty*, or *of information*, because it is additive (as any measure ought to be) in the following sense. Let π', π'' characterize two statistically independent sets Z' and Z''; that is, the joint occurrence $z=(z'$ and $z'')$ of given messages from the two sets occurs with probability

$$\pi_z = \pi'_{z'} \cdot \pi''_{z''} ;$$

then, by the definition (8.3.1) of the distribution parameter H,

$$(8.3.2) \qquad H(\pi) = H(\pi') + H(\pi'') .$$

Similar additivity properties are derived for certain related distribution parameters (such as 'uncertainty removed by transmission', of which more later). Since $H(\pi)$ measures, at least in the limit, the average length of a sequence of *bi*nary dig*its*, the measurement unit of 'uncertainty' (or its negative, 'information') is called, briefly, a *bit*, following a suggestion of J. W. Tukey.

It is not clear, however, for what economic purpose one should measure uncertainty, or information. Because of the additive property (8.3.2) of the distribution parameter H, specialists in various fields (mathematics, statistics, psychology) expressed enthusiasm: the subtle, intangible concept of information has now become measurable "in a way similar to that as money is used in everyday life" [46]. Indeed a paper currency bill can be measured by the number of dollars it represents, and thus by the amount of some useful commodity at a given price. But it can be also measured (a peso and a hundred peso bill alike) in square inches of its area. If I use it for papering my walls, the latter not the former measurement is appropriate.

Somewhat anticipating the subsequent more detailed discussion, note that a distribution parameter such as $H(\pi)$ cannot alone determine the information value of a system. For $H(\pi)$ depends only on the distribution π, not on the benefit function β. To be sure, the special assumption (8.1.1) of equal penalty for all communication errors does remove variations of the benefit function. This fact may have been the source of misunderstandings about the economic significance of the number of bits gained or lost, regardless of the use the decision-maker can make of them. If a general fidelity criterion (presumably reflecting the decision-maker's needs) is introduced, $H(\pi)$ fails to determine the information value of the system.

What *is* economically important about $H(\pi)$ is its meaning as the greatest lower bound of the expected length of a code word, given the distribution π. For, the shorter a code word the less is, presumably, the time needed to transmit it, digit by digit; and therefore, for reasons just stated in Section 8.2, the larger the expected benefit.[33]

On the other hand, note that, to bring the expected length of code words down close to its lower limit, $H(\pi)$, one may have to wait till a very long sequence of messages (T large) is piled up. The resulting delay may offset the acceleration due to the shortening of code words. In addition, there are storage costs. Like other entropy formulas, to be dealt with later in this section, $H(\pi)$ loses economic significance unless messages flow in at a fast rate, see Section 8.7.

We can now refer to the 'four-link' chain (b) of Section 3.3. Messages to be sent are stored, encoded, transmitted, decoded. The benefit will depend on the messages to be sent and on the decoded messages; the expected benefit will depend on the probability distribution π characterizing the source (i.e., the messages to be sent) and on the Markov matrices characterizing consecutive processings. Costs and delays arise at each processing link, and their distribution (and hence expectation) depends, too, on π and those Markov matrices.

However, the four-link chain is merely a part of the total information system. Benefit depends on events and actions. Events are transformed, by inquiry, into observations ('data'). These are the messages to be sent, the initial inputs of the communication system; and its final output, the decoded messages, are transformed into actions by applying strategies. We have thus added two links, one at each end of the communication chain. It remains true that the probability distribution (and hence the expectation) of benefits, costs, and delays depends on the initial distribution π (now attached to events, not to messages received) and on the successive Markov matrices.

Alternatively, we can also regard a communication system as a special case of the general information system; viz., one in which the processing of events into data and the processing of decoded messages into action are characterized by identity transformations and by zero-costs and zero-delays.

8.4. *Noisy Channel: Transmission Rate and Capacity*

To concentrate on the properties of a channel, it will be convenient to reinterpret our notation again. Let us now designate channel inputs by z in Z, and its outputs by y in Y, analogous to the 'events' and 'observations' of Sections 4–6. Channel inputs z, the digits of the encoded message, occur with probabilities π_z. Channel outputs, y, the digits received at the channel's end, occur, for a given z, with conditional probabilities $p(y|z)=\eta_{zy}$, elements of the Markov matrix η, called the channel matrix. The channel is noiseless if η is the identity matrix. The joint probability of z and y and the marginal probability of y are, respectively

$$p(z, y) = \pi_z \eta_{zy}$$
$$p(y) = \sum_{z \in Z} \pi_z \eta_{zy} .$$

It will be convenient to give a special symbol, δ_{yz} (an element of the Markov matrix $\delta = [\delta_{yz}]$) to the posterior probability of z, given y. Clearly δ depends on π and η:

$$\delta_{yz} = p(z \mid y) = p(z, y)/p(y)$$
$$= \pi_z \eta_{zy} / \sum_{u \in Z} \pi_u \eta_{uy} .$$

We may call 'uncertainty about z, retained after digit y was received through the channel', the expression

$$H(Z \mid y) = -\sum_z \delta_{yz} \log \delta_{yz} ,$$

and to call its expectation

$$(8.4.1) \qquad -\sum_y p(y)\, H(Z \mid y) = H(Z \mid Y),$$

the '*uncertainty retained*', in L. Breiman's [7] suggestive language. It is clear from its definition that $H(Z|Y)$ depends only on the probability distributions π and η, and we want to emphasize this by writing occasionally

$$H(Z \mid Y) \equiv G(\pi, \eta).$$

The quantity (never negative)

$$H(Z) - H(Z \mid Y) \equiv I(Z, Y) \equiv I(Y, Z) \tag{8.4.2}$$

has been called '*uncertainty removed*' or '*amount of information transmitted*'. Because of the symmetry with respect to Z, Y, which is easily shown (but is not relevant for our purposes) $I(Y, Z)$ has also been called 'mutual information'.[34] Clearly it depends on π and η only. This is brought out if we rewrite (8.4.2) thus:

$$H(\pi) - G(\pi, \eta) = J(\pi, \eta), \tag{8.4.3}$$

Shannon's 'generalized first theorem' states that $J(\pi, \eta)$ is the greatest lower bound of the expected number of binary digits, needed to identify (by appropriately decoding the digit sequence received) each digit put through the channel. Thus $J(\pi, \eta)$ is measured in bits per digit.

In Section 8.2, the speed of a channel, v digits per time unit (say) was introduced. If we multiply it by $J(\pi, \eta)$ bits per digit, we obtain

$$v(\text{digits/time}) \times J(\pi, \eta)\,(\text{bits/digit}) = v \cdot J(\pi, \eta)\,(\text{bits/time}), \tag{8.4.4}$$

a quantity called *transmission rate*. Some confusion is present in textbooks though certainly not in engineering practice, by choosing the time unit so as to make $v=1$ for convenience, and not stating this very explicitly. Yet the distinction between 'uncertainty removed' and 'uncertainty removed per time unit' is of economic importance.

If transmission matrix η undergoes garbling, in the formal sense of our Section 5.2, the number $J(\pi, \eta)$ of bits per digit decreases.[35] Thus variations of 'uncertainty removed' affect expected benefit in the case of possible garbling. But another factor affecting expected benefit is the delay in transmission, due to decreasing the factor v, not $J(\pi, \eta)$. An accurate but slow transmission may have the same value to the user as an inaccurate but fast one.

By (8.4.4) the transmission rate depends on v, π, and η. If v and η are kept constant but π varies over the set of all probability vectors of order m, the transmission rate will vary, and its maximum is called the *capacity of the channel.* It depends on v and η (and thus also on m, the number of rows in η). [However, in theoretical discussion v is often put=1, making the capacity, denoted by C, depend on η only.] In our notation we have, for any v

$$\max_{\pi} J(\pi, \eta)\, v = C(\eta)\cdot v \quad \text{bits per time unit}.$$

8.5. *Capacity and Cost*

It can be presumed that the cost of channel increases with v. It is also usually assumed, I think, that channel cost increases with $C(\eta)$. This assumption was used in Section 7.9, where a formula for $C(\eta)$ was given for η binary and $v=1$. However, it is not too clear why two channels with two different matrices η, η' should require equal costs (of construction, maintenance and operation) whenever $C(\eta)=C(\eta')$. For example, formula (7.9.1) yields approximately (see Figure 6)

$$\text{(8.5.1)} \quad C\begin{pmatrix} .82 & .18 \\ .18 & .82 \end{pmatrix} = .32 = C\begin{pmatrix} .5 & .5 \\ 1 & 0 \end{pmatrix}.$$

The matrix on the right is exemplified by a channel which transmits every 'no' without fault, but transforms a 'yes' into a 'no' half of the time: "You will send me a word (through a rather unreliable messenger) only if you decide to come." It is not clear why the use of such a channel should equal in cost the use of a somewhat more reliable messenger who mistakes a 'yes' for a 'no', or conversely, about one time out of six, as in the matrix on the left; and should be more costly than a messenger who makes the mistake one time out of five.

8.6. *Does Informativeness Always Increase with 'Information Transmitted?'*

The answer is no. Let ϕ be any convex function of a nonnegative variable. One such function is

$$\text{(8.6.1)} \quad \phi_0(x) = x \ln x, \quad 0 \leqslant x \leqslant 1,$$

since $\phi_0''(x)=1/x>0$. The following has been proved:[36]

THEOREM: If $\eta^{(1)}=[\eta_{zy}^{(1)}]$ and $\eta^{(2)}=[\eta_{zy}^{(2)}]$ are two information matrices then $\eta^{(1)} > \eta^{(2)}$ if and only if, for any convex function ϕ,

$$(8.6.2) \quad \sum_{y^{(1)}} p(y^{(1)}) \sum_z \phi(\delta_{y^{(1)}z}) \geqslant \sum_{y^{(2)}} p(y^{(2)}) \sum_z \phi(\delta_{y^{(2)}z}),$$

where, as in Section 8.4, p. $(y^{(k)})$ and $\delta_{y^{(k)}z}$ are, respectively, the marginal probability of $y^{(k)}$ and the posterior probability of z, given $y^{(k)}$; both depend on the distribution π and $\eta^{(k)}$. Consider now the particular convex function ϕ_0 defined in (8.6.1). By the definitions of Section 8.4,

$$-\sum_y p(y) \sum_z \phi_0(\delta_{yz}) = G(\pi, \eta)/\ln 2$$

where $\eta = [\eta_{zy}]$. It follows from the preceding theorem that

$$G(\pi, \eta^{(1)}) \leqslant G(\pi, \eta^{(2)}) \quad \text{if} \quad \eta^{(1)} > \eta^{(2)};$$

it also follows that the converse is not true since the theorem requires condition (8.6.2) to hold for all convex functions and not just for ϕ_0. It further follows, by (8.4.3), that the condition

$$J(\pi, \eta^{(1)}) \geqslant J(\pi, \eta^{(2)})$$

is necessary but not sufficient for $\eta^{(1)}$ to be more informative than $\eta^{(2)}$. This means that there exist distributions π and benefit functions (fidelity criteria) β such that an increase in J, the information transmitted, can be consistent with a decrease in the expected benefit.

8.7. *Efficient Coding, Given a Fidelity (Benefit) Function*

Let us continue with the notations of Section 8.4. A channel is characterized by speed v, and by a Markov matrix η, which transforms channel inputs z in Z (occurring with probabilities π_z) into channel outputs y in Y. Now, the channel is a processing link intermediary between two others. On the one hand, at its exit, outputs must be decoded; and, as before, we identify, in the context of communication theory, the results of decoding (decoded messages) with benefit-relevant actions a in A (where the sets A and Z are identical), and, hence, identify the decoding transformation with the strategy α. On the other hand, the benefit-relevant events are not the channel inputs but the messages to be sent. These are transformed into channel inputs by a processing called encoding, possibly preceded by storing, as indicated in Section 8.3. Neglect storing for a moment (i.e., assume it to be characterized by identity transformation, zero costs and zero delays) and denote the messages to be sent by s in S, and their probability distribution by σ. Denote by w the speed of inflow of these messages. An encoding Markov matrix ε (possibly noiseless) transforms S into Z; and clearly σ and ε completely determine the distribution π on Z. To be feasible, an encoding matrix ε is conditioned on some costs and delays, as is the decoding matrix α. These costs and delays are presumably increasing with the length of code words, and also with the number of code words (size of 'dictionary'). The pair (ε, α) is called *code*.

Given σ and the benefit (fidelity) function β on $A \times S$, we can express the expected benefit thus, analogous to (4.6.3):

$$(8.7.1) \quad B_{\sigma\beta}(\eta, \varepsilon, \alpha) = \sum_{s, z, y, a} \beta(a, s)\, \sigma_s \varepsilon_{sz} \eta_{zy} \alpha_{ya} \,.$$

Let Z and Y have m and n elements, respectively, and denote by M_{mn} the set of all Markov matrices of order $m \times n$.

It is in these terms[37] consonant with general economics of information that I shall try to express the main results of Shannon [51], more general and appropriate, for the reasons stated, than those of his original paper [50]. Let B^* be some expected benefit, disregarding any losses due to communication delays. Of course, B^* cannot exceed the expected benefit obtained under perfect information, i.e., with a noiseless channel with a speed not less than that of the inflow of messages, using the best code. Nor can B^* be less than the expected benefit under null-information. Define

$$\begin{aligned} Q &= Q_\beta(B^*, \sigma, \varepsilon, \alpha) \text{ (bits per digit)} \\ &= \min_{\eta'} J(\sigma, \eta') \text{ subject to} \end{aligned}$$

$$B_{\sigma\beta}(\eta', \varepsilon, \alpha) \geqslant B^*, \quad \eta' \in M_{mn}$$

That is, given the benefit function β and the probabilities σ of the messages sent, Q is the least amount of information that needs to be transmitted in order to achieve an expected benefit not less than B^*, using any code (ε, α) and a varying channel matrix η' of order $m \times n$. Now let an available channel have matrix η of that order, and speed v, and let the messages flow in at a speed w (digits per time unit). It was proved by Shannon that, if

$$v \cdot C(\eta) \geqslant w \cdot Q_\beta(B^*, \sigma, \varepsilon, \alpha),$$

then, for every σ, η and every positive k, there exists a code (ε, α) such that

$$(8.7.2) \quad B_{\sigma\beta}(\eta, \varepsilon, \alpha) \geqslant B^* - k\,.$$

Thus, the expected benefit can be brought up arbitrarily close to the desired one provided an appropriate code is used and the channel capacity is appropriately large.[38]

More precisely, for each positive k there exists a number $N(k)$, and a sequence of codes $(\varepsilon_1, \alpha_1), \ldots, (\varepsilon_n, \alpha_n), \ldots$ such that if $n > N(k)$ then (8.7.2) holds. For k small the code $(\varepsilon_n, \alpha_n)$ will, in general, require long words, making it necessary to wait for long sequences of messages before encoding and sending them. As discussed earlier (Sections 8.2, 8.3), long code words cause delays. Long sequences of messages presuppose storing. Therefore, to realize a good code for a small k, it is not possible to neglect (as we have done at the beginning of this section) the storage of messages that must precede their encoding. And this introduces additional delays, resulting in diminished benefits (Section 6). *Unless messages come in very fast, the entropy amounts H, G, J lose economic relevance.*

8.8. *Demand for Communications Links*

The cost of each processing link (storing, encoding, transmitting, decoding) will depend on the characteristics of its transformation matrix but it may also, in general, vary with its inputs, as in Section 2.1. Thus the expected cost of encoding will depend on probabilities σ_s of the various messages to be encoded; the expected cost of transmitting will depend on the $\sigma_s \varepsilon_{sz}$; and that of decoding, on the $\sigma_s \varepsilon_{sz} \eta_{zy}$. And similarly with expected delays. This is simplified if, as in Section 7.8, the cost and delay of each processing depends on the transformation characterizing it $(\varepsilon, \eta, \alpha)$ but not on the input; and if the same is assumed of delays. The sum of costs of the links is then subtracted from the expected benefit; and the latter is affected by the delays in the several links, especially because of the diminution of expected benefit, caused by the obsolescence of actions (here: decodings), as in Section 6.

However, most of the existing literature lets each link be associated, not with its costs and delays, but with characteristics such as channel capacity, length of the code word, and size of the code dictionary. A question such as the following is asked:

Given the channel capacity, the (expected) word length, and the code size, how large an expected fidelity can be achieved?[39]

Answering such a question would not really provide the set of communication systems efficient from the point of view of a given user, who is characterized by a fidelity function and a probability distribution of messages to be sent. We remarked in Section 8.5 that two channels with equal capacity (and speed) need not have equal cost. As to the length (or more generally, the expected length) of code words, it causes delays; and these influence expected utility to the user, not by being added to costs but through a complicated effect on expected benefit, especially by making decisions obsolete, as we have just remarked. Expected utility cannot be decomposed additively into expected benefit, channel capacity and (expected) word length; that is, utility is not linear in these quantities. (Similar considerations would apply to the size of code.) Yet without such additivity, answers to a question like the one just formulated would not provide the set efficient from a given user's point of view (see Appendix A).

In a sense, the set of non-dominated quadruples (expected fidelity, channel capacity, expected word length, code size) is the result of a crude 'averaging' over all users. Delays, being undesirable for all users, are replaced by what amounts to an additive cost, as a make-do. This gives a rough guidance to the supplier of the communication links in estimating the demand for them. The demand of the individual user (if he is 'rational') is rather different, and hence that crude average cannot represent the aggregate demand.

9. Market for information

9.1. *Demand for Systems and Sub-Systems*

Return now to the general outline of purposive processing chains (and networks, for that matter) that we gave in Sections 2 and 3, with special regard to information systems. The individual user (meta-decider) can achieve a given sequence of transformations only at certain costs and with certain delays (or, more generally, a certain probability distribution of costs and delays). Subject to these constraints, he should maximize the expected benefit simultaneously with respect to all of the transformations, just like an ideal plant designer decides simultaneously about the size and composition of the personnel as well as of the machine park, the warehouses and the transportation facilities! This is, of course, hardly ever achieved in reality.[40] The humbler meta-decider makes his choices separately for each of several sub-systems; this is what the term 'sub-optimization' is often intended to mean, I believe. Hopefully, he partitions the total system in such a way that the complementarity between sub-systems (with regard to expected benefit) is small.

The failure to maximize over all system components simultaneously is just one of many allowances for 'lack of rationality' that must be made before we claim a modicum of descriptive validity to aggregating the demands of individual users into the total demand for system components of various kinds, given the constraints.

9.2. *The Supply Side*

The 'demand side' of the market, the relation associating the set of constraints with the set of demands, depends on the benefit functions β and the probability distributions π characterizing individual users. The 'supply side' is the relation between those constraints and the supplies, and depends on the 'production conditions' ('technology') characterizing each supplier. As usual, the economist is almost completely ignorant of technology.

Let me conclude with three, rather casual, remarks on these production conditions.

9.3. *Standardization*

In many cases, it does not pay to produce 'on order'. Mass production may be cheaper. This may explain why our Sunday newspaper is so bulky (it gives all things to all subscribers), and why our telephones have such a high fidelity. The individual user is 'forced' to purchase information services which, for him, would be wasteful if they were not so cheap.

9.4. *Packaging*

In our scheme, inquiry was presented as a component separate from storing the data, encoding as separate from transmission, etc. The producer of automata and control mechanisms may find it cheaper to produce them jointly, in fixed 'packages'. This, again, imposes constraints on the user, similar to those of standardization.

9.5. *Man vs Machine*

The competition between machines and human nerves (not muscles) is much discussed today. Some symbol-manipulating services consist in many-to-one mapping, variously called 'sorting' and 'pattern-recognition'. Encoding and decoding are of this nature, but not the (generally noisy) transmission. To be sure, we have, in Section 8, characterized encoding and decoding by Markov matrices, thus allowing for 'randomized codes'. Such codes have been used for the convenience of mathematical proofs. But, as in any one-person game, there exists an optimal non-randomized choice. Except to allow for (non-rational) error-making encoders and decoders, we may as well consider these activities as many-to-one mappings. We can imagine the encoder to partition a set of visible or audible stimuli, including verbal sentences, into equivalence classes, variously called 'patterns' and 'meanings'. These are translated, in turn, into the language of channel inputs and outputs, and then decoded back into 'patterns' or 'meanings'. Even when we are little concerned with transmission noise – newspaper misprints or slips of the tongue, – the problem of the best code remains: what is the best way to make the receiver (a listener or reader, for example) to 'understand' the sender (a lecturer or writer)? The sender must encode into a well-chosen set of patterns, (an 'effective style' of speech, or writing, for example), such that the receiver would be able to recognize them, and respond to them by benefit-maximizing actions.

We are told by psycholinguists – e.g., Miller [39] – that man's effectiveness as a channel (and also as a storage facility) is poor compared with inanimate equipment such as telephones (and record tapes). But his coding ability seems superb in many cases. It is variously called 'insight', 'judgment', 'ability to recognize a Gestalt (pattern)'....

APPENDIX A: REQUIREMENT OF COMMENSURABLE CRITERIA

In the text, utility was defined on each pair 'event, action'. It is sometimes useful to introduce an additional concept – the *result*, r (also called consequence) of the given pair 'event, action', and to define utility as a function of the result. The result need not be numerical. For example, the result's values can be 'getting cured; dying; continuing in ill health'.

When the result is a numerical vector, and utility is monotone increasing in each of its components, we call each component a (desirable) criterion.[41] Thus

$$\text{action} = a\,; \qquad \text{event} = z\,;$$
$$\text{result } r = (r_1, \ldots, r_n), \text{ with every } r_i \text{ numerical}\,;$$
$$r_i = \rho_i(a, z) \text{ (}i\text{th 'result function')}\,;$$
$$\text{utility } u = v(r_1, \ldots, r_n)\,;$$
$$v(r_1, \ldots, r_n) > v(r_1', \ldots, r_n') \quad \text{if}$$
$$r_i > r_i' \quad \text{for some} \quad i, \qquad r_i \geqslant r_i' \quad \text{for all} \quad i.$$

Consider a case when $n=1$: suppose, e.g., the decision-maker maximizes the expected utility of money profit. The unique component of the criterion vector is then a dollar amount. It is well known that, in this case, expected utility is not necessarily monotone in expected money profit (independently of some other parameters of the distribution of money profit such as variance) unless utility is linear in money.

Before we extend to the case of n components, note, as an example, that the pair '*minus* cost, numerical benefit' constitutes a vector consisting of two criteria. In Section 8.8 the following criteria, used in communication theory, were listed: fidelity criterion; length of code word; size of code; capacity of channel (provided of course that the last three numbers be replaced by their negatives). Given the distribution π of events z, the action a will result in some joint distribution of $r_1, \ldots, r_n$, to be denoted by

$$\pi^a(r_1, \ldots, r_n)\,.$$

Consequently, action a will yield expected utility

$$\text{(A.1)} \qquad E_a(u) = \sum_{r_1 \ldots r_n} v(r_1, \ldots, r_n)\, \pi^a(r_1, \ldots, r_n)\,.$$

Given the action a, and thus the joint distribution π^a, the marginal probability distribution of a particular criterion, for example of r_1, will be denoted by

$$\pi^a(r_1) \equiv \sum_{r_2 \ldots r_n} \pi^a(r_1, \ldots, r_n)\,;$$

no ambiguity results from using the same symbol – here π^a – for two different functions, made distinguishable by their different arguments, in parentheses.

Then the expected value of r_i, given action a, is

$$(\text{A.2}) \qquad E_a(r_i) \equiv \sum_{r_i} r_i \pi^a(r_i).$$

The vector of expected criterion values will be denoted by

$$[E_a] = [E_a(r_1), \ldots, E_a(r_n)].$$

Given two actions a and b, we say, as usual, that $[E_a]$ dominates $[E_b]$, and write $[E_a]$ *dom* $[E_b]$, if

$$\begin{aligned} E_a(r_i) &\geqslant E_b(r_i), \quad \text{all} \quad i \\ E_a(r_i) &> E_b(r_i), \quad \text{some} \quad i. \end{aligned}$$

We shall then also say that action a dominates b with *respect to criterion expectations.*

Suppose that

$$(\text{A.3}) \qquad E_a(u) > E_b(u) \quad \text{whenever} \quad [E_a] \ \ dom \ \ [E_b].$$

Clearly this is equivalent to saying that expected utility $E_a(u)$ is a monotone increasing function of the expected criterion values $E_a(r_1), \ldots, E_a(r_n)$. If this is the case then, and only then, the feasible action a^* (say) that maximizes each of the $E_a(r_i)$ will also maximize $E_a(u)$.

Suppose the utility function v is not known; but condition (A.3), or, equivalently, the monotonicity of $E_a(u)$ with respect to the criterion expectations $E_a(r_1), \ldots, E_a(r_n)$ is known to hold. Then, while it is not possible to determine an optimal action one can at least eliminate all actions that are dominated by some feasible action. The remaining subset of feasible actions will be then, as usual, called the *efficient set.*

Consider now the case

$$u = v(r) = r_1 + r_2 + \cdots + r_n;$$

then by (A.1),

$$E_a(u) = \sum_{r_1 \ldots r_n} r_1 \pi^a(r_1, \ldots, r_n) + \cdots + \sum_{r_1 \ldots r_n} r_n \pi^a(r_1, \ldots, r_n);$$

then by (A.2)

$$E_a(u) = \sum_{r_1} r_1 \pi^a(r_1) + \cdots + \sum_{r_n} r_n \pi^a(r_n) =$$
$$= E_a(r_1) + \cdots + E_a(r_n),$$

an obvious result ('Expectation of sum = sum of expectations'). We shall now prove

THEOREM. Expected utility is monotone in expected criterion values if and only if utility is linear in the criteria. Clearly, the conclusion of this theorem ('the expected utility is monotone in expected criterion values') could be replaced by the following equivalent propositions:

(1) If action a dominates action b with respect to expected criterion values then a is preferred to b,

(2) The efficient set consists of all those feasible actions which are not dominated, with respect to expected criterion values, by any feasible action.

(3) An action that maximizes, over the set of feasible actions, the expected value of each criterion, is optimal.

By substituting any of these three sentences for the conclusion of the theorem, we obtain three theorems equivalent to it.

The 'if' part of the theorem is obvious since a sum is a monotone increasing function of its components. It is unfortunate that the 'only if' part is also true. For it follows that unless it is known that utility is additive, the computation of expected criterion values loses much of its usefulness: an action b dominated by some other action a with respect to the expected criteria may still be preferable to a, and may indeed be optimal, unless of course some further conditions are known to exist [e.g., distributions $\pi^a(r)$, $\pi^b(r), \ldots$ yielded by all feasible actions are known to belong to some special class – Gaussian, for example].

I shall now give a proof (suggested orally by Roy Radner) of the 'only if' part of the preceding theorem. Consider three vectors

$$r^0 = (r_1^0, \ldots, r_n^0),$$
$$r' = (r_1', \ldots, r_n'),$$
$$\bar{r} = (\bar{r}_1, \ldots, \bar{r}_n),$$

where $\bar{r}_i = \alpha r_i^0 + (1-\alpha) r_i'$ (all i), and $0<\alpha<1$. That is, $\bar{r}$ is a convex combination of r^0 and r' (geometrically, $\bar{r}$ is represented by a point on a straight line between r^0 and r'). Let two actions, a and b, result, respectively, in the following two joint distributions:

$$\pi^a(r): \pi^a(r_1^0, \ldots, r_n^0) = \alpha, \quad \pi^a(r_1', \ldots, r_n') = 1 - \alpha;$$
$$\pi^b(r): \pi^d(\bar{r}_1, \ldots, \bar{r}_n) = 1.$$

Then for every $i = 1, \ldots, n$, by (A.2)

$$E_a(r_i) = \alpha r_i^0 + (1-\alpha) r_i',$$
$$E_b(r_i) = 1 \cdot \bar{r}_i = \alpha r_i^0 + (1-\alpha) r_i'.$$

Hence

$$E_b(r_i) = E_a(r_i), \quad \text{all} \quad i.$$

On the other hand, by (A.1)

$$E_a(u) = \alpha v(r^0) + (1-\alpha) v(r')$$
$$E_b(u) = v(\alpha r^0 + (1-\alpha) r').$$

Let the expected utility of any action be monotone in the expected criterion values (resulting from that action). Then, since $E_b(r_i) = E_a(r_i)$ for all i, we must have

$$E_a(u) = E_b(u),$$
$$\alpha v(r^0) + (1-\alpha) v(r') = v(\alpha r^0 + (1-\alpha) r').$$

This is possible only if the function v on the space of vectors r is linear, i.e., if there exist $w_i (i = 0, 1, \ldots, n)$ such that

$$v(r_1, \ldots, r_n) = w_0 + \sum_1^n w_i r_i.$$

It is then often said that the criteria are 'commensurable' (among each other and with utility itself). A most common case is to convert them in dollars, under the (sometimes tacit) assumption that utility is linear in dollars.

APPENDIX B (to Section 7.5)

To prove (7.5.10), write $\partial a_j / \partial p_i \equiv a_{ji}$. Differentiate V_y in (7.5.8) with respect to $p_i (=\eta_{ii})$, using (7.5.8′):

$$\partial V_i/\partial p_i = V_i'(a_i)\, a_{ii} + \gamma_i(a_i) = 0 + \gamma_i(a_i)$$
$$\partial V_j/\partial p_i = V_j'(a_j)\, a_{ji} - \gamma_i(a_j) = 0 - \gamma_i(a_j)\,; \quad i \neq j\,;$$

and since $V = V_1 + V_2$,

$$\partial V/\partial p_1 = \gamma_1(a_1) - \gamma_1(a_2)\,; \qquad \partial V/\partial p_2 = -\gamma_2(a_1) + \gamma_2(a_2)\,;$$

then by (7.5.11) and writing $\gamma_i'(a_j) = \gamma_{ij}$,

$$w_{11} = \gamma_{11}a_{11} - \gamma_{12}a_{21} \qquad w_{12} = \gamma_{11}a_{12} - \gamma_{12}a_{22}$$
$$w_{21} = -\gamma_{21}a_{11} + \gamma_{22}a_{21} \qquad w_{22} = -\gamma_{21}a_{12} + \gamma_{22}a_{22}\,;$$

(it will be confirmed presently that $w_{12} = w_{21}$). To evaluate the a_{ji}, differentiate with respect to p_i the Equations (7.5.8′) which are identities in the a_j:

$$\partial V_1'/\partial p_1 = 0 = V_1'' \cdot a_{11} + \gamma_{11}$$
$$\partial V_1'/\partial p_2 = 0 = V_1'' a_{12} - \gamma_{21}$$
$$\partial V_2'/\partial p_1 = 0 = V_2'' \cdot a_{21} - \gamma_{12}$$
$$\partial V_2'/\partial p_2 = 0 = V_2'' a_{22} - \gamma_{22}\,;$$

solve for the a_{ji}, writing for brevity

$$V_j'' = 1/k_j < 0, \quad j = 1, 2 \text{ [by (7.5.8″)]}\,;$$

then

$$a_{jj} = -k_j\gamma_{jj}\,; \qquad a_{ji} = k_j\gamma_{ij}, \quad i \neq j\,;$$
$$w_{11} = -\gamma_{11}^2 k_1 - \gamma_{12}^2 k_2 \qquad w_{22} = -\gamma_{21}^2 k_1 - \gamma_{22}^2 k_2 > 0$$
$$w_{12} = \gamma_{11}\gamma_{21}k_1 + \gamma_{12}\gamma_{22}k_2 = w_{21}$$
$$w_{11}w_{22} - w_{12}^2 = k_1 k_2 (\gamma_{11}\gamma_{22} - \gamma_{12}\gamma_{21})^2 > 0,$$

thus establishing condition (7.5.10), and completing the proof.

NOTES

* This article, invited by the Journal of the American Statistical Association, is an expanded version of a paper presented at a session of the Econometric Society, December 1969. Research for this article was supported partially by the Office of Naval Research and the National Science Foundation. An earlier version appears in the forthcoming book, *Frontiers of Quantitative Economics* (Michael Intriligator, ed.), North-Holland Publishing Co., Amsterdam. The author is grateful to Carlo Brumat, James MacQueen,

Michel Pham-Huu-Tri and other members of the Western Management Science Institute for helpful discussions.

[1] See Marschak [34], [34a], papers addressed to wider audiences and, in essence, revised here in a somewhat more precise fashion. For some earlier results, see [33].

[2] For the case of a 'discrete source', See Section 8.1 below.

[3] In the quoted paper, he also says that another paper [10] (strongly influenced by Ramsey's, De Finetti's and Savage's logic of expected utility) "gives an exposition of my view on the nature of inductive logic which is clearer and from my present point of view more adequate than that which I gave in my book," viz, in [8].

[4] See [5] for an extension of the concept of stochastic transformation to infinite sets.

[5] Example: let $x=1, 2, 3$; $y=1, 2$; and let

$$[\eta_{xy}] = \begin{pmatrix} 1 & 0 \\ 0 & 1 \\ 0 & 1 \end{pmatrix}; \quad \text{then} \quad \eta(1) = 1; \qquad \eta(2) = \eta(3) = 2.$$

[6] I refer to the work of F. P. Ramsey, B. De Finetti, L. J. Savage, accepted in recent years by professional logicians R. Carnap and R. C. Jeffrey. For a survey see [35]; also, regarding Carnap and regarding the relation of probability to frequency see [36]. That certain observed behavior is not really inconsistent with the expected utility rule if cost or feasibility of storing or other processing is accounted for, was brilliantly shown by S. Winter [55]. Among the many merits of Raiffa's delightful introduction to the field [45] is his forceful emphasis on the need for and the possibility of training people for consistency.

[7] Elsewhere, B was called 'expected gross payoff', see [38].

[8] On the other hand, in most statistical writings, our environmental variable z is generalized, as follows. The event (or, in the case of continued processing, a time-sequence of events) is replaced by a probability distribution called 'hypothesis', so that our π becomes a distribution on the space of probability distributions of some variable v. However, this complicated description of the problem is equivalent, and can be reduced, to the original problem, with v playing the role of the event z. We shall, therefore, not pursue this further.

[9] In statistical literature the negative of β is called the loss function, and the negative of B is called risk. As M. Loève remarked to this writer, "we statisticians minimize losses, you economists maximize profits," – which is clearly the same thing.

[10] Contrast Examples 1–3 with Example 4 in [29, Section 1.2]. See also Pratt [42a]. The author is indebted to M. DeGroot and W. Kruskal for discussions of this question.

[11] A terminological note: in some earlier writings [30, 38], information value of an inquiry η was defined as the difference

$$V(\eta) - V(1),$$

which, by (5.3.1) is never negative. Thus the value of null-information was chosen as the origin to measure information values. The present terminology is simpler.

[12] In Figure 2, the unit square represents the set $H_{2\times2}$ (say) of all inquiry matrices of order 2×2. The corresponding essential set $H_{2\times2}/e$ is, then, in 1-1 correspondence with the set consisting of all points above the main diagonal and an arbitrary point on that diagonal.

[13] See also [15, Section 8.4]. Chapters 6–7 of [48] are also relevant.

[14] Several papers by Blackwell and also some earlier work by Bohnenblust, Shapley

and Sherman are summarized, as far as 'informativeness' is concerned, in Chapter 12 of [6]. See also [37].

15 In [37] 'garbling' was defined by a stronger condition, viz., the statistical dependence of y' on y only; that is, by the requirement that, for all z, y, y',

$$(5.2.3) \qquad p(y' \mid y, z) = p(y' \mid y),$$

where $p(s \mid t)$ denotes the conditional probability of s given, t. Since the left side of (5.2.3) is identical with $p(y, y' \mid z)/p(y \mid z)$, the requirement is equivalent to

$$(5.2.4) \qquad p(y, y' \mid z) = p(y' \mid y) \cdot p(y \mid z);$$

and this implies, by summing over y, a weaker condition

$$\eta' = \eta \Gamma,$$

where $\Gamma = [\gamma_{yy'}]$, $\gamma_{yy'} = p(y' \mid y)$. The present 'garbing' condition (5.2.2) is still weaker as it does not involve z. *Added in 1974.* In a later paper [59], it is called 'quasi-garbling'.

16 Example:

$$\eta = \begin{pmatrix} .6 & .3 & .1 \\ .2 & .1 & .7 \end{pmatrix}; \quad G = \begin{pmatrix} 1 & 0 \\ 1 & 0 \\ 0 & 1 \end{pmatrix}; \quad \eta' = \begin{pmatrix} .9 & .1 \\ .3 & .7 \end{pmatrix}.$$

17 For a possibly more instructive, direct proof, see [38, Chapter II, Section 6].

18 It can be also shown that this ordering is strong over the subset of H_m/e that consists of square non-singular matrices. For the general case, however, David Rosenblatt (in a personal communication for which I am greatly indebted) has constructed η, η' (each square and singular) such that

$$\eta > \eta', \quad \eta' > \eta; \quad \text{and not:} \quad \eta e \eta'.$$

19 Further analysis, using some special classes of environment distributions π and benefit functions β is given in Chapter 7 of [38].

20 See [4, 32, 41].

21 As stipulated in Section 3.3 we continue to speak, for brevity, of 'inquiries' instead of 'information matrices' even when we may be, in fact, concerned with the stochastic transformation η characterizing the whole information processing chain except its last link (decision).

22 If we considered inquiry costs fixed, the comparison between expected utilities (net benefits) of inquiries would not be affected by putting $b_1 = b_2 = V^{\max} = 0$. This is usually done in statistics.

23 These are 'multiple decisions', treated by Ferguson [17, Chapter 6] with somewhat different purposes.

24 By (7.5.6), the specified functions $\gamma_z(a)$ are consistent with our example of the farmer optimizing the proportion of wet to dry acreage, provided

$$\pi_1 = \pi_2 = \tfrac{1}{2}$$
$$g_w(x) = g_d(x) = x(3 - x)/4; \qquad f_w(x) = f_d(x) = 3x(3 - x)/4.$$

This implies, for each crop and each weather condition, 'decreasing marginal returns to land'.

25 The author is grateful to M. DeGroot and T. Ferguson for discussing this matter with him.

26 See, e.g., [3], Theorem 3.3.3 (p. 56) and problem 3.7 (p. 304).

27 For, since both V and C are symmetric functions of p_1, p_2 we must have $p_1 = p_2$ at

the point of tangency. Using (8.5.1) (for $C=.32$) and (7.5.13) we have approximately

$$C(.82, .82) = C(.50, 1.00) = C(1.00, .50)\,, \quad \text{but}$$
$$V(.82, .82) = V(.58, 1.00) = V(1.00, .58);$$

thus a C-curve is less flat than the V-curve touching it. See also Figures 4 and 6.

28 In general, an interior optimum would exist if the determinant

$$\begin{vmatrix} 0 & c_1 & c_2 \\ c_1 & w_{11} & w_{12} \\ c_2 & w_{21} & w_{22} \end{vmatrix}$$

is positive, where $c_i = \partial C/\partial p_i$, $w_{ij} = \partial^2 V/\partial p_i \partial p_j$. See, e.g., [47, p.378].

29 See [33, Equation (55)]. The example given in that paper has n stocks in a portfolio and a sample of m of them. With population infinite the sample size would be convex in p (instead of exhibiting an inflection), so that the example would not add much to that of the preceding section.

30 See note 8.

31 These ideas have not yet penetrated the bulk of literature, certainly not the textbooks on communication theory. But see, more recently, [24, 42].

32 The clearest formulation of such an efficient set is given by Wolfowitz [56], in the context of optimal coding for a noisy channel. See Section 8.8 below. It seems that the assumption of utility linear in its criteria is implicit in the discussion of optimal design in many fields of engineering. See e.g., [16].

33 Wolfowitz [56] writes that the function H should

'for convenience and brevity have a name. However, we shall draw no implicit conclusions from its name, and shall use only such properties of H as we shall explicitly prove. In particular, we shall not erect any philosophical systems on H as a foundation. One reason for this is that we shall not erect any philosophical systems at all, and shall confine ourselves to the proof of mathematical theorems,'

namely, theorems on optimal coding. The present writer, though guided by economic rather than mathematical interest, tends to agree.

34 H. Theil [54] uses the difference $H(Z)-H(Z\mid Y)$ to measure, for example, the discrepancy between the predicted and the actual composition of a balance sheet, the national income, or some other total. Of course, this measure can be used outside of economics as well; and it is related to information mainly because the same formula has been used in the theory of communication as developed by C. Shannon and others. This explains the difference in content between Theil's studies and those presented here, in spite of the similarity of titles.

35 It is easily seen that, in fact, when the channel is noiseless (i.e., η is an identity matrix) then $G(\pi, \eta)=0$, $J(\pi, \eta)=H(\pi)$. That is, for given π, uncertainty retained is at its minimum, and uncertainty removed reaches its maximum, when the channel is noiseless. See also Section 8.6.

36 See [6], Part 4 of Theorem 12.2.2; and [14].

37 To translate into Shannon's notation, substitute i for s; j for a; d_{ij} (distortion measure') for $-\beta(a, s)$; D(='average distortion') for $-B$ (='minus expected benefit') and $R(D^*)$ for $Q(B^*)$. The formulation is due to M. Pham-Huu-Tri.

38 When the benefit function and expected benefit are the simple ones of (8.1.1), (8.1.2), (i.e., all errors are equally undesirable), $B_{\sigma\beta}=-p_e$, J is minimized at $\eta'=1$ (null-information, Sec.4.9), $Q=H(\sigma)$ and the result is reduced to the 'Fundamental Theorem for

Discrete Channel with Noise' in Shannon's original paper [50]: an appropriate code can make the error probability arbitrarily small, provided $v \cdot C(\eta) \geqslant w \cdot H(\sigma)$.

[39] This is the formula given by Wolfowitz [56], but generalized in two respects: by introducing a general fidelity criterion instead of an equal penalty for all errors; and by permitting the code words to vary in length, thus presumably increasing coding efficiency. I must acknowledge a great debt to Wolfowitz's clear presentation of the economic problem.

[40] For an attempt to deal more formally with the limitations of the meta-decider ('organizer'), see [38, Chapter 9].

[41] In fact, a suggestion has been made to replace the commodity space of usual economic theory by a space of criteria that may 'explain' the consumers' preferences: e.g., a car becomes a bundle of criteria such as speed, mileage per gallon of fuel, etc. See [27].

BIBLIOGRAPHY

[1] Anderson, N. G., 'Computer Interfaced Fast Analyzers', *Science* **166** (1969), 317–24.

[2] Arrow, K. J. and Enthoven, A. C., 'Quasi-Concave Programming', *Econometrica* (1961), 779–800.

[3] Ash, R., *Information Theory*, John Wiley and Sons, Inc., New York, 1965.

[4] Bellman, R., *Adaptive Control Processes: A Guided Tour*, Princeton University Press, Princeton, N.J., 1961

[5] Blackwell, D., 'Equivalent Comparisons of Experiments', *Annals of Mathematical Statistics* **24** (1953), 265–72.

[6] Blackwell, D. and Girshick, A., *Theory of Games and Statistical Decisions*, John Wiley and Sons, Inc., New York, 1954.

[7] Breiman, L., 'Discrete Signaling and Coding Systems', in E. Beckenbach (ed.), *Conceptual Bases of Communication*, John Wiley and Sons, Inc., New York, 1970.

[8] Carnap, R., *Logical Foundations of Probability*, University of Chicago Press, Chicago, 1950.

[9] Carnap, R., and Bar-Hillel, Y., 'An Outline of a Theory of Semantic Information', Research Laboratory of Electronics, MIT Technical Report 247, Cambridge, 1952 (reprinted in Y. Bar-Hillel, *Language and Information*, Addison-Wesley, Reading, Mass., 1964).

[10] Carnap, R., 'The Aim of Inductive Logic', in P. Suppes and A. Tarski (eds), *Logic, Methodology, and Philosophy of Science*, Stanford University Press, Stanford, 1962.

[11] Carnap, R., 'Probability and Content Measure', in P. Feyerabend and G. Maxwell (eds.), *Mind, Matter and Method: Essays in Philosophy and Science in Honor of M. Feigl*, University of Minnesota Press, 1966.

[12] Chernoff, H., 'Optimal Stochastic Control', in G. Dantzig and A. F. Veinott (eds.), *Mathematics of the Decision Sciences*, Part 2, American Mathematical Society, 149–72, 1968.

[13] Cramér, H., *Mathematical Methods of Statistics*, Princeton University Press, Princeton, N.J. 1946.

[14] DeGroot, M. H., 'Uncertainty, Information and Sequential Experiments', *Annals of Mathematical Statistics* (1962), 404–419.

[15] DeGroot, M. H., *Optimal Statistical Decisions*, McGraw-Hill Book Co., New York, 1970.

[16] English, J. M. (ed.), *Cost Effectiveness: Economic Evaluation of Engineering Systems*, John Wiley and Sons, Inc., New York, 1968.

[17] Ferguson, Th. S., *Mathematical Statistics. A Decision Theoretic Approach*, Academic Press, New York, 1967.

[18] Good, I. J., *Probability and the Weighing of Evidence*, Hafner Publishing Co., New York, 1950.

[19] Good, I. J., 'Weight of Evidence, Corroboration, Explanatory Power, Information, and the Utility of Experiments', *Journal of the Royal Statistical Society*, Ser. B, (1960), 319–31.

[20] Good, I. J. and Toulmin, G. H., 'Coding Theorems and Weight of Evidence', *Journal of the Institute of Mathematical Applications* (1968), 94–105.

[21] Hirshleifer, J., 'Notes on the Private and Social Value of Information', *Amer. Econ. Rev.*, **61** (1971), 561–74.

[22] Howard, R. A., 'Information Value Theory', *IEEE Transactions in Systems Science and Cybernetics*, Vol. SSC-2, No. 1 (1966), 22–34.

[23] Hurwicz, L., 'Optimality and Informational Efficiency in Resource Allocation Processes' in K. Arrow *et al.* (eds.), *Mathematical Methods in the Social Sciences*, Stanford University Press, Stanford, 1960, 27–46.

[24] Jellinek, F., *Probabilistic Information Theory*, McGraw-Hill Book Co., New York, 1968.

[25] Karlin, S., *Mathematical Methods and Theory in Games, Programming, and Economics*, Addison-Wesley, Reading, Mass., 1959.

[26] Koopmans, T. C., 'Stationary Ordinal Utility and Impatience', *Econometrica* (1960), 287–309.

[27] Lancaster, J., 'Change and Innovation in the Technology of Consumption', *American Economic Review* (1966).

[28] LaValle, J., 'On the Cash Equivalents and Information Evaluation in Decisions under Uncertainty,' *Journal of American Statistical Association* **63** (1968).

[29] Lehmann, E., *Testing Statistical Hypotheses*, John Wiley and Sons, Inc., New York, 1959.

[30] Marschak, J., 'Towards an Economic Theory of Information and Organization', 1954, *Selected Essays*, 20.

[31] Marschak, J., 'Remarks on the Economics of Information', 1960, *Selected Essays*, 23.

[32] Marschak, J., Adaptive Programming', 1963, *Selected Essays*, 11.

[33] Marschak, J., 'Problems on Information Economics', 1964, *Selected Essays*, 25.

[34] Marschak, J., 'Economics of Inquiring, Communicating, Deciding', 1968, *Selected Essays*, 30.

[34a] Marschak, J., 'Optimal Symbol-Processing: A Problem in Individual and Social Economics', *Behavioral Science* (1971), 202–17.

[35] Marschak, J., 'Decision-Making: Economic Aspects', 1968, *Selected Essays*, 16.

[36] Marschak, J., 'The Economic Man's Inductive Logic', 1970, *Selected Essays*, 17.

[37] Marschak, J. and Miyasawa, K., 'Economic Comparability of Information Systems', 1968, *Selected Essays*, 29.

[38] Marschak, J. and Radner, R., *Economic Theory of Teams*, Cowles Foundation Monograph 22, Yale University Press, 1972.

[39] Miller, G. A., *The Psychology of Communication*, Basic Books, New York, 1967.

[40] Miller, G. A., and Chomsky, N., 'Finitary Models of Language Users', *Handbook of Mathematical Psychology*, Vol. 2, John Wiley and Sons, Inc., New York, 1963.

[41] Miyasawa, K., 'Information Structures in Stochastic Programming Problems', *Management Science* (1968), 275–91.

[42] Pham-Huu-Tri, H. M., 'Processing and Transmitting Information, Given a Payoff Function', Working Paper No. 143, Western Management Science Institute, University of California, Los Angeles (Ph.D. dissertation), 1968.
[42a] Pratt, J., 'Review of Lehmann' [29]. *Journal of the American Statistical Association*, 1961, 163–167.
[43] Radner, R., 'Equilibre des Marchés à Terme et au Comptant en Cas d'Incertitude', *Cahiers d'Econométrie*, No. 9 (1967), 30–47.
[44] Radner, R., 'Competitive Equilibrium Under Uncertainty', *Econometrica* **36**, No. 1 (1968), 31–58.
[45] Raiffa, H., *Decision Analysis*, Addison-Wesley, Reading, Mass. 1968.
[46] Rényi, A., 'Statistics Based on Information Theory', Paper presented at the European Meeting of Statisticians, London, 1966, (mimeographed).
[47] Samuelson, P., *Foundations of Economic Analysis*, Harvard University Press, Boston, 1948.
[48] Savage, L. J., *The Foundations of Statistics*, John Wiley and Sons, Inc., New York 1954. Revised: Dover, 1972.
[49] Savage, L. J., 'Bayesian Statistics', in R. E. Machol and P. Gray (eds.), *Recent Developments in Information and Decision Processes*, Macmillan Co., New York, 1962.
[50] Shannon, C. E., 'The Mathematical Theory of Communication', *Bell System Technical Journal* (two papers, reproduced in the book of same title, by Shannon and Weaver, University of Illinois Press, 1949).
[51] Shannon, C. E., 'Coding Theorems for a Discrete Source with a Fidelity Criterion', in R. E. Machol (ed.), *Information and Decision Processes*, McGraw-Hill Book Co., New York, 1960, 93–126.
[52] Stigler, G., 'The Economics of Information', *Journal of Political Economy* (June 1961).
[53] Stigler, G., 'Information in the Labor Market', *Journal of Political Economy* (October 1962), supplement.
[54] Theil, H., *Economics and Information Theory*, Rand-McNally, New York, 1967.
[55] Winter, S. G., 'Binary Choice and the Supply of Memory', *Working Papers in Mathematical Economics and Econometrics*, No. 97. Berkeley, 1966.
[56] Wolfowitz, J., *Coding Theorems of Information Theory*, Springer-Verlag, Berlin, 1961.

Added in 1974

[57] Marschak, J., 'Prior and Posterior Probabilities and Semantic Information', in G. Menges (ed.), *Information, Inference, and Decision*, D. Reidel, Dordrecht, 1974, 167–180.
[58] Marschak, J., 'Information, Decision, and the Scientist', in C. Cherry (ed.), *Pragmatic Aspects of Human Communication*, D. Reidel, Dordrecht, 1974, 145–178.
[59] Marschak, J., 'Optimal Systems for Information and Decision', 1972, *Selected Essays*, 32.
[60] Marschak, J., 'Economics of Organizational Systems', in M. Marois (ed.), *Man and Computer*, North-Holland, 1974.

OPTIMAL SYSTEMS FOR INFORMATION AND DECISION

(1972)

1. Introduction

'Optimal' means the same as 'economical'. My talk might be entitled: 'Economics of producing, storing, transporting and using knowledge'. Optimal ways to *produce* and *use* knowledge (sometimes called 'optimal design of experiment') have been studied by statisticians such as Neyman and Pearson (1928–32), Wald (1950), Blackwell (1953), De Groot (1962, 1968). The study of economical codes for *storing* and *transporting* knowledge was introduced by Shannon (1948), and this optimality aspect of communication theory was emphasized by the Yagloms (1960, esp. Ch. IV, Section 1) and Wolfowitz (1961). The traditional separation between the economics of communication and of statistical decision is, in general, 'sub-optimal'. A precise estimate based on a large statistical sample may be not worth its cost if it is garbled or outdated by the time it reaches the decision-maker, owing to the low capacity or deficient coding in communication. Using well-established theorems, I shall try to show how the expected benefit and cost of an information-and-decision system depend on the choice of its links.

We shall thus distinguish between the system's *expected benefit* (its 'value in use', i.e., the least upper bound on the price that the organizer, i.e., the buyer or renter of the system should be willing to pay); and the system's *expected cost* (the greatest lower bound that the sellers of its various components are willing to charge).

Another important contrast is that between the storage and communication costs, which (similar to the cost of storing and transporting commodities) are, by and large, additive and independent of content; and the costs of inquiring and deciding, which do not have these properties.

2. Purposive symbol-processing systems

Define a finite sequence of sets

$$(X^0, X^1, \ldots, X^n) = X$$

with generic elements $x^i \in X^i$, $i = 0, \cdots, n$. All sets X^i are assumed finite for simplicity, and are interpreted thus:

$$X^i \text{ consists of} \begin{cases} \text{events,} & i = 0 \\ \text{symbols,} & 1 < i < n \\ \text{actions,} & i = n. \end{cases}$$

Define a sequence (chain) of 'processors'

$$(P^1, \ldots, P^n) = P \in \mathscr{P}$$
$$P^i = \langle X^{i-1}, X^i, \varphi^i, d^i, \kappa^i \rangle.$$

X^{i-1}, X^i are, respectively, the sets of inputs and outputs of P^i.

The Markov matrix φ^i is the transpose of the matrix of conditional probabilities, $[p(x^i \mid x^{i-1})]$ (say) and is called a stochastic transformation, degenerating in the special, deterministic case (with a unit element in each row) into an ordinary function, $X^{i-1} \to X^i$, also to be denoted by φ^i. κ^i is the '*cost function*' per time unit, from X^{i-1} onto non-negative reals (in 'cost units' such as dollars per time unit). As in the usual accounting practice, it consists of a constant component (depreciation and maintenance of equipment, other long-term commitments) and a random variable component depending on the input processed. d^i, a non-negative real (in time units) is the *delay* between inputs and outputs of P^i.

$\mathscr{P}$ denotes the sets of conceivable (not necessarily feasible) sequences P of processors. We write similarly

$$(\varphi^1, \ldots, \varphi^n) = \varphi \in \Phi$$
$$(\kappa^1, \ldots, \kappa^n) = \kappa \in \mathscr{K}$$
$$(d^1, \ldots, d^n) = d \in \mathscr{D}.$$

Hence $\mathscr{P}$ is the cartesian product

$$\mathscr{P} = \Phi \times \mathscr{K} \times \mathscr{D}$$

Given to the organizer (buyer) of a system is, to begin with, the *feasible* subset

$$\mathscr{P}_f \subset \mathscr{P};$$

for example, he is aware that he has to trade off high speed (a low d^i) for high cost (κ^i), or for low 'precision' (a property of φ^i, also called 'informativeness': see Section 4).

Also *given* to the organizer are

π, a *probability* function on X^0, represented for convenience by a diagonal matrix (non-negative, with trace = 1); and

β, the *benefit* function from $X^0 \times X^n$ onto the reals (in dollars per action), conveniently represented by a matrix, $\beta = [\beta_{x_n x_0}]$. There is no loss of generality in eliminating repeated rows and columns of β, thus defining X^0 and X^n as the sets of 'benefit-relevant' events and actions, respectively (Marschak, 1963); and also eliminating dominated rows of β (corresponding to 'inadmissible actions'). Clearly, the *expected benefit* earned *per action* is

$$(1) \qquad B = \text{trace } \pi\varphi^1 \ldots \varphi^n \beta \equiv B_{\pi\beta}(\varphi),$$

with the givens in the subscript. On the other hand, *expected cost* spent *per time unit* is

$$(2) \qquad K = \sum E[\kappa^i(x^{i-1})] \equiv K_\pi(\varphi, \kappa).$$

If for simplicity we disregard the queueing problem by assuming [in the language of network theory: e.g., Iri (1969)] that 'the flows do not stagnate', so that

$$d^i = \bar{d}, \quad \text{all} \quad i,$$

then we can define *expected utility per time unit* as

$$(3) \qquad B_{\pi\beta}(\varphi)/\bar{d} - K_\pi(\varphi, \kappa) \equiv U_{\pi\beta}(\varphi, \kappa, \bar{d}),$$

conceiving the utility function of benefit and cost simply as the difference between them (admittedly a special case). [In case the delay $\bar{d}$ is long, or the equipment is very durable, one must introduce discounting for time. Note also the effect of delays on B (*not* K) whenever they cause loss in informativeness: see Section 4.] Under our assumptions, *the problem* is then, by the definition of expected utility as the maximand for a consistent choicemaker [see, e.g., Savage (1954)]:

$$(4) \qquad \max_{(\varphi, \kappa, \bar{d}) \in \mathscr{P}_f} U_{\pi\beta}(\varphi, \kappa, \bar{d}).$$

The notations of this section may be reinterpreted, and some assumptions relaxed, to allow greater generality. More general than a chain is a network of processors. This would permit to describe, for example, an organization with a well-defined objective (benefit) function, the incentives to a given member being represented by a cost function. A network can be reduced to a chain by defining the states (of the outside world *and* of the system) at time-points $i-1$ and i as the inputs x^{i-1} and outputs x^i of the ith processor. This would take care of feedbacks. It is also possible to reinterpret an event, an action, and any intermediate output as a time-sequence and also to include among possible actions that of 'getting new information'; sequential sampling is a special case of such 'learning while earning'. For events to remain independent of actions, X^0 can be also interpreted as a set of unknown and rival 'laws of nature': an interval for a physical constant, a statistical parameter space. Another generalization is, even to permit the collection of the in- and output sets of all processors to vary: for example, the chooser of a system may be able to choose between business enterprises belonging to different industries!

Among important assumptions that need to be relaxed is the finiteness of the in- and output; and the neglecting of the queueing problem. Yet, the following Sections will have to introduce less rather than more generality.

3. Expected utility of inquiring

In this and the subsequent sections, and on the Diagram[1], the notations of Section 2 will be replaced by more specific ones, using the following correspondence:

$x^0 \in X^0 \to z \in Z$: events;
$\varphi^1 \to \eta$: inquiring;
$\kappa^1 \to \kappa_\eta$: cost of inquiring;
$x^1 \in X^1 \to y \in Y$: observed data (or, possibly, estimates, diagnoses);

$\varphi^n \to \alpha$: deciding;
$\kappa^n \to \kappa_\alpha$: cost of deciding;
$x^n \in X^n \to a \in A$: actions.

(See the Diagram for further notations.)

Essentially, statistical decision theory considers only two processors: inquiring and deciding. This can be stated formally in two alternative ways:
either (a) $\varphi^1 = \eta$, $\varphi^i =$ identity matrix, $1 < i < n$;
or (b) $\varphi^1 \varphi^2 \ldots \varphi^{n-1} = \eta$.

In the first case, communication is neglected and the statistician concentrates on the comparative advantages of alternative methods of sampling and of producing estimates on which decisions are based. In the second case, action is taken in response to a 'message received', the terminal output of a chain or network of processors – observing, storing, encoding, transmitting, decoding – jointly characterized by a stochastic transformation η and by total cost and delay. Although possibly neglecting sampling details, the second case, too, can be said to capture much of the contents of the statistical decision theory. In any case, this theory (though not all statistical practice) makes two further assumptions, making the cost of deciding, and the delays, constant:

$$\kappa_\alpha = 0 \text{ (or a constant)}; \qquad \bar{d} = 1 \text{ (or a constant} > 0).$$

With the decision cost neglected, all functions from Y onto A ('pure strategies') as well as their mixtures become available. The set of optimal decision rules includes then at least one pure strategy. Hence the set of transformations α can be reduced to deterministic ones. The expected utility is by (3)

$$U_{\pi\beta}(\eta, \alpha) = B_{\pi\beta}(\eta, \alpha) - K_\pi(\eta, \kappa_\eta),$$

to be maximized, by (4), with respect to η, κ_η, α subject to the feasibility of (η, κ_η) (and with no constraint on α, any function $Y \to A$). Define the *value of information* and use (1) (see also McGuire, 1972):

$$(5) \qquad V_{\pi\beta}(\eta) \equiv V(\eta) \equiv \max_\alpha B_{\pi\beta}(\eta, \alpha) \equiv \max_\alpha \text{trace } \pi\eta\beta$$

$$(6) \qquad \max_{\eta, \kappa_\eta, \alpha} U_{\pi\beta}(\eta, \alpha) = V(\eta) - \min_{\eta, \kappa_\eta} K_\pi(\eta, \kappa_\eta).$$

If Z consists of m events, all the considered matrices η have m rows. If these are all identical ($\eta_{zy} = \lambda_y$, all z), η is called *null-information.* If η is an identity matrix, it is called *complete information.* All null-information matrices can be shown to have the same value, viz.,

$$(7) \qquad \max_{a \in A} \sum_z \beta_{az}\pi_{zz} \equiv V^{\min} \leqslant V(\eta) \leqslant \sum_z (\max_z \beta_{az})\, \pi_{zz} \equiv V(I),$$

for all η with the same number of rows. The difference

$$(8) \qquad G(\eta) \equiv V(\eta) - V^{\min} \geqslant 0,$$

will be called 'gain due to information η'. The following example illustrates the *non-additivity* of information gains, *contrasted with the additivity of the transmission rate* (mutual information), a parameter of the joint distribution $\pi\eta$ of Z and Y which we shall denote by

$$(9) \qquad R_\pi(\eta) \equiv H(Z) + H(Y) - H(Z \times Y),$$

where, given the probabilities p_t, $t \in T$, $H(T) \equiv -\sum p_t \log p_t$, also conveniently denoted by $H(p)$. Define the Markov matrices η^1, η^2, η^{12} by their typical entries

$$\eta^1_{z,y^1} = p(y^1 \mid z), \eta^2_{z,y^2} = p(y^2 \mid z), \eta^{12}_{z,y^1y^2} = p(y^1, y^2 \mid z)$$

and let y^1, y^2 be independent. Given the distribution π of z, a real valued function $F_\pi(\eta)$ is additive only if

$$(10) \qquad F_\pi(\eta^{12}) = F_\pi(\eta^1) + F_\pi(\eta^2).$$

Thus $R_\pi(\eta)$ is known to be additive. But the gain $G_{\pi\beta}(\eta)$ (for β fixed) need not be. For example,[2] let event $z=(z_1, z_2)$ be a pair of independent random variables with

$$Pr(z_i = 1) = 1 - Pr(z_i = 0) = \pi_1 = 1 - \pi_0 < \tfrac{1}{2}; \quad i = 1, 2,$$

where $z_i=1$ (0) means fire (no fire) in suburb i. The possible fire danger is 1 money (or, better, utility) unit. To fix ideas let the expense of alerting 1 fire brigade be $=\pi_1$ (i.e., adjusted to the risk). Denote the number of alerted brigades (the *action*) by $a=0, 1, 2$ and neglect the expense of putting out the fire, once alerted. Then the matrix of losses (the negative of the *benefits*), $[-\beta_{az}]$, has the following entries, row by row:

$$-\beta_{0z} = z_1 + z_2; \qquad -\beta_{1z} = \pi_1 + z_1 z_2; \qquad -\beta_{2z} = 2\pi_1;$$

the probabilities of the events (1, 1), (1, 0), (0, 1), (0, 0) are, respectively: π_1^2, $\pi_1\pi_0$, $\pi_1\pi_0$, π_0^2. Assuming negligible decision costs, only pure strategies α need be considered. Now define four information systems, each with a different (and deterministic) transformation η; and compute for each η

$$\text{its value } V_{\pi\beta}(\eta) = \max \mathsf{E}_{zy}(\beta_{\alpha(y),z}) = \mathsf{E}_{zy}(\beta_{\alpha^*(y),z}),$$

say,

and also its gain $G_{\pi\beta}(\eta) = V_{\pi\beta}(\eta) - V_{\pi\beta}^{\min}$ and the transmission rate $R_\pi(\eta)$:

Information system η:	'Complete', η^{12}	'Partial', η^1	'Partial', η^2	'Null', η^0
Message received, $y=\eta(z)$	(z_1, z_2)	z_1	z_2	constant
Optimal strategy, $a=\alpha^*(y)$	z_1+z_2	1	1	1
Value, $V_{\pi\beta}(\eta)$	$-2\pi_1^2$	$-\pi_1(1+\pi_1)$	$-\pi_1(1+\pi_1)$	$-\pi_1(1+\pi_1)$
Gain, $G_{\pi\beta}(\eta)$	$\pi_1\pi_0$	0	0	0
Transmission rate $R_\pi(\eta)$	$2H(\pi)$	$H(\pi)$	$H(\pi)$	0

Note that η^1 and η^2 are 'useless', calling as they do for the same optimal constant action ($a=1$) as does η^0. They yield no gain, although η^1 (or η^2) adds information on one variable, z^1 (or z^2), to the information at η^0. With η^{12}, information on still another variable is added. The function $G_{\pi\beta}$ (or G for brevity) is not additive: $G(\eta^{12}) > G(\eta^1)+G(\eta^2)$. Super-additivity (and also sub-additivity) of the values in use (demand prices) occurs in other economic fields and is called complementarity (possibly negative): the value of a cow with a barn is larger than the value of cow without a barn (in a city apartment, for example!) *plus* the value of a barn without a cow. A bag of fertilizer and 10 bushels of seeds have greater value together than the sum of their separate values.

On the other hand, the cost of transporting that bag and those bushels together is indeed (by and large) equal to the sum of the costs of transporting them separately. Similarly, the economic significance of the additivity of transmission rates is due to the fact that $R_\pi(\eta)$ measures (in the limit of long sequences of messages) the expected number of required code symbols, and this is, by and large, proportional to the cost of communication; and the cost of communicating two independent sequences would be equal to the sum of communicating them separately.

Unlike the costs of transportation, costs of production are, in general, non-additive. In our example, the cost of observing (as distinct from that of communicating about) fires in several suburbs may or may not equal the sum over separate observations. In statistical decision theory, sampling cost may be proportional to sample size but the choice of optimization procedures will depend on whether or not the expected utility $U_{\pi\beta}(\eta)$ is a concave function of sample size (case of 'decreasing returns'): see Marschak (1971).

Another property of transportation costs is their (approximate) independence on contents: it costs about the same to transport over a given distance 100 pounds of seeds or of fertilizer. Similarly, communication costs do not depend on whether the message belongs to one or another equivalence class of messages with the same 'meaning'; nor (economically more important!) on whether it belongs to a given (more inclusive) class of messages calling for the same optimal action. [This corresponds presumably to the distinction between 'semantic' and 'pragmatic' theories, as formulated by Cherry (1957) and others. Optimization is, then, 'pragmatic'.] Thus $R_\pi(\eta)$ does not depend on β. But $V_{\pi\beta}(\eta)$ does. Detailed and accurate information on trivial matters may be, on the average, less valuable than rough information on matters of life and death. This was clearly stated, e.g., in the very introductions to the main works of Shannon (1949) and Brillouin (1960). [Still, misunderstandings do occur; see, e.g., Charkewitch, 1960]. To illustrate, let $a=(a_1, a_2)$, $z=(z_1, z_2)$, where

$$z_1 = \begin{matrix}1\\0\end{matrix} \quad \text{if operation} \quad \begin{matrix}\text{succeeds}\\\text{doesn't}\end{matrix};$$

$$a_1 = \begin{matrix}1\\0\end{matrix} \quad \text{means:} \quad \begin{matrix}\text{operate}\\\text{don't}\end{matrix}; \quad \eta^1(z) = y_1 = z_1$$

$$z_2 = \begin{matrix}1\\0\end{matrix} \quad \text{if stock} \quad \begin{matrix}\text{rises}\\\text{doesn't}\end{matrix};$$

$$a_2 = \begin{matrix}1\\0\end{matrix} \quad \text{means:} \quad \begin{matrix}\text{buy}\\\text{don't}\end{matrix}; \quad \eta^2(z) = y_2 = z_2 .$$

Let $Pr(z_1=1)\equiv\pi_1>P(z_2=1)=\frac{1}{2}$. Then $R_\pi(\eta^1)<R_\pi(\eta^2)$; but β may be such that $V_{\pi\beta}(\eta^1)>V_{\pi\beta}(\eta^2)$. Let $\beta_{az}=\sum_1^2 k_i\cdot\delta_{a_iz_i}$ (Kronecker delta), with $k_1>k_2>0$. Then the optimal response to message y_i $(i=1, 2)$ is: $a_i=y_i$, $a_j=1$ $(j\neq i)$. Hence

$$V_{\pi\beta}(\eta^1) = k_1 + \tfrac{1}{2}k_2 > V_{\pi\beta}(\eta^2) = \pi_1 k_1 + k_2 \quad \text{iff} \quad \frac{k_1}{k_2} > \frac{1}{2(1-\pi_1)} .$$

Thus, although under our assumptions less information bits are conveyed by correct prediction of the outcome of surgical rather than stock market action, the former prediction is more valuable, provided surgical success has sufficiently high relative importance and sufficiently low probability.

4. Partial Ordering by Informativeness

Let the typical entries of matrices η, η' be $\eta_{zy}=p(y|z)$ and $\eta'_{zy'}=p(y'|z)$, respectively. Define the following conditions on any pair η, η' with the same number of rows:

(*g*) $\eta g \eta'$ (η is 'garbled', or 'cascaded' into η') means: $p(y'|y, z) = p(y'|y)$.

(*q*) $\eta q \eta'$ (η is 'quasi-garbled' into η') means:[3] $\exists$ a Markov matrix q with $\eta' = \eta q$.

($>$) $\eta > \eta'$ (η is 'more informative' than η') means: $V_{\pi\beta}(\eta) \geqslant V_{\pi\beta}(\eta')$, all π, β.

(*R*) $\eta R \eta'$ (η has no lower transmission rate than η) means: $R_\pi(\eta) \geqslant R_\pi(\eta')$, all π.

It has been shown (Blackwell, 1953) that (*q*) and ($>$) are equivalent. Moreover,

$$(11) \qquad (g) \mapsto\!\!\!\Rightarrow (q) \Leftrightarrow (>) \mapsto\!\!\!\Rightarrow (R),$$

where $(a) \mapsto\!\!\!\Rightarrow (b)$ means: (*b*) if, but not only if, (*a*). Whenever (*q*) is not satisfied there exist (π, β) and (π', β') such that

$$V_{\pi\beta}(\eta) > V_{\pi\beta}(\eta') \quad \text{and} \quad V_{\pi'\beta'}(\eta') > V_{\pi\beta}(\eta),$$

as already illustrated. Thus ($>$) orders the information systems only partially. When the matrix q is deterministic the relation $\eta q \eta'$ can be read 'η is coarsened (contracted) into η''. It follows immediately from (11) that lengthening memory (or any addition of detail) cannot decrease informativeness. And it can be shown that increasing obsolescence (increasing delay) of complete information about event-sequences cannot decrease informativeness, provided the sequences are Markovian (see Marschak and Radner, 1972).

5. Case when Decision Cost is not Negligible

If κ_α is not negligible, the optimization problem cannot be reduced to that stated in (5), (6) but becomes, more generally, as in (4),

$$\max_{(\eta, \kappa_\eta, \alpha, \kappa_\alpha) \in \mathscr{P}_f} [B_{\pi\beta}(\eta, \alpha) - K_\pi(\eta, \kappa_\eta, \kappa_\alpha)],$$

where $\mathscr{P}_f$ is some *feasible set* of quadruples $(\eta, \kappa_\eta, \alpha, \kappa_\alpha)$. In particular, some α can occur only in combination with κ_α infinite; such strategies themselves are then often called non-feasible. It is also possible that a mixed strategy is cheaper than some of its components and cannot therefore be disregarded (as was done in Section 3). It may be implemented by an error-making decider, whether man or machine (not to be confused with the 'organizer', our 'rational' chooser of an optimal information system in $\mathscr{P}_f$, not of a single action in A) to be chosen by the organizer in preference to an expensive error-free one.

It is therefore important to note the results obtained by Perez (1964) who concerned himself with the 'average risk', i.e., the negative of our 'expected benefit' $B_{\pi\beta}(\eta, \alpha)$, with α generally mixed – and not only with the 'Bayes risk' which is the negative of our 'information value', $V_{\pi\beta}(\eta)$. An upper bound on the difference between the expected benefits of (η, α) and (η', α') [a lower bound is obtained by interchanging the two pairs] is given by

$$[B_{\pi\beta}(\eta, \alpha) - B_{\pi\beta}(\eta', \alpha')] \leqslant \\ \leqslant [2B_{\beta^2\pi}(\eta', \alpha') \cdot H(\pi\eta\alpha\beta \mid \pi\eta'\alpha'\beta)]^{1/2},$$

using our notations and adjusting to our context (Perez considers varying π, and not only η, α); where $\beta^2(a, z) = (\beta(a, z))^2$, and $H(p|p')$ stands for the 'equivocation' $\equiv H(p) - R_p(p')$. Note that the latter expression depends not only on the compared joint probability distributions $\pi\eta$, $\pi\eta'$ but also on $\alpha\beta$, $\alpha'\beta$ characterizing decisions and benefits.

What do we know about decision cost κ_α? While the inquiry cost, κ_η, is reasonably transparent at least in the case of statistical sampling (including quality control), I wish I knew of some systematic work on the cost of deciding and its 'technology', as exemplified by the number of required computer operations and by psycho-physiological observations of problem-solving behavior. Bongard (1963) may be mentioned here as one who tried to justify the entropy formula as a measure of the average 'degree of difficulty of a problem'. He appeals to an 'intuitive feeling' that the 'difficulty' is roughly proportional to the expected logarithm of the number of search acts. This psychological hypothesis reminds one of Daniel Bernoulli's (1738) logarithmic utility of monetary wealth which inspired G. Th. Fechner (1859) to postulate subjective 'sensations' as logarithms of the intensity of a physical stimulus: mathematically attractive but without supportive evidence.

6. Expected Benefit and Cost of Communication

Essentially, communication theory is isolated out of a comprehensive theory of information and decision by a device analogous to (a) of Section 3, page 345. Using the notations of our Diagram[1], assume

(12) $\eta = \alpha =$ identity matrix; or, alternatively, if messages are decoded directly into the language (set) of actions,

(12a) $\eta = \delta =$ identity matrix.

In much of the literature, a restriction is also imposed upon the benefit function by assuming

$$\beta_{az} = \begin{matrix} 0 \\ -1 \end{matrix} \text{ if } a \begin{matrix} = \\ \neq \end{matrix} z, \tag{13}$$

so that, by (12) or (12a), expected benefit is the negative of the probability of communication error. It is more interesting in our context, not to use restriction (13) but to follow the more general and recent approach of Shannon (1960) anticipated in his earlier work (1949) for continuous message sets only. He has called the negative of our β_{az} the 'distortion measure'. His example: to receive message 'all's well!' when the message sent is 'emergency!' is a much worse distortion than the converse. In our terminology, to optimize a communication system is to maximize expected utility, i.e., the expected difference between benefit and cost, per time unit, as in (3). As on our Diagram, let the transmission channel have a Markov matrix τ, of order $m \times n$, say. Using R for transmission rate as before, define its capacity

(14) $C(\tau) \equiv \max_{\lambda \in \Lambda} R_\lambda(\tau)$ bits per letter,

where Λ is the set of all probability vectors of order m. It would be more conforming with the usual economic terminology to call capacity the quantity

(15) $vC(\tau)$ bits per time unit,

where v is the channel speed, i.e., the number of letters received per time unit. Presumably, the higher (15) the higher the *cost*, constant per time unit, of maintenance and depreciation. [It seems, in fact, that, for fixed v, channels with equal $C(\tau)$ are assumed to be equally expensive, even in a case like

$$C\begin{pmatrix} .89 & .11 \\ .11 & .89 \end{pmatrix} \cong .32 \cong C\begin{pmatrix} 1 & 0 \\ \frac{1}{2} & \frac{1}{2} \end{pmatrix}.]$$

On the other hand, the expected *benefit* per letter, $B_{\lambda\beta}(\tau, \gamma)$, will depend on the matrix τ and the code $\gamma \equiv (\sigma, \delta)$ (see Diagram); the expected benefit per time unit is decreased, as in (3), by delays; and these depend on the number of letters, w (say) sent per time unit. No expected benefit per letter can exceed that for τ noiseless (an identity matrix), $B^{\max}$, say, analogous to the value $V^{\max}$ of complete information in (7). For a preassigned expected benefit B^*, and a given code γ, define

(16) $Q_{\lambda\beta}(B^*, \gamma)$ bits per letter $\equiv \text{Max}_\tau R_\lambda(\tau)$
taken over all $(m \times n)$-Markov matrices,
subject to $B^* \leqslant B_{\lambda\beta}(\tau, \gamma) \leqslant B^{\max}$.

Shannon proved that for any positive ε there exists a number $N(\varepsilon)$ and a sequence of codes $\gamma_1, \ldots, \gamma_{M(\varepsilon)}, \ldots$ such that, if $M(\varepsilon) > N(\varepsilon)$ then

(17) $B^* - B_{\lambda\beta}(\tau, \gamma_{M(\varepsilon)} \leqslant \varepsilon,$

provided the channel capacity and speed is sufficiently large in the sense that

(18) $w \cdot Q_{\lambda\beta}(B^*, \gamma_{M(\varepsilon)} \leqslant v \cdot C(\tau).$

[It can be verified that when the benefit function is that of (13), then the left side of (17) becomes the probability of error and that of (18) becomes $w \cdot H(\lambda)$ as in the 'Fundamental Theorem for Discrete Channel with Noise' of Shannon's original paper (1949).]

However, large capacity entails high constant cost per time unit; and the required code $\gamma_{M(\varepsilon)}$ may cause long delays in coding, as well as in the storage preliminary to encoding large 'blocks' of messages. Thus, while increasing the benefit per letter, $\gamma_{M(\varepsilon)}$ may result in a decreased expected utility.

7. Concluding remark

The 'economic' interpretation of the theory of statistics and of information is not the only possible one. In the context of statistical inference, Sir Ronald Fisher (1955) was unhappy about the modern Russians' "ideal that research in pure science can and should be geared to technological performance" and disliked the American fashion "to confuse the process appropriate for drawing conclusions with those aimed at... saving money." And a leader in information mathematics, A. Renyi (1965) stated the difference between the 'pragmatic' interest of J. Wolfowitz in optimal coding, and his own 'axiomatic' approach that seeks "to find all the expressions which possess (those) postulated properties which a reasonable measure of information should satisfy." The latter approach is also that of S. Kullback's (1959) book on our subject. But in the present Colloquium on Optimization Techniques no apologies are needed for the approach used in this paper.

The support given by the Western Management Science Institute and the National Science Foundation and the Office of Naval Research is gratefully acknowledged.

NOTES

[1] See Figure 1, *Selected Essays*, 31.

[2] If our *y* and *z* are parameters describing, respectively, the estimated and the actual distribution of some variable, our example would contradict the additivity desideratum imposed by I. J. Good (1969) on the 'utility of asserting' an estimated distribution, different from the actual one.

[3] This terminology seems preferable to that used in earlier publications.

BIBLIOGRAPHY

Bernoulli, D., Exposition of a New Theory on the Measurement of Risk, 1738; English translation, *Econometrica*, **22** (1954).

Blackwell, D., 'Equivalent Comparisons of Experiments', *Ann. Math. Stat.*, **24** (1953).

Bongard, M., 'On the Concept of 'Useful Information', *Problemy Kibernetiki*, **9** (1963).

Brillouin, L., *Science and Information Theory*, Academic Press, 1960.

Charkewitch, A., 'On Value of Information', *Problemy Kibernetiki* **4** (1960).

Cherry, C., *On Human Communication*, Wiley 1957.

DeGroot, M., 'Uncertainty, Information, and Sequential Experience', *Ann. Math. Stat.* **33** (1962). *Optimal Statistical Decisions*, McGraw-Hill, 1970.

Fechner, G. Th., *Elemente der Psychophysik*. Leipzig, 1859.

Fisher, R., 'Statistical Methods and Scientific Induction', *J. Royal Stat. Soc. B*, **17** (1955).

Good, I. J., 'What Is the Use of a Distribution?' *Multivariate Analysis*, Vol. 2, Academic Press, 1969.

Kullback, S., *Information Theory and Statistics*, Wiley, 1959.

Marschak, J., 'The Payoff-Relevant Description of States and Acts', (1963), *Selected Essays*, 13; 'Economics of Information Systems', (1971), *Selected Essays*, 31.

Marschak, J. and Miyasawa, K., 'Economic Comparability of Information Systems', *Selected Essays*, 29.

Marschak, J. and Radner, R., *Economic Theory of Teams*, Yale University Press, 1972.

McGuire, C. B., 'Comparisons of Information Structures', *Decision and Organization* (ed. by R. Radner and C. B. McGuire), North-Holland Publishing Co., 1971.

Neyman, J. and Pearson, E., *Joint Statistical Papers* 1928–38. Republished by University of California Press, 1967.

Perez, A., 'Information Theory Methods in Reducing Complex Decision Problems', *Trans. 4. Prague Conf. Inform. Theory*, Prague, 1967.

Renyi, A., 'On the Foundations of Information Theory', *Bul. Internat. Stat. Inst.* **33** (1965).

Savage, L. J., *The Foundations of Statistics*, Wiley, 1954.

Shannon, C., *The Mathematical Theory of Communication* Illinois Univ. Press (with W. Weaver), 1949; 'Coding, Theorems for a Discrete Source with a Fidelity Criterion', *Information and Decision Processes* (ed. by R. E. Machol). McGraw-Hill, 1960.

Wald, A., *Statistical Decision Functions*, Wiley, 1950.

Wolfowitz, J.; *Coding Theorems of Information Theory*, Springer, 1961.

Yaglom, A. and I., *Probability and Information*, 2nd ed. (in Russian), Fizmat., 1960.

INDEX OF NAMES

INDEX OF SUBJECTS

THEORY AND DECISION LIBRARY

An International Series in the Philosophy and Methodology of the Social and Behavioral Sciences

Editors:

1. GÜNTER MENGES (ed.), *Information, Inference, and Decision.* 1974, viii + 195 pp.
2. ANATOL RAPOPORT (ed.), *Game Theory as a Theory of Conflict Resolution.* 1974, v + 283 pp.
3. MARIO BUNGE (ed.), *The Methodological Unity of Science.* 1973, viii + 264 pp.
4. COLIN CHERRY (ed.), *Pragmatic Aspects of Human Communication*, 1974, ix + 178 pp.
5. FRIEDRICH RAPP (ed.), *Contributions to a Philosophy of Technology. Studies in the Structure of Thinking in the Technological Sciences.* 1974, xv + 228 pp.
6. WERNER LEINFELLNER and ECKEHART KÖHLER (eds.), *Developments in the Methodology of Social Science.* 1974, x + 430 pp.

ECONOMIC INFORMATION, DECISION, AND PREDICTION

SELECTED ESSAYS: VOLUME III

THEORY AND DECISION LIBRARY

AN INTERNATIONAL SERIES

IN THE PHILOSOPHY AND METHODOLOGY OF THE

SOCIAL AND BEHAVIORAL SCIENCES

VOLUME 7

JACOB MARSCHAK

ECONOMIC INFORMATION, DECISION, AND PREDICTION

Selected Essays: Volume III

PART III
Money and Other Assets

PART IV
Economic Measurements

PART V
Contributions to the Logic of Economics

D. REIDEL PUBLISHING COMPANY
DORDRECHT : HOLLAND / BOSTON : U.S.A.
LONDON : ENGLAND

Library of Congress Catalog Card Number 74–81940

Volume I: ISBN 90–277–0544–5
ISBN 90–277–1195–X (pbk.)
Volume II: ISBN 90–277–0545–3
ISBN 90–277–1196–8 (pbk.)
Volume III: ISBN 90–277–0546–1
ISBN 90–277–1197–6 (pbk.)

Published by D. Reidel Publishing Company,
P.O. Box 17, 3300 AA Dordrecht, Holland.

Sold and distributed in the U.S.A. and Canada
by Kluwer Boston Inc., Lincoln Building,
160 Old Derby Street, Hingham, MA 02043, U.S.A.

In all other countries, sold and distributed
by Kluwer Academic Publishers Group,
P.O. Box 322, 3300 AH Dordrecht, Holland.

D. Reidel Publishing Company is a member of the Kluwer Group.

0–1195–0580–468
0–1196–0580–468
0–1197–0580–468

Printed in The Netherlands

CONTENTS

PART V: CONTRIBUTIONS TO THE LOGIC OF ECONOMICS

CONTENTS OF VOLUMES I AND II

VOLUME I

VOLUME II

PART II: ECONOMICS OF INFORMATION AND ORGANIZATION

ACKNOWLEDGEMENTS

Essay 33 first appeared in *Econometrica*, Vol. 6, No. 4, pp. 311–325 (October 1938) and is reprinted here by permission of Yale University.

Essay 34 (co-author: Helen Makower) first appeared in *Economica*, New Series, Vol. V, pp. 261–288 (1938) and was reprinted with slight revisions in *Readings in Price Theory*, Part III, Chapter 14, pp. 283–310 (ed. by American Economic Association, and published by Irwin, Chicago). Reprinted here by permission of *Economica*.

Essay 35 first appeared in *Social Research*, Vol. 8, No. 1, pp. 41–62 (February 1941) and is reprinted here by permission of *Social Research*.

Essay 36 first appeared in *Social Research*, Vol. 8, No. 4, pp. 469–478 (November 1941) and is reprinted here by permission of *Social Research*.

Essay 37 first appeared in *American Economic Review*, Vol. 39, No. 3, pp. 182–195 (May 1949) and is reprinted here by permission of the American Economic Association.

Essay 38 first appeared in *Metroeconomica*, Vol. 2, pp. 71–100 (1950) and is reprinted here by permission of *Metroeconomica*.

Essay 39 first appeared in *Econometrica*, Vol. 18, No. 2, pp. 176–177 (April 1950) and is reprinted here by permission of Yale University.

Essay 40 first appeared in *Cahiers du Seminaire d'Économétrie*, No. 3 (ed. by René Roy), pp. 103–111, Centre National de la Recherche Scientifique, Paris (1954) and is reprinted here by permission.

Essay 41 first appeared in *The Economic Journal*, Vol. 44, No. 173, pp. 146–151 (March 1934) and is reprinted here by permission of the Royal Economic Society.

Essay 42 was first read to the Manchester Statistical Society in the 1935–36 Session and was later printed in the report on Group Meetings, pp. 57–64, and is reprinted here by permission of the Manchester Statistical Society.

Essay 43 first appeared in *Economica*, New Series, Vol. 3, pp. 221–226 (May 1936) and is reprinted here by permission of *Economica*.

Essay 44 first appeared in *The Review of Economic Statistics*, Vol. 21,

No. 4, pp. 161–170 (November 1939) and is reprinted here by permission of *The Review of Economic Statistics*.

Essay 45 first appeared in *Studies in Mathematical Economics and Econometrics* in Memory of Henry Schultz (ed. by O. Lange, F. McIntyre and T. O. Yntema), pp. 135–150, University of Chicago Press (1942) and is reprinted here by permission of The University of Chicago Press.

Essay 46 first appeared in *The Review of Economic Statistics*, Vol. 25, No. 1, pp. 40–48 (February 1943) and is reprinted here by permission of *The Review of Economic Statistics*.

Essay 47 (co-author: William H. Andrews) first appeared in *Econometrica*, Vol. 12, Nos. 3/4, pp. 143–205 (July/October 1944) and is reprinted here by permission of Yale University.

Essay 48 first appeared in *American Economic Review*, Vol. 37, No. 2, pp. 81–84 (May 1947) and is reprinted here by permission of the American Economic Association.

Essay 49 first appeared in *Studies in Econometric Method* (ed. by W. C. Hood and T. C. Koopmans), Chap. 1, pp. 1–26, Wiley, 1953 (reprinted by Yale University Press, 1970). Reprinted here by permission of John Wiley and Sons, Inc.

Essay 50 first appeared in *Econometrica*, Vol. 10, No. 1, pp. 61–74 (January 1942) and is reprinted here by permission of Yale University.

Essay 51 first appeared in *American Economic Review*, Vol. 35, No. 3, pp. 368–381 (June 1945) and is reprinted here by permission of the American Economic Association.

Essay 52 was first presented at the Conference on Business Cycles, November 25–27, 1949 and published in the report by the National Bureau of Economic Research, New York, 1951, and is reprinted here by permission of the National Bureau of Economic Research.

Essay 53 first appeared in *So Much Alive*, The Life and Work of Wladimir S. Woytinsky (ed. by Emma S. Woytinsky), Vanguard Press, New York, 1962 and is reprinted here by permission of Vanguard Press and Emma S. Woytinsky.

Essay 54 first appeared in *Synthese*, Vol. 20, No. 4, pp. 483–488 (December 1969) and is reprinted here by permission of the editor, Jaakko Hintikka, and the publisher, D. Reidel, Dordrecht.

Essay 55 first appeared in *Festschrift für Walter G. Waffenschmidt* (ed. by H. J. Niedereichholz), Verlag Anton Hain, Meisenheim am Glan, 1972, 127–132 and is reprinted here by permission of Verlag Anton Hain.

PART III

MONEY AND OTHER ASSETS

INTRODUCTORY NOTE

Part Three is mostly dedicated to making the theory of money consistent with the theory of optimal decisions in perfect (or, more generally, imperfect) commodity markets under conditions of certainty (or, more generally, uncertainty) about the future. Decisive is the existence of 'transaction' costs (e.g., advertising, brokerage) for commodities: they are less 'marketable', or 'liquid', than money. This phenomenon occupied the author rather early (1924). Essay 38 comes to grips with the resulting discontinuities and inequality constraints, not accessible to the calculus of traditional economics. Modern 'programming' tools would make the solution more elegant.

The studies included in Part Three led the author naturally to decision problems of Part One; the resulting overlap is described in the Introductory Note to that Part. These studies – for example, Essay 37 – led also to the information problems of Part Two; and some more recent ideas presented in that Part – for example, the value and cost of obsolete messages, in Essay 31 – would improve some of the early analysis in Part Three. Note also that the public policy discussion of Essay 35 deals with 'non-rational' decisions of both the public and the policymaker: an 'anthropological' approach urged but little used in Part One.

In the last few years, the incorporating of monetary into general economics advanced vigorously. I may mention F. H. Hahn (1971), J. Hirshleifer (1972), J. Niehans (1971), J. Ostroy (1973), R. M. Starr (1972). Such work presupposes an understanding, not only of the role of information in the markets of goods and services; but also of the marketing of information itself – a subject only broached by the author in Part Two. Also, he has explicitly neglected (Essay 38) the phenomenon of moneyless economy, or barter, and the analysis of its comparative social ('Paretian') efficiency: a task undertaken by some of those recent authors.

REFERENCES

Hahn, F. H. (1971), 'Equilibrium with Transaction Costs', *Econometrica* **39**, 417–40.

Hirshleifer, J. (1972), 'Liquidity, Uncertainty, and the Accumulation of Information', in *Uncertainty and Expectations in Economics:* Essays in Honour of G. L. S. Shackle (ed. by C. F. Carter and J. L. Ford), pp. 136–47, Blackwell, Oxford.

Marschak, J. (1924), 'Die Verkehrsgleichung', *Archiv fuer Sozialwissenschaft* **52**, 344–83.

Niehans, J. (1971) 'Money and Barter in General Equilibrium with Transaction Costs', *American Economic Review* **61**, 773–83.

Ostroy, J. (1973), 'The Informational Efficiency of Monetary Exchange', *American Economic Review* **63**, 597–610.

Starr, R. M. (1972), 'Exchange in Barter and Money Economies', *Quarterly Journal of Economics* **86**, 290–302.

33

MONEY AND THE THEORY OF ASSETS*

(1938)

1. The scope

There has been until recently little connection between what is usually taught as Monetary Theory and the General Theory of Prices (or Value). Furthermore, there is little connection between the two compartments of Monetary Theory: the Theory of the 'Equation of Exchange' with its underlying concepts, Price Level, Velocity of Circulation, Real Income, etc., on the one hand and, on the other, the Theory of Credit and Banking. The Babylonian lack of common language between the two compartments of Monetary Theory is well illustrated by the fact that, while 'Exchange Value of Money' (Wicksell, Robertson) is defined as the reciprocal of the Price Level, the term Price of Money is often used to designate interest rates on short loans – although usually economists agree to use Exchange Value of a thing and Price of a thing as equivalent terms. In neither of the two compartments of Monetary Theory is much use made of the fundamentals of economic theory. The Price Level is treated as if it had nothing to do with prices. The velocity of circulation has been, thanks to the Cambridge School, associated with cash holdings instead of being left in the air; but the next step, to treat cash holdings on the same lines on which holdings of any other Stocks are treated in the General Theory of Prices, has been made by few economists only, of whom Dr. Hicks is the most outstanding.[1] Similarly, the Interest Rate of the treatises on Banking and Trade Cycle seems to be ashamed of any connection with its less adventurous and 'dynamic' but more scholarly relation, the Interest Rate of the marginal productivity theory: the parentage is casually mentioned, if at all, in a few hurried phrases only.

F. Divisia has suggested[2] to add the Equation of Exchange to the Paretian system of equations. This makes it possible to determine the absolute and not only the relative prices of goods if the velocity of circulation is given. But we may refuse to regard the velocity of circulation as given because we want to find the factors determining it, or determining

Walras' *encaisse desirée*, just as we look for the factors determining the desired quantity of houses, stocks of materials in the factory or in a housewife's larder, securities, bills, or any other balance-sheet items. We do not want the Velocity of Circulation to save the situation like a *deus ex machina.* Yet there is the difficulty that money is neither a production good nor a consumers' good, and the technique used to explain the causation of quantities and prices of such goods may not apply to money unless we find some way of generalizing the concepts used.

Recently, the rigid (i.e., given) velocity of circulation has been discarded, and the cash holdings expressed as a function of the interest rate, a kind of demand function. Mr. Keynes' 'liquidity preference' is a great step forward, provided it is not taken to be simply another word for the old and mysterious 'love of money'; provided that it yields itself to a further rational analysis.

The desire to treat monetary problems and indeed, more generally, problems of investment with the tools of a properly generalized Economic Theory is not merely one of aesthetics or disciplinarianism – although the example of the gradual unification of the various forms of Energy in Nineteenth Century Physics might in itself encourage the search for unity. The unsatisfactory state of Monetary Theory as compared with general Economics is due to the fact that the principle of determinateness so well established by Walras and Pareto for the world of perishable consumption goods and labour services has never been applied with much consistency to durable goods and, still less, to claims (securities, loans, cash). To do this requires, first, an extension of the concept of human *tastes*: by taking into account not only men's aversion for waiting but also their desire for safety, and other traits of behaviour not present in the world of perfect certainty as postulated in the classical static economics. Second, the *production conditions*, assumed hereto to be objectively given, become, more realistically, mere subjective expectations of the investors – and *all* individuals are investors (in any but a timeless economy) just as all market transactions are investments. The problem is: to explain the objective quantities of goods and claims held at any point of time, and the objective market prices at which they are exchanged, given the subjective tastes and expectations of the individuals at this point of time.

2. PROCEDURE[3]

Our procedure is as follows: we recapitulate the theory of economic determinateness[4] properly generalised so as to include the case of joint demand and supply (which will be found to be important later). We treat perfect competition as a special, imperfect competition as a general case. We then gradually extend the meaning of the symbols so as to take account of uncertainty and ignorance. At no stage do we assume a 'timeless' economy – an assumption which has always made the economics of production extremely vague.

For each of the r individuals in the market there are two sets of unknowns: (1) his best accessible balance sheet, or best accessible collection of m present *assets* $a, b, \ldots$; and (2) his best accessible consumption plan, or best combination of n future consumption items $x, y, \ldots$ which we shall call for brevity '*yields*', because unfortunately 'consumptions' would be ungrammatical. A further set of unknowns are (3) the m market *prices* of assets: p (of a), q (of b), etc.

The yields, or amounts consumed, $x, y, \ldots$, differ either in quality or with respect to the time interval in which the consumption takes place. Thus, x may be first year's milk consumption, y second year's milk consumption, z first year's meat consumption, etc. Yields cannot be stocked or exchanged. Assets are stocks of either goods or claims. Assets are thus a wider concept than 'producers' goods' or indeed than any goods in stock. Yields, on the other hand, are not stocks of consumers' goods, but flows of amounts consumed. Assets are items (positive or negative) in a balance sheet; yields are items in a family budget. By buying and selling assets in the market the individual arranges his present balance sheet in the time point 1 so as to be able to enjoy the best accessible consumption plan, i.e., the most satisfactory series of family budgets for the time intervals 1–2, 2–3, etc. The yields $x, y, \ldots$ refer thus to the future. The assets $a, b, \ldots$ as well as their prices $p, q, \ldots$ refer to the present. It is not necessary to introduce here the concept of 'future assets'. Exchanges in the market of "futures" can be regarded as exchanges of present claims.

It is seen that the assets are 'jointly demanded'; the significance of an asset to the investor depends on what other items he has on his balance sheet. And a given balance sheet enables him to receive not one yield but a whole set of mutually dependent yields; yields are 'jointly supplied'.

3. The Crusoe Case

Certain rudimentary features of the system can be studied already in the case of an isolated producer-consumer. There are here n unknowns only: the yields $x, y, \ldots$. The assets $a, b, \ldots$ are fixed since there is no exchange; but the individual can choose between various consumption plans. His *tastes* are given by the utility function

$$U(x, y, \ldots)$$

(or any monotonically increasing function of U), which has to be maximized, subject to the restricting *transformation condition*

$$(3.1) \qquad T(x, y, \ldots; a, b, \ldots) = 0,$$

which describes what consumption plans the individual expects to be accessible with the given asset collection. Equating to zero the complete differential of U, and comparing it to the complete differential of T, we obtain $n-1$ equations of the type

$$(3.2) \qquad U_x/U_y = T_x/T_y, \quad \text{(yield substitution equations)},$$

which together with (3.1) give a determinate system.[5] The left-hand side of (3.2) may be called rate of preference between x and y (e.g., rate of time preference if x and y are amounts of milk to be consumed in two periods); it depends on tastes. The right-hand side may be called transformation rate between x and y, i.e., the rate at which x and y can be substituted for one another if assets and all other yields are kept constant: it depends on transformation (in Crusoe case, production) conditions. The two rates are equal 'in equilibrium'.

It will be noticed that the transformation condition, $T(x, y, \ldots; a, b, \ldots) = 0$, describes the case of joint supply *and* joint demand. Each combination of m assets (= each balance sheet) can produce an n-dimensional set of yield combinations (= consumption plans). To select from this set the best consumption plan is, for the individual, 'a matter of taste' as shown by the condition $U = \max$. If there is only one consumption good (and only one time period), the function T degenerates into the 'production function' treated in the theory of distribution, wages, etc.: the case of joint supply only. If $a, b, \ldots$ (as in the Crusoe case) are fixed, T is identical with Irving Fisher's 'opportunity function'.[6]

4. A MAN IN THE MARKET

Next, let us consider the case of a producer exchanging assets at given prices $p, q, \ldots$. The unknowns are: m asset quantities $a, b, \ldots$ and n yields $x, y, \ldots$.

The transformation condition $T(x, y, \ldots; a, b, \ldots) = 0$ describes again all the consumption plans which are accessible to a present possessor of the amounts $a, b, \ldots$ of the assets, according to his judgement. The individual can realize these plans not only by future production (as in the Crusoe case) but also by future buying and selling of assets. The transformation condition thus depends, not only on the expected technical conditions (including future inventions, weather, etc.) but also on the expected future market prices. We are thus concerned not only with 'productive' but also with 'speculative' stocks of goods and claims, i.e., those to be sold later.

Writing a_0, $b_0, \ldots$ for the initial quantities of assets (now to be distinguished from the unknown best amounts $a, b, \ldots$), we have

$$(4.1) \qquad T(x, y, \ldots; a, b, \ldots) = 0, \quad \text{(transformation equation)},$$
$$(4.2) \qquad p(a - a_0) + q(b - b_0) + \cdots = 0, \quad \text{(balance equation)},$$

and the requirement that $U(x, y, \ldots)$ should be a maximum. Differentiating,

$$U_x dx + U_y dy + \cdots = 0$$
$$T_x dx + T_y dy + \cdots + T_a da + T_a db = 0$$
$$pda + qdb + \cdots = 0.$$

Keeping the assets constant and letting only two yields vary at a time we get, as before, $n-1$ *equations of the type*

$$(4.3) \qquad U_x/U_y = T_x/T_y, \quad \text{(yield-substitution equations)}.$$

Keeping, on the other hand, yields constant and varying two assets at a time, we get $m-1$ equations of the type

$$(4.4) \qquad p/q = T_a/T_b, \quad \text{(asset-substitution equations)}.$$

We have thus $m+n$ equations for the same number of unknowns. The Equation (4.4) shows that 'in equilibrium' the price ratio between two assets is equal to their rate of transformation. It is more usual to state that 'prices of production goods are proportionate to their marginal productivities' but the latter have seldom been defined so as to cover the case of joint demand and joint supply. Consider the derivative dT/da which is obtained from (4.1) if all yields but only one asset are regarded as variable:

$$\frac{dT}{da} = T_a + T_x \frac{dx}{da} + T_y \frac{dy}{da} + \cdots = 0;$$

similarly

$$\frac{dT}{db} = T_b + T_x \frac{dx}{db} + T_y \frac{dy}{db} + \cdots = 0.$$

Therefore, and in consequence of (4.3),

$$\frac{T_a}{T_b} = \frac{U_x \frac{dx}{da} + U_y \frac{dy}{da} + \cdots}{U_x \frac{dx}{db} + U_y \frac{dy}{db} + \cdots},$$

so that we can write, instead of (4.4), the following 'marginal productivity theorem':

$$\text{(4.4')} \qquad \frac{p}{q} = \frac{U_x \frac{dx}{da} + U_y \frac{dy}{da} + \cdots}{U_x \frac{dx}{db} + U_y \frac{dy}{db} + \cdots}, \qquad \text{(marginal productivity equations).}$$

The numerator in the right-hand part of the last equation may be called for brevity the 'marginal productivity' of the asset a; although a more precise name would be 'the utility of the best accessible combination of marginal yields of the asset a'; or 'the asset's largest possible contribution to the total utility of the consumption plan'.

Let x and y be the amounts of some definite item in the family budgets of two successive years; and suppose that the asset a contributes to nothing but the consumption of this item in the first year, while the asset b contributes the same amount to the consumption of the second year only. (These are, in fact, the assumptions tacitly made in the usual explanation of the interest rate as the 'price of waiting'.) We have then $dx/da = dy/db$; $dx/db = dy/da = 0$; while terms involving dz, etc., vanish.

It follows from (4.4′) that $p/q = U_x/U_y$, i.e., the price ratio is equal to the time-preference rate. The expression $(U_x/U_y - 1)$ is occasionally called the subjective rate of interest (for the two years concerned), and it must be equal, in equilibrium, to the market rate of interest $(p/q - 1)$. The assumptions made do not, however, apply in reality, except in the case of the lending of a consumption good, to be repaid *in one single lump*. In general there is no simple relationship between the market price of assets and the preference rates between yields (of which the preference, for a given kind of yield, between two given years is a special case). There is, therefore, strictly, no single 'market rate of interest'.

The usual assumptions are unrealistic also for the further reason that loans are seldom made in the form of consumption goods. The thing borrowed and lent is *cash*. Let, then, our asset a be 'present cash', and our asset b be 'a claim on next year's cash'. The ratio p/q between the present prices of these two assets depends not only (as in the preceding paragraph) on the preference rates such as U_y/U_x but also on the comparative size of the marginal yields dx/da, dy/db; in the preceding paragraph these were assumed equal; but in the present meaning of a and b they depend on the money prices of consumption goods in the two years. This influence of the expected price tendency of goods upon the present price of loans (or, loosely, upon the 'market rate of interest') has been discussed in detail by Irving Fisher [7] and others.

Let a still be present cash; but let b be, not a present claim on future cash, but some present commodity stock. The numerator in (4.4′) is again the smaller, the higher the expected money prices of consumption goods: the well-known 'flight from money into things' in times of expected inflation.[8]

The equation (4.4′) shows that the system may become inconsistent (and therefore, in the economists' language, no equilibrium possible) if the preference rates U_x/U_y, etc., as well as the ratios $(dx/da)/(dx/db)$, etc., are constant. Preference rates are variable if there is some "law of changing (e.g., diminishing), marginal utilities"; while the ratios $(dx/da)/(dx/db)$, etc. are variable if there is some 'law of changing (e.g., diminishing) returns'. The latter must be generalized so as to include – in accordance with the definition of the transformation function – not only yields from production but also from speculation. The condition that $(dx/da)/(dx/db)$ should depend on a, b implies in this case that the investor must not assume the future market to be perfect; while the constancy of p/q assumed in this section implies a perfect present market. A speculator with a constant time-preference ('patience') rate would pile up 'infinite' commodity stocks if he could buy spot and sell forward in perfect markets and was sure that future commodity prices will exceed present ones. In reality this limiting case is precluded not only by the imperfection of markets, both future and present, but also by uncertainty: limitations which we shall study later.

In the Crusoe case no utility was, of course, provided by holding cash. Under the assumptions of the present section cash holding receives some explanation in so far as cash may be held, even in conditions of certainty, to benefit from an expected *fall* of commodity prices. It has been shown how this affects the price of cash both in terms of commodities and of loans. This speculative aspect of cash holding is, however, obviously insufficient to explain it in general.

5. Price formation in a perfect market

In the preceding section the asset prices $p, q, \dots$ of the assets $a, b, \dots$ were regarded as data given to the individual. Their formation can now be explained by the tastes, transformation conditions, and initial assets of all (say r) individuals in the market. The unknowns are: mr assets, nr yields, m prices; total, $mr+nr+m$. There are $(m+n)r$ equations of the types discussed in Section 4: r transformation equations (4.1), r balance equations (4.2), $r(n-1)$ yield-substitution equations (4.3), and either $r(m-1)$ asset-substitution equations (4.4) or $r(m-1)$ marginal-productivity equations (4.4′). In addition, there are m equations of the type

(5.1) $\sum(a-a_0)=0$, etc., (clearing-of-the-market equations),

the summation being performed over the r individuals. One of the equations of the type (5.1) is redundant because multiplying each by the corresponding price and adding we get the sum of all balance equations of the type (4.2). On the other hand, assuming a to be the numéraire, the equation

(5.2) $p=1$

makes the necessary total, $mr+nr+m$ equations.

The contents of this section are well known but had to be briefly restated, as a link with the further discussion.

6. Imperfect present market

The preceding sections did not exclude the imperfection (in the investor's eyes) of the *future* market: it was, indeed, indicated that it is more realistic to assume it, which simply meant that the transformation function $T(x, y, \ldots; a, b, \ldots)$ was nonlinear everywhere: imperfection of the future market (prices decreasing as sales increase) was treated as a case of 'decreasing returns'. If we had introduced the concept of 'future assets' we could have distinguished formally between future exchange and future production; but this advantage would only have been gained at the expense of a much more complicated notation which I prefer to avoid at present. It suffices to remember always that the transformation function has been generalised so as to include under yields x, y,... all possible future consumption, whether made possible by future physical transformation or by future exchange.

The preceding sections did, however, assume the *present* market to be perfect. The rates of exchange between assets are, in a perfect market, independent of amounts exchanged. The linear 'balance equation' (cf. 4.2)

$$(6.1) \qquad pa+qb+\cdots-(pa_0+qb_0+\cdots)=0, \quad \text{(balance equation)},$$

expresses the fact that each individual's receipts equal his expenditure in terms of any one asset chosen as a numéraire. In conditions of perfect competition, (6.1) can, however, also be interpreted as a 'market equation': the partial derivatives of its left-hand side taken at any point $(a, b, \ldots)$ with respect to a or b, etc., are proportionate to the respective prices. In conditions of imperfect competition, (6.1) remains valid as a balance equation; $p, q, \ldots$ being interpreted as the market prices actually paid for the total amounts bought – 'average revenues'. But it ceases to be valid as a 'market equation' because the prices become dependent on the amounts $a, b, \ldots$; they become proportionate to functions, say, $p^*(a, b, c, \ldots)$, $q^*(a, b, c, \ldots)$ instead of $p, q, \ldots$. The market plane becomes a more general market surface. The individual has to choose not one out of the family of all 'market planes' (6.1) through the initial point, but one of the family of 'market surfaces' through the initial point, say

(6.2) $M(\mu, a, b, c, \ldots) - M(\mu, a_0, b_0, c_0, \ldots) = 0$, (market equation),

where $M = \int (p^* da + q^* db + \cdots)$, (assuming the right-hand side integrable). The r parameters μ (one for each individual) are new unknowns of the system which remains determined because r new equations (6.2) have been added. Thus, if the forms of the M-functions are given, the μ's (and, therefore, the relevant market surfaces for each individual) are determined by the tastes, initial assets, and transformation conditions of all individuals. The form of each M-function is determined by other data than those enumerated and is loosely described as the individual's 'bargaining power', his 'strategic position', etc. (In a perfect market, M degenerates into a linear form.) Substituting partial derivatives ('marginal revenues') M_a, $M_b, \ldots$ for p, $q, \ldots$ in the Equations (4.4) or (4.4′) we get now

(6.3) $M_a/M_b = T_a/T_b$, (asset-substitution equations),

or

(6.3′) $$\frac{M_a}{M_b} = \frac{U_x \dfrac{dx}{da} + U_y \dfrac{dy}{da} + \cdots}{U_x \dfrac{dx}{db} + U_y \dfrac{dy}{db} + \cdots},$$ (marginal-productivity equations)

The Equations (6.1) to (6.3) or (6.3′), together with (4.1), (5.1), and (5.2), constitute a determinate system.

For the problem of asset holdings, and in particular cash holdings, the imperfection of the present market is mainly relevant in connection with 'decreasing selling costs': selling costs are expenses to improve the bargaining power (i.e., to straighten a market function); if they decrease, per unit of amount sold, with increasing sales, small sales will be avoided and stocks accumulated: e.g., stocks of cash waiting for investment. Stocks (of cash or, say, wheat) due to the different timing of receipts and outgoings are cases of the same type.

7. Uncertainty

Since, in the actual uncertain world, the future production situation (technique, weather, etc.) and future prices are not known, the transformation equation $T(a, b, \ldots; x, y, \ldots) = 0$ is not strictly valid so long as it means that, in the mind of the producer, to each combination of assets there corresponds one and only one n-dimensional set of yield combinations. It is more correct to assume (although this assumption will also be revised later) that to each combination of assets there corresponds, in his mind, an n-dimensional joint probability distribution of the yields. Thus, instead of assuming an individual who thinks he knows the future events we assume an individual who thinks he knows the probabilities of future events. We may call this situation the situation of a game of chance, and consider it as a better although still incomplete approximation to reality, and to relevant monetary problems, than the usual assumption that people believe themselves to be prophets.

We may, then, use the previous formal set-up if we reinterpret the notation: x, y,... shall mean, not future yields, but parameters (e.g., moments and joint moments) of the joint probability distribution of future yields. Thus, x may be interpreted as the mathematical expectation of first year's meat consumption, y may be its standard deviation, z may be the correlation coefficient between meat and salt consumption in a given year, t may be the third moment of milk consumption in second year, etc. We know of the economic relevance of certain of these parameters: e.g., in our illustration, x, z, and, in many cases, t are positive utilities, while y is a disutility: people usually like to eat more, rather than less, meat; they dislike (with the exception of passionate gamblers) situations in which the amounts of meat can be anything within a wide range; they like meat consumption to be accompanied by salt consumption; and (witness football pools) they like 'long odds', i.e., high positive skewness of yields. It is sufficiently realistic, however, to confine ourselves, for each yield, to two parameters only: the mathematical expectation ('lucrativity') and the coefficient of variation ('risk'); while it would be definitely unrealistic (as pointed out in Keynes' *Treatise on Probability* as well as by Irving Fisher, A. C. Pigou, S. Florence, and J. R. Hicks), to confine ourselves to the mathematical expectation only.

The system of our Sections 3–6 holds good with this new interpretation. The unknowns are: the present quantities and prices of assets, and the parameters of yield distributions. The data are: initial balance sheets, tastes of men (in terms of lucrativities and risks of various yields), and transformation conditions (expressed in terms of assets, and of the lucrativities and risks of various yields). As before, the rate of preference (or aversion) between x and y (say between risk and lucrativity of meat) equals, in equilibrium, their rate of transformation; and the price of each asset is proportionate to its marginal productivity, the latter being redefined as the utility of the best set of its marginal contributions to various parameters (e.g., to risk or lucrativity of meat, salt, etc.).

This application of the methods of the general price theory to the conditions of uncertainty is obviously relevant to monetary theory because of the relatively low risk which is usually attached to money. Cash always produces constant (namely zero) dividends; and, if it is disposed of, the consumption made thus possible depends on commodity prices only. Bonds also produce constant dividends; but the consumption made possible by selling a bond depends not only on commodity prices (in terms of cash) but also on loan prices (in terms of cash). Finally, with shares both prices and dividends vary. The marginal contribution of cash to the variability of future yields (i.e., consumption amounts) is therefore smaller than that of shares (and also plants, etc.) or even bonds (or houses, landed property, etc.).[9] A change in tastes in the sense of increasing risk aversion leads to decreasing prices of relatively risky assets, or to hoarding, or to both. The same result can be due to changes of transformation conditions in the sense of an increasing expected variability of yields (for given amounts of assets), i.e., to increased 'insecurity feeling'.

8. Plasticity, saleability, liquidity

Suppose the individual has fixed his present assets, as determined by the conditions described in the previous section. It can be shown that the range of variations of the *best* yields compatible with the assets thus fixed is the larger (1) the larger the dispersion of the probability distribution of *possible* yields, (2) the greater the difficulty of substitution between the various yields, as measured by the curvature of the transformation function, (3) the larger the curvature of the indifference lines. We shall confine ourselves to a simple case of two kinds of yields only, say x and y.

Let the assets $a, b, \ldots$ assume their best present values. For yields, use the notation of the sections previous to 7. Express the random character of the transformation relationship between the yields x and y($a, b, \ldots$ being fixed) not by using means and coefficients of variation, but by using a *random term h*, thus

$$(8.1) \qquad y = f(x+h).$$

As h assumes various values with given probabilities, the best values of x and y, as required by the taste condition $U(x, y) = \max$, also change. They must satisfy the condition – cp. (3.2) –

$$(8.2) \qquad \frac{d}{dx} f(x+h) = -\frac{U_x}{U_y}.$$

Writing for brevity $-U_x/U_y = v(x, y)$, we have from (8.1) and (8.2)

$$v[x, f(x+h)] = f'(x+h).$$

Differentiating completely and separating the terms in dx and dh

$$(8.3) \qquad dx = dh \left[-1 + \frac{\dfrac{\partial v}{\partial x}}{\dfrac{\partial v}{\partial x} + \dfrac{\partial v}{\partial f} f'(x+h) - f''(x+h)} \right].$$

The fraction on the right-hand side has a positive numerator because $|v|$, the numerical value of the exchange ratio of x in terms of y, usually decreases as x increases. Since, on the other hand, $|v|$ increases with increasing y, and because of the law of diminishing returns, the denominator appears to be a sum of positive terms

$$\left(\frac{\partial v}{\partial x} + \frac{\partial v}{\partial f} \cdot v \right) \quad \text{and} \quad [-f''(x+h)],$$

and is larger than the numerator. Hence dx/dh lies between -1 and 0, approaching -1 as the numerical value of $f''(x+h)$, i.e., the curvature of the transformation line, increases, or the sum of the two other terms of the denominator, i.e., the curvature of the indifference line, increases, or both.

If, therefore, the addition of a unit of some asset in forming a present balance sheet makes the curvature $f''(x)$ larger than the addition of a unit of some other asset, the risk contributed by the former is larger, and its marginal productivity (in the sense of Section 7), accordingly, smaller.

With a given dispersion of the transformation function (i.e., given degree of 'insecurity feeling') – measured, e.g., by the mean square root of the values of the random shifts (such as h), the price of the asset a is affected by the magnitude $(d/da)[f''(x)]$. Its reciprocal may be called 'plasticity' of an asset: the easiness of manoeuvring into and out of various yields after the asset has been acquired. When plasticity is due to the fact that the future market of this asset is perfect, we may call it 'saleability': the more imperfect the future market of an asset the more difficult it is to sell it in order to adapt the yields consequent upon its acquisition to the transformation conditions as they take actual shape in the course of time.

The future market of cash is probably less imperfect than that of most assets. Cash is 'universally acceptable' or has at least a very wide market. Cash is therefore held partly for the special purpose of future manoeuvring. Holdings of cash and its price in terms of other assets must therefore be larger the larger the dispersion of the estimates of future transformation conditions.

Money's saleability, or plasticity, is probably meant when people use the word 'liquid' – as opposed to 'frozen'. Yet the other property of cash already mentioned in Section 7 – the low variability of its price, due to the low variability of its contribution to yields – is also important, and it may be useful to indicate the two properties by the single word 'liquidity', admitting, however, that it denotes a bundle of two measurable properties and is therefore itself not measurable.

Future adjustment of yields can be performed by physical transformation of assets, as well as by selling and buying assets: saleability is not the only form of plasticity. Stocks of raw materials are more plastic than those of finished goods because they are more easily put into various physical shapes according to needs.[10]

9. Degree of Knowledge

In the preceding two sections, the individual was assumed to know the relevant probabilities: the parameters of the transformation function as defined were assumed to be known. But this knowledge of probabilities – a situation approached in the games of chance – is a limiting case only. In reality the man does not regard himself as enabled by his experience to assign definite probabilities to each yield combination. Let the form of the transformation function (8.1) depend on a set of parameters S. For each set of values, say, S_1 assigned to these parameters there can be stated a probability $P(\mathsf{E} \mid \mathsf{S}_1)$ that the actual observed facts E (e.g., the crops and outputs, prices, etc., of the past, or any other information available) would have happened if S_1 was true. We obtain thus a likelihood function $L(\mathsf{S})$ of the variable set S, viz.,

$$L(\mathsf{S}) = P(\mathsf{E} \mid \mathsf{S}).$$

If knowledge is small, the function does not show any conspicuous peaks: a set of parameters, S_1, may be nearly as much in agreement with the facts E as some other set, say, S_2 in its neighbourhood, i.e. $P(\mathsf{E} \mid \mathsf{S}_1)$ may be nearly equal to $P(\mathsf{E} \mid \mathsf{S}_2)$. Greater knowledge means a concentration of the most likely rival hypotheses within a narrow region. Characteristic parameters can be used to measure this: e.g., the steepness of $L(\mathsf{S})$ near its maximum, or some measure analogous to measures of dispersion, or Dr. Neyman's 'confidence limits', etc.

This may be the *rationale* of Professor Knight's important distinction between 'risk' and 'uncertainty': the former is a known parameter of a probability distribution, the latter, the lack of knowledge of this (or any other) parameter.[11]

The importance of this from the point of view of economic theory lies in the distinction between gambler and entrepreneur. Some assets may produce higher known risks than others, and gamblers may develop a higher preference for them than other people. On the other hand, some assets may contribute to the yields – their mean values as well as their variabilities – in a less-known way than others; and 'entrepreneurs' have a higher preference for them than other people. Càsh is usually regarded as an asset, the future productivity of which is definitely zero, and the future price of which (in terms of consumption goods) is assumed to remain known. Cash holdings grow whenever the prevailing preferences are either nonentrepreneurial or non-gambling.

10. Static Rewards and Dynamic Losses

The above discussion has not included any statement as to whether the transformation functions expected by each individual have proved right or wrong in the next point of time after his 'present' best collection of assets has been formed. Usually the forecasts will have proved more or less wrong; the total utility of each individual will have proved smaller than it would have been if he had known the future: these will be *dynamic losses* – (or malinvestment losses) – the larger, the less the man's skill (or luck) in forecasting. In what way dynamic losses influence the man's further revision of his expectations and thus affect the equilibrium of the day after tomorrow (as perhaps suggested by Mr. Keynes' phrase of 'profits and losses being the mainspring of action'), is a problem in Economic Dynamics where the causation of changes of data (tastes, expectations, present market conditions) is to be studied.

Dynamic losses resulting from the change in data have clearly little to do with 'static rewards' accruing to any individual whose tastes or expectations are different from those of the mass of other men. If meat abstinence is scarce, vegetarians profit by low prices of vegetables; a man who has a small time preference, or a small risk aversion, or optimistic ideas about future transformation, or an entrepreneurial taste for 'dark horses' in times when these attitudes are scarce gets higher total utility than in times when they are common: the assets for which he is relatively more keen than others are cheaper, in terms of other assets, than in times when everyone develops those characteristics.

It follows from the preceding discussion that hoarding of cash is 'rewarded' in those times. On the other hand, risk aversion, pessimistic transformation functions, and lack of either knowledge or entrepreneurial spirit, although analytically distinguishable, usually go, in fact, together, and all make for 'cheap money'.

NOTES

* *Added in 1973:* For the author's later views on the subject matter of Sections 7–9, the reader is referred to 'Role of Liquidity under Complete and Incomplete Information', 1949, *Selected Essays*, 37; and 'Decision-Making: Economic Aspects', 1968, *Selected Essays*, 16, esp. Sections 5–6.

[1] *Economica*, 1935. See also the interesting article by P. Rosenstein-Rodan, *Economica*, 1936.

[2] *Économie Rationelle*.

[3] Cp. Makower and Marschak, 'Assets, Prices and Monetary Theory', 1938, *Selected Essays*, 34.

[4] We prefer this term to 'economic equilibrium' as the stability of a given system of quantities *in time* is not implied. For brevity only, we shall occasionally use expressions like 'the *equilibrium amount a* of an asset' to mean 'the amount which satisfies the set of determining equations'; taking the point of view of the individual concerned we may also use, instead, the expression 'the *best accessible amount* of an asset'.

[5] We shall not give the well-known discussion of second derivatives and the conditions under which a maximum, and not a minimum, is obtained.

[6] R. G. D. Allen calls this rudimentary T a 'transformation function' (*Mathematical Analysis for Economists*, pp. 121–124). He also treats the usual 'production function' but he does not give a general function involving several production and several consumers' goods. Pareto (*Manuel*, App. 78) introduces a set of equations (in our notation): $a = F(x, y, \ldots)$, $b = G(x, y, \ldots)$; but these may become incompatible if there are more production goods than consumption goods.

[7] In the concluding part of his *Theory of Interest*.

[8] The 'self-acceleration' of inflation follows from the above only if an additional, dynamic assumption holds true: that the expected price change has the same sign as the preceding one.

[9] This is sometimes expressed by using the concept of a market rate of interest: the price of a share or bond is said to vary 'owing' to fluctuations in the interest rate; (the price of a share varying also on account of fluctuations in dividends). Since the 'market rate of interest' is only another word for relative asset prices (see Section 4), this is a tautology rather than an explanation.

[10] To distinguish formally between the two kinds of plasticity would imply the treatment of 'future assets' as variables of the system. We have found it unnecessary to use that more complicated approach.

[11] We prefer to use 'lack of knowledge' for Prof. Knight's 'uncertainty' and to reserve the latter term for its ordinary use, viz., for expressing the fact that not all probabilities – even if known – equal 1 (and therefore not all dispersions equal 0).

34

ASSETS, PRICES AND MONETARY THEORY

(1938)

Co-author: HELEN MAKOWER

1. *Introduction*[1]

In order to understand what determines people's cash holdings and the prices of goods in terms of cash, we have to discuss more generally the causes making people hold idle stocks – of which cash balances are a particular case. This necessitates the application of Equilibrium Theory generalised to take account of time, imperfect competition and uncertainty. Our procedure is as follows.

Sections 2–7 give the theory of prices and quantities of assets generalised to take account of time. The case of joint demand together with joint supply[2] is presented: a number of consumption goods or *yields* are produced by the combination of a number of production goods, or *assets*. This takes us rather far back into the theory of marginal productivity and utility: we have to give a broader version of that theory, since the usual versions treat of joint demand without joint supply or vice versa.[3] It has seemed worth while to do this spade-work deep down in the foundations of equilibrium theory; for it enables us to build the theory of asset prices upon something less uncanny than a sheep producing quite on its own supplies of meat and wool ready for consumption; or a combination of assets producing an output (with no by-products) at one blow, and then collapsing instantly on to the scrap-heap.

The generalisation of the theory from one which is applicable to a riskless economy only, to one which applies also to a hazardous world, is given in Sections 8–10. Sections 11–14 order assets according to some fundamental characteristics, such as safety and future saleability, etc. In Sections 15–18 the theory is applied to cash holdings, and a link is forged between the Quantity Theory of Money, the Theory of Interest, and the Theory of Asset Prices.

We may distinguish the following types of *data* for each individual:

Tastes;

Initial resources;

Transformation conditions;

Market conditions.

It will be shown that these data determine the following *unknown quantities* (also called equilibrium [4] quantities):

Prices of assets;

Quantities of assets exchanged and possessed by each individual in equilibrium;

Quantities of yields consumed in the future.

I. CERTAINTY

2. *Assets and Yields*

Yields are *flows* while assets are *stocks*. Yields are consumed but not exchanged; assets are exchanged but not consumed.[5] Yields may differ not only in quality but also in the time at which they accrue.

Assets are physical goods or claims which give rise to yields. Debts are negative assets. There are only present assets, not future assets. Dealings in futures can be treated as dealings in present claims. Futures are present claims on future yields. We shall call a collection of assets a *property*, or balance sheet. The problem is, what property will each individual possess after having exchanged on the market, given the initial property with which he comes to the market, and given also his tastes and the transformation and market conditions.

It must be borne in mind that yields are here defined as amounts consumed. In the particular case where there is only one quality of yield, or else a bundle of fixed composition, we might define 'investment' during a year as the discounted value of the yield series expected from a property as it is at the year's end *minus* the discounted value of the yield series expected from the property as it is at the year's beginning (the term discounted will be defined below, Section 3). Investment thus defined may be negative; it is then usually called disinvestment or wear and tear. 'Net yield', or income, would then be the sum of consumption and investment (or consumption *minus* wear and tear), and therefore consumption, or gross yield, is net yield *minus* investment (or *plus* wear and tear). In reality, however, there are many qualities of yield. Consequently it is not in general possible to define either investment or net yield without recourse to some artificial index numbers which break down whenever relative quantities change considerably. However, it is not necessary for us to use these concepts here: the quantities fundamental for our discussion are the various yields – by which we always mean *gross* yields – and the various assets.

Thus in the case of a loan the lender's yield in a given year is his consumption of the amount repaid to him, irrespective of how much represents 'interest' (or net yield) and how much 'amortisation' (or disinvestment). Or, if the share is sold, the yield is the ultimate consumption of the proceeds from the sale. Hence yields depend not only on physical transformation but also on future exchange. The appreciation of an asset which is to be sold must affect the yield in some year or years.

3. *Tastes*

Individuals' tastes refer to consumption. They are expressed by indicating the order of preference for all conceivable combinations of yields. Each individual tries to maximise the satisfaction he gets from the consumption of all the yields derived from all his assets. His satisfaction, or 'utility', depends upon the size, physical quality and time distribution of his yields.

For each individual enjoying given quantities of yields there are definite rates at which he would be willing to substitute a small amount of any one yield (say milk in the first year) for any other yield (milk in the second or third year, or meat in the first, second or third year, etc.). These *rates of preference* are ratios between marginal utilities. They vary with the quantities of yields enjoyed (so-called 'law of decreasing marginal utility'). The rates of preference enable us to express any bundle of yields – certain amounts of milk and meat in the first and second year – in terms of an equivalent amount of a single yield, say milk in the first year. If two yields differ not in quality but in time only, the rates of preference are called *time preference rates* (impatient people have high time preference rates). The translation of any future yield into an equivalent amount of present yield will be called *discounting*. It will be convenient to use this term in a wide sense, to describe the translation of any kind of yield at any time into some kind of present yield, by means of the time and quality preference rates. The yield selected as *standard yield* (e.g., present consumption of 1 lb. of bread) is, of course, arbitrary. By discounting a bundle of future yields we obtain the present value of the bundle.

People do not exchange yields, they exchange assets. Prices are exchange ratios between assets. Yet people have no direct preferences for assets, but only for things consumed. The link between yields and assets is provided by the *Transformation Conditions*.

4. *Transformation Conditions*

By a *bundle of yields* we mean a series of yields of various qualities in different intervals of time. Transformation conditions tell us all the possible bundles of yields which can be got in the future from any given property, either by physical transformation or by exchange.

In general there is no meaning in the phrase 'productivity of an asset' independently of other assets. The increase of yields due to the addition of an asset depends upon the other assets with which it is combined. If a coal-washing plant is brought into a sugar factory it will make less difference to the yield than if the same plant is installed in connection with a coal mine.

The ratio at which it would be possible to substitute one asset for another while keeping yields unaltered, we shall call the *rate of transformation of assets*. This rate usually changes with the quantity of the asset that is substituted (the so-called 'law of varying returns'). The larger the decrease in the rate of transformation accompanying a given change in the quantity transformed, the less transformable is the one asset into the other. (In the limiting case where the rate is constant, there would be perfect transformability.)

Similarly, the rate at which it would be possible to substitute one yield for another, without altering the assets, we shall call the *rate of transformation of yields*.

The transformation conditions are subjective in the sense that they are people's estimates. They need not be correct nor need they be the same for different individuals. Yet their being subjective does not mean that we are already concerned with an uncertain economy. Until Section 8 we shall assume that every individual thinks he knows exactly the yields accruing from given properties.

5. *The Individual's Equilibrium*

A. *Crusoe*. Since an isolated individual cannot exchange, he cannot alter his initial property, which is therefore identical with his equilibrium property. But he can choose between various bundles of yields which can be produced from his property. His satisfaction will only be at a maximum when his preference rate for yields is equal to the transformation rate for yields. Thus the condition of equilibrium is that the rate at which he is *willing* to substitute yields must be equal to the rate at which he is *able* to substitute them.

B. *A Producer in a Perfect Market*. The individual in a perfect market regards prices as given to him and as uninfluenced by the quantities he sells. In equilibrium he will choose such a combination of assets, and with this combination he will produce such a bundle of yields, as will make (i) his rate of preference equal to the transformation rate for yields, (ii) the rate of transformation of assets equal to the ratio of market prices. The first condition also applies to Crusoe, but the second does not.

The equilibrium requirement can be put in the familiar way, in terms of marginal productivity, provided only that we define marginal productivity more generally than is done in the usual marginal productivity theory, where it is assumed that there is only one product. As has been seen, an asset may contribute a variety of alternative bundles of yields. The marginal productivity of an asset is the most preferred bundle of yields (properly discounted by using preference rates and thus expressed in terms of standard yield) of all those bundles which may result from the addition of one unit of an asset to the existing property. When we say that in equilibrium the price of each asset is proportionate to its marginal productivity, we mean that it is proportionate to the utility of its most preferred bundle of yields.

One asset – say £ 1 cash – may be chosen as a numéraire, i.e., its price taken as unity. The numéraire must not be confused with the standard yield – say present consumption of 1 lb. of bread – which is the yield (not an asset!) the marginal utility of which is taken as unity.

Since the future yields contributed at the margin by an asset depend not only on production, but also on the proceeds of future sales, the term marginal productivity is employed in a more general sense than usual.

C. *A Producer in an Imperfect Market*. In the present passage and in Section 6B we give the analysis of equilibrium in an imperfect market.[6] This makes the theory more realistic. But it is not essential to the main argument and may be omitted by the reader. Only the concept of market imperfection is required for the later discussion, when we deal with future saleability as a property of cash.

We can generalise the analysis of the individual's equilibrium in a perfect market so as to cover also imperfect markets, by introducing the concept of *market conditions*. Market conditions describe the way in which price varies as the individual increases the quantity he sells. The 'initial price' is the price obtained if he sells a very small quantity. The ratio between total quantities exchanged is the *average price*. The *marginal price* is the exchange ratio between small quantities in the neighbourhood of the equilibrium point. Prices actually charged on the market are in general average, not marginal, prices. Only in a perfect market is the average price equal to the initial (and also to the marginal) price. Thus the case where the market is perfect represents one special market condition. The individual in an imperfect market regards the way in which prices vary with quantity sold, as given to him. Once the initial price is given, his equilibrium is fixed by his initial resources, his tastes, and his transformation conditions. He will sell that quantity which makes the ratio of the marginal prices equal to the ratio of the marginal transformation rates.[7]

6. *The Market in Equilibrium*

A. *A Perfect Market.* When in the preceding section we assumed perfect markets, that is, dealt with an individual who regarded prices as uninfluenced by his own sales, we took the prices as given. Maintaining, to begin with, the restricting assumption of a perfect market, we shall now see how prices themselves are determined by the tastes, transformation conditions and initial resources of every individual. For each conceivable exchange ratio between a pair of assets (goods or claims), there are definite quantities of each asset which each individual would be willing to buy or sell. Only that exchange ratio can obtain in the market for which the double condition is satisfied: that, for each asset, the total quantity people are willing to buy equals the total quantity other people are willing to sell (clearing of the market); and that each person's receipts, expressed in terms of any one asset, equal his expenditure.

B. *An Imperfect Market.*[8] This statement of the way in which prices are determined can be generalised, so as to make it applicable also to the case where the market conditions of each individual are not perfect, but instead some other market conditions are given, in general different for each person. For each conceivable initial price, there are definite quantities which each individual would be willing to exchange – namely those which equalise the ratio of marginal prices to the ratio of transformation rates. These quantities imply also definite average prices. As in the case of the perfect market, the quantities and prices which each individual spends must be compatible with the quantities and prices selected by all other individuals. This gives the same double condition as before: total quantities bought and sold must be equal for each asset; expenditure must equal receipts for each individual.[9]

Suppose we add to our property an asset, some quantity of which is going to be sold at some definite time in the future. If the market is imperfect (few buyers) the future selling price and therefore the discounted yield from the present property is lower than if the market were perfect. We may compare the asset's discounted marginal contribution to the yield of the property with what this marginal contribution would be if the market for the asset were perfect. This difference between the two can be reduced, i.e., the market can be made more perfect, by advertising (in the wide sense of the word including, e.g., brokerage). Advertising will be pushed to the point where its cost equals the gain from perfecting the market.

In general the extent to which the imperfection of the market is reduced by advertisement depends on how long the seller waits between advertising and selling. By waiting longer he gets in touch with more buyers. But on the other hand the yields will have to be discounted more heavily for time (see Section 3). He will select that waiting interval which maximizes the sum of his discounted yields.[10]

7. *Interest Rate, Determinacy, and Equilibrium*

We have shown how the quantities of assets exchanged and possessed, together with their prices, are determined. It may be asked why no mention has been made of the rate of interest. As yields are not in general exchanged in the market, no 'price of present yield in terms of future yield' can be found in the market. Individuals' subjective time preference rates refer to yields; they are not equalised in the market.

Instead of saying that a one-year loan of £ 100 with guaranteed interest of £ 7 p.a. costs to-day £ 104, we may, if we like, say that the rate of interest is 3 per cent. This is an application of the formula (Section 5B): price is proportionate to the discounted value of the marginal gross yield.[11] Only it should be remembered that this 'rate of interest' refers simply to the price of one asset (cash) in terms of another (one-year loan). If the loan runs for more than a year we can still define the rate of interest as that percentage which, given the yields, would, if used to discount yields in all years, give the actual price of the loan in terms of cash. It is in this sense that 'the market rate of interest' is sometimes calculated from the yield and the price of consols. Clearly this calculated interest rate is quite distinct from individuals' preference rates. It is a function (a kind of mean) of the various preference rates for different years, for each individual. Obviously this mean may be the same for all individuals although no two individuals have the same time-preference rate for any given pair of years.

The data of our analysis – tastes, transformation conditions, initial resources and market conditions – are subjective, in the sense that they are estimates made by individuals. On the other hand the prices of assets and the quantities exchanged, which are unknowns of our system, are objective. At any given moment there are definite prices and quantities of assets which are consistent with the set of data. We sometimes call these the equilibrium prices and quantities. But it must be understood that by equilibrium we merely mean determinacy. There is absolutely no guarantee that the prices and quantities will persist through time. Suppose even that the data do not change, i.e., that people do not revise their estimates. Then, in the first place, the quantities and prices as determined in the first moment of time will in general not persist in the later moments, because people's plans for the future will usually incorporate quantities which vary through time. In the second place, even if we could assume that people plan for unvarying quantities, the fact that the plans of the various individuals need not be compatible will mean that quantities which had been planned in the past are not maintained; for the market for assets must always be cleared. Finally, the data usually do change: people continually revise their estimates in the light of experience. Thus prices and quantities tend to change continually, although they are determinate at each moment.

To talk of a 'natural rate of interest' is an over-simplification. But we could define a natural system of prices in a way which might correspond to the situation that economists have in mind when they talk of the natural rate of interest. A natural system of asset prices would be a system which can remain stable through time. We have just shown that the data at any given time, though fixing equilibrium in the sense of a determinate system of prices, do not by any means imply a stable system either of prices or of quantities. The question of conditions of stability is essentially dynamic and requires a study of the causes determining the data themselves.

II. UNCERTAINTY

8. *Definitions*

We have assumed so far that there is certainty. We have now to enquire what are the data in an uncertain world.[12]

People do not know, they can only guess at, the yields they will be able to get from their properties, whether by productive activity or by future exchange. The yields must be expressed as an array of more or less probable quantities, that is as a frequency distribution,[13] or more strictly a system of yields must be expressed by a joint frequency distribution.

At least two characteristics are usually used to describe approximately a frequency distribution: some measure of average and some measure of variability or dispersion. Measures of average are, for instance, the most probable value (mode), the mathematical expectation (mean or actuarial value), the mid-point between the extreme values, etc. As a measure of dispersion the difference between the extreme possible values (range) divided by the average may be used, or alternatively the coefficient of variation (i.e., the standard deviation divided by the mean).[14] Thus for example, an investor may think that a security will most probably yield £5; but that it may yield £6 and it may yield nothing. The mode is then £5, the range £6. Or he may think it equally probable that a security will yield £2 and £6. The actuarial value or mean is then £4, the standard deviation is £2, and the coefficient of variation, ·5.

9. *Tastes in an Uncertain World*

It was assumed earlier that a person's satisfaction depends upon the size, quality and time-distribution of his yields. But for 'size' we must now substitute the two characteristics of the frequency distribution. People like yields with a high actuarial value – they like *lucrativity*.[15] And further, the dispersion of yields is relevant. If two expected yields of a given quality accruing in a given year have the same mean (or actuarial) value, most people prefer the one whose values do not usually deviate strongly from the mean. That is, people usually prefer safe yields and dislike risky ones. The *risk*, a disutility, may be measured by the coefficient of variation of yield; or alternatively, the *safety*, a utility, can be measured by the coefficient of variation taken with a negative sign.

Just as there are rates of preference between any two yields differing in time or quality, so also there are rates of preference between the mean and the dispersion of yield: we may call these rates *safety preferences*. 'Audacious' people have a low safety preference. They would give up a lot of safety in exchange for a small increase in mean or lucrativity.[16] Using the individual's safety preference rate, in addition to his quality and time preference rates, we can express any expected bundle of yields in terms of a standard unit of yield, namely present lucrativity of a given quality. We can again, as in Section 2, call this process discounting – in this case, discounting for risk.

10. *Marginal Lucrativity and Safety*

Our previous results can now be applied to the world of uncertainty. For this generalisation we simply have to substitute for the word 'yields' the words 'lucrativities and safeties of yields'. An investor with a given property can choose between various bundles of lucrativities and safeties of yields. This is the generalised way of stating the transformation conditions. As before, an asset's contribution to yield is in general not independent of other assets. This is illustrated by Investment Trusts. The object of an Investment Trust is to increase the safety of the whole property by properly mixing the risks attached to various assets. A gas share added to a holding of electricity shares has a greater marginal safety than if it is added to a holding of gas shares.

It is now possible to extend the concept of marginal productivity so as to make it apply to an uncertain economy. We shall call this generalised concept *marginal contribution*: an asset's marginal contribution is the most preferred bundle of lucrativities and safeties, properly discounted, resulting from the addition of one unit of the asset to a given property. Asset prices are proportionate to marginal contributions. The price of the asset chosen as numéraire is unity. The lucrativity of one unit of the standard yield is also unity.

As an illustration, suppose a person's property consists mainly of plant. Let us first consider in what way the addition of more plant will affect expected yields. Let the most preferred contribution of the added plant be: nine units of lucrativity (discounted for time) and an amount of safety which, discounted for time and risk, is one unit of lucrativity. Suppose now that, instead of more plant, a house is added to the property and that the best yield-bundle consists of a smaller amount of lucrativity, 3, together with a larger amount of safety, say 7. The two assets then make contributions of equal value, viz., 10 lucrativity units. Therefore their present prices must be equal: the higher lucrativity of the plant is offset by its lower safety.

It now becomes clear why changes in interest rates do not materially affect investment plans, even long-term investment plans, except in the cases of housing and public utilities. The increase in lucrativity due to saving on interest payments is only one of the considerations relevant to the borrower: there is also the effect on safety. Whereas in the case of housing and public utilities the latter effect may be very small, in the case of industrial investments there may be such a large unfavorable effect on the safety of the yields from the whole property that the gain in lucrativity is outweighed by the loss in safety.

We have shown that the interest rate can be defined as the result of an arithmetical operation on the price and gross yield of a (safe) loan, like consols. The situation is analogous if we consider discounting for risk instead of for time. 'The risk premium' would be that quantity which, if used to discount each successive unit of risk, would give the actual price of a (non-durable) asset. If, however, the asset is both durable and risky, the definition collapses: there is an indefinite number of pairs of interest and risk premia which, if applied in discounting a given yield series, will result in a given price. Asset prices are still perfectly determinate; but the interest rate and the risk premium are now indeterminate – we must abandon them, and we do so without regret. The fact that 'interest rate' and 'risk premium' vaguely suggest to us time-preference and safety-preference does not constitute a recommendation for them. The interest rate is not in general identical with any time-preference rate (see Section 7) and, for analogous reasons, the risk premium is not identical with any safety-preference rate.

11. *Classification of Assets*

We may group together familiar types of actual assets – like money, shares, plant – according to the ways in which they contribute to lucrativities and safeties. We shall start with simplified conditions and then introduce imperfection of the market and uncertainty.

A. *Certainty with a Perfect Market.* In a certain world with a perfect market the marginal contributions of assets are simply their marginal productivities. All stocks are *productive* stocks. Asset prices are proportionate to these productivities. The quantities of stocks of each kind of asset held are such as to make asset prices proportionate to their marginal productivities.

It may appear that some stocks would be held in a world of certainty without contributing to productivity. For instance, an ounce of crude tin may be held simply because it is not worth while blowing-in the blast furnace. This, however, does not constitute any exception to our rule. Because of the high costs of melting small quantities, the marginal product of tin under process would be less than the marginal product of the idle stock of crude tin. What may be called *discontinuity stocks* are only an extreme case of this same phenomenon: they are therefore also a variety of productive stock. Crops ripen at a definite season. The reason why wheat is held over winter is that it is extremely expensive to grow wheat out of season, in hothouses. Ore from overseas arrives discontinuously in big ship-loads. It is cheaper to keep some ore in stock than to have it delivered in small canoes whenever it is wanted.

Thus, in a world of certainty with perfect market conditions all stocks are lucrative stocks or, more specifically, productive stocks.

B. *Certainty with an Imperfect Market.* With an imperfect market some stocks may be acquired because their price is expected to rise in the future. Such stocks will be called *speculative*. Their acquisition contributes to lucrativity through exchange. In the absence of uncertainty speculative stocks can only exist if the market is imperfect. For in a perfect market with full certainty (Section 4) speculation would defeat its own end: any investor who, on going to the market, saw a possibility of speculative gains, would, by his own purchases, push up the present price to that level which he expected the future price to reach. Therefore in equilibrium no one could be expecting speculative gains. In an imperfect market, however, the investor would not push his purchases so far. He would take into account the effect of his own purchases upon price.

As a common term for speculative and productive stocks we may use the expression 'lucrative stocks'. As in the case of a perfect market, stocks may also be held owing to the high costs of investing small quantities – where by 'investing' we now mean not only transforming physically but also exchanging in the market. Such stocks are merely a kind of lucrative stocks. In an imperfect market advertising costs arise. High brokerage charges may make the marginal product of a share with a low dividend greater than that of a share with a higher dividend.

This kind of consideration would explain the existence of some minimum stocks of cash even in the absence of uncertainty. Provided income does not accrue exactly at the same times and in the same quantities as expenditures are made, people will keep cash balances; for the cost of investing very small balances is prohibitive.

C. *Uncertainty with a Perfect Market.* In a certain world, then, assets are valued in proportion to their marginal productivities. With the introduction of uncertainty the price-relations become different. Assets are valued in proportion to what we have defined as their marginal contributions. Some assets become more highly valued, and are acquired in larger quantities, than they would be in a world of certainty. Those parts of stocks which would not have been acquired in a certain economy are usually called non-productive. Some kinds of assets which are familiar in the world as we know it would hardly be held at all in the absence of uncertainty. The considerations determining people's asset-holdings in an uncertain world are reviewed below.

(i) Lucrative Stocks. Assets can contribute to lucrativity either by physical transformation or by exchange. Those assets acquired because of their contribution to lucrativity without recourse to the market are *productive stocks*. They would exist in a certain as well as in an uncertain world.

Assets may be acquired because they are expected to contribute to lucrativity through future exchange. Such assets are *speculative*. They may always exist in an uncertain world; in a certain world they can only exist if the market is imperfect.

(ii) Safe Stocks. Some assets are acquired because, without future exchange, they contribute to safety (i.e., reduce the dispersion of yields) more than others. Such assets may be called *safe in production*.

Further, there are assets which are acquired because their future prices are more certain than those of others (i.e., have a smaller dispersion). The small dispersion of price will make their yields after sale (consumed proceeds) less dispersed than those of other assets. Such assets may be called *safe in exchange*; they are sometimes described by the phrase 'store of value'. Thus money has often been called a store of value by economists who abstract from the experiences of inflation.

In so far as the yield-expectations of the various persons are based partly on the same objective facts and are therefore to some extent similar, assets with certain prices are usually those whose yield is known with some precision. Therefore assets which are safe in production are usually also safe in exchange and can be kept as stores of value. For instance the yield, and hence the price, of a bond is not subject to large dispersion; so that bonds are partly kept as a store of value.

D. *An Uncertain Economy with an Imperfect Market*. The introduction of market imperfection into an uncertain economy gives rise to a distinction between assets which will be more and those which will be less *saleable*.

12. *Future Saleability*

The future saleability of any asset to a given investor depends upon two factors: the estimated degree of imperfection of the future market and the frequency distribution of expected future sales.[17]

A picture will be difficult to sell – it will be hard to find buyers; advertising costs will be high. On the other hand it will be easy to sell a single Imperial Chemicals Share of similar value. To meet a contingency, it will be easier to manoeuvre if the future market is perfect.

When an investor adds an asset of the kind A to his property, he does not know exactly how much of it he will sell out later. If it should turn out that his best policy is to sell a small quantity, say α, of A, he would get a small quantity, say β, of B in exchange. But if he should sell 2α, 3α, or 4α, etc., then he would get 2β, 3β, 4β, etc., *only if* the future market is perfect (if the A's are single shares, for instance). In an imperfect market, like that for pictures or for whole blocks of shares, he would get less than 2β, 3β, 4β, etc. It follows that for any given amount of A retained the seller will have less of B, the less perfect the market. He will therefore get smaller yields from the whole property the less perfect the market. The investor assigns probabilities to each event: selling none of A; selling α of A; selling 2α of A, etc. To this frequency distribution of amounts of A sold there corresponds a frequency distribution of yields from the property. The actuarial value of the expected yields from the property (its lucrativity) is evidently higher the less imperfect the market. An asset's marginal contribution is thus highest in a perfect market. The reduction in its marginal contribution – and hence in its price in terms of the numéraire – due to future market imperfection depends both on the degree of imperfection and on the form of the frequency distribution of expected sales. This reduction may be called the asset's future unsaleability, and the reciprocal its future saleability.

Our definition of saleability does not imply that an asset is exchanged against one other asset only; it may, of course, be exchanged against a number of assets. The rate at which different quantities of A will in the future be exchanged against other assets, taken in conjunction with the probabilities of the respective exchanges, determines the asset's marginal contribution and hence also its saleability.

It follows from our definition that saleability depends not only upon future market conditions but also on the frequency distribution of the quantities which the individual thinks it possible he may sell. The smaller the dispersion of these quantities, the greater is the asset's saleability. When times become more uncertain the dispersion increases. This, by introducing the possibility of large sales which entail large price-reductions, not only increases the dispersion of future yields, but also reduces their actuarial value. Therefore increased uncertainty will decrease the marginal contributions of assets with future imperfect markets. As uncertainty increases people try to reduce their holdings of such assets, with the result that their prices fall relatively to those of other assets: a phenomenon known as hoarding of liquid [18] assets takes place.

It should be clear from the above that saleability is not a new kind of utility additional to lucrativity and safety. Saleability is a reduction in price due to reductions in lucrativity caused by uncertainty and the imperfection of the future market.

In Section 10 we considered for illustration two assets having the same price but differing in respect to the ways in which this price was built up. Table I extends this illustration. As before, the safety preference rate has been used to express safety in lucrativity units. The table refers to a single investor.

Let us compare first the figures under the heading 'With Perfect Market'. There, plant appears more lucrative than shares and both are more lucrative than cash. The lucrativity may be derived via production or speculation (see Section 11). On the other hand houses, bonds and cash have the highest safety, either because of stable yields or stable prices. They are stores of value. Consider now also the figures under the heading 'Actual': we see that the fact that certain markets are more perfect than others increases the lucrativity of easily saleable assets – namely shares, bonds and cash – relatively to others.

TABLE I

	Lucrativity		Safety (Discounted)		Asset's Marginal contribution (lucrativity+safety		Difference
	Actual	With perfect market	Actual	With perfect market	Actual	With perfect market	
Plant	9	20	1	3	10	23	13
House	3	12	7	11	10	23	13
Shares	9	9	1	1	10	10	0
Bonds	3	3	7	7	10	10	0
Cash	1	1	9	9	10	10	0

It may be worth recalling again that the saleability or unsaleability of an asset must be distinguished from its appreciation (or depreciation). Depreciation is the excess of the future price over the present price. Saleability is the reciprocal of the difference between an asset's actual present price and the price which it would have at present if the market in which it may be sold in the future were perfect. Speculative stocks are thus distinct from saleable stocks.[19] Further, saleability is sometimes described as the relationship between the selling price and the time which the seller must wait in order to get it. If an example is chosen where 'the selling price' includes appreciation (or depreciation) saleability and speculation will again be confused. If, however, an example is chosen where there is no appreciation or depreciation, the influence of time on the selling price is due to the seller's finding more buyers (compare the concluding paragraph of Section 6). In this case the price-time schedule describes the imperfection of the market and therefore, *given the frequency distribution of expected sales*, it determines the degree of saleability.

13. *Future Plasticity*[20]

The investor can meet an emergency either by exchanging or by physical transformation. In the first case manoeuvring is easier the more perfect the future market for the asset, i.e., the less the rate of exchange will vary with the quantity exchanged. Analogously, manoeuvring by physical transformation is easier the more substitutable the asset, i.e., the less the rate of transformation will vary with the quantity transformed. The investor does not know exactly what quantities of assets he will substitute by physical transformation. If he should substitute a small amount, α, of an asset A for another asset B, he would get a small quantity, say β, of B. If, however, he should substitute 2α, 3α, 4α, etc., of A he will generally get less than 2β, 3β, 4β respectively of B. The rate at which he will be able to increase the quantity of one asset at the expense of another is not generally constant; it will depend on the quantity substituted (Section 4). If the rate of substitution varies strongly with the quantity substituted, the elasticity of substitution is small; if the ratio varies little the elasticity of substitution is large. In the limiting case, where the rate is constant, the elasticity of substitution is infinite. Just as we found when dealing with saleability, so here an asset's marginal contribution is found by assigning to each possible amount of A substituted, the probability that this amount will be substituted. With a given set of contingencies, the less the rate of substitution is expected to vary with the amount substituted, the greater the asset's marginal contribution – because the investor reckons to be able to manoeuvre with a smaller sacrifice of yields. An asset's future 'unplasticity' can be measured by the difference between what its price would be if its elasticity of substitution were infinite, and its actual price. The reciprocal of this quantity is the asset's future *plasticity*.[21]

The fact that an asset has a relatively perfect market and high elasticity of substitution for all other assets would not, in itself, be sufficient to cause people to hold stocks of this asset if there were no uncertainty about the future. But if there is uncertainty then, for every given frequency distribution of contingencies, future saleability is greater the more perfect the market, and future plasticity is greater the greater the elasticity of substitution.[22]

The reason why producers find it profitable to hold large stocks of raw cotton, but not to hold large stocks of finished cotton goods, is that it is easier to transform raw cotton into a large range of alternative products. It must of course be remembered that an asset's marginal contribution, and therefore its plasticity, depends on the other assets possessed by the investor. Even raw cotton has no particular advantages of high plasticity to a tin-smelting firm.

We could now add the assets raw cotton and cotton goods to Table I as follows (see Table II).

TABLE II

	Lucrativity		Safety (discounted)		Asset's marginal contribution (lucrativity + safety)		Difference
	Actual	With perfect market or substitutability	Actual	With perfect market or substitutability	Actual	With perfect market or substitutability	
Raw Cotton	2	2	8	8	10	10	0
Cotton Goods	2	3	8	9	10	12	2

14. *Types of Asset: Summary*

Assets may be classified according to the reasons which make people acquire and keep them. These reasons, which also determine the asset prices, may be different in perfect and imperfect markets, and, again, in certain and uncertain economies; also, of course, an asset may be kept for several reasons at a time.

In a world of certainty with a perfect market, assets are kept only for their productivity. If the market is imperfect they may also be kept as speculative stocks. In both cases they are kept for lucrativity. What we have called 'discontinuity stocks' are a special case of lucrative stocks: they arise from the prohibitive costs of investing small quantities, i.e., transforming them into other assets either physically or by exchange.

In an uncertain economy stocks are held not only for their lucrativity (in production or exchange) but also for their safety: and again, stocks may be safe in production or in exchange. In an uncertain world, with a given set of contingencies, prices and/or quantities are lower the less perfect the market and the less physically transformable the asset is expected to be in the future.

III. MONEY AND OTHER ASSETS

15. *Cash-Holdings*

Let us consider, in the light of the preceding discussion, what determines people's cash-holdings.

Cash cannot be held for productivity. It may be held speculatively, if prices are expected to fall: postponed expenditure may be expected to add more to the utility derived from the property than the utility obtainable by present expenditure on consumption.

Owing to the high cost of investing small quantities, cash may also be held without expectation of a fall in prices. This is important because of the intervals which usually exist between an investor's receipt of income and his various expenditures. Thus cash-holdings due to such intervals appear as a special – and important – case of lucrative stocks.

The two above reasons for holding cash might exist even in the absence of uncertainty. They are, however, not the most important or characteristic reasons for holding cash. In fact many other assets are kept for the same reasons to at least as large an extent as cash. People frequently hold goods for appreciation in terms of other goods. Also raw materials often lie in stock because of the high cost of investing small quantities;

whenever delivery is made discontinuously and does not exactly synchronise with outgoings, there will be stocks.

There are, however, two qualities which, in the eyes of investors, cash possesses in an especially high degree. These are safety and future saleability.

In times of monetary stability cash is held because it is safe in exchange – at least it is believed to be so by those who forget the experiences of inflation. This is the quality of money which economists have often described as a 'store of value'.

Second, cash possesses in a high degree the property of future saleability. This may be illustrated by contrasting cash with houses. When an investor sells out his house-property, he is likely by his own action to depress the price of houses in terms of other goods, because there are relatively few buyers of houses. When he "sells out" his cash he does not noticeably depress its price in terms of other goods, because there are many buyers of cash. The saleability of cash is presumably what was meant by economists when they praised it as a 'good medium of exchange' owing to its universal, or almost universal, acceptability.[23] It does not matter, of course, whether the saleability of cash is due to law or custom. The market for cash is more nearly perfect than that for other assets.

It is clear that the future saleability of cash has nothing to do with appreciation (Section 12). Cash may still be saleable even when it is depreciating.

These two properties, safety and future saleability, which money possesses in a higher degree than many other assets, are often lumped together under the name of 'liquidity'. Those assets are said to be liquid which are in some way like cash. Thus liquidity is used to denote 'being like cash'. But since the two properties do not necessarily go together, two terms are required in order to avoid ambiguity.

It may occur to the reader that the term liquidity might be chosen to denote future saleability:[24] the word would indeed suggest the fact that money is easily transformable (on the market) into other assets and is thus an effective instrument for manoeuvring. This terminology would be justified by the metaphorical allusion conveyed by the word 'liquid' and its opposite 'frozen': liquids change shape more easily than solids. However, 'liquidity' has so often been used to cover all properties of money indiscriminately that it seems better not to use it for any of the separate properties of money. We thus resign ourselves to giving up 'liquidity' as a measurable concept: it is, like the price level, a bundle of measurable properties.

16. *'The Velocity of Circulation'. 'The Liquidity Position'*

Once the factors determining cash-holdings have been analysed it would be mere arithmetic to take the ratio of cash-holdings to income – the well-known Cambridge k; or its reciprocal – the notorious Income Velocity of Circulation; or the proportion of cash-holdings to other items in the balance sheet – the so-called liquidity position of firms.

In fact these derived magnitudes become unnecessary tools if we have direct access to the fundamental variables: asset holdings of all kinds including cash; prices; yields (i.e., quantities consumed). In order to explain prices it is not necessary to bring cash-holdings into relation with income. The very concept of income can be dispensed with and has not been used here. The quantities we need are the amounts of various commodities and services consumed in various time intervals, and the asset holdings. To introduce the concept income would be merely to reduce the amounts consumed, and the changes in asset holdings, to a single quantity by the use of some ill-defined index-numbers. This would again be mere arithmetic, and not even very sound arithmetic. For certain purposes the reduction of the multiplicity of yields and assets to imaginary entities like consumption and investment is a useful statistical approximation; but it is an approximation which is inapplicable in practice whenever there are any considerable changes in relative prices or quantities. Such an approximation ought therefore not to be fundamental to our theory.

Similarly, the liquidity position can be described as the ratio of cash to total wealth only at the cost of neglecting important qualitative distinctions between various assets, both positive and negative.

Short-hand measures, however essential for statistical purposes, are no substitute for the causal analysis undertaken here.

17. *The Rationale of 'The Interest Rate' and 'The Price Level'*

To have first explicitly approached money as one among many assets is an important service rendered by Dr. Hicks to modern economic theory.[25] The present analysis shows the connection between two aspects of monetary theory which textbooks usually put into watertight compartments: the theory of the price-level of commodities in terms of money, and the theory of the interest rate. The first aspect is treated under captions such as 'The Quantity Theory of Money', 'The Equation of Exchange', 'The Velocity of Circulation', and 'The Value of Money'. The second compartment works with concepts like 'The Price of Loans', 'The Price of Waiting', 'Liquidity Premium', and sometimes – rather unclearly related to 'The Value of Money' of the first compartment – 'The Price of Money'. But in fact one and the same thing is treated in the two compartments. Given tastes, transformation conditions and market conditions, as defined above, the quantity of cash held, and its price in terms of each of the other assets, are simultaneously determined. These other assets may be commodities bought for immediate consumption, goods bought as a source of future consumption, or claims. In discussing the value of money one or other of these groups of assets has been isolated by writers. The prices of immediate consumption goods have been singled out and submitted to arithmetical operations of index-number computation; prices of other goods like raw materials, houses and land being sometimes added in, sometimes excluded, the so-called price level was obtained. On the other hand claims were bundled together – with or without an admixture of houses and land – and their prices described under the rubric 'Interest Rate'. Or sometimes separate bundles of claims, classified according to their duration, were made up, and a kind of average 'short-term interest rate' and average 'long-term interest rate' were calculated. The difference between the short- and long-term rate was vaguely associated with the risk premium, although the measurement of the price of risk obviously presupposes the fixing of a unit of risk, which was not done.

Strictly speaking, there is a multiplicity of asset prices. We may, however, depart from this purist standpoint and venture out into approximations, grouping or ranking assets in whatever way is relevant to the problem in hand; but then we must always remember that this procedure implies the use of the concept of a 'representative investor' with given expectations and tastes. Bearing this in mind we may, for instance, isolate the influence of risk on price by comparing two asset-groups which differ from each other little except in respect to their (marginal) safety. Similarly, if we can find two asset-groups differing little except in respect to the year in which their yield accrues, we can roughly isolate the influence of the time of yield upon price – always assuming that investors' expectations are sufficiently uniform to allow us to interpret them as the expectations of the 'representative investor'. This is the rationale of the market rate of interest and the market risk premium.

Similarly, indices of 'real income' are used as approximate measures of total utilities. Assets have no utilities, and there is, strictly, no market price which expresses the ratio of utilities of two yields. Yields are not traded, and assets, which are traded, give rise in general to bundles of yields. However, an approximation to the ratio of the utilities of two yields is given by the relative prices of two assets with negligible future yields and negligible risk – i.e., of two so-called non-durable consumption goods. Still assuming that all investors have the same expectations and tastes, and that gross yields do not vary very much in time or quality, an approximate measure of the relative utilities of the yields from two properties, or from all the properties in two economies could be obtained. We could then take as our measure simply the annual yield or (as yields are not traded) the annual quantity of consumption goods bought. This measure is probably at the back of economists' minds when they say that in order to measure real income we must use, not some general index, but an index of the cost of living. All indices are, however, only simplifications which are more or less liable to become unusable in the real world, owing to the non-uniformity of tastes and expectations, the inconstancy of the yield-flow through time and its variability in composition. We must therefore have a theory which does not collapse at the introduction of a touch of realism.

18. *Changing Data*

Changes in (relative) prices and in quantities of assets, including cash, may be due to changes in any of the data, viz., to changes in tastes, changes in transformation conditions or changes in market conditions. It will be remembered that all these data are subjective, and changes in them may be due to mere changes in mood. Individuals' tastes may shift – for instance, safety preferences may decline. People will then reduce their reserves of cash and other safe assets; they will dishoard and drive up prices of, say, shares in terms of bonds and cash. On the other hand, a revision of the estimates of transformation conditions will cause the choice of yield-bundles which the investors regard as open to them, to change. For example, they may reduce their estimate of the difference in safety between, say, cash, bank notes, call money, bonds, on the one hand, and houses, durable plant, shares, on the other. In this case again the price of cash and the other assets in the first group will fall relatively to the prices of the second group. Further, if for any reason people's estimates of the degree of perfection in the market for, say, houses, increases, the price of houses will rise; there will be dishoarding of cash, etc. If all yields become less safe the prices of saleable and plastic assets will rise relatively to those of others. Empirically, it is very difficult to ascribe dishoarding to a change in one particular type of data.

We can regard banks as individuals, and consider an increase in the note issue or in bank deposits as a result of decreased safety preference, or revision of estimated data, on the part of the banks. As before, there will result a rise in the price of other assets in terms of money. These considerations provide a link between the Quantity Theory of Money and the Theory of Asset Prices.

We have described how prices and quantities of assets at any given moment are determined by the data at that moment. In particular we have tried to show how the explanation of money prices and cash balances is to be found in the general theory of asset prices and quantities. A dynamic analysis, which is an explanation of the time sequence of prices or quantities, has not been attempted. Dynamic analysis implies additional hypotheses about how the data at one moment depend upon prices and quantities in preceding moments. It presupposes an inquiry, of the kind undertaken here, into the mechanism by which prices and quantities at each moment are determined by the data at that moment.

NOTES

1 This article reconsiders certain ideas which were treated by one of the present authors in a memorandum on Investment circulated privately in 1935 and in a paper read at the 1935 Meeting of the Econometric Society. A mathematical version of the article is to appear shortly in *Econometrica*: [J. Marschak, 'Money and the Theory of Assets', *Selected Essays*, 33]. See also the Report of the Colorado Springs Conference for Research in Economics, 1937. The subject was also treated by the writers in an unpublished thesis called *The Theory of Value on the Capital Market*. It will be noticed that in the present discussion of Value and the Capital Market, neither the word Capital nor the word Value appears. It

was found better to base the discussion on prices and assets, which are measurable quantities.

[2] In Marshall's sense. *Principles*, Book V, Chap. VI.

[3] Loans repayable in a lump sum and stocks of consumers' goods represent as nearly as possible cases where there is no element of joint supply or joint demand. The theory of prices and quantities in an economy where one asset always produces one yield is given by Irving Fisher *(Theory of Interest)*. For most items in a balance sheet, however, this simplification breaks down. Even the marginal productivity theory of prices of factors of production is a special case, because it assumes only one yield jointly produced by many factors.

[4] See, however, below Section 7.

[5] Instead of contrasting production goods and consumption goods we shall for the purpose of our analysis contrast assets and yields, the former being stocks, the latter consumed flows. The treatment of what might appear to be cross cases presents no serious difficulty: the service 'dwelling accommodation' is a consumption flow, or yield. On the other hand labour is regarded as the stock of services of the labourer over the period for which the worker is signed on, that is as an asset.

[6] Pietri-Tonelli *(La Spéculation de Bourse)* also treats imperfect competition in the capital market. Our method seems, however, to be more in tune with the General Equilibrium approach.

[7] Geometrically, the relationship between the price of an asset and the quantity sold by an individual can be represented in the Marshallian way, as a Demand curve drawn in a system of co-ordinates measuring horizontally the quantity of an asset sold and vertically its price in terms of another asset. The initial price is given by the intercept of the curve on the vertical axis. When market conditions are given, the initial price fixes the whole curve.

The alternative way of representing graphically the relationship between prices and quantities sold is Pareto's (and Fisher's) way. Here each co-ordinate measures the quantity of one asset retained after exchange. The line connecting the point representing the initial quantities with other points accessible by exchange is called the market line (or surface) and the marginal price at any point is given by the slope of the line. The initial price is the slope at the point representing the initial quantities. If market conditions are given, the initial price fixes the whole *allure* of the market line.

In a Marshallian figure a perfect market is shown by a horizontal straight line, an imperfect market by a falling curve. In the Paretian system a perfect market is shown by a straight line (always falling), an imperfect one by a curve (always falling and concave downwards). The degree of perfection of the market can be roughly measured by the elasticity of the demand curve confronting an individual or firm, or by the curvature of the market line. Strictly, this concept of measurable perfection of the market only applies if the elasticity is constant all along the line.

[8] As mentioned above, this passage may be omitted by the more impatient reader.

[9] We may now give the geometrical interpretation of the way in which prices themselves, as well as quantities of assets, are determined. Each market line (or demand curve) corresponds to the series of marginal prices, starting with the initial price, which may confront the individual as he proceeds to exchange increasing quantities. Only one line, for each individual, is eligible when initial resources, transformation conditions and tastes are given. Which line is thus eligible is determined by the double condition given in the text. Thus market conditions are a whole bundle or family of curves, going through the initial point, and having some given property. In the special case of perfect competition they degenerate

into a bundle of straight market lines (or a set of horizontal linear demand curves). Constant (finite) elasticity is an example of an imperfect market condition. But a market condition is a more general property than elasticity. Any other property common to a family of curves can give a market condition.

[10] An interesting unpublished paper on this subject by W. Hasler was mimeographed for the London, Cambridge and Oxford Joint Seminar. Mr. Hasler depicts the equilibrium time for the seller to wait in a diagram, where the axes measure time and price. Equilibrium is shown as the point of tangency between an indifference line (for present and future yields) and the schedule connecting time and price.

The schedule of the prices that can be fetched after various waiting intervals depicts the ease with which an asset can be sold. But it does not help to explain the size of cash-holdings. We shall therefore not apply the term saleability to it. Saleability, in the sense in which this term will be used here to explain cash-holdings and other idle stocks, is a property which, although connected with market conditions, only arises in an uncertain world.

[11] The present price of 100 units of the loan is: £ $104 = 0 + 107/(1.03)^1$.
The present price of 100 units of cash is: £ $100 = 100 + 0/(1.03)^1$.
Therefore the price ratio is 104/100.

[12] We appreciate the importance of Professor Knight's distinction between risk and uncertainty. It seems that we may interpret Professor Knight's 'risk' as the dispersion of the frequency distribution of alternative future events, and his 'uncertainty' as the degree of ignorance about this frequency distribution. For the first concept we too shall use the term *risk*; as to the second, we find it more convenient to call it *degree of ignorance*.

This enables us to reserve the term *uncertainty* to denote the fact that risk exists, i.e., that no event is assigned the probability 1 (and therefore the dispersion is greater than zero). This seems consistent with the ordinary use of the word 'uncertainty'. In the roulette room we are not ignorant about the probabilities which are to be assigned to the various alternative events; yet there is uncertainty even there about each single event.

On the other hand the fact that in ordinary life, outside games of chance, the frequency distributions are not exactly known, we denote as *ignorance*. A discussion of how, in the light of the Theory of Inference, we may measure the degree of ignorance, and how it affects the prices and holdings of assets, must be left for another occasion.

[13] Compare I. Fisher, *Capital and Interest*, 1906, App. to Chap. XVI, p. 10. A. C. Pigou, *Economics of Welfare*, 1920, App. I. P. S. Florence, *Statistical Methods in Economics and Political Science*, 1929, Chap. XVIII, p. 4. J. R. Hicks, *Economica*, May 1931 and February 1935. Leyden meeting of Econometric Society, 1933 (reported in *Econometrica*, 1934). K. Menger, *Zeitschrift für Nationalökonomie*, 1934.

[14] Our analysis is not dependent upon any particular measures selected to represent the probability distributions. Mode and range are less accurate than, for instance, the moments used in statistical work. But perhaps they correspond better to the vague way people think about expected yields.

We might, further, introduce a third characteristic of the frequency curve, its asymmetry. The economic relevance of this is mentioned in the next footnote. It may be measured by the difference between mean and mode, or between midpoint and mode (−2 in the first example cited at the end of Section 8).

The analysis need not be confined to two or three characteristics, or parameters, but can be extended to any number (e.g., any number of moments). And instead of using a finite number of parameters we could use the full description of the probability distribution, stating the probabilities ascribed to each infinitely small range of values, or using the form of the function as a whole. The analysis would be unaltered in principle.

Further, as mentioned in the text, it is, strictly, the joint distribution of all yields rather than distributions of the separate yields which matter. This would mean using, in addition to the parameters attached to each variable (mean, dispersion, etc.), the parameters connecting them, such as correlation coefficients. In fact people are not indifferent as to whether there is association between simultaneous plenty and scarcity of different types of yields produced by the property in any one year (or any given quality of yields in successive years). However we shall not pursue this refinement here.

[15] In a world of certainty there is only one possible value for the yield which is therefore its own actuarial value.

[16] It seems also (cf. Professor Pigou, Professor Sargant Florence, Dr. Hicks) that people are not indifferent about the asymmetry of the probability distribution: of two equally lucrative and equally safe properties, the one offering a small chance of a very large gain is often preferred. Football pools are popular. 'Long-odds enthusiasts' are willing to accept a considerably lower average in order to get a slightly more (positively) skew distribution.

[17] We speak of 'future' saleability simply in order to emphasise that we are concerned only with *future* contingent exchanges. In our terminology there is no such thing as 'present saleability'. The ease with which an asset can be sold in the present market (Section 5C) is not relevant to saleability in our sense. This will become clear in the present section.

[18] We should say 'saleable' (Section 15 *sub finem*).

[19] This distinction is not always clearly made. See, for instance, 'The Concept of Liquidity', A. M. Neumann, *Review of Economic Studies*, 1935.

[20] This section deals with physical transformation of assets and is therefore irrelevant to monetary theory. It is, however, important for the general theory of assets.

[21] In our terminology there is no such thing as present plasticity. The reason why we sometimes use the adjective 'future' is the same as in the case of saleability. (See note 17.)

[22] In geometrical terms, given the frequency distribution of expected sales or transformation, saleability depends on the curvature of the market line, and plasticity, in an exactly analogous way, on the curvature of the transformation line.

[23] See Jevons, *Money*, 1875. Wicksell, *Lectures on Political Economy*, Vol. 2, Introduction. Marshall, *Money, Credit and Commerce*, Book I, Chap. I. Mises, *The Theory of Money and Credit*, Part I, Chap. I, etc.

[24] As in *Kapitalbildung* (by J. Marschak and W. Lederer), pp. 8–10.

[25] *Economica*, 1935. 'A Suggestion for Simplifying the Theory of Money'.

35

LACK OF CONFIDENCE*

(1941)

As the armament effort depletes the ranks of the unemployed, fills the floor space of factories, threatens to clog the railroad tracks with moving materials, people become conscious of one economic danger – inflation. They say, with justification, that if – in a time when the nation's resources are fully used – the consumers and the peacetime firms maintain or increase their spending, while the production of armaments is also maintained and increased, the prices of commodities will rise. Their rise will throw overboard all cost calculations, thus favoring the speculator at the expense of the carefully planning entrepreneur; will expropriate the middle class in so far as it consists of savers or of people with fixed money incomes; will penalize the workers, who are usually unable to adjust their incomes to rising prices. Injustice and political upheaval will threaten to frustrate the defense effort.

Aware of these dangers, leading economists are unanimous in asking for measures which can prevent them. J. M. Keynes, who has suggested compulsory restriction of British consumption during this war, has found a good many adherents in this country. Although in the summer of 1940 he expressed the view that American productive resources are too large to make the Keynes plan really necessary in the United States,[1] present opinion here is less optimistic, concerned as it is with dangerous bottlenecks, with obstructions to a smooth development of the armament program. The mere number of the unemployed does not tell the tale: not all, not even a large part, of the idle men and machines happen to be men and machines of the type needed at the start of armament. In reality, the resources as a whole may soon be worked to capacity, even if some of them have to stay idle for a long time.

Can one hope that this inflation consciousness means at the same time deflation consciousness? Have people realized the important task of modern economic policy, the ironing out of unemployment fluctuations? Do they see that the counterpart of the restriction of consumption and peacetime investment and of the need for increased taxes – which are necessary in times of threatening inflation – is, in times of slump and unused resources, the encouragement of consumption and investment and the reduction of taxes? Beware of short memory. The depression left us only a few months ago. The next one may come like the thief in the night. Have we learned to think in terms of flexible economic policies? If one's vision, backward and forward, is not limited to a couple of years, it should be worth while to train one's mind, and the minds of one's neighbors, to the view that both 'inflationary policy' and 'deflationary policy' are good when in season, harmful when out of season. But powerful prejudices make this training difficult.

1. On some tabus

A large part of human behavior is controlled by tabus – so, at least, we are told by anthropologists. Economists are students of human behavior. They would go wrong if they neglected the tabus. The market for cowhides in India, for kosher meat in Brooklyn, for fish in Catholic countries, is affected by religious prohibitions. Chinese fields have, or had, their boundaries determined by necromantic rules which designate the most propitious sites for ancestors' graves.

In the summer of 1931 the ratio of the German Reichsbank's gold to the volume of paper currency fell, and approached more and more closely the legal limit of 40 percent, foreign gold having been withdrawn from Germany. Authorities induced people to use more silver and less paper, as if that made much difference. The president of the Reichsbank took airplane visits to the heads of sister institutions in other parts of Europe, in the hope of borrowing gold. All this happened because he and other authorities *believed that people believed* that a ratio of 39.9 percent, as compared with 40.1 percent, was a catastrophe. Such a belief, if it existed, could not of course be met by a revision of the law. President Hans Luther was probably not himself obsessed by that supersition. He probably knew that although a certain amount of gold was necessary for Germany's international payments, and a certain amount of paper was necessary to keep German business going, at a given price level, the ratio of the two was not much more than a convention. He, and the officials, bankers and financial writers who advised him, merely believed that other people believed a certain unreasonable thing. In this the leaders proved wrong.

Events after the unsuccessful flight showed that the feared tabu did not exist with the people. No catastrophe occurred.

There are, then, actual and imaginary tabus. I can be surrounded by lunatics. Or I can imagine I am surrounded by lunatics. Leaders of economic policy have occasionally been in both these situations.

To increase the aggregate national consumption for this generation and for the next one or two (or ten) is not the only thing the economic statesman has to think of. He has not merely to think of economic matters, even if an equal, or a just, distribution of the aggregate income – which certainly is his second important task – be considered a purely 'economic' problem. He has also to think of other values, more or less established: he will try not to hurt liberty and not to encroach upon property, the first of which is to some, the second to others, sweeter than life itself. To insure continuity he will give a wide berth to measures which courts may deem illegal – even where legality conflicts with welfare. He will, true enough, fight bad or antiquated laws; but he will abstain from fighting if his aim is not feasible. It may not be feasible in the face of powerful interests. It may not be feasible in the face of a widespread prejudice.

Thus Prejudice has to enter the calculations of applied economics, along with the written Law, or with Interests; along with Liberty, Property, Justice; along with the economist's own standards, Production and Distribution. Prejudice deserves its capital letter, as well as those loftier principles of the century of enlightenment: the statesman will do well to take account of the actual tabus. But he will do well to rid himself, and as many of his colleagues as possble, of imaginary tabus.

In regard to the purely economic questions, one remark will prove useful later: it is probably easier to increase production than to change distribution, especially in times of unemployment. The figures on the relative shares which go to labor and capital are quite obstinate. In the period 1929 through 1939 the share of wages and salaries in the national income of this country fluctuated only slightly around the fraction two-thirds. The real national income itself fell by more than a third from 1929 to 1932, and had regained that lost portion by 1939. Thus the depression took away from the employees, and the recovery gave them back, an amount equal to that enjoyed by all the rest of the community during the depression. From depression to recovery the employees increased their total real income by one-half. This is natural. National income increases either because resources previously idle have become employed, or because employed resources are put to improved uses. In either case there is an increase both in wage payments and in the incomes of entrepreneurs. To be sure, technical inventions can be conceived which raise the marginal product of capital but not of labor (or vice versa), but such inventions do not seem to have prevailed enough to change distribution conspicuously, compared with the gain in total production. Moreover, when idle resources still exist, the income going to any group can be increased much more effectively by reducing the idleness of men and machines than by transferring income from one group to another by any of the current methods – least of all by establishing high wage rates or interest rates, somewhat more efficiently by appropriate taxation and social expenditure. In current politics the fight for relative income shares, especially by fixing high income rates for the services of either labor or capital, has had an appeal out of proportion to its economic effect. A prejudice is at work.

It may well be that the prejudice is even an 'imaginary' one, and that masses do not really have the preferences imputed to them by leaders. Has it not turned out, in Blum's France and Hitler's Germany, that reemployment is more appreciated than high wage rates?

2. Losses cause, profits cure, unemployment

I am now using the word 'losses' (meaning aggregate losses of all entrepreneurs taken together) where some would be inclined to use 'oversaving' or 'excess of savings over investments'. By doing so it is possible to avoid esoteric discussions, or rather to use their results without bothering the reader too much with them.[2] That losses cause, profits cure, unemployment, at least if they persist for some time, does not, however, follow from mere definitions. It is a description of plausible (not to say rational) behavior, fairly well confirmed by observation. The plausible causal chain is: high and persistent current profits lead men to expect, with some probability, high future profits; high profit expectations lead them to increase their production (the opposite being the case if they have been experiencing losses). Empirical tests of the influence of current profits on production (omitting the immeasurable intermediate link, profit expectations) have been amply supplied, for example by J. Tinbergen.

Aggregate current profits must increase with increasing government expenditure, and decrease with increasing government revenue, other things being equal. This is so because expenditures of the government, in so far as they are not offset by taxes, increase the aggregate receipts of entrepreneurs without increasing their aggregate expenses. But this generalization, while it applies with equal force to the expansion of the navy, the parkways or the galleries of modern American art, and to the reduction of sales taxes or of income taxes, requires a few qualifications.[3]

When government increases its expenditures, not only profits but also wage rates will increase – wage rates in the construction industries and in the industries supplying them with materials, because of direct government demand; wage rates in general because of increased spending on the part of those who hitherto had no employment, or had low profits. Increased wage rates may thus partly offset, or more than offset (so runs the argument), the new receipts of some firms, especially those that directly compete with the government for labor, materials or customers, and are at the same time at the mercy of monopolistic colleagues who may succeed in absorbing, by means of higher prices, the better part of the public espenditure. To this I would answer that more accurate study is needed in regard to the actual extent to which market imperfections can, and do, affect the benefits of public expenditure, not only in their distribution but also in their amount; but the fact itself, that government expenditure increases profits, cannot be denied. As to wage rates, it should be remembered that the ratio of wage rates to prices (which alone matters in the calculation of profits) is usually at its highest in the slump: it is reasonable to expect (again apart from monopolies) that wage rates, even if they are bolstered up by public expenditure, will lag behind prices.

With these qualifications – which, it is clear, reduce themselves to a plea against momopolies – the entrepreneurial class as a whole is benefited by public deficits (or, more generally, by any reduction in public surpluses). If it is true that high profits cure unemployment, entrepreneurs should, in times of idle resources, advocate public deficits, or reduced public surpluses, both in their own and in the general interest. If they do not, and yet do not protest loudly against price monopolies, then either the dictum 'high profits cure unemployment' must be qualified, or there is a clear case of 'tabu'.

The salutary effect of public deficits in times of idle resources – and their harmful effect in times of strained resources – should be true regardless of whether the deficit is caused by high expenditures or by low taxes. An effect similar to that of public deficits is produced also by increased exports caused by war orders of foreign countries: the belligerents, in the last resort, pay either in promissory notes which will never be honored, or in some metal which, for one reason or another, it is impossible to use. The pile of metal or of foreign notes may be a more or less useful monument than the schools, ships or roads, remaining after the processes started by public expenditure have accomplished themselves. But in either case the remnant, whether useful or futile, is merely a by-product (although, of course, a useful one is preferable). The important thing is, in both cases, that the lifting of aggregate profits has led to the expectation of future profits and thus to higher employment (or, when 'full' employment is reached, to inflation).

This cannot be answered by saying that public deficits, or reduced public surpluses, while increasing current profits, necessarily lower future ones by the amount of taxes which the entrepreneurs themselves will later have to pay to support the debt service of the government. This argument begs the question. It tacitly assumes that the effect in question has already failed to materialize. It assumes, in fact, that the addition to annual future profits (taken at gross value, that is, before taxation) which is brought about by current entrepreneurial receipts being increased through public orders and through entrepreneurs' own additional investments, is necessarily smaller – as soon as public spending is discontinued – than the annual interest and repayment charges on the public debt. But even if this were true, and if there were no favorable turn of the cycle as a result of external causes such as foreign wars – even if all the increase of (gross) profits in a given year were exactly equal to the public debt contracted in that year, and none was due to the entrepreneurs' own increased activities caused by improved expectations – even in such an extreme case it would take, at the low interest rates characteristic of slumps, more than a couple of decades until the charges on accumulated public debt outweighed the additional current profits due to fresh debts.

The argument against public deficits in times of unemployment must therefore assume that fresh public debts, while admittedly adding their own amount to some receipts of entrepreneurs, destroy other receipts.

This has, indeed, been said: accumulation of public debts, or fear of such accumulation, tends to diminish private investments. Why? Because public deficits kill confidence. In this form the argument becomes interesting. It introduces a term, confidence, which, unlike profits, income, production, monopoly, has seldom, in the more popular economic literature, been submitted to rational scrutiny, unless we count the verbiage, in textbooks and editorials, about 'psychological factors' (as if there were any economics outside of psychological factors). Closer analysis is needed.

The same result – appeal to the confidence factor – is obtained if we try to meet the argument of impending future taxes by postulating very low or zero interest on public debts, or if we go further and suppose government spending to be done *à fonds perdus*, and not to take at all the legal form of borrowing and thus not generate future repayments. The government borrowing we have been considering is, of course, in addition to and not in place of any private borrowing. Therefore its replacement by spending *à fonds perdus* does not change the immediate effect of public spending on profits and production. But, it is said, entrusting government with such powers ruins confidence. Again we are faced with a subject matter singularly neglected by traditional economic analysis.

The influence of public deficits on prices – the danger of inflation [4] – has been another important argument against public deficits as an instrument of employment policy. At present few reasonable people believe that this argument applies with greater force to deficits which do not take the form of debts than to those which do take that form. Collateral, of whatever kind, does not keep prices from rising if additional money appears in the market and does not meet there additional goods. The point is that until full use of resources is reached, additional money does meet additional goods. This distinguishes the Roosevelt deficits before 1940 from those of Louis XVI and from all war deficits. This makes it necessary to watch carefully that the deficits are discontinued as soon as resources approach full utilization, or the 'bottlenecks' are reached. This, in fact, is the substance of the 'compensatory spending' principle, the negative part of which will soon become more topical than the positive, as the armament boom takes its course.

There may be plenty of labor, or land, or plant space, but not of the kind which the public or private spenders of additional money are anxious to acquire; and the reshaping of these resources may be impossible or costly or slow. An increase in prices ensues: it is, in fact, that very increase in prices which forecasters of business improvement so keenly await after the slump has endured for some time. Whether the first spender who breaks the spell is a private or a public body does not matter very much. If it is a public body writers sometimes scorn such 'artificial' measures and predict that their effects will be short-lived. But is not every work of men 'artificial'? Have these writers never crossed bridges, artificial links between two separate points? Obviously, however, this reasoning is bringing us back to the subject of 'confidence'.

3. 'Optimism' and 'confidence'

We have seen that the link between the cause – high current profits – and the effect – increased employment – is plausibly provided by 'high expected profits'. But what are 'expected profits'? In our uncertain world nobody can be sure of earning in a given future year, from a given investment or industrial venture, a perfectly fixed and exact amount. This is true even if we think of profits in terms of dollars, disregarding possible price changes; it is still more true if the entrepreneur or investor thinks in terms of real goods.

The eighteenth century, however fascinated by exact and unfailing laws of nature, nevertheless contributed also to the study of events which are merely probable. It even studied human behavior with regard to such events. The classical rational Gambler stands beside Economic Man, or rather is himself an Economic Man, endowed with this additional rule of action: expected amounts of money, or goods, can be treated as exact amounts if we multiply them by their probabilities. A high but uncertain profit is equivalent to a moderate but certain one. More generally, if various alternative profits, or losses, are expected with various respective probabilities, form their weighted average, using probabilities as weights. The swarm of uncertain alternative profits, or losses, promised by a given venture would prompt the gambler to exactly the same actions as he would follow if he were offered, with perfect certainty, the amount measured by that weighted average, technically called the 'expected value' of a venture, a stake, an asset.

This rule of behavior, if true, does not, of course, lose any of its economic importance if it is added that any two men's evaluations of a given venture's probabilities are different, and purely subjective. The optimist may ascribe to the same venture a higher 'expected value' than a pessimist, even if both have the same sources of information. This does not make the evaluations less effective economically. The effect of Hinduism on the packers' business is the same whether beef eating has or has not the consequences in future life which that philosophy asserts. If more people than before become optimistic with regard to a given type of assets, that is, if people assign increased probabilities to higher, and decreased probabilities to lower, profits (or, of course, to losses), the demand for these assets grows at the expense of other assets, and their relative price increases. It is in this sense that the 'expected profits' or, technically, the 'expected value' of profits from industrial enterprises lead to an extension of plant, hence to increased employment and incidentally to higher prices of industrial stocks.

Students of Mr. Keynes the economist have paid too little attention to the very provocative criticism to which, in his early *Treatise on Probabilities*, he subjected the eighteenth century type of behavior analysis which we have just expounded and which was, in substance, followed by Alfred Marshall, his teacher.[5] Keynes has two objections: first, probabilities, of which we speak as determinants of human actions, are not numbers but vaguely estimated 'degrees of certainty', and therefore there is no calculation of 'expected values'; second, even if probabilities were subject to calculation by acting men, actions would be determined also by other considerations.

As to the first objection, it seems to me that the 'vagueness' which it emphasizes means really three different things: (a) the acting man does not and cannot make exact calculations; (b) degrees of certainty – the only probability concept general enough to apply to human actions – are non-measurable since they represent ranks, not numbers; (c) the individual, except in games of chance, has no knowledge of probabilities involved.

To (a) I would answer that we know well that investors are not actuaries; nor are housewives accountants. Any chapter of economic theory starts from simplified and idealized behavior patterns and treats the results as mere approximations. This has nothing to do with the special problem of uncertainties and expectations.

To (b): the 'classical' relation between prices and expected values which was given above can easily be generalized to include Keynes' more general probability concept, using tools similar to those applied in economic theory where 'utility' too is recognized as a rank, not a number.

To (c): this objection is perhaps the one made also by F. H. Knight in his *Risk, Uncertainty and Profit*: it must be recognized that an individual may estimate two assets as having the same expected value, yet be aware that the two estimates have different degrees of reliability according to the different types of information at his disposal. Thus the objection calls for the use of additional concepts (reliability), analogous to those developed by the modern theory of statistical inference; but it does not make older ones useless. I must apologize for my brevity here, but I think I have stated the case fairly.[6]

As to Keynes' second objection – the insufficiency of 'expected values' as a description of investors' action – I fully agree with It. In line with Irving Fischer (who stated this as early as 1906), A. C. Pigou, J. R. Hicks, I would say that the investor, when visualizing the range of alternative losses or profits which may arise in case he buys a given asset, is not concerned merely with some average (be it the 'expected value' in the technical sense, or some other form of average); he is concerned also, for example, with the dispersion of the profits, in whatever way this may be measured (the standard deviation, the difference between the highest and the lowest possible profit or ome other measure). He may also be interested in other considerations, such as the more or less 'long odds', but we may omit them here. Dispersion may be taken as a measure of 'risk'; its reciprocal would measure the 'safety' of an asset. The tendency to put a high estimate on the expected values of profits (or some other average) we have called 'optimism'. The tendency to estimate a low dispersion of profits – low risks – may be called 'confidence'. (For the purpose of this acticle, however, I shall use this term also to denote a high degree of reliability of estimates; the distinction between the two uses is important – see above under (c) – but it can, I think, be disregarded here.)

I would not contend that this terminology is exactly the one used at present in political speeches or in the press. What the men of affairs have in mind when they speak of 'lack of confidence' is probably sometimes 'pessimism', sometimes lack of 'confidence' in our sense. Their complaint may be that any profits which may be expected are rather low, if not negative ('pessimism'); or it may be that, while high profits are possible, high losses are equally possible, because of the dependence of business on the decisions of a government which, with equal probability, may either continue or discontinue its policy of public works: 'lack of confidence'. It seems useful to make the distinction between these complaints if we wish to find their rational meaning and cure.

There is another important concept mixed up in discussions involving confidence, and one that also needs to be clearly defined and distinguished. We shall see that it is a useful concept. It may be designated as 'audacity' or 'venturesomeness' – the willingness to sacrifice a given amount of 'safety' for a given amount of 'expected profits'. If, between two points of time, expectations have remained the same, that is, if people have retained unchanging optimism and confidence, the changing relation between the prices of risky assets and of comparatively safe assets (in the sense defined above) can be taken as an indicator of changing 'audacity'. As is well known (it is a matter of arithmetic), this price ratio can be represented also by the discrepancy between the yields of the two types of assets – say, stocks and bonds – the so-called risk premium. In general, however, this interesting quantity will reflect not only people's love for high profits in comparison with their hate of risk, but also their expectations concerning the amounts of profit and risk embodied in a given line of action, of investment. Every price ratio for two given goods depends not only on the relative demand, or tastes, for these goods, but also on their relative supply, or what people think is their relative supply. In the case of investments, and of their price ratios as expressed by 'risk premiums', demand and supply of 'expected profits' and of 'safety' are both reflected in the statistical data; and if both have undergone changes during the period the mixture is not easy to disentangle.

In any case it will be useful to remember that the relative yields, or prices, of stocks, bonds, land, raw materials, machines, bank deposits or any other form of investment, change either because people become more, or less, optimistic or confident with regard to respective profits from these various assets; or because they become more, or less, 'venturesome'. People may begin to shun buying or expanding industrial plant or contracting for raw materials or labor, either because they think profits will be lower, or more uncertain, than hitherto; or because, even if they have the same expectations as before, they begin to prefer better sleep and higher safety to the industrial yields which are always relatively more risky, even if on the average higher, than yields from bonds or time deposits. Briefly, either hopes change or tastes change.

4. The rationale of mistrust

Of the several ways in which public deficits have been associated with 'lack of confidence', in the broad and vague popular usage of that term, a few have been mentioned above under the heading 'Losses Cause, Profits Cure, Unemployment'. It was pointed out in that section that public spending in excess of tax revenue, superimposed upon private spending or consumption of investment goods, can be effected either by borrowing, with or without interest, or *à fonds perdus*. If there are idle productive resources current profits will increase in either case. But the expectation of future profits – so runs the argument if reduced to its rational nucleus – will develop unfavorably because public spending as such is detrimental to confidence. Confidence is destroyed if the government borrows and thus piles up a huge debt. Confidence is also destroyed if the government spends money which it prints itself. Finally, regardless of the method used, confidence is destroyed because businessmen cannot gear themselves to a level of national income 'artificially' raised by public spending, since that spending may be discontinued at any time.

The first cause of confidence destruction – fear of large debt figures – is not convincing, and this regardless of whether 'confidence' is taken to mean high average expected profits (what I have called 'optimism') or a narrow spread or high reliability of the estimates of expected profits (what I have called 'confidence'). It is not clear why people should let the public debt affect their expectations at all. It has been shown that this cannot be explained by the fear of taxes, as taxes could be offset, if not by added profits (the real object of successful public spending) then by fresh borrowing. Nor can the fear of rising prices be adduced, since this fear does not seem to be alleged in the case of private booms. The inflation argument is, of course, very serious when resources are fully employed, as in wartime, or when armaments are being built. But it does not weigh during a slump. It seems that the explanation must be sought not in the fact of borrowing itself but in some other policies of the borrowing government, which inspire the investors with mistrust.

It is true that a logically perfect answer, not burdened like the preceding ones by a *petitio principii*, or by an appeal to extraneous factors, might be this: fear of public debt is a fact; it is not justified rationally, but, for historical reasons, it is deeply rooted in the hearts of the millions. They carry in their blood the memory of bad kings who, to escape the check of Parliament (or was it a Witenagemot?), borrowed from Jews and Lombards and plunged the country into unprofitable wars. The trouble is that this does not seem to be true. From Napoleon to Hitler the English have bravely and without interruption sustained their debt. Few people study treasury figures. We have here not an actual but an imaginary tabu.

The same seems true of the explanation of confidence destruction which refers to spending *à fonds perdus*. The inflation argument applies here with little more force than in the case of government borrowing. As soon as bullish sentiment is aroused there are probably few inhibitions which make borrowing from banks a less feasible matter than investing one's own liquid capital. It is therefore hardly relevant whether, during the slump, the dollar amount of annual purchases within the nation is being raised by using stale bills and accounts dormant in banks, or by using freshly printed paper; and, in the latter case, it does not matter whether a reserve bank or the Treasury attaches its signature. As before, unused production reserves are a guarantee (so long as they exist) against a rapid price rise. As compared with borrowing, spending *à fonds perdus* removes, it is true, one or two checks on the executive power: it removes the necessity for an agreement between two public servants, the head of the Treasury and the head of the central bank; it removes the worries about debt charges, which are subject to quarrels with the legislature not once but every year. Even more forcefully than in the case of borrowing, the citizen who loves liberty will hate to remove those checks. A citizen who loves not liberty but profits, or their safety, will not care about these matters, unless he expects the particular person or group that has executive power to use it in a way which will diminish profits, or make them less certain. Thus again the argument reduces itself to a discussion not of public deficits on their own merits, but of other economic and social policies which a given government pursues. And again the alternative answer, an appeal to the existence of a mass tabu, a mass panic caused by figures of fiduciary circulation, does not seem to be proved by facts.

Third explanation: public deficits destroy confidence because they may at any time be unexpectedly discontinued. Here 'confidence' obviously refers to the spread of expected profits, the unreliability of profit estimates: it is identical with the technical use of the word, suggested in the preceding section. The argument is logically correct and seems to be confirmed by facts: why else could the armament program cheer up the stock market whereas WPA, financed by the same methods and the same government, failed to do so?

But this 'discontinuation' argument needs reformulation. What determines entrepreneurs' receipts and profits is not the amount of public spending but the sum of public and private spending, the national income. Suppose the government intends to keep total spending constant (or to increase it slowly) by cutting down or raising its own expenditure whenever private spending (on either consumption or investment goods) rises or slackens. Suppose this policy is known to the public and is expected to be maintained. There is no reason why government spending, timed in this way, should make profit calculations uncertain, compared with a situation (too well known for many decades) in which national income fluctuates violently. Writers friendly to the present administration have in recent years introduced the term 'compensatory spending', which I understand to describe just the policy indicated in this paragraph. A presidential message even named a figure of national income which it was thought desirable and possible to reach and maintain. If the masses of entrepreneurs and investors have not been apprised of the essence of this policy, or have not given faith to it, some fault must have been committed by the information agencies of the administration, or of its opponents.[7] But that fault is not inherent in the principle of 'compensatory spending' itself.[8]

It seems that an additional, equally extraneous, reason has lessened the appeal of the 'compensatory' principle. Influential friends of that policy have believed, and declared, that private spending on consumption and investment goods will never in the future be at a level sufficient to maintain a high national income without being constantly supplemented by public spending. The proportion of the latter in the total income must therefore be not fluctuating or intermittent but constant or even growing. Whether this belief is justified or not, its declaration certainly does not affect the economic working of the compensatory spending policy as such. But it belongs among those aspects of the administration upon which, as we have seen, all the objections against public spending concentrate when freed from logical and factual errors. An 'unfavorable social climate'[9] does affect expectations and decisions of business.

Besides, it does not seem to me that the prophets of 'mature economy' have successfully and scientifically made their case. It is true that savings increase more rapidly than income: American family budgets indicate that if aggregate consumer income increased from 50 to 60 billion dollars (at the prices of 1935–36), about 26 percent of the additional income would be saved, that is, withheld from consumption; and that if income increased from 70 to 80 billion, 32 percent of the addition would be saved. To maintain an increased national income, investments must increase more than proportionately. If they do not, losses arise and are subtracted from the national income.

But to prove that it is impossible to expect adequate investments from private enterprise alone, two groups of facts should be established: the prospects for profitable investments; and the responsiveness of the entrepreneurs to any given profit expectations.

For the first group, prospective profits from housing (taking account of the number of families, including immigrants, and of changes in tastes) should be studied along with armaments, with the inventions which modern wars profusely foster, and with exports. I don't know that conclusive studies have been made. The second group of facts should answer an even more difficult and subtle question: has the 'venturesomeness', the 'audacity', of men diminished? That is, are they prepared now, more than before, to sacrifice a high but uncertain profit for a low but safe one? A very strong desire to shift to other shoulders, even at the expense of profits, the responsibility for estimating the duration of wars has motivated the recent struggle around the depreciation allowances on armament profits. If this is a correct interpretation, it may indeed indicate a somewhat lowered 'audacity', and strengthen the case of 'mature economy'.

But the evidence is too scanty. Remember how quickly, in very recent years, sociologists revised the trends of population in which they firmly believed a few years before! How unexpectedly gold production took a course opposite to that forecast by the best experts! And the question of the future demand for capital is no less intricate than that of the monetary and mining techniques responsible for gold vagaries; the factors determining entrepreneurs' psychology from generation to generation are no less subtle than the obscure factors making for the spread or decline of birth control. Non liquet.

5. Conclusions

We have failed to find rational reasons why, in times of unused resources, compensatory spending should of itself have an unfavorable effect on any man's profit expectations – either on his 'optimism' or on his 'confidence'. Only because of other aspects of a government's policy can such a connection be conceived: aspects disagreeable to entrepreneurs and therefore making them believe that the executive power which "is increasing and has increased, ought to be diminished." For other reasons than those of economic interest this belief will be shared by many – by all those, in fact, who, for freedom's sake, acclaim Cincinnatus repelling the enemy but are pleased and grateful when he returns to his fields. And, in addition, there are considerations of general economic welfare which give strength to some criticisms of the government's economic policy. These, however, are independent of the considerations which center around the question of public deficits.

As was mentioned above, it is probably easier, especially in the presence of idle reserves, to increase the total national income than to change distribution. Consequently it is easier to raise the total income of a given group by raising national income (fuller use of resources) than by attempting to affect the relative share of that group. The latter attempt may even frustrate the former. To increase wage rates or – what comes to the same thing – to tax the employer in proportion to the number of people he employs (social security tax) is not a means of increasing employment. Even the best instrument of income equalization, the progressive income tax, is not free from an objection: it depresses the expected values (in the technical sense discussed above) of risky investments, that is, the investments with widely spread possible yields, and thus, by penalizing industrial daring in favor of hoarding, it may curtail employment. This is probably offset by the increased consumption of the poor (the employed ones, to be sure), but the example indicates the difficulties that are inherent in any equalization policy as compared with those that accompany a straight policy of reemployment.

Yet it was for his equalization policies that Gracchus was killed in a bathtub filled with snakes. Today hate is softened, maybe, into 'lack of confidence'. Whatever its form, it is not, from the point of view of economic policy, a good thing to provoke. Even from the point of view of the poor alone it is not wise to attempt to redistribute a good which the same measures cause to decrease in aggregate value. It may be, of course, that what is lost through the hate of the rich is gained in the love of the poor, for the poor, it is said, ask for higher wage rates, if only because they don't know better. It was indicated above, however, that even this is not probable; recent experience disproves it and points to unemployment, more than wage rates, as the real concern of the industrial masses in these years.

If it is true that public spending, in times of unused productive resources, cannot in itself destroy the 'optimism', the 'confidence', the 'venturesomeness', of investors, whereas a policy of income equalization can, and if it is true that public spending, so long as these attitudes of investors are maintained, can raise employment and thus the income of all, including the poor, whereas an equalization policy cannot, then the statesman whose goal is high national income will in times like ours try more urgently to meet the people's need for reemployment than their desire for equality.

The statesman will, of course, apply other standards in addition to those of economics. He will revise our purely economic finding in accordance with the requirements of justice, the ties of law, the balance of interests. He will not omit from his consideration the existence of powerful prejudices, time-honored or merely silly. But he will free himself of prejudices of his own. And he will try in addition to enlighten and educate public opinion to the best of his powers.

A nation "only asks to be told what is necessary," says Keynes, trying in an accessible and lucid little book to shed rational light on the mysteries of war financing.[10] And Hugh Dalton, another Englishman who has had influence beyond the circle of his students, wrote years ago, "Against unreasonable panic, stimulated by misunderstanding and even by deliberate misrepresentation, there can be no guarantee and no defense except in argument and education. It is not difficult, however, to remove all causes of reasonable panic."[11]

NOTES

* This article was first drafted in the autumn of 1940. The development of armament production in the past months would change the emphasis of presentation but would not, it is believed, affect the theoretical structure or the long-run considerations.

1 'The United States and the Keynes Plan', in *New Republic* **103** (July 29, 1940).

2 If we disregard the replacement of equipment and stocks, which merely causes payments between entrepreneurs, aggregate receipts consist of people's purchases of consumer goods, and of people's purchases of new investment goods, the latter designated as 'investment'. Thus receipts=consumption+investment. National income is devoted either to consumption or to saving; therefore national income=consumption+saving. National income is usually defined as consisting of incomes paid by entrepreneurs to others for their services (costs), and the incomes of the entrepreneurs themselves (profits, positive or negative). With the national income so defined, receipts are identical with national income, and therefore, from the two equations above, investment is found to be identical with saving; consequently 'oversaving' is impossible by definition. On the other hand, if profits were not included in (or losses not subtracted from) national income, the latter would be identical with costs. Again comparing the two equations we see that the excess of costs over receipts (that is, losses) is the same thing as the difference between saving and investment, or 'oversaving'; and similarly, profits are then another word for 'overinvestment'. Thus the concepts 'oversaving' and 'overinvestment' depend on a somewhat odd definition of national income, from which entrepreneurs are excluded (while their consumption still constitutes, as in usual language, a part of national consumption). If this definition is not accepted, oversaving or undersaving does not exist; if it is accepted oversaving is the same thing as losses, and undersaving the same thing as profits. Why, then, not simply use these unambiguous notions – the difference between receipts and costs – regardless of definitional squabbles?

This hare was started by Mr. Keynes, and economists, including Mr. Keynes, have worked hard to catch him.

3 These points were discussed in the spring of 1940 in the meetings of a group in which, besides members, assistants and students of the Graduate Faculty, Mr. Clinton Davidson, Mr. Milton Friedman, Mr. George Terborgh, Mr. I. de Vegh and Mr. Simon N. Whitney were the main participants. To all of them, and to Mr. A. Halasi, who read and gave valuable comments on the manuscript, I express my gratitude; but I do not wish to give the impression that the formulations in the text represent their agreed opinion.

4 "In itself an unbalanced budget is of no moment, and if it represents income-creating expenditures may even be a harbinger of returning prosperity; but in the French mind unbalanced budgets were associated with inflation, a falling franc, and instability" (Benjamin Higgins, 'The Economic War Since 1918', in *War in the Twentieth Century* (ed. by Willard Waller), New York, 1940, p. 173).

5 See, for example, *Principles of Economics*, Mathematical Appendix, notes ix and xxiv.

6 See J. Marschak, 'Money and the Theory of Assets', 1938, *Selected Essays*, 33; Helen Makower and J. Marschak, 'Assets, Prices and Monetary Theory', 1938, *Selected Essays*, 34. The latter article cites some of the literature, partly mentioned below.

7 One opponent has gone so far as to pervert the idea of a constant national income into its very opposite: 'Life on a flying trapeze'.

8 The *Economic Record* of the National Industrial Conference Board (Vol. 1, no. 7, August 31, 1939) gives an account of the various modes and names ('pump-priming',

'compensatory spending' and the like) which public spending has assumed in the course of recent years.

[9] This term has been very effectively used by J. Schumpeter to describe and explain important phases of the economic history of Europe and the United States, especially after 1919. The concept is particularly convincing in his discussion of the very problem we are treating here. Why, for example, have identical measures of the Hoover and the Roosevelt administrations produced such different results? Why was the RFC regarded as 'helping the capitalists' and the WPA as 'helping the workers', although their economic effects should be practically the same? See Schumpeter, *Business Cycles* (New York, 1939), Vol. 2, pp. 942, 983ff.

[10] *How to Pay for War* (London, 1940) p. vi.

[11] *Principles of Public Finance* (London, 1924) p. 203.

36

WICKSELL'S TWO INTEREST RATES

(1941)

Any economic theory tries to explain certain observed facts, such as quantities, prices, incomes, outputs, etc., by certain other observed facts – in particular, by observed behavior of men in given situations. For example, the quantity of a good sold in the market, and its price, are explained by certain behavior characteristics of buyers (the 'demand equation' or curve) and certain characteristics of the sellers (the 'supply equation' or curve). The question of monetary equilibrium studied by Dr. Neisser in his article[1] requires explanation of the following four magnitudes: annual national savings (S)[2]; annual national money income (Y); rate of interest (R); and quantity of money (M).

The explanation is given by the behavior of the following men, or of men in the following situations: behavior of savers (supply equation for capital); behavior of borrowers, mainly entrepreneurs (demand equation for capital); behavior of cashholders in general (the so-called liquidity preference equation); and behavior of the monetary authorities which, for the purposes of this type of discussion are identified with the 'banking system' or, for brevity, 'banks'. Distinctions between the various links in the banking system could be made, and reflected in more behavior equations; but that would be irrelevant here.

For example, the following approximations are plausible and can be used, for the sake of this discussion, without further refinements:

Behavior of savers: $S = mY + bR - g$, where m, b and g are constants, m certainly positive (the marginal propensity to save), b probably but not necessarily positive. Although it is probable that m is not really a constant but grows with the income, this fact is not relevant here; the linear relationship will suffice as an approximation.

Behavior of borrowers: $S = nY - cR + h$, where the constants n, c, are positive with great plausibility, especially c.

Behavior of cashholders: We need not specify it here, and may write down as a general 'liquidity preference equation', $M = f(Y, R)$.

Behavior of banks: Two extreme alternatives can be studied: banks fixing a certain supply of money, say a constant μ; or aiming at maintaining a fixed interest rate, say ρ_0. Thus, the fourth equation is either $M=\mu$ (a constant), or $R=\rho_0$ (a constant). Somewhat loosely, people speak in the first case of a rigid, in the second of an 'elastic' supply of money by the banking system.

The great merit of J. R. Hicks and his remarkable article on 'Mr. Keynes and the Classics' [3] which Neisser mentions in the last section of his article, lies in his clear enumeration of *the first three behavior equations*, in a general form which he illustrates geometrically. As always in the case of more than two variables, such illustration has its pedagogical limits – as proved perhaps by the fact that the article has not received the attention it deserves. Further, the behavior of banks need not be specified in an equation of its own (the fourth) as long as we discuss, for example, Keynes' theory alone, where the 'rigid' policy is indeed assumed. But since Wicksell assumes (according to Hicks) the opposite policy when he tries to explain inflation and deflation by the interest rate which the banks choose to maintain, any comparison between Keynes and Wicksell requires the statement of a specified behavior equation for banks. With four variables and equations, the advantages of graphical presentation become still more blurred. Some simple algebra may prove helpful, both to restate and to develop Hicks' suggestions – this, at least, is the impression I have gathered in reading the more recent publications on the subject, such as those criticized by Neisser.

What is the influence of interest rate on money income? Let us express money income in terms of interest rate. To do this, let us first subtract the 'borrowers' equation' from the 'savers' equation'. We obtain

$$\text{(A)} \qquad (m-n)\,Y+(b+c)\,R=g+h;$$

this must hold good for any simultaneous values of income Y and of interest rate R. Call their initial values – that is, the values which they had before a certain bank policy was started – Y_0 and R_0 respectively. Then

$$\text{(B)} \qquad (m-n)\,Y_0+(b+c)\,R_0=g+h$$

On the other hand, when the 'elastic' bank policy is being applied, and the interest rate is maintained at a fixed level – namely, $R=\rho_0$ – it follows from equation (A) that

$$\text{(C)}\qquad (m-n)\,Y+(b+c)\,\rho_0=g+h$$

Subtracting (B) from (C) we find the following proportion:

$$\text{(D)}\qquad \frac{Y-Y_0}{R_0-\rho_0}=\frac{b+c}{m-n}$$

That value of the money income Y which satisfies all the behavior equations will also satisfy this proportion. If the expression on its right-hand side, $(b+c)/(m-n)$, could always be assumed to be positive, our result would mean this: if at some point of time, when the money income and the interest rate have, respectively, the values Y_0 and R_0 (which we call initial values), the banks begin to adjust the money supply in such a way as to keep the interest rate at some fixed level, then the resulting money income will exceed the initial money income if the new interest rate is fixed below the initial one; but new money income will fall short of the initial money income if the new interest rate is fixed at a higher level than the initial one. In other words, we have 'inflation' or 'deflation' of money income according to whether the banks decide to fix the interest rate below or above the rate which prevailed before their action.

This result is seen to depend on the assumption that the expression $(b+c)/(m-n)$ is positive. Before taking up this assumption for further scrutiny, a few remarks may help to explain our provisional result.

First, the rise in money income need not mean a proportionate rise of prices, unless all resources are fully employed; it is probable, but of no importance here, that Wicksell had just this case in mind.

Second, the actual quantity of money M which the banks have to supply in order to fix the interest rate at the desired level ρ, is determined by the fourth equation of our system, the 'liquidity preference equation' which describes the behavior of cashholders, but which we need not study here.

Third, the initial value of the money income, Y_0, and its final value, Y, are both equilibrium values, because they both satisfy all the behavior equations: these values are different because one of the behavior equations – the behavior of banks – is not the same at the initial and at the final time-point. Initially, it is the quantity of money which is given: $M=\mu$ (a constant); but as soon as the banks fix the interest, the interest rate is given, and the money supply becomes a variable.

Fourth, as with incomes, so with interest rates: both interest rates, the initial (R_0) and the final, or fixed, rate ($R=\rho_0$), are equilibrium rates in the sense that each of them satisfies a system of behavior equations; the system satisfied by the initial rate contains as its 'banks' behavior equation' the equation $M=\mu$, while the system satisfied by the fixed interest rate has, instead, the equation $R=\rho_0$.

Fifth, it seems hard to maintain that Wicksell's 'money rate' can mean anything but our ρ_0 and that his 'natural rate' can mean anything but our R_0. At least, I do not know of any other logically tenable interpretation. One does come across interpretations where the "natural rate" is itself a variable (a 'schedule' as the economists say), not, as here, a constant. If it is then said that, in the case of 'cumulative inflation' (which we shall treat presently and which is a peculiarly Wicksellian construct) the banks maintain the market rate below that variable, it is implied that the market rate itself varies; but then there is no need to 'explain' the lack of equilibrium, the 'cumulation', since all the magnitudes are supposed to change anyway. Wicksell may have expressed himself vaguely on occasion but he has seldom talked nonsense.

Sixth, the 'natural' rate need not be understood as "the interest rate as it would be in a moneyless economy" – an interpretation suggested by some authors. It is not necessary to postulate artificially such economy. It suffices to postulate a state in which the quantity of money is given.

Seventh, it may be useful to emphasize that the tools used here are essentially those of 'comparative statics', not of dynamics; the behavior equations used here enable us to compare the 'initial' and the 'final' equilibrium situations, but not to study the path of transition. In a sense, however, this analysis points beyond 'comparative statics', by constructing, as a special case, Wicksell's cumulative inflation, when equilibrium is never reached. This case is obtained when some of the roots of the system of equations become infinite. To study the case we must come back to our $(b+c)/(m-n)$.[4]

Looking back to our original four behavior equations we see that b measured the reaction of savers, and c (taken with a negative sign) the reaction of borrowers, to changes in the interest rate. There is little doubt that c is positive, although recent investigations tend to show that – outside the fields of housing and public utilities, highly durable and comparatively predictable investments involving a high ratio of interest cost to the total cost of product, not offset by the risk premium – the coefficient is smaller than economists have been used to thinking.[5] As to b, which measures the influence of interest on capital supply, much has been said by Marshall and since Marshall to show that it is probably somewhere in the neighborhood of zero, a high interest rate encouraging the savings of some people, but discouraging others or leaving them indifferent.[6] Since c is, at any rate, positive, and b, if negative, numerically small, $b+c$ is, most likely, positive. Consider now the denominator of our fraction, $m-n$. The marginal propensity to save, m, is positive; and n – which we may call the 'marginal propensity to borrow' – is probably also positive since, at a given interest rate, entrepreneurs would borrow more when the national income is large than when it is small – the reason for such behavior lying plausibly in higher profit expectations or, more precisely, in the larger aggregate value of possible investments promising a given rate of profits. As it is difficult to decide which of the two positive magnitudes, m or n, is larger, we do not really know whether the expression $(b+c)/(m-n)$ is positive or negative. We do not know, therefore, whether the expression $(T-Y_0)/(R_0-\rho_0)$ is positive or negative. In other words, in order that the lowering of the interest rate should result in an increased money income, the marginal propensity to save must be larger than the increase of borrowings associated with a unit increase of money income. Of course, if the influence of money income on borrowing is altogether neglected ($n=0$), $m-n$ is positive, and the inflationary effect of lower interest rates is again assured. This may have been Wicksell's view of the facts. It does not seem general enough to cover all the facts.

Whether a given interest rate policy is accompanied by inflation or deflation of money income depends thus on whether n, the marginal propensity to borrow, exceeds or falls short of m, the marginal propensity to save. In Figure 1 m is fixed at .2, while n is given, alternatively, the values .1 (in the left-hand part of the diagram) and .3 (in the right-hand part).[7] The initial positions are indicated by the intersection of solid lines, while the dotted lines intersect at the new equilibrium. It is seen that when the marginal propensity to borrow is low, relatively to the marginal propensity to save, the income inflation is associated with a lowering of the interest rate. But when marginal propensity to borrow is high, the interest rate is raised, not lowered, although money income has had the

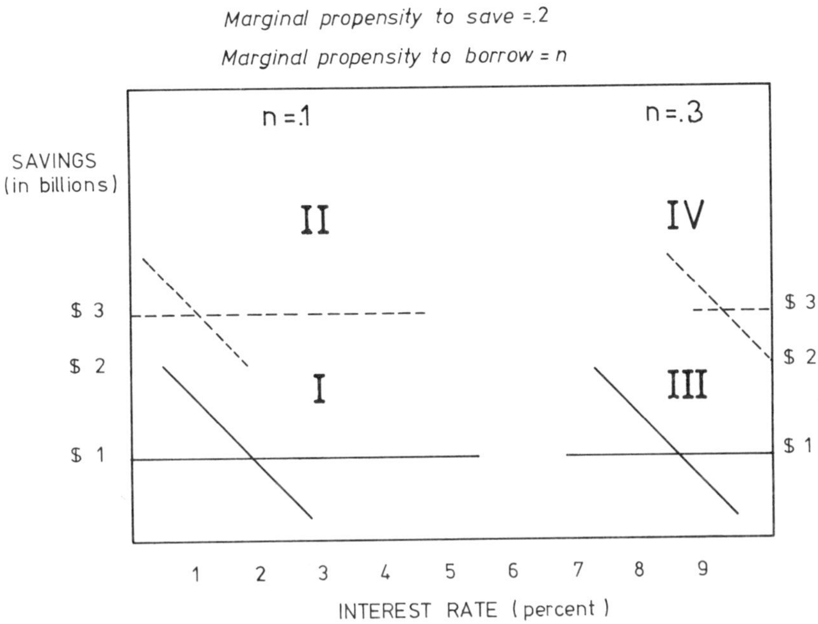

Fig. 1. Charts I and III describe the case when income = $ 30 billion.
Charts II and IV describe the case when income = $ 40 billion.

same increase as in the previous case: high money income may result in borrowing so intense as to push the interest rate up in spite of increased capital supply.

Wicksell's limiting case, the cumulative inflation or deflation, is approached if $m-n$, while remaining positive, becomes smaller and smaller. The new equilibrium income[8] Y, then increases beyond bounds, or 'tends to infinity'. A somewhat more realistic approach to the phenomenon is obtained by discarding the assumption of an 'absolutely elastic' money supply, and by assuming instead that the banks, rather than supplying any amounts of money required to keep the interest rate at the level fixed in advance, increase the interest rate gradually as the inflation proceeds. For example, one might take account of Irving Fisher's point that banks must raise the interest rate during the inflation lest they take real losses on their loans, because of money depreciation. Let, for example, the banks follow the rule

$$\text{(E)} \qquad R = \rho_0 + k(Y - Y_0)$$

increasing the interest rate linearly with the money income. Here ρ_0 is the interest rate set by the banks at the beginning of their inflationary (or deflationary) policy, and k indicates the increment which they allow to the interest rate as the money income rises by one unit. Operations similar to those before but replacing ρ_0 by the right-hand term of (E) lead to transforming the proportion (D) into a more general one:

$$\text{(F)} \qquad (Y - Y_0):(R_0 - \rho_0) = 1:\left(\frac{m-n}{b+c} + k\right)$$

The smaller k is – that is, the more slowly the banks adjust the interest rate to growing money incomes, or the more 'elastic' the money supply – the larger the new equilibrium money income. Again, Wicksell's cumulative inflation (or deflation) appears as a limiting case, as k approaches 0 and as m and n approach each other. As usual – and as too often overlooked in economic theory – the limiting case can easily mislead if we do not know from which side we approach it, that is, if we do not know the intermediate cases. If we simply put $m = n$ and $k = 0$ in the last equation, we cannot tell whether the expressions on each side of it represent a positive or a negative infinity. To be able to associate low interest rates with inflation and high interest rates with deflation, it must be assumed that the banks do raise the rate in inflation (that is, that k is positive); and that the savers' reaction to growing money income is either stronger than the borrowers' ($m - n > 0$), or at least not enough weaker to make the expression on the right-hand side of Equation (F) negative.

Conclusions

(1) Wicksell's 'natural' and 'market' rates of interest can best be interpreted as the rates satisfying, respectively, each of two systems of behavior equations: the one – call it rigid – characterized by the banks' supplying a given amount of money; the other – call it elastic – characterized by the banks' supplying the amounts of money required either to keep the interest rate at a desired level or, more generally, to start from a desired level and gradually shift the rate in response to the changing money income.

(2) If the banks change their behavior from the rigid to the elastic type, the rate prevailing just before the change – which by definition is a 'natural' rate – can be called the 'initial' rate; this rate (R_0) must be compared, in the Wicksellian argument, with the rate (ρ_0) which the banks fix when they begin their new policy. The comparison is, thus, one between two constants, or data, of the situation.

(3) The statement that there is inflation or deflation according to whether the natural rate is larger or smaller than the market rate requires, to be true, that the expressions on the right-hand side of (D) or – in a more general case – of (F) should be positive. This implies, in turn, that the reaction (n) of borrowers (entrepreneurs) to changing money income is small in relation either to the marginal propensity to save (m), or to the rate (k) at which banks adjust the interest rate in response to money income changes. It is possible that Wicksell simply neglected n, that he assumed away any influence of money income on aggregate borrowings.

(4) An unlimited 'cumulative inflation' (or deflation) must be conceived as a limiting case, as the borrowers' reaction to money income (n) becomes more and more nearly equal to, but never larger than, the marginal propensity to save (m); while the banks' money supply becomes more and more elastic (k approaches 0).

(5) Cumulative inflation or deflation does not continue, in reality, indefinitely. It is stopped, for example, by some adjustment of the interest rate. The concept of indefinitely continuing inflation has a propaedeutic rather than descriptive value. Whether the direction of the income change, be it unlimited or limited in its amount, can always be validly explained in the Wicksellian way by the discrepancy between the two interest rates, depends on the actual numerical values of the involved behavior parameters; these measure the reaction of borrowers and savers to changes in money income and the interest rate, and the reaction of banks to changes in income. As indicated, Wicksell's theory may be invalidated if the borrowers respond very strongly to changes in the national money income.

NOTES

1 Hans Neisser, 'Monetary Equilibrium and the Natural Rate of Interest', *Social Research*, **8**, November 1941, 469–78.

2 National savings are equal to national investments if the national income is defined so

as to include all kinds of entrepreneurial incomes. This is explained in Neisser's article. See also my article, 'Lack of Confidence', (1941) *Selected Essays*, 35, note 2.

[3] *Econometrica* **5** (April 1937).

[4] Readers familiar with the differentiation of implicit functions find in a footnote to Hicks' article (on p. 157) the expression which, in the case of linear relationships, is identical with the fraction $(b+c)/(m-n)$ with which we must deal at some length here. We have arrived at it by solving explicitly the equations involved – a method which will be more easily understood by economic readers but which presupposes, of course, arbitrarily simple functions.

[5] See *Oxford Economic Papers*, Nos. 1 and 3: reports by Meade and Andrews and articles by Henderson and Sayers based on an inquiry by the Oxford Economists' Research Group; and J. Franklin Ebersole, 'The Influence of Interest Rates upon Entrepreneurial Decisions in Business', *Harvard Business Review* **17**, No. 1 (Autumn 1938).

[6] Alfred Marshall, *Principles of Economics* (8th ed., London 1936) book IV, chapter 7, §9; E. A. Radice, *Savings in Great Britain, 1922-1935* (Oxford 1939). For the relative importance of the 'Böhm-Bawerk effect', 'Carver effect' and 'Marshall effect' of the interest rate on savings supply, see my papers presented at the Manchester Statistical Society in 1936 and at the Cowles Commission for Research in Economics, Colorado Springs, 1937. See also P. H. Douglas, *The Theory of Wages* (New York 1934).

[7] The other parameters were assumed as follows: $b=h=0$, $c=1$, $g=5$. Accordingly, the capital supply curves (horizontal lines) are $S=\$1$ billion or $S=\$3$ billion respectively, when money income is at $30 or $40 billion. The capital demand curves (sloping lines) are: (I) $S=3-R$; (II) $S=4-R$; (III) $S=9-R$; (IV) $S=12-R$, each of these four cases corresponding to a given money income ($30 or $40 billion) and to a given marginal propensity to borrow ($n=.1$ or $.3$).

[8] *Added in 1973.* P. Samuelson ('A Fundamental Multiplier Identity', *Econometrica* **11** (1943), 221–226) points out that $m-n\leqslant 0$ is sufficient for cumulative inflation or deflation.

37

ROLE OF LIQUIDITY UNDER COMPLETE AND INCOMPLETE INFORMATION*

(1949)

1. It is proposed to study how the demand of rationally acting men for a commitment (an asset or a contract) depends on its liquidity under various degrees of available information.

1.1. While the actual behavior of men is not rational, the implications of rational behavior, or the so-called 'pure economic theory', deserve study for two reasons: (1) as a possible first approximation to the description of actual behavior; (2) as a set of practical norms, to be used by firms or governments.

2. Liquidity

Let x_0, x_1 = rates of input of a certain service (in man-hours, machine-hours, etc.) in 'years' 0 and 1 respectively. If $x_1 > x_0$, and the asset or contract that yields the service is expanded, a price, P, is to be paid, per unit of input added. If $x_1 < x_0$, and the asset or contract that yields the service is reduced, a certain amount, Pl is released, per unit of input subtracted. The ratio $l (0 \leqq l \leqq 1)$ will be called liquidity. Of the cases drawn on Chart I, we shall consider line *bb* as sufficiently realistic, though *cc* is somewhat more general.

2.1. *Special Forms*

2.1.1. Liquidity as *marketability* of an asset. Here Pl = second hand or scrap value of a machine (per machine-hour at maximum rate of use); the selling price of a (nonstandardized) real estate after advertising or agent costs, etc. In perfect market (single shares, bonds; grains) $l = 1$. Note (on Chart I) that continuous line *dd* ordinarily used for monopoly does not meet our case as well as do cases *bb* or *cc*: the transition from the buying to the selling role involves a break!

2.1.2. Liquidity as *physical convertibility* of an asset. Here $l = 1$ implies costless change of physical form or location. For raw materials, l is larger than for finished goods.

2.1.3. *Liquidity of contracts.* Here $l<1$ if the dissolution of contract entails legal penalty or some other cost.

2.1.4. Liquidity and *nondurability.* It follows that if the contract's term is not longer than one 'year', its liquidity $l=1$; and $l<1$ otherwise. Similarly, a plant with durability exceeding one 'year' has $l<1$.

2.1.5. Thus liquidity is a physical or institutional property of an asset or contract, similar to the proportion of raw material in a final product. It is the ratio of two contemporary prices and therefore independent of any price changes in the time between the buying and the selling of an asset, or between entering and dissolving a contract.[1]

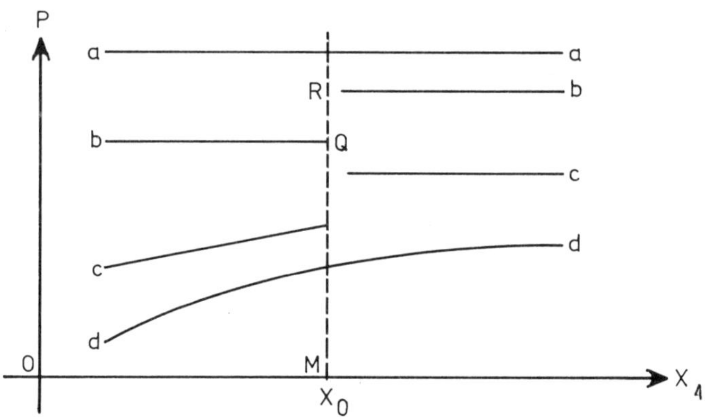

Chart I

P=price (per input unit) paid or retained by firm
x_1=input rate in year 1
x_0=initial input rate

aa: perfect liquidity: $l=1$
bb: imperfect liquidity (admitting discontinuity): $l=MQ/MR$=constant<1
cc: ditto, l variable<1
dd: imperfect liquidity (continuous case).

2.2. We shall assume a single kind of input (or a bundle of inputs tied by constant proportions between quantities and between prices; but see also 4.5). We shall regard it, at its buying price, as the *numéraire*; i.e., put $P \equiv 1$.

2.2.1. If one drops this assumption, or at least admits preference for present versus future profits, then liquidity must be defined, not as a ratio between two money costs, but as a ratio between two marginal utilities (a 'marginal rate of substitution'). See also 5.4.1, 5.4.1.2.

2.3. *Horizon* might be extended beyond two time units ('years') but this would not alter the essential results.

2.4. The *initial input* x_0 is identical with *investment*, up to a proportionality factor; viz., the maximum number of input-units (machinehours, etc.) per year.

3. Degrees of information

For brevity, the words 'the firm knows' will be used instead of 'the firm believes it knows'. Suppose it considers a set $[u]$ of alternative events $u_1, u_2, \ldots$. Denote by $[p]$ the set of probabilities $p_1, p_2, \ldots$ of these events. We can then distinguish four degrees of information about $[u]$ (besides obvious mixed cases):

3.1. The firm does not know $[p]$.

3.2. As above, but it knows data permitting it to estimate $[p]$.

3.3. The firm knows $[p]$.

3.4. As in 3.3, and every element of $[p]$ is either 0 or 1.

3.5. The degrees 3.4, 3.3 we call *complete information*; in particular, degree 3.4 constitutes *certainty*. The degrees 3.1, 3.2 we call *incomplete information* (at least one of them seems to be what F. H. Knight calls 'uncertainty'); in particular, degree 3.1 will be called *ignorance*.

3.5.1. Note that the extreme highest and lowest degrees of information do not involve probabilities; while the two intermediate degrees involve probabilities. We can thus distinguish between stochastic and non-stochastic cases of complete information; and similarly for incomplete information. The non-stochastic cases can be considered as special cases of the corresponding stochastic ones (e.g., by letting all variances vanish).

3.5.2. In both stochastic cases (3.2, 3.3) information is *sequential*: more is known in year 1 than in year 0. As will be seen, it may pay to postpone investment (i.e., to have a smaller x_0) and wait for more information.

3.5.3. Note that all probabilities involved are *subjective.*

3.6. The model can be extended to the case when probabilities are *degrees of belief* not depending on observed frequencies; provided the firm can make choices between bets.

3.7. Extension to '*ordinal probabilities*' is possible but will not be discussed here.

3.8. The rational man (1.1) maximizes the expected (=mean) value of utility.[2]

4. Effect of liquidity on demand in case of certainty

4.1. The firm *knows* (as in 3.4) that x input units will produce in years 0 and 1, a revenue of, respectively, $\rho_0(x)$ and $\rho_1(x)$. Write $x_1 - x_0 \equiv y$. The firm chooses, at beginning of year 0, those values of x, y that maximize two years' profit $z = z_0 + z_1$ where $z_0 = \rho_0(x_0) - x_0$; $z_1 = \rho_1(x_0 + y) - x_0 -$ $- qy$, where $q = 1$ if $y \geqq 0$; $q = l$ if $y < 0$.

4.2. *Problem:* Investigate the effect of l upon x and y for a given change in the revenue function.

4.2.1. Assume a one-parametric 'shift' in revenue function, thus:

$\rho_1(x) = \rho_0(x + u)$ (i.e., total cost needed to produce a given revenue is changed by a constant).

4.2.2. We might, instead, assume a multiplicative not additive 'shift' and write for the revenue of the second year, $u \cdot \rho_0(x+y)$. Variations in u might be due to changes in production, as well as in the price-ratio between input and output. The latter case was suggested by A. G. Hart in 'Risk, Uncertainty, and the Unprofitability of Compounding Probabilities' (in *Studies in Mathematical Economics and Econometrics*, in memory of Henry Schultz, 1942). The results are in essence the same as those obtained under assumptions 4.2.1. The most general case is $\rho_1(x) = \rho_0(x) + \delta\rho_0(x)$, where δ indicates functional variation. (See Kenneth May, 'Technological Change and Aggregation', *Econometrica*, 1947.)

4.2.3. Assume, as on Chart II, that marginal revenue function is linear,

$$\rho_0'(x) = b - x/c; \quad \rho_1'(x) = b - (x+u)/c; \quad c > 0.$$

On Charts II–IV, $b=4$, $c=1$.

4.2.4. From now on we write x for x_0; $x+y$ for x_1; and ρ for ρ_0.

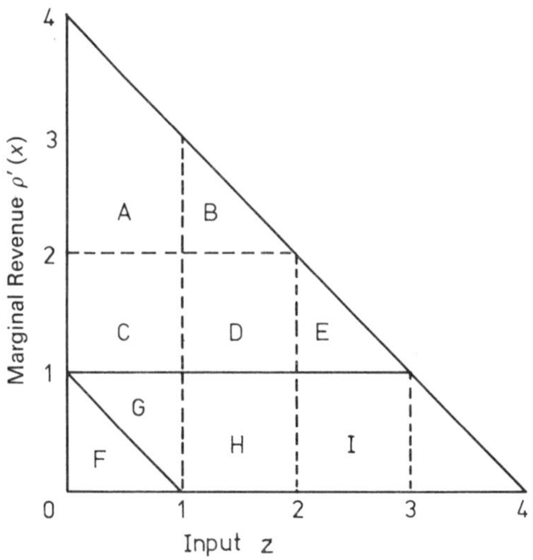

Chart II

Best inputs and profits under perfect liquidity and illiquidity.

It is known that marginal revenue function represented by line 44 in year 0 will shift by 3 input units (to line 11) in year 1. Input price = 1 throughout.

Case $l=1$ (perfect liquidity)
  Best inputs: $x_0=3$, $x_1=0$;
  Profits: $z_0=A+B+C+D+E$
  $z_1=0$
Case $l=0$ (perfect illiquidity)
  If again $x_0=3$, $x_1=0$, then
  Profits: $z_0=A+B+C+D+E$
  $z_1=-(F+G+H+I)$
  A better (in fact, the best[a]) choice is:
  $x_0=2$, $x_1=1$; then
  Profits: $z_0=A+B+C+D$
  $z_1=-(G+H)$. Then total profit (z_0+z_1) exceeds that of previous choice by $(F+I-E)$.

[a] See Chart IIIB, with $u=3$.

4.3. The problem becomes: '$\hat{x}$, $\hat{y}$ are values of x, y that maximize

$$z(x, y)=a+bx-x^2/2c+a+b(x+y+u)-$$
$$-(x+y+u)^2/2c-2x-qy,$$

where $q=1$ if $y\geqq 0$; $q=l$ if $y<0$; $a=$constant.
  Express $\hat{x}$, $\hat{y}$ as functions of both u and l'.

4.3.1. Especially, show that, given the shift $u>0$ (decrease in total cost for given revenue), $\hat{x}$ is smaller when $l=0$ than when $l=1$: Chart II.

4.4. Solution of 4.3. Putting $\partial z/\partial x=\partial z/\partial y=0$, solve for x, y, when $y\neq 0$:

$$y=y(u, q)=2c(1-q)-u$$
$$x=x(u, q)=c(b-2+q).$$

When $y=0$, see (γ) below.
  Case 1. Perfect liquidity: $l=1$, hence $q=1$.

$$\left.\begin{aligned}\hat{x}&=x(u, 1)=c(b-1)\\ \hat{y}&=y(u, 1)=-u\end{aligned}\right\}\text{ See Chart IIIA.}$$

  Case 2. Imperfect liquidity (See Chart III B): $0\leqq l<1$.
(α) for values of u such that $y(u, 1)\geqq 0$:

$$\hat{y}=y(u, 1)=-u, \quad \text{as in Case 1}$$
$$\hat{x}=x(u, 1)=c(b-1), \quad \text{as in Case 1}$$
$$u\leqq 0;$$

(β) for values of u such that $y(u, 1)<0$ and that even $y(u, l)<0$:

$$\hat{y}=y(u, 1)=2c(1-l)-u$$
$$\hat{x}=x(u, 1)=c(b-2+l)$$
$$u>2c(1-l)>0.$$

(γ) for values of u such that $y(u, 1)<0\leqq y(u, 1)$:

$$\hat{y}=0,$$
$$\frac{\partial z(x, 0)}{\partial x}=0, \qquad \hat{x}=c(b-1)-u/2$$
$$0<u\leqq 2c(1-l).$$

4.4.1. Meaning of the intervals (α), (β), (γ) in terms of *capacity*:

In (α) the shift of revenue function calls for an increase in input after year 0. This means also an increase in capacity as the asset acquired or contract made at the beginning of year 0 was such as to suit the initial input $\hat{x}$.

In (β) the shift calls for decrease of input. In this case, if the second-hand price of the asset $=0$, part of capacity created in year 0 may remain unused during year 1; that is, it was not absurd to plan in year 0 for unused capacity in year 1.

In (γ) the shift in revenue function would call for decrease of input if the second hand price equaled the price of new equipment; but with a lower, or even zero, second hand price it is preferable to start with smaller capacity in year 0 and to maintain it unchanged, and fully used, in year 1.

4.5. Problem of *several* (n) kinds of inputs (and, correspondingly, several kinds of assets or contracts), each having different liquidity l^i $(i=1,\ldots, n)$. Find the best initial inputs (proportional to investments) $\hat{x}^i$ and the best increments $\hat{y}_1^i$, $\hat{y}_2^i$ for successive years 1, 2,... as functions of l^i and of a known shift u in the revenue function. It is conjectured that (as on Chart III B), $\partial\hat{x}^i/\partial l^i\geqq 0$.

4.6. We conclude that differences in the liquidity of various assets affect the relative demand for them even under conditions of certainty. Examples: till money, and pipe-line stocks held to provide for predicted changes (seasonal or otherwise) in production and market conditions.

5. Effect of liquidity on demand in the general case of complete information (3.3)

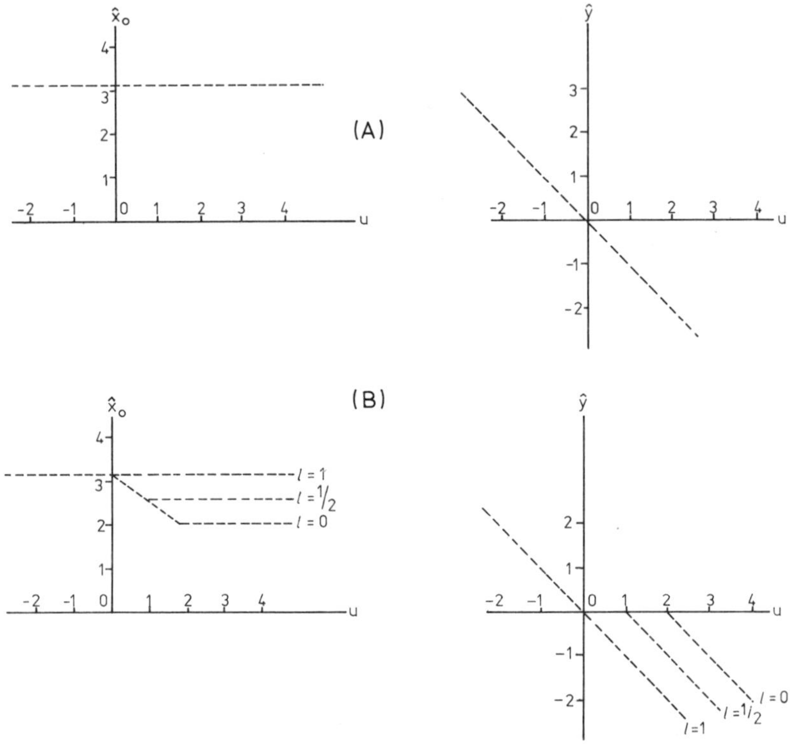

Chart III

Optimal initial input ($\hat{x}_0$) and optimal change in input ($\hat{y}$) as functions of a known shift (u) in revenue function.

(A): Perfect liquidity ($l = 1$)

(B): Varying degrees of liquidity ($l = 0, \frac{1}{2}, 1$).

5.1. Notation: Lower case letters: nonrandom variables (quantities and functions)

Capital letters: variables that are in general random

Italic letters: quantities (mostly)

Greek letters: functions (mostly)

5.2. At the beginning of year 0, the revenue function $\rho(x)$ for that year is known, but the revenue function for the next year is random. Specifically, replace equation in 4.2.1 by the following:

$$\rho_1(x) = \rho(x+U)$$

where the 'random shift' U has probability density function $\phi(U)$.

5.3. We shall assume $\mathrm{E}U=0$ and denote $\mathrm{E}U^2$ by σ^2. We shall discuss how the best investment (best initial input) $\hat{x}$ depends upon liquidity l and upon riskiness σ^2 of the contract or asset in question.

5.4. The two-years' profit z in 4.3 becomes

$$Z = Z(x, Y) = \rho(x) - x + \rho(x+Y+U) - x - QY,$$

where $Q=1$ if $Y \geqq 0$; $Q=l$ if $Y<0$. Here Y, and therefore Q, is random, because the choice of best value for Y, to be made at beginning of year 1, will depend upon the value which the shift U will have taken by then. At the beginning of year 0, the firm determines:

(a) the ('best') value $\hat{x}$ of x, and

(b) the ('best') function $\hat{\eta}(\ )$, –

such that if $x=\hat{x}$ and $Y=\hat{\eta}(U)$, then the expectation $\mathrm{E}Z$ has a maximum, i.e.

$$\mathrm{E}Z[\hat{x}, \hat{\eta}(U)] \geqq \mathrm{E}Z[x, \eta(U)]$$

for any x, η (cf. 4.3), or

$$\mathrm{E}Z[\hat{x}, \hat{\eta}(U)] = \mathrm{Max}_x\ \mathrm{Max}_\eta\ \mathrm{E}Z.$$

5.4.1. $Z = Z_1 + Z_2$ is used here as a simple case of utility function of money profits instead of a more general one, say $\omega(Z_1, Z_2)$: cf. 2.2.1. Expanding ω into Taylor series (as in Marshall, *Principles*, Math. Appendix IX) we approximate $\mathrm{E}\omega$ by a linear combination of EZ, the variances of Z_1 and Z_2 (sometimes called 'risks'), their correlation, etc. The firm is thus concerned with higher moments and not only with the means of profits. This does not contradict 3.8.

5.4.1.1. In the expansion just mentioned, the coefficient of the variance of Z_i $(i=1,2)$ is $\partial^2\omega/\partial Z_i^2$. Only if this is negative, i.e., if the marginal utility of profit decreases with profit, is there 'risk aversion' (cf. Friedman and Savage, *Journal of Political Economy*, 1948).

5.4.1.2. Further generalization of the utility function might make it dependent on other commodities besides money – e.g. honor (for a firm's manager), consumers' goods (for the householder).

5.4.1.3. However, the simple utility function $\omega(Z_1, Z_2) = Z_1 + Z_2 = Z$ and hence the maximizing of EZ, will suffice to illustrate the main propositions of this paper.

5.4.1.4. The behavior in 5.4 is equivalent to the Neumann-Morgenstern optimal strategy.

5.4.1.5. We have here 'sequential information' – the particular value taken by U becomes known after the end of year 0. The result of 5.3 will mean that if liquidity of the asset is low, it may pay to wait with investment (i.e., to invest in another, more liquid asset), pending further information.

5.5. We shall show that

$$\text{(5.5.1)} \qquad \text{Max}_x \, \text{Max}_\eta \, \text{E}Z[x, \eta(U)] = \text{Max}_x \text{E} \, \text{Max}_\eta Z[x, \eta(U)];$$

for this, it suffices to show that

$$\text{(5.5.2)} \qquad \text{Max}_\eta \text{E}Z[x, \eta(U)] = \text{E} \, \text{Max}_\eta Z[x, \eta(U)].$$

Suppose that

$$\text{(5.5.3)} \qquad \text{Max}_\eta Z[x, \eta(U)] = Z[x, \hat{\eta}(U)];$$

that is, for any U, x, η

$$Z[x, \hat{\eta}(U)] \geqq Z[x, \eta(U)];$$

multiplying by $\phi(U)$ (nonnegative) and summing over U,

$$\text{E}Z[x, \hat{\eta}(U)] \geqq \text{E}Z[x, \eta(U)],$$
$$\text{E}Z[x, \hat{\eta}(U)] = \text{Max}_\eta \text{E}Z[x, \eta(U)];$$

This, by (5.5.3) is equivalent to (5.5.2); hence (5.5.1) is proved.

5.6. Therefore, to find $\hat{x}$, $\hat{\eta}$, we proceed as follows: solve

(5.6.1) $\partial Z(x, Y)/\partial Y = 0$

for Y, obtaining $Y = \hat{\eta}(U)$, which involves x. Substituting,

(5.6.2) $\mathrm{E}Z(x, Y) = \mathrm{E}Z[x, \hat{\eta}(U)] = \mathrm{E}Z,$

now a function of x only. Then solve for x the equation

(5.6.3) $d\mathrm{E}Z/dx = 0;$

it will be satisfied by $x = \hat{x}$

5.7. Apply this to the case of linear marginal revenue function (4.2.3.) The problem in 4.3 becomes:

"Write $Y \equiv \eta(U; l)$; $V = x + Y + U$; then $\hat{x}$ and $\hat{\eta}(U; l)$ are a constant and a function that maximize $\mathrm{E}Z(x, Y)$, where

$$Z(x, Y) = a + bx - x^2/2c + a + bV - V^2/2c - 2x - QY,$$

where $Q = 1$ if $\eta(U, l) \geqq 0$; $Q = l$ if $\eta(U, l) < 0$; and $\mathrm{E}U = 0$.

Express $\hat{x}$ as a function of liquidity l and of the parameters of the probability function $\phi(U)$, such as the variance, $\sigma^2 = \mathrm{E}U^2$, of random shifts of the revenue function. In particular, find the signs of $\partial\hat{x}/\partial l$ and $\partial\hat{x}/\partial\sigma$."

5.8. Proceeding as in (5.6.1), we obtain, for the three intervals analogous to those in 4.4:

(α) for $U \leqq c(b-1) - x$:
$\hat{\eta}(U) = c(b-1) - x - U;$ $\quad V = c(b-1);$ $\quad Q = 1.$

(β) for $U \geqq c(b-l) - x$:
$\hat{\eta}(U) = c(b-l) - x - U;$ $\quad V = c(b-l);$ $\quad Q = l.$

(γ) for $c(b-1) - x < U < c(b-l) - x$:
$\hat{\eta}(U) = 0;$ $\quad V = x + U;$

5.9. Proceeding further, as in (5.6.2), (5.6.3):

$$d\mathrm{E}Z/dx = b - 2 - \hat{x}/c + \int_{m_1}^{m_l} [b - (\hat{x} + U)/c]\, \phi(U)\, dU +$$

$$+\int_{-\infty}^{m_1} \phi(U)\,dU + \int_{m_l}^{\infty} l\phi(U)\,dU = 0,$$

where $m_l = (b-l)\,c - \hat{x}$, $m_1 = (b-1)\,c - \hat{x}$.

5.9.1. *Note:* At perfect liquidity $l = 1$, the equation in 5.9 yields

$$\hat{x} = (b-1)\,c,$$

independent of the random shifts, and identical with the solution in 4.4, Case 1.

5.9.2. On Chart IV, the equation in 5.9 is plotted for $\phi(U)$ normal and for $l = 0$ and $l = 1$: $\hat{x}$ is expressed as a function of σ.

5.10. To find the sign of $\partial\hat{x}/\partial l$, differentiate the equation in 5.9 with respect to l, and write for the cumulative probability function

$$\int_{-\infty}^{m} \phi(U)\,dU = \psi(m) \geqq 0.$$

We obtain

$$(\partial\hat{x}/\partial l)\cdot[1 + \psi(m_l) - \psi(m_1) + c\phi(m_1)] = c\psi(m_l);$$

and since $c > 0$, and $m_1 < m_l$, $\psi(m_1) < \psi(m_l)$, $\partial\hat{x}/\partial l \geqq 0$.

That is, initial investment increases with liquidity.

5.11. It can be further shown that investment $\hat{x}$ decreases with increasing variance of the random shift. By introducing $U^* = U/\sigma$, a random variable with zero mean, unit variance and probability density function $\phi^*(U^*)$, Herman Chernoff has shown that for continuous distribution functions,

$$\frac{\partial\hat{x}}{\partial\sigma} = -\int_{n_1}^{n_l} U^*\phi^*(U^*)\,dU^* \Big/ \left[1 + \int_{n_1}^{n_l} \phi^*(U^*)\,dU^*\right] \leqq 0,$$

where $n_i = m_i/\sigma$ $(i = 1, l)$. (The equality sign applies when $l = 1$: see 5.9.1).

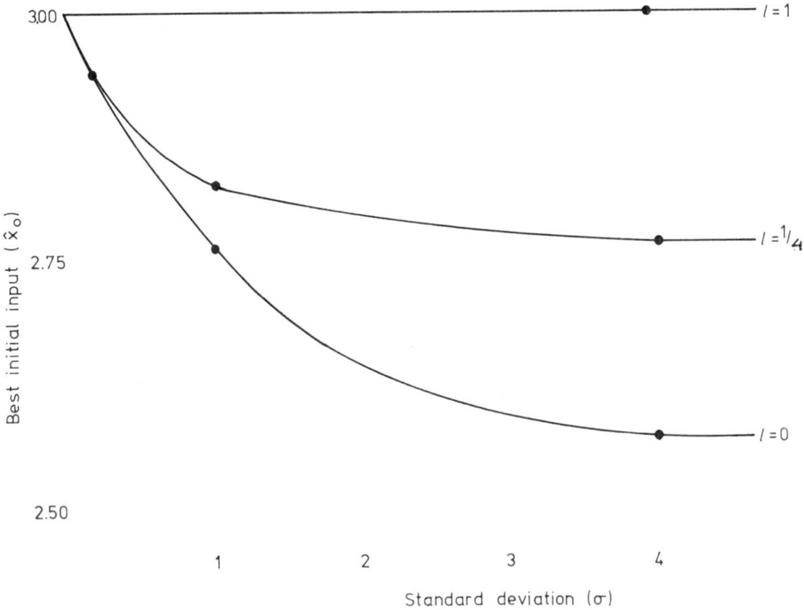

Chart IV

Dependence of best initial input (x_0) upon liquidity (l) of the asset or contract, and upon the known standard deviation (σ) of the probability distribution (known to be normal, with zero mean) of a future shift in the production function.

5.12. Chernoff has shown, moreover, that investment $\hat{x}$ is bounded as follows:

(5.12.1) as $\sigma \to 0$, $\hat{x} \to c(b-1)$;
(5.12.2) as $\sigma \to \infty$, $x \to c[b-2+l+(1-l)\psi^*(0)]$,

where $\psi^*(m) = \int_{-\infty}^{m} \psi^*(U^*)\, dU^*$, so that, for symmetrical functions, $\psi^*(0) = 1/2$.

While (5.12.1) simply repeats the result obtained in the case of certainty (4.4: Case 2, for $u=0$), the result (5.12.2) is interesting: as the variance of the random shift increases indefinitely, investment does not fall to zero; for example, if $l=0$ and the distribution is symmetrical, $\hat{x}$ approaches $(b-3/2)\,c$. (See Chart IV for the more special case of normal distribution and for $b=4$, $c=1$.)

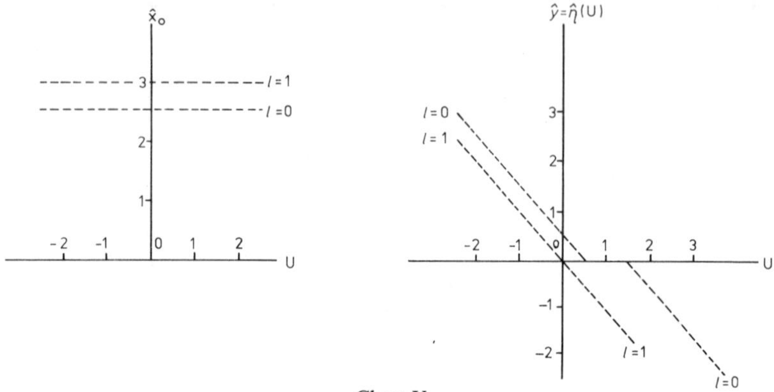

Chart V

Limiting values of best initial input $\hat{x}_0$ and best change in input $\hat{y}=\hat{\eta}(U)$ as functions of a random shift U, symmetrically distributed with zero mean,[a] and with standard deviation increasing indefinitely ($\sigma\rightarrow\infty$); two alternative degrees of liquidity ($l=0$; 1) of the asset or contract in question are assumed.

[a] *Note:* Since this chart is constructed for mean $U=0$, it can be compared with the case of certainty ($\sigma=0$) plotted on Chart III, for $u=0$ only. The comparison is as follows:

$$\begin{array}{lll} \sigma=0;\ 0\leqq l\leqq 1: & \hat{x}_0=3, & \hat{y}=0 \\ \sigma\rightarrow\infty;\ l=1 & \hat{x}_0=3, & \hat{y}=\hat{\eta}(0)=0 \\ \sigma\rightarrow\infty;\ l=0 & \hat{x}_0=2\frac{1}{2}, & \hat{y}=\hat{\eta}(0)=\frac{1}{2} \end{array}$$

6. The case of ignorance

6.1. We proceed now to the cases of incomplete information, and begin with the simple, non-stochastic one: the case of ignorance (3.4, 3.5.1). Consider two examples:

6.1.1. The firm knows the revenue function $\rho(\ )$, the liquidity l of the asset or contract in question, and a set $[u]$ of values, that the shift u of the revenue function can take; but it has no information from which to estimate probabilities attached to each of these values. It has to choose x, y.

6.1.2. Same as before but, instead of a set $[u]$ of constants, the firm knows that $\phi(U)$, the probability distribution of the random shift U, has zero mean and is normal, and that standard deviation σ is an element of a set $[\sigma]$ of constants.

6.1.3. The two cases 6.1.1 and 6.1.2 can be considered as special cases of the following: The form and all but one parameters of $\phi(U)$ are known. In case 6.1.1, $\sigma=0$, and EU is unknown; in 6.1.2, E$U=0$, and σ is unknown.

6.2. If the unknown conditions (u, σ) were determined by a rational opponent in a game, a rational choice by our firm, in case 6.1.1, would be as was shown by von Neumann and Morgenstern: it would 'minimax the loss', i.e., make a choice of x, y such as to obtain:

$$\mathrm{Min}_{x,y}\ \mathrm{Max}_u[-z(x, y; u)];$$

and, in case 6.1.2, it would 'minimax the expected value of the loss',

$$\mathrm{Min}_{x,\eta}\ \mathrm{Max}_\sigma[-\mathrm{E}Z(x, \eta(U); \sigma)].$$

6.2.1. In words: In a game, choose a policy (x and y, or x and η) such that, even if the unknown conditions (u or σ) should turn out to be the ones most adverse to this policy, the expected gain (z or EZ) would be at least as large as the expected gain that would result from any other policy, and from conditions most adverse to that other policy.

6.3. If conditions are not determined by an inimical rational opponent, there is no reason for this maxim of behavior. L. J. Savage has suggested (orally) that not the loss but the 'regret' (or 'miss') be minimaxed. In the case 6.1.1, the 'regret', r is the difference between the gain actually obtained and the gain that would be obtained if choice had been made in full knowledge of conditions. We shall work out this case.

6.4. We define regret:

$$\begin{aligned} r &= \mathrm{Max}_{x,y}\, z(x, y; u) - z(x, y; u) = r(x, y, u) \\ &= z(\hat{x}, \hat{y}; u) - z(x, y; u). \end{aligned}$$

The firm chooses x, y so as to achieve

$$\mathrm{Min}_{x,y}\ \mathrm{Max}_{u \text{ in } [u]}\, r(x, y, u) = r(\hat{x}, \hat{y}, \bar{u}), \text{ say.}$$

We are interested in the effect of liquidity l upon best investment, $\hat{x}$. Obviously if $l=1$, or if u cannot take positive values the case is identical with 4.4, Case 1: the best investment in this case will be called $\hat{x}_\alpha$. Consider now the case $l=0$ and show that then the regret will be minimax at a certain value of $x, \hat{x} \leqq x_\alpha$: investment in an illiquid asset is equal to or smaller than that in a liquid one, all other things being equal.

6.4.1. Suppose first that $[u]$ consists of two values only: u_α in the interval (α), and u_β in the interval (β), as defined in 4.4; $u_\alpha \leqq 0$, $u_\beta > 2c$. Then, using the respective optimal inputs (call them $\hat{x}_\alpha$, $\hat{y}_\alpha$; $\hat{x}_\beta$, $\hat{y}_\beta$), given in 4.4, we can compute the corresponding maximum profits, $\hat{z}_\alpha$, $\hat{z}_\beta$, and hence obtain the regrets, $r_\alpha = \hat{z}_\alpha - z_\alpha$, $r_\beta = \hat{z}_\beta - z_\beta$. The difference

$$r_\alpha - r_\beta = u_\alpha - c + \rho(x+y+u_\beta) - \rho(x+y+u_\alpha),$$

is an increasing function of $x+y$. It vanishes when $x+y$ has a certain value, w (say), depending on u_α, u_β. Therefore $r_\alpha >, <, = r_\beta$ according as $x+y >, <, = w$. Minimax regret is therefore found as follows: minimize r_α for the cases $x+y>w$; minimize r_β for the cases $x+y<w$; then choose the smaller of the two minima. Note that r_α can itself have two minima, one at some $y \geqq 0$, and one at some $y<0$; and similarly for r_β. It turns out that all minima considered are either at $x=\hat{x}_\alpha=c(b-1)$ or at $x=\hat{x}_\beta=c(b-2)$. And, depending on the size of the possible shifts u_α, u_β, either $\hat{x}_\alpha$ or $\hat{x}_\beta$ yields the smallest of the minima. Therefore the minimax regret is obtained at an investment value which is $\leqq \hat{x}_\alpha$, and thus best investment under illiquidity is smaller than or equal to the best investment under full liquidity.

6.4.2. This result is easily shown to be true also in the more general case: when $[u]$ contains any number of elements, belonging to all three intervals defined in 4.4: (α), (β), and the intermediate interval (γ). Again, minimax regret will be obtained when investment is either $\hat{x}_\alpha$ or $\hat{x}_\beta$: the possibility of events of intermediate kind (γ) has no effect!

6.4.2.1. It follows that, for example, a rational man ignorant of the probabilities of three alternative events should *not*, in general, apply the rule that each of these events has probability $\frac{1}{3}$. Thus the classical doctrine (Laplace) which declared events with unknown probabilities equiprobable cannot be a guide to action.

7. The General Case of Incomplete Information

7.1. We now modify the example 6.1.2 as follows:

The firm knows the revenue function ρ_0, the liquidity l of the asset or contract in question, and knows that $\phi\ (U)$, the distribution of random shifts, is normal with zero-mean. In addition, it can obtain, in the year 0, certain data, to be denoted by D_0, that are related to the future random shifts U. For example, the numbers D_0 may be sample previews of crops. Denote the (unknown) joint distribution of D_0, U by $\delta(D_0, U)$. In particular, δ may be characterized by variances and regression coefficients. To choose a policy means to decide how to react to information D_0, i.e., what functions ξ, ε will yield optimal initial investment $\hat{X}=\xi(D_0)$ and optimal increment in year 1, $Y=\varepsilon(D_0)$, determined on the basis of information in year 0. Applying the principles of 6.4, we have to choose ξ, ε so as to obtain

$$\mathrm{Min}_{\xi,\varepsilon}\ \mathrm{Max}_{\delta}(\mathrm{Max}_{\xi,\varepsilon}\mathrm{E}Z-\mathrm{E}Z),$$

where $Z=Z[\xi(D_0), \varepsilon(D_0)]$ and $\delta(U, D_0)$ is an unknown joint distribution function.

7.2. Again, it is conjectured that if the optimal decision functions – say, $\hat{\xi}$, $\hat{\varepsilon}$ – are actually evaluated for our economic examples, they will turn out to depend on liquidity.

7.3. In 7.1, the only data considered were those available at beginning of year 0, D_0. Actually, further data, say D_1, will become available in the course of that year. Then D_1 must be included as argument in the joint distribution function δ and in the decision function ε. This will affect the optimal values of ξ, ε.

7.3.1. In particular, it will probably turn out that if the liquidity of the asset is low, it is advantageous (i.e., it will 'minimax the regret') to have less of it during the year 0, in order to *wait for additional information.* The fact of 'sequential information' (3.5.2) is likely to be of importance for the theory of liquidity as was already seen in the (stochastic) case of complete information (5.4.1.5).

7.4. This section (7) merely outlines a program. Its problem is, in fact, identical with the general theory of statistical inference, interpreted as the theory of a choice of action rather than choice of hypotheses. (The statistician is merged with the entrepreneur.) This is the approach of Abraham Wald (continuing the work of J. Neyman and E. Pearson); for most recent writings, see Wald, 'Foundations of a General Theory of Sequential Decision Functions', *Econometrica*, 1948; and Arrow, Blackwell, and Girshick: 'Bayes and Minimax Solutions of Sequential Decision Problems' (to be published in *Econometrica*).

NOTES

* With acknowledgments to Messrs. K. Arrow and H. Chernoff, of the Cowles Commission for Research in Economics and to Mr. James Tobin. The paper will be reprinted as Cowles Commission Paper, New Series, No. 37.

1 G. H. Evans has privately made the interesting suggestion of describing a commitment as more or less 'reversible'. The older term 'liquid' (as opposed to 'frozen') has the advantage of being universally used. It alludes to the ability of liquid bodies, to change their form freely: cash (and to a lesser extent a share, a bond, or a stock of raw materials) is freely transformed into other assets.

2 See 'Measurable Utility and the Theory of Assets' (mimeographed: Cowles Commission Discussion Paper, Economics 226, 226A), presented at Madison meeting of Econometric Society, 1948; abstract in *Econometrica*, 1949; von Neumann and Morgenstern, *Theory of Games and Economic Behavior*, Section 3.6, and Appendix to Second Edition.

38

THE RATIONALE OF THE DEMAND FOR MONEY AND OF 'MONEY ILLUSION'*

(1950)

ABSTRACT. Consider the following propositions: (1) Each individual maximizes a utility function that depends only on the amounts of various goods he will consume during a period that begins after the marketing date and during which no further exchanges takes place; (2) The *numéraire* (i.e., the thing whose price is fixed at unity) is neither a consumption nor a production good; (3) At least one individual has positive money stock. Condition (1) defines a 'static' or 'uniperiod' model; (2) defines paper money; (3) excludes the regimes of 'money-of-account'.

Jointly, these three conditions imply: (4) Prices of consumption goods that would clear the (perfect) market are infinite. That is, market equilibrium is not compatible with (1), (2), (3) taken jointly. This was proved mathematically in Patinkin's first article and verbally by Phipps. It is difficult to understand why either of them could think they disagree.

Now replace (3) by: (3′) All money stocks are zero. (1), (2), (3′) jointly imply: (4′) Prices (also called absolute prices) of consumption goods are indeterminate; their ratios (so-called relative prices) are determinate and finite. Leontief's paper consists, in effect, in describing such a system: the regime of money-of-account.

Since in the system (1), (2), (3′), (4′) money stocks are zero, this system cannot be supplemented by the so-called equation of exchange making positive absolute prices proportional to the total money stock. This contradiction is present in what Hickman described as the 'classical' combination of a theory of formation of relative prices (determined in the 'commodity-sector' where utilities are maximized and markets cleared) with the equation of exchange (or 'monetary sector'), in a regime of paper money.

To reconcile finite and determinate absolute prices of consumers' goods with positive stocks of paper money, one can drop the 'static' condition (1). Replace it by: (1′) Each individual maximizes a utility function which depends not only on present but also on future consumption flows; he will be able to exchange stocks of goods and of money at future marketing dates. If some but not all individuals expect the prices of all goods to fall, these individuals will demand positive money stocks; at the same time the prices of goods will be determinate, positive, and finite.

This implies sharp alternations between an individual's bearish 'flight into money' and bullish 'flight into (certain) goods'. More realistic, smooth fluctuations of stocks are obtained if we introduce market imperfection, including transaction costs. If barter is excluded, one can define 'illiquidity' of a good as the slope of the marginal money revenue and marginal money outlay curve of the individual considered, respectively, as a seller and a buyer of this good. The individual demand for stocks of various goods and of money, given expected shifts in that curve, will depend on their degrees of illiquidity: for speculative purchase to be followed by resale, a relatively 'liquid' good (and money in particular) is preferred.

It is neither necessary nor sufficient to introduce uncertainty in order to explain positive stocks of money and the smooth fluctuation of these stocks.

Any system that admits positive demand for paper money stocks has also to admit that a change in the absolute prices of goods (the cheapening or appreciation of paper money in terms of goods) induces the individual to change his holdings of money relative to his holding and consumption of goods. Hence, there is 'money illusion' in all systems except that of money-of-account.

1. The problem outlined

A. Unlike precious metals, paper money is neither a consumption nor a production good. The classical theory of market equilibrium was developed at a time when metallic money prevailed. It fails to relate the desired quantity of paper money and the exchange ratios between paper money and various commodities (the 'absolute' prices of commodities) to assumptions of rational (utility-maximizing) behavior. As a makeshift, an 'equation of exchange' was used by later authors [1]. It appealed to the alleged existence of an 'institutional' constant (velocity of circulation) superimposed upon the assumption of rational behavior of individuals. More recently, this makeshift device was generalized, and slightly rationalized, into Keynes' 'liquidity preference' equation [2]. Like the rest of macro-economics, this equation is still in need of being related to assumptions of rational behavior. Should the 'liquidity preference equation' and other Keynesian equations have purely empirical claims, these would be hard to establish: the observed time series of the relevant variables (quantity of money, interest rate, price level, consumption, national income and, possibly, its distribution) are no doubt consistent with a large number of equation-systems other than the Keynesian one [3].

B. Patinkin [1] has proved – in a manner to be somewhat modified in our Section 2 below – the inconsistency of traditional microeconomics with positive quantities of paper money. After having contributed this important criticism, he has not attempted to give a better microeconomics improved upon Walras and Pareto.

Instead, Patinkin [2] followed [4] the more superficial approach of Cassel whose aggregate demand and supply equations emerge from nowhere. Had these equations been derived from the maximization of each individual's utility subject to the limitation of his and the society's resources these limitations would result in certain restrictions upon the macroeconomic system. Unless one derives these restrictions precisely, the consistency and determinacy of the system cannot be discussed.

C. Questions like the following arise in a paper money system: Why can a unit of a thing that cannot be used by anyone either as a consumption or as a production good, acquire for the individual more than a zero amount of any useful thing? Yet, does not exactly this happen when goods are bought for paper money at prices that are less than infinite? Why is the desired stock of such money positive and not zero? In short: how can positive stocks of paper money be consistent with finite prices of physical goods? What explains the demand for paper money?

D. A related question is that of 'money illusion'. If the prices of all consumption goods (and of labor, the negative of the consumption good 'leisure') are multiplied by a constant, should this affect the demands for various goods on the part of a rational, i.e., a utility-maximizing consumer? Do his decisions depend on the prices of consumption goods or on the ratios of these prices? It is often stated that the latter must be the case; to respond to an equiproportional change in the prices of all consumption goods (including leisure) is irrational, a 'money illusion'. Note that the question itself is meaningful only in a regime of paper money. If money were a consumption good (gold, cattle) it would be impossible to change the prices of *all* physical goods in the same proportion since the price of money must, by definition, remain equal to one.

E. The following question is usually associated with, but is not identical with, that of 'money illusion'. Under a regime of paper money, does the market consisting of utility-maximizing individuals determine the absolute prices of physical goods, or only their ratios? In the latter case, the observed fact that absolute prices have determinate values would have to be explained by some relationship outside of the market – e.g., by the government's fixing the price of one of the physical goods. Suppose a certain theory seemed internally consistent under the assumption that absolute prices were determined in the market. If this assumption is disproved, the theory reveals itself as internally inconsistent; because if, before the assumption was disproved, the theory was internally consistent and therefore contained as many independent equations as it had variables, now the equations will outnumber the variables by one.

F. If there is no money illusion, i.e., if price-ratios and not absolute prices govern the single individual, there is at least an intuitive presumption (subject to a mathematical confirmation or rejection) that the market determines price-ratios rather than absolute prices. Accordingly, some theories, to remain consistent, have to admit 'money illusion' (possibly as a human habit rather than a utility maximizing behavior) on the part of at least one group of decision makers – be it the workers or their unions (as explicitly assumed by Keynes)[5], or be it the consumers[6], the entrepreneurs, the banks, or the fiscal authorities.

G. In what follows, Section 2 discusses the inconsistency of paper money with positive money stocks in a static model. Sections 3–4 are devoted to the microeconomic determination of the demand for paper money, and of the ratios of exchange of paper money against goods (so-called absolute prices). The essential steps beyond Walras-Pareto would be the following:

(a) One has to remove the assumption that the individual is concerned with only one marketing date. It will be shown that in the resulting more general, '*multi-period*' *or dynamic model*, stocks appear in an 'essential' way (i.e., they are not necessarily proportional to flows);

(b) One has to introduce *market imperfections, transaction costs*, and the property of money as the *legal tender*;

(c) One may introduce *uncertainty*.

H. Of these three steps, step (a), the formation of a simple dynamic model is made in Section 3. This step is sufficient to explain the occurrence of positive stocks of money, but is not sufficient to explain why the money stock of an individual takes values other than either zero or the money equivalent of all the resources. Step (b), the introduction of market imperfection and the legal tender is made in Section 4. This step is sufficient for an explanation of continuous money stocks, even (contrary to the prevailing opinion) without introducing uncertainty. Accordingly, step (c), introduction of probabilities would merely add an (important) touch of reality.

I. A further step towards reality would be to introduce *lending* (and borrowing) or, more generally, claims (and liabilities) of all kinds. There are analogies, from the point of view of a single individual, between claims and physical assets. Therefore it would be convenient to introduce the more familiar phenomenon of *production* before treating claims.

J. Further, one would have to remove the assumption that the market is cleared instantaneously, and to develop the *rationale* of the actions of individuals with uncertain information that tend, in the course of a time-consuming process, to diminish the difference between demand and supply.

K. These steps would develop a rational theory of the market, itself a necessary basis for a rational theory of the relation between economic aggregates, and of their movement through time. The currently popular set of aggregative equations, such as the 'consumption function', 'investment function', 'equation of exchange' (or of 'liquidity preference'), etc., does seem rather arbitrary, and lacking a theoretical foundation [7].

In the present paper, however, we confine ourselves to steps (a) and (b) listed in G above.

2. A STATIC MODEL OF PURE EXCHANGE ECONOMY

A. We shall call a '*good*' or '*commodity*' anything that can be demanded in nonzero quantities. Let there be A individuals and N goods. The ath individual ($a=1,\ldots, A$) enters the market with the *initial* quantity $\bar{x}_{na}$ of the nth good ($n=1,\ldots, N$). He leaves it with a *desired* quantity x_{na}. The difference $x_{na}-\bar{x}_{na}$ is his *demand* for this good; this expression can also be called his 'negative supply', or the 'excess of his demand over his supply', or his 'net demand' for the nth good. The sum $\sum_{a=1}^{A} (x_{na}-\bar{x}_{na})$ is best called '*aggregate net demand*'.

B. We shall call a '*consumption good*' a good that enters the utility function of at least one individual. Dollar bills, factories, and bonds are goods but not consumption goods; (but factories and bonds will not be considered in a pure exchange economy).

C. A 'flow' is the rate of use of a 'stock', per unit of time. We shall formulate a static model in terms of 'flows'. It will be presently seen (in E) that its reformulation in terms of 'stocks' does not add anything essential. The same will not be true of a dynamic model (Sections 3 and 4).

D. We shall first assume all goods to be consumers goods, and let the ath individual maximize his utility function of the N flows,

$$(2.1) \qquad u^a(x_{1a},\ldots, x_{Na}),$$

subject to his 'budget restriction'

$$(2.2) \qquad \sum_{n=1}^{N} (\bar{x}_{na}-x_{na})\, p_n=0, \quad a=1,\ldots, A.$$

Using a Lagrange multiplier λ, we differentiate with respect to each x_{na} the expression

$$u^a(x_{1a},\ldots, x_{Na})+\lambda \sum_{n=1}^{N} (\bar{x}_{na}-x_{na})\, p_n,$$

and equate each partial derivative to zero. We obtain, denoting by u_{na} ('marginal utility') the partial derivative of u^a with respect to its nth argument,

$$(2.3) \qquad u_{na}/u_{Na}=p_n/p_N; \quad n=1,\ldots, N-1; \quad a=1,\ldots, A.$$

These $N-1$ equations together with (2:2) determine, for any given set of the $N-1$ price ratios $p_1/p_N,\ldots, p_{N-1}/p_N$, the N desired flows $x_{1a},\ldots, x_{Na}$. Thus the individual's demand $(x_{na}-\bar{x}_{na})$ for the nth good depends on the $N-1$ price ratios. Bargaining goes on (i.e., prices and exchanged quantities are subjected to trial-and-error adjustments, not further analyzed in this theory) till 'the market is cleared', i.e., till the aggregate demand for each commodity balances its aggregate supply; its aggregate net demand vanishes:

$$(2.4) \qquad \sum_{a=1}^{A} (\bar{x}_{na}-x_{na})=0, \quad n=1,\ldots, N.$$

The system (2.2–4) contains $N-1+NA$ independent equations since Equations (2.2) together with the first $N-1$ equations in (2.4) yield the Nth Equation in (2.4). This number of independent equations equals the number of the following variables: $N-1$ price ratios plus NA demands.

If, now, the Nth consumption good is used as a numéraire, an extra equation is added:

$$(2.5) \qquad P_N = 1,$$

permitting to determine the N absolute prices instead of the $N-1$ price ratios.

E. The well known model just given[8] has certain tacitly implied properties of great importance. Marketing takes place on a single date. The individual's satisfaction is not affected by flows other than those determined on that date; and no distinction is made by the individual between the different post-market dates at which consumption may take place. Suppose such an individual plans for a period of θ time units (a 'horizon', possibly his whole life). Suppose he enters the market with $\bar{x}_{na}$ initial flow units of a certain kind (future daily housing or heating services of a house or of a pile of coal, future daily labor services or annual crops) and leaves it with x_{na} desired flow units. We can then also say, under the assumption of the static model, that he enters the market with $\bar{y}_{na}$ stock units (rooms, coal calories, expected man-years of labor or bushels of grain) and leaves the market with y_{na} stock units, where

$$(2.6) \qquad \bar{y}_{na}/\bar{x}_{na} = y_{na}/x_{na} = \theta \quad \text{time units.}$$

Because of this proportionality, a static model can be said to admit stocks 'in a non-essential way only'.

F. Suppose the Nth good is paper money. Equations (2.2), (2.4), (2.5) still hold. But the utility function (2.1) is replaced by

$$(2.7) \qquad u^a(x_{1a}, \ldots, x_{N-1,a}); \quad \text{hence}$$

$$(2.8) \qquad u_{Na} = 0.$$

Return for a moment to a system with non-paper money. Assume that there is no 'universal satiety': that is, $u_{na} \neq 0$ for at least one individual a and one consumption good $n \neq N$. Then, by (2.3), (2.5), its absolute price,

$$(2.9) \qquad p_n = u_{na}/u_{Na}, \quad n = 1, \ldots, N,$$

approaches infinity as u_{Na} approaches zero. It follows that in a static model with paper money, prices of consumption goods are bid up indefinitely. No equilibrium can be reached.

G. A more complete solution is arrived at (and was in essence, obtained by Patinkin [1]) if one introduces new restrictions. Returning first again to the system in which the numéraire is a consumption good, observe that in a static model no debts, or servicing of debts, can exist. Hence all stocks and flows are non-negative:

$$(2.10') \qquad x_{na} \geqslant 0, \quad n=1,\ldots, N.$$

To maximize (2.1) subject to (2.2) and (2.10′) rewrite the latter restriction thus:

$$(2.10) \qquad x_{na} - (r_{na})^2 = 0, \quad n=1,\ldots, N,$$

where the r is known to be real. The ath individual maximizes with respect to x_{na}, r_{na} $(n=1,\ldots, N)$ the expression

$$(2.11) \qquad u + \lambda \sum_n (\bar{x}_{na} - x_{na})\, p_n + \sum_n \mu_{na}(x_{na} - (r_{na})^2),$$

where the prices p are given, and the λ, μ_n $(n=1,\ldots, N)$ are Lagrange multipliers. We obtain

$$\begin{aligned} &(2.12) \qquad u_{na} + \mu_{na} = \lambda p_n, \\ &(2.13) \qquad \mu_{na} r_{na} = 0 \end{aligned} \qquad n=1,\ldots, N.$$

Eliminate μ_{na}, r_{na} from (2.10), (2.12), 2.13):

$$\lambda p_n = u_{na} + 0/\sqrt{x_{na}}, \quad n=1,\ldots, N.$$

Hence, for any two goods – say n, N –

$$(2.14) \qquad \frac{p_n}{p_N} = \frac{u_{na} + 0/\sqrt{x_{na}}}{u_{Na} + 0/\sqrt{x_{Na}}}.$$

This is a more general equation than the usual marginal utility theorem (2.3). It reduces to that theorem if the optimal flows x_{na}, x_{Na} of the two goods are known to be non-zero.

H. If N is paper money, and the optimal flow of n is non-zero, then $u_{Na}=0$, $p_N=1$, $x_{na}\neq 0$; therefore (2.14) becomes

$$(2.15)\qquad p_n=\frac{u_{na}}{(0/\sqrt{x_{Na}})}.$$

If $x_{Na}\neq 0$ we again obtain – as in (2.9) – an infinite price for any consumption good n [unless the flow of that consumption good is zero: see (2.14)]. But, in addition, we have to consider the possibility that $x_{Na}=0$, i.e., that the optimal flow [and hence – by (2.6) – the optimal stock] of money is zero for all individuals; then, by (2.4)

$$(2.16)\qquad \sum_{a=1}^{A}\bar{x}_{Na}=0;$$

and since $\bar{x}_{Na}\geqslant 0$ for every a, (2.16) implies that $\bar{x}_{Na}=0$ for every a. Hence, paper money occurs not physically but only as *'money of account'*. The denominator on the right side of (2.15), and therefore the whole expression, becomes indeterminate, permitting finite though indeterminate prices for consumption goods. Under this regime, every consumption good with a positive optimal flow can be assigned in the equilibrium any finite absolute price compatible with the requirement that the ratio between the prices of any two such consumption goods – say p_n/p_m – be equal to the ratio of their marginal utilities: see (2.14), replacing N by m, with $x_n>0$, $x_m>0$. But if 'money of account' is replaced by paper money with positive physical stocks, finite equilibrium prices of consumption goods with positive flows become impossible[9].

I. This agrees with common sense. Individuals endowed with physical stocks of useless money will try to dispose of it: its price relative to that of useful things will tend to zero[10]; or, in other words, the price of useful things in terms of money will tend to infinity. If, on the other hand, no physical stocks of money exist, no such bidding of money against consumption goods takes place. Their prices may well be finite; but there is no reason for one rather than another set of (finite) prices to establish themselves in the market provided that the prices of different consumption goods are proportional to their marginal utilities for all individuals. If the prices 2, 3, 5,… (say) satisfy this latter condition, the prices 4, 6,

10,... or 6, 9, 15,... will also satisfy it, and any of these price-sets will be an equilibrium price-set under the regime of 'money of account'.

J. Economic literature contains occasionally a distinction between the 'commodity-sector' of the economy – the system of equations (2.2)–(2.4) derived from utility-maximization under limited resources – and the 'monetary sector' which is not derived from utility-maximization and consists of an 'equation of exchange'. It is then stated for a paper-money economy that while the commodity-sector determines only the relative prices of consumption goods, their absolute prices are fixed by the 'equation of exchange', i.e., a relation between a certain average of prices and the stock of money[11].

However, such an equation is meaningless in a static model of a paper-money economy since, as we have seen, such a model admits finite commodity prices only when the money stock is zero. In the subsequent sections we shall see that, in a non-static model, each individual's optimal stock of money (and of other goods) is indeed related to prices. This relation may give the *rationale* of any 'equation of exchange'. The latter would follow from, and will not be superimposed upon, the equations derived from the maximization of utility under given constraints.

K. The static model is the usual model of the general equilibrium theory. We can now answer, with respect to this model, the questions asked in 1C. The coexistence of paper money and determinate and finite prices of consumption goods is not consistent with this model. This answer rules out the question whether in such a model the equilibrium demand for a consumption good is or is not homogenous of zero degree in absolute prices: the model itself excludes equilibrium. (The question is similar to this one: If a rectangle has five angles, is their sum 360° or 450°?).

L. However, the question of 'money illusion' is not meaningless in a regime of 'money-of-account'. This regime can be actually described by the equations of Section 2D, in N consumption goods if we replace (2.5) by

$$p_N = c, \tag{2.17}$$

where c is a constant arbitrarily fixed by some authority. c is a certain number of units of money-of-account. Money-of-account is not itself a 'good' as defined in 2A. However, if one insists, we can number money-of-account as the $N+1$th 'good' but then enter it in none but the following two equations, that will replace (2.17):

$$(2.17') \qquad p_N/p_{N+1}=c\,; \qquad p_{N+1}=1.$$

We can now make, with reference to a 'money-of-account' regime, two distinct statements, each of which is sometimes called the 'absence of money illusion' (they answer, respectively, the questions put in 1D and 1E above).

(i) By (2.1)–(2.3), the optimal flows chosen by an individual depend on his utility function, initial flows, and the *ratios* between consumption goods' prices; they do not depend on c;

(ii) By (2.1)–(2.4), the utility functions and initial flows of all individuals determine the *price-ratios* but leave the *prices* undetermined.

Later, in 3T–3U, similar questions about 'money illusion' will again arise meaningfully; and, again, in 4N–4O. But the answers will be different.

3. A SIMPLE DYNAMIC MODEL[12]

A. We shall now introduce the expectation of changing – viz., falling – prices as a simple but far from satisfactory explanation for the desire to hold paper money. It will be seen that such a model has important unrealistic features, not due to the paper money's lack of immediate utility but to other properties of the model. Modifications will be introduced in Section 4 that will make the model more realistic.

B. Suppose the individual plans for a finite sequence of time intervals devoted alternately to marketing and to consumption. The marketing intervals are negligible in length[13]. The length of each consumption interval is used as time unit. As in 2E, denote flows by x and stocks retained by y. Stocks sold will be denoted by z. Considering now the plan of the ath individual regarding nth consumption good (possibly leisure), we can omit the subscripts a, n for brevity; we shall indicate time by a superscript. The individual plans at time 0 for a succession of marketing dates (interspersed with consumption periods) ending at time T, the 'horizon'. See (3.1).

$\bar{y}$ is the *'initial stock'*, a non-negative quantity possessed by the individual before the marketing date 0. On this date, exchanges will be made. They will result in the individual's retaining a non-negative *optimal stock* y^0 which may be larger or smaller than $\bar{y}$. Thus the *amount sold*, $z = \bar{y} - y^0$ may be negative, zero, or positive. A non-negative optimal quantity x^0, not larger than the retained stock y^0, will be *consumed* during the interval (0.1). Hence, a non-negative stock $y^0 - x^0$ will be brought to market at date 1. And so on.

(3.1)

Date of marketing	Stocks brought	Stocks re-tained	Stocks sold	At price	Period of consump-tion	Con-sumed
0	y	y^0	$z^0 = y - y^0$	p^0	(0, 1)	x^0
1	$y^0 - x^0$	y^1	$z^1 = y^0 - x^0 - y^1$	p^1	(1, 2)	x^1
–	–	–	–	–	–	–
t	$y^{t-1} - x^{t-1}$	y^t	$z^t = y^{t-1} - x^{t-1} - y^t$	p^t	$(t, t+1)$	x^t
–	–	–	–	–	–	–
$T-1$	$y^{T-2} - x^{T-2}$	y^{T-1}	$z^{T-1} = y^{T-2} - x^{T-2} - y^{T-1}$	p^{T-1}	$(T-1, T)$	x^{T-1}
T	$y^{T-1} - x^{T-1}$	y^T	$z^T = y^{T-1} - x^{T-1} - y^T$	p^T	–	–

For at least one good, there are assumed to exist at least two dates at which its prices are different.

The initial stock $\bar{y}_{na}$ (we re-introduce the subscripts now) is given to the individual. He tries to retain, sell (or buy) and consume, respectively the following optimal quantities of $n = 1, \ldots, N$:

$$(3.2) \quad \begin{cases} \text{stocks retained:} & y_{na}^0, y_{na}^1, \ldots, y_n^{T-1}, y_{na}^T \\ \text{stocks sold:} & z_{na}^0, z_{na}^1, \ldots, z_{na}^{T-1}, z_{na}^T \end{cases}$$

$$(3.3) \quad \{\text{consumption flows:} \quad x_{na}^0, x_{na}^1, \ldots, x_{na}^{T-1}.$$

C. The individual's satisfaction depends on the *consumption flows* (3.3) in each of the T considered periods; but it also depends on the *final stocks* y_{na}^T. To be sure, he is indifferent to the particular way in which he or his heirs will arrange their consumption in the future following the instant T. But he is not indifferent as to the resources evaluated at the prices of instant T – with which he or his heir will start that future. The second and third column headings of the Plan (3.1) have to be interpreted, with respect to the last line, as follows: 'Stocks Brought (Retained)' means 'Stocks Brought (Retained) if Trading would take Place'. Accordingly, we include the quantities y_{na}^T into the argument of the utility function of the a-th individual, which we write thus:

$$(3.4) \qquad u^a(x_{1a}^0, \dots, x_{Na}^0, \dots, x_{1a}^{T-1}, \dots, x_{Na}^{T-1}, y_{1a}^T, \dots, y_{Na}^T).$$

We shall write for every n: $\partial u^a / \partial x_{na}^t = u_{na}^t$ $(t=0, \dots, T-1)$; $\partial u^a / \partial y_{na}^T = u_{na}^T$.

D. The Plan (3.1) must satisfy the following conditions – analogous to (2.2), – each stating that stocks brought to the market are exchanged, at certain prices, for stocks with which the next consumption period is started: for every a,

$$(3.5) \qquad \sum_{n=1}^{N} z_{na}^t p_{na}^t = 0, \quad t=0, \dots, T;$$

where for every a and n, the quantities x, y and z are connected by the identities given in the column 'stocks sold' of the Plan (3.1)

$$(3.6) \qquad \begin{cases} z_{na}^0 = \bar{y}_{na} - y_{na}^0 \\ z_{na}^t = y_{na}^{t-1} - x_{na}^{t-1} - y_n^t, \quad t=1, \dots, T. \end{cases}$$

Note that the prices p_n settled at instant 0 are the same for all individuals; but the expected prices p_{na}^t, $t>0$, will, in general, vary from one man to another. The expected prices need not clear the market; but the prices of instant 0 must be such as to have the market cleared [analogous to (2.4)]:

$$(3.6') \qquad \sum_{a=1}^{A} z_{na}^0 = 0, \quad n=1, \dots, N.$$

E. We rule out negative consumption flows, by entering not labor but leisure. For the present model we also rule out liabilities, i.e., negative stocks (see 1I above). The stocks and flows obey therefore the following inequalities, already stated in our comments following the Plan (3.1):

$$(3.7') \qquad y_{na}^t - x_{na}^t \geqslant 0; \quad x_{na}^t \geqslant 0; \quad y_{na}^T \geqslant 0; \quad n=1, \dots, N; \quad t=0, \dots, T-1.$$

They can be rewritten thus:

$$\left.\begin{array}{ll} (3.7) & x_{na}^t-(r_{na}^t)^2=0 \\ (3.8) & y_{na}^t-x_{na}^t-(s_{na}^t)^2=0 \\ (3.9) & y_{na}^T-(r_{na}^T)^2=0, \end{array}\right\}, \quad \begin{array}{l} t=0,\ldots,T-1 \\ n=1,\ldots,N. \end{array}$$

where the r, s, are known to be real.

F. Each of the optimal stocks and flows listed in (3.2), (3.3) is determined by the ath individual as a function of the following givens: his N initial stocks $\bar{y}_{na}$, the prices p_n^0 that clear the market at date 0, and the expected prices p_{na}^t, $t=1,\ldots,T$. For each set of these givens, optimal stocks and flows are obtained by maximizing (3.4) subject to the conditions (3.5), (3.6), (3.7), (3.8), (3.9). Omit the index a (indicating the individual) for brevity and maximize with respect to x_n^t, y_n^t, y_n^T, z^t, z^T, r_n^t, r_n^T, s_n^t $(t=0,\ldots,T-1;$ $n=1,\ldots,N)$, in the order stated, the following expression:

$$(3.10') \quad u+\sum_{t=0}^{T}\lambda^t\sum_n z_n^t p_n^t+\sum_n \kappa_n^0(\bar{y}_n-y_n^0-z_n^0)+ \\ +\sum_{t=1}^{T}\kappa_n^t(y_n^{t-1}-x_n^{t-1}-y_n^t-z_n^t)+\sum_n\sum_{t=0}^{T-1}\mu_n^t(x_n^t-(r_n^t)^2)+ \\ +\sum_n\mu_n^T(y_n^T-(r_n^T)^2)+\sum_n\sum_{t=0}^{T-1}\nu_n^t(y_n^t-x_n^t-(s_n^t)^2),$$

where the κ, λ, μ, ν, with appropriate sub- and superscripts are Lagrange multipliers, and summation $\sum_n$ is from 1 through N. Equating the partial derivatives to zero, we obtain:

$$0=u_n^t-\kappa_n^{t+1}+\mu_n^t-\nu_n^t=-\kappa_n^t+\kappa_n^{t+1}+\nu_n^t= \\ =u_n^T-\kappa_n^T+\mu_n^T=\lambda^t p_n^t-\kappa_n^t=\lambda^T p_n^T-\kappa_n^T= \\ =\mu_n^t r_n^t=\mu_n^T r_n^T=\nu_n^t s_n^t; \quad t=0,\ldots,T-1.$$

Rearranging,

$$u_n^t+\mu_n^t=\lambda^t p_n^t=\lambda^{t+l}p_n^{t+1}+\nu_n^1=\kappa_n^t; \\ u_n^T+\mu_n^T=\lambda^T p_n^T=\kappa_n^T; \\ \mu_n^t r_n^t=\mu_n^T r_n^T=\nu_n^t s_n^t=0; \quad t=0,\ldots,T-1.$$

With the help of (3.7)–(3.9) we can eliminate the κ, r, s and obtain, for every $n(=1,\ldots,N)$,

$$
\begin{aligned}
&u_n^t+\mu_n^t=\lambda^t p_n^t={}^{t+1}p_n^{t+1}+v_n^t, \quad t=0,\ldots,T-1;\\
(3.10'')\quad &\mu_n^t=0/\sqrt{x_n^t},\ v_n^t=0/\sqrt{y_n^t-x_n^t}, \quad t=0,\ldots,T-1;\\
&u^T+\mu_n^T=\lambda^T p_n^T, \quad \mu_n^T=0/\sqrt{y_n^T}.
\end{aligned}
$$

Eliminating the $T+1\lambda$'s from these $N(4T+2)$ equations, we obtain the following equations for the ath individual (we re-introduce the a-subscript in order to count, in 3G below, the unknowns and equations of the whole market),

$$
\begin{aligned}
&(3.11)\quad \mu_{na}^t=0/\sqrt{x_{na}^t}, \qquad \mu_{na}^T=0/\sqrt{y_{na}^T}, \qquad v_{na}^t=0/\sqrt{y_{na}^t-x_{na}^t},\\
&(3.12)\quad u_{na}^{t+1}+\mu_{na}^{t+1}=u_{na}^t+\mu_{na}^t-v_{na}^t, \quad n=1,\ldots,N; \quad t=0,\ldots,T-1;\\
&(3.13)\quad p_{na}^t/p_{Na}^t=(u_{na}^t+\mu_{na}^t)/(u_{Na}^t+\mu_{Na}^t), \quad n=1,\ldots,N-1; \quad t=0,\ldots,T.
\end{aligned}
$$

Equations (3.11) imply, jointly with (3.7′), for $t=0,\ldots,T-1$:

$$
\begin{aligned}
(3.14)\quad &\text{if}\ \ x_{na}^t>0, \quad \mu_{na}^t=0; \quad \text{therefore if}\ \ \mu_{na}^t\neq 0, \quad x_{na}^t=0;\\
&\text{if}\ \ y_{na}^T>0, \quad \mu_{na}^T=0; \quad \text{therefore if}\ \ \mu_{na}^T\neq 0, \quad y_{na}^T=0;\\
&\text{if}\ \ y_{na}^t>x_{na}^t, \quad v_{na}^t=0; \quad \text{therefore if}\ \ v_{na}^t\neq 0, \quad y_{na}^t=x_{na}^t.
\end{aligned}
$$

G. Analogous to the procedure in 2D, we consider first the ath individual, with all prices given to him. We have the following:

Equations		Unknowns (where $t=0,\ldots,T-1$)	
(3.5):	$T+1$	x_{na}^t:	NT
(3.6):	$(T+1)N$	y_{na}^t, y_{na}^T:	$N(T+1)$
(3.11):	$N(2T+1)$	z_{na}^t, z_{na}^T:	$N(T+1)$
(3.12):	NT	μ_{na}^t, μ_{na}^T:	$N(T+1)$
(3.13):	$(N-1)(T+1)$	v_{na}^t:	NT
Total:	$N(4T+3)$		$N(4T+3)$

Thus z_{na}^0 is determined for each individual $a(=1,\ldots,A)$ and each good $n(=1,\ldots,N)$ as a function of all prices for all marketing dates. The clearing-of-the-market condition (3.6′) for the date 0 provides N further equations; of these, however, one is redundant because of (3.5). The remaining $N-1$ equations of (3.6′) determine the set of $N-1$ price-ratios p_n^0/p_N^0 $(n=1,\ldots,N-1)$ for the date 0; this set is the same for all individuals. As already stated in 3D the subsequent (expected) price ratios p^t_{na}/p^t_{Na}, $t>0$, are not necessarily common to all inviduals and need not clear the market. These expected price-ratios, the initial stocks $\bar{y}_{na}$, and the utility functions u^a constitute the initial conditions (the givens) for the market as a whole.

H. Equations (3.11)–(3.13) repeat, for each period, the generalized marginal utility proposition (2.14) of the static model. But, because (3.12) connects each pair of successive dates we can now study, in addition, the effect of expected price changes. We shall assume all prices positive and finite, and show that in a dynamic model such prices are consistent with both maximized utilities and positive stocks of paper money.

I. Note that the expression $y^t_{na}-x^t_{na}$ in (3.11) is the stock brought to market at date $t+1$: see (3.1). When $y^t_{na}-x^t_{na}>0$, the stock retained at date t exceeds the consumption needs of the ensuing period $(t, t+1)$. When $y^t_{na}=x^t_{na}$ we say that the stock is 'unloaded'. In this case the individual retains only as much of the nth good as is needed for his immediate consumption during the period $(t, t+1)$; the possible needs of later periods will be satisfied by later repurchases.

J. We have, by (3.12)–(3.13),

$$(3.15)\qquad p^{t+1}_{na}/p^{t+1}_{Na}=(u^t_{na}+\mu^t_{na}-v^t_{na})/(u^t_{Na}+\mu^t_{Na}-v^t_{Na}),$$
$$n=1,\ldots,N-1;\quad t=0,\ldots,T-1.$$

Suppose that, at date t, neither n nor N is 'unloaded'; that is, $y^t_{na}>x^t_{na}$ and $y^t_{Na}>x^t_{Na}$. Then by (3.13), (3.12), (3.15), $p^t_{na}/p^t_{Na}=p^{t+1}_{na}/p^{t+1}_{Na}$. Therefore if $p^t_{na}/p^t_{Na}\neq p^{t+1}_{na}/p^{t+1}_{Na}$ then $y^t_{na}=x^t_{na}$ or [14] $y^t_{Na}=x^t_{Na}$. That is, if the individual expects the prices of two goods to change in different proportions, then he unloads the stock of at least one of them.

K. The individual never unloads the stocks of all goods (excepting the trivial case when all sales are zero from the next market date on). For, if not all sales are zero, then, since all prices are positive, (3.5) implies that some sales must be positive and some negative. But this would be contradicted if $y^{t-1}_n=x^{t-1}_n$ $(t=1,\ldots,T)$ for all n, since then by (3.6), (3.7'), $z^t_n=-y^t_n\leqslant 0$ for all n. Hence the stocks of at least one good are not unloaded.

L. We shall now show that if no two prices are expected to change in the same proportion from time t to $t+1$ then the stocks of all goods are unloaded at the time t in favor of one. For, if for any pair of goods – say $m, n=1, \ldots, N$ – the prices are expected to change in different proportions, then by 3J, at least one of these two goods is unloaded. Hence, there can be at most one good, say q, such that its stocks are not unloaded. But since we have just seen in 3K that there must be at least one such good, it follows that all stocks are unloaded at the time t in favor of a single good. This good thus 'absorbs all resources' of the individual as of date t, apart from those needed for immediate consumption[15]; provided all prices are expected to change in different proportions.

M. This agrees with the common sense of speculation. Suppose that I am sure, at time t, that all prices will change during the next period in different proportions, and that the qth good will rise in a larger proportion than all other goods. In this case, my best plan, for the marketing date t, is to reduce my possessions of all these goods down to the amounts required for consumption during the ensuing interval $(t, t+1)$ by exchanging against stocks of the qth good; and to resell, at date $t+1$, as much of this good as will be needed, at the then prevailing prices, to acquire other goods, for consumption and possibly (depending on the prices expected for time $t+2$) for speculation.

N. Note, however, that this 'common sense' argument does not explain (as do the equations) what determines the amount of consumption.

O. In general, the set of all goods can be split into two or more subsets, each consisting of goods whose prices are expected to change in the same proportion (a subset may have one or more elements). The stocks in all the subsets but one will be unloaded in favor of the remaining subset. We forego the formal proof of two intuitively obvious propositions: (1) that the favored subset consists of goods whose prices are expected to rise in a higher proportion than the prices of all other goods; and (2) that the individual has no preference as between the possible distributions of stocks (not needed for consumption) between the various goods forming the favored subset.

P. Thus, the dynamic model defined in 3B implies that all resources of an individual (apart from those providing for immediate consumption) are invested, at any time, in stocks of the one good (or of the several goods) promising the highest proportionate rise of price. The shift of all resources from one kind of stocks to another depends on changes in relative prices, however slight these changes may be. This instability can be regarded as an idealization of phenomena such as the alternating 'flight into commodities' or 'flight into money'. These terms were coined, I believe, in Germany during the inflation of the 20-ies and the deflation of the 30-ies. These phenomena do not presuppose paper money: 'flight into commodities' occurred also in times of 'gold inflation'.

Q. If the Nth good is a numéraire, $p^t_{Na}=1$ for every individual, a, and every market date, $t=0,\ldots, T$. If, in addition, this numéraire is paper money, the partial derivative of utility with respect to money flow in every consumption period, $\partial u^a/\partial x^t_{Na}\equiv u^t_{Na}=0$, $t=0,\ldots, T-1$; also, its partial derivative with respect to the *final* money stock, $\partial u^a/\partial x^T_{Na}\equiv u^T_{Na}=0$: the individual's satisfaction deriving from the prospect of ending with (or leaving to his heirs) a sum of paper money is entirely due to this paper money being convertible, at the prices of the horizon date T, into consumption goods. Thus (3.13), (3.15) become, respectively, for every consumption good $n=1,\ldots, N-1$,

$$(3.16)\qquad p^t_{na}=(u^t_{na}+\mu^t_{na})/\mu^t_{Na},\quad t=0,\ldots, T$$

$$(3.17)\qquad p^{t+1}_{na}=(u^t_{na}+\mu^t_{na}-v^t_{na})/(\mu^t_{Na}-v^t_{Na}),\quad t=0,\ldots, T-1.$$

The implications of (3.16) simply extend those of the static model to all *flows* of paper money and to its *final stocks.* Since there exists at least one consumption good n $(<N)$ such that, for $t=0,\ldots, T-1$, $u^t_{na}>0$, $x^t_{na}>0<p^t_{na}<\infty$, therefore, by (3.14), $\mu^t_{na}=0$, and $\mu^t_{Na}\neq 0$; hence the paper money flow $x^t_{Na}=0$. Similarly, the existence of a consumption good with a positive final stock $(y^T_{na}>0)$ that affects the individual's satisfaction $(u^T_{na}>0)$ implies that the final paper money stock $y^T_{Na}=0$[16]. However, (3.17) implies that the *stocks of paper money at previous dates,* $t=0,\ldots, T-1$, need not all vanish. This distinguishes the dynamic model from the static model, in which all stocks were final (and proportional to corresponding flows).

R. By applying to (3.16), (3.17) the same reasoning as in 3J–3O (with $p^t_{Na}=1=p^T_N$, $x^t_{Na}=0=y^T_{Na}$, $t=0,\ldots, T-1$), we find that positive stocks of paper money are consistent with finite prices of all consumption goods for every t if, and only if, $p^{t+1}_{na}\leqslant p^t_{na}$ for all consumption goods n ($<N$) such that $p^t_{na}>0$. Whenever this condition is satisfied – i.e., whenever the (absolute) price of no consumption good is expected to rise at the next market date – the individual invests all his resources (apart from immediate consumption needs) in paper money or in other goods whose price expects to remain unchanged. Whenever the price of at least one consumption good is expected to rise, the individual reduces his paper money stock to zero. Thus, the paper money stocks he brings to the market jump in an unstable and discontinuous fashion, sometimes vanishing and sometimes equalling the money equivalent of all his resources.

S. All stocks to be retained by the individual at the market dates $t>0$ are planned stocks. No clearing-of-the-market condition exists for these dates. It is different with the date $t=0$. For any good (including N, paper money), the equilibrium stocks y^0_{na} ($a=1,\ldots, A$) are actually retained by the individuals and must obey the condition [see (3.6′), (3.6)]

$$(3.18)\qquad \sum_{a=1}^{A} y^0_{na}=\sum_{a=1}^{A} \bar{y}_{na}, \quad n=1,\ldots, N.$$

Suppose that, at time 0, every individual expects the price of every consumption good to rise by time 1: $p^1_{na}>p^0_{na}$, $a=1,\ldots, A$; $n<N$. Then, as we have just seen in 3R, $y^0_{Na}=0$ for every a. Hence by (3.18), the total money stock $\sum_a^{A=1}\bar{y}_{Na}=0$, and since $\bar{y}_{Na}\geqslant 0$, we have $\bar{y}_{Na}=0$ for every a; moreover, since $x^t_{Na}=0$ for every a and t, it is seen from the (3.6), (3.7′) that the planned money stocks y^t_{Na} must also vanish. We conclude that unless there is disagreement between at least two individuals about the direction of the price change of at least one commodity between the dates 0 and 1, the actual or planned possession of positive stocks of paper money is not consistent, under conditions of our model, with finite prices and maximized utilities.

T. We can now resume the questions of 'money illusion' raised in Section 1 and already discussed in 2K–2L for classical static models.

This time we have a model in which positive stocks of money are consistent with finite determinate prices.

The budget restriction Equations (3.5) are not, in general, homogenous in the prices of consumption goods. They can be rewritten thus:

$$(3.19) \qquad \sum_{n=1}^{N-1} z_{na}^t p_{na}^t + z_{Na}^t = 0,$$

for every a and t. As we have seen in 3Q, the planned final paper money stock $y_{Na}^T = 0$ for every a; and since the initial stock $\bar{y}_{Na} > 0$ for at least one individual, this individual must have [because of (3.6), and because all $x_{Na}^t = 0$] $z_{Na}^t \neq 0$ for at least one date, say $t = t'$. Hence (3.19) is, for $t = t'$, non-homogenous in the prices p_{na}^t. If all prices are multiplied by $k > 0$, the $z_{na}^{t'}$ will change, depending on k.

We are particularly interested in the effect of an equiproportional change in the current prices, $p_1^0, \ldots, p_{N-1}^0$. If z_{Na}^0 is non-zero, we have the case just discussed, with $t' = 0$. But suppose $z_{Na}^0 = 0$. If only the current, but not also the expected prices change in the same proportion, then the ratio p_{na}^1 / p_{na}^0, $n < N$, changes; and the values of the x, y, z that satisfy the Equations (3.16), (3.17) for $t = 0$, will, in general, have to change. If, on the other hand, not only the current but also all expected prices are multiplied by k, then let $t = t'$ be a marketing date for which $z_{Na}^{t'} \neq 0$. We have seen that such a date must exist, and that the $z_{na}^{t'}$ depend on k. We shall not pursue the matter further for the particular (and unrealistic) model of this section. Suffice it to conclude that, in general, at least some of the individual's decisions must be affected by an equiproportional change of current prices, even if accompanied by a similar change in expected prices.

Moreover, unless no individual changes his money stock at time 0, the budget restriction (3.19) is non-homogeneous in current prices for at least one individual; hence, the market determines absolute prices and not only price ratios.

U. To sum up Section 3: the assumptions of the dynamic model of this section are sufficient to explain, by a consistent system of equations, the existence of positive paper money stocks desired by individuals, the rationale of the 'money illusion' of individuals, and the determination of absolute prices. But the model is highly unrealistic as it implies that stocks of money, as well as of consumption goods, fluctuate in a discontinuous fashion under the impact of ever so slight expected price changes.

4. Introducing illiquidity

A. In the dynamic model of Section 3, no *perfect knowledge* of the future was assumed. It was merely assumed that the ath individual ($a=1,\ldots,A$) *thinks* that he has perfect knowledge of future prices beginning at date 1 and including the horizon date T. At the marketing date 0, the set of current equilibrium prices $p_1^0,\ldots,p_{N-1}^0$ is established, common to all individuals. This set depends on the, generally differing, expectations of future prices by different individuals, and on their utility functions and initial stocks. The price set $p_{1a}^1,\ldots,p_{N-1,a}^1$, that the ath individual ($a==1,\ldots,A$) has expected for the next marketing date 1 will, in general, not coincide with the price set which will clear the market when that date arrives (and which will be common to all individuals). Even if the individuals do not then revise their price expectations for the marketing dates $2, 3,\ldots, T$ in the light of some new experience, they have at any rate to revise the price-set for the date 1, lest the demands and supplies remain unequalized. Similarly, when the marketing date 2 arrives, the ath individual will, in general, have to revise his price-set for that date. And so on.

B. However, the model of Section 3 assumed a *perfect market*, in the following sense: The ath individual ($a=1,\ldots,A$) considers the prices $p_n^0, p_{na}^1,\ldots,p_{na}^T$ ($n=1,\ldots,N$) as given to him, independent of his actions.

We now weaken this condition. Note that in the previous model the 'budget restrictions' (3.5) of the ath individual are the only restrictions upon his utility maximization that involve prices:

$$\sum_{n=1}^{N} z_{na}^t p_{na}^t=0\,;\quad t=0,\ldots,T. \tag{4.1}$$

Since the z's are related by (3.6) to the stocks brought to the market, the budget restrictions determine, for each commodity and marketing date, the set of quantities that are within a's reach, given his initial stocks and the expectations of prices. In a more general case this set of quantities might be determined by equations

$$(4.2) \qquad B_a^t(z_{1a}^t, \ldots, z_{Na}^t) = 0\,; \quad t = 0, \ldots, T,$$

where for each date t, the function B_a^t describes the 'market conditions' expected by the individual. While the condition (4.1) can be represented, in the space of the z's, by a hyperplane through the origin, the condition (4.2) – if it does not degenerate into (4.1), which is its limiting case – is represented by a hypersurface which contains the origin and which is convex if viewed from the negative orthant. This property reflects the existence of a 'cost of transaction', in a model which (thus maintaining some limitations of Section 3) is not concerned with specific transactions between single pairs (or triplets, etc.) of individuals, that make up the marketing process. It considers only the net acquisitions or sacrifices (the z's) of each individual, resulting from the bargaining in the market. The convexity of (4.2) expresses then the fact that, whenever – as the net result of marketing – the individual has exchanged one commodity against another (say 1 against 2), he had to sacrifice, in addition, positive amounts of at least one of the N commodities: the so called transaction cost (in money paid to advertising agents or brokers, or in one's own leisure, etc.). The commodity thus sacrificed may itself be commodity 1 or 2. Thus in Figure 1, $N=2$, and the straight line AA represents the budget restriction

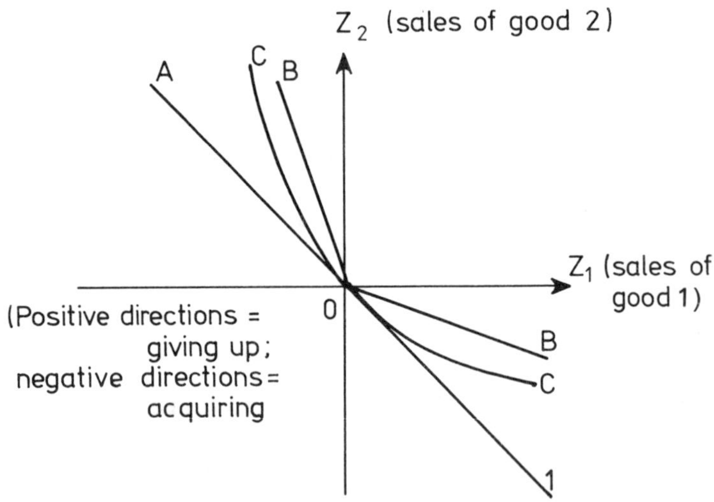

Fig. 1. Curves describing alternative market conditions.

in a perfect market, (4.1). The broken line BB (convex if viewed from the negative quadrant) represents the budget restrictions (4.2) when, per unit of commodity 1 given up or acquired, a constant amount of commodity 2 is acquired or given up – the same as in the case AA; but when, in addition, a constant transaction cost is incurred, by always giving up a further amount of commodity 2. We can measure the total amount of commodity 2, paid (received) by the individual to (from) one or more other individuals *per unit* of commodity 1, as the slope of the line drawn from the origin to the point (z_1, z_2) on the curve. If this slope, the 'price including transaction cost', increases (decreases) with the amount of commodity 1 acquired (given up), the budget restriction (4.2) is represented by a curve such as CC: the individual is a monopsonistic buyer (monopolistic seller) of commodity 2, relative to commodity 1[17].

C. For $N > 2$ the economic interpretation of properties of the functions B_a^t, if treated in full generality, becomes more complicated than is justified by the limited purposes of this article[18]. We shall give the general budget restriction (4.2) a special form: for every a and t,

$$(4.3) \qquad \sum_{n}^{N=1} R_{na}^t(z_{na}^t) = 0\,; \quad R_{Na}(z_{Na}) = z_{Na}.$$

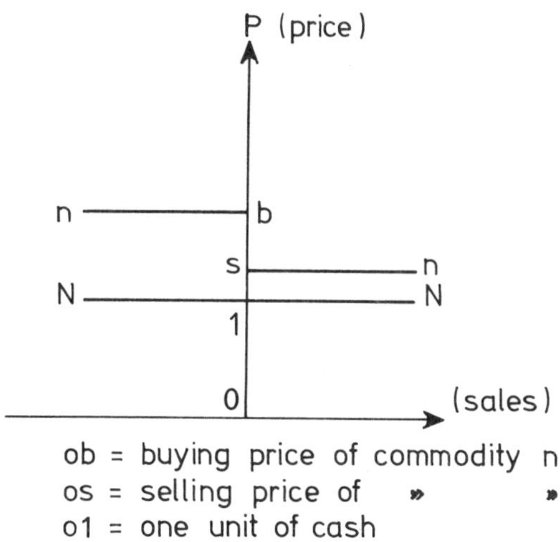

Fig. 2. Demand curves for a consumption good (nbsn) and for cash (NN).

The quantity $R^t_{na}(z^t_{na})$, for $n<N$, is the revenue received (and its negative is the outlay paid) for the nth commodity, in exchange for the Nth commodity. (4.3) is satisfied if every commodity, when exchanged, is exchanged only against the Nth commodity. The latter is the 'universal means of payment'. A condition sufficient for the validity of (4.3) is, that no barter is permitted to take place. We can think of this as an institutional restriction. Thus, we shall not try here to explain the absence (or any existing extent) of barter in a society as a consequence of utility maximization by its members, combined with certain conditions – physical or institutional, but not including a prohibition of barter – which make certain transactions more costly than others[19].

D. It is convenient, and possibly clarifying, to define now the concepts of a (variable) price and of marginal revenue. In Figure 2 we have plotted the prices (omitting subscript a and superscript t).

(4.4) $p_n \equiv R_n(z_n)/z_n;\ z_n \gtrless 0;\quad n=1,\ldots,N;$ hence by (4.3)

(4.5) $p_N = 1.$

The broken line, *nbsn*, is implied by the same assumption as the broken line *BB* in Figure 1. The ordinates *ob* and *os* are, respectively, the buying and the selling price of the commodity $n(<N)$ after payment of trans-

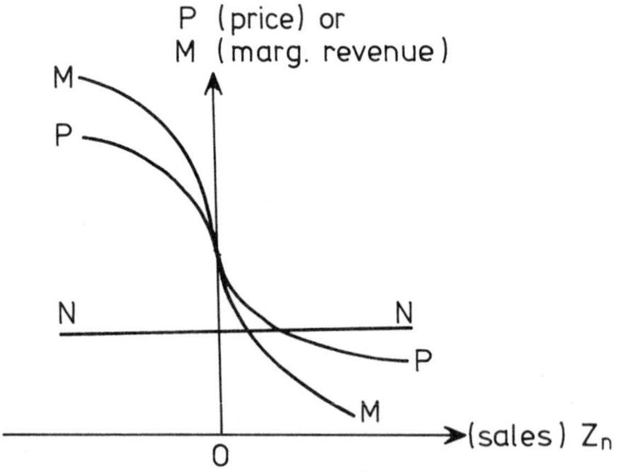

Fig. 3. Demand curve (PP) and marginal revenue curve (MM) for a consumption good; demand and marginal revenue curve for cash (NN).

action cost, constant per unit of transaction. To avoid, in our pure exchange model, the discussion of production goods such as advertising services or brokers' services we can interpret here the positive difference between buying and selling prices by the fact that if one has to sell in a hurry, he cannot recoup the price he had paid. The line NN represents Equation (4.5): N is money.

E. It was shown in an earlier paper[20] that the positive excess of the buying over the selling price of a commodity – as in Figure 2 – affects unfavorably its optimal stock held by a profit-maximizing firm. The present paper's problem is analogous. Since the mathematical analysis is tedious owing to the discontinuity of this price function, we shall use, instead, in the present paper, an approximation that is continuous and differentiable everywhere: the curve PP in Figure 3. The possibly strong difference between the conditions of a buyer and those of a seller can be reproduced by making the negative slope in the neighborhood of $z_n=0$, as large in absolute value as we like, yet maintaining this slope finite. At the same time a non-positive (rather than zero) slope is maintained for all finite values of z_n, thus generalizing constant unit transaction costs into possibly increasing ones. In general, the curve reproduces imperfect competition: its segment for all $z_n>0$ is the 'demand curve *to* the monopolist'; its segment for all $z_n<0$ is the 'demand curve *of* the monopsonist'. [In Figure 1, the corresponding curve for the budget restriction (4.2) is CC]. The slope of PP can be made as near zero – i.e., the market can be regarded as nearly perfect – as we like, provided $|z_n|$ is sufficiently large.

F. Marginal revenue is defined by

(4.6) $M_n=M_n(z_n)=dR_n(z_n)/dz_n,\ z_n\gtrless 0,\quad n=1,\ldots,N;$ *hence by* (4.3)

(4.7) $M_N=1.$

A function $M_n(z_n)$, for $n<N$ is represented in Figure 3 by the curve MM.

Since $dp_n/dz_n\leqslant 0$, $M_n=p_n+z_n\cdot dp_n/dz_n=p_n(1+z_n dp_n/p_n dz_n)\leqslant p_n$ for z_n positive; $M_n\geqslant p_n$ for z_n negative. The absolute value of the (negative) elasticity $z_n\ dp_n/p_n\ dz_n$ or simply the slope dp_n/dz_n has been used as a measure of market imperfection, with respect to the individual monopolist or monopsonist. We notice that, for the universal means of payment, this measure vanishes; while it can be said – at least in the neighborhood of $z_n = 0$ – to be particularly large for commodities involving a high cost of selling. In this sense, we can identify the degree of market imperfection especially in the vicinity of $z_n = 0$ with the degree of *'illiquidity'*, which is zero for money and is larger than zero (and depends on the quantity sold) for goods that are difficult to sell. Line NN in Figure 3 represents both Equations (4.5) and (4.7). But remember that this interpretation is possible because of a simplifying but asymmetrical institutional assumption (made in 4C) which excluded barter, i.e., introduced an universal means of payment. Without this assumption (i.e., with money defined merely as a numéraire by $p_N = 1$) a numerically high elasticity $z_n dp_n / p_n dz_n$ might be interpreted equally well as a market imperfection for the commodity n or for the commodity N (the numéraire) or both; in fact, the elementary theory of imperfect markets would cease to be serviceable, and we would need the more general approach outlined in 4B above.

G. The givens of the perfect market model of Section 3 were, for the ath individual: his N initial stocks $\bar{y}_{na}$, his utility function u^a, the N prices of zero-instant p_n^0 (common to all individuals), and the NT expected prices $p_{na}^1, \ldots, p_{na}^T$. In the imperfect market model, the set of prices p_n^0, $p_{na}^1, \ldots, p_{na}^T$, for a given a, is replaced by as many revenue functions $R_{na}^0, \ldots, R_{na}^T$.

For the market as a whole, the perfect model considered as the givens: the AN initial stocks, the A utility functions, and the ANT expected prices. The imperfect market model considers as the givens; the AN initial stocks, the A utility functions, and the $AN(T+1)$ revenue functions. *The latter do not form an independent set.* Their forms and parameters are restricted by the condition (3.6′) that the market be cleared. This is another way of saying that, in the market, one man's strength is another man's weakness. For $A < 5$, the Theory of Games has begun to discuss these restrictions. We need not try here to develop this discussion.

H. We have replaced the expression in (4.1) $\sum_{n=1}^{N} z_{na}^t p_{na}^t$, linear in the z, by a non-linear expression, $\sum_{n=1}^{N} R_{na}^t(z_{na}^t)$. Both mean the sum of (positive and negative) revenues of the individual at the marketing date t, expressed in terms of a single commodity, the numéraire. In the present model, these revenues are not only expressed mathematically but also collected (or paid out, if negative) in units of the numéraire which has become now the universal means of payment, barter being excluded. Substituting appropriately in (3.5), (3.10), we find that in (3.10″) constant prices p_{na} $(t=0,\ldots, T)$ must be replaced by marginal revenues $M^t_{na}(z^t_{na})$. Then, since $M^t_{Na}(z^t_{Na})=1$ for every t, (3.13), (3.15) become for $n=1,\ldots, N-1$

$$(4.8) \qquad M^t_{na}(z^t_{na})=(u^t_{na}\ldots\mu^t_{na})/(u_{Na}+\mu^t_{Na}), \quad t=0,\ldots, T$$

$$(4.9) \qquad M^{t+1}_{na}(z^{t+1}_{na})=(u^t_{na}+\mu^t_{na}-v^t_{na})/(u^t_{Na}+\mu^t_{Na}-v^t_{Na}), \quad t=0,\ldots, T-1.$$

I. From (4.8) it follows that if two commodities m, n $(=1,\ldots, N)$ have positive consumption flows, and hence $\mu^t_{ma}=\mu^t_{na}=0$, then their marginal utilities are proportional to their marginal revenues: a 'generalized law of marginal utilities' [compare here (2.14)].

J. If the universal means of payment is paper money, $u^t_{Na}=0$, $t=0,\ldots, T$. There exists at least one consumption good n $(<N)$ such that $M^t_{na}>0$, $u^t_{na}>0$, and $x^t_{na}>0$, and hence $\mu^t_{na}=0$. Therefore $\mu^t_{Na}>0$, $x^t_{na}>0=y^T_{Na}$, $t=0,\ldots, T-1$. That is, again, as in 3Q, there cannot be positive flows or positive *final* stocks of paper money[21].

K. On the other hand, positive stocks of money for $t<T$ are possible, and we shall show that, different from those of Section 3, they need not jump between zero and the absorption of all resources, but may change continuously. We shall show it for a general case of paper or non-paper money. It will suffice to prove that, in the present model, it is possible to have changing and finite prices for all consumption goods without the 'unloading' of stocks occurring for any goods, including money. That is, the stocks of every good may exceed current consumption needs (and, hence, the stocks of the 'good', paper money, may be always positive). Suppose that for every $n=1,\ldots, N$, and $t=0,\ldots, T-1$, $y^t_{na}>x^t_{na}$. Then by (3.14) $v^t_{na}=0$. Therefore by (4.9), (4.8).

$$(4.10) \qquad M^t_{na}(z^t_{na})=M^{t+1}_{na}(z^{t+1}_{na}), \quad n=1,\ldots, N, \quad t=0,\ldots, T-1; \quad \text{hence}$$

$$(4.11) \qquad M^0_{na}(z^0_{na})=M^1_{na}(z^1_{na})=\ldots=M^T_{na}(z^T_{na}), \quad \text{for every} \quad n.$$

If markets were perfect, with no transaction costs, marginal revenues would be identical with prices, and (4.11) would imply the expectation of unchanging prices, i.e., would bring us back to the static model of Section 2. Under conditions of the present model, however, marginal revenues are not equal to prices; and the rule (4.11), telling the individual to equalize over time the marginal revenue for each good is consistent with expectations of changing prices, provided the marginal revenue functions are expected to change. These expectations have thus been shown to be consistent with stocks of single goods that can exceed current consumption needs (can exceed zero, in case the good is paper money) yet do not absorb all the resources of the individual.

L. The result (4.11) gives a hint as to how one might approach the general problem of the effect of transaction cost and market imperfection upon the size of investment in a commodity; although, because of the limited scope of this paper, we can deal only with investments for speculation and future consumption, neglecting production and lending. Moreover, the result (4.11) was obtained under two simplifying assumptions, made in 4C and 4E respectively: that barter is excluded, and that (Figure 3), at any time t, the demand curves for the nth good and the ath individual in his capacity as either a buyer or a seller can be approximated by a single continuous and differentiable curve, $p_{na}^t\,(z_{na}^t)$. Accordingly, there is a continuous and differentiable curve of marginal revenues and outlays, $M_{na}^t(z_{na}^t)$, for the whole range of possible sales or purchases. Dropping the subscripts n, a, for brevity, expand

$$(4.12) \qquad M^t(z^t) = \alpha^t + \beta^t z^t + \cdots,$$

where α^t, β^t are, respectively, the values of $M^t(z^t)$ and dM^t/dz^t approached as z^t approaches 0 from either the positive or the negative direction. Assume that transaction cost (or market imperfection in the neighborhood of $z=0$) exists; then $\beta^t < 0$. To fix the ideas, put $t=0$ or 1. Then by (4.11), (4.12)

$$(4.13) \qquad \alpha^0 + \beta^0 z^0 + \cdots = \alpha^1 + \beta^1 z^1 + \cdots.$$

Consider now the following special case: the givens of the problem are such that the individual's best plan involves buying a certain positive amount z of the commodity at time 0, and selling the same amount at time 1:

$$0 < z = -z^0 = z^1.$$

Substituting for z^0, z^1 in (4.13) and neglecting higher terms,

$$z=(\alpha^0-\alpha^1)/(\beta^0+\beta^1).$$

Or, since the β's are negative,

$$z=\frac{\alpha^1-\alpha^0}{|\beta^0+\beta^1|}. \tag{4.14}$$

Since $z>0$, we conclude:

(1): $\alpha^1>\alpha^0$, i.e., speculative buying of a given commodity implies an expected upward shift in its marginal revenue curve. This corresponds to the expected price rise of the perfect market case treated in Section 3, but with two important differences: In the perfect market case, speculative buying had to imply (a) that for no other commodity a stronger proportionate price rise was expected; and (b) that the stocks of all goods with a weaker expected proportionate price rise, were unloaded. Transaction costs and market imperfection remove such implications and make it rational to speculate simultaneously in commodities whose marginal revenues, for given quantities, will rise in different proportions.

(2): The larger the absolute value $|\beta^0+\beta^1|$ for a given commodity, the smaller is its amount z that the individual invests in speculation; and note that the β's – the slopes of the marginal revenue curves near $z=0$ – can characterize both the transaction costs, and the market imperfections for small sales and purchases. (It is also easily seen that β is proportional to the usual measure of market imperfection, dp/dz, apart from a second order term. We omit here a discussion of corresponding elasticity measures, given in 4F above, which would be necessary for inter-commodity comparisons). Thus an increase in transaction costs for a given commodity would drive the speculator out of it, and into stocks of commodities with more nearly horizontal marginal revenue curves – especially but not exclusively into stocks of the universal means of payment (whose marginal revenue curve is exactly horizontal).

These results are illustrated in Figure 4, where for simplicity the slopes $\beta^0=\beta^1=\beta$ (say). On each of the two diagrams, the lines M^0 and M^1 are portions of the marginal revenue (or marginal outlay) curve, at the dates 0 and 1 respectively. Their intercepts $0\alpha^0$, $0\alpha^1$ are the same for the corresponding curves on the upper and the lower diagram; and $0\alpha^1>0\alpha^0$. On each diagram we find a quantity $AB=BC$ such that the marginal revenues on the two successive dates are equal: $AK = CL$. The quantity $AB = BC$ ($= z$, say) is the amount bought and sold in speculation. We see that z is larger on the lower diagram – the one where the absolute value of the slope β is smaller, i.e., where the transaction cost (or market imperfection) is smaller.

M. In reviewing now the equations of our dynamic model – with paper

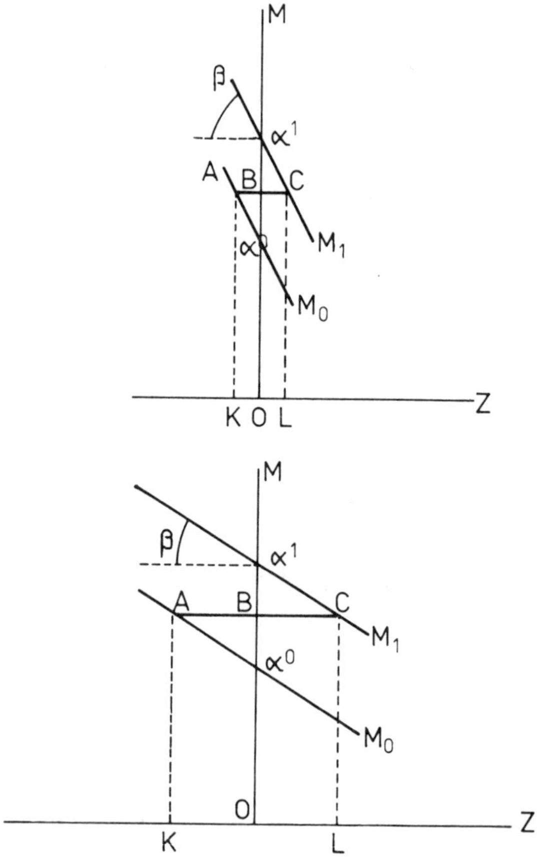

Fig. 4. Unfavorable effect of illiquidity (slope β) of a good upon its amount ($AB = BC$) bought and re-sold.
OZ: Axis of quantities; OM: Axis of marginal revenues.
M_0 and M_1: Marginal revenue curves at times 0 and 1, respectively.
Top: a less liquid good. Bottom: a more liquid good.

money, market imperfection and no barter – we shall make use of demand functions of the individuals (expressing the price as a function of the demand *of* a buyer or *to* a seller) $p_{na}^t = f_{na}^t(z_{na}^t)$, as these functions are most familiar from economic literature. The functions f_{na}^t are related to the revenue functions R_{na}^t and the marginal revenue functions M_{na}^t by the identities – [see (4.4), (4.6)] –

$$(4.15) \qquad R_{na}^t(z_{na}^t) = z_{na}^t f_{na}^t(z_{na}^t)$$

$$(4.16) \qquad M_{na}^t(z_{na}^t) = dR_{na}/dz_{na}^t,$$

for every a, t, and $n < N$. Moreover, for every a, t – [see (4.5), (4.7)] –

$$(4.17) \qquad f_{Na}^t(z_{Na}^t) = M_{Na}^t(z_{Na}^t) = 1.$$

For each individual a, and every t, the budget restriction is [see (4.3)]

$$(4.18) \qquad \sum_{n=1}^{N-1} z_{na}^t f_{na}^t(z_{na}^t) + z_{Na}^t = 0.$$

Discarding, for the purposes of the present paper, the occurrence of consumption goods with zero-flows (such cases lead to a tedious study of inequalities and 'corner solutions' similar to that of Section 3), and remembering that $u_{Na}^t = 0$, $\mu_{Na}^t > 0$ for every a, t (see 4J), we obtain, by (4.8), for every a, t

$$(4.19) \qquad \frac{M_{1a}^t(z_{na}^t)}{u_{1a}^t(X_a)} = \cdots = \frac{M_{N-1,a}^t(z_{N-1,a}^t)}{u_{N-1,a}^t(X_a)} = \mu_{Na}^t > 0,$$

where X_a is the set of all consumption flows and final stocks of the individual. If we do not discard the possibility that stocks can be 'unloaded' we have by (4.8), (4.9), (3.14),

$$(4.20) \qquad M_{na}^{t+1}(z_{na}^{t+1})/M_{na}^t(z_{na}^t) = \left(1 - \frac{v_{na}^t}{u_{na}^t}\right) \Big/ \left(1 - \frac{v_{Na}^t}{\mu_{na}^t}\right),$$

for every a, $t < T$, and $n < N$; where

$$(4.21) \qquad v_{na}^t = 0/\sqrt{y_{na}^t - x_{na}^t}, \quad n < N,$$

$$(4.22) \qquad v_{Na}^t = 0/\sqrt{y_{Na}^t};$$

the identities connecting the y with the x and z are given in (3.5). Finally, there is the clearing-of-the-market requirement for date 0

$$(4.23)\qquad \sum_{a=1}^{A} z_{na}^{0}=0, \quad n=1,\ldots, N;$$

this involves a restriction upon the current demand functions f_{na}^{0} (see 4G).

N. We may now ask whether, in the generalized model of this section, the individual has 'money illusion': will the quantities of stocks sold and retained by the individual, and his consumption flows, remain unchanged if either all current prices or all current as well as all expected prices change in the same proportion? Note that now it is not the expected prices p_{na}^{t}, $t>0$ but the demand functions f_{na}^{t}, $t>0$ that are given to the individual (subject however to the restrictions upon the f_{na}^{0} mentioned in 4M and required to clear the market). An equiproportional change in the prices of all consumption goods must be understood as a change in the prices for given quantities bought or sold by the individual, i.e., as the multiplication of all demand functions f_{na}^{t}, $(n<N)$ by a constant, say $k(>0)$. Because of the definitions (4.15), (4.16) this is equivalent to multiplying by k all functions M_{na}^{t} $(n<N)$.

As in 3T, the z_{Na}^{t} of the individual a (the successive changes in his money stock) cannot vanish for all marketing dates t: for he starts with a stock $y_{Na}^{0}>0$, and plans to end up with $y_{Na}^{T}=0$. Hence his budget restriction (4.18) is non-homogenous in the prices $f_{na}^{t}(z_{na}^{t})$ for at least one date, say $t=t'$. Thus the quantities $z_{na}^{t'}$ will depend on the multiplier k. In particular, if $t'=0$, i.e., if the individual changes his money stock at date 0, his demands z_{na}^{0} will depend on the multiplier k, both when k is applied only to all current demand functions f_{na}^{0}, $n<N$, or when it is applied to the whole sequence of demand functions, $f_{na}^{0},\ldots, f_{na}^{T}$, $n<N$. Suppose, on the other hand that $t'>0$. Consider the equations (4.11) which result from (4.20)–(4.22) if the case of unloading is neglected[22]. If the multiplier k is applied only to the functions M_{na}^{0} but not to the later marginal revenue functions M_{na}^{t} $(t>0)$, the system of equations that contains (4.11) will not be, in general, satisfied unless the z_{na}^{t} for all t, including $t=0$, are changed. If, on the other hand, the whole sequence of marginal revenue functions is multiplied by k, then the change in $z_{na}^{t'}$ will in general involve, because of (4.11), also a change in the z_{na}^{0}. It is thus rational, in a dynamic market, to have 'money illusion'.

O. Since we conceive of each demand function f_{na}^{t} as a univalued one, the givens of the system that determine the demands z_{na}^t, determine also the absolute prices $p_{na}^t = f_{na}^t(z_{na}^t)$. The question asked in 1E must be re-adapted to fit the imperfect market situation. We have to ask whether the set of demands (z), flows (x) and stocks (y) of all individuals that is consistent with certain utility functions (u^a), initial stocks $(\bar{y})$ and demand functions (f), and that clears the market of date 0, will also clear that market when either all demand functions, or possibly only the demand functions of date 0 (f_{na}^0 for every a, $n<N$), are multiplied by a constant. We have seen in 4N that this is not the case.

5. Summary

A. The most general among the models that were treated explicitly in this paper is characterized by the same Plan (3.1) as in the perfect market model, but with the column of successive prices, p_{na}^t, replaced by a column of successive marginal revenue functions, $M_{na}^t(z_{na}^t)$. These functions belong to the givens of the problem, together with the utility functions u^a and the initial stocks $\bar{y}_{na}$. The unknowns are the stocks z_{na}^t that the individual plans to sell, the stocks y_{na}^t that he plans to retain, and the consumption flows x_{na}^t. The marketing dates are $t=0,\ldots, T$; the goods are $n=1,\ldots, N$, with N being the universal means of payment, i.e., $M_{Na}^t(z_{Na}^t)=1$, for all a and t.

Special, mutually independent, assumptions taken singly or in combinations, modify this general model into more special ones. These assumptions are:

(I) Perfect market: $dM_{na}^t/dz_{na}^t=0$ for all n, a, t.
(II) Paper Money: $u_{Na}^t=0$ for all a, t.
(III) Static case: $T=0$.

The implications of assumption (II), when it is introduced singly into the general model, were studied in Section 4. The implications of (I), alone or in combination with (II), were discussed in Section 3. In Section 2, assumptions (I) and (III) were introduced jointly, and treated both in the absence and in the presence of assumption (II). In all cases, we tried to find whether, and under what conditions, positive stocks of paper money are consistent with utility maximization and with positive and finite prices of consumption goods. We found this consistency present in the dynamic case with market imperfections (or transaction costs), i.e., when assumptions (I) and (III) are not made. When assumption (I) is introduced, only discontinuous and unstable stocks of paper money are seen to be justifiable. When, in addition, assumption (III) is introduced, positive and finite prices of consumption goods imply zero stocks of paper money; i.e., a regime of money-of-account.

B. Important omissions were registered as we went along. Not only did we disregard uncertainty, production and lending (1H–1I); we decreed the exclusion of barter (4C); we compressed the bargaining process into an instant of time (3B) and glossed over the nature of interdependence between marginal revenue functions of various individuals (4G); and, for reasons of mathematical simplicity, we approximated the discontinuous phenomenon of transaction costs (and the finite difference between selling and buying price) by piecing together in a continuous fashion the demand curve *of* a buyer and that *to* a seller (4E).

C. Using the expressions of the older economic literature the results obtained so far can be also summarized as follows: It was shown in Section 2 (confirming the finding of Patinkin [1]) that the existence of paper money is not explained by its function as a *numéraire*, a unit of price measurement. In Section 3, the *'store of value'* function of money was investigated but was not proved sufficient to explain paper money stocks that take values other than 0 or the money equivalent of all resources. In Section 4, money was viewed (in addition to being the numéraire, and to 'store value' in expectation of favorable prices) as the *universal means of payment* ('legal tender'), and all other goods were assumed to have imperfect markets. Under these conditions continuous positive stocks of paper money were explained. Note that it was not necessary to introduce uncertainty.

D. Of all models studied, 'money illusion' was absent only in a model involving 'money-of-account'. Wherever positive stocks of money were present, we had also 'money illusion': the change of all prices in relation to money did affect the quantities of goods held or consumed by the individual.

This agrees with common sense. If people hold money stocks this holding must give them some advantages. Therefore, if the prices of all non-money goods change in relation to the price of money (though not necessarily in relation to each other), it may be advantageous to change the stock of money held – and, therefore, to change other quantities involved, i.e., stocks retained and sold, and the consumption flows, of some or all non-money goods. Thus 'money illusion' is rational. We had better not call it illusion!

BIBLIOGRAPHY

Dantzig, George B. [1]: 'Programming of Interdependent Activities; II. Mathematical Model', *Econometrica* (1949).
Divisia, F. [1]: *Economique Rationelle*, 1928.
Fossati, Eraldo [1]: *Elementi di economia razionale*, Vol. 1, 1950.
Haavelmo, T. [1]: *The Notion of Price Homogeneity*, Oslo, 1949 (mimeographed).
Hickman, W. Braddock [1]: 'The Determinacy of Absolute Prices in the Classical Economic Theory', *Econometrica* (1950).
Hicks, J. R. [1]: 'Mr. Keynes and the Classics', *Econometrica* (1937).
Hurwicz, Leonid [1]: 'Theory of the Frim and of Investment', *Econometrica* (1946).
Klein, L. R. [1]: *The Keynesian Revolution*, New York, 1947.
Leontief, W. [1]: 'The Fundamental Assumption of Mr. Keynes' Monetary Theory of Unemployment', *Quarterly Journal of Economics* **51** (1936–37). [2]: 'The Consistency of the Classical Theory of Money and Prices', *Econometrica* (1950).
Marschak, J. [1]: 'Money and the Theory of Assets', *Selected Essays*, 33. [2]: 'Money Illusion and Demand Analysis', *Selected Essays*, 46. [3]: 'The Role of Liquidity Under Complete and Incomplete Information', (1949) *Selected Essays*, 37.
Pareto, V. [1]: *Manuel d'Economie Politique*, Seconde Edition, Paris, 1927.
Patinkin, D. [1]: 'Relative Prices, Say's Law and the Demand for Money', *Econometrica* (1948). [2]: 'The Indeterminacy of Absolute Prices in Classical Economic Theory', *Econometrica* (1949).
Phipps, Cecil G. [1]: 'A Note on Patinkin's "Relative Prices"', *Econometrica* (1950).
Stigler, G. [1]: 'Review of P. Samuelson's "Foundations of Economic Analysis"', *Journal of the American Statistical Association* (1948), 604–5.
Tinbergen, Jan and Polak, J. J. [1]: *The Dynamics of Business Cycles*, Chicago, 1950.
Wicksell, K. [1]: *Lectures on Political Economy*, London, 1934.

NOTES

* Presented at the Meeting of Econometric Society in New York City, December 1949. Acknowledgments are due to Donald Fort for his valuable remarks in class discussions back in 1946; to Karl Brunner and William Hood for their comments on earlier versions of the present paper; and to Milton Friedman and Leonid Hurwicz for suggestions. *Added in 1974*. The recent work of Jurg Niehans is relevant.

[1] E.g., Divisia [1].

[2] See Hicks [1].

[3] For an attempt to derive a macroeconomic system from the assumption that individuals

maximize their utilities or profits see Klein [1], Technical Appendix pp. 192–199.

4 Patinkin is aware of the loss of information due to this neglect of microeconomic assumptions: [2], footnotes 19, 20; [1], footnote 3. See Eraldo Fossati [1], Chapter X and Appendix.

5 The importance of this assumption was first pointed out by Leontief [1], I believe.

6 For an empirical attempt see Marschak [2].

7 There is truth in G. Stigler's [1], remark that "Most discussions of dynamic economies... would better be entitled 'What I know about Differential and Difference Equations'... The economics... is appallingly absent."

8 For example, Pareto [1], Appendice, 63; Wicksell [1], pp. 66–67.

9 I believe the model discussed by Leontief [2] in his criticism of Patinkin is, in fact, a 'money-of-account' model.

10 This common sense is well stated in a paper by Phipps [1] who disagrees with Patinkin on the form but not, I think, on the substance.

11 For a succinct statement of this point of view see Hickman [1].

12 The author hesitates between calling this a 'dynamic' or a 'multiperiod' model. In the best known dynamic economic models, expectations are not given (as they are in our model) but are themselves functions of current observations made by the individual – see, for example, Tinbergen [1], pp. 103–104; Hurwicz [1], p. 120. However, in recent writings on planning – e.g., by Dantzig [1], p. 205 – a 'dynamic' plan contains all expectation constants as given at the time of planning, like in the present model: see the price column of our (3.1). The term 'multi-period' model would not quite meet the need, as our model may contain just one period of consumption (but two marketing dates).

13 That is, we do not study here the time-consuming adjustment in the market: see 1J above.

14 We use 'or' in the sense of 'and/or' as distinct from 'either-or'.

15 Or, to put it in a different way: this single good absorbs all resources of the individual as of date $t+1$.

16 As pointed out in 3D the plans of individuals need not be mutually consistent except for the condition that the market of date 0 be cleared. Thus, $y_{Na}^{T}=0$ for every a does not contradict the fact that the initial aggregate money stock is positive.

17 Cf. Marschak [1], Section 6, for an earlier attempt on these lines.

18 It is possible, but outside of our scope here – see 1I above – to interpret (4.2) so as to include production conditions along with market conditions. Note also that brokers' services mentioned above are production goods, and these are again outside of the scope of the paper.

19 If one limits oneself – as we have done in this paper – to consumption goods, the most important case which we are excluding by our institutional assumption of an economy without barter is probably that of exchanging food and lodging for domestic services. More modern and more important examples involve claims and production goods: the exchange of shares and real properties between industrial corporations. Thus the question – raised but not answered by Wicksell [1], p. 67 – as to how the extent of barter is determined by market equations, apart from legal restrictions, remains an important one.

20 Marschak [3].

21 The positive quantity

$$\mu_{Na}^{t}=u_{na}^{t}/M_{na}^{t}, \quad n=1,\ldots,N-1,$$

can be called 'the marginal utility of paper money' for the ath individual.

22 Unloading was a rule, rather than an exception, in the model of Section 3; but it is not essential for the present model, and we may leave its analysis aside.

OPTIMAL INVESTMENT OF A FIRM

(1950)

NOTATIONS, DEFINITIONS, ASSUMPTIONS. (1) Use Latin capitals for random variables. Denote the vector of *assets* held by a firm by $a \equiv [a_g] \equiv (a_1, \ldots, a_n)$, and its *profit* by $Y \equiv Y(a)$. Then, at $a=0$, $Y=0$; and write $\partial Y/\partial a_g \equiv Y_g$, $\partial^2 Y/\partial a_g \partial a_h \equiv Y_{gh}$, $(g, h=1, \ldots, n)$. Expand $Y = \sum a_g Y_g + + \frac{1}{2} \sum \sum a_g a_h Y_{gh} + \cdots$. Write $\mathscr{E} Y \equiv m_Y$: $\mathscr{E}(Y-\mu_Y)^2 \equiv m_{YY}$; $\mathscr{E} Y_g \equiv q_g \equiv$ the mean of the *marginal profitability of* the gth asset; its variance and covariances are $\mathscr{E}(Y_g - q_g)(Y_h - q_h) \equiv q_{gh}$, $(g, h=1, \ldots, n)$.

(2) Assume that *complementarity* $Y_{gh} = \text{const.} \equiv y_{gh}$, $(g, h \equiv 1, \ldots, n)$. Then the profit function $Y(a)$ is approximately characterized by the vector $[q_g]$ and the two matrices $\|q_{gh}\|$, $\|y_{gh}\|$.

(3) *Effective utility function* $u(Y) \equiv u_2[u_1(Y)]$ where $u_1(Y) \equiv$ profit after taxes, and u_2 is the subjective utility function.

(4) Expand $v \equiv \mathscr{E} u(Y) = u(m_Y) + u''(m_Y) \cdot m_{YY}/2 + \cdots$. Hence approximately, for v given, $dm_Y/dm_{YY} = -\frac{1}{2} u''(m_Y)/u'(m_Y) \equiv \rho \equiv$ risk *aversion.* (If $u = u_1$, $\rho =$ *tax progressivity*; if $u = u_2$, $2\rho =$ *flexibility of marginal utility of profit, multiplied by profit.*)

(5) *Rational behavior:* maximize v subject to constraints such as (in a simple case) $\sum a_g p_g = k$ (borrowing limit), where p_g are constant prices.

PROBLEM I. Find desirable properties of assets. $\rho > 0$, and, by (5) p_g is proportional to $\partial v/\partial a_g$ and therefore, by (4), also to the quantity $(q_g + \sum y_{gh} a_h - 2\rho \sum q_{gh} a_h)$. Hence high values are desired for q_g, y_{gh}, y_{gg}, $-q_{gh}$, $-q_{gg}$. Examples: comparisons between insurance companies and specialized and diversified investment trusts and producers.

PROBLEM II. Let $X \equiv X(a) \equiv$ the firm's physical output. In the national interest, maximize $\mathscr{E} X$ by choosing an appropriate profit-after-tax schedule, $u_1(Y)$, provided the expectation of tax revenue has a fixed level, c.

Simplifying assumptions: $u = u_1$ for any Y; $n = 2$; $0 \leqslant a_1 =$ risky plant; $0 \leqslant a_2 =$ riskless bonds. $X = X(a_1)$, $X'(a_1) > 0$; $Y = a_1 Y_1 + a_1^2 y_{11}/2 + a_2 y_2$

approximately, where y_{11}, y_2 (constant interest), and the mean and variance of Y_1 are known. Put $p_1 = p_2 = 1$. Then by (5),

$$(\alpha) \qquad a_1 \leqslant k,$$

$$(\beta) \qquad \mathscr{E}u[Y(a_1)] \geqslant \mathscr{E}u[Y(a_1{}^*)] \quad \text{for any} \quad a_1^*, \quad 0 \leqslant a_1^* \leqslant k.$$

To find a function u that maximizes a_1 (and hence X), subject to (α), (β), and subject to

$$(\gamma) \qquad \mathscr{E}[Y - u(Y)] = c,$$

is a problem in the calculus of variations. A solution was given for a quadratic tax schedule admitting negative taxes, and with $u(0)=0$. Instead, some or all of the following conventional constraints upon the tax schedule might be used: for $Y>0$, $u \leqslant Y$, $0<u'<1$, $u''<0$; and for $Y \leqslant 0$, $u(Y) = Y$.

PROBLEM III. Let $Y^{(\tau)} \equiv$ *sequence of profits* in τ years, 0 through $\tau - 1$. Generalize Problem I by substituting $Y^{(t)}$ for Y (t='horizon'), and by redefining a as a matrix of *decision functions* ('strategy') $a \equiv \| a_g^{(\tau)} [Y^{(\tau)}] \|$, where $g = 1, \ldots, n$; $\tau = 1, \ldots, t$. The best value of a will depend on parameters $[q_g]$, $\|q_{gh}\|$, $\|y_{gh}\|$ [defined in (2) and properly generalized] and on additional asset properties, viz. the mutual conversion costs (illiquidities).

PROBLEM IV. Same as Problem III, but the parameters just mentioned are not known in advance. The materialized sequence $Y^{(\tau)}$ serves as a statistical sample of growing size.

40

MONNAIE ET LIQUIDITÉ DANS LES MODÈLES MACROÉCONOMIQUES ET MICROÉCONOMIQUES*

(1954)

On a reconnu, ces dernières années, que la politique monétaire peut affecter non seulement le niveau des prix, mais aussi le niveau de la production. On a reconnu aussi que la politique fiscale peut non seulement affecter la position budgétaire du Gouvernement (revenu et dettes), et intervenir dans la distribution des charges, mais aussi influencer le revenu réel de la nation dans son ensemble.

Les domaines monétaire et fiscal constituent d'ailleurs des champs d'action en quelque sorte classiques de la politique publique, qu'elle soit gouvernementale ou semi-gouvernementale (dans le cas où la Banque Centrale n'est pas complètement indépendante). A ces domaines s'ajoute aujourd'hui celui des salaires; le système des conventions collectives est un système de règlementation des salaires qui, s'il ne relève pas, d'une façon générale et directe de l'action gouvernementale, n'en relève pas moins de la 'politique publique'; il est entendu que l'action des syndicats patronaux ou ouvriers affecte le bien-être général puisqu'elle influence, non seulement les taux des salaires nominaux et les revenus de ceux qui sont directement intéressés, mais aussi le niveau général de l'emploi et des prix.

Les modèles macroéconomiques se rapportent justement à ces questions et ont en conséquence grandement attiré l'attention de ceux qui ont pour tâche ou pour vocation de conseiller le gouvernement ou l'opinion. Nous considérerons comme 'contrôlables' les paramètres suivant d'un modèle macroéconomique: la quantité de monnaie (ou bien le taux d'intérêt ou le cours des valeurs d'Etat, s'ils sont fixés par les pouvoirs publics ou les autorités monétaires); un système de taux d'impôts; les dépenses gouvernementales et un système de taux des salaires. Les paramètres (ou relations) qui ne sont pas contrôlés experiment les attitudes psychologiques du consommateur, de l'entrepreneur, du travailleur, quand ils réagissent aux changements dans leurs revenus, dans leurs biens et dans les prix des biens et services. Ces équations (relations) macroéconomiques sont obtenues à partir des équations microéconomiques, par agrégation. Celle-ci est réalisée, en principe, en faisant intervenir la loi de distribution des attitudes des individus.

Le modèle macroéconomique contiendra trois sortes de variables: les paramètres contrôlés $y(y_1,\ldots,y_n)$, les paramètres non contrôlés $z(z_1,\ldots,z_p)$, et finalement les variables endogènes, ou dépendantes $x(x_1,\ldots,x_m)$. On veut savoir comment les variables endogènes (tels que le niveau des prix, de la production, etc. ...) sont influencées par un changement voulu des paramètres contrôlés, les paramètres non-contrôlés étant donnés. Le nombre d'équations est égal à m:

$$(1) \qquad F_i(x,y,z)=0 \quad i=1,\ldots,m.$$

Le 'conseiller' veut déterminer l'influence d'un changement de y_j sur x_i (par exemple). Si on suppose la différentiabilité, on obtient l'ensemble d'équations linéaires:

$$(2) \qquad \sum_{i=1}^{m} \frac{\partial F_h}{\partial x_i}\frac{dx_i}{dy_j}=0 \quad h=1,\ldots,m$$

On obtiendra une solution de la forme:

$$(3) \qquad \frac{dx_i}{dy_j}=G_{ij} \quad (x_1,\ldots,x_m;\, y_1,\ldots,y_n;\, z_1,\ldots,z_p).$$

Nous prendrons pour exemple quelques modèles suggérés par les discussions relatives aux théories de J. M. Keynes. Ces exemples nous montreront d'ailleurs comment les modèles mathématiques servent à clarifier certaines difficultés logiques que l'on rencontre dans les débats économiques. Nous commencerons par un modèle dans lequel toutes les quantités économiques sont 'réelles', c'est-à-dire ne dépendant pas du choix de l'unité monétaire. Nous désignerons les quantités réelles par des lettres latines minuscules, et les fonctions par des lettres grecques; les lettres surlignées se rapporteront aux paramètres contrôlés.

Désignons par e le niveau de l'emploi, par e_1 la main d'oeuvre demandée et par e_2 la main d'oeuvre offerte. Désignons par s le taux réel des salaires. Supposons que le revenu national réel, r, ne dépende que du niveau de l'emploi, en négligeant l'influence lente de l'accroissement du capital et du progrès technique: Soit $r=\rho(e)$; la dérivée $\rho'(e)$ est alors le produit marginal du travail. Si les entrepreneurs maximisent leurs profits, leur demande de main d'oeuvre est telle que $s=\rho'(e_1)$. Quant à l'offre de main d'oeuvre, on aura $s=\sigma(e_2)$ où la fonction traduit le comportement des travailleurs et dépend de leur évaluation relative du loisir et des biens. Supposons encore que la somme totale, d, des dépenses réelles des consommateurs et des entrepreneurs ne dépende que de la somme totale de leurs revenus réels, soit $d=\delta(r)$. Désignons enfin par $\bar{g}$ la dépense réelle du gouvernement, le seul paramètre contrôlé de ce modèle hypothétique très simplifié. Les paramètres non-contrôlés sont les paramètres des fonctions δ, σ, ρ; celles-ci reflètent les conditions psychologiques et techniques ou, plus précisément, la loi de distribution des attitudes psychologiques des consommateurs, entrepreneurs, ouvriers ainsi que la distribution du niveau technique des entreprises. On se demande quelle serait l'influence d'un changement de $\bar{g}$ (les fonctions δ, σ, ρ étant fixées) sur chacune des six variables endogènes: e, e_1, e_2, r, s, d. Par exemple, on veut déterminer $de/d\bar{g}$ étant donné le système d'équations:

$$
\text{(I)} \quad
\begin{array}{ll}
(4) & r=\rho(e) \\
(5) & s=\rho'(e_1) \\
(6) & s=\sigma(e_2) \\
(7) & d=\delta(r) \\
(8) & e=e_1 \\
(9) & e=e_2 \\
(10) & d+\bar{g}=r
\end{array}
$$

Les équations (4)–(7) ont déjà été proposées dans le courant du texte. (8) et (9) expriment les conditions d'équilibre du marché du travail. Le deuxième membre de (10) est la valeur réelle des produits venant sur le marché (égale à la somme totale des revenus réels individuels), tandis que le premier membre de (10) est la valeur réelle de la demande de ces produits. L'équation (10) exprime donc la condition d'équilibre du marché des articles de consommation, des outils et des armements. Notons encore une fois que, dans (4), on néglige les influences lentes de l'accroissement des capitaux et du progrès technique; et ajoutons que dans (8), (9), (10) on considère négligeable le délai nécessaire à la réalisation de l'équilibre de l'offre et de la demande.

Les équations du système (I) sont incompatibles: il y a six variables (endogènes), et sept équations indépendantes pour les déterminer. Au fond des choses, les discussions suscitées par la théorie Keynésienne ('J. M. Keynes contre J. B. Say') peuvent être interprétées comme des tentatives plus ou moins conscientes de construire des systèmes d'équations compatibles. On peut construire un grand nombre de tels systèmes. Tout d'abord, on doit choisir ceux qui s'accordent avec les observations empiriques; mais, même compte tenu de cette restriction, la liberté de choix demeure encore considérable.

La solution 'classique' est d'introduire le taux d'intérêt, *i*, dans l'équation (7) qui devient ainsi:

$$(7') \qquad d = \delta^*(r, i)$$

le nombre des variables devient alors égal au nombre des équations. On peut considérer, en effet, le taux d'intérêt comme une des variables qui déterminent la demande des outils ainsi que l'épargne (et, partant, la consommation). Nous reviendrons sur cette idée plus loin. Pour le moment, nous proposerons d'autres modifications, pour expliquer surtout le phénomène du 'chômage involontaire', c'est-à-dire l'existence d'une différence positive entre e_2 et e_1.

Une modification réaliste du système (I) consiste à remplacer (8) et (9) par une équation plus générale:

$$(11) \qquad e = \min(e_1, e_2)$$

Nos institutions impliquent en effet que l'emploi actuel n'excède ni l'offre ni la demande de main d'oeuvre (l'occupation des usines par les ouvriers est interdite aussi bien que l'esclavage); tandis que l'expérience de chômages prolongés rend douteuse l'existence d'un mécanisme établissant rapidement les égalités $e = e_1 = e_2$.

Une autre façon de remplacer le système (I) par un système d'équations compatibles est de nier que le niveau des prix soit sans influence sur la détermination du niveau de l'emploi et d'autres variables économiques 'réelles'. Par exemple, on pourrait nier que les ouvriers fassent des calculs leur permettant de comparer l'utilité des biens à celle du loisir; on pourrait alors supposer que l'offre de la main d'oeuvre dépend, non du taux réel des salaires, mais du taux nominal sP en désignant par P le niveau des prix. L'équation (6) serait alors remplacée par:

(12) $sP = \sigma^*(e_2)$

ou, d'une façon plus générale, par

(13) $\sigma^{**}(e_2, s, P) = 0$

tout en conservant l'idée que l'offre et la demande s'équilibrent, c'est-à-dire, en maintenant (8) et (9). On disposerait alors d'un nombre égal de variables endogènes (*y* compris *P*) et d'équations indépendantes. Il me semble qu'une partie des écrivains post-Keynésiens tend, en effet, à accepter l'équation (12). Mais si, en même temps, pour expliquer le chômage, ils cessent d'admettre l'équilibre du marché du travail et remplacent (8) et (9) par (11) – ou plus simplement, rejettent (9) tout en conservant (8) – le système devient indéterminé.

Pour remédier à cela, quelques économistes, également en sympathie avec Keynes, ont porté l'accent sur un phénomène tout différent, à savoir la fixation du taux de salaire nominal comme résultat des conventions collectives, le taux nominal demeurant indépendant des intentions des ouvriers pris individuellement. Cela revient à introduire, non seulement une nouvelle variable endogène *P* mais aussi un nouveau paramètre contrôlé – désignons-le par $\bar{S}$. L'équation (9) est alors remplacée par:

(14) $Ps = \bar{S}$

(nous utiliserons des lettres majuscules pour des quantités qui dépendent du choix de l'unité monétaire). En admettant cette modification du modèle, des écrivains Keynésiens rejoignent M. Rueff dans son explication du chômage par la rigidité des salaires.

Si on est décidé à introduire le niveau des prix *P* pour pallier l'insuffisance du nombre des variables dépendantes dans le système (I), il n'y a pas de raison pour introduire *P* seulement dans l'équation qui décrit les goûts des ouvriers (équation (6) remplacée par (12) ou (13)): on peut se demander si le comportement des consommateurs, des acheteurs d'outils, et de l'Etat, ne doit pas être conçu en termes des valeurs monétaires plutôt qu'en termes de quantités 'réelles'. L'Etat fixe-t-il dans son budget une somme de $\bar{G}$ Milliards de francs ou la quantité des mitrailleuses à mettre en service. Si le niveau des prix monte au cours d'une année l'état change-t-il $\bar{G}$ ou $\bar{g}$? De même, la demande réelle du consommateur dépend-elle de son revenu réel r? de son revenu nominal rP? ou n'est-elle pas éventuellement une fonction de P et r distincte de leur produit rP? Ces considérations conduiraient à remplacer (7) et (10) par

$$(15)\qquad d=\delta^*(r, P)$$

$$(16)\qquad d+\frac{\bar{G}}{P}=r.$$

Dans les modèles précédents, la monnaie ne figurait pas. Or, on peut considérer la quantité $\bar{M}$ de monnaie comme un paramètre contrôlé. Si M est l'encaisse désirée par le public et s'il y a équilibre monétaire, on a:

$$(17)\qquad M=\bar{M}$$

$$(18)\qquad M=\mu(rP)$$

On notera que 'l'équation d'échange' traditionnelle n'est qu'un cas particulier de (18), avec M proportionnel à rP. Le système (I) s'accroit alors de deux équations et de deux variables endogènes (M et P) et, par conséquent, demeure incompatible. Pour obtenir un système compatible on peut proposer d'autres modifications que celles que nous avons envisagées plus haut. On peut introduire une variable endogène additionnelle i, le taux d'intérêt, qui a une influence sur la demande d des outils et des articles de consommation figurant dans (15) ainsi que sur l'encaisse désirée M figurant dans (18). On remplace dont (15) et (18) par:

$$(19)\qquad d=\delta^{**}(r, P, i)\quad \text{et}$$

$$(20)\qquad M=\mu^*(rP, i)$$

On voit que (19) est plus générale que (7′).

Nous avons proposé plusieurs modifications permettant chacune de remplacer le système (I) par un système d'équations compatibles. Dans le tableau I qui, d'ailleurs, est incomplet, chaque colonne correspond à un système bien déterminé; les '+' se réfèrent aux équations composant le système donné. Le tableau I est suivi par un sommaire des variables endogènes et des paramètres contrôlés, indiquant aussi les systèmes qui contiennent ces variables et paramètres.

Si on considère les fonctions telles que ρ, ρ', σ etc, comme différentiables pour toutes les valeurs possibles de leurs arguments, on détermine sans difficulté les dérivées des variables endogènes par rapport aux para-

TABLEAU I

Equations	Systèmes II	III	IV	V	VI	VII
(4) $r=\varrho(e)$	+	+	+	+	+	+
(5) $s=\varrho'(e_1)$	+	+	+	+	+	+
(6) $s=\sigma(e_2)$	+	+				
(13) $\sigma^{**}(e_2, s, P)=0$			+	+	+	+
(14) $sP=\bar{S}$				+	+	+
(7) $d=\delta(r)$		+	+	+		
(7′) $d=\delta^*(r, i)$	+					
(15) $d=\delta^{**}(r, P)$					+	
(19) $d=\delta^{***}(r, P, i)$						+
(8) $e=e_1$	+		+	+	+	+
(9) $e=e_2$	+		+			
(11) $e=\min(e_1, e_2)$		+				
(10) $d+\bar{g}=r$	+	+	+	+		
(16) $d+(\bar{G}/P)=r$					+	+
(17) $M=\bar{M}$						+
(20) $M=\mu^*(rP, i)$						+
Nombre d'équations (= nombre de variables endogènes)	7 dont i	6	7 dont P	7 dont P	7 dont P	9 dont P, i, M

Variables endogènes	Systèmes					
r = revenu réel	II	III	IV	V	VI	VII
e = main d'oeuvre employée	II	III	IV	V	VI	VII
e_1 = main d'oeuvre demandée	II	III	IV	V	VI	VII
e_2 = main d'oeuvre offerte	II	III	IV	V	VI	VII
s = taux de salaire réel	II	III	IV	V	VI	VII
d = dépense totale	II	III	IV	V	VI	VII
P = niveau des prix	IV	V	VI	VII		
i = taux d'intérêt	II	VII				
M = encaisse désirée	VII					

Paramètres controlés	Systèmes			
$\bar{S}$ = taux de salaire nominal fixé par les conventions collectives	V	VI	VII	
$\bar{M}$ = quantité de monnaie fixée par les autorités bancaires	VII			
$\bar{g}$ = dépense gouvernementale réelle	II	III	IV	V
$\bar{G}$ = dépense gouvernementale nominale	VI	VII		

mètres contrôlés (voir équations (2) et (3)) par exemple:

$$(21) \qquad \frac{dr}{dg}, \frac{dr}{d\bar{M}}, \frac{dr}{d\bar{S}}; \qquad \frac{dP}{d\bar{g}}, \frac{dP}{d\bar{M}}, \frac{dP}{d\bar{S}}.$$

On pourrait directement estimer ces dérivées par les procédés statistiques habituels (régression de r par rapport à $\bar{g}$, $\bar{M}$ et $\bar{S}$), à partir des données historiques si on pouvait observer dans le passé une suite suffisamment longue de changements significatifs des paramètres contrôlés. Mais si de tels changements ont été rares la méthode directe n'est pas applicable. Il faut alors estimer les fonctions 'structurelles' ρ, σ, δ etc. (pour cela, on se servira encore des données historiques, mais aussi d'autres données telles que des budgets familiaux, des résultats d'enquêtes sur les attitudes des entrepreneurs, etc). On obtiendra ainsi, d'une façon indirecte – voir équation (2) – des dérivées présentant un intérêt pratique telles que (21). C'est un de ces cas où la pratique présuppose la théorie.

Il ne nous est pas possible de poursuivre en détail la détermination des dérivées (21) à partir des modèles tels que II–VII. (Il est d'ailleurs nécessaire de remarquer que des fonctions telles que ρ et, peut-être μ, ne remplissent pas partout la condition de différentiabilité. En effet la variable e n'est pas défine pour des valeurs supérieures à ε (la main d'oeuvre physique disponible; ε est un paramètre non contrôlé.) C'est la raison pour laquelle il faut distinguer nettement entre le cas où $\varepsilon - e = 0$ ('emploi complet') et le cas où $\varepsilon - e > 0$. La quantité $\varepsilon - e$ peut être appelée le 'chômage physique', à distinguer du 'chômage involontaire', soit $e_2 - e_1$.

Un caractère fondamental des modèles macro-économiques est le rôle joué par l'absence ou la présence de 'l'illusion monétaire', une expression due à feu Irving Fisher. Nous avons vu que les dérivées (21) dépendent du fait, par exemple, que les consommateurs (les entrepreneurs ou les ouvriers) sont ou ne sont pas indifférents entre une hausse de 5% de la valeur monétaire de leurs revenus (et de leurs capitaux, quoique cette dernière variable n'ait pas figuré dans nos modèles précédents) et une baisse de 5% des prix des biens qu'ils achètent. Ils le sont dans les systèmes I et II; ils ne le sont pas dans tous les systèmes III–VII de notre tableau. Il semble que beaucoup de modèles macro-économiques proposés en économie 'littéraire' pour autant qu'on peut exactement préciser leur contenu, sont de la nature du système I et, partant, sont incompatibles.

C'est une raison suffisante (bien qu'elle ne soit pas la seule) pour analyser les éléments à partir desquels sont construits les modèles macro-économiques; à savoir, les équations de comportement individuel. En particulier, on peut chercher à vérifier si le phénomène de 'l'illusion monétaire' (loin d'être seulement une "aberration psychologique") peut exister quand chaque individu maximise son utilité ou, dans des conditions plus générales d'incertitude, son utilité moyenne ('espérance morale').

Ceci conduit à la question suivante: Qu'est-ce qui détermine 'l'encaisse désirée'? en supposant que chacun maximise son utilité moyenne sous réserve de certaines conditions restrictives. Pareilles conditions figurent les conditions initiales dans lesquelles l'individu se trouve, aussi bien que ses prédictions sur le futur.

Dans des conditions strictement statiques, on ne peut donner aucune explication à une demande non nulle de stocks de papier-monnaie; et on démontre aisément que le système ne détermine que les prix relatifs, et que 'l'illusion monétaire' est nécessairement absente.

Cependant si l'on suppose que le futur différera du présent et que chaque individu est subjectivement certain du futur (ce qui ne veut pas dire qu'il ait objectivement raison), on trouve, dans des conditions de concurrence parfaite, une explication pour des stocks non-nuls de monnaie (ainsi que d'autres biens) dans le désaccord entre les individus sur les prix futurs; il s'agit alors des stocks spéculatifs: on investit en monnaie si on attend une baisse des prix des marchandises. Ceci toutefois ne donne pas une explication du fait, qu'à tout moment donné, les ressources d'un individu ne sont pas investies en totalité dans un seul élément d'actif (notamment la monnaie), à savoir dans l'élément d'actif dont l'individu attend la hausse la plus forte en prix relatifs.

Une explication plus satisfaisante est obtenue si on introduit le concept 'd'illiquidité' (ou de 'coût de transaction') d'un élément d'actif. Le problème peut être discuté dans les conditions de certitude ou d'incertitude. Pour la seconde hypothèse, qui constitue le cas le plus général, l'exemple suivant est suggéré.

Supposons que j'envisage de louer un certain équipement de x kilowatt pour une durée de deux années au prix $=1$ par kilowatt-année, et que j'envisage la possibilité d'y ajouter Y kilowatts (au même prix par kilowatt-année) au début de l'année suivante et pour la durée de cette année. J'obtiendrai alors x kilowatt-années au cours de la première année, et $x+Y$

au cours de la seconde. Ou, en modifiant légèrement cet exemple, supposons que j'achète x unités d'un équipement qui durera deux années et qu'au début de la seconde année j'achète Y unités (Y positif) ou vende $-Y$ unités (Y négatif). Y est une quantité aléatoire (j'utiliserai des lettres majuscules pour de telles quantités) car elle dépend d'évènements qui ne sont pas prévus au début de la première année. Soit $\rho(x)$ la fonction revenu dans la première année. Dans la seconde année, elle subira un changement aléatoire, disons: une translation U, pour fixer les idées, de telle sorte que le revenu sera $\rho(x+Y+U)$. Si Y est négatif, j'obtiendrai, pour la vente de chaque kilowatt d'équipement, non pas le prix 1, mais le prix $\lambda \leqslant 1$, étant la 'liquidité' de l'élément d'actif considéré. Le revenu net pour deux ans est:

$$\begin{aligned} & Z=\rho(x)+\rho(x+Y+U)-2x-QY \\ (22) \qquad & Q=1 \quad \text{si} \quad Y\geqslant 0 \\ & =\lambda \quad \text{si} \quad Y<0. \end{aligned}$$

Z est donc une fonction non linéaire de Y; le choix de Y sera effectué quand j'apprendrai la valeur de U, au commencement de la seconde année. Y est une fonction de U, ayant λ pour paramètre: $Y=\eta(U;\lambda)$ c'est ma 'règle d'action'. Ma 'stratégie la meilleure', $x=\hat{x}$, $\eta=\hat{\eta}$ maximisera l'espérance mathématique de Z.

Nous voudrions savoir, en particulier, comment $\hat{x}$ dépend de la liquidité et de la loi de distribution de U. Un exemple, où ρ est quadratique et la distribution de U Gaussienne, montre que l'investissement x, (c'est-à-dire ma demande pour cet élément d'actif particulier) est une fonction croissante de sa liquidité λ, et une fonction décroissante de l'écart-type de U.

Ces considérations tendent à montrer que si la monnaie est de tous les biens celui qui a la liquidité la plus élevée (le coût de transaction le plus bas), l'encaisse désirée des individus rationnels dépend de la nature des distributions de probabilités des évènements futurs et croit avec l'incertitude.

Ces considérations expliquent qu'il puisse exister une demande non-nulle de stocks de papier-monnaie et montrent que 'l'illusion monétaire' a un fondement rationnel; aussi serait-il préférable de ne pas l'appeler une 'illusion'.

Les coûts de transaction ont été reconnus par les hommes d'affaires aussi bien que par les théoriciens comme un facteur important dans la détermination des stocks de biens autres que la monnaie. La théorie des stocks optimum montre de quelle façon ceux-ci sont déterminés par le coût de transaction et par la loi de probabilité des courbes exprimant la demande en fonction du temps (un processus stochastique).

Les coûts de transactions sont incompatibles avec une concurrence parfaite. De plus, alors qu'ils sont aisément traités dans le cadre de la théorie d'une seule firme, les coûts de transaction créent des difficultés quand on veut expliquer la formation des prix sur le marché. Quelques tentatives dans cette direction ont été faites mais la solution complète n'est pas encore en vue. C'est, en fait, une partie du problème général du 'marchandage' entre un nombre fini d'individus.

NOTE

* Presenté au Seminaire d'Econometrie conduit par M. René Roy, en 1952.

L'auteur est très reconnaissant à M. Arnold Harberger de l'Université de Chicago pour ses conseils précieux, et à M. André Laurent qui a fait la révision du texte français.

Différents aspects des problèmes abordés dans cet article ont été traités par l'auteur d'une façon plus détaillée dans les publications suivantes:

(1) *Income, Employment and Price Level.* Notes of Lectures given at the University of Chicago in 1948 and 1949, 95 pp., Augustus Kelly, New York, 1951.

(2) 'Economic Measurements for Policy and Prediction', 1953, *Selected Essays*, 49.

(3) 'The Rationale of the Demand for Money and the Money Illusion', 1950, *Selected Essays*, 38.

(4) 'The Role of Liquidity under Complete and Incomplete Information', 1949, *Selected Essays*, 37.

(5) 'Optimal Inventory Policy', (en collaboration avec K. Arrow et T. Harris), 1951, *Selected Essays*, 19.

PART IV

ECONOMIC MEASUREMENTS

INTRODUCTORY NOTE

The author's attempts at measuring economic magnitudes and relations, mainly those relevant to the aggregate production rate, wealth, and money (the early publications (1932, 1933, 1934), some in cooperation with Walter Lederer (1932, 1936), or the Essays 42, 44 of the present Part Four) have preceded and, in fact, forced on him a critical concern with both the fundamentals of economic theory and the choice of useful methods of measurement. Now, the fundamental 'micro-economic' relations reflect individual behavior and social institutions. And to be useful for economic policy which may change some of the past relations, these must be measured – even though controlled experiments are seldom feasible.

Accordingly, Essay 44 is concerned with 'aggregating' the data on individual behavior. So is Essay 46; and its subject, the 'money illusion' was later submitted to 'micro'-theoretical analysis (Essay 38 in Part Three). In Essay 47, the theory of production is 'disaggregated', and it is attempted to estimate a system of 'structural' behavior equations, simultaneous and stochastic. The need for such measurements was stated early in Essays 43, 45, stimulated by Ragnar Frisch (1933, 1934). Later work on appropriate statistical tools was stimulated by Trygve Haavelmo (1943, 1944). The essential solution given by H. B. Mann and Abraham Wald (1943) was later developed by the team under T. C. Koopmans' leadership (1950, 1953); the author's paper (1951) and Essays 48, 49, 54 are in the same spirit. Later writings on Econometric Tools are listed after Essay 54, assigned to Part Five as a contribution to the logic of economics.

REFERENCES

Frisch, Ragnar (1933), *Pitfalls in the Construction of Statistical Demand Curves*, H. Buske, Leipzig.

Frisch, Ragnar (1934), *Statistical Conference Analysis by Means of Complete Regression Systems*, Economic Institute, Oslo University.

Haavelmo, Trygve (1943), 'The Statistical Implications of a System of Simultaneous Equations', *Econometrica* **11**, 1–12.

Haavelmo, Trygve (1944), *The Probability Approach in Econometrics*, Supplement to *Econometrica*, **12**.

Hood, Wm. C. and Koopmans, T. C. (eds.) (1953), *Studies in Econometric Methods*, Cowles Commission Monograph No. 14, Wiley, New York (reproduced by Yale University Press, 1970).

Koopmans, T. C. (ed.) (1950), *Statistical Inference in Dynamic Economics*, Cowles Commission Monograph No. 10, Wiley, New York.

Marschak, J. (1932), 'Substanzverluste', *Archiv fuer Sozialwissenschaft und Sozialpolitik*, **67**, 129–45.

Marschak, J. (1933), 'Volksvermoegen und Kassenbedarf', *Archiv f. Sozialwiss.* **68**, 385–419.

Marschak, J. (1934), 'Economic Parameters in a Stationary Society with Monetary Circulation', *Econometrica* **2**, 91–111.

Marschak, J. (1951), 'Statistical Inference from Non-Experimental Observations', *Proceedings, International Statistical Conferences 1947*, **3**, 289–98.

Marschak, J. and Lederer, W. (1932b), 'Groessenordnungen des deutschen Geldsystems', *Archiv f. Sozialwiss.* **67**, 385–403.

Marschak, J. and Lederer, W. (1936), *Kapitalbildung*, Wm. Hodge and Co., London.

A NOTE ON THE PERIOD OF PRODUCTION

(1934)

The December issue of the *Economic Journal* contains two extremely interesting contributions, by Mr. C. H. P. Gifford and Mr. Martin Hill, to the problem of measuring the 'length of the period of production'. As has been pointed out by both authors, this notion is not without significance for the understanding of recent discussions on business cycles. A few further remarks may be permitted.[1]

The definition of the length of the period given by Mr. Gifford seems to be all the more valuable as it proves, if duly modified, to be identical with another interesting economic magnitude, viz. the ratio of the total value of existing commodities ('stocks') to the value of the current income (or consumption) 'flow'. Slightly modifying Mr. Gifford's notation let $V(x)$ be the number of units of services added per unit of time at time $t-x$ on commodities consumed at time t, and $L(x)$ be the cost of the joint product of these services and of all those added in the preceding stages of production. Then $L(O)$, which corresponds to L in Mr. Gifford's notation, is the total cost of the finished products consumed per time unit; it is identical, in a stationary society, with the total income. Obviously

$$(1) \qquad V(x) = -\frac{dL(x)}{dx} > 0$$

$$(2) \qquad L(x_1) = -\int_{x_1}^{\infty} V dx > 0$$

$$L(O) = -\int_{0}^{\infty} V dx > 0,$$

$$(3) \qquad L(\infty) = 0;$$

Mr. Gifford defines (*mutatis mutandis*) the length of production R as the average of the consumption-distances x weighted according to the respective amounts of services applied:

(4)[2] $$R=\frac{\int_0^\infty xV dx}{\int_0^\infty V dx}=\frac{-\int_0^\infty xV dx}{L(O)}$$

It is easy to show that the numerator of the last fraction is equal to the total value of existing commodities, if a stationary society is assumed. In fact, commodities which are being produced at a consumption-distance x and are moving to the consumption-distance $x-dx$ form stocks whose value (=value of product per time unit multiplied by the stock duration) is $L(x)\,dx$; the total value K of all stocks is therefore:

(5) $$K=\int_0^\infty L(x)\,dx$$

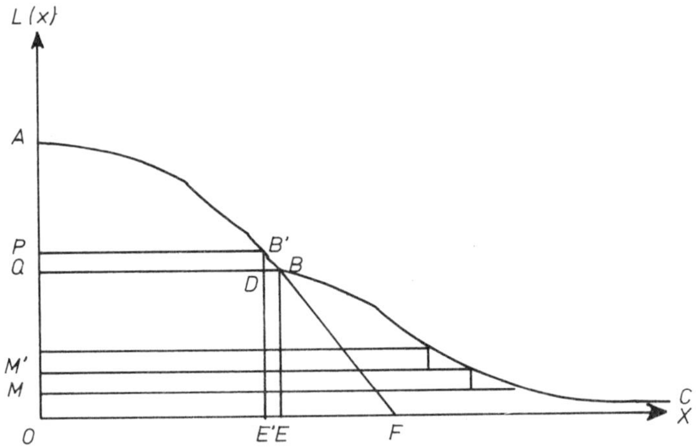

Fig. 1.

Curve ABC='function of manufacture': $L=L(x)$.
Length BE=product flow at consumption-distance OE.
Length AO=product flow at consumption-distance OE zero (=total consumption).
Area $BEE'B'$=stocks between the consumption-distances OE and OE'.
Area $AO...CA$=stocks between the consumption-distances O and ∞ (=total stocks).
The slope of $B'B$=labour added per time-unit at cons.-distance OE.
Length $PQ=B'D$=labour added at the interval between OE and OE'.

Since K, the total value of stocks, must be finite, the area limited by $L(x)$ and the positive parts of the co-ordinate axes (see Figure 1) does not change if the axes are interchanged:

$$K=\int_{x=0}^{\infty} L(x)\,dx=\int_{L=L(\infty)}^{L(O)} xdL(x)=-\int_{x=0}^{\infty} xdL(x).^{3}$$

It follows then, by (4), (1) and (5) that

$$R=\frac{-\int_0^\infty xVdx}{\int_0^\infty Vdx}=\frac{K}{L(O)},$$

so that the 'average delay' of Mr. Gifford is identical with the ratio of stocks to income, so long as stationary conditions are assumed.[4]

Our definition differs, however, from Mr. Gifford's in so far as our $L(x)$ contains labour as well as capital services; Mr. Gifford considers labour only. Let $L(x)$ consist of $l(x)$ labour and $m(x)$ capital services and put $\lambda=\int_x^\infty l(x)\,dx$ and $\mu=\int_x^\infty m(x)\,dx$. Then Mr. Gifford's length of production is $R_1=\lambda(0)/l(o)$, our length of production is $R_2=(\lambda(o)\ldots\mu(o))/(l(o)+m(o))$, and the capital per head is $R_3=(\lambda(o)+\mu(o))/l(o)$. Let the the interest rate be I. By solving the equation

$$m(x)=I\lambda(x)+I\mu(x)$$

with respect to m we find

$$m(x)=[C-\int_x^\infty Ie^{Ix}l(x)\,dx]^{-Ix},$$

C being a constant. We may, thus, express R_1, R_2 and R_3 in terms of a common argument $l(x)$ *i.e.* in terms of the time-distribution of labour only. We may also transform R_1 in R_2 or R_3, etc.

Modifying Mr. Gifford's definition in our way we may easily apply it to both cases given by Mr. Martin Hill, in the same issue of the *Economic Journal*, and considered by him as examples of two different 'methods of reckoning'. Mr. Hill's statement that, although in a stationary society, 'the periods yielded by the two methods of reckoning may not be of identical length, their behaviour will correspond' (p. 603), requires further elucidation. I think that in a stationary society both methods yield exactly identical results. In the first example (p. 600), drawn from Böhm-Bawerk, 'if the production of a commodity requires in all 100 days of labour, of which one day was spent 10 years before the completion of the commodity, another 9 years before, others respectively 8, 7, 6, 5, 4, 3, 2, and 1 years before, while the remaining 90 days were expended immediately before the completion, its average production period is $(10+9+\cdots+1+0)/100=0.55$ year'.

This reckoning corresponds exactly to our definition if we substitute as we ought to, say, 'commodity consumed per month', and labour-days applied per month' for 'commodity' and 'labour-days'. The same result, viz. 0.55 year will be yielded if we calculate the ratio of stocks to consumption measuring in labour-days labour and capital services alike: the denominator is the same as before (100 labour-days per month); and so is the numerator, since the value of stocks in each stage is the product per month multiplied by the stock duration, and the sum of the values of all stocks is therefore (beginning with the remotest stage) (1 labour day/month) × 1 year) + (2 labour days/month) × 1 year) + ⋯ + (10 (labour days/month) × 1 year) = 55 (labour days × year/month); the ratio is then 55/100 years.

In Mr. Hill's second case, 'the simple case of a tool required at a final stage of production (*e.g.* the awl of a cobbler), produced in a day and expected to make a uniform productive contribution for 5 years, the average period of production in respect of the original factors which produced the tool would be $2\frac{1}{2}$ years' (p. 602). The difference between this case and the preceding one seems to be this: we have in case 2 a large period of wearing-out (5 years) and a negligible period of investment (1 day), whereas case 1 only took account of investment and altogether neglected the wearing-out. This difference is, however, only an apparent one. It disappears if we adequately represent stocks of durable goods and services spent on their replacement. Imagine – in accordance with case 2 – a society drawing its whole amount of satisfaction out of the use of durable consumption goods (houses). Considering the houses as stocks of future satisfaction and assuming the duration of a house is 100 years, we shall represent the *new* houses by narrow horizontal strips (see diagram) with a height equal to the annual wear-and-tear OM and a breadth equal to 100 years; the strip representing the 1-year-old houses has then a height $OM' = OM$ and a breadth 99 years, etc. The curve limiting the total area corresponds then, in a stationary society, to our function $L(x)$; its ordinate at any consumption-distance x is the value of those already existing particles of satisfaction which will be consumed, per unit of time, after x units of time have elapsed. The absolute value of the first derivative $dL/dx = V(x)$ is the amount of services spent per unit of time in replacing the worn-out particles by new ones which will be consumed after a given elapse of time x. We may apply to this case the same definition of the length of production as before: either a weighted average of the amounts of factors spent on different stages, or a ratio of total stocks to total consumption. The results will be identical. In the instance chosen by Mr. Hill there is 'a uniform productive contribution' of the durable goods in question; in other words, the rate of wearing-out is constant; or, in other words again, all 'ages' of durable goods are at any given moment equally represented in the consumption; 1 per cent, of all families live in new houses, 1 per cent, live in 1-year-old houses, etc. $L(x)$ is then a straight line; or, if the property $L(\infty) = O$ is to be maintained (as it should be if the whole production of society is considered), the condition of 'uniform contributions' must be replaced by 'nearly uniform contributions' (neglecting the remotest stages of production); $L(x)$ is then approximately a straight line, and the area limited by it and by the axes is (approximately) the triangle known by Jevons. The average length of production, *i.e.* the ratio of the area to the height, is then (approximately) $\frac{1}{2}$ length of duration. In the general case, however, the wearing-out, and consequently the replacement work, do not go on at uniform rates. For example, if the time-shape of the wearing-out process is expressed by the figures of case 1, then the replacement work is distributed through time in the same way as the investment work in case 1, and the resulting average length of production is the same, viz. 0.55 year. In a sense, *all* work done in a stationary society is replacement work.

Obviously the average length of production

$$\frac{\int_{\infty}^{0} L(x)\,dx}{L(O)}$$

is only one and a very insufficient characteristic of the function $L(x)$. More complete information about the stock-distribution and distribution of services over the maturity-stages is given by the function $L(x)$ itself (as shown by our diagram), or by its first derivative $V(x)$ (as shown by Mr. Gifford's diagram, p. 613). Even this information is, of course, very limited. It postulates a homogeneous 'congeries' of goods (D. H. Robertson), neglecting all differences in the durability of individual goods and consequently ignoring the influence of quasi-rents upon prices of 'stocks'. The capitalised quasi-rents may considerably alter the properties of the curve $L(x)$. A further deformation of the function $L(x)$ may be due – as pointed out by Mr. Hill – to the wrong expectancies of the entrepreneurs, which lead to a discrepancy between consumption and replacement; the consequent congestion of commodity stocks (durable and nondurable) in certain stages may even destroy the monotonic decreasing character of $L(x)$ as expressed by (1). Finally, there is a distinction (of degree) between specific and non-specific goods, a further source of differences in the speed of adaptation. Thus the stationary scheme cannot cover dynamic facts; but the deviations of the facts from the scheme may be in themselves a symptom and a measure of certain dynamic phenomena even though not their explanation.[5]

NOTES

[1] I owe much to Dr. Fritz London (Oxford).

[2] Professor Pigou's definition of the period of production as "the time interval between the centre of gravity of labour employed and the... sale of the finished product" is probably adequately expressed by the formula of Mr. Gifford, which has indeed a certain analogy with the formula for one co-ordinate of the centre of gravity. (Cf. *Theory of Unemployment*, p. 57.)

[3] More strictly, the economic fact of K's being finite means that the function $L(x)$ must have, in addition to the properties (1) and (3), the property

$$L(x) < \frac{1}{x^{1+a}},$$

where $a(>0)$ may be made as small as we please; therefore

$$\lim_{x\to\infty} [xL(x)] = 0,$$

and by (3),

$$[xL(x)]_0^\infty = 0;$$

$$K = \int_{x=0}^{\infty} L(x)\,dx = [xL(x)]_0^\infty - \int_{L=L(O)}^{L(\infty)} x dL(x) = -\int_{x=0}^{\infty} x dL(x)$$

[4] In terms of our diagram, the same area $ABC\ldots xO$ is obtained whether we sum up the infinitesimal areas of the type $PQBB'$ (*i.e.* the "values added" multiplied by the corresponding consumption-distances) or the infinitesimal areas of the type $E'EBB'$ (*i.e.* the stocks).

[5] The writer has tried elsewhere to show the importance of the 'function of manufacture' $L(x)$ and its predictable (seasonal, etc.) and unpredictable fluctuations through time for the determination of the money volume of a nation ('Economic Parameters in a Stationary Society with Monetary Circulation', *Econometrica*, January 1934). For purposes of monetary analysis, the fluctations of non-durable stocks alone are statistically measurable; with durable goods, the fluctuations of the amortisation rates are likely to be surpassed by fluctuations of the capitalised quasi-rents owing to changes of the market interest rate and of the risk premium. This makes a statistical evaluation of that part of the money-volume which is needed to provide for fluctuations of wear-and-tear, impracticable.

42

MEASUREMENTS IN THE CAPITAL MARKET*

(1935/6)

Out of the many measurement problems involved in that complicated and elusive thing, the capital market, I have selected two as the most familiar: (1) What is the most likely response of the savers to changes in incomes and the interest rate ('Supply elasticity of savings'); (2) What is the relationship between the magnitudes designated as savings, or the non-consumed part of the income; investments or increments of the total stock of goods; increments of the value of this stock; and increcrements of the total amount of claims ('Savings and Investments')?

1. Supply elasticity of savings

The following are some of the elementary effects of a change of interest rate on savings. (1) Positive effects: (a) the '*Carver effect*' – rise of interest rate causes increase of the incomes of the interest-receivers, i.e., of the rich, i.e., of the main savers, at the expense of the non-saving classes; (b) the '*Böhm-Bawerk effect*' – more future goods are bought if their price falls, i.e., if the interest rate rises. (2) Negative effects: the '*Marshall effect*' – rise of interest rate makes smaller annual savings sufficient to secure (a) a desired capital, (b) a desired income. Paul Douglas, who summarised some of these contradictory theories, tried to test them by computing the correlation coefficient between parallel time-series of interest rates and savings. The small correlation coefficient he obtained does not necessarily prove Knight's theory that savings are fully independent of interest rates. Yet it suggests that the various elementary effects tend to cancel each other. To check this, and to avoid the pitfalls of the correlation method applied to time-series, I shall treat the elementary effects separately and show the way they work together. The evaluation is based on long-term reactions only.

Carver effect. If m is the ratio of interest to total income, and s_i the elasticity of savings with respect to income, then obviously a 1% increase in the interest rate causes an increase of savings by ms_i per cent.

For statistical evaluations, see Appendix I. The American data are based on family samples, the German on the Inland Revenue Statistics.[1] The Carver component was, therefore, 0.6 in U.S.A., and 0.1 in Germany. This estimate would be reduced if we could take account of the decrease in the incomes and savings of wage-earners caused by increase of the interest rate.

Marshall effect. If a given capital sum is to be accumulated in t years, the increase of the interest rate by 1% decreases the necessary annual savings in the ratio

$$(1+1.01r)^t-(1+r)^t=1+0.01rt \text{ approx.}$$

The 'Marshallian' component 'a' of the supply elasticity of savings is thus $-rt$. If not a given capital, but a given income is aimed at, the component is equal to $-(1+rt)$, as can be easily shown (Marshallian component 'b').

The values of the Marshallian components are, with interest rate 3%, and $t=10$ years, -0.3, or -1.3 respectively. Thus the negative Marshallian effect may partly compensate, or more than compensate the positive Carver effect.

Böhm's effect. The demand elasticity of savings with respect to the interest rate (incomes being constant) is easily shown to be equal rt times the demand elasticity of future goods with respect to their price in terms of present goods, i.e., with respect to

$$\left[\frac{1}{(1+r)^t}\right].$$

This latter elasticity can be expressed, in its turn, in accordance with Hicks-Allen's general formula (*Economica*, 1934) as a weighted average of 'income-elasticity' s_i and the 'elasticity of substitution' (δ) between between present and future goods; the weights being proportionate to savings and consumption expenditure respectively (k and $1-k$).

The co-operation of Carver's effect, Marshall's effect 'a', and Böhm's effect is shown (in the Appendix II) to obey the formula

$$s_r=m\cdot s_i-r\cdot t+r\cdot t\,[k\cdot s_i+(1-k)\,\delta]$$
$$(0.3)\,(1.85)-(0.03)\,(10)+(0.3)\,[(0.2)\,(1.85)+(0.8)\,\delta]$$

The numerical values have been inserted in the way of a plausible example and are partly based on American figures. They give approximately $\frac{1}{3}+\frac{1}{4}\delta$; or, with Marshall's 'b' – effect – $\frac{2}{3}+\frac{1}{4}\delta$. The remaining unknown is δ, the elasticity of substitution between future and present goods. If the level of satisfaction is to remain unchanged while the interest rate increases by one point (i.e., the price of future goods decreases from, say, 97 per cent. to 96 per cent. units of present goods), by how many per cent. is the consumption to decrease? δ is probably very small; if it is less than $\frac{2}{3}$, the aggregate effect is expressed by an elasticity lying within the range $0 \pm \frac{1}{2}$. Yet, δ becomes considerable, if the substitution between home and foreign investments is considered.

It is not claimed that all possible effects are exhausted by this presentation.

2. Savings and Investments

The non-consumed part of the income is identical in value to the increment of goods, provided that all values are based on the expectations prevailing in the same point of time. This is in accordance with the definition of the capital value as discounted sum of future gross yields. Let us first assume that the expectations do not change. I is the capital value in the beginning and end of the year 1, initial and final capital respectively, the difference being caused by physical changes in the capital, but not by changes of expectations; 'yield 1' is 'expected gross yield during year 1'; etc.; r_1, r_2, are the expected interest rates.

$$\text{Initial Capital} = \frac{\text{yield 1}}{1+r_1} + \frac{\text{yield 2}}{(1+r_1)(1+r_2)} + \cdots$$

$$\text{Final Capital} = \frac{\text{yield 2}}{1+r_2} + \frac{\text{yield 3}}{(1+r_2)(1+r_3)} + \cdots$$

Multiply the first equation by $(1+r_1)$ and compare the right-hand term with the second equation:

$\therefore$ Initial Capital + Interests on it = yield 1 + Final Capital.
$\therefore$ Final Capital − Initial Capital = Interests minus yield 1.
$\therefore$ Increment of Capital = 'Income' − 'Consumption' = 'Savings'.

The gross yield of an asset is, of course, identical with the consumption rate. Thus savings are equal capital increment so long as the market price of each asset is kept equal to the sum of discounted values of future yields. All these measurements are in money units. The usc of 'physical units' is dangerous unless the proportions of different commodities are reasonably constant.

Next assume that expectations have changed during the year; the above equations must then be written for 'prospective' and for 'retrospective' values separately. First define the investments, starting from the four different capital values:

	Prospective	Retrospective	Differences
Initial	100	120	Revaluation of initial capital 20
Final	110	135	Revaluation of final capital 25
Differences:	Prospective Investment 10	Retrospective Investment 15	

Equations:

Prospective Income = Prospective Consumption + Prospective Investment.

Retrospective Income = Retrospective Consumption + Retrospective Investment.

Difference: 'Profits' = Consumed profits + Invested profits.

In a simple case where the expectations of yields, but not the expectations of the interest rate have changed, profits are identical with interests on the revaluation amount. The revaluation amount itself (change of 'goodwill') is never contained in dynamic profits and is consequently not a part of (retrospective) income. The 'difference between savings and investment' in Mr. Keynes' 'Treatise' (of 1930) was possibly a difference between prospective and retrospective investments – unless it was the result of a comparison between the capital investments in two different periods.

Statistical analysis of savings. Two methods are used: (1) Increment of goods. Stocks of short duration are naturally free from large revaluations. Comparability of physical units and existence of competitive markets permits of computing both initial and final capital amounts, at prospective or retrospective prices. This is not possible with highly diversified and not competitive durable goods ('going concerns'). Usual method: gross investments minus depreciation. The latter is arbitrary except in the case of qualitatively identical replacement in which case depreciation is the difference between final and initial capital in absence of repairs. In general, to each imaginable time-series of desirable yields corresponds a different depreciation.

(2) Increment of claims (sometimes called 'money savings') with internal savings of enterprises added. This sum can approach the actual savings if only those increments of claims or internal savings are included which accompany net increments of goods. The gross figures of internal savings often contain positive, or at least (with cautious accountants) negative revaluations; capital issues, even if corrected for vendor's shares, conversions, etc., may still contain revaluations; bank deposits may increase when a new loan is made to finance, not commodity increments, but commodity revaluation, or consumption. It is likely that the claims' method gives positive errors during booms and negative during depressions. But this has little to do with profits or losses, which are, at most, interests on revaluation but not the revaluation itself. The comparison of estimates of 'money savings' (including undistributed profits) with the increments of capital goods has been tried by different authors (e.g., *Institut fuer Konjunkturforschung, Sonderheft* 22; C. Clark, *National Income*, pp. 136–138). It does not seem to yield useful results.

APPENDIX I. EVALUATION OF 'CARVER'S EFFECT'

1 Income group	2 Income per family	3 Savings per family	4 Ratio interest to income	5 Ratio savings to total savings	6 Remarks, results
I. Germany, 1926/7 (Wagemann's data)					
000 M.	000 M.	M.	%	%	
100–	200	100000	27	12.3	*Results:*
50–	58.4	17909	19	6.0	$s_i = 1.5$
16–	25.3	3684	6	10.7	$m = 6.6$
8–	11.5	881	3	7.1	Carver's effect
5–	6.9	519	5	9.1	$= 0.1$
3–	4.2	258	3	12.6	
0–	1.8	90	1	42.2	
II. U.S.A., 1929 (Brooking's Institution's data): Non-Farmers					
000 $	000 $ [c])	$ [c])	% [a]	% [b])	Remarks:
1000–	3650	2400000	52	17.1	[a] 'Non-occupational
250–	420	235000	44	11.6	incomes' reduced
100–	135	67500	39	7.5	by 27% for specu-
50–	63	29800	35	8.2	lative gains.
20–	30	11800	30	13.0	[b] Incomes below
15–	17.20	6600	24	14.1	3000 $ omitted.
10–	12.06	4270			[c] Averages for 3 up-
9–	9.47	2720	18	11.7	per classes less
8–	8.37	2240			reliable.
7–	7.46	1720			
6–	6.46	1320			
5–	5.46	990	14	9.8	*Results:*
4.5–	4.74	780			$s_i = 1.85$
4–	4.24	620			$m = 31.5$
3.5–	3.74	510	12	7.0	Carver's effect
3–	3.23	400			$= 0.6$

N.B. The income-elasticity of savings (s_i) was found by fitting a straight line to the logarithms of family incomes and savings (col. 2 and 3). In Germany, savings were found from Inland Revenue data as differences between capitalised revenues from capital in two successive years. ('Kapitalbildung und Steuersystem': Konferenz von Eilsen (ed. by Colm and Neisser), Berlin, 1930: Wagemann's contribution on p. 187 seq; table on p. 201). For U.S.A., v. 'America's Capacity to Consume', p. 261, pp. 218–221, p. 96. Groupings according to earnings from capital only were adjusted by Wagemann into groups of total incomes. Similarly, we had to adjust (by graphical interpolation) the table of the Brookings' Institution (p. 221) from 'earning classes' to groups of total incomes. American incomes below $3000 were omitted because below that limit 'non-occupational income' was almost negligible. Such as there was came chiefly from home ownership and from work at odd jobs, i.e., was not interest on capital. A similar omission of the lowest income-group (below 3000 M.) from the German table would make $m = 10.9$ and Carver's effect $= 0.16$.

APPENDIX II

s = savings.
s_i = elasticity of savings' supply with respect to income.
s_r = elasticity of savings' supply with respect to interest rate.
r = interest rate.
i = income = wages + r. capital.
t = accumulation time.
f = future value of savings = $f(i, r)$.
m = ratio of interests to income.
k = ratio of savings to income.
δ = elasticity of substitution between present and future goods.

$$se^{rt} = f \quad (1); \qquad \frac{\partial f}{\partial i} \cdot \frac{i}{f} = s_i \quad (2); \qquad \frac{di}{dr} = \frac{mi}{r} \quad (3).$$

Differentiate (1) with respect to r:

$$\frac{ds}{dr} e^{rt} + ste^{rt} = \frac{\partial f}{\partial i} \cdot \frac{di}{dr} + \frac{\partial f}{\partial r}.$$

Multiply by r/s, and consider (2) and (3).

$$\frac{ds}{dr} \frac{r}{s} e^{rt} + rte^{rt} = \frac{fms_i}{s} + \frac{\partial f}{\partial r} \frac{r}{s},$$

or, by (1):

$$s_r e^{rt} + rte^{rt} = ms_i e^{rt} + \frac{\partial f}{\partial r} \frac{r}{s} \quad (4).$$

Now, the demand elasticity for future goods

$$-\frac{\partial f}{\partial (e^{-rt})} \cdot \frac{e^{-rt}}{f} = ks_i + (1-k)\,\delta.$$

$$\therefore \frac{\partial f}{\partial r} = ste^{rt} \left[ks_i + (1-k)\,\delta\right].$$

and from (4)

$$s_r = -rt + ms_i + rt\left[ks_i + (1-k)\,\delta\right].$$

NOTES

* Presented at a Group Meeting of The Manchester Statistical Society.

[1] The elasticity s_i is not very different in the two countries (1.85 and 1.5 respectively). But the average ratio of interests to total incomes, weighted according to the contribution of each income-group to total savings, is much larger in U.S.A.

43

AN EMPIRICAL ANALYSIS OF THE LAWS OF DISTRIBUTION*

(1936)

When Goethe visited, in 1786, the amphitheatre of Verona, he meditated on its crater shape:

> Whenever something spectacular happens in an open place and everybody rushes to see it those at the back try, in every possible way, to climb higher than those in front: they jump on benches, roll barrels together, drive up carts, bridge the gaps with planks, swarm on to a near-by hill, and thus in no time a crater is formed. If the spectacle often occurs on the same spot some light structure is put up. (*Italienische Reise*.)

Here the crater-like shape of the amphitheatre appears as one of those 'empty boxes', which any generalising, *a priori* description of rational activities of massed men purports to construct. Thus, the falling 'normal' demand curve, the ascending long-run supply curve, etc., have been called 'empty boxes'. But, after all, they are not absolutely empty. Either simply because they are not absolutely *a priori* but contain precisely that amount of our empirical knowledge of human behaviour which we have put into them, or because (as, I believe, modern Phenomenology thinks) to be *a priori* is, even outside the domain of mathematical intuition, not necessarily the same as to be void of new contents. Whatever the case may be, we certainly learn from Pure Economics a few things not altogether banal. The *first* thing worth knowing is the 'determinateness' of a system. We learn (by a process of thought which, in its mathematical transcription, reduces to the counting of 'unknowns' and of equations) whether a problem is 'fully explained', i.e. whether a given set of conditions fully determine the set of facts to be explained, so that none of the given conditions is superfluous and no further ones are needed. That certain conditions are likely to produce certain human reactions, this is of course a postulate akin to Goethe's statement that "those at the back try to climb over those in the front." Certainly we are not rich in reasonable postulates of this sort. We know, e.g., that a prospect of high profits in the future tends to increase the entrepreneurs' activity in the present. But we have no well founded answer to the more important question, how often the entrepreneurs conclude from high profits realised in the past that high profits will accrue in the future. We know almost nothing of the direction (let alone the amount) in which the interest-rate influences the supply of capital, or the wage-rate the supply of labour. We know, therefore, sometimes very little about the solutions of a system even if we are able to state whether it is a determinate one. Yet we can, in most cases, exhaust the list of possible alternative postulates – e.g. by calling up that all-exhaustive triad. 'More, Less, and Equal' – and arrive thus at a list of possible alternative solutions.

Therefore, with or without those postulates which aspire at being immediate and infallible messengers of a banal Truth – with or without this well-fed but uninteresting Bourgeoisie – the *second* task of Pure Economics can be performed: the investigation of the *signs*. We analyse the rate of change of one magnitude with respect to another; if it is positive, we have an increasing, otherwise a decreasing, or a constant, function. We analyse the sign of the rate of change of this rate of change in order to see whether the function at its turning point is at its maximum (which, in Economics, in many cases means stable equilibrium), or at its minimum (which often means an unstable equilibrium). The answer we find in the 'box' will be categorical or optional according to whether the postulates which we had put into it were categorical or optional.

Hier stock' ich schon. No further does Pure Economics lead. If its results are optional, which of the alternatives is the most probable? But even if some solutions are categorical, as far as signs are concerned; even if we know that certain forces, when considered in isolation, always produce, *ceteris paribus*, effects in a certain and not in an opposite direction, knowledge of this sort still leaves us as helpless as before, when we try to find the direction (let alone the amount) of the composite results of mutually opposed forces. What we really need to know is the numerical values, not only the signs, of our magnitudes. Now, even for the first two tasks we have described, viz. the study of determinateness and of signs, the common knowledge of human behaviour does not always supply sufficient raw material. For the *third* task, the *numerical* analysis, an extension of our knowledge of facts is simply indispensable.

Two sorts of amphitheatrically-shaped diagrams have become, in recent times, more popular among economists than they were before. The one deals with the subjective, the other with the objective data of the economic system. The 'indifference-map' describes the state of a man's taste in terms of all the commodities at his choice; the 'productivity-map' describes the state of technique, i.e. the possible amounts of production in terms of all the accessible factors of production. These maps are less familiar to the readers of Marshall than the 'elasticities'. The latter measure the ratios between mutually connected relative changes of two magnitudes: such as the demand and the price; or the supply and the cost; or the quantity of a factor used and of the output produced. Elasticities can be easily obtained from the 'maps', which are indeed a more comprehensive method of description.

Professor Douglas' book, in its first two parts, is a bold attempt to find, by the use of statistical data, the shape of the production map – and, hence, the magnitude of the elasticity of the product with respect to either capital or labour – for U.S.A. in 1890–1922; for Massachusetts 1890–1926; and for New South Wales 1901–1927. For the two American areas he gets $\frac{3}{4}$ and $\frac{1}{4}$ as the elasticities of the product with respect to labour and capital respectively; for New South Wales the figures are $\frac{2}{3}$ and $\frac{1}{3}$. "During the period from 1890 to 1922 an increase of 1 per cent in the quantity of labour in manufacturing in the United States, with the quantity of capital constant, would normally lead to an increase of $\frac{3}{4}$ per cent in physical product," etc.[1] The main statistical source was the Census of Production, but further subsidiary sources (for interpolating between the census years, etc.) were also used.

If, or so long as, the formula is true, it is possible to calculate from it, for each given amount of capital and of working population, not only the total product but also the rates of marginal returns to labour and capital, i.e. the wage-rate and (as Professor Douglas thinks) the interest-rate.[2] Thus the influence of the wage-rate demanded on the amount of labour employable, i.e. the demand function for labour, can be derived from the formula for the above 'production map'. And, similarly, Professor Douglas claims to have derived a demand function for what he calls capital.

Thus, the production map and its derivates, the *demand* functions for labour and capital, are the result of Part I (theoretical) and Part II (numerical) of his work. It is duly completed, in Part III, by an admirable, theoretical and numerical analysis of the *supply* side of the factors of production. He studies the short-run supply of labour (response of the proportion employed, and of the hours of work, to wage-rates); the long-run supply of labour (response of the population movement to wage-rates); and the supply of savings in response to interest-rates, and of natural resources. The brilliant critical summaries of the discussions of the relationship between poverty and fertility, and between interest-rate and thrift, can hardly be surpassed in both comprehensiveness and clearness.

No doubt, some further relationships not included in Professor Douglas' list might prove relevant to a still more realistic description of the equilibrium of the factors of production. E.g. the effect of the income-distribution on the quantities of different goods consumed, and, therefore, on the shape of the production function, ought to be studied. Further, Professor Douglas' assumption of perfect competition between entrepreneurs – and, accordingly, the general form of his formula, which is based on this assumption – should be treated as a first approximation only. Finally, the analysis of equilibrium should be supplemented by the analysis of disequilibria lest certain facts correctly observed by politicians (e.g. the fact that the poor are in general the non-hoarders) should remain for all their practical importance, a mere 'disturbing factor' to economic experts. Yet, the bold plan of Professor Douglas is well rounded-off in itself because it does embrace a set of conditions – the demand and supply functions – which, taken by themselves, would fully determine the facts in question, viz., labour and capital employed, amount produced, wage- and interest-rates. Readers not versed in equilibrium theories will learn from the mere architecture of this book that many of the popular theories of wages are half-theories, or, to use Marshall's simile, half-scissors.

Pure theory has helped Professor Douglas to select carefully the necessary number of relationships for a given number of unknowns. His production map itself is, at least partly, taken from a box of pure theory. It is based on the theorem advanced by Wicksteed and others and perfected by Wicksell (and recently by Dr. Hicks): that under free competition between entrepreneurs the 'returns to the scale' (as distinct from the returns to a single factor) must, in equilibrium, be constant. If this were not the case too large enterprises would be split up in smaller ones, and the enterprises too small would merge together to larger ones. A double amount of all factors must, therefore, result in a double product. This theorem limits the field of possible production functions to the 'homogeneous linear' ones, i.e. to functions which double if all their independent variables double. Out of this still indefinite field Professor Douglas selects, for the sake of convenience, those with elasticities independent of the amounts, i.e. the functions of the type $P = b \cdot L^k C^{1-k}$. Ultimately he finds, by the 'method of least squares', that $k = \frac{3}{4}$ suits better than any other value the facts for U.S.A.

The reasoning thus consists of three steps: a theoretical selection; a further selection from the point of view of convenience; and a final selection, by statistical methods.

The first, or theoretical, step of Professor Douglas, viz. the use of the 'box' called 'constant returns to scale' provokes a theoretical objection. Capital, in a sense of the total value of physical goods used in production, can hardly be considered as a strictly independent variable, since it depends on the way in which the invested labour is distributed in time. It is nearer the truth to regard as independent factors of production all the different amounts of labour invested at different times (*cf.* Wicksell, *Lectures*, Vol. I, pp. 203–4). If, then, we assume, with Professor Douglas, free entry into industry, we should say that the product is a 'homogeneous linear function' of these separate labour-amounts; and a mathematical expression of this in terms of the variables, total labour and 'capital' (the latter being the value of all labour amounts invested in the existing stock of goods *plus* compound interest on them) would *not* lead to a homogeneous linear function of these two variables. The above formula loses therefore a great deal of its *a priori* plausibility.[3] Yet this objection is of less weight for fixed capital than for circulating capital. In fact the fixed capital reflects changes in the time-distribution of labour rather slowly, and thus (think of railways and harbours!) tends to approach 'land'. And, as Professor Douglas (although not very consistently and for not very clear reasons) excludes the circulating capital at least from the more important of his statistical calculations, the objection does not in itself invalidate his results.

If Professor Douglas' theoretical step can, therefore, be vindicated, at least as a first approximation, this is even more true of his assumption of independent elasticities. It would be futile, with the data at our disposal, to attempt any more ambitious degree of approximation.

Our more substantial objection refers, however, to Professor Douglas' third step: his insertion of numerical values into his formula by 'fitting curves' to statistical data. Such a 'fitting' is always based on the assumption that the observed variations of data are due, in substance, *not* to changes in the relationship itself (which is under study), but to changes in some other relationships.[4] Accordingly, in Part II of Professor Douglas' book a function is 'fitted' to the figures of production, 'capital', and employed labour under the implicit assumption that their changes are due, not to changes in technical structure (which is indeed the function to be found), but to *other* changes, viz. the changes of some causes (movement of population, of savings, etc.) determining the supply of labour and capital at given reward-rates. In Part III, however, the supply of labour, and of savings, undergoes a similar procedure of 'fitting'. It rests, again, on a similar assumption: that supply functions themselves (which are the functions to be found) remain unmoved, the changes in the figures being provoked from the demand side only, i.e. in the first resort (so long as we deal with 'statics' only and ignore the vagaries of the entrepreneurs' mood): by changes of production-technique.

Again, even this objection does not perhaps decide the final fate of Professor Douglas' method, but only calls for certain safeguards. Strictly speaking, the 'fitting of curves' to statistical data may apply, even if the relationships under consideration are not absolutely stable but only relatively more stable in comparison with all the other relationships. As different data are used in Professor Douglas' production (and demand) analysis and in his analysis of the supply of factors, it is perhaps not impossible to find sets of data which in one case show relatively more violent shifts of supply, and in the other relatively more violent shifts of demand. The relationships described would then, of course, belong to two different states of equilibrium. But this is all right. It is logically obvious that if we should set out to describe all the relationships constituting *one* equilibrium state we should not be able to find statistical time-series, since a time-series always implies some changes. If we find a formula for the production function in U.S.A., 1890–1922, on the assumption of stable technique we cannot supplement it by a labour demand formula, which would assume, for the same area and period, an unstable technique. But we can try the latter assumption for some other area and period.

It should be clear from this discussion that 'econometric' functions can never have the ambition to be as eternal as Dante's Gate. Those functions are nothing else than short-hand records of massed historical facts. And they have a value as forecasting instruments only in so far – yes, in so far as history *does* repeat itself.

NOTES

* *The Theory of Wages*, by Paul H. Douglas, Professor of Economics in the University of Chicago. The Macmillan Company, New York, 1934; xviii+502 pp., with a Statistical Appendix and a Bibliography.

[1] Professor Douglas' formula, for U.S.A., is

$$P = 1.01\, L^{3/4} C^{1/4} \text{ (approximately)};$$

where P is the total physical product, L the amount of labour employed and C the amount of physical capital in existence; the average amounts of each of these magnitudes for a certain basic period being taken as arbitrary units.

[2] The theoretical total shares of labour and capital in the total income then work out, by easy algebra, equal to the respective elasticities – i.e., in U.S.A.: $\frac{3}{4}$ and $\frac{1}{4}$ of the product – which result Professor Douglas tries to check by income-statistics.

[3] Incidentally, Professor Douglas' attempt to check it by using income-statistics (see last footnote) rests on Thünen's conception of the interest-rate as the rate of marginal returns on physical capital. This idea is, however, not compatible with Wicksell's capital analysis as reported above. Professor Douglas' check appears to me, therefore, theoretically less convincing than to him.

[4] Cf. E. Working: 'What Do Statistical Demand Curves Show?', *Quarterly Journal of Economics*, 1927. R. Frisch: *Pitfalls in the Statistical Construction of Demand and Supply Curves*, Leipzig, 1933.

44

PERSONAL AND COLLECTIVE BUDGET FUNCTIONS*

(1939)

I. THE PROBLEM

The elasticity of demand, with respect to income, for a single commodity or for consumers' goods in general (the latter elasticity being closely related to the 'marginal propensity to consume') has recently given rise to much discussion.[1] These concepts primarily refer to the behavior of a single person or family, but they are also used to describe the relation between national income and demand. The individual and collective concepts are closely related. For example, Mr. Keynes bases his propositions regarding the interdependence of national saving and national income (the theory of the 'multiplier') on certain "psychological laws" or assumptions related to the individual. Now, it is not certain that in all circumstances all or some propositions concerning individual behavior can be simply repeated, with 'community' substituted for 'individual'. The connecting link is, of course, the income-distribution. Yet the exact form of the connection, although studied in the past by several writers,[2] is often slurred over by others. As many economists have been interested recently in the family budget data and their application to questions of national economy, it may be found convenient to have the relations between the properties of 'personal' and 'collective' budget functions[3] set out somewhat systematically.

Let r and R be, respectively, the individual[4] and the national income; let x be the consumption of a given commodity by the individual, and X its aggregate consumption. With population assumed constant, the functions

$$x = x(r) \quad \text{and} \quad X = X(R)$$

may be called the 'personal' and the 'national' budget functions for the commodity considered. It is more general, however, to call $X(R)$ the 'collective' budget function to cover cases where the aggregate income and consumption are not those of the whole nation but only of a section of it, such as 'non-relief native-born whites living in communities of 2500 or more inhabitants', or 'families with less than \$10000 income', etc.

Analogous pairs of functions can be constructed also for the total expenditure of a person or a community on all consumption goods; or for the savings of a person and a community; or for the labor effort offered, etc. The formal set-up is much the same. Therefore, the propositions will be stated in terms of a single commodity, except when a special statement in terms of total consumption expenditure presents some interest.

It requires time for consumers to adapt their budgets to a changed income. The symbols X and R must, therefore, be regarded as referring to different points of time, separated by a lag. Little is known as yet of the actual magnitude of the lag.

A practical difficulty is the precariousness of the family budget materials for higher incomes. Extrapolation may prove dangerous unless checked by other material, such as estimates of total consumption of the commodity considered, or of the plausible limits which the function or certain characteristics of it (such as the derivatives) approach as incomes increase, etc. These checks are, however, not always directly available, although we may hope for improvement. In any case the small number of the very rich will always make it inevitable to describe their behavior within large margins of error, and to calculate the effect of that error on any estimate of the national budget function. This effect is the smaller, the less the consumption changes with income; it is, therefore, the smallest in the case of necessary consumption goods not having substitutes.

II. THE 'STANDARD' CASE: ALL INCOMES CHANGE PROPORTIONALLY

The total amount X consumed by the community is the weighted sum of the amounts consumed by the individuals at the various income-levels, each weight being the proportion of the income-receivers of a given income-level in the total population. From a given personal budget function, an infinite number of collective budget functions can be derived according to how the relative income-shares are supposed to behave. We may regard as a simplest or 'standard' case the proportional change of all incomes, and consider the general case later.

Figures 1 and 2 are designed with special reference to savings. They may, however, well serve to illustrate the graphical proceeding by which any 'standard' collective budget function can be obtained by combining the personal budget function with the data on the income-distribution. The bar-diagram in Figure 1 and the curve on the same chart must be thought of as drawn on separate sheets and superimposed.[5] The bar-diagram shows the income-distribution at a certain initial situation (at which the collective income per family was $2410). The position of each

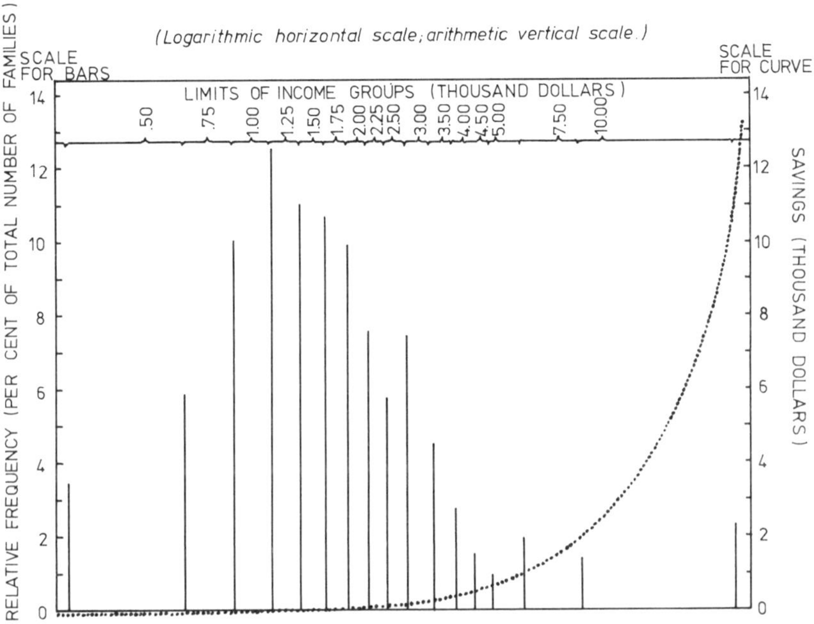

Fig. 1. Savings and relative frequency of non-relief native-born white families with various incomes.

On the horizontal scale, the bars represent 'average family income within an income group'; the curve represents family income'.

The vertical scale measures 'relative frequency of the income group' and 'savings (probably exaggerated for incomes above $ 10 000)'.

bar on the horizontal (logarithmic) axis corresponds to the average income of a given income-group in the initial situation. The height of each bar measures the group's relative size in per cent of the total number of families, i.e., the weight to be assigned to each income group. The curve, on the other hand, represents the personal budget function. Shift the bar diagram to the right by an amount corresponding to, say, a ten per cent increase of all incomes. Read off the personal budget curve the consumption amounts corresponding to each bar and weight them by the heights of the bars. The weighted sum gives the collective consumption at a per-family income of $ 2410 plus ten per cent, the relative income-shares being supposed unchanged. By shifting thus the bar-diagram to the right or left to new positions and forming the weighted sums, the whole collective

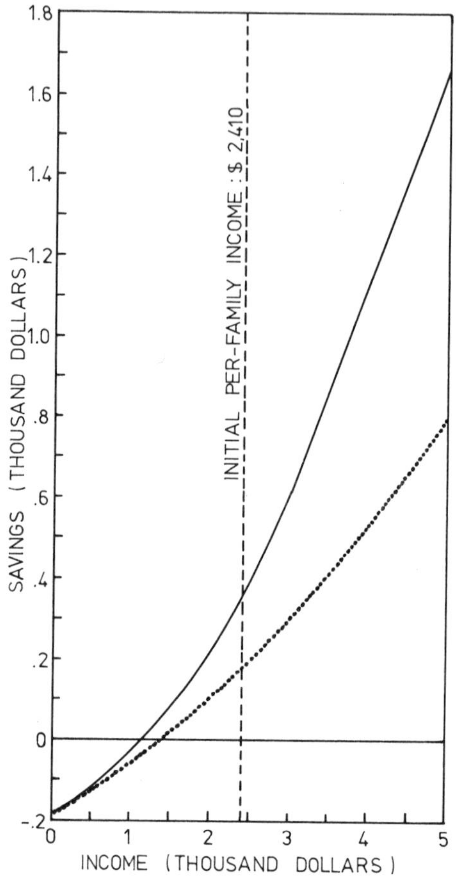

Fig. 2. Income and Savings.

The lower curve represents 'family income and savings'; the upper curve, 'average income per family and average savings per family'.

In constructing the upper curve it was assumed that all incomes were initially distributed as in Figure 1, and then always changed proportionally.

budget curve $X(R)$ can be traced.[6] It is shown in Figure 2 (upper curve) and compared with the personal budget curve $x(r)$ (lower curve).

If in the initial situation the per-family income is R_1, the proportion (relative frequency) of families having an income r is $f(r)$, and the highest and lowest incomes considered are m and n respectively; and if the personal budget function is $x(r)$, then the collective 'standard' budget function is the weighted sum, or integral,

$$X(R) = \int_n^m x\left(r \cdot \frac{R}{R_1}\right) f(r)\,dr. \tag{2.1}$$

If, instead of smoothing the budget data graphically, we succeed in fitting a curve of a given mathematical form, the procedure becomes very simple; e.g., the curve $x(r)$ in Figure 1, and also in Figure 2, is a parabola

$$x = c + br + ar^2 \tag{2.2}$$

Now, by definition,

$$\int_n^m f(r)\,dr = 1 \tag{2.3}$$

and

$$\int_n^m rf(r)\,dr = R_1 \tag{2.4}$$

Hence, applying (2.1) to (2.2) we obtain

$$\begin{aligned} X &= \int_n^m \left(c + br\frac{R}{R_1} + ar^2\frac{R^2}{R_1^2}\right) f(r)\,dr \\ &= c + bR + aR^2\,\frac{\int_n^m r^2 f(r)\,dr}{R_1^2}. \end{aligned} \tag{2.5}$$

Thus a parabolic personal budget curve yields a parabolic collective standard budget curve, whatever the income-distribution function; two of its coefficients (the intercept and the slope at zero-income) are the same as in the personal budget curve, while the third is easily obtained by summing the squares of incomes (regarding the mean of each income-class as representative of the class).[7]

As another example, let the personal budget function be approximated (as in the writings of Mrs. Gilboy, Mr. and Mrs. Stone, and of others) by a 'curve of constant elasticity η', i.e., assume

$$x = r^\eta \cdot k \tag{2.6}$$

where k is the quantity consumed (or saved) when income $=1$. Hence we obtain, inserting in (2.1)

$$\begin{aligned} X &= \int_n^m kr^\eta \frac{R^\eta}{R_1^\eta} f(r)\,dr = \\ &= R^\eta \cdot K, \quad \text{where} \quad K = \frac{k}{R_1^\eta}\int_n^m r^\eta f(r)\,dr. \end{aligned} \tag{2.7}$$

Thus, if constant elasticity is assumed for the personal budget function, the collective standard budget function has the same constant elasticity; while the other coefficient (value of X at average income 1) of the collective standard budget function is larger (smaller) than the corresponding coefficient of the personal budget function in the same proportion in which the average consumption per family is larger (smaller) than the consumption of a family having average income; larger if $\eta > 1$, smaller if $\eta < 1$.

Data on the actual aggregate savings, or on the national consumption of a given commodity, help to check or correct the supposed personal budget curve. For example, in Figure 2 the average savings of 'native-born white families in communities with 2500 or more inhabitants' would amount to nearly $400 when the income has the average value it had in 1935–36, i.e., $2410. This proportion (nearly $\frac{1}{6}$) is, according to other available sources, certainly too high. Instead of extrapolating the parabola, some other assumptions must be tried for the upper income-classes: e.g., the marginal propensity of families to save – the slope of the curve $x(r)$ – may be assumed to stop increasing from a certain income-level on; or it may be assumed to tend to a certain limit as income grows indefinitely. To satisfy this, the curve $x(r)$ may be built up of two curves adjoining each other; or a single curve may be found to display satisfactorily the properties which the savings of the rich are supposed to have.[8]

III. THE GENERAL CASE: INCOMES DO NOT CHANGE PROPORTIONALLY

The 'standard' collective budget function, based on the assumption that all incomes change in the same proportion, is a useful point of departure. In the general case, however, the various initial incomes must be assumed to move in various proportions, as shown (under hypothetical assumption) in Figure 3. (For simplicity, the case of negative incomes is left out.)

Here the initial average income per family (R_1) is used as a unit of income measurement. The upper curve shows the amount (l) which is received by those who initially received twice the average income, when the average has increased or decreased by a given amount. The lower curve deals similarly with those who initially received $\frac{3}{4}$ of the per-family income. A whole family of such curves is needed. Its characteristics may either be imposed from outside, i.e., when the influence of a given change in income distribution due to taxation or wages-policy[9] is discussed; or the attempt may be made to find whether the participation of various incomes in general fluctuations of prosperity shows any regularity. Attempts to find cyclical variations[10] of certain parameters of the income distribution other than the average income seem promising and might throw light on the factual nature of the 'participation curves' shown in Figure 3. The slope of a participation curve represents the 'marginal

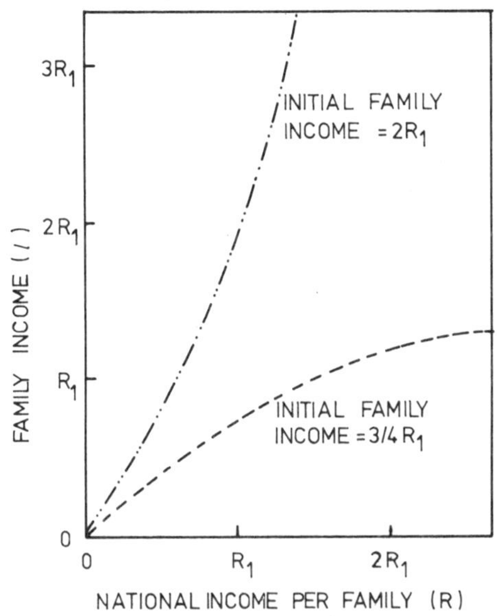

Fig. 3. Hypothetical changes of the incomes of two families when national income changes ('participation curves'). Unit: R_1 = initial income per family.

proportion' of a given personal income in a small change of the per-family income. In the 'standard' case, all participation curves are straight lines through the origin, and the 'marginal proportion' coincides with the 'initial proportion' of a given income to the per-family income. If changes in distribution are not imposed from outside, the 'marginal proportions' are probably positive everywhere (barring the Marxian 'absolute Verelendung').

These marginal proportions weighted by the initial relative frequencies of the various incomes may be called marginal income-shares; they must add up to 1; hence, if the rich men's 'marginal proportions' are larger (smaller) than 1, the poor men's must be smaller (larger) than 1, for any given increase in the per-family income. Similarly, if the elasticity of personal income with respect to national income is more (less) than 1 with the rich, it must be smaller (larger) than 1 with the poor. Now, if it is true, as often suggested, that the poor participate in the general increase of prosperity to a smaller extent than the rich, it means that the marginal proportion, as well as the elasticity of their income with respect to the average income, is smaller than 1. This hypothesis of the 'inequality increasing with prosperity' is indicated in Figure 3.[11] It will be attempted below to show how the behavior of the generalized collective budget function depends on marginal proportions, elasticities, and other properties of the participation-functions. In practical work, however, it is often sufficient to approximate the national budget function by considering separately large social sections of the community – for instance, (a) the poor, (b) the middle class, (c) the rich – and applying the methods of the 'standard' case separately to each of them, neglecting differences in the proportionate income-changes *within* each section. Collective standard budget functions for the several sections are thus obtained, and may be summed to form the national budget function.

If a change in the average income from the initial amount R_1 to R is accompanied by a change of a given personal income from r to l, then l is a function of r and R/R_1.

$$l = l\left(r, \frac{R}{R_1}\right);$$

in the 'standard' case, this function is simply a product

$$l = r \cdot \frac{R}{R_1}$$

as used, e.g., in (2.1). The generalized budget function is

$$X(R) = \int_n^m x\left[l\left(r, \frac{R}{R_1}\right)\right] f(r)\, dr; \tag{3.1}$$

it is thus defined with reference to the initial income-distribution $f(r)$ and to the function

l describing the participation of various initial personal incomes in the changes of national income. This function has the following properties: $l(r, 0)=0$, $l(r, 1)=r$; and

$$\int_n^m lf(r)\,dr=R \tag{3.2}$$

The 'marginal proportion' and the elasticity of a given personal income with respect to the average income are defined, respectively, as $\partial l/\partial R$ and $\eta_l \equiv (\partial l/\partial R)\cdot(R/l)$, both positive. The 'marginal share' is $(\partial l/\partial R)\,f(r)$. Differentiating (3.2) with respect to R,

$$\int_n^m \frac{\partial l}{\partial R} f(r)\,dr=1, \quad \text{and therefore} \tag{3.3}$$

$$\int_n^m \left(\frac{\partial l}{\partial R}\cdot\frac{R}{l}\right)\cdot\frac{l}{R} f(r)\,dr = \int_n^m \eta_l\cdot\frac{l}{R} f(r)\,dr=1, \tag{3.4}$$

i.e., [because of (2.3) and (3.2)] both the weighted mean of 'marginal proportions' and the weighted mean of 'elasticities' of various incomes with respect to the average income equal 1, the weights being, in the former case, the initial income-frequencies, and in the latter, the actual income-shares. Barring discontinuity, it follows that there exist for any given value of R and within the limits m and n, such values of r ($r=s$ and $r=t$, say) as to render, respectively, $\partial l/\partial R=1$ and $\eta_l=1$. Hence, $\partial l/\partial R$ is smaller or larger than unity for $r>s$, and η_l is smaller or larger than unity for $r>t$, according to whether $\partial l/\partial R$ falls or rises with r, i.e., according to whether $\partial^2 l/\partial r \partial R$ is positive or negative. The assumption of 'inequality increasing with prosperity', i.e., $\partial^2 l/\partial r \partial R>0$ (as in Figure 3) thus implies that both marginal proportion and elasticity of very high incomes with respect to the average are higher than unity; whereas they are below unity for the incomes of the poor. These statements will be applied presently.

IV. MARGINAL PROPENSITY TO CONSUME

The derivative, with respect to the income, of the consumption as a whole has been called 'marginal propensity' to consume. This term may be applied to both persons and communities, and also extended to the consumption of single commodities, or to savings. It will be proved that the collective marginal propensity is the weighted average of the personal marginal propensities, the weights being the marginal shares of the various incomes. In the standard case, the marginal coincide with the initial income-shares. The collective standard marginal propensity to save, when the income-distribution was as in Figure 1, is 36 per cent, if the personal budget-curve is as fitted by Dr. Mendershausen. (The marginal propensities to save are on this 'personal' curve approximately 18 per cent at

\$2000, 28 per cent at \$5000, 45 per cent at \$10000.) As its steepness is, however, exaggerated in the upper income-brackets (see above), this must be an overestimate.

Differentiate (3.1) with respect to R to obtain the collective marginal propensity:

$$X'(R) = \frac{dX}{dR} = \int_n^m x'(l) \cdot \frac{\partial l}{\partial R} f(r)\, dr. \tag{4.1}$$

Here $X'(R)$ is the collective, and $x'(l)$ the personal marginal propensity; $\partial l/\partial R\, f(r)$ is the marginal income-share corresponding to the initial income r. In the 'standard' case, $l = r \cdot (R/R_1)$, and

$$X'(R) = \int_n^m x'\left(r \cdot \frac{R}{R_1}\right) \frac{r}{R_1} f(r)\, dr; \tag{4.2}$$

the weight $(r/R_1)\, f(r)$ is the initial income-share for r. Another proof, for the special case of a community consisting of two persons only, was given by Staehle.[12]

It follows that if the personal marginal propensities are contained between certain limits, the collective marginal propensity, being a weighted mean, cannot lie outside these limits. Since, for the individual's expenditure on all his consumption we can reasonably state[13] that the marginal propensity lies between 0 and 1, it follows that for the community as well the marginal propensity also lies between 0 and 1. The same is true of the marginal propensity to save since it is equal to one minus the marginal propensity to consume. (For a single commodity, however, the corresponding limits may not always be valid, e.g., in the case of commodities of poorer quality, consumed by poorer people only.)

It also follows that if with increasing income the personal marginal propensity approaches a limit, the national marginal propensity approaches the same limit. In the case of consumption as a whole, this limit is likely to lie between .5 and 0 and depends much on the prevailing taxation system.

It further follows that if the personal budget function is exactly linear (i.e., its marginal propensity constant along the line), the collective budget function must also be linear, with the same slope. If the personal budget function is only approximately linear (as in Bowley-Allen's work), the collective budget function may be curved because of the existing inequality of incomes; this will be shown below.

In the 'standard' case, the collective budget function corresponding to a linear personal budget function is represented by an identical (and not merely parallel) straight line. Because, if the personal budget function is $a_0 + a_1 r$, the collective standard budget function is

$$\int_n^m \left(a_0 + a_1 r \cdot \frac{R}{R_1}\right) f(r)\, dr = a_0 + a_1 R \tag{4.3}$$

[Compare also (2.3), (2.4)....][14]

V. ELASTICITY OF CONSUMPTION WITH RESPECT TO INCOME

While the marginal propensities of a personal and of a collective budget function lie within the same limits so that a 'psychological low' stated for individuals can be applied to communities, the same is not always true of further characteristics of the functions, such as elasticities, second derivatives, etc.

It will be proved that the collective elasticity of consumption with respect to income is, in the standard case, the average of personal elasticities of consumption with respect to income weighted by the individuals' shares in the total consumption of the commodity in question. In the *general* case, the same weights have to be applied not directly to the personal elasticities of consumption with respect to income (η_x) but to their products with the elasticities of personal income with respect to average income (η_l).

Write $\eta_x \equiv (dx/dl) \cdot (l/x)$ for the elasticity of consumption with respect to income l; and [as in (3.4)] $\eta_l \equiv (\partial l/\partial R) \cdot (R/l)$ for the elasticity of personal with respect to average income. Then the collective elasticity of consumption with respect to income

$$\frac{dX}{dR} \cdot \frac{R}{X} = \frac{R}{X} \cdot \int_n^m \frac{dx}{dl} \cdot \frac{\partial l}{\partial R} \cdot f(r)\, dr = \int_n^m \eta_x \eta_l \cdot \frac{x}{X} f(r)\, dr,$$

while

$$\int_n^m \frac{x}{X} f(r)\, dr = 1 \text{ [cp. (3.1)]}$$

For the 'standard' case put $\eta_l = 1$. The standard case, confined to a community of two persons, has been discussed by Dr. Staehle.[15]

To find H, the per-head national income at which the consumption of the luxury by the community begins, substitute H for R in (4.4) and equate $X(H)$ to zero. Hence

$$H = -\frac{a_0 u(h)}{a_1 z(h)} = h \cdot \frac{u(h)}{z(h)}$$

$$\frac{H}{h}=\frac{u(h)}{z(h)}$$

Thus there is a simple correspondence between the shape of the Lorenz curve and the relative positions of the individual and average income at which the consumption of a given luxury begins. (For non-linear functions the reasoning can be extended, using higher derivatives and moments discussed below.)

The following two propositions are therefore true in the standard case:

If the personal budget function has constant elasticity, the collective standard budget function has the same constant elasticity.[16]

If the elasticity of the personal budget function varies within certain limits or approaches a certain limit indefinitely, the elasticity of the (standard) collective budget function has the same properties.

This is, however, not necessarily true in a general case, i.e., when the incomes do not change all in the same proportion. The elasticity of the collective budget function is then – as stated above – not an average of the elasticities of personal budget functions but the average of the products of their elasticities and the 'elasticities of personal incomes with respect to average income'. Now, we have seen in Section III that the postulate of 'inequality increasing with prosperity' implies that the very poor must have elasticities of personal with respect to average income smaller than 1. It follows therefore, for those commodities in which these poor have a major share, that if the elasticity of personal budgets with regard to a given commodity is smaller than 1, the elasticity of the collective budget is also likely to be smaller than 1; but if the former is larger than 1, the latter may be either larger or smaller than 1.

Thus, a 'psychological law' conceived for an individual need not hold for the community. This has been rightly pointed out, in a general form, by Mrs. Gilboy and Dr. Staehle who criticized Mr. Keynes. However, in the particular case considered, the criticism does not prove to be final, because Mr. Keynes' case is the first and not the second of the cases just stated. Mr. Keynes postulates (footnote 2, p. 126 of the *General Theory*) that the proportion of consumption to income decreases as wealth increases. This implies that the elasticity of consumption with respect to income is less than unity.[17] This 'psychological law' will thus hold for the community if inequality increases with prosperity and if those poor whose income has elasticity with respect to the average income smaller than 1 have a major share in the people's consumption. This assumption very likely corresponds to facts in a modern community.

VI. FURTHER PROPERTIES

If the statement that marginal propensity decreases as income increases is true for the individual, is it also true for the community? Not necessarily, unless all incomes move in the same proportion ('standard case') or unless certain other postulates are made about the redistribution of income. In the standard case, it is further true that the collective marginal propensity changes faster with the per-family income than the personal marginal propensity changes with personal income; the faster, the larger the inequality of incomes. Income inequality renders the collective budget line more curved.

Differentiating again (4.1), we have, in the general case,

$$X''(R) = \int_n^m x''(l) \cdot \left(\frac{\partial l}{\partial R}\right)^2 f(r)\, dr + \int_n^m x'(l) \frac{\partial^2 l}{\partial R^2} f(r)\, dr \tag{6.1}$$

The first term on the right-hand side does have the same sign as $x''(l)$, but $X''(R)$ may still have an opposite sign, because of the second term; it depends on the proportion of those people who have $\partial^2 l/\partial R^2 < 0$ (and therefore have the elasticity $(\partial l/\partial R)\cdot(R/l) < 1$ [cf. note 10]) and on their marginal propensity $x'(l)$. If both are large, $x''(l) < 0$ may imply $d^2X/dR^2 < 0$, so that this 'psychological law' would indeed apply to the community.

For the 'standard' case, substituting $l = r \cdot R/R_1$ in (6.1) – or differentiating (4.2) directly –

$$X''(R) = \int_n^m x''\left(r \cdot \frac{R}{R_1}\right) \cdot \frac{r^2}{R_1^2} f(r)\, dr, \tag{6.2}$$

so that in this case the collective marginal propensity increases or decreases with income if the personal marginal propensity increases or decreases.

The above proposition about the influence of income-inequality on curvature assumes the curvature x'' constant throughout the personal budget curve. Then (6.2) can be written

$$X''(R) = x'' \cdot \frac{\mu_2}{R_1^2} = x'' \cdot \left(1 + \frac{\sigma^2}{R_1^2}\right); \tag{6.3}$$

(remembering that R_1 is the mean income). μ_2 (the second moment of the income-distribution about zero) or σ (the standard deviation) can be used as measures of inequality.

It is further seen that the k-th derivative of the standard budget function is analogous to (6.2), with k substituted for 2. At zero income, it is

$$X^{(k)}(0) = x^{(k)}(0) \cdot \tag{6.4}$$

Therefore, if the personal function $x(r)$ can be expanded into a polynomial with coefficients $a_0 \ldots a_n$, the corresponding coefficients of the standard collective function $X(R)$ will be:

$$\left.\begin{aligned} A_0 &= a_0 \\ A_1 &= a_1 \end{aligned}\right\} \text{cf. also (4.3) and (2.5)}$$

$$A_2 = \tfrac{1}{2}a_2\left(1 + \frac{\sigma^2}{R_1^2}\right)$$

$$A_3 = \tfrac{1}{6}a_3\left(1 + 3\frac{\sigma^2}{R_1^2} + \frac{m_3}{R_1^3}\right)$$

where m_3, the third moment about the mean, can measure the skewness of the income-distribution and is negative.

Because of (6.4) the personal budget curve $x(r)$ touches the collective standard budget curve $X(R)$ where the two curves cross the consumption axis (cf. Figure 2). At small incomes, $X(R)$ lies below $x(r)$ but the two curves may meet again at a higher income. If the coefficient of r^3 in $x(r)$ is positive (negative) and the higher terms are negligible, the point of intersection is the higher (lower) the skewer the income distribution. This is seen by equating $\sum_0^3 a_i r^i = \sum_0^3 A_i r^i$ and using (6.5).

An important characteristic of the budget curve for the total consumption expenditure is the 'critical income' – the income at which consumption equals income so that there is no saving or dissaving. The national critical income would establish itself if there were no investments; losses would induce entrepreneurs to contract output until the critical income is reached. Does the national average critical income lie below or above the personal critical income (which can be found from family budgets and seems to lie in U.S. in 1935–36, at about \$1400)? In the case of linear budget functions, the two critical incomes coincide; and in the case of parabolae, the national average critical income lies below the personal critical income (11 per cent below in Figure 2). In a general case, however, the relative position depends, among other things, on the skewness of the income-distribution.

VII. EMPIRICAL METHODS

The preceding section must not lead to the impression that the approximation of the personal budget function $x(r)$ by polynomials, and the calculation of successive moments for the income-distribution function $f(r)$, are essential for actual numerical work. In fact, even if no assumption as to the analytical form of $x(r)$ is made, the national budget function $X(R)$ can be obtained, by smoothing empirically $x(r)$ and calculating the sum of products $x(l)\,f(r)$ for various values of l. This was shown in section two, above, for the standard case ($l = r(R/R_1)$) but can be easily extended to any other case. Or, $x(r)$ can be approximated by some formula other than a polynomial, e.g., a convenient personal budget function for the consumption as a whole,

$$x = a + br + cr^k \; (a > 0,\ 1 > b > 0,\ 1 > k > 0,\ c > 0),$$

gives, in the standard case,

$$X = a + bR + cR^k R_1^{-k} \int_n^m r^k f(r)\, dr,$$

thus requiring merely the computation of $r^k f(r)$ for various income intervals [cf. also (2.7)]. Again, it may be convenient to express $f(r)$ by an analytical function such as Pareto's, Gibrat's, etc., or by several such functions used separately for each of a few large income-groups. But it is not really necessary and need not be attempted if the approximations are poor.

No *a priori* form need be assumed for any of the functions used: the personal budget function, the income-distribution function, and the 'participation function' characterizing the way in which distribution changes with prosperity. If, however, some analytical form has been found to express the personal budget function (or if it can be expressed by two or more analytical functions, joining each other), then this will also fix the choice of those characteristics of the income-distribution which are economically relevant in the case of the commodity in question (e.g., the parameter $\int_n^m r^k f(r)\, dr$ in the example just used); use of such relevant parameters is preferable to the use of arbitrary indices of income-concentration chosen independently of the consumer's behavior.

VIII. SUMMARY

From the 'personal budget function' (relationship between income and consumption of an individual) and the income-distribution function, a 'collective budget function' can be derived. For both the 'standard' case (proportionate changes of all incomes) and 'general' case (any changes of incomes), certain corresponding properties of the 'personal' and 'national' budget function were discussed. The marginal propensities (= first derivatives) of the personal and the collective budget functions have identical limits; hence, a 'psychological law' saying that the individual's marginal propensity to consume lies between 0 and 1 (Keynes, *General Theory*, p. 115) would also apply to the community. The same is not in general true of propositions concerning the limits of the elasticity and of the curvature of budget functions. Yet it is true if all incomes move in the same proportion; so that in this case if, for example, elasticity < 1, or curvature < 0 for a person, the same is valid for the community (as in Keynes' *General Theory*, p. 126). The limits just given for elasticity and curvature are also valid for the community if valid for the individual, even where the incomes do not move in proportion but (as is plausible) become increasingly unequal when prosperity increases, provided the poor have a sufficiently large share in the aggregate consumption.

NOTES

* Paragraphs in small print contain proofs and may be omitted by the nonmathematical reader. I am indebted to Miss P. Armstead and Mr. P. S. King, of the Food Research Institute, Stanford University, for drawing charts and for general help; and to the administration of the Institute for providing me with facilities for work. I am grateful to Mr. W. A. Wallis, National Bureau of Economic Research, for valuable comments.

[1] Of more recent publications of a statistical character see in particular: Elizabeth W. Gilboy, *Quarterly Journal of Economics* **53** (1938) 120–40 and *Review of Economic Statistics* **21** (1939) 69–74; H. Staehle, *Review of Economic Statistics* **19** (1937) 133–43 and **20** (1938) 134–41; R. and W. M. Stone, *Review of Economic Studies* **6** (1938) 1–24; J. J. Polak, *Review of Economic Statistics* **21** (1939) 1–12.

[2] See, for example, H. Staehle, *Review of Economic Statistics* **19** (1937) 134 and **20** (1938) 141; J. Wisnievsky's article (*Econometrica* (1935) 411–15) as well as Staehle's contributions must be added to the list.

[3] Analogous to Edgeworth's collective demand functions.

[4] 'Individual', 'person', and 'family' are used as synonyms in this article. The families dealt with in the empirical example consist of husband, wife, with or without children. Methods to allow for the influence of the family size (by introducing it as a separate independent variable, or by using 'consumption units' etc.) are familiar. See, for instance, Bowley and Allen, *Family Income and Expenditure* (London, 1935).

[5] Both curves refer to 'native-born white non-relief families living in communities of 2500 or more inhabitants in the U.S'. They are based on the figures of the official Consumer Purchases Study. The curve was fitted by Dr. Horst Mendershausen and kindly communicated to the author (savings being defined as the net change in assets or liabilities). I am indebted to Dr. Mendershausen for discussions of both material and method relevant to the calculation of budget functions for savings.

[6] The weighting itself can also be done graphically if *double* logarithmic paper is used and the bars indicating the income-distribution drawn downward instead of upward. Applying the logarithmic scale to measure the vertical distance between the lower end of each bar and the personal budget curve, we get the necessary products without performing numerical multiplication. This cannot be done in the case of savings because of the negative values (dissaving) at lower incomes.

[7] The coefficients of Mendershausen's personal budget parabola (lower curve of Figure 2) are – if incomes and savings are measured in thousands of dollars – as follows: $a = .01696$; $b = .11108$; $c = -.18492$. If the income-distribution of Figure 1 is applied, the coefficient of R^2 in the corresponding standard collective budget parabola (2.5) (lower curve in Figure 2) is .05182.

[8] Neither (2.2) nor (2.5) is particularly suited to picture the theoretical properties of the budget functions for savings; however, the discussion of possible alternatives for this and other budget items may be profitably postponed until data for actual numerical work are fully available. When calculating the collective budget curve from a 'spliced' personal budget curve, an error in the neighborhood of the juncture is introduced which is, however, negligible except for large income changes.

[9] As in this author's earlier writings; see *Die Arbeit*, 1927 ('Volkswirtschaftliche Funktion hoher Löhne') and 1928 ('Löhne und Ersparnisse').
[10] Professor W. L. Crum has discussed cyclical variations in Pareto's α (*Review of Economic Statistics* (November, 1935) 116–30). Mr. Rufus S. Tucker (*Quarterly Journal of Economics* (August, 1938) 547–87) studied fluctuations of α (with some additional material) and of the ratio of the average to mode. Dr. Hans Staehle (*op. cit.*) measured changes of β, an index of concentration proposed in its present form by Dr. Mendershausen.
[11] The elasticity is measured by the ratio, at any point, of the slope of the curve's tangent to the slope of a straight line through the origin. Hence the curves concave (convex) to the horizontal axis on the chart have elasticities smaller (larger) than 1. This is a property of all curves passing through the origin, and having both variables positive.
[12] *Review of Economic Statistics* **19** (1937), 138.
[13] Mr. Keynes (*General Theory of Employment, Interest, and Money*, pp. 114–15) calls this statement a 'psychological law': "Our normal psychological law that, when the real income of the community increases or decreases, its consumption will increase or decrease but not so fast, can... be translated... into the propositions that ΔC_w and ΔY_w have the same sign, but $\Delta Y_w > \Delta C_w$, where C_w is the consumption [and Y_w the income – J. M.] in terms of wage-units." In actual numerical illustrations, Mr. Keynes gives another additional interpretation of his above expression 'but not so fast', viz., "As wealth increases dC/dY diminishes, but C/Y also diminishes" (p. 126, footnote 2). This involves the second derivative and the elasticity and will be discussed below. There is some ambiguity as to which of the statements is *the* 'psychological law': e.g., Mr. Holden (*Quarterly Journal of Economics* (February, 1938) 283) criticizes $dC/dY<1$ and $d^2C/dY^2>0$, while Mrs. Gilboy criticizes $dC/dY \cdot Y/C<1$ (*Quarterly Journal of Economics* (November, 1938) 120, 137). As pointed out to me by Mr. E. S. Shaw, page 97 and, to some extent, page 251 of Mr. Keynes' book show that he does not assign too much importance to the latter two varieties. Yet the subject in general is worth a little thought as the collective budget functions (for various single items of the budget) are at least as important as the much discussed demand functions.
[14] The case of a linear budget function deserves particular attention as a convenient simplification; in addition, it has been found by Bowley and Allen to be in many cases a good empirical approximation. Care must be taken, however, in correctly interpreting its economic meaning. At zero-income, a positive value for the total consumption expenditure of an individual (or a negative value for his savings) means so much deficit and has economic meaning. Again, for a single commodity there can be a positive intercept of a linear budget function with the consumption axis; such commodities have been called 'necessities' by Bowley-Allen. There is, however, no sense in talking of 'negative' consumption. For Bowley-Allen's 'luxuries', a linear personal budget function $x(r)$ should be defined, strictly speaking, as

$$\begin{aligned} x &= a_0 + a_1 r \quad (r \geqslant h) \\ x &= 0 \quad\quad\quad\; (r < h), \end{aligned}$$

where $h = -a_0/a_1$ is the income at which the consumption of the given luxury by an individual begins to be appreciable. Hence, applying (2.1):

$$X(R) = \int_h^m x\left(r \cdot \frac{R}{R_1}\right) f(r)\, dr = \int_h^m \left(a_0 + a_1 \frac{R}{R_1} r\right) f(r)\, dr$$

$$\therefore X(R) = a_0 u(h) + a_1 z(h) R \tag{4.4}$$

where $u(h)$ and $z(h)$ are the coordinates of the well-known Lorenz curve showing respectively the proportion of people having incomes above h, and the proportion of the aggregate income of these people to the national income:

$$u(h)=\frac{\int_h^m f(r)\,dr}{\int_n^m f(r)\,dr}; \qquad z(h)=\frac{\int_h^m rf(r)\,dr}{\int_n^m rf(r)\,dr}; \qquad \frac{u(h)}{z(h)}<1$$

[15] *Econometrica* **2** (1934), 357.

[16] Cf. also the discussion of (2.6), (2.7) above.

[17] If
$$\frac{d\left(\dfrac{x}{r}\right)}{dr}\equiv\frac{r\dfrac{dx}{dr}-x}{r^2}\leqslant 0, \quad \frac{dx}{dr}\leqslant\frac{x}{r}, \quad \text{hence} \quad \eta_x\equiv\frac{dx}{dr}\bigg/\frac{x}{r}\leqslant 1.$$

Also, conversely: if $\eta_x\leqslant 1$, $\dfrac{d\left(\dfrac{x}{r}\right)}{dr}\leqslant 0.$

45

ECONOMIC INTERDEPENDENCE AND STATISTICAL ANALYSIS*

(1942)

I. CONDITIONS OF INDUCTIVE STUDY

Economic equations derived from experience, like Henry Schultz's demand curves for agricultural commodities, have, or strive to attain, this practical importance: they should make it possible to estimate the values which one of the variables, the 'predictand' (e.g., demand), will assume when other variables, the 'predictors' (e.g., income and price), are made to assume given values.[1] There is, however, a proviso, silently admitted in this as in any other inductive work, whether quantitative or not. If we use the word 'magnitude' in a broad sense to include characteristics which can assume the values 'presence' or 'absence' but which cannot be measured; and if we use the words 'observation period' and 'prediction period' so as to include observations and predictions not only over time but, for example, within and between geographical areas (or any other groupings), then we can formulate the proviso as follows.

Let y be the predictand, let $x_1, \ldots, x_n$ be used by the investigator as predictors, and let $a_1, a_2, \ldots$ denote 'all other magnitudes in the world'; some, but not all, of the a's enter the proposed relationship explicitly and are called its parameters. Then every a either must remain constant or its variations must have no significant influence on the value of y. This must be true both during the observation period and during the prediction period.

If the condition is not fulfilled during the observation period, the relationship between y and the x's is a 'spurious' one. If the condition is fulfilled during the observation period but not during the prediction period, the case is called 'lack of homogeneousness' or of 'uniformity' as between the two periods. It is assumed in all inductive work that the investigator tries his best to take over all the relevant factors into the 'x' group – to use, in other words, a 'complete list of factors' – and it is also assumed that the world is not so utterly chaotic and capricious as to make the list of x's infinitely long, even if a comparatively short time (or space, or any other characteristic which may reasonably be connected with some important factors) lies between observation period and prediction period. Those historians who sincerely believe that history does not repeat itself must resign themselves to a selective description of single events. Economists have not, in general, thus resigned themselves. Even where the description of 'economic institutions' militantly opposes theory, the existence of 'invariants' is assumed, and, in fact, the interest is centered on 'standing rules' ('institutions').

II. INTERDEPENDENCE

When a single economic equation – a 'demand curve', for example – is used to predict y (demand) for given values of the x's (price, income), the causes determining in turn the x's themselves are not considered: the x's may change because of the weather or because of the government – causes which economists choose to regard as extraneous to their field – or the explanation may be found without recourse to such extraneous fields.[2] In the latter case an equation like Schultz's is regarded as a part of an economic 'dynamic system' of equations.

The interdependence between a single empirically found economic equation and the other equations of the system seems, at first sight, both to enhance the importance and to endanger the validity of each single equation. Its importance and interest are increased because economists try to use it not only for the explanation and prediction of the behavior of the 'predictand' contained in this equation but also for the explanation of the behavior of all the other variables of the system: for the 'Verification of Business Cycles Theories'.[3] At the same time, the fact of interdependence causes many workers in the field to subject every single empirical equation to serious doubts: some pitfalls in statistical research on economic data are credited to economic interdependence.

The present article leads, however, to the following conclusion: the single empirical equations are less useful or necessary for the empirical analysis of the system than it is sometimes thought; while, at the same time, the fact of interdependence is not necessarily fatal to the validity of such single equations for the purpose of prediction.

III. TINBERGEN VERSUS MITCHELL

Tinbergen's verification of business-cycle theories is performed in these steps:

(1) A system of economically meaningful and plausible equations (the theory to be tested) is set up. Their number must equal the number of variables (excluding time).

(2) For the equations other than identities the numerical values of parameters (such as elasticities, lags, etc.) are estimated either by the regression analysis of time series or from other sources – technological recipes, interviews. In the process some of the theoretically plausible equations are weeded out if contradicted by facts.

(3) From the system of equations, with numerical parameters inserted, all variables are eliminated except one – say, x. Thus a difference equation is obtained which explains the value of x at any given point of time by earlier values of x. For example, if linear relationships were assumed throughout, we obtain

$$(1) \qquad x(t) = A_0 + A_1 x(t-1) + A_2 x(t-2) + \cdots.$$

Here x is an implicit function of time. The empirical coefficients $A_0, A_1, \ldots$ are thus obtained in the process of elimination. That is, they are the result of certain operations on those numbers which either the regression analysis or other methods have yielded at stage 2.

(4) From the Equation (1) the equation of the cycle is derived: x is expressed as an explicit function of time. This is, in the simplest cases, a sum of sine functions (damped, undamped, or antidamped) and of pure exponential functions.

(5) The cycles thus derived are compared with the existing time series.

A few important objections, or corrections, can be and have been advanced.

(a) A regression coefficient is an estimate only: in economics its error may be very considerable. To obtain the equation (1), regression coefficients obtained in step 2, are operated upon as if they were exact numbers. In principle it should be possible to supplement the operations on the estimates by operations on errors, although the existing formulas for the error of a given function are merely approximations (except in the simplest cases). Would it not be simpler, however, to abstain from regression analysis at the early step 2 and to postpone the estimation of the A's until step 3? The resulting equation will be similar to (1) but with coefficients A_0, A_1, unknown (although some relationship between them may be known owing to the insertion of the data from 'interviews', etc., into the theoretical equations). Similar equations, with coefficients B_0, $B_1, \ldots, C_0, C_1$, can be obtained for the other variables – y, and z. These unknown coefficients can then, in principle, be estimated by statistical methods, although their exact distribution from sample to sample has not yet been found (see below, Section VI).

(b) More than one equation of the cycle may correspond to a given Equation (1); also, conversely, more than one Equation (1), and consequently more than one system of theoretical equations may correspond to a given form of the cycle. The former fact has been well known and gave to the economists a somewhat doubtful latitude in choosing their cycles. The latter fact is perhaps less well known.[4] Yet, both do not altogether preclude the possibility of testing hypotheses of the economic theory of business cycles in the light of experience: the observations do restrict the class of viable hypotheses, even if it is impossible to reduce the number of such hypotheses to one.

But the result relevant for our discussion is this: to 'explain' the cycle it is unnecessary and, because of errors of regression, even dangerous to compute elasticities, etc., first, and to obtain, by operating on them, the equation of the cycle. It is safer to solve the system of theoretical equations in the abstract and to fill in the numerical data in Equations (1) (or into the equations of the cycle) for each separate variate directly from the historical data. Does not this mean that the theoretical system should be directly confronted with Mitchell's empirical cycles for separate variables, omitting the intermediary (Schultz's or similar) single empirical relationships?

These relationships are important when partial decisions must be taken. But they do not help to establish the interdependent system as a whole. Some people think they are rendered meaningless by the existence of the system. To this question we proceed in the next two sections.

IV. VARIATE PARAMETERS

Suppose you fit a curve to a scatter of points representing prices and consumed quantities of a commodity. How do you know whether your curve is the demand or the supply curve? A restatement of answers given earlier by E. Working (1927),[5] R. Frisch (1933),[6] and others is also given on pages 72–81 of Schultz's *The Theory and Measurement of Demand*, although in a somewhat loose form. The answer is, briefly: the fitted curve approximates closer that of the two theoretical curves which has undergone smaller changes during the observation period. As the simplest example, consider the case of straight lines, subject to parallel shifts only. Write, for the tth observation

$$(2) \qquad Y_t = aX_t + U_t; \qquad Y_t = \beta X_t + V_t,$$

where Y_t and X_t are quantity and price, and U_t and V_t measure the varying intercepts of the two curves with the Y-axis, while the slopes α and β remain constant; U and V are variate parameters. Which of the two non-variate parameters, the slope α or the slope β comes closer to the empirical regression coefficient, say, b_{yx} of Y on X? Solving (2) with respect to X_t and Y_t and subtracting from the respective means, we obtain (lower-case letters denote deviations of X, Y, U, V from their respective means; subscript t dropped for brevity):

$$(3) \qquad x = \frac{u-v}{\beta-\alpha}, \qquad y = \frac{u\beta - v\alpha}{\beta-\alpha}$$

$$\therefore b_{yx} = \frac{\sum xy}{\sum x^2} = \frac{\sum [u^2\beta + v^2\alpha - uv(\beta+\alpha)]}{\sum (u^2+v^2-2uv)}$$

$$\therefore \frac{b_{yx}-\alpha}{\beta - b_{yx}} = \frac{\sum u^2 - \sum uv}{\sum v^2 - \sum uv} = \left(\frac{\sigma_u}{\sigma_v} - r_{uv}\right) \Big/ \left(\frac{\sigma_v}{\sigma_u} - r_{uv}\right),$$

where σ_u and σ_v are standard deviations, and r_{uv} is the correlation coefficient, of the 'shifts'. It is seen from (3) that the regression coefficient is nearer to the slope of the demand than to that of the supply curve, if the former is more 'stable' than the latter.[7] (In the case of independent shifts, $r_{uv}=0$; the differences of the two slopes and the regression coefficient are then in exact proportion to the variances of the respective shifts.) In the limiting case one of the curves (e.g., the first one) is completely fixed: inserting $u=0$ into (3), we get $b_{yx}=\alpha$ exactly. Graphically, all points of the scatter are intersections of the fixed and the 'shifting' curve; consequently, they all lie on the fixed curve. If *both* curves are fixed, $u=v=0$, and b_{yx} becomes indeterminate. Graphically, if none of the curves is subject to shifts, the 'scatter' of their intersection points reduces to one single point; and there is an infinite number of straight lines through one point.

The initial question, and the answer to it, can be generalized in various important directions. The most vigorous work on the subject has been done by Ragnar Frisch. Current debates on the foundations of the econometric methods and on the statistical time series have suggested to the present writer that complete clarity on the subject is certainly still far from universal and that a systematic and elementary treatment may be of some use if only to point out where the unsolved questions seem to lie.

A set of observed values of m variables $x_1, \ldots, x_m$ can be looked upon as a solution of m equations. The observed ith set, for example, may be the solution of a system of m equations

$$(4) \qquad f_j(x_1, \ldots, x_m; a_{i1}^j, a_{i2}^j, \ldots, a_{is_j}^j)=0, \quad (j=1, \ldots, m)$$

where the a's designate parameters. Some of these equations may be postulated from theory while others express environmental conditions or (which is the same thing) causations unknown or irrelevant to theory. If the observed values vary from set to set, this must be due to changes in at least one parameter. Graphically, if none of the parameters changes from set to set, the 'scatter' of, say, n observation points

$$(x_{i1}, x_{i2}, \ldots, x_{im}) \quad (i=1, \ldots, n)$$

reduces to one single point – the point of intersection of the m surfaces (4).

Suppose, then, that not all m equations (4) are 'fixed'. Then two questions arise. (1) Which are the equations (say, p of them in all) with the relatively stable parameters? (2) Supposing that these p equations have been identified, what are the conditions making possible the evaluation of their parameters?

The answer to the first question is sometimes provided from additional sources of information. For example, it may be taken that the equation connecting wheat consumption, wheat price, and national income is subject to negligible changes of the parameters involved, compared with the equation which expresses wheat crops as a function of price: because the weather which affects wheat crops fluctuates more strongly than the taste for this necessary and well-established component of human diet. Such an assumption is additional to the information embodied in the statistics of prices, quantities, and incomes (used for the derivation of the equations themselves) and cannot be derived from those statistics.[8]

V. LOST DIMENSIONS

Unlike the first question (location of shifting parameters) the second question (possibility of measuring the stable parameters) is capable of an answer based on the nature of the theoretical system itself.

A simple case has been discussed at the beginning of the preceding section. As far as I know, more complicated cases have not been studied in similar detail, nor would such study present much interest here. The principles which we are going to discuss will be sufficiently elucidated by studying an extreme case, namely, by assuming that all parameters of the 'stable' equations should remain strictly constant through the observations, while some or all parameters of any other equations change from observation to observation. Instead of estimating the parameters by the method of least squares or otherwise, we shall have to find them by exact solution. Graphically, we shall assume the points of the scatter to lie *exactly* on some of the theoretical surfaces; the surfaces will not have to be 'fitted to' but to be drawn through the observed points. This simplifies considerably the presentation of what follows. It means, for example, that, instead of discussing the 'normal equations' formed to obtain regression coefficients from the observations, we shall study directly the theoretical equations, with observed values substituted for the variables ('observation equations'). The somewhat conventional technicalities of the correlation analysis, irrelevant to our main purpose, are thus cleared out of the way.[9]

The problem treated at the beginning of Section IV, is thus reduced to this: of the two equations of the system, one – say the first one – is stable. Find its parameters. (Obviously, one observation is sufficient to find the one unknown parameter.) When extended to more than two variables, our problem assumes additional features. Consider first this example, not uncommon in economics:

$$(5)\qquad \begin{aligned} z &= ax+by+c \\ z &= g\log x+h\log y+k, \end{aligned}$$

these being two 'stable' equations in three variables; the third equation of the system has changing parameters and need not be written down explicitly. Regarding the parameters a, b, c, g, h, and k as unknown, we can find them from the six observation equations:

$$\begin{aligned} z_i &= ax_i + by_i + c \\ z_i &= g \log x_i + h \log y_i + k. \end{aligned} \qquad (i = 1, 2, 3)$$

We can, thus, draw a plane through the observations (x_i, y_i, z_i) and, independently, another plane through $(\log x_i, \log y_i, z_i)$.

As the next example, suppose that we have derived from theoretical considerations the system

$$\text{(6)} \qquad \begin{aligned} z &= a \log x + b \log y + c \\ z &= g \log x + h \log y + k. \end{aligned}$$

By substituting the observed values and solving with respect to the parameters, we draw again a plane through points $(z_i, \log x_i, \log y_i)$; but which of the two planes visualized by theory have we fitted, the one involving the coefficients a, b, c, or the one involving g, h, k? The question is similar to the one posed in an earlier part of the article, where the scatter was reduced to a point; here it is reduced to a line (straight line in the coordinates z, $\log x$, $\log y$). There is an infinite number of straight lines through a point and of planes through a straight line.

We have chosen on purpose an example where the original variables appear in equations in a nonlinear form; in this example, however, the case reduces itself, by a simple transformation of coordinates, to a linear one – to the problem of multicollinearity studied in detail in Frisch's *Statistical Confluence Analysis.* By extension, system (6) may be called 'multiconform'.

The case can, however, be stated more generally. Consider, for example, these two stable equations in three variables:

$$\text{(7)} \qquad \begin{aligned} (x-g)^2 + (y-h)^2 + (z-k)^2 - r^2 &= 0 \\ x + ay + bz + c &= 0. \end{aligned}$$

Geometrically, the scatter points lie on the intersection of a sphere and a plane; that is, they lie on a circle. Now, given this circle, there can obviously be only one plane on which that circle can lie; but there is an infinite number of spheres passing through that circle (the Arctic Circle may be the Equator of some smaller Earth overlapping ours). The scatter is too poor in dimensions to enable constructing the sphere. Thus, geometrical intuition tells us that the coefficients g, h, k, and r cannot be found, while the coefficients a, b, and c can. As to the analytical test: by the conditions of our problem all the observation equations are compatible; it suffices, therefore, to pick out, in accordance with the number of the unknown parameters, four observation equations for the sphere:

$$(x_i-g)^2+(y_i-h)^2+(z_i-k)^2-r^2=0 \quad (i=1,\ldots,4)$$

and three observation equations for the plane:

$$x_i+ay_i+bz_i+c=0, \quad (i=1,2,3)$$

all other observations being redundant.

First consider the observation equations of the sphere. If the left-hand term of one of these equations – say, the first one – can be represented as the function of some of the remaining ones (i.e., if the left-hand terms are dependent functions), the first equation is redundant, and the system is indeterminate. To find whether the left-hand terms are, in fact, dependent, the following theorem can be used: the Jacobian determinant of m functions in m variables vanishes if and only if the functions are dependent. A Jacobian is a determinant each element of which is the partial derivative of one of the m functions, taken with respect to one of the m variables. On differentiating the observation equations of the sphere with respect to its unknown parameters, we have to see whether the determinant vanishes, i.e., whether (identifying it by its diagonal)

$$|-2(x_i-g),\ -2(y_i-h),\ -2(z_i-k),\ -2r|=0. \quad (i=1,\ldots,4)$$

Dividing each column by -2 and substituting (from the observation equations of the plane) $x_i=-(ay_i+bz_i+c)$, we obtain

$$|-ay_i-bz_i-c-g,\ y_i-h,\ z_i-k,\ r|. \quad (i=1,\ldots,4)$$

The first column is reduced to a column of zeros if the other three columns are multiplied, respectively, by a, b, and $(ah+bk+c+g)/r$, and added to the first. Thus, if the observation equations of the plane are to be satisfied, the observation equations of the sphere form an indeterminate system, and the parameters g, h, k, and r cannot be found. But the parameters of the plane – a, b, c – can: the Jacobian for the observation equations of the plane is (differentiating with respect to a, b, c):

$$|y_i \quad z_i \quad 1|. \qquad (i=1,2,3)$$

This does not vanish, even when the observation equations of the sphere are satisfied.

We can now give a more general formulation.

Suppose that, of the *m theoretical Equations* (4) in m economic variables, p equations $(0<p<m)$ are identified as having stable parameters only. Then n sets of observations yield each p sets of *observation equations*, each set consisting of n equations. The pn observation equations are:

$$f_{ji}(x_{i1}, x_{i2}, \ldots, x_{im}; a_1^j, \ldots, a_{s_j}^j)=0, \quad (i=1,\ldots,n; j=1,\ldots,p)$$

s_j being the number of parameters.

If $m=2$, $p=1$, and the only condition for the parameters to be obtainable from observations is $s_1 \leqq n$.

But if $m>2$, $p \geqq 1$, and it becomes possible that whatever the number of observations as compared with the number of parameters, some of the sets of the observation equations become dependent and therefore indeterminate. This is shown by the vanishing of one or more of the Jacobians:

$$\left|\frac{\partial f_{ji}}{\partial a_k^j}\right|. \quad (j=1,\ldots,p;\ i=1,\ldots,s_j;\ k=1,\ldots,s_j)$$

Each such Jacobian refers to one of the p sets of observation equations but *must be evaluated by taking into account all the other sets.*

If $m=2$, then $p=1$, and the question of dependence of observation equations does not arise, although the question of identifying the stable equation of the system does. Therefore, when dealing with examples in two variables, the problem of variate parameters is easily understood, but the more general problem of 'lost dimensions' keeps out of sight.

The results apply, of course, also to linear systems, or those transformable into linear ones – like in (6); the Jacobian of a set of linear observation equations in its reduced form (in $m+1$ variables and parameters)

(B) $$x_{i0}+b_1x_{i1}+\cdots+b_mx_{im}+b_0=0 \quad (i=1,\ldots,m+1)$$

is the determinant $|x_{i1}, \ldots, x_{im}1|$. If another set of linear observation equations, in the same variables,

$$\text{(A)} \qquad x_{i0}+a_1x_{i1}+\cdots+a_mx_{im}+a_0=0 \quad (i=1,\ldots,m+1)$$

is to be satisfied together with the first, the above determinant vanishes, as is seen by multiplying its columns by (b_1-a_1), $(b_2-a_2),\ldots,$ and adding together, thus forming a new last column whose elements, as is seen by subtracting (A) from (B), are equal to zero. The vanishing determinant is, of course, common to both systems (A) and (B), and so the parameters of neither of them can be found.

Geometrically, the intersection of two planes is a straight line, but there is an infinite number of planes going through the same straight line.[10] Suppose, however, that one of the planes is tied to some condition; for example, it must be parallel to one of the coordinate planes or inclined to it at some given angle. There is only one such plane going through the line given by the equations. Analytically, this is the case if one of the coefficients in (B), say b_1, is known. While the determinant of the observation equations (A) has still the same form and vanishes for the same reason as before, the determinant of the observation system (B) becomes shorter by a row and column (because the term b_1x_{i1} is now a constant):

$$|x_{i2},\ldots,x_{im}1| \quad (i=1,\ldots,m)$$

and does not vanish.

Such cases frequently occur in practice, especially when the coefficient of one of the variables is known to be zero in one of the stable theoretical equations, so that the variable does not appear at all in that equation. Suppose, for example, the demand to depend linearly on price x and income y, and the supply to depend linearly on price x only, and both the demand and the supply equations to be 'stable' compared with the missing third equation of the system. Equating demand = supply = z (say), we have (using again the reduced form)

$$z=ax+by+c$$
$$z=gx+h.$$

The supply equation (a plane parallel to the y-axis) can be found, but not the other one.

When scrutinizing a system of economic equations, like Tinbergen's, it is not correct to discard it (as some critics do) on the sweeping accusation of the 'interdependence of variables'. As far as I see, the various theoretical systems used in his work stand the test of dimensionality. The same is true of at least some of the simpler attempts made by Schultz. He argues that the supply (z) of agricultural commodities probably responds not to current prices (x) but to prices of the preceding year (x'). Suppose both the demand equation $z=F(x)$, and the supply equation $z=f(x')$ are linear; no loss of dimensions need be feared, unless further relationships exist. In each of the two equations the coefficient of one of the variables, a different one in each case, has a known value, viz., zero, as in the preceding paragraph.

When the relationships involved are not linear in the variables but are linear in parameters and can therefore be made linear in variables by transformation, as in the cases (5) and (6) above, the same rule will apply: in equations where some parameters have a known value, others can be found, provided that the known parameters are not the coefficients of the same variable in any two equations. Also, if, in the example (7) (where the function involved is not a linear one), of the four parameters of the sphere one is given a priori, the other three can be found. This is easily shown by testing the Jacobians of the observation equations or by geometrical construction ('through a given circle draw a sphere of a given radius r' or 'through a given circle draw a sphere the center of which has distance g from the yz-plane').

Thus, in the case of linear and certain nonlinear relationships, the addition of one further variable with an unknown parameter makes the equation where this addition is made indeterminable. If the additional variable is 'time', we obtain the rule – as in Section IV which now appears as a special case – that the "unstable" equations are not determinable. Whether the rule can be extended to wider classes of equations[11] would be a problem of some practical importance, as it would make it unnecessary, in those cases, to evaluate the Jacobians of observation equations in order to find whether the parameters can be determined.

VI. CORRELATION BETWEEN AND WITHIN TIME SERIES

There is at present a strong reaction among economists against the over-optimistic application of statistical methods to economic time series. The difficulties are, of course, due not to some mystical property of 'time' but to the interdependence within the economic system. The dangers, not always clearly distinguished, are of two kinds: (1) dangers due to unsuspected additional relationships and (2) dangers due to relationships which, although assumed by the investigator, do not fit the framework of the sampling theory in its present form. The former type of dangers was described as 'spurious correlation' and presented as such by Pearson and by Yule;[12] the latter was treated in Yule's article on 'nonsense correlations'.[13]

(1) Suspicion of 'spurious correlation' is expressed, for example, in Keynes's criticism of Tinbergen's method:

> Must we push our preliminary analysis to the point at which we are confident that the different factors are substantially independent of one another?... If we are using factors which are not wholly independent, we lay ourselves open to the extraordinary difficult and deceptive complications of 'spurious' correlation.... My mind goes back to the days when Mr. Yule sprang a mine under the contraptions of optimistic statisticians by the discovery of spurious correlation. In plain terms, it is evident that if what is really the same factor is appearing in several places under different disguises, a free choice of regression coefficients can lead to strange results.[14]

The last sentence suggests that Keynes has in mind the case discussed above (Section V) as the case of lost dimensions. Pearson's and Yule's emphasis was somewhat different. They chose as the simplest example the correlation between x and y when these variates have as a common factor a variate z. Obviously, a similar situation exists when z is not a common factor but a common additive or, still simpler, when $x=y+z$; this latter case has, in fact, been often used to explain the logical origin of the correlation coefficient,[15] because in this case the square of the correlation coefficient r^2 measures the 'proportion of the variance of x explained by y'.[16]

The point about 'spurious correlation' is not the *existence* of some common cause but its *unsuspected* existence. If, on the contrary, the existence of the common cause is the very hypothesis we are testing (or a part of it) then there is nothing spurious about the correlation. As already stated, the investigator takes into account all the factors which may affect each predictand, grouping them into a system of theoretically meaningful relations. The danger of 'lost dimensions' would, but need not always, arise if there is more than one relation between the variables, but this is another question (Section V).

(2) A different question is the difficulty to apply ordinary sampling analysis in its present form to sequences of not independent observations. This serial interdependence may, again, be the result of the very relations the economist studies as his hypotheses. For example, if the supply of a given year determines the current price (demand function) but is itself determined by the price of the preceding year (supply function), then there is a relationship holding for any two successive prices. We saw in Section III that relations of this kind (Equation (1)) may constitute the very hypotheses the economist wants to test. The parameters of such a theoretical or 'true' relation are the parameters he has to estimate. The attention of economic statisticians has been too often absorbed by the question of 'removing' these relations.

Suppose, then, the variable – for example, price – has, in any two successive years, the values x_t and x_{t+1} obeying the simple relation

$$x_{t+1} = \beta x_t + \varepsilon_t, \quad (t = 1, \ldots, n) \tag{8}$$

where the 'error' ε_t is uncorrelated with x_t. The coefficient β is the unknown proportion which must, on theoretical grounds, exist between the expectation of the price in a given year and the actual price in the preceding year. The statistical problem is to estimate β from the observed series of prices in $n+1$ years.

We note that the regression coefficient of x_{t+1} on x_t,

$$b = \frac{\sum (x_t - \bar{x})(\beta x_t - \beta \bar{x} + \varepsilon_t - \bar{\varepsilon})}{\sum (x_t - \bar{x})^2} =$$

$$= \beta + \frac{\sum (x_t - \bar{x})(\varepsilon_t - \bar{\varepsilon})}{\sum (x_t - \bar{x})^2} = \beta + b_{\varepsilon x},$$

does approach the true value as the number of observations increases and the value which the term $b_{\varepsilon x}$ on the right-hand side can exceed with any given probability, approaches zero (because of non correlation between ε and x): b is a 'consistent' estimate of β. Further, the sample regression coefficient b is distributed around β in the same way as the sample regression coefficient ($b_{\varepsilon x}$) of ε on x is distributed around zero. But this distribution is not the distribution proper to the sample regression coefficient in the classical case. The difference can be illustrated on the following simple model. Imagine an indefinitely large number of urns, each bearing on the outside one of the existing integer numbers, positive or negative, no number being repeated. Each urn contains an indefinite number of slips inscribed, for the urn r, with the numbers $\beta r+\varepsilon$, where ε is a normally distributed random number with zero mean, and a variance which is the same for all urns. If we choose n urns, record the value x_r of the slip drawn from any urn r, and calculate the regression coefficient between x_r and r for the sample of n drawings, and if, for the same n urns, such samples are repeated indefinitely, then the various regression coefficients will be distributed around β in the classical way. Suppose, however, that merely the first urn is the same in each sample, while the other urns are chosen in the following way: The number written on the slip drawn from the first urn (i.e., x_1) will be the number of the second urn, etc., each successive urn being determined by the number on the slip drawn from the preceding one. We have, then, our relationship (8): the urn number, which is the expectation of the slip number, is made to depend on the observed previous slip number. I do not know whether the distribution of sample regression coefficients in this and generalized cases has been studied; and whether other, more appropriate estimates have been considered. In the interest of economic work such studies would be highly desirable.[17]

If the errors in (8) were all zero, that equation would describe the 'true path' (or 'trend'?) of x through time. The path is exponential for $\beta>0$, and periodical – with a period of 4 time units – if $\beta<0$: as is familiar to the students of the "cobweb" in economics. Similarily, if instead of (8), we had

$$x_{t+1}=x_t+\alpha+\varepsilon_t, \quad (t=1,\ldots,n;\ \alpha \text{ constant})$$

the trend would be linear. A consistent estimate of the rate of increase α is $a=(1/n)\sum_1^n(x_{t+1}-x_t)$.

So long as the trend, or path, is the very relationship we are trying to estimate, there is nothing dangerous in the fact of the serial interdependence, except the fact that the relevant statistical distributions await the mathematician who would calculate them.[18]

VII. SUMMARY

To test theories describing the interdependence of economic variables, empirical equations of the Schultz type are not a useful tool. On the other hand, their use for prediction and policy – assuming a reasonable degree of uniformity in the economic world – is not as endangered by the economic interdependence and the nature of time series as is sometimes felt. The problems of 'variate parameters' and the more general one of 'lost dimensions' are studied. The meaning of "spurious correlation" is discussed; the difficulties inherent in series of interdependent observations are shown to be due merely to the present lack of knowledge of the relevant statistical distributions.

NOTES

* From *Studies in Mathematical Economics and Econometrics, Volume in Memory of Henry Schultz*, edited by O. Lange, F. McIntyre, and T. O. Yntema, University of Chicago Press.

The article could not have been written without the stimulating influence of talks with T. Haavelmo. Acknowledgments are due also to O. Lange, J. Mosak, and A. Wald with each of whom several important points were discussed. The article was written in March, 1940.

[1] The terms 'predictand' and 'predictors' are H. Hotelling's, I believe.

[2] Of course, these delimitations need not be hard and fast (see, e.g., Schumpeter, *Business Cycles*, chap. 1).

[3] J. Tinbergen, *Statistical Testing of Business-Cycle Theories* (2 vols., Geneva, 1939).

[4] Ragnar Frisch, 'Statistical versus Theoretical Relations in Economic Macrodynamics' (mimeographed, 1938).

[5] *Quarterly Journal of Economics*, 1927.

[6] *Pitfalls in the Statistical Construction of Demand and Supply Curves* (Leipzig, 1933).

[7] The problem of variate parameters must be clearly distinguished from the problem of 'fitting a line when both variables are subject to error' (see A. Wald in *Report of Fifth Annual Research Conference, Cowles Commission* [Chicago, 1939], p. 25; R. G. D. Allen in *Economica*, 1939; see Sec. VI of this paper).

[8] If measurable indicators could be introduced to represent 'weather' and 'tastes' (e.g., humidity and temperature for 'weather' and some physiological characteristics of people for 'tastes'), some idea as to the relative violence of the shifts in the respective parameters might be gained. Or, one can go further and use those indicators themselves as new variables of the system. In this augmented system, the demand and supply equations, each of them richer in variables than before, would be reckoned as 'stable', while all shifts would be located in the equations which would describe the causation of humidity or of tastes and could be left out of the economic analysis.

[9] See, however, n. 10.

[10] Instead of studying the interdependence between linear *observation equations* (B) as above, Ragnar Frisch studied the interdependence between the linear *normal equations* resulting from the assumption that the sum of squares of the left-hand terms of (B) is minimum. If the normal equations are dependent (collinear), the correlation determinant (i.e., the determinant whose elements are simple correlations between the variables) must vanish. In the 'exact' case, discussed in the text, the sums of squares are zero and therefore

minimum; and the correlation determinant vanishes. In the practice of 'fitting' it never vanishes exactly.

[11] It has been pointed out to me by T. Haavelmo that such an extension is by no means obvious. See his paper presented at the Research Conference of the Cowles Commission, Colorado Springs, 1940.

[12] K. Pearson, 'On a Form of Spurious Correlation Which May Arise When Indices Are Used in the Measurement of Organs', *Proceedings of the Royal Society of London*, 1897; G. U. Yule, *Introduction to the Theory of Statistics* (1927), chap. xi.

[13] 'Why Do We Sometimes Get Nonsense-Correlations between Time Series?', *Journal of the Royal Statistical Society*, 1926.

[14] *Economic Journal*, September, 1939, pp. 561–62.

[15] G. Darmois, *Statistique et applications*, p. 129; M. Ezekiel, *Methods of Correlation Analysis*, p. 375.

[16] A useful approximation formula for the general case is given by B. S. Yastremsky: If $x=x(z, u)$ and $y(z, v)$, where u and v are independent of each other and of z, then the correlation coefficient

$$r_{xy}=x_z y_z \sigma_z^2 / \sqrt{(x_z^2\sigma_z^2+x_u^2\sigma_u^2)\,(y_z^2\sigma_z^2+y_v^2\sigma_v^2)},$$

where x_z, x_u, y_z, and y_v are partial derivatives, and the σ's denote the standard deviations. (Yastremsky and Chotimsky, *Theory of Mathematical Statistics* [in Russian] [Moscow, 1930], pp. 357–59.)

[17] Cf. J. Neyman, *Lectures and Conferences on Mathematical Statistics* (Washington, 1938), pp. 109–24; M. M. Flood, 'Recursive Methods and the Analysis of Time Series', Cowles Commisson for Research in Economics, *Report of Fourth Annual Research Conference* (Chicago, 1938).

[18] Of this nature is also the problem treated in Yule's article on 'nonsense-correlations'. The correlation coefficient between $\sin t$ and $\sin(t+\text{lag})$ has a U-shaped distribution if the samples are taken over small parts of the cycle: the probability of a comparatively wrong estimate of the correlation coefficient is higher than the probability of a comparatively correct estimate. This shows, incidentally, the danger implied in the method of estimating the true time lag by choosing the one which makes the correlation coefficient a maximum. But better methods could be devised.

46

MONEY ILLUSION AND DEMAND ANALYSIS*

(1943)

I

'We should not indulge in high hopes of producing rapidly results of immediate use to economic policy or business practice. Our aims are first and last scientific. We do not stress the numerical aspect just because we think that it leads right up to the core of the burning questions of the day, but rather because we expect, from constant endeavor to cope with the difficulties of numerical work, a wholesome discipline, the suggestion of new points of view, and helps in building up the economic theory of the future. But we believe, of course, that indirectly the quantitative approach will be of great practical consequence. The only way to a position in which our science might give positive advice on a large scale to politicians and businessmen, leads through quantitative work. For as long as we are unable to put our arguments into figures, the voice of our science, although occasionally it may help to dispel gross errors, will never be heard by practical men. They are, by instinct, econometricians all of them, in their distrust of anything not amenable to exact proof.'[1]

In recent months, the present writer has had the opportunity of listening to discussions of practical men on the question: To reduce the demand for consumers' goods, which of two measures is more effective, a tax on incomes at the source (withholding tax) or a sales-tax? I have heard contradictory opinions, all based on purported knowledge of 'the worker's' or 'the housewife's' psychology. Some said that a thinner pay envelope would duly impress the would-be spender; others endowed the price tag with stronger deterrent powers.

A suitable 'null-hypothesis', to be tested by facts, would be the following: If an individual's income and all prices change in the same proportion, he continues to consume the same amount of various goods as before. Actual observations deviate from this pattern. But if the deviations are so small that they might have arisen, with large preassigned probability, from chance, we shall say that they are insignificant and that the null-hypothesis is correct; we shall conclude that a small proportionate reduction of the individual's income will, apart from chance fluctuations, have the same effect as the rise of all prices in the same proportion; and the choice between the two forms of taxation will have to be made on other grounds, such as the speed and cheapness of collection. If, on the other hand, facts do deviate from the null-hypothesis significantly, we shall be able to substitute for it other hypotheses; to estimate the extent by which given changes in income and/or in any or all prices would affect individual demand for various commodities; and, hence, to estimate the relative effect on total demand of withholding taxes and sales taxes, whether imposed as flat rates, or diversified and graduated according to commodities or income-levels. The problem is familiar as 'Analysis of (individual) demand'.

For the economist, our 'null-hypothesis' has an additional interest on the grounds (1) that it is a necessary (though not sufficient) condition of rational behavior, defined as using one's income to one's best satisfaction, (2) that it supplies a justification for using 'deflators' in economic statistics and for discussing the demand relationships in terms of so called 'real' incomes and prices, and (3) that it is incompatible with important theories of unemployment.

(1) If the prices of various 'commodities' (consumers' services or goods, other physical assets, claims) are $p_1, \ldots, p_n$, and the individual wants to spend his income r to his best satisfaction, he will buy such quantities $x_1, \ldots, x_n$ as will obey the 'Slutsky equation' (now familiar to economists, owing to the work of Allen, Hicks, and Schultz) for any pair of commodities:

$$\frac{\partial x_i}{\partial p_k} + \frac{\partial x_i}{\partial r} x_k = \frac{\partial x_k}{\partial p_i} + \frac{\partial x_k}{\partial r} x_i$$

Each of the quantities demanded (x_i, x_k) is regarded as a function of income and of all prices. The relationship follows from the condition that the 'satisfaction index', U, should be maximum, subject to the identity $r = \sum p_i x_i$, where U is defined as the preference rank given to a combination of purchases $x_1, \ldots, x_n$ so that combinations with higher rank are preferred to those with lower rank.[2]

If β_i denotes the income-proportion spent on the commodity i, ε_i its demand elasticity with respect to income, and η_{ik} its demand elasticity with respect to the price of commodity k, then the following three relationships hold in the neighborhood of the most satisfactory combination:[3]

(1) $$\sum_i \beta_i \varepsilon_i = 1$$

(2) $$\sum_i \beta_i \eta_{ik} = \beta_k$$

$$(3) \qquad \sum_k \eta_{ik} = -\varepsilon_i$$

The first two follow from the identity $r = \sum p_i x_i$, differentiating partially with respect to r or p_k. The third is obviously identical with our 'null-hypothesis'; it is obtained from the other two relationships and the Slutsky equation after multiplying the latter by $p_i p_k / r$ and summing over commodities.

(2) If the hypothesis is true, the physical amount demanded, x_i, is not affected if both the income and each of the prices are divided by the same number ('deflator'), e.g., by the 'cost of living'. To divide them by one of the prices is particularly useful; in this way, the number of variables, and of coefficients to be determined in order to estimate the effect of a change of prices and incomes on demand, is diminished by one. For example, the demand for food can be represented, not as a function of income, food-price, and non-food-price, but as a function of income/food-price and of non-food-price/food-price, provided, of course, that within each of the two commodity-groups the prices of single commodities do not move entirely out of step, thus making the group price-indices meaningless. The diminution of the number of variables raises the reliability of estimates.[4]

(3) Finally, when considering the connection of our problem with business cycles, we may point out that Irving Fisher expressed the opinion that people are more sensitive to changes in money income than to changes in prices, and that he considered the consequent failure to adjust interest rates to rising prices as one cause of inflationary profits. J. M. Keynes' theory is based on similar observations, referring both to the demand for goods and to the supply of labor. This has been ably pointed out by W. Leontief[5] who suggested, in particular, two directions in which Keynes' theory can differ from our 'null-hypothesis': (a) the demand for a commodity can depend on present prices and income in a way incompatible with the hypothesis; (b) the demand can depend on past instead of (or along with) present prices and incomes. We shall presently investigate a generalized demand function, taking account of both possibilities.

II

In the remainder of the article, a method will be described which pools 'budget data' and 'market data', and thus uses as much information as possible to estimate the individual demand function. In addition to providing a test for the hypothesis formulated in the preceding section, the individual demand function can be used to forecast the aggregate demand of all individuals for any given national income, distributed in any given way, and for any set of prices.

Recently, various government agencies have estimated the aggregate hypothetical demand of a given commodity as the weighted sum of the amounts consumed by the average family in each income-bracket, the weights being the hypothetical frequencies assigned to each bracket.

Such weighted sum (line $\bar{g}$ in Figure 1, p. 217) must, however, be considered only as a first approximation to the actual consumption, because of the presumable influence of prices. To estimate the effects, not only of changing incomes but also of changing prices (due, e.g., to sales taxes, parity legislation, ceilings, production costs, cartelization, etc.), the weighted sum (which we shall call 'hypothetical consumption') must be corrected, the correction term, either additive or multiplicative, being a function of prices. The method aims essentially at estimating the correction term. In effect, the method tries to express the individual demand as a function of both income and prices, and to forecast aggregate demand as a sum of individual demands.

From the straightforward multiple regression of the aggregate demand on prices and aggregate income[6] the method differs mainly by using more information. Incidentally, it minimizes the danger (already mentioned above) of spurious estimates, by eliminating at the start the influence of one variable, the income. This is (because of the high serial correlation of the income series) of particular importance when income at more than one point of time is discussed.[7] Finally, considerable advantage is gained by obtaining the individual demand function; the aggregate demand function is unable to tell the effect that is produced by a deliberate redistribution of incomes.

The procedure consists of nine steps, listed below and explained further in remarks (a)–(i), in Section III. The data used are (1) the consumption (in dollars or in physical amounts) and income-distribution data of the National Resources Committee's study of Consumers' Income and Purchases, which refers to the year 1936; (2) the time series, 1920–40, for consumption per head, for national income paid out to individuals, per head, or 'mean income' (subtract veterans' bonus in 1931 and 1936), and for prices.

Step 1. If the income per head in a given bracket of the budget study is r, and the corresponding consumption of the studied commodity, per head, is x_r, plot a continuous curve ('Engel curve') through all the known points (r, x_r).

Step 2. Using the relative income-frequencies of the brackets in the year of the budget study (1936), form the weighted average of all x_r's. This figure is the per-head consumption in 1936. It need not tally exactly with the corresponding figure as derived from production, and other, statistics (time series of consumption). If the discrepancy is large, however, the question must be asked whether this discrepancy can be regarded either as reasonably constant or as furnishing a reasonably constant proportion of the consumption;[8] if this is not the case, the data must be judged insufficient for the application of the method. The discrepancy may be due not only to some bias or other errors in the sampling but also to differences in definition and, in particular, to processing waste, vagueness of estimated retail trade margins, different behavior of single individuals and of institutional inmates as compared with families, etc. In general, the discrepancy is likely to be proportionate to the total; but judgment must be made separately for each commodity.

Step 3. Suppose now that the mean income has increased 10 per cent over that of 1936, in such a way that all individual incomes have risen in the same proportion. Call the assumption of a proportionate change of all incomes the 'standard case'. What will be the 'standard hypothetical consumption' per head if the mean income is 110 per cent of that of 1936? Obtain the answer by reading off the Engel curve the consumption amounts corresponding to $1.1r$ for each of the several brackets, r, weighting them with the relative income-frequencies of 1936, and adding together the weighted amounts. Express the result as a percentage of the consumption of 1936 (derived in Step 1), and plot it as the ordinate against the abscissa 110. In a similar way, form the ordinates corresponding to mean incomes 120, 130, 90, 80, etc. (where income of 1936 = 100); connect all the points plotted; call the abscissae m (mean income), and the ordinates, $\bar{g}$ ('standard hypothetical consumption').

Step 4. Express the mean income in the years 1930,..., 1940 as a percentage of the figure for 1936. Read off the 'standard hypothetical consumption curve' (see Step 3) the ordinates corresponding to each of these years. Call the time series thus obtained, $\bar{g}_t$.

Step 5. Form a time series of the actual consumption per head in each of the years 1920,..., 1940, expressed as a percentage of the figure for 1936. Call the series, $\bar{x}_t$.

Step 6. Form either a series $\bar{y}_t = \bar{x}_t - \bar{g}_t$ ('absolute excess consumption') or a series $\bar{z}_t = \log \bar{x}_t - \log \bar{g}_t$ ('logarithmic excess consumption').

Step 7. Express the relevant prices (denoted below as $p, p', \ldots$), using those of 1936 as units. The 'relevant prices' are, in general, the price of the commodity studied (say, meat); the prices of its most important substitutes (eggs) or complements; the price-index of the whole commodity-group (food) excluding the commodities just mentioned; the remaining part of the cost-of-living index; possibly an index of bond prices or interest rates to allow for the substitution between spending and saving in forms other than cash.

Step 8. Compute the regression equations of the absolute or logarithmic excess consumption ($\bar{y}_t$ or $\bar{z}_t$) on the logarithms of the prices:

$$\text{(1a)} \qquad \text{either} \quad \bar{y} = a \log p + a' \log p' + \cdots$$
$$\text{(1b)} \qquad \text{or} \quad \bar{z} = b \log p + b' \log p' + \cdots$$

Denoting the Engel curve as $\bar{g}(r)$ (no analytical expression is needed to replace this empirical curve), the individual demand function[9] is – according to whether we choose (1a) or (1b) above –

$$\text{(2a)} \qquad \text{either} \quad x = \bar{g}(r) + a \log p + a' \log p' + \cdots$$
$$\text{(2b)} \qquad \text{or} \quad \log x = \log \bar{g}(r) + b \log p + b' \log p' + \cdots$$

The price-elasticities are

$$\text{either} \quad a \cdot \frac{.43}{x}; \quad a' \cdot \frac{.43}{x}, \quad \text{etc.} \quad (.43 = \log_{10} e)$$

$$\text{or} \quad b; \quad b', \quad \text{etc.}$$

The income-elasticity is

$$\text{either} \quad \frac{d\bar{g}(r)}{d \log r} \cdot \frac{.43}{x}$$

$$\text{or} \quad \frac{d \log \bar{g}(r)}{d \log r}$$

and is obtained directly (without Steps 2–8) from the slope of the Engel curve plotted on simple or double logarithmic scale; or, to give proper weights to the various incomes, it is preferable to measure the slope of the 'hypothetical standard consumption curve', $\bar{g}(m)$, (described in Step 3) over the range of actually observed mean incomes; this slope proves in many cases quite constant.

Step 9. To forecast actual consumption for any given future year, with any given national income and its distribution, and any given set of prices, proceed as follows:

9.1: Compute the hypothetical consumption per head ($\bar{g}$) for that year, by reading off the Engel curve the consumption of each bracket, weighting by the given income-frequencies of that year, and adding.

9.2: From the given set of prices compute the excess consumption ($\bar{y}_t$ or $\bar{z}_t$). Add it to the hypothetical consumption, or to its logarithm. The result is the actual consumption per head, or its logarithm. Then multiply the consumption per head by the expected population.

III

(a) All calculations can be made 'per consumer unit', 'per head', or (for food) per 'equivalent adult'. The Budget studies of the National Resources Committee give the average family size by income-brackets. Although this average size may change in time, refinements to allow for these changes would hardly alter the ultimate result.

(b) Besides subtracting the veterans' bonus, direct taxes might also be subtracted from national income paid out to individuals, and all operations might be made in terms of the remaining ('disposable') income. This refinement may have some effect for years with heavy taxation.

(c) All calculations in Steps 1–4 can be made separately for farmers and non-farmers, and the figures of their 'standard hypothetical consumption' added. This procedure is necessary if the Engel curves are very different. For the forecast (Step 9.1), again the 'hypothetical consumptions' must be computed separately for farmers and non-farmers and added, before proceeding to Step 9.2.

(d) The 'standard case' assumption (Step 3) is made because of the lack of data on income-distribution in the past. Note that no such assumption is to be made for the future; see Step 9. The error involved in assuming the standard case does not seem to affect the result (i.e., the price-elasticities) considerably. To estimate the size of the error in the case of meat, we used the OPA-Income Distribution estimate for 1941 and drew an alternative (non-standard) hypothetical consumption curve, using an interpolation formula for the income-distribution in years other than 1935–36 and 1941. We found that the elasticity with respect to the price of meat changed by less than .1. A similar deviation, but in the opposite direction, was found when the interpolation was based on D. L. Wickens' sample of income-distribution among urban tenants in 1929 and 1933.[10]

(e) The relevant prices $p, p', \ldots$ may happen to be intercorrelated to an extent strongly diminishing the reliability of the estimated coefficients. This will be shown by the standard errors, but only if the intercorrelation is not masked by errors in the prices themselves. One advantage of the method consists in eliminating one variable – income – before proceeding to correlation analysis.

(f) The wider assumptions satisfied by equations (1b), (2b) are that the individual demand can be expressed, with sufficient precision, as either a sum or a product of two independent functions $g(r)$ and, say, $f(p, p', \ldots)$. Further, in actual practice $f(\ )$ or its logarithm often turns out to be linear in the logarithms of prices; but such an assumption is not necessary, and the preliminary inspection of the scatter diagram (graphical method) may suggest another assumption as to the form of $f(\ )$. But even the more general assumption mentioned – i.e., individual demand being the sum or product of $g(r)$ with an arbitrary $f(p, p', \ldots)$ – is not strictly necessary for the application of the method. One can, instead, assume, for example,

$$x = g(r) + f(p, p', \ldots) + k \log p \log r$$

or use any other additional term consisting of known functions with unknown parameters. This refinement is necessary only if the simpler set-up proves insufficient in the sense of giving too low correlation coefficients, or a non-random time series of residuals. But even in that case, it may be preferable to measure first the effect of *past* incomes. See remark (h).

(g) Whether to choose the additive or the multiplicative set-up (i.e., formulae 1a, 2a, or 1b, 2b) depends partly on the judgment regarding the discrepancy mentioned at Step 2. If the discrepancy (which will affect the constant term of the result) is thought to remain nearly constant in amount, the additive set-up is preferable; if it is thought to remain constant as a proportion of the actual consumption, the multiplicative set-up is preferable.

(h) The individual demand function can also be expressed in terms not of current income but of income at two past points of time, e.g. (measuring time from 1935–36 as the origin and using H. Barger's series of quarterly income estimates),[11]

$$x_t = c_i \log r_{t-i} + c_j \log r_{t-j} + a \log p + \cdots.$$

Thus the 'stickiness of habits' (often mentioned as an argument against the applicability of budget studies) can be accounted for if, for every pair of lags, i, j, $(i, j \geqq 0)$ the coefficients c_i, c_j are found. Denoting by m_t the mean income in the year t, and assuming the 'standard case', it is easy to show that, independently of i and j, the sum $c_i + c_j = d\bar{g}_t / d \log m_t =$ the slope of the hypothetical consumption curve, plotted on appropriate scales; c_j can be found as a regression coefficient in $(\bar{x}_t - \bar{h}_t) = c_j n_t + a \log p + \cdots$ where $\bar{h}_t$ can be read off as the hypothetical consumption corresponding to a mean income m_{t-i}/m_{-i}; while n_t is the logarithm of the ratio $m_{t-j} \cdot m_{-i} / m_{t-i} \cdot m_{-j}$. We may choose that pair of lags (i, j) which gives to the above equation the closest fit. Since every point in the past is likely to influence the present demand, it is more satisfactory to describe demand as a function of two past incomes rather than of one, particularly in view of the turning points of the business cycle, when, e.g., a high income may be associated with both higher and lower preceding incomes. Our procedure helps to obtain the size and weights of two representative income lags without using the income-variable more than once in the same regression equation; this diminishes the danger of spurious estimation. (To avoid the same danger with regard to past prices, we would need budget data for more than one year.)

The above equation can be conveniently written as

$$x_t = (c_i + c_j) \log r_{t-i} + c_j \log \frac{r_{t-j}}{r_{t-i}} + a \log p + \cdots; \quad (i < j),$$

showing the dependence of demand on a late income and on the income-change between the later and the earlier point of time. As $(c_i + c_j)$ does not depend on the lags chosen and is approximately equal to the income-elasticity which is shown in Table I, Table II will show c_j only.

(i) The method is equally applicable to physical amounts and to dollar amounts. It can, in the latter case, take account of consumers' shifts from lower to higher qualities under the influence of changing incomes and prices. Consumption adjusted for quality shifts is obtained by dividing the average price of all qualities (price-index for the commodity as a whole) into the dollar expenditure, and may be called 'real expenditure'. In many cases, the Budget studies give data for both physical consumption and expenditure; and time series of both types are often available.

TABLE I

Real expenditure[a] for meat per equivalent adult

(Based on the following data: Budget study, 1936[b]; time series, 1920–40.)

Set no.	Elasticities with respect: To the prices of: Meat p_M	Other food p_F	Non-food p_N	To the income	Sum of price elasticities	Correlation coefficient[f]	Forecast[g] for 1941 (actual = *100*) [h]	[i]
				From budgets[b c]				
1	−.424 ±.043			non-farmers +.498; farmers +.361; all[d] +.467	−.424 ±.043	.909	100.7 ±3.3	103.2 ±3.3
2	−.604 ±.042	+.200 ±.035			−.404 ±.027	.966	98.4 ±2.0	100.8 ±2.0
3	−.554 ±.038		+.341 ±.066		−.213 ±.049	.963	99.2 ±2.1	101.6 ±2.1
4	−.598 ±.044	+.126 ±.062	+.158 ±.108		−.314 ±.067	.969	98.6 ±2.0	101.0 ±2.1
				By direct regression				
5	−.502 ±.063		+.370 ±.080	+.412 ±.073	−.132[e] ±.105	.920	99.8 ±2.7	

[a] Money expenditure divided by a price index covering main meat qualities.
[b] Unused in Set No. 5.
[c] Income range: $\frac{3}{4}$ to $\frac{5}{4}$ of 1936 income.
[d] Farmers and non-farmers, weighted by meat expenditure of 1936.
[e] Sum of price and income elasticities: +.280 ±.054.
[f] Adjusted for the number of variables.
[g] Last digit of standard error inexact.
[h] Using income distribution for 1941 estimated by the Office of Price Administration.
[i] Assuming for 1941 same Lorenz curve as in 1935–36.

TABLE II

Effect of past incomes on real expenditure for meat per equivalent adult

(Based on the following data: Budget study, 1936; quarterly time series, 1923–38[a])

Correlation coefficient[b]	Two lags (quarters)	Elasticity[c] with respect		
		To the relative income rise (non-farmers)[d]	To the prices of	
			Meat	Eggs
.983	6; 7	+.51	−.67	+.13
.982	6; 8	+.56	−.80	+.18
.981	5; 7	+.52	−.75	+.16
.980	7; 8	+.53	−.69	+.14
.980	5; 6	+.48	−.65	+.13
.980	1; 7	+.47	−.72	+.16
.950	0; 0	–	−.51	+.05

[a] H. Barger, *Outlay and Income in the United States, 1921–1938* (National Bureau of Economic Research, New York, 1942).

[b] Adjusted for the number of variables and observations.

[c] At the meat expenditure level of 1936.

[d] For farmers, multiply this column by about .7.

For forecasts of sales values, the second type (dollars) is necessary; but for forecasts of shipping space or acreage required, the first type (bushels) is more important.

IV

Figure 1 illustrates the combining of budget and market data: from the former, the 'hypothetical consumption', $\bar{g}$, is built up; the remainder ('excess') is explained by relevant prices, using ordinary regression. The 'multiplicative' set-up[12] (Equation (2b), Section II) has been used; the regression coefficients are price-elasticities. For convenience, a scale in units of the 1936 real expenditure has been provided on the right-hand margin. The results, based on 1920–40 market series and 1936 budgets, have been used to make a forecast for 1941.

The figure corresponds to set 3 of Table I. In this table, sets 1–4 combine budget data with various price-variables. In set 5, budget data are disregarded and a straightforward regression of the total real expenditure on prices and income is applied. The similarity of the coefficients of set

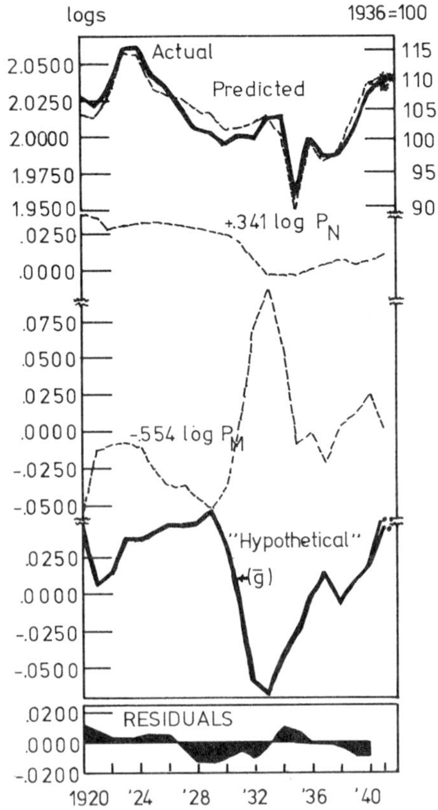

Fig. 1. Real expenditure for meat per equivalent adult. (See Table 1, Set Number 3, and footnotes, particularly the first.)
* Using income distribution for 1941 estimated by the Office of Price Administration.
** Assuming for 1941 same Lorenz curve as in 1935–36.

5 with those of the analogous set 3 is remarkable; but it does not always occur, and, for reasons stated, higher reliability must be assigned to the method that does not neglect budget data. In fact, meat price happens to be strongly correlated with the income effect (see figure); hence the usefulness of eliminating the latter before proceeding to regression analysis.

The income-elasticity of demand for meat would, then, seem numerically higher (especially in the case of non-farmers) than the sum of its price-elasticities; and the existence of 'money illusion' on this particular market would seem confirmed. Note also that the elasticity of meat demand with respect to meat price seems to lie between .5 and .6, nearer to the higher limit; and its income-elasticity lies, on the average of the whole population, between .4 and .5, again nearer the higher limit. The formulae give a forecast for 1941 in satisfactory agreement with facts. Much less reliable, on the other hand, are the estimates of the elasticity of meat demand with respect to the prices of other goods and services.

Set 4 uses more variables than the preceding sets; but the standard errors of their estimated coefficients become dangerously high, presumably because of correlation between these prices in the past. In so far as the observed prices themselves may be subject to error, their past linear dependence may not show itself in correlation and in consequent high standard errors of regression coefficients. Other tests may be needed (bunch maps).[13] It may be necessary to abstain from splitting our commodity groups into smaller ones although, from the economic point of view, there may be little meaning in, say, the 'elasticity with respect to non-food price' unless the prices of various non-food commodities and services have retained, on the whole, fixed proportions. Unfortunately, the case of proportionality, which would justify our not splitting the 'non-food' group, is only a special case of linear dependence; and, if rent is linearly dependent on but not proportionate to, say, the price of furniture, then it is statistically dangerous to use the two as separate variables; while it is economically meaningless not to do so if we want to measure their influence.

For the particular problem in hand – to test whether the sum of price-elasticities is numerically equal to income-elasticity – this difficulty is not quite so decisive: the sum of the regression coefficients changes only slowly as variables are being split up. Nor is their usefulness in forecasting affected, provided the dependence between the variables is held to be due to causes that are likely to persist.[14] The price-elasticity of the main commodity also remains sufficiently stable, for practical purposes, as new variables are added.

In Table II the effect of past incomes, in the form of a pair of 'distributed lags', is shown as explained in remark (h), Section III. The case without lags is shown in the last line of the table; others have been chosen because of high resulting correlation coefficients.

The case without lags shows the price-elasticity of meat similar to that of Table I. But the rate of income change does seem to affect the price-elasticity estimate. However, further analysis will be necessary.

V

The pooling of data from various sources is a feature of economic statistics; witness estimates of national income, or of capital formation. If we had access to the individual cards (one for each sampled family) of the Budget study, the budget and market observations that we have used could be analyzed in the following way, disregarding, for brevity, the bias in the sample, mentioned at Step 2, Section II. Assume the demand of the individual i in the year t to be

$$\phi(r_{it}, p_t, p'_t) + e_{it},$$

where ϕ, a function linear in its parameters, is common to all individuals during the whole period, while e_{it} is a random variable with expected value zero. Our data can, then, be represented by this system of observation equations:

$$x_{iT} = \phi(r_{iT}, p_T, p'_T) + e_{iT} \begin{cases} i = 1, \dots n & \text{(size of sample)} \\ T = 1935\text{–}36 \end{cases}$$

$$N\bar{x}_t = \sum_r \phi(r, p_t, p'_t)\, N_r + \sum_k e_{kt}$$

N_r = Number of families having income r
$k = 1, \dots N$ (number of families in U.S.A.)
$t = 1920, \dots, 1940$
$r = \$1000, \$2000, \dots$ (say)

Under the assumptions just made, the parameters of the 'demand function' $\phi(\ )$ can be estimated as those making the sum of squares, $\sum_i e_{iT}^2 + \sum_i (\sum_k e_{kt})^2$, a minimum. Similar principles would apply if we used still further data: a budget sample for another year, the retail sales data, by states, of the Distribution Census,[15] etc.

The method we actually had to use can be regarded as a modification of this general one, necessary because of the deficient form in which the budget data are available; instead of individual family cards, we have income and consumption averages for each income bracket. We had to neglect any random deviations which may not have cancelled out in these averages; and we had to regard the empirical curve interpolated between the bracket averages as the exact function $\phi(r, p_T, p'_T)$. (The error thus caused might be estimated if the data were published in the form of correlation tables, or if at least the standard deviations and the correlation of the sampled incomes and consumptions were published.[16] With large samples, the error is hardly considerable.) The procedure was further simplified by the choice of a particular class of functions, as explained in remark (f), above.

'Pooling' is the answer to the discussion as to whether 'budget' or 'market' methods of demand analysis are preferable. In work of this kind "metaphysical acerbity and sweeping verdicts will vanish," as Professor Schumpeter early foresaw. Nor can, thus far, any sweeping verdict be made on the question asked at the beginning of this article. Yet with the material now at hand, we can venture the statement that a reduction of money incomes (especially those of non-farmers) is likely to have a somewhat stronger effect on the real expenditure on meat than would a proportionate rise in the price of meat, accompanied by a proportionate rise in the price of other foods and/or in other living costs. The use of budget data for one year in addition to market time series does improve the reliability of a demand forecast and, to a lesser degree, of the estimated elasticities. But to estimate a larger number of price elasticities for separate commodities and obtain, among other things, a more definite test of our null-hypothesis, further additional dates will be desirable.

NOTES

* Published in an issue of the *Review of Economic Statistics* dedicated to Joseph Schumpeter.

The fundamental critical analysis of sources and the preparation of basic series as well as of final tables was done by George Garvy, while A. Kisselgof did the computing work. Both worked under a grant from the Rockefeller Foundation to the Graduate Faculty of the New School for Social Research. Thanks are also due to Trygve Haavelmo and Abraham Wald for criticisms and suggestions; and to D. H. Leavens, Emma Manning, and Mildred Titus of the Cowles Commission for the computations of Table II. A brief exposition of the method used was given in two papers at meetings of the Econometric Society: see the abstracts in *Econometrica*, **10** (1942), 92–93 and 162–73. Professor Schumpeter first encouraged the author in these studies.

1 Joseph Schumpeter, 'The Common Sense of Econometrics', *Econometrica* **1** (1933), 12.

2 See, for example, J. R. Hicks, *Value and Capital* (Oxford, 1939), Mathematical Appendix, Equation (7.2).

[3] See J. Marschak, 'Demand Elasticities Reviewed,' *Econometrica*, **11** (January, 1943).
[4] See Section III, remark (e), and Section IV.
[5] W. Leontief, 'The Fundamental Assumption of Mr. Keynes' Monetary Theory of Unemployment', *Quarterly Journal of Economics* **51** (1936–37), 192–97. See also G. Haberler, *Prosperity and Depression* (Geneva and New York, 1941, 3rd edition), Part III, p. 460.
[6] For a recent example, see J. Tinbergen, 'Does Consumption Lag Behind Incomes?', this *Review of Economic Statistics* **24** (1942), 1–8.
[7] See Section III, remark (h).
[8] See also Section III, remark (g).
[9] (1a) is obtained from (2a) by averaging all individuals and remembering the definitions. (1b) is obtained from (2b) in a similar way, after taking antilogarithms. As explained in remark (f), below, the method applies to a much wider class of functions. Over a small range of changes, the choice of the function is of limited importance. The use of logarithms of economic variables may often make the distribution of random terms of regression equations more near to normal, and the application of standard error formulae more justifiable. To test the 'null-hypothesis' of Section I, the set-ups used here are particularly convenient, as is seen from the simple form of the elasticities given presently. The demand function (2a) and the demand function corresponding to (2b) are homogeneous of zero degree if the elasticities sum up to zero.
[10] D. L. Wickens, *Residential Real Estate* (National Bureau of Economic Research, New York, 1941).
[11] Harold Barger, *Outlay and Income in the United States, 1921–1938* (National Bureau of Economic Research, New York, 1942). The 'additive' set-up chosen in the text and analogous to (2a) rather than (2b) of the previous discussion permits of using separate data, and calculating separate lag-coefficients, for farmers and non-farmers.
[12] The additive set-up gives almost identical results.
[13] See, e.g., J. Tinbergen, *Statistical Testing of Business-Cycle Theories* (Geneva, 1939), Vol. 1, pp. 27–33, and 141–46. There is reason to believe that price data are subject to smaller errors than consumption data. This gives additional credibility to the 'classical' regression coefficients shown in the table.
[14] The forecast, i.e., the sum of regression coefficients *weighted* by the prices of a given year, is not affected by the linear relation between the prices. And the *unweighted* sum of the regression coefficients (the magnitude which we are estimating to test our null-hypothesis) does not, as a rule, differ from the weighted sum.
[15] Used with promising results by W. Draeger.
[16] See also P. S. Dwyer, 'Grouping Methods', *Annals of Mathematical Statistics* (1942).

RANDOM SIMULTANEOUS EQUATIONS AND THE THEORY OF PRODUCTION* **

(1944)

Co-author: W. H. ANDREWS

INTRODUCTION

§1. To describe and measure causation, the economist cannot perform experiments. That is, he cannot choose one variable as 'dependent', and, while keeping the other, 'independent', ones under control (i.e., while making them assume deliberately chosen sets of values), watch the values taken by the dependent, i.e., uncontrolled variable. The economist has no independent variables at his disposal because he has to take the values of all variables as they come, produced by a mechanism outside his control. This mechanism is expressed by a system of simultaneous equations, as many of them as there are variables. The experimenter can isolate one such equation, substituting his own action for all the other equations. The economist cannot.

For example, in agricultural experimentation preassigned quantities of fertilizers are added to the soil of various plots, and the yields compared. Substitute 'firms' for 'plots', and 'labor, capital' for 'nitrate, phosphate'. Can the economist measure the effect of changing amounts of labor and capital on the firm's output – the 'production function' – in the same way in which the agricultural research worker measures the effect of changing amounts of fertilizers on the plot's yield? He cannot because the manpower and capital used by each firm is determined by the firm, not by the economist. This determination is expressed by a system of functional relationships; the production function, in which the economist happens to be interested, is but one of them. Suppose, for example, that each firm chooses its labor and capital amounts so as to make profit as large as possible; but has no influence on prices (perfect competition). Writing[1] x_0 for net output (product value minus the value of raw materials and depreciation), x_1 for labor, x_2 for capital used, and p_0, p_1, p_2, for the corresponding prices, we have – subject to more detailed explanations which will be given in Section I – the 'production equation', say

$$(1) \qquad x_0 = \phi(x_1, x_2).$$

Since profit $= p_0x_0 - p_1x_1 - p_2x_2$, its assumed maximization with respect to labor and to capital, respectively, gives the 'marginal-productivity equations'

$$(2), (3) \qquad \partial x_0/\partial x_1 = p_1/p_0, \qquad \partial x_0/\partial x_2 = p_2/p_0.$$

Thus, the quantities x_1 and x_2 are determined (just as x_0 is) by the equation characteristic of the firm, not by the fiat of the experimenter. x_1 and x_2 are not 'independent variables' because they are not under control. The economist is confronted not only with the single equation (1) in which he may be interested; but with a system of three equations none of which he can ignore.

The single equation – say, one analogous to (1) – which an agricultural experimenter would be able to isolate in his case, is a 'stochastic', or 'random' one: the yield obtained from a given plot with a given combination of fertilizers is, in general, not exactly equal to the yield obtained with the same combination of fertilizers applied to another plot; or at least the yields as measured with necessarily imperfect instruments will not be exactly equal. This is ascribed to the combined work of numerous unidentifiable causes to which each individual plot is exposed ('erratic' factors) or to which at least each measuring action of the observer is exposed ('errors of measurement'). These causes are comparable to the causes affecting the drawing of lots from urns, though the drawing scheme need not be the simple one of successive independent drawings from an urn in which the lots are distributed in some simple way. It suffices to assume, quite generally, that when the identifiable causes (amounts of fertilizers) are fixed, the individual measurements will take, owing to the nonidentifiable causes, certain values with certain, though possibly unknown, probabilities; that is, those values would tend to occur in certain, though possibly unknown, proportions if the number of observations could be increased indefinitely. Accordingly, the relationship expressing the yield as a function of the amounts of fertilizers used will be a 'random' function: it will change from plot to plot (or from measurement to measurement) and can be represented as a function that has at least one 'random parameter', i.e., a parameter that assumes different values with certain, though possibly unknown probabilities.

Similar assumptions can be made (and are made, consciously or not) in the statistical work relating to economics. For example, the production function (1) will change, even within the same industry, from firm to firm and from year to year, depending on the technical knowledge, the will, effort, and luck of a given entrepreneur: these factors can be summarized as 'technical efficiency', and may be represented by one or more random parameters. If a single parameter, say ε_f, suffices to characterize the 'technical efficiency' of a firm f, while the production function is in all other respects similar for all firms, we may write for this firm

$$(1') \qquad x_0 = \phi(x_1, x_2, \varepsilon_f)$$

or

$$x_0 = \phi_f(x_1, x_2).$$

The simple form (1′) states that the production functions of various firms belong to a one-parameter family, the changing parameter being ε_f, the 'technical efficiency'. It is further clear that Equations (2), (3), involving as they do the derivatives of the function ϕ, are also random equations. As will be explained in the next chapter, they will be random for other reasons, too: differences in the prices paid or received by various firms (if we drop, as we realistically must, the assumption of perfect competition); differences in what may be called 'economic efficiency' of various firms, i.e., the ability or willingness to choose, or luck in choosing the most profitable combination of resources. This will be taken up in Section I (especially §§11 *et seq.*) where the functions and concepts will be further specified, for purposes of both illustration and statistical manageability. We shall write here quite generally the random equations taking the place of (2), (3), by introducing further random parameters η_f, θ_f,

$$(2'), (3') \qquad \partial x_0/\partial x_1 = \lambda(\eta_f, p_1/p_0), \qquad \partial x_0/\partial x_2 = \kappa(\theta_f, p_1/p_0),$$

where $\lambda(\ )$ and $\kappa(\ )$ are certain functions common to all firms.

Our object, so far, has been to state the similarity and difference between measuring the effect of changing fertilizer amounts on the yield of experimental plots, and measuring the effect of changing labor and capital amounts on the output of freely deciding firms. The similarity: in both cases we deal with random equations. The difference: in the case of a firm we have a system of such equations; in the case of experimental plots, a single equation can be isolated.

Let there be $v+1$ variables $x_0, x_1, \ldots, x_v$ connected by $(v+1)$ equations involving s random parameters $\pi_1, \ldots, \pi_s$. If the observations are not controlled, call the values taken by the random parameters in the kth observation (year, firm, plot), $\pi_{1k}, \ldots, \pi_{sk}$ $(k=1, \ldots, n)$. The observed values $x_{0k}, \ldots, x_{vk}$ of the variables must, then, satisfy a system of equations, say

$$f_i(x_{0k}, \ldots, x_{vk}; \pi_{1k}, \ldots, \pi_{sk})=0, \quad (i=0, \ldots, v;\ k=1, \ldots, n).$$

This is the economist's situation.

If, on the other hand, all variables but one (say, x_0) are controlled, the above $v+1$ equations are replaced by the following:

$$f_0(x_{0k}, \ldots, x_{vk}; \pi_{1k}, \ldots, \pi_{sk})=0,$$
$$x_{1k}=c_{1k}, \ldots, x_{vk}=c_{vk} \quad (k=1, \ldots, n),$$

where $c_{1k}, \ldots, c_{vk}$ are constants assigned by the experimenter. He may change them from experiment to experiment; but, unlike the random parameters (the π's), the c's are considered constant from sample to sample. They determine the conditions of the experiment; any fluctuations in x_0, while the c's are fixed, are ascribed to changes in the π's. This is the agricultural research worker's situation.[2]

§2. The importance of simultaneous random equations for economic research has been recently emphasized by Haavelmo [21], [22]. Section II of the present article will illustrate the application of methods suggested by him and by Mann and Wald [31]. Their work has brought further clarification to the older debate on "pitfalls in the statistical construction of demand and supply curves" (Frisch [18]) and on "what do statistical demand curves show?" (Working [50]). That discussion was started at least as early as 1910, when Pigou [36] had to recapitulate economic theory to explain the fact that the "statistical demand curve" for steel, i.e., the curve fitted (by H. L. Moore [34]) to the data on price and consumption of steel was an increasing one; and to point out that it could in no sense claim to be a demand curve. L. R. Klein [28] made an analogous point in discussing relationships between investment and income.

Discussion of the pioneer work of Paul H. Douglas [8]–[16] points in the same direction. Bronfenbrenner [3], [10], and Reder [38], gave the name of "interfirm production functions" to functions fitted to the data on the output, manpower, and capital of a number of individual firms. They raised doubt whether these functions can be identified with the production function as understood by economists.[3]

As the lessons of the discussion on demand functions are better known, and yet do not seem to have been fully applied in the more recent discussion on production functions, those lessons may be usefully recalled in this introduction. Suppose, then, the per-head consumption (q) and the price (p) of a commodity has been measured in some of the 48 states of the Union. Suppose the commodity to be perishable, hence its stocks negligible, i.e., consumption = demand = supply. In general, each of the states will show a different price and a different consumption per head. These differences will be ascribed to each state's having a somewhat different demand and supply curve compared with that of any other state. Write for the state k

(4) $q = D_k(p)$ (demand curve),
(5) $q = S_k(p)$ (supply curve).

This determines the observed pair of values p, q for each state, as shown on a scatter diagram in the (p, q)-plane. We can also regard k as the number assigned to a state after they had been arranged in some – e.g., alphabetical – order:

(4′), (5′) $q = D(p, k), \quad q = S(p, k)$,

and can regard the scatter diagram as representing a function (discontinuous and, in general, multivalued)

(6) $q = q(p)$, say,

obtained from (4′), (5′) by eliminating k: this is, in fact, what the construction of a scatter diagram amounts to. A continuous function, say,

(7) $q = q^*(p)$,

fitted by some method (e.g., by least squares) to the observed pairs (p, q) was called, unhappily, the statistical demand function; or, in analogy to the recent discussion on 'interfirm production functions', the fitted function $q^*(p)$ would be called, equally unhappily, 'interstate demand function'. Only under certain well-defined conditions has it any more affinity with the demand function than with the other relationship of the system, the supply function. In particular, the following is obvious, regardless of the method of fitting used: if all observed states have the same demand curve, or the same supply curve, that curve will coincide with the 'fitted' curve (7).[4] (If neither the supply nor the demand curve varies from state to state, the scatter diagram reduces to one point). In general, however, (7) cannot be regarded as an estimate of either. It is a 'mongrel' curve.

If both the demand and the supply curve vary from state to state, the problem 'to determine *the* demand (or supply) curve' obviously needs reformulation. Vaguely, what we are looking for is some 'true' or 'average' demand (or supply) curve, from which the demand (and supply) curves of individual states happen to deviate more or less. More precisely: we consider all such individual demand curves as belonging to the same family of curves, only differing from each other with respect to one or more random parameters; so that (4′), (5′) can be rewritten, for example, thus:

$$(8), (9) \qquad q = D(p, \varepsilon_k), \qquad q = S(p, \eta_k).$$

If, as a more specific assumption, the random parameters enter additively, we may write, say,

$$q = D^0(p) + \varepsilon_k, \qquad q = S^0(p) + \eta_k;$$

we may assume that in the long run the positive and negative 'shifts', ε_k, of demand will cancel out; or, more precisely, that their algebraic sum, weighted with the respective probabilities, i.e., the expectation $E\varepsilon_k = 0$. Similarly, $E\eta_k = 0$. In this case, the functions $D^0(p)$ and $S^0(p)$ above can indeed be called, in a well-defined sense, the 'average' demand and supply functions. After having assumed some specific form (say, polynomial) for each of these two functions, the problem would be to find the 'best estimate' (in some well-defined sense, such as: unbiased, efficient, etc.) of each of their parameters. The practical purpose is to 'predict' for any given price the limits which the demand (or supply) will be unlikely to trespass – 'unlikely' being meant in the sense of some preassigned probability. This requires that, in addition to the estimates of the parameters of the 'average' functions $D^0(p)$, $S^0(p)$, some further quantities be computed, such as the variances and covariances of the random parameters ε_k and η_k. The problem is thus analogous to the familiar one arising in the case of one single random equation.

The estimated functions $D^0(p)$, $S^0(p)$ are different from the 'mongrel' function $q^*(p)$ in (7). However, the latter also serves the purpose of 'prediction', but in quite a different sense. If the price is to be changed by deliberate action and not as the result of fluctuating demand and supply conditions described by the random quantities ε_k, η_k, then to predict the ensuing change in demand we need the 'average' demand function $D^0(p)$ together with the other quantities just described (such as the variances and covariances of the random terms). But if no interference with the previously observed set of causes is intended, and we want merely to predict the demanded and supplied quantities that accompany a given price when those causes are at work, the 'mongrel' function will do just this. In this case, the economist is called (as he often is) to act like a meteorologist. But if he is called to act like an engineer, i.e., to advise upon the likely results of some deliberate action (of a government, or a firm), he will have to determine functions of the kind $D^0(p)$, $S^0(p)$, separately for each of the simultaneous equations of the system. This point has been forcefully made by Haavelmo [21], [22].[5]

§3. We return now to the equations of firms: (1′), (2′), (3′). Eliminating f from a set of such equations – analogous to (4′), (5′) or to (8), (9) – gives a scatter diagram in the (x_0, x_1, x_2)-space, and a 'mongrel' surface fitted to it by some method would serve the purpose of 'meteorological' prediction. It will tell us what likely production we shall expect from a firm whose technical and economic efficiency and other characteristics are such as to make it hire a given amount of manpower and capital. This is different from the 'engineering' type of question: how much will a firm produce, if a certain amount of labor and capital is forced upon it. The latter question is answered by the parameters of the random Equation (1′) taken by itself, not by the 'mongrel' function that results from all three random Equations (1′), (2′), (3′). In particular, we can derive from (1′) the 'elasticity of output with respect to labor' of an 'average' firm. This cannot be derived from the 'mongrel' surface fitted to the (x_0, x_1, x_2)-values of the observed firms, since the change in the observed x_0-value accompanying the change in the observed x_1- and x_2-values is not the result of fixing first one, then another pair of values of x_1 and x_2, each to be regarded as constant in repeated samples. Rather (as can be seen formally by solving the three equations with respect to x_0, x_1, x_2) each of the three variables x_0, x_1, x_2 changes as the result of variations in the random features ε, η, θ, from firm to firm.

If we desire to estimate the value of x_0 associated with given values of x_1 and x_2, using past observations on x_0, x_1, and x_2 and assuming all three to be determined by the same set of random causes as before (a 'meteorological' type of prediction), the least-squares method applied to a single equation of the system provides, under certain conditions, and in a certain well-defined sense, the 'best' estimate of x_0.[6] If, on the other hand, we desire to estimate the value of x_0 if x_1 and x_2 should be determined not by that set of random causes which existed in the past but by deliberate action ('engineering' type of prediction), then we have to estimate the coefficients in the Equation (1′). For this, a method suggested by Haavelmo [21] and elaborated by Mann and Wald [31] can be applied, provided certain conditions are satisfied.

The agricultural researcher can control his experiments and can influence the growth of plants. The meteorologist cannot make experiments, nor does he want to influence weather. The economist cannot make experiments, yet is expected to advise how to influence events. This is why his data are the result of simultaneous random equations; and why he is interested in the parameters of each such equation.

I. HYPOTHESIS

§4. We shall first consider firms producing the same commodity. We shall not assume perfect competition. We shall denote by x_0, x_1, x_2 the annual physical output (in tons or bushels, etc.), the manpower, and the capital of a firm. Correspondingly, p_0, p_1, and p_2 mean the price of the firm's product, and the wage rate and the interest rate it pays. Furthermore, the firm's revenue will be denoted by y_0, its pay roll by y_1, and its annual interest charge by y_2; in other words,

$$(1.1) \qquad y_j = x_j p_j, \quad j = 0, 1, 2.$$

In addition to the identities (1.1) the existence of the following four relationships is *postulated*:

(1.2)	$x_0 = \phi(x_1, x_2)$,	the production function,
(1.3)	$y_0 = y_0(x_0)$,	the revenue function,
(1.4)	$y_1 = y_1(x_1)$,	the outlay function for labor,
(1.5)	$y_2 = y_2(x_2)$,	the outlay function for interest.

We further have the following definitions and inequalities (economic reasons for the latter will be stated presently):

(1.6) $$\alpha_i = \frac{\partial \phi}{\partial x_i} \cdot \frac{x_i}{x_0} > 0,$$

(1.7) $$\beta_i = \frac{dy_i}{dx_i} \cdot \frac{x_i}{y_i} \geqq 1,$$

(1.8) $$\beta_0 = \frac{dy_0}{dx_0} \cdot \frac{x_0}{y_0} \leqq 1 \quad (i = 1, 2).$$

§5. α_1 and α_2 are called the elasticities of output with respect to labor and to capital; they are nonnegative, as the adding of labor or capital cannot normally decrease output. If, in addition, ϕ is homogeneous of degree r, i.e., if for any λ and any initial values x_1', x_2',

$$\phi(\lambda x_1', \lambda x_2') = \lambda^r \phi(x_1', x_2') = \lambda^r \cdot \text{constant} = \psi(\lambda) \quad \text{(say)},$$

then it follows that

$$r = \frac{d\psi(\lambda)}{d\lambda} \cdot \frac{\lambda}{\psi(\lambda)},$$

so that r can be called 'elasticity of output with respect to the scale of operation'; λ is here used as a measure of the scale of operation, and can be defined only if the production factors are employed in a fixed proportion x_1'/x_2'. Increasing, constant, or decreasing returns to scale[7] are then defined by:

$$r \gtreqless 1, \quad \text{respectively.}$$

On the other hand (Euler's Theorem) if ϕ is homogeneous of degree r,

(1.8a) $$\frac{\partial \phi}{\partial x_1} x_1 + \frac{\partial \phi}{\partial x_2} x_2 = r\phi(x_1, x_2);$$

therefore, dividing by x_0, we have

$$(1.9) \qquad \alpha_1+\alpha_2=r \gtreqless 1.$$

§6. The inequality signs in (1.7), (1.8) follow from the nature of the demand function for a firm's product and the supply functions of labor and capital to the firm. In general, a firm can raise the demand price of its product by restricting its output:

$$\frac{dp_0}{dx_0} \leqq 0; \quad \text{hence} \quad \beta_0 \leqq 1,$$

the equality sign referring to a limiting case called perfect competition.[8] Furthermore a firm can, in general, lower the wage rate or the interest rate it has to pay, by hiring fewer workers or borrowing less capital:

$$\frac{dp_i}{dx_i} \geqq 0; \quad \text{hence} \quad \beta_i \geqq 1 \quad (i=1,2),$$

the equality sign referring to the limiting case called perfect competition in the market in which the firm hires labor (or borrows capital).

§7. So far, the market of the firm's product has been described as being either in perfect or imperfect competition; this includes the case of the firm's monopoly. In the markets of the factors, the firm appears either in perfect or imperfect competition as a buyer; this includes the case of the firm's monopsony. But the buyers of the product and the sellers of labor and capital are assumed to be in perfect competition only, thus excluding for example, the case of bargaining between a labor union and an employers' union. This assumption can be dropped later.

§8. The firm's profit is defined as

$$(1.10) \qquad \pi=y_0-y_1-y_2.$$

If the firm adjusts instantaneously the quantities x_1, x_2 of the hired factors so as to make profit a maximum (an assumption which also will be dropped later), the following 'first-order conditions' must be satisfied

$$(1.11), (1.12) \qquad \frac{\partial \pi}{\partial x_1}=0, \qquad \frac{\partial \pi}{\partial x_2}=0;$$

the inequalities forming the 'second-order conditions' for maximum profits will be discussed in Appendix 1.

The three identities (1.1), the production Equation (1.2), the revenue and outlay Equations (1.3)–(1.5), the profit definition (1.10), and the two 'equilibrium' (i.e., profit-maximizing) Equations (1.11), (1.12) are ten equations to determine the ten variables, i.e., the quantity, money value, and price of output, manpower, and capital services, respectively; and the size of profit.

§9. These equations can be naturally extended to cases of more than two productive resources. Further, a simplification is possible if some of the resources (e.g. the 'raw materials') are always used in a fixed proportion to output so that, for example, $x_3/x_0=k$ (a constant). The production function – say, $x_0=\phi(x_1, x_2, x_3)=\phi(x_1, x_2, kx_0)$ can then be replaced by a simpler one, $x_0=\psi(x_1, x_2)$.[9] If, furthermore, perfect competition in raw materials is assumed in the sense that $p_3/p_0=l$ (a constant), it is permissible to use 'net output value' $=p_0x_0-p_3x_3=y_0(1-kl)$ instead of y_0, and, correspondingly, $y_0(1-kl)/p_0=x_0(1-kl)$ instead of x_0. This change in the units used, and the assumptions underlying it, have so far been made in all empirical work (see Section III); it can be avoided if all the firms studied produce a single, reasonably standardized commodity, making the comparison of physical outputs possible.

§10. By use of the definitions (1.6)–(1.8), the equilibrium Equations (1.11), (1.12) can be rewritten in the form

$$(1.11'), (1.12') \quad \beta_0 y_0 \alpha_i - \beta_i y_i = 0,$$

$$(1.13), (1.14) \quad \alpha_i \frac{\beta_0}{\beta_i} = \frac{y_i}{y_0} = w_i \quad (i=1, 2),$$

where w_i is defined as the proportionate share of the firm's pay roll (or interest charge) in its revenue. If there is perfect competition in all three markets, $\beta_0=\beta_1=\beta_2=1$ and therefore

$$(1.15), (1.16) \quad \alpha_i = w_i \quad (i=1, 2);$$

under perfect competition, the share of labor (or capital) in the firm's revenue is equal to the corresponding output elasticity, provided the equilibrium equations are valid, i.e., provided the profit is maximized. Conversely, each of the Equations (1.15), (1.16) implies perfect competition in the market of the product and in the market of one of the productive resources since, because of (1.6)–(1.8), $\beta_0 = \beta_i$ $(i=1, 2)$ only if both $=1$.[10]

Equations (1.13), (1.14) can also be rewritten thus

$$\frac{\partial x_0}{\partial x_i} = \frac{p_i}{p_0} \cdot \frac{\beta_i}{\beta_0} \quad (i=1, 2),$$

which in the case of perfect competition becomes

$$\text{(1.17), (1.18)} \quad \frac{\partial x_0}{\partial x_i} = \frac{p_0}{p_i} \quad (i=1, 2),$$

the familiar 'marginal-productivity theorem'.

§11. For reasons of statistical manageability the case will be tried in which the elasticities defined in (1.6), (1.7), (1.8) are all independent of x_0, x_1, x_2. This gives the four relationships (1.2) to (1.5) the form

$$\text{(1.19)} \quad x_0 = a_0 x_1^{\alpha 1} x_2^{\alpha 2} \quad \text{(a homogeneous function of degree } \alpha_1 + \alpha_2\text{)},$$

and

$$\text{(1.20)–(1.22)} \quad y_j = b_j x^{\beta j} \quad (j=0, 1, 2);$$

or, if the logarithm of a quantity is denoted by the corresponding capital letter,

$$\text{(1.23)} \quad X_0 = \alpha_1 X_1 + \alpha_2 X_2 + A_0,$$
$$\text{(1.24)–(1.26)} \quad Y_j = \beta_j X_j + B_j \quad (j=0, 1, 2).$$

As far as we know, (1.19), or (1.23), was for the first time suggested and applied by Cobb and Douglas [5].

§12. The relationships (1.2) to (1.5) will be regarded as random relationships in the sense explained in the Introduction. They will be assumed to involve parameters that vary from firm to firm and from year to year in such a way as to approximate the results of some scheme of (not necessarily independent) drawings from urns. One can also say – without claiming full rigor for this statement – that the value taken, in the case of a given firm in a given year, by any of the 'random' parameters is assumed to be the combined effect of a large number of causes (not necessarily independent of each other), of which none has an influence considerably surpassing the influence of each of the other causes. It is a matter of judgment which of the parameters should be regarded as random. In the work of Douglas, the production function was specified in the form (1.19) or its equivalent (1.23) with the object of estimating the parameters α_1 and α_2.[11] These are, in effect, assumed not to vary from firm to firm or from year to year. The only remaining parameter in the production function is a_0 (or A_0). Unless each firm in each year obeys exactly the same production function, this parameter must be considered a random one. Its value will depend on the technical knowledge, the will, effort, and luck of a given entrepreneur in a given year, as can be summarized in the word '*technical efficiency*': with any given pair of amounts of labor and capital the firm, in a given year, will produce a larger (smaller) output than another firm, or than the same firm in another year, if the corresponding value of a_0 is larger (smaller). Locating thus all the 'randomness' of the production function in the parameter a_0, or A_0, we must rewrite (1.23) in the form

$$X_{0f}=\alpha_1 X_{1f}+\alpha_2 X_{2f}+A_{0f},$$

where the new subscript f is used to identify the particular firm and year (or, if only one year is used, the particular firm). By assumption, α_1 and α_2 are free from this subscript.

Similarly, unless the revenue functions and the outlay functions of all firms in all years coincide, some or all of the β's and b's (or B's) in the above equations will be considered random (and accordingly supplied with the f-subscript).

In addition, not all entrepreneurs may have the same urge,[12] or ability, or luck to choose the most profitable combinations of production factors: even if entrepreneur A be technically as efficient as B, he may have smaller '*economic efficiency*': the combination of resources which A will choose may bring his profit not as close to the possible maximum as the combination chosen by B. Accordingly, the Equations (1.11), (1.12) [or their equivalents (1.13), (1.14); and, under perfect competition, also (1.15), (1.16) or (1.17), (1.18)] will not be satisfied exactly. Another cause of their failure to be satisfied exactly may be the absence of perfect competition among the buyers of the product or among the sellers of productive resources (§7).

§13. Let us use the particular case of the simple Equations (1.19)–(1.22) or their equivalents (1.23)–(1.26): each of the parameters will, in general, vary from firm to firm (and from year to year). With this understanding we shall continue, for brevity, to have the firm subscripts omitted. If the assumptions of §§7 and 8 were valid, we could rewrite the profit-maximizing Equations (1.11′), (1.12′) in the form (denoting logarithms by capital letters):

$$Y_0 = Y_i - \log(\alpha_i \beta_0/\beta_i) \quad (i=1, 2);$$

but if profits are not exactly maximized, or if there is bilateral monopoly, we shall have in general

$$(1.27), (1.28) \quad Y_0 = Y_i - \log(\alpha_1 \beta_0/\beta_i) - C_i \quad (i=1, 2).$$

where C_1 and C_2 are random parameters depending on the firm's 'economic efficiency' and on the degree of competition between its customers, or workers, or creditors. The six Equations (1.23) to (1.28) determine for each firm the six variables

$$X_j,\ Y_j \quad (j=0, 1, 2).$$

We may eliminate any three variables. In particular we can obtain the following systems:[13]

(I) Variables: X_0, X_1, X_2 (i.e., output and resources measured in their respective units):

$$(1.29) \quad \begin{aligned} &X_0 - \alpha_1 X_1 - \alpha_2 X_2 = A_0, \\ &X_0 - \frac{\beta_i}{\beta_0} X_1 = D_i \quad (i=1, 2). \end{aligned}$$

(II) Variables Y_0, Y_1, Y_2 (i.e., dollar values of output and of resources used):

$$(1.30) \quad \begin{aligned} &Y_0 - \alpha_1 \frac{\beta_0}{\beta_1} Y_1 - \alpha_2 \frac{\beta_0}{\beta_2} Y_2 = E_0, \\ &Y_0 - Y_i = F_i. \quad (i=1, 2). \end{aligned}$$

(III) Variables Y_0, X_1, X_2 (i.e., output measured in dollars, resources measured in their respective units):

$$(1.31)\qquad \begin{aligned}&Y_0-\alpha_1\beta_0X_1-\alpha_2\beta_0X_2=G_0,\\&Y_0-\beta_iX_i=H_i\quad(i=1,2),\end{aligned}$$

where the capital letters on the right-hand side denote the following linear functions of the parameters A_0, B_0, B_i, C_i $(i=1,2)$:

$$(1.32)\qquad \begin{aligned}&G_0=A_0\beta_0+B_0,\quad F_i=-C_i-\log\alpha_i\frac{\beta_0}{\beta_i},\\&E_0=G_0-\alpha_1\frac{\beta_0}{\beta_1}B_1-\alpha_2\frac{\beta_0}{\beta_2},\qquad H_i=B_i+F_i\quad(i=1,2),\\&D_i=-(H_i+B_0)/\beta_0.\end{aligned}$$

§14. The general form of production, revenue, and outlay functions has so far been assumed common to all firms (viz., linear in the logarithms of all variables). To make the hypothesis a statistical one we have to specify it still further. We want to estimate certain parameters. As a general case, consider n firms, p years, q parameters, all of the parameters being random. Let K_{fgh} be the value which the parameter k_h had in the year g for the firm f. We can consider K_{fgh} as a value assumed by a certain random variable called, say, k_{fgh}; we may denote its expectation, or mean value, by Ek_{fgh} and its variance $E(k_{fgh}-Ek_{fgh})^2$ by $\sigma_{fgh,fgh}$. We can further consider the joint distribution of all such npq random variables and denote their covariance $E(k_{fgh}-Ek_{fgh})(k_{f'g'h'}-Ek_{f'g'h'})$ by $\sigma_{fgh,f'g'h'}$ $(f,f'=1,\ldots,n;\ g,g'=1,\ldots,p;\ h,h'=1,\ldots,q)$. The statistical problem would be to estimate the mean values, the variances, and the covariances of the npq variables, from the observed values such as X_{0fg}, X_{1fg}, X_{2fg} $(f=1,\ldots,n;\ g=1,\ldots,p)$, and from any other available knowledge.

As a stronger assumption, we may assume that all parameters k_h $(h=1,\ldots,q)$ have in a given year g the same expected value for all firms (at least within one and the same industry); or have, for any firm, the same expected value in any year; or, if both hypotheses are combined

$$\begin{aligned}&Ek_{fgh}=Ek_{f'g'h'}=Ek_h\quad\text{(say)}\\&(h=1,\ldots,q;\ f,f'=1,\ldots,n;\ g,g'=1,\ldots,p);\end{aligned}$$

further, if the value taken by any random parameter is noncorrelated with the values taken by the same or other parameters at another time or in another firm, we have

$$\sigma_{fgh,f'g'h_1} = \sigma_{hh_1} \cdot \delta_{ff'} \delta_{gg'}$$
$$(h, h_1 = 1, \ldots, q;\ f, f' = 1, \ldots, n;\ g, g' = 1, \ldots, p),$$

where $\delta_{ff'}$ is 1 or 0 according as $f = f'$ or $\neq f'$ (and similarly for $\delta_{gg'}$); and where σ_{hh_1} can be called the covariance (the same for all firms and years) between the two parameters k_h and k_{h_1}. If such assumptions are made, the statistical problem is to estimate the q mean values Ek_h ($h = 1, \ldots, q$), their q variances, and their $q(q-1)/2$ covariances or correlation coefficients. The assumptions involve intertemporal and interfirm independence (in the sense of noncorrelation) between the parameters. The assumptions exclude 'contagion', and thus exclude 'heredity' or serial correlation (e.g., in time series), which is a particular, one-dimensional type of contagion. But they do not imply (what in our particular case would be impermissible, as we shall see) that all parameters involved in the equations of a single firm in a given year are noncorrelated among themselves. Further, if we deal only with observations made in one and the same year, the assumption of intertemporal noncorrelation need not be made (and the g-subscript might have been omitted in the discussion just presented).

§15. By assuming the relevant economic functions to be linear in the logarithms we were led to equations systems I, II, III, describing certain random relationships prevailing in a firm. The assumptions just made permit us to regard all the parameters involved – i.e., all the magnitudes other than the X's and Y's – as jointly distributed random variables, the joint distribution having the same mean values, variances, and covariances for each firm. The X's and Y's are uniquely determined functions of those parameters and are therefore also random variables, obeying the same joint distribution for every firm. Therefore every observation of the values such as X_{0f}, X_{1f}, X_{2f} for any firm f can be regarded as a triplet of (generally nonindependent) drawings from three urns.

Under these assumptions, every symbol in the equation systems I, II, or III should be provided with an f-subscript, and the problem would be to estimate the mean values, variances, and covariances of all parameters, each regarded as a random variable. The limitations of the statistical tools available at present make it, however, necessary to restrict the problem still further. We have to restrict our hypotheses to systems of equations linear in the unknown parameters; further, no random parameter may appear in other than additive form. (The same limitations are also known to apply to the least-squares method.) Consequently, if system I is used, α_1, α_2, and the ratios β_1/β_0, β_2/β_0 must be regarded as constants, and only A_0, D_1, D_2 are permitted to vary. Therefore, we can only estimate on the left-hand side of the equations certain 'average' elasticities of the firms' output with respect to labor or capital; and certain 'average' relative degrees of the firms' monopsony and monopoly.[14] If system II is used, we can estimate the coefficients of Y_1 and Y_2; they are 'average' output elasticities, 'corrected for average imperfect competition in two markets'. Finally, if the system III is used, the parameters which can be estimated on the left-hand side are $\alpha_1\beta_0$, $\alpha_2\beta_0$, β_1, β_2: i.e., the 'average' output elasticities corrected for possible monopoly in the product market; and the 'average' degrees of monopsony in each of the resources markets.

The right-hand terms of the equations, on the other hand, can be regarded as random parameters. It is necessary to estimate their expectations, variances, and covariances.

§16. Consider, in particular, system III,[15] i.e., the equations (1.31) and definitions (1.32). Denote the expectation of the three random terms on the right-hand side of (1.31) by

$$E(G_0)=\gamma_0, \quad E(H_1)=\gamma_1, \quad E(H_2)=\gamma_2,$$

and write

$$G_{0f}-\gamma_0=\varepsilon_{0f}, \quad H_{1f}-\gamma_1=\varepsilon_{1f}, \quad H_{2f}-\gamma_2=\varepsilon_{2f}; \tag{1.33}$$

consequently

$$E(\varepsilon_j)=0 \quad (j=0,1,2).$$

Write further $Y_0=z_0$, $X_i=z_i$,

$$\beta_0\alpha_i=\alpha_i' \quad (i=1,2).$$

Our system becomes

$$\begin{aligned} \gamma_0+z_{0f}-\alpha_1' z_{1f}-\alpha_2' z_{2f}&=\varepsilon_{0f}, \\ \gamma_1+z_{0f}-\beta_1 z_{1f} \qquad\qquad &=\varepsilon_{1f}, \\ \gamma_2+z_{0f} \qquad\qquad -\beta_2 z_{2f}&=\varepsilon_{2f}, \end{aligned} \tag{1.34}$$

where the α's, β's, γ's are constants, while the z's and ε's are random variables, and $E(\varepsilon_j)=0$ $(j=0, 1, 2)$. The covariance σ_{jk} between ε_j and ε_k is independent of f. The problem is to estimate from $3n$ observations z_{jf} $(j=0, 1, 2; f=1, \ldots, n)$ the seven constants and the six variances and covariances of the ε's,

$$\sigma_{jk}=E\varepsilon_j\varepsilon_k \quad (j, k=0, 1, 2). \tag{1.35}$$

This problem is obviously a special case of the following more general one:

$$\gamma_j+\sum_{k=1}^{v} \gamma_{jk}z_{kf}=\varepsilon_{jf} \quad (j=0, \ldots, v); \tag{1.36}$$

the case treated in Part II of Mann and Wald's article [31] is still more general, as it admits of serial correlation: there z_{kf} depends on $z_{k,f-1}$, $z_{k,f-2}, \ldots, z_{h,f-1}, \ldots$ (f denoting time, for example).

§17. Since, by §6, β_0 is smaller than or equal to one, the constants α_1' and α_2' in (1.34) are smaller than or equal to the output-elasticities α_1 and α_2: equal if there is perfect competition in the product market. If the "average" value of β_0 in the industry considered is known (as a piece of separate information), the output elasticities can be derived from α_1' and α_2'.

§18. Further, under perfect competition in the product market, B_0 in (1.24) and (1.32) is a constant and therefore the deviations of G_0 and A_0 from their means are equal, and ε_{0f} can be regarded as a measure of the technical efficiency of firm f, expressed as the deviation from the common logarithm of the geometric mean of all possible values of technical efficiency. If, with a given amount of labor and capital, firm f produces k times more than firm f', then $\varepsilon_{0f}-\varepsilon_{0f}'=\log_{10}k$. In particular, let f be the best firm, defined as the worst of the $1\frac{1}{2}$°/₀₀ best *possible* firms; and let f' be the worst firm defined as the best of the $1\frac{1}{2}$°/₀₀ worst *possible* firms. If technical efficiency (or 'goodness') were normally distributed[16] the difference $\varepsilon_{0f}-\varepsilon_{0f'}$ would be about six times larger than the standard deviation of technical efficiency:

$$\varepsilon_{0f}-\varepsilon_{0f'}=\log_{10}k=6\sqrt{\sigma_{00}} \quad \text{approximately.}$$

Thus, if $k=4$, $\sigma_{00}=[(\log_{10}4)/6]^2=0.01$ approximately. This kind of judgment presupposes not only that the distribution of (logarithmic) technical efficiency is not too far from normal, but also that β_0 is not too far from unity. If more knowledge is available on these points, it can be used in obvious ways. At any rate, tentative limits – say, constants c_{00} and c'_{00} – can be set up so that

$$(1.37) \qquad 0 \leqq c'_{00} \leqq \sigma_{00} \leqq c_{00}.$$

§19. As to the terms ε_1 and ε_2, they depend, by definition – (1.32), (1.33) – on the firm's supply curve for labor (or capital) and on the firm's economic efficiency. At the same time, by (1.25)–(1.26),

$$H_i = Y_0 - \beta_i X_i = B_i - (Y_i - Y_0) \quad (i=1,2).$$

Hence if B_1 and B_2 (that is, in the case of perfect competition, the wage rate and interest rate) do not vary from firm to firm, we have

$$(1.38) \qquad \varepsilon_i = -\log w_i + \text{const.} \quad (i=1,2),$$

where w_i, as in (1.13), is the share of pay roll, or of the interest charge, in the output value. Since $E\varepsilon_0=0$, we have $\sigma_{0i}=E\varepsilon_0\varepsilon_1=-E\varepsilon_0 \log w_i$ ($i=$ $=1,2$). We may form judgment regarding the correlation coefficients

$$\rho_{01}=\sigma_{01}/\sqrt{\sigma_{00}\sigma_{11}} \quad \text{and} \quad \rho_{02}=\sigma_{02}/\sqrt{\sigma_{00}\sigma_{02}}.$$

Presumably ρ_{01} is positive and ρ_{02} negative, i.e., large positive values of ε_0 are accompanied by large negative values of $\log w_1$ and by large positive values of $\log w_2$. Of two entrepreneurs in the same industry, the one who knows how to extract the highest production out of any given combination of labor and capital was (at least in the last few generations), more likely than not, the one who mechanized production more. Again, we may set trial limits such as

$$(1.39) \qquad \rho_{01} \geqq c_{01} \text{ (a constant)} > 0,$$
$$(1.40) \qquad \rho_{02} \leqq c_{02} \text{ (a constant)} < 0.$$

There is presumably also positive correlation between the technical efficiency ε_0 and the ratio of profits to net output, say w. This fact can be utilized if the output measured (Y_0) is net output, so that $w_1+w_2+w=1$.

Expanding $\log w_i$ about Ew_i, we have

$$\log w_i = \log[Ew_i + (w_i - Ew_i)] =$$
$$= \log Ew_i + \frac{w_i - Ew_i}{Ew_i} - \frac{1}{2}\left(\frac{w_i - Ew_i}{Ew_i}\right)^2 + \cdots;$$

if the quadratic and higher terms are dropped we have, since $E\varepsilon_0 = 0$,

$$\sigma_{0i} = -\frac{E\varepsilon_0 w_i}{Ew_i} \quad (i = 1, 2);$$

multiplying by Ew_i, adding up, and using the fact that $w_1 + w_2 = 1 - w$, we obtain the equation

$$\sigma_{01} Ew_1 + \sigma_{02} Ew_2 = E\varepsilon_0 w.$$

The expression on the right-hand side is positive if the profit rate w is positively correlated with technical efficiency. Approximating Ew_1 and Ew_2 by the arithmetic averages – say $\bar{w}_1$, $\bar{w}_2$ – known from data, use the inequality

$$(1.41) \qquad \sigma_{01}\bar{w}_1 + \sigma_{02}\bar{w}_2 > c > 0$$

as another boundary condition.

Under perfect competition, for B_i $(i = 1, 2)$ to be constant from firm to firm means (since β_i has to be supposed constant) that the supply curves of labor, or of capital, to all firms of an industry are identical (under perfect competition they are all horizontal). To the extent that this is not true, the interpretation (1.38) of the residual terms ε_1 and ε_2 will not be exact, and the boundaries just outlined will be shifted: by how much will, again, be a matter of judgment.

§20. Finally, a boundary condition is also provided by the sufficient conditions for profit maximization,

$$(4.7') \qquad \alpha_1 \frac{\beta_0}{\beta_1} + \alpha_2 \frac{\beta_0}{\beta_2} < 1,$$

proved in Appendix 1, §39. If this is not satisfied, Equations (1.11), (1.12), or their equivalents (1.11′), (1.12′) may give conditions for minimum instead of maximum profits. Figure 3 on p. 264 shows the corresponding boundary lines, in the plane (α_1', α_2'):

$$\frac{\alpha_1'}{\beta_1}+\frac{\alpha_2'}{\beta_2}=1, \tag{1.43}$$

for certain values of β_1, β_2. Only regions enclosed by this boundary line and the axes are economically eligible. This statement, however, need not apply exactly, as soon as the assumption of exact profit maximization is dropped – as in (1.27), (1.28).[17]

II. STATISTICAL METHOD

§21. To estimate the parameters of a single equation, viz., the first Equation in (1.34), the least-squares method requires the computation of second moments (sample variances and covariances) m_{jk} of the observed values of the variables measured from the sample means:

$$\begin{aligned} m_{jk} &= \frac{1}{n}\sum_{f=1}^{n}(z_{jf}-\bar{z}_j)(z_{kf}-\bar{z}_k), \\ \bar{z}_j &= \frac{1}{n}\sum_{f=1}^{n} z_{jf} \qquad (j, k=0, 1, 2). \end{aligned} \tag{2.1}$$

To estimate the parameters of a system of simultaneous equations by applying Haavelmo's principle, we have to start with essentially the same numerical computations.

To explain the application of that method to our economic case, it will prove useful to start by considering relationships between the moments m_{jk} and the unknowns of the problem. This will also bring out clearly the meaning of the 'mongrel functions' (as we call them in the Introduction) fitted by least squares to one of a number of simultaneous equations, while neglecting the others. Denote by s_{jk} the sample variances and covariances of the random terms ε_{jf}:

$$\begin{aligned} s_{jk} &= \frac{1}{n}\sum_{f=1}^{n}(\varepsilon_{jf}-\bar{\varepsilon}_j)(\varepsilon_{kf}-\bar{\varepsilon}_k), \\ \bar{\varepsilon}_j &= \frac{1}{n}\sum_{f=1}^{n} \varepsilon_{jf} \qquad (j, k=0, 1, 2). \end{aligned} \tag{2.2}$$

Then by (1.34)

$$
(2.3)\quad
\begin{aligned}
s_{00} &= m_{00} + \alpha_1'^2 m_{11} + \alpha_2'^2 m_{22} - 2\alpha_1' m_{01} - 2\alpha_2' m_{02} + 2\alpha_1 \alpha_2 m_{12},\\
s_{01} &= m_{00} - \beta_1 m_{01} - \alpha_1' (m_{01} - \beta_1 m_{11}) - \alpha_2' (m_{02} - \beta_1 m_{12}),\\
s_{02} &= m_{00} - \beta_2 m_{02} - \alpha_1' (m_{01} - \beta_2 m_{12}) - \alpha_2' (m_{02} - \beta_2 m_{22}),\\
s_{11} &= m_{00} + \beta_1^2 m_{11} - 2\beta m_{01},\\
s_{22} &= m_{00} + \beta_2^2 m_{22} - 2\beta_2 m_{02},\\
s_{12} &= m_{00} + \beta_1 \beta_2 m_{12} - \beta_1 m_{01} - \beta_2 m_{02}.
\end{aligned}
$$

The m's are all known from observations. For the diagrams which follow, the following m's were computed from data of the U.S.A. Census of Manufactures, 1909 [45].

TABLE I
Moments of observations (m_{jk}) used in Figures 1 and 2 (U.S.A., 1909)[a]

	$j=0$	1	2
$k=0$	0.1354	0.1381	0.1481
1		0.1507	0.1478
2			0.1925

[a] The nature and shortcomings of data are explained in Section III, especially §27. The moments were weighted according to the number of firms in each industry, the available data giving industrial totals only: see Formulas (3.3).

The first of the Equations (2.3) can be represented by a family of ellipses in the (α_1', α_2')-plane, one ellipse for each value of the sample variance s_{00}. These are shown in solid lines (—) on Figure 1. At the point A the ellipse shrinks to a single point, and s_{00}, the sample variance of the random term ε_0 has assumed its smallest possible value. But s_{00} is just the magnitude that is minimized when the least-squares method is applied to estimate the coefficients in the first equation in (1.34). Hence the co-ordinates of point A are the least-squares estimates of α_1' and α_2' for a mongrel equation of production. We shall call these estimates a_1 and a_2 (see for example Tables II and III).

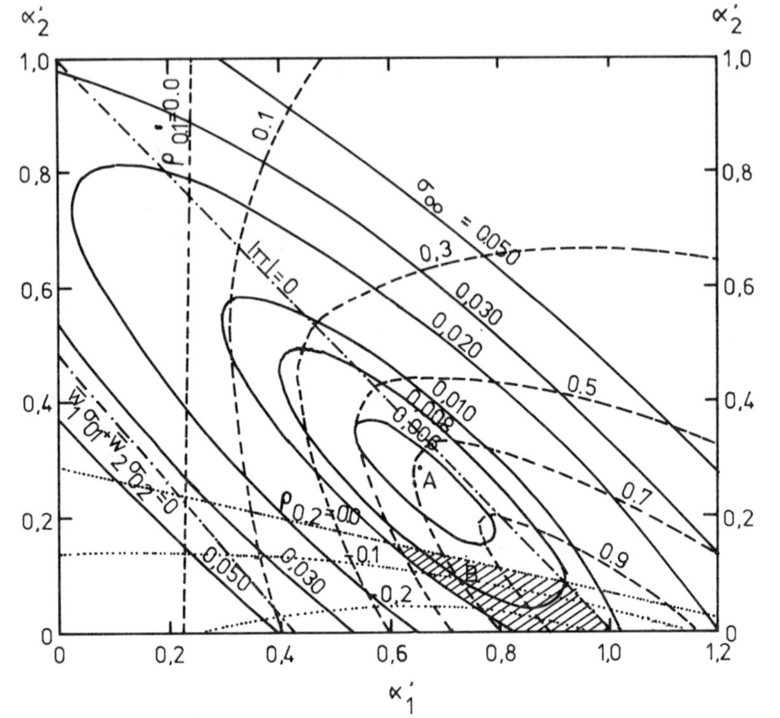

Fig. 1. The effect of various side conditions on the parameters α_1' and α_2' when $\beta_1=\beta_2=1$ (U.S.A., 1909). Point A indicates the 'single-equation' estimates of the parameters and the shaded area covers the estimates compatible with certain economic considerations. (Greek letters π and ϱ are used instead of the corresponding Latin letters s and r discussed in §21. The reasons are given in §22.) For details, see §37.

The second of the Equations (2.3) can be represented, for any given value of β_1, as a family of parallel and straight lines in the (α_1', α_2') plane, one line for each value of s_{01}. These are not drawn on Figure 1. Instead, if we write r_{01} for the sample correlation coefficient,

$$r_{01}=s_{01}/\sqrt{s_{00}s_{11}},$$
$$s_{01}^2=r_{01}^2 s_{00}s_{11};$$

this equation is quadratic in α_1', α_2' since, by (2.3), s_{01} is linear in α_1', α_2', s_{00} is quadratic in, and s_{11} is independent of α_1', α_2'. However, s_{01} ands_{11} depend on β_1. We have thus, for any given value of β_1, a system of conics

TABLE II

Some single-equation estimates (a_1 and a_2) of output elasticities (a_1 and a_2 are followed by their standard errors; $\bar{w}_1$ = national ratio of payroll to net output)

Reference[a]	Place	Type of Study[b]	Date	a_1	a_2	$a_1 + a_2$	$\bar{w}_1$
[5]	U.S.A.	*T*	1899–1922	0.750[c]	–	[j]	–
[8]	Massachusetts	*T*	1890–1926	0.743	–	[j]	–
	New South Wales	*T*	1901–1927	0.650	–	[j]	–
[9]	Victoria	*T*	1907–1929	0.71	–	[j]	–
				±0.065			
				0.837	0.230	1.067	
				±0.342	±0.166		
[10]	U.S.A.[d]	*C*	1909	0.742	0.319	1.061	0.676
				±0.045	±0.043		
[11]	Victoria	*C*	1910–1911	0.74	0.25	0.99	0.64
				±0.08	±0.11		
		C	1923–1924	0.62	0.30	0.92	0.65
				±0.08	±0.10		
		C	1927–1928	0.59	0.27	0.86	0.68
				±0.07	±0.09		
	Australia	*C*	1934–1935	0.64	0.36	0.99	0.61
				±0.04	±0.04		
	New South Wales	*C*	1933–1934	0.65	0.34	0.99	0.51
				±0.04	±0.03		
[12]	U.S.A.[e]	*C*	1919	0.76	0.25	1.01	0.60
[13]	Australia[f]	*C*	1912	0.50	0.48	0.98	0.54
				±0.05	±0.04		
	[f]	*C*	1922–1923	0.61	0.46	1.07	0.54
				±0.06	±0.05		
	[f]	*C*	1926–1927	0.60	0.36	0.96	0.57
				±0.06	±0.05		
	[f]	*C*	1936–1937	0.50	0.50	1.00	0.51
				±0.05	±0.04		
			average	0.53	–	–	0.54
	[g]	*C*	1912	0.52	0.47	0.99	0.54
				±0.05	±0.05		
	[g]	*C*	1922–1923	0.53	0.49	1.02	0.54
				±0.05	±0.05		
	[g]	*C*	1926–1927	0.59	0.34	0.93	0.57
				±0.06	±0.04		

Table II (Continued)

	[g]	*C*	1936–1937	0.49 ±0.04	0.49 ±0.04	0.98	0.51
			average	0.53	–	–	0.54
[14]	U.S.A.	*C*	1914	0.612 ±0.027	0.359 ±0.025	0.971	0.586
[15]	U.S.A.	*C*	1904	0.647 ±0.023	0.311 ±0.022	0.958	0.635
	[h]	*C*	1904	0.654 ±0.022	0.312 ±0.021	0.966	0.635
[16]	Canada[i]	*C*	1923	0.48 ±0.038	0.48 ±0.035	0.96	0.50
	[i]	*C*	1927	0.46 ±0.039	0.52 ±0.036	0.98	0.48
	[i]	*C*	1935	0.50 ±0.044	0.52 ±0.040	1.02	0.40
	[i]	*C*	1937	0.43 ±0.041	0.58 ±0.036	1.01	0.52
			average	0.468	0.525	0.992	0.475
[4]	New Zealand	*T*	1915–1935	0.483	–	[j]	–

[a] With the exception of [4] (Clark) the references are to papers by Douglas and his collaborators [5] and [8]–[16] listed at the end of the present article and arranged according to the date of the publication.
[b] T=intertemporal study (based on time series of national totals); C=interindustrial ('cross-section') study.
[c] $a_1=0.67$ fits better for 1899–1916.
[d] Cf. also Table III.
[e] Output includes depreciation, hence low $\bar{w}_1$.
[f] Averages per plant (but moments of logarithms unweighted).
[g] Industry aggregates (not divided by number of firms).
[g] Includes proprietors and firm members under 'labor'.
[i] Depreciation apparently not deducted.
[j] $a_1+a_2=1$ by assumption.

in the (α_1', α_2') plane, each conic corresponding to one value of the sample correlation coefficient r_{01} regardless of the value of s_{00}. For the case $\beta_1=1$, such system of conics is shown on Figure 1 in dashed lines (---): each of the hyperbolae corresponds to one value of r_{01} (positive or zero); as r_{01} grows they become ellipses; and finally shrink to a point when

$r_{01}=1$; then $\alpha_1'=1$, $\alpha_2'=0$. To the case $r_{01}=0$ corresponds a straight line.

An analogous family of conics, shown in dotted lines (.....), corresponds on Figure 1 to changing values of r_{02} (negative or zero), at $\beta_2=1$.

Figure 1 helps thus to understand how the same pair of "single-equation" least-squares estimates a_1, a_2 of α_1', α_2' (shown in point A) is compatible with very different combinations of true values of α_1', α_2'. For example, the combination of true values shown in point B is compatible with their least-squares estimate shown in point A provided the sample variance $s_{00}=0.008$, and the sample correlation coefficient $r_{01}=0.7$ (these two conditions are seen to imply also $r_{02}=-0.1$). The least-squares estimate of α_1', α_2' approaches the true values as the sample variance s_{00} diminishes; it becomes exact when s_{00} reaches its minimum.

TABLE III

Effect of weighting and of other procedures on some single-equation estimates of output elasticities (a_1, a_2) and their sums
(Estimates are followed by their standard errors)

U.S. 1909[a] (cf. Table II, Ref. [10])	a_1	a_2	a_1+a_2
Bronfenbrenner-Douglas: 90 industries			
Total-capital figures			
Industry aggregates			
Moments unweighted	0.742	0.319	1.061
	±0.045	±0.043	±0.027
Fixed-capital figures			
Industry aggregates			
Moments unweighted	0.857	0.083	0.940
	±0.045	±0.035	±0.031
Andrews: 85 industries reclassified			
Industry aggregates			
Moments unweighted	0.707	0.261	0.968
	±0.039	±0.034	±0.023
Industry averages per firm			
Moments unweighted	0.677	0.281	0.958
	±0.043	±0.034	±0.020
Moments weighted	0.656	0.266	0.922
	±0.042	±0.037	±0.021

[a] Weighting of moments (of logarithms) discussed in §25; 'industrial totals' vs. 'industrial averages') in §28, sub. (3). For the reclassification of industries and the use of capital figures, see note 23.

Figure 2 is a magnification of part of the area of Figure 1, with a different selection of conics. It also shows the effect of changing the values of β_1 and β_2. It follows from (2.3) that the family of s_{00}-ellipses (and hence the position of the least-squares estimate) is not affected (only one such ellipse was drawn: $s_{00}=0.010$). The change in β_1 or β_2 does affect, however, the position of r_{01}- or r_{02}-conics, respectively.

§22. Figures 1 and 2 also show what would be the implications of certain boundary conditions. For example, if the sample correlation coefficient $r_{01}>0$, the true (α_1', α_2') point must lie below and to the right of the line $r_{01}=0$; if $s_{00}\leqq 0.01$, the true value (α_1', α_2') must lie on or within the ellipse $s_{00}=0.01$, etc. Such inequalities must run in terms of the *sample* variances (Latin letters, s and r) because the s_{jk}'s in (2.3) are functions of sample variances, as defined in (2.2). On the other hand, the boundary conditions derived from economic considerations, as in §§18–20, relate

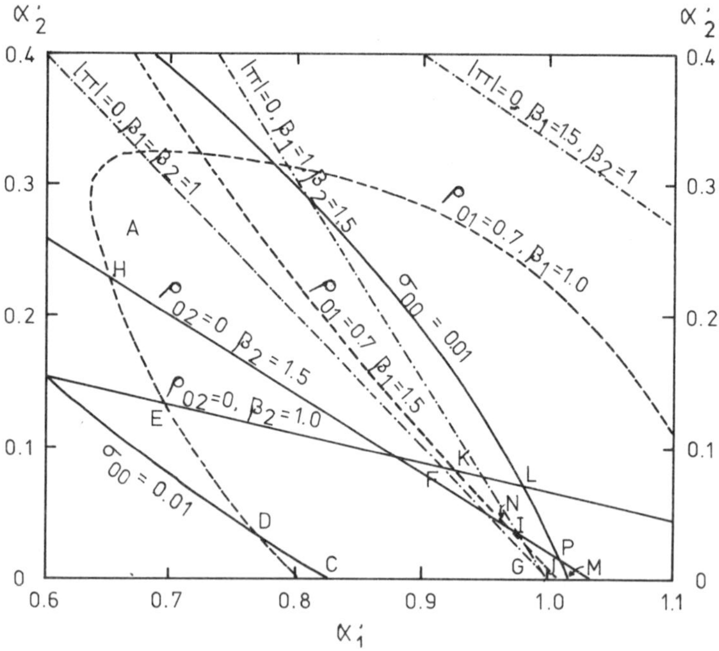

Fig. 2. The effect of the side conditions, $\sigma_{00}=0.01$ and $\varrho_{01}=0.7$ and of various values of the β's on the parameters α_1' and α_2' (U.S.A., 1909). For details, see §37.

to *true* variances (Greek letters, σ and ρ), as defined in, or derived from, (1.35). If it were possible to regard the sample variances as estimates of true variances, and to substitute them for the latter, boundary conditions derived from economic considerations could be used to define regions of eligible estimates of the set of parameters α_1', α_2', β_1, β_2: i.e., regions that would contain all such estimates of the set as are compatible (1) with the observations on economic data; (2) with other economic considerations. The observations would provide the moments m_{jk} from which the conics on diagrams such as Figures 1 and 2 are calculated; other economic considerations would provide the boundaries for the combinations (α_1', α_2') compatible with any given pair of values (β_1, β_2).

Using a procedure indicated by Mann and Wald [31], we shall see in Appendix 3, that it is indeed permissible, when the sample is large, to replace the true variances and correlation coefficients σ_{jk}, ρ_{jk} by their sample values s_{jk}, r_{jk}, since the latter are consistent estimates of the former. Therefore, the procedure just described is permissible. In applying it, an error of a given size will be the less probable the larger the sample.

III. DATA AND FINDINGS

§23. In formulating the economic hypothesis (Chapter I) we considered individual firms belonging to one and the same industry. The only study known to us where data of this kind were used to estimate (by the least-squares method) output elasticities with respect to productive resources, is that of Tintner [44]. It is based on 609 records of Iowa farms for 1942.

The census authorities of U.S.A., Australia, and Canada who supplied the published data on which Paul H. Douglas' studies [8]–[16] were based, had, of course, collected their material factory by factory. If the material had then been grouped to show, for certain industries, the trivariate distribution of firms by size of net output, labor, and capital it would be possible to make studies of those industries by the methods outlined in the two previous chapters, even though original ungrouped data (individual firm sheets) were not available. Instead, the published material is of a different kind. It gives, for each industry, the aggregate net output, the labor and the capital, and the number of firms. In addition, univariate distributions of firms by size of manpower or by net output are given for each industry.[18]

To study the relationship between the three variables – net output, labor, capital – Douglas suggested applying the least-squares method to the data on *aggregates* of firms: the aggregate of all manufacturing firms of a country in each year ('intertemporal' studies: [5], [8], [9]); the aggregate of all manufacturing firms of each of the 48 states of the Union (interstate 'cross-section' studies); the aggregate of all firms in each industry (interindustrial 'cross-section' studies: [10]–[16]).

§24. In all three cases, the aim is the same: to estimate the production function – more specifically, some 'average values' (§15) of the output elasticities – of the *individual firm.* It is the firm, not the country, state, or industry, that chooses the resources and (more or less) tries to maximize the profit.[19] The 'production function' for an *aggregate* of firms cannot even be defined unless one postulates that the (bivariate) distribution of firms by manpower and by capital used changes from aggregate to aggregate in some well-defined way. Consider the firms belonging to an aggregate g ($g=1,\ldots,p$; g thus denoting either – as in §14 – time, or state, or industry) and having from x_1 to x_1+dx_1 workers and x_2 to x_2+dx_2 dollars of capital. Let the proportion of those firms to all firms be $n_g(x_1, x_2)\,dx_1dx_2$. Then the average labor per firm ($\bar{x}_{1g}$), and the average capital per firm ($\bar{x}_{2g}$), in the aggregate g are

$$\bar{x}_{ig}=\int_0^\infty\int_0^\infty x_i n_g(x_1, x_2)\,dx_1dx_2 \quad (i=1, 2;\ g=1,\ldots, p).$$

If the production function, assumed to be common to all firms of all aggregates, is $x_0=\phi(x_1, x_2)$, the output ($\bar{x}_{0g}$) per firm of aggregate g is

$$\bar{x}_{0g}=\int_0^\infty\int_0^\infty \phi(x_1, x_2)\,n_g(x_1, x_2)\,dx_1dx_2 \quad (g=1,\ldots, p).$$

It is thus clear that the relationship between $\bar{x}_{0g}$, $\bar{x}_{1g}$, and $\bar{x}_{2g}$ will depend not only on the production function ϕ but also on the way in which the distribution function n_g changes from aggregate to aggregate. For example, if g denotes time ($g=1,\ldots, p$) and the growth or fluctuations of a country's manufactures has proceeded in such a way that every firm has always changed its manpower and capital in the same proportion as other firms, then, using the per-firm labor, capital, and output in some basic year 0 as units of labor, capital, and output, we have[20] $x_{ig}/\bar{x}_{ig} = x_{i0}/\bar{x}_{i0}$ $(i=1, 2)$, and therefore

$$\bar{x}_{0g} = \int_0^\infty \int_0^\infty \phi(x_1 \bar{x}_{1g}, x_2 \bar{x}_{2g})\, n_{0g}(x_1, x_2)\, dx_1 dx_2 = \Phi(\bar{x}_{1g}, \bar{x}_{2g}) \quad (g=1,\ldots, p), \tag{3.1}$$

a relationship between labor, capital, and output per firm that might be termed 'collective production function' but that would take another form if the distribution of firms by the size of manpower and capital changed in some other way than the one just assumed. In particular if the production function for individual firms has the form

$$x_0 = a_0 x_1^{\alpha_1} x_2^{\alpha_2}, \tag{1.19}$$

(3.1) becomes

$$\bar{x}_{0g} = \alpha_0 \bar{x}_{1g}^{\alpha_1} \bar{x}_{2g}^{\alpha_2} \quad (g=1,\ldots, p), \tag{3.2}$$

where the constant α_0 depends on the initial distribution:

$$\alpha_0 = a_0 \int_0^\infty \int_0^\infty x_1^{\alpha_1} x_2^{\alpha_2} n_0(x_1, x_2)\, dx_1 dx_2\,;$$

thus the output-elasticities α_1, α_2 are in this case the same in the individual and in the 'collective' production function.

§25. The assumption of proportionate fluctuations of manpower (and of capital) in all firms from year to year is difficult to visualize, especially when old firms disappear and new ones, perhaps more numerous, are added. It is still less possible to apply that assumption in comparing aggregates as widely differing in the number of firms as single 'industries'.

Such comparison becomes easier if the above assumption is replaced by the following: that all firms in a given aggregate have the same output, manpower, and capital. If the aggregate g consists of n_g firms, the measuring of the three averages $\bar{x}_{0g}$, $\bar{x}_{1g}$, $\bar{x}_{2g}$ is assumed equivalent to the measuring of the three variables on identical n_g firms. Accordingly, when, e.g., the moments of those averages (or, say, of their logarithms) are computed, each product must be weighted by n_g, the number of firms in a given industry. For example, for 'interindustrial cross-section' studies the operations to be performed on the census data – either to apply the least-squares method, or the method suggested in Section II and assuming (1.19) – are as follows. Given, for each industry g ($g=1,\ldots,p$) the total labor x'_{1g}, capital x'_{2g}, net output value y'_{0g}, and the number of firms n_g, form the averages

$$\bar{y}_{0g}=y'_{0g}/n_g, \qquad \bar{x}_{ig}=x'_{ig}/n_g \quad (i=1,2;\ g=1,\ldots,p);$$

find the logarithms

$$\log_{10}\bar{y}_{0g}=z_{0g}, \qquad \log_{10}\bar{x}_{ig}=z_{ig} \quad (i=1,2;\ g=1,\ldots,p).$$

Write $n=\sum_{g=1}^{p} n_g$ and compute the weighted means $\bar{z}_j=(1/n)\sum_{g=1}^{p} n_g z_{jg}$ $(j=0,1,2)$ and the weighted moments

$$m_{jk}=\frac{1}{n}\sum_{g=1}^{p} n_g(z_{jg}-\bar{z}_j)(z_{kg}-\bar{z}_k) \quad (j,k=0,1,2). \tag{3.3}$$

§26. The assumption that all firms in an industry are identical is a makeshift called for by the fact that data on single firms collected by census authorities have not been published in the form of trivariate distributions for each industry. Using this assumption it is impossible, in particular, to construct confidence limits around the estimates of parameters since the size of the sample is not known: the information provided by the industrial averages for p (say 80 or 100) industries is larger than that which would be provided by p firms picked at random; but it is smaller than the information that would be provided by a trivariate grouped distribution; and the latter is smaller than the information that would be provided by separate data on all $n=\sum_{g=1}^{p} n_g$ $(=100000$, say, or thereabouts) firms. On the other hand, even the lowest of these figures, p, is rather large. The imperfection of our knowledge of certain constants such as c_{00}, c_{01}, or c_{02} in §§18 and 19 (limits of the variance of technical efficiency; limits of its correlation with manpower and with capital), imposes on the final estimates much wider limits than the confidence limits constructed for, say, size of sample $=100$ and for any given set of mutually compatible values of those constants.

§27. However, even if individual data for all firms (or a trivariate grouped distribution) were published, making the makeshift of §25 unnecessary, it would be probably preferable to study each industry separately. The hypothesis of §15 – that α_1 and α_2 do not vary from firm to firm, while a_0 is a random parameter – is essential to the application of the least-squares method as well as to the method outlined in Section II. This hypothesis, however, is difficult to maintain for all firms of all industries. Though a_0 (and consequently ε_0) need not be distributed normally to permit the application of either method; and though the technological differences between the 80 or so industries can be regarded as random, yet the ensuing, presumably multimodal, distribution (strong clustering of the values of a_0 around certain magnitudes characteristic of each industry) may produce great inaccuracies[21] – though perhaps not much greater than those due to the imperfection of our knowledge of the boundary constants, such as c_{00}, c_{01}, c_{02}. If a firm's belonging to a given industry is regarded as a 'systematic' rather than a 'random' cause, and is, accordingly, studied by properly isolating it – i.e., by studying each industry separately, perhaps after a preliminary analysis of variance as a guide to such separation – more accurate results are obtained. For the analogous reason, the 'intertemporal' studies cannot render reliable estimates unless one isolates the factor time by introducing a proper trend. This is an alternative to isolating each year (as is done in the 'cross-section studies'); but in either case the systematic variations from industry to industry will spoil the accuracy even if the systematic variations from year to year have been removed.

The computations and diagrams of Chapter II were based on figures of the U.S.A. Census of Manufactures for 1909 [45] using the assumption that all firms belonging to one industry were identical. Because this assumption is dubious and because of systematic variations as between industries, the results are probably very inaccurate. They mainly serve the purpose of showing the kind of uncertainty that would prevail in these studies even if the data by individual firms were available, and the assumption of 'identical firms' unnecessary. In addition, Figures 1 and 2 help to illustrate the relationship between the least-squares 'single-equation' estimates and the true values of output elasticities.

§28. Some of the 'single-equation' least-squares estimates of output elasticities, computed by Douglas and others from census data, are listed in Table II.[22] One has to keep in mind that:

(1) in some earlier studies – e.g., [5], [8], [9] – the systematic effect of a time trend was not eliminated;

(2) in some earlier studies, the coefficients α_1 and α_2 were bound by the a priori condition of 'constant returns to scale', $\alpha_1+\alpha_2=1$; this does not seem justified (see Appendix 1, §43);

(3) the dividing of aggregate output, labor, and capital of a year or an industry by the number of firms was not performed except in later studies;

(4) when such dividing was done, the computed moments were not weighted though they should be (see §25).

Table III takes up in somewhat more detail one of the results listed in Table II, viz., U.S.A. 1909 [10]. The effect is shown (1) of dividing or not dividing each industrial aggregate by the number of firms in the industry; (2) of computing weighted or unweighted moments of the logarithms. (As explained in §25, the correct procedure is to divide the industrial aggregates and to weight the moments of logarithms.) We have applied one further adjustment. Some of the industrial groupings used by Bronfenbrenner and Douglas [10] were rather heterogeneous composites of Census items. To make the assumption of 'identical firms in each industry' more plausible, the list had to be revised.[23] It is from these revised data that the weighted moments (§21, Table I) were computed by formula (3.3), and used for the construction of Figures 1 and 2.

§29. In this and the following sections, the two main findings of Douglas and his collaborators will be analyzed. It is claimed by those authors that: (1) the sum a_1+a_2 – the sum of the least-squares estimates – tends to be close to 1; (2) a_1 tends to be close to the national ratio of pay rolls to net output, $\bar{w}_1$.

From these findings, conclusions were drawn regarding the prevalence of perfect competition in the industry. This may mean (1) absence of monopoly in the markets of products (§6); (2) rapid free entry into or exit out of industry, of firms having nonzero profits (Appendix 1, §§41 seq.); (3) absence of monopsony in the labor market (§6); (4) absense of monopsony in the capital market (§6); (5) absence of monopolistic arrangements among customers, among workers, or among lenders (§7).

We shall first analyze whether, or under what conditions, any of these economic implications do follow from the above two findings, granted the statistical reliability of those findings. We shall then (§34) come back to the statistical question.

It should be kept in mind that whether the conclusions as to the prevalence of perfect competition be justified or not, the estimation of output elasticities (α_1, α_2) and of the other parameters involved [β_j; $\sigma_{jk}(j, k=0, 1, 2)$] has theoretical interest and particular importance as a tool of policy of firms and of governments. Hence the importance of the statistical question implied.

§30. To begin with (see §17), a_1 and a_2 are estimates not of the output elasticities α_1 and α_2 but of the 'output elasticities corrected for monopoly', viz., of $\alpha_1' = \alpha_1 \beta_0$ and $\alpha_2' = \alpha_2 \beta_0$. This follows from equations (1.31) which must be applied when the data used are: output (or net output) in dollars, labor in men, capital in dollars.[24] To obtain, instead, the estimates of α_1 and α_2 one would have to use equations (1.29): but this would imply that output is measured in physical, not in money units (hence independent of prices, i.e., of degree of monopoly) – a kind of data possible for interfirm studies in certain one-commodity industries, but not for a study embracing different industries. Since β_0 is equal to or smaller than one, the presence of imperfect competition in the market of the products of at least some of the industries studied makes α_1' and α_2' lower than the true output elasticities.

§31. The first of the two findings listed in §29 must therefore (granted the statistical reliability of the estimates) be written in the form

$$(3.4) \qquad (\alpha_1 + \alpha_2)\,\beta_0 = 1.$$

If it were known that $\beta_0 = 1$, equation (3.4) would indeed mean that the production function assumed common to all firms is homogeneous of first degree: 'constant returns to scale' at any combination of resources. This would not in itself imply the absence of monopoly in the markets of products; nor the absence of monopsony in the markets of resources; nor the rapidity of 'free entry and exit'. But if those monopolies and monopsonies were absent, the homogeneity, of first degree, of the production function of each firm would indeed imply necessarily, though it is not implied by (see Appendix 1, §§42–43), the absence of profits and losses; and this absence, in turn, is implied by (though does not necessarily imply) instantaneous 'free entry and exit'. The question thus arises whether the data yield, in addition to (3.4), also $\beta_0=\beta_1=\beta=1$, i.e., the absence of firms' monopolies and monopsonies in the three markets.

§32. The absence of monopsony in at least one of the markets concerned, viz., the absence of monopsony for labor, has, in fact, been inferred from the second finding, viz., from a_1 being close to the national ratio of pay rolls to net output. Still granting that a_1 is a reliable approximation of $\alpha_1'=\alpha_1\beta_0$, let us formulate the finding more precisely:

$$(3.5)\qquad \alpha_1\beta_0=\frac{\sum_{f=1}^{n} y_{1f}}{\sum_{f=1}^{n} y_{0f}}\equiv\frac{\sum_{f=1}^{n} w_{1f}y_{0f}}{\sum_{f=1}^{n} y_{0f}}\equiv\bar{w}_1 \quad \text{(say)},$$

a weighted average of the ratios (w_{1f}) of each firm's pay roll to each firm's net output value. On the other hand, for each such individual ratio we know, rewriting (1.13) for the firm f, that, if it has its profit at a maximum,

$$(3.6)\qquad \alpha_1\beta_0=\beta_1 w_{1f}.$$

The finding (3.5) together with the assumption of maximized profits would lead thus to

$$(3.7)\qquad \beta_1=\frac{\bar{w}_1}{w_{1f}}.$$

Thus, if all profits were maximized, and if all the individual pay-roll shares w_{1f} were equal (and hence equal to their weighted average $\bar{w}_1$), it would have been proved that

$$\beta_1=1,$$

i.e., absence of monopsony for labor. Unfortunately, to assume that all w_{1f} are equal is not realistic. A look at the Census figures shows great fluctuations even between industrial averages of w_{1f}. Even after all industries are grouped into large complexes, there remain strong fluctuations of the average labor shares (w_1), as seen, for example, from the following calculations of Bronfenbrenner and Douglas for U.S.A., 1909 [10]: Clothing and textiles, $w_1=0.69$; Foods and beverages, $w_1=0.56$; Metals and machinery, $w_1=0.73$. Fluctuations among single firms are, of course, larger: it is likely (§19) that, within an industry, the more efficient firms have lower values of w_{1f} than the technically less efficient ones. Thus (3.7) would imply that β_1, too, fluctuates from firm to firm, stronger monopsony being accompanied by lower labor share and correlated with higher technical efficiency. Alternatively, one may doubt the exact validity of (3.7) – even while still granting statistical reliability to the finding (3.5) – because (3.7) is based on the assumption of exactly maximized profits, which cannot be granted and need not be made in realistic studies (§§12, 13).

§33. To sum up: granted the statistical reliability of the claimed two findings, i.e., granted that

$$(3.4) \qquad (\alpha_1+\alpha_2)\,\beta_0=1 \quad \text{(approximately)},$$

and

$$(3.5) \qquad \alpha_1\beta_0=\bar{w}_1 \quad \text{(approximately)},$$

the following inferences can be made, provided there is no monopoly in product markets ($\beta_0=1$): (1) all production functions are homogeneous of first degree; (2) if there is no monopsony in the resources markets ($\beta_0=\beta_1=\beta_2=1$), there is 'free entry and exit'; (3) either the degree of labor monopsony varies strongly from industry to industry (and firm to firm), fluctuating around unity; or the profits are not maximized. These inferences have, however, to compete with another one, viz., the statistical reliability of the findings may be doubted.

§34. First of all, the degree of approximation in (3.4) and (3.5) is not very satisfactory. This is seen from Tables II and III. The sum a_1+a_2 does deviate from 1, and a_1 does deviate from $\bar{w}_1$ considerably if account is taken of the standard error.

These deviations might become either larger or smaller if the necessary revisions (enumerated in §28) were made in the calculations.

§35. Moreover, we should remember that the assumption that α_1, α_2

(though not A_0) are the same for all firms is due only to the limitation of our statistical tools (§15). What is actually computed are certain 'average' values of these parameters. Therefore, even if it should be true that estimates of α_1 and α_2 added up to 1, this would imply 'constant returns to scale' only in the sense that if some firms have increasing returns, these are, on the whole, offset by others having decreasing returns. The proportion of firms to have 'almost' constant returns to scale will be the smaller, the more strongly the values of α_1 and α_2 fluctuate from firm to firm – thus making hypotheses such as (1.23) [the one used in the least-squares estimates and also used as part of our own hypothesis (1.31)] with A_0 as the only random parameter, more and more erroneous.

On the other hand, another limitation, not of statistical tools, but (a more accidental one) of available published data, has made it necessary, in the studies of Douglas as well as in our own illustration, to assume that all firms within an industry are identical (§25).

§36. The two particular assumptions mentioned in §35 are needed for our estimates not less than for those of Douglas and his collaborators. But we have removed certain further assumptions that are tacitly made when the 'single-equation' method is applied, and that need not be made. This is seen in our Figures 1 and 2. For example, the 'single-equation' least-squares estimate becomes worse and worse the stronger the variation of technical efficiency from firm to firm (or firm industry to industry), as measured by the sample variance s_{00} which can be used as an approximation (being a consistent estimate) of the population variance σ_{00} (§§21–22).

Furthermore, the sample correlations r_{01} and r_{02} are both nonnegative at the point A whose co-ordinates are the least-squares estimates a_1, a_2. This fact is not due to the particular data on which Figure 1 is based; it can be derived from (2.3), substituting for α'_1, α'_2 their 'single-equation' least-squares estimates a_1, a_2.[25] As the sample covariances can be used as approximations (being consistent estimates) of the population covariances, the population correlation coefficients ρ_{01}, ρ_{02} are likely to be nonnegative if the least-squares estimates a_1, a_2 happen to coincide with the true values of α'_1, α'_2. Economic considerations (§19) make it probable, however, that ρ_{01} is positive but ρ_{02} *negative*. This would throw doubt on any estimate of α'_1, α'_2 represented by a point lying far above the line $\rho_{02}=0$. To be sure, the hypothesis $\rho_{02}<0$ is only approximate: it is the less exact, the stronger the differences between the firms' supply curves (which are all horizontal under perfect competition).

§37. Consider now Figure 1. It is based on the assumption that labor and capital markets are perfect ($\beta_1=\beta_2=1$). Using first the considerations of §18: if the 'best' firm as there defined is technically at the most 4 times more efficient than the worst, and if a Gibrat distribution of technical efficiency is assumed, then $\sigma_{00}=0.010$, and the consistent estimate of α_1', α_2' will lie on or within the corresponding ellipse. As our 'firms' are actually industrial averages (§§25–26), the ratio 4:1 is perhaps a reasonable upper limit. The next larger ellipse on Figure 1, $\sigma_{00}=0.020$, would correspond to a ratio $10^{6\sqrt{\sigma_{00}}}:1=7:1$ which some estimators may prefer as a more cautious upper limit.

Using now the considerations of §19: if $\rho_{01}>0$ and $\rho_{02}<0$, the consistent estimates of α_1', α_2' must lie within the triangle formed by the lines $\rho_{01}=0$, $\rho_{02}=0$, and the horizontal axis (since $\alpha_2'>0$). Together with the elliptic boundary ($\sigma_{00}=0.010$) just discussed, this will reduce the region to the southeastern part of the ellipse. The other boundary derived in §19, viz., Equation (1.41), does not prove effective as it practically coincides, in the relevant part of the figure, with one of the larger ellipse. ($\bar{w}_1=0.68$, assumed profit $\bar{w}=0.10$, so that $\bar{w}_2=0.22$.)

Finally, the condition of §20 is, under perfect competition, that of nonincreasing returns (and maximized profits). A straight line (denoted by $|\pi|=0$), sloping at $-45°$ to both axes, chops another bit off the ellipse. The resulting region is shaded.

On Figure 2, four alternative assumptions (the same as on Figure 3) have been made as to the size of β_1 and β_2; and, in addition to the assumptions of the preceding paragraphs, it was assumed $\rho_{01}\geqq 0.7$. The resulting regions are:

If	$\beta_1=\beta_2=1$,	*CDEFGC*,
If	$\beta_1=1$, $\beta_2=1.5$	*CDEHIGC*,
If	$\beta_1=1.5$, $\beta_2=1$	*JKLMJ*,
If	$\beta_1=\beta_2=1.5$	*JNPMJ*.

It appears that the region of values of α_1', α_2' compatible with the data and with certain economic considerations shrinks as β_1 increases. One might thus be able to form a judgment as to the upper limits of β_1; in the case of a single industry these would be indicative of the degrees of monopsony in the labor market. However, the economic considerations would need further treatment before such judgment is made. For example (as follows from the reasoning of § 19), the bounding lines $\rho_{01}=0$, $\rho_{02}=0$ must themselves be modified as the markets become more imperfect and the supply curves to single firms less similar.

Naturally, the region of consistent estimates of the set of parameters α_1', α_2', β_1, β_2, compatible with the data as well as with other information we have is the narrower, the more precise that information: that is, the narrower the inequalities such as thus suggested in §§ 18–20.[26] With information vague, the region is wide, and the conclusions, on the whole, of a negative type. For actual applications a still wider region would have to be used: a confidence interval would have to be constructed around every estimation point. This could not be done here, because, when using industrial averages instead of single firms, we were ignorant about what to consider the size of the sample (§ 26).

If data on the output and used resources of individual firms of a single industry become available, the method outlined in Chapter II and resulting so far in Figures 1 and 2 will become more promising for three reasons: (1) the assumption 'all firms in an industry are identical' will be dropped; (2) it will become possible, at least in the case of one-commodity industries, to apply hypothesis (1.29) and estimate α_1, α_2 instead of $\alpha_1\beta_0$, $\alpha_2\beta_0$; (3) for a given single industry, the knowledge of the variability of technical efficiency, and of its correlation with labor, capital, and profit share can be more precise than for all industries, so that the region of consistent estimates can be narrowed down; (4) confidence intervals can be constructed, the size of sample being equal to the number of firms.

With the type of data used here (and also used by Douglas and his collaborators) the discussion was necessarily critical and illustrative. Douglas' estimates listed in Table II do exhibit a stability from one year to another which presumably would not be much affected by applying corrections as in Table III. Since the probabilities of the least-squares estimates are functions of the parameters of the joint distribution of output, labor, and capital – i.e., functions of the α's, as well as of the variances and covariances of the random components (such as technical and economic efficiency) – the stability of Douglas' results suggest that those parameters change only slowly. This promises significant results as soon as better data are available for the estimation of those parameters.

IV. APPENDIX 1. DECREASING, INCREASING, AND CONSTANT RETURNS TO SCALE

§38. It is often believed that, for 'a priori reasons', the production function must belong to a certain class. Such restrictions are derived from the assumption of maximized profits and perfect competition in the markets of products as well as resources; to these assumptions sometimes is added the assumption of instantaneous wiping out of profits and losses by free entry of firms into profit-making, free exit of firms out of loss-making industries. In the empirical work, outlined in the preceding chapters, no such assumptions need be made though some of them may be tested. However, the questions have played a role in the theory and statistical study of production. They deserve clarification if only to establish how these various assumptions are related.

In Section I, only the first-order conditions for a maximum profit of a firm were stated:

$$(1.11), (1.12) \qquad \frac{\partial \pi}{\partial x_1}=0, \qquad \frac{\partial \pi}{\partial x_2}=0.$$

These conditions are necessary for the profit to be at a maximum, i.e., to exceed the profits in all points of the neighborhood. However, these conditions are also compatible with profits being at a minimum, or being at an 'improper maximum',[27] and with still other situations. In other words, the vanishing of the first-order derivatives of the profit is necessary but not sufficient for a proper maximum.

Denoting now the second derivatives $\partial^2\pi/\partial x_h \partial x_i$ by π_{hi} $(i=1, 2)$, there exist, for a proper maximum of π, the following *necessary* conditions

$$(4.1), (4.2), (4.3) \qquad \pi_{11} \leqq 0, \qquad \pi_{22} \leqq 0, \qquad |\pi| \geqq 0$$

where $|\pi|$ is the determinant $\pi_{11}\pi_{22}-\pi_{12}^2$. There exist the following *sufficient* conditions (to be taken together):

$$(4.4), (4.5) \qquad \pi_{11}<0, \qquad |\pi|>0$$

(from the latter two follows also $\pi_{22}<0$).

(4.1)–(4.5) will be seen in the next sections to imply, in the case of a firm, that, if the output of and the quantities of resources used by the firm are determined by its making profits a maximum, and if there is perfect competition in the markets of its product as well as of its resources, the firm's production function must not show *increasing* returns to scale; if it shows *decreasing* returns to scale, while all the necessary first-order conditions are satisfied, the proper maximum of profit is secured. This leaves open (until §42) the case of *constant* returns to scale. The three cases were defined in §5.

§39. Let us start with the special case (1.19)–(1.22), used in the present article as an empirical approximation: the case of constant output elasticities (α_1, α_2) and constant elasticities of revenue and of outlays ($\beta_0, \beta_1, \beta_2$). Then the profit

$$\pi \equiv b_0 \cdot (a_0 x_1^{\alpha_1} x_2^{\alpha_2})^{\beta_0} - b_1 x_1^{\beta_1} - b_2 x_2^{\beta_2}.$$

If the necessary first-order conditions, $\partial\pi/\partial x_1 = \partial\pi/\partial x_2 = 0$, are satisfied, the necessary second-order conditions (4.1)–(4.3) become[28]

$$(4.6) \qquad (\beta_0 \alpha_i - \beta_i) \leqq 0 \quad (i=1, 2),$$
$$\beta_1 \beta_2 - \beta_0 \cdot (\alpha_1 \beta_2 + \alpha_2 \beta_1) \geqq 0.$$

From §6 and from these inequalities we have (since $\alpha_1, \alpha_2, \beta_1, \beta_2$ are all positive)

$$(4.7) \qquad \alpha_1 \frac{\beta_0}{\beta_1} + \alpha_2 \frac{\beta_0}{\beta_2} \leqq 1.$$

If $\beta_0 = \beta_1 = \beta_2 = 1$, i.e., if there exists perfect competition in all three markets, the sufficient condition (4.7) becomes

$$(4.8) \qquad \alpha_1 + \alpha_2 \leqq 1,$$

i.e., increasing returns to scale are excluded.

If, instead of combining the necessary first-order conditions with the necessary second-order conditions (4.1)–(4.3), we combine the necessary first-order conditions with the sufficient second-order conditions (4.4), (4.5), we obtain, as sufficient conditions for proper maximum of profits, the same propositions as (4.6), (4.7), (4.8), but with the equality signs dropped:

$$(4.7') \qquad \alpha_1 \frac{\beta_0}{\beta_1} + \alpha_2 \frac{\beta_0}{\beta_2} < 1 ;$$

and, under perfect competition in all three markets,

$$(4.8') \qquad \alpha_1 + \alpha_2 < 1 ;$$

i.e., under perfect competition, the vanishing of the first-order derivatives of profit of a firm with decreasing returns to scale ensures proper maximum profits.

Figure 3 illustrates these results. The axes are $\alpha_1' = \alpha_1 \beta_0$ and $\alpha_2' = \alpha_2 \beta_0$. Those points in the (α_1', α_2')-plane which lie neither in the area bounded by the axes and by the straight line with intercepts β_1, β_2, nor on that straight line itself, are not compatible with profit maximization. The equation of the straight line is

$$(1.43) \qquad \frac{\alpha_1'}{\beta_1} + \frac{\alpha_2'}{\beta_2} = 1 .$$

In the case of perfect competition in all three markets the excluded area is that bounded by line (a) which has equation $\alpha_1 + \alpha_2 = 1$. That is, the returns to scale must not be increasing. In a somewhat more general case $\beta_1 = \beta_2$ $(= \beta$, say$)$ $\geqq \beta_0$, we have $\alpha_1 + \alpha_2 \leqq \beta / \beta_0$, and since $\beta / \beta_0 \geqq 1$, increasing returns to scale are possible (i.e., compatible with maximum profits). The line (b) illustrates at the same time the case $\beta_0 = 1$, $\beta_1 = \beta_2 = \frac{3}{2}$ (perfect competition in the sale of the product); or the case $\beta_0 = \frac{2}{3}$, $\beta_1 =$ $= \beta_2 = 1$ (perfect competition in the purchase of the factors); or a case like $\beta_0 = \frac{8}{9}$, $\beta_1 = \beta_2 = \frac{4}{3}$ (imperfect competition in all three markets, with the two outlay elasticities equal). In all these cases the sum $\alpha_1 + \alpha_2 \leqq \frac{3}{2}$. Still more general is a case (c) when all three elasticities are unequal: the sum $\alpha_1 + \alpha_2$ is $\leqq \beta_1 / \beta_0$, or $\leqq \beta_2 / \beta_0$, whichever is larger. Other cases, (d) and (e), are also shown on Figure 3 as well as on Figure 2.

This exclusion of a certain area represents a necessary condition (4.7) for a proper maximum. We further have the sufficient condition (4.7'): if the point lies neither in the excluded area *nor on the boundary line*, and the necessary conditions (vanishing of first derivative) are satisfied, proper maximum profits are assured. The boundary line represents, under per-

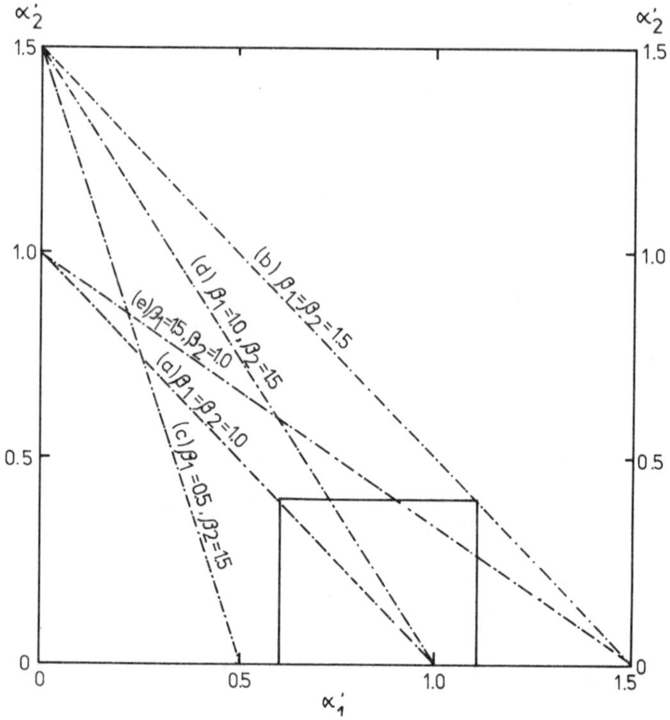

Fig. 3. Boundary lines for profit maxima, $|\pi|=0$, under varying degrees of labor and capital monopsony. $\alpha_1'/\beta_1+\alpha_2'/\beta_2=1$, $(\alpha_1'=\alpha_1\beta_0,\ \alpha_2'=\alpha_2\beta_0)$. (Small rectangle represents field of Figure 2.)

fect competition, the case of *constant returns*: they leave the sufficient conditions unfulfilled.

§40. Dropping now our special case (1.19)–(1.22), we can conveniently treat the general case (1.2)–(1.5) by introducing the 'elasticities of elasticities',

$$\alpha_{hi}=\frac{\partial\alpha_h}{\partial x_i}\cdot\frac{x_i}{\alpha_h}\quad(h,i=1,2),$$

and writing further

$$\beta_j^*=\beta_j+\frac{d\beta_j}{dx_j}\cdot\frac{x_j}{\beta_j}\quad(j=0,1,2).$$

From definitions we have

$$\text{(4.9)} \qquad \frac{\alpha_{12}}{\alpha_2}=\frac{\alpha_{21}}{\alpha_1}\equiv\alpha \quad \text{(say)}.$$

If profit is maximized, we obtain by straightforward differentiation the following restrictions upon the functions involved (necessary conditions; or, if equality signs are dropped, sufficient conditions)

$$\text{(4.10)} \qquad \begin{aligned} &\beta_0\cdot(\alpha_i\beta_0^*-\beta_i^*+\alpha_{ii})\leqq 0 \quad (i=1,2),\\ &(\alpha_1\beta_0^*-\beta_1^*+\alpha_{11})(\alpha_2\beta_0^*-\beta_2^*+\alpha_{22})-\alpha_1\alpha_2(\beta_0^*+\alpha)^2\geqq 0.\end{aligned}$$

These inequalities have to take the place of (4.6), (4.7) which had already shown, for the special case then considered, that under imperfect competition increasing returns to scale are compatible with maximum profits. Those special inequalities can be derived from the general ones (4.10), by making the α_i and β_i constant, so that $\alpha_{hi}=\alpha=0$, $\beta_j^*=\beta_j$ $(h, i=1,2; j=0,1,2)$.

Another important case (which includes the special case just mentioned) is that of a production function homogeneous of degree $\alpha_1+\alpha_2=$ $=r=$const. [see Equation (1.9)], the α's being, in general, not indepent of the x's. Differentiating (1.9) with respect to x_1 or x_2, we have, by (4.9),

$$\frac{\alpha_{11}}{\alpha_2}=\frac{\alpha_{22}}{\alpha_1}=-\alpha,$$

and, by (4.10), if $\beta_0=\beta_1=\beta_2=1$ (perfect competition),

$$\begin{aligned} &\alpha_1-1-\alpha_2\alpha\leqq 0,\\ &\alpha_2-1-\alpha_1\alpha\leqq 0,\\ &(1-r)(\alpha r+1)\geqq 0.\end{aligned}$$

Adding the first two inequalities gives $(1-r)\geqq-(\alpha r+1)$, so that in the third inequality the factors cannot both be negative; hence

$$\begin{aligned} 1-r&\geqq 0,\\ \alpha_1+\alpha_2&\leqq 1.\end{aligned}$$

Again [as in the special case (4.8)], this restriction upon the production function (exclusion of increasing returns to scale) would not be obtained if at least one of the three markets was imperfect.

§41. If it is assumed that firms enter or leave the industry instantaneously in response to positive or negative profits, an additional equation is provided:

$$(4.11) \qquad \pi_f = 0 \quad (f = 1, \ldots, n),$$

making thus for each firm the number of equations [29] larger by one than the number of variables. The system thus becomes inconsistent unless certain further restrictions are imposed upon the functions involved. As the process of the entry and exit of firms involves interrelationships among firms, it is necessary to set up the system of equations for the economy as a whole. No generality is lost, for the purpose at hand, if all (n) firms are supposed to produce the same commodity (identified by subscript 0). Before the condition of zero profits is introduced, we have the following determinate system ($f = 1, \ldots, n$; $j = 0, 1, 2$; $i = 1, 2$), where the last column refers to the single-firm system of equations in Section I:

(4.12)	$3n$ identities	$y_{jf} = p_{jf} x_{jf}$	(1.1),
(4.13)	n identities	$\pi_f = y_{0f} - y_{1f} - y_{2f}$	(1.10),
(4.14)	$3n$ revenue and outlay equations	$y_{jf} = y_{jf}(x_{jf})$	(1.3)–(1.5),
(4.15)	n production equations	$x_{0f} = \phi_f(x_{1f}, x_{2f})$	(1.2),
(4.16)	$2n$ equilibrium equations	$\dfrac{\partial \pi_f}{\partial x_{if}} = 0$	(1.11)–(1.12).

This system of $10n$ equations and unknowns reproduces exactly that given in Section I for one firm. If perfect competition is assumed, in the sense that firms receive (and pay) the same prices, and no single firm can affect them, the number of unknown prices is reduced by $3(n-1)$; and the $3n$ revenue and outlay equations have to be replaced by 3 equations of aggregate demand (and supply): say [30]

$$(4.17) \qquad p_j = F_j\left(\sum_{f=1}^{n} x_{jf}\right) \quad (j = 0, 1, 2).$$

We can then present the system more compactly, eliminating the y's (revenues and outlays) and performing the differentiation in (4.16):

$$\begin{aligned} &(4.18) \qquad \pi_f = p_0 x_{0f} - p_1 x_{1f} - p_2 x_{2f}, \\ &x_{0f} = \phi_f(x_{1f}, x_{2f}) \qquad (f=1,\ldots,n), \\ &\frac{p_i}{p_0} = \frac{\partial \phi_f}{\partial x_i} \qquad (j=0,1,2;\ i=1,2), \\ &p_j = F_j\left(\sum_{f=1}^{n} x_{jf}\right). \end{aligned}$$

§42. If, now, the condition of 'free entry' is added,

$$(4.11) \qquad \pi_f = 0 \quad (f=1,\ldots,n),$$

the system has n equations more than unknowns. It becomes inconsistent unless such restrictions are imposed upon the production functions and other functions involved, as would make n equations derivable from the rest of the system.

Economists have looked for such restrictions, discussing in particular the case of perfect competition, i.e., the case when (4.14) is replaced by (4.17). It was suggested that the conditions of perfect competition and maximum profits can be reconciled with the condition of zero profits if all production functions ϕ_f $(f=1,\ldots,n)$ are homogeneous of first degree, i.e., the returns to scale are constant. However, other restrictions on the functions involved might be imposed instead.[31]

§43. If all n production functions ϕ_f are homogeneous of first degree, and Equations (4.18) are satisfied, profits π_f $(f=1,\ldots,n)$ vanish identically by Euler's theorem (1.8a). In this case the n equations (4.11) do not make the system inconsistent. But the production functions being homogeneous of first degree make the system indeterminate. This is seen by rewriting the production function for each firm (dropping the subscript f for brevity) in the form $x_0 = x_2 \cdot g(x_1/x_2)$ and defining $u = x_1/x_2$, $v = x_0/x_2$. The first three lines in (4.18) become

$$\begin{aligned} &(4.19) \qquad \frac{\pi}{p_0 x_2} = v - \frac{p_1}{p_0} u - \frac{p_2}{p_0}, \\ &v = g(u), \\ &\frac{p_1}{p_0} = g'(u), \quad \frac{p_2}{p_0} = g(u) - u g'(u). \end{aligned}$$

The last two equations in (4.19) impose a restriction on prices; if this is satisfied, one of these two equations becomes redundant, and (4.19) determines the ratios u and v, and the profit $(=0)$, but not the x's themselves. These remain still indeterminate when the n individual firms' systems (4.19) are supplemented by the 3 Equations (4.17) of aggregate demand and supply.

The amount of resources and product being indeterminate, the question whether the profit is at its maximum loses much of its meaning. To be sure, the same formal property of the homogeneous linear function ϕ that makes the system indeterminate renders also the sufficient conditions for profit maximum unsatisfied. The determinant $|\phi|=|\partial^2\phi/\partial x_h \partial x_i|$ is the Jacobian of the system of equations $p_0\phi_i - p_i = 0$, and its vanishing shows the system indeterminate. On the other hand the determinant $|\pi|=|\partial^2\pi/\partial x_h \partial x_i| = p_0 |\phi|$; and its vanishing indicates that the profit need not be at the maximum.[32]

Now consider profit as a function of the ratio $u=x_1/x_2$, denoting by $\hat{u}$ the 'equilibrium' value of $\hat{u}$, i.e. the value that satisfies the last two equations in (4.19). Will this ratio be the most profitable one? We have

$$\frac{\pi}{p_0 x_2} = g(u) - ug'(\hat{u}) - g(\hat{u}) + \hat{u}g'(\hat{u})$$

(so that, as would be expected, $\pi=0$ when $u=\hat{u}$). If, now, u varies while x_2 remains constant,

$$\frac{1}{p_0 x_2} \cdot \frac{d\pi}{du} = g'(u) - g'(\hat{u})$$

(so that, as would be expected, $d\pi/du=0$ when $u=\hat{u}$); and, still varying u while x_2 remains constant, we have

$$\frac{1}{p_0 x_2} \cdot \frac{d^2\pi}{du^2} = g''(u);$$

thus, if u varies while x_2 remains constant, $d^2\pi/du^2$ has (when $u=\hat{u}$) the same sign as $g''(u)$. The same can be shown, at the point $u=\hat{u}$, if u varies while x_1 remains constant in the two successive differentiations; or when u varies while first x_1 and then x_2 (or vice versa) are kept constant. Hence, at the point $u=\hat{u}$, $\pi(u)$ has a maximum (or minimum, or neither) if $g(u)$

has a maximum (or minimum, or neither). For example, if in our special case (1.19) the production function is made homogeneous of first degree,

$$\alpha_1 + \alpha_2 = 1,$$
$$x_0 = a_0 x_1^{\alpha_1} x_2^{\alpha_2} = a_0 x_2 u^{\alpha_1},$$
$$g(u) = a_0 u^{\alpha_1},$$
$$g''(u) = \alpha_1(\alpha_1 - 1) = -\alpha_1 \alpha_2 < 0 \quad \text{(by 1.6)};$$

hence π is larger when $u = \hat{u}$ than at other neighboring values of u.[33] With some other production functions, also homogeneous of first degree, $g''(u)$ might have been positive, making profit a minimum at the 'equilibrium' ratio of resources used; or zero, and requiring further investigation.

To sum up: making all production functions homogeneous of the first degree does in general render perfect competition and profit maximization consistent with zero profits inferred from 'free entry', but makes the system indeterminate: only the ratios between the amounts of resources used by each firm and not those amounts themselves can be determined. And it depends on further properties of the production functions assumed, whether those ratios are indeed the most (or perhaps, e.g., the least) profitable ones.

It was also shown that other restrictions, having nothing to do with "constant returns", may be imposed upon the functions involved and render the system consistent.

Finally and probably most important: the whole problem of reconciling perfect competition, profit maximization, and instantaneous wiping out of profits hardly arises in reality. A workable empirical hypothesis must not be based on any of these three. It is especially hard to believe that the functions involved would 'adjust themselves' to the appropriate shapes with such rapidity, or that the profits and losses would vanish so quickly that the statistician's survey would record 'long-run' functions and the absence of profits and losses.[34]

The 'constant returns to scale' is a tricky boundary case which, as so often in economics, is too much used in classrooms because of its mistaken theoretical simplicity. The real interest of nondecreasing returns to scale lies in this: in theory they would preclude maximum profits under perfect competition; nevertheless, they may occur or even prevail in actual fact. Therefore the deviations of profits from their maxima and the deviations of prices from competitive ones (and the causes of such deviations) must be studied empirically. In the present study, the existence of such deviations was, in fact, not excluded.

V. APPENDIX 2: CRITICAL NOTE

§44. The gist of the recent discussion on 'interfirm production functions' would have lent itself to easier understanding if the authors had explicitly formulated the simultaneous random equations constituting the economist's hypothesis on firms' behavior. Mr. Reder's argument in [38] seems to indicate correctly that the hypothesis must consist of equations listed in our Introduction as (1), (2), (3) – preferably in a generalized form admitting of imperfect competition. He correctly states (in his last footnote) that the equations involved will vary from firm to firm. This seems contradicted, however, by his assumption (in introducing the article) that the production function "is known with complete accuracy, i.e., the values which its parameters take are not affected by random fluctuations. This assumption is made in order to simplify our discussion which is primarily theoretical". If this means (in contradiction to his footnote just mentioned) that all firms have the same production function, then, as illustrated in our Introduction in the case of demand and supply functions, the production function will exactly coincide with the 'empirical' (or 'interfirm') function. On the other hand, if all functions involved vary from firm to firm, the quantities of output, labor, and capital will not trace out a single surface (or, at constant capital, a single curve, whose derivative with respect to L is curve ww' on Reder's diagram), unless some additional constraints on the form of their variation are imposed. Presumably, the surface (or curve, or its derivative: Reder's curve, ww') is obtained by fitting it to the scatter diagram traced out by those variations, and is a 'mongrel' surface. This lack of clarity seems to be due to the attempt to make the discussion 'primarily theoretical', in the sense of omitting explicit treatment of random fluctuations. However, Reder's analysis seems to point in the right direction.

§45. Bronfenbrenner's [3] interpretation of the 'empirical production function' (i.e., the function fitted to the data on output, labor, and capital of a number of firms) seems different. He seems to consider the empirical equation not as a 'mongrel equation' at all; but rather as one of the equations of the system. The system he suggests consists, for each firm, of our Equations (1), (2), (3), correctly assumed to change from firm to firm; and, in addition, of the equations, one for each firm, expressing the absence of profits,

$$(5.1) \qquad x_0 p_0 = x_1 p_1 + x_2 p_2,$$

and, further, of two aggregate supply equations, one for each production factor (cf. §§41–42 above). Thus perfect competition is assumed not only in the sense of the prices being independent of any single firm's action; but also in the sense of instantaneous free entry or exit of firms, destroying instantaneously profits and losses. (As shown above, such a system, to be consistent, implies certain restrictions upon the functions involved.) Equation (5.1) which expresses this assumption, does not seem to contain, in Bronfenbrenner's view (if we interpret him correctly), any terms fluctuating from firm to firm. Hence the empirically fitted function must exactly coincide with (5.1). We do not think this is realistic. Entry and exit of firms, and the consequent wiping out of profits and losses (and the adjustment of the functions involved, to make the system consistent), can hardly be regarded as rapid enough to ensure, at any time, actual absence of profits and losses among the statistically observed firms. If, therefore, the "zero-profits" equation can be included at all in the system of equations describing a firm, with a random term to denote a profit (or loss), that random term is certainly subject to strong fluctuations from firm to firm. There is, therefore, little likelihood that a function fitted, e.g., by the least squares, would give even an approximation of the equation (5.1).[35]

VI. APPENDIX 3: CONSISTENT ESTIMATES OF PARAMETERS OF SYSTEMS OF LINEAR EQUATIONS WITHOUT TIME LAGS

§46. At the end of §22 it was stated that the sample variances and covariances s_{jk} are consistent estimates of the corresponding true values σ_{jk}. This statement will now be elaborated on the lines of [31] with respect to the general case (1.36), which is more symmetrical and therefore easier to handle than our special case (1.34).

It is required to estimate γ_j, γ_{jk}, σ_{jk} ($j, k=0, 1,\ldots, v$) in the equations

$$(1.36)\qquad \gamma_j+\sum_{k=0}^{v}\gamma_{jk}z_k=\varepsilon_j \quad (j=0,\ldots, v),$$

using n sets of observed values $(z_{0f},\ldots, z_{vf})$ $(f=1,\ldots, n)$. No assumption is made as to the form of the distribution of the ε_j's, except that (1) the random sets $(\varepsilon_{0f},\ldots,\varepsilon_{vf})$, $(\varepsilon_{0f'},\ldots,\varepsilon_{vf'}),\ldots,$ affecting the sets of observations numbered f, $f',\ldots,$ are independently distributed, each having the same distribution, and $E(\varepsilon_j)=0$ for all values of j; (2) that all moments of ε_j are finite; and (3) that $|\sigma_{jk}|\neq 0$.

Write

$$|\sigma|=\text{determinant } |\sigma_{jk}|,\ \|\sigma^{jk}\|=\|\sigma_{jk}\|^{-1},$$
$$|\gamma|=\text{absolute value of the determinant } |\gamma_{jk}|,$$ [36]

$$(6.1)\qquad q_{jk}=\frac{1}{n}\sum_{f=1}^{n}\varepsilon_{jf}\varepsilon_{kf}.$$ [37]

Form the expression

$$(6.2)\qquad L=\log|\gamma|+\tfrac{1}{2}\log|\sigma|^{-1}-\tfrac{1}{2}\sum_{j=0}^{v}\sum_{k=0}^{v}\sigma^{jk}q_{jk},$$

the logarithm (apart from a constant) of the likelihood function of a normal distribution.[38] Suppose that, from knowledge additional to the observations, we have w relationships

$$(6.3)\qquad F_u(\gamma_0,\ldots,\gamma_v,\gamma_{00},\ldots,\gamma_{vv},\sigma_{00},\ldots,\sigma_{vv})=0 \quad (u=1,\ldots, w).$$

Further use symbol $P_n(A)$ for the words 'probability that, when the sample has size n, A is true'.

It has been proved that *the values* $\gamma_j=\hat{\gamma_j}$, $\gamma_{jk}=\hat{\gamma_{jk}}$, $\sigma_{jk}=\hat{\sigma_{jk}}$ *that make L the highest maximum, subject to the side conditions* (6.3) *are consistent estimates of the γ's and σ's*; i.e., for any positive η, the probabilities

$$P_n(|\gamma_j-\hat{\gamma_j}|\leqq\eta),\ P_n(|\gamma_{jk}-\hat{\gamma_{jk}}|\leqq\eta),\ P_n(|\sigma_{jk}-\hat{\sigma_{jk}}|\leqq\eta),$$

all have limit 1 as $n\to\infty$.

If the joint probability distribution of the ε_j's is normal, these estimates are maximum-likelihood estimates. For that reason, according to a well-known theorem (see Wilks [49], pp. 138–139), they are consistent estimates. If the distribution of the ε_j's is not normal, the estimates are not maximum-likelihood estimates, but may be called, because of the method of their derivation, 'quasi-maximum-likelihood estimates'. In this case, their consistency has been proved by Mann and Wald [31], Part II, even under conditions more general than those here assumed (see last sentence of our § 16).

We have to differentiate L with respect to γ_g, γ_{gh}, and σ^{gh} $(g, h=0,\ldots, v)$; the latter is more convenient than differentiation with respect to σ_{jk} as it gives at once (the sign ^ indicating the values that maximize L)

$$\text{(6.4)} \qquad \left(\frac{\partial L}{\partial \sigma^{gh}}\right)^{\wedge} = \tfrac{1}{2}(2-\delta_{gh})\,(\sigma_{gh}^{\wedge} - q_{gh}^{\wedge}) = 0 \quad (g, h=0,\ldots, v),$$

$$\text{(6.5)} \qquad \sigma_{jk}^{\wedge} = q_{jk}^{\wedge} \quad (j, k=0,\ldots, v);$$

or in matrix form

$$\text{(6.5a)} \qquad \|\sigma^{\wedge}\| = \|q^{\wedge}\|.$$

For the other derivatives, we shall need the identities – from definitions (2.2), (6.1) –:

$$\text{(6.6)} \qquad q_{jk} = s_{jk} + \bar{\varepsilon}_j \bar{\varepsilon}_k,$$

$$\text{(6.7)} \qquad s_{jk} = \sum_{p=0}^{v} \sum_{q=0}^{v} \gamma_{jp} m_{pq} \gamma_{kq},$$

$$\text{(6.7a)} \qquad \|s\| = \|\gamma\| \cdot \|m\| \cdot \|\gamma\|'.$$

Hence by (6.6)

$$\frac{\partial q_{jk}}{\partial \gamma_g} = \frac{\partial \bar{\varepsilon}_j}{\partial \gamma_g}\,\bar{\varepsilon}_k + \frac{\partial \bar{\varepsilon}_k}{\partial \gamma_g}\,\bar{\varepsilon}_j = \delta_{jg}\bar{\varepsilon}_k + \delta_{kg}\bar{\varepsilon}_j,$$

$$\text{(6.8)} \qquad \left(\frac{\partial L}{\partial \gamma_g}\right)^{\wedge} = -\tfrac{1}{2}\sum_j \sum_k \sigma^{jk\wedge}\,\frac{\partial q_{jk}}{\partial \gamma_g} =$$

$$= -\tfrac{1}{2}\left(\sum_k \sigma^{gk}\bar{\varepsilon}_k^{\wedge} + \sum_j \sigma^{jg\wedge}\,\bar{\varepsilon}_j^{\wedge}\right)$$

$$= -\sum_k \sigma^{gk\wedge}\,\bar{\varepsilon}_k^{\wedge} = 0 \quad (g=0,\ldots, v),$$

a system of $(v+1)$ homogeneous linear equations in $\bar{\varepsilon}_k^{\wedge}$ $(k=0,\ldots, v)$. Since its determinant σ^{-1} is not zero,

$$(6.9) \qquad \bar{\varepsilon}_k^{\wedge} = 0 \quad (k = 0, \ldots, v);$$

hence by (6.6)

$$(6.10) \qquad \|q^{\wedge}\| = \|s^{\wedge}\|,$$

and by (1.36) and (2.1)

$$(6.11) \qquad \gamma_j^{\wedge} = -\sum_{k=0}^{v} \gamma_{jk}^{\wedge} \bar{z}_k,$$

which is the usual kind of equation for estimating the constant term. Finally, to obtain $\partial L/\partial\gamma_{gh}$, calculate, by (6.6), (6.9),

$$\begin{aligned}\left(\frac{\partial q_{jk}}{\partial \gamma_{gh}}\right) = \left(\frac{\partial s_{jk}}{\partial \gamma_{gh}}\right)^{\wedge} + \frac{\partial \bar{\varepsilon}_j}{\partial \gamma_{gh}} \bar{\varepsilon}_k^{\wedge} + \frac{\partial \bar{\varepsilon}_k}{\partial \gamma_{gh}} \bar{\varepsilon}_h^{\wedge} = \\ = \left(\frac{\partial s_{jk}}{\partial \gamma_{gh}}\right)^{\wedge} \quad \text{by (6.9)} = \\ = \sum_p \sum_q (\delta_{gj}\delta_{hp} m_{pq} \gamma_{kq}^{\wedge} + \delta_{gk}\delta_{hq} m_{pq} \gamma_{jp}^{\wedge}) = \\ = \sum_q \delta_{gj} m_{hq} \gamma_{kq}^{\wedge} + \sum_p \gamma_{jp}^{\wedge} m_{ph} \delta_{gk};\end{aligned}$$

hence

$$\left(\frac{\partial}{\partial \gamma_{gh}} \sum_j \sum_k \sigma^{jk} q_{jk}\right)^{\wedge} = 2 \sum_k \sum_q \sigma^{gk\wedge} \gamma_{kq}^{\wedge} m_{qh},$$

$$(6.12) \qquad \left(\frac{\partial L}{\partial \gamma_{gh}}\right)^{\wedge} = \gamma^{hg\wedge} - \sum_k \sum_q \sigma^{gk\wedge} \gamma_{kq}^{\wedge} m_{qh} = 0,$$

$$(6.12\text{a}) \qquad (\|\gamma^{\wedge}\|')^{-1} - \|\sigma^{\wedge}\|^{-1} \cdot \|\gamma^{\wedge}\| \cdot \|m\| = 0.$$

If there were no side conditions (6.3), the unknown γ's and σ's would have to be determined from (6.5), (6.11), and (6.12). However, this would be impossible since equations (6.12) are not independent of the rest. This is seen from the above matrix equations. We have by (6.5a), (6.7a), (6.10),

$$(6.13) \qquad \begin{aligned}\|\sigma^{\wedge}\| = \|q^{\wedge}\| = \|s^{\wedge}\| = \|\gamma^{\wedge}\| \cdot \|m\| \cdot \|\gamma^{\wedge}\|', \\ \|\sigma^{\wedge}\| - \|\gamma^{\wedge}\| \cdot \|m\| \cdot \|\gamma^{\wedge}\|' = 0.\end{aligned}$$

Premultiplying this by $\|\sigma^{\wedge}\|^{-1}$ and postmultiplying by $(\|\gamma^{\wedge}\|')^{-1}$, we obtain (6.12a).[39] The system contains as many dependent equations as there are unknown γ_{jk}'s.[40]

§47. If we have as many side conditions (6.3) as there are unknown γ_{jk}'s (counting also each known σ_{jk} as one side condition), the necessary conditions for the maximum of L are of the form

$$\left(\frac{\partial L}{\partial \theta_t} + \sum_{u=1}^{w} \lambda_u \frac{\partial F_u}{\partial \theta_t}\right)^{\wedge} = 0,$$

$$F_u^{\wedge} = 0 \quad (t=1, \ldots, w';\ u=1, \ldots, w),$$

where the θ's denote w' unknown consistent estimates (all σ's and some γ's) and where the λ's are Lagrange multipliers. If the number of side conditions is exactly equal to the number of unknown γ_{jk}'s, then one solution is provided by all λ's being zero, since we then obtain the equations

$$\left(\frac{\partial L}{\partial \theta_t}\right)^{\wedge} = 0, \qquad F_u = 0 \quad (t=1, \ldots, w';\ u=1, \ldots, w), \tag{6.14}$$

of which the first group is equivalent to (6.4), (6.8), and implies (6.12), so that we have the system

$$\sigma_{jk}^{\wedge} = \sum_{p=0}^{v} \sum_{q=0}^{v} \gamma_{jp}^{\wedge} m_{pq} \gamma_{kq}^{\wedge}, \tag{6.15}$$

$$\gamma_j^{\wedge} = -\sum_{p=0}^{v} \gamma_{jp}^{\wedge} \bar{z}_p,$$

$$F_u^{\wedge} = 0 \quad (j, k=0, \ldots, v;\ u=1, \ldots, w).$$

The problem has thus become that of a nonrestricted maximum of L, regarded as a function of σ's only. For any set of γ's, the Equations (6.15) will provide a set of σ's such as will satisfy the necessary conditions for L maximum, or minimum. We have to see whether such a set of σ's makes L a maximum (and not, for example, a minimum); and whether this maximum is higher than other maxima, to fulfill the consistency property of the maximum-likelihood estimates.

§48. To show that the roots of (6.15) make L a maximum we have to show that the matrix

$$\left\| \frac{\partial^2 L}{\partial \sigma^{gh} \partial \sigma^{rs}} \right\| = \left\| (2-\delta_{gh}) \frac{\partial \sigma_{gh}}{\partial \sigma^{rs}} \right\| \quad \text{[by (6.4)]}$$

is negative definite, as it will be shown later (§49) that L will then be a maximum for the problem. We may omit a discussion of the constant terms γ_j as trivial.

Differentiate with respect to σ^{rs} the identity

$$\|\sigma\| \cdot \|\sigma\|^{-1} = I,$$

$$\frac{\partial \|\sigma\|}{\partial \sigma^{rs}} \cdot \|\sigma\|^{-1} + \|\sigma\| \cdot \frac{\partial \|\sigma\|^{-1}}{\partial \sigma^{rs}} = 0,$$

$$\frac{\partial \|\sigma\|}{\partial \sigma^{rs}} \cdot \|\sigma\|^{-1} = - \|\sigma\| \cdot \|\eta\|,$$

where any element of $\|\eta\|$ is one when $j=r$, $k=s$, and is zero otherwise;

$$\frac{\partial \|\sigma\|}{\partial \sigma^{rs}} = - \|\sigma\| \cdot \|\eta\| \cdot \|\sigma\|,$$

$$\frac{\partial^2 L}{\partial \sigma^{gh} \partial \sigma^{rs}} = -\tfrac{1}{2}(2-\delta_{gh})(2-\delta_{rs})(\sigma_{gr}\sigma_{hs} + \sigma_{hr}\sigma_{gs}) =$$

$$= -a_{gh,rs}, \quad \text{say.}^{41}$$

If $g=h$, and $r=s$, $a_{gh,rs} = \sigma_{gr}\sigma_{hs}$;
If $g \neq h$, and $r=s$, $a_{gh,rs} = \sigma_{gr}\sigma_{hs} + \sigma_{hr}\sigma_{gs}$;
if $g=h$, and $r \neq s$, $a_{gh,rs} = \sigma_{gr}\sigma_{hs} + \sigma_{hr}\sigma_{gs}$;
if $g \neq h$, and $r \neq s$, $a_{gh,rs} = 2\sigma_{gr}\sigma_{hs} + 2\sigma_{hr}\sigma_{gs}$.

Let matrix $A = \|a_{gh,rs}\|$. Construct another matrix $B = \|b_{gh,rs}\|$ as follows: in the (g, h)th row and the (r, s)th column place the element $\sigma_{gr}\sigma_{hs}$. Then A can be obtained from B in the following way: if $h > g$, add the (h, g)th row to the (g, h)th row and delete the (h, g)th row; if $s > r$, add the (s, r)th row to the (r, s)th row and delete the (s, r)th row. The resulting matrix is A. Hence A is a diagonal minor of a Hermitian matrix cogredient with B. Therefore, if we succeed in proving that B is positive definite, it will follow that A is also positive definite,[42] and therefore $\|\partial^2 L / \partial \sigma^{gh} \partial \sigma^{rs}\|$ negative definite.

It remains to prove that the matrix B, whose elements are of the form

$\sigma_{gr}\sigma_{hs}$, is positive definite. This follows from the assumptions of §46: the random sets $\{\varepsilon_{jf}\}$, $\{\varepsilon_{kf'}\}$ $(j, k=0, \ldots, v)$, are independently distributed, and $|\sigma_{jk}| \neq 0$. Since a moment matrix can be either positive definite or singular, the latter condition implies that $\|\sigma_{jk}\|$ is positive definite. On the other hand, the independence of the random ε-sets implies that

$$E(\varepsilon_{gf}\varepsilon_{hf'})(\varepsilon_{rf}\varepsilon_{sf'}) = E\varepsilon_{gf}\varepsilon_{rf} \cdot E\varepsilon_{hf'}\varepsilon_{sf'} = \sigma_{gr}\sigma_{hs},$$

so that B, too, can be considered a moment matrix. Since $|\sigma_{jk}| \neq 0$, each of the sets $\{\varepsilon_{jf}\}$, $\{\varepsilon_{kf'}\}$ is linearly independent. Hence the sets $\{\varepsilon_{jk}\varepsilon_{kf'}\}$ are linearly independent and therefore $|B| = |\sigma_{gr}\sigma_{hs}| \neq 0$, and B, too, is positive definite.

§49. It follows from the results of §46 that, whenever $\sigma_{jk} = s_{jk}$ $(j, k=0, \ldots, v)$ L has the same constant value $L^\wedge$, whatever the values of the γ's. We have then, in fact, by (6.2)

$$L^\wedge = \log|\gamma^\wedge| + \tfrac{1}{2}\log|\sigma^\wedge|^{-1} - \tfrac{1}{2}\sum_{j=0}^{r}\sum_{k=0}^{r}\sigma^{jk\wedge}q_{jk}^\wedge;$$

but since by (6.13),

$$|\sigma^\wedge| = |q^\wedge| = |s^\wedge| = |\gamma^\wedge| \cdot |m| \cdot |\gamma^\wedge| = |\gamma^\wedge|^2 \cdot |m|,$$

$$L^\wedge = -\tfrac{1}{2}\log|m| - \frac{(v+1)}{2}. \tag{6.16}$$

Since, by §48, $\|\partial^2 L/\partial\sigma^{jk}\partial\sigma^{pq}\|$ is negative definite, $L^\wedge$ is a maximum with respect to the σ's. We shall show it is the highest maximum. Denote by δ the set of σ_{jk}'s, and by γ the set of *unknown* γ_{jk}'s. Denote by $\mathbf{s}$ the set of s_{jk}'s; and since each s_{jk} is a function of γ_{jk}'s (6.7) we can write

$$\mathbf{s} = \mathbf{s}(\gamma).$$

Whenever $\delta = s(\gamma)$, $L = L^\wedge$:

$$L(\delta, \gamma) = L[\mathbf{s}(\gamma), \gamma] = L^\wedge.$$

Change γ to γ'; and change δ to δ'. Then either $\delta' = \mathbf{s}(\gamma')$, in which case $L(\delta', \gamma') = L^\wedge$. Or $\delta' \neq \mathbf{s}(\gamma')$, in which case, by §48, $L(\delta', \gamma') < L^\wedge$. This can be extended to the boundaries of the δ-region, i.e., wherever $\|\sigma_{jk}\|$ and hence $\|\partial^2 L/\partial\sigma^{jk}\partial\sigma^{pq}\|$ is definite. In that region $L < L^\wedge$ if $\delta \neq \mathbf{s}(\gamma)$, and $L = L^\wedge$ if $\delta = \mathbf{s}(\gamma)$.

§50. In our particular case, (1.34), the unknown parameters are:

$\gamma_0, \gamma_1, \gamma_2$, corresponding to the γ_j's of the general case;

six covariances σ_{rk} $(j, k=0, 1, 2)$, corresponding to the σ_{jk}'s of the general case;

four coefficients $\alpha'_1, \alpha'_2, \beta_1, \beta_2$, corresponding to the γ_{jk}'s of the general case.

We should thus need four side conditions to obtain a system corresponding to (6.15) and have

$$F_u=0 \qquad (u=1,\dots,4),$$

$$\sigma_{\hat{jk}} = \sum_{p=0}^{2} \sum_{q=0}^{2} \gamma_{\hat{jp}} m_{pq} \gamma_{\hat{kq}} \qquad (j, k=0, 1, 2),$$

$$\gamma_{\hat{j}} = -\sum_{p=0}^{2} \gamma_{\hat{jp}} \bar{z}_p .$$

In the second group of equations one will recognize the Equations (2.3), with $\sigma^\wedge$'s replacing the s's, and where $\gamma_{\hat{jp}}$'s become the estimates of the coefficients of z's in (1.34), forming the matrix

$$(6.17) \qquad \begin{matrix} 1 & -\alpha_1'^{\wedge} & -\alpha_2'^{\wedge} \\ 1 & -\beta_{\hat{1}} & 0 \\ 1 & 0 & -\beta_{\hat{2}} \end{matrix} = \|\gamma_{\hat{jk}}\| .$$

Of the four side conditions two can be given by

$$(6.18) \qquad \begin{aligned} &\beta_1=c_1 \text{ (a constant)}, \\ &\beta_2=c_2 \text{ (a constant)}; \end{aligned}$$

that is, we can combine trial values to β_1 and β_2. Four such combinations were tried (see Figure 2; the second combination falls outside of the relevant area):

$$\beta_1=\beta_2=1; \quad \beta_1=\beta_2=1.5;$$
$$\beta_1=1, \quad \beta_2=1.5; \quad \beta_1=1.5, \quad \beta_2=1.$$

In addition we have several inequalities, derived in §§18, 19, 20 from economic considerations. We can use any of them in the form of equalities: e.g., from (1.37)[43]

$$\sigma_{\hat{00}}=c_{00}-d^2,$$

where d is an arbitrary real number. As d changes, the solutions move within a region bounded by the condition

$$\sigma_{00}^{\wedge} = c_{00}\,; \tag{6.19}$$

i.e., (since $\sigma_{00}^{\wedge} = s_{00}^{\wedge}$), by the ellipse

$$\begin{aligned} c_{00} = m_{00} + \alpha_1'^{\wedge 2} m_{11} + \alpha_2'^{\wedge 2} m_{22} - \\ - 2\alpha_1'^{\wedge} m_{01} - 2\alpha_2'^{\wedge} m_{02} + 2\alpha_1'^{\wedge}\alpha_2'^{\wedge} m_{02}, \end{aligned} \tag{6.20}$$

corresponding to the first of the Equations (2.3). Similarly with the other inequalities of §§ 18–20.

Since by § 49 the condition $\sigma_{jk} = s_{jk}$ makes the likelihood function the highest maximum regardless of the values of the α's and β's, any number of additional inequalities can be imposed as further side conditions.[44] If the four or more side conditions become incompatible with the observations, the boundary will not form a region on the diagram. This may be just what we want to know: for example, certain values of β_1 (labor monopsony as measured by the elasticity of a firm's pay roll with respect to its manpower) may not be compatible with: (1) the observed values of labor, capital, and output, as resulting in the computed moments m_{jk} and hence in the curves of the Figures 1 and 2: (2) other economic considerations resulting in the boundary lines.

On the other hand, insofar as we do get regions of compatible estimates of our parameters, judgment may be formed about the limits within which our parameter sets may lie. This is done in § 37 but merely as an illustration: the shortcomings of data, described in Section III, are too large.

§ 51. The results of Mann and Wald would, furthermore, permit, for any chosen significance level, the construction of confidence regions, one for each set of side *equations* (not inequalities) (6.3). If one or more nonlinear equations – such as (6.20) – occur in the system, we have, in general, one or more pairs of sets of roots, each set giving the same maximum value $L^{\wedge}$ to L (§ 49). Hence, we shall have two or more sets of consistent estimates (e.g., two points of intersections between ellipse and straight line): and confidence regions would have to be built around each of them. Correspondingly, the boundaries of the regions based on certain (two or more) inequalities will be widened somewhat.

As explained in §26, published data on manufacturing industries are such as make it difficult to decide what is the number measuring the size of the sample to be properly inserted into the confidence-region formula. In the example used, this number (at least 85) is probably large enough to make consistent estimates useful, and hence to make the construction of regions like those in our diagrams useful enough. But it is not certain enough to make it worth while to compute numerically the confidence regions around each set of estimates.

NOTES

* Cowles Commission Papers, New Series, No. 5. References in square brackets [ ] are to the list at the end of the article. Textbook references are provided whenever mathematical theories are used not contained in Allen [2].

** Mr. Dickson H. Leavens, Cowles Commission, supplied painstaking editorial help, in addition to laying out computations and drawing diagrams. T. Koopmans, Cowles Commission, read and criticized large parts of the manuscript. Thanks are due to Abraham Wald, Columbia University, for unfailing interest and aid in questions of statistical method. Herman Rubin, Cowles Commission, provided several important proofs. Leonid Hurwicz, Cowles Commission, gave valuable suggestions. *Added in 1973.* See now Mark Nerlove, *Estimation and Identification of Cobb-Douglas Production Functions*. Rand McNally, 1965.

[1] This notation is more symmetrical than the usual one (P, L, C for product, labor, capital); it will both simplify the statistical symbols which will follow (covariances, etc.) and permit of an easy extension to the case of three or more productive resources. Some changes in notation will be needed later to distinguish between physical output; (gross) revenue; net revenue ('net output'): see § §4 and 9.

[2] Solving the *single* random equation of the agricultural example, $f_0=0$, with respect to x_{vk}, we have, say

$$x_{0k}=\phi_0(x_{1k},\dots,x_{vk};\pi_{1k},\dots,\pi_{sk})\quad(k=1,\dots,n);$$

consider the particular case

$$x_{0k}=\sum_{i=1}^{v}\beta_i y_{ik}+\pi_k,\quad(k=1,\dots,n),$$

where each y is some known function of the corresponding x, the β's are unknown constants, and the π_k is a single random parameter. In this situation the least-squares method is applicable to estimate the unknown constant parameters $\beta_1,\dots,\beta_v$ of a single random equation. The least-squares estimate of β_i – say, b_i $(i=1,\dots,v)$ is an 'unbiased linear estimate' of β_i. It is linear because b_i is a linear function of the observed values of x_0; it is unbiased because the expectation $E(b_i)=\beta_i$. Moreover, the set of estimates $b_i,\dots,b_v$ is at least as efficient as any other set of unbiased estimates, say $b'_1,\dots,b'_v$, in the sense that $E(b_i-\beta_i)^2\leq E(b'_i-\beta_i)^2$, $(i=1,\dots,v)$. From what has been said it is clear that these virtues of the least-squares estimate are not sufficient for the economist concerned with estimating the parameters of his *system* of random equations.

See, for example, David and Neyman [6]; Hotelling [27]. Certain further conditions

(linear independence of the observations) must be satisfied but need not be treated here.
[3] See Appendix 2.
[4] Schultz [39], pp. 72–81. As an example, assume that both the demand and supply function of any observed state k are linear

$$q_k = ap_k + \varepsilon_k, \qquad q_k = bp_k + \eta_k, \quad a \neq b;$$

by choosing a proper origin let $\sum \varepsilon_k = \sum \eta_k = 0$, where $\sum$ stands for summation over observed states. The straight line fitted by least squares to the observations, with q as the 'dependent' variable, has slope $\sum q_k p_k / \sum p_k^2 = c$ (say). On the other hand, using the above equations to express q_k and p_k in terms of ε_k, η_k, we have:

$$p_k = (\eta_k - \varepsilon_k)/(a-b), \qquad q_k = (a\eta_k - b\varepsilon_k)/(a-b),$$

$$c = \frac{a \sum \eta_k^2 + b \sum \varepsilon_k^2 - (a+b) \sum \eta_k \varepsilon_k}{\sum \eta_k^2 + \sum \varepsilon_k^2 - 2 \sum \eta_k \varepsilon_k}.$$

Hence, for c to be equal to a, it is sufficient (though not necessary) that $\varepsilon_k = 0$ for every observed k.

Some formal properties of the least-squares (or, better, 'single-equation') estimate of the parameters of production functions will be treated in §21, where the reasoning has a purpose analogous to that of this note.
[5] We have so far purposely omitted the specific complications arising out of 'contagion' between separate observations, as is especially the case with observations following each other in time. Also, we have purposely simplified the example by assuming that all relevant quantities other than q and p were completely represented by the catch-all random terms ε_k, η_k. In actual work, one would, of course, take care to measure such variables as per-head income, cost level, etc., of each state, and introduce them into the system.
[6] As in note 2, to §1 above, x_0 must be assumed a function of x_1 and x_2, linear in its coefficients. Then the predicted values x_0^* of the dependent variable x_0, based on least-squares estimates of those coefficients, will be an unbiased linear estimate: linear because such estimates of the coefficients are linear functions of the observed values of x_0; and unbiased because the expectation $E(x_0^*) = x_0$. Moreover, x_0^* is at least as efficient as any other unbiased linear estimate of x_0 – say x_0' – in the sense that the expectation $E(x_0 - x_0^*)^2 \leqq E(x_0 - x_1')^2$.
[7] This point will return under 'findings' (especially §§29–31, 33–42) and in Appendix I.
[8] If the elasticity of demand to the firm (algebraic value) $(dx_0/dp_0)(p_0/x_0)$ is η_0, we have clearly $\beta_0 = 1 + 1/\eta_0$; and similarly for the labor and capital supply elasticities to the firm. If firms of the same industry are compared, each β (or rather $|\beta - 1|$) can be used to measure the degree of monopoly, or monopsony, in the respective market.
[9] A more general case of 'limitational' resources would be $x_0 = \psi(x_1, x_2) = \chi(x_3)$. See N. Georgescu-Roegen [19].
[10] This point will be taken up again under 'findings' (especially §§29–30, 32–34).
[11] In some of Douglas' computations 'constant returns to scale' (i.e. $\alpha_1 + \alpha_2 = 1$) were assumed a priori, leaving only one of the α's to be estimated. See below, Table II and the reference in note 7 above.
[12] For a theory of entrepreneurial 'tastes' see T. de Scitovszky [40].
[13] In accordance with §9, Y_0 will usually mean the logarithm of the *net* output value.
[14] See §6, note 8, for a more precise interpretation of the β's.
[15] This system, with Y_0 standing for the logarithm of *net* output value (see §9) is based on data used so far in most of the empirical work, as listed in Section III. However, the

method discussed in the present and the next Section (II), applies, with obvious modifications, to the systems I and II as well.

[16] For a given amount of labor and capital, the logarithm of output would then be normally distributed: a 'Gibrat distribution', not uncommon in economies. See L. Gibrat [20].

[17] On Figures 1, 2 and 3 the boundary line dividing profit maxima from profit minima is denoted by $|\pi|=0$. This is in accordance with §38 where

$$|\pi|=\frac{\partial^2\pi}{\partial x_1^2}\cdot\frac{\partial^2\pi}{\partial x_2^2}-\left(\frac{\partial^2\pi}{\partial x_1\partial x_2}\right)^2,$$

no particular form being assumed for the production function. If our special case (1.19) is assumed, leading to the linear system (1.34), the condition (4.7′) can be also written in the form

$$(1.42) \qquad |\gamma|<0,$$

$|\gamma|$ being the determinant of the coefficients in (1.34),

$$\begin{matrix} 1 & -\alpha_1' & -\alpha_2' \\ 1 & -\beta_1 & 0 \\ 1 & 0 & -\beta_2 \end{matrix}.$$

[18] The authors have also attempted to use bivariate distributions (labor and net output) which may be derived from some tables of the U.S. Census of Manufactures for 1909 [45]. This attempt required a number of additional hypotheses and did not appreciably alter the illustrative results outlined in §37.

[19] This has been emphasized by Durand [17].

[20] This corresponds to the 'standard case' in the discussion of 'collective budget functions', i.e., functions connecting per-head consumption with per-head income and naturally depending on the way in which income distribution changes. The standard case implies an unchanging 'Lorenz curve'. See Marschak [32], [33].

[21] We have no proof for this assertion, however.

[22] In our notation, a_1 and a_2 are the least-squares estimates of elasticities of net output with respect to labor and capital, respectively. In Douglas' notation, $a_1=k$, $a_2=j$. Further, our $\bar{w}_1$ equals, in Douglas' notation, W/P, where W=national pay roll and P=national net output of manufactures.

[23] Of the 90 'industries' used by Douglas and Bronfenbrenner, 22 had to be regarded as mere composites. We have listed, instead, 86 industries each representing a single Census item, [45] p. 186, and each employing 10000 or more wage-earners. One industry (locomotives not made by railroad companies) was omitted since it did not appear in one of the Census tables from which data were used. Of the remaining 85 industries, 63 duplicate exactly those of Bronfenbrenner-Douglas, while 22 form part of their 'composite' items. Those items included in addition 50 other (small) industries.

To compute net output, Bronfenbrenner and Douglas used the Census figure of 'value added' after adjusting for various items the most important of which was depreciation. These adjustments were taken over for convenience and comparability. Where one of the 85 industries was part of the Bronfenbrenner-Douglas 'composites', the same adjustment was applied as had been applied by them to the whole group.

Bronfenbrenner and Douglas used two alternative series for capital: the total-capital series, taken directly from the Census for 1909, [45], pp. 507ff; and a series for fixed capital only. The latter was obtained by multiplying total capital by the ratio, fixed capital:

total capital, from the 1904 Census (since breakdown of capital was not given in 1909). We used the total-capital series.

24 Reder seems to have in mind the same criticism: [38], p. 261 under 1.

25 Write $|m|$ = determinant $|m_{00}m_{11}m_{22}|$; $\|m^{ij}\| = \|m_{ij}\|^{-1}$. Then $a_i = -m^{0i}/m^{00}$ $(i=1, 2)$. Inserting into the second equation in (2.3), we have

$$s_{01}m^{00} = \sum_{j=0}^{2} m_{0j}m^{0j} - \beta_1 \sum_{j=0}^{2} m_{1j}m^{0j} = 1;$$

hence $s_{01} = s_{02} = 1/m^{00}$ which is nonnegative, as $|m|$ is a moment determinant. Therefore both r_{01} and r_{02} are nonnegative.

26 The use of such boundary conditions has exactly the same logical meaning as the use, very common in recent economics, of series of plausible alternative assumptions or combinations of assumptions. See, for example, Pigou [37], Machlup [30], Slichter [41].

27 See note 33 for a geometrical example.

28 In differentiating, use the fact that $\partial x_0/\partial x_1 = \alpha_1 x_0/x_1$, where $x_0 = \alpha_0 x_1^{\alpha_1} x_2^{\alpha_2}$.

29 These were given in § §4–8 with the firm subscript omitted.

30 To express the fact that demand and supply functions F_j depend on the aggregate incomes of workers and of lenders, these quantities can be included in the parentheses in (4.17) without changing the number of equations. On the other hand, the system breaks down if bilaterally imperfect competition is introduced.

31 As an illustration consider production functions in one variable (x_1) only (say, labor, all firms having the same capital; or labor and caiital in fixed proportions, etc.): output $x_{0f} = \phi_f(x_{1f})$ $(f=1, \ldots, n)$. Further, under perfect competition, $p_1 = F(\sum x_{1f})$, $p_0 = F_0(\sum x_{0f})$, as in (4.17). Then, if profits are both zero and maximum, we have

$$\frac{p_1}{p_0} = \frac{\partial \phi_f}{\partial x_{1f}} = \frac{x_{0f}}{x_{1f}} \quad (f=1, \ldots, n).$$

Assume each ϕ_f to pass through the origin and have a point of inflexion in the positive quadrant: such S-shaped production curves, corresponding to a U-shaped average-cost curve, are often set up – Knight [29], Bronfenbrenner [3] – and can be approximated – Allen [2] – by a cubic,

$$x_{0f} = a_f x_{1f}^3 + b_f x_{1f}^2 + c_f x_{1f}.$$

This gives x_{1f} the equilibrium value $-b_f/2a_f$ and imposes n conditions upon the parameters of the functions involved, viz.,

$$\frac{d_1}{4a_1} = \cdots = \frac{d_n}{4a_n} = \frac{F(-\sum b_f/2a_f)}{-F_0(\sum b_f d_f/8a_f^2)},$$

where $d_f = b_f^2 - 4a_f c_f$ $(f=1, \ldots, n)$. Further if $d^2\pi_f/dx_{1f}^2 < 0$, then $b_f > 0$ is a sufficient condition for maximum profits.

Bronfenbrenner's Figure 1 – [3], p. 36 – well illustrates the necessity for some such restrictions: not every set of S-shaped production curves will have the property that all of them will touch the same straight line; and not every price ratio p_1/p_0 represented by the slope of that straight line will clear the market. In presenting the system of equations, however, Bronfenbrenner, while counting the n profits as unknowns, omits to count the n profit-defining identities – (4.13) above – as equations; thus failing to make clear that, in the absence of special restrictions, the 'free entry' postulate makes the system inconsistent.

[32] For the second result see Mosak [35], Durand [17]. Hicks [26] ("Dans le cas d'une fonction de production homogène et du premier degré, l'ensemble de notre analyse s'effondre") points out that the property $|\phi|=0$ makes it necessary to change the definition of the elasticity of substitution. However, the 'effondrement' is even more radical.

It is easily seen that the Jacobian of the market system (4.18) also vanishes if $|\phi|=0$.

[33] To illustrate geometrically, think of undersea reefs: let profit be represented by the altitude above sea level, and let the amounts of the factors used be represented by longitude and latitude respectively. If the production function is homogeneous of the first degree and $g''(u)<0$, then the highest attainable profits (zero) lie on a horizontal ridge just touching at all its points the sea surface. The ridge is a straight line which goes through the point where latitude, longitude, and altitude are all zero. All points of the ridge are equally high, viz., zero above sea level. Hence, the fact that the highest altitude (profit) is chosen by the entrepreneur determines the ratio of longitude to latitude (direction of the ridge on a map: ratio of labor used to capital used) but not their absolute amounts. But if $g''(u)>0$ we shall have not a reef but a boat touching with its keel the surface of a (quicksilver) sea: zero profits will be lowest, not highest profits.

Under imperfect competition, the condition of constant returns is generalized into $|\pi|=0$ in (4.3) or into the second equation in (4.10) (dropping the inequality sign). If the production function is linear in the logarithms of the x's, this condition becomes (4.7′) and is the same as the condition $|\gamma|=0$, cf. (1.42). See notes 17 and 36.

[34] The nonnecessity of assuming constant returns to scale was pointed out by Wicksell [48], as reported by the historians of the problem, Hicks [24] and Stigler [42]. These two authors also hint only briefly in their more recent work, [25], [26], [43] at the awkward implications of that assumption. A definitive critical history of the subject will require thorough counting and interpretation of the equations and inequalities involved: even Pareto and Walras do not seem to have settled that count to mutual satisfaction: cf. Walras [46].

[35] Unfortunately, certain statements of Bronfenbrenner make it very difficult to understand him. It seems to us that to interpret the 'interfirm' function as coinciding with (5.1) is not compatible with Reder's interpretation of it as what we have called a 'mongrel' function. Yet, Bronfenbrenner expresses partial agreement with Reder, and merely points out that monopsony in the labor market, which Reder (in our opinion, rightly) regards as compatible with Douglas' empirical findings, is not thus compatible. Those empirical findings had stated that the regression coefficient of $\log x_0$ on $\log x_1$ happened to come close to the ratio of the aggregate pay roll of all firms to their aggregate output (cf. our §32). Supposing that this ratio was nearly the same for all firms, this finding would indeed imply absence of monopsony, provided the empirical regression function did really represent the production function. But if the empirical function is thought to be (5.1) then Douglas' finding would follow in any case, regardless of absence or presence of monopsony, since from (5.1)

$$\partial \log x_0/\partial \log x_1 = (\partial x_0/\partial x_1)\,(x_1/x_0) = p_1 x_1/p_0 x_0 .$$

Bronfenbrenner's use of those findings leaves us, therefore, uncertain whether,after all, the empirical equation is, in his opinion, (1), or (5.1), or a 'mongrel' one. Also, though the explanation he gives verbally to his Figure 1 leaves little doubt that (5.1) must be meant [represented in the (x_0, x_1)-plane by a straight line through the origin, with slope p_1/p_0] his algebraic expressions again create doubt: cf. [3], p. 40, equation (7) and the accompanying text.

[36] Conditions (1) and (3) above are not compatible with $|\gamma|=0$, e.g., the case of 'constant returns' under perfect competition is excluded; cf. second paragraph of note 33.

Condition (1) follows from § 14.

[37] Thus, while s_{jk} in (2.2) is the mean sum-product of ε's in the sample, measured from the sample means, q_{jk} is the mean sum-product of ε's in the sample measured from zero (i.e., from the population means since $E\varepsilon_k=0$). Finally σ_{jk} is the mean sum-product of ε's in the population, measured from zero. Symbols $s^\wedge$, $q^\wedge$, $\sigma^\wedge$ are used when all parameters have such values as would make L in (6.2) a maximum. Typographical limitations prevented the use of symbols like $\hat{u}$.

[38] The density of the normal joint probability distribution of the ε_{jf}'s ($j=0,\ldots,v$; $f=1,\ldots,n$) is – see, for example, Wilks [49]:

$$C|\sigma|^{-n/2}\exp\left(-\tfrac{1}{2}\sum_{j=0}^{v}\sum_{k=0}^{v}\sum_{f=1}^{v}\sigma^{jk}\varepsilon_{jf}\varepsilon_{kf}\right)d\varepsilon_{01}\ldots d\varepsilon_{vn}=$$

$$=C|\sigma|^{-n/2}\exp\left(-\frac{n}{2}\sum_{j=0}^{v}\sum_{k=0}^{v}\sigma^{jk}q_{jk}\right)d\varepsilon_{01}\ldots d\varepsilon_{vn},$$

where C is a constant. To transform this into the joint distribution density of the z_{jf}'s ($j=0,\ldots,v$; $f=1,\ldots,n$) we have to multiply by the absolute value of the Jacobian of our Equation (1.36) (for $f=1,\ldots,n$), i.e., by the absolute value of

$$\frac{\partial(\varepsilon_{01},\ldots,\varepsilon_{vn})}{\partial(z_{01},\ldots,z_{vn})}=|\gamma|^n.$$

Thus the product

$$C\cdot|\gamma|^n\cdot|\sigma|^{-n/2}\exp\left(-\frac{n}{2}\sum_{j=0}^{v}\sum_{k=0}^{v}\sigma^{jk}q_{jk}\right) \tag{6.2a}$$

gives the likelihood function to be maximized. Its logarithm (apart from a constant) is L in (6.2).

[39] See, for example, Aitken [1].

[40] "It is impossible to have estimates of all the parameters... on the basis of observations alone. However, if we have some a priori knowledge as to (their) values, then it may be possible to estimate all the unknown parameters." Mann and Wald [31], p. 201.

[41] The proof that follows and that in § 49 are due to Herman Rubin, Cowles Commission.

[42] See, for example, Wedderburn [47], p. 100, Theorem 17.

[43] See, for example, Hancock [23].

[44] If there exists a point $x'=(x_1',x_2',\ldots,x_n')$ where a function $f(x)=f(x_1,x_2,\ldots,x_n)$ under the restrictions

(i) $\phi_a(x)=0 \quad (a=1,\ldots,A), \qquad \psi_b(x)\geqq 0 \quad (b=1,\ldots,B),$

reaches an absolute maximum, and if that point x' is found to satisfy certain additional restrictions

(ii) $\psi_c(x)\geqq 0 \quad (c=1,\ldots,C),$

then evidently every point x'' where an absolute maximum of $f(x)$ under the combined restrictions

(iii) $\phi_a(x)=0, \qquad \psi_b(x)\geqq 0, \qquad \psi_c(x)\geqq 0,$

is reached, is a point where $f(x)$ reaches an absolute maximum restricted by (i) only, and which satisfies (ii), and conversely (H. Rubin).

BIBLIOGRAPHY

[1] A. C. Aitken, *Determinants and Matrices*, Second edition, Interscience Publishers, New York, 1942, 135 pp.

[2] R. G. D. Allen, *Mathematical Analysis for Economists*, Macmillan, London, 1938, 548 pp.

[3] M. Bronfenbrenner, 'Production Functions: Cobb-Douglas, Interfirm, Intrafirm', *Econometrica* **12** (January, 1944) 35–44.

[4] Colin Clark, *The Conditions of Economic Progress*, Macmillan, London, 1940, 504 pp.; esp. references to work of Max Brown on New Zealand, pp. 384–385, 407.

[5] Charles W. Cobb and Paul H. Douglas, 'A Theory of Production', *American Economic Review* **18**, Supplement (March, 1928) 139–165.

[6] F. N. David and J. Neyman, 'Extension of the Markoff Theorem on Least Squares', *Statistical Research Memoirs* **11** (1938) 105–116.

[7] Harold T. Davis, *The Theory of Econometrics*, The Principia Press, Bloomington, Indiana, 1941, 482 pp., esp. pp. 159ff.

[8] Paul H. Douglas, *The Theory of Wages*, Macmillan, New York, 1934, 639 pp., esp. pp. 113–158, 159–166 (Massachusetts), 167–172 (New South Wales).

[9] Paul H. Douglas (with Marjorie L. Handsaker), 'The Theory of Marginal Productivity Tested by Data for Manufacturing in Victoria', *Quarterly Journal of Economics* **52** (November, 1937) 1–36; (February, 1938) 215–254.

[10] Paul H. Douglas (with M. Bronfenbrenner), 'Cross-Section Studies in the Cobb-Douglas Function', *Journal of Political Economy* **47** (December, 1939) 761–785.

[11] Paul H. Douglas (with Grace T. Gunn), 'Further Measurements of Marginal Productivity', *Quarterly Journal of Economics* **54** (May, 1940) 399–428.

[12] Paul H. Douglas (with Grace T. Gunn), 'The Production Function for American Manufacturing in 1919', *American Economic Review* **31** (March, 1941) 67–80.

[13] Paul H. Douglas (with Grace T. Gunn), 'The Production Function for Australian Manufacturing', *Quarterly Journal of Economics* **56** (November, 1941) 108–129.

[14] Paul H. Douglas (with Grace T. Gunn), 'The Production Function for American Manufacturing for 1914', *Journal of Political Economy* **50** (August, 1942) 595–602.

[15] Paul H. Douglas (with Patricia Daly and Ernest Olson), 'The Production Function for Manufacturing in the United States, 1904', *Journal of Political Economy* **51** (February, 1943) 61–65.

[16] Paul H. Douglas (with Patricia Daly), 'The Production Function for Canadian Manufactures', *Journal of American Statistical Association* **39** (June, 1943) 178–186.

[17] David Durand, 'Some Thoughts on Marginal Productivity, with Special Reference to Professor Douglas' Analysis', *Journal of Political Economy* **45** (December, 1937) 740–758.

[18] Ragnar Frisch, *Pitfalls in the Statistical Construction of Demand and Supply Curves*, Veröffentlichungen der Frankfurter Gesellschaft für Konjunkturforschung, Neue Folge, Heft 5, Leipzig, Buske, 1933, 39 pp.

[19] N. Georgescu-Roegen, 'Fixed Coefficients of Production and the Marginal Productivity Theory', *Review of Economic Studies* **3** (October, 1935) 40–49.

[20] R. Gibrat, *Les inégalités économiques*, Sirey, Paris, 1931, 296 pp.

[21] Trygve Haavelmo, 'The Statistical Implications of a System of Simultaneous Equations', *Econometrica* **11** (January, 1943) 1–12.

[22] Trygve Haavelmo, 'The Probability Approach in Econometrics', *Econometrica* **12**, Supplement (July, 1944) 118 pp.; also issued as Cowles Commission Papers, New Series, No. 4.

[23] Harris Hancock, *Theory of Maxima and Minima*, Ginn, Boston, 1917, 193 pp., esp. pp. 149ff.
[24] J. R. Hicks, *The Theory of Wages*, Macmillan, London, 1935, 247 pp., esp. Appendix, pp. 233–239.
[25] J. R. Hicks, 'Distribution and Economic Progress, A Revised Version', *Review of Economic Studies* **4** (October, 1936) 1–12, esp. Equation (30.3), pp. 2–3.
[26] J. R. Hicks, *Théorie mathématique de la valeur en régime de libre concurrence*, Hermann, Paris, 1937, 55 pp., esp. p. 47.
[27] Harold Hotelling, 'Problems of Prediction', *American Journal of Sociology* **48** (July, 1942) 61–76.
[28] Lawrence R. Klein, 'Pitfalls in the Statistical Determination of the Investment Schedule', *Econometrica* **11** (July–October, 1943) pp. 246–258.
[29] Frank H. Knight, *Risk, Uncertainty and Profit*, Houghton Mifflin, Boston, 1921, 381 pp. (reprinted by London School of Economics, 1933), esp. pp. 100–101.
[30] Fritz Machlup, *International Trade and the National Income Multiplier*, Blakiston, Philadelphia, 1943, 237 pp.
[31] H. B. Mann and Abraham Wald, 'On the Statistical Treatment of Linear Stochastic Difference Equations', *Econometrica* **11** (July–October, 1943) 173–220.
[32] J. Marschak, 'Personal and Collective Budget Functions', (1939), *Selected Essays*, 44.
[33] J. Marschak, 'Income Inequality and Demand Studies: A Note', *Econometrica* **11** (April, 1943) 163–166.
[34] H. L. Moore, *Economic Cycles: Their Law and Cause*, Macmillan, New York, 1914, 149 pp., esp. Chapters IV and V.
[35] Jacob L. Mosak, 'Interrelations of Production, Price, and Derived Demand', *Journal of Political Economy* **46** (December, 1938) 761–787, esp. p. 772, footnote 8.
[36] A. C. Pigou, 'A Method of Determining the Numerical Value of Elasticities of Demand', *Economic Journal* **20** (1910), 636–640; and revised in his *Economics of Welfare*, Fourth edition, Appendix II, pp. 782–788, Macmillan, London, 1932.
[37] A. C. Pigou, *The Theory of Unemployment*, Macmillan, London, 1933, 319 pp.
[38] M. W. Reder, 'An Alternative Interpretation of the Cobb-Douglas Function', *Econometrica* **11** (July–October, 1943) 259–264.
[39] Henry Schultz, *The Theory and Measurement of Demand*, The University of Chicago Press, Chicago, 1938, 817 pp.
[40] T. de Scitovszky, 'A Note on Profit Maximisation and Its Implications', *Review of Economic Studies* **11** (Winter, 1943) 57–60.
[41] Sumner H. Slichter, 'Present Savings and Postwar Markets', *Harvard Business Review* **22** (Autumn, 1943) Part 2, 73 pp.
[42] George J. Stigler, *Production and Distribution Theories, The Formative Period*, Macmillan, New York, 1941, 392 pp., especially Chapter XII, 'Euler's Theorem and the Marginal Productivity Theory', pp. 320–387.
[43] George J. Stigler, *The Theory of Competitive Price*, Macmillan, New York, 1942, 197 pp., esp. p. 130.
[44] Gerhard Tintner, 'A Note on the Derivation of Production Functions from Farm Records', *Econometrica* **12** (January, 1944) 26–34.
[45] United States Department of Commerce, Bureau of the Census, *Thirteenth Census of the United States Taken in the Year 1910*, Vol. VIII, *Manufactures, 1909*, Washington, 1913, 845 pp.
[46] Léon Walras, *Éléments d'économie politique pure*, Pichon, Paris, 1926, 498 pp., esp. pp. 374–376 and footnote.

[47] J. H. M. Wedderburn, *Lectures on Matrices*, American Mathematical Society, New York, Colloquium Publications, Vol. XVII, 1934, 200 pp.
[48] Knut Wicksell, *Lectures on Political Economy*, Vol. I, Routledge, London, 1935, 299 pp., esp. pp. 127ff.
[49] S. S. Wilks, *Mathematical Statistics*, Princeton University Press, Princeton, 1943, 284 pp., esp. §3.23, and §6.24.
[50] Elmer J. Working, 'What Do Statistical 'Demand Curves' Show?', *Quarterly Journal of Economic* **41** (1927) 212–235.

48

ECONOMIC STRUCTURE, PATH, POLICY, AND PREDICTION*

(1947)

I. POLICY AND PREDICTION

(1) Knowledge is called useful if it helps to choose the *best policy* (action).

(2) Best policy depends on (a) the things which one values as goals (e.g., for a firm, profit; for a government, national income, or budget surplus, etc.); (b) noncontrolled conditions (e.g., for a firm, weather and government policy; for a government, weather). The best policy is an action that maximizes (a), given (b).

(3) To choose the best policy, it is necessary to predict (a) the effect of alternative policies under any given noncontrolled conditions; (b) the future noncontrolled conditions.

(4) Thus, all useful knowledge implies prediction; and knowledge useless at one time may become useful later when new goals and conditions present themselves.

(5) In human affairs (but also in large parts of technology), to predict is, in general, to estimate, for given conditions and for a given probability level, a probable range of the results of a given policy. This range is wide if the observations are few or subject to large errors, or if structural relations (see II) are subject to large random disturbances.

II. STOCHASTIC ECONOMIC STRUCTURE AND PATH

(6) The probabilistic character of economic prediction is due to the chance ('stochastic') character of economic *structural relations*.

(7) Each of the structural relations describes either (a) human behavior (of a specified group of people), e.g., consumers' demand depends on their current and past income, assets, prices and on a 'random disturbance', the latter being the aggregate effect of numerous, separately insignificant factors; or (b) technology, e.g., crops depend on acreage, labor, fertilizers, humidity, and a random disturbance; or (c)

legal rules, e.g., price ceilings, tax laws, bank reserve regulations. Economic structure is fully described by these relations provided the character of the random disturbances (e.g., their variances, covariances) is given.

(8) The number of structural relations must equal the number of economic (or nonautonomous) variables. In addition, structural relations contain noneconomic (or autonomous) variables. At any time, the probable range of values which an economic variable can take depends on the following conditions: (a) the economic structure; (b) the values of noneconomic variables.

(9) Conditions can be noncontrolled (see 2 and 3 above) or controlled. Policies and controlled conditions are identical. Thus a policy fixes either some of the structural relations, or some of the noneconomic variables. However, certain government actions may lie outside of government control. For example, certain parts of the budget (interest on national debt) are determined by past values of certain variables; and tax rates may reflect political shifts which, in turn, are partly determined by economic conditions at or before election time. Such nonautonomous government actions will not be classified as policies; and relations stating what determines such actions may have to be included among structural relations (possibly using information gathered by political scientists). On the other hand, government policy may consist in deliberately invalidating such relations of the past and in fixing autonomously variables that were previously governed by structure.

The deliberate introduction of 'automatisms' into the economic structure is a particular kind of policy; for example, adopting the legal rule that a change of level of employment or prices by given amounts should be followed by a certain change (stated in advance) in tax rates or public expenditures, with the object of stabilizing employment or prices; or the Bank of England's old rule to raise discount rate when gold flows out.

(10) The path which an economic variable follows through time depends therefore on (a) economic structure and (b) on noneconomic variables.

Depending on the character of random disturbances the probable range of deviations from the most probable path will be larger or smaller; the most probable path may show *oscillations* if some of the structural relations are dynamic, e.g., if they contain time-lags or rates of change or acceleration – as in the case of 'cobwebs'.

III. THE NEED FOR STRUCTURAL ESTIMATION

(11) Predictions for a future period, based on observations during a past period, are of different kinds according to whether both or one or none of the types of conditions 8 a, b changes within and between the two periods.

(12) In particular, if structure is known to remain in the future what it was in the past, and if the noneconomic variables have constant values through both periods, the path of each variable would be predictable from the past, apart from random disturbances. In the presence of random disturbances, the problem is analogues to that of weather prediction.

(13) If structure is known to be retained but the noneconomic variables have assumed and are going to assume changing though known values, it is possible to estimate for each current economic variable its dependence ('regression') on all noneconomic ones and on the past ('lagged') economic ones, and to apply this relation to the future. One can thus estimate the effect of policies that consist in controlling certain variables (tax rates, bank reserve ratios).

(14) Finally, if structure is known to change in a given way, the prediction of the effect of this change requires the estimation of the original structure. In this case the study of past relations 7 a, b, c, is necessary.

(15) Case 14 applies also with regard to the particular policy of introducing 'automatisms' (see 9 above) of the most effective kind. For example, to fix in advance the best possible schedule relating tax rates to the unemployment and prices of the previous month, it is necessary to know the lags and elasticities in the consumption equation and in other structural relations at a time when no such legal schedules were in operation. Only when such new device has operated long enough can structural estimation be replaced by the more 'mechanical' type of predictions described in 12 and 13.

IV. ECONOMIC THEORY, STATISTICS, AND MATHEMATICS

(16) The statistical estimation of the structural relations 7 a, b, c is the

'filling of empty boxes of economic theory'. The theory is a set of hypotheses. Most of these hypotheses state which variables enter which structural equations, or state certain inequalities (e.g., regarding the signs or relative sizes of certain elasticities). They are based, essentially, on experience independent of the material which is to be used in estimation. This experience includes statements on rational (i.e., utility-maximizing) behavior and on deviations from it, on a plausible psychology of anticipations, on technological data, etc.

(17) Economic theory is useful in the case 14 and useless in the cases 12 and 13. It can be presumed, however, that cases 12 and 13 seldom occur in practice. In particular, any policy that changes one or more of the structural relations of the past, gives rise to case 14, and necessitates structural estimation for prediction purposes. Structural estimation may seem useless until a structural change is expected or intended: it comes in very useful then. Thus practice requires theory.

(18) All the foregoing statements are concerned with the logic of economic knowledge and its uses. This logic is the same whether or not mathematical symbols are used. However, mathematical presentation is of great help in testing the internal consistency of a theory (see 8 on the number of relations and variables); and it is hardly avoidable when the appropriate estimation methods are to be chosen and applied.

(19) After stating the hypotheses about the structure, one may find that a certain collection of data will permit prediction only in the form of such a wide range of values as to make it useless for policy choice (since a wide range of policies will appear to yield equally good results). For this, mathematics cannot be blamed; it will merely reveal what otherwise might remain concealed. Mathematics does not suppress any information available for other methods; and it makes clearer when and how additional information must be used (e.g., extending time series, supplementing them by cross-section data including attitude surveys, etc.).

NOTE

* Presented at the annual meeting of the American Economic Association, 1946.

ECONOMIC MEASUREMENTS FOR POLICY AND PREDICTION*

(1953)

1. Useful knowledge

Knowledge is useful if it helps to make the best decisions.

To illustrate useful knowledge we shall take an example from the century-old elementary economics of the firm and of taxation. Such examples are admittedly crude (or, if the reader prefers, neat) compared with the complex actual world since their very purpose is to isolate the essentials of a problem by 'idealizing reality'. Later sections (beginning with Section 5) will deal with ways of eliminating at least some of the legitimate realistic objections.

What kinds of knowledge are useful (A) to guide a monopolistic firm in its choice of the most profitable output level and (B) to guide the government in its choice of the rate of excise tax on the firm's product? Let q represent quantity produced and sold per unit of time; p, price including tax; θ, tax per unit of product; γ, total cost of producing and selling q units. To fix ideas, suppose that the demand for the product of the firm is known to be (approximately) a linear function of the price and that all costs are known to consist of fixed charges. (This is almost the case with hydroelectric plants.) Write for the demand curve

$$(1) \qquad p=\alpha-\beta q \quad (\alpha, \beta>0).$$

The firm's profit (net revenue) per unit of time is

$$(2) \qquad r=(p-\theta)\, q-\gamma,$$

or, using (1),

$$(3) \qquad r=(\alpha-\theta-\beta q)\, q-\gamma=-\beta q^2+(\alpha-\theta)\, q-\gamma.$$

CASE A: If the firm knows α, β, and θ, it can use equation (3) to compute the difference between the profits that would be attained at any two alternative output levels. To choose the most profitable output of all, it therefore suffices to know α, β, and θ. It happens in our example, as in most discussions of classical economics, that the functions involved are differentiable,[1] so that the best output level, say $q=\hat{q}$, can be found by putting $dr/dq=0$. Hence

$$(4) \qquad \hat{q}=(\alpha-\theta)/2\beta.$$

CASE B: Assume that the government knows that the firm maximizes its profit. What other knowledge is useful to the government? This depends on its aims:

CASE B_1: Suppose, first, that the government, which collects from the firm the tax revenue T,

$$(5) \qquad T=\theta\hat{q},$$

wants to maximize this revenue by the proper choice of the excise-tax rate θ. Now, by Equations (4) and (5),

$$(6) \qquad T=\theta(\alpha-\theta)/2\beta.$$

Therefore, if the government knows α, it can compute the ratio between the tax revenues resulting from fixing any two alternative excise rates. This ratio is independent of β. Hence, to make the best decision (i.e., to choose the value of θ that will bring in the highest tax revenue) it is sufficient for the government to know α. In fact, the best value of θ is $\hat{\theta}=\alpha/2$.

CASE B_2: Suppose, on the other hand, that the government wants to goad the monopolist into maximum production, provided that a fixed tax revenue $T=T^*$ can be collected. The best tax rate is found by solving the (quadratic) equation (6) for θ with T^* substituted for T. The equation will have two real roots, say θ_1 and θ_2 (which, in a limiting case, may coincide), provided that T^* is not too large. Since, by Equation (4), $\hat{q}$ is larger the smaller θ is, and since the government was assumed to be interested in high output, it will choose the smaller of the two real roots, say $\theta_1<\theta_2$. If T^* exceeds a certain level T_0, the roots will be not real (i.e., a tax revenue $T^*>T_0$ is unattainable). We thus conclude that if the government knows α and β it can choose the best value of θ for any desired and attainable level T^* of tax revenue.

We can sum up as follows:

CASE A: Desired: maximum r. Decision variable: q. Useful knowledge: the form of relations (1) and (2) and the values of the parameters α, β, θ.

CASE B_1: Desired: maximum T. Decision variable: θ. Useful knowledge: the fact that profits are maximized, the form of (1) and (2), and the value of α.

CASE B_2: Desired: maximum q for given $T = T^*$. Decision variable: θ. Useful knowledge: same as in Case B_2, plus the knowledge of β.

2. Structure

In all of our examples so far, useful knowledge pertains to certain economic relations. In Case A the firm has to know something about relations (1) and (2). Relation (1), the demand equation, describes the behavior of buyers. The form and the coefficients (α, β) of this relation depend on social and psychological facts, such as the frequency distribution of consumers by tastes, family size, income, etc. Relation (2), the profit equation, registers the institutional fact that the tax rate is fixed at θ, and the fact (reflecting the technology of the firm as well as the price and durability of its plant and the interests and rents stipulated in its contracts) that the total cost consists of given fixed charges, γ. With respect to the decision problem of Case A, relations (1) and (2) are called *structural relations* and are said to constitute the *structure*; they involve constants (α, β, θ, γ) called *structural parameters.* In Case B the assumed structure includes, in addition to (1) and (2), the assumption of profit maximization, which results in relation (4); and definition (5) may also be counted as part of the structure. If (1) or (2) or both had included a definite pattern of change – say, a linear trend – this would also be a part of the structure.

In each of the problems studied the form of the structural relations and the values of some (not necessarily all) of their parameters prove to constitute useful knowledge. However, we shall presently see that under certain conditions other kinds of knowledge, possibly more easily attained, are sufficient to make the choice of the best decision possible.

3. Maintained structure and change of structure

We shall show that the knowledge of structure is not necessary if the structure is not expected to have changed by the time the decision takes its effect.[2] Again consider Case A. Assume that the form of the structural relations (1) and (2) and the values of coefficients α, β, γ are known to have been unchanged in the past and to continue unchanged in the future, and make three alternative assumptions about the tax rate θ:

CASE A′: θ has not changed in the past and is not expected to change.

CASE A″: θ has not changed in the past but is expected to change in a known way.

CASE A‴: θ has changed in the past.

Suppose that in the firm's past experience, of which it has records, it had tried out varying levels of output q and obtained varying profits r. In Case A′ it can tabulate the observations of q and r in the form of a schedule, or fit an empirical curve, and use the table or the curve to predict future profit r for any given output q. It can therefore choose its most profitable output without knowing any of the structural parameters α, β, γ, θ.

True, knowledge of the form (not the parameters) of relation (3) may help in filling the gaps in the empirical schedule (if the observations are few) by suggesting that a quadratic rather than some other relation be fitted to the data on r and q. Remember that output q was assumed to be controlled by the firm independently of any other variables and to determine, for given values of the structural parameters (α, β, γ, θ), both the profit r and the price p. Accordingly, r and p are said to be 'jointly dependent' on q, an 'independent' variable. Independent variables are also called 'exogenous' ('autonomous', 'external'); and the jointly dependent variables, 'endogenous' ('induced', 'internal').[3] There are as many jointly dependent variables as there are structural relations – in our case, two. Solving the structural relations (1) and (2) for the two jointly dependent variables we obtain the 'reduced form' of the system: two relations predicting, respectively, p and r from q. In our case the relation predicting p happens to coincide with one of the structural relations [viz.,

(1)]. The other equation of the reduced form (viz., the one predicting r) is a quadratic-equation,

$$r=\lambda q^2+\mu q+v, \tag{7}$$

say, whose coefficients are related to the coefficients of the structural equations as follows:

$$\lambda=-\beta, \quad \mu=\alpha-\theta, \quad v=-\gamma. \tag{8}$$

If the structural relations (1) and (2) are assumed to retain in the future the same (linear) form and the same values of parameters as in the observed past, the firm can predict r for a given q by fitting a quadratic Equation (7) to past observations on output and profit. It can thus determine empirically the parameters λ, μ, v of the reduced form without having to pay any attention to the manner [described by equations (8)] in which these parameters are related to the demand and cost conditions. In fact, as already mentioned, the firm may display an even stronger disregard for 'theory'. If the number of observations is large while the firm's confidence in the linearity of the relations (1) and (2) and hence in the quadratic nature of (7) is small, it may prefer to rely altogether on some purely empirical fit.

Case A″ is different. Although the same schedule as in Case A′ will describe the past relation between output and profit, this schedule will not help in choosing the most profitable output under the new tax rate. If the firm could conduct a series of experiments under the new tax rate, varying the outputs and observing the profits, it could discard the old schedule and construct a new one to be used in decision-making. But such experiments take time.[4] In our case these experiments are not necessary if the firm knows, in addition to the old observations, the form of relations (1) and (2) and both the old and the new tax rates, say θ and θ^*. Then the old schedule will be the reduced-form equation (7). The firm obtains the coefficients of (7) empirically from old observations. It knows them to be related to the structural parameters, by Equations (8). Under the new tax rate θ^* the coefficient μ will be replaced by $\mu^*=\alpha-\theta^*$, while λ and v will not be affected. Hence the new relation between profits and outputs will be

$$r=\lambda q^2+(\mu+\theta-\theta^*)\,q+v. \tag{9}$$

The new schedule can thus be obtained by the firm from the old one by inserting the known tax change in a well-defined way.

We see that, in the case of a foreseen change in structure, the purely empirical projection of observed past regularities into the future cannot be used in decision-making. But knowledge of past regularities becomes useful if supplemented by some knowledge (not necessarily complete knowledge) of the past structure and of the way it is expected to change. In our case we can replace the old, empirically obtained schedule (7) by the new, not observed schedule (9) if we know (a) the mathematical form (viz., quadratic) of these schedules and the role played in them by the tax rate [this knowledge is derived from the knowledge of the form (not the coefficients) of the structural relations (1) and (2)], and (b) the amount of change of tax rate, $\theta^* - \theta$. Having thus obtained (9), and maximizing r, we can determine the best output, $q = \hat{q}$. In terms of the tax change and of the coefficients of the old, empirical profit schedule (8),

$$\hat{q} = (\theta^* - \theta - \mu)/2\lambda.$$

We now come to Case A‴, in which the tax rate θ was observed to vary independently in the past, θ being similar in this respect to the output q. In this case, both q and θ are exogenous variables, while α, β, γ are, as before, structural parameters and r is endogenous. From past observations on q, θ, and r, the firm can derive a double-entry table or fit an empirical surface to predict the profit r for any specified output q and tax rate θ. As in Case A′, it is not necessary to know the structural parameters, although knowledge of the form of the structural relations helps to interpolate gaps in the empirical table. Specifically, profit r is related to q and θ by an equation of the form

$$(10) \qquad r = -\theta q + \lambda q^2 + \pi q + v,$$

whose parameters are related to the structural parameters as follows:

$$(11) \qquad \lambda = -\beta, \qquad \pi = \alpha, \qquad v = -\gamma.$$

If the firm has confidence in the form of the structural Equations (1) and (2), it will be helped by the knowledge that Equation (10) involves a product term $(-\theta q)$ in the two exogenous variables and a term (λq^2) quadratic in q. Thus, Case A‴ is analogous to A′ except that the reduced form now involves two exogenous variables (q, θ) instead of one (q).

Suppose, however, that a change in the social and psychological conditions is expected to change the demand Equation (1). Suppose, for example, that the slope of the demand curve, which had maintained a constant value β during the past observations, is expected to obtain a new value, β^*, while the tax rate θ and the output q had both undergone observed variations during the observation period. With the demand curve thus changed, the coefficient λ in Equations (10) and (11) will be replaced by $\lambda^* = \lambda + (\beta - \beta^*)$. Therefore, the old reduced-form equation (10) cannot be used to predict profits r from given values of tax rate θ and output q and to decide upon the best output level $\hat{q}$ unless one knows, in addition, the amount by which the demand parameter β is going to change. This case is analogous to Case A″, with β now playing the role that was played in Case A″ by θ, while q and θ play the role previously played by q alone.

To sum up: (a) for purposes of decision-making it is always necessary to know past and future values of all exogenous variables (i.e., of variables that determine the outcome in question and that were observed to change in the past); (b) if conditions that have not changed in the past are expected to change in the future, some knowledge of such conditions (called 'structure') and of the nature of their change is necessary for decision-making.

The choice of the best decision presupposes that two or more alternative future values are tentatively assigned to a decision variable. If the decision variable has varied in the past, it is called an exogenous variable; if it has not, it is usually called a structural parameter. In Case A′, A″, and A‴, q, an exogenous variable, was such a decision variable. In Case B of Section 1 the tax rate θ was a decision variable, the government being the decision-maker. If θ has varied in the past, and is thus an exogenous variable, the government has to know these variations in order to choose the best decision on the basis of past relations between θ and the quantity that it tries to maximize. If θ has not varied in the past (for example, if θ was zero) and the government now tries to fix it at its best value, a structural change is planned. To determine the effect of such a change the government has to know something about the past structure. This knowledge may require more than the knowledge of the past tax rate itself. For example, it is seen from Equation (6) that if the tax is to be introduced for the first time, the choice of the tax rate that will maximize the tax revenue will require knowledge of α, a parameter of the demand equation.

4. Controlled and uncontrolled changes

We have noted that a decision variable can be either a structural parameter or an exogenous variable. Structural parameters and exogenous variables that are decision variables can be called 'controlled' variables, as distinct from 'uncontrolled' variables (both exogenous and endogenous) and parameters. For example, the legally fixed quantity θ is uncontrolled from the point of view of the firm, though controlled from the point of view of the government. The psychological and social factors determining α and β and the technological and economic factors determining γ were here considered uncontrolled, though a different hypothesis (e.g., involving the effects of an advertising campaign designed to change buyers' tastes) might have been discussed instead.

In predicting the effect of its decisions (policies) the government thus has to take account of exogenous variables, whether controlled by it (the decisions themselves, if they are exogenous variables) or uncontrolled (e.g., weather), and of structural changes, whether controlled by it (the decisions themselves, if they change the structure) or uncontrolled (e.g., sudden changes in people's attitudes, in technology, etc.). An analogous statement would apply to the firm except that, for it, government decisions belong to the category of uncontrolled variables.

5. Some definitions extended

We shall now proceed, as promised in Section 1, to generalize our examples to meet realistic objections. One such objection is that in practice the decision is frequently qualitative, not quantitative. For example, the firm may have to decide in which of a limited number of eligible locations – each of them near a fuel source, say – it should build a plant; the government has to decide whether to abolish or continue rent control; etc. Such cases look superficially different from Cases A and B_1, treated in Section 1, where the decision-maker had to choose among a large (possibly infinite) number of values of a (possibly continuous) variable. Note, however, that in Case B_2 the choice had to be made between only two values (θ_1 and θ_2). In every case the decisionmaker compares the outcome of alternative decisions, and these may or may not form a continuous set. It is obviously not essential whether the alternatives are identified as quantities (as in the examples of the previous sections), or by city names (as in the case of location choice), or by the words 'yes' or 'no' (as in the choice between maintaining and abolishing rent control). In every case the choice goes to the decision that promises the best outcome.

The extension applies, in fact, to all the variables (including the structural parameters), which we had previously introduced as continuous quantities. It has been claimed, for example, that in the interwar period businessmen's willingness to invest in plant and equipment depended, other things being equal, on whether the national administration happened to be Democratic or Republican. Should an economist take this hypothesis seriously, there is nothing against his regarding the party label of the administration as a two-valued variable and trying to explain certain 'shifts' in the investment schedule as a function of that variable.

Similarly, fluctuations in the supply of a commodity according to the four seasons of the year can be conveniently treated by introducing into the supply schedule a four-valued exogenous variable called season. This is a more rational approach than the usual mechanical 'seasonal adjustment' of individual time series, which does not use available knowledge as to which particular structural relations (such as the technological supply schedule for crops or buildings or the demand schedule for winter clothes) are affected by seasons.

Finally, consider a structural change[5] that (unlike the changes discussed in previous sections) consists, not in changing a certain continuous parameter, such as the coefficient α of the demand Equation (1), but in scrapping one equation and replacing it by another. Let the two equations be, respectively, $F=0$ and $F^*=0$, where F and F^* are functions involving, in general, several endogenous and exogenous variables and certain parameters. Form the equation $\delta F+(1-\delta) F^*=0$, where δ is a new structural parameter with the following values: $\delta=1$ before the change, $\delta=0$ afterwards. Then structural change is expressed by a change in the value of δ.

These examples show that our previous description of structures and decisions in terms of variables (including parameters) is general enough if the concepts are properly interpreted. The corresponding generalization of mathematical operations involved is, in principle, feasible.

Some readers may find it more convenient to give the set of exogenous variables and structural parameters a more general name: 'conditions'. Similarly, the set of jointly dependent variables can be renamed 'result'. Conditions that undergo changes during the period of observation correspond to 'exogenous variables'. Conditions that remain constant throughout the observation period but may or may not change in the future constitute the 'structure'. Conditions that can be controlled are called 'decisions'. Given the conditions, the result is determined. The decision-maker ranks the various achievable results according to his preferences: some results are more desirable than others. The best decision consists in fixing controlled conditions so as to obtain the most desirable of all results consistent with given noncontrolled conditions.

For the economy as a whole, endogenous variables can be roughly identified with what are often called 'economic variables'. These are usually the quantities (stocks or flows) and prices of goods and services, or their aggregates and averages, such as national income, total investment, price level, wage level, and so on. The exogenous variables and the structural parameters are, roughly, 'noneconomic variables' (also called 'data' in the economic literature) and may include the weather and technological, psychological, and sociological conditions as well as legal rules and political decisions. But the boundary is movable. Should political science ever succeed in explaining political situations (and hence legislation itself) by economic causes, institutional variables like tax rates would have to be counted as endogenous.[6]

6. The Technician and the Policy-Maker

Outcomes of alternative decisions are ranked according to their desirability by the policy-maker, not by the technician.

Returning to Case B of Section 1, suppose, for example, that the government desires both a high tax revenue and a high level of production of the taxed commodity. The endogenous variable that is being maximized is thus neither the tax revenue (as in Case B_1) nor the output (as in Case B_2) but a function of the two; for example, this function may be

$$U = T + \omega \hat{q}, \tag{12}$$

where ω, a positive number, indicates the "weight" attached to the production aim relative to the aim of collecting revenue. The statement that the government maximizes U is a special case of the statement, made in Section 5, that the government ranks the possible results – here the possible pairs of values of T and $\hat{q}$ – according to its preferences. We find that the best value of θ, in this sense, is $\hat{\theta}=(\alpha-\omega)/2$.

We can imagine a division of labor between the government (or some other decision-maker) and the technician. The latter is relieved of the responsibility of knowing the 'utility function' such as (12). The technician is merely asked to evaluate the effects of alternative decisions (tax rates θ) separately upon $\hat{q}$ and T, as in Equations (4) and (5). Clearly, knowledge of the structural coefficients α, β is useful for this purpose. This knowledge is even necessary if the tax is introduced for the first time (or if α, β, θ had all been constant throughout the observed past). The technician will thus try to estimate α and β. The decision-maker, on the other hand, need not formulate his own utility function – $U(T, \hat{q})$, say – completely and in advance. It suffices for him to make the choice only between the particular pairs of values of $(T, \hat{q})$ that the technician tells him will result from setting the tax at various considered levels.

An additional example will illustrate this role of the technician as separated from the decision-maker. The government (or the legislator) considers the possibility of guaranteeing some fixed price for a farm product. The technician is asked how many bushels will have to be purchased for storage at public expense at any given guaranteed price. Suppose that the technician knows the supply and demand functions which have so far determined the price in a free market:

$$\begin{aligned} &q^s=\alpha^s+\beta^s p, \\ (13) \qquad &q^d=\alpha^d-\beta^d p, \\ &q^s-q^d=0, \end{aligned}$$

where q^s is the quantity supplied and q^d is the quantity demanded by private people, and where p is the (varying) price at which demand and supply were equalized in previous years. Under the intended legislation this system would be replaced by

$$\begin{aligned} &q^s=\alpha^s+\beta^s \bar{p}, \\ (14) \qquad &q^d=\alpha^d-\beta^d \bar{p}, \\ &q^s-q^d=g, \end{aligned}$$

where q^s and q^d are, as before, the supply and demand of private people, and where g is the amount to be purchased by the government when the price is fixed at $\bar{p}$. Hence

$$(15) \qquad g = (\alpha^s - \alpha^d) + (\beta^s + \beta^d)\, \bar{p}.$$

If the technician can estimate the parameters (α^s, β^s, α^d, β^d) of the supply and demand equations, he can tell what alternative pairs of values of g and $\bar{p}$ are available for the policy-maker's choice. We can say that the latter maximizes some utility function $U(g, \bar{p})$ over the set of those available pairs of values. But this function is of no concern to the technician.[7]

7. Random shocks and errors

Exact structural relations such as Equations (1) and (2) are admittedly unrealistic. Even if, in describing the behavior of buyers, we had included, in addition to the price and to the quantity demanded, a few more variables deemed relevant (such as the national income, the prices of substitutes, etc.), an unexplained residual would remain. It is called 'disturbance', or 'shock', and can be regarded as the joint effect of numerous separately insignificant variables that we are unable or unwilling to specify but presume to be independent of observable exogenous variables. Similarly, numerous separately insignificant variables add up to produce errors in the measurement of each observable variable (observation errors). Shocks and errors can be regarded as random variables. That is, certain sizes of shocks and observation errors are more probable than others. Their joint probability distribution (i.e., the schedule or formula giving the probability of a joint occurrence of given sizes of shocks and errors) may be regarded as another characteristic of a given economic structure, along with the structural relations and parameters we have treated so far.

If at least some of the variables are subject to observation errors it is impossible to predict exactly what the observed value of each of the endogenous variables will be when the observed values of exogenous variables, together with the structure, are given. But it is possible to make a prediction in the form of a probability statement. The probability that the observation on a certain endogenous variable will take a certain value, or will fall within a certain range of values, can be stated, provided that the probability distribution of observation errors of the variables is known. Similarly, no exact predictions, but, in general, only probability statements, can be made if at least one of the structural relations is subject to random disturbances (shocks), even if all observations are exact. Few economic observations are free of errors; few economic relations are free of shocks. The quantities that we want to predict (viz., the endogenous variables) are therefore random variables. Prediction consists in stating the probability distribution of these variables.[8]

As an example, replace the supply and the demand equations in (13) and (14) by equations involving shocks (random 'shifts', in the economist's language) u^s and u^d but not errors of observation. In particular, Equations (14) become

$$(16)\qquad \begin{aligned} q^s &= \alpha^s + \beta^s \bar{p} + u^s, \\ q^d &= \alpha^d - \beta^d \bar{p} + u^d, \\ q^s - q^d &= g; \end{aligned}$$

accordingly, Equation (15) must be replaced by

$$(17)\qquad g = (\alpha^s - \alpha^d) + (\beta^s + \beta^d)\,\bar{p} + (u^s - u^d).$$

Suppose that the shocks are known to have the following joint distribution (as already remarked, it must be independent of the observable exogenous variables; that is, in our case, independent of $\bar{p}$):

$$(18)\qquad \begin{aligned} &\text{the probability that } u^s = 1 \text{ and } u^d = 1 \text{ is } \tfrac{3}{6}, \\ &\text{the probability that } u^s = 1 \text{ and } u^d = -5 \text{ is } \tfrac{1}{6}, \\ &\text{the probability that } u^s = -2 \text{ and } u^d = 1 \text{ is } \tfrac{2}{6}. \end{aligned}$$

Then $(u^s - u^d)$ is distributed as follows:

$$(19)\qquad \begin{aligned} (u^s - u^d) &= 0 \text{ with probability } \tfrac{3}{6}, \\ (u^s - u^d) &= 6 \text{ with probability } \tfrac{1}{6}, \\ (u^s - u^d) &= -3 \text{ with probability } \tfrac{2}{6}. \end{aligned}$$

That is, to predict the amount g which the government will have to purchase if it fixes the price at $\bar{p}$, the technician will use the same function of $\bar{p}$ as in Equation (15), *plus* a random quantity which takes values 0, 6, or -3, with respective probabilities $\tfrac{3}{6}$, $\tfrac{1}{6}$, $\tfrac{2}{6}$. Our example shows how, given the values of exogenous variables ($\bar{p}$ in our case) and given the structure [which now includes the probability distribution of shocks u^s,

u^d along with the structural relations (16) and their parameters], the technician can state the probability distribution of each endogenous variable (g in our case). He can state with what probability each endogenous variable will take any specified value, or a value that will belong to any specified set of numbers or any specified interval.

Instead of a discrete probability distribution of u^d and u^s, such as (18), we might have assumed a continuous probability distribution. For example, let u^d and u^s be jointly normally distributed, with zero means, with a correlation coefficient $\rho=0.6$, and with respective standard deviations $\sigma_d=3$ and $\sigma_s=5$ crop units. Then the term u^s-u^d in (17) has a normal distribution with zero mean and with variance equal to σ_d^2+ $+\sigma_s^2-2\rho\sigma_d\sigma_s=16$ and standard deviation equal to $\sqrt{16}=4$. Hence the odds are approximately 1:2 that the necessary government purchase g will have to exceed or fall short of the value given in (15) by more than 4 units.[9] The values of α^s, α^d, β^s, β^d, σ_s, σ_d, ρ constitute the structure, assuming that the structural equations (16) are linear and that the distribution of u^s and u^d is normal. The knowledge of the structure permits the prediction of the endogenous variable g, given the exogenous variable $\bar{p}$.

Such is the nature of statistical prediction. It is perhaps not too well understood in parts of economic literature. Too often economic theory is formulated in terms of exact relations (similar to alleged laws of natural science), with the frustrating consequence that it is always contradicted by facts. If the numerous causes that cannot be accounted for separately are appropriately accounted for in their joint effect as random disturbances or as measurement errors, statistical prediction in a well-defined sense becomes possible.

This is not to say that the interval within which a variable is predicted to fall with a given probability may not be large. If it is so large that widely differing policies appear to yield equally desirable results, the prediction becomes useless as a means of choosing the best decision. However, provided the technician has used the best available data and the most plausible assumptions, he cannot be blamed for the disturbances inherent in complex processes such as human behavior, weather, crops, new inventions, and for the errors that have occurred in measuring their manifestations. It is quite possible that some of the structural relations of our economy are, by their very nature, subject to strong random fluctuations. Should it be true, for example, that the investment decisions of entrepreneurs are essentially made in imitation of the decisions of a very few leaders who, in turn, are affected by conditions of their personal lives as much as by economic considerations, then the prediction of aggregate investment could be made only within a very large prediction interval, unless one is content with assigning a very small probability to the success of the prediction. This fact would merely be a consequence of a certain structural characteristic of the economy, and the technician would merely have recorded it faithfully.

Note that any function of endogenous variables, and therefore also the utility of a given policy [such as U in Equation (12)], now becomes a random variable. Its distribution depends on the structural relations, on the distribution of disturbances and errors, and on the values of exogenous variables, the structural relations and exogenous variables being partly controlled by the policy-maker himself. He will prefer certain probability distributions of utility to others and will choose the best decision accordingly. In particular, he can choose that decision which maximizes the long-run average (the mathematical expectation) of utility. This may result in his preferring policies with a narrow range of possible outcomes to policies with a wide range of possible outcomes; that is, he may 'play for safety'.

8. The Need for Structural Estimation

The results of Section 3 extend themselves with added force to the now generalized probabilistic (stochastic, statistical) concept of economic structure. The determination of relevant unknowns will now be called 'estimation'.[10] Generalizing the example used in Section 3, replace the demand and profit Equations (1) and (2) and the resulting reduced-form Equation (7) by, respectively,

$$(1') \qquad p=\alpha-\beta q+u,$$
$$(2') \qquad r=(p-\theta)\, q-\gamma+v,$$
$$(7') \qquad r=\lambda q^2+\mu q+\nu+w,$$

where u, v, w are random shocks and where, corresponding to Equations (8) of Section 3,

$$(8') \qquad \lambda=-\beta, \quad \mu=\alpha-\theta, \quad \nu=-\gamma, \quad w=uq+v.$$

The shock variables u, v represent, respectively, random shifts in demand behavior and in the total cost and are independent of exogenous variables such as q and θ. As an example, u and v may depend partly on random fluctuations of the general price level (so that u and v are correlated) and partly on numerous other causes specific to the demand or to the cost formation. Let u, v be normally distributed with zero means, and call their variances σ_u^2 and σ_v^2 and their correlation coefficient ρ. Then w, the random term in the reduced-form Equation (7′), will be, by (8′), normally distributed with zero mean and with variance

$$\sigma_w^2 = q^2\sigma_u^2 + \sigma_v^2 + 2q\rho\sigma_u\sigma_v. \tag{20}$$

Suppose, as before, that a certain change in the structure (viz., a known change in the tax rate θ) is expected by the firm. It has to choose the best new level for its output. This may be defined as the output level that yields, under the new tax rate, the highest mathematical expectation of the profit (or, more generally, the highest mathematical expectation of some utility function of profit, possibly giving different weights to a dollar lost and a dollar gained). To find the best new output level we need to know, as in Section 3, the relation that will correspond to (7′) under the new structure. (This knowledge will now have to include the distribution of w in addition to some of the coefficients λ, μ, ν). The case for estimating the old structure and inserting its known change, and against relying upon experiments to be made under the new structure, is now even stronger than it was in Section 3, where all relations were assumed to be exact.[11] Even though we have assumed that the firm knows the (quadratic) form of Equation (7′) and that it knows the (normal) form of the distribution of w for given q, it will not suffice now to have just as many observations under the new structure as there are unknown parameters of the reduced form. To achieve a degree of precision necessary for practical action one may need a large number of observations on q and r under the new structure. This number is larger, the larger σ_w. Therefore, by (20), the larger the quantities σ_u, σ_v, ρ, and q are, the more observations are needed. The required delay would impede the making of decisions. On the other hand, the old structure (the old tax rate) may have prevailed during a long enough period to make possible a sufficiently precise estimation of the old structural equations (1′) and (2′) (i.e., of their coefficients and of the distribution of parameters σ_u, σ_v, ρ) from data on

r, p, and q. Hence λ, μ (under the old as well as the new value of θ), and v can be estimated, by (8′), and the standard deviation for any given q can be estimated, by (20).[12]

It is not claimed, to be sure, that the available data for the past always provide a large enough sample to estimate the old structure with precision that is sufficient for practical decision. In fact, it will be remembered from the previous section that the random disturbances of some economic relationships may well be so large as to make even the full knowledge of the old structure (including the knowledge of the distribution of those disturbances) useless for practical decisions. In this case even an infinitely large sample would be useless. All that is claimed in the present section is this: Whenever a given change in structure is expected or intended, the attempt to predict the outcome of alternative decisions under the new structure without taking into account experience collected under the old structure is either so lacking in precision or so wasteful of time as to be useless. It is more promising, though not always practicable, to base the choice of best policy upon an estimate of the old structure and on the knowledge of its expected or intended change.

9. THE TIME PATH OF ECONOMIC VARIABLES; DYNAMIC STRUCTURES

We are usually interested in predicting the values of economic variables, not only for a single point or interval of time, but for a whole succession of such points or intervals. We are interested in the path of the variable through time. As often pointed out by economists, the properties of the path (for example, the intensity of the oscillations, or the rate of growth, of income) are of direct concern to the individual or the nation.

Suppose that the exogenous variables and/or the structure will undergo specified changes during the future period in question, and disregard for a moment any disturbances and errors. Then the value of each endogenous variable, being at any time exactly determined by exogenous variables, will change throughout the period in the manner prescribed by the relevant equation of the reduced form, such as Equation (7) or (15).

Now introduce disturbances, such as u and v in (1′) and (2′), or u^s and u^d in (16), and errors of measurement. Assume either that their probability distribution, which can be regarded as a characteristic of the structure, is unchanged throughout the period or that it will undergo specified changes. Then the relevant equation of the reduced form will also involve random fluctuations, as exemplified in (7′) or in (17). Thus, for each future point of time it will be possible to make a statistical prediction as discussed in Section 7.

So far we have discussed changes in the exogenous variables or in the structure and the presence of random disturbances and errors as the only explanations of the change of economic variables over time. If this were true, no economic trends or oscillations of endogenous economic variables would be generated except by trends and oscillations in specifiable exogenous variables (such as climate, population, technology, domestic political balance, the state of foreign economies, armaments, wars, demobilizations) or else by random variations of the joint effect of numerous other external forces for which we are unable to account separately. Accordingly, in the examples studied so far, all observed values of endogenous variables would remain constant if the exogenous variables and the structure did not change and if disturbances and errors were not present. All paths would be straight lines parallel to the time axis.

Many economists have been dissatisfied with this picture of economic changes. Many if not most business cycle theories imply that economic fluctuations would take place even if external conditions remained constant and no random shocks existed.

This is consistent with the observation, neglected in all of our previous examples, that relations describing human behavior, technology, or legal rules must often involve not only a set of contemporary variables but also their rates of change (time derivatives, or differences between successive values of a variable) or their cumulated values (integrals or sums over time). For example, net investment may be related to the rate of change in annual consumption and also to the existing capacity (i.e., to the cumulated past net investment). To give another example, building construction lags behind building plans, and both may play a role in a system of structural relations. Even supposing that the exogenous variables and the structure are constant and that random disturbances are absent, such a system would generate variations of endogenous variables through time. The paths of these variables will depend on their initial values and in general will not be parallel to the time axis, except possibly for a particular set of initial values (called 'equilibrium values') which, if attained, are maintained. We call a structure that would admit variations of observed endogenous variables, even if exogenous variables did remain constant and if there existed no random disturbances, a 'dynamic structure'.

As an example, we may modify the market system (13) into the 'cobweb' case familiar to economists and often used to illustrate the so-called 'period analysis' of business cycles.[13] Suppose that the suppliers of grain determine output in response to the price that prevails one year before the harvest, and suppose that the demanders set the price at which they are willing to absorb the whole (perishable) crop immediately after harvest. Thus, transactions take place only once a year, and the prices and quantities obey the following relations:

(21) $q_t = \alpha^s + \beta^s p_{t-1}$ (behavior of suppliers),
(22) $p_t = \alpha^d + \beta^d q_t$ (behavior of demanders),

where the subscript indicates time. Let $\alpha^s = 0$, $\beta^s = 2$, $\alpha^d = 1$, $\beta^d = -\frac{1}{4}$, and suppose that the initial crop $q_0 = 1$. By previous definitions (Section 3), these five quantities can be regarded as structural parameters or, equally well, as exogenous variables that happen to remain constant during the whole period in question. The two endogenous variables, p_t and q_t, will trace certain paths, or time schedules, that we can obtain as follows. By Equation (22), $p_0 = 1 - \frac{1}{4}q_0 = \frac{3}{4}$. Then, by (21), $q_1 = 2p_0 = \frac{3}{2}$; by (22), $p_1 = 1 - \frac{1}{4}q_1 = \frac{5}{8}$; by (21), $q_2 = 2p_1 = \frac{5}{4}$; and so on. In our numerical case q_t and p_t happen to oscillate around $\frac{4}{3}$ and $\frac{2}{3}$, respectively, approaching these constants as time goes on ('damped oscillations'):

	t	0	1	2	3	$\ldots \to \infty$
(23)	q_t	1	48/32	40/32	41/32	$\ldots \to 4/3$
	p_t	24/32	20/32	22/32	21/32	$\ldots \to 2/3$.

(Note that if, at some time $t = T$, the price and quantity were to be artificially set at $\frac{2}{3}$ and $\frac{4}{3}$, respectively, then the demand Equation (22) would be satisfied. Also, by putting $t = T, T+1, \ldots$ in (21) and (22), we see that $q_T = q_{T+1} = q_{T+2} = \cdots$, and $p_T = p_{T+1} = p_{T+2} = \cdots$. That is, the values $\frac{2}{3}$ and $\frac{4}{3}$, if attained, are maintained. They are the equilibrium price and quantity.)

The time schedule (23) expresses each endogenous variable as a function of time, a discrete function in our case. We have been able to predict the values of endogenous variables at each point of time from their values in the preceding point of time, using the fact that in Equation (21) an endogenous variable was related to the lagged value of another endogenous variable. Another method for obtaining the time schedule (23) is to transform (21) and (22) into equations expressing each endogenous variable in terms of its own previous value, predicting q_1 from q_0, q_2 from q_1, etc. These equations are

(24) $$q_t = \delta + \varepsilon q_{t-1},$$
(25) $$p_t = \gamma + \varepsilon p_{t-1},$$

where $\varepsilon = \beta^d \beta^s$, $\gamma = \alpha^d + \beta^d \alpha^s$, $\delta = \alpha^s + \beta^s \alpha^d$. Note, moreover, that if we replace t by $t-1$, Equation (24) becomes $q_{t-1} = \delta + \varepsilon q_{t-2}$. Hence, substituting into the original (24), we have $q_t = \delta\ (1+\varepsilon) + \varepsilon^2 q_{t-2}$; and, by repeating the procedure, $q_t = \delta(1+\varepsilon+\varepsilon^2) + \varepsilon^3 q_{t-3}$, and, in general,

(26) $$q_t = \delta(1+\varepsilon+\cdots+\varepsilon^{n-1}) + \varepsilon^n q_{t-n} \quad (n=1, 2, \ldots).$$

Thus, the current value of an endogenous variable can be predicted from any of its preceding values. In more general cases it can be predicted from combinations of these values. The form (24), (25) into which we have put the dynamic structural system (21), (22) exemplifies a set of 'final equations', in Tinbergen's terminology.[14] Each final equation is a difference equation (or, in other cases, a differential, or possibly a mixed difference-differential-integral equation), possibly of high order, in a single variable, with a corresponding time schedule or path, such as those in (23), as its solution.

As still another, and the most direct, way to obtain the time schedule (23), we can express q_t (or p_t) in a form[15] involving only the initial values of the endogenous variables. In (26), put $n=t$:

(27) $$q_t = \delta \cdot \frac{1-\varepsilon^t}{1-\varepsilon} + \varepsilon^t q_0.$$

Using (27), q_t is predicted from the following quantities, considered as given: the structural parameters, which determine δ, ε; the initial value q_0; and time.[16] In fact, (27) is the equation of the time schedule for q_t in (23); it is the solution of the 'final equation' (24). Equation (27), together with the analogous one for price p_t, corresponds to the reduced form previously defined for static systems, since Equation (27), like (7) or (13), relates an endogenous (or jointly dependent) variable to the independent quantities only. However, we have already mentioned other forms that can be used in a dynamic system to predict the future value of an endogenous variable. As the reader will remember, those other forms included as given the lagged values of the endogenous variable to be predicted or of other endogenous variables.

We can now readmit changes of exogenous variables in our example. Suppose that the intercept α^d of the demand curve is not a constant but a variable depending on the size of the population, and therefore determined outside of our system (21), (22). Suppose that α^d takes successive values $\alpha_0^d, \alpha_1^d, \ldots$ The demand equation (22) is replaced by

$$(28) \qquad p_t = \alpha_t^d + \beta^d q_t.$$

The 'final equations' change accordingly; (24) becomes

$$(29) \qquad q_t = \delta_t + \varepsilon q_{t-1},$$

where $\delta_t = \alpha^s + \beta^s \alpha_{t-1}^d$. The reduced-form Equation (27) becomes

$$(30) \qquad q_t = \delta_t + \varepsilon \delta_{t-1} + \cdots + \varepsilon^{t-1} \delta_1 + \varepsilon^t q_0.$$

It is now, of course, impossible to predict the endogenous variable q from the constants (ε and q_0) only; one has to take account also of all the past values of the exogenous variables (δ and therefore α^d) if one uses the reduced-form Equation (30). Alternatively, one can take into account only some of those past values but must then employ as additional predictors the past values of the predicted endogenous variable [as in (29)] or of other endogenous variables [as in (28) when combined with (21)].

Changes in exogenous variables will, of course, affect the time schedules of the endogenous variables. This fact is generally recognized in the case of annual seasons. But it is not always recognized with sufficient clarity by those who try to discover longer wave-like (so-called cyclical) regularities of the paths of economic variables without first eliminating the effects of noneconomic variables,[17] or try to predict future waves from the past ones without regard for possible changes in the noneconomic conditions.

Let us now replace observable exogenous influences by nonobservable random disturbances. Modify our example (21), (22) by letting the supply equation undergo random shifts. That is, replace α^s in (21) by $\alpha^s + u^s$, where u^s is a nonobservable random variable which we shall, to begin with, assume to have an unchanging probability distribution. For example, u_t^s may measure the effect of weather on crops in the year t, and we assume that weather in one year is independent of that in any of the preceding years but has the same probability distribution; this is a situation similar to that in which lots are drawn from a sequence of urns, lots of a given kind being present in each urn in the same proportion. To fix ideas, let this distribution be normal, with zero mean and variance σ_u^2. The distribution is now a part of the structure, which is described, in addition, by the following equations, with fixed values attached to each parameter denoted by a Greek letter and also to the initial values q_0, p_0:

(31) $q_t = \alpha^s + \beta^s p_{t-1} + u_t^s$ (behavior of suppliers),

(32) $p_t = \alpha^d + \beta^d q_t$ (behavior of demanders).

The 'final equations'[18] (difference equations in single endogenous variables) (24) and (25) now become 'stochastic' (i.e., involve random variables). In particular, Equation (24) is replaced by

(33) $q_t = \delta + \varepsilon q_{t-1} + u_t^s$.

Each successive value of q is a random variable whose distribution depends on the value actually taken by q at the preceding point (or, generally, points) of time. The path of q (and also of p), instead of being a sequence of constants as in (23), has become a 'stochastic process'. The equation of the path [viz., the reduced-form equation (27)] now becomes a 'stochastic equation'. The reader will easily obtain, by the same recurrent procedures as before,

(34) $$q_t = \delta \cdot \frac{1-\varepsilon^t}{1-\varepsilon} + \varepsilon^t q_0 + w_t,$$

where

(35) $$w_t = u_t^s + \varepsilon u_{t-1}^s + \cdots + \varepsilon^{t-1} u_1^s.$$

Since u_1^s, $u_2^s, \ldots$ all have zero means, so has, by (35), w_t, the random component of q_t. Since u_1^s, $u_2^s, \ldots$ were assumed independent, the variance of w_t (and therefore of q_t) is the sum of the variances of u_t^s, $\varepsilon u_{t-1}^s, \ldots$ and is therefore equal to

$$(36) \qquad \sigma_{w_t}^2 = \sigma_u^2 (1-\varepsilon^{2t})/(1-\varepsilon^2).$$

As t increases, this variance approaches a constant, provided that the absolute value of ε is smaller than one. (In our numerical example, $\varepsilon = -\frac{1}{2}$ and $\sigma_{w_t}^2$ approaches $\frac{4}{3}\sigma_u^2$.) But q_t itself does not approach any equilibrium value. In this and other respects the path actually described by each endogenous variable will differ from the path (23) generated by the corresponding nonstochastic structure (21), (22). In fact, a stochastic structure may generate explosive oscillations even though the corresponding nonstochastic structure [such as (21), (22), with $\beta^s\beta^d = \varepsilon = 1$] produces oscillations with a constant amplitude.[19]

However, the prediction procedure is similar to that of the nonstochastic case if the concept of prediction is appropriately modified (as in Section 7) in the sense of stating the probability that, at a given time, the endogenous variable in question will fall within a given interval. Analogously to the nonstochastic case, predictions can be made either from the structural quantities only [as in (34) and (36), where the predictors are δ, ε, q_0, and σ_u^2]; or from the past values of the endogenous variable that is being predicted [as in (33)]; or, more generally, from the past values of all endogenous variables.

If we now reintroduce changes in exogenous variables (such as α^d in a previous example), these will have to enter the equations used for prediction. In fact, under the conditions stated so far, the past values of endogenous variables play the same role as exogenous variables in that they are independent of present random shocks. In this case both the exogenous and the lagged endogenous variables determine the current values of the endogenous variables but are independent of them. They are, accordingly, called 'predetermined', while the current endogenous variables are called 'jointly dependent'.[20]

This similarity between exogenous and lagged endogenous variables ceases to exist, however, if we drop our assumption that successive random shocks (the random supply shifts u_1^s, u_2^s,... due to weather in our example) are independent. If, for example, we consider not annual but daily weather records, the independence of successive shocks may have to be ruled out. Instead, these shocks u_1^s, u_2^s,... themselves may constitute a stochastic process, each shock depending on one or more of its predecessors. Since the lagged endogenous variable q_{t-1} depends on the shock u^s_{t-1}, and this is correlated with u^s_t, q_{t-1} is not independent of u^s_t. Therefore q_{t-1} is not predetermined. It is determined, jointly with $q_1, \ldots, q_{t-2}, q_t, q_{t+1}, \ldots$, by the exogenous variables, the coefficients of the structural equations [such as (31) and (32)], and the joint distribution of successive shocks entering all of the structural equations.[21] Whenever we use weekly or even quarterly instead of annual time series, we must be wary of predictions that use lagged endogenous variables as though they were exogenous.

The conclusions of the previous sections can now be generalized to the case of structures that are both stochastic and dynamic. Policy consists in changing those elements of the structure and those exogenous variables that are under the policy-maker's control. Given the values of the uncontrollable features of the structure and of the uncontrollable exogenous variables, the technician's task is to predict which stochastic processes will be generated by the various proposed policies. The variables that are thus predicted are the potentially observable (and hence possibly erroneous, because of measurement errors) values of some economic quantities of interest to the policy-maker. To make his best decision, the policy-maker ranks these alternative outcomes according to his preferences. For example, his objectives may include high income averaged over time, but also small intensity of variations in time, and, in addition, a high degree of predictability (small prediction intervals for a given probability level). These objectives may conflict, so he will rank the various combinations of average income, stability, predictability, etc. [for example, by ascribing to them weights analogous to 1 and w in (12)].

As in the cases treated earlier, knowledge of past structure is necessary if the policies under consideration and the expected changes of uncontrolled conditions involve not only changes in exogenous variables but also changes in the structure itself.

10. 'Steering wheel' and automatisms

To the extent to which economic fluctuations are regarded as an evil, policies can be suggested that will dampen such fluctuations. Through an appropriate change of controlled exogenous variables or controlled structural parameters, the jerky path described by national income and other economic aggregates in the last hundred years or so may be replaced by a smoother one in the future. In particular, jumps due to sudden changes of exogenous variables or to rare, but nonetheless possible, large random disturbances may be counteracted by the construction of appropriate 'shock-absorbers', If the existing structure is known, one can attempt to find the extent to which a given and feasible change in the institutional characteristics of the structure would affect certain properties of the oscillatory path of an important economic variable, such as the wave frequency, or the so-called damping ratio between the amplitudes of two successive waves in the absence of new impulses. In this way Tinbergen [1939, p. 169] tried to measure the effect of increasing or decreasing the (properly defined) rigidity of wages or of prices upon the shape of the business fluctuations.

Economic history knows remarkable examples of stabilizing institutions. Possibly the best known is the unwritten law that is said to have ruled the conduct of the Bank of England during the nineteenth century. Any serious change in the balance of payments, as indicated by the outflow or inflow of gold, was counteracted by changes in the discount rate. More recently, in the discussion of the stabilization of employment and of the price level, institutional rules were proposed that would obligate the monetary or fiscal authorities to take specified measures that would nip deflations and inflations in the bud.

It has been argued that the formulation of such rules need not presuppose any knowledge of economic structure or, in particular, of its numerical characteristics. As Lerner [1941] put it, the motorist, ignorant of the car mechanism, steers his wheel quite successfully, responding instantaneously to changes in the surface and the direction of the road. Other economists have even suggested what we may call 'pilotless' devices. Thus, income tax receipts, at a tax rate fixed once and for all, will rise and fall with money income, thus counteracting inflation or deflation. (Such automatisms have been called, e.g., by Hart [1945], 'built-in flexibilities'.) Again, it has been argued that the knowledge of economic structure is not necessary if one wants to stabilize the economy by such devices.

Our previous conclusions (Sections 3 and 8) can be applied. There is a difference between changing the exogenous variables and changing the structure. If a certain rule of fiscal or monetary action in response to changes in national income or in price level has been tried out long enough, in various doses and with various delays, such experience can indeed suffice to determine when and how intensely the measure should be applied. If income tax has been operating in various situations and at various tax rates, it is possible to estimate the tax rate that would best fulfill the task of damping fluctuations of national income. In such cases we have merely to fit an empirical relation between, say, bank-reserve ratios or income-tax rates, on the one hand, and some measure of the violence of price or national income fluctuations on the other. The case is then indeed analogous to that of Lerner's motorist, or, for that matter, to the case of the firm that (as in Section 3) collected experience on the effect of output upon profit without ever bothering to explain this effect by the existing behavior of buyers, the cost structure, and the rate of the excise tax on the firm's product.

Suppose, however, that the institution in question is to be introduced for the first time. To fix in advance the rule of monetary action that will stabilize prices and national income most quickly and effectively, even within a large margin of error, it is necessary to know, for example, the lags and elasticities involved in the relation describing consumers' response to changes in national income, prices, cash balances, etc., and the lags and elasticities involved in other structural relations at a time when the institution was not in force. To experiment with the institution would require too much trial and error.[22]

11. Mathematics and prediction

All of the foregoing was concerned with the logic of economic knowledge and of its uses. This logic is the same whether or not mathematical symbols are used. However, mathematical presentation is of great help in testing whether a set of structural relations proposed by a theorist is internally consistent and whether it can be determined numerically from observations. Mathematical presentation is hardly avoidable when appropriate statistical methods are to be applied to observations in order to estimate the structure or (if no structural change is envisaged) to estimate its reduced form.

As stated in Section 7, the technician cannot be blamed if a certain kind of data results in a predicted range of values that is so wide, or has such a small probability attached to it, as to be useless. The mathematical method and result will merely reveal what otherwise might remain concealed. Mathematics does not suppress any information available for other methods, and it makes clearer when and how additional information must be used – for example, to extend the time series, to supplement them by cross-section data such as attitude surveys, or to insert additional knowledge on technology and institutions.

12. Conclusion[23]

This paper has been concerned with the type of knowledge useful or necessary for determining the best policy. In particular, the circumstances were stated under which the choice of best policy requires the knowledge of 'structure'. Structure was defined as a set of conditions which did not change while observations were made but which might change in the future. If a specified change of structure is expected or intended, prediction of variables of interest to the policy-maker requires some knowledge of past structure. It follows that if among the policies considered there are some that involve structural changes, then the choice of the policy best calculated to achieve given ends presupposes knowledge of the structure that has prevailed before.

In economics, the conditions that constitute a structure are (1) a set of relations describing human behavior and institutions as well as technological laws and involving, in general, nonobservable random disturbances and nonobservable random errors of measurement; (2) the joint probability distribution of these random quantities.

Economic theories try to explain observed facts by postulating plausible human behavior under given institutional and technological conditions. To be consistent with facts, they should also introduce random disturbances and errors. Thus every economic theory susceptible to factual tests must describe a structure or a class of structures.

It follows that a theory may appear unnecessary for policy decisions until a certain structural change is expected or intended. It becomes necessary then. Since it is difficult to specify in advance what structural changes may be visualized later, it is almost certain that a broad analysis of economic structure, later to be filled out in detail according to needs, is not a wasted effort.

Thus, practice requires theory.

NOTES

* From Cowles Commission Monograph 14: *Studies in Econometric Methods*, edited by W. C. Hood and T. C. Koopmans, Wiley 1953. Republished, Yale University Press, 1970.

1 But see Section 5.

2 See Chapter II, Section 8, of this monograph and Hurwicz [1950b].

3 A slight change in definition will be convenient later, when dynamic systems with lagged endogenous variables are introduced. See Section 9.

4 Strictly speaking, if the form of the new schedule is known, one needs only as many observations as there are unknown parameters of the schedule. Thus, three observations, and therefore a delay of three accounting periods, will suffice to determine the new quadratic schedule that replaces (7) when the tax rate is changed. If the form of the new schedule is not known, the output that results in maximum profit under the changed schedule can be found by trial and error, the number of necessary trials depending on the firm's skill in hitting from the beginning an output level near the optimal one and in varying the output level by amounts not too large and not too small. This skill is equivalent to some approximate knowledge of the properties of the new schedule – Equation (9) of the text – in the neighborhood of the optimal point and is therefore enhanced if the firm has approximately the kind of knowledge to be discussed presently (viz., some knowledge of old structural relations and of the change they have undergone).

However, the full significance of the delay that occurs when, without knowing the structure, one estimates empirically a new reduced-form schedule (such as the relation between the dependent variable r and the independent variable q after the tax rate θ has changed) cannot be gauged by the reader as long as we deal with the artificial assumption of *exact* economic relations such as constitute the usual economic theory. When, beginning with Section 7, random disturbances of relations and errors in the measurement of variables are introduced, the time-saving aspect of the knowledge of structural relations will appear in a more realistic light. See Section 8.

5 For example, the introduction of price control, which will be discussed in Section 6, consists in scrapping the equation $q^s - q^d = 0$ in (13) and replacing it by the equation $p - \bar{p} = 0$.

6 See Koopmans [1950c].

7 In the above case of 'protecting the farm income', g is nonnegative and $\bar{p}$ is chosen to be at least equal to the price p that satisfies Equations (13) of the free market. Equations (13) and (14) can also describe the introduction of rent control, with $\bar{p} \leqslant p$ and with government-financed housing being denoted by $-g$.

8 See Hurwicz [1950b] and Haavelmo [1944, Chapter VI].

9 When the sample is small, this calculation must be modified somewhat to account for errors of estimation in σ_d, σ_s, ρ. We disregard this here as technical and irrelevant to our discussion.

10 See Chapters VI and VII of this monograph.

11 See note 4.

12 For some other aspects of experiments vs. nonexperimental observations, see Marschak [1947a, p. 292ff.]

13 See Leontief [1934], Lundberg [1937], and Samuelson [1947, Chapter XI].

14 *Added in 1973*. See now Theil and Boot [1962].

15 The form (24) (25) has been also called 'separated' and the form (27), 'resolved'. [Marschak, 1950, Sections 2.4.5, 2.5.3.]

16 The equilibrium values are obtained, for $-1 < \varepsilon < 0$, by putting $t = \infty$ Thus, in our

numerical case ($\varepsilon = \beta^d \cdot \beta^s = -\frac{1}{2}$, $\delta = 2$), we obtain $q_\infty = \frac{4}{3}$, which confirms (23). If $\varepsilon = -1$, the oscillation has constant amplitude; if $\varepsilon < -1$, the oscillation is 'explosive'. If $\varepsilon > 0$, the path is nonoscillatory but converges to a constant if $\varepsilon < 1$. Thus, equilibrium values for q exist only if $|\varepsilon| < 1$.

[17] See Marschak [1949].

[18] This is the 'separated form' of note 14.

[19] See Frisch [1933a] and Hurwicz [1945].

[20] Compare footnote 3. See Koopmans [1950c, Table, p. 406].

[21] In our example this joint distribution involves only $u_1^s, \ldots, u_t^s, \ldots$. The properties of this distribution, such as, for example, the ('serial') correlation coefficient between successive pairs u_{t-1}^s, u_t^s, must be considered part of the structure.

[22] James Angell [1947, p. 291] sees here "the familiar problem of taking the right compensatory action *promptly* enough and in the right degree.... How much change in what indices should be the signal for how big a change in what fiscal and monetary operations, to offset or reverse a process of undesired general change which is *already* under way? Not only the nature of the actually current movement but the effects of the compensation measures themselves... must be gauged... if the result is not to be merely the imposition of a new set of 'artificial' or 'induced' fluctuations on those already operating."

[23] See Marschak [1947b]. *Added in 1973*: See Theil [1961].

BIBLIOGRAPHY

Angell, James, Review of *Planning and Paying for Full Employment* (ed. by Abba P. Lerner and Frank D. Graham), and *Economic Policy for Full Employment*, by Alvin H. Hansen, *Review of Economic Statistics* **29** (November, 1947) 290–292.

Frisch, Ragnar, 'Propagation Problems and Impulse Problems in Dynamic Economics', in *Economic Essays in Honour of Gustav Cassel*, George Allen & Unwin, London, 1933, pp. 171–205.

Haavelmo, Trygve, 'The Statistical Implications of a System of Simultaneous Equations', *Econometrica* **11** (January, 1943) 1–12.

Haavelmo, Trygve, 'The Probability Approach in Econometrics', *Econometrica* **12**, Supplement (July, 1944) 118 pp. (reprinted as Cowles Commission Paper, New Series, No. 4).

Hart, Albert, ''Model Building' and Fiscal Policy', *American Economic Review* **35** (September, 1945) 531–558.

Hurwicz, Leonid, 'Aspects of the Theory of Economic Fluctuations' (abstract), *Econometrica* **13** (January, 1945) 79.

Hurwicz, Leonid, 'Generalization of the Concept of Identification', Chapter IV in *Statistical Inference in Dynamic Economic Models*, Cowles Commission Monograph 10 (T. C. Koopmans, ed.), John Wiley & Sons, Inc., New York, 1950, pp. 245–257.

Hurwicz, Leonid, 'Prediction and Least Squares', Chapter VI in *Statistical Inference in Dynamic Economic Models*, Cowles Commission Monograph 10 (T. C. Koopmans, ed.), John Wiley & Sons, Inc., New York, 1950, pp. 266–300.

Koopmans, Tjalling C., 'When Is an Equation System Complete for Statistical Purposes?', Chapter XVII in *Statistical Inference in Dynamic Economic Models*, Cowles Commission Monograph 10 (T. C. Koopmans, ed.), John Wiley & Sons, Inc., New York, 1950, pp. 393–409.

Leontief, W. W., 'Verzoegerte Angebotsanpassung', *Zeitschrift für Nationalökonomie* (1934) 670–676.

Lerner, Abba P., 'The Economic Steering Wheel', *The University Review* (University of Kansas City), June, 1941.

Lundberg, Erik, *Studies in the Theory of Economic Expansion*, P. S. King, London, 1937, 265 pp.

Marschak, J., 'Economic Interdependence and Statistical Analysis', 1942, *Selected Essays*, 45.

Marschak, J., 'Statistical Inference from Nonexperimental Observations: An Economic Example', presented September 10, 1947; *Proceedings of the International Statistical Conferences*, International Statistical Institute, Washington, D.C., 1951, Vol. III, pp. 289–298.

Marschak, J., 'Economic Structure, Path, Policy, and Prediction', 1947, *Selected Essays*, 48.

Marschak, J., 'Comment on Mitchell', 1949, *Selected Essays*, 52.

Marschak, J., 'Statistical Inference in Economics: An Introduction', Chapter I in *Statistical Inference in Dynamic Economic Models*, Cowles Commission Monograph 10 (T. C. Koopmans, ed.), John Wiley & Sons, Inc., New York, 1950, pp. 1–50.

Theil, H., *Economic Forecasts and Policy*, 2nd ed. North-Holland, 1961.

Theil, H. and Boot J. C. G., 'The Final Form of Econometric Equation Systems', *Review of the International Statistical Institute* **30** (1962), 136–152.

Tinbergen, Jan, *Statistical Testing of Business-Cycle Theories*, Vol. II: *Business Cycles in the United States of America*, 1919–1932, League of Nations, Geneva, 1939.

PART V

CONTRIBUTIONS TO THE LOGIC OF ECONOMICS

INTRODUCTORY NOTE

As Tjalling Koopmans used to say, the Cowles Commission was 'spreading the gospel': namely, the conviction that economic measurements had to be based on 'theories', i.e., on systems of – generally probabilistic – relations (equations, inequalities) describing human behavior and institutions; that appropriate statistical tools should use such theories, partly as '*a priori* constraints' (often indispensable for a structure to be 'identifiable'), and partly as hypotheses to be tested. And, perhaps most important: the conviction that mathematical language might help to dispel much of the confusion habitual in the discussion of economics, due to the systems' complexity. This is the main concern of the present Part Five.

The new Annals published by the National Bureau of Economic Research (1972ff), on whose precincts the gospel of needs for theory and for mathematical language was preached, testify perhaps to the mission's belated success. How the mathematical language spread over wider fields of social science is reported by F. Mosteller (1974). How it helps social scientists to communicate with each other and with those of other disciplines is described in the concluding Essay 55 (such interdisciplinary communication was also attempted in the earlier Essays 18, 26, 27).

Recently, in papers (1974c, d), cited in the Introductory Note to Part Two, the author attempted to approach, as an economist, the logic of any empirical research as that of an 'optimal meta-decision': a simultaneous choice of a 'worthwhile problem'; of its partition into hypotheses; of the source of data; and of the decision rule as to which hypothesis to accept or whether to choose a new problem. However, he has not applied this approach to economics, his own field, so far.

REFERENCES

Mosteller, F. (1974), 'The Role of the Social Science Research Council in the Advance of Mathematics in the Social Sciences', *Items*, **28**, 17–24, Social Science Research Council, New York.

Annals of Economic and Social Measurement, (1972ff), Journal of Computers, Information Retrieval and Research Methodology, National Bureau of Economic Research, New York.

IDENTITY AND STABILITY IN ECONOMICS: A SURVEY*

(1942)

Stability is one of the desiderata of economic policy. We extol virtues of a 'well-equilibrated economy', discuss the necessity of 'restoring the equilibrium between agriculture and industry', or 'between sensitive and insensitive prices'. We deplore 'instability of business', or the 'disequilibrium of international payments'. The econometrician wants to use such terms with more precision.

I. EXAMPLES OF IDENTITIES AND EQUILIBRIUM CONDITIONS

The existing state of literature makes it necessary to deal first with a somewhat obvious preliminary distinction: the distinction between identical equations and equations expressing conditions of equilibrium. Economists have sometimes failed to make the distinction clear enough (to their readers or to themselves), thus causing confusion.

EXAMPLE ONE: 'The balance of payments must always balance'.

> As a matter of fact, the sum total of a nation's trade, debits and credits, whether visible or invisible, must *always* balance. And this remains true, whether a policy of contracting or expanding trade is followed. If it did not, a country would forever be becoming more indebted to other nations, or the reverse. Creditor countries would not for long tolerate this state of affairs, unless the debtor country met its interest and amortization obligations. ... How are these obligations met? How is international trade *in the long run* kept in balance? [Italics mine.]

This is from the *Report on International Economic Relations*, published in 1934 by the Minnesota University Press (p. 20). From the enumeration of items (pp. 18–19), it is seen that the "sum total of a nation's trade, debits and credits, whether visible or invisible", includes loans and their repayment; it is correct to say that such a "sum total... must always balance," and therefore it is not correct to ask why it is "in the long run kept in balance." The latter question would have a meaning if applied, for example, to the current items only; but it has no meaning, if all items are included.

A similar ambiguity is found in J. E. Meade's very complete and up-to-date *Introduction to Economic Analysis and Policy* (pp. 308, 312):

> If all the items in the Balance of Payments are properly recorded, the total of all the items on the receipts side valued in dollars must be equal to the total of all the items on the payments side valued in dollars. This is in reality an obvious but none the less important fact... just as sales are equal purchases... In order to discuss... the mechanism which insures that a country's Balance of Payments is in equilibrium, we must outline the factors which determine the size of the different items.

Here again: if the equality is true by definition, there is no sense in explaining a 'mechanism which insures' its validity. [*Added in 1973.* I believe Meade's more recent work is not open to this criticism].

If an identity is not satisfied, the system is logically inconsistent. If a condition of equilibrium is not satisfied, the system may be logically consistent but is nonpersistent in time. To prove an identity (supposing it is not immediately evident to the reader), it can be shown that its nonvalidity would imply the validity of some proposition whose inconsistency with the initial definitions is more immediately evident – though it is largely a matter of choice as to which propositions should be selected as immediately evident and as definitions.[1] To prove an equilibrium condition, on the other hand, it must be shown that its nonvalidity implies a situation which cannot endure in time. In the one case, we have the 'reductio ad absurdum'; in the other, what may be called the 'reductio ad nonperseverantem'.[2]

In actual fact, the theorists of international trade do not make much use of the identity they proclaim. Rather, they establish, and try to prove, equilibrium conditions, such as the following:

(a) Net loans of a country = 0;

(b) Net gold movements out of a non-gold-producing country = 0. (a) and (b) together imply the condition that

(c) Sales less purchases of goods and services (including gold sales by gold producers) = 0.

The validity of (a) and (b) taken together is a more stringent requirement than (c); it is in this stringent form that the stability condition of 'balanced current accounts' must be put, since a country cannot go on indefinitely lending out of a limited gold reserve (or repaying in gold a debt larger than the gold reserve). Yet, even in this stringent form, the requirement of balanced current accounts is not sufficient for equilibrium: the money value of each of these accounts is the product of 'physical quantity' times 'home price' times 'foreign-exchange rate'. It is possible that the product is constant, but its single factors are not – as, for example, in the case of a country which manages to pay for its imports by exporting growing quantities at a steadily depreciating exchange rate. Thus, the equilibrium requirements are

(d) Rate of change of each single price = 0;
(e) Rate of change of foreign-exchange rates = 0;
(f) Rate of change of each single physical amount = 0.

In actual practice small subdivisions of current accounts are neglected, and approximations, using price indices and indices of physical volume, are regarded as sufficient. If a price index is used covering all prices including those of tourist accommodation, shipping services, and the like, then condition (f) becomes redundant, since it is then implied in (a), (b), (d), and (e).

Conditions (d), (e), (f) are the same as in the ordinary commodity markets without loans: equilibrium is reached when both price and quantity sold cease to change. In the absence of loans, or gifts, or theft, the condition 'value of sales = value of purchases' becomes an identity; the stability conditions are: prices and quantities are constant.

As an alternative formulation of conditions of international equilibrium, J. E. Meade uses the following one: stability is reached when the amount of dollars which foreigners *wish* to buy is equal to the amount of dollars Americans *wish* to sell (Meade's italics).[3] The amounts actually bought and sold are identical, but the amounts which people wish to buy and sell are equal only in equilibrium. This approach is identical to that of '*ex ante*' and '*ex post*' magnitudes recently introduced into economic discussions. The buyers, or sellers, however, do not wish to buy, or sell, fixed quantities irrespective of prices. Rather, their behavior (or 'wishes') is described, say, by demand functions and supply functions. The coincidence of 'wishes' – which, then, must coincide not only with regard to physical amounts or sales values only, but also to prices – of buyers and sellers is the same as the requirement that all the behavior equations should be satisfied simultaneously. Instead of the dynamic requirement that all rates of change should vanish, we have here another variety of conditions of economic equilibrium: each static behavior equation[4] is such a condition.

EXAMPLE TWO: The equation of exchange is often regarded as an identity. However, Mr. Keynes writes on 'The United States and the Keynes Plan'[5]

... an adequate war effort will require some diversion of the production effort which provided previously for private consumption. Thus a larger purchasing power will face a smaller volume of purchaseable goods. If nothing is done about it, the sure consequence must be a rise in prices until the smaller volume of goods sells for an amount of money equal to the larger volume of purchasing power. *In this way the equilibrium is restored.* [Italics mine.]

If the price level is denoted by P, the volume of transactions by T, and the quantity of money by M, then $V = PT/M$ is the definition of V, the velocity of circulation, and as such is valid, whether in equilibrium or not; but the equilibrium condition is that V should have a certain constant value, say V_0, depending on the duration of customary payment periods, etc. $V = V_0$ is, again, a static behavior equation.

EXAMPLE THREE. 'Saving and investment'.

Mrs. Joan Robinson, in her *Introduction to The Theory of Unemployment*, says (pp. 9–10):

All incomes are derived either from producing consumption goods or from producing investment goods. And all income either is spent on consumption goods or is saved. The income derived from production of consumption goods is equal to the income spent on consumption goods. In short, the rate of savings is equal to the rate of investment.

Yet, to this statement of an identity following from definitions, is added the following description of a process in time:

How then does it come about that, on the balance, individuals always decide to save just as much as entrepreneurs decide to invest?... What happens when investment increases?... Then... incomes increase, savings increase with income... Saving is equal to investment because investment leads to a state of affairs in which people want to save. [And (p. 16)]: When investment increases incomes rise to the point at which saving increases equally.

Here 'investment = savings' is not an identity any more; it is an equilibrium condition; but it could only lose its character as an identity because the definitions have been silently changed (just as in Example One the term 'all items' sometimes included, sometimes excluded, the item 'loans'). Let y denote the sum of all incomes except entrepreneurial windfall profits (or losses); let p denote such profits; let i = investment, and

c = consumption. Then, identically, as explained in the first quotation of Mrs. Robinson's reasoning,

$$y+p=c+i,$$

and therefore,

$$i=(y+p)-c.$$

Now, saving is defined as

$$s=\text{income}-\text{consumption}.$$

Subtracting from the above,

$$i-s=(y+p)-\text{income}.$$

Therefore, identically, either

$$i-s=0$$

or

$$i-s=p,$$

according to whether income is defined as

$$\text{income}=y+p$$

or as

$$\text{income}=y.$$

Under the first definition of income, any diminution of investment while consumption and nonwindfall incomes are constant means identically an equal diminution of windfall profits (the entrepreneurs' receipts are smaller than before while their payments are the same), and therefore an equal diminution of total income, and therefore of savings, since the latter are defined as nonconsumed income. 'Undersaving', 'oversaving' are by definition impossible. But, they become possible under the second definition of income; under that definition they are equal to windfall profits (losses). That they should be zero, is, then, not an identity but a condition of equilibrium. In other words, it is assumed that windfall profits (losses) cannot endure, because their existence gives rise (in time) to processes which tend to annihilate them. Thus the equilibrium condition is

$$p=0,$$

regardless of whether income is defined so as to include or not to include p. However, under the second definition – but not under the first – p is identically equal to $i-s$, and therefore the stability condition can also be written as

$$i-s=0.$$

We do not see that much advantage arises from this second formulation of equilibrium, based as it is on a rather artificial definition of income.[6] In any case, it is important to explain just what is meant by that variable, p (windfall profits, identical, under a certain definition of income, with undersaving), which has the property to tend toward zero. From the above quotations, it seems that p must be defined as that part of the entrepreneur's income which has the property of stimulating output if p is positive, and of depressing output if it is negative:

$$dy_t/dt=f(p_{t-\theta}), \quad f(0)=0, \quad f(a)/a>0,$$

for any nonnull value of a; t is time; θ is a time lag.

As long as the lag and the fluctuation are not further specified, the equation can be regarded as a definition of p, the windfall profits (or 'undersaving'). The equation becomes a (dynamic) behavior equation when θ and f are specified. The processes described by Mrs. Robinson, Keynes, and others can be probably represented in the simplest way by the following dynamic model, where s'' and s' are, respectively, the savings out of windfall profits and out of other incomes, $s=$ the total investments, or savings, and h and g describe the 'propensity to save' functions appropriate to windfall and nonwindfall income respectively:

$$\begin{aligned} dy_t/dt &= f(p_{t-\theta}), \\ s' &= g(y), \\ s'' &= h(p), \\ s &= s'+s''. \end{aligned}$$

This determines y as a function of time, given its initial value y_0 at a time when the total saving was fixed (say, by decision of the public-works authorities) at a constant amount s. By substitution,

$$dy_t/dt = k(y_{t-\theta}),$$

where the form of the function k depends on the other three functions involved. On them, and on the lag θ will depend whether, on solving the last equation, we shall or shall not obtain a time function for y tending to vanish, e.g., a damped oscillation. We do get such a function (without oscillation) if, to fix the ideas, we give to the functions involved the following simplest specifications (omitting the time lags), where the parameters b, m, n are all positive:

$$dy/dt = bp, \quad s' = my - n, \quad s'' = p, \quad s' + s'' = s;$$

this yields the solution

$$\text{in terms of } p\text{: } p(t) = p_0 e^{-bmt};$$

$$\text{in terms of } y\text{: } y(t) = \frac{s+n}{m}(1 - e^{-bmt}) + y_0 e^{-bmt}.$$

As t increases,

p approaches 0,
y approaches $(s+n)/m$.

Thus, windfall profits tend to disappear the faster, the larger b (sensitivity of entrepreneurs to windfall profits) and the larger m (marginal propensity to save). When this ('equilibrium') stage is reached, the national income is the larger, the larger the total investment, s (supposed here to be fixed from the start by authorities), and the smaller the marginal propensity to save, m. Also, in equilibrium, $dy/dt = 0$. Furthermore, the equilibrium value (say, Y) of y has the property $dY/ds = 1/m$, Mr. Keynes' multiplier. It is seen in our example that the multiplier (or its reciprocal) while determining the size of the equilibrium income for a given size of investments, does at the same time also determine the path of the income through time. The 'path' approach to the 'multiplier' concept was, in fact, the one originally used by Mr. R. F. Kahn when he discovered the multiplier in his article on public works (*Economic Journal*, 1931) where he described how "one man put to work on the road" would *gradually* induce the employment of two or three. His dynamics (e.g., the specification of speeds and lags involved) were, however, somewhat vague, and when the multiplier again appeared, in Mr. Keynes' book, it was in connection with equilibrium values only. Yet, it is the dynamic assumption (stimulation of output by windfall profits) which gives Keynes' system its sense, even if the details of the path are left out of consideration.[7]

II. EQUILIBRIUM AND DETERMINATENESS

If all the variables of the system refer to the same point of time (which implies that neither lags nor derivatives occur in the equations), the system is called static. If it has a finite number of real and finite roots, the behavior equations of such a system are themselves equilibrium conditions: when all the variables have the values given by the roots of the system, all the behavior equations are satisfied, and no individual has cause to move to another position, i.e., to another set of values. Wicksell's 'cumulative inflation' is an example of *disequilibrium* which takes place if the parameters of a system do not allow of finite roots of some of the variables.[8] In such a case we can test stability without analyzing the path of the variables through time. Wicksell assumes, in effect, four equations:

$$(1)\quad \begin{cases} \text{Behavior of banks: } R = r_0\,; \\ \text{Behavior of savers: } S = mY + bR + g\,; \\ \text{Behavior of entrepreneurs: } S = nY - cR + h\,; \\ \text{Behavior of money holders: } M = f(Y, R)\,; \end{cases}$$

where the variables are: the national savings (in money units), S, identically equal to investments; the national money income, Y; the interest rate, R; and the quantity of money, M. On the other hand, r_0 is a *constant* number, viz., the interest level which the banks have, at time 0, decided to maintain, by supplying appropriate amounts of money; these amounts are determined by the fourth equation, describing the 'liquidity preference' of money-holders; a relationship which we can here leave unspecified. Subtract the 'entrepreneurs'' equation from the 'savers'' equation:

$$(2a)\qquad (m-n)\,Y + (b+c)\,R = g + h\,;$$

this also holds true for the initial values of Y and R; say Y_0 and R_0:

$$(2b)\qquad (m-n)\,Y_0 + (b+c)\,R_0 = g + h\,;$$

on the other hand, substituting into (2a) from the 'banks' equation' we get:

(2c) $(m-n)\,Y+(b+c)\,r_0=g+h.$

We obtain from the last two equations

(2d) $Y-Y_0=(R_0-r_0)\,(b+c)/(m-n).$

Now, m, n, c, and in all probability b (at least in Wicksell's description of the capital market) are positive. The Equation (2d) shows therefore that, provided $m>n$, the equilibrium money income will be above the initial money income, if the banks maintain an interest rate higher than the initial one, i.e., higher than the rate which prevailed before the banks becan to increase the supply of money.[9] In particular, as $m-n$ approaches zero while remaining positive, the equilibrium income, Y, rises indefinitely. Therefore, if the reactions of enterpreneurs and of savers to changes in national income (the parameters m and n) are sufficiently near each other, a low market rate, compared with the initial rate, implies indefinite inflation of the money income. A somewhat more realistic set-up is obtained by giving up the hypothesis of the banks' maintaining a completely rigid money rate regardless of advancing inflation; and regarding the rigid policy as a limiting case only. Let the banking policy be

$$R=r_0+k(Y-Y_0),\quad k \text{ a positive constant};$$

(taking, for example, account of Irving Fisher's point that banks must raise the interest rate in inflation, lest they should make losses on their loans owing to money depreciation). We shall then obtain, instead of (2d), a more general equation

$$Y-Y_0=(R_0-r_0):\left(k+\frac{m-n}{b+c}\right).$$

The smaller k, the larger Y for any given money rate r_0; the requirement that $m-n$ should be positive is replaced by a less stringent one. Wicksell's cumulative inflation appears as a limiting case, as k approaches 0, and m approaches n.

Thus the examination of the roots of a static system may reveal conditions of disequilibrium.[10] In our case, with linear equations only, we obtained conditions of infinite roots, or of roots too large to indicate a practically attainable or maintainable situation. (With nonlinear equations, a similar interpretation might be given to imaginary roots.) On the other hand, the case where numerator and denominator are zero can be interpreted as an indeterminate equilibrium, analogous to the case of a ball lying on a table. Such investigations of roots of a static system, to find its conditions of equilibrium, have also been applied in the analysis of duopoly and of bilateral monopoly.

The implication, however, that a determinate system is also an equilibrium does not apply when variables refer to different points of time. In general x_{ik} may denote the value of the variable x expected at the time i to be attained at the time k. In the particular case $i=k$, we have the *actual* value of x at the time k; but if $i>k$, we have the *expected* value. Dynamic models subject to statistical verifications have usually to be confined to actual values at different points of time. In that case it is obvious that the determinateness of the system, time being counted as a variable, does not imply the perseverance of its roots through time; while, if time is not counted as a variable the determinateness of the system means, of course, that each variable can be expressed as a function of time. In the economic theory, however, in its general form as theory of assets, we have also to deal with 'expected' values, and the special case is of importance where i is constant (the same for all variables of the system) but k is not. The determinateness of such a system (of which it is doubtful whether it should be called static or not) means that, given the data of the system (such as the tastes, the expected production and exchange conditions, and so on, separately for each individual) the finite values of the variables actually attained at the time point i (the prices and quantities of all assets) can be explained. But it does not mean that those values will persist through time: as i assumes higher values expectations must be revised in the light of realizations, if only because the expectations of different individuals have proved to be incompatible with each other.[11]

III. STABILITY AND THE PATH

Any behavior equation expressing the individual's behavior in terms of economic variables, such as amounts and prices $x, y, \ldots$, say $f(x, y, \ldots)=0$, means that combinations of values of these variables which satisfy the equation are preferred by the individual to, or bring him more satisfaction than, other combinations. It must, therefore, be possible to derive any behavior equation from the conditions that some expression $F(x, y, \ldots)$ which measures satisfaction, or some monotonically increasing function of it, should be maximized, subject to the validity of all the other equations of the system. Whether we use behavior equations, such as demand curves, whether we write $F = \max$, a requirement from which they are derived, in both cases we formulate equilibrium conditions; just as by requiring that the potential energy of a system of bodies should be at its minimum, we require implicitly that the total work done by small displacements should be zero. The former requirement is stricter, however, since the latter is fulfilled whether the potential is at its minimum or at its maximum, i.e., in the case of both stable and unstable equilibria.

For the stable equilibrium of the market as a whole to be achieved, the satisfaction of each individual should be at its maximum, constrained by other conditions, among which are the similar requirements for *other* individuals. Attempts have been made to translate this proposition from the language of individual preference maps into the language of aggregate demand and supply functions. The attempts, however, have not so far seemed successful. We arrive, under certain conditions, to opposite stability conditions, according to whether we deal with 'output adjusters' or 'price adjusters'. Let $p =$ price, and in particular, $p' =$ demand price, $p'' =$ supply price; let $X =$ quantity, and in particular, $X' =$ demand quantity, $X'' =$ supply quantity.

Price adjusters[12] act as follows:

(1) if, at a given price, $X' - X'' > 0$, price rises; (2) its rise pulls $X' - X''$ down;

Output adjusters act as follows:

(1) if, at a given output, $p' - p'' > 0$, output increases; (2) its rise pulls $p' - p''$ down.

Let the demand and supply equations be, respectively

$$X' = a - bp' \quad \text{and} \quad X'' = m + np'' \quad (b \text{ positive}),$$

and express the *second halves* of the above propositions on the behavior of price adjusters and output adjusters:

Price adjusters:	Output adjusters:
$\dfrac{d}{dp}(X' - X'') < 0,$	$\dfrac{d}{dX}(p' - p'') < 0,$

$$p' = p'' = p, \qquad X' = X'' = X,$$

$$X' - X'' = a - m - p(b+n), \qquad p' - p'' = \frac{a}{b} + \frac{m}{n} - X\left(\frac{1}{b} + \frac{1}{n}\right),$$

$$\text{Therefore } b+n > 0. \qquad \text{Therefore } \frac{1}{b} + \frac{1}{n} > 0.$$

We have assumed b positive (decreasing demand curve); if n is also positive (increasing supply curve), the results for the case of price adjusters and output adjusters are consistent. But if n is negative (decreasing supply curve) they are not. In that case, in the market of price adjusters stability is ensured if $b > |n|$; but in the market of output adjusters it is ensured if $b < |n|$.

This analysis of the *second halves* of the above alternative behavior propositions shows that, in the cases assumed by Marshall and Walras respectively, the condition that a sloping down supply curve should yet permit of a stable equilibrium assumes diametrically opposite forms: Marshall requires that it should fall more steeply, whereas Walras requires that it should be less steep, than the demand curve.

However, let us consider the *first halves*. They are dynamic and can be written, in the simplest case, using positive coefficients r and s:

Price adjusters:	Output adjusters:
$dp/dt = (X' - X'')\, r;$	$dX/dt = (p' - p'')\, s;$

which, in connection with the above demand and supply equations leads (indicating initial values by zero subscripts) to

$$X' - X'' = (X_0' - X_0'')\, e^{-rt\lambda}, \qquad p' - p'' = (p_0' - p_0'')\, e^{-st\mu},$$

where

$$\lambda = b + n; \qquad \mu = \frac{1}{b} + \frac{1}{n},$$

$$p = \frac{a-m}{\lambda}(1 - e^{-rt\lambda}) + p_0 e^{-rt\lambda},$$

$$X = \frac{\frac{a}{b} + \frac{m}{n}}{\mu}(1 - e^{-st\mu}) + X_0 e^{-st\mu}.$$

Thus, the discrepancy of supply and demand, or of supply prices and demand prices, will tend to disappear if λ or μ, respectively, are positive. But this is the same stability condition we obtained discussing the second (static) halves of the behavior propositions. And, as before, if n is negative the stability conditions in the price-adjuster and in the output-adjuster case are of opposite nature. Also, the values which, with λ or μ positive, the price and the quantity approach as time goes on are simply the solutions of the static demand and supply equations given above (as can be seen by inspecting the solutions of the differential equations.)

By an analysis similar to the one given here, P. Samuelson is led to the conclusion that "the definition of stability of a comparative statical system rests implicitly upon the introduction of dynamical considerations.... In order for the analysis of comparative statics to be useful, it must be generalized to include the determination of the dynamical path of the system in and out of equilibrium."[13]

It is clear that the knowledge of the dynamical path is sufficient for the knowledge of the point to which the path leads. But is the former knowledge always necessary for the latter? Granted that Mr. Hicks has not succeeded in deducing the stability conditions in the market from the principle of maximum satisfaction, simultaneous for all the individuals,[14] yet it has not been proved that the task is impossible.

Whether or not static considerations can, in some cases, suffice to test a system's stability, it has been seen in the previous sections that it is of more general applicability to inspect the dynamic path.

A well-known example is that of the 'cobweb.' Here, as in the previous section, much depends on whether the buyers or sellers are supposed to adjust prices or quantities. Suppose first that buyers adjust prices, and sellers quantities. Measuring prices p and quantities x from an origin chosen so as to make the constant terms vanish, and denoting by k and l adjustment lags (both positive) we may write, say,

Demand:	Supply:
$p_t = \frac{1}{b} x_{t-k}$,	$x_t = m p_{t-l}$.

Hence

$$x_t = \frac{m}{b} x_{t-l-k},$$

leading to an oscillation the exponential factor of which has the index

$$\frac{\log |m| - \log |b|}{k+l}.$$

Thus, in this case it will depend on the slopes m and b, whether the oscillation is or is not a damped one. Suppose, however, that buyers and not only sellers are price adjusters, i.e., write

Demand:	Supply:
$x_t = bp_{t-k}$,	$x_t = mp_{t-l}$.

Hence

$$x_t = \frac{m}{b}\, x_{t-l+k};$$

the exponential factor has in this case the index

$$\frac{\log |m| - \log |b|}{k-l},$$

the sign of which depends not only, as before, on the relative size of the slopes of the demand and supply curves but also on the relative size of the time lags necessary for the adjustments by buyers and sellers respectively.

Similar examples are provided in the analysis of duopoly which has recently been presented (by Smithies) not merely in the form of successive steps by which each duopolist reacts to the last action of the other, but in the form of time functions. It may be more general both in the case of the cobweb and of duopoly, to assume, not constant time lags irrespective of the position at which the individual finds itself, but adjustment velocities changing according to the position of the point. (Cf. such proposals for duopoly, Frisch's 'Notion de la force dans l'équilibre économique', *Economic Tijdskrift*, 1931.)

NOTES

* Paper presented at the meeting of the Econometric Society in New Orleans, December 28, 1940.

[1] See, for example, Ernst Mach's rearrangement of Newton's Laws, in *Die Entwicklung der Mechanik*, Vienna, 1912, Chapter II, 7.

[2] The analogy (not identity) between the 'proof' of the principle of virtual displacements and the 'reductio ad absurdum' is pointed out, for example, in Haas' *Theoretical Physics*, pp. 63–64 (second English edition).
[3] E. Meade, *Introduction to Economic Analysis and Policy*, p. 309. On the ambiguities of the '*ex ante*' concepts, see A. P. Lerner in *Economica*, 1939.
[4] See below, Section III.
[5] *The New Republic*, July 29, 1940. A similar statement also in the *Report on Current Economic Condition* of the London and Cambridge Economic Service, July, 1940.
[6] As is well known, Mr. Keynes followed the 'second' definition of income (exclusion of windfall profits from income) in his *Treatise* of 1930, but emphatically abandoned it, in favor of the first definition, in his *General Theory* of 1936. However, he occasionally relapses, in important places of the book, into speaking of 'savings = investment' as of an equilibrium condition, thus silently switching over to the other definition of income: "An increment of investment... cannot occur unless the public are prepared to increase their savings.... The public will not do this unless their aggregate income... is increasing. Thus their effort to consume a part of their increased income will stimulate output *until* the new level of income provides a margin of saving sufficient to correspond to increased investment." [Italics mine] *General Theory of Employment, Interest, and Money*, p. 117.
[7] See A. H. Hansen and P. A. Samuelson, *Review of Economic Statistics*, 1939, for more complete statements. See also my article, 'Family Budgets and the So-called Multiplier', in *Canadian Journal of Economics*, 1939; and P. A. Samuelson, 'The Theory of Pump-Priming Reëxamined', *American Economic Review* **30** (September, 1940) 492–506.
[8] We follow the interpretation given to Wicksell by Hicks, in his article 'Mr. Keynes and the Classics', *Econometrica* **5** (April, 1937) especially p. 158. (*Added in 1973*.) See also J. Marschak, 'Wicksell's Two Interest Rates', (1941), *Selected Essays*, 36, and P. Samuelson's weaker sufficient condition for cumulative inflation, in 'Fundamental Multiplier Identity', *Econometrica*, **11** (1943), 221–226.
[9] It is seen that r_0 is Wicksell's market rate, and R_0 his 'natural' rate. I do not know of any other logically tenable interpretation. One does come across interpretations where the 'natural rate' is itself a variable, not – as in ours – a constant. If it is then said that banks maintain the market rate below that variable, it is implied that the market rate itself varies; but then there is no need to 'explain' the lack of equilibrium, since anyhow all the magnitudes are supposed to change.
[10] For another example see my 'Money and the Theory of Assets', 1938, *Selected Essays*, 33: if marginal utilities and costs are both independent of outputs, the system becomes, in general, inconsistent. This includes the case of a speculator who has a constant time preference and a certainty that prices will grow: he will then pile up infinite stocks.
[11] Cf. Hicks, *Value and Capital*, Oxford, 1939, Chapter X; Makower and Marschak, 'Assets, Prices and Monetary Theory', 1938, *Selected Essays*, 34.
[12] The 'price adjusters' type is the one discussed by Walras and recently by Hicks. The 'output adjuster' type was discussed by Marshall. Hicks thinks (*Value and Capitals*, p. 63, footnote) that Marshall's reasoning applies to the case of monopoly, while his applies to the case of perfect competition. Actually we can think of monopolistic sellers who are price adjusters, and, of course, of monopolistic buyers who are (Hotelling, *Economic Journal* (1929) 41–42). *Added in 1974*. More recently, the Marshall-Walras contrast has been studied by Axel Leijonhufvud.

[13] Cowles Commission for Research in Economics, *Report of Sixth Annual Research Conference on Economics and Statistics at Colorado Springs, July 1–26, 1940*, p. 44.
[14] In his Mathematical appendix to Ch. V of *Value and Capital*, Hicks merely takes over from the nonmathematical text the condition that "a rise in price makes supply larger than demand": pp. 62–63, 315. It is significant that R. G. D. Allen's *Mathematical Analysis for Economists* omits any discussion of the stable equilibrium for *an industry* as distinct from *a firm*.

51

A CROSS SECTION OF BUSINESS CYCLE DISCUSSION: A REVIEW OF 'READINGS'* **

(1945)

> The purpose of the criticism... was not so much that the people did not like what [the painter] was doing as that they wanted to know exactly what was in his mind. – A Bell for Adano

The task of Professors Ellis and Haberler, and of the committees over which they presided, was like the task of directors of an art gallery, cramped into a small house and open to a wide public. The collection must be small yet representative, therefore broad. It must be broad but not shallow, that is, every piece must be significant. But, while significant, no piece should puzzle the busy layman who strays into the gallery to rest and enjoy.

The editors could not have accomplished the task more perfectly. As one revives in one's memory a twenty years' crop of blue, green, and red economic periodicals, one finds that no bouquet could be gathered with more taste and sense of proportion – yes, with more love. This impression is strengthened by Professor Somers's excellently classified bibliography of some 800 articles 'on business cycle theories'. About one in every forty of these articles has been reprinted in the volume under review. I doubt very much that more than one or two substitutions could be suggested to make the selection more weighty or more representative.

The volume is so representative that any reader interested in the progress of economics is rightly tempted to regard it as a sample of the present state of our discipline. What results have been achieved? What tools are being handed to the next generation (for the volume is also intended as a textbook) for further achievement?

I

I hear that the progress of seismology may be due, in the main, either to better instruments and theories, or to frequent earthquakes. In our case, the earthquakes did most of the job. The 1930's experienced depression. The 1940's experienced full employment. To be sure, the present volume contains little evidence of the direct utilization by economists of those contemporary experiences (an exception is an article by John Williams, 1941; while the factual material used in Alvin Hansen's article, 1939, chosen for the volume happens to refer to population and other trends rather than cycles). Yet it is difficult to imagine that the revolution in our outlook has been due to the tools: they are too blunt! or to the theories: they are too inarticulate! This has happened: the greatest among us, and especially the genius of Keynes, have sensed history and have had the courage and intuition to recast theory accordingly.[1] The historical facts have been so forceful that no particularly clear and consistent theory and almost no measurements were needed to carry the conviction, or at least the feeling, that old economics could not explain all the facts and ought not to direct all policies.

Rather symptomatically, the field of discussion itself has not been clearly defined. The present volume, for example, purports to deal with 'business cycle theory'. Yet, as in many university courses of the same name, much more is attempted in its component articles than explaining business fluctations. There is, of course, no harm in a name, provided distinct matters are named distinctly. Four articles (by Schumpeter, 1935; Kondratieff, 1926; Mitchell, 1923; and Tinbergen, 1940) do attempt to explain, or at least describe, the phenomenon of quasi-periodical changes in economic variables; they form the volume's Part I (Over-All Picture of the Business Cycle and Method of Analysis). Part VI on Special Commodity Cycles contains Mordecai Ezekiel's article, 1938, on the cobweb theorem. Of the remaining sixteen articles, hardly more than four or five deal with the trade cycles proper[2], or at least with the process of adjustments (or explosions: so-called cumulative processes) in response to external trends or shocks: in short, with economic dynamics.[3] Faithfully and fairly reflecting the present state of discussion, the bulk of the volume is devoted, in essence, to the static question: *viz.*, assuming that equilibrium is always reached somehow, what will it be under given conditions? For example: assuming that the money value of the supply of all goods (identical with the total money income earned in their production) has somehow reached equality with the money value of the demand for all goods, what will be the money value of this supply (another word for money income),[4] if the wage rate, or the interest rate, or the rate of investment has a given size? This is the kind of discussions inaugurated by Lord Keynes's discoveries, of which J. R. Hicks said: "The *General Theory of Employment* is a useful book. But it is neither the beginning nor the end of economic dynamics."[5]

It is true that the discussion cannot help stumbling upon dynamic relations. For example, 'cumulative processes' are described. Or, to take another example, the relationship between income and consumption is ascribed to a 'multiplier principle' working over a hypothetical sequence of undefined 'periods', during which sequence of periods the variables converge to certain values called equilibrium values. A third example of rudimentary dynamics is the Robertsonian 'day', used by many authors of this volume: an undefined period of time introduced to justify giving different names (savings and investment) to two dated values of what is regarded as one and the same variable. To be sure, a truly dynamic theory will not neglect hypotheses which those authors may have in mind: the hypothesis, for example, that a divergence between two certain quantities leads to processes which increase the divergence (as in the case of 'cumulative' processes of Wicksell and his school), or decrease it (as in the case of Mr. Kahn's multiplier theory in which the difference between actual employment and the employment compatible with a given total demand gradually fades out); or the hypothesis that a significant time-lag separates consumption decisions from income changes. But, to apply such hypotheses seriously, the concepts and relations must be stated with greater precision than that given them by the original authors and by most of the interpreters. The present ambiguities are well illustrated by Fritz Machlup, 1939, who lucidly enumerates and classifies the various 'periods' confused by various authors. The prevailing carelessness in discussing processes suggests that it is the equilibrium values and not the process of reaching them (nor the question of whether they are reached at all) that has interested most economists, at least after Keynes's book of 1936 was read and digested. This is also shown by Somers's bibliography of 'business cycle theory': hardly one-sixth of the listed articles deal with the explanation of business fluctuations.[6]

II

Across the distinction between statics and dynamics cuts another one: that between aggregative or 'macro'-economics, and the 'micro'-economics of a single firm or household. The contributions of the volume are essentially macro-economic. Some contributors (Schumpeter, Mitchell, Williams, Haberler) emphasize the error involved in unduly sweeping aggregation. But this has been so far almost entirely negative criticism. Little has been done to indicate the size of the error under various types of aggregation and, hence, to find the 'optimal' extent and method of aggregation; though probably nobody but a purist will deny that *some* aggregation, and hence *some* error, is inevitable because a theory in a million variables can be neither verified nor applied. The relation between 'micro'- and 'macro'-propositions, *e.g.*, between the individual's and the community's 'marginal propensity to consume' (a distinction emphasized by Haberler, p. 198) depends, of course, on the frequency-distributions involved: in this case, on the income-distribution in particular. As another example: Mitchell observes that the changing dispersion of profits has cyclical features.[7] This suggests that two frequency-moments of profits (dispersion and average) and not only one (average) must be studied. Such studies bridge the gap between 'micro'- and 'macro'-economics.

There exists, in fact, an awkward gap: that between the theorems which the undergraduate is taught to derive from the rational behavior of single firms and consumers, either in perfect or imperfect markets, and the rather crude and sudden assumptions of the 'macro'-discussion on, say, 'investments as a whole'. How is the formula 'investments are high when profits are high' linked with the formula 'a firm employs as many machines as would make the value of their marginal product equal to the marginal expense'? (To use the last formula makes investments depend, *inter alia*, on the ratio of machine prices to wage rates.) Or: How is the rise of costs during, but not before, the latter part of the boom (Mitchell, p. 50) connected with the production and cost functions of firms? If such links are not established, the theory of the firm as taught in colleges may degenerate into a 'mark of a gentleman's education' like the fencing and archery taught to would-be mandarins. Yet this need not happen: rationality of firms' behavior is probably not a bad first approximation and can be well utilized in realistic analyses of the economy as a whole.

III

To say that the bulk of the volume, or of the discussion it reflects, is on macro-statics does not mean that the book or the discussion is useless. New equilibrium values corresponding to changed conditions, including changed policies, are *sometimes* reached so quickly that useful policy can *sometimes* be performed without paying much attention to the adjustment process. Thus, considerable practical knowledge can be derived from a relatively simple theory.

Unfortunately, the usefulness of macro-statics has been lowered by the crudity of our tools. We are spending too much time on misunderstandings, and we misunderstand each other because we talk carelessly. That our concepts are not unambiguous is well known from the savings-investment controversy (of which the volume contains top specimens in the articles by Ohlin, 1937; Friedrich Lutz, 1938, and Lerner). Had there been more attempts to measure the quantities under discussion economists might have found themselves compelled to more precision. Williams's plea to give a systematic place to 'monetary' *versus* 'realized' savings – both measurable – is a case in point (although his distinction between 'oversaving' and 'underinvestment' is again a puzzle). Another case in point is the Robertsonian 'day'. If it had 24 hours, the difference between the values of any variable taken 'yesterday' and 'today' would be trifling except on a Black Friday; and it is not too meticulous to ask just how long, approximately, is the lag in question. It is, in fact, the lag of spending habits behind changing incomes that matters: an empirically given amount of time, not an arbitrarily chosen unit of time-measurement.[8] As an alternative, the theorists may have in mind a relation, with or without time-lag, between a variable and the rate of change, per arbitrary unit of time, of another variable. (Examples of such relations will be given in the next section.)

These doubts of a sympathetic reader are given here merely to suggest that some current concepts and assumptions could well bear a fresh and unambiguous restatement.

The volume contains a well-known article by Oscar Lange, 1939. It expounds the relevant behavior relations (economists' 'schedules') with a degree of clarity which other static articles of the volume have attained only in regard to certain accounting identities such as are specified in articles by Ohlin, Lerner, and Lutz. By counting relations of both kinds, it can be seen whether one has really explained what determines the variables (if there are as many of them as there are independent relations); or only given a half-theory, like the half-scissors of Marshall's simile (if the variables are more numerous than independent relations); or, thirdly, whether one has perhaps contradicted oneself (if there are more variables than there are independent relations). People afraid of symbols can describe each relation in words like 'consumption depends on income', then count all such sentences and thus reach those rather important results. People who do not despise God's gift of equations can easily get even more interesting results. Hicks (in an article already quoted and similar to Lange's in scope) has used such a static system to study the effect of changing interest rate; one could similarly study the complete effect of (much discussed, rarely clarified) cuts of wage rates.[9]

IV

Yet, even the clearest static theories usually have one misty spot. They assume equilibrium between, say, the supply of and demand for a single commodity; or between the value of all goods produced (another word for national income) and the value of all goods demanded. This implies unchanged inventories. This assumption tempts one to use the same symbols for supply and for demand, neglecting to state the assumption itself as a separate relation. Actually the relation is seldom valid. Under the names of inflationary (or deflationary) gaps we have recently familiarized ourselves with aggregate-demand-supply differences of spectacular dimensions. These differences show up in the depletion (or rise) of inventories and later cause a change in prices and in production.

The existence and the dynamic effects of excess demand or supply were well known to the founders of modern market theory such as Walras and Marshall.[10] To explain the reaching of market equilibrium, they referred to the fact that excess demand (or supply) caused a rise (or fall) in price: a relation between a variable and the rate of change of another variable. Together with the two static relations (demand and supply schedules), this dynamic one constituted the market theory of a single commodity. Three and not two relations are, in fact, necessary to explain the movement (of which the convergence to equilibrium is one possibility) of the three variables, supply, demand, and price. This did not easily fit the two-dimensional blackboards of our classrooms and was consequently forgotten. Yet, a market theory consisting of the three propositions 'demand depends on price', 'supply depends on price', 'excess supply makes the price fall', is both clearer and nearer the truth than a market theory in which the third (dynamic) sentence is replaced, without further explanation, by 'demand equals supply'. Strictly, the latter sentence is only correct if the price falls and the consequent adjustment of demand and supply (hence, of inventories) is infinitely rapid: a special, limiting case. The suppressed and replaced sentence helps to describe just this process of adjustment.

National money income which, for the theory of a single commodity, is taken as an exogenous cause of 'shifts of demand schedule', becomes an endogenous variable (i.e., one to be explained) in problems of employment of national resources. National money income is the sum of all money incomes earned, and is therefore another word for the money value of total supply. Again, the equation 'total supply = total demand' is only approximately true; quite unlike the equation 'total supply = total income', which is an accounting identity. The total demand (for consumption goods *plus* investment goods) is therefore not identically equal to total income. To be sure, no harm arises from thinking otherwise, as long as equilibrium is assumed to have been reached somehow: no different consequences arise from the proposition 'supply is assumed to equal demand' than from the proposition 'supply is another word for demand'. But the confusion shows up as soon as one approaches the facts, the changing inventories, changing prices.[11] One has then to discard the 'supply = demand' assumption, and to substitute for it, say, 'supply = demand *plus* a random quantity', the latter quantity being an accidental (and exogenous) failure of producers to adjust inventories; or going further, one may substitute for it a dynamic relation such as 'excess supply slows down supply' (possibly including again, in addition, a random quantity). The savings-investment controversy would not have been so tiresome and inconclusive if, at the time of the controversy, the contributors to the volume under review (this includes Messrs. Lutz, Lerner and Lange) had made clear that the proposition 'money value of aggregate demand = money value of aggregate supply', far from being an accounting identity, was not even true, except as a limiting case –

viz., the case of infinitely quick adjustments – of some more general dynamic statement. Professor Samuelson's dynamic restatement, on somewhat similar lines,[12] of the Keynes-Hicks-Lange system might well have deserved inclusion in the volume and would supplement Ezekiel's discussion of the cobweb, a form of dynamics of single commodity markets. By facing dynamic facts, full understanding is reached of the nature of the static model.

V

In the volume under review, two or three simplified dynamic models (involving an equal number of relations and endogenous variables) and half-models (e.g., a single relation in two or more endogenous variables) are discussed articulately: such are the works of Ezekiel, Samuelson and J. M. Clark. They do not claim to explain the business cycle. Authors who have tried to do so faced a more difficult problem, yet applied more deficient tools. The criticism which Tinbergen in his reprinted article makes of most business-cycle theories applies to his neighbors in the volume: Schumpeter, Mitchell, Hawtrey. Are they not, in Tinbergen's words, "telling stories, not making theory"? The relations they have in mind may be sufficient to explain the cycles, but this is difficult to check because the system of relations is not clearly stated. They may be too numerous, or there may be not enough of them. Even if there are just as many relations as variables, the relations may or may not be able to explain turning points, i.e., periodic movements instead of non-periodical 'cumulative processes' or of non-periodical convergence toward equilibrium. The method chosen is to tell how one situation breeds another, and many striking facts are observed and plausibly interpreted from step to step. But the reader, aware of the many simultaneous, entangled threads of economic causation, is left to puzzle why, at any juncture of the story, one particular thread is chosen and not any of the others. One is merely made to feel, with Tony Lumpkins's genteel but vague friend, that there is some 'concatenation accordingly'.

Tinbergen's methodological article does therefore fulfill an important function in the volume. Unfortunately, the article itself does not illustrate Tinbergen's economics. Specific economic relations had to be treated in that article cursorily and formally. It would be useful to acquaint students with Tinbergen's actual hypotheses, and to provoke criticisms. For example, they might ask (as we did above, in Section II) for a fuller use of the results provided by the theory of single firms; or they might suggest getting at the economic causation of some of the trends which Tinbergen imposes from outside – e.g., reduce some trends to the fact that resources or markets approach exhaustion.

VI

As mentioned earlier, empirical tests or measurements appear in the volume rather casually. Kondratieff's statistical-historical article on long waves is an exception. This is an empirical discovery, with little pretense of a theory. The author forcefully rejects exogenous explanations (inventions, wars, new markets, increase of gold stocks are, to him, themselves caused by the economic conditions); but he does not try to give an endogenous one.

The great merit of Tinbergen's approach is, of course, the knitting together of theory and measurements. His tests by fact are indeed necessary since the number of possible, logically watertight theories is infinite. This is not to say that the tests are sufficient: as in all science, we can only narrow down the set of possible hypotheses by rejecting some of them; we can never be sure that we have hit the uniquely true one. But is it not important enough that, for example, Tinbergen (p. 81) has shown the 'acceleration principle', so attractive to theorists, to be of doubtful account in actual fact?

Tinbergen estimates, separately for each economic relation, the size of parameters such as 'marginal propensities', price-elasticities of demand, time-lags, etc. The size of those parameters makes the system periodic (with wave frequency of plausible size), or otherwise. With the exception of time-lags, the parameters are estimated by the partial regression coefficients (familiar to statistical workers) of the single relations. The student will, however, be misled by Tinbergen's statement, now five years old, that "Various pitfalls in this field have recently been discussed... fairly completely... it is now more useful to apply the method to concrete cases" (p. 81). Recent researches have shown that estimates of parameters, obtained by separately fitting each of the theoretical equations to the data, are, in general, biased estimates if the data are of non-experimental origin. This is the economist's case. His data are produced by the interplay of simultaneously valid relations. He does not have any controlled variables. Accordingly, other more general and more suitable methods are being developed;[13] though in certain cases, especially where lags and exogenous variables are involved, the old method may also lead to correct results.

VII

Whether macro- or micro-economics; statics or dynamics; purely hypothetical or empirically tested, no economic theory – however interesting or true – is really useful if it does not help policy. To nip depressions in the bud, is it necessary to know why they arise? We know that a large total demand would guarantee full employment of resources – if not immediately, then after some reasonable time needed for adjustments. Let us, then, keep total demand at the desired level, correcting it upward or downward whenever it slips down or up. This is the policy of the steering wheel.[14] It dispenses with both theories and measurements of business cycles. All that is necessary is to watch current (not past) facts pertinent to employment, and to act quickly. It is not necessary to know the causes of the trouble or of its alleged periodicity. If the room is too hot we open the window though the trouble may have been caused by the radiator, not the window; nor need we ask ourselves whether the room warms up and cools off periodically, and why. To practical man, this short-cut is precious. It is interesting to note[15] how, since the publication of the *General Theory of Employment* by a statesman-economist, the output of articles on business cycles proper has slowed down. Except for the finishing of a few monuments started before the day of revelation, and excepting the work of harmless econometric drudges, victims of despised 'scientism', the professional interest shifted to macro-statics!

It is not too conceited to call this shift a boon to mankind, involving as it did a change in the attitude of administrators and, though much slower, a change in public opinion. Certain tenets of fiscal and monetary policy, rational in their time but mere magic taboos under changed circumstances, are giving place to new rules, appropriate to higher productivity levels. There is disagreement about details only: about the way to circumvent this or that prejudice, or the feasibility of dispelling it;

about the distribution of benefits of the policy between the various classes; and about the probability that the steering wheel will have to be resorted to more often or less often. Robertson's article, 1940, classifies the tastes or fears at the base of those disagreements; articles of Williams, 1941, and of J. M. Clark, 1939, are examples of understanding and weighing the difficulties. The principle itself is, if possible, even more generally accepted now than if was five years ago: witness the current discussion of post-war employment.

We do not think, however, that the general acceptance of the (static) principle of effective demand, and of the steering wheel policies implied in it, makes business cycles theories, economic dynamics useless. Cars must not only be steered, but also repaired and built. A car must not be built to swing wildly and to require exasperated steering at every turn or slope of the road. A system able to absorb or 'dampen' external impacts is more 'stable' than one whose 'damping-ratio' is small (Tinbergen, p. 79). That ratio is a well-defined quantity. (It is, roughly speaking, another way of measuring the speed with which equilibrium is approached.) It depends, of course, on the structural characteristics of the system, i.e., on its parameters such as the various elasticities, lags, reaction velocities, etc. Would a lowering of the elasticity of labor supply (i.e., a higher flexibility of wages) make the system more stable or less stable, and by how much? What effects on the stability of the system have the current regulations on bank reserves? on dealing in securities? on governmental storage of agricultural commodities? These are problems in comparative dynamics, just as the effect of a changed consumption propensity, or of changed government spending, on the equilibrium income, are problems in comparative statics. The latter studies the factors affecting the equilibrium values; the former reveals the factors affecting the speed with which equilibrium values are reached. Both kinds of factors can be instruments of a policy that aims at high and stable income for the nation.

To answer the problems of dynamics, one has to go into the past and learn from previous fluctuations: one has to have business-cycle theories. In addition, one has to study the past even if one merely wants to 'steer the wheel': to avoid a drunken course of the car, one has to estimate in advance the presumable effect of various external, or 'spontaneous' changes in the structure of production or demand (Neisser,

1934), or the effect of, say, profits on investments. But it is erroneous to think that these relations can be measured in isolation (see end of Section VI). Therefore, even if applied statics should be the only aim, the necessary empirical study of economic relations would imply the study of the dynamic system of the economy as a whole. If, however, in addition to steering the wheel of the system we want the system to have a stable structure, we need the knowledge of what makes systems stable or sharply fluctuating. Hence, in both cases, theory of business cycles is needed.

VIII

Economic theories are made to explain what determines quantities such as prices, or employment, or interest rates at any given time. Any economic theory therefore involves relations between quantities. If economic policy applies theory it uses these relations: it tries to give some of the quantities, such as the national income, desired value by influencing other, more directly controllable quantities, such as tax rates. A theory involving false relationships cannot help, and may harm, policy. A theory that consists of vaguely stated relationships can help only if the relationships meant were true and, by an accident, happened to be understood as they were meant; or if the relationships meant were false but, by an accident, have been misunderstood in an appropriate way. More useful than to rely on such accidents is to have theories as true as possible, and to formulate them clearly.

To be true, a theory must be logically, or internally, consistent and must not contradict facts. (Although necessary, these conditions are of course not sufficient.) A theory about the determination of quantities can in general be expressed by a system of relations such as equations or inequalities, and the implications of such a system can be studied by rules of mathematics. If, in addition to being internally consistent, a theory about quantities wishes to claim consistency with facts, measurements must be made. In economics, measurements must in general be statistical estimates because numerous factors exist that cannot and need not be identified separately and that combine themselves into 'random' influences. Economic propositions (except for definitions or identities) are in general statistical, i.e., they state that certain occurrences are more probable than others. An economic theory is in agreement with facts if it does not assign a high probability to occurrences which, in reality, prove to happen but rarely.[16]

Ill-defined concepts, relations, and systems of relations (called theories) can be more easily extirpated or improved, and the logical consistency and empirical reliability of propositions about quantities are more easily tested if mathematical tools are used. Occidental humanity has developed mathematics for those very purposes.

Economics is far flung and borders on law and ethics, psychology and history, on human biology and on technology. To reason by methods other than mathematical ones and to ascertain facts without statistics is legitimate or necessary in some of those fields or nearer their borders. Economic theory is not the only and perhaps not the most useful part of economics. Propositions of legal economics about the existing institutions, and statements of sociology or political science as to how institutions change, may be more reliable, and hence more useful, than the essentially quantitative propositions of economic theory and economic statistics about man's probable behavior in matters of supply and demand of goods and services. Nevertheless, propositions of the latter kind have been shown to possess some moderate degree of reliability, and this is why any sort of economic theory can exist at all. Why, then, neglect the tools appropriate to quantitative relations and thus diminish whatever usefulness economic theory may have? There is nothing inhuman about stating that, in given conditions, men behave in moderately persistent ways; there is nothing frivolous in counting men and measuring their ways. True, the Lord did punish David for taking a census: but that was a long time ago.[17]

A giant can do with a hammer the work of a steamhammer. Ricardo and Keynes, using numerical examples and the short-cuts of powerful intuition, have achieved great things; but I doubt that a third name (Menger? Marx?) could be added to these. Marshall probably arrived at, and most certainly tested, his conclusions by mathematics. By hiding his tools in appendices, Marshall bowed to an old belief, a self-deception, I think: that in economics clear reasoning can be replaced by delightfully Ciceronian discourse and that the resulting agreement of minds is due to conviction rather than respect. Robertson's (1938, pp. 315, 312) purpose is "to give an account of events in language as nearly as possible approaching that of *Reading without Tears*." ... "Latterly several helpful attempts have been made to express precisely in mathematical terms some of the points at issue. Has a stage now been reached when it is possible to sum the whole position up broadly in more ordinary language, indicating in a general way what departments of the whole tangled controversy seem to be primarily concerned with words and methods, and what with more substantial issues? I do not know, but I should like... to make the attempt."

As one who has perused *Readings in Business Cycle Theory* I must confess: this was not *reading without tears*. It was strenuous reading. If we study economics to remember the names of authors, their characteristic terms and phrases, conflicts and misunderstandings, and perhaps the social and psychological setting of those conflicts, a volume like the present one is both pleasant and useful: an admirable art gallery. But if economics is not about economists and their words and feelings but about how to explain or influence facts, then to extract economic knowledge from the articles of the volume is a most difficult task. A giant's disciple says (Lerner, p. 164): "Mr. Keynes' presentation [of the multiplier concept] cannot escape the suspicion of the lack of clarity." In the course of our present article we had cause to complain similarly of other authors. To read about triangles yet shed no tears, give us Euclid, not Cicero.

Precise language would make reading and writing slower, no doubt. Yet in the long run time would be saved. Do we not (and our students) read and write too hastily, anyhow? Do we not, just because of that haste, read and write too much? Economists praise the fruits of patience: the bee in the seal of the Royal Economic Society is there to buzz the glory of 'roundabout processes'. Even non-economists know that to get along in England or in the United States it pays to learn some modest English. Our students begin to realize that, to master quantitative relationships that make up economic theory, it pays to learn some modest mathematics. The econometricians may not have been such harmless drudges after all.

The *Readings* reflect excellently the discussion of the last twenty years. The discussion was moved by momentous events and has achieved important results. The results were obtained by intuition rather than clear thought. The problems still unsolved are naturally the more complicated ones. Nevertheless, no better tools may perhaps be needed for their solution if – but only if! – the coming generation again produces a genius of intuition. But what if it does not?

NOTES

* *American Economic Review*, **35** (1945).

** *Readings in Business Cycle Theory*, selected by a Committee of the American Economic Association, Volume II of the Blakiston Series of Republished Articles on Economics, with a Preface by Howard S. Ellis, chairman, General Committee on Republications; an Introduction by Gottfried Haberler, chairman, Selection Committee; and a Bibliography of Articles on Business Cycle Theory compiled by Harold M. Somers.

When referred to for the first time, the articles included in the volume will, in general, be quoted only by the author's name and the year of first publication. Page numbers refer to the pages of the volume, not to those of the original publications.

[1] R. L. Klein, *The Keynesian Revolution* (unpublished thesis, Massachusetts Institute of Technology, 1944).

[2] Hawtrey, 1926.

[3] J. M. Clark, 1917, and P. A. Samuelson, 1939, on the acceleration principle; J. M. Clark, 1939, on 'compensatory devices'; F. A. Hayek, 1935, on price expectations, monetary disturbances and maladjustments.

[4] By 'demand' and 'supply' we mean the variable quantities demanded or supplied, not the functional relations between each of those variables and other variables such as prices. If the latter terminology were accepted, we should have to replace the simple expressions 'demand equals supply', 'demand exceeds supply by a given amount', etc., by more cumbersome ones. The relevance of those expressions for dynamic analysis will appear below.

[5] J. R. Hicks, 'Mr. Keynes and the Classics; a Suggested Interpretation', *Econometrica* **5**, No. 2 (Apr., 1937), 147–59. Among the authors included in the present volume, the distinction is recognized by Ellis, 1940 (p. 406); but also by Lerner, 1939 (p. 167), who says: "Mr. Keynes's greatest fault is perhaps his failure to point out with sufficient emphasis that he is in the main concerned with equilibrium analysis." Haberler, 1936, seems to go even further and to accuse Keynes of feeding us not even with statics but with 'barren' identities. This is another misunderstanding, and reveals Keynes's second greatest fault, *viz.* (to paraphrase Mr. Lerner), "his failure to point out with sufficient emphasis that he is not concerned with mere accounting": some parts of the *General Theory* (although not as often as does the *Treatise* with its 'Fundamental Equations'), do merely state identities; but not all relations of Keynes's theories are identities! See the present author's 'Identity and Stability in Economics: A Survey', *Selected Essays*, 50.

[6] These articles are mostly classified under I: Over-all Discussions and Development of Business-Cycle Theory (54 titles); and II: Dynamic and Econometric Business-Cycle Analysis (65 titles). Of the first group, only 14 were published after 1937; of the second, 36! (See below, Section VII of this review.)

[7] "As prosperity approaches its heights… a sharp contrast develops between the business prospects of different enterprises" (p. 56).

[8] Mr. Robertson would probably agree with the second, but perhaps not the first, part of this sentence. See his *Essays in Monetary Theory* (London, 1940), p. 83.

[9] The technique, known as 'differentiating implicit functions' is useful in economics because the functions ('schedules') involved are seldom known except for some general features, like the signs of derivatives. Hicks, *Econometrica* **5**, 157, footnote. See also my article

on 'Wicksell's Two Interest Rates' (*Social Research* **8**, No. 4 (Nov., 1941) for the use of an elementary technique which assumes linear relations.

[10] In his *Principles*, though not in his *Pure Theory of Foreign Trade*, Marshall preferred to study the (dynamic) effects of the difference between demand price and supply price. See P. A. Samuelson, 'The Stability of Equilibrium: Comparative Statics and Dynamics', *Econometrica* **9**, No. 2 (Apr., 1941), especially pp. 102–05.

[11] Macro-theories of unemployed resources often choose to neglect prices and to discuss the deflationary gap in terms of deflation of physical supply only. We have assumed this simplistic attitude in the rest of the paragraph merely for brevity's sake.

[12] Samuelson, *Econometrica* **9**, especially pp. 113 *seq.*

[13] See Trygve Haavelmo, 'The Statistical Implications of a System of Simultaneous Equations', *Econometrica* **11**, No. 1 (Jan., 1943). See also the introduction to J. Marschak and W. H. Andrews, 'Random Simultaneous Equations and the Theory of Production', *Selected Essays*, 47.

[14] A. P. Lerner, 'Economics of the Steering Wheel', *University of Kansas City Bulletin*, 1941.

[15] See note 6 for some figures.

[16] Trygve Haavelmo, 'The Probability Approach in Econometrics', *Econometrica* **12** (1944), suppl.; also issued as Cowles Commission Paper, New Series, No. 4.

[17] II Samuel, 24.

52

COMMENT ON MITCHELL*

(1951)

Empirical economics is at its very beginnings. Without Wesley Mitchell's faith and encouragement it would not have made even the little progress achieved so far. One possible contribution towards continuing this progress is to help in gaining a clear idea of Mitchell's own propositions. We must translate them, if necessary, into terms that are as unequivocal as possible and that might yield themselves to well defined, or definable, empirical tests. After sketching such a tentative translation, I shall discuss the types of information that were or could be employed to either state or test hypotheses on business cycles. In doing so, I shall give especial attention to the role which general insight into human behavior and institutions plays in Mitchell's posthumous piece of work[1], the way in which such insight might be best combined with statistical time series, and the use that can be made of the knowledge so combined.

I

When, in Chapter 2 of the *Progress Report*, Mitchell tries to "develop a working definition of business cycles" he states, in effect, a hypothesis – the hypothesis that such cycles exist: "Business cycles are a type of fluctuations *found* [my italics] in the aggregate economic activity of nations that organize their work mainly in business enterprises." The definition and the subsequent text (Ch. 2 and 3) go on to describe properties of this type of fluctuation. To prepare the ground for a formal restatement of these rather complicated properties we may first give the hypothesis a deliberately simplified form. It is admittedly not Mitchell's; but it helps to introduce some of the relevant concepts. Our simplified hypothesis is:

> In a society consisting mainly of business enterprises, and apart from seasonal and small random influences, certain economic variables are periodic functions of time; the period length is the same for all these variables; for each variable, each period contains exactly one peak and one trough. (It follows that for any two variables the distance in time [the 'lag'] between the corresponding peaks is constant.)

The phrase *apart from random influences* that we have just used is often encountered in business cycle literature. We must define it and thus get it out of our way. It seems that a statement S $(a, b, \ldots)$ made about the variables $a, b, \ldots$ is usually called 'true apart from random influences' if there exists a true statement S^* $(a, b, \ldots; u, v, \ldots)$ about $a, b, \ldots$ *and* about some, generally unobservable, random variables $u, v, \ldots$, such that, if $u, v, \ldots$ vanished, S^* would become identical with S; symbolically, $S\ (a, b, \ldots) = S^*\ (a, b, \ldots; O, O, \ldots)$. As to the term "random variable" itself, it is used to describe any variable such that a fixed probability can be assigned to the occurrence of any specified range of its values. The more special phrase 'S is true apart from *small* random influences' should also be defined, but I shall not try to do so here. Lack of time forces me also to assume that the phrase 'apart from seasonal influences' has the same precise meaning for everyone, although this is probably untrue. Unfortunately, this omission is not altogether trivial in our context: since Mitchell often operates on data for periods shorter than a year, his definition of seasonal influences, necessarily implied in his method of eliminating them, may affect the conclusions.

Mitchell's actual hypothesis is more complicated than the one I have stated. It is weaker inasmuch as the constant period length is replaced by a variable (possibly random) period length, restricted, however, in the case of the United States, by certain specified properties. Here is one tentative formulation:

> In the United States, and apart from seasonal and small random influences, there exists a sequence of intervals that is common to all economic variables and has the following properties: (1) each interval lasts from 2 to 12 years and overlaps its successor by 3 months; (2) each interval contains, for each variable, exactly 3 turning points, of which 2 are near the ends of the interval; (3) the time lag between two nearest peaks (troughs) for any two variables retains its sign (+, −, 0) throughout the sequence of intervals; (4) this time lag is zero for a large proportion of pairs of variables.

The style of Mitchell's presentation does not make it easy to discuss whether this translation is faithful. Supposing it gives the gist of his findings, it is not easy to define and discuss the tests (or the estimation methods) used. Let us assume that the translation is correct in essence, and grant that the tests are valid and the estimates (lengths of intervals and lags) are satisfactory for practical purposes. Notice that the hypothesis thus accepted is implied in any of a number of hypotheses about some 'mechanism' generating the observed set of economic time series. One such 'mechanism' is this:

> There exists a variable (called 'general business activity') whose value at any point of time depends, apart from random influences, upon one or more of its preceding values. (Such a function of time is called a 'stochastic process'.) Apart from random influences, each observable economic variable is a certain, possibly lagged, function of the general business activity.

Tentatively, I think it is justifiable to say that Mitchell implicitly accepted this last hypothesis. The operations actually proposed by Mitchell to derive the general business activity for a given point of time consist essentially in expressing each variable as a relative deviation from its observed average over time; in findings lags by direct inspection of turning points; and in averaging the properly lagged relative deviations over all variables for a given point of time. This suggests that the hypothesis in the investigator's mind was even stronger than the one just stated. For example, a possible justification for those operations might be the following hypothesis: each variable, adjusted for its characteristic lag and divided by its average, is proportional to 'general business activity', apart from an additive random term, whose average (mathematical expectation) over time for a given variable is zero, and whose average over all variables for a given time is also zero. It is not denied that some alternative proposition might be constructed that would lead to the same operations. But many passages of the book suggest, in fact, that Mitchell often regarded each properly adjusted and calibrated time series of economic variables as a drawing (not necessarily an independent one) from a random universe of which the 'general business activity' is the mean. In addition, he often expresses himself as if he regarded each cycle (the 2 to 12 year time intervals) as a drawing from a random universe, or, in his words, a 'unit of a species'. Provided these 'units' are not assumed to be mutually independent, this view is consistent with the hypothesis that 'general business activity' constitutes a stochastic process; although the cutting up of the process into intervals defined by selected turning points is probably not the most efficient start for estimating its properties. Moreover, it is not clear from actual arithmetical operations whether our proviso, that the successive cycles must not be treated as independent drawings, was fully heeded. If it was not, the mechanism assumed must have been a more special one than the one I stated tentatively.

However, the existence of a 'general business activity' of which the observed economic variables are random and lagged functions is only a sufficient, not a necessary condition for the validity of Mitchell's finding of 2 to 12 years intervals, possessing certain properties with respect to economic variables. Among many other mechanisms that would imply the same properties of the observed time series, the following simple ones may be mentioned: The observable variables are mutually connected by a number of lagged relationships, apart from random influences (such is the familiar 'cobweb'). Or: Apart from random influences, the observable stocks of some commodities depend on certain variables which in turn depend on the rate of change of the flows of those commodities. In listening to this, you are rightly thinking of dynamic econometric models, systems of differential or difference equations. At this point, I do not argue their advantages.

To be sure, Mitchell does state that "general business activity" is merely a "nebulous congeries". It is a formal construct, a unifying index. We must be clear, however, that such an index does not add anything to our knowledge unless its changes are indeed assumed to govern the changes in the economic variables that interest us. (This was well discussed in Keynes' *Treatise* of 1930, when he criticized Jevons and his followers for pursuing the mirage of a 'true' general price level.) To change the field, suppose for a moment that pulse, temperature, blood pressure and composition, metabolism, etc. were each a function (apart from random influences) of the same variable – the 'general health' of the individual. The pulse, the temperature, etc. would then indeed reflect, every one of them, the state of health; and an appropriate average ('index') compounded from those measurements would reflect it still better, by virtue of reducing the random influences. As a matter of fact, however, those measurements are never compounded into a single index, because they are never thought of as reflecting a single 'general health'. Instead, a physiological theory consists of relations between a number of variables, some of which are more easily measurable than others. If these relations are known, the values – current or future – of variables that are not easily measurable but are deemed important may be estimated from a set of easy current measurements, such as temperature taking.

The physiologist tries to improve his knowledge of those relations, and the practitioner uses them.

II

Similarly, the economist should try to improve his knowledge of relations among economic variables. From what sources? Economic time series are not our only source. Astronomical time series were not the only source for Newton's explanation of planetary motions. His other source was the experiments, such as Galileo's, on falling bodies. And either source would remain silent if he had not asked it to confirm or reject his basic hypothesis, the law of gravity. In the economist's case, time series are supplemented by the knowledge of responses of individual households and firms, by the knowledge of human institutions and technologies; and we have to approach all those sources with some hypotheses in mind. (Mitchell was doubtless aware of this, yet he often seems to recommend the use of hypotheses on human behavior and sources other than time series merely as a check, an afterthought, a 'this-is-what-we-should-expect'.)

When you survey New York from the top of the Empire State Building, you see a procession of beetles, moving, stopping, moving, stopping. After a few glances at the street and at your watch, you will obtain a good 'cyclical pattern' of stops and moves. If, in addition, you pay attention to colors, you may find that the proportion of red to green beetles in any given section of the avenue also fluctuates in time, though probably with less pronounced cyclicity; but that the occurrence of red and green lights at certain points of the avenue is indeed rigidly cyclical and is strongly correlated (almost without a lag) with the stops and moves of the beetles at these same points. Solid empirical knowledge! But how much more certain and useful it would become if you knew, in addition to your time series, another set of facts: that both the beetles and the lights are controlled by men like you; that few auto drivers have reason to drive in reverse; and that there exists a certain agreement (an institution) between the drivers and those who control the lights. Thus fortified, the knowledge of the tower watchman becomes more certain because he can foresee the circumstances under which the cycles may change their character, e.g., become longer at night. His knowledge becomes more useful also because he will now stop studying the color composition of vehicles, as irrelevant; and because he will be able, instead, to make sensible recommendations from his vantage point. For example, knowing now that the lights determine the moves of beetles (and not conversely) he may recommend a change in the rhythm of lights so as to ensure smoother traffic; or, if he has friends among drivers, he may tell them what speed they should maintain to miss red lights all along the avenue. He can thus be likened to the economist called upon by the government or advising a single firm. Of such an economist it is often said that, in addition to generalizations drawn from empirical time series he has used 'economic theory'. This is an unfortunate terminology, suggesting a false distinction between theory and empirical knowledge. I prefer to say that economics becomes more secure and more useful if, in addition to time series, we use all other available information, including our insight into the plausible behavior of human beings, especially when they are our fellow-countrymen and contemporaries, and our knowledge of human institutions and techniques.

Mitchell saw the need for using our knowledge of human behavior and institutions. But one may question whether he used it, or intended to use it, in the most efficient way. After a frankly mechanical, though time-consuming, manipulation of the 800 observed series, he interprets the results – the lags, the comparative amplitudes – often to state that "none of the findings seems surprising" (Ch. 7). Sometimes the check is performed on mere identities and is therefore essentially a check on the consistency of data – as when the series of wage rates and weekly working hours are compared with their product, the series of weekly earnings. When, on the other hand, the empirical results were checked not against identities but against verifiable implications of plausible human behavior, these implications were seldom thought through exhaustively – either because time ran short or, more likely, because Mitchell genuinely underestimated the logical intricacy of the economic system. In Mitchell's words (Ch. 5):

When the analysis is written out in full it becomes a long chain of commonplace observations upon familiar experiences. Department stores sell more goods in expansion because income payments to individuals have increased. Less butter is produced because families buy more milk as their incomes rise; the flow of milk cannot be increased as rapidly as consumption grows, so less milk is turned into butter. Essentially similar reasoning can be extended to all sectors of economy.

The butter example shows that more careful reasoning would be necessary. Must a rise in income lead necessarily to an increase in milk consumption and a consequent fall in butter consumption (the total flow of milk being constant for physical reasons)? Why not to a rise in butter consumption and a fall in milk consumption? It is worth while to pause here. As a simple hypothesis, let us grant that the total milk flow is a technological datum, subject to slow and negligible changes only. Dairies will change the ratio of butter to milk in response to the changing ratio between the price of butter and of milk – presumably increasing the former ratio if the latter ratio increases. Given a family's real income, number of children, etc., the ratio of its butter demand to its milk demand will presumably fall as the ratio between the two prices rises. Hence for a given aggregate real income (and its distribution by income, family size, etc.) we can plot both the quantity-ratio supplied and the quantity-ratio demanded against the price-ratio (see Figure 1).

As real income rises, the 'demand curve' will shift – but in which direction? In other words: does increased income induce consumers to raise or to diminish their demand for butter relative to milk? Mitchell's empirical result implies that they will reduce it. But could this answer be obtained also from 'commonplace observation on familiar experiences'? I think not. There would be nothing incompatible with common sense if the consumers responded in the opposite way. Contrary to his own opinion, Mitchell's result – that milk consumption grows and falls with income – is *not* trivial. As we have seen, it appears trivial only if

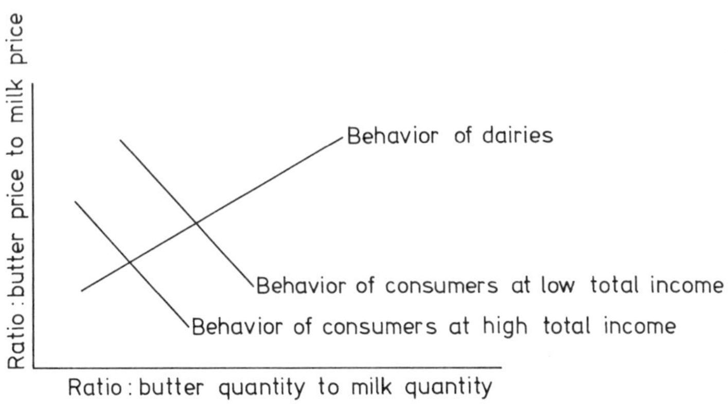

Fig. 1.

we refuse to puzzle over the human responses and institutions beneath the surface of economic figures. Systems of simultaneous relationships tentatively describing the economic intercourse (and exemplified, albeit in an unduly simple form, on our graph) suggest also ways for checking a given empirical result with other data. In our case, for example, one sees the importance of bringing in additional time series, viz., butter and milk prices (their ratio should fall with rising income if the hypothesis is correct); one sees how the data on family budgets and the production records of dairies, both commercial and experimental, might be used. This is not all. If we succeed in formulating our findings in terms of numerically specified human responses, e.g., if the demands for milk and butter are expressed as numerical functions of income and the prices, predictions can be made about the effect of institutional or technological changes: we can estimate the effect of artificial price fixation, say, or of a change in freight or tariff rates, etc. Such questions cannot be answered if we content ourselves with the finding that milk consumption rises with income. It is in this sense that prediction presupposes explanation.

As a second example of Mitchell's attitude to our knowledge of, or hypotheses on, human behavior, I shall use his section, Reference-Cycle Amplitudes of Prices and Production (Ch. 7). He writes:

> We know that increases in supply tend to depress prices and that increases in demand tend to raise them; but how will prices behave in a cyclical expansion when both supply and demand rise, or in a contraction when both supply and demand shrink? It is in this theoretically indeterminate form that price problems confront students of business cycles. What to expect we learn from experience: most prices rise and fall with the cyclical tides of business activity most of the time – not always.

In this case, unlike that of milk consumption, knowledge of human behavior that we may have independently of time series is recognized by Mitchell as indeterminate with regard to the question asked. Hence, the empirical findings cannot be trivial. But his empirical analysis does not seem to me to have been organized in a way that would most efficiently supplement the knowledge of human behavior by available time series or other statistical data. The first sentence of the passage just quoted suggests that the demand curve and/or the supply curve (each expressing the response of a specified social group to a change in price) are shifted by changes in consumers' income, profit expectations, etc.;

changes that are reflected, although only imperfectly, in the general index of business activity, and hence in the position of the observation time-point on the 'reference cycle' axis. An effort might be made to purify the index from irrelevant components. For example, one might replace it, in the case of the demand for food, by variables deemed to determine consumers' decisions: for example, real income, but hardly carloadings or bond rates. For the demand for steel or cement, or for the supply of food, other determining variables would be chosen. One would then attempt to estimate, for a given commodity or group of commodities, the dependence of demand on price (the Marshallian demand curve) as well as on other factors relevant to buyers' decisions (and causing measurable 'shifts' of the Marshallian demand curve). If similar attempts were made on the supply side, one would obtain an explanation of the changes of both price and quantity of the commodity through time, and in relation to other variables. For example, suppose the supply curve is positively sloped and the demand curve negatively sloped; and suppose we have found from various data that, in response to changes in real income, in profits, and in other variables concealed in the general business index, the demand curve reacts by stronger shifts than the supply curve, e.g., that a given price, a billion dollar change in income raises the quantity demanded by a million bushels and the quantity supplied by only half a million bushels. Then we would have explained the direction, and even the size, of the changes that the price of the commodity, and its quantity bought and sold, undergo in response to given changes in the relevant components of the business index, and hence (a less interesting question) in the index itself. To obtain this explanation, time series had to be combined with additional knowledge; hence the explanation would be, in general, more secure than if we had used time series only. The explanation would also be more useful in that it would enable us to predict the results of given changes of the assumed institutions or technologies. For example, a given invention or an excise tax will change the supply curve in a specifiable fashion; the redistribution of income in favor of the poor would affect the demand curve in a certain way; price fixation by government removes the equality between quantity demanded and quantity supplied, and so on. If the system of economic relationships valid under old institutions and technologies was properly estimated, and if the assumed change in institution or technology is well defined, the resulting change in the prices and quantities can be estimated in advance.

In his empirical analysis of prices and quantities Mitchell, following F. C. Mills, takes a different route. He makes little use of the knowledge of human behavior contained in the first sentence of his own statement quoted above. Instead, he counts the number of price or production series that rise or fall with a rising business index or, in another terminology, have 'positive' or 'inverted' timing (there are also series with 'neutral' or 'irregular' timing). The cases are counted separately for contraction and expansion periods. The counting is done separately also for farm products and for other products; for goods with administered prices and other goods; and for durable, nondurable, and semidurable goods. This classification, based on knowledge of technology and institutions, is no doubt significant. But it is not followed by a corresponding purification of the business index – the 'nebulous congeries' – to exclude factors irrelevant to the particular commodity group; more important still, the classification of goods is not followed by the distinction between the decisions of producers and those of consumers (and possibly of others, such as dealers or lenders), decisions that are certainly determined by different sets of factors and not by the same 'nebulous congeries'. The method of counting signs, instead of operating on the amounts, of changes of variables, is probably an unnecessarily coarse, hence inefficient way of using available figures, even if one takes account of its labor saving advantages; and when these signs cannot be regarded as independent drawings from a homogeneous universe, counting may lead to biased inferences. Finally, even supposing that all inferences were correct and that a certain true pattern describing the simultaneous changes of the business index, the price of the commodity and its quantity, were discovered for the past, what use could be made of this knowledge? In the future the three variables just mentioned will be observed simultaneously so that the need for predicting one variable from another, or from the other two will not arise – apart from the special case when, for external reasons, the observation on one variable becomes available, e.g., published, earlier than on another one. More important, the pattern does not enable us to predict how a given, well specified change in institutions or technology would affect any of the variables studied in the past; for such prediction requires the knowledge of demand and supply curves (and of their shifts under given changes in income, etc.) under the old conditions, and the specification of the institutional or technological change in terms of such curves (and of their shifts).

Institutional changes have, of course, taken place also in the past. In fact, some are listed among the 800 times series used by Mitchell; for example, this list includes several series on public construction work. These, says Mitchell,

> have irregular timing, because governments do not build for profit to themselves. Just why they time the letting of contracts... as they do is a question that has many answers – pressing needs for more schoolrooms, sanitary requirements, ... local pride, political jobbery, and so on.

This means that, in another terminology, public construction works are 'exogenous variables': they are not determined by, though they may determine, economic variables. Most likely, various other aspects of the governmental fiscal and monetary policy, tax rates and expenditures, the monetary gold stock, tariffs, supported bond prices or farm prices, the volume of government stored products, arbitrated wage rates, the size of the armed forces, are exogenous or at least are partly determined by exogenous variables. Exogenous variables may be regarded as parameters, the 'givens', of the economic system that have undergone observable changes in the past. Other parameters may not have changed in the past. All parameters of the system may undergo changes in the future. The practical problem is to predict the effect of a given change in parameters upon the economic variables; for example, to predict the effect of increasing armaments, decreasing a tax rate, or introducing or removing price control.

Mitchell discusses whether to exclude public construction works, administered prices, and similarly 'irregular' time series when computing the index of general activity, and decides that to do so would distort the facts. To me the question itself seems irrelevant but it helps to understand Mitchell's general attitude towards economic facts and policies. It seems to me that a wave pattern that can describe American business cycles at a time when public expenditures equalled a tenth of national income is unlikely to have much predictive value for a time when public expenditures equal a fifth or a fourth of national income; nor can it help to predict how a given change in public expenditures or in administered prices and wages, etc. can affect national income or any other economic variable. To Mitchell, effects of changes in these or similar parameters appear negligible, thus enabling his 'cyclical procession' to roll on majestically like the planets. Although Mitchell does occasionally urge (Ch. 7) that the nation needs "economic 'know how'" viz., "to use its resources at tolerably full capacity year in and year out," he is not particularly concerned with how policies have affected or can affect the course of economic time series; nor is it clear how his analysis might help to answer such questions.

Perhaps we face here a difference between generations. Mitchell's thought is in the grand manner of the masters of the nineteenth century, including Marx: economic laws of the capitalist society are inexorable (as long as it exists), with little place left for deliberate changes. If this were true, there would indeed be no need for looking beyond the surface of the recorded wave-like movements; suffice it to know – and this merely as a matter of curiosity – that they will repeat themselves. But if those movements do depend on human institutions, they will change in response to institutional changes. To find how these movements change their character, we have to study more closely how economic variables are determined. But to this question, time series alone give no answer; other knowledge, in particular that of human decisions and institutions, has to be added. Thus, our interest in combining time series with 'economic theory' goes hand in hand with our belief that economic laws, far from being inexorable, depend on habits, institutions, and policies. Perhaps this generation has learned it from the experience of recent upheavals. "To find out how business cycles come to differ from one another as much as they patently do... remains for later times and other hands," says Mitchell. It is in keeping with the memory of a courageous and persistent thinker that those 'other hands' try to dig deeper, in order to find more.

NOTES

* Presented after Arthur Burns' address that opened the Conference on Business Cycles held under the auspices of Universities – National Bureau Committee for Economic Research, November 25–27, 1949. A Reply by Arthur Burns followed.

[1] Wesley Mitchell, *What Happens During Business Cycles: A Progress Report*, National Bureau of Economic Research, New York, 1951.

53

WLADIMIR WOYTINSKY AND ECONOMIC THEORY*

(1962)

I

As a schoolboy of seventeen, Woytinsky started a book, *Market and Prices. Theory of Consumption, Market and Market Prices.* The manuscript was submitted one year later to Tugan-Baranovsky, one of Russia's leading economists. Without knowing the author's age and identity, the professor advised that it be published. Having then learned that Woytinsky had just graduated from high school, Tugan-Baranovsky sent him a letter of introduction to his publisher. By the time the book was published early in 1906, with Tugan-Baranovsky's preface,[1] Woytinsky had entered the University, delivered a seminar paper on 'The Historical Premises of Political Economy', and had his inspiring discussions of the subtler aspects of value theory with B. W. Raitz, a friend who died early and to whose memory the book is dedicated. But 1905–1906 were also years of revolution. While the book on economic theory was being printed, or soon afterwards, Woytinsky – as 'Sergei Petrov', in worker's cap and high boots – organized a large number of the unemployed of the Russian capital. He actually succeeded in having public works set up by the St. Petersburg municipality. Were his efforts inspired by Louis Blanc's example of the Paris revolution of 1848, so well known then to every Russian reader of Marx? Or was he simply led by good common sense?

Good common sense and warm concern with live human beings and their social order combined in young Woytinsky's book with the gift for generalization, simplification, and abstraction, necessary to analyze complex psychological and sociological facts such as consumption choices and the formation of prices. As time went on, his sharp eye caught growing masses of facts. His innate intuition (already evident in his early work) processed the observed facts into predictions and recommendations of the greatest social import. He proved right in the German deflation crisis of 1932, with his unorthodox recommendations for employment through public spending. He proved again right in the United States of 1944 with his lonely forecast of successful postwar adjustment, and therefore the advice against public spending. His belief in good judgment and common sense grew, and his interest in abstractions faded.

Almost half a century after young Woytinsky's theoretical book, an article by him on 'Limits of Mathematics in Statistics' was published (*The American Statistician*, 1954). The title is indicative of the mature man's aversion to the abstract. I shall compare the book and the article. This should be of interest to any student of human thought.

II

The book consists of a methodological Introduction and of two parts: I. Consumption; II. Market.

In his methodological remarks the author takes issue with the two opposing schools that determined the academic climate of those days: (a) the marginalist school (Jevons and Boehm-Bawerk), at grips with (b) the German historicists – with the shadow of Marx hovering over the combatants. It is remarkable that the budding Social-Democrat is quite immune to Marxist economic theory: the theory of prices expounded by Woytinsky is not the labor theory of value. Woytinsky shared with the marginal-utility school the basically psychological approach, and the emphasis on consumer's choice rather than on labor's effort. What he rejects in that school – along with its neglecting the imperfections of the market – is the unhistorical postulation of universal, eternal properties of the economic man. His sarcasm about imputing London Stock Exchange *mores* to Polynesian natives does have a good dose of Marxian style, though often relieved by Russian folk humor. Marxian in style are also the ironic characterizations of the modern businessman. The young son of a mathematics professor could not have had much contact with business, other than in his capacity of a highly observant shopper, and it is astonishing how many stimulating, concrete, and original hypotheses on market phenomena he has derived from that limited material. Finally, Woytinsky's allusions to the labor movement – as when attacking the wage-fund theory that proclaims labor unions helpless to raise living standards – could never have been written by a marginalist professor, though it was probably in harmony with the tone of the Russian university seminars of the turn of the century.

In his drive toward greater realism, Woytinsky declares his intention to make the approach of the utility school more historical and more psychological than that of his predecessors – more historical, by explicitly confining the scope of the theory to the modern industrial society, and by accepting constraints on the theory that are dictated by the actual state of that society. For example, we have to accept the fact that the prices for a commodity are never completely equalized by competition in a market. Further, he tries to make economic theory more psychological, by giving up claims to explain all human decisions and transactions – claims that make the theory so general as to be tautological – and by trying to derive economic postulates from the empirical analysis of the actual process of satisfaction of desires. Most of this analysis is carried out by introspection. Yet the lion's claw of the future social statistician shows itself whenever Woytinsky finds appropriate materials. Accordingly, he makes ready use of the then available German Consumers' Surveys (of Engel and of Schwabe) to discuss the quantitative relation between income and various branches of consumption – the income-elasticity of demand, as one would say now. To derive what is now called price-elasticity of demand he juxtaposes Russian grain prices and harvest figures.

As with most thinkers of great passion, young Woytinsky's methodological remarks, often sarcastic and often amusing, do not fully agree with his own practice. Tugan-Baranovsky points this out in his wise preface: in spite of Woytinsky's criticism of "... abstraction, he does use not only abstract but even mathematical methods." It is also true, however, that, as Tugan-Baranovsky hastened to add, "the author strives to build his decision on an empirical foundation, as close to life as possible: his abstractions do not hang in the air, they are grounded in historical soil. This distinguishes them favorably from many constructions of the psychological [so-called marginalist; J. M.] school."

III

You will presumably change your demand for a given commodity if your income, the price of that commodity, or other prices, change. These quantitative relationships are, in principle, observable. If known, they would help to predict the total demand for each commodity, given all incomes and all prices. Or, alternatively, to predict all prices, given the incomes and the supplies (e.g., grain harvests) that are available and must be consumed sooner or later. In setting himself this task, Woytinsky hastened to define its necessary limits, with scholarly humility and his usual common sense. Fearless and lusty in attacking theories and theorists, the young economist had a wise and cautious respect for fact and was aware of the enormous complexity of the human decision process. No two individuals behave similarly, even in response to identical changes in environment; and nobody is strictly consistent from one day to another. Any statement about consumption can be made only in terms of statistical averages. And this is good enough because, for purposes of broad social policy, it is the statistical averages that matter, not the individual or short-run deviations. His statistical instinct helped Woytinsky to raise consumption theory from the speculative to the empirical domain. I believe this approach was then, on the whole, rather novel. Certainly Woytinsky stated it less casually and with more force than many of his predecessors. The probabilistic, statistical philosophy that today permeates the physical and biological sciences not less than the science of Man, was not so common fifty-five years ago: the faith in deterministic laws of nature still held sway, certainly in the high school curriculum and in Marxist student circles.

As already indicated, he used German consumers' surveys and Russian grain statistics. He needed them to trace the (average) relationships between income and consumption, and between prices and consumption. As a first approximation, he suggested relationships of a form that implies, in modern economic lingo, 'constant elasticity', a term unknown to Woytinsky. If, whenever a variable changes by 1%, another one changes by k%, economists say that the latter variable has, with respect to the former, an elasticity of size k (mathematicians call it the logarithmic derivative). If k is the same at all levels of the two variables, the second variable is proportional to the k-th power of the first. Woytinsky tries to show how well his simplifying hypothesis fits the facts: i.e., how little the elasticity k changes as his variables (income and demand, or price and demand) change. The apparatus of modern correlation theory was not at his disposal then but his rough and ready tests, similar to those still current in many laboratories and clinics, were impressive enough for his time and purposes. He wants to describe economic relationships as simply as possible. If his formulas fit the facts, a single number, different for each commodity, suffices for the prediction of the relative change in demand that would be caused by a given relative change in income. Another single number would characterize in a similar way the relation between relative changes in the demand for and the price of a commodity. Woytinsky is cautious enough to claim such predictability, not for every single commodity, but for broad groups only – such as food, shelter, etc.

He is particularly interested in a still broader classification: the dichotomy of goods into necessities and luxuries. The demand for luxuries is more sensitive (more elastic) with respect to changes in income as well as in prices. He uses a certain numerical boundary (k equal to 1 in absolute value) to delimit the two commodity groups. This may seem arbitrary. But Woytinsky tries to give a substantive, not merely formal, interpretation of his definitions, by contrasting un-postponable, biological needs with the needs for display and imitation. On such matters, Woytinsky's mathematics become intertwined with his sociological sarcasm, appropriately a Veblenesque one. To be sure, Woytinsky did not know Veblen's work and could not have heard the slogan of 'conspicuous consumption', but, quite independently, he got its substance. Unlike Veblen, he used these concepts to give content and precision to economic theory (which Veblen found so uncongenial and dull). Thus he derived a wealth of statements about the differential effects of fashion and of advertisement upon luxuries and upon necessities.

Cautious about the predictability of each man's behavior, Woytinsky was also cautious about men's influence on one another. Yet a useful hypothesis must be simple. Demand was assumed proportional to a fixed power of (say) income. This power (the demand elasticity), is, according to Woytinsky, an inherent, constant property of the particular commodity for a given man. But the coefficient of proportionality can be changed by fashion, advertisement, etc. Advertisement shifts the level of demand without changing its elasticity. And the total effect is different for luxuries as contrasted with necessities, and is studied in many an interesting detail.

Underlying the observable data on consumption and on its reactions to income changes, price changes, and fashion and advertisement, there is a theory of 'utility', an explanatory construct that eludes direct observation other than introspection. The theory assumes, in essence, that man's preferences are broadly consistent. He ranks the various alternatives open to him – in particular, he ranks the various alternative ways (the 'budgets') in which he can distribute his income among different purchases – in an order of preferences that does not vary substantially from one day to another. The preference rank of a given alternative budget is called the total utility (of the budget), and the increment of total utility due to adding a unit of a commodity is that commodity's marginal utility. The budget that is preferred to all other budgets feasible at a given income is reached by the consumer when he cannot improve his situation by shifting one dollar of his income from one commodity to another. Hence the marginal utility of a dollar's worth of every commodity is the same, as soon as the consumer has chosen his best budget. Thus, if the consumer has made his best choice of the budget, his marginal utilities of the various commodities are proportional to their prices. Woytinsky expounds this logical implication of the consistency assumption. He then replaces it by a much more special, stronger postulate, in an attempt to give a deductive underpinning to his statistical results. He assumes that the marginal utility of a good depends on the quantity of that good only; and that this dependence is again one with constant elasticity. The marginal utility of a good is thus assumed to be proportional to a (negative) power of its quantity; and this power is larger (in absolute value) for luxuries than for necessities. Woytinsky seems to have believed that this postulate was sufficient and necessary for his statistical finding that the elasticities of demand with respect to income and to price were almost constant. Actually, the postulate contradicts those findings. This can be shown by using the more complete mathematical results obtained ten years later by Woytinsky's countryman and contemporary, Evgeniy Slutsky.[2] But we must note that Woytinsky was not alone in thinking that the relationship between demand, income, and marginal utility must be reflected in a simple way in the relationship between demand, income, and price. A similar view was advanced two years later in the well-known book of Joseph Schumpeter[3], though the latter was less specific as to the form (constant elasticities) of those relationships; he did not have to be more specific, as he did not attempt statistical analysis of facts.

IV

As Woytinsky's study proceeds from the single consumer to the aggregate of consumers in the market, his special postulates help to simplify his tools. Under his conditions, it is possible to operate on the 'market marginal utility', defined as the (geometric) average of the marginal utilities of a commodity to the various individuals. Woytinsky tackles what is now called the 'aggregation problem' – deriving quantitative relations in the market from individual behavior relations – in a probabilistic spirit, by making a certain simplifying assumption about the probability that the marginal utility of a commodity to a given individual exceeds a given level. It is remarkable that Woytinsky made no reference at all to the distribution of incomes, an important datum used for the same task by Pareto (1895), an author not then known in Russia.

More important than these technical matters is Woytinsky's lively and fruitful criticism of an 'antiquated superstition' of economists: their belief that competition quickly equalizes prices over an entire geographically defined market. He puts his finger on the imperfections of the actual market, a phenomenon that came into the focus of economic theory some twenty-five years later, with E. Chamberlin and Joan Robinson. He pays rather passing attention to monopolies and cartels, a matter that was shortly to become, in Rudolf Hilferding's hands, the central point of revived Marxist economics. Instead, he concentrated on the imperfections in the buyers' information which can be exploited by advertisement; and on differentiation of the product's quality through inessentials such as packaging, the store's furnishings, etc. He gives a vivid analysis of the retail market; he knew, of course, less about manufacturing or mining, and it has been in Woytinsky's nature to rely on immediate, own evidence. The retail market has a 'cellular structure': because of transportation costs, the consumers' inertia, and their lack of information, each store represents a 'cell' of the market, with its own customers and its fairly independent prices calculated so as to maximize profit, given a limited stock. But the territorial boundaries between the 'cells' become diffuse as some of the stores begin to attract customers from afar by advertisement and secondary advantages. The complete equalization of prices (even allowing for those additional, now so-called 'selling costs') takes time. In fact, because of intervening changes in environment, price equalization is never achieved. Woytinsky also discusses the time that it takes for a price change to affect total market demand: because of the prestige value of luxuries, consumers of luxuries do not complain to one another about a price rise, but consumers of necessities do. This difference in the flow of communications (a fashionable topic today!) is reflected in the resulting demand and final prices.

Woytinsky's direct insight is remarkable. He trusts his immediate observation of the crowds of buyers, scurrying through the city's streets or congregating in the stores, appraising the goods in windows and on counters, gaping at ads, gossiping with envy or condescension. His own common sense and his power of observation enable him to stand up to doctrinaire dogma and to disprove it.

V

Some fifty years later, he wrote the article 'Limits of Mathematics in Statistics': a paean for common sense, intuition, and good judgment, a cold shower on simplifying hypotheses and airy speculations. He does not object to mathematical statistics, a branch of mathematics. He does attack the superficial belief in mathematical magic when the purpose is to study social phenomena.

He scorns extrapolations. "If a formula can be projected into the future, it must be at least as good when projected into the past. I have seen no regression formula that could stand this test."

He uses striking examples. Many population forecasts have failed grotesquely. "A population forecast is nothing more than the numerical expression of our judgment about the probable behavior of people in the field of reproduction. In this realm a superb mathematical technique, a host of statistical clerks, and a battery of calculating machines are no substitute for intuition."

Total consumption expenditure had been predicted as a function of national income and sometimes of a few other variables. A total of 118 such 'consumption functions' were turned out, 93 of these for the United States (21 of them by Woytinsky himself, who "concocted [them] with the only objective of reducing the whole procedure ad absurdum"). Most of those functions [not all. J.M.] led to an enormous underestimation of future consumption and hence to erroneous forecasts of postwar unemployment. "Actually, in order to use the consumption function or any other crystal ball in economic forecasting, you must have an opinion on the trend of events. If your opinion is sound, there is a fair chance that you will pick the formula which later will be vindicated; if your judgment is poor, you will gamble on a wrong formula."

Apart from the disturbing influence of variables which only a man of good judgment can assess, there is also the inherent unreliability of most data on social and economic statistics. Woytinsky recalls and recommends the effort of Stamp and Gini (who dealt with the national income estimates of various countries), to classify such data according to the degree of reliability. This measure has almost nothing to do with the reliability of estimates from unbiased random samples, as studied in mathematical statistics. We do not know Woytinsky's further thoughts on this matter, which touches upon deeper problems in inductive logic.

"The realm of statistics ... is the world of human relations and human behavior. It is full of life and for this reason full of confusion and contradiction. Every time we try to measure the phenomena of this world, we discover that like all living things they defy precise measurement ... and yet without quantitative analysis we cannot understand and appraise them. Mathematical devices are necessary in this work but the mathematical laws which control the Euclidian Universe cannot be extended to human relations. Their quantitative analysis requires more than mathematical skill and familiarity with the field from which the data come. It requires imagination and intuition. Such an analysis is an art more than a science."

The present writer suspects that not all modern biologists would agree about the inherently non-mathematical nature of 'living things.' And, as illustrated by Woytinsky's own strivings in his youth, the very 'confusion' of economic phenomena calls for the clarity of concepts and relations that can be provided by good logic and mathematics. Shall we entrust ourselves only to innate intuition (which few people have) or to experience (which only old people have), and not attempt teachable ways of explaining the world? If Wladimir Woytinsky were still alive, I would ask him about his work of 1906 and 1954, and what happened in between. He would not compromise. And I would enjoy to the full the glow of his loving irony, his tales of pedantic stupidities, his accent on human needs, his pungent characterizations of our reality, his bright hopes, and his unyielding concern with what is true and is truly important.

NOTES

* From *So Much Alive: The Life and Work of W. S. Woytinsky*, edited by Emma S. Woytinsky, Vanguard Press, New York, 1962.

[1] *Market and Prices. Theory of Consumption, Market and Market Prices* (translated by Emma S. Woytinsky), August M. Kelly, New York, 1964.

[2] Slutsky and Woytinsky never met. Slutsky's scientific work did not compete with political action as did Woytinsky's. His brush with Tsarist authorities was more mild and casual. Expelled temporarily from Kiev University, Slutsky studied in Germany and by 1914 was able to return and to teach. His 'Sulla Teoria del Bilancio del Consumatore' (*Giornale degli Economisti*, 1915) was unnoticed by most economists until after its results were rediscovered by John R. Hicks and R. G. D. Allen in 1934, to become the core of modern mathematical economics of consumption. Slutsky died a member of the Soviet Academy of Sciences, respected for his work in mathematical statistics, aloof from politics and economics alike.

Using the assumption that the marginal utility of a commodity depends on the quantity of this commodity only (first part of Woytinsky's postulate), Irving Fisher (1927) and Ragnar Frisch (1932) outlined a method for reconstructing the utility function from statistical data on demand at given incomes and prices. This was outdated with the rediscovery of Slutsky's more general theory; and a more general approach to estimating the utility function from statistical data was outlined by Abraham Wald in 1940.

In an unpublished longhand note, Woytinsky dropped the first part of his postulate, and replaced the second part by making the utility of a good linearly dependent on its quantity and the quantity of a second good.

[3] J. Schumpeter, *Das Wesen und der Hauptinhalt der theoretischen Nationaloekonomie*, Leipzig, 1908.

54

ON ECONOMETRIC TOOLS*

(1969)

Why should the tools of inductive inference differ from one empirical discipline to another? In a deeper sense, the tools do not differ. Econometrics shares its logical foundations with psychometrics and biometrics and, for that matter, with meteorology and even with experimental physics. Two or more sets of jointly asserted propositions about observable facts (*not* about mathematics or logic or ethics) are compared to determine which set is, in some sense, in better correspondence with facts. In Harold Hotelling's terminology each set of propositions, or hypotheses, contains a subset which is 'considered' (tested) and its complement which is 'maintained' (assumed) for the purposes of an individual piece of empirical inquiry. Econometric usage (perhaps since Mann and Wald, 1943) attaches the name 'prior' to the maintained propositions, thus extending that old philosophical term to propositions which, although not subjected to test in the particular research piece in question, may well have been derived from previous observations. The 'prior' propositions give 'specification' (R. A. Fisher's term) of a part, not all, of the properties of the studied phenomena – for example, the form of some functions and possibly the sign, the range, or even the exact numerical value of some of their parameters. To take a crude example, proportionality between two observable variables may be asserted *a priori*, but the choice between rival candidates for the proportionality constant (e.g., between the various estimates of the economists' 'velocity of circulation of money') will depend on facts. To be sure, nothing can prevent additional facts from discrediting a prior assumption itself. Predictions based on data for a certain set of years, or cities, or firms, or families, are tested against other data. The comparison may render the prior assumptions quite suspect, and a search for different ones must ensue.

Other words for maintained, or prior, or assumed propositions are: constraints, boundary conditions. Some constraints will be maintained with stubbornness, others will be sacrificed with ease. An econometrician may have no qualms about replacing a linear by a quadratic trend. On the other hand he will try to maintain his *a priori* assumption that a fall in the price of 'all fats considered together' cannot decrease the demand for them; though he will be less insistent in assuming the same for margarine alone, especially in the case of a poor country where the saving resulting from lowered margarine prices may transfer consumers' demand from margarine (an 'inferior good') to butter.

The reader will see from these examples that at least a part of prior assumptions is 'taken from economic theory': a body of propositions partly derived from postulates of rational (so-called 'economic') behavior of consumers and producers, but amended and supplemented by everyday experience, broad historical knowledge, occasionally also specialized knowledge of the technology of industrial and agricultural processes, of the psycho-sociology of marketing, etc.

It may be worth noting that Thomas Bayes 'prior probabilities' reintroduced recently in some statistical and econometric discussion also define a constraint in the sense just described; and they can affect the results of calculations from data quite considerably if the sample is small – as it often is with economic data. Some logical and, inevitably, psychological problems involved in prior 'judgments' are treated in Shelley and Bryan (1964), a collection of essays of which the one by F. J. Anscombe deals with the Bayesian approach.

Some social scientists including econometricians denote the set of prior propositions by the term 'model'. I believe this usage is not generally accepted by philosophers of science. But there is hardly much disagreement about the general principle of testing by observations and the usual practice of not testing all propositions at once.

The methodological agreement between social and natural sciences was enhanced when, in the latter, statistical propositions replaced some deterministic ones. To be sure, the existence of random 'errors of observation' has been long recognized and dealt with. But more recently, especially since the advent of genetics and statistical physics, the phenomenon itself has been described in probabilistic terms. If all that is asserted in science is a probability distribution, many social hypotheses, even the historical theory presented in *War and Peace*, can claim admission.

So much for common foundations. What about the differences? Does empirical economics have any particular properties that call for special 'econometric' methods? Two such properties have been stated. Both are peculiar to economics only in degree but not in essence. First, the standards of the economist's profession require that his empirical results be useful for practical policy, at least over short horizons. Second, many of his prior assumptions are based on vague 'judgment' and introspection, rarely amenable to controlled experiment.

The economist is asked to predict how some specified changes (or the absence of changes) in the 'environment' will affect 'economic variables'. These variables represent actions of people in their various economic roles: as producers of, or bidders for, consumers goods, labor, materials, loans, etc. These action variables are supposed to be 'endogenous' – that is, to depend on, but not to determine in turn, the environment. Of particular interest are those changes of environment that are deliberate and are called 'policies', and those economic variables that are a given policy-maker's 'decision criteria', such as the levels of national production and of prices in the case of a government's decisions or the level of profit in the case of a single firm. To specify endogenous and exogenous variables is itself a prior assumption. Less ambitious than Marx, Spengler, or Toynbee, the economist avoids the risk of constructing self-contained social models. He makes, for example, the convenient (yet surely not totally safe) assumption that the growth of population, or the foreign or fiscal policy of a government, influences, but is not influenced by, say, national income. Even then, however, his list of such, allegedly exogenous, 'non-economic' variables is usually very incomplete, leaving a great deal of 'unexplained variance' of the economic ones. Only quite recently have economists, pressed by practical needs of economic development of different countries, begun to specify and to study the economic relevance of political and sociological variables – see, for example, Adelman and Morris (1967).

To predict the effects of a given policy change the economist can seldom rely on experiments. He cannot emulate the engineer's 'dry runs'. Nor is it easy to synthesize those effects by using help (of psychologists, for example) of the kind offered to meteorologists by physicists who are able to study one variable at a time, controlling all others. He cannot set up a laboratory experiment to study the behavioral responses of representatives of each economic group to changes that would simulate the actions of other groups or changes in the common environment.

So far, the economist's main observations have been historical data. Yet he cannot assign future validity to the patterns of the past. For policy change may consist in changing the very mechanism by which the environment influences economic variables. He must therefore peek in the interior of the notorious 'black box' that operated in the past, and describe policy changes as specific changes of that interior.

In his use of historical data, the economist is also helped by occasional surveys of the expenditures and plans of sampled consumers, producers, etc. Most importantly, he makes full use of his common sense. He is certain, for example, that consumers do not consult steel production statistics before purchasing groceries, and that hog raisers are concerned with the price of corn and of hogs, not of copper. Any knowledge of technology, of legal or habitual constraints, and of the relevant time lags of people's responses must be incorporated.

The study of economic time sequences can be said to deal with:

(i) An 'endogenous' n-tuple $y(t)=[y_i(t);\ i=1,\dots,n]$ and an 'exogenous' m-tuple $z(t)=[z_j(t);\ j=1,\dots,m]$ of functions of time. For example, $y_1(t)$ may be the rate of savings at time t, and $z_3(t)$ may be a tax rate at time t.

(ii) n functions $\phi_i(i=1,\dots,n)$, each having as its argument the quantities

$$[y(t-\lambda),\ z(t-\mu)],$$

where λ and μ are 'time lag' variables ranging from zero to infinity.

(iii) A joint probability distribution $F[u(t)]$ of the n-tuple $u(t)$ of functions of time ('random shocks') defined by

$$u_i(t)\equiv y_i(t)-\phi_i[y(t-\lambda),\ z(t-\mu)] \quad i=1,\dots,n.$$

The values of the $m+n$ functions $y(t)$ and $z(t)$ are observed from time to time. Alternatively, in a more elaborate view occasionally taken from psychologists and sociologists, $y(t)$ and $z(t)$ are 'latent' but are statistically related to 'manifest' observables in some partly known fashion. (In the simplest case each latent variable differs from a corresponding observable by an additive 'error' which enters the distribution function F jointly with the 'shocks.')

A *partial* specification of the $n+1$ functions $F, \phi_1,\dots,\phi_n$ constitutes a 'model'. When *fully* specified – or rather estimated – in the light of facts, they constitute a 'structure'. These 'structural functions', together with the exogenous variables $z(t)$, represent the environment. Some changes of environment are deliberate policies. These policies can consist in changing some of the structural functions in a specified way (e.g., when a free market is replaced by rationing or price control of a commodity) or in fixing some of the exogenous variables. It is because of the former type of environmental changes that we need the knowledge of 'structure' that prevailed in the observed past. We are then able to formulate the transition to a new structure. But those functions cannot, in general, be obtained ('identified' is the technical term) from observations unless some restrictions are assumed *a priori*. Without sufficient restrictions an infinity of structures may be consistent with a given set of observations.

An important type of such prior restrictions is this: For a given i, the function ϕ_i is independent of $y_k(t-\lambda), z_j(t-\mu)(k=1,\ldots, n; j=1,\ldots, m)$ except for a few specified pairs (k, λ), (j, μ). For example, if ϕ_i is linear, all its coefficients are zero, except a few specified ones. Thus the builders' supply of housing will depend, among a few other things, on the interest rate charged on their borrowings, with a time lag (determined by construction technology, customs, and legal regulations) which is ascertainable from experts. The consumers' demand for housing depends on other things, with other time lags. Some of these lags are well known, others very little known.

I submit that very often economists have made more, or stronger, prior assumptions than can be justified by solid knowledge or are needed to make the model identifiable. For example, in many economic models the assumed lags are the first few integers (in years or months). Such arbitrary choice may be quite unrealistic. The choice of time lags not ascertainable from other sources should, at least in part, become a matter of estimation from observed time sequences instead of being imposed *a priori*.

It may be useful to refer here to recent exciting applications of spectral analysis to economics. These have not been concerned, so far, with estimating economic 'structures' needed to predict effects of certain policies. To use my earlier phrase, they 'assign future validity to the patterns of the past' and have neglected the use of much of available economic 'prior knowledge'. On the other hand, spectral analysis might help to do away with the unrealistic time lags so cavalierly chosen by practicing econometricians. The frequencies of the major component oscillations of endogenous variables (given the exogenous ones), which can presumably be revealed by such analysis, should be closely related to the prevailing time lags. Is there a way to combine 'prior knowledge' of economic models with techniques of spectral analysis?

The historical nature of data is not peculiar to economics alone: consider meteorology. Nor is the stress on policy applications: consider engineering. That these two features occur together is somewhat more distinctive for, though still not unique to, economics. Only by following in some detail the actual work of econometricians can one get the peculiar flavor. This work is of course of interest to economists. But it should also interest students of scientific method when applied to nonexperimental data for practical decision purposes – a problem that arises especially, but not exclusively, in social sciences.

NOTE

* The paper is an adaptation and extension of the Foreword (entitled 'Remarks on Econometric Tools') written by the author for Carl F. Christ's *Econometric Models and Tools*, John Wiley & Sons, Inc., New York 1966. The publisher's permission to use the Foreword is gratefully acknowledged. Of other relevant expositions in book form published after 1960, the reader will find useful those by Goldberger, Johnston, Klein, Malinvaud, and Theil.

BIBLIOGRAPHY

Adelman, I. and C. T. Morris, *Society, Politics, and Economic Development. A Quantitative Approach*, The Johns Hopkins Press, Baltimore, 1967.

Christ, C. F., *Econometric Models and Methods*, Wiley, New York, 1966.

Goldberger, A. S., *Econometric Theory*, Wiley, New York, 1964.

Johnston, J., *Econometric Methods*, McGraw-Hill, New York, 1963.

Klein, L. R., *An Introduction to Econometrics*, Prentice-Hall, Englewood Cliffs, N.J., 1962.

Malinvaud, E., *Statistical Methods in Econometrics*, Rand McNally, Chicago, and North-Holland Publ. Co., Amsterdam, 1966.

Mann, H. B. and Wald, A., 'On the Statistical Treatment of Linear Stochastic Difference Equations', *Econometrica* **11** (1943) 173–200.

Shelley, M. W. and Bryan, G. L., (eds.), *Human Judgments and Optimality*, Wiley, New York, 1964.

Theil, H., *Applied Economic Forecasting*, Rand McNally, Chicago, and North-Holland Publ. Co., Amsterdam, 1966.

55

INTERDISCIPLINARY DISCUSSIONS ON MATHEMATICS IN BEHAVIORAL SCIENCES

(1972)

Both Pareto and Waffenschmidt started as engineers. What is fashionably called 'optimization' to-day, coincides with the engineer's 'efficiency'. But 'optimal' is also identical with 'economical'. These words denote the most desirable use of limited possibilities ('resources'). A language common to economics and engineering – that of mathematics – was applied by Pareto and by Waffenschmidt. In later life each shifted to 'sociology'. Indeed, the traditional economics of marketable commodities is but one aspect of society and its functions, of its history and policy. This has been, of course, the point of view of Adam Smith and John Stuart Mill, of the German *Kameralisten* and Karl Marx. The specialization of economists in the last 100 years was probably a good thing. It favored the development of adequate tools. But it could not last. To a specialized economist, population and politics and panics are 'exogenous variables'. He assumes that demographers, politologists, psychologists will deal with them. But, in fact, he does not present them with his problems and ask a psychologist what is known about decision-making under stress; nor does he give a politologist the explicit task of relating tax systems to power distribution. Lack of communication makes the division of labor sub-optimal. The latter days' trend, back to integrated social science, is due, in part, to the needs of our time. The development of non-industrial countries, new approaches to military, diplomatic, urban planning, the control of environment, all increasingly confluent, have called for joint efforts of social scientists. Even wider cooperation is called for – with biologists and physical scientists. Joint effort requires communication and a common language.

It has been often remarked that each of the various social sciences has developed a separate jargon. Yet not only do they share a common object of study but there is a commonalty of method, too. This has been recognized for a long time as far as the testing of hypotheses from statistical data is concerned; thus, most social scientists agree on what they mean, for example by 'variance', when analyzing statistical data.

More recently, it has become more and more apparent that social scientists can learn from each other and from scholars in other fields, not only how to test but also how to construct hypotheses. In many cases, this business of 'model building' can be, and has been, unified across the whole field of social sciences by the use of a common language: that of logical and mathematical symbolism. Techniques for formulating unambiguous propositions, (possibly but not necessarily quantitative ones), and for establishing logical relations between them (the 'axiomatic' approach) have become known to many social scientists. Even more special techniques such as graph theory, stochastic processes, spectral analysis have been borrowed from other fields. Conversely (as with the ancient problems of insurance risks or with the new field of games of strategy and of mathematical programming) behavioral scientists have occasionally infected not only each other but also mathematicians and engineers: just as, in earlier generations, Malthus infected Darwin, jury procedures inspired Poisson, and Daniel Bernoulli's logarithmic utility begat Fechner's logarithmic sensation.

The goal-oriented, 'policy-making' feature is rightly dominant in social sciences. Is this perhaps what my teacher Heinrich Rickert had in mind so many years ago? Though he would probably not share my belief that this ('optimizing') feature makes it useful for social scientists to understand the logical and mathematical workings of the engineer's mind.

Mathematical language has also made it easier to study those social science problems that are either formally analogous or substantively related to the work of their neighbors in fields such as brain research, or ecology and evolution, or the theory of information.

An Interdisciplinary Colloquium on the Application of Mathematics in the Behavioral Sciences, University of California at Los Angeles (UCLA), is now in its 12th year. Its activities may be of some interest to the readers of this *Festschrift* (who will have noted that I use 'behavioral' and 'social' sciences interchangeably).

The fields with which the topics can be roughly identified, and the number of respective sessions of the colloquium were, in the period October 1960–June 1971, as follows: Mathematics, Statistics and Computer Science, 38; Economics, 36; Psychology, 28; Engineering, 15;

Biology and Medicine, 9; Philosophy incl. Logic, 7; Linguistics, 6; Sociology, 4; Political Science, 2; Musicology, 1. (Total, 146, or about 12 sessions a year). The colloquium chairman, an economist, is advised by an interdepartmental committee in which most of these fields are represented.

It was assumed that members of the audience did use some mathematics in their work, and were not afraid of the blackboard. To ensure better mutual understanding, the speaker is asked to hand out an outline, in which his concepts, notations and propositions were stated as clearly as possible; and it is the chairman's duty to encourage the audience to interrupt the speaker if (and only if) further clarification is needed. Using mathematics as the esperanto accessible to all participants, technical terms like the economists' 'elasticity' or the psychologists' 'threshold' are clarified in less than a minute! Note also that 'mathematics' does deal with non-quantitative concepts, for it embraces logic and set theory. The colloquium would be useful even if its only effect were training in clear thinking. But it may have achieved more than that.

To illustrate the colloquium's activities let me state in more detail, and roughly categorize, the topics of the year 1970/71, also giving the affiliation of those discussants who cared to submit written comments for circulation, usually a week or two after the session.

COLLOQUIUM SESSIONS, 1970–71, ROUGHLY GROUPED

1. *Constructing and Testing of Models Describing Individual Behavior*

'A System for Perception and Memory', D. A. Norman (Psychology, University of California at San Diego). Comments by a logician, a psychiatrist, an economist.

'Experiments on the Use of Imprecise Information in Decision Making', N. C. Dalkey (Logic, RAND Corporation). Comments by a management scientist.

'Probabilistic Analysis of Choice', A. Tversky (Psychology, University of Jerusalem). Comments by a psychologist, an economist, a management scientist.

'Multidimensional Preferences', by L. G. Cooper (Management, UCLA). Comments by two psychologists.

2. *Construction and Testing of Models Describing Social Behavior*

'Simulation of Urban Politics', F. and I. Adelman (Economics, Northwestern University). Comments by an economist and a lawyer.

'Bayesian and Non-Bayesian Inference in Econometrics', A. Zellner (Economics, University of Chicago), Comments by two mathematicians, two economists.

'Developmental Behavior of Complex Systems', C. H. Waddington (Genetics, University of Edinburgh). (Session co-sponsored with the Brain Research Institute, the Departments of Psychology and of Psychiatry, the Institute for Environmental and Evolutionary Biology, and the School of Architecture and Urban Planning).

3. *Models for Optimization or Stabilization*

'Racial Discrimination in the Job Market: The Role of Information and Search', J. McCall (Economics, UCLA). Comments by two economists.

'Resource Allocation on a University Campus: An Analytical Approach', A. M. Geoffrion (Management Science, UCLA). Comments by two management scientists, one economist.

'Decentralized Control of Large-Scale Economic Systems', M. Aoki (Engineering, UCLA). Comments by an economist.

'An Economist's View of Biological Interaction', C. Tullock (Economics and Public Choice, Virginia Polytechnic Institute). Comments by economists.

'Gaming, Simulation, Game Theory', M. Shubik (Economics, Yale University).

'Games and Economic Equilibrium: Some Unsolved Problems', R. Aumann (Mathematics, University of Jerusalem).

4. *Logic of Measurement*

'Measurement Structures', D. H. Krantz (Psychology, University of Michigan). Comments by an economist and a psychologist.

At its annual meeting at the end of the academic year, the colloquium's interdepartmental committee suggested as both desirable and possible:

(a) to add (as was done, in part, in some of the previous years) speakers from anthropology, education, linguistics, political science, sociology, to the extent that mathematics has been used in these disciplines in nontrivial, significant ways; (b) to give added emphasis to serious applications (as distinct from fads) in fields such as social budgeting, urban planning, interspecies ecology, and the economics of public goods and bads.

The attendance of a session averaged 39, ranging from 16 to 83 (almost exactly the same extremes as on the average of the preceding 10 years). About 8% were staff members of some local 'think-tanks' – RAND Corporation, Systems Development Corporation – and other private or public non-academic institutions. The remainder were faculty members or advanced students of UCLA and other campuses of the University of California, or other institutions of higher learning in Southern California, – notably the University of Southern California and some State Colleges. The academic departments most strongly represented in the audience were: Economics, 20%; Management Science, 18%; Psychology and Education, 15%; Engineering and Physical Sciences, 10%; Biology and Medicine, 6%; Mathematics and Computer Sciences, 5%; Anthropology and Linguistics, 5%; Political Science and Sociology, 2%; Geography, 1%, of the total attendance.

We estimate that about one third of the attending UCLA members were registered as students of various departments. There were two kinds of students; a hard core, mostly candidates for advanced degrees; and those attracted by a prominent visitor. The latter type students came in droves just for some particular session, mostly following the suggestion of their teacher who presumably felt it to be useful for their education. It is difficult to say whether or not this type of attendance is of less significance than the hard-core attendance by research students who have found the general trend of the colloquium congenial to their own development. For that matter, the attendance and participation by faculty members is also a part of the never-ending educational process vital to the community of scholars.

During the eleven years of its existence, the colloquium seems to have filled a real niche in the intellectual life of UCLA. This may have been due both to the increasing role of mathematics in the social sciences, and to the resurgence of a 'generalist' interest (term due to Fred Mosteller, the Harvard statistician), almost a revival of XVIII Century encyclopedism. Suffice it to mention, on the one hand, the expansion of old and the appearance of several new journals in mathematical economics and econometrics; in mathematical psychology and psychometrics; in formal logic and linguistics; in systems analysis and its applications to social problems. On the other hand, the intellectual posture of men like Bertrand Russell and Norbert Wiener has become widely accepted. The current success of *Science* and *Scientific American* and the current attempts to redirect aerospace engineers towards socio-economic problems are also worth mentioning. All this makes the continuation of the colloquium desirable and possible.

Some ideas of the colloquium were explicitly transplanted to the University of Helsinki, Finland, by Professor G. H. von Wright, formerly visiting professor of philosophy at UCLA – transplanted and modified, of course. Any such transplanting would be done, if at all, *mutatis mutandis*, depending on the active persons. At UCLA itself, the colloquium chairmanship is likely to devolve from an economist to a psychologist, with a probable shift of emphasis from problems of optimal information, decision and organization to those of perception, possibly bordering on physiology. An engineer or computer scientist would center the interdisciplinary discussion in a different manner, and a historian of science in a still different one. In fact, one can visualize a shift to... philosophy, – in the spirit of German universities of half-a-century ago, when philosophy was supposed to provide foundations for all knowledge; yea, for men's life itself.

What, then, about the colloquium's emphasis on mathematics? I had already indicated that clear thinking need not be quantitative; nor should we prefer trivial knowledge, even if based on large samples, to deep insights tentatively stated without too much statistics. Still, what about my hunch, stated earlier, that the current trend favors clear thinking, needed to solve many practical problems of to-day's society? Don't we witness, on the contrary, a revival of 'anti-intellectualism', a search for other ways of expression. Indeed, between the *siècle de la raison* of the encyclopedists and the *siècle de la science* of the last four generations or so, there was the interruption through Romanticism, much needed and enriching in its time, no doubt. Some of those problems that challenge the society to-day may indeed be brought closer to solution by a revision of goals and values, with less haste and more contemplation, less science and more poetry. Yet, it is impossible for me to imagine that, in the long run, hunger, wars and pollution will leave us if we just reject the gift of clear and patient thinking.

INDEX OF NAMES

INDEX OF SUBJECTS

THEORY AND DECISION LIBRARY

An International Series in the Philosophy and Methodology
of the Social and Behavioral Sciences

Editors:

GERALD EBERLEIN, *University of Saarland*

WERNER LEINFELLNER, *University of Nebraska*

1. GÜNTER MENGES (ed.), *Information, Inference, and Decision.* 1974, viii + 195 pp.

2. ANATOL RAPOPORT (ed.), *Game Theory as a Theory of Conflict Resolution.* 1974, v + 283 pp.

3. MARIO BUNGE (ed.), *The Methodological Unity of Science.* 1973, viii + 264 pp.

4. COLIN CHERRY (ed.), *Pragmatic Aspects of Human Communication.* 1974, ix + 178 pp.

5. FRIEDRICH RAPP (ed.), *Contributions to a Philosophy of Technology. Studies in the Structure of Thinking in the Technological Sciences.* 1974, xv + 228 pp.

6. WERNER LEINFELLNER and ECKEHART KÖHLER (eds.), *Developments in the Methodology of Social Science.* 1974, x + 430 pp.